North American Industry Classification System (NAICS)

Reprint

United States 2017 Edition

Includes

U.S. Small Business Administration Table of Size Standards matched to the 2017 NAICS SBA size standards date August 19, 2019

The upper black band is for the NAICS and the lower band is for the SBA Table of Size Standards. You can use these to quickly navigate to the section of this volume you are interested in.

edited by
Brian Greul

The North American Industry Classification System (NAICS) is the standard used by Federal statistical agencies in classifying business establishments for the purpose of collecting, analyzing, and publishing statistical data related to the U.S. business economy. It is a joint work between the Untied States, Canada, and Mexico that allows a high level of comparability between the countries. The NAICS officially replaced the SIC (Standard Industrial Classification) system in 1997.

The publisher has included the SBA Size Standards Table as an appendix at the back of this book to assist users of the data.

Should you have suggestions or feedback on ways to improve this book please send email to Books@OcotilloPress.com

If you would like to order a copy of this book as a 3 ring punched looseleaf print please contact Books@OcotilloPress.com

---

Edited 2021 Ocotillo Press
ISBN 978-1-954285-07-1

Printed in the United States of America

Ocotillo Press
Houston, TX 77017
Books@OcotilloPress.com

NORTH AMERICAN INDUSTRY CLASSIFICATION SYSTEM

United States, 2017

EXECUTIVE OFFICE OF THE PRESIDENT
OFFICE OF MANAGEMENT AND BUDGET

Foreword

The Instituto Nacional de Estadística y Geografía (INEGI) of Mexico, Statistics Canada, and the United States Office of Management and Budget, through its Economic Classification Policy Committee, have jointly updated the system of classification of economic activities that makes the industrial statistics produced in the three countries comparable. The North American Industry Classification System (NAICS) revision for 2017 is scheduled to go into effect for reference year 2017 in Canada and the United States, and 2018 in Mexico. NAICS was originally developed to provide a consistent framework for the collection, analysis, and dissemination of industrial statistics used by government policy analysts, by academics and researchers, by the business community, and by the public. Revisions for 2017 were made to account for our rapidly changing economies.

Classifications serve as a lens through which to view the data they classify. NAICS is the first industry classification system that was developed in accordance with a single principle of aggregation, the principle that producing units that use similar production processes should be grouped together. NAICS also reflects, in a much more explicit way, the enormous changes in technology and in the growth and diversification of services that have marked recent decades. Though NAICS differs from other industry classification systems, the three countries continue to strive to create industries that do not cross two-digit boundaries of the United Nations' International Standard Industrial Classification of All Economic Activities (ISIC).

The actual classification reveals only the tip of the work carried out by dedicated staff from INEGI, Statistics Canada, and U.S. statistical agencies. It is through their efforts, painstaking analysis, and spirit of accommodation that NAICS has emerged as a harmonized international classification of economic activities in North America.

Preface

The North American Industry Classification System (NAICS) represents a continuing cooperative effort among Statistics Canada, Mexico's Instituto Nacional de Estadística y Geografía (INEGI), and the Economic Classification Policy Committee (ECPC) of the United States, acting on behalf of the Office of Management and Budget, to create and maintain a common industry classification system. With its inception in 1997, NAICS replaced the existing classification of each country—the Standard Industrial Classification (1980) of Canada, the Mexican Classification of Activities and Products (1994), and the Standard Industrial Classification (1987) of the United States. Since 1997, the countries have collaborated in producing five-year revisions to NAICS in order to keep the classification system current with changes in economic activities.

The North American Industry Cla ssification System is unique among industry classifications in that it is constructed within a single conceptual framework. Economic units that have similar production processes are classified in the same industry, and the lines drawn between industries demarcate, to the extent practicable, differences in production processes. This supply-based, or production-oriented, economic concept was adopted for NAICS because an industry classification system is a framework for collecting and publishing information on both inputs and outputs, for statistical uses that require that inputs and outputs be used together and be classified consistently. Examples of such uses include measuring productivity, unit labor costs, and the capital intensity of production, estimating employment-output relationships, constructing input-output tables, and other uses that imply the analysis of production relationships in the economy. The classification concept for NAICS leads to production of data that facilitate such analyses.

In the design of NAICS, attention was given to developing production-oriented classifications for (a) new and emerging industries, (b) service industries in general, and (c) industries engaged in the production of advanced technologies. These special emphases are embodied in the particular features of NAICS, discussed below. These same areas of special emphasis account for many of the differences between the structure of NAICS and the structures of industry classification systems in use elsewhere. NAICS provides enhanced industry comparability among the three North American Free Trade Agreement (NAFTA) trading partners, while also increasing compatibility with the two-digit level of the International Standard Industrial Classification (ISIC, Rev. 4) of the United Nations.

NAICS divides the economy into 20 sectors. Industries within these sectors are grouped according to the production criterion. A key feature of NAICS is the Information sector that groups industries that primarily create and disseminate a product subject to copyright. The NAICS Information sector brings together those activities that transform information into a commodity that is produced and distributed, and activities that provide the means for distributing those products, other than through traditional wholesale-retail distribution channels. Industries included in this sector are telecommunications; broadcasting; newspaper, book, and periodical publishing; motion picture and sound recording industries; libraries; and other information services.

Another feature of NAICS is a sector for Profes sional, Scientific, and Technical Services that comprises establishments engaged in activities where human capital is the major input. The industries within this sector are each defined by the expertise and training of the service provider. The sector includes such industries as offices of lawyers, engineering services, architectural services, advertising agencies, and interior design services.

A sector for Arts, Entertainment, and Recreation includes a wide range of establishments that operate facilities or provide services to meet varied cultural, entertainment, and recreational interests of their patrons.

Another key sector, Health Care and Social Assi stance, recognizes the merging of the boundaries of health care and social assistance. The industries in this sector are arranged in an order that reflects the range and extent of health care and social assistance provided. Some important industries are family planning centers, outpatient mental health and substance abuse centers, and continuing care retirement communities.

In the Manufacturing sector, an important subsector, Computer and Electronic Product Manufacturing, brings together industries producing electronic products and their components. The manufacturers of computers, communications equipment, and semiconductors, for example, are grouped into the same subsector because of the inherent technological similarities of their production processes, and the likelihood that these technologies will continue to converge in the future. NAICS acknowledges the importance of these electronic industries, their rapid growth over the past several decades and the likelihood that these industries will, in the future, become even more important in the economies of the three North American countries.

This NAICS structure reflects the levels at which data comparability was agreed upon by the three countries' statistical agencies. The boundaries of all the sectors of NAICS are delineated. In most sectors, NAICS provides for comparability at the industry (five-digit) level. However, for one of the three subsectors in Mining, Quarrying, and Oil and Gas Extraction, one of the three industry groups in Utilities, one of the ten industry groups in Construction, two of the four subsectors in Finance and Insurance, one of the three industry groups in the Real Estate subsector, and two of the four subsectors in Other Services (except Public Administration), three-country comparability occurs either at the industry group (four-digit) or subsector (three-digit) level. For these sectors or subsectors, differences in the economies of the three countries prevent full comparability at the NAICS industry level. For Retail Trade, Wholesale Trade, and Public Administration, the three countries' statistical agencies have agreed, at this time, only on the boundaries of the sector (two-digit level). Below the agreed upon level of comparability, each country may add additional detailed industries, as necessary to meet national needs, provided that this additional detail aggregates to the NAICS level.

The United States has adopted the revised clas sification in their statistical programs for the reference year beginning in 2017.

Acknowledgments

This 2017 revision of the North American Industry Classification System (NAICS) was an immense undertaking requiring the time, energy, creativity, and cooperation of numerous people and organizations throughout the three countries. The work that has been accomplished is a testament to the individual and collective willingness of many persons and organizations both inside and outside the government to contribute to the development of NAICS. Within the United States, NAICS was revised under the guidance of the Office of Management and Budget by the Economic Classification Policy Committee (ECPC). Members of the ECPC were **Dennis Fixler** and **Edward T. Morgan**, Bureau of Economic Analysis, U.S. Department of Commerce; **William G. Bostic, Jr.** (retired) and **John B. Murphy** (Chair), Bureau of the Census, U.S. Department of Commerce; **David Talan**, Bureau of Labor Statistics, U.S. Department of Labor; and ex officio, **Paul Bugg** (retired), Office of Management and Budget.

In addition to the parties listed above, OMB would like to acknowledge the dedicated staff of the Classification Development Branch at the Bureau of the Census. This staff was responsible for researching, summarizing, and making preliminary recommendations to the ECPC for comments received from the public on 2017 NAICS revisions; for preparing documents summarizing the ECPC position for use in negotiations with Canada and Mexico; and for preparing all of the manuscript files for the published manual. It was their hard work and dedication that resulted in

Contents

Foreword 1
Preface 3
Acknowledgments 5
Explanation of Symbols 11
Introduction 13
NAICS United States Structure 25
Frequently Asked Questions About Economic Classifications 77

Part I. Titles and Descriptions of Industries 79
Sector 11. Agriculture, Forestry, Fishing and Hunting 81
Subsector 111. Crop Production 81
Subsector 112. Animal Production and Aquaculture 92
Subsector 113. Forestry and Logging 98
Subsector 114. Fishing, Hunting and Trapping 99
Subsector 115. Support Activities for Agriculture and Forestry 100
Sector 21. Mining, Quarrying, and Oil and Gas Extraction 105
Subsector 211. Oil and Gas Extraction 105
Subsector 212. Mining (except Oil and Gas) 106
Subsector 213. Support Activities for Mining 115
Sector 22. Utilities 119
Subsector 221. Utilities 119
Sector 23. Construction 123
Subsector 236. Construction of Buildings 123
Subsector 237. Heavy and Civil Engineering Construction 127
Subsector 238. Specialty Trade Contractors 131
Sector 31-33. Manufacturing 143
Subsector 311. Food Manufacturing 144
Subsector 312. Beverage and Tobacco Product Manufacturing 164
Subsector 313. Textile Mills 167
Subsector 314. Textile Product Mills 169
Subsector 315. Apparel Manufacturing 172
Subsector 316. Le ather and Allied Product Manufacturing 175

Subsector 335. Electrical Equipment, Appliance, and Component Manufacturing 276
Subsector 336. Transportation Equipment Manufacturing 286
Subsector 337. Furn iture and Related Product Manufacturing 299
Subsector 339. Miscellaneous Manufacturing 304
Sector 42. Wholesale Trade 313
Subsector 423. Merchant Wholesalers, Durable Goods 313
Subsector 424. Merchant Wholesalers, Nondurable Goods 330
Subsector 425. Wholes ale Electronic Markets and Agents and Brokers 342
Sector 44-45. Retail Trade 345
Subsector 441. Motor Vehicle and Parts Dealers 346
Subsector 442. Furniture and Home Furnishings Stores 349
Subsector 443. Electronics and Appliance Stores 352
Subsector 444. Bu ilding Material and Garden Equipment and Supplies Dealers 353
Subsector 445. Food and Beverage Stores 356
Subsector 446. Health and Personal Care Stores 360
Subsector 447. Gasoline Stations 362
Subsector 448. Clothing and Clothing Accessories Stores 363
Subsector 451. Sporting Goods, Hobby, Musical Instrument, and Book Stores 367
Subsector 4 52. General Merchandise Stores 370
Subsector 4 53. Miscellaneous Store Retailers 372
Subsector 454. Nonstore Retailers 377
Sector 48-49. Transportation and Warehousing 379
Subsector 481. Air Transportation 379
Subsector 482. Rail Transportation 383
Subsector 483. Water Transportation 384
Subsector 484. Truck Transportation 386
Subsector 485. Transit and Ground Passenger Transportation 389
Subsector 486. Pipeline Transportation 394
Subsector 487. S cenic and Sightseeing Transportation 395
Subsector 488. Support Activities for Transportation 397
Subsector 491. Postal Service 403
Subsector 492. Couriers and Messengers 404
Subsector 493. Warehousing and Storage 405
Sector 51. Information 409
Subsector 511. Publishing Industries (except Internet) 410
Subsector 512. Motion Picture and Sound Recording Industries 414
Subsector 515. Broadcasting (except Internet) 419
Subsector 517. Telecommunications 421
Subsector 518. Data Processing, Hosting, and Related Services 425

Subsector 522. Cr edit Intermediation and Related Activities 430
Subsector 523. S ecurities, Commodity Contracts, and Other Financial Investments and Related Activities 435
Subsector 524. Insurance Carriers and Related Activities 440
Subsector 525. Fund s, Trusts, and Other Financial Vehicles 445
Sector 53. Real Estate and Rental and Leasing 449
Subsector 531. Real Estate 449
Subsector 532. Rental and Leasing Services 453
Subsector 533. Lessors of Nonfinancial Intangible Assets (except Copyrighted Works) 459
Sector 54. Professional, Scien tific, and Technical Services 461
Subsector 541. Profe ssional, Scientific, and Technical Services 461
Sector 55. Management of Companies and Enterprises 485
Subsector 551. Management of Companies and Enterprises 485
Sector 56. Administrative and Support and Waste Management and Remediation Services 489
Subsector 561. Administrative and Support Services 489
Subsector 562. Wast e Management and Remediation Services 505
Sector 61. Educational Services 513
Subsector 611. Educational Services 513
Sector 62. Health Care and Social Assistance 523
Subsector 621. Ambulatory Health Care Services 523
Subsector 622. Hospitals 53 3
Subsector 623. Nu rsing and Residential Care Facilities 534
Subsector 624. Social Assistance 538
Sector 71. Arts, Entertainment, and Recreation 543
Subsector 711. Performin g Arts, Spectator Sports, and Related Industries 543
Subsector 712. Museums, Historical Sites, and Similar Institutions 549
Subsector 713. Amusement, Gambling, and Recreation Industries 551
Sector 72. Accommodation and Food Services 557
Subsector 721. Accommodation 557
Subsector 722. Food Services and Drinking Places 560
Sector 81. Other Services (e xcept Public Administration) 567
Subsector 811. Repair and Maintenance 567
Subsector 812. Personal and Laundry Services 576
Subsector 813. Religious, Grantmaking, Civic, Professional, and Similar Organizations 583
Subsector 814. Private Households 590
Sector 92. Public Administration ....

Subsector 925. Administration of Housing Programs, Urban Planning, and Community Development 599
Subsector 926. Administration of Economic Programs 599
Subsector 927. Space Research and Technology 601
Subsector 928. Nati onal Security and International Affairs 602

Part II. List of Short Titles 605
Abbreviations and Acronyms 639

Part III. Appendixes 641
A. A. 2017 NAICS United States Matched to 2012 NAICS United States (Changes Only)

Explanation of Symbols

In NAICS United States Structure

Symbol	Explanation
T	Canadian, Mexican, and United States industries are comparable

In Part I, Titles and Descriptions of Industries

Symbol	Explanation
T	Canadian, Mexican, and United States industries are comparable

In Appendix A

Symbol	Explanation
N	New NAICS industry for 2017
*	Part of 2012 NAICS United States industry

In Appendix B

Symbol	Explanation
pt.	Part of 2017 NAICS United States industry

Introduction

Background

In 1937, the Central Statistical Board established an Interdepartmental Committee on Industrial Classification ''to develop a plan of classification of various types of statistical data by industries and to promote the general adoption of such classification as the standard classification of the Federal Government.''[1] The List of Industries for manufacturing was first available in 1938, with the List of Industries for nonmanufacturing following in 1939. These Lists of Industries became the first Standard Industrial Classification (SIC) for the United States. The SIC was developed for use in the classifi cation of establishments by type of activity in which they are primarily engaged; for purposes of facilitating the collection, tabulation, presentation, and analysis of data relating to establishments; and for promoting uniformity and comparability in the presentation of statistical data collected by various agencies of the United States Government, State agencies, trade associations, and private research organizations. The SIC covered the entire field of economic activities by defining industries in accordance with the composition and structure of the economy.

Since the inception of the SIC in the 1930's, the system was periodically revised to reflect the economy's changing industrial composition and organization. The last revision of the SIC was in 1987.

Rapid changes in both the U.S. and worl d economies brought the SIC under increasing criticism. In 1991, an International Conference on the Classification of Economic Activities was convened in Williamsburg, Virginia, to provide a forum for responding to such criticism and to explore new approaches to classifying economic activity. In July 1992, the Office of Management and Budget (OMB) established the Economic Classification Policy Committee (ECPC) and charged it with a ''fresh slate'' examination of economic classifications for statistical purposes. The ECPC prepared a number of issue papers regarding classification, consulted with outside users, and ultimately joined with Mexico's Instituto Nacional de Estadística, Geografía e Informática (now the Instituto Nacional de Estadística y Geografía) (INEGI) and Statistics Canada to develop the North American Industry Classification System (NAICS), which replaced the 1987 U.S. SIC and the classification systems of Canada (1980 SIC) and Mexico (1994 Mexican Classification of Activities and Products (CMAP)).

The dynamic nature of world economies conti nues to affect classification systems. The creators of NAICS agreed that the classification system should be reviewed every five years, and revised as appropriate to reflect the changing economies of the three countries. The U.S. statistical programs implemented NAICS for the first time in 1997. NAICS was revised in 2002, 2007, and 2012. This 2017 NAICS revision was undertaken to achieve one main goal—to modify or create industries to reflect new, emerging, or changing activities and technologies.

The impact of NAICS on various countries has brought about a renewed effort for additional convergence with the many industry classifications used throughout the world. Future revisions of NAICS will continue to strive for greater global comparability.

[1]Pearce, Esther, History of the Standard Industrial Classification, Executive Office of the President, Office of

Purpose of NAICS

NAICS is an industry classification system that groups establishments into industries based on the similarity of their production processes. It is a comprehensive system covering all economic activities. There are 20 sectors and 1,057 industries in 2017 NAICS United States.

NAICS was initially developed and subsequently revised by Mexico's INEGI, Statistics Canada, and the U.S. ECPC (the latter acting on behalf of OMB) to provide common industry definitions for Canada, Mexico, and the United States that will facilitate economic analyses of the economies of the three North American countries. The statistical agencies in the three countries produce information on inputs and outputs, industrial performance, productivity, unit labor costs, and employment. NAICS, which is based on a production-oriented concept, ensures maximum usefulness of industrial statistics for these and similar purposes.

NAICS United States is used by U.S. statistical agencies to facilitate the collection, tabulation, presentation, and analysis of data relating to establishments; and to provide uniformity and comparability in the presentation of statistical data describing the U.S. economy. NAICS United States is designed for statistical purposes. Although the classification also may be used for various administrative, regulatory, and taxation purposes, the requirements of government agencies that use it for nonstatistical purposes played no role in its development or subsequent revision.

Development of NAICS as a Replacement for the U.S. SIC

The U.S. ECPC established by OMB in 1992 was chaired by the Bureau of Economic Analysis, U.S. Department of Commerce, with representatives from the Bureau of the Census, U.S. Department of Commerce, and the Bureau of Labor Statistics, U.S. Department of Labor. The ECPC was asked to examine economic classifications for statistical purposes and to determine the desirability of developing a new industry classification system for the United States based on a single economic concept. On March 31, 1993, OMB published a **Federal Register** notice (58 FR 16990-17004) announcing the intention to revise the SIC for 1997, the establishment of the ECPC, and the process for revising the SIC.

In July 1994, OMB announced plans to develop a new industry classification system in cooperation with Mexico's INEGI and Statistics Canada. The new system—NAICS—replaced the U.S. SIC. The concepts of the new system and the principles upon which NAICS was to be developed were announced in a July 26, 1994, **Federal Register** notice (59 FR 38092-38096) and were as follows:

1. NAICS will be erected on a production-ori ented or supply-based conceptual framework. This means that producing units that use identical or similar production processes will be grouped together in NAICS.
2. The system will give special attention to de veloping production-oriented classifications for (a) new and emerging industries, (b) service industries in general, and (c) industries engaged in the production of advanced technologies.
3. Time series continuity will be maintained to the greatest extent possible. However, changes in the economy and proposals from data users must be considered. In addition, adjustments will be required for sectors where the United States, Canada, and Mexico have incompatible industry

classification definitions in order to produce a common industry system for all three North American countries.

4. The system will strive for compatibility with the two-digit level of the International Standard Industrial Classification of All Economic Activities (ISIC, Rev. 3) of the United Nations.

The structure of NAICS was developed in a series of meetings among the three countries. Public proposals for individual industries from all three countries were considered for acceptance if the proposed industry was based on the production-oriented concept of the system. In the United States, public comments also were solicited as groups of subsectors of NAICS were completed and agreed upon by the three countries. The ECPC published the proposed industries for those subsectors in a series of five successive **Federal Register** notices, in 1995 and 1996, asking for comments from interested data users.

Revision of NAICS for 2017

OMB published a notification of potential revision to NAICS for 2017 in a May 22, 2014, **Federal Register** notice (79 FR 29626-29629). This notice solicited comments on: 1) new and emerging industries for consideration in potential revisions to NAICS for 2017; 2) the electronic dissemination of NAICS 2017; and 3) updating the structure of the oil and gas industries for NAICS 2017. This notice also provided an update on the treatment of manufacturing units that outsource all transformation activities. In addition, OMB published a notification regarding implementation of the Factoryless Goods Producer (FGP) classification in NAICS 2017 in an August 8, 2014, **Federal Register** notice (79 FR 46558-46559). This notice stated the directive of the August 17, 2011, **Federal Register** notice (76 FR 51240-51243) was no longer in force, to allow for additional research, testing, and evaluation of FGPs.

After considering all proposals from the public, consulting with a number of U.S. data users and industry groups, and undertaking extensive discussions with Statistics Canada and Mexico's Instituto Nacional de Estadística y Geografía (INEGI), the ECPC formulated a set of recommendations for revisions to NAICS for 2017. OMB published a solicitation of public comments on these recommendations in an August 4, 2015, **Federal Register** notice (80 FR 46480-46484). After reviewing comments to that notice and conducting further consultation with data users and industry groups, OMB decided to adopt the ECPC recommendations presented in the August 4, 2015, notice. OMB published a notice of final decisions regarding NAICS revisions for 2017 in an August 8, 2016, **Federal Register** notice (81 FR 52584).

Conceptual Framework

NAICS is erected on a production-oriented or supply-based conceptual framework that groups establishments into industries according to similarity in the processes used to produce goods or services. A production-oriented industry classification system ensures that statistical agencies in the three countries can produce information on inputs and outputs, industrial performance, productivity, unit labor costs, employment, and other statistics and structural changes occurring in each of the three economies.

When an industry is defined on a production-oriented concept, producing units within the industry's boundaries share a basic production process; they use closely similar technology. In the language of economics, producing units within an industry share the same production functions; producing units in different industries have different production functions. The boundaries between industries thus demarcate, in principle, differences in production processes and production technologies.

The reasoning behind the three countries' deci sion to base NAICS on a production-oriented concept is summarized as follows: An industry is a grouping of economic activities. Though it inevitably groups the products of the economic activities that are included in the industry definition, it is not solely a grouping of products; put another way, an industry groups producing units. Accordingly, an industry classification system provides a framework for collecting data on inputs and outputs together.

The uses of economic data that require that data on inputs and outputs be used together and be collected on the same basis include production analyses, productivity measurement, and studying input usage and input intensities. The North American statistical agencies developed NAICS using a production-oriented concept as the framework for two reasons: (1) an industry classification system groups producing units, not products or services; and (2) groupings of producing units permit the collection of data on inputs and outputs on a comparable basis, which is required for production-oriented analysis, but do not facilitate a comprehensive collection of data on the total output of any particular good or service, which is required for market-oriented analysis. Thus, the efficient organizing concept of an industry classification system is production-oriented rather than market-oriented.

Structure of NAICS

The structure of NAICS is hierarchical. The first two digits of the structure designate the NAICS sectors that represent general categories of economic activities.

NAICS classifies all economic activities into 20 sectors. The NAICS sectors, their two-digit codes, and the distinguishing activities of each are:

11 Agriculture, Forestry, Fishing and Hunting—Activities of this sector are growing crops, raising animals, harvesting timber, and harvesting fish and other animals from farms, ranches, or the animals' natural habitats.

21 Mining, Quarrying, and Oil and Gas Extraction—Activities of this sector are extracting naturally occurring mineral solids, such as coal and ore; liquid minerals, such as crude petroleum; and gases, such as natural gas; and beneficiating (e.g., crushing, screening, washing, and flotation) and other preparation at the mine site, or as part of mining activity.

22 Utilities—Activities of this sector are generating, transmitting, and/or distributing electricity, gas, steam, and water and removing sewage through a permanent infrastructure of lines, mains, and pipe.

23 Construction—Activities of this sector are erecting buildings and other structures (including additions); heavy construction other than buildings; and alterations, reconstruction, installation, and maintenance and repairs.

31-33 Manufacturing—Activities of this sector are the mechanical, physical, or chemical transformation of materials, substances, or components into new products.

42 Wholesale Trade—Activities of this sector are selling or arranging for the purchase or sale of goods for resale; capital or durable nonconsumer goods; and raw and intermediate materials and supplies used in production, and providing services incidental to the sale of the merchandise.

44-45 Retail Trade—Activities of this sector are retailing merchandise generally in small quantities to the general public and providing services incidental to the sale of the merchandise.

48-49 Transportation and Warehousing—Activities of this sector are providing transportation of passengers and cargo, warehousing and storing goods, scenic and sightseeing transportation, and supporting these activities.

51 Information—Activities of this sector are distributing information and cultural products, providing the means to transmit or distribute these products as data or communications, and processing data.

52 Finance and Insurance—Activities of this sector involve the creation, liquidation, or change in ownership of financial assets (financial transactions) and/or facilitating financial transactions.

53 Real Estate and Rental and Leasing—Activities of this sector are renting, leasing, or otherwise allowing the use of tangible or intangible assets (except copyrighted works), and providing related services.

54 Professional, Scientific, and Technical Services—Activities of this sector are performing professional, scientific, and technical services for the operations of other organizations.

55 Management of Companies and Enterprises—Activities of this sector are the holding of securities of companies and enterprises, for the purpose of owning controlling interest or influencing their management decisions, or administering, overseeing, and managing other establishments of the same company or enterprise and normally undertaking the strategic or organizational planning and decision-making role of the company or enterprise.

56 Administrative and Support and Waste Management and Remediation Services—Activities of this sector are performing routine support activities for the day-to-day operations of other organizations.

61 Educational Services—Activities of this sector are providing instruction and training in a wide variety of subjects.

62 Health Care and Social Assistance—Activities of this sector are providing health care and social assistance for individuals.

71 Arts, Entertainment, and Recreation—Activities of this sector are operating or providing services to meet varied cultural, entertainment, and recreational interests of their patrons.

72 Accommodation and Food Services—Activities of this sector are providing customers with lodging and/or preparing meals, snacks, and beverages for immediate consumption.

81 Other Services (except Public Administration)—Activities of this sector are providing services not elsewhere specified, including repairs, religious activities, grantmaking, advocacy, laundry, personal care, death care, and other personal services.

92 Public Administration—Activities of this sector are administration, management, and oversight of public programs by Federal, State, and local governments.

NAICS uses a six-digit coding system to identif y particular industries and their placement in this hierarchical structure of the classification system. The first two digits of the code designate the sector, the third digit designates the subsector, the fourth digit designates the industry group, the fifth digit designates the NAICS industry, and the sixth digit designates the national industry. A zero as the sixth digit generally indicates that the NAICS industry and the U.S. industry are the same.

The subsectors, industry groups, and NAICS industries, in accord with the conceptual principle of NAICS, are production-oriented combinations of establishments. However, the production distinctions become more narrowly defined as one moves down the hierarchy.

NAICS agreements permit each country to de signate detailed industries, below the level of a NAICS industry, to meet national needs. The United States has such industry detail in many places in the classification system to recognize large, important U.S. industries that cannot be recognized in the other countries because of size, specialization, or organization of the industry.

Typically the level at which comparable data w ill be available for Canada, Mexico, and the United States is the five-digit NAICS industry; for some sectors (or subsectors or industry groups) however, the three countries agreed upon the boundaries at a higher level of detail rather than the detailed industry structure (five-digit). There is agreement at the sector level for Wholesale Trade; Retail Trade; and Public Administration. There is agreement either at the industry group (four-digit) or subsector (three-digit) level for one of the three subsectors in the Mining, Quarrying, and Oil and Gas Extraction sector, one of the three industry groups in the Utilities sector, one of the ten industry groups in the Construction sector, two of the four subsectors in the Finance and Insurance sector, one of the three industry groups in the Real Estate subsector, and two of the four subsectors in the Other Services (except Public Administration) sector.

Differences in the economies of the three countries or time constraints necessitated establishing comparability at a higher level of detail for the sectors and subsectors noted above. For each of these sectors, except Wholesale Trade and Public Administration, Canada and the United States have agreed upon an industry structure and hierarchy to ensure comparability of statistics between those two countries. Canada and the United States also have established the same national detail (six-digit) industries where possible, adopting the same codes to describe comparable industries. For this reason, the numbers of the U.S. industries may not be consecutive. In a few cases, it was necessary for the United States to use all of the numbers available to establish its six-digit detail so that the same six-digit codes do not necessarily represent comparable industries in the U.S. and Canada.

NAICS with U.S. detail is known as NAIC S United States, while Canada and Mexico produce six-digit detail and publish that detail as NAICS Canada and NAICS (SCIAN in Spanish) Mexico.

Definition of an Establishment

NAICS is a classification system for establishments. The establishment as a statistical unit is defined as the smallest operating entity for which records provide information on the cost of resources—materials, labor, and capital—employed to produce the units of output. The output may be sold to other establishments and receipts or sales recorded, or the output may be provided without explicit charge, that is, the good or service may be ''sold'' within the company itself.

The establishment, in NAICS United States, is generally a single physical location where business is conducted or where services or industrial operations are performed (for example, a factory, mill, store, hotel, movie theater, mine, farm, airline terminal, sales office, warehouse, or central administrative office). There are cases where records identify distinct and separate economic activities performed at a single physical location (e.g., shops in a hotel). These retailing activities, operated out of the same physical location as the hotel, are identified as separate establishments and classified in the Retail Trade sector, while the hotel is classified in the Accommodation subsector. In such cases, each activity is treated as a separate establishment provided: (1) no one industry description in the classification includes such combined activities;
(2) separate reports can be prepared on the number of employees, their wages and salaries, sales or receipts, and expenses; and (3) employment and output are significant for both activities.

Exceptions to the single location exist for physically dispersed operations, such as construction, transportation, and telecommunications. For these activities the individual sites, projects, fields, networks, lines, or systems of such dispersed activities are not normally considered to be establishments. The establishment is represented by those relatively permanent main or branch offices, terminals, stations, and so forth, that are either (1) directly responsible for supervising such activities, or (2) the base from which personnel operate to carry out these activities.

Although an establishment may be identical with the enterprise (company), the two terms should not be confused. An enterprise (company) may consist of more than one establishment. Such multiunit enterprises may have establishments in more than one industry in NAICS. If such enterprises have a separate establishment primarily engaged in providing headquarters services, these establishments are classified in Sector 55, Management of Companies and Enterprises. Although all establishments have output, they may or may not have receipts. In large enterprises, it is not unusual for establishments to exist to solely serve other establishments of the same enterprise (auxiliary, or enterprise support, establishments). In such cases, these units often do not collect receipts from the establishments they serve. This type of support (captive) activity is found throughout the economy and involves goods-producing activities as well as services. Units that carry out support activities for the enterprise to which they belong are classified, to the extent feasible, according to the NAICS code related to their own activity. This means that warehouses providing storage facilities for their own enterprise are classified as warehouses. For certain analytical purposes, an alternative code may be assigned corresponding to the activity of the enterprise that they support.

Determining an Establishment's Industry Classification

An establishment is classified in an industry when its primary activity meets the definition for that industry. Because establishments may perform more than one activity, it is necessary to determine procedures for identifying the primary activity of the establishment.

In most cases, if an establishment is engaged in more than one activity, the industry code is assigned based on the establishment's principal product or group of products produced or distributed, or services rendered. Ideally, the principal good or service should be determined by its relative share of current production costs and capital investment at the establishment. In practice, however, it is often necessary to use other variables such as revenue, shipments, or employment as proxies for measuring significance.

There are two types of combined activities that are given special attention in NAICS. They are vertical integration and joint production. These combined activities have an economic basis and occur in both goods-producing and services-producing sectors. In some cases, there are efficiencies to be gained from combining certain activities in the same establishment. Some of these combinations occur so commonly or frequently that their combination can be treated as a third activity in its own right and explicitly classified in a specific industry.

One approach to classifying these activities woul d be to use the primary activity rule, that is, whichever activity is largest. However, the fundamental principle of NAICS is that establishments that employ the same production process should be classified in the same industry. If the premise that the combined activities correspond to a distinct third activity is accepted, then using the primary activity rule would place establishments performing the same combination of activities in different industries, thereby violating the production principle of NAICS. A second reason for NAICS recognizing combined activities is to improve the stability of establishment classification, both over time and among the various agencies that implement the classification. An establishment should remain classified in the same industry unless its production process changes, and different agencies should code the same establishment or type of establishment in the same way. A consistent treatment of establishments with combined activities is more likely if they are classified to a single industry.

Vertical integration involves consecutive stages of fabrication or production processes in which the output of one step is the input of the next. In general, establishments are classified based on the final process in a vertically integrated production environment, unless specifically identified as classified in another industry. For example, paper may be produced either by establishments that first produce pulp and then consume that pulp to produce paper or by those establishments producing paper from purchased pulp. NAICS explicitly specifies that both of these types of paper-producing processes should be classified in NAICS 32212, Paper Mills, the final step in paper manufacturing, rather than in NAICS 32211, Pulp Mills. In other cases, NAICS specifies that vertically integrated establishments are classified in the industry representing the first stage of the manufacturing process. For example, steel mills that make steel and also perform other activities such as producing steel castings are classified in NAICS 33111,

Iron and Steel Mills and Ferroalloy Manufacturing, the first stage of the manufacturing process.

The joint production of goods or services repres ents the second type of combined activities. For example, automobile dealers both sell and repair autos; automotive parts dealers may both sell parts and repair automobiles; and musical instrument stores may both sell and rent instruments. In the Manufacturing sector, establishments may make two different products such as men's suits and women's suits, activities that are classified in two different NAICS United States detailed industries. In general, receipts/sales and revenue data are used as a proxy to determine primary activity for these establishments. The assumption is that the activity generating the most receipts is also the activity using the most resources and most indicative of the production process.

In some cases, however, these combined activit ies have been assigned to a specific NAICS industry. Most of these activities involve either the sale and repair of goods or the sale and rental of goods in the same establishment. For example, establishments that both sell automobile parts and repair automobiles are classified in NAICS 44131, Automotive Parts and Accessories Stores, and music stores that both sell and rent musical instruments are classified in NAICS 45114, Musical Instrument and Supplies Stores. In other cases, specific industries are identified for these combined activities, such as NAICS 44711, Gasoline Stations with Convenience Stores.

Classification rules related to the agreement to permit individual country detail at the six-digit level for NAICS sometimes result in less comparable NAICS industries at the five-digit level and above. For example in NAICS, the assignment of the industry code is at the most detailed level of the classification (the six-digit U.S. detail code), except for Agriculture. That is, if the value of an establishment's production consists of 30 percent from computers, 30 percent from computer storage devices, and 40 percent from semiconductors and related devices, it is classified in U.S. detail industry 334413, Semiconductor and Related Device Manufacturing, that is aggregated to NAICS 33441, Semiconductor and Other Electronic Component Manufacturing, the level that comparable information is shown for all three countries. If the classification for the above example were at the five-digit NAICS level, that establishment would be classified in NAICS 33411, Computer and Peripheral Equipment Manufacturing. There would then be more comparable information at the NAICS level, but it would be impossible to classify this establishment to a U.S. detail six-digit industry.

In Agriculture, however, NAICS coding begins at the top of the structure and continues down to the most detailed level (the six-digit U.S. detail code). The existence of a 50 percent rule in Agriculture and the presence of combination industries based on families of related agricultural products with none accounting for 50 percent or more of production require a top down coding procedure rather than coding at the most detailed level first as is done in the balance of the classification.

Use of Reporting Units Other than Establishments

NAICS is based on the economic principle that establishments should be grouped together based on their production processes. The NAICS definition of the establishment ensures that, at some level, "establishments": (1) identify the most refined (generally smallest) individual entity possible; (2) can provide the information needed when surveying economic activity; and (3) when aggregated, approximate the statistical universe of economic activity. Each economic survey program, in practice, determines whether the establishment is the most appropriate reporting unit to meet the three criteria listed above with respect to the program's objectives. If not, an alternative reporting unit is identified.

For example, an economic survey of employment or wage data may choose the establishment—generally a physical location—as the reporting unit. Physical locations generally have records for the number of employees and their wages readily available. Therefore, it is reasonable to expect that separate wage and employment data are available for each switching station in a multiunit telecommunications carrier enterprise and the physical location is a logical choice for the reporting unit.

If the economic survey collects output data, the individual switching stations would not have the total number of telephone calls or a complete accounting of inputs and outputs of the multiunit telecommunications carrier. If a telephone call is routed through three different switching stations and the price is determined at a fourth location, all of the related locations would need to be merged into an alternative reporting unit to measure the volume and value of the output. In this case, the physical location is not an appropriate reporting unit. The level of aggregation of physical units required to create reporting units will vary greatly depending on the business activity being studied. To efficiently define reporting units, statistical surveys need to evaluate the characteristics of the activities being studied and the organizational structure of the entities producing goods or services. In some cases, the physical location is appropriate, sometimes units will need to be grouped based on homogeneous production characteristics or geographical groupings, and in other cases, the enterprise (company) may form the most appropriate reporting unit.

The practical variation in reporting unit definitions affects comparability of data. A count of units defined as physical locations will be different from a count of units defined based on the need for complete input and output records in the telecommunications industries. It is critical that each data provider clearly identify the reporting unit definition used when presenting summary statistics. The analysis of statistical data from a variety of sources requires the transparency of clearly defined reporting units.

While the reporting unit definition can vary, NAICS is a classification system for establishments and is based on grouping establishments with similar production function characteristics.

Comparison of NAICS to the International Standard Industrial Classification of All Economic Activities (ISIC)

Recognizing the need for international comparability of economic statistics, the United Nations (UN) first adopted an International Standard Industrial Classification system in 1948. Revisions to the ISIC structure and codes were adopted by the UN's Statistical Commission in 1958, 1968, 1989, 2002, and 2007.[2]

Similar to NAICS, ISIC was designed primarily to provide classifications for grouping activities (rather than enterprises or firms), and the primary focus for the ISIC classification system is the kind of activity in which establishments or other statistical entities are engaged. The main criteria employed in delineating divisions and groups (the two- and three-digit categories, respectively) of ISIC are: (a) the character of the goods and services produced; (b) the uses to which the goods and services are put; and (c) the inputs, the process, and the technology of production.

[2] International Standard Industrial Classification of All Economic Activities, Statistical Papers, Series M, No. 4, Rev. 4, United Nations, New York, 2008.

The third classification criterion of the ISIC is the conceptual foundation of NAICS, and thus, NAICS is aligned more closely with ISIC than was the 1987 SIC system. However, there are differences between the NAICS and ISIC classification schemes. Most important, perhaps, is the single (production process) conceptual framework of NAICS. As noted elsewhere, this is unique among industry classifications.

ISIC, Rev. 4, groups economic activity into 21 broad Sections, 88 Divisions, 238 Groups, and 420 Classes. In the coding system, Sections are distinguished by the letters A through U, and the Divisions, Groups, and Classes are identified as the two-digit, three-digit, and four-digit groupings, respectively. As was the case with 2007 NAICS, the most recent revision of ISIC also focused on improvements to the detail in services sections.

In the development and subsequent revision of NAICS industries, the statistical agencies of the three countries strove to create industries that did not cross ISIC two-digit boundaries. The 2007 revisions of the NAICS and ISIC increased comparability beyond previous levels. Similar to the 2012 NAICS revision, this 2017 NAICS revision maintains a similar level of comparability with ISIC, Rev. 4.

2017 NAICS United States Structure

The following page contains a summary table of the 2017 NAICS United States structure. This table shows the counts of subsectors, industry groups, industries, and United States detail industries for each of the NAICS sectors.

Following the summary table is a complete listing of the 2017 NAICS United States structure. This list displays the codes and official full titles for the sectors, subsectors, industry groups, industries, and United States detail industries. A "T" superscript on the title indicates a level at which Canada, Mexico, and the United States formally agreed to maintain comparability. Detail below that level may or may not be comparable to detail for one or both of the other countries.

Part II of this manual contains a list of short titles that are recommended for use when space limitations preclude the use of the full titles for the dissemination of data classified using NAICS.

2017 NAICS United States Structure

Sector	Name	Subsectors (3-digit)	Industry Groups (4-digit)	NAICS Industries (5-digit)	6-digit Industries		
					U.S. Detail	Same as 5-digit	Total
11	Agriculture, Forestry, Fishing and Hunting	5	19	42	32	32	64
21	Mining, Quarrying, and Oil and Gas Extraction	3	5	11	24	4	28
22	Utilities	1	3	6	10	4	14
23	Construction	3	10	28	4	27	31
31-33	Manufacturing	21	86	180	265	95	360
42	Wholesale Trade	3	19	71	0	71	71
44-45	Retail Trade	12	27	57	17	49	66
48-49	Transportation and Warehousing	11	29	42	25	32	57
51	Information	6	11	25	12	19	31
52	Finance and Insurance	5	11	31	15	26	41
53	Real Estate and Rental and Leasing	3	8	17	11	13	24
54	Professional, Scientific, and Technical Services	1	9	35	20	29	49
55	Management of Companies and Enterprises	1	1	1	3	0	3
56	Administrative and Support and Waste Management and Remediation Services	2	11	29	25	19	44
61	Educational Services	1	7	12	7	10	17
62	Health Care and Social Assistance	4	18	30	16	23	39
71	Arts, Entertainment, and Recreation	3	9	23	3	22	25
72	Accommodation and Food Services	2	6	10	8	7	15
81	Other Services (except Public Administration)	4	14	30	30	19	49
92	Public Administration	8	8	29	0	29	29
	Total	**99**	**311**	**709**	**527**	**530**	**1057**

Sector 11--Agriculture, Forestry, Fishing and Hunting[T]

111 Crop Production[T]

1111 Oilseed and Grain Farming[T]

11111 Soybean Farming[T] 111110
Soybean Farming
11112 Oilseed (except Soybean) Farming[T]
111120 Oilseed (except Soybean) Farming
11113 Dry Pea and Bean Farming[T]
111130 Dry Pea and Bean Farming
11114 Wheat Farming[T]
111140 Wheat Farming
11115 Corn Farming[T]
111150 Corn Farming
11116 Rice Farming[T]
111160 Rice Farming
11119 Other Grain Farming[T]
111191 Oilseed and Grain Combination Farming
111199 All Other Grain Farming

1112 Vegetable and Melon Farming[T] 11121 Veg-

etable and Melon Farming[T] 111211 Potato
Farming
111219 Other Vegetable (except Potato) and Melon Farming

1113 Fruit and Tree Nut Farming[T]

11131 Orange Groves[T]
111310 Orange Groves
11132 Citrus (except Orange) Groves[T]
111320 Citrus (except Orange) Groves
11133 Noncitrus Fruit and Tree Nut Farming[T]
111331 Apple Orchards
111332 Grape Vineyards
111333 Strawberry Farming
111334 Berry (except Strawberry) Farming
111335 Tree Nut Farming
111336 Fruit and Tree Nut Combination Farming
111339 Other Noncitrus Fruit Farming

1114 Greenhouse, Nursery, and Floriculture Production[T]

11141 Food Crops Grown Under Cover[T]
111411 Mushroom Production
111419 Other Food Crops Grown Under Cover
11142 Nursery and Floriculture Production[T]
111421 Nursery and Tree Production
111422 Floriculture Production

1119 Other Crop Farming[T]

11191 Tobacco Farming[T]
111910 Tobacco Farming
11192 Cotton Farming[T]
111920 Cotton Farming
11193 Sugarcane Farming[T]
111930 Sugarcane Farming

11194 Hay Farming[T]
111940 Hay Farming
11199 All Other Crop Farming[T]
111991 Sugar Beet Farming
111992 Peanut Farming
111998 All Other Miscellaneous Crop Farming

112 Animal Production and Aquaculture[T]

1121 Cattle Ranching and Farming[T]
11211 Beef Cattle Ranching and Farming, including Feedlots[T]
112111 Beef Cattle Ranching and Farming
112112 Cattle Feedlots
11212 Dairy Cattle and Milk Production[T]
112120 Dairy Cattle and Milk Production
11213 Dual-Purpose Cattle Ranching and Farming[T]
112130 Dual-Purpose Cattle Ranching and Farming

1122 Hog and Pig Farming[T] 11221 Hog
and Pig Farming[T]
112210 Hog and Pig Farming

1123 Poultry and Egg Production[T] 11231
Chicken Egg Production[T] 112310
Chicken Egg Production
11232 Broilers and Other Meat Type Chicken Production[T]
112320 Broilers and Other Meat Type Chicken Production
11233 Turkey Production[T]
112330 Turkey Production
11234 Poultry Hatcheries[T]
112340 Poultry Hatcheries
11239 Other Poultry Production[T]
112390 Other Poultry Production

1124 Sheep and Goat Farming[T]
11241 Sheep Farming[T]
112410 Sheep Farming
11242 Goat Farming[T]
112420 Goat Farming

1125 Aquaculture[T]
11251 Aquaculture[T]
112511 Finfish Farming and Fish Hatcheries
112512 Shellfish Farming
112519 Other Aquaculture

1129 Other Animal Production[T]
11291 Apiculture[T]
112910 Apiculture
11292 Horses and Other Equine Production[T]
112920 Horses and Other Equine Production
11293 Fur-Bearing Animal and Rabbit Production[T]
112930 Fur-Bearing Animal and Rabbit Production
11299 All Other Animal Production[T]
112990 All Other Animal Production

113 Forestry and Logging[T]

1131 Timber Tract Operations[T] 11311
Timber Tract Operations[T]
113110 Timber Tract Operations

1132 Forest Nurseries and Gathering of Forest Products[T] 11321
Forest Nurseries and Gathering of Forest Products[T] 113210 Forest Nurseries and Gathering of Forest Products

1133 Logging[T]
11331 Logging[T]
113310 Logging

114 Fishing, Hunting and Trapping[T]

1141 Fishing[T]
11411 Fishing[T]
114111 Finfish Fishing
114112 Shellfish Fishing
114119 Other Marine Fishing

1142 Hunting and Trapping[T] 11421
Hunting and Trapping[T]
114210 Hunting and Trapping

115 Support Activities for Agriculture and Forestry[T]

1151 Support Activities for Crop Production[T] 11511
Support Activities for Crop Production[T] 115111 Cotton Ginning
115112 Soil Preparation, Planting, and Cultivating
115113 Crop Harvesting, Primarily by Machine
115114 Postharvest Crop Activities (except Cotton Ginning)
115115 Farm Labor Contractors and Crew Leaders
115116 Farm Management Services

1152 Support Activities for Animal Production[T] 11521
Support Activities for Animal Production[T] 115210 Support Activities for Animal Production

1153 Support Activities for Forestry[T] 11531
Support Activities for Forestry[T] 115310 Support Activities for Forestry

Sector 21--Mining, Quarrying, and Oil and Gas Extraction[T]

211 Oil and Gas Extraction[T]

2111 Oil and Gas Extraction[T]
21112 Crude Petroleum Extraction
211120 Crude Petroleum Extraction
21113 Natural Gas Extraction
211130 Natural Gas Extraction

212 Mining (except Oil and Gas)[T]

2121 Coal Mining[T]

21211 Coal Mining[T]
212111 Bituminous Coal and Lignite Surface Mining
212112 Bituminous Coal Underground Mining
212113 Anthracite Mining

2122 Metal Ore Mining[T] 21221

Iron Ore Mining[T]
212210 Iron Ore Mining
21222 Gold Ore and Silver Ore Mining[T]
212221 Gold Ore Mining
212222 Silver Ore Mining
21223 Copper, Nickel, Lead, and Zinc Mining[T]
212230 Copper, Nickel, Lead, and Zinc Mining
21229 Other Metal Ore Mining[T]
212291 Uranium-Radium-Vanadium Ore Mining
212299 All Other Metal Ore Mining

2123 Nonmetallic Mineral Mining and Quarrying[T]

21231 Stone Mining and Quarrying[T]
212311 Dimension Stone Mining and Quarrying
212312 Crushed and Broken Limestone Mining and Quarrying
212313 Crushed and Broken Granite Mining and Quarrying
212319 Other Crushed and Broken Stone Mining and Quarrying
21232 Sand, Gravel, Clay, and Ceramic and Refractory Minerals Mining and Quarrying[T]
212321 Construction Sand and Gravel Mining
212322 Industrial Sand Mining
212324 Kaolin and Ball Clay Mining
212325 Clay and Ceramic and Refractory Minerals Mining
21239 Other Nonmetallic Mineral Mining and Quarrying[T]
212391 Potash, Soda, and Borate Mineral Mining
212392 Phosphate Rock Mining
212393 Other Chemical and Fertilizer Mineral Mining
212399 All Other Nonmetallic Mineral Mining

213 Support Activities for Mining[T]

2131 Support Activities for Mining[T] 21311

Support Activities for Mining[T] 213111
Drilling Oil and Gas Wells
213112 Support Activities for Oil and Gas Operations
213113 Support Activities for Coal Mining
213114 Support Activities for Metal Mining
213115 Support Activities for Nonmetallic Minerals (except Fuels) Mining

Sector 22--Utilities[T]

221 Utilities[T]

2211 Electric Power Generation, Transmission and Distribution[T]

22111 Electric Power Generation[T]

221111 Hydroelectric Power Generation
221112 Fossil Fuel Electric Power Generation
221113 Nuclear Electric Power Generation
221114 Solar Electric Power Generation
221115 Wind Electric Power Generation
221116 Geothermal Electric Power Generation
221117 Biomass Electric Power Generation
221118 Other Electric Power Generation
22112 Electric Power Transmission, Control, and Distribution[T]
221121 Electric Bulk Power Transmission and Control
221122 Electric Power Distribution

2212 Natural Gas Distribution[T] 22121
Natural Gas Distribution[T]
221210 Natural Gas Distribution

2213 Water, Sewage and Other Systems[T]
22131 Water Supply and Irrigation Systems
221310 Water Supply and Irrigation Systems
22132 Sewage Treatment Facilities
221320 Sewage Treatment Facilities
22133 Steam and Air-Conditioning Supply
221330 Steam and Air-Conditioning Supply

Sector 23--Construction[T] 236

Construction of Buildings[T]

2361 Residential Building Construction[T] 23611
Residential Building Construction[T]
236115 New Single-Family Housing Construction (except For-Sale Builders)
236116 New Multifamily Housing Construction (except For-Sale Builders)
236117 New Housing For-Sale Builders
236118 Residential Remodelers

2362 Nonresidential Building Construction[T] 23621
Industrial Building Construction[T] 236210
Industrial Building Construction
23622 Commercial and Institutional Building Construction[T]
236220 Commercial and Institutional Building Construction

237 Heavy and Civil Engineering Construction[T]

2371 Utility System Construction[T]
23711 Water and Sewer Line and Related Structures Construction[T]
237110 Water and Sewer Line and Related Structures Construction
23712 Oil and Gas Pipeline and Related Structures Construction[T]
237120 Oil and Gas Pipeline and Related Structures Construction
23713 Power and Communication Line and Related Structures Construction[T]
237130 Power and Communication Line and Related Structures Construction

2372 Land Subdivision[T] 23721
Land Subdivision[T] 237210
Land Subdivision

2373 Highway, Street, and Bridge Construction[T] 23731 Highway, Street, and Bridge Construction[T] 237310 Highway, Street, and Bridge Construction

2379 Other Heavy and Civil Engineering Construction[T] 23799 Other Heavy and Civil Engineering Construction[T] 237990 Other Heavy and Civil Engineering Construction

238 Specialty Trade Contractors[T]

2381 Foundation, Structure, and Building Exterior Contractors[T]

23811 Poured Concrete Foundation and Structure Contractors
238110 Poured Concrete Foundation and Structure Contractors
23812 Structural Steel and Precast Concrete Contractors
238120 Structural Steel and Precast Concrete Contractors
23813 Framing Contractors
238130 Framing Contractors
23814 Masonry Contractors
238140 Masonry Contractors
23815 Glass and Glazing Contractors
238150 Glass and Glazing Contractors
23816 Roofing Contractors
238160 Roofing Contractors
23817 Siding Contractors
238170 Siding Contractors
23819 Other Foundation, Structure, and Building Exterior Contractors
238190 Other Foundation, Structure, and Building Exterior Contractors

2382 Building Equipment Contractors[T]

23821 Electrical Contractors and Other Wiring Installation Contractors[T]
238210 Electrical Contractors and Other Wiring Installation Contractors
23822 Plumbing, Heating, and Air-Conditioning Contractors[T]
238220 Plumbing, Heating, and Air-Conditioning Contractors
23829 Other Building Equipment Contractors[T]
238290 Other Building Equipment Contractors

2383 Building Finishing Contractors[T]

23831 Drywall and Insulation Contractors[T]
238310 Drywall and Insulation Contractors
23832 Painting and Wall Covering Contractors[T]
238320 Painting and Wall Covering Contractors
23833 Flooring Contractors[T]
238330 Flooring Contractors
23834 Tile and Terrazzo Contractors[T]
238340 Tile and Terrazzo Contractors
23835 Finish Carpentry Contractors[T]
238350 Finish Carpentry Contractors
23839 Other Building Finishing Contractors[T]
238390 Other Building Finishing Contractors

2389 Other Specialty Trade Contractors[T] 23891 Site Preparation Contractors[T] 238910 Site Preparation Contractors 23899 All Other Specialty Trade Contractors[T] 238990 All Other Specialty Trade Contractors

Sector 31-33--Manufacturing[T] 311

Food Manufacturing[T]

3111 **Animal Food Manufacturing[T]** 31111 Animal Food Manufacturing[T] 311111 Dog and Cat Food Manufacturing 311119 Other Animal Food Manufacturing

3112 **Grain and Oilseed Milling[T]**
31121 Flour Milling and Malt Manufacturing[T]
311211 Flour Milling
311212 Rice Milling
311213 Malt Manufacturing
31122 Starch and Vegetable Fats and Oils Manufacturing[T]
311221 Wet Corn Milling
311224 Soybean and Other Oilseed Processing
311225 Fats and Oils Refining and Blending
31123 Breakfast Cereal Manufacturing[T]
311230 Breakfast Cereal Manufacturing

3113 **Sugar and Confectionery Product Manufacturing[T]**
31131 Sugar Manufacturing[T]
311313 Beet Sugar Manufacturing
311314 Cane Sugar Manufacturing
31134 Nonchocolate Confectionery Manufacturing[T]
311340 Nonchocolate Confectionery Manufacturing
31135 Chocolate and Confectionery Manufacturing[T]
311351 Chocolate and Confectionery Manufacturing from Cacao Beans
311352 Confectionery Manufacturing from Purchased Chocolate

3114 **Fruit and Vegetable Preserving and Specialty Food Manufacturing[T]**
31141 Frozen Food Manufacturing[T]
311411 Frozen Fruit, Juice, and Vegetable Manufacturing
311412 Frozen Specialty Food Manufacturing
31142 Fruit and Vegetable Canning, Pickling, and Drying[T]
311421 Fruit and Vegetable Canning
311422 Specialty Canning
311423 Dried and Dehydrated Food Manufacturing

3115 **Dairy Product Manufacturing[T]**
31151 Dairy Product (except Frozen) Manufacturing[T]
311511 Fluid Milk Manufacturing
311512 Creamery Butter Manufacturing
311513 Cheese Manufacturing
311514 Dry, Condensed, and Evaporated Dairy Product Manufacturing
31152 Ice Cream and Frozen Dessert Manufacturing[T]
311520 Ice Cream and Frozen Dessert Manufacturing

3116 **Animal Slaughtering and Processing[T]** 31161 Animal Slaughtering and Processing[T]
311611 Animal (except Poultry) Slaughtering
311612 Meat Processed from Carcasses
311613 Rendering and Meat Byproduct Processing
311615 Poultry Processing

3117 **Seafood Product Preparation and Packaging**[T] 31171 Seafood Product Preparation and Packaging[T] 311710 Seafood Product Preparation and Packaging

3118 **Bakeries and Tortilla Manufacturing**[T]
31181 Bread and Bakery Product Manufacturing[T]
311811 Retail Bakeries
311812 Commercial Bakeries
311813 Frozen Cakes, Pies, and Other Pastries Manufacturing
31182 Cookie, Cracker, and Pasta Manufacturing[T]
311821 Cookie and Cracker Manufacturing
311824 Dry Pasta, Dough, and Flour Mixes Manufacturing from Purchased Flour
31183 Tortilla Manufacturing[T]
311830 Tortilla Manufacturing

3119 **Other Food Manufacturing**[T] 31191 Snack Food Manufacturing[T]
311911 Roasted Nuts and Peanut Butter Manufacturing
311919 Other Snack Food Manufacturing
31192 Coffee and Tea Manufacturing[T]
311920 Coffee and Tea Manufacturing
31193 Flavoring Syrup and Concentrate Manufacturing[T]
311930 Flavoring Syrup and Concentrate Manufacturing
31194 Seasoning and Dressing Manufacturing[T]
311941 Mayonnaise, Dressing, and Other Prepared Sauce Manufacturing
311942 Spice and Extract Manufacturing
31199 All Other Food Manufacturing[T]
311991 Perishable Prepared Food Manufacturing
311999 All Other Miscellaneous Food Manufacturing

312 Beverage and Tobacco Product Manufacturing[T]

3121 **Beverage Manufacturing**[T]
31211 Soft Drink and Ice Manufacturing[T]
312111 Soft Drink Manufacturing
312112 Bottled Water Manufacturing
312113 Ice Manufacturing
31212 Breweries[T]
312120 Breweries
31213 Wineries[T]
312130 Wineries
31214 Distilleries[T]
312140 Distilleries

3122 **Tobacco Manufacturing**[T] 31223 Tobacco Manufacturing
312230 Tobacco Manufacturing

313 Textile Mills[T]

3131 **Fiber, Yarn, and Thread Mills**[T] 31311 Fiber, Yarn, and Thread Mills[T] 313110 Fiber, Yarn, and Thread Mills

3132 Fabric Mills[T]
31321 Broadwoven Fabric Mills[T]
313210 Broadwoven Fabric Mills
31322 Narrow Fabric Mills and Schiffli Machine Embroidery[T]
313220 Narrow Fabric Mills and Schiffli Machine Embroidery
31323 Nonwoven Fabric Mills[T]
313230 Nonwoven Fabric Mills
31324 Knit Fabric Mills[T]
313240 Knit Fabric Mills

3133 Textile and Fabric Finishing and Fabric Coating Mills[T]
31331 Textile and Fabric Finishing Mills[T]
313310 Textile and Fabric Finishing Mills
31332 Fabric Coating Mills[T]
313320 Fabric Coating Mills

314 Textile Product Mills[T]

3141 Textile Furnishings Mills[T]
31411 Carpet and Rug Mills[T]
314110 Carpet and Rug Mills
31412 Curtain and Linen Mills[T]
314120 Curtain and Linen Mills

3149 Other Textile Product Mills[T]
31491 Textile Bag and Canvas Mills[T]
314910 Textile Bag and Canvas Mills
31499 All Other Textile Product Mills[T]
314994 Rope, Cordage, Twine, Tire Cord, and Tire Fabric Mills
314999 All Other Miscellaneous Textile Product Mills

315 Apparel Manufacturing[T]

3151 Apparel Knitting Mills[T]
31511 Hosiery and Sock Mills[T]
315110 Hosiery and Sock Mills
31519 Other Apparel Knitting Mills[T]
315190 Other Apparel Knitting Mills

3152 Cut and Sew Apparel Manufacturing[T]
31521 Cut and Sew Apparel Contractors
315210 Cut and Sew Apparel Contractors
31522 Men's and Boys' Cut and Sew Apparel Manufacturing
315220 Men's and Boys' Cut and Sew Apparel Manufacturing
31524 Women's, Girls', and Infants' Cut and Sew Apparel Manufacturing
315240 Women's, Girls', and Infants' Cut and Sew Apparel Manufacturing
31528 Other Cut and Sew Apparel Manufacturing
315280 Other Cut and Sew Apparel Manufacturing

3159 Apparel Accessories and Other Apparel Manufacturing[T] 31599 Apparel Accessories and Other Apparel Manufacturing[T] 315990 Apparel Accessories and Other Apparel Manufacturing

316 Leather and Allied Product Manufacturing[T]

3161 Leather and Hide Tanning and Finishing[T] 31611 Leather and Hide Tanning and Finishing[T] 316110 Leather and Hide Tanning and Finishing

3162 Footwear Manufacturing[T] 31621 Footwear Manufacturing[T]
316210 Footwear Manufacturing

3169 Other Leather and Allied Product Manufacturing[T] 31699 Other Leather and Allied Product Manufacturing[T] 316992 Women's Handbag and Purse Manufacturing 316998 All Other Leather Good and Allied Product Manufacturing

321 Wood Product Manufacturing[T]

3211 Sawmills and Wood Preservation[T] 32111 Sawmills and Wood Preservation[T] 321113 Sawmills
321114 Wood Preservation

3212 Veneer, Plywood, and Engineered Wood Product Manufacturing[T] 32121 Veneer, Plywood, and Engineered Wood Product Manufacturing[T] 321211 Hardwood Veneer and Plywood Manufacturing 321212 Softwood Veneer and Plywood Manufacturing 321213 Engineered Wood Member (except Truss) Manufacturing 321214 Truss Manufacturing
321219 Reconstituted Wood Product Manufacturing

3219 Other Wood Product Manufacturing[T]
32191 Millwork[T]
321911 Wood Window and Door Manufacturing
321912 Cut Stock, Resawing Lumber, and Planing
321918 Other Millwork (including Flooring)
32192 Wood Container and Pallet Manufacturing[T]
321920 Wood Container and Pallet Manufacturing
32199 All Other Wood Product Manufacturing[T]
321991 Manufactured Home (Mobile Home) Manufacturing
321992 Prefabricated Wood Building Manufacturing
321999 All Other Miscellaneous Wood Product Manufacturing

322 Paper Manufacturing[T]

3221 Pulp, Paper, and Paperboard Mills[T]
32211 Pulp Mills[T]
322110 Pulp Mills
32212 Paper Mills[T]
322121 Paper (except Newsprint) Mills
322122 Newsprint Mills
32213 Paperboard Mills[T]
322130 Paperboard Mills

3222 Converted Paper Product Manufacturing[T] 32221 Paperboard Container Manufacturing[T]

322211 Corrugated and Solid Fiber Box Manufacturing
322212 Folding Paperboard Box Manufacturing
322219 Other Paperboard Container Manufacturing
32222 Paper Bag and Coated and Treated Paper Manufacturing[T]
322220 Paper Bag and Coated and Treated Paper Manufacturing
32223 Stationery Product Manufacturing[T]
322230 Stationery Product Manufacturing
32229 Other Converted Paper Product Manufacturing[T]
322291 Sanitary Paper Product Manufacturing
322299 All Other Converted Paper Product Manufacturing

323 Printing and Related Support Activities[T]

3231 Printing and Related Support Activities[T]
32311 Printing[T]
323111 Commercial Printing (except Screen and Books)
323113 Commercial Screen Printing
323117 Books Printing
32312 Support Activities for Printing[T]
323120 Support Activities for Printing

324 Petroleum and Coal Products Manufacturing[T]

3241 Petroleum and Coal Products Manufacturing[T]
32411 Petroleum Refineries[T]
324110 Petroleum Refineries
32412 Asphalt Paving, Roofing, and Saturated Materials Manufacturing[T]
324121 Asphalt Paving Mixture and Block Manufacturing
324122 Asphalt Shingle and Coating Materials Manufacturing
32419 Other Petroleum and Coal Products Manufacturing[T]
324191 Petroleum Lubricating Oil and Grease Manufacturing
324199 All Other Petroleum and Coal Products Manufacturing

325 Chemical Manufacturing[T]

3251 Basic Chemical Manufacturing[T] 32511 Petrochemical Manufacturing[T] 325110 Petrochemical Manufacturing 32512 Industrial Gas Manufacturing[T] 325120 Industrial Gas Manufacturing 32513 Synthetic Dye and Pigment Manufacturing[T] 325130 Synthetic Dye and Pigment Manufacturing 32518 Other Basic Inorganic Chemical Manufacturing[T] 325180 Other Basic Inorganic Chemical Manufacturing 32519 Other Basic Organic Chemical Manufacturing[T] 325193 Ethyl Alcohol Manufacturing
325194 Cyclic Crude, Intermediate, and Gum and Wood Chemical Manufacturing
325199 All Other Basic Organic Chemical Manufacturing

3252 Resin, Synthetic Rubber, and Artificial and Synthetic Fibers and Filaments Manufacturing[T]
32521 Resin and Synthetic Rubber Manufacturing[T]
325211 Plastics Material and Resin Manufacturing
325212 Synthetic Rubber Manufacturing

32522 Artificial and Synthetic Fibers and Filaments Manufacturing[T]
325220 Artificial and Synthetic Fibers and Filaments Manufacturing

3253 Pesticide, Fertilizer, and Other Agricultural Chemical Manufacturing[T]
32531 Fertilizer Manufacturing[T]
325311 Nitrogenous Fertilizer Manufacturing
325312 Phosphatic Fertilizer Manufacturing
325314 Fertilizer (Mixing Only) Manufacturing
32532 Pesticide and Other Agricultural Chemical Manufacturing[T]
325320 Pesticide and Other Agricultural Chemical Manufacturing

3254 Pharmaceutical and Medicine Manufacturing[T] 32541 Pharmaceutical and Medicine Manufacturing[T] 325411 Medicinal and Botanical Manufacturing 325412 Pharmaceutical Preparation Manufacturing 325413 In-Vitro Diagnostic Substance Manufacturing 325414 Biological Product (except Diagnostic) Manufacturing

3255 Paint, Coating, and Adhesive Manufacturing[T]
32551 Paint and Coating Manufacturing[T] 325510 Paint and Coating Manufacturing 32552 Adhesive Manufacturing[T] 325520 Adhesive Manufacturing

3256 Soap, Cleaning Compound, and Toilet Preparation Manufacturing[T]
32561 Soap and Cleaning Compound Manufacturing[T]
325611 Soap and Other Detergent Manufacturing
325612 Polish and Other Sanitation Good Manufacturing
325613 Surface Active Agent Manufacturing
32562 Toilet Preparation Manufacturing[T]
325620 Toilet Preparation Manufacturing

3259 Other Chemical Product and Preparation Manufacturing[T]
32591 Printing Ink Manufacturing[T]
325910 Printing Ink Manufacturing
32592 Explosives Manufacturing[T]
325920 Explosives Manufacturing
32599 All Other Chemical Product and Preparation Manufacturing[T]
325991 Custom Compounding of Purchased Resins
325992 Photographic Film, Paper, Plate, and Chemical Manufacturing
325998 All Other Miscellaneous Chemical Product and Preparation Manufacturing

326 Plastics and Rubber Products Manufacturing[T]

3261 Plastics Product Manufacturing[T]
32611 Plastics Packaging Materials and Unlaminated Film and Sheet Manufacturing[T]
326111 Plastics Bag and Pouch Manufacturing
326112 Plastics Packaging Film and Sheet (including Laminated) Manufacturing
326113 Unlaminated Plastics Film and Sheet (except Packaging) Manufacturing
32612 Plastics Pipe, Pipe Fitting, and Unlaminated Profile Shape Manufacturing[T]
326121 Unlaminated Plastics Profile Shape Manufacturing
326122 Plastics Pipe and Pipe Fitting Manufacturing
32613 Laminated Plastics Plate, Sheet (except Packaging), and Shape Manufacturing[T]
326130 Laminated Plastics Plate, Sheet (except Packaging), and Shape Manufacturing

32614 Polystyrene Foam Product Manufacturing[T]
326140 Polystyrene Foam Product Manufacturing
32615 Urethane and Other Foam Product (except Polystyrene) Manufacturing[T]
326150 Urethane and Other Foam Product (except Polystyrene) Manufacturing
32616 Plastics Bottle Manufacturing[T]
326160 Plastics Bottle Manufacturing
32619 Other Plastics Product Manufacturing[T]
326191 Plastics Plumbing Fixture Manufacturing
326199 All Other Plastics Product Manufacturing

3262 Rubber Product Manufacturing[T]
32621 Tire Manufacturing[T]
326211 Tire Manufacturing (except Retreading)
326212 Tire Retreading
32622 Rubber and Plastics Hoses and Belting Manufacturing[T]
326220 Rubber and Plastics Hoses and Belting Manufacturing
32629 Other Rubber Product Manufacturing[T]
326291 Rubber Product Manufacturing for Mechanical Use
326299 All Other Rubber Product Manufacturing

327 Nonmetallic Mineral Product Manufacturing[T]

3271 Clay Product and Refractory Manufacturing[T]
32711 Pottery, Ceramics, and Plumbing Fixture Manufacturing[T]
327110 Pottery, Ceramics, and Plumbing Fixture Manufacturing
32712 Clay Building Material and Refractories Manufacturing[T]
327120 Clay Building Material and Refractories Manufacturing

3272 Glass and Glass Product Manufacturing[T] 32721
Glass and Glass Product Manufacturing[T] 327211 Flat
Glass Manufacturing
327212 Other Pressed and Blown Glass and Glassware Manufacturing
327213 Glass Container Manufacturing
327215 Glass Product Manufacturing Made of Purchased Glass

3273 Cement and Concrete Product Manufacturing[T]
32731 Cement Manufacturing[T]
327310 Cement Manufacturing
32732 Ready-Mix Concrete Manufacturing[T]
327320 Ready-Mix Concrete Manufacturing
32733 Concrete Pipe, Brick, and Block Manufacturing[T]
327331 Concrete Block and Brick Manufacturing
327332 Concrete Pipe Manufacturing
32739 Other Concrete Product Manufacturing[T]
327390 Other Concrete Product Manufacturing

3274 Lime and Gypsum Product Manufacturing[T]
32741 Lime Manufacturing[T]
327410 Lime Manufacturing
32742 Gypsum Product Manufacturing[T]
327420 Gypsum Product Manufacturing

3279 Other Nonmetallic Mineral Product Manufacturing[T]
32791 Abrasive Product Manufacturing[T]
327910 Abrasive Product Manufacturing
32799 All Other Nonmetallic Mineral Product Manufacturing[T]

327991 Cut Stone and Stone Product Manufacturing
327992 Ground or Treated Mineral and Earth Manufacturing
327993 Mineral Wool Manufacturing
327999 All Other Miscellaneous Nonmetallic Mineral Product Manufacturing

331 Primary Metal Manufacturing[T]

3311 Iron and Steel Mills and Ferroalloy Manufacturing[T] 33111 Iron and Steel Mills and Ferroalloy Manufacturing[T] 331110 Iron and Steel Mills and Ferroalloy Manufacturing

3312 Steel Product Manufacturing from Purchased Steel[T]
33121 Iron and Steel Pipe and Tube Manufacturing from Purchased Steel[T]
331210 Iron and Steel Pipe and Tube Manufacturing from Purchased Steel
33122 Rolling and Drawing of Purchased Steel[T]
331221 Rolled Steel Shape Manufacturing
331222 Steel Wire Drawing

3313 Alumina and Aluminum Production and Processing[T] 33131 Alumina and Aluminum Production and Processing[T] 331313 Alumina Refining and Primary Aluminum Production 331314 Secondary Smelting and Alloying of Aluminum 331315 Aluminum Sheet, Plate, and Foil Manufacturing 331318 Other Aluminum Rolling, Drawing, and Extruding

3314 Nonferrous Metal (except Aluminum) Production and Processing[T] 33141 Nonferrous Metal (except Aluminum) Smelting and Refining[T] 331410 Nonferrous Metal (except Aluminum) Smelting and Refining 33142 Copper Rolling, Drawing, Extruding, and Alloying[T] 331420 Copper Rolling, Drawing, Extruding, and Alloying 33149 Nonferrous Metal (except Copper and Aluminum) Rolling, Drawing,
Extruding, and Alloying[T]
331491 Nonferrous Metal (except Copper and Aluminum) Rolling, Drawing, and Extruding
331492 Secondary Smelting, Refining, and Alloying of Nonferrous Metal (except Copper and Aluminum)

3315 Foundries[T]
33151 Ferrous Metal Foundries[T]
331511 Iron Foundries
331512 Steel Investment Foundries
331513 Steel Foundries (except Investment)
33152 Nonferrous Metal Foundries[T]
331523 Nonferrous Metal Die-Casting Foundries
331524 Aluminum Foundries (except Die-Casting)
331529 Other Nonferrous Metal Foundries (except Die-Casting)

332 Fabricated Metal Product Manufacturing[T]

3321 Forging and Stamping[T] 33211
Forging and Stamping[T]
332111 Iron and Steel Forging
332112 Nonferrous Forging
332114 Custom Roll Forming
332117 Powder Metallurgy Part Manufacturing

332119 Metal Crown, Closure, and Other Metal Stamping (except Automotive)

3322 Cutlery and Handtool Manufacturing^T 33221
Cutlery and Handtool Manufacturing^T
332215 Metal Kitchen Cookware, Utensil, Cutlery, and Flatware (except Precious) Manufacturing
332216 Saw Blade and Handtool Manufacturing

3323 Architectural and Structural Metals Manufacturing^T
33231 Plate Work and Fabricated Structural Product Manufacturing^T
332311 Prefabricated Metal Building and Component Manufacturing
332312 Fabricated Structural Metal Manufacturing
332313 Plate Work Manufacturing
33232 Ornamental and Architectural Metal Products Manufacturing^T
332321 Metal Window and Door Manufacturing
332322 Sheet Metal Work Manufacturing
332323 Ornamental and Architectural Metal Work Manufacturing

3324 Boiler, Tank, and Shipping Container Manufacturing^T 33241
Power Boiler and Heat Exchanger Manufacturing^T 332410
Power Boiler and Heat Exchanger Manufacturing 33242 Metal Tank (Heavy Gauge) Manufacturing^T 332420 Metal Tank (Heavy Gauge) Manufacturing
33243 Metal Can, Box, and Other Metal Container (Light Gauge) Manufacturing^T
332431 Metal Can Manufacturing
332439 Other Metal Container Manufacturing

3325 Hardware Manufacturing^T 33251
Hardware Manufacturing^T
332510 Hardware Manufacturing

3326 Spring and Wire Product Manufacturing^T 33261
Spring and Wire Product Manufacturing^T 332613
Spring Manufacturing
332618 Other Fabricated Wire Product Manufacturing

3327 Machine Shops; Turned Product; and Screw, Nut, and Bolt Manufacturing^T
33271 Machine Shops^T
332710 Machine Shops
33272 Turned Product and Screw, Nut, and Bolt Manufacturing^T
332721 Precision Turned Product Manufacturing
332722 Bolt, Nut, Screw, Rivet, and Washer Manufacturing

3328 Coating, Engraving, Heat Treating, and Allied Activities^T 33281
Coating, Engraving, Heat Treating, and Allied Activities^T 332811 Metal Heat Treating
332812 Metal Coating, Engraving (except Jewelry and Silverware), and Allied Services to Manufacturers
332813 Electroplating, Plating, Polishing, Anodizing, and Coloring

3329 Other Fabricated Metal Product Manufacturing^T
33291 Metal Valve Manufacturing^T 332911
Industrial Valve Manufacturing
332912 Fluid Power Valve and Hose Fitting Manufacturing
332913 Plumbing Fixture Fitting and Trim Manufacturing

332919 Other Metal Valve and Pipe Fitting Manufacturing
33299 All Other Fabricated Metal Product Manufacturing^T
332991 Ball and Roller Bearing Manufacturing
332992 Small Arms Ammunition Manufacturing
332993 Ammunition (except Small Arms) Manufacturing
332994 Small Arms, Ordnance, and Ordnance Accessories Manufacturing
332996 Fabricated Pipe and Pipe Fitting Manufacturing
332999 All Other Miscellaneous Fabricated Metal Product Manufacturing

333 Machinery Manufacturing^T

3331 Agriculture, Construction, and Mining Machinery Manufacturing^T

33311 Agricultural Implement Manufacturing^T
333111 Farm Machinery and Equipment Manufacturing
333112 Lawn and Garden Tractor and Home Lawn and Garden Equipment Manufacturing
33312 Construction Machinery Manufacturing^T
333120 Construction Machinery Manufacturing
33313 Mining and Oil and Gas Field Machinery Manufacturing^T
333131 Mining Machinery and Equipment Manufacturing
333132 Oil and Gas Field Machinery and Equipment Manufacturing

3332 Industrial Machinery Manufacturing^T 33324 Industrial Machinery Manufacturing^T 333241 Food Product Machinery Manufacturing 333242 Semiconductor Machinery Manufacturing 333243 Sawmill, Woodworking, and Paper Machinery Manufacturing 333244 Printing Machinery and Equipment Manufacturing 333249 Other Industrial Machinery Manufacturing

3333 Commercial and Service Industry Machinery Manufacturing^T 33331 Commercial and Service Industry Machinery Manufacturing^T 333314 Optical Instrument and Lens Manufacturing 333316 Photographic and Photocopying Equipment Manufacturing 333318 Other Commercial and Service Industry Machinery Manufacturing

3334 Ventilation, Heating, Air-Conditioning, and Commercial Refrigeration Equipment Manufacturing^T

33341 Ventilation, Heating, Air-Conditioning, and Commercial Refrigeration Equipment Manufacturing^T
333413 Industrial and Commercial Fan and Blower and Air Purification Equipment Manufacturing
333414 Heating Equipment (except Warm Air Furnaces) Manufacturing 333415 Air-Conditioning and Warm Air Heating Equipment and Commercial and Industrial Refrigeration Equipment Manufacturing

3335 Metalworking Machinery Manufacturing^T 33351 Metalworking Machinery Manufacturing^T 333511 Industrial Mold Manufacturing
333514 Special Die and Tool, Die Set, Jig, and Fixture Manufacturing
333515 Cutting Tool and Machine Tool Accessory Manufacturing
333517 Machine Tool Manufacturing
333519 Rolling Mill and Other Metalworking Machinery Manufacturing

3336 Engine, Turbine, and Power Transmission Equipment Manufacturing^T 33361 Engine, Turbine, and Power Transmission Equipment Manufacturing^T

333611 Turbine and Turbine Generator Set Units Manufacturing
333612 Speed Changer, Industrial High-Speed Drive, and Gear Manufacturing
333613 Mechanical Power Transmission Equipment Manufacturing
333618 Other Engine Equipment Manufacturing

3339 Other General Purpose Machinery Manufacturing[T]
33391 Pump and Compressor Manufacturing[T]
333912 Air and Gas Compressor Manufacturing
333914 Measuring, Dispensing, and Other Pumping Equipment Manufacturing
33392 Material Handling Equipment Manufacturing[T]
333921 Elevator and Moving Stairway Manufacturing
333922 Conveyor and Conveying Equipment Manufacturing
333923 Overhead Traveling Crane, Hoist, and Monorail System Manufacturing
333924 Industrial Truck, Tractor, Trailer, and Stacker Machinery Manufacturing
33399 All Other General Purpose Machinery Manufacturing[T]
333991 Power-Driven Handtool Manufacturing
333992 Welding and Soldering Equipment Manufacturing
333993 Packaging Machinery Manufacturing
333994 Industrial Process Furnace and Oven Manufacturing
333995 Fluid Power Cylinder and Actuator Manufacturing
333996 Fluid Power Pump and Motor Manufacturing
333997 Scale and Balance Manufacturing
333999 All Other Miscellaneous General Purpose Machinery Manufacturing

334 Computer and Electronic Product Manufacturing[T]

3341 Computer and Peripheral Equipment Manufacturing[T] 33411 Computer and Peripheral Equipment Manufacturing[T] 334111 Electronic Computer Manufacturing 334112 Computer Storage Device Manufacturing
334118 Computer Terminal and Other Computer Peripheral Equipment Manufacturing

3342 Communications Equipment Manufacturing[T]
33421 Telephone Apparatus Manufacturing[T]
334210 Telephone Apparatus Manufacturing
33422 Radio and Television Broadcasting and Wireless Communications Equipment Manufacturing[T]
334220 Radio and Television Broadcasting and Wireless Communications Equipment Manufacturing
33429 Other Communications Equipment Manufacturing[T]
334290 Other Communications Equipment Manufacturing

3343 Audio and Video Equipment Manufacturing[T] 33431 Audio and Video Equipment Manufacturing[T] 334310 Audio and Video Equipment Manufacturing

3344 Semiconductor and Other Electronic Component Manufacturing[T] 33441 Semiconductor and Other Electronic Component Manufacturing[T] 334412 Bare Printed Circuit Board Manufacturing 334413 Semiconductor and Related Device Manufacturing 334416 Capacitor, Resistor, Coil, Transformer, and Other Inductor Manufacturing 334417 Electronic Connector Manufacturing 334418 Printed Circuit Assembly (Electronic Assembly) Manufacturing 334419 Other Electronic Component Manufacturing

3345 Navigational, Measuring, Electromedical, and Control Instruments Manufacturing[T]

33451 Navigational, Measuring, Electromedical, and Control Instruments Manufacturing[T]

334510 Electromedical and Electrotherapeutic Apparatus Manufacturing 334511 Search, Detection, Navigation, Guidance, Aeronautical, and Nautical System and Instrument Manufacturing

334512 Automatic Environmental Control Manufacturing for Residential, Commercial, and Appliance Use

334513 Instruments and Related Products Manufacturing for Measuring, Displaying, and Controlling Industrial Process Variables

334514 Totalizing Fluid Meter and Counting Device Manufacturing 334515 Instrument Manufacturing for Measuring and Testing Electricity and Electrical Signals

334516 Analytical Laboratory Instrument Manufacturing

334517 Irradiation Apparatus Manufacturing

334519 Other Measuring and Controlling Device Manufacturing

3346 Manufacturing and Reproducing Magnetic and Optical Media[T] 33461 Manufacturing and Reproducing Magnetic and Optical Media[T] 334613 Blank Magnetic and Optical Recording Media Manufacturing 334614 Software and Other Prerecorded Compact Disc, Tape, and Record Reproducing

335 Electrical Equipment, Appliance, and Component Manufacturing[T]

3351 Electric Lighting Equipment Manufacturing[T] 33511 Electric Lamp Bulb and Part Manufacturing[T] 335110 Electric Lamp Bulb and Part Manufacturing 33512 Lighting Fixture Manufacturing[T]

335121 Residential Electric Lighting Fixture Manufacturing 335122 Commercial, Industrial, and Institutional Electric Lighting Fixture Manufacturing

335129 Other Lighting Equipment Manufacturing

3352 Household Appliance Manufacturing[T]

33521 Small Electrical Appliance Manufacturing[T]

335210 Small Electrical Appliance Manufacturing

33522 Major Household Appliance Manufacturing[T]

335220 Major Household Appliance Manufacturing

3353 Electrical Equipment Manufacturing[T] 33531 Electrical Equipment Manufacturing[T]

335311 Power, Distribution, and Specialty Transformer Manufacturing

335312 Motor and Generator Manufacturing

335313 Switchgear and Switchboard Apparatus Manufacturing

335314 Relay and Industrial Control Manufacturing

3359 Other Electrical Equipment and Component Manufacturing[T]

33591 Battery Manufacturing[T]

335911 Storage Battery Manufacturing

335912 Primary Battery Manufacturing

33592 Communication and Energy Wire and Cable Manufacturing[T]

335921 Fiber Optic Cable Manufacturing

335929 Other Communication and Energy Wire Manufacturing

33593 Wiring Device Manufacturing[T]

335931 Current-Carrying Wiring Device Manufacturing
335932 Noncurrent-Carrying Wiring Device Manufacturing
33599 All Other Electrical Equipment and Component Manufacturing[T]
335991 Carbon and Graphite Product Manufacturing
335999 All Other Miscellaneous Electrical Equipment and Component Manufacturing

336 Transportation Equipment Manufacturing[T]

3361 Motor Vehicle Manufacturing[T]
33611 Automobile and Light Duty Motor Vehicle Manufacturing[T]
336111 Automobile Manufacturing
336112 Light Truck and Utility Vehicle Manufacturing
33612 Heavy Duty Truck Manufacturing[T]
336120 Heavy Duty Truck Manufacturing

3362 Motor Vehicle Body and Trailer Manufacturing[T] 33621 Motor Vehicle Body and Trailer Manufacturing[T] 336211 Motor Vehicle Body Manufacturing 336212 Truck Trailer Manufacturing 336213 Motor Home Manufacturing 336214 Travel Trailer and Camper Manufacturing

3363 Motor Vehicle Parts Manufacturing[T]
33631 Motor Vehicle Gasoline Engine and Engine Parts Manufacturing[T]
336310 Motor Vehicle Gasoline Engine and Engine Parts Manufacturing
33632 Motor Vehicle Electrical and Electronic Equipment Manufacturing[T]
336320 Motor Vehicle Electrical and Electronic Equipment Manufacturing
33633 Motor Vehicle Steering and Suspension Components (except Spring) Manufacturing[T]
336330 Motor Vehicle Steering and Suspension Components (except Spring) Manufacturing
33634 Motor Vehicle Brake System Manufacturing[T]
336340 Motor Vehicle Brake System Manufacturing
33635 Motor Vehicle Transmission and Power Train Parts Manufacturing[T]
336350 Motor Vehicle Transmission and Power Train Parts Manufacturing
33636 Motor Vehicle Seating and Interior Trim Manufacturing[T]
336360 Motor Vehicle Seating and Interior Trim Manufacturing
33637 Motor Vehicle Metal Stamping[T]
336370 Motor Vehicle Metal Stamping
33639 Other Motor Vehicle Parts Manufacturing[T]
336390 Other Motor Vehicle Parts Manufacturing

3364 Aerospace Product and Parts Manufacturing[T] 33641 Aerospace Product and Parts Manufacturing[T] 336411 Aircraft Manufacturing
336412 Aircraft Engine and Engine Parts Manufacturing
336413 Other Aircraft Parts and Auxiliary Equipment Manufacturing
336414 Guided Missile and Space Vehicle Manufacturing
336415 Guided Missile and Space Vehicle Propulsion Unit and Propulsion Unit Parts Manufacturing
336419 Other Guided Missile and Space Vehicle Parts and Auxiliary Equipment Manufacturing

3365 Railroad Rolling Stock Manufacturingᵀ 33651
Railroad Rolling Stock Manufacturingᵀ 336510 Railroad Rolling Stock Manufacturing

3366 Ship and Boat Buildingᵀ 33661 Ship and Boat Buildingᵀ
336611 Ship Building and Repairing
336612 Boat Building

3369 Other Transportation Equipment Manufacturingᵀ 33699
Other Transportation Equipment Manufacturingᵀ 336991 Motorcycle, Bicycle, and Parts Manufacturing
336992 Military Armored Vehicle, Tank, and Tank Component Manufacturing
336999 All Other Transportation Equipment Manufacturing

337 Furniture and Related Product Manufacturingᵀ

3371 Household and Institutional Furniture and Kitchen Cabinet Manufacturingᵀ
33711 Wood Kitchen Cabinet and Countertop Manufacturingᵀ
337110 Wood Kitchen Cabinet and Countertop Manufacturing
33712 Household and Institutional Furniture Manufacturingᵀ
337121 Upholstered Household Furniture Manufacturing
337122 Nonupholstered Wood Household Furniture Manufacturing
337124 Metal Household Furniture Manufacturing
337125 Household Furniture (except Wood and Metal) Manufacturing
337127 Institutional Furniture Manufacturing

3372 Office Furniture (including Fixtures) Manufacturingᵀ 33721
Office Furniture (including Fixtures) Manufacturingᵀ 337211 Wood Office Furniture Manufacturing
337212 Custom Architectural Woodwork and Millwork Manufacturing
337214 Office Furniture (except Wood) Manufacturing
337215 Showcase, Partition, Shelving, and Locker Manufacturing

3379 Other Furniture Related Product Manufacturingᵀ
33791 Mattress Manufacturingᵀ
337910 Mattress Manufacturing
33792 Blind and Shade Manufacturingᵀ
337920 Blind and Shade Manufacturing

339 Miscellaneous Manufacturingᵀ

3391 Medical Equipment and Supplies Manufacturingᵀ 33911
Medical Equipment and Supplies Manufacturingᵀ 339112 Surgical and Medical Instrument Manufacturing 339113 Surgical Appliance and Supplies Manufacturing 339114 Dental Equipment and Supplies Manufacturing 339115 Ophthalmic Goods Manufacturing 339116 Dental Laboratories

3399 Other Miscellaneous Manufacturingᵀ 33991 Jewelry and Silverware Manufacturingᵀ 339910 Jewelry and Silverware Manufacturing 33992 Sporting and Athletic Goods Manufacturingᵀ 339920 Sporting and Athletic Goods Manufacturing

33993 Doll, Toy, and Game Manufacturing[T]
339930 Doll, Toy, and Game Manufacturing
33994 Office Supplies (except Paper) Manufacturing[T]
339940 Office Supplies (except Paper) Manufacturing
33995 Sign Manufacturing[T]
339950 Sign Manufacturing
33999 All Other Miscellaneous Manufacturing[T]
339991 Gasket, Packing, and Sealing Device Manufacturing
339992 Musical Instrument Manufacturing
339993 Fastener, Button, Needle, and Pin Manufacturing
339994 Broom, Brush, and Mop Manufacturing
339995 Burial Casket Manufacturing
339999 All Other Miscellaneous Manufacturing

Sector 42--Wholesale Trade[T]

423 Merchant Wholesalers, Durable Goods

4231 Motor Vehicle and Motor Vehicle Parts and Supplies Merchant Wholesalers
42311 Automobile and Other Motor Vehicle Merchant Wholesalers
423110 Automobile and Other Motor Vehicle Merchant Wholesalers
42312 Motor Vehicle Supplies and New Parts Merchant Wholesalers
423120 Motor Vehicle Supplies and New Parts Merchant Wholesalers
42313 Tire and Tube Merchant Wholesalers
423130 Tire and Tube Merchant Wholesalers
42314 Motor Vehicle Parts (Used) Merchant Wholesalers
423140 Motor Vehicle Parts (Used) Merchant Wholesalers

4232 Furniture and Home Furnishing Merchant Wholesalers
42321 Furniture Merchant Wholesalers
423210 Furniture Merchant Wholesalers
42322 Home Furnishing Merchant Wholesalers
423220 Home Furnishing Merchant Wholesalers

4233 Lumber and Other Construction Materials Merchant Wholesalers 42331
Lumber, Plywood, Millwork, and Wood Panel Merchant Wholesalers
423310 Lumber, Plywood, Millwork, and Wood Panel Merchant Wholesalers
42332 Brick, Stone, and Related Construction Material Merchant Wholesalers
423320 Brick, Stone, and Related Construction Material Merchant Wholesalers
42333 Roofing, Siding, and Insulation Material Merchant Wholesalers
423330 Roofing, Siding, and Insulation Material Merchant Wholesalers
42339 Other Construction Material Merchant Wholesalers
423390 Other Construction Material Merchant Wholesalers

4234 Professional and Commercial Equipment and Supplies Merchant Wholesalers
42341 Photographic Equipment and Supplies Merchant Wholesalers
423410 Photographic Equipment and Supplies Merchant Wholesalers
42342 Office Equipment Merchant Wholesalers
423420 Office Equipment Merchant Wholesalers
42343 Computer and Computer Peripheral Equipment and Software Merchant Wholesalers
423430 Computer and Computer Peripheral Equipment and Software Merchant Wholesalers
42344 Other Commercial Equipment Merchant Wholesalers
423440 Other Commercial Equipment Merchant Wholesalers

42345 Medical, Dental, and Hospital Equipment and Supplies Merchant Wholesalers
423450 Medical, Dental, and Hospital Equipment and Supplies Merchant Wholesalers
42346 Ophthalmic Goods Merchant Wholesalers
423460 Ophthalmic Goods Merchant Wholesalers
42349 Other Professional Equipment and Supplies Merchant Wholesalers
423490 Other Professional Equipment and Supplies Merchant Wholesalers

4235 Metal and Mineral (except Petroleum) Merchant Wholesalers 42351 Metal Service Centers and Other Metal Merchant Wholesalers
423510 Metal Service Centers and Other Metal Merchant Wholesalers
42352 Coal and Other Mineral and Ore Merchant Wholesalers
423520 Coal and Other Mineral and Ore Merchant Wholesalers

4236 Household Appliances and Electrical and Electronic Goods Merchant Wholesalers
42361 Electrical Apparatus and Equipment, Wiring Supplies, and Related Equipment Merchant Wholesalers
423610 Electrical Apparatus and Equipment, Wiring Supplies, and Related Equipment Merchant Wholesalers
42362 Household Appliances, Electric Housewares, and Consumer Electronics Merchant Wholesalers
423620 Household Appliances, Electric Housewares, and Consumer Electronics Merchant Wholesalers
42369 Other Electronic Parts and Equipment Merchant Wholesalers
423690 Other Electronic Parts and Equipment Merchant Wholesalers

4237 Hardware, and Plumbing and Heating Equipment and Supplies Merchant Wholesalers
42371 Hardware Merchant Wholesalers
423710 Hardware Merchant Wholesalers
42372 Plumbing and Heating Equipment and Supplies (Hydronics) Merchant Wholesalers
423720 Plumbing and Heating Equipment and Supplies (Hydronics) Merchant Wholesalers
42373 Warm Air Heating and Air-Conditioning Equipment and Supplies Merchant Wholesalers
423730 Warm Air Heating and Air-Conditioning Equipment and Supplies Merchant Wholesalers
42374 Refrigeration Equipment and Supplies Merchant Wholesalers
423740 Refrigeration Equipment and Supplies Merchant Wholesalers

4238 Machinery, Equipment, and Supplies Merchant Wholesalers 42381 Construction and Mining (except Oil Well) Machinery and Equipment Merchant Wholesalers
423810 Construction and Mining (except Oil Well) Machinery and Equipment Merchant Wholesalers
42382 Farm and Garden Machinery and Equipment Merchant Wholesalers
423820 Farm and Garden Machinery and Equipment Merchant Wholesalers
42383 Industrial Machinery and Equipment Merchant Wholesalers
423830 Industrial Machinery and Equipment Merchant Wholesalers
42384 Industrial Supplies Merchant Wholesalers
423840 Industrial Supplies Merchant Wholesalers
42385 Service Establishment Equipment and Supplies Merchant Wholesalers
423850 Service Establishment Equipment and Supplies Merchant Wholesalers

42386 Transportation Equipment and Supplies (except Motor Vehicle) Merchant Wholesalers
423860 Transportation Equipment and Supplies (except Motor Vehicle) Merchant Wholesalers

4239 Miscellaneous Durable Goods Merchant Wholesalers
42391 Sporting and Recreational Goods and Supplies Merchant Wholesalers
423910 Sporting and Recreational Goods and Supplies Merchant Wholesalers
42392 Toy and Hobby Goods and Supplies Merchant Wholesalers
423920 Toy and Hobby Goods and Supplies Merchant Wholesalers
42393 Recyclable Material Merchant Wholesalers
423930 Recyclable Material Merchant Wholesalers
42394 Jewelry, Watch, Precious Stone, and Precious Metal Merchant Wholesalers
423940 Jewelry, Watch, Precious Stone, and Precious Metal Merchant Wholesalers
42399 Other Miscellaneous Durable Goods Merchant Wholesalers
423990 Other Miscellaneous Durable Goods Merchant Wholesalers

424 Merchant Wholesalers, Nondurable Goods

4241 Paper and Paper Product Merchant Wholesalers 42411 Printing and Writing Paper Merchant Wholesalers
424110 Printing and Writing Paper Merchant Wholesalers
42412 Stationery and Office Supplies Merchant Wholesalers
424120 Stationery and Office Supplies Merchant Wholesalers
42413 Industrial and Personal Service Paper Merchant Wholesalers
424130 Industrial and Personal Service Paper Merchant Wholesalers

4242 Drugs and Druggists' Sundries Merchant Wholesalers 42421 Drugs and Druggists' Sundries Merchant Wholesalers
424210 Drugs and Druggists' Sundries Merchant Wholesalers

4243 Apparel, Piece Goods, and Notions Merchant Wholesalers
42431 Piece Goods, Notions, and Other Dry Goods Merchant Wholesalers
424310 Piece Goods, Notions, and Other Dry Goods Merchant Wholesalers
42432 Men's and Boys' Clothing and Furnishings Merchant Wholesalers
424320 Men's and Boys' Clothing and Furnishings Merchant Wholesalers
42433 Women's, Children's, and Infants' Clothing and Accessories Merchant Wholesalers
424330 Women's, Children's, and Infants' Clothing and Accessories Merchant Wholesalers
42434 Footwear Merchant Wholesalers
424340 Footwear Merchant Wholesalers

4244 Grocery and Related Product Merchant Wholesalers 42441 General Line Grocery Merchant Wholesalers 424410 General Line Grocery Merchant Wholesalers 42442 Packaged Frozen Food Merchant Wholesalers 424420 Packaged Frozen Food Merchant Wholesalers 42443 Dairy Product (except Dried or Canned) Merchant Wholesalers 424430 Dairy Product (except Dried or Canned) Merchant Wholesalers 42444 Poultry and Poultry Product Merchant Wholesalers 424440 Poultry and Poultry Product Merchant Wholesalers 42445 Confectionery Merchant Wholesalers 424450 Confectionery Merchant Wholesalers 42446 Fish and Seafood Merchant Wholesalers 424460 Fish and Seafood Merchant Wholesalers

42447 Meat and Meat Product Merchant Wholesalers
424470 Meat and Meat Product Merchant Wholesalers
42448 Fresh Fruit and Vegetable Merchant Wholesalers
424480 Fresh Fruit and Vegetable Merchant Wholesalers
42449 Other Grocery and Related Products Merchant Wholesalers
424490 Other Grocery and Related Products Merchant Wholesalers

4245 Farm Product Raw Material Merchant Wholesalers
42451 Grain and Field Bean Merchant Wholesalers
424510 Grain and Field Bean Merchant Wholesalers
42452 Livestock Merchant Wholesalers
424520 Livestock Merchant Wholesalers
42459 Other Farm Product Raw Material Merchant Wholesalers
424590 Other Farm Product Raw Material Merchant Wholesalers

4246 Chemical and Allied Products Merchant Wholesalers
42461 Plastics Materials and Basic Forms and Shapes Merchant Wholesalers
424610 Plastics Materials and Basic Forms and Shapes Merchant Wholesalers
42469 Other Chemical and Allied Products Merchant Wholesalers
424690 Other Chemical and Allied Products Merchant Wholesalers

4247 Petroleum and Petroleum Products Merchant Wholesalers
42471 Petroleum Bulk Stations and Terminals
424710 Petroleum Bulk Stations and Terminals
42472 Petroleum and Petroleum Products Merchant Wholesalers (except Bulk Stations and Terminals)
424720 Petroleum and Petroleum Products Merchant Wholesalers (except Bulk Stations and Terminals)

4248 Beer, Wine, and Distilled Alcoholic Beverage Merchant Wholesalers
42481 Beer and Ale Merchant Wholesalers
424810 Beer and Ale Merchant Wholesalers
42482 Wine and Distilled Alcoholic Beverage Merchant Wholesalers
424820 Wine and Distilled Alcoholic Beverage Merchant Wholesalers

4249 Miscellaneous Nondurable Goods Merchant Wholesalers
42491 Farm Supplies Merchant Wholesalers
424910 Farm Supplies Merchant Wholesalers
42492 Book, Periodical, and Newspaper Merchant Wholesalers
424920 Book, Periodical, and Newspaper Merchant Wholesalers
42493 Flower, Nursery Stock, and Florists' Supplies Merchant Wholesalers
424930 Flower, Nursery Stock, and Florists' Supplies Merchant Wholesalers
42494 Tobacco and Tobacco Product Merchant Wholesalers
424940 Tobacco and Tobacco Product Merchant Wholesalers
42495 Paint, Varnish, and Supplies Merchant Wholesalers
424950 Paint, Varnish, and Supplies Merchant Wholesalers
42499 Other Miscellaneous Nondurable Goods Merchant Wholesalers
424990 Other Miscellaneous Nondurable Goods Merchant Wholesalers

425 Wholesale Electronic Markets and Agents and Brokers

4251 Wholesale Electronic Markets and Agents and Brokers
42511 Business to Business Electronic Markets 425110 Business to Business Electronic Markets 42512 Wholesale Trade Agents and Brokers 425120 Wholesale Trade Agents and Brokers

Sector 44-45--Retail Trade[T] 441 Mo-

tor Vehicle and Parts Dealers

4411 **Automobile Dealers** 44111
New Car Dealers
441110 New Car Dealers
44112 Used Car Dealers
441120 Used Car Dealers

4412 **Other Motor Vehicle Dealers** 44121
Recreational Vehicle Dealers
441210 Recreational Vehicle Dealers
44122 Motorcycle, Boat, and Other Motor Vehicle Dealers
441222 Boat Dealers
441228 Motorcycle, ATV, and All Other Motor Vehicle Dealers

4413 **Automotive Parts, Accessories, and Tire Stores**
44131 Automotive Parts and Accessories Stores
441310 Automotive Parts and Accessories Stores
44132 Tire Dealers
441320 Tire Dealers

442 Furniture and Home Furnishings Stores

4421 **Furniture Stores** 44211
Furniture Stores
442110 Furniture Stores

4422 **Home Furnishings Stores** 44221
Floor Covering Stores
442210 Floor Covering Stores
44229 Other Home Furnishings Stores
442291 Window Treatment Stores
442299 All Other Home Furnishings Stores

443 Electronics and Appliance Stores

4431 **Electronics and Appliance Stores**
44314 Electronics and Appliance Stores
443141 Household Appliance Stores
443142 Electronics Stores

444 Building Material and Garden Equipment and Supplies Dealers

4441 **Building Material and Supplies Dealers**
44411 Home Centers
444110 Home Centers
44412 Paint and Wallpaper Stores
444120 Paint and Wallpaper Stores
44413 Hardware Stores
444130 Hardware Stores
44419 Other Building Material Dealers
444190 Other Building Material Dealers

4442 Lawn and Garden Equipment and Supplies Stores
44421 Outdoor Power Equipment Stores
444210 Outdoor Power Equipment Stores
44422 Nursery, Garden Center, and Farm Supply Stores
444220 Nursery, Garden Center, and Farm Supply Stores

445 Food and Beverage Stores

4451 Grocery Stores
44511 Supermarkets and Other Grocery (except Convenience) Stores
445110 Supermarkets and Other Grocery (except Convenience) Stores
44512 Convenience Stores
445120 Convenience Stores

4452 Specialty Food Stores
44521 Meat Markets
445210 Meat Markets
44522 Fish and Seafood Markets
445220 Fish and Seafood Markets
44523 Fruit and Vegetable Markets
445230 Fruit and Vegetable Markets
44529 Other Specialty Food Stores
445291 Baked Goods Stores
445292 Confectionery and Nut Stores
445299 All Other Specialty Food Stores

4453 Beer, Wine, and Liquor Stores 44531
Beer, Wine, and Liquor Stores
445310 Beer, Wine, and Liquor Stores

446 Health and Personal Care Stores

4461 Health and Personal Care Stores
44611 Pharmacies and Drug Stores
446110 Pharmacies and Drug Stores
44612 Cosmetics, Beauty Supplies, and Perfume Stores
446120 Cosmetics, Beauty Supplies, and Perfume Stores
44613 Optical Goods Stores
446130 Optical Goods Stores
44619 Other Health and Personal Care Stores
446191 Food (Health) Supplement Stores
446199 All Other Health and Personal Care Stores

447 Gasoline Stations

4471 Gasoline Stations
44711 Gasoline Stations with Convenience Stores
447110 Gasoline Stations with Convenience Stores
44719 Other Gasoline Stations
447190 Other Gasoline Stations

448 Clothing and Clothing Accessories Stores

4481 Clothing Stores 44811 Men's
Clothing Stores

448110 Men's Clothing Stores
44812 Women's Clothing Stores
448120 Women's Clothing Stores
44813 Children's and Infants' Clothing Stores
448130 Children's and Infants' Clothing Stores
44814 Family Clothing Stores
448140 Family Clothing Stores
44815 Clothing Accessories Stores
448150 Clothing Accessories Stores
44819 Other Clothing Stores
448190 Other Clothing Stores

4482 Shoe Stores 44821
Shoe Stores
448210 Shoe Stores

4483 Jewelry, Luggage, and Leather Goods Stores
44831 Jewelry Stores
448310 Jewelry Stores
44832 Luggage and Leather Goods Stores
448320 Luggage and Leather Goods Stores

451 Sporting Goods, Hobby, Musical Instrument, and Book Stores

4511 Sporting Goods, Hobby, and Musical Instrument Stores
45111 Sporting Goods Stores
451110 Sporting Goods Stores
45112 Hobby, Toy, and Game Stores
451120 Hobby, Toy, and Game Stores
45113 Sewing, Needlework, and Piece Goods Stores
451130 Sewing, Needlework, and Piece Goods Stores
45114 Musical Instrument and Supplies Stores
451140 Musical Instrument and Supplies Stores

4512 Book Stores and News Dealers 45121
Book Stores and News Dealers 451211
Book Stores
451212 News Dealers and Newsstands

452 General Merchandise Stores

4522 Department Stores 45221
Department Stores
452210 Department Stores

4523 General Merchandise Stores, including Warehouse Clubs and Supercenters
45231 General Merchandise Stores, including Warehouse Clubs and Supercenters
452311 Warehouse Clubs and Supercenters 452319 All Other General Merchandise Stores

453 Miscellaneous Store Retailers

4531 Florists 45311
Florists
453110 Florists

4532 Office Supplies, Stationery, and Gift Stores
45321 Office Supplies and Stationery Stores
453210 Office Supplies and Stationery Stores
45322 Gift, Novelty, and Souvenir Stores
453220 Gift, Novelty, and Souvenir Stores

4533 Used Merchandise Stores 45331
Used Merchandise Stores
453310 Used Merchandise Stores

4539 Other Miscellaneous Store Retailers
45391 Pet and Pet Supplies Stores
453910 Pet and Pet Supplies Stores
45392 Art Dealers
453920 Art Dealers
45393 Manufactured (Mobile) Home Dealers
453930 Manufactured (Mobile) Home Dealers
45399 All Other Miscellaneous Store Retailers
453991 Tobacco Stores
453998 All Other Miscellaneous Store Retailers (except Tobacco Stores)

454 Nonstore Retailers

4541 Electronic Shopping and Mail-Order Houses 45411
Electronic Shopping and Mail-Order Houses
454110 Electronic Shopping and Mail-Order Houses

4542 Vending Machine Operators 45421
Vending Machine Operators
454210 Vending Machine Operators

4543 Direct Selling Establishments
45431 Fuel Dealers
454310 Fuel Dealers
45439 Other Direct Selling Establishments
454390 Other Direct Selling Establishments

Sector 48-49--Transportation and Warehousing[T]

481 Air Transportation[T]

4811 Scheduled Air Transportation[T] 48111 Scheduled Air Transportation[T] 481111 Scheduled Passenger Air Transportation 481112 Scheduled Freight Air Transportation

4812 Nonscheduled Air Transportation[T] 48121
Nonscheduled Air Transportation[T]
481211 Nonscheduled Chartered Passenger Air Transportation
481212 Nonscheduled Chartered Freight Air Transportation
481219 Other Nonscheduled Air Transportation

482 Rail Transportation[T]

4821 Rail Transportation[T] 48211 Rail Transportation[T]
482111 Line-Haul Railroads
482112 Short Line Railroads

483 Water Transportation[T]

4831 Deep Sea, Coastal, and Great Lakes Water Transportation[T] 48311 Deep Sea, Coastal, and Great Lakes Water Transportation[T] 483111 Deep Sea Freight Transportation 483112 Deep Sea Passenger Transportation 483113 Coastal and Great Lakes Freight Transportation 483114 Coastal and Great Lakes Passenger Transportation

4832 Inland Water Transportation[T] 48321 Inland Water Transportation[T] 483211 Inland Water Freight Transportation 483212 Inland Water Passenger Transportation

484 Truck Transportation[T]

4841 General Freight Trucking[T]
48411 General Freight Trucking, Local[T]
484110 General Freight Trucking, Local
48412 General Freight Trucking, Long-Distance[T]
484121 General Freight Trucking, Long-Distance, Truckload
484122 General Freight Trucking, Long-Distance, Less Than Truckload

4842 Specialized Freight Trucking[T]
48421 Used Household and Office Goods Moving[T]
484210 Used Household and Office Goods Moving
48422 Specialized Freight (except Used Goods) Trucking, Local[T]
484220 Specialized Freight (except Used Goods) Trucking, Local
48423 Specialized Freight (except Used Goods) Trucking, Long-Distance[T]
484230 Specialized Freight (except Used Goods) Trucking, Long-Distance

485 Transit and Ground Passenger Transportation[T]

4851 Urban Transit Systems[T] 48511 Urban Transit Systems[T]
485111 Mixed Mode Transit Systems
485112 Commuter Rail Systems
485113 Bus and Other Motor Vehicle Transit Systems
485119 Other Urban Transit Systems

4852 Interurban and Rural Bus Transportation[T] 48521 Interurban and Rural Bus Transportation[T] 485210 Interurban and Rural Bus Transportation

4853 Taxi and Limousine Service[T]
48531 Taxi Service[T] 485310 Taxi Service

48532 Limousine Service^T
485320 Limousine Service

4854 School and Employee Bus Transportation^T 48541
School and Employee Bus Transportation^T 485410
School and Employee Bus Transportation

4855 Charter Bus Industry^T 48551
Charter Bus Industry^T
485510 Charter Bus Industry

4859 Other Transit and Ground Passenger Transportation^T 48599
Other Transit and Ground Passenger Transportation^T 485991
Special Needs Transportation
485999 All Other Transit and Ground Passenger Transportation

486 Pipeline Transportation^T

4861 Pipeline Transportation of Crude Oil^T 48611
Pipeline Transportation of Crude Oil^T 486110
Pipeline Transportation of Crude Oil

4862 Pipeline Transportation of Natural Gas^T 48621
Pipeline Transportation of Natural Gas^T 486210
Pipeline Transportation of Natural Gas

4869 Other Pipeline Transportation^T
48691 Pipeline Transportation of Refined Petroleum Products^T
486910 Pipeline Transportation of Refined Petroleum Products
48699 All Other Pipeline Transportation^T
486990 All Other Pipeline Transportation

487 Scenic and Sightseeing Transportation^T

4871 Scenic and Sightseeing Transportation, Land^T 48711
Scenic and Sightseeing Transportation, Land^T 487110 Scenic and Sightseeing Transportation, Land

4872 Scenic and Sightseeing Transportation, Water^T 48721
Scenic and Sightseeing Transportation, Water^T 487210 Scenic and Sightseeing Transportation, Water

4879 Scenic and Sightseeing Transportation, Other^T 48799
Scenic and Sightseeing Transportation, Other^T 487990
Scenic and Sightseeing Transportation, Other

488 Support Activities for Transportation^T

4881 Support Activities for Air Transportation^T
48811 Airport Operations^T
488111 Air Traffic Control
488119 Other Airport Operations
48819 Other Support Activities for Air Transportation^T
488190 Other Support Activities for Air Transportation

4882 Support Activities for Rail TransportationT 48821 Support Activities for Rail TransportationT 488210 Support Activities for Rail Transportation

4883 Support Activities for Water TransportationT
48831 Port and Harbor OperationsT
488310 Port and Harbor Operations
48832 Marine Cargo HandlingT
488320 Marine Cargo Handling
48833 Navigational Services to ShippingT
488330 Navigational Services to Shipping
48839 Other Support Activities for Water TransportationT
488390 Other Support Activities for Water Transportation

4884 Support Activities for Road TransportationT
48841 Motor Vehicle TowingT
488410 Motor Vehicle Towing
48849 Other Support Activities for Road TransportationT
488490 Other Support Activities for Road Transportation

4885 Freight Transportation ArrangementT 48851 Freight Transportation ArrangementT 488510 Freight Transportation Arrangement

4889 Other Support Activities for TransportationT 48899 Other Support Activities for TransportationT 488991 Packing and Crating
488999 All Other Support Activities for Transportation

491 Postal ServiceT

4911 Postal ServiceT
49111 Postal ServiceT
491110 Postal Service

492 Couriers and MessengersT

4921 Couriers and Express Delivery ServicesT 49211 Couriers and Express Delivery ServicesT 492110 Couriers and Express Delivery Services

4922 Local Messengers and Local DeliveryT 49221 Local Messengers and Local DeliveryT 492210 Local Messengers and Local Delivery

493 Warehousing and StorageT

4931 Warehousing and StorageT 49311 General Warehousing and StorageT 493110 General Warehousing and Storage 49312 Refrigerated Warehousing and StorageT 493120 Refrigerated Warehousing and Storage 49313 Farm Product Warehousing and StorageT 493130 Farm Product Warehousing and Storage

49319 Other Warehousing and Storage[T]
493190 Other Warehousing and Storage

Sector 51--Information[T]

511 Publishing Industries (except Internet)[T]

5111 Newspaper, Periodical, Book, and Directory Publishers[T]

51111 Newspaper Publishers[T]
511110 Newspaper Publishers
51112 Periodical Publishers[T]
511120 Periodical Publishers
51113 Book Publishers[T]
511130 Book Publishers
51114 Directory and Mailing List Publishers[T]
511140 Directory and Mailing List Publishers
51119 Other Publishers[T]
511191 Greeting Card Publishers
511199 All Other Publishers

5112 Software Publishers[T]

51121 Software Publishers[T]
511210 Software Publishers

512 Motion Picture and Sound Recording Industries[T]

5121 Motion Picture and Video Industries[T]

51211 Motion Picture and Video Production[T]
512110 Motion Picture and Video Production
51212 Motion Picture and Video Distribution[T]
512120 Motion Picture and Video Distribution
51213 Motion Picture and Video Exhibition[T]
512131 Motion Picture Theaters (except Drive-Ins)
512132 Drive-In Motion Picture Theaters
51219 Postproduction Services and Other Motion Picture and Video Industries[T]
512191 Teleproduction and Other Postproduction Services
512199 Other Motion Picture and Video Industries

5122 Sound Recording Industries[T]

51223 Music Publishers[T]
512230 Music Publishers
51224 Sound Recording Studios[T]
512240 Sound Recording Studios
51225 Record Production and Distribution[T]
512250 Record Production and Distribution
51229 Other Sound Recording Industries[T]
512290 Other Sound Recording Industries

515 Broadcasting (except Internet)[T]

5151 Radio and Television Broadcasting[T]

51511 Radio Broadcasting[T]
515111 Radio Networks
515112 Radio Stations

51512 Television Broadcasting[T]
515120 Television Broadcasting

5152 Cable and Other Subscription Programming[T] 51521 Cable and Other Subscription Programming[T] 515210 Cable and Other Subscription Programming

517 Telecommunications[T]

5173 Wired and Wireless Telecommunications Carriers[T] 51731 Wired and Wireless Telecommunications Carriers[T] 517311 Wired Telecommunications Carriers
517312 Wireless Telecommunications Carriers (except Satellite)

5174 Satellite Telecommunications[T] 51741 Satellite Telecommunications[T]
517410 Satellite Telecommunications

5179 Other Telecommunications[T] 51791 Other Telecommunications[T]
517911 Telecommunications Resellers
517919 All Other Telecommunications

518 Data Processing, Hosting, and Related Services[T]

5182 Data Processing, Hosting, and Related Services[T] 51821 Data Processing, Hosting, and Related Services[T] 518210 Data Processing, Hosting, and Related Services

519 Other Information Services[T]

5191 Other Information Services[T]
51911 News Syndicates[T]
519110 News Syndicates
51912 Libraries and Archives[T]
519120 Libraries and Archives
51913 Internet Publishing and Broadcasting and Web Search Portals[T]
519130 Internet Publishing and Broadcasting and Web Search Portals
51919 All Other Information Services[T]
519190 All Other Information Services

Sector 52--Finance and Insurance[T] 521

Monetary Authorities-Central Bank[T]

5211 Monetary Authorities-Central Bank[T] 52111 Monetary Authorities-Central Bank[T] 521110 Monetary Authorities-Central Bank

522 Credit Intermediation and Related Activities[T]

5221 Depository Credit Intermediation
52211 Commercial Banking 522110 Commercial Banking

52212 Savings Institutions
522120 Savings Institutions
52213 Credit Unions
522130 Credit Unions
52219 Other Depository Credit Intermediation
522190 Other Depository Credit Intermediation

5222 Nondepository Credit Intermediation
52221 Credit Card Issuing
522210 Credit Card Issuing
52222 Sales Financing
522220 Sales Financing
52229 Other Nondepository Credit Intermediation
522291 Consumer Lending
522292 Real Estate Credit
522293 International Trade Financing
522294 Secondary Market Financing
522298 All Other Nondepository Credit Intermediation

5223 Activities Related to Credit Intermediation 52231
Mortgage and Nonmortgage Loan Brokers
522310 Mortgage and Nonmortgage Loan Brokers
52232 Financial Transactions Processing, Reserve, and Clearinghouse Activities
522320 Financial Transactions Processing, Reserve, and Clearinghouse Activities
52239 Other Activities Related to Credit Intermediation
522390 Other Activities Related to Credit Intermediation

523 Securities, Commodity Contracts, and Other Financial Investments and Related Activities[T]

5231 Securities and Commodity Contracts Intermediation and Brokerage[T]
52311 Investment Banking and Securities Dealing
523110 Investment Banking and Securities Dealing
52312 Securities Brokerage
523120 Securities Brokerage
52313 Commodity Contracts Dealing
523130 Commodity Contracts Dealing
52314 Commodity Contracts Brokerage
523140 Commodity Contracts Brokerage

5232 Securities and Commodity Exchanges[T] 52321
Securities and Commodity Exchanges[T] 523210 Securities and Commodity Exchanges

5239 Other Financial Investment Activities[T]
52391 Miscellaneous Intermediation
523910 Miscellaneous Intermediation
52392 Portfolio Management
523920 Portfolio Management
52393 Investment Advice
523930 Investment Advice
52399 All Other Financial Investment Activities
523991 Trust, Fiduciary, and Custody Activities
523999 Miscellaneous Financial Investment Activities

524 Insurance Carriers and Related Activities[T]

5241 Insurance Carriers[T]
52411 Direct Life, Health, and Medical Insurance Carriers
524113 Direct Life Insurance Carriers
524114 Direct Health and Medical Insurance Carriers
52412 Direct Insurance (except Life, Health, and Medical) Carriers
524126 Direct Property and Casualty Insurance Carriers
524127 Direct Title Insurance Carriers
524128 Other Direct Insurance (except Life, Health, and Medical) Carriers
52413 Reinsurance Carriers
524130 Reinsurance Carriers

5242 Agencies, Brokerages, and Other Insurance Related Activities[T]
52421 Insurance Agencies and Brokerages
524210 Insurance Agencies and Brokerages
52429 Other Insurance Related Activities
524291 Claims Adjusting
524292 Third Party Administration of Insurance and Pension Funds
524298 All Other Insurance Related Activities

525 Funds, Trusts, and Other Financial Vehicles

5251 Insurance and Employee Benefit Funds
52511 Pension Funds
525110 Pension Funds
52512 Health and Welfare Funds
525120 Health and Welfare Funds
52519 Other Insurance Funds
525190 Other Insurance Funds

5259 Other Investment Pools and Funds
52591 Open-End Investment Funds
525910 Open-End Investment Funds
52592 Trusts, Estates, and Agency Accounts
525920 Trusts, Estates, and Agency Accounts
52599 Other Financial Vehicles
525990 Other Financial Vehicles

Sector 53--Real Estate and Rental and Leasing[T]

531 Real Estate[T]

5311 Lessors of Real Estate[T] 53111 Lessors of Residential Buildings and Dwellings 531110 Lessors of Residential Buildings and Dwellings 53112 Lessors of Nonresidential Buildings (except Miniwarehouses) 531120 Lessors of Nonresidential Buildings (except Miniwarehouses) 53113 Lessors of Miniwarehouses and Self-Storage Units 531130 Lessors of Miniwarehouses and Self-Storage Units 53119 Lessors of Other Real Estate Property 531190 Lessors of Other Real Estate Property

5312 **Offices of Real Estate Agents and Brokers**[T] 53121 Offices of Real Estate Agents and Brokers[T] 531210 Offices of Real Estate Agents and Brokers

5313 **Activities Related to Real Estate**[T] 53131 Real Estate Property Managers
531311 Residential Property Managers
531312 Nonresidential Property Managers
53132 Offices of Real Estate Appraisers
531320 Offices of Real Estate Appraisers
53139 Other Activities Related to Real Estate
531390 Other Activities Related to Real Estate

532 Rental and Leasing Services[T]

5321 **Automotive Equipment Rental and Leasing**[T]
53211 Passenger Car Rental and Leasing[T]
532111 Passenger Car Rental
532112 Passenger Car Leasing
53212 Truck, Utility Trailer, and RV (Recreational Vehicle) Rental and Leasing[T]
532120 Truck, Utility Trailer, and RV (Recreational Vehicle) Rental and Leasing

5322 **Consumer Goods Rental**[T]
53221 Consumer Electronics and Appliances Rental[T]
532210 Consumer Electronics and Appliances Rental
53228 Other Consumer Goods Rental[T]
532281 Formal Wear and Costume Rental
532282 Video Tape and Disc Rental
532283 Home Health Equipment Rental
532284 Recreational Goods Rental
532289 All Other Consumer Goods Rental

5323 **General Rental Centers**[T] 53231 General Rental Centers[T]
532310 General Rental Centers

5324 **Commercial and Industrial Machinery and Equipment Rental and Leasing**[T] 53241 Construction, Transportation, Mining, and Forestry Machinery and Equipment Rental and Leasing[T]
532411 Commercial Air, Rail, and Water Transportation Equipment Rental and Leasing
532412 Construction, Mining, and Forestry Machinery and Equipment Rental and Leasing
53242 Office Machinery and Equipment Rental and Leasing[T]
532420 Office Machinery and Equipment Rental and Leasing
53249 Other Commercial and Industrial Machinery and Equipment Rental and Leasing[T]
532490 Other Commercial and Industrial Machinery and Equipment Rental and Leasing

533 Lessors of Nonfinancial Intangible Assets (except Copyrighted Works)[T]

5331 **Lessors of Nonfinancial Intangible Assets (except Copyrighted Works)**[T] 53311 Lessors of Nonfinancial Intangible Assets (except Copyrighted Works)[T] 533110 Lessors of Nonfinancial Intangible Assets (except Copyrighted Works)

Sector 54--Professional, Scientific, and Technical Services[T] 541

Professional, Scientific, and Technical Services[T]

5411 Legal Services[T]
54111 Offices of Lawyers[T]
541110 Offices of Lawyers
54112 Offices of Notaries[T]
541120 Offices of Notaries
54119 Other Legal Services[T]
541191 Title Abstract and Settlement Offices
541199 All Other Legal Services

5412 Accounting, Tax Preparation, Bookkeeping, and Payroll Services[T]
54121 Accounting, Tax Preparation, Bookkeeping, and Payroll Services[T]
541211 Offices of Certified Public Accountants
541213 Tax Preparation Services
541214 Payroll Services
541219 Other Accounting Services

5413 Architectural, Engineering, and Related Services[T]
54131 Architectural Services[T]
541310 Architectural Services
54132 Landscape Architectural Services[T]
541320 Landscape Architectural Services
54133 Engineering Services[T]
541330 Engineering Services
54134 Drafting Services[T]
541340 Drafting Services
54135 Building Inspection Services[T]
541350 Building Inspection Services
54136 Geophysical Surveying and Mapping Services[T]
541360 Geophysical Surveying and Mapping Services
54137 Surveying and Mapping (except Geophysical) Services[T]
541370 Surveying and Mapping (except Geophysical) Services
54138 Testing Laboratories[T]
541380 Testing Laboratories

5414 Specialized Design Services[T]
54141 Interior Design Services[T]
541410 Interior Design Services
54142 Industrial Design Services[T]
541420 Industrial Design Services
54143 Graphic Design Services[T]
541430 Graphic Design Services
54149 Other Specialized Design Services[T]
541490 Other Specialized Design Services

5415 Computer Systems Design and Related Services[T] 54151 Computer Systems Design and Related Services[T] 541511 Custom Computer Programming Services 541512 Computer Systems Design Services 541513 Computer Facilities Management Services 541519 Other Computer Related Services

5416 Management, Scientific, and Technical Consulting Services[T]
54161 Management Consulting Services[T]
541611 Administrative Management and General Management Consulting Services
541612 Human Resources Consulting Services
541613 Marketing Consulting Services
541614 Process, Physical Distribution, and Logistics Consulting Services
541618 Other Management Consulting Services
54162 Environmental Consulting Services[T]
541620 Environmental Consulting Services
54169 Other Scientific and Technical Consulting Services[T]
541690 Other Scientific and Technical Consulting Services

5417 Scientific Research and Development Services[T]
54171 Research and Development in the Physical, Engineering, and Life Sciences[T]
541713 Research and Development in Nanotechnology
541714 Research and Development in Biotechnology (except Nanobiotechnology)
541715 Research and Development in the Physical, Engineering, and Life Sciences (except Nanotechnology and Biotechnology)
54172 Research and Development in the Social Sciences and Humanities[T]
541720 Research and Development in the Social Sciences and Humanities

5418 Advertising, Public Relations, and Related Services[T]
54181 Advertising Agencies[T]
541810 Advertising Agencies
54182 Public Relations Agencies[T]
541820 Public Relations Agencies
54183 Media Buying Agencies[T]
541830 Media Buying Agencies
54184 Media Representatives[T]
541840 Media Representatives
54185 Outdoor Advertising[T]
541850 Outdoor Advertising
54186 Direct Mail Advertising[T]
541860 Direct Mail Advertising
54187 Advertising Material Distribution Services[T]
541870 Advertising Material Distribution Services
54189 Other Services Related to Advertising[T]
541890 Other Services Related to Advertising

5419 Other Professional, Scientific, and Technical Services[T] 54191 Marketing Research and Public Opinion Polling[T] 541910 Marketing Research and Public Opinion Polling 54192 Photographic Services[T] 541921 Photography Studios, Portrait 541922 Commercial Photography 54193 Translation and Interpretation Services[T] 541930 Translation and Interpretation Services 54194 Veterinary Services[T] 541940 Veterinary Services
54199 All Other Professional, Scientific, and Technical Services[T]
541990 All Other Professional, Scientific, and Technical Services

Sector 55--Management of Companies and Enterprises[T] 551

Management of Companies and Enterprises[T]

5511 **Management of Companies and Enterprises[T]** 55111 Management of Companies and Enterprises[T] 551111 Offices of Bank Holding Companies 551112 Offices of Other Holding Companies 551114 Corporate, Subsidiary, and Regional Managing Offices

Sector 56--Administrative and Support and Waste Management and Remediation Services[T]

561 Administrative and Support Services[T]

5611 **Office Administrative Services[T]** 56111 Office Administrative Services[T] 561110 Office Administrative Services

5612 **Facilities Support Services[T]** 56121 Facilities Support Services[T]
561210 Facilities Support Services

5613 **Employment Services[T]**
56131 Employment Placement Agencies and Executive Search Services[T]
561311 Employment Placement Agencies
561312 Executive Search Services
56132 Temporary Help Services[T]
561320 Temporary Help Services
56133 Professional Employer Organizations[T]
561330 Professional Employer Organizations

5614 **Business Support Services[T]**
56141 Document Preparation Services[T]
561410 Document Preparation Services
56142 Telephone Call Centers[T]
561421 Telephone Answering Services
561422 Telemarketing Bureaus and Other Contact Centers
56143 Business Service Centers[T]
561431 Private Mail Centers
561439 Other Business Service Centers (including Copy Shops)
56144 Collection Agencies[T]
561440 Collection Agencies
56145 Credit Bureaus[T]
561450 Credit Bureaus
56149 Other Business Support Services[T]
561491 Repossession Services
561492 Court Reporting and Stenotype Services
561499 All Other Business Support Services

5615 **Travel Arrangement and Reservation Services[T]**
56151 Travel Agencies[T] 561510 Travel Agencies

56152 Tour Operators[T]
561520 Tour Operators
56159 Other Travel Arrangement and Reservation Services[T]
561591 Convention and Visitors Bureaus
561599 All Other Travel Arrangement and Reservation Services

5616 Investigation and Security Services[T]
56161 Investigation, Guard, and Armored Car Services[T]
561611 Investigation Services
561612 Security Guards and Patrol Services
561613 Armored Car Services
56162 Security Systems Services[T]
561621 Security Systems Services (except Locksmiths)
561622 Locksmiths

5617 Services to Buildings and Dwellings[T]
56171 Exterminating and Pest Control Services[T]
561710 Exterminating and Pest Control Services
56172 Janitorial Services[T]
561720 Janitorial Services
56173 Landscaping Services[T]
561730 Landscaping Services
56174 Carpet and Upholstery Cleaning Services[T]
561740 Carpet and Upholstery Cleaning Services
56179 Other Services to Buildings and Dwellings[T]
561790 Other Services to Buildings and Dwellings

5619 Other Support Services[T]
56191 Packaging and Labeling Services[T]
561910 Packaging and Labeling Services
56192 Convention and Trade Show Organizers[T]
561920 Convention and Trade Show Organizers
56199 All Other Support Services[T]
561990 All Other Support Services

562 Waste Management and Remediation Services[T]

5621 Waste Collection 56211
Waste Collection
562111 Solid Waste Collection
562112 Hazardous Waste Collection
562119 Other Waste Collection

5622 Waste Treatment and Disposal 56221 Waste Treatment and Disposal 562211 Hazardous Waste Treatment and Disposal 562212 Solid Waste Landfill 562213 Solid Waste Combustors and Incinerators 562219 Other Nonhazardous Waste Treatment and Disposal

5629 Remediation and Other Waste Management Services
56291 Remediation Services 562910 Remediation Services 56292 Materials Recovery Facilities 562920 Materials Recovery Facilities 56299 All Other Waste Management Services

562991 Septic Tank and Related Services
562998 All Other Miscellaneous Waste Management Services

Sector 61--Educational Services[T]

611 Educational Services[T]

6111 Elementary and Secondary Schools[T] 61111 Elementary and Secondary Schools
611110 Elementary and Secondary Schools

6112 Junior Colleges[T]
61121 Junior Colleges[T]
611210 Junior Colleges

6113 Colleges, Universities, and Professional Schools[T] 61131 Colleges, Universities, and Professional Schools[T] 611310 Colleges, Universities, and Professional Schools

6114 Business Schools and Computer and Management Training[T]
61141 Business and Secretarial Schools[T]
611410 Business and Secretarial Schools
61142 Computer Training[T]
611420 Computer Training
61143 Professional and Management Development Training[T]
611430 Professional and Management Development Training

6115 Technical and Trade Schools[T] 61151 Technical and Trade Schools[T] 611511 Cosmetology and Barber Schools 611512 Flight Training 611513 Apprenticeship Training 611519 Other Technical and Trade Schools

6116 Other Schools and Instruction[T]
61161 Fine Arts Schools[T] 611610 Fine Arts Schools
61162 Sports and Recreation Instruction[T]
611620 Sports and Recreation Instruction
61163 Language Schools[T]
611630 Language Schools
61169 All Other Schools and Instruction[T]
611691 Exam Preparation and Tutoring
611692 Automobile Driving Schools
611699 All Other Miscellaneous Schools and Instruction

6117 Educational Support Services[T] 61171 Educational Support Services[T] 611710 Educational Support Services

Sector 62--Health Care and Social Assistance[T] 621

Ambulatory Health Care Services[T]

6211 Offices of Physicians[T]
62111 Offices of Physicians[T]
621111 Offices of Physicians (except Mental Health Specialists)
621112 Offices of Physicians, Mental Health Specialists

6212 Offices of Dentists[T]
62121 Offices of Dentists[T]
621210 Offices of Dentists

6213 Offices of Other Health Practitioners[T]
62131 Offices of Chiropractors[T]
621310 Offices of Chiropractors
62132 Offices of Optometrists[T]
621320 Offices of Optometrists
62133 Offices of Mental Health Practitioners (except Physicians)[T]
621330 Offices of Mental Health Practitioners (except Physicians)
62134 Offices of Physical, Occupational and Speech Therapists, and Audiologists[T]
621340 Offices of Physical, Occupational and Speech Therapists, and Audiologists
62139 Offices of All Other Health Practitioners[T]
621391 Offices of Podiatrists
621399 Offices of All Other Miscellaneous Health Practitioners

6214 Outpatient Care Centers[T] 62141
Family Planning Centers[T]
621410 Family Planning Centers
62142 Outpatient Mental Health and Substance Abuse Centers[T]
621420 Outpatient Mental Health and Substance Abuse Centers
62149 Other Outpatient Care Centers[T]
621491 HMO Medical Centers
621492 Kidney Dialysis Centers
621493 Freestanding Ambulatory Surgical and Emergency Centers
621498 All Other Outpatient Care Centers

6215 Medical and Diagnostic Laboratories[T] 62151
Medical and Diagnostic Laboratories[T] 621511
Medical Laboratories 621512 Diagnostic Imaging
Centers

6216 Home Health Care Services[T] 62161
Home Health Care Services[T]
621610 Home Health Care Services

6219 Other Ambulatory Health Care Services[T]
62191 Ambulance Services[T]
621910 Ambulance Services
62199 All Other Ambulatory Health Care Services[T]
621991 Blood and Organ Banks
621999 All Other Miscellaneous Ambulatory Health Care Services

622 Hospitals[T]

6221 General Medical and Surgical Hospitals[T] 62211
General Medical and Surgical Hospitals[T] 622110 General Medical and Surgical Hospitals

6222 Psychiatric and Substance Abuse Hospitals^T 62221
Psychiatric and Substance Abuse Hospitals^T 622210 Psychiatric and Substance Abuse Hospitals

6223 Specialty (except Psychiatric and Substance Abuse) Hospitals^T 62231
Specialty (except Psychiatric and Substance Abuse) Hospitals^T 622310 Specialty (except Psychiatric and Substance Abuse) Hospitals

623 Nursing and Residential Care Facilities^T

6231 Nursing Care Facilities (Skilled Nursing Facilities)^T 62311
Nursing Care Facilities (Skilled Nursing Facilities)^T 623110
Nursing Care Facilities (Skilled Nursing Facilities)

6232 Residential Intellectual and Developmental Disability, Mental Health, and Substance Abuse Facilities^T
62321 Residential Intellectual and Developmental Disability Facilities^T
623210 Residential Intellectual and Developmental Disability Facilities
62322 Residential Mental Health and Substance Abuse Facilities^T
623220 Residential Mental Health and Substance Abuse Facilities

6233 Continuing Care Retirement Communities and Assisted Living Facilities for the Elderly^T
62331 Continuing Care Retirement Communities and Assisted Living Facilities for the Elderly^T
623311 Continuing Care Retirement Communities
623312 Assisted Living Facilities for the Elderly

6239 Other Residential Care Facilities^T 62399
Other Residential Care Facilities^T 623990 Other Residential Care Facilities

624 Social Assistance^T

6241 Individual and Family Services^T 62411
Child and Youth Services^T 624110
Child and Youth Services
62412 Services for the Elderly and Persons with Disabilities^T
624120 Services for the Elderly and Persons with Disabilities
62419 Other Individual and Family Services^T
624190 Other Individual and Family Services

6242 Community Food and Housing, and Emergency and Other Relief Services^T
62421 Community Food Services^T
624210 Community Food Services
62422 Community Housing Services^T
624221 Temporary Shelters
624229 Other Community Housing Services
62423 Emergency and Other Relief Services^T
624230 Emergency and Other Relief Services

6243 Vocational Rehabilitation Services^T 62431
Vocational Rehabilitation Services^T 624310 Vocational Rehabilitation Services

6244 **Child Day Care Services[T]** 62441
Child Day Care Services[T]
624410 Child Day Care Services

Sector 71--Arts, Entertainment, and Recreation[T] 711 Per-forming Arts, Spectator Sports, and Related Industries[T]

7111 **Performing Arts Companies[T]**
71111 Theater Companies and Dinner Theaters[T]
711110 Theater Companies and Dinner Theaters
71112 Dance Companies[T]
711120 Dance Companies
71113 Musical Groups and Artists[T]
711130 Musical Groups and Artists
71119 Other Performing Arts Companies[T]
711190 Other Performing Arts Companies

7112 **Spectator Sports[T]** 71121
Spectator Sports[T]
711211 Sports Teams and Clubs
711212 Racetracks
711219 Other Spectator Sports

7113 **Promoters of Performing Arts, Sports, and Similar Events[T]**
71131 Promoters of Performing Arts, Sports, and Similar Events with Facilities[T]
711310 Promoters of Performing Arts, Sports, and Similar Events with Facilities
71132 Promoters of Performing Arts, Sports, and Similar Events without Facilities[T]
711320 Promoters of Performing Arts, Sports, and Similar Events without Facilities

7114 **Agents and Managers for Artists, Athletes, Entertainers, and Other Public Figures[T]**
71141 Agents and Managers for Artists, Athletes, Entertainers, and Other Public Figures[T]
711410 Agents and Managers for Artists, Athletes, Entertainers, and Other Public Figures

7115 **Independent Artists, Writers, and Performers[T]** 71151
Independent Artists, Writers, and Performers[T] 711510 Independent Artists, Writers, and Performers

712 Museums, Historical Sites, and Similar Institutions[T]

7121 **Museums, Historical Sites, and Similar Institutions[T]**
71211 Museums[T]
712110 Museums
71212 Historical Sites[T]
712120 Historical Sites
71213 Zoos and Botanical Gardens[T]
712130 Zoos and Botanical Gardens
71219 Nature Parks and Other Similar Institutions[T]
712190 Nature Parks and Other Similar Institutions

713 Amusement, Gambling, and Recreation Industries^T

7131 Amusement Parks and Arcades^T 71311
Amusement and Theme Parks^T 713110
Amusement and Theme Parks 71312
Amusement Arcades^T 713120 Amusement
Arcades

7132 Gambling Industries^T
71321 Casinos (except Casino Hotels)^T
713210 Casinos (except Casino Hotels)
71329 Other Gambling Industries^T
713290 Other Gambling Industries

7139 Other Amusement and Recreation Industries^T
71391 Golf Courses and Country Clubs^T
713910 Golf Courses and Country Clubs
71392 Skiing Facilities^T
713920 Skiing Facilities
71393 Marinas^T
713930 Marinas
71394 Fitness and Recreational Sports Centers^T
713940 Fitness and Recreational Sports Centers
71395 Bowling Centers^T
713950 Bowling Centers
71399 All Other Amusement and Recreation Industries^T
713990 All Other Amusement and Recreation Industries

Sector 72--Accommodation and Food Services^T

721 Accommodation^T

7211 Traveler Accommodation^T
72111 Hotels (except Casino Hotels) and Motels^T
721110 Hotels (except Casino Hotels) and Motels
72112 Casino Hotels^T
721120 Casino Hotels
72119 Other Traveler Accommodation^T
721191 Bed-and-Breakfast Inns
721199 All Other Traveler Accommodation

7212 RV (Recreational Vehicle) Parks and Recreational Camps^T 72121
RV (Recreational Vehicle) Parks and Recreational Camps^T 721211 RV
(Recreational Vehicle) Parks and Campgrounds 721214 Recreational
and Vacation Camps (except Campgrounds)

7213 Rooming and Boarding Houses, Dormitories, and Workers' Camps^T
72131 Rooming and Boarding Houses, Dormitories, and Workers' Camps^T
721310 Rooming and Boarding Houses, Dormitories, and Workers' Camps

722 Food Services and Drinking Places^T

7223 Special Food Services^T 72231 Food
Service Contractors^T 722310 Food
Service Contractors

72232 Caterers[T]
722320 Caterers
72233 Mobile Food Services[T]
722330 Mobile Food Services

7224 Drinking Places (Alcoholic Beverages)[T] 72241 Drinking Places (Alcoholic Beverages)[T] 722410 Drinking Places (Alcoholic Beverages)

7225 Restaurants and Other Eating Places[T] 72251 Restaurants and Other Eating Places[T] 722511 Full-Service Restaurants 722513 Limited-Service Restaurants 722514 Cafeterias, Grill Buffets, and Buffets 722515 Snack and Nonalcoholic Beverage Bars

Sector 81--Other Services (except Public Administration)[T]

811 Repair and Maintenance[T]

8111 Automotive Repair and Maintenance[T]

81111 Automotive Mechanical and Electrical Repair and Maintenance[T]
811111 General Automotive Repair
811112 Automotive Exhaust System Repair
811113 Automotive Transmission Repair
811118 Other Automotive Mechanical and Electrical Repair and Maintenance
81112 Automotive Body, Paint, Interior, and Glass Repair[T]
811121 Automotive Body, Paint, and Interior Repair and Maintenance
811122 Automotive Glass Replacement Shops
81119 Other Automotive Repair and Maintenance[T]
811191 Automotive Oil Change and Lubrication Shops
811192 Car Washes
811198 All Other Automotive Repair and Maintenance

8112 Electronic and Precision Equipment Repair and Maintenance[T] 81121 Electronic and Precision Equipment Repair and Maintenance[T] 811211 Consumer Electronics Repair and Maintenance 811212 Computer and Office Machine Repair and Maintenance 811213 Communication Equipment Repair and Maintenance 811219 Other Electronic and Precision Equipment Repair and Maintenance

8113 Commercial and Industrial Machinery and Equipment (except Automotive and Electronic) Repair and Maintenance[T]

81131 Commercial and Industrial Machinery and Equipment (except Automotive and Electronic) Repair and Maintenance[T]
811310 Commercial and Industrial Machinery and Equipment (except Automotive and Electronic) Repair and Maintenance

8114 Personal and Household Goods Repair and Maintenance[T] 81141 Home and Garden Equipment and Appliance Repair and Maintenance[T] 811411 Home and Garden Equipment Repair and Maintenance 811412 Appliance Repair and Maintenance 81142 Reupholstery and Furniture Repair[T] 811420 Reupholstery and Furniture Repair

81143 Footwear and Leather Goods Repair[T]
811430 Footwear and Leather Goods Repair
81149 Other Personal and Household Goods Repair and Maintenance[T]
811490 Other Personal and Household Goods Repair and Maintenance

812 Personal and Laundry Services[T]

8121 Personal Care Services
81211 Hair, Nail, and Skin Care Services
812111 Barber Shops
812112 Beauty Salons
812113 Nail Salons
81219 Other Personal Care Services
812191 Diet and Weight Reducing Centers
812199 Other Personal Care Services

8122 Death Care Services
81221 Funeral Homes and Funeral Services
812210 Funeral Homes and Funeral Services
81222 Cemeteries and Crematories
812220 Cemeteries and Crematories

8123 Drycleaning and Laundry Services
81231 Coin-Operated Laundries and Drycleaners
812310 Coin-Operated Laundries and Drycleaners
81232 Drycleaning and Laundry Services (except Coin-Operated)
812320 Drycleaning and Laundry Services (except Coin-Operated)
81233 Linen and Uniform Supply
812331 Linen Supply
812332 Industrial Launderers

8129 Other Personal Services
81291 Pet Care (except Veterinary) Services
812910 Pet Care (except Veterinary) Services
81292 Photofinishing
812921 Photofinishing Laboratories (except One-Hour)
812922 One-Hour Photofinishing
81293 Parking Lots and Garages
812930 Parking Lots and Garages
81299 All Other Personal Services
812990 All Other Personal Services

813 Religious, Grantmaking, Civic, Professional, and Similar Organizations[T]

8131 Religious Organizations 81311
Religious Organizations
813110 Religious Organizations

8132 Grantmaking and Giving Services 81321 Grantmaking and Giving Services 813211 Grantmaking
Foundations 813212 Voluntary Health Organizations
813219 Other Grantmaking and Giving Services

8133 **Social Advocacy Organizations** 81331 Social Advocacy Organizations 813311 Human Rights Organizations
813312 Environment, Conservation and Wildlife Organizations
813319 Other Social Advocacy Organizations

8134 **Civic and Social Organizations** 81341 Civic and Social Organizations
813410 Civic and Social Organizations

8139 **Business, Professional, Labor, Political, and Similar Organizations**
81391 Business Associations
813910 Business Associations
81392 Professional Organizations
813920 Professional Organizations
81393 Labor Unions and Similar Labor Organizations
813930 Labor Unions and Similar Labor Organizations
81394 Political Organizations
813940 Political Organizations
81399 Other Similar Organizations (except Business, Professional, Labor, and Political Organizations)
813990 Other Similar Organizations (except Business, Professional, Labor, and Political Organizations)

814 Private Households[T]

8141 **Private Households[T]**
81411 Private Households[T]
814110 Private Households

Sector 92--Public Administration[T]

921 Executive, Legislative, and Other General Government Support

9211 **Executive, Legislative, and Other General Government Support**
92111 Executive Offices
921110 Executive Offices
92112 Legislative Bodies
921120 Legislative Bodies
92113 Public Finance Activities
921130 Public Finance Activities
92114 Executive and Legislative Offices, Combined
921140 Executive and Legislative Offices, Combined
92115 American Indian and Alaska Native Tribal Governments
921150 American Indian and Alaska Native Tribal Governments
92119 Other General Government Support
921190 Other General Government Support

922 Justice, Public Order, and Safety Activities

9221 **Justice, Public Order, and Safety Activities**
92211 Courts
922110 Courts
92212 Police Protection
922120 Police Protection

92213 Legal Counsel and Prosecution
922130 Legal Counsel and Prosecution
92214 Correctional Institutions
922140 Correctional Institutions
92215 Parole Offices and Probation Offices
922150 Parole Offices and Probation Offices
92216 Fire Protection
922160 Fire Protection
92219 Other Justice, Public Order, and Safety Activities
922190 Other Justice, Public Order, and Safety Activities

923 Administration of Human Resource Programs

9231 Administration of Human Resource Programs
92311 Administration of Education Programs
923110 Administration of Education Programs
92312 Administration of Public Health Programs
923120 Administration of Public Health Programs
92313 Administration of Human Resource Programs (except Education, Public Health, and Veterans' Affairs Programs)
923130 Administration of Human Resource Programs (except Education, Public Health, and Veterans' Affairs Programs)
92314 Administration of Veterans' Affairs 923140 Administration of Veterans' Affairs

924 Administration of Environmental Quality Programs

9241 Administration of Environmental Quality Programs 92411 Administration of Air and Water Resource and Solid Waste Management Programs
924110 Administration of Air and Water Resource and Solid Waste Management Programs
92412 Administration of Conservation Programs
924120 Administration of Conservation Programs

925 Administration of Housing Programs, Urban Planning, and Community Development

9251 Administration of Housing Programs, Urban Planning, and Community Development
92511 Administration of Housing Programs
925110 Administration of Housing Programs
92512 Administration of Urban Planning and Community and Rural Development
925120 Administration of Urban Planning and Community and Rural Development

926 Administration of Economic Programs

9261 Administration of Economic Programs 92611 Administration of General Economic Programs 926110 Administration of General Economic Programs 92612 Regulation and Administration of Transportation Programs 926120 Regulation and Administration of Transportation Programs

92613 Regulation and Administration of Communications, Electric, Gas, and Other Utilities
926130 Regulation and Administration of Communications, Electric, Gas, and Other Utilities
92614 Regulation of Agricultural Marketing and Commodities
926140 Regulation of Agricultural Marketing and Commodities
92615 Regulation, Licensing, and Inspection of Miscellaneous Commercial Sectors
926150 Regulation, Licensing, and Inspection of Miscellaneous Commercial Sectors

927 Space Research and Technology

9271 Space Research and Technology 92711 Space Research and Technology
927110 Space Research and Technology

928 National Security and International Affairs

9281 National Security and International Affairs
92811 National Security
928110 National Security
92812 International Affairs
928120 International Affairs

Frequently Asked Questions About Economic Classifications

1. What is the purpose of an industry classification system?
    - An industry classification system facilitates the collection, tabulation, presentation, and analysis of data relating to establishments and ensures that data about the U.S. economy published by U.S. statistical agencies are uniform and comparable. NAICS ensures that such data are uniform and comparable among Canada, Mexico, and the United States.

1. What is an establishment?
    - An establishment is generally a single, physical location at which economic activity occurs (e.g., store, factory, farm, etc.). An enterprise consists of one or more locations that are more than 50 percent owned by the same entity performing the same or different types of economic activities. Each establishment of that enterprise is assigned a NAICS code, based on its own primary activity.

1. How can I determine the correct NAICS code for my business?
    - To determine the correct NAICS code for your establishment, first identify the primary business activity. Then refer either to: 1) the NAICS United States Structure near the beginning of the manual to search the titles from the 2-digit level down through the 6-digit, more detailed level, to find the appropriate code; or 2) the Alphabetic Index at the back of the book to search alphabetically for the primary activity and its corresponding code. Next, turn to the industry description of the specified code in Part I of the manual, read the full description of the industry (including the narrative, cross-references, and illustrative examples), and determine if that description fits the activities of your establishment. Electronic references are available at census.gov/naics.

1. Who assigns NAICS codes to businesses and how?
    - There is no central government agency with the role of assigning, monitoring, or approving NAICS codes for establishments. Different agencies maintain their own lists of business establishments to meet their own programmatic needs. These different agencies use their own methods for assigning NAICS codes to the establishments on their lists. Statistical agencies assign one NAICS code to each establishment based on its primary activity. For example, the Social Security Administration assigns a NAICS code to new businesses based on information provided on their application for an Employer Identification Number. The Census Bureau generally assigns NAICS codes to businesses on its list of establishments based on information provided by the business on a survey or census report form. The Bureau of Labor Statistics initially assigns NAICS codes based on business activity information provided on an application for unemployment insurance.

1. How do I apply for a NAICS code?
    - A business does not 'apply' for a NAICS code. As explained above, statistical agencies generally assign NAICS codes based on information provided by a business on an application form, an administrative report, or on a survey or census report form.

6. How can I get a new NAICS code created for my type of business?
    - □ Every five years NAICS is reviewed for potential revisions, so that the classification system can keep pace with the changing economy. This is the only time that new NAICS codes can be considered. The Office of Management and Budget (OMB), through its Economic Classification Policy Committee (ECPC), will solicit public comments regarding changes to NAICS through a notice published in the **Federal Register**. The notice will provide details of the format in which comments should be submitted, how and to whom they should be submitted, and the deadline for submission. Generally, the comment period will close 90 days after publication of the notice. During that time, suggestions for new and emerging industries can be submitted to the ECPC. The next scheduled review of NAICS will be for a potential 2022 revision.

6. What is the relationship between NAICS and the Small Business Administration's (SBA) size standards?
    - □ NAICS categories do not distinguish between small and large business, or between for-profit and non-profit. The Small Business Administration (SBA) develops size standards for each NAICS category. To find more information about the SBA size standards, or when the SBA will update their size standards to reflect 2017 NAICS revisions, visit the SBA Web site at www.sba.gov/size/indexsize.html. You may also contact SBA's Office of Size Standards on 202-205-6618 or via email to sizestandards@sba.gov.

8. How do the NAICS codes affect federal procurement and regulatory activities, such as those carried out by the Environmental Protection Agency, OSHA, the Department of Defense, and the General Services Administration?
    - □ NAICS was developed specifically for the collection and publication of statistical data to foster the comparability of economic estimates for Canada, Mexico, and the United States. The NAICS categories and definitions were not developed to meet the needs of procurement and/or regulatory applications. However, other federal agencies and other organizations have adopted NAICS for procurement and regulatory purposes even though it does not entirely fit their specific needs. For questions regarding these agencies' use of the NAICS system, contact the specific agency. "

For answers to other NAICS questions, you may visit the NAICS Web site at census.gov/naics.

Part I

Titles and Descriptions of Industries

Sector 11--Agriculture, Forestry, Fishing and Hunting[T]

The Sector as a Whole

The Agriculture, Forestry, Fishing and Hunting sector comprises establishments primarily engaged in growing crops, raising animals, harvesting timber, and harvesting fish and other animals from a farm, ranch, or their natural habitats.

The establishments in this sector are often described as farms, ranches, dairies, greenhouses, nurseries, orchards, or hatcheries. A farm may consist of a single tract of land or a number of separate tracts which may be held under different tenures. For example, one tract may be owned by the farm operator and another rented. It may be operated by the operator alone or with the assistance of members of the household or hired employees, or it may be operated by a partnership, corporation, or other type of organization. When a landowner has one or more tenants, renters, croppers, or managers, the land operated by each is considered a farm.

The sector distinguishes two basic activities: agricultural production and agricultural support activities. Agricultural production includes establishments performing the complete farm or ranch operation, such as farm owner-operators and tenant farm operators. Agricultural support activities include establishments that perform one or more activities associated with farm operation, such as soil preparation, planting, harvesting, and management, on a contract or fee basis.

Excluded from the Agriculture, Forestry, Fishing and Hunting sector are establishments primarily engaged in agricultural research and establishments primarily engaged in administering programs for regulating and conserving land, mineral, wildlife, and forest use. These establishments are classified in Industry 54171, Research and Development in the Physical, Engineering, and Life Sciences; and Industry 92412, Administration of Conservation Programs, respectively.

111 Crop Production[T]

Industries in the Crop Production subsector grow crops mainly for food and fiber. The subsector comprises establishments, such as farms, orchards, groves, greenhouses, and nurseries, primarily engaged in growing crops, plants, vines, or trees and their seeds.

The industries in this subsector are grouped by similarity of production activity, including biological and physiological characteristics and economic requirements, the length of growing season, degree of crop rotation, extent of input specialization, labor requirements, and capital demands. The production process is typically completed when the raw product or commodity grown reaches the "farm gate" for market, that is, at the point of first sale or price determination.

Establishments are classified in the Crop Production subsector when crop production (i.e., value of crops for market) accounts for one-half or more of the establishment's total agricultural production. Within the subsector, establishments are classified in a specific industry when a product or industry family of products (i.e., oilseed and grain farming, vegetable and melon farming, fruit and tree nut farming) account for one-half or more of the establishment's agricultural production. Establishments with one-half or more crop production with no one product or family of products of an industry accounting for one-half of the establishment's agricultural production are treated as general combination crop farming and are classified in Industry 11199, All Other Crop Farming.

Industries in the Crop Production subsector include establishments that own, operate, and manage and those that operate and manage. Those that manage only are classified in Subsector 115, Support Activities for Agriculture and Forestry. Establishments that raise aquatic plants in controlled or selected aquatic environments are classified in Subsector 112, Animal Production and Aquaculture.

1111 Oilseed and Grain Farming[T]

This industry group comprises establishments primarily engaged in (1) growing oilseed and/or grain crops and/or (2) producing oilseed and grain seeds. These crops have an annual life cycle and are typically grown in open fields.

11111 Soybean Farming[T] See industry description for 111110.

T—Canadian, Mexican, and United States industries are comparable.

111110 Soybean Farming

This industry comprises establishments primarily engaged in growing soybeans and/or producing soybean seeds.

Cross-References.

Establishments engaged in growing soybeans in combination with grain(s) with the soybeans or grain(s) not accounting for one-half of the establishment's agricultural production (value of crops for market) are classified in U.S. Industry 111191, Oilseed and Grain Combination Farming.

11112 Oilseed (except Soybean) Farming[T] See industry description for 111120.

111120 Oilseed (except Soybean) Farming

This industry comprises establishments primarily engaged in growing fibrous oilseed producing plants and/or producing oilseed seeds, such as sunflower, safflower, flax, rape, canola, and sesame.

Cross-References. Establishments primarily engaged in--

- Growing soybeans--are classified in Industry 111110, Soybean Farming; and
- Growing oilseed(s) in combination with grain(s) with no one oilseed (or family of oilseeds) or grain(s) (or family of grains) accounting for one-half of the establishment's agricultural production (value of crops for market)--are classified in U.S. Industry 111191, Oilseed and Grain Combination Farming.

11113 Dry Pea and Bean Farming[T] See industry description for 111130.

111130 Dry Pea and Bean Farming

This industry comprises establishments primarily engaged in growing dry peas, beans, and/or lentils.

Cross-References.

Establishments primarily engaged in growing fresh green beans and peas are classified in U.S. Industry 111219, Other Vegetable (except Potato) and Melon Farming.

11114 Wheat Farming[T] See industry description for 111140.

111140 Wheat Farming

This industry comprises establishments primarily engaged in growing wheat and/or producing wheat seeds.

Cross-References.

Establishments growing wheat in combination with oilseed(s) with the wheat or oilseed(s) not accounting for one-half of the establishment's agricultural production (value of crops for market) are classified in U.S. Industry 111191, Oilseed and Grain Combination Farming.

11115 Corn Farming[T] See industry description for 111150.

T—Canadian, Mexican, and United States industries are comparable.

111150 Corn Farming

This industry comprises establishments primarily engaged in growing corn (except sweet corn) and/or producing corn seeds.

Cross-References. Establishments primarily engaged in--

- Growing sweet corn--are classified in U.S. Industry 111219, Other Vegetable (except Potato) and Melon Farming; and
- Growing corn in combination with oilseed(s) with the corn or oilseed(s) not accounting for one-half of the establishment's production (value of crops for market)--are classified in U.S. Industry 111191, Oilseed and Grain Combination Farming.

11116 Rice Farming[T] See industry description for 111160.

111160 Rice Farming

This industry comprises establishments primarily engaged in growing rice (except wild rice) and/or producing rice seeds.

Cross-References. Establishments primarily engaged in--

- Growing wild rice--are classified in U.S. Industry 111199, All Other Grain Farming; and
- Growing rice in combination with oilseed(s) with the rice or oilseed(s) not accounting for one-half of the establishment's agricultural production (value of crops for market)--are classified in U.S. Industry 111191, Oilseed and Grain Combination Farming.

11119 Other Grain Farming[T]

This industry comprises establishments primarily engaged in (1) growing grain(s) and/or producing grain seeds (except wheat, corn, and rice) or (2) growing a combination of grain(s) and oilseed(s) with no one grain (or family of grains) or oilseed (or family of oilseeds) accounting for one-half of the establishment's agricultural production (i.e., value of crops for market). Combination grain(s) and oilseed(s) establishments may produce oilseed(s) and grain(s) seeds and/or grow oilseed(s) and grain(s).

Illustrative Examples:

Barley farming
Rye farming
Milo farming
Sorghum farming
Oat farming
Wild rice farming
Oilseed and grain combination farming

Cross-References. Establishments primarily engaged in--

- Growing wheat--are classified in Industry 11114, Wheat Farming;
- Growing corn (except sweet corn)--are classified in Industry 11115, Corn Farming;
- Growing sweet corn--are classified in Industry 11121, Vegetable and Melon Farming; and
- Growing rice (except wild rice)--are classified in Industry 11116, Rice Farming.

111191 Oilseed and Grain Combination Farming

This U.S. industry comprises establishments engaged in growing a combination of oilseed(s) and grain(s) with no one oilseed (or family of oilseeds) or grain (or family of grains) accounting for one-half of the establishment's

---

T—Canadian, Mexican, and United States industries are comparable.

agricultural production (value of crops for market). These establishments may produce oilseed(s) and grain(s) seeds and/or grow oilseed(s) and grain(s).

Cross-References.

Establishments engaged in growing one grain (or family of grains) or oilseed (or family of oilseeds) accounting for one-half of the establishment's agricultural production (i.e., value of crops for market) are classified in Industry Group 1111, Oilseed and Grain Farming, accordingly by the prominent grain(s) or oilseed(s) grown.

111199 All Other Grain Farming

This U.S. industry comprises establishments primarily engaged in growing grains and/or producing grain(s) seeds (except wheat, corn, rice, and oilseed(s) and grain(s) combinations).

Illustrative Examples:

Barley farming
Sorghum farming
Oat farming
Wild rice farming
Rye farming

Cross-References. Establishments primarily engaged in--

- Growing wheat--are classified in Industry 111140, Wheat Farming;
- Growing corn (except sweet corn)--are classified in Industry 111150, Corn Farming;
- Growing rice (except wild rice)--are classified in Industry 111160, Rice Farming;
- Growing sweet corn--are classified in U.S. Industry 111219, Other Vegetable (except Potato) and Melon Farming; and
- Growing a combination of grain(s) and oilseed(s) with no one grain (or family of grains) or oilseed (or family of oilseeds) accounting for one-half of the establishment's agricultural production (value of crops for market)--are classified in U.S. Industry 111191, Oilseed and Grain Combination Farming.

1112 Vegetable and Melon Farming[T]

11121 Vegetable and Melon Farming[T]

This industry comprises establishments primarily engaged in one or more of the following: (1) growing vegetable and/or melon crops; (2) producing vegetable and/or melon seeds; and (3) growing vegetable and/or melon bedding plants. The crops included in this industry have an annual growth cycle and are grown in open fields. Climate and cultural practices limit producing areas but often permit the growing of a combination of crops in a year.

Cross-References. Establishments primarily engaged in--

- Growing sugar beets--are classified in Industry 11199, All Other Crop Farming;
- Growing vegetables and melons under glass or protective cover--are classified in Industry 11141, Food Crops Grown Under Cover;
- Growing dry peas and beans--are classified in Industry 11113, Dry Pea and Bean Farming;
- Growing corn (except sweet corn)--are classified in Industry 11115, Corn Farming;
- Canning, pickling, and/or drying (artificially) vegetables--are classified in Industry 31142, Fruit and Vegetable Canning, Pickling, and Drying; and
- Growing fruit on trees and other fruit-bearing plants (except melons)--are classified in Industry Group 1113, Fruit and Tree Nut Farming.

T—Canadian, Mexican, and United States industries are comparable.

111211 Potato Farming

This U.S. industry comprises establishments primarily engaged in growing potatoes and/or producing seed potatoes.

Cross-References.

Establishments primarily engaged in canning or drying potatoes are classified in Industry 31142, Fruit and Vegetable Canning, Pickling, and Drying.

111219 Other Vegetable (except Potato) and Melon Farming

This U.S. industry comprises establishments primarily engaged in one or more of the following: (1) growing melons and/or vegetables (except potatoes; dry peas; dry beans; field, silage, or seed corn; and sugar beets); (2) producing vegetable and/or melon seeds; and (3) growing vegetable and/or melon bedding plants.

Illustrative Examples:

Carrot farming
Squash farming
Green bean farming
Tomato farming
Watermelon farming
Melon farming (e.g., cantaloupe, casaba, honeydew, watermelon)
Vegetable (except potato) farming
Pepper farming (e.g., bell, chili, green, red, sweet peppers)

Cross-References. Establishments primarily engaged in--

- Growing potatoes, including sweet potatoes and yams--are classified in U.S. Industry 111211, Potato Farming;
- Growing sugar beets--are classified in U.S. Industry 111991, Sugar Beet Farming;
- Growing vegetables and melons under glass or protective cover--are classified in U.S. Industry 111419, Other Food Crops Grown Under Cover;
- Growing dry peas and beans--are classified in Industry 111130, Dry Pea and Bean Farming;
- Growing corn (except sweet corn)--are classified in Industry 111150, Corn Farming;
- Canning, pickling, and/or drying (artificially) vegetables--are classified in Industry 31142, Fruit and Vegetable Canning, Pickling, and Drying; and
- Growing fruit on trees and other fruit-bearing plants (except melons)--are classified in Industry Group 1113, Fruit and Tree Nut Farming.

1113 Fruit and Tree Nut Farming[T]

This industry group comprises establishments primarily engaged in growing fruit and/or tree nut crops. The crops included in this industry group are generally not grown from seeds and have a perennial life cycle.

11131 Orange Groves[T] See industry description for 111310.

111310 Orange Groves

This industry comprises establishments primarily engaged in growing oranges.

11132 Citrus (except Orange) Groves[T] See industry description for 111320.

T—Canadian, Mexican, and United States industries are comparable.

111320 Citrus (except Orange) Groves

This industry comprises establishments primarily engaged in growing citrus fruits (except oranges).

Illustrative Examples:

Citrus groves (except oranges)
Mandarin groves
Grapefruit groves
Tangelo groves
Lemon groves
Tangerine groves

Cross-References.

Establishments primarily engaged in growing oranges are classified in Industry 111310, Orange Groves.

11133 Noncitrus Fruit and Tree Nut Farming[T]

This industry comprises establishments primarily engaged in one or more of the following: (1) growing noncitrus fruits (e.g., apples, grapes, berries, peaches); (2) growing tree nuts (e.g., pecans, almonds, pistachios); or (3) growing a combination of fruit(s) and tree nut(s) with no one fruit (or family of fruit) or family of tree nuts accounting for one-half of the establishment's agricultural production (i.e., value of crops for market).

Cross-References. Establishments primarily engaged in--

- Harvesting berries or nuts from native and non-cultivated plants--are classified in Industry 11321, Forest Nurseries and Gathering of Forest Products; and
- Canning and/or drying (artificially) fruit--are classified in Industry 31142, Fruit and Vegetable Canning, Pickling, and Drying.

111331 Apple Orchards

This U.S. industry comprises establishments primarily engaged in growing apples.

Cross-References.

Establishments engaged in growing apples in combination with tree nut(s) with the apples or family of tree nuts not accounting for one-half of the establishment's agricultural production (i.e., value of crops for market) are classified in U.S. Industry 111336, Fruit and Tree Nut Combination Farming.

111332 Grape Vineyards

This U.S. industry comprises establishments primarily engaged in growing grapes and/or growing grapes to sun dry into raisins.

Cross-References. Establishments primarily engaged in--

- Drying grapes artificially--are classified in U.S. Industry 311423, Dried and Dehydrated Food Manufacturing; and
- Growing grapes in combination with tree nut(s) with the grapes or family of tree nuts not accounting for one-half of the establishment's agricultural production (i.e., value of crops for market)--are classified in U.S. Industry 111336, Fruit and Tree Nut Combination Farming.

111333 Strawberry Farming

This U.S. industry comprises establishments primarily engaged in growing strawberries.

T—Canadian, Mexican, and United States industries are comparable.

Cross-References.

Establishments engaged in growing strawberries in combination with tree nut(s) with the strawberries or family of tree nuts not accounting for one-half of the establishment's agricultural production (i.e., value of crops for market) are classified in U.S. Industry 111336, Fruit and Tree Nut Combination Farming.

111334 Berry (except Strawberry) Farming

This U.S. industry comprises establishments primarily engaged in growing berries.

Illustrative Examples:

Berry (except strawberries) farming
Cranberry farming
Blackberry farming
Currant farming
Blueberry farming
Raspberry farming

Cross-References. Establishments primarily engaged in--

- Growing strawberries--are classified in U.S. Industry 111333, Strawberry Farming;
- Harvesting berries from native and non-cultivated bushes or vines--are classified in Industry 113210, Forest Nurseries and Gathering of Forest Products; and
- Growing berries in combination with tree nut(s) with the berries or family of tree nuts not accounting for one-half of the establishment's agricultural production (i.e., value of crops for market)--are classified in U.S. Industry 111336, Fruit and Tree Nut Combination Farming.

111335 Tree Nut Farming

This U.S. industry comprises establishments primarily engaged in growing tree nuts.

Illustrative Examples:

Almond farming
Pistachio farming
Filbert farming
Tree nut farming
Macadamia farming
Walnut farming
Pecan farming

Cross-References. Establishments primarily engaged in--

- Growing coconut and coffee--are classified in U.S. Industry 111339, Other Noncitrus Fruit Farming; and
- Growing tree nut(s) in combination with fruit(s) with no one fruit (or family of fruit or of tree nuts) accounting for one-half of the establishment's agricultural production (i.e., value of crops for market)--are classified in U.S. Industry 111336, Fruit and Tree Nut Combination Farming.

111336 Fruit and Tree Nut Combination Farming

This U.S. industry comprises establishments primarily engaged in growing a combination of fruit(s) and tree nut(s) with no one fruit (or family of fruit) or family of tree nuts accounting for one-half of the establishment's agricultural production (i.e., value of crops for market).

Cross-References.

Establishments engaged in growing fruit(s) or the family of tree nut(s) accounting for one-half of the establishment's agricultural production (i.e., value of crops for market) are classified in Industry Group 1113, Fruit and Tree Nut Farming, accordingly by the prominent fruit(s) or tree nut(s) grown.

T—Canadian, Mexican, and United States industries are comparable.

111339 Other Noncitrus Fruit Farming

This U.S. industry comprises establishments primarily engaged in growing noncitrus fruits (except apples, grapes, berries, and fruit(s) and tree nut(s) combinations).

Illustrative Examples:

Apricot farming
Fig farming
Banana farming
Noncitrus fruit farming
Cherry farming
Peach farming
Coffee farming
Pineapple farming
Date farming
Prune farming

Cross-References. Establishments primarily engaged in--

- Growing apples--are classified in U.S. Industry 111331, Apple Orchards;
- Growing grapes including sun drying of grapes into raisins--are classified in U.S. Industry 111332, Grape Vineyards;
- Growing strawberries--are classified in U.S. Industry 111333, Strawberry Farming;
- Growing berries (except strawberries)--are classified in U.S. Industry 111334, Berry (except Strawberry) Farming;
- Drying fruit artificially--are classified in U.S. Industry 311423, Dried and Dehydrated Food Manufacturing; and
- Growing noncitrus fruit(s) in combination with tree nut(s) with no one fruit (or family of fruits) or family of tree nuts accounting for one-half of the establishment's agricultural production (i.e., value of crops for market)--are classified in U.S. Industry 111336, Fruit and Tree Nut Combination Farming.

1114 Greenhouse, Nursery, and Floriculture Production[T]

This industry group comprises establishments primarily engaged in growing crops of any kind under cover and/or growing nursery stock and flowers. "Under cover" is generally defined as greenhouses, cold frames, cloth houses, and lath houses. The crops grown are removed at various stages of maturity and have annual and perennial life cycles. The nursery stock includes short rotation woody crops that have growth cycles of 10 years or less.

11141 Food Crops Grown Under Cover[T]

This industry comprises establishments primarily engaged in growing food crops (e.g., fruits, melons, tomatoes) under glass or protective cover.

Cross-References.

Establishments primarily engaged in growing vegetable and melon bedding plants are classified in Industry 11121, Vegetable and Melon Farming.

111411 Mushroom Production

This U.S. industry comprises establishments primarily engaged in growing mushrooms under cover in mines underground, or in other controlled environments.

111419 Other Food Crops Grown Under Cover

This U.S. industry comprises establishments primarily engaged in growing food crops (except mushrooms) under glass or protective cover.

T—Canadian, Mexican, and United States industries are comparable.

Illustrative Examples:

Alfalfa sprout farming, grown under cover
Melon farming, grown under cover
Vegetable farming, grown under cover
Hydroponic crop farming
Fruit farming, grown under cover

Cross-References.

Establishments primarily engaged in growing mushrooms under cover are classified in U.S. Industry 111411, Mushroom Production.

11142 Nursery and Floriculture Production[T]

This industry comprises establishments primarily engaged in (1) growing nursery and floriculture products (e.g., nursery stock, shrubbery, cut flowers, flower seeds, foliage plants) under cover or in open fields and/or (2) growing short rotation woody trees with a growing and harvesting cycle of 10 years or less for pulp or tree stock (e.g., cut Christmas trees, cottonwoods).

Cross-References. Establishments primarily engaged in--

- Growing vegetable and melon bedding plants--are classified in Industry 11121, Vegetable and Melon Farming;
- Operating timber tracts (i.e., growing cycle greater than 10 years)--are classified in Industry 11311, Timber Tract Operations; and
- Retailing nursery, tree stock, and floriculture products primarily purchased from others--are classified in Industry 44422, Nursery, Garden Center, and Farm Supply Stores.

111421 Nursery and Tree Production

This U.S. industry comprises establishments primarily engaged in (1) growing nursery products, nursery stock, shrubbery, bulbs, fruit stock, sod, and so forth, under cover or in open fields and/or (2) growing short rotation woody trees with a growth and harvest cycle of 10 years or less for pulp or tree stock.

Cross-References. Establishments primarily engaged in--

- Growing vegetable and melon bedding plants--are classified in Industry 11121, Vegetable and Melon Farming;
- Operating timber tracts (i.e., growing cycle greater than 10 years)--are classified in Industry 113110, Timber Tract Operations; and
- Retailing nursery, tree stock, and floriculture products primarily purchased from others--are classified in Industry 444220, Nursery, Garden Center, and Farm Supply Stores.

111422 Floriculture Production

This U.S. industry comprises establishments primarily engaged in growing and/or producing floriculture products (e.g., cut flowers and roses, cut cultivated greens, potted flowering and foliage plants, and flower seeds) under cover and in open fields.

Cross-References.

Establishments primarily engaged in retailing floriculture products primarily purchased from others are classified in Industry 444220, Nursery, Garden Center, and Farm Supply Stores.

T—Canadian, Mexican, and United States industries are comparable.

1119 Other Crop Farming[T]

This industry group comprises establishments primarily engaged in (1) growing crops (except oilseed and/or grain; vegetable and/or melon; fruit and tree nut; and greenhouse, nursery, and/or floriculture products), such as tobacco, cotton, sugarcane, hay, sugar beets, peanuts, agave, herbs and spices, and hay and grass seeds, or (2) growing a combination of crops (except a combination of oilseed(s) and grain(s) and a combination of fruit(s) and tree nut(s)).

11191 Tobacco Farming[T] See industry description for 111910.

111910 Tobacco Farming

This industry comprises establishments primarily engaged in growing tobacco.

11192 Cotton Farming[T] See industry description for 111920.

111920 Cotton Farming

This industry comprises establishments primarily engaged in growing cotton.

Cross-References.

Establishments primarily engaged in ginning cotton are classified in U.S. Industry 115111, Cotton Ginning.

11193 Sugarcane Farming[T] See industry description for 111930.

111930 Sugarcane Farming

This industry comprises establishments primarily engaged in growing sugarcane.

11194 Hay Farming[T] See industry description for 111940.

111940 Hay Farming

This industry comprises establishments primarily engaged in growing hay, alfalfa, clover, and/or mixed hay.

Cross-References. Establishments primarily engaged in--

- Growing grain hay--are classified in Industry Group 1111, Oilseed and Grain Farming; and
- Growing grass and hay seeds--are classified in U.S. Industry 111998, All Other Miscellaneous Crop Farming.

11199 All Other Crop Farming[T]

This industry comprises establishments primarily engaged in (1) growing crops (except oilseeds and/or grains; vegetables and/or melons; fruits and/or tree nuts; greenhouse, nursery, and/or floriculture products; tobacco; cotton; sugarcane; or hay) or (2) growing a combination of crops (except a combination of oilseed(s) and grain(s); and a combination of fruit(s) and tree nut(s)) with no one crop or family of crops accounting for one-half of the establishment's agricultural production (i.e., value of crops for market).

T—Canadian, Mexican, and United States industries are comparable.

Illustrative Examples:

Agave farming
Spice farming
General combination crop farming (except oilseed and grain; vegetables and melons; fruit and nut combinations) Tea farming
Hay seed farming
Maple sap gathering
Peanut farming
Sugar beet farming
Grass seed farming

Cross-References. Establishments primarily engaged in--

- Growing oilseeds and/or wheat, corn, rice, or other grains--are classified in Industry Group 1111, Oilseed and Grain Farming;
- Growing vegetables and/or melons--are classified in Industry Group 1112, Vegetable and Melon Farming;
- Growing fruits and/or tree nuts--are classified in Industry Group 1113, Fruit and Tree Nut Farming;
- Growing greenhouse, nursery, and/or floriculture products--are classified in Industry Group 1114, Greenhouse, Nursery, and Floriculture Production;
- Growing tobacco--are classified in Industry 11191, Tobacco Farming;
- Growing cotton--are classified in Industry 11192, Cotton Farming;
- Growing sugarcane--are classified in Industry 11193, Sugarcane Farming;
- Growing hay--are classified in Industry 11194, Hay Farming; and
- Growing algae, seaweed, or other aquatic plants--are classified in Industry 11251, Aquaculture.

111991 Sugar Beet Farming

This U.S. industry comprises establishments primarily engaged in growing sugar beets.

Cross-References.

Establishments primarily engaged in growing beets (except sugar beets) are classified in U.S. Industry 111219, Other Vegetable (except Potato) and Melon Farming.

111992 Peanut Farming

This U.S. industry comprises establishments primarily engaged in growing peanuts.

111998 All Other Miscellaneous Crop Farming

This U.S. industry comprises establishments primarily engaged in one of the following: (1) growing crops (except oilseeds and/or grains; vegetables and/or melons; fruits and/or tree nuts; greenhouse, nursery, and/or floriculture products; tobacco; cotton; sugarcane; hay; sugar beets; or peanuts); (2) growing a combination of crops (except a combination of oilseed(s) and grain(s); and a combination of fruit(s) and tree nut(s)) with no one crop or family of crops accounting for one-half of the establishment's agricultural production (i.e., value of crops for market); or (3) gathering tea or maple sap.

Illustrative Examples:

Agave farming
Mint farming
General combination crop farming (except oilseed and grain; vegetables and melons; fruit and tree nut combinations)
Hay seed farming
Grass seed farming
Hop farming
Spice farming

T—Canadian, Mexican, and United States industries are comparable.

Cross-References. Establishments primarily engaged in--

- Growing oilseeds and/or wheat, corn, rice, or other grains--are classified in Industry Group 1111, Oilseed and Grain Farming;
- Growing vegetables and/or melons--are classified in Industry Group 1112, Vegetable and Melon Farming;
- Growing fruits and/or tree nuts--are classified in Industry Group 1113, Fruit and Tree Nut Farming;
- Growing greenhouse, nursery, and/or floriculture products--are classified in Industry Group 1114, Greenhouse, Nursery, and Floriculture Production;
- Growing tobacco--are classified in Industry 111910, Tobacco Farming;
- Growing cotton--are classified in Industry 111920, Cotton Farming;
- Growing sugarcane--are classified in Industry 111930, Sugarcane Farming;
- Growing hay--are classified in Industry 111940, Hay Farming;
- Growing sugar beets--are classified in U.S. Industry 111991, Sugar Beet Farming;
- Growing peanuts--are classified in U.S. Industry 111992, Peanut Farming; and
- Growing algae, seaweed, or other aquatic plants--are classified in U.S. Industry 112519, Other Aquaculture.

112 Animal Production and Aquaculture[T]

Industries in the Animal Production and Aquaculture subsector raise or fatten animals for the sale of animals or animal products and/or raise aquatic plants and animals in controlled or selected aquatic environments for the sale of aquatic plants, animals, or their products. The subsector includes establishments, such as ranches, farms, and feedlots, primarily engaged in keeping, grazing, breeding, or feeding animals. These animals are kept for the products they produce or for eventual sale. The animals are generally raised in various environments, from total confinement or captivity to feeding on an open range pasture.

The industries in this subsector are grouped by important factors, such as suitable grazing or pasture land, specialized buildings, type of equipment, and the amount and types of labor required. Establishments are classified in the Animal Production and Aquaculture subsector when animal production (i.e., value of animals for market) accounts for one-half or more of the establishment's total agricultural production. Establishments with one-half or more animal production with no one animal product or family of animal products of an industry accounting for one-half of the establishment's agricultural production are treated as combination animal farming classified in Industry 11299, All Other Animal Production.

1121 Cattle Ranching and Farming[T]

This industry group comprises establishments primarily engaged in raising cattle, milking dairy cattle, or feeding cattle for fattening.

11211 Beef Cattle Ranching and Farming, including Feedlots[T]

This industry comprises establishments primarily engaged in raising cattle (including cattle for dairy herd replacements), or feeding cattle for fattening.

Cross-References. Establishments primarily engaged in--

- Milking dairy cattle--are classified in Industry 11212, Dairy Cattle and Milk Production; and
- Operating stockyards for transportation and not buying, selling, or auctioning livestock--are classified in Industry 48899, Other Support Activities for Transportation.

112111 Beef Cattle Ranching and Farming

This U.S. industry comprises establishments primarily engaged in raising cattle (including cattle for dairy herd replacements).

T—Canadian, Mexican, and United States industries are comparable.

Cross-References.

Establishments primarily engaged in milking dairy cattle are classified in Industry 112120, Dairy Cattle and Milk Production.

112112 Cattle Feedlots

This U.S. industry comprises establishments primarily engaged in feeding cattle for fattening.

Cross-References.

Establishments primarily engaged in operating stockyards for transportation and not buying, selling, or auctioning livestock are classified in U.S. Industry 488999, All Other Support Activities for Transportation.

11212 Dairy Cattle and Milk Production[T] See industry description for 112120.

112120 Dairy Cattle and Milk Production

This industry comprises establishments primarily engaged in milking dairy cattle.

Cross-References. Establishments primarily engaged in--

- Raising dairy herd replacements--are classified in U.S. Industry 112111, Beef Cattle Ranching and Farming; and
- Milking goats--are classified in Industry 112420, Goat Farming.

11213 Dual-Purpose Cattle Ranching and Farming[T] See industry description for 112130.

112130 Dual-Purpose Cattle Ranching and Farming

This industry comprises establishments primarily engaged in raising cattle for both milking and meat production.

Cross-References. Establishments primarily engaged in--

- Milking dairy cattle--are classified in Industry 112120, Dairy Cattle and Milk Production;
- Raising cattle or feeding cattle for fattening--are classified in Industry 11211, Beef Cattle Ranching and Farming, including Feedlots; and
- Operating stockyards for transportation and not buying, selling, or auctioning livestock--are classified in U.S. Industry 488999, All Other Support Activities for Transportation.

1122 Hog and Pig Farming[T]

11221 Hog and Pig Farming[T] See industry description for 112210.

112210 Hog and Pig Farming

This industry comprises establishments primarily engaged in raising hogs and pigs. These establishments may include farming activities, such as breeding, farrowing, and the raising of weanling pigs, feeder pigs, or market size hogs.

T—Canadian, Mexican, and United States industries are comparable.

Cross-References.

Establishments primarily engaged in operating stockyards for transportation and not buying, selling, or auctioning livestock are classified in U.S. Industry 488999, All Other Support Activities for Transportation.

1123 Poultry and Egg Production[T]

This industry group comprises establishments primarily engaged in breeding, hatching, and raising poultry for meat or egg production.

11231 Chicken Egg Production[T] See industry description for 112310.

112310 Chicken Egg Production

This industry comprises establishments primarily engaged in raising chickens for egg production. The eggs produced may be for use as table eggs or hatching eggs.

Cross-References.

Establishments primarily engaged in raising chickens for the production of meat are classified in Industry 112320, Broilers and Other Meat Type Chicken Production.

11232 Broilers and Other Meat Type Chicken Production[T] See industry description for 112320.

112320 Broilers and Other Meat Type Chicken Production

This industry comprises establishments primarily engaged in raising broilers, fryers, roasters, and other meat type chickens.

Cross-References.

Establishments primarily engaged in raising chickens for egg production are classified in Industry 112310, Chicken Egg Production.

11233 Turkey Production[T] See industry description for 112330.

112330 Turkey Production

This industry comprises establishments primarily engaged in raising turkeys for meat or egg production.

11234 Poultry Hatcheries[T] See industry description for 112340.

112340 Poultry Hatcheries

This industry comprises establishments primarily engaged in hatching poultry of any kind.

11239 Other Poultry Production[T] See industry description for 112390.

T—Canadian, Mexican, and United States industries are comparable.

112390 Other Poultry Production

This industry comprises establishments primarily engaged in raising poultry (except chickens for meat or egg production and turkeys).

Illustrative Examples:

Duck production
Ostrich production
Emu production
Pheasant production
Geese production
Quail production

Cross-References. Establishments primarily engaged in--

- Raising aviary birds, such as parakeets, canaries, and love birds--are classified in Industry 112990, All Other Animal Production;
- Raising chickens for egg production--are classified in Industry 112310, Chicken Egg Production;
- Raising broilers and other meat type chickens--are classified in Industry 112320, Broilers and Other Meat Type Chicken Production;
- Raising turkeys--are classified in Industry 112330, Turkey Production; and
- Raising swans, peacocks, flamingos or other "adornment birds"--are classified in Industry 112990, All Other Animal Production.

1124 Sheep and Goat Farming[T]

This industry group comprises establishments primarily engaged in raising sheep, lambs, and goats, or feeding lambs for fattening.

11241 Sheep Farming[T] See industry description for 112410.

112410 Sheep Farming

This industry comprises establishments primarily engaged in raising sheep and lambs, or feeding lambs for fattening. The sheep or lambs may be raised for sale or wool production.

Cross-References.

Establishments primarily engaged in operating stockyards for transportation and not buying, selling, or auctioning livestock are classified in U.S. Industry 488999, All Other Support Activities for Transportation.

11242 Goat Farming[T] See industry description for 112420.

112420 Goat Farming

This industry comprises establishments primarily engaged in raising goats.

1125 Aquaculture[T]

11251 Aquaculture[T]

This industry comprises establishments primarily engaged in the farm raising and production of aquatic animals or plants in controlled or selected aquatic environments. These establishments use some form of intervention in the rearing process to enhance production, such as holding in captivity, regular stocking, feeding, and protecting from predators, pests, and disease.

T—Canadian, Mexican, and United States industries are comparable.

Cross-References.

Establishments primarily engaged in the catching or taking of fish and other aquatic animals from their natural habitat are classified in Industry 11411, Fishing.

112511 Finfish Farming and Fish Hatcheries

This U.S. industry comprises establishments primarily engaged in (1) farm raising finfish (e.g., catfish, trout, goldfish, tropical fish, minnows) and/or (2) hatching fish of any kind.

Cross-References.

Establishments primarily engaged in the catching or taking of finfish from their natural habitat are classified in U.S. Industry 114111, Finfish Fishing.

112512 Shellfish Farming

This U.S. industry comprises establishments primarily engaged in farm raising shellfish (e.g., crayfish, shrimp, oysters, clams, mollusks).

Cross-References.

Establishments primarily engaged in the catching or taking of shellfish from their natural habitat are classified in U.S. Industry 114112, Shellfish Fishing.

112519 Other Aquaculture

This U.S. industry comprises establishments primarily engaged in (1) farm raising of aquatic animals (except finfish and shellfish) and/or (2) farm raising of aquatic plants. Alligator, algae, frog, seaweed, or turtle production is included in this industry.

Cross-References. Establishments primarily engaged in--

- Miscellaneous fishing activities, such as catching or taking of terrapins, turtles, and frogs from their natural habitat--are classified in U.S. Industry 114119, Other Marine Fishing;
- Farm raising finfish--are classified in U.S. Industry 112511, Finfish Farming and Fish Hatcheries;
- Farm raising shellfish--are classified in U.S. Industry 112512, Shellfish Farming; and
- Growing hydroponic crops--are classified in U.S. Industry 111419, Other Food Crops Grown Under Cover.

1129 Other Animal Production[T]

This industry group comprises establishments primarily engaged in raising animals and insects (except cattle, hogs and pigs, poultry, sheep and goats, and aquaculture) for sale or product production. These establishments are primarily engaged in raising one of the following: bees, horses and other equines, rabbits and other fur-bearing animals, and so forth, and producing products, such as honey and other bee products. Establishments primarily engaged in raising a combination of animals with no one animal or family of animals accounting for one-half of the establishment's agricultural production (i.e., value of animals for market) are included in this industry group.

11291 Apiculture[T] See industry description for 112910.

T—Canadian, Mexican, and United States industries are comparable.

112910 Apiculture

This industry comprises establishments primarily engaged in raising bees. These establishments may collect and gather honey; and/or sell queen bees, packages of bees, royal jelly, bees' wax, propolis, venom, pollen, and/or other bee products.

11292 Horses and Other Equine Production[T] See industry description for 112920.

112920 Horses and Other Equine Production

This industry comprises establishments primarily engaged in raising horses, mules, donkeys, and other equines.

Cross-References.

- Establishments primarily engaged in equine boarding are classified in Industry 115210, Support Activities for Animal Production; and
- Equine owners entering horses in racing or other spectator sporting events are classified in U.S. Industry 711219, Other Spectator Sports.

11293 Fur-Bearing Animal and Rabbit Production[T] See industry description for 112930.

112930 Fur-Bearing Animal and Rabbit Production

This industry comprises establishments primarily engaged in raising fur-bearing animals including rabbits. These animals may be raised for sale or for their pelt production.

Cross-References.

Establishments primarily engaged in the trapping or hunting of wild fur-bearing animals are classified in Industry 114210, Hunting and Trapping.

11299 All Other Animal Production[T] See industry description for 112990.

112990 All Other Animal Production

This industry comprises establishments primarily engaged in (1) raising animals (except cattle, hogs and pigs, poultry, sheep and goats, aquaculture, apiculture, horses and other equines; and fur-bearing animals including rabbits) or (2) raising a combination of animals, with no one animal or family of animals accounting for one-half of the establishment's agricultural production (i.e., value of animals for market).

Illustrative Examples:

Bird production (e.g., canaries, parakeets, parrots)
Laboratory animal production (e.g., rats, mice, guinea pigs)
Combination animal farming (except dairy, poultry)
Companion animals production (e.g., cats, dogs)
Worm production
Deer production
Llama production

Cross-References. Establishments primarily engaged in--

- Raising cattle, dairy cattle, or feeding cattle for fattening--are classified in Industry Group 1121, Cattle Ranching and Farming;
- Raising hogs and pigs--are classified in Industry Group 1122, Hog and Pig Farming;

T—Canadian, Mexican, and United States industries are comparable.

- Raising poultry and raising poultry for egg production--are classified in Industry Group 1123, Poultry and Egg Production;
- Raising sheep and goats--are classified in Industry Group 1124, Sheep and Goat Farming;
- Animal aquaculture--are classified in Industry 11251, Aquaculture;
- Raising bees--are classified in Industry 112910, Apiculture;
- Raising horses and other equines--are classified in Industry 112920, Horses and Other Equine Production; and
- Raising fur-bearing animals including rabbits--are classified in Industry 112930, Fur-Bearing Animal and Rabbit Production.

113 Forestry and Logging[T]

Industries in the Forestry and Logging subsector grow and harvest timber on a long production cycle (i.e., of 10 years or more). Long production cycles use different production processes than short production cycles, which require more horticultural interventions prior to harvest, resulting in processes more similar to those found in the Crop Production subsector. Consequently, Christmas tree production and other production involving production cycles of less than 10 years, are classified in the Crop Production subsector.

Industries in this subsector specialize in different stages of the production cycle. Reforestation requires production of seedlings in specialized nurseries. Timber production requires natural forest or suitable areas of land that are available for a long duration. The maturation time for timber depends upon the species of tree, the climatic conditions of the region, and the intended purpose of the timber. The harvesting of timber (except when done on an extremely small scale) requires specialized machinery unique to the industry. Establishments gathering forest products, such as gums, barks, balsam needles, rhizomes, fibers, Spanish moss, and ginseng and truffles, are also included in this subsector.

1131 Timber Tract Operations[T]

11311 Timber Tract Operations[T] See industry description for 113110.

113110 Timber Tract Operations

This industry comprises establishments primarily engaged in the operation of timber tracts for the purpose of selling standing timber.

Cross-References. Establishments primarily engaged in--

- Acting as lessors of land with trees as real estate property--are classified in Industry 531190, Lessors of Other Real Estate Property;
- Growing short rotation woody trees (i.e., growing and harvesting cycle is 10 years or less)--are classified in U.S. Industry 111421, Nursery and Tree Production; and
- Cutting timber--are classified in Industry 113310, Logging.

1132 Forest Nurseries and Gathering of Forest Products[T]

11321 Forest Nurseries and Gathering of Forest Products[T] See industry description for 113210.

113210 Forest Nurseries and Gathering of Forest Products

This industry comprises establishments primarily engaged in (1) growing trees for reforestation and/or (2) gathering forest products, such as gums, barks, balsam needles, rhizomes, fibers, Spanish moss, ginseng, and truffles.

T—Canadian, Mexican, and United States industries are comparable.

Cross-References. Establishments primarily engaged in--

- Gathering tea and maple sap--are classified in U.S. Industry 111998, All Other Miscellaneous Crop Farming; and
- Processing maple syrup into other products--are classified in Industry 31199, All Other Food Manufacturing.

1133 Logging[T]

11331 Logging[T] See industry description for 113310.

113310 Logging

This industry comprises establishments primarily engaged in one or more of the following: (1) cutting timber; (2) cutting and transporting timber; and (3) producing wood chips in the field.

Cross-References. Establishments primarily engaged in--

- Trucking timber without cutting timber--are classified in Industry 484220, Specialized Freight (except Used Goods) Trucking, Local; and
- Producing wood chips in sawmills--are classified in U.S. Industry 321113, Sawmills.

114 Fishing, Hunting and Trapping[T]

Industries in the Fishing, Hunting and Trapping subsector harvest fish and other wild animals from their natural habitats and are dependent upon a continued supply of the natural resource. The harvesting of fish is the predominant economic activity of this subsector and it usually requires specialized vessels that, by the nature of their size, configuration and equipment, are not suitable for any other type of production, such as transportation. Hunting and trapping activities utilize a wide variety of production processes and are classified in the same subsector as fishing because the availability of resources and the constraints imposed, such as conservation requirements and proper habitat maintenance, are similar.

1141 Fishing[T]

11411 Fishing[T]

This industry comprises establishments primarily engaged in the commercial catching or taking of finfish, shellfish, or miscellaneous marine products from a natural habitat, such as the catching of bluefish, eels, salmon, tuna, clams, crabs, lobsters, mussels, oysters, shrimp, frogs, sea urchins, and turtles.

Cross-References. Establishments primarily engaged in--

- Farm raising finfish, shellfish or other marine animals and plants--are classified in Industry 11251, Aquaculture; and
- Gathering and processing seafood into canned seafood products--are classified in Industry 31171, Seafood Product Preparation and Packaging.

114111 Finfish Fishing

This U.S. industry comprises establishments primarily engaged in the commercial catching or taking of finfish (e.g., bluefish, salmon, trout, tuna) from their natural habitat.

T—Canadian, Mexican, and United States industries are comparable.

Cross-References. Establishments primarily engaged in--

- Farm raising finfish--are classified in U.S. Industry 112511, Finfish Farming and Fish Hatcheries; and
- Gathering and processing (known as "floating factory ships") seafood into canned seafood products--are classified in Industry 311710, Seafood Product Preparation and Packaging.

114112 Shellfish Fishing

This U.S. industry comprises establishments primarily engaged in the commercial catching or taking of shellfish (e.g., clams, crabs, lobsters, mussels, oysters, sea urchins, shrimp) from their natural habitat.

Cross-References.

Establishments primarily engaged in farm raising shellfish are classified in U.S. Industry 112512, Shellfish Farming.

114119 Other Marine Fishing

This U.S. industry comprises establishments primarily engaged in the commercial catching or taking of marine animals (except finfish and shellfish).

Cross-References. Establishments primarily engaged in--

- Animal or plant aquaculture (except finfish and shellfish)--are classified in U.S. Industry 112519, Other Aquaculture;
- The commercial catching or taking of finfish from their natural habitat--are classified in U.S. Industry 114111, Finfish Fishing; and
- The commercial catching or taking of shellfish from their natural habitat--are classified in U.S. Industry 114112, Shellfish Fishing.

1142 Hunting and Trapping[T]

11421 Hunting and Trapping[T] See industry description for 114210.

114210 Hunting and Trapping

This industry comprises establishments primarily engaged in one or more of the following: (1) commercial hunting and trapping; (2) operating commercial game preserves, such as game retreats; and (3) operating hunting preserves.

Cross-References. Establishments primarily engaged in--

- Operating nature preserves--are classified in Industry 712190, Nature Parks and Other Similar Institutions; and
- Farm raising rabbits and other fur-bearing animals--are classified in Industry 112930, Fur-Bearing Animal and Rabbit Production.

115 Support Activities for Agriculture and Forestry[T]

Industries in the Support Activities for Agriculture and Forestry subsector provide support services that are an essential part of agricultural and forestry production. These support activities may be performed by the agriculture or forestry producing establishment or conducted independently as an alternative source of inputs required for the production process for a given crop, animal, or forestry industry. Establishments that primarily perform these activities independent of the agriculture or forestry producing establishment are in this subsector.

T—Canadian, Mexican, and United States industries are comparable.

1151 Support Activities for Crop Production[T] 11511

Support Activities for Crop Production[T]

This industry comprises establishments primarily engaged in providing support activities for growing crops.

Aerial crop dusting or spraying (i.e., using specialized or dedicated aircraft)
Farm management services
Cotton ginning
Planting crops
Cultivating services
Vineyard cultivation services

Cross-References. Establishments primarily engaged in--

- Performing crop production that are generally known as farms, orchards, groves, or vineyards (including tenant farms)--are classified in the appropriate crop industry within Subsector 111, Crop Production;
- Providing support activities for forestry--are classified in Industry 11531, Support Activities for Forestry;
- Landscaping and horticultural services, such as lawn and maintenance care and ornamental shrub and tree services--are classified in Industry 56173, Landscaping Services;
- Land clearing, land leveling, and earth moving for terracing, ponds, and irrigation--are classified in Industry 23891, Site Preparation Contractors;
- Artificially drying and dehydrating fruits and vegetables--are classified in Industry 31142, Fruit and Vegetable Canning, Pickling, and Drying;
- Stemming and redrying tobacco--are classified in Industry 31223, Tobacco Manufacturing;
- Providing water for irrigation--are classified in Industry 22131, Water Supply and Irrigation Systems; and
- Buying farm products, such as fruits or vegetables, for resale to other wholesalers or retailers, and preparing them for market or further processing--are classified in Industry 42448, Fresh Fruit and Vegetable Merchant Wholesalers.

115111 Cotton Ginning

This U.S. industry comprises establishments primarily engaged in ginning cotton.

115112 Soil Preparation, Planting, and Cultivating

This U.S. industry comprises establishments primarily engaged in performing a soil preparation activity or crop production service, such as plowing, fertilizing, seed bed preparation, planting, cultivating, and crop protecting services.

Cross-References. Establishments primarily engaged in--

- Mulching and seeding burned forests from the air in support of reforestation or on an emergency basis--are classified in Industry 115310, Support Activities for Forestry;
- Land clearing, land leveling, and earth moving for terracing, ponds, and irrigation--are classified in Industry 238910, Site Preparation Contractors; and
- Providing water for irrigation--are classified in Industry 221310, Water Supply and Irrigation Systems.

115113 Crop Harvesting, Primarily by Machine

T—Canadian, Mexican, and United States industries are comparable.

Cross-References. Establishments primarily engaged in--

- Providing personnel for manual harvesting--are classified in U.S. Industry 115115, Farm Labor Contractors and Crew Leaders; and
- Providing farm management services (i.e., on a contract or fee basis) and arranging or contracting crop mechanical or manual harvesting operations for the farm(s) they manage--are classified in U.S. Industry 115116, Farm Management Services.

115114 Postharvest Crop Activities (except Cotton Ginning)

This U.S. industry comprises establishments primarily engaged in performing services on crops, subsequent to their harvest, with the intent of preparing them for market or further processing. These establishments provide postharvest activities, such as crop cleaning, sun drying, shelling, fumigating, curing, sorting, grading, packing, and cooling.

Cross-References. Establishments primarily engaged in--

- Ginning cotton--are classified in U.S. Industry 115111, Cotton Ginning;
- Custom grain grinding for animal feed--are classified in U.S. Industry 311119, Other Animal Food Manufacturing;
- Artificially drying and dehydrating fruits and vegetables--are classified in U.S. Industry 311423, Dried and Dehydrated Food Manufacturing;
- Stemming and redrying tobacco--are classified in Industry 312230, Tobacco Manufacturing;
- Buying farm products for resale to other wholesalers or retailers and preparing them for market or further processing--are classified in Industry 424480, Fresh Fruit and Vegetable Merchant Wholesalers; and
- Providing farm management services (i.e., on a contract or fee basis) and arranging or contracting postharvesting crop activities for the farm(s) they manage--are classified in U.S. Industry 115116, Farm Management Services.

115115 Farm Labor Contractors and Crew Leaders

This U.S. industry comprises establishments primarily engaged in supplying labor for agricultural production or harvesting.

Cross-References. Establishments primarily engaged in--

- Providing machine harvesting--are classified in U.S. Industry 115113, Crop Harvesting, Primarily by Machine; and
- Providing farm management services (i.e., on a contract or fee basis) and arranging or contracting farm labor for the farm(s) they manage--are classified in U.S. Industry 115116, Farm Management Services.

115116 Farm Management Services

This U.S. industry comprises establishments primarily engaged in providing farm management services on a contract or fee basis usually to citrus groves, orchards, or vineyards. These establishments always provide management and may arrange or contract for the partial or the complete operations of the farm establishment(s) they manage. Operational activities may include cultivating, harvesting, and/or other specialized agricultural support activities.

Cross-References.

Establishments primarily engaged in crop production that are generally known as farms, orchards, groves, or vineyards (including tenant farms), are classified in the appropriate crop industry within Subsector 111, Crop Production.

T—Canadian, Mexican, and United States industries are comparable.

1152 Support Activities for Animal Production[T]

11521 Support Activities for Animal Production[T] See industry description for 115210.

115210 Support Activities for Animal Production

This industry comprises establishments primarily engaged in performing support activities related to raising livestock (e.g., cattle, goats, hogs, horses, poultry, sheep). These establishments may perform one or more of the following: (1) breeding services for animals, including companion animals (e.g., cats, dogs, pet birds); (2) pedigree record services; (3) boarding horses; (4) dairy herd improvement activities; (5) livestock spraying; and (6) sheep dipping and shearing.

Cross-References.

Establishments primarily engaged in raising companion animals (e.g., cats, dogs, pet birds) for sale are classified in Industry 112990, All Other Animal Production.

1153 Support Activities for Forestry[T]

11531 Support Activities for Forestry[T] See industry description for 115310.

115310 Support Activities for Forestry

This industry comprises establishments primarily engaged in performing particular support activities related to timber production, wood technology, forestry economics and marketing, and forest protection. These establishments may provide support activities for forestry, such as estimating timber, forest firefighting, forest pest control, treating burned forests from the air for reforestation or on an emergency basis, and consulting on wood attributes and reforestation.

Cross-References. Establishments primarily engaged in--

- Public administration and conservation of forest lands--are classified in Industry 924120, Administration of Conservation Programs; and
- Individual activities as part of a restoration project--are classified according to the primary activity.

T—Canadian, Mexican, and United States industries are comparable.

Sector 21--Mining, Quarrying, and Oil and Gas Extraction[T]

The Sector as a Whole

The Mining, Quarrying, and Oil and Gas Extraction sector comprises establishments that extract naturally occurring mineral solids, such as coal and ores; liquid minerals, such as crude petroleum; and gases, such as natural gas. The term mining is used in the broad sense to include quarrying, well operations, beneficiating (e.g., crushing, screening, washing, and flotation), and other preparation customarily performed at the mine site, or as a part of mining activity.

The Mining, Quarrying, and Oil and Gas Extraction sector distinguishes two basic activities: mine operation and mining support activities. Mine operation includes establishments operating mines, quarries, or oil and gas wells on their own account or for others on a contract or fee basis. Mining support activities include establishments that perform exploration (except geophysical surveying) and/or other mining services on a contract or fee basis (except mine site preparation and construction of oil/gas pipelines).

Establishments in the Mining, Quarrying, and Oil and Gas Extraction sector are grouped and classified according to the natural resource mined or to be mined. Industries include establishments that develop the mine site, extract the natural resources, and/or those that beneficiate (i.e., prepare) the mineral mined. Beneficiation is the process whereby the extracted material is reduced to particles that can be separated into mineral and waste, the former suitable for further processing or direct use. The operations that take place in beneficiation are primarily mechanical, such as grinding, washing, magnetic separation, and centrifugal separation. In contrast, manufacturing operations primarily use chemical and electrochemical processes, such as electrolysis and distillation. However, some treatments, such as heat treatments, take place in both the beneficiation and the manufacturing (i.e., smelting/refining) stages. The range of preparation activities varies by mineral and the purity of any given ore deposit. While some minerals, such as petroleum and natural gas, require little or no preparation, others are washed and screened, while yet others, such as gold and silver, can be transformed into bullion before leaving the mine site. Mining, beneficiating, and manufacturing activities often occur in a single location. Separate receipts will be collected for these activities whenever possible. When receipts cannot be broken out between mining and manufacturing, establishments that mine or quarry nonmetallic minerals, and then beneficiate the nonmetallic minerals into more finished manufactured products are classified based on the primary activity of the establishment. A mine that manufactures a small amount of finished products will be classified in Sector 21, Mining, Quarrying, and Oil and Gas Extraction. An establishment that mines whose primary output is a more finished manufactured product will be classified in Sector 31-33, Manufacturing.

211 Oil and Gas Extraction[T]

Industries in the Oil and Gas Extraction subsector operate and/or develop oil and gas field properties. Such activities may include exploration for crude petroleum and natural gas; drilling, completing, and equipping wells; operating separators, emulsion breakers, desilting equipment, and field gathering lines for crude petroleum and natural gas; and all other activities in the preparation of oil and gas up to the point of shipment from the producing property. This subsector includes the production of crude petroleum, the mining and extraction of oil from oil shale and oil sands, the production of natural gas, sulfur recovery from natural gas, and recovery of hydrocarbon liquids. Establishments in this subsector include those that operate oil and gas wells on their own account or for others on a contract or fee basis. Establishments primarily engaged in providing support services, on a contract or fee basis, required for the drilling or operation of oil and gas wells (except geophysical surveying and mapping, mine site preparation, and construction of oil/gas pipelines) are classified in Subsector 213, Support Activities for Mining.

2111 Oil and Gas Extraction[T]

21112 Crude Petroleum Extraction

See industry description for 211120.

T—Canadian, Mexican, and United States industries are comparable.

211120 Crude Petroleum Extraction

This industry comprises establishments primarily engaged in (1) the exploration, development, and/or the production of petroleum from wells in which the hydrocarbons will initially flow or can be produced using normal or enhanced drilling and extraction techniques or (2) the production of crude petroleum from surface shales or tar sands or from reservoirs in which the hydrocarbons are semisolids. Establishments in this industry operate oil wells on their own account or for others on a contract or fee basis.

Cross-References. Establishments primarily engaged in--

- Performing oil field services for operators on a contract or fee basis--are classified in Industry 21311, Support Activities for Mining; and
- Refining crude petroleum into refined petroleum and liquid hydrocarbons--are classified in Industry 324110, Petroleum Refineries.

21113 Natural Gas Extraction
See industry description for 211130.

211130 Natural Gas Extraction

This industry comprises establishments primarily engaged in (1) the exploration, development, and/or the production of natural gas from wells in which the hydrocarbons will initially flow or can be produced using normal or enhanced drilling and extraction techniques or (2) the recovery of liquid hydrocarbons from oil and gas field gases. Establishments primarily engaged in sulfur recovery from natural gas are included in this industry.

Cross-References. Establishments primarily engaged in--

- Performing gas field services for operators on a contract or fee basis--are classified in Industry 21311, Support Activities for Mining;
- Manufacturing acyclic and cyclic hydrocarbons from refined petroleum or converting refined petroleum into liquid hydrocarbons (i.e., petrochemicals)--are classified in Industry 325110, Petrochemical Manufacturing;
- Refining crude petroleum into refined petroleum and liquid hydrocarbons--are classified in Industry 324110, Petroleum Refineries; and
- Recovering helium from natural gas--are classified in Industry 325120, Industrial Gas Manufacturing.

212 Mining (except Oil and Gas)[T]

Industries in the Mining (except Oil and Gas) subsector primarily engage in mining, mine site development, and beneficiating (i.e., preparing) metallic minerals and nonmetallic minerals, including coal. The term “mining” is used in the broad sense to include ore extraction, quarrying, and beneficiating (e.g., crushing, screening, washing, sizing, concentrating, and flotation), customarily done at the mine site.

Beneficiation is the process whereby the extracted material is reduced to particles which can be separated into mineral and waste, the former suitable for further processing or direct use. The operations that take place in beneficiation are primarily mechanical, such as grinding, washing, magnetic separation, centrifugal separation, and so on. In contrast, manufacturing operations primarily use chemical and electrochemical processes, such as electrolysis, distillation, and so on. However some treatments, such as heat treatments, take place in both stages: the beneficiation and the manufacturing (i.e., smelting/refining) stages. The range of preparation activities varies by mineral and the purity of any given ore deposit. While some minerals, such as petroleum and natural gas, require little or no preparation, others are washed and screened, while yet others, such as gold and silver, can be transformed into bullion before leaving the mine site.

Establishments in the Mining (except Oil and Gas) subsector include those that have complete responsibility for operating mines and quarries (except oil and gas wells) and those that operate mines and quarries (except oil and gas wells) for others on a contract or fee basis. Establishments primarily engaged in providing support services, on a

T—Canadian, Mexican, and United States industries are comparable.

contract or fee basis, required for the mining and quarrying of minerals are classified in Subsector 213, Support Activities for Mining.

2121 Coal Mining[T]

21211 Coal Mining[T]

This industry comprises establishments primarily engaged in one or more of the following: (1) mining bituminous coal, anthracite, and lignite by underground mining, auger mining, strip mining, culm bank mining, and other surface mining; (2) developing coal mine sites; and (3) beneficiating (i.e., preparing) coal (e.g., cleaning, washing, screening, and sizing coal).

Cross-References. Establishments primarily engaged in--

- Manufacturing coke oven products in coke oven establishments--are classified in Industry 32419, Other Petroleum and Coal Products Manufacturing; and
- Manufacturing coal products in steel mills--are classified in Industry 33111, Iron and Steel Mills and Ferroalloy Manufacturing.

212111 Bituminous Coal and Lignite Surface Mining

This U.S. industry comprises establishments primarily engaged in one or more of the following: (1) surface mining of bituminous coal and lignite; (2) developing bituminous coal and lignite surface mine sites; (3) surface mining and beneficiating (e.g., cleaning, washing, screening, and sizing) of bituminous coal; or (4) beneficiating (e.g., cleaning, washing, screening, and sizing coal), but not mining, bituminous coal.

Cross-References. Establishments primarily engaged in--

- Manufacturing coke oven products in coke oven establishments--are classified in U.S. Industry 324199, All Other Petroleum and Coal Products Manufacturing;
- Underground mining of bituminous coal--are classified in U.S. Industry 212112, Bituminous Coal Underground Mining; and
- Mining and/or beneficiating anthracite coal--are classified in U.S. Industry 212113, Anthracite Mining.

212112 Bituminous Coal Underground Mining

This U.S. industry comprises establishments primarily engaged in one or more of the following: (1) underground mining of bituminous coal; (2) developing bituminous coal underground mine sites; and (3) underground mining and beneficiating of bituminous coal (e.g., cleaning, washing, screening, and sizing coal).

Cross-References. Establishments primarily engaged in--

- Manufacturing coke oven products in coke oven establishments--are classified in U.S. Industry 324199, All Other Petroleum and Coal Products Manufacturing;
- Surface mining and/or beneficiating of bituminous coal or lignite--are classified in U.S. Industry 212111, Bituminous Coal and Lignite Surface Mining; and
- Mining and/or beneficiating anthracite coal--are classified in U.S. Industry 212113, Anthracite Mining.

212113 Anthracite Mining

This U.S. industry comprises establishments primarily engaged in one or more of the following: (1) mining anthracite coal; (2) developing anthracite coal mine sites; and (3) beneficiating anthracite coal (e.g., cleaning, washing, screening, and sizing coal).
T—Canadian, Mexican, and United States industries are comparable.

Cross-References. Establishments primarily engaged in--

- Manufacturing coke oven products in coke oven establishments--are classified in U.S. Industry 324199, All Other Petroleum and Coal Products Manufacturing;
- Surface mining and/or beneficiating bituminous coal or lignite--are classified in U.S. Industry 212111, Bituminous Coal and Lignite Surface Mining; and
- Underground mining of bituminous coal--are classified in U.S. Industry 212112, Bituminous Coal Underground Mining.

2122 Metal Ore Mining[T]

This industry group comprises establishments primarily engaged in developing mine sites or mining metallic minerals, and establishments primarily engaged in ore dressing and beneficiating (i.e., preparing) operations, such as crushing, grinding, washing, drying, sintering, concentrating, calcining, and leaching. Beneficiating may be performed at mills operated in conjunction with the mines served or at mills, such as custom mills, operated separately.

21221 Iron Ore Mining[T] See industry description for 212210.

212210 Iron Ore Mining

This industry comprises establishments primarily engaged in (1) developing mine sites, mining, and/or beneficiating (i.e., preparing) iron ores and manganiferous ores valued chiefly for their iron content and/or (2) producing sinter iron ore (except iron ore produced in iron and steel mills) and other iron ore agglomerates.

Cross-References.

Establishments primarily engaged in manufacturing pig iron ore are classified in Industry 331110, Iron and Steel Mills and Ferroalloy Manufacturing.

21222 Gold Ore and Silver Ore Mining[T]

This industry comprises establishments primarily engaged in developing the mine site, mining, and/or beneficiating (i.e., preparing) ores valued chiefly for their gold and/or silver content. Establishments primarily engaged in the transformation of the gold and silver into bullion or dore bar in combination with mining activities are included in this industry.

Cross-References.

Establishments primarily engaged in manufacturing gold or silver bullion or dore bar without mining are classified in Industry 33141, Nonferrous Metal (except Aluminum) Smelting and Refining.

212221 Gold Ore Mining

This U.S. industry comprises establishments primarily engaged in developing the mine site, mining, and/or beneficiating (i.e., preparing) ores valued chiefly for their gold content. Establishments primarily engaged in transformation of the gold into bullion or dore bar in combination with mining activities are included in this industry.

Cross-References.

Establishments primarily engaged in manufacturing gold bullion or dore bar without mining are classified in Industry 331410, Nonferrous Metal (except Aluminum) Smelting and Refining.

T—Canadian, Mexican, and United States industries are comparable.

212222 Silver Ore Mining

This U.S. industry comprises establishments primarily engaged in developing the mine site, mining, and/or beneficiating (i.e., preparing) ores valued chiefly for their silver content. Establishments primarily engaged in transformation of the silver into bullion or dore bar in combination with mining activities are included in this industry.

Cross-References.

Establishments primarily engaged in manufacturing silver bullion or dore bar without mining are classified in Industry 331410, Nonferrous Metal (except Aluminum) Smelting and Refining.

21223 Copper, Nickel, Lead, and Zinc Mining[T] See industry description for 212230.

212230 Copper, Nickel, Lead, and Zinc Mining

This industry comprises establishments primarily engaged in developing the mine site, mining, and/or beneficiating (i.e., preparing) ores valued chiefly for their copper, nickel, lead, or zinc content. Beneficiating includes the transformation of ores into concentrates. Establishments primarily engaged in recovering copper concentrates by the precipitation, leaching, or electrowinning of copper ore are included in this industry.

Cross-References. Establishments primarily engaged in--

- Refining copper concentrates--are classified in Industry 331410, Nonferrous Metal (except Aluminum) Smelting and Refining; and
- Developing the mine site, mining, and/or beneficiating iron and manganiferous ores valued for their iron content--are classified in Industry 212210, Iron Ore Mining.

21229 Other Metal Ore Mining[T]

This industry comprises establishments primarily engaged in developing the mine site, mining, and/or beneficiating (i.e., preparing) metal ores (except iron and manganiferous ores valued for their iron content, gold ore, silver ore, copper, nickel, lead, and zinc ore).

Illustrative Examples:

Antimony ores mining and/or beneficiating
Tantalum ores mining and/or beneficiating
Columbite ores mining and/or beneficiating
Tungsten ores mining and/or beneficiating
Ilmenite ores mining and/or beneficiating
Uranium-radium-vanadium ores mining and/or beneficiating
Molybdenum ores mining and/or beneficiating

Cross-References. Establishments primarily engaged in--

- Developing the mine site, mining, and/or beneficiating iron and manganiferous ores valued chiefly for their iron content--are classified in Industry 21221, Iron Ore Mining;
- Developing the mine site, mining, and/or beneficiating ores valued chiefly for their gold or silver content--are classified in Industry 21222, Gold Ore and Silver Ore Mining;
- Developing the mine site, mining, and/or beneficiating ores valued chiefly for their copper, nickel, lead, or zinc content--are classified in Industry 21223, Copper, Nickel, Lead, and Zinc Mining; and
- Enriching uranium--are classified in Industry 32518, Other Basic Inorganic Chemical Manufacturing.

T—Canadian, Mexican, and United States industries are comparable.

212291 Uranium-Radium-Vanadium Ore Mining

This U.S. industry comprises establishments primarily engaged in developing the mine site, mining, and/or beneficiating (i.e., preparing) uranium-radium-vanadium ores.

Cross-References.

Establishments primarily engaged in enriching uranium are classified in Industry 325180, Other Basic Inorganic Chemical Manufacturing.

212299 All Other Metal Ore Mining

This U.S. industry comprises establishments primarily engaged in developing the mine site, mining, and/or beneficiating (i.e., preparing) metal ores (except iron and manganiferous ores valued for their iron content, gold ore, silver ore, copper, nickel, lead, zinc, and uranium-radium-vanadium ore).

Illustrative Examples:

Antimony ores mining and/or beneficiating
Rare earth metal ores mining and/or beneficiating
Columbite ores mining and/or beneficiating
Tantalum ores mining and/or beneficiating
Ilmenite ores mining and/or beneficiating
Tungsten ores mining and/or beneficiating
Molybdenum ores mining and/or beneficiating

Cross-References. Establishments primarily engaged in--

- Developing the mine site, mining, and/or beneficiating iron and manganiferous ores valued for their iron content--are classified in Industry 212210, Iron Ore Mining;
- Developing the mine site, mining, and/or beneficiating ores valued chiefly for their gold or silver content--are classified in Industry 21222, Gold Ore and Silver Ore Mining;
- Developing the mine site, mining, and/or beneficiating ores valued chiefly for their copper, nickel, lead, or zinc content--are classified in Industry 212230, Copper, Nickel, Lead, and Zinc Mining; and
- Developing the mine site, mining, and/or beneficiating uranium-radium-vanadium ores--are classified in U.S. Industry 212291, Uranium-Radium-Vanadium Ore Mining.

2123 Nonmetallic Mineral Mining and Quarrying[T]

This industry group comprises establishments primarily engaged in developing mine sites, or in mining or quarrying nonmetallic minerals (except fuels). Also included are certain well and brine operations, and preparation plants primarily engaged in beneficiating (e.g., crushing, grinding, washing, and concentrating) nonmetallic minerals.

Beneficiation is the process whereby the extracted material is reduced to particles which can be separated into mineral and waste, the former suitable for further processing or direct use. The operations that take place in beneficiation are primarily mechanical, such as grinding, washing, magnetic separation, and centrifugal separation. In contrast, manufacturing operations primarily use chemical and electrochemical processes, such as electrolysis and distillation. However, some treatments, such as heat treatments, take place in both the beneficiation and the manufacturing (i.e., smelting/refining) stages. The range of preparation activities varies by mineral and the purity of any given ore deposit. While some minerals, such as petroleum and natural gas, require little or no preparation, others are washed and screened, while yet others, such as gold and silver, can be transformed into bullion before leaving the mine site.

21231 Stone Mining and Quarrying[T]

This industry comprises (1) establishments primarily engaged in developing the mine site, mining or quarrying dimension stone (i.e., rough blocks and/or slabs of stone), or mining and quarrying crushed and broken stone and/or

T—Canadian, Mexican, and United States industries are comparable.

(2) preparation plants primarily engaged in beneficiating stone (e.g., crushing, grinding, washing, screening, pulverizing, and sizing).

Cross-References. Establishments primarily engaged in--

- Producing lime--are classified in Industry 32741, Lime Manufacturing; and
- Quarrying and dressing dimension stone--are classified in Industry 32799, All Other Nonmetallic Mineral Product Manufacturing.

212311 Dimension Stone Mining and Quarrying

This U.S. industry comprises establishments primarily engaged in developing the mine site and/or mining or quarrying dimension stone (i.e., rough blocks and/or slabs of stone).

Cross-References.

Establishments primarily engaged in dressing dimension stone and manufacturing stone products are classified in U.S. Industry 327991, Cut Stone and Stone Product Manufacturing.

212312 Crushed and Broken Limestone Mining and Quarrying

This U.S. industry comprises (1) establishments primarily engaged in developing the mine site, mining or quarrying crushed and broken limestone (including related rocks, such as dolomite, cement rock, marl, travertine, and calcareous tufa) and (2) preparation plants primarily engaged in beneficiating limestone (e.g., grinding or pulverizing).

Cross-References. Establishments primarily engaged in--

- Producing lime--are classified in Industry 327410, Lime Manufacturing; and
- Mining or quarrying bituminous limestone--are classified in U.S. Industry 212319, Other Crushed and Broken Stone Mining and Quarrying.

212313 Crushed and Broken Granite Mining and Quarrying

This U.S. industry comprises (1) establishments primarily engaged in developing the mine site, and/or mining or quarrying crushed and broken granite (including related rocks, such as gneiss, syenite (except nepheline), and diorite) and (2) preparation plants primarily engaged in beneficiating granite (e.g., grinding or pulverizing).

212319 Other Crushed and Broken Stone Mining and Quarrying

This U.S. industry comprises: (1) establishments primarily engaged in developing the mine site and/or mining or quarrying crushed and broken stone (except limestone and granite); (2) preparation plants primarily engaged in beneficiating (e.g., grinding and pulverizing) stone (except limestone and granite); and (3) establishments primarily engaged in mining or quarrying bituminous limestone and bituminous sandstone.

Illustrative Examples:

Bituminous limestone mining and/or beneficiating
Marble crushed and broken stone mining and/or beneficiating
Bituminous sandstone mining and/or beneficiating
Sandstone crushed and broken stone mining and/or beneficiating

Cross-References. Establishments primarily engaged in--

- Mining or quarrying crushed and broken limestone--are classified in U.S. Industry 212312, Crushed and Broken Limestone Mining and Quarrying; and

T—Canadian, Mexican, and United States industries are comparable.

- Mining or quarrying crushed and broken granite--are classified in U.S. Industry 212313, Crushed and Broken Granite Mining and Quarrying.

21232 Sand, Gravel, Clay, and Ceramic and Refractory Minerals Mining and Quarrying[T]

This industry comprises (1) establishments primarily engaged in developing the mine site and/or mining, quarrying, dredging for sand and gravel, or mining clay (e.g., china clay, paper clay and slip clay) and (2) preparation plants primarily engaged in beneficiating (e.g., washing, screening, and grinding) sand and gravel, clay, and ceramic and refractory minerals.

Cross-References. Establishments primarily engaged in--

- Calcining, dead burning, or otherwise processing (i.e., beyond basic preparation) clay or refractory minerals--are classified in Industry 32799, All Other Nonmetallic Mineral Product Manufacturing;
- Shaping, molding, baking, burning, or hardening nonclay ceramics, clay and nonclay refractories, and structural clay products--are classified in Industry 32712, Clay Building Material and Refractories Manufacturing; and
- Shaping, molding, glazing, and firing pottery, ceramics, and plumbing fixtures--are classified in Industry 32711, Pottery, Ceramics, and Plumbing Fixture Manufacturing.

212321 Construction Sand and Gravel Mining

This U.S. industry comprises establishments primarily engaged in one or more of the following: (1) operating commercial grade (i.e., construction) sand and gravel pits; (2) dredging for commercial grade sand and gravel; and (3) washing, screening, or otherwise preparing commercial grade sand and gravel.

Cross-References.

Establishments primarily engaged in mining industrial grade sand are classified in U.S. Industry 212322, Industrial Sand Mining.

212322 Industrial Sand Mining

This U.S. industry comprises establishments primarily engaged in one or more of the following: (1) operating industrial grade sand pits; (2) dredging for industrial grade sand; and (3) washing, screening, or otherwise preparing industrial grade sand.

Cross-References.

Establishments primarily engaged in mining commercial (i.e., construction) grade gravel are classified in U.S. Industry 212321, Construction Sand and Gravel Mining.

212324 Kaolin and Ball Clay Mining

This U.S. industry comprises (1) establishments primarily engaged in developing the mine site and/or mining kaolin or ball clay (e.g., china clay, paper clay, and slip clay) and (2) establishments primarily engaged in beneficiating (i.e., preparing) kaolin or ball clay.

Cross-References.

Establishments primarily engaged in calcining, dead burning, or otherwise processing (i.e., beyond basic preparation) kaolin and ball clay are classified in U.S. Industry 327992, Ground or Treated Mineral and Earth Manufacturing.

T—Canadian, Mexican, and United States industries are comparable.

212325 Clay and Ceramic and Refractory Minerals Mining

This U.S. industry comprises establishments primarily engaged in one or more of the following: (1) mining clay (except kaolin and ball), ceramic, or refractory minerals; (2) developing the mine site for clay, ceramic, or refractory minerals; and (3) beneficiating (i.e., preparing) clay (except kaolin and ball), ceramic, or refractory minerals.

Illustrative Examples:

Bentonite mining and/or beneficiating
Fuller's earth mining and/or beneficiating
Common clay mining and/or beneficiating
Magnesite mining and/or beneficiating
Feldspar mining and/or beneficiating
Nepheline syenite mining and/or beneficiating
Fire clay mining and/or beneficiating
Shale (except oil shale) mining and/or beneficiating

Cross-References. Establishments primarily engaged in--

- Shaping, molding, baking, burning, or hardening clay and nonclay refractories, and structural clay products--are classified in Industry 327120, Clay Building Material and Refractories Manufacturing;
- Developing the mine site, mining, and/or beneficiating kaolin or ball clay--are classified in U.S. Industry 212324, Kaolin and Ball Clay Mining; and
- Shaping, molding, glazing, and firing pottery, ceramics, and plumbing fixtures--are classified in Industry 327110, Pottery, Ceramics, and Plumbing Fixture Manufacturing.

21239 Other Nonmetallic Mineral Mining and Quarrying[T]

This industry comprises establishments primarily engaged in developing the mine site, mining, and/or milling or otherwise beneficiating (i.e., preparing) nonmetallic minerals (except coal, stone, sand, gravel, clay, ceramic, and refractory minerals).

Illustrative Examples:

Barite mining and/or beneficiating
Phosphate rock mining and/or beneficiating
Borate, natural, mining and/or beneficiating
Potash mining and/or beneficiating
Peat mining and/or beneficiating
Rock salt mining and/or beneficiating

Cross-References. Establishments primarily engaged in--

- Mining or quarrying dimension stone--are classified in Industry 21231, Stone Mining and Quarrying;
- Mining or quarrying sand, gravel, clay, and ceramic and refractory minerals--are classified in Industry 21232, Sand, Gravel, Clay, and Ceramic and Refractory Minerals Mining and Quarrying;
- Calcining, dead burning, or otherwise processing (i.e., beyond basic preparation) minerals, such as talc, mica, feldspar, barite, and soapstone--are classified in Industry 32799, All Other Nonmetallic Mineral Product Manufacturing;
- Manufacturing boron compounds and potassium salts--are classified in Industry 32518, Other Basic Inorganic Chemical Manufacturing;
- Manufacturing table salt--are classified in Industry 31194, Seasoning and Dressing Manufacturing;
- Manufacturing salt (except table salt)--are classified in Industry 32599, All Other Chemical Product and Preparation Manufacturing; and
- Manufacturing phosphoric acid, superphosphates, or other phosphatic fertilizer materials--are classified in Industry 32531, Fertilizer Manufacturing.

212391 Potash, Soda, and Borate Mineral Mining

This U.S. industry comprises establishments primarily engaged in developing the mine site, mining and/or milling, or otherwise beneficiating (i.e., preparing) natural potassium, sodium, or boron compounds. Drylake brine

T—Canadian, Mexican, and United States industries are comparable.

operations are included in this industry, as well as establishments engaged in producing the specified minerals from underground and open pit mines.

Cross-References. Establishments primarily engaged in--

- Manufacturing sodium carbonate, boron compounds, and/or potassium salts--are classified in Industry 325180, Other Basic Inorganic Chemical Manufacturing; and
- Manufacturing table salt--are classified in U.S. Industry 311942, Spice and Extract Manufacturing.

212392 Phosphate Rock Mining

This U.S. industry comprises establishments primarily engaged in developing the mine site, mining, milling, and/or drying or otherwise beneficiating (i.e., preparing) phosphate rock.

Cross-References.

Establishments primarily engaged in manufacturing phosphoric acid, superphosphates, or other phosphatic fertilizer materials are classified in U.S. Industry 325312, Phosphatic Fertilizer Manufacturing.

212393 Other Chemical and Fertilizer Mineral Mining

This U.S. industry comprises establishments primarily engaged in developing the mine site, mining, milling, and/or drying or otherwise beneficiating (i.e., preparing) chemical or fertilizer mineral raw materials (except potash, soda, boron, and phosphate rock).

Illustrative Examples:

Barite mining and/or beneficiating
Rock salt mining and/or beneficiating
Celestite mining and/or beneficiating
Sulfur mining and/or beneficiating
Fluorspar mining and/or beneficiating

Cross-References. Establishments primarily engaged in--

- Mining and/or milling or otherwise beneficiating natural potassium, sodium, or boron compounds--are classified in U.S. Industry 212391, Potash, Soda, and Borate Mineral Mining;
- Manufacturing industrial salt--are classified in U.S. Industry 325998, All Other Miscellaneous Chemical Product and Preparation Manufacturing;
- Mining, milling, drying, and/or sintering or otherwise beneficiating phosphate rock--are classified in U.S. Industry 212392, Phosphate Rock Mining; and
- Manufacturing table salt--are classified in U.S. Industry 311942, Spice and Extract Manufacturing.

212399 All Other Nonmetallic Mineral Mining

This U.S. industry comprises establishments primarily engaged in developing the mine site, mining and/or milling, or otherwise beneficiating (i.e., preparing) nonmetallic minerals (except stone, sand, gravel, clay, ceramic, refractory minerals, and chemical and fertilizer minerals).

Illustrative Examples:

Gypsum mining and/or beneficiating
Soapstone mining and/or beneficiating
Mica mining and/or beneficiating
Talc mining and/or beneficiating
Pyrophyllite mining and/or beneficiating

T—Canadian, Mexican, and United States industries are comparable.

Cross-References. Establishments primarily engaged in--

- Mining or quarrying stone--are classified in Industry 21231, Stone Mining and Quarrying;
- Mining, quarrying, or beneficiating sand, gravel, clay, and ceramic and refractory minerals--are classified in Industry 21232, Sand, Gravel, Clay, and Ceramic and Refractory Minerals Mining and Quarrying;
- Mining, quarrying, or beneficiating natural potash, soda, and borate--are classified in U.S. Industry 212391, Potash, Soda, and Borate Mineral Mining; and
- Mining and/or milling or otherwise beneficiating phosphate rock--are classified in U.S. Industry 212392, Phosphate Rock Mining.

213 Support Activities for Mining[T]

Industries in the Support Activities for Mining subsector group establishments primarily providing support services, on a contract or fee basis, required for the mining and quarrying of minerals and for the extraction of oil and gas. Establishments performing exploration (except geophysical surveying and mapping) for minerals, on a contract or fee basis, are included in this subsector. Exploration includes traditional prospecting methods, such as taking core samples and making geological observations at prospective sites.

The activities performed on a contract or fee basis by establishments in the Support Activities for Mining subsector are also often performed in-house by mining operators. These activities include taking core samples, making geological observations at prospective sites, excavating slush pits and cellars, and such oil and gas operations as spudding in, drilling in, redrilling, directional drilling, and well surveying; running, cutting, and pulling casings, tubes, and rods; cementing and shooting wells; perforating well casings; acidizing and chemically treating wells; cleaning out, bailing, and swabbing wells; and operating oil and gas field gathering lines.

2131 Support Activities for Mining[T]

21311 Support Activities for Mining[T]

This industry comprises establishments primarily engaged in providing support services, on a contract or fee basis, required for the mining and quarrying of minerals and for the extraction of oil and gas. Drilling, taking core samples, and making geological observations at prospective sites (except geophysical surveying and mapping) for minerals, on a contract or fee basis, are included in this industry.

Cross-References. Establishments primarily engaged in--

- Performing geophysical surveying and mapping services for minerals (i.e., coal, metal ores, oil and gas, and nonmetallic minerals) on a contract or fee basis--are classified in Industry 54136, Geophysical Surveying and Mapping Services;
- Mining, quarrying, and/or beneficiating on a contract or fee basis--are classified in Subsector 212, Mining (except Oil and Gas), based on the mineral mined;
- Operating oil and gas field properties on a contract or fee basis--are classified in Subsector 211, Oil and Gas Extraction, based on the activity;
- Oil and gas pipeline and related structures construction and repair--are classified in Industry 23712, Oil and Gas Pipeline and Related Structures Construction;
- Site preparation and related construction activities on a contract or fee basis--are classified in Industry 23891, Site Preparation Contractors; and
- Mining machinery and equipment repair and maintenance--are classified in Industry 81131, Commercial and Industrial Machinery and Equipment (except Automotive and Electronic) Repair and Maintenance.

213111 Drilling Oil and Gas Wells

This U.S. industry comprises establishments primarily engaged in drilling oil and gas wells for others on a contract or fee basis. This industry includes contractors that specialize in spudding in, drilling in, redrilling, and directional drilling.

T—Canadian, Mexican, and United States industries are comparable.

Cross-References. Establishments primarily engaged in--

- Performing exploration (except geophysical surveying and mapping) services for oil and gas on a contract or fee basis--are classified in U.S. Industry 213112, Support Activities for Oil and Gas Operations; and
- Performing geophysical surveying and mapping services for oil and gas on a contract or fee basis--are classified in Industry 541360, Geophysical Surveying and Mapping Services.

213112 Support Activities for Oil and Gas Operations

This U.S. industry comprises establishments primarily engaged in performing support activities on a contract or fee basis for oil and gas operations (except site preparation and related construction activities). Services included are exploration (except geophysical surveying and mapping); excavating slush pits and cellars, well surveying; running, cutting, and pulling casings, tubes, and rods; cementing wells, shooting wells; perforating well casings; acidizing and chemically treating wells; and cleaning out, bailing, and swabbing wells.

Cross-References. Establishments primarily engaged in--

- Contract drilling for oil and gas--are classified in U.S. Industry 213111, Drilling Oil and Gas Wells;
- Operating oil and gas field properties on a contract or fee basis--are classified in Industry Group 2111, Oil and Gas Extraction;
- Performing geophysical surveying and mapping services for oil and gas on a contract or fee basis--are classified in Industry 541360, Geophysical Surveying and Mapping Services;
- Oil and gas pipeline and related structures construction and repair--are classified in Industry 237120, Oil and Gas Pipeline and Related Structures Construction;
- Inspecting pipelines--are classified in Industry 541990, All Other Professional, Scientific, and Technical Services;
- Site preparation and related construction activities on a contract or fee basis--are classified in Industry 238910, Site Preparation Contractors; and
- Mining machinery and equipment repair and maintenance--are classified in Industry 811310, Commercial and Industrial Machinery and Equipment (except Automotive and Electronic) Repair and Maintenance.

213113 Support Activities for Coal Mining

This U.S. industry comprises establishments primarily engaged in providing support activities for coal mining (except site preparation and related construction activities) on a contract or fee basis. Exploration for coal is included in this industry. Exploration includes traditional prospecting methods, such as taking core samples and making geological observations at prospective sites.

Cross-References. Establishments primarily engaged in--

- Performing geophysical surveying and mapping services for coal on a contract or fee basis--are classified in Industry 541360, Geophysical Surveying and Mapping Services;
- Operating coal mines or quarries on a contract or fee basis--are classified in Industry 21211, Coal Mining, based on the type of coal mined; and
- Site preparation and related construction activities on a contract or fee basis--are classified in Industry 238910, Site Preparation Contractors.

213114 Support Activities for Metal Mining

This U.S. industry comprises establishments primarily engaged in providing support activities (except site preparation and related construction activities) on a contract or fee basis for the mining and quarrying of metallic minerals and for the extraction of metal ores. Exploration for these minerals is included in this industry.
Exploration (except geophysical surveying and mapping services) includes traditional prospecting methods, such as taking core samples and making geological observations at prospective sites.

T—Canadian, Mexican, and United States industries are comparable.

Cross-References. Establishments primarily engaged in--

- Performing geophysical surveying and mapping services for metallic minerals on a contract or fee basis--are classified in Industry 541360, Geophysical Surveying and Mapping Services;
- Operating metallic mineral mines or quarries on a contract or fee basis--are classified in Industry Group 2122, Metal Ore Mining, based on the type of ore mined; and
- Site preparation and related construction activities on a contract or fee basis--are classified in Industry 238910, Site Preparation Contractors.

213115 Support Activities for Nonmetallic Minerals (except Fuels) Mining

This U.S. industry comprises establishments primarily engaged in providing support activities, on a contract or fee basis, for the mining and quarrying of nonmetallic minerals (except fuel) and for the extraction of nonmetallic minerals (except site preparation and related construction activities). Exploration for these minerals is included in this industry. Exploration (except geophysical surveying and mapping services) includes traditional prospecting methods, such as taking core samples and making geological observations at prospective sites.

Cross-References. Establishments primarily engaged in--

- Performing geophysical surveying and mapping services for nonmetallic minerals on a contract or fee basis--are classified in Industry 541360, Geophysical Surveying and Mapping Services;
- Operating nonmetallic mineral mines or quarries on a contract or fee basis--are classified in Industry Group 2123, Nonmetallic Mineral Mining and Quarrying, based on the type of mineral mined or quarried; and
- Site preparation and related construction activities on a contract or fee basis--are classified in Industry 238910, Site Preparation Contractors.

T—Canadian, Mexican, and United States industries are comparable.

Sector 22--Utilities[T]

The Sector as a Whole

The Utilities sector comprises establishments engaged in the provision of the following utility services: electric power, natural gas, steam supply, water supply, and sewage removal. Within this sector, the specific activities associated with the utility services provided vary by utility: electric power includes generation, transmission, and distribution; natural gas includes distribution; steam supply includes provision and/or distribution; water supply includes treatment and distribution; and sewage removal includes collection, treatment, and disposal of waste through sewer systems and sewage treatment facilities.

Excluded from this sector are establishments primarily engaged in waste management services classified in Subsector 562, Waste Management and Remediation Services. These establishments also collect, treat, and dispose of waste materials; however, they do not use sewer systems or sewage treatment facilities.

221 Utilities[T]

Industries in the Utilities subsector provide electric power, natural gas, steam supply, water supply, and sewage removal through a permanent infrastructure of lines, mains, and pipes. Establishments are grouped together based on the utility service provided and the particular system or facilities required to perform the service.

2211 Electric Power Generation, Transmission and Distribution[T]

This industry group comprises establishments primarily engaged in generating, transmitting, and/or distributing electric power. Establishments in this industry group may perform one or more of the following activities: (1) operate generation facilities that produce electric energy; (2) operate transmission systems that convey the electricity from the generation facility to the distribution system; and (3) operate distribution systems that convey electric power received from the generation facility or the transmission system to the final consumer.

22111 Electric Power Generation[T]

This industry comprises establishments primarily engaged in operating electric power generation facilities. These facilities convert other forms of energy, such as water power (i.e., hydroelectric), fossil fuels, nuclear power, and solar power, into electrical energy. The establishments in this industry produce electric energy and provide electricity to transmission systems or to electric power distribution systems.

Cross-References.

Establishments primarily engaged in operating trash incinerators that also generate electricity are classified in Industry 56221, Waste Treatment and Disposal.

221111 Hydroelectric Power Generation

This U.S. industry comprises establishments primarily engaged in operating hydroelectric power generation facilities. These facilities use water power to drive a turbine and produce electric energy. The electric energy produced in these establishments is provided to electric power transmission systems or to electric power distribution systems.

221112 Fossil Fuel Electric Power Generation

This U.S. industry comprises establishments primarily engaged in operating fossil fuel powered electric power generation facilities. These facilities use fossil fuels, such as coal, oil, or gas, in internal combustion or combustion turbine conventional steam process to produce electric energy. The electric energy produced in these establishments is provided to electric power transmission systems or to electric power distribution systems.

T—Canadian, Mexican, and United States industries are comparable.

221113 Nuclear Electric Power Generation

This U.S. industry comprises establishments primarily engaged in operating nuclear electric power generation facilities. These facilities use nuclear power to produce electric energy. The electric energy produced in these establishments is provided to electric power transmission systems or to electric power distribution systems.

221114 Solar Electric Power Generation

This U.S. industry comprises establishments primarily engaged in operating solar electric power generation facilities. These facilities use energy from the sun to produce electric energy. The electric energy produced in these establishments is provided to electric power transmission systems or to electric power distribution systems.

221115 Wind Electric Power Generation

This U.S. industry comprises establishments primarily engaged in operating wind electric power generation facilities. These facilities use wind power to drive a turbine and produce electric energy. The electric energy produced in these establishments is provided to electric power transmission systems or to electric power distribution systems.

221116 Geothermal Electric Power Generation

This U.S. industry comprises establishments primarily engaged in operating geothermal electric power generation facilities. These facilities use heat derived from the Earth to produce electric energy. The electric energy produced in these establishments is provided to electric power transmission systems or to electric power distribution systems.

221117 Biomass Electric Power Generation

This U.S. industry comprises establishments primarily engaged in operating biomass electric power generation facilities. These facilities use biomass (e.g., wood, waste, alcohol fuels) to produce electric energy. The electric energy produced in these establishments is provided to electric power transmission systems or to electric power distribution systems.

Cross-References.

Establishments primarily engaged in operating trash disposal incinerators that also generate electricity are classified in U.S. Industry 562213, Solid Waste Combustors and Incinerators.

221118 Other Electric Power Generation

This U.S. industry comprises establishments primarily engaged in operating electric power generation facilities (except hydroelectric, fossil fuel, nuclear, solar, wind, geothermal, biomass). These facilities convert other forms of energy, such as tidal power, into electric energy. The electric energy produced in these establishments is provided to electric power transmission systems or to electric power distribution systems.

Cross-References. Establishments primarily engaged in--

- Operating trash disposal incinerators that also generate electricity--are classified in U.S. Industry 562213, Solid Waste Combustors and Incinerators;
- Operating hydroelectric power generation facilities--are classified in U.S. Industry 221111, Hydroelectric Power Generation;
- Operating fossil fuel powered electric power generation facilities--are classified in U.S. Industry 221112, Fossil Fuel Electric Power Generation;
- Operating nuclear electric power generation facilities--are classified in U.S. Industry 221113, Nuclear Electric Power Generation;

T—Canadian, Mexican, and United States industries are comparable.

- Operating solar electric power generation facilities--are classified in U.S. Industry 221114, Solar Electric Power Generation;
- Operating wind electric power generation facilities--are classified in U.S. Industry 221115, Wind Electric Power Generation;
- Operating geothermal electric power generation facilities--are classified in U.S. Industry 221116, Geothermal Electric Power Generation; and
- Operating biomass electric power generation facilities--are classified in U.S. Industry 221117, Biomass Electric Power Generation.

22112 Electric Power Transmission, Control, and Distribution^T

This industry comprises establishments primarily engaged in operating electric power transmission systems, controlling (i.e., regulating voltages) the transmission of electricity, and/or distributing electricity. The transmission system includes lines and transformer stations. These establishments arrange, facilitate, or coordinate the transmission of electricity from the generating source to the distribution centers, other electric utilities, or final consumers. The distribution system consists of lines, poles, meters, and wiring that deliver the electricity to final consumers.

Cross-References.

Establishments primarily engaged in generating electric energy are classified in Industry 22111, Electric Power Generation.

221121 Electric Bulk Power Transmission and Control

This U.S. industry comprises establishments primarily engaged in operating electric power transmission systems and/or controlling (i.e., regulating voltages) the transmission of electricity from the generating source to distribution centers or other electric utilities. The transmission system includes lines and transformer stations.

Cross-References. Establishments primarily engaged in--

- Generating electric energy--are classified in Industry 22111, Electric Power Generation; and
- Distributing electricity to final consumers--are classified in U.S. Industry 221122, Electric Power Distribution.

221122 Electric Power Distribution

This U.S. industry comprises electric power establishments primarily engaged in either (1) operating electric power distribution systems (i.e., consisting of lines, poles, meters, and wiring) or (2) operating as electric power brokers or agents that arrange the sale of electricity via power distribution systems operated by others.

Cross-References. Establishments primarily engaged in--

- Generating electric energy--are classified in Industry 22111, Electric Power Generation; and
- Transmitting electricity between generating sources or distribution centers--are classified in U.S. Industry 221121, Electric Bulk Power Transmission and Control.

2212 Natural Gas Distribution^T

22121 Natural Gas Distribution^T See industry description for 221210.

T—Canadian, Mexican, and United States industries are comparable.

221210 Natural Gas Distribution

This industry comprises: (1) establishments primarily engaged in operating gas distribution systems (e.g., mains, meters); (2) establishments known as gas marketers that buy gas from the well and sell it to a distribution system; (3) establishments known as gas brokers or agents that arrange the sale of gas over gas distribution systems operated by others; and (4) establishments primarily engaged in transmitting and distributing gas to final consumers.

Cross-References. Establishments primarily engaged in--

- Pipeline transportation of natural gas from process plants to local distribution systems--are classified in Industry 486210, Pipeline Transportation of Natural Gas; and
- Retailing liquefied petroleum (LP) gas via direct selling--are classified in Industry 454310, Fuel Dealers.

2213 Water, Sewage and Other Systems[T]

This industry group comprises establishments primarily engaged in: (1) operating water treatment plants and/or water supply systems; (2) operating sewer systems or sewage treatment facilities; or (3) providing steam, heated air, or cooled air.

22131 Water Supply and Irrigation Systems
See industry description for 221310.

221310 Water Supply and Irrigation Systems

This industry comprises establishments primarily engaged in operating water treatment plants and/or operating water supply systems. The water supply system may include pumping stations, aqueducts, and/or distribution mains. The water may be used for drinking, irrigation, or other uses.

22132 Sewage Treatment Facilities
See industry description for 221320.

221320 Sewage Treatment Facilities

This industry comprises establishments primarily engaged in operating sewer systems or sewage treatment facilities that collect, treat, and dispose of waste.

Cross-References. Establishments primarily engaged in--

- Operating waste treatment or disposal facilities (except sewer systems or sewage treatment facilities)--are classified in Industry 56221, Waste Treatment and Disposal;
- Pumping (i.e., cleaning) septic tanks and cesspools--are classified in U.S. Industry 562991, Septic Tank and Related Services; and
- Cleaning and rodding sewers and catch basins--are classified in U.S. Industry 562998, All Other Miscellaneous Waste Management Services.

22133 Steam and Air-Conditioning Supply
See industry description for 221330.

221330 Steam and Air-Conditioning Supply

This industry comprises establishments primarily engaged in providing steam, heated air, or cooled air. The steam distribution may be through mains.

T—Canadian, Mexican, and United States industries are comparable.

Sector 23--Construction[T]

The Sector as a Whole

The Construction sector comprises establishments primarily engaged in the construction of buildings or engineering projects (e.g., highways and utility systems). Establishments primarily engaged in the preparation of sites for new construction and establishments primarily engaged in subdividing land for sale as building sites also are included in this sector.

Construction work done may include new work, additions, alterations, or maintenance and repairs. Activities of these establishments generally are managed at a fixed place of business, but they usually perform construction activities at multiple project sites. Production responsibilities for establishments in this sector are usually specified in (1) contracts with the owners of construction projects (prime contracts) or (2) contracts with other construction establishments (subcontracts).

Establishments primarily engaged in contracts that include responsibility for all aspects of individual construction projects are commonly known as general contractors, but also may be known as design-builders, construction managers, turnkey contractors, or (in cases where two or more establishments jointly secure a general contract) joint-venture contractors. Construction managers that provide oversight and scheduling only (i.e., agency) as well as construction managers that are responsible for the entire project (i.e., at risk) are included as general contractor type establishments. Establishments of the "general contractor type" frequently arrange construction of separate parts of their projects through subcontracts with other construction establishments.

Establishments primarily engaged in activities to produce a specific component (e.g., masonry, painting, and electrical work) of a construction project are commonly known as specialty trade contractors. Activities of specialty trade contractors are usually subcontracted from other construction establishments, but especially in remodeling and repair construction, the work may be done directly for the owner of the property.

Establishments primarily engaged in activities to construct buildings to be sold on sites that they own are known as for-sale builders, but also may be known as speculative builders or merchant builders. For-sale builders produce buildings in a manner similar to general contractors, but their production processes also include site acquisition and securing of financial backing. For-sale builders are most often associated with the construction of residential buildings. Like general contractors, they may subcontract all or part of the actual construction work on their buildings.

There are substantial differences in the types of equipment, work force skills, and other inputs required by establishments in this sector. To highlight these differences and variations in the underlying production functions, this sector is divided into three subsectors.

Subsector 236, Construction of Buildings, comprises establishments of the general contractor type and for-sale builders involved in the construction of buildings. Subsector 237, Heavy and Civil Engineering Construction, comprises establishments involved in the construction of engineering projects. Subsector 238, Specialty Trade Contractors, comprises establishments engaged in specialty trade activities generally needed in the construction of all types of buildings.

Force account construction is construction work performed by an enterprise primarily engaged in some business other than construction for its own account, using employees of the enterprise. This activity is not included in the construction sector unless the construction work performed is the primary activity of a separate establishment of the enterprise. The installation and the ongoing repair and maintenance of telecommunications and utility networks is excluded from construction when the establishments performing the work are not independent contractors. Although a growing proportion of this work is subcontracted to independent contractors in the Construction sector, the operating units of telecommunications and utility companies performing this work are included with the telecommunications or utility activities.

236 Construction of Buildings[T]

The Construction of Buildings subsector comprises establishments primarily responsible for the construction of buildings. The work performed may include new work, additions, alterations, or maintenance and repairs. The on-site assembly of precut, panelized, and prefabricated buildings and construction of temporary buildings are included in this subsector. Part or all of the production work for which the establishments in this subsector have responsibility may be subcontracted to other construction establishments--usually specialty trade contractors.

T—Canadian, Mexican, and United States industries are comparable.

Establishments in this subsector are classified based on the types of buildings they construct. This classification reflects variations in the requirements of the underlying production processes.

2361 Residential Building Construction[T]

23611 Residential Building Construction[T]

This industry comprises establishments primarily responsible for the construction or remodeling and renovation of single-family and multifamily residential buildings. Included in this industry are residential housing general contractors (i.e., new construction, remodeling, or renovating existing residential structures), for-sale builders and remodelers of residential structures, residential project construction management firms, and residential design-build firms.

Cross-References. Establishments primarily engaged in--

- Performing specialized construction work on houses and other residential buildings, generally on a subcontract basis--are classified in Subsector 238, Specialty Trade Contractors;
- Performing manufactured (mobile) home set up and tie-down work--are classified in Industry 23899, All Other Specialty Trade Contractors; and
- Constructing and leasing residential buildings on their own account--are classified in Industry 53111, Lessors of Residential Buildings and Dwellings.

236115 New Single-Family Housing Construction (except For-Sale Builders)

This U.S. industry comprises general contractor establishments primarily responsible for the entire construction of new single-family housing, such as single-family detached houses and town houses or row houses where each housing unit (1) is separated from its neighbors by a ground-to-roof wall and (2) has no housing units constructed above or below. This industry includes general contractors responsible for the on-site assembly of modular and prefabricated houses. Single-family housing design-build firms and single-family construction management firms acting as general contractors are included in this industry.

Cross-References. Establishments primarily engaged in--

- Building single-family houses on their own account for sale as speculative builders or merchant builders--are classified in U.S. Industry 236117, New Housing For-Sale Builders;
- Remodeling or repairing existing houses and other residential buildings--are classified in U.S. Industry 236118, Residential Remodelers;
- Performing manufactured (mobile) home set up and tie-down work--are classified in Industry 238990, All Other Specialty Trade Contractors;
- Performing specialized construction work on houses and other residential buildings, generally on a subcontract basis--are classified in Subsector 238, Specialty Trade Contractors; and
- Constructing and leasing residential buildings on their own account--are classified in Industry 531110, Lessors of Residential Buildings and Dwellings.

236116 New Multifamily Housing Construction (except For-Sale Builders)

This U.S. industry comprises general contractor establishments primarily responsible for the construction of new multifamily residential housing units (e.g., high-rise, garden, town house apartments, and condominiums where each unit is not separated from its neighbors by a ground-to-roof wall). Multifamily design-build firms and multifamily housing construction management firms acting as general contractors are included in this industry.

Cross-References. Establishments primarily engaged in--

- Building multifamily buildings on their own account for sale as speculative builders or merchant builders--are classified in U.S. Industry 236117, New Housing For-Sale Builders;

T—Canadian, Mexican, and United States industries are comparable.

- Remodeling or repairing existing multifamily housing and other residential buildings--are classified in U.S. Industry 236118, Residential Remodelers;
- Performing specialized construction work on multifamily housing and other residential buildings, generally on a subcontract basis--are classified in Subsector 238, Specialty Trade Contractors; and
- Constructing and leasing residential buildings on their own account--are classified in Industry 531110, Lessors of Residential Buildings and Dwellings.

236117 New Housing For-Sale Builders

This U.S. industry comprises establishments primarily engaged in building new homes on land that is owned or controlled by the builder rather than the homebuyer or investor. The land is included with the sale of the home. Establishments in this industry build single-family and/or multifamily homes. These establishments are often referred to as merchant builders, but are also known as production or for-sale builders.

Cross-References. Establishments primarily engaged in--

- Building single-family houses for others as general contractors--are classified in U.S. Industry 236115, New Single-Family Housing Construction (except For-Sale Builders);
- Building multifamily residential buildings for others as general contractors--are classified in U.S. Industry 236116, New Multifamily Housing Construction (except For-Sale Builders);
- Remodeling or repairing existing houses and other residential buildings, either for others or on own account for sale--are classified in U.S. Industry 236118, Residential Remodelers;
- Performing specialized construction work on houses or other residential buildings, generally on a subcontract basis--are classified in Subsector 238, Specialty Trade Contractors; and
- Constructing and leasing residential buildings on their own account--are classified in Industry 531110, Lessors of Residential Buildings and Dwellings.

236118 Residential Remodelers

This U.S. industry comprises establishments primarily responsible for the remodeling construction (including additions, alterations, reconstruction, maintenance, and repairs) of houses and other residential buildings, single-family and multifamily. Included in this industry are remodeling general contractors, for-sale remodelers, remodeling design-build firms, and remodeling project construction management firms.

Cross-References. Establishments primarily engaged in--

- Building single-family houses for others as general contractors--are classified in U.S. Industry 236115, New Single-Family Housing Construction (except For-Sale Builders);
- Building multifamily buildings for others as general contractors--are classified in U.S. Industry 236116, New Multifamily Housing Construction (except For-Sale Builders);
- Building houses or other residential buildings, on their own account for sale as speculative builders or merchant builders--are classified in U.S. Industry 236117, New Housing For-Sale Builders;
- Remodeling nonresidential buildings--are classified in Industry Group 2362, Nonresidential Building Construction, based on the type of structure being remodeled;
- Performing specialized construction work on houses or other residential buildings, generally on a subcontract basis--are classified in Subsector 238, Specialty Trade Contractors; and
- Constructing and leasing residential buildings on their own account--are classified in Industry 531110, Lessors of Residential Buildings and Dwellings.

2362 Nonresidential Building Construction[T]

This industry group comprises establishments primarily responsible for the construction (including new work, additions, alterations, maintenance, and repairs) of nonresidential buildings. This industry group includes nonresidential general contractors, nonresidential for-sale builders, nonresidential design-build firms, and nonresidential project construction management firms.

T—Canadian, Mexican, and United States industries are comparable.

23621 Industrial Building Construction[T] See industry description for 236210.

236210 Industrial Building Construction

This industry comprises establishments primarily responsible for the construction (including new work, additions, alterations, maintenance, and repairs) of industrial buildings (except warehouses). The construction of selected additional structures, whose production processes are similar to those for industrial buildings (e.g., incinerators, cement plants, blast furnaces, and similar nonbuilding structures), is included in this industry. Included in this industry are industrial building general contractors, industrial building for-sale builders, industrial building design-build firms, and industrial building construction management firms.

Illustrative Examples:

Assembly plant construction
Furnace, industrial plant, construction
Cannery construction
Mine loading and discharging station construction
Cement plant construction
Paper or pulp mill construction
Chemical plant (except petrochemical) construction
Pharmaceutical manufacturing plant construction
Factory construction
Steel mill construction
Food processing plant construction
Waste disposal plant (except sewage treatment) construction

Cross-References. Establishments primarily engaged in--

- Constructing oil refineries and petrochemical plants--are classified in Industry 237120, Oil and Gas Pipeline and Related Structures Construction;
- Constructing water treatment plants, sewage treatment plants, and pumping stations for water and sewer systems--are classified in Industry 237110, Water and Sewer Line and Related Structures Construction;
- Constructing power generation plants (except hydroelectric)--are classified in Industry 237130, Power and Communication Line and Related Structures Construction;
- Constructing industrial warehouses--are classified in Industry 236220, Commercial and Institutional Building Construction; and
- Performing specialized construction work on industrial buildings, generally on a subcontract basis--are classified in Subsector 238, Specialty Trade Contractors.

23622 Commercial and Institutional Building Construction[T] See industry description for 236220.

236220 Commercial and Institutional Building Construction

This industry comprises establishments primarily responsible for the construction (including new work, additions, alterations, maintenance, and repairs) of commercial and institutional buildings and related structures, such as stadiums, grain elevators, and indoor swimming facilities. This industry includes establishments responsible for the on-site assembly of modular or prefabricated commercial and institutional buildings. Included in this industry are commercial and institutional building general contractors, commercial and institutional building for-sale builders, commercial and institutional building design-build firms, and commercial and institutional building project construction management firms.

Illustrative Examples:

Airport building construction
Office building construction
Arena construction
Parking garage construction
Barrack construction
Prison construction
Farm building construction
Radio and television broadcast studio construction
Fire station construction
Grain elevator or bin construction

T—Canadian, Mexican, and United States industries are comparable.

Religious building (e.g., church, synagogue, mosque, temple) construction
Restaurant construction
Hospital construction
School building construction
Hotel construction
Shopping mall construction
Indoor swimming facility construction
Warehouse construction (e.g., commercial, industrial, manufacturing, private)

Cross-References. Establishments primarily engaged in--

- Constructing structures that are integral parts of utility systems (e.g., storage tanks, pumping stations) or are used to produce products for these systems (e.g., power plants, refineries)--are classified in Industry Group 2371, Utility System Construction, based on the type of construction project;
- Performing specialized construction work on commercial and institutional buildings, generally on a subcontract basis--are classified in Subsector 238, Specialty Trade Contractors; and
- Constructing buildings on their own account for rent or lease--are classified in Industry Group 5311, Lessors of Real Estate.

237 Heavy and Civil Engineering Construction[T]

The Heavy and Civil Engineering Construction subsector comprises establishments whose primary activity is the construction of entire engineering projects (e.g., highways and dams), and specialty trade contractors, whose primary activity is the production of a specific component for such projects. Specialty trade contractors in the Heavy and Civil Engineering Construction subsector generally are performing activities that are specific to heavy and civil engineering construction projects and are not normally performed on buildings. The work performed may include new work, additions, alterations, or maintenance and repairs.

Specialty trade activities are classified in this subsector if the skills and equipment present are specific to heavy or civil engineering construction projects. For example, specialized equipment is needed to paint lines on highways. This equipment is not normally used in building applications so the activity is classified in this subsector. Traffic signal installation, while specific to highways, uses much of the same skills and equipment that are needed for electrical work in building projects and is therefore classified in Subsector 238, Specialty Trade Contractors. Construction projects involving water resources (e.g., dredging and land drainage) and projects involving open space improvement (e.g., parks and trails) are included in this subsector. Establishments whose primary activity is the subdivision of land into individual building lots usually perform various additional site-improvement activities (e.g., road building and utility line installation) and are included in this subsector.

Establishments in this subsector are classified based on the types of structures that they construct. This classification reflects variations in the requirements of the underlying production processes.

2371 Utility System Construction[T]

This industry group comprises establishments primarily engaged in the construction of distribution lines and related buildings and structures for utilities (i.e., water, sewer, petroleum, gas, power, and communication). All structures (including buildings) that are integral parts of utility systems (e.g., storage tanks, pumping stations, power plants, and refineries) are included in this industry group.

23711 Water and Sewer Line and Related Structures Construction[T] See industry description for 237110.

237110 Water and Sewer Line and Related Structures Construction

This industry comprises establishments primarily engaged in the construction of water and sewer lines, mains, pumping stations, treatment plants, and storage tanks. The work performed may include new work, reconstruction, rehabilitation, and repairs. Specialty trade contractors are included in this industry if they are engaged in activities primarily related to water, sewer line, and related structures construction. All structures (including buildings) that are integral parts of water and sewer networks (e.g., storage tanks, pumping stations, water treatment plants, and sewage treatment plants) are included in this industry.

T—Canadian, Mexican, and United States industries are comparable.

Illustrative Examples:

Distribution line, sewer and water, construction
Sewer main, pipe and connection, construction
Fire hydrant installation
Storm sewer construction
Irrigation systems construction
Water main and line construction
Sewage disposal plant construction
Pumping station, water and sewage system, construction
Water system storage tank and tower construction
Reservoir construction
Water treatment plant construction
Water well drilling, digging, boring, or sinking (except water intake wells in oil and gas fields)

Cross-References.

Establishments primarily engaged in constructing marine facilities (e.g., ports), flood control structures, dams, or hydroelectric power generation facilities are classified in Industry 237990, Other Heavy and Civil Engineering Construction.

23712 Oil and Gas Pipeline and Related Structures Construction[T] See industry description for 237120.

237120 Oil and Gas Pipeline and Related Structures Construction

This industry comprises establishments primarily engaged in the construction of oil and gas lines, mains, refineries, and storage tanks. The work performed may include new work, reconstruction, rehabilitation, and repairs. Specialty trade contractors are included in this industry if they are engaged in activities primarily related to oil and gas pipeline and related structures construction. All structures (including buildings) that are integral parts of oil and gas networks (e.g., storage tanks, pumping stations, and refineries) are included in this industry.

Illustrative Examples:

Distribution line, gas and oil, construction
Oil refinery construction
Gas main construction
Petrochemical plant construction
Gathering line, gas and oil field, construction
Natural gas pipeline construction
Pumping station, gas and oil transmission, construction
Storage tank, natural gas or oil, tank farm or field, construction
Natural gas processing plant construction

Cross-References. Establishments primarily engaged in--

- Building chemical plants (except petrochemical) and similar process or batch facilities--are classified in Industry 236210, Industrial Building Construction;
- Oil well rig building, repairing, and dismantling, on a contract basis--are classified in U.S. Industry 213112, Support Activities for Oil and Gas Operations;
- Inspecting pipelines--are classified in Industry 541990, All Other Professional, Scientific, and Technical Services; and
- Mining machinery and equipment repair and maintenance--are classified in Industry 811310, Commercial and Industrial Machinery and Equipment (except Automotive and Electronic) Repair and Maintenance.

23713 Power and Communication Line and Related Structures Construction[T] See industry description for 237130.

237130 Power and Communication Line and Related Structures Construction

This industry comprises establishments primarily engaged in the construction of power lines and towers, power plants, and radio, television, and telecommunications transmitting/receiving towers. The work performed may include new work, reconstruction, rehabilitation, and repairs. Specialty trade contractors are included in this

T—Canadian, Mexican, and United States industries are comparable.

industry if they are engaged in activities primarily related to power and communication line and related structures construction. All structures (including buildings) that are integral parts of power and communication networks (e.g., transmitting towers, substations, and power plants) are included.

Illustrative Examples:

Alternative energy (e.g., geothermal, ocean wave, solar, wind) structure construction
Power line stringing
Cellular phone tower construction
Radio transmitting tower construction
Co-generation plant construction
Satellite receiving station construction
Communication tower construction
Nuclear power plant construction
Telephone line stringing
Electric light and power plant (except hydroelectric) construction
Transformer station and substation, electric power, construction
Electric power transmission line and tower construction
Underground cable (e.g., cable television, electricity, telephone) laying

Cross-References. Establishments primarily engaged in--

- Constructing hydroelectric generating facilities--are classified in Industry 237990, Other Heavy and Civil Engineering Construction;
- Constructing broadcast studios and similar nonresidential buildings--are classified in Industry 236220, Commercial and Institutional Building Construction;
- Performing electrical work within buildings--are classified in Industry 238210, Electrical Contractors and Other Wiring Installation Contractors;
- Line slashing or cutting (except maintenance)--are classified in Industry 238910, Site Preparation Contractors;
- Installing and maintaining communication transmission lines performed by telecommunications companies--are classified in Subsector 517, Telecommunications;
- Locating underground utility lines prior to digging--are classified in Industry 561990, All Other Support Services; and
- Tree and brush trimming for overhead utility lines--are classified in Industry 561730, Landscaping Services.

2372 Land Subdivision[T]

23721 Land Subdivision[T] See industry description for 237210.

237210 Land Subdivision

This industry comprises establishments primarily engaged in servicing land and subdividing real property into lots, for subsequent sale to builders. Servicing of land may include excavation work for the installation of roads and utility lines. The extent of work may vary from project to project. Land subdivision precedes building activity and the subsequent building is often residential, but may also be commercial tracts and industrial parks. These establishments may do all the work themselves or subcontract the work to others. Establishments that perform only the legal subdivision of land are not included in this industry.

Cross-References. Establishments primarily engaged in--

- Constructing buildings, for sale, on lots they subdivide--are classified based on the type of construction project, in Industry Group 2361, Residential Building Construction, or Industry Group 2362, Nonresidential Building Construction;
- Installing roads on a subcontract basis for land subdividers--are classified in Industry 237310, Highway, Street, and Bridge Construction;

T—Canadian, Mexican, and United States industries are comparable.

- Installing utilities on a subcontract basis for land subdividers--are classified in Industry Group 2371, Utility System Construction;
- Preparing land owned by others for building construction--are classified in Industry 238910, Site Preparation Contractors;
- Constructing buildings, for rent or lease, on lots they subdivide--are classified in Industry Group 5311, Lessors of Real Estate;
- Subdividing and servicing land for cemetery development--are classified in Industry 812220, Cemeteries and Crematories; and
- Legal subdivision of land without land preparation--are classified elsewhere in the classification system based on the primary activity of the establishment.

2373 Highway, Street, and Bridge Construction[T]

23731 Highway, Street, and Bridge Construction[T] See industry description for 237310.

237310 Highway, Street, and Bridge Construction

This industry comprises establishments primarily engaged in the construction of highways (including elevated), streets, roads, airport runways, public sidewalks, or bridges. The work performed may include new work, reconstruction, rehabilitation, and repairs. Specialty trade contractors are included in this industry if they are engaged in activities primarily related to highway, street, and bridge construction (e.g., installing guardrails on highways).

Illustrative Examples:

Airport runway construction
Highway line painting
Causeway construction
Painting traffic lanes or parking lot lines
Culverts, highway, road, and street, construction
Pothole filling, highway, road, street, or bridge
Elevated highway construction
Resurfacing, highway, road, street, or bridge
Guardrail construction
Sign erection, highway, road, street, or bridge

Cross-References. Establishments primarily engaged in--

- Constructing tunnels--are classified in Industry 237990, Other Heavy and Civil Engineering Construction;
- Highway lighting and signal installation--are classified in Industry 238210, Electrical Contractors and Other Wiring Installation Contractors;
- Painting bridges--are classified in Industry 238320, Painting and Wall Covering Contractors;
- Road decommissioning or removing culverts or bridges--are classified in Industry 238910, Site Preparation Contractors; and
- Constructing parking lots, private driveways, sidewalks, or erecting billboards--are classified in Industry 238990, All Other Specialty Trade Contractors.

2379 Other Heavy and Civil Engineering Construction[T]

23799 Other Heavy and Civil Engineering Construction[T] See industry description for 237990.

237990 Other Heavy and Civil Engineering Construction

This industry comprises establishments primarily engaged in heavy and civil engineering construction projects (excluding highway, street, bridge, and distribution line construction). The work performed may include new work, reconstruction, rehabilitation, and repairs. Specialty trade contractors are included in this industry if they are engaged in activities primarily related to heavy and civil engineering construction projects (excluding highway, street, bridge, distribution line, oil and gas structure, and utilities building and structure construction). Construction

T—Canadian, Mexican, and United States industries are comparable.

projects involving water resources (e.g., dredging and land drainage), development of marine facilities, and projects involving open space improvement (e.g., parks and trails) are included in this industry.

Illustrative Examples:

Channel construction
Land drainage contractors
Dam construction
Marine construction
Dock construction
Microtunneling contractors
Dredging (e.g., canal, channel, ditch, waterway)
Nuclear waste disposal site construction
Earth retention system construction
Flood control project construction
Park ground and recreational open space improvement construction Railroad construction
Golf course construction
Subway construction
Horizontal drilling (e.g., cable, pipeline, sewer installation)
Trenching, underwater
Hydroelectric generating station construction
Tunnel construction

Cross-References. Establishments primarily engaged in--

- Constructing water mains, sewers, and related structures--are classified in Industry 237110, Water and Sewer Line and Related Structures Construction;
- Constructing oil and gas pipelines and related structures--are classified in Industry 237120, Oil and Gas Pipeline and Related Structures Construction;
- Constructing power and communication transmission lines and related structures--are classified in Industry 237130, Power and Communication Line and Related Structures Construction;
- Constructing highways, streets, and bridges--are classified in Industry 237310, Highway, Street, and Bridge Construction;
- Trenching (except underwater) or removing dams, dikes, and other heavy and civil engineering constructions--are classified in Industry 238910, Site Preparation Contractors; and
- Inspecting pipelines--are classified in Industry 541990, All Other Professional, Scientific, and Technical Services.

238 Specialty Trade Contractors[T]

The Specialty Trade Contractors subsector comprises establishments whose primary activity is performing specific activities (e.g., pouring concrete, site preparation, plumbing, painting, and electrical work) involved in building construction or other activities that are similar for all types of construction, but that are not responsible for the entire project. The work performed may include new work, additions, alterations, maintenance, and repairs. The production work performed by establishments in this subsector is usually subcontracted from establishments of the general contractor type or for-sale builders, but especially in remodeling and repair construction, work also may be done directly for the owner of the property. Specialty trade contractors usually perform most of their work at the construction site, although they may have shops where they perform prefabrication and other work. Establishments primarily engaged in preparing sites for new construction are also included in this subsector.

There are substantial differences in types of equipment, work force skills, and other inputs required by specialty trade contractors. Establishments in this subsector are classified based on the underlying production function for the specialty trade in which they specialize. Throughout the Specialty Trade Contractors subsector, establishments commonly provide both the parts and labor required to complete work. For example, electrical contractors supply the current-carrying and noncurrent-carrying wiring devices that are required to install a circuit. Plumbing, heating, and air-conditioning contractors also supply the parts required to complete a contract.

Establishments that specialize in activities primarily related to heavy and civil engineering construction that are not normally performed on buildings, such as the painting of lines on highways, are classified in Subsector 237, Heavy and Civil Engineering Construction.

Establishments that are primarily engaged in selling construction materials are classified in Sector 42, Wholesale Trade, or Sector 44-45, Retail Trade, based on the characteristics of the selling unit.

T—Canadian, Mexican, and United States industries are comparable.

2381 Foundation, Structure, and Building Exterior Contractors[T]

This industry group comprises establishments primarily engaged in the specialty trades needed to complete the basic structure (i.e., foundation, frame, and shell) of buildings. The work performed may include new work, additions, alterations, maintenance, and repairs.

23811 Poured Concrete Foundation and Structure Contractors
See industry description for 238110.

238110 Poured Concrete Foundation and Structure Contractors

This industry comprises establishments primarily engaged in pouring and finishing concrete foundations and structural elements. This industry also includes establishments performing grout and shotcrete work. The work performed may include new work, additions, alterations, maintenance, and repairs.

Illustrative Examples:

Concrete pouring and finishing
Gunite contractors
Concrete pumping (i.e., placement)
Mud-jacking contractors
Concrete work (except paving)
Shotcrete contractors
Footing and foundation concrete contractors

Cross-References. Establishments primarily engaged in--

- Constructing or paving streets, highways, and public sidewalks--are classified in Industry 237310, Highway, Street, and Bridge Construction;
- Concrete sealing, coating, waterproofing, or dampproofing--are classified in Industry 238390, Other Building Finishing Contractors; and
- Paving residential driveways, commercial parking lots, and other private parking areas--are classified in Industry 238990, All Other Specialty Trade Contractors.

23812 Structural Steel and Precast Concrete Contractors
See industry description for 238120.

238120 Structural Steel and Precast Concrete Contractors

This industry comprises establishments primarily engaged in (1) erecting and assembling structural parts made from steel or precast concrete (e.g., steel beams, structural steel components, and similar products of precast concrete) and/or (2) assembling and installing other steel construction products (e.g., steel rods, bars, rebar, mesh, and cages) to reinforce poured-in-place concrete. The work performed may include new work, additions, alterations, maintenance, and repairs.

Illustrative Examples:

Concrete product (e.g., structural precast, structural prestressed) installation Rebar contractors
Erecting structural steel
Reinforcing steel contractors
site
Structural steel contractors
Precast concrete panel, slab, or form installation

Cross-References.
Placing and tying reinforcing rod at a construction

Establishments primarily engaged in pouring concrete at the construction site for building foundations or structural

T—Canadian, Mexican, and United States industries are comparable.

23813 Framing Contractors
See industry description for 238130.

238130 Framing Contractors

This industry comprises establishments primarily engaged in structural framing and sheathing using materials other than structural steel or concrete. The work performed may include new work, additions, alterations, maintenance, and repairs.

Illustrative Examples:

Building framing (except structural steel)
Post framing contractors
Foundation, building, wood, contractors
Steel framing contractors
Framing contractors
Wood frame component (e.g., truss) fabrication on site

Cross-References. Establishments primarily engaged in--

- Finish carpentry--are classified in Industry 238350, Finish Carpentry Contractors; and
- Installing structural steel, precast concrete framing, or structural elements--are classified in Industry 238120, Structural Steel and Precast Concrete Contractors.

23814 Masonry Contractors
See industry description for 238140.

238140 Masonry Contractors

This industry comprises establishments primarily engaged in masonry work, stone setting, bricklaying, and other stone work. The work performed may include new work, additions, alterations, maintenance, and repairs.

Illustrative Examples:

Block laying
Marble, granite, and slate, exterior, contractors
Bricklaying
Masonry pointing, cleaning, or caulking
Concrete block laying
Stucco contractors
Foundation (e.g., brick, block, stone), building, contractors

Cross-References. Establishments primarily engaged in--

- Erecting the basic structure of buildings by pouring concrete--are classified in Industry 238110, Poured Concrete Foundation and Structure Contractors;
- Interior marble, granite, and slate work--are classified in Industry 238340, Tile and Terrazzo Contractors; and
- Laying precast stones or bricks for patios, sidewalks, and driveways; or paving residential driveways, commercial parking lots and other private parking areas--are classified in Industry 238990, All Other Specialty Trade Contractors.

23815 Glass and Glazing Contractors
See industry description for 238150.

238150 Glass and Glazing Contractors

This industry comprises establishments primarily engaged in installing glass panes in prepared openings (i.e., glazing work) and other glass work for buildings. The work performed may include new work, additions, alterations, maintenance, and repairs.

~~T—Canadian, Mexican, and Unit~~ed States industries are comparable.

Illustrative Examples:

Decorative glass and mirror installation
Glazing contractors
Glass cladding installation
Stained glass installation
Glass coating and tinting (except automotive) contractors
Window pane or sheet installation
Glass installation (except automotive) contractors

Cross-References. Establishments primarily engaged in--

- Installing prefabricated window units--are classified in Industry 238350, Finish Carpentry Contractors; and
- The replacement, repair, and/or tinting of automotive glass--are classified in U.S. Industry 811122, Automotive Glass Replacement Shops.

23816 Roofing Contractors
See industry description for 238160.

238160 Roofing Contractors

This industry comprises establishments primarily engaged in roofing. This industry also includes establishments treating roofs (i.e., spraying, painting, or coating) and installing skylights. The work performed may include new work, additions, alterations, maintenance, and repairs.

Illustrative Examples:

Painting, spraying, or coating, roof
Sheet metal roofing installation
Shake and shingle, roof, installation
Skylight installation

Cross-References. Establishments primarily engaged in--

- Installing roof trusses and sheathing attached to trusses--are classified in Industry 238130, Framing Contractors; and
- Installing downspouts, gutters, fascia, and soffits--are classified in Industry 238170, Siding Contractors.

23817 Siding Contractors
See industry description for 238170.

238170 Siding Contractors

This industry comprises establishments primarily engaged in installing siding of wood, aluminum, vinyl, or other exterior finish material (except brick, stone, stucco, or curtain wall). This industry also includes establishments installing gutters and downspouts. The work performed may include new work, additions, alterations, maintenance, and repairs.

Illustrative Examples:

Downspout, gutter, and gutter guard installation
Fascia and soffit installation
Siding (e.g., vinyl, wood, aluminum) installation

Cross-References. Establishments primarily engaged in--

- Installing brick, stone, or stucco building exterior finish materials--are classified in Industry 238140, Masonry Contractors;
- Installing curtain wall--are classified in Industry 238190, Other Foundation, Structure, and Building Exterior Contractors; and

---

T—Canadian, Mexican, and United States industries are comparable.

- Installing sheet metal duct work--are classified in Industry 238220, Plumbing, Heating, and Air-Conditioning Contractors.

23819 Other Foundation, Structure, and Building Exterior Contractors
See industry description for 238190.

238190 Other Foundation, Structure, and Building Exterior Contractors

This industry comprises establishments primarily engaged in building foundation and structure trades work (except poured concrete, structural steel, precast concrete, framing, masonry, glass and glazing, roofing, and siding). The work performed may include new work, additions, alterations, maintenance, and repairs.

Illustrative Examples:

Curtain wall, metal, installation
Forms for poured concrete, erecting and dismantling
Welding, on-site, contractors
Ornamental metal work installation
Fire escape installation
Decorative steel and wrought iron work installation

Cross-References. Establishments primarily engaged in--

- Poured concrete foundation and structure work--are classified in Industry 238110, Poured Concrete Foundation and Structure Contractors;
- Installation of structural steel or precast concrete building components--are classified in Industry 238120, Structural Steel and Precast Concrete Contractors;
- Framing buildings--are classified in Industry 238130, Framing Contractors;
- Masonry work--are classified in Industry 238140, Masonry Contractors;
- Glass and glazing work--are classified in Industry 238150, Glass and Glazing Contractors;
- Installing or repairing roofs--are classified in Industry 238160, Roofing Contractors;
- Installing siding--are classified in Industry 238170, Siding Contractors; and
- Fireproofing buildings--are classified in Industry 238310, Drywall and Insulation Contractors.

2382 Building Equipment Contractors[T]

This industry group comprises establishments primarily engaged in installing or servicing equipment that forms part of a building mechanical system (e.g., electricity, water, heating, and cooling). The work performed may include new work, additions, alterations, maintenance, and repairs. Contractors installing specialized building equipment, such as elevators, escalators, service station equipment, and central vacuum cleaning systems, are also included.

23821 Electrical Contractors and Other Wiring Installation Contractors[T] See industry description for 238210.

238210 Electrical Contractors and Other Wiring Installation Contractors

This industry comprises establishments primarily engaged in installing and servicing electrical wiring and equipment. Contractors included in this industry may include both the parts and labor when performing work. These contractors may perform new work, additions, alterations, maintenance, and repairs.

Illustrative Examples:

Airport runway lighting contractors
Fiber optic cable (except transmission line) contractors
Alarm system (e.g., fire, burglar), electric, installation only
Highway, street, and bridge lighting and electrical signal installation
Audio equipment (except automotive) installation contractors
Home automation system installation

T—Canadian, Mexican, and United States industries are comparable.

Lighting system installation
Cable television hookup contractors
Telecommunications equipment and wiring (except transmission line) installation contractors
Computer and network cable installation
Traffic signal installation
Environmental control system installation
Cable splicing, electrical or fiber optic

Cross-References. Establishments primarily engaged in--

- Installing and maintaining telecommunications lines by telecommunications companies--are classified in Subsector 517, Telecommunications;
- Constructing power and communication transmission lines--are classified in Industry 237130, Power and Communication Line and Related Structures Construction; and
- Burglar and fire alarm installation combined with sales, maintenance, or monitoring services--are classified in U.S. Industry 561621, Security Systems Services (except Locksmiths).

23822 Plumbing, Heating, and Air-Conditioning Contractors[T] See industry description for 238220.

238220 Plumbing, Heating, and Air-Conditioning Contractors

This industry comprises establishments primarily engaged in installing and servicing plumbing, heating, and air-conditioning equipment. Contractors in this industry may provide both parts and labor when performing work. The work performed may include new work, additions, alterations, maintenance, and repairs.

Illustrative Examples:

Cooling tower installation
Heating, ventilation, and air-conditioning (HVAC) contractors
Duct work (e.g., cooling, dust collection, exhaust, heating, ventilation) installation
Lawn sprinkler system installation
Fire sprinkler system installation
Mechanical contractors
Fireplace, natural gas, installation
Refrigeration system (e.g., commercial, industrial, scientific) installation
Furnace installation
Sewer hookup and connection, building

Cross-References. Establishments primarily engaged in--

- Installing electrical controls for HVAC systems--are classified in Industry 238210, Electrical Contractors and Other Wiring Installation Contractors;
- Duct cleaning--are classified in Industry 561790, Other Services to Buildings and Dwellings; and
- Installing septic tanks--are classified in Industry 238910, Site Preparation Contractors.

23829 Other Building Equipment Contractors[T] See industry description for 238290.

238290 Other Building Equipment Contractors

This industry comprises establishments primarily engaged in installing or servicing building equipment (except electrical, plumbing, heating, cooling, or ventilation equipment). The repair and maintenance of miscellaneous building equipment is included in this industry. The work performed may include new work, additions, alterations, maintenance, and repairs.

Illustrative Examples:

Automated and revolving door installation
Lightning protection equipment (e.g., lightning rod) installation
Boiler and pipe insulation installation
Machine rigging
Commercial-type door installation

T—Canadian, Mexican, and United States industries are comparable.

Millwrights
Conveyor system installation
Overhead door, commercial- or industrial-type, installation
Dismantling large-scale machinery and equipment
Revolving door installation
Elevator installation
Satellite dish, household-type, installation
Escalator installation
Vacuum cleaning system, built-in, installation
Gasoline pump, service station, installation

Cross-References. Establishments primarily engaged in--

- Manufacturing industrial equipment with incidental installation--are classified in Sector 31-33, Manufacturing; and
- Repair and maintenance of commercial refrigeration equipment or production equipment--are classified in Industry 811310, Commercial and Industrial Machinery and Equipment (except Automotive and Electronic) Repair and Maintenance.

2383 Building Finishing Contractors[T]

This industry group comprises establishments primarily engaged in the specialty trades needed to finish buildings. The work performed may include new work, additions, alterations, maintenance, and repairs.

23831 Drywall and Insulation Contractors[T] See industry description for 238310.

238310 Drywall and Insulation Contractors

This industry comprises establishments primarily engaged in drywall, plaster work, and building insulation work. Plaster work includes applying plain or ornamental plaster, and installation of lath to receive plaster. The work performed may include new work, additions, alterations, maintenance, and repairs. Establishments primarily engaged in providing firestop services are included in this industry.

Illustrative Examples:

Acoustical ceiling tile and panel installation
Lathing contractors
Drop ceiling installation
Plastering (i.e., ornamental, plain) contractors
Drywall contractors
Soundproofing contractors
Firestop contractors
Fresco (i.e., decorative plaster finishing) contractors
Taping and finishing drywall
Gypsum board installation
Wall cavity and attic space insulation installation

Cross-References. Establishments primarily engaged in--

- Applying stucco--are classified in Industry 238140, Masonry Contractors; and
- Insulating pipes and boilers--are classified in Industry 238290, Other Building Equipment Contractors.

23832 Painting and Wall Covering Contractors[T]
See industry description for 238320.

238320 Painting and Wall Covering Contractors

This industry comprises establishments primarily engaged in interior or exterior painting or interior wall covering. The work performed may include new work, additions, alterations, maintenance, and repairs.

Illustrative Examples:

Bridge painting
Paperhanging or removal contractors

~~T—Canadian, Mexican, and Unit~~ed States industries are comparable.

House painting
Ship painting contractors
Paint and wallpaper stripping
Wallpaper hanging and removal contractors

Cross-References. Establishments primarily engaged in--

- Painting lines on highways, streets, and parking lots--are classified in Industry 237310, Highway, Street, and Bridge Construction;
- Roof painting--are classified in Industry 238160, Roofing Contractors; and
- Installing wood paneling--are classified in Industry 238350, Finish Carpentry Contractors.

23833 Flooring Contractors[T] See industry description for 238330.

238330 Flooring Contractors

This industry comprises establishments primarily engaged in the installation of resilient floor tile, carpeting, linoleum, and hardwood flooring. The work performed may include new work, additions, alterations, maintenance, and repairs.

Illustrative Examples:

Carpet, installation only
Resilient floor tile or sheet (e.g., linoleum, rubber, vinyl), installation only
Vinyl flooring contractors
Resurfacing hardwood flooring
Hardwood flooring, installation only
Floor laying, scraping, finishing, and refinishing

Cross-References. Establishments primarily engaged in--

- Laying concrete flooring--are classified in Industry 238110, Poured Concrete Foundation and Structure Contractors;
- Installing fireproof flooring--are classified in Industry 238310, Drywall and Insulation Contractors;
- Installing stone or ceramic floor tile--are classified in Industry 238340, Tile and Terrazzo Contractors; and
- Selling and installing carpet and other flooring products as retail establishments--are classified in Sector 44-45, Retail Trade.

23834 Tile and Terrazzo Contractors[T] See industry description for 238340.

238340 Tile and Terrazzo Contractors

This industry comprises establishments primarily engaged in setting and installing ceramic tile, stone (interior only), and mosaic and/or mixing marble particles and cement to make terrazzo at the job site. The work performed may include new work, additions, alterations, maintenance, and repairs.

Ceramic tile installation
Mosaic work
Mantel, marble or stone, installation
Tile (except resilient) laying and setting
Stone flooring installation
Marble, granite, and slate, interior installation contractors

Cross-References. Establishments primarily engaged in--

- Exterior marble, granite, and slate work--are classified in Industry 238140, Masonry Contractors;

T—Canadian, Mexican, and United States industries are comparable.

- Manufacturing precast terrazzo products--are classified in Industry 327390, Other Concrete Product Manufacturing; and
- Installing, without selling resilient floor tile--are classified in Industry 238330, Flooring Contractors.

23835 Finish Carpentry Contractors[T] See industry description for 238350.

238350 Finish Carpentry Contractors

This industry comprises establishments primarily engaged in finish carpentry work. The work performed may include new work, additions, alterations, maintenance, and repairs.

Illustrative Examples:

Built-in wood cabinets constructed on site
Molding or trim, wood or plastic, installation
Countertop, residential-type, installation
Paneling installation
Door and window frame construction
Garage door, residential-type, installation
Prefabricated kitchen and bath cabinet, residential-type, installation
Ship joinery contractors
Millwork installation
Window and door, residential-type, of any material, prefabricated, installation

Cross-References. Establishments primarily engaged in--

- Installing skylights--are classified in Industry 238160, Roofing Contractors;
- Framing--are classified in Industry 238130, Framing Contractors; and
- Building custom kitchen and bath cabinets (except freestanding) in a shop--are classified in Industry 337110, Wood Kitchen Cabinet and Countertop Manufacturing.

23839 Other Building Finishing Contractors[T] See industry description for 238390.

238390 Other Building Finishing Contractors

This industry comprises establishments primarily engaged in building finishing trade work (except drywall, plaster, and insulation work; painting and wall covering work; flooring work; tile and terrazzo work; and finish carpentry work). The work performed may include new work, additions, alterations, maintenance, and repairs.

Illustrative Examples:

Bathtub refinishing, on-site
Fabricating metal cabinets or countertops on site
Closet organizer system installation
Modular furniture system attachment and installation
Concrete coating, glazing, or sealing
Trade show exhibit installation and dismantling
Countertop and cabinet, metal (except residential-type), installation
Waterproofing contractors
Drapery fixture (e.g., hardware, rods, tracks) installation
Window shade and blind installation

Cross-References. Establishments primarily engaged in--

- Installing drywall, plaster, or insulation--are classified in Industry 238310, Drywall and Insulation Contractors;
- Installing or removing paint or wall coverings--are classified in Industry 238320, Painting and Wall Covering Contractors;
- Installing or repairing wood floors, resilient flooring, and carpet--are classified in Industry 238330, Flooring Contractors;

T—Canadian, Mexican, and United States industries are comparable.

- Setting tile or performing terrazzo work--are classified in Industry 238340, Tile and Terrazzo Contractors; and
- Finish carpentry--are classified in Industry 238350, Finish Carpentry Contractors.

2389 Other Specialty Trade Contractors[T]

This industry group comprises establishments primarily engaged in site preparation activities and in specialized trades (except foundation, structure, and building exterior contractors; building equipment contractors; and building finishing contractors). The specialty trade work performed includes new work, additions, alterations, maintenance, and repairs.

23891 Site Preparation Contractors[T] See industry description for 238910.

238910 Site Preparation Contractors

This industry comprises establishments primarily engaged in site preparation activities, such as excavating and grading, demolition of buildings and other structures, and septic system installation. Earthmoving and land clearing for all types of sites (e.g., building, nonbuilding, mining) is included in this industry. Establishments primarily engaged in construction equipment rental with operator (except cranes) are also included.

Illustrative Examples:

Blasting, building demolition
Foundation digging (i.e., excavation)
Concrete breaking and cutting for demolition
Foundation drilling contractors
Cutting new rights of way
Grading construction sites
Demolition, building and structure
Line slashing or cutting (except maintenance)
Dewatering contractors
Septic system contractors
Dirt moving for construction
Trenching (except underwater)
Equipment rental (except crane), construction, with operator
Underground tank (except hazardous) removal
Excavating, earthmoving, or land clearing contractors
Wrecking, building or other structure

Cross-References. Establishments primarily engaged in--

- Earth retention or underwater trenching--are classified in Industry 237990, Other Heavy and Civil Engineering Construction;
- Crane rental with operator--are classified in Industry 238990, All Other Specialty Trade Contractors;
- Overburden removal as an activity prior to mineral removal from quarries or open pit mines--are classified in Sector 21, Mining, Quarrying, and Oil and Gas Extraction;
- Drilling oil and gas field water intake wells--are classified in U.S. Industry 213111, Drilling Oil and Gas Wells;
- Dismantling tanks in oil fields--are classified in U.S. Industry 213112, Support Activities for Oil and Gas Operations;
- Construction equipment rental without an operator--are classified in U.S. Industry 532412, Construction, Mining, and Forestry Machinery and Equipment Rental and Leasing;
- Tree and brush trimming for overhead utility lines--are classified in Industry 561730, Landscaping Services; and
- Nuclear power plant decommissioning and environmental remediation work, such as the removal of underground steel tanks for hazardous materials--are classified in Industry 562910, Remediation Services.

23899 All Other Specialty Trade Contractors[T] See industry description for 238990.

T—Canadian, Mexican, and United States industries are comparable.

238990 All Other Specialty Trade Contractors

This industry comprises establishments primarily engaged in specialized trades (except foundation, structure, and building exterior contractors; building equipment contractors; building finishing contractors; and site preparation contractors). The specialty trade work performed includes new work, additions, alterations, maintenance, and repairs.

Illustrative Examples:

Billboard erection
Outdoor swimming pool construction
Cleaning building interiors during and immediately after construction
Paver, brick (e.g., driveway, patio, sidewalk), installation
Crane rental with operator
Paving, residential and commercial driveway and parking lot
Sandblasting building exteriors
Fence installation
Scaffold erecting and dismantling
Interlocking brick and block installation
Steeplejack work
Manufactured (mobile) home set up and tie-down work
Driveway paving or sealing

Cross-References. Establishments primarily engaged in--

- Foundation, structure, and building exterior work--are classified in Industry Group 2381, Foundation, Structure, and Building Exterior Contractors;
- Installing, repairing, or maintaining building mechanical systems--are classified in Industry Group 2382, Building Equipment Contractors;
- Finishing buildings--are classified in Industry Group 2383, Building Finishing Contractors;
- Paving public highways, streets, and roads--are classified in Industry 237310, Highway, Street, and Bridge Construction;
- Construction equipment rental with an operator (except cranes) or preparing land for building construction--are classified in Industry 238910, Site Preparation Contractors;
- Construction equipment rental without an operator--are classified in U.S. Industry 532412, Construction, Mining, and Forestry Machinery and Equipment Rental and Leasing;
- Radon testing--are classified in Industry 541380, Testing Laboratories;
- Power washing and other building exterior cleaning (except sandblasting)--are classified in Industry 561790, Other Services to Buildings and Dwellings; and
- Environmental remediation work, such as asbestos abatement--are classified in Industry 562910, Remediation Services.

T—Canadian, Mexican, and United States industries are comparable.

Sector 31-33--Manufacturing[T]

The Sector as a Whole

The Manufacturing sector comprises establishments engaged in the mechanical, physical, or chemical transformation of materials, substances, or components into new products. The assembling of component parts of manufactured products is considered manufacturing, except in cases where the activity is appropriately classified in Sector 23, Construction.

Establishments in the Manufacturing sector are often described as plants, factories, or mills and characteristically use power-driven machines and material handling equipment. However, establishments that transform materials or substances into new products by hand or in the worker's home and those engaged in selling to the general public products made on the same premises from which they are sold, such as bakeries, candy stores, and custom tailors, may also be included in this sector. Manufacturing establishments may process materials or may contract with other establishments to process their materials for them. Both types of establishments are included in manufacturing. The materials, substances, or components transformed by manufacturing establishments are raw materials that are products of agriculture, forestry, fishing, mining, or quarrying as well as products of other manufacturing establishments. The materials used may be purchased directly from producers, obtained through customary trade channels, or secured without recourse to the market by transferring the product from one establishment to another, under the same ownership.

The new product of a manufacturing establishment may be finished in the sense that it is ready for utilization or consumption, or it may be semi-finished to become an input for an establishment engaged in further manufacturing. For example, the product of the alumina refinery is the input used in the primary production of aluminum; primary aluminum is the input to an aluminum wire drawing plant; and aluminum wire is the input for a fabricated wire product manufacturing establishment.

The subsectors in the Manufacturing sector generally reflect distinct production processes related to material inputs, production equipment, and employee skills. In the machinery area, where assembling is a key activity, parts and accessories for manufactured products are classified in the industry of the finished manufactured item when they are made for separate sale. For example, a replacement refrigerator door would be classified with refrigerators and an attachment for a piece of metalworking machinery would be classified with metalworking machinery. However, components, input from other manufacturing establishments, are classified based on the production function of the component manufacturer. For example, electronic components are classified in Subsector 334, Computer and Electronic Product Manufacturing, and stampings are classified in Subsector 332, Fabricated Metal Product Manufacturing.

Manufacturing establishments often perform one or more activities that are classified outside the Manufacturing sector of NAICS. For instance, almost all manufacturing has some captive research and development or administrative operations, such as accounting, payroll, or management. These captive services are treated the same as captive manufacturing activities. When the services are provided by separate establishments, they are classified in the NAICS sector where such services are primary, not in manufacturing.

The boundaries of manufacturing and the other sectors of the classification system can be somewhat blurry. The establishments in the Manufacturing sector are engaged in the transformation of materials into new products. Their output is a new product. However, the definition of what constitutes a new product can be somewhat subjective. As clarification, the following activities are considered manufacturing in NAICS:

Milk bottling and pasteurizing;
Water bottling and processing;
Fresh fish packaging (oyster shucking, fish filleting);
Apparel jobbing (assigning materials to contract factories or shops for fabrication or other contract operations) as well as contracting on materials owned by others;
Printing and related activities;
Ready-mix concrete production;
Leather converting;
Grinding lenses to prescription;
Wood preserving;
Electroplating, plating, metal heat treating, and polishing for the trade; Lapidary work for the trade;
Fabricating signs and advertising displays;
Rebuilding or remanufacturing machinery (i.e., automotive parts); Ship repair and renovation;
Machine shops; and
Tire retreading.

T—Canadian, Mexican, and United States industries are comparable.

Conversely, there are activities that are sometimes considered manufacturing, but which for NAICS are classified in another sector (i.e., not classified as manufacturing). They include:

1. 1. Logging, classified in Sector 11, Agriculture, Forestry, Fishing and Hunting, is considered a harvesting operation;
2. 2. Beneficiating ores and other minerals, classified in Sector 21, Mining, Quarrying, and Oil and Gas Extraction, is considered part of the activity of mining;
3. 3. Constructing structures and fabricating at the construction site by contractors are classified in Sector 23, Construction;
4. 4. Breaking bulk and redistributing in smaller lots, including packaging, repackaging, or bottling products, such as liquors or chemicals; assembling computers on a custom basis; sorting scrap; mixing paints to customer order; and cutting metals to customer order, classified in Sector 42, Wholesale Trade, or Sector 44-45, Retail Trade, produce a modified version of the same product, not a new product; and
5. 5. Publishing and the combined activity of publishing and printing, classified in Sector 51, Information, transform information into a product for which the value to the consumer lies in the information content, not in the format in which it is distributed (i.e., the book or software compact disc).

311 Food Manufacturing[T]

Industries in the Food Manufacturing subsector transform livestock and agricultural products into products for intermediate or final consumption. The industry groups are distinguished by the raw materials (generally of animal or vegetable origin) processed into food products.

The food products manufactured in these establishments are typically sold to wholesalers or retailers for distribution to consumers, but establishments primarily engaged in retailing bakery and candy products made on the premises not for immediate consumption are included.

Establishments primarily engaged in manufacturing beverages are classified in Subsector 312, Beverage and Tobacco Product Manufacturing.

3111 Animal Food Manufacturing[T]

31111 Animal Food Manufacturing[T]

This industry comprises establishments primarily engaged in manufacturing food and feed for animals from ingredients, such as grains, oilseed mill products, and meat products.

Cross-References. Establishments primarily engaged in--

- Slaughtering animals for feed--are classified in Industry 31161, Animal Slaughtering and Processing; and
- Manufacturing vitamins and minerals for animals--are classified in Industry 32541, Pharmaceutical and Medicine Manufacturing.

311111 Dog and Cat Food Manufacturing

This U.S. industry comprises establishments primarily engaged in manufacturing dog and cat food from ingredients, such as grains, oilseed mill products, and meat products.

Cross-References. Establishments primarily engaged in--

- Manufacturing food for animals (except dog and cat)--are classified in U.S. Industry 311119, Other Animal Food Manufacturing;
- Slaughtering animals for feed--are classified in Industry 31161, Animal Slaughtering and Processing; and
- Manufacturing vitamins and minerals for dogs and cats--are classified in Industry 32541, Pharmaceutical and Medicine Manufacturing.

T—Canadian, Mexican, and United States industries are comparable.

311119 Other Animal Food Manufacturing

This U.S. industry comprises establishments primarily engaged in manufacturing animal food (except dog and cat) from ingredients, such as grains, oilseed mill products, and meat products.

Cross-References. Establishments primarily engaged in--

- Manufacturing dog and cat foods--are classified in U.S. Industry 311111, Dog and Cat Food Manufacturing;
- Slaughtering animals for feed--are classified in Industry 31161, Animal Slaughtering and Processing; and
- Manufacturing vitamins and minerals for animals--are classified in Industry 32541, Pharmaceutical and Medicine Manufacturing.

3112 Grain and Oilseed Milling[T]

This industry group comprises establishments primarily engaged in milling flour or meal from grains or vegetables, manufacturing malt, wet milling corn and other vegetables, crushing oilseeds and tree nuts, refining and/or blending vegetable oils, and manufacturing breakfast cereals.

31121 Flour Milling and Malt Manufacturing[T]

This industry comprises establishments primarily engaged in one or more of the following: (1) milling flour or meal from grains or vegetables; (2) preparing flour mixes or doughs from flour milled in the same establishment; (3) milling, cleaning, and polishing rice; and (4) manufacturing malt from barley, rye, or other grains.

Cross-References. Establishments primarily engaged in--

- Preparing breakfast cereals from flour milled in the same establishment--are classified in Industry 31123, Breakfast Cereal Manufacturing;
- Crushing soybeans or wet milling corn and vegetables--are classified in Industry 31122, Starch and Vegetable Fats and Oils Manufacturing;
- Manufacturing prepared flour mixes or doughs from flour ground elsewhere--are classified in Industry 31182, Cookie, Cracker, and Pasta Manufacturing;
- Brewing malt beverages--are classified in Industry 31212, Breweries;
- Mixing purchased dried and dehydrated ingredients with purchased rice--are classified in Industry 31199, All Other Food Manufacturing;
- Drying and/or dehydrating ingredients and packaging them with purchased rice--are classified in Industry 31142, Fruit and Vegetable Canning, Pickling, and Drying; and
- Manufacturing malt extract and syrups--are classified in Industry 31194, Seasoning and Dressing Manufacturing.

311211 Flour Milling

This U.S. industry comprises establishments primarily engaged in (1) milling flour or meal from grains (except rice) or vegetables and/or (2) milling flour and preparing flour mixes or doughs.

Cross-References. Establishments primarily engaged in--

- Preparing breakfast cereals from flour milled in the same establishment--are classified in Industry 311230, Breakfast Cereal Manufacturing;
- Manufacturing prepared flour mixes or doughs from flour ground elsewhere--are classified in U.S. Industry 311824, Dry Pasta, Dough, and Flour Mixes Manufacturing from Purchased Flour;
- Milling rice or cleaning and polishing rice--are classified in U.S. Industry 311212, Rice Milling;
- Wet milling corn and vegetables--are classified in U.S. Industry 311221, Wet Corn Milling; and

T—Canadian, Mexican, and United States industries are comparable.

- Crushing soybeans and extracting soybean oil--are classified in U.S. Industry 311224, Soybean and Other Oilseed Processing.

311212 Rice Milling

This U.S. industry comprises establishments primarily engaged in one of the following: (1) milling rice; (2) cleaning and polishing rice; or (3) milling, cleaning, and polishing rice. The establishments in this industry may package the rice they mill with other ingredients.

Cross-References. Establishments primarily engaged in--

- Drying and/or dehydrating ingredients and packaging them with purchased rice--are classified in U.S. Industry 311423, Dried and Dehydrated Food Manufacturing; and
- Mixing purchased dried and/or dehydrated ingredients with purchased rice--are classified in U.S. Industry 311999, All Other Miscellaneous Food Manufacturing.

311213 Malt Manufacturing

This U.S. industry comprises establishments primarily engaged in manufacturing malt from barley, rye, or other grains.

Cross-References. Establishments primarily engaged in--

- Brewing malt beverages--are classified in Industry 312120, Breweries; and
- Manufacturing malt extract and syrups--are classified in U.S. Industry 311942, Spice and Extract Manufacturing.

31122 Starch and Vegetable Fats and Oils Manufacturing[T]

This industry comprises establishments primarily engaged in one or more of the following: (1) wet milling corn and vegetables; (2) crushing oilseeds and tree nuts; (3) refining and/or blending vegetable oils; (4) manufacturing shortening and margarine; and (5) blending purchased animal fats with vegetable fats.

Cross-References. Establishments primarily engaged in--

- Manufacturing table syrups from corn syrup and starch base dessert powders--are classified in Industry 31199, All Other Food Manufacturing;
- Reducing maple sap to maple syrup--are classified in Industry 11199, All Other Crop Farming;
- Milling flour or meal from grains and vegetables--are classified in Industry 31121, Flour Milling and Malt Manufacturing;
- Wet milling corn to produce nonpotable ethyl alcohol--are classified in Industry 32519, Other Basic Organic Chemical Manufacturing;
- Rendering or refining animal fats and oils--are classified in Industry 31161, Animal Slaughtering and Processing; and
- Manufacturing laundry starches--are classified in Industry 32561, Soap and Cleaning Compound Manufacturing.

311221 Wet Corn Milling

This U.S. industry comprises establishments primarily engaged in wet milling corn and other vegetables (except to make ethyl alcohol). Examples of products made in these establishments are corn sweeteners, such as glucose, dextrose, and fructose; corn oil; and starches (except laundry).

T—Canadian, Mexican, and United States industries are comparable.

Cross-References. Establishments primarily engaged in--

- Refining and/or blending corn oil from purchased oils--are classified in U.S. Industry 311225, Fats and Oils Refining and Blending;
- Manufacturing sweetening syrups from corn syrup and starch base dessert powders--are classified in U.S. Industry 311999, All Other Miscellaneous Food Manufacturing;
- Reducing maple sap to maple syrup--are classified in U.S. Industry 111998, All Other Miscellaneous Crop Farming;
- Milling (except wet milling) corn--are classified in U.S. Industry 311211, Flour Milling;
- Wet milling corn to produce nonpotable ethyl alcohol--are classified in U.S. Industry 325193, Ethyl Alcohol Manufacturing; and
- Manufacturing laundry starches--are classified in U.S. Industry 325612, Polish and Other Sanitation Good Manufacturing.

311224 Soybean and Other Oilseed Processing

This U.S. industry comprises establishments primarily engaged in crushing oilseeds and tree nuts, such as soybeans, cottonseeds, linseeds, peanuts, and sunflower seeds. Examples of products produced in these establishments are oilseed oils, cakes, meals, and protein isolates and concentrates.

Cross-References. Establishments primarily engaged in--

- Wet milling corn and other vegetables--are classified in U.S. Industry 311221, Wet Corn Milling; and
- Refining and/or blending vegetable, oilseed, and tree nut oils from purchased oils--are classified in U.S. Industry 311225, Fats and Oils Refining and Blending.

311225 Fats and Oils Refining and Blending

This U.S. industry comprises establishments primarily engaged in one or more of the following: (1) manufacturing shortening and margarine from purchased fats and oils; (2) refining and/or blending vegetable, oilseed, and tree nut oils from purchased oils; and (3) blending purchased animal fats with purchased vegetable fats.

Cross-References. Establishments primarily engaged in--

- Refining and/or blending corn oil made by wet corn milling--are classified in U.S. Industry 311221, Wet Corn Milling;
- Refining and/or blending oilseed and tree nut oils in crushing mills--are classified in U.S. Industry 311224, Soybean and Other Oilseed Processing; and
- Rendering or refining animal fats and oils--are classified in Industry 31161, Animal Slaughtering and Processing.

31123 Breakfast Cereal Manufacturing[T] See industry description for 311230.

311230 Breakfast Cereal Manufacturing

This industry comprises establishments primarily engaged in manufacturing breakfast cereal foods.

Cross-References. Establishments primarily engaged in--

- Manufacturing nonchocolate-coated granola bars and other types of breakfast bars--are classified in Industry 311340, Nonchocolate Confectionery Manufacturing;
- Manufacturing chocolate-coated granola bars from purchased chocolate--are classified in U.S. Industry 311352, Confectionery Manufacturing from Purchased Chocolate;

T—Canadian, Mexican, and United States industries are comparable.

- Manufacturing chocolate-coated granola bars from cacao beans--are classified in U.S. Industry 311351, Chocolate and Confectionery Manufacturing from Cacao Beans; and
- Manufacturing coffee substitutes from grain--are classified in Industry 311920, Coffee and Tea Manufacturing.

3113 Sugar and Confectionery Product Manufacturing[T]

This industry group comprises (1) establishments that process agricultural inputs, such as sugarcane, beet, and cacao, to give rise to a new product (sugar or chocolate) and (2) those that begin with sugar and chocolate and process these further.

31131 Sugar Manufacturing[T]

This industry comprises establishments primarily engaged in manufacturing raw sugar, liquid sugar, and refined sugar from sugarcane, raw cane sugar and sugar beets.

Cross-References. Establishments primarily engaged in--

- Manufacturing corn sweeteners by wet milling corn--are classified in Industry 31122, Starch and Vegetable Fats and Oils Manufacturing;
- Manufacturing table syrups from corn syrup and starch base dessert powders--are classified in Industry 31199, All Other Food Manufacturing;
- Reducing maple sap to maple syrup or maple sugar--are classified in Industry 11199, All Other Crop Farming; and
- Manufacturing synthetic sweeteners (i.e., sweetening agents), such as saccharin and sugar substitutes (i.e., synthetic sweetener blended with other ingredients)--are classified in Subsector 325, Chemical Manufacturing.

311313 Beet Sugar Manufacturing

This U.S. industry comprises establishments primarily engaged in manufacturing refined beet sugar from sugar beets.

Cross-References. Establishments primarily engaged in--

- Manufacturing raw cane sugar and/or refined cane sugar--are classified in U.S. Industry 311314, Cane Sugar Manufacturing;
- Manufacturing corn sweeteners by wet milling corn--are classified in U.S. Industry 311221, Wet Corn Milling;
- Manufacturing table syrups from corn syrup--are classified in U.S. Industry 311999, All Other Miscellaneous Food Manufacturing;
- Reducing maple sap to maple syrup or maple sugar--are classified in U.S. Industry 111998, All Other Miscellaneous Crop Farming; and
- Manufacturing synthetic sweeteners (i.e., sweetening agents), such as saccharin and sugar substitutes (i.e., synthetic sweetener blended with other ingredients)--are classified in Subsector 325, Chemical Manufacturing.

311314 Cane Sugar Manufacturing

This U.S. industry comprises establishments primarily engaged in (1) processing sugarcane and/or (2) refining cane sugar from raw cane sugar.

Cross-References. Establishments primarily engaged in--

- Manufacturing beet sugar--are classified in U.S. Industry 311313, Beet Sugar Manufacturing;

T—Canadian, Mexican, and United States industries are comparable.

- Manufacturing corn sweeteners by wet milling corn--are classified in U.S. Industry 311221, Wet Corn Milling;
- Reducing maple sap to maple syrup or maple sugar--are classified in U.S. Industry 111998, All Other Miscellaneous Crop Farming;
- Manufacturing table syrups from corn syrup--are classified in U.S. Industry 311999, All Other Miscellaneous Food Manufacturing; and
- Manufacturing synthetic sweeteners (i.e., sweetening agents), such as saccharin and sugar substitutes (i.e., synthetic sweetener blended with other ingredients)--are classified in Subsector 325, Chemical Manufacturing.

31134 Nonchocolate Confectionery Manufacturing[T] See industry description for 311340.

311340 Nonchocolate Confectionery Manufacturing

This industry comprises establishments primarily engaged in manufacturing nonchocolate confectioneries. Included in this industry are establishments primarily engaged in retailing nonchocolate confectionery products not for immediate consumption made on the premises.

Cross-References. Establishments primarily engaged in--

- Manufacturing chocolate confectioneries from cacao beans--are classified in U.S. Industry 311351, Chocolate and Confectionery Manufacturing from Cacao Beans;
- Manufacturing chocolate confectioneries from chocolate made elsewhere--are classified in U.S. Industry 311352, Confectionery Manufacturing from Purchased Chocolate;
- Retailing confectioneries not for immediate consumption made elsewhere--are classified in U.S. Industry 445292, Confectionery and Nut Stores;
- Preparing and selling confectioneries for immediate consumption--are classified in U.S. Industry 722515, Snack and Nonalcoholic Beverage Bars; and
- Roasting, salting, drying, cooking, or canning nuts and seeds--are classified in U.S. Industry 311911, Roasted Nuts and Peanut Butter Manufacturing.

31135 Chocolate and Confectionery Manufacturing[T]

This industry comprises establishments primarily engaged in (1) manufacturing chocolate and chocolate confectioneries from cacao beans or (2) manufacturing chocolate confectioneries from chocolate produced elsewhere. Included in this industry are establishments primarily engaged in retailing chocolate confectionery products not for immediate consumption made on the premises from chocolate made elsewhere.

Cross-References. Establishments primarily engaged in--

- Manufacturing, not for immediate consumption, nonchocolate confectioneries--are classified in Industry 31134, Nonchocolate Confectionery Manufacturing;
- Retailing confectioneries not for immediate consumption made elsewhere--are classified in Industry 44529, Other Specialty Food Stores; and
- Preparing and selling confectioneries for immediate consumption--are classified in Industry 72251, Restaurants and Other Eating Places.

311351 Chocolate and Confectionery Manufacturing from Cacao Beans

This U.S. industry comprises establishments primarily engaged in shelling, roasting, and grinding cacao beans and making chocolate cacao products and chocolate confectioneries.

T—Canadian, Mexican, and United States industries are comparable.

Cross-References. Establishments primarily engaged in--

- Manufacturing, not for immediate consumption, chocolate confectioneries from chocolate made elsewhere--are classified in U.S. Industry 311352, Confectionery Manufacturing from Purchased Chocolate;
- Manufacturing, not for immediate consumption, nonchocolate candies--are classified in Industry 311340, Nonchocolate Confectionery Manufacturing;
- Preparing and selling confectioneries for immediate consumption--are classified in U.S. Industry 722515, Snack and Nonalcoholic Beverage Bars; and
- Retailing confectioneries not for immediate consumption made elsewhere--are classified in U.S. Industry 445292, Confectionery and Nut Stores.

311352 Confectionery Manufacturing from Purchased Chocolate

This U.S. industry comprises establishments primarily engaged in manufacturing chocolate confectioneries from chocolate produced elsewhere. Included in this industry are establishments primarily engaged in retailing chocolate confectionery products not for immediate consumption made on the premises from chocolate made elsewhere.

Cross-References. Establishments primarily engaged in--

- Manufacturing chocolate confectioneries from cacao beans--are classified in U.S. Industry 311351, Chocolate and Confectionery Manufacturing from Cacao Beans;
- Manufacturing, not for immediate consumption, nonchocolate confectioneries--are classified in Industry 311340, Nonchocolate Confectionery Manufacturing;
- Retailing confectioneries not for immediate consumption made elsewhere--are classified in U.S. Industry 445292, Confectionery and Nut Stores; and
- Preparing and selling confectioneries for immediate consumption--are classified in U.S. Industry 722515, Snack and Nonalcoholic Beverage Bars.

3114 Fruit and Vegetable Preserving and Specialty Food Manufacturing[T]

This industry group includes (1) establishments that freeze food and (2) those that use preservation processes, such as pickling, canning, and dehydrating. Both types begin their production process with inputs of vegetable or animal origin.

31141 Frozen Food Manufacturing[T]

This industry comprises establishments primarily engaged in manufacturing frozen fruit, frozen juices, frozen vegetables, and frozen specialty foods (except seafood), such as frozen dinners, entrees, and side dishes; frozen pizza; frozen whipped toppings; and frozen waffles, pancakes, and french toast.

Cross-References. Establishments primarily engaged in--

- Manufacturing frozen dairy specialties--are classified in Industry 31152, Ice Cream and Frozen Dessert Manufacturing;
- Manufacturing frozen bakery products--are classified in Industry 31181, Bread and Bakery Product Manufacturing;
- Manufacturing frozen seafood products--are classified in Industry 31171, Seafood Product Preparation and Packaging; and
- Manufacturing frozen meat products--are classified in Industry 31161, Animal Slaughtering and Processing.

311411 Frozen Fruit, Juice, and Vegetable Manufacturing

This U.S. industry comprises establishments primarily engaged in manufacturing frozen fruits; frozen vegetables; and frozen fruit juices, ades, drinks, cocktail mixes and concentrates.

T—Canadian, Mexican, and United States industries are comparable.

Cross-References.

Establishments primarily engaged in manufacturing frozen specialty foods are classified in U.S. Industry 311412, Frozen Specialty Food Manufacturing.

311412 Frozen Specialty Food Manufacturing

This U.S. industry comprises establishments primarily engaged in manufacturing frozen specialty foods (except seafood), such as frozen dinners, entrees, and side dishes; frozen pizza; frozen whipped topping; and frozen waffles, pancakes, and french toast.

Cross-References. Establishments primarily engaged in--

- Manufacturing frozen dairy specialties--are classified in Industry 311520, Ice Cream and Frozen Dessert Manufacturing;
- Manufacturing frozen bakery products--are classified in U.S. Industry 311813, Frozen Cakes, Pies, and Other Pastries Manufacturing;
- Manufacturing frozen fruits, frozen fruit juices, and frozen vegetables--are classified in U.S. Industry 311411, Frozen Fruit, Juice, and Vegetable Manufacturing;
- Manufacturing frozen meat products--are classified in Industry 31161, Animal Slaughtering and Processing; and
- Manufacturing frozen seafood products--are classified in Industry 311710, Seafood Product Preparation and Packaging.

31142 Fruit and Vegetable Canning, Pickling, and Drying[T]

This industry comprises establishments primarily engaged in manufacturing canned, pickled, and dried fruits, vegetables, and specialty foods. Establishments in this industry may package the dried or dehydrated ingredients they make with other purchased ingredients. Examples of products made by these establishments are canned juices; canned baby foods; canned soups (except seafood); canned dry beans; canned tomato-based sauces, such as catsup, salsa, chili sauce, spaghetti sauce, barbeque sauce, and tomato paste; pickles and relishes; jams and jellies; dried soup mixes and bouillon; and sauerkraut.

Cross-References. Establishments primarily engaged in--

- Manufacturing canned dairy products--are classified in Industry 31151, Dairy Product (except Frozen) Manufacturing;
- Manufacturing canned seafood soups and seafood products--are classified in Industry 31171, Seafood Product Preparation and Packaging;
- Manufacturing canned meat products--are classified in Industry 31161, Animal Slaughtering and Processing;
- Milling rice and packaging it with other ingredients or manufacturing vegetable flours and meals--are classified in Industry 31121, Flour Milling and Malt Manufacturing;
- Manufacturing dry pasta and packaging it with other ingredients--are classified in Industry 31182, Cookie, Cracker, and Pasta Manufacturing;
- Mixing purchased dried and/or dehydrated potatoes, rice, and pasta and packaging them with other purchased ingredients; mixing purchased dried and/or dehydrated ingredients for soup mixes and bouillon; and manufacturing canned puddings--are classified in Industry 31199, All Other Food Manufacturing;
- Manufacturing dry salad dressing and dry sauce mixes--are classified in Industry 31194, Seasoning and Dressing Manufacturing; and
- Manufacturing canned fruit and vegetable drinks, cocktails, and ades--are classified in Industry 31211, Soft Drink and Ice Manufacturing.

T—Canadian, Mexican, and United States industries are comparable.

311421 Fruit and Vegetable Canning

This U.S. industry comprises establishments primarily engaged in manufacturing canned, pickled, and brined fruits and vegetables. Examples of products made in these establishments are canned juices; canned jams and jellies; canned tomato-based sauces, such as catsup, salsa, chili sauce, spaghetti sauce, barbeque sauce, and tomato paste; and pickles, relishes, and sauerkraut.

Cross-References. Establishments primarily engaged in--

- Manufacturing canned baby foods, canned soups (except seafood), and canned specialty foods (except seafood)--are classified in U.S. Industry 311422, Specialty Canning;
- Manufacturing canned seafood soups and canned seafood products--are classified in Industry 311710, Seafood Product Preparation and Packaging;
- Manufacturing canned meat products--are classified in Industry 31161, Animal Slaughtering and Processing; and
- Manufacturing canned fruit and vegetable drinks, cocktails, and ades--are classified in U.S. Industry 312111, Soft Drink Manufacturing.

311422 Specialty Canning

This U.S. industry comprises establishments primarily engaged in manufacturing canned specialty foods. Examples of products made in these establishments are canned baby food, canned baked beans, canned soups (except seafood), canned spaghetti, and other canned nationality foods.

Cross-References. Establishments primarily engaged in--

- Manufacturing canned dairy products--are classified in U.S. Industry 311514, Dry, Condensed, and Evaporated Dairy Product Manufacturing;
- Manufacturing canned fruits, canned vegetables, and canned juices--are classified in U.S. Industry 311421, Fruit and Vegetable Canning;
- Manufacturing canned seafood soups and canned seafood products--are classified in Industry 311710, Seafood Product Preparation and Packaging;
- Manufacturing canned meat products--are classified in Industry 31161, Animal Slaughtering and Processing; and
- Manufacturing canned puddings--are classified in U.S. Industry 311999, All Other Miscellaneous Food Manufacturing.

311423 Dried and Dehydrated Food Manufacturing

This U.S. industry comprises establishments primarily engaged in (1) drying (including freeze-dried) and/or dehydrating fruits, vegetables, and soup mixes and bouillon and/or (2) drying and/or dehydrating ingredients and packaging them with other purchased ingredients, such as rice and dry pasta.

Cross-References. Establishments primarily engaged in--

- Milling rice and packaging it with other ingredients--are classified in U.S. Industry 311212, Rice Milling;
- Manufacturing dry pasta and packaging it with other ingredients--are classified in U.S. Industry 311824, Dry Pasta, Dough, and Flour Mixes Manufacturing from Purchased Flour;
- Manufacturing vegetable flours and meals--are classified in U.S. Industry 311211, Flour Milling;
- Mixing purchased dried and/or dehydrated potatoes, rice, and pasta, and packaging them with other purchased ingredients, and mixing purchased dried and/or dehydrated ingredients for soup mixes and bouillon--are classified in U.S. Industry 311999, All Other Miscellaneous Food Manufacturing; and
- Manufacturing dry salad dressing and dry sauce mixes--are classified in U.S. Industry 311942, Spice and Extract Manufacturing.

T—Canadian, Mexican, and United States industries are comparable.

3115 Dairy Product Manufacturing[T]

This industry group comprises establishments that manufacture dairy products from raw milk, processed milk, and dairy substitutes.

31151 Dairy Product (except Frozen) Manufacturing[T]

This industry comprises establishments primarily engaged in one or more of the following: (1) manufacturing dairy products (except frozen) from raw milk and/or processed milk products; (2) manufacturing dairy substitutes (except frozen) from soybeans and other nondairy substances; and (3) manufacturing dry, condensed, concentrated, and evaporated dairy and dairy substitute products.

Cross-References. Establishments primarily engaged in--

- Manufacturing cheese-based salad dressings--are classified in Industry 31194, Seasoning and Dressing Manufacturing;
- Manufacturing margarine or margarine-butter blends--are classified in Industry 31122, Starch and Vegetable Fats and Oils Manufacturing;
- Manufacturing frozen whipped toppings--are classified in Industry 31141, Frozen Food Manufacturing; and
- Manufacturing ice cream, frozen yogurt, and other frozen dairy desserts--are classified in Industry 31152, Ice Cream and Frozen Dessert Manufacturing.

311511 Fluid Milk Manufacturing

This U.S. industry comprises establishments primarily engaged in (1) manufacturing processed milk products, such as pasteurized milk or cream and sour cream and/or (2) manufacturing fluid milk dairy substitutes from soybeans and other nondairy substances.

Cross-References. Establishments primarily engaged in--

- Manufacturing dry mix whipped toppings, canned milk, and ultra high temperature milk--are classified in U.S. Industry 311514, Dry, Condensed, and Evaporated Dairy Product Manufacturing;
- Manufacturing frozen whipped toppings--are classified in U.S. Industry 311412, Frozen Specialty Food Manufacturing; and
- Manufacturing ice cream and frozen yogurt and other frozen desserts--are classified in Industry 311520, Ice Cream and Frozen Dessert Manufacturing.

311512 Creamery Butter Manufacturing

This U.S. industry comprises establishments primarily engaged in manufacturing creamery butter from milk and/or processed milk products.

Cross-References.

Establishments primarily engaged in manufacturing margarine or margarine-butter blends are classified in U.S. Industry 311225, Fats and Oils Refining and Blending.

311513 Cheese Manufacturing

This U.S. industry comprises establishments primarily engaged in (1) manufacturing cheese products (except cottage cheese) from raw milk and/or processed milk products and/or (2) manufacturing cheese substitutes from soybean and other nondairy substances.

T—Canadian, Mexican, and United States industries are comparable.

Cross-References. Establishments primarily engaged in--

- Manufacturing cheese-based salad dressings--are classified in U.S. Industry 311941, Mayonnaise, Dressing, and Other Prepared Sauce Manufacturing; and
- Manufacturing cottage cheese--are classified in U.S. Industry 311511, Fluid Milk Manufacturing.

311514 Dry, Condensed, and Evaporated Dairy Product Manufacturing

This U.S. industry comprises establishments primarily engaged in manufacturing dry, condensed, and evaporated milk and dairy substitute products.

Cross-References. Establishments primarily engaged in--

- Manufacturing fluid milk products--are classified in U.S. Industry 311511, Fluid Milk Manufacturing;
- Manufacturing creamery butter--are classified in U.S. Industry 311512, Creamery Butter Manufacturing; and
- Manufacturing cheese products--are classified in U.S. Industry 311513, Cheese Manufacturing.

31152 Ice Cream and Frozen Dessert Manufacturing[T] See industry description for 311520.

311520 Ice Cream and Frozen Dessert Manufacturing

This industry comprises establishments primarily engaged in manufacturing ice cream, frozen yogurts, frozen ices, sherbets, frozen tofu, and other frozen desserts (except bakery products).

Cross-References. Establishments primarily engaged in--

- Manufacturing frozen bakery products--are classified in U.S. Industry 311813, Frozen Cakes, Pies, and Other Pastries Manufacturing; and
- Manufacturing ice cream and ice milk mixes--are classified in U.S. Industry 311514, Dry, Condensed, and Evaporated Dairy Product Manufacturing.

3116 Animal Slaughtering and Processing[T]

31161 Animal Slaughtering and Processing[T]

This industry comprises establishments primarily engaged in one or more of the following: (1) slaughtering animals; (2) preparing processed meats and meat byproducts; and (3) rendering and/or refining animal fat, bones, and meat scraps. This industry includes establishments primarily engaged in assembly cutting and packing of meats (i.e., boxed meats) from purchased carcasses.

Cross-References. Establishments primarily engaged in--

- Manufacturing canned meat for baby food--are classified in Industry 31142, Fruit and Vegetable Canning, Pickling, and Drying;
- Manufacturing meat-based animal feeds from carcasses--are classified in Industry 31111, Animal Food Manufacturing;
- Blending purchased animal fats with vegetable fats--are classified in Industry 31122, Starch and Vegetable Fats and Oils Manufacturing;
- Manufacturing canned and frozen specialty foods containing meat, such as nationality foods (e.g., enchiladas, pizza, egg rolls) and frozen dinners--are classified in Industry Group 3114, Fruit and Vegetable Preserving and Specialty Food Manufacturing;
- Drying, freezing, or breaking eggs--are classified in Industry 31199, All Other Food Manufacturing; and

T—Canadian, Mexican, and United States industries are comparable.

- Cutting meat (except boxed meat)--are classified in Industry 42447, Meat and Meat Product Merchant Wholesalers.

311611 Animal (except Poultry) Slaughtering

This U.S. industry comprises establishments primarily engaged in slaughtering animals (except poultry and small game). Establishments that slaughter and prepare meats are included in this industry.

Cross-References. Establishments primarily engaged in--

- Processing meat and meat byproducts (except poultry and small game) from purchased meats--are classified in U.S. Industry 311612, Meat Processed from Carcasses;
- Slaughtering and/or processing poultry and small game--are classified in U.S. Industry 311615, Poultry Processing;
- Rendering lard and other animal fats and oils, bones, and meat scraps--are classified in U.S. Industry 311613, Rendering and Meat Byproduct Processing; and
- Manufacturing canned and frozen specialty foods containing meat, such as nationality foods (e.g., enchiladas, egg rolls, pizza) and frozen dinners--are classified in Industry Group 3114, Fruit and Vegetable Preserving and Specialty Food Manufacturing.

311612 Meat Processed from Carcasses

This U.S. industry comprises establishments primarily engaged in processing or preserving meat and meat byproducts (except poultry and small game) from purchased meats. This industry includes establishments primarily engaged in assembly cutting and packing of meats (i.e., boxed meats) from purchased meats.

Cross-References. Establishments primarily engaged in--

- Slaughtering animals (except poultry and small game)--are classified in U.S. Industry 311611, Animal (except Poultry) Slaughtering;
- Slaughtering poultry and small game--are classified in U.S. Industry 311615, Poultry Processing;
- Rendering lard and other animal fats and oils, bones, and meat scraps--are classified in U.S. Industry 311613, Rendering and Meat Byproduct Processing;
- Manufacturing canned meats for baby food--are classified in U.S. Industry 311422, Specialty Canning;
- Manufacturing meat-based animal feeds from carcasses--are classified in Industry 31111, Animal Food Manufacturing;
- Manufacturing canned and frozen specialty foods containing meat, such as nationality foods (e.g., enchiladas, egg rolls, pizza) and frozen dinners--are classified in Industry Group 3114, Fruit and Vegetable Preserving and Specialty Food Manufacturing; and
- Cutting meat (except boxed meat)--are classified in Industry 424470, Meat and Meat Product Merchant Wholesalers.

311613 Rendering and Meat Byproduct Processing

This U.S. industry comprises establishments primarily engaged in rendering animal fat, bones, and meat scraps.

Cross-References.

Establishments primarily engaged in blending purchased animal fats with vegetable fats are classified in U.S. Industry 311225, Fats and Oils Refining and Blending.

311615 Poultry Processing

This U.S. industry comprises establishments primarily engaged in (1) slaughtering poultry and small game and/or (2) preparing processed poultry and small game meat and meat byproducts.
T—Canadian, Mexican, and United States industries are comparable.

Cross-References. Establishments primarily engaged in--

- Slaughtering animals (except poultry and small game) and/or preparing meats--are classified in U.S. Industry 311611, Animal (except Poultry) Slaughtering;
- Preparing meat and meat byproducts (except poultry and small game) from purchased meats--are classified in U.S. Industry 311612, Meat Processed from Carcasses;
- Rendering animal fats and oils, bones, and meat scraps--are classified in U.S. Industry 311613, Rendering and Meat Byproduct Processing;
- Canning poultry and small game for baby food--are classified in U.S. Industry 311422, Specialty Canning;
- Producing poultry-based animal feeds from carcasses--are classified in Industry 31111, Animal Food Manufacturing;
- Manufacturing frozen meat and poultry products, such as nationality foods (e.g., enchiladas, egg rolls, pizza) and frozen dinners--are classified in U.S. Industry 311412, Frozen Specialty Food Manufacturing; and
- Drying, freezing, and breaking eggs--are classified in U.S. Industry 311999, All Other Miscellaneous Food Manufacturing.

3117 Seafood Product Preparation and Packaging[T]

31171 Seafood Product Preparation and Packaging[T] See industry description for 311710.

311710 Seafood Product Preparation and Packaging

This industry comprises establishments primarily engaged in one or more of the following: (1) canning seafood (including soup); (2) smoking, salting, and drying seafood; (3) eviscerating fresh fish by removing heads, fins, scales, bones, and entrails; (4) shucking and packing fresh shellfish; (5) processing marine fats and oils; and (6) freezing seafood. Establishments known as “floating factory ships” that are engaged in the gathering and processing of seafood into canned seafood products are included in this industry.

3118 Bakeries and Tortilla Manufacturing[T]

This industry group comprises establishments primarily engaged in one of the following: (1) manufacturing fresh and frozen bread and other bakery products; (2) retailing bread and other bakery products not for immediate consumption made on the premises from flour, not from prepared dough; (3) manufacturing cookies, crackers, and dry pasta; (4) manufacturing prepared flour mixes or dough from flour ground elsewhere; or (5) manufacturing tortillas.

31181 Bread and Bakery Product Manufacturing[T]

This industry comprises establishments primarily engaged in manufacturing fresh and frozen bread and other bakery products.

Cross-References. Establishments primarily engaged in--

- Manufacturing cookies and crackers--are classified in Industry 31182, Cookie, Cracker, and Pasta Manufacturing;
- Preparing and selling bakery products (e.g., cookies, pretzels) for immediate consumption--are classified in Industry 72251, Restaurants and Other Eating Places;
- Retailing bakery products not for immediate consumption made elsewhere--are classified in Industry 44529, Other Specialty Food Stores; and
- Manufacturing pretzels (except soft)--are classified in Industry 31191, Snack Food Manufacturing.

T—Canadian, Mexican, and United States industries are comparable.

311811 Retail Bakeries

This U.S. industry comprises establishments primarily engaged in retailing bread and other bakery products not for immediate consumption made on the premises from flour, not from prepared dough.

Cross-References. Establishments primarily engaged in--

- Retailing bakery products not for immediate consumption made elsewhere--are classified in U.S. Industry 445291, Baked Goods Stores;
- Preparing and selling bakery products (e.g., cookies, pretzels) for immediate consumption--are classified in U.S. Industry 722515, Snack and Nonalcoholic Beverage Bars;
- Manufacturing fresh or frozen breads and other fresh bakery (except cookies and crackers) products--are classified in U.S. Industry 311812, Commercial Bakeries; and
- Manufacturing cookies and crackers--are classified in U.S. Industry 311821, Cookie and Cracker Manufacturing.

311812 Commercial Bakeries

This U.S. industry comprises establishments primarily engaged in manufacturing fresh and frozen bread and bread-type rolls and other fresh bakery (except cookies and crackers) products.

Cross-References. Establishments primarily engaged in--

- Retailing bread and other bakery products not for immediate consumption made on the premises from flour, not from prepared dough--are classified in U.S. Industry 311811, Retail Bakeries;
- Manufacturing frozen bakery products (except bread)--are classified in U.S. Industry 311813, Frozen Cakes, Pies, and Other Pastries Manufacturing;
- Preparing and selling bakery products (e.g., cookies, pretzels) for immediate consumption--are classified in U.S. Industry 722515, Snack and Nonalcoholic Beverage Bars;
- Retailing bakery products not for immediate consumption made elsewhere--are classified in U.S. Industry 445291, Baked Goods Stores;
- Manufacturing cookies and crackers--are classified in U.S. Industry 311821, Cookie and Cracker Manufacturing; and
- Manufacturing pretzels (except soft)--are classified in U.S. Industry 311919, Other Snack Food Manufacturing.

311813 Frozen Cakes, Pies, and Other Pastries Manufacturing

This U.S. industry comprises establishments primarily engaged in manufacturing frozen bakery products (except bread), such as cakes, pies, and doughnuts.

Cross-References. Establishments primarily engaged in--

- Manufacturing frozen breads--are classified in U.S. Industry 311812, Commercial Bakeries;
- Retailing bakery products not for immediate consumption made on the premises from flour, not from prepared dough--are classified in U.S. Industry 311811, Retail Bakeries;
- Preparing and selling bakery products (e.g., cookies, pretzels) for immediate consumption--are classified in U.S. Industry 722515, Snack and Nonalcoholic Beverage Bars;
- Manufacturing cookies and crackers--are classified in U.S. Industry 311821, Cookie and Cracker Manufacturing; and
- Retailing bakery products not for immediate consumption made elsewhere--are classified in U.S. Industry 445291, Baked Goods Stores.

T—Canadian, Mexican, and United States industries are comparable.

31182 Cookie, Cracker, and Pasta Manufacturing[T]

This industry comprises establishments primarily engaged in one of the following: (1) manufacturing cookies and crackers; (2) preparing flour and dough mixes and dough from flour ground elsewhere; and (3) manufacturing dry pasta. The establishments in this industry may package the dry pasta they manufacture with other ingredients.

Cross-References. Establishments primarily engaged in--

- Preparing and selling bakery products (e.g., cookies, pretzels) for immediate consumption--are classified in Industry 72251, Restaurants and Other Eating Places;
- Retailing bakery products not for immediate consumption made elsewhere--are classified in Industry 44529, Other Specialty Food Stores;
- Manufacturing bakery products (e.g., bread, cookies, pies)--are classified in Industry 31181, Bread and Bakery Product Manufacturing;
- Milling flour and preparing flour mixes or doughs--are classified in Industry 31121, Flour Milling and Malt Manufacturing;
- Manufacturing canned pasta specialties--are classified in Industry 31142, Fruit and Vegetable Canning, Pickling, and Drying;
- Manufacturing fresh pasta--are classified in Industry 31199, All Other Food Manufacturing;
- Manufacturing pretzels (except soft)--are classified in Industry 31191, Snack Food Manufacturing;
- Mixing purchased dried and/or dehydrated ingredients with purchased dry pasta--are classified in Industry 31199, All Other Food Manufacturing; and
- Drying and/or dehydrating ingredients and packaging them with purchased dry pasta--are classified in Industry 31142, Fruit and Vegetable Canning, Pickling, and Drying.

311821 Cookie and Cracker Manufacturing

This U.S. industry comprises establishments primarily engaged in manufacturing cookies, crackers, and other products, such as ice cream cones.

Cross-References. Establishments primarily engaged in--

- Preparing and selling bakery products (e.g., cookies, pretzels) for immediate consumption--are classified in U.S. Industry 722515, Snack and Nonalcoholic Beverage Bars;
- Retailing bakery products not for immediate consumption made elsewhere--are classified in U.S. Industry 445291, Baked Goods Stores;
- Manufacturing bakery products (e.g., breads, cookies, pies)--are classified in Industry 31181, Bread and Bakery Product Manufacturing; and
- Manufacturing pretzels (except soft)--are classified in U.S. Industry 311919, Other Snack Food Manufacturing.

311824 Dry Pasta, Dough, and Flour Mixes Manufacturing from Purchased Flour

This U.S. industry comprises establishments primarily engaged in (1) manufacturing dry pasta and/or (2) manufacturing prepared flour mixes or dough from flour ground elsewhere. The establishments in this industry may package the dry pasta they manufacture with other ingredients.

Cross-References. Establishments primarily engaged in--

- Milling flour and preparing flour mixes or doughs--are classified in U.S. Industry 311211, Flour Milling;
- Manufacturing fresh pasta--are classified in U.S. Industry 311991, Perishable Prepared Food Manufacturing;
- Manufacturing pasta specialties--are classified in Industry Group 3114, Fruit and Vegetable Preserving and Specialty Food Manufacturing;

T—Canadian, Mexican, and United States industries are comparable.

- Mixing purchased dried and/or dehydrated ingredients with purchased dry pasta--are classified in U.S. Industry 311999, All Other Miscellaneous Food Manufacturing; and
- Drying and/or dehydrating ingredients packaged with purchased dry pasta--are classified in U.S. Industry 311423, Dried and Dehydrated Food Manufacturing.

31183 Tortilla Manufacturing[T] See industry description for 311830.

311830 Tortilla Manufacturing

This industry comprises establishments primarily engaged in manufacturing tortillas.

Cross-References. Establishments primarily engaged in--

- Manufacturing canned nationality foods using tortillas--are classified in U.S. Industry 311422, Specialty Canning;
- Manufacturing frozen nationality foods using tortillas--are classified in U.S. Industry 311412, Frozen Specialty Food Manufacturing; and
- Manufacturing tortilla chips--are classified in U.S. Industry 311919, Other Snack Food Manufacturing.

3119 Other Food Manufacturing[T]

This industry group comprises establishments primarily engaged in manufacturing food (except animal food; grain and oilseed milling; sugar and confectionery products; preserved fruits, vegetables, and specialty foods; dairy products; meat products; seafood products; and bakery products and tortillas). This industry group includes industries with different production processes, such as snack food manufacturing; coffee and tea manufacturing; concentrate, syrup, condiment, and spice manufacturing; and, in general, an entire range of other miscellaneous food product manufacturing.

31191 Snack Food Manufacturing[T]

This industry comprises establishments primarily engaged in one or more of the following: (1) salting, roasting, drying, cooking, or canning nuts; (2) processing grains or seeds into snacks; (3) manufacturing peanut butter; and (4) manufacturing potato chips, corn chips, popped popcorn, pretzels (except soft), pork rinds, and similar snacks.

Cross-References. Establishments primarily engaged in--

- Manufacturing crackers--are classified in Industry 31182, Cookie, Cracker, and Pasta Manufacturing;
- Manufacturing unpopped popcorn--are classified in Industry 31199, All Other Food Manufacturing;
- Manufacturing chocolate or candy-coated nuts and candy-covered popcorn--are classified in Industry Group 3113, Sugar and Confectionery Product Manufacturing; and
- Manufacturing soft pretzels--are classified in Industry 31181, Bread and Bakery Product Manufacturing.

311911 Roasted Nuts and Peanut Butter Manufacturing

This U.S. industry comprises establishments primarily engaged in one or more of the following: (1) salting, roasting, drying, cooking, or canning nuts; (2) processing grains or seeds into snacks; and (3) manufacturing peanut butter.

Cross-References.

Establishments primarily engaged in manufacturing chocolate or candy-coated nuts and candy-covered popcorn are classified in Industry Group 3113, Sugar and Confectionery Product Manufacturing.

T—Canadian, Mexican, and United States industries are comparable.

311919 Other Snack Food Manufacturing

This U.S. industry comprises establishments primarily engaged in manufacturing snack foods (except roasted nuts and peanut butter).

Illustrative Examples:

Corn chips and related corn snacks manufacturing
Popped popcorn (except candy-covered) manufacturing
Pork rinds manufacturing
Potato chips manufacturing
Pretzels (except soft) manufacturing
Tortilla chips manufacturing

Cross-References. Establishments primarily engaged in--

- Manufacturing cookies and crackers--are classified in U.S. Industry 311821, Cookie and Cracker Manufacturing;
- Manufacturing candy-covered popcorn and nonchocolate granola bars--are classified in Industry 311340, Nonchocolate Confectionery Manufacturing;
- Salting, roasting, drying, cooking, or canning nuts and seeds--are classified in U.S. Industry 311911, Roasted Nuts and Peanut Butter Manufacturing;
- Manufacturing unpopped popcorn--are classified in U.S. Industry 311999, All Other Miscellaneous Food Manufacturing; and
- Manufacturing soft pretzels--are classified in U.S. Industry 311812, Commercial Bakeries.

31192 Coffee and Tea Manufacturing[T] See industry description for 311920.

311920 Coffee and Tea Manufacturing

This industry comprises establishments primarily engaged in one or more of the following: (1) roasting coffee; (2) manufacturing coffee and tea concentrates (including instant and freeze-dried); (3) blending tea; (4) manufacturing herbal tea; and (5) manufacturing coffee extracts, flavorings, and syrups.

Cross-References.

Establishments primarily engaged in bottling and canning iced tea are classified in U.S. Industry 312111, Soft Drink Manufacturing.

31193 Flavoring Syrup and Concentrate Manufacturing[T] See industry description for 311930.

311930 Flavoring Syrup and Concentrate Manufacturing

This industry comprises establishments primarily engaged in manufacturing flavoring syrup drink concentrates and related products for soda fountain use or for the manufacture of soft drinks.

Cross-References. Establishments primarily engaged in--

- Manufacturing chocolate syrup--are classified in Industry 31135, Chocolate and Confectionery Manufacturing;
- Manufacturing flavoring extracts (except coffee and meat) and natural food colorings--are classified in U.S. Industry 311942, Spice and Extract Manufacturing;
- Manufacturing coffee extracts and/or coffee-based syrups--are classified in Industry 311920, Coffee and Tea Manufacturing;

T—Canadian, Mexican, and United States industries are comparable.

- Manufacturing liquid meat extracts from slaughtered or purchased carcasses--are classified in Industry 31161, Animal Slaughtering and Processing;
- Manufacturing canned gravies by mixing liquid meat extracts with other ingredients--are classified in U.S. Industry 311422, Specialty Canning;
- Manufacturing powdered drink mixes (except coffee, tea, chocolate, or milk based), table syrup from corn syrup, or sweetening syrups (except pure maple)--are classified in U.S. Industry 311999, All Other Miscellaneous Food Manufacturing;
- Reducing maple sap to maple syrup--are classified in U.S. Industry 111998, All Other Miscellaneous Crop Farming; and
- Manufacturing natural nonfood colorings--are classified in U.S. Industry 325199, All Other Basic Organic Chemical Manufacturing.

31194 Seasoning and Dressing Manufacturing[T]

This industry comprises establishments primarily engaged in one or more of the following: (1) manufacturing dressings and sauces, such as mayonnaise, salad dressing, vinegar, mustard, horseradish, soy sauce, tarter sauce, Worcestershire sauce, and other prepared sauces (except tomato-based and gravies); (2) manufacturing spices, table salt, seasoning, and flavoring extracts (except coffee and meat), and natural food colorings; and (3) manufacturing dry mix food preparations, such as salad dressing mixes, gravy and sauce mixes, frosting mixes, and other dry mix preparations.

Cross-References. Establishments primarily engaged in--

- Manufacturing catsup and other tomato-based sauces--are classified in Industry 31142, Fruit and Vegetable Canning, Pickling, and Drying;
- Mixing purchased dried and/or dehydrated potato, rice, and pasta and packaging them with other purchased ingredients, and manufacturing prepared frosting--are classified in Industry 31199, All Other Food Manufacturing;
- Drying and/or dehydrating ingredients for dry soup mixes and bouillon--are classified in Industry 31142, Fruit and Vegetable Canning, Pickling, and Drying;
- Mixing purchased dried and/or dehydrated ingredients for dry soup mixes and bouillon--are classified in Industry 31199, All Other Food Manufacturing;
- Manufacturing industrial salts--are classified in Industry 32599, All Other Chemical Product and Preparation Manufacturing;
- Manufacturing flavoring syrups (except chocolate and coffee-based syrups)--are classified in Industry 31193, Flavoring Syrup and Concentrate Manufacturing;
- Manufacturing synthetic food colorings--are classified in Industry 32513, Synthetic Dye and Pigment Manufacturing;
- Manufacturing natural organic colorings for nonfood uses--are classified in Industry 32519, Other Basic Organic Chemical Manufacturing;
- Manufacturing coffee extracts--are classified in Industry 31192, Coffee and Tea Manufacturing;
- Manufacturing liquid meat extracts from slaughtered or purchased carcasses--are classified in Industry 31161, Animal Slaughtering and Processing; and
- Manufacturing canned liquid gravies--are classified in Industry 31142, Fruit and Vegetable Canning, Pickling, and Drying.

311941 Mayonnaise, Dressing, and Other Prepared Sauce Manufacturing

This U.S. industry comprises establishments primarily engaged in manufacturing mayonnaise, salad dressing, vinegar, mustard, horseradish, soy sauce, tarter sauce, Worcestershire sauce, and other prepared sauces (except tomato-based and gravy).

T—Canadian, Mexican, and United States industries are comparable.

Cross-References. Establishments primarily engaged in--

- Manufacturing catsup and other tomato-based sauces--are classified in U.S. Industry 311421, Fruit and Vegetable Canning;
- Manufacturing dry salad dressing and dry sauce mixes--are classified in U.S. Industry 311942, Spice and Extract Manufacturing; and
- Manufacturing canned liquid gravies--are classified in U.S. Industry 311422, Specialty Canning.

311942 Spice and Extract Manufacturing

This U.S. industry comprises establishments primarily engaged in (1) manufacturing spices, table salt, seasonings, flavoring extracts (except coffee and meat), and natural food colorings and/or (2) manufacturing dry mix food preparations, such as salad dressing mixes, gravy and sauce mixes, frosting mixes, and other dry mix preparations.

Cross-References. Establishments primarily engaged in--

- Manufacturing catsup and other tomato-based sauces--are classified in U.S. Industry 311421, Fruit and Vegetable Canning;
- Manufacturing mayonnaise, dressings, and prepared sauces (except tomato-based and gravy)--are classified in U.S. Industry 311941, Mayonnaise, Dressing, and Other Prepared Sauce Manufacturing;
- Manufacturing canned liquid gravies--are classified in U.S. Industry 311422, Specialty Canning;
- Manufacturing industrial salts--are classified in U.S. Industry 325998, All Other Miscellaneous Chemical Product and Preparation Manufacturing;
- Drying and/or dehydrating ingredients for dry soup mixes and bouillon--are classified in U.S. Industry 311423, Dried and Dehydrated Food Manufacturing;
- Mixing purchased dried and/or dehydrated ingredients for dry soup mixes and bouillon--are classified in U.S. Industry 311999, All Other Miscellaneous Food Manufacturing;
- Manufacturing flavoring syrups (except chocolate and coffee-based syrups)--are classified in Industry 311930, Flavoring Syrup and Concentrate Manufacturing;
- Mixing purchased dried and/or dehydrated potato, rice, and pasta and packaging them with other purchased ingredients, and manufacturing prepared frosting--are classified in U.S. Industry 311999, All Other Miscellaneous Food Manufacturing;
- Manufacturing coffee extracts and/or coffee-based syrups--are classified in Industry 311920, Coffee and Tea Manufacturing;
- Manufacturing liquid meat extracts from slaughtered or purchased carcasses--are classified in Industry 31161, Animal Slaughtering and Processing;
- Manufacturing synthetic food colorings--are classified in Industry 325130, Synthetic Dye and Pigment Manufacturing; and
- Manufacturing natural organic colorings for nonfood uses--are classified in U.S. Industry 325199, All Other Basic Organic Chemical Manufacturing.

31199 All Other Food Manufacturing[T]

This industry comprises establishments primarily engaged in manufacturing food (except animal food; grain and oilseed milling; sugar and confectionery products; preserved fruits, vegetables, and specialty foods; dairy products; meat products; seafood products; baked goods and tortillas; snack foods; coffee and tea; flavoring syrups and concentrates; seasonings; and dressings). Included in this industry are establishments primarily engaged in mixing purchased dried and/or dehydrated ingredients, including those mixing purchased dried and/or dehydrated ingredients for soup mixes and bouillon.

Illustrative Examples:

Baking powder manufacturing
Cut or peeled fresh vegetables manufacturing
Dessert puddings manufacturing
Egg substitutes manufacturing
Sweetening syrups (except pure maple) manufacturing

T—Canadian, Mexican, and United States industries are comparable.

Fresh pasta manufacturing
Fresh pizza manufacturing
Honey processing
Popcorn (except popped) manufacturing
Powdered drink mixes (except chocolate, coffee, tea, or milk based) manufacturing

Cross-References. Establishments primarily engaged in--

- Manufacturing animal foods--are classified in Industry Group 3111, Animal Food Manufacturing;
- Milling grains and oilseeds--are classified in Industry Group 3112, Grain and Oilseed Milling;
- Manufacturing sugar and confectionery products--are classified in Industry Group 3113, Sugar and Confectionery Product Manufacturing;
- Preserving fruit, vegetables, and specialty foods--are classified in Industry Group 3114, Fruit and Vegetable Preserving and Specialty Food Manufacturing;
- Manufacturing dairy products--are classified in Industry Group 3115, Dairy Product Manufacturing;
- Manufacturing meat products--are classified in Industry Group 3116, Animal Slaughtering and Processing;
- Manufacturing seafood products--are classified in Industry Group 3117, Seafood Product Preparation and Packaging;
- Manufacturing bakery products and tortillas--are classified in Industry Group 3118, Bakeries and Tortilla Manufacturing;
- Manufacturing snack foods--are classified in Industry 31191, Snack Food Manufacturing;
- Manufacturing coffee and tea--are classified in Industry 31192, Coffee and Tea Manufacturing;
- Manufacturing flavoring syrups and concentrates (except chocolate and coffee-based)--are classified in Industry 31193, Flavoring Syrup and Concentrate Manufacturing;
- Manufacturing seasonings and dressings--are classified in Industry 31194, Seasoning and Dressing Manufacturing;
- Milling rice and packaging it with other ingredients--are classified in Industry 31121, Flour Milling and Malt Manufacturing;
- Manufacturing dry pasta and packaging it with other ingredients--are classified in Industry 31182, Cookie, Cracker, and Pasta Manufacturing; and
- Drying and/or dehydrating ingredients and packaging them with other purchased ingredients--are classified in Industry 31142, Fruit and Vegetable Canning, Pickling, and Drying.

311991 Perishable Prepared Food Manufacturing

This U.S. industry comprises establishments primarily engaged in manufacturing perishable prepared foods, such as salads, sandwiches, prepared meals, fresh pizza, fresh pasta, and peeled or cut vegetables.

311999 All Other Miscellaneous Food Manufacturing

This U.S. industry comprises establishments primarily engaged in manufacturing food (except animal food; grain and oilseed milling; sugar and confectionery products; preserved fruits, vegetables, and specialties; dairy products; meat products; seafood products; bakeries and tortillas; snack foods; coffee and tea; flavoring syrups and concentrates; seasonings and dressings; and perishable prepared food). Included in this industry are establishments primarily engaged in mixing purchased dried and/or dehydrated ingredients including those mixing purchased dried and/or dehydrated ingredients for soup mixes and bouillon.

Illustrative Examples:

Baking powder manufacturing
Cake frosting, prepared, manufacturing
Dessert puddings manufacturing
Sweetening syrups (except pure maple) manufacturing
Egg substitutes manufacturing
Gelatin dessert preparations manufacturing
Honey processing
Powdered drink mixes (except chocolate, coffee, tea, or milk based) manufacturing Popcorn (except popped) manufacturing
Yeast manufacturing

T—Canadian, Mexican, and United States industries are comparable.

Cross-References. Establishments primarily engaged in--

- Manufacturing animal foods--are classified in Industry Group 3111, Animal Food Manufacturing;
- Milling grains and oilseeds--are classified in Industry Group 3112, Grain and Oilseed Milling;
- Manufacturing sugar and confectionery products--are classified in Industry Group 3113, Sugar and Confectionery Product Manufacturing;
- Preserving fruit, vegetable, and specialty foods--are classified in Industry Group 3114, Fruit and Vegetable Preserving and Specialty Food Manufacturing;
- Manufacturing dairy products--are classified in Industry Group 3115, Dairy Product Manufacturing;
- Manufacturing meat products--are classified in Industry Group 3116, Animal Slaughtering and Processing;
- Manufacturing seafood products--are classified in Industry Group 3117, Seafood Product Preparation and Packaging;
- Manufacturing bakery products and tortillas--are classified in Industry Group 3118, Bakeries and Tortilla Manufacturing;
- Manufacturing snack foods--are classified in Industry 31191, Snack Food Manufacturing;
- Manufacturing coffee and tea--are classified in Industry 31192, Coffee and Tea Manufacturing;
- Manufacturing flavoring syrups and concentrates (except coffee-based)--are classified in Industry 31193, Flavoring Syrup and Concentrate Manufacturing;
- Manufacturing seasonings and dressings--are classified in Industry 31194, Seasoning and Dressing Manufacturing;
- Manufacturing perishable prepared foods--are classified in U.S. Industry 311991, Perishable Prepared Food Manufacturing;
- Milling rice and packaging it with other ingredients--are classified in U.S. Industry 311212, Rice Milling;
- Manufacturing dry pasta and packaging it with ingredients--are classified in U.S. Industry 311824, Dry Pasta, Dough, and Flour Mixes Manufacturing from Purchased Flour; and
- Drying and/or dehydrating ingredients and packaging them with other purchased ingredients--are classified in U.S. Industry 311423, Dried and Dehydrated Food Manufacturing.

312 Beverage and Tobacco Product Manufacturing[T]

Industries in the Beverage and Tobacco Product Manufacturing subsector manufacture beverages and tobacco products. The Beverage Manufacturing industry group includes three types of establishments: (1) those that manufacture nonalcoholic beverages; (2) those that manufacture alcoholic beverages through the fermentation process; and (3) those that produce distilled alcoholic beverages. Ice manufacturing, while not a beverage, is included with nonalcoholic beverage manufacturing because it uses the same production process as water purification.

In the case of activities related to the manufacture of beverages, the structure follows the defined production processes. Brandy, a distilled beverage, is not placed under distillery product manufacturing, but rather under winery product manufacturing since the production process used in the manufacturing of alcoholic grape-based beverages produces both wines (fermented beverage) and brandies (distilled beverage).

The Tobacco Manufacturing industry group includes two types of establishments: (1) those engaged in redrying and stemming tobacco and (2) those that manufacture tobacco products, such as cigarettes and cigars.

3121 Beverage Manufacturing[T]

This industry group comprises establishments primarily engaged in manufacturing soft drinks and ice; purifying and bottling water; and manufacturing brewery, winery, and distillery products.

31211 Soft Drink and Ice Manufacturing[T]

This industry comprises establishments primarily engaged in one or more of the following: (1) manufacturing soft drinks; (2) manufacturing ice; and (3) purifying and bottling water.

T—Canadian, Mexican, and United States industries are comparable.

Cross-References. Establishments primarily engaged in--

- Canning fruit and vegetable juices--are classified in Industry 31142, Fruit and Vegetable Canning, Pickling, and Drying;
- Manufacturing soft drink bases--are classified in Industry 31193, Flavoring Syrup and Concentrate Manufacturing;
- Manufacturing nonalcoholic cider--are classified in Industry 31194, Seasoning and Dressing Manufacturing;
- Manufacturing dry ice--are classified in Industry 32512, Industrial Gas Manufacturing;
- Manufacturing milk based drinks--are classified in Industry 31151, Dairy Product (except Frozen) Manufacturing;
- Manufacturing nonalcoholic beers--are classified in Industry 31212, Breweries;
- Manufacturing nonalcoholic wines--are classified in Industry 31213, Wineries; and
- Bottling purchased purified water--are classified in Industry 42449, Other Grocery and Related Products Merchant Wholesalers.

312111 Soft Drink Manufacturing

This U.S. industry comprises establishments primarily engaged in manufacturing soft drinks and artificially carbonated waters.

Cross-References. Establishments primarily engaged in--

- Canning fruit and vegetable juices--are classified in U.S. Industry 311421, Fruit and Vegetable Canning;
- Manufacturing fruit syrups for flavoring--are classified in Industry 311930, Flavoring Syrup and Concentrate Manufacturing;
- Manufacturing nonalcoholic cider--are classified in U.S. Industry 311941, Mayonnaise, Dressing, and Other Prepared Sauce Manufacturing;
- Purifying and bottling water (except artificially carbonated and flavored water)--are classified in U.S. Industry 312112, Bottled Water Manufacturing;
- Manufacturing milk based drinks--are classified in U.S. Industry 311511, Fluid Milk Manufacturing;
- Manufacturing nonalcoholic beers--are classified in Industry 312120, Breweries; and
- Manufacturing nonalcoholic wines--are classified in Industry 312130, Wineries.

312112 Bottled Water Manufacturing

This U.S. industry comprises establishments primarily engaged in purifying and bottling water (including naturally carbonated).

Cross-References. Establishments primarily engaged in--

- Manufacturing artificially carbonated or flavored waters--are classified in U.S. Industry 312111, Soft Drink Manufacturing; and
- Bottling purchased purified water--are classified in Industry 424490, Other Grocery and Related Products Merchant Wholesalers.

312113 Ice Manufacturing

This U.S. industry comprises establishments primarily engaged in manufacturing ice.

Cross-References.

Establishments primarily engaged in manufacturing dry ice are classified in Industry 325120, Industrial Gas Manufacturing.
T—Canadian, Mexican, and United States industries are comparable.

31212 Breweries[T] See industry description for 312120.

312120 Breweries

This industry comprises establishments primarily engaged in brewing beer, ale, lager, malt liquors, and nonalcoholic beer.

Cross-References. Establishments primarily engaged in--

- Bottling purchased malt beverages--are classified in Industry 424810, Beer and Ale Merchant Wholesalers; and
- Manufacturing malt--are classified in U.S. Industry 311213, Malt Manufacturing.

31213 Wineries[T] See industry description for 312130.

312130 Wineries

This industry comprises establishments primarily engaged in one or more of the following: (1) growing grapes and manufacturing wines and brandies; (2) manufacturing wines and brandies from grapes and other fruits grown elsewhere; and (3) blending wines and brandies.

Cross-References.

Establishments primarily engaged in bottling purchased wines are classified in Industry 424820, Wine and Distilled Alcoholic Beverage Merchant Wholesalers.

31214 Distilleries[T] See industry description for 312140.

312140 Distilleries

This industry comprises establishments primarily engaged in one or more of the following: (1) distilling potable liquors (except brandies); (2) distilling and blending liquors; and (3) blending and mixing liquors and other ingredients.

Cross-References. Establishments primarily engaged in--

- Manufacturing nonpotable ethyl alcohol--are classified in U.S. Industry 325193, Ethyl Alcohol Manufacturing;
- Bottling liquors made elsewhere--are classified in Industry 424820, Wine and Distilled Alcoholic Beverage Merchant Wholesalers; and
- Manufacturing brandies--are classified in Industry 312130, Wineries.

3122 Tobacco Manufacturing[T]

31223 Tobacco Manufacturing
See industry description for 312230.

312230 Tobacco Manufacturing

This industry comprises establishments primarily engaged in (1) stemming and redrying tobacco and/or (2) manufacturing cigarettes or other tobacco products.

T—Canadian, Mexican, and United States industries are comparable.

Illustrative Examples:

Chewing tobacco manufacturing
Cigar manufacturing
Cigarettes manufacturing (except electronic)
Snuff manufacturing
Prepared pipe tobacco manufacturing
Tobacco leaf processing and aging

Cross-References. Establishments primarily engaged in--

- Manufacturing tobacco pipes or electronic cigarettes--are classified in U.S. Industry 339999, All Other Miscellaneous Manufacturing;
- Manufacturing electronic cigarette vapor refills--are classified in U.S. Industry 325998, All Other Miscellaneous Chemical Product and Preparation Manufacturing;
- Selling leaf tobacco as merchant wholesalers that also engage in stemming tobacco--are classified in Industry 424940, Tobacco and Tobacco Product Merchant Wholesalers; and
- Selling leaf tobacco as agents or brokers that also engage in stemming tobacco--are classified in Industry 425120, Wholesale Trade Agents and Brokers.

313 Textile Mills[T]

Industries in the Textile Mills subsector group establishments that transform a basic fiber (natural or synthetic) into a product, such as yarn or fabric that is further manufactured into usable items, such as apparel, sheets, towels, and textile bags for individual or industrial consumption. The further manufacturing may be performed in the same establishment and classified in this subsector, or it may be performed at a separate establishment and be classified elsewhere in manufacturing.

The main processes in this subsector include preparation and spinning of fiber, knitting or weaving of fabric, and the finishing of the textile. The NAICS structure follows and captures this process flow. Major industries in this flow, such as preparation of fibers, weaving of fabric, knitting of fabric, and fiber and fabric finishing, are uniquely identified. Texturizing, throwing, twisting, and winding of yarn contain aspects of both fiber preparation and fiber finishing and are classified with preparation of fibers rather than with finishing of fibers.

NAICS separates the manufacturing of primary textiles and the manufacturing of textile products (except apparel) produced from purchased primary textiles, such as fabric. The manufacturing of textile products (except apparel) from purchased fabric is classified in Subsector 314, Textile Product Mills, and apparel from purchased fabric is classified in Subsector 315, Apparel Manufacturing.

Excluded from this subsector are establishments that weave or knit fabric and make garments. These establishments are included in Subsector 315, Apparel Manufacturing.

3131 Fiber, Yarn, and Thread Mills[T]

31311 Fiber, Yarn, and Thread Mills[T] See industry description for 313110.

313110 Fiber, Yarn, and Thread Mills

This industry comprises establishments primarily engaged in one or more of the following: (1) spinning yarn; (2) manufacturing thread of any fiber; (3) texturizing, throwing, twisting, and winding purchased yarn or manmade fiber filaments; and (4) producing hemp yarn and further processing into rope or bags.

Cross-References.

Establishments primarily engaged in manufacturing artificial and synthetic fibers and filaments and texturizing these filaments are classified in Industry 325220, Artificial and Synthetic Fibers and Filaments Manufacturing.

T—Canadian, Mexican, and United States industries are comparable.

3132 Fabric Mills[T]

This industry group comprises establishments primarily engaged in one of the following: (1) weaving broadwoven fabrics and felts (except tire fabrics and rugs); (2) weaving or braiding narrow fabrics; (3) making fabric-covered elastic yarn and thread; (4) manufacturing Schiffli machine embroideries; (5) manufacturing nonwoven fabrics and felts; (6) knitting weft (i.e., circular) and warp (i.e., flat) fabric; (7) knitting and finishing weft and warp fabric; (8) manufacturing lace; or (9) manufacturing, dyeing, and finishing lace and lace goods.

31321 Broadwoven Fabric Mills[T] See industry description for 313210.

313210 Broadwoven Fabric Mills

This industry comprises establishments primarily engaged in weaving broadwoven fabrics and felts (except tire fabrics and rugs). Establishments in this industry may weave only, weave and finish, or weave, finish, and further fabricate fabric products.

Cross-References. Establishments primarily engaged in--

- Weaving widths specifically constructed for cutting to narrow widths--are classified in Industry 313220, Narrow Fabric Mills and Schiffli Machine Embroidery;
- Weaving or tufting carpet and rugs--are classified in Industry 314110, Carpet and Rug Mills; and
- Making tire cord and tire fabrics--are classified in U.S. Industry 314994, Rope, Cordage, Twine, Tire Cord, and Tire Fabric Mills.

31322 Narrow Fabric Mills and Schiffli Machine Embroidery[T] See industry description for 313220.

313220 Narrow Fabric Mills and Schiffli Machine Embroidery

This industry comprises establishments primarily engaged in one or more of the following: (1) weaving or braiding narrow fabrics in their final form or initially made in wider widths that are specially constructed for narrower widths; (2) making fabric-covered elastic yarn and thread; and (3) manufacturing Schiffli machine embroideries. Establishments in this industry may weave only; weave and finish; or weave, finish, and further fabricate fabric products.

31323 Nonwoven Fabric Mills[T] See industry description for 313230.

313230 Nonwoven Fabric Mills

This industry comprises establishments primarily engaged in manufacturing nonwoven fabrics and felts. Processes used include bonding and/or interlocking fibers by mechanical, chemical, thermal, or solvent means, or by combinations thereof.

31324 Knit Fabric Mills[T] See industry description for 313240.

313240 Knit Fabric Mills

This industry comprises establishments primarily engaged in one of the following: (1) knitting weft (i.e., circular) and warp (i.e., flat) fabric; (2) knitting and finishing weft and warp fabric; (3) manufacturing lace; or (4) manufacturing, dyeing, and finishing lace and lace goods. Establishments in this industry may knit only; knit and finish; or knit, finish, and further fabricate fabric products (except apparel).

T—Canadian, Mexican, and United States industries are comparable.

Cross-References.

Establishments primarily engaged in knitting apparel are classified in Industry Group 3151, Apparel Knitting Mills.

3133 Textile and Fabric Finishing and Fabric Coating Mills[T]

This industry group comprises establishments primarily engaged in one of the following: (1) finishing textiles, fabrics, and apparel; (2) converting fabrics and textiles by buying fabric goods in the grey, having them finished on contract, and selling them at wholesale; or (3) coating, laminating, varnishing, waxing, and rubberizing textiles and apparel.

31331 Textile and Fabric Finishing Mills[T] See industry description for 313310.

313310 Textile and Fabric Finishing Mills

This industry comprises (1) establishments primarily engaged in finishing textiles, fabrics, and apparel and (2) establishments of converters who buy fabric goods in the grey, have them finished on contract, and sell at wholesale. Finishing operations include: bleaching, dyeing, printing (e.g., roller, screen, flock, plisse), stonewashing, and other mechanical finishing, such as preshrinking, shrinking, sponging, calendering, mercerizing, and napping; as well as cleaning, scouring, and the preparation of natural fibers and raw stock.

Cross-References. Establishments primarily engaged in--

- Coating or impregnating fabrics--are classified in Industry 313320, Fabric Coating Mills;
- Knitting or knitting and finishing fabric--are classified in Industry 313240, Knit Fabric Mills;
- Manufacturing and finishing apparel--are classified in Subsector 315, Apparel Manufacturing;
- Weaving and finishing fabrics--are classified in Industry Group 3132, Fabric Mills;
- Manufacturing and finishing rugs and carpets--are classified in Industry 314110, Carpet and Rug Mills; and
- Printing on apparel--are classified in Industry 32311, Printing.

31332 Fabric Coating Mills[T] See industry description for 313320.

313320 Fabric Coating Mills

This industry comprises establishments primarily engaged in coating, laminating, varnishing, waxing, and rubberizing textiles and apparel.

Cross-References.

Establishments primarily engaged in dyeing and finishing textiles are classified in Industry 313310, Textile and Fabric Finishing Mills.

314 Textile Product Mills[T]

Industries in the Textile Product Mills subsector group establishments that make textile products (except apparel). With a few exceptions, processes used by these establishments are generally cut and sew (i.e., purchasing fabric and cutting and sewing to make nonapparel textile products, such as sheets and towels).

T—Canadian, Mexican, and United States industries are comparable.

3141 Textile Furnishings Mills[T]

This industry group comprises establishments primarily engaged in (1) manufacturing woven, tufted, and other carpets and rugs and (2) manufacturing household textile products from purchased materials. The household textile products may be made on a stock or custom basis for sale to individual retail customers.

31411 Carpet and Rug Mills[T] See industry description for 314110.

314110 Carpet and Rug Mills

This industry comprises establishments primarily engaged in (1) manufacturing woven, tufted, and other carpets and rugs, such as art squares, floor mattings, needlepunch carpeting, and door mats and mattings, from textile materials or from twisted paper, grasses, reeds, sisal, jute, or rags and/or (2) finishing carpets and rugs.

31412 Curtain and Linen Mills[T] See industry description for 314120.

314120 Curtain and Linen Mills

This industry comprises establishments primarily engaged in manufacturing household textile products, such as curtains, draperies, linens, bedspreads, sheets, tablecloths, towels, and shower curtains, from purchased materials. The household textile products may be made on a stock or custom basis for sale to individual retail customers.

Cross-References. Establishments primarily engaged in--

- Weaving broadwoven fabrics--are classified in Industry 313210, Broadwoven Fabric Mills;
- Manufacturing lace curtains on lace machines--are classified in Industry 313240, Knit Fabric Mills;
- Manufacturing textile blanket, wardrobe, and laundry bags--are classified in Industry 314910, Textile Bag and Canvas Mills; and
- Manufacturing mops--are classified in U.S. Industry 339994, Broom, Brush, and Mop Manufacturing.

3149 Other Textile Product Mills[T]

This industry group comprises establishments primarily engaged in making textile products (except carpets and rugs, curtains and draperies, and other household textile products) from purchased materials.

31491 Textile Bag and Canvas Mills[T] See industry description for 314910.

314910 Textile Bag and Canvas Mills

This industry comprises establishments primarily engaged in manufacturing textile bags or other canvas and canvas-like products, such as awnings, sails, tarpaulins, and tents from purchased textile fabrics or yarns.

Illustrative Examples:

Covers (e.g., boat, swimming pool, truck) made from purchased fabrics
Laundry bags made from purchased woven or knitted materials
Seed bags made from purchased woven or knitted materials
Textile bags made from purchased woven or knitted materials

Cross-References. Establishments primarily engaged in--

- Manufacturing plastic bags--are classified in U.S. Industry 326111, Plastics Bag and Pouch Manufacturing;

T—Canadian, Mexican, and United States industries are comparable.

- Manufacturing canvas blinds and shades--are classified in Industry 337920, Blind and Shade Manufacturing;
- Manufacturing women's handbags and purses of leather or other material (except precious metal)--are classified in U.S. Industry 316992, Women's Handbag and Purse Manufacturing; and
- Manufacturing luggage--are classified in U.S. Industry 316998, All Other Leather Good and Allied Product Manufacturing.

31499 All Other Textile Product Mills[T]

This industry comprises establishments primarily engaged in manufacturing nonapparel textile products (except carpet, rugs, curtains, linens, bags, and canvas products) from purchased materials. This industry includes establishments primarily engaged in decorative stitching such as embroidery or other art needlework on textile products, including apparel.

Illustrative Examples:

Batts and batting (except nonwoven fabrics) manufacturing
Carpet cutting and binding
Diapers (except disposable) made from purchased materials
Fishing nets made from purchased materials
Embroidering on textile products or apparel for the trade
Ropes (except wire rope) manufacturing
Sleeping bags manufacturing
Tire cord and fabric, all materials, manufacturing
Twines manufacturing

Cross-References. Establishments primarily engaged in--

- Manufacturing yarns and thread--are classified in Industry 31311, Fiber, Yarn, and Thread Mills;
- Manufacturing carpets and rugs--are classified in Industry 31411, Carpet and Rug Mills;
- Manufacturing apparel--are classified in Subsector 315, Apparel Manufacturing;
- Manufacturing curtains and linens--are classified in Industry 31412, Curtain and Linen Mills; and
- Manufacturing textile bags and canvas products--are classified in Industry 31491, Textile Bag and Canvas Mills.

314994 Rope, Cordage, Twine, Tire Cord, and Tire Fabric Mills

This U.S. industry comprises establishments primarily engaged in (1) manufacturing rope, cable, cordage, twine, and related products from all materials (e.g., abaca, sisal, henequen, cotton, paper, jute, flax, manmade fibers including glass) and/or (2) manufacturing cord and fabric of polyester, rayon, cotton, glass, steel, or other materials for use in reinforcing rubber tires, industrial belting, and similar uses.

Cross-References.

Establishments primarily engaged in spinning yarns and filaments are classified in Industry 313110, Fiber, Yarn, and Thread Mills.

314999 All Other Miscellaneous Textile Product Mills

This U.S. industry comprises establishments primarily engaged in manufacturing textile products (except carpets and rugs; curtains and linens; textile bags and canvas products; rope, cordage, and twine; and tire cords and tire fabrics) from purchased materials. These establishments may further embellish the textile products they manufacture with decorative stitching. Establishments primarily engaged in adding decorative stitching such as embroidery or other art needlework on textile products, including apparel, on a contract or fee basis for the trade, are included in this industry.

T—Canadian, Mexican, and United States industries are comparable.

Illustrative Examples:

Batts and batting (except nonwoven fabrics) manufacturing
Embroidering on textile products or apparel for the trade
Fishing nets made from purchased materials
Carpet cutting and binding
Sleeping bags manufacturing
Diapers (except disposable) made from purchased materials
Textile fire hoses made from purchased materials
Dust cloths made from purchased fabric
Weatherstripping made from purchased textiles

Cross-References. Establishments primarily engaged in--

- Manufacturing yarns and thread--are classified in Industry 313110, Fiber, Yarn, and Thread Mills;
- Manufacturing carpets and rugs--are classified in Industry 314110, Carpet and Rug Mills;
- Manufacturing curtains and linens--are classified in Industry 314120, Curtain and Linen Mills;
- Manufacturing textile bags and canvas products--are classified in Industry 314910, Textile Bag and Canvas Mills; and
- Manufacturing rope, cordage, twine, tire cord, and tire fabrics--are classified in U.S. Industry 314994, Rope, Cordage, Twine, Tire Cord, and Tire Fabric Mills.

315 Apparel Manufacturing[T]

Industries in the Apparel Manufacturing subsector group establishments with two distinct manufacturing processes: (1) cut and sew (i.e., purchasing fabric and cutting and sewing to make a garment) and (2) the manufacture of garments in establishments that first knit fabric and then cut and sew the fabric into a garment. The Apparel Manufacturing subsector includes a diverse range of establishments manufacturing full lines of ready-to-wear apparel and custom apparel: apparel contractors, performing cutting or sewing operations on materials owned by others; jobbers, performing entrepreneurial functions involved in apparel manufacturing; and tailors, manufacturing custom garments for individual clients. Knitting fabric, when done alone, is classified in the Textile Mills subsector, but when knitting is combined with the production of complete garments, the activity is classified in the Apparel Manufacturing subsector.

3151 Apparel Knitting Mills[T]

This industry group comprises establishments primarily engaged in knitting apparel or knitting fabric and then manufacturing apparel. This industry group includes jobbers performing entrepreneurial functions involved in knitting apparel and accessories. Knitting fabric, without manufacturing apparel, is classified in Subsector 313, Textile Mills.

31511 Hosiery and Sock Mills[T] See industry description for 315110.

315110 Hosiery and Sock Mills

This industry comprises establishments primarily engaged in knitting or knitting and finishing hosiery and socks.

Cross-References. Establishments primarily engaged in--

- Manufacturing orthopedic hosiery--are classified in U.S. Industry 339113, Surgical Appliance and Supplies Manufacturing;
- Manufacturing slipper socks from purchased socks--are classified in Industry 316210, Footwear Manufacturing; and
- Finishing apparel products only--are classified in Industry 313310, Textile and Fabric Finishing Mills.

31519 Other Apparel Knitting Mills[T] See industry description for 315190.

T—Canadian, Mexican, and United States industries are comparable.

315190 Other Apparel Knitting Mills

This industry comprises establishments primarily engaged in one of the following: (1) knitting underwear, outerwear, and/or nightwear; (2) knitting fabric and manufacturing underwear, outerwear, and/or nightwear; or (3) knitting, manufacturing, and finishing knit underwear, outerwear, and/or nightwear.

Cross-References. Establishments primarily engaged in--

- Manufacturing outerwear, underwear, and nightwear from purchased fabric--are classified in Industry Group 3152, Cut and Sew Apparel Manufacturing; and
- Finishing apparel products only--are classified in Industry 313310, Textile and Fabric Finishing Mills.

3152 Cut and Sew Apparel Manufacturing[T]

This industry group comprises establishments primarily engaged in manufacturing cut and sew apparel from woven fabric or purchased knit fabric. Included in this industry group is a diverse range of establishments manufacturing full lines of ready-to-wear apparel and custom apparel: apparel contractors, performing cutting or sewing operations on materials owned by others; jobbers, performing entrepreneurial functions involved in apparel manufacturing; and tailors, manufacturing custom garments for individual clients. Establishments weaving or knitting fabric, without manufacturing apparel, are classified in Subsector 313, Textile Mills.

31521 Cut and Sew Apparel Contractors
See industry description for 315210.

315210 Cut and Sew Apparel Contractors

This industry comprises establishments commonly referred to as contractors primarily engaged in (1) cutting materials owned by others for apparel and accessories and/or (2) sewing materials owned by others for apparel and accessories.

Cross-References. Establishments primarily engaged in--

- Manufacturing men's and boys' apparel from purchased fabric--are classified in Industry 315220, Men's and Boys' Cut and Sew Apparel Manufacturing;
- Manufacturing women's, girls', and infants' apparel from purchased fabric--are classified in Industry 315240, Women's, Girls', and Infants' Cut and Sew Apparel Manufacturing;
- Manufacturing all other cut and sew apparel from purchased fabric--are classified in Industry 315280, Other Cut and Sew Apparel Manufacturing;
- Manufacturing apparel accessories from purchased fabric--are classified in Industry 315990, Apparel Accessories and Other Apparel Manufacturing; and
- Embroidering apparel on a contract or fee basis for the trade--are classified in U.S. Industry 314999, All Other Miscellaneous Textile Product Mills.

31522 Men's and Boys' Cut and Sew Apparel Manufacturing
See industry description for 315220.

315220 Men's and Boys' Cut and Sew Apparel Manufacturing

This industry comprises establishments primarily engaged in manufacturing men's and boys' cut and sew apparel from purchased fabric. Men's and boys' clothing jobbers, who perform entrepreneurial functions involved in apparel manufacture, including buying raw materials, designing and preparing samples, arranging for apparel to be made from their materials, and marketing finished apparel, are included.

T—Canadian, Mexican, and United States industries are comparable.

Cross-References. Establishments primarily engaged in--

- Cutting and/or sewing materials owned by others for men's and boys' apparel--are classified in Industry 315210, Cut and Sew Apparel Contractors;
- Knitting men's and boys' apparel or knitting fabric and manufacturing men's and boys' apparel--are classified in Industry Group 3151, Apparel Knitting Mills; and
- Manufacturing fur or leather apparel and team athletic uniforms--are classified in Industry 315280, Other Cut and Sew Apparel Manufacturing.

31524 Women's, Girls', and Infants' Cut and Sew Apparel Manufacturing
See industry description for 315240.

315240 Women's, Girls', and Infants' Cut and Sew Apparel Manufacturing

This industry comprises establishments primarily engaged in manufacturing women's, girls', and infants' apparel from purchased fabric. Women's, girls', and infants' clothing jobbers, who perform entrepreneurial functions involved in apparel manufacture, including buying raw materials, designing and preparing samples, arranging for apparel to be made from their materials, and marketing finished apparel, are included.

Cross-References. Establishments primarily engaged in--

- Knitting women's, girls', and infants' apparel or knitting fabric and manufacturing women's, girls', and infants' apparel--are classified in Industry Group 3151, Apparel Knitting Mills;
- Manufacturing unisex outerwear garments, such as T-shirts, sweatshirts, and sweat pants that are sized without reference to specific gender (i.e., adult S, M, L, XL)--are classified in Industry 315220, Men's and Boys' Cut and Sew Apparel Manufacturing;
- Cutting and/or sewing materials owned by others for women's, girls', and infants' apparel--are classified in Industry 315210, Cut and Sew Apparel Contractors;
- Manufacturing fur or leather apparel and team athletic uniforms--are classified in Industry 315280, Other Cut and Sew Apparel Manufacturing; and
- Manufacturing cloth diapers--are classified in U.S. Industry 314999, All Other Miscellaneous Textile Product Mills.

31528 Other Cut and Sew Apparel Manufacturing
See industry description for 315280.

315280 Other Cut and Sew Apparel Manufacturing

This industry comprises establishments primarily engaged in manufacturing cut and sew apparel from purchased fabric (except men's, boys', women's, girls', and infants' apparel). Clothing jobbers for these products, who perform entrepreneurial functions involved in apparel manufacture, including buying raw materials, designing and preparing samples, arranging for apparel to be made from their materials, and marketing finished apparel, are included. Examples of products made by these establishments are fur or leather apparel, sheep-lined clothing, team athletic uniforms, band uniforms, academic caps and gowns, clerical vestments, and costumes.

Cross-References. Establishments primarily engaged in--

- Manufacturing men's and boys' apparel from purchased fabric--are classified in Industry 315220, Men's and Boys' Cut and Sew Apparel Manufacturing;
- Manufacturing women's, girls', and infants' apparel from purchased fabric--are classified in Industry 315240, Women's, Girls', and Infants' Cut and Sew Apparel Manufacturing;
- Knitting apparel or knitting fabric and manufacturing apparel--are classified in Industry Group 3151, Apparel Knitting Mills;
- Cutting and/or sewing materials owned by others for apparel--are classified in Industry 315210, Cut and Sew Apparel Contractors;

T—Canadian, Mexican, and United States industries are comparable.

- Manufacturing fur and leather mittens and gloves--are classified in Industry 315990, Apparel Accessories and Other Apparel Manufacturing; and
- Dyeing and dressing furs--are classified in Industry 316110, Leather and Hide Tanning and Finishing.

3159 Apparel Accessories and Other Apparel Manufacturing[T]

31599 Apparel Accessories and Other Apparel Manufacturing[T] See industry description for 315990.

315990 Apparel Accessories and Other Apparel Manufacturing

This industry comprises establishments primarily engaged in manufacturing apparel and accessories (except apparel knitting mills, cut and sew apparel contractors, men's and boys' cut and sew apparel, women's, girls', and infants' cut and sew apparel, and other cut and sew apparel). Jobbers, who perform entrepreneurial functions involved in apparel accessories manufacture, including buying raw materials, designing and preparing samples, arranging for apparel accessories to be made from their materials, and marketing finished apparel accessories, are included. Examples of products made by these establishments are belts, caps, gloves (except medical, sporting, safety), hats, and neckties.

Cross-References. Establishments primarily engaged in--

- Cutting and/or sewing materials owned by others for apparel accessories--are classified in Industry 315210, Cut and Sew Apparel Contractors;
- Manufacturing paper hats and caps--are classified in U.S. Industry 322299, All Other Converted Paper Product Manufacturing;
- Manufacturing plastics or rubber hats and caps (except bathing caps)--are classified in Subsector 326, Plastics and Rubber Products Manufacturing;
- Manufacturing athletic gloves, such as boxing gloves, baseball gloves, golf gloves, batting gloves, and racquetball gloves--are classified in Industry 339920, Sporting and Athletic Goods Manufacturing;
- Manufacturing metal fabric, metal mesh, or rubber gloves--are classified in U.S. Industry 339113, Surgical Appliance and Supplies Manufacturing;
- Knitting apparel, mittens, gloves, hats, and caps or knitting fabric and manufacturing apparel, mittens, gloves, hats, and caps--are classified in Industry Group 3151, Apparel Knitting Mills;
- Cutting and/or sewing materials owned by others for apparel--are classified in Industry 315210, Cut and Sew Apparel Contractors;
- Manufacturing men's and boys' underwear and outerwear from purchased fabric--are classified in Industry 315220, Men's and Boys' Cut and Sew Apparel Manufacturing;
- Manufacturing women's, girls', and infants' underwear and outerwear from purchased fabric--are classified in Industry 315240, Women's, Girls', and Infants' Cut and Sew Apparel Manufacturing; and
- Manufacturing other apparel from purchased fabric and manufacturing fur and leather apparel--are classified in Industry 315280, Other Cut and Sew Apparel Manufacturing.

316 Leather and Allied Product Manufacturing[T]

Establishments in the Leather and Allied Product Manufacturing subsector transform hides into leather by tanning or curing and fabricating the leather into products for final consumption. This subsector also includes the manufacture of similar products from other materials, including products (except apparel) made from "leather substitutes," such as rubber, plastics, or textiles. Rubber footwear, textile luggage, and plastics purses or wallets are examples of "leather substitute" products included in this subsector. The products made from leather substitutes are included in this subsector because they are made in similar ways leather products are made (e.g., luggage). They are made in the same establishments, so it is not practical to separate them.

The inclusion of leather and hide tanning and finishing in this subsector is partly because it is a relatively small industry that has few close neighbors as a production process, partly because leather is an input to some of the other products classified in this subsector, and partly for historical reasons.

T—Canadian, Mexican, and United States industries are comparable.

3161 Leather and Hide Tanning and Finishing[T]

31611 Leather and Hide Tanning and Finishing[T] See industry description for 316110.

316110 Leather and Hide Tanning and Finishing

This industry comprises establishments primarily engaged in one or more of the following: (1) tanning, currying, and finishing hides and skins; (2) having others process hides and skins on a contract basis; and (3) dyeing or dressing furs.

3162 Footwear Manufacturing[T]

31621 Footwear Manufacturing[T] See industry description for 316210.

316210 Footwear Manufacturing

This industry comprises establishments primarily engaged in manufacturing footwear (except orthopedic extension footwear).

Illustrative Examples:

Athletic shoes manufacturing
Ballet slippers manufacturing
Cleated athletic shoes manufacturing
Shoes, children's and infants' (except orthopedic extension), manufacturing
Shoes, men's (except orthopedic extension), manufacturing
Shoes, women's (except orthopedic extension), manufacturing

Cross-References.

Establishments primarily engaged in manufacturing orthopedic extension footwear are classified in U.S. Industry 339113, Surgical Appliance and Supplies Manufacturing.

3169 Other Leather and Allied Product Manufacturing[T]

31699 Other Leather and Allied Product Manufacturing[T]

This industry comprises establishments primarily engaged in manufacturing leather products (except footwear and apparel) from purchased leather or leather substitutes (e.g., fabric, plastics).

Illustrative Examples:

Billfolds, all materials, manufacturing
Boot and shoe cut stock and findings, leather, manufacturing
Dog furnishings (e.g., collars, leashes, harnesses, muzzles), manufacturing
Luggage, all materials, manufacturing
Shoe soles, leather, manufacturing
Purses, women's, all materials (except metal), manufacturing
Toilet kits and cases (except metal) manufacturing
Watch bands (except metal) manufacturing
Welders' jackets, leggings, and sleeves, leather, manufacturing

Cross-References. Establishments primarily engaged in--

- Manufacturing leather apparel--are classified in Industry 31528, Other Cut and Sew Apparel Manufacturing;

T—Canadian, Mexican, and United States industries are comparable.

- Manufacturing leather gloves, mittens, belts, and apparel accessories--are classified in Industry 31599, Apparel Accessories and Other Apparel Manufacturing;
- Manufacturing footwear--are classified in Industry 31621, Footwear Manufacturing;
- Manufacturing nonleather soles--are classified elsewhere based on the primary input material;
- Manufacturing small articles made of metal carried on or about the person--are classified in Industry 33991, Jewelry and Silverware Manufacturing; and
- Manufacturing leather gaskets--are classified in Industry 33999, All Other Miscellaneous Manufacturing.

316992 Women's Handbag and Purse Manufacturing

This U.S. industry comprises establishments primarily engaged in manufacturing women's handbags and purses of any material (except precious metal).

Cross-References.

Establishments primarily engaged in manufacturing precious metal handbags and purses are classified in Industry 339910, Jewelry and Silverware Manufacturing.

316998 All Other Leather Good and Allied Product Manufacturing

This U.S. industry comprises establishments primarily engaged in manufacturing leather products (except footwear, handbags, purses, and apparel) from purchased leather or leather substitutes (e.g., fabric, plastics).

Illustrative Examples:

Billfolds, all materials, manufacturing
Boot and shoe cut stock and findings, leather, manufacturing
Coin purses (except metal) manufacturing
Dog furnishings (e.g., collars, leashes, harnesses, muzzles) manufacturing
Key cases (except metal) manufacturing
Luggage, all materials, manufacturing
Leather belting for machinery (e.g., flat, solid, twisted, built-up) manufacturing
Shoe soles, leather, manufacturing
Toilet kits and cases (except metal) manufacturing
Watch bands (except metal) manufacturing
Welders' jackets, leggings, and sleeves, leather, manufacturing

Cross-References. Establishments primarily engaged in--

- Manufacturing handbags and purses--are classified in U.S. Industry 316992, Women's Handbag and Purse Manufacturing;
- Manufacturing leather apparel--are classified in Industry 315280, Other Cut and Sew Apparel Manufacturing;
- Manufacturing leather gloves, mittens, belts, and apparel accessories--are classified in Industry 315990, Apparel Accessories and Other Apparel Manufacturing;
- Manufacturing footwear--are classified in Industry 316210, Footwear Manufacturing;
- Manufacturing nonleather soles--are classified elsewhere based on the primary input material;
- Manufacturing small articles made of metal carried on or about the person--are classified in Industry 339910, Jewelry and Silverware Manufacturing; and
- Manufacturing leather gaskets--are classified in U.S. Industry 339991, Gasket, Packing, and Sealing Device Manufacturing.

321 Wood Product Manufacturing[T]

Establishments in the Wood Product Manufacturing subsector manufacture wood products, such as lumber, plywood, veneers, wood containers, wood flooring, wood trusses, manufactured homes (i.e., mobile homes), and prefabricated wood buildings. The production processes of the Wood Product Manufacturing subsector include sawing, planing, shaping, laminating, and assembling wood products starting from logs that are cut into bolts, or

T—Canadian, Mexican, and United States industries are comparable.

lumber that then may be further cut, or shaped by lathes or other shaping tools. The lumber or other transformed wood shapes may also be subsequently planed or smoothed, and assembled into finished products, such as wood containers. The Wood Product Manufacturing subsector includes establishments that make wood products from logs and bolts that are sawed and shaped, and establishments that purchase sawed lumber and make wood products. With the exception of sawmills and wood preservation establishments, the establishments are grouped into industries mainly based on the specific products manufactured.

3211 Sawmills and Wood Preservation[T]

32111 Sawmills and Wood Preservation[T]

This industry comprises establishments primarily engaged in one or more of the following: (1) sawing dimension lumber, boards, beams, timber, poles, ties, shingles, shakes, siding, and wood chips from logs or bolts; (2) sawing round wood poles, pilings, and posts and treating them with preservatives; and (3) treating wood sawed, planed, or shaped in other establishments with creosote or other preservatives to prevent decay and to protect against fire and insects. Sawmills may plane the rough lumber that they make with a planing machine to achieve smoothness and uniformity of size.

Cross-References. Establishments primarily engaged in--

- Operating portable chipper mills in the field--are classified in Industry 11331, Logging;
- Manufacturing wood products (except round wood poles, pilings, and posts) and treating them with preservatives--are classified elsewhere in Subsector 321, Wood Product Manufacturing, based on the related production process;
- Manufacturing veneer from logs and bolts or manufacturing engineered lumber and structural members other than solid wood--are classified in Industry 32121, Veneer, Plywood, and Engineered Wood Product Manufacturing; and
- Planing purchased lumber or manufacturing cut stock or dimension stock (i.e., shapes) from logs or bolts--are classified in Industry 32191, Millwork.

321113 Sawmills

This U.S. industry comprises establishments primarily engaged in sawing dimension lumber, boards, beams, timbers, poles, ties, shingles, shakes, siding, and wood chips from logs or bolts. Sawmills may plane the rough lumber that they make with a planing machine to achieve smoothness and uniformity of size.

Cross-References. Establishments primarily engaged in--

- Planing purchased lumber or manufacturing cut stock or dimension stock (i.e., shapes) from logs or bolts--are classified in Industry 32191, Millwork;
- Manufacturing veneer from logs or bolts--are classified in Industry 32121, Veneer, Plywood, and Engineered Wood Product Manufacturing; and
- Operating portable chipper mills in the field--are classified in Industry 113310, Logging.

321114 Wood Preservation

This U.S. industry comprises establishments primarily engaged in (1) treating wood sawed, planed, or shaped in other establishments with creosote or other preservatives, such as alkaline copper quat, copper azole, and sodium borates, to prevent decay and to protect against fire and insects and/or (2) sawing round wood poles, pilings, and posts and treating them with preservatives.

T—Canadian, Mexican, and United States industries are comparable.

Cross-References.

Establishments primarily engaged in manufacturing wood products (except round wood poles, pilings, and posts) and treating them with preservatives are classified elsewhere in Subsector 321, Wood Product Manufacturing, based on the related production process.

3212 Veneer, Plywood, and Engineered Wood Product Manufacturing[T]

32121 Veneer, Plywood, and Engineered Wood Product Manufacturing[T]

This industry comprises establishments primarily engaged in one or more of the following: (1) manufacturing veneer and/or plywood; (2) manufacturing engineered wood members; and (3) manufacturing reconstituted wood products. This industry includes manufacturing plywood from veneer made in the same establishment or from veneer made in other establishments, and manufacturing plywood faced with nonwood materials, such as plastics or metal.

Illustrative Examples:

Fabricated structural wood members manufacturing
Laminated structural wood members manufacturing
Medium density fiberboard (MDF) manufacturing
Oriented strandboard (OSB) manufacturing
Particleboard manufacturing
Plywood manufacturing
Reconstituted wood sheets and boards manufacturing
Roof trusses, wood, manufacturing
Veneer mills
Waferboard manufacturing

Cross-References. Establishments primarily engaged in--

- Manufacturing veneer and further processing that veneer into wood containers or wood container parts in the same establishment--are classified in Industry 32192, Wood Container and Pallet Manufacturing;
- Manufacturing prefabricated wood buildings or wood sections and panels for buildings--are classified in Industry 32199, All Other Wood Product Manufacturing; and
- Manufacturing solid wood structural members, such as dimension lumber and timber from logs or bolts in sawmills--are classified in Industry 32111, Sawmills and Wood Preservation.

321211 Hardwood Veneer and Plywood Manufacturing

This U.S. industry comprises establishments primarily engaged in manufacturing hardwood veneer and/or hardwood plywood.

Cross-References. Establishments primarily engaged in--

- Manufacturing veneer and further processing that veneer into wood containers or wood container parts--are classified in Industry 321920, Wood Container and Pallet Manufacturing;
- Manufacturing softwood veneer and softwood plywood--are classified in U.S. Industry 321212, Softwood Veneer and Plywood Manufacturing; and
- Manufacturing reconstituted wood sheets and boards--are classified in U.S. Industry 321219, Reconstituted Wood Product Manufacturing.

321212 Softwood Veneer and Plywood Manufacturing

This U.S. industry comprises establishments primarily engaged in manufacturing softwood veneer and/or softwood plywood.

T—Canadian, Mexican, and United States industries are comparable.

Cross-References. Establishments primarily engaged in--

- Manufacturing veneer and further processing that veneer into wood containers or wood container parts--are classified in Industry 321920, Wood Container and Pallet Manufacturing;
- Manufacturing hardwood veneer and hardwood plywood--are classified in U.S. Industry 321211, Hardwood Veneer and Plywood Manufacturing; and
- Manufacturing reconstituted wood sheets and boards--are classified in U.S. Industry 321219, Reconstituted Wood Product Manufacturing.

321213 Engineered Wood Member (except Truss) Manufacturing

This U.S. industry comprises establishments primarily engaged in manufacturing fabricated or laminated wood arches and/or other fabricated or laminated wood structural members.

Illustrative Examples:

Finger joint lumber manufacturing
I-joists, wood, fabricating
Laminated veneer lumber (LVL) manufacturing
Parallel strand lumber manufacturing
Timbers, structural, glue laminated or pre-engineered wood, manufacturing

Cross-References. Establishments primarily engaged in--

- Manufacturing prefabricated wood buildings or wood sections and panels for buildings--are classified in U.S. Industry 321992, Prefabricated Wood Building Manufacturing;
- Manufacturing wood trusses--are classified in U.S. Industry 321214, Truss Manufacturing; and
- Manufacturing solid wood structural members, such as dimension lumber and timber from logs or bolts--are classified in U.S. Industry 321113, Sawmills.

321214 Truss Manufacturing

This U.S. industry comprises establishments primarily engaged in manufacturing laminated or fabricated wood roof and floor trusses.

Cross-References.

Establishments primarily engaged in manufacturing wood I-joists are classified in U.S. Industry 321213, Engineered Wood Member (except Truss) Manufacturing.

321219 Reconstituted Wood Product Manufacturing

This U.S. industry comprises establishments primarily engaged in manufacturing reconstituted wood sheets and boards.

Illustrative Examples:

Medium density fiberboard (MDF) manufacturing
Oriented strandboard (OSB) manufacturing
Particleboard manufacturing
Reconstituted wood sheets and boards manufacturing

Cross-References. Establishments primarily engaged in--

- Manufacturing softwood plywood--are classified in U.S. Industry 321212, Softwood Veneer and Plywood Manufacturing; and
- Manufacturing hardwood plywood--are classified in U.S. Industry 321211, Hardwood Veneer and Plywood Manufacturing.

T—Canadian, Mexican, and United States industries are comparable.

3219 Other Wood Product Manufacturing[T]

This industry group comprises establishments primarily engaged in manufacturing wood products (except establishments operating sawmills and wood preservation facilities; and establishments manufacturing veneer, plywood, or engineered wood products).

32191 Millwork[T]

This industry comprises establishments primarily engaged in manufacturing hardwood and softwood cut stock and dimension stock (i.e., shapes); wood windows and wood doors; and other millwork including wood flooring. Dimension stock or cut stock is defined as lumber and worked wood products cut or shaped to specialized sizes. These establishments generally use woodworking machinery, such as jointers, planers, lathes, and routers to shape wood.

Cross-References. Establishments primarily engaged in--

- Manufacturing dimension lumber, boards, beams, timbers, poles, ties, shingles, shakes, siding, and wood chips from logs and bolts--are classified in Industry 32111, Sawmills and Wood Preservation;
- Fabricating millwork at the construction site--are classified in Industry 23835, Finish Carpentry Contractors; and
- Manufacturing wood furniture frames and finished wood furniture parts--are classified in Industry 33721, Office Furniture (including Fixtures) Manufacturing.

321911 Wood Window and Door Manufacturing

This U.S. industry comprises establishments primarily engaged in manufacturing window and door units, sash, window and door frames, and doors from wood or wood clad with metal or plastics.

Cross-References.

Establishments primarily engaged in fabricating wood windows or wood doors at the construction site are classified in Industry 238350, Finish Carpentry Contractors.

321912 Cut Stock, Resawing Lumber, and Planing

This U.S. industry comprises establishments primarily engaged in one or more of the following: (1) manufacturing dimension lumber from purchased lumber; (2) manufacturing dimension stock (i.e., shapes) or cut stock; (3) resawing the output of sawmills; and (4) planing purchased lumber. These establishments generally use woodworking machinery, such as jointers, planers, lathes, and routers to shape wood.

Cross-References. Establishments primarily engaged in--

- Manufacturing dimension lumber, boards, beams, timbers, poles, ties, shingles, shakes, siding, and wood chips from logs or bolts--are classified in U.S. Industry 321113, Sawmills;
- Manufacturing wood stairwork, wood molding, wood trim, and other millwork--are classified in U.S. Industry 321918, Other Millwork (including Flooring); and
- Manufacturing wood furniture frames and finished wood furniture parts--are classified in U.S. Industry 337215, Showcase, Partition, Shelving, and Locker Manufacturing.

321918 Other Millwork (including Flooring)

This U.S. industry comprises establishments primarily engaged in manufacturing millwork (except wood windows, wood doors, and cut stock).

T—Canadian, Mexican, and United States industries are comparable.

Illustrative Examples:

Clear and finger joint wood moldings manufacturing
Decorative wood moldings (e.g., base, chair rail, crown, shoe) manufacturing
Ornamental woodwork (e.g., cornices, mantel) manufacturing
Planing mills, millwork
Stairwork (e.g., newel posts, railings, stairs, staircases), wood, manufacturing
Wood flooring manufacturing
Wood shutters manufacturing

Cross-References. Establishments primarily engaged in--

- Manufacturing wood windows and doors--are classified in U.S. Industry 321911, Wood Window and Door Manufacturing; and
- Manufacturing cut stock, resawing lumber, and/or planing purchased lumber--are classified in U.S. Industry 321912, Cut Stock, Resawing Lumber, and Planing.

32192 Wood Container and Pallet Manufacturing[T] See industry description for 321920.

321920 Wood Container and Pallet Manufacturing

This industry comprises establishments primarily engaged in manufacturing wood pallets, wood box shook, wood boxes, other wood containers, and wood parts for pallets and containers.

Cross-References.

Establishments primarily engaged in manufacturing wood burial caskets are classified in U.S. Industry 339995, Burial Casket Manufacturing.

32199 All Other Wood Product Manufacturing[T]

This industry comprises establishments primarily engaged in manufacturing wood products (except establishments operating sawmills and wood preservation facilities; and establishments manufacturing veneer, plywood, engineered wood products, millwork, wood containers, or pallets).

Illustrative Examples:

Mobile homes manufacturing
Panels, prefabricated wood building, manufacturing
Prefabricated wood buildings manufacturing
Sections, prefabricated wood building, manufacturing
Wood dowels manufacturing
Wood handles (e.g., broom, handtool, mop) manufacturing

Cross-References. Establishments primarily engaged in--

- Operating sawmills or preserving wood--are classified in Industry 32111, Sawmills and Wood Preservation;
- Manufacturing veneer, plywood, and engineered wood products--are classified in Industry 32121, Veneer, Plywood, and Engineered Wood Product Manufacturing;
- Manufacturing millwork--are classified in Industry 32191, Millwork;
- Manufacturing wood containers, pallets, and wood container parts--are classified in Industry 32192, Wood Container and Pallet Manufacturing;
- Manufacturing travel trailers with self-contained facilities for storage of water and waste--are classified in Industry 33621, Motor Vehicle Body and Trailer Manufacturing; and
- Fabricating wood buildings or wood sections and panels for buildings at the construction site, or setting up manufactured homes (i.e., mobile homes) at the construction site--are classified in Sector 23, Construction.

T—Canadian, Mexican, and United States industries are comparable.

321991 Manufactured Home (Mobile Home) Manufacturing

This U.S. industry comprises establishments primarily engaged in making manufactured homes (i.e., mobile homes) and nonresidential mobile buildings. Manufactured homes are designed to accept permanent water, sewer, and utility connections and although equipped with wheels, they are not intended for regular highway movement.

Cross-References. Establishments primarily engaged in--

- Manufacturing prefabricated wood buildings not equipped with wheels--are classified in U.S. Industry 321992, Prefabricated Wood Building Manufacturing;
- Manufacturing travel trailers with self-contained facilities for storage of water and waste--are classified in U.S. Industry 336214, Travel Trailer and Camper Manufacturing; and
- Setting up manufactured homes (i.e., mobile homes) at the construction site--are classified in Industry 238990, All Other Specialty Trade Contractors.

321992 Prefabricated Wood Building Manufacturing

This U.S. industry comprises establishments primarily engaged in manufacturing prefabricated wood buildings and wood sections and panels for prefabricated wood buildings.

Cross-References. Establishments primarily engaged in--

- Fabricating wood buildings or wood sections and panels for buildings at the construction site--are classified in Sector 23, Construction;
- Making manufactured homes (i.e., mobile homes)--are classified in U.S. Industry 321991, Manufactured Home (Mobile Home) Manufacturing; and
- Setting up manufactured homes (i.e., mobile homes) at the construction site--are classified in Industry 238990, All Other Specialty Trade Contractors.

321999 All Other Miscellaneous Wood Product Manufacturing

This U.S. industry comprises establishments primarily engaged in manufacturing wood products (except establishments operating sawmills and preservation facilities; establishments manufacturing veneer, engineered wood products, millwork, wood containers, pallets, and wood container parts; and establishments making manufactured homes (i.e., mobile homes) and prefabricated buildings and components).

Illustrative Examples:

Cabinets (i.e., housings), wood (e.g., sewing machines, stereo, television), manufacturing
Cork products (except gaskets) manufacturing
Kiln drying lumber
Shoe trees manufacturing
Wood dowels manufacturing
Wood extension ladders manufacturing
Wood handles (e.g., broom, handtool, mop), manufacturing
Wood kitchenware manufacturing
Wood stepladders manufacturing
Wood toilet seats manufacturing
Wood toothpicks manufacturing

Cross-References. Establishments primarily engaged in--

- Operating sawmills and preserving wood--are classified in Industry 32111, Sawmills and Wood Preservation;
- Manufacturing veneer and engineered wood products--are classified in Industry 32121, Veneer, Plywood, and Engineered Wood Product Manufacturing;
- Manufacturing millwork--are classified in Industry 32191, Millwork;
- Manufacturing boxes, box shook, wood containers, pallets, and wood parts for containers--are classified in Industry 321920, Wood Container and Pallet Manufacturing;

~~T—Canadian, Mexican, and Unit~~ed States industries are comparable.

- Making manufactured homes (i.e., mobile homes)--are classified in U.S. Industry 321991, Manufactured Home (Mobile Home) Manufacturing; and
- Manufacturing prefabricated wood buildings or wood sections and panels for buildings--are classified in U.S. Industry 321992, Prefabricated Wood Building Manufacturing.

322 Paper Manufacturing[T]

Industries in the Paper Manufacturing subsector make pulp, paper, or converted paper products. The manufacturing of these products is grouped together because they constitute a series of vertically connected processes. More than one is often carried out in a single establishment. There are essentially three activities. The manufacturing of pulp involves separating the cellulose fibers from other impurities in wood or used paper. The manufacturing of paper involves matting these fibers into a sheet. The manufacturing of converted paper products involves converting paper and other materials by various cutting and shaping techniques and includes coating and laminating activities.

The Paper Manufacturing subsector is subdivided into two industry groups, the first for the manufacturing of pulp and paper and the second for the manufacturing of converted paper products. Paper making is treated as the core activity of the subsector. Therefore, any establishment that makes paper (including paperboard), either alone or in combination with pulp manufacturing or paper converting, is classified as a paper or paperboard mill. Establishments that make pulp without making paper are classified as pulp mills. Pulp mills, paper mills and paperboard mills comprise the first industry group.

Establishments that make products from purchased paper and other materials make up the second industry group, Converted Paper Product Manufacturing. This general activity is then subdivided based, for the most part, on process distinctions. Paperboard container manufacturing uses corrugating, cutting, and shaping machinery to form paperboard into containers. Paper bag and coated and treated paper manufacturing establishments cut and coat paper and foil. Stationery product manufacturing establishments make a variety of paper products used for writing, filing, and similar applications. Other converted paper product manufacturing includes, in particular, the conversion of sanitary paper stock into such things as tissue paper and disposable diapers.

An important process used in the Paper Bag and Coated and Treated Paper Manufacturing industry is lamination, often combined with coating. Lamination and coating make a composite material with improved properties of strength, impermeability, and so on. The laminated materials may be paper, metal foil, or plastics film. While paper is often one of the components, it is not always. Lamination of plastics film to plastics film is classified in Subsector 326, Plastics and Rubber Products Manufacturing, because establishments that do this often first make the film. The same situation holds with respect to bags. The manufacturing of bags from plastics only, whether or not laminated, is classified in Subsector 326, Plastics and Rubber Products Manufacturing, but all other bag manufacturing is classified in this subsector.

Excluded from this subsector are photosensitive papers. These papers are chemically treated and are classified in Industry 32599, All Other Chemical Product and Preparation Manufacturing.

3221 Pulp, Paper, and Paperboard Mills[T]

This industry group comprises establishments primarily engaged in manufacturing pulp, paper, or paperboard.

32211 Pulp Mills[T] See industry description for 322110.

322110 Pulp Mills

This industry comprises establishments primarily engaged in manufacturing pulp without manufacturing paper or paperboard. The pulp is made by separating the cellulose fibers from the other impurities in wood or other materials, such as used or recycled rags, linters, scrap paper, and straw.

Cross-References. Establishments primarily engaged in--

- Manufacturing both pulp and paper--are classified in Industry 32212, Paper Mills; and
- Manufacturing both pulp and paperboard--are classified in Industry 322130, Paperboard Mills.

T—Canadian, Mexican, and United States industries are comparable.

32212 Paper Mills[T]

This industry comprises establishments primarily engaged in manufacturing paper from pulp. These establishments may manufacture or purchase pulp. In addition, the establishments may convert the paper they make. The activity of making paper classifies an establishment into this industry regardless of the output.

Cross-References. Establishments primarily engaged in--

- Manufacturing pulp without manufacturing paper--are classified in Industry 32211, Pulp Mills;
- Manufacturing paperboard--are classified in Industry 32213, Paperboard Mills;
- Converting paper without manufacturing paper--are classified in Industry Group 3222, Converted Paper Product Manufacturing; and
- Manufacturing photographic sensitized paper from purchased paper--are classified in Industry 32599, All Other Chemical Product and Preparation Manufacturing.

322121 Paper (except Newsprint) Mills

This U.S. industry comprises establishments primarily engaged in manufacturing paper (except newsprint and uncoated groundwood paper) from pulp. These establishments may manufacture or purchase pulp. In addition, the establishments may also convert the paper they make.

Cross-References. Establishments primarily engaged in--

- Manufacturing newsprint and uncoated groundwood paper--are classified in U.S. Industry 322122, Newsprint Mills;
- Converting paper without manufacturing paper--are classified in Industry Group 3222, Converted Paper Product Manufacturing;
- Manufacturing paperboard--are classified in Industry 322130, Paperboard Mills;
- Manufacturing pulp without manufacturing paper--are classified in Industry 322110, Pulp Mills; and
- Manufacturing photographic sensitized paper from purchased paper--are classified in U.S. Industry 325992, Photographic Film, Paper, Plate, and Chemical Manufacturing.

322122 Newsprint Mills

This U.S. industry comprises establishments primarily engaged in manufacturing newsprint and uncoated groundwood paper from pulp. These establishments may manufacture or purchase pulp. In addition, the establishments may also convert the paper they make.

Cross-References. Establishments primarily engaged in--

- Manufacturing paper (except newsprint and uncoated groundwood)--are classified in U.S. Industry 322121, Paper (except Newsprint) Mills;
- Converting paper without manufacturing paper--are classified in Industry Group 3222, Converted Paper Product Manufacturing;
- Manufacturing paperboard--are classified in Industry 322130, Paperboard Mills; and
- Manufacturing pulp without manufacturing paper--are classified in Industry 322110, Pulp Mills.

32213 Paperboard Mills[T] See industry description for 322130.

322130 Paperboard Mills

This industry comprises establishments primarily engaged in manufacturing paperboard (e.g., can/drum stock, container board, corrugating medium, folding carton stock, linerboard, tube) from pulp. These establishments may manufacture or purchase pulp. In addition, the establishments may also convert the paperboard they make.

T—Canadian, Mexican, and United States industries are comparable.

Cross-References. Establishments primarily engaged in--

- Manufacturing pulp without manufacturing paperboard--are classified in Industry 322110, Pulp Mills;
- Converting paperboard without manufacturing paperboard--are classified in Industry Group 3222, Converted Paper Product Manufacturing; and
- Manufacturing insulation board and other reconstituted wood fiberboard--are classified in U.S. Industry 321219, Reconstituted Wood Product Manufacturing.

3222 Converted Paper Product Manufacturing[T]

This industry group comprises establishments primarily engaged in converting paper or paperboard without manufacturing paper or paperboard.

32221 Paperboard Container Manufacturing[T]

This industry comprises establishments primarily engaged in converting paperboard into containers without manufacturing paperboard. These establishments use corrugating, cutting, and shaping machinery to form paperboard into containers. Products made by these establishments include boxes, corrugated sheets, pads, pallets, paper dishes, and fiber drums and reels.

Cross-References. Establishments primarily engaged in--

- Manufacturing similar items of plastics materials--are classified in Industry Group 3261, Plastics Product Manufacturing;
- Manufacturing paperboard and converting paperboard into containers--are classified in Industry 32213, Paperboard Mills;
- Manufacturing egg cartons, food trays, and other food containers from molded pulp--are classified in Industry 32229, Other Converted Paper Product Manufacturing;
- Manufacturing paper and converting paper into containers--are classified in Industry 32212, Paper Mills; and
- Manufacturing paper bags without manufacturing paper--are classified in Industry 32222, Paper Bag and Coated and Treated Paper Manufacturing.

322211 Corrugated and Solid Fiber Box Manufacturing

This U.S. industry comprises establishments primarily engaged in laminating purchased paper or paperboard into corrugated or solid fiber boxes and related products, such as pads, partitions, pallets, and corrugated paper without manufacturing paperboard. These boxes are generally used for shipping.

Cross-References. Establishments primarily engaged in--

- Manufacturing setup paperboard boxes (except corrugated or laminated solid fiber boxes)--are classified in U.S. Industry 322219, Other Paperboard Container Manufacturing;
- Manufacturing folding paperboard boxes (except corrugated or laminated solid fiber boxes)--are classified in U.S. Industry 322212, Folding Paperboard Box Manufacturing; and
- Manufacturing paperboard and converting paperboard into boxes--are classified in Industry 322130, Paperboard Mills.

322212 Folding Paperboard Box Manufacturing

This U.S. industry comprises establishments primarily engaged in converting paperboard (except corrugated) into folding paperboard boxes without manufacturing paper and paperboard.

T—Canadian, Mexican, and United States industries are comparable.

Cross-References. Establishments primarily engaged in--

- Manufacturing setup paperboard boxes (except corrugated or laminated solid fiber boxes) or milk cartons--are classified in U.S. Industry 322219, Other Paperboard Container Manufacturing;
- Manufacturing corrugated and solid fiber boxes--are classified in U.S. Industry 322211, Corrugated and Solid Fiber Box Manufacturing;
- Manufacturing paperboard and converting paperboard into containers--are classified in Industry 322130, Paperboard Mills;
- Manufacturing paper and converting paper into containers--are classified in Industry 32212, Paper Mills; and
- Manufacturing paper bags--are classified in Industry 322220, Paper Bag and Coated and Treated Paper Manufacturing.

322219 Other Paperboard Container Manufacturing

This U.S. industry comprises establishments primarily engaged in converting paperboard into paperboard containers (except corrugated, solid fiber, and folding paperboard boxes) without manufacturing paperboard.

Illustrative Examples:

Fiber cans and drums (i.e., all-fiber, nonfiber ends of any material) made from purchased paperboard
Milk cartons made from purchased paper or paperboard
Sanitary food containers (except folding) made from purchased paper or paperboard
Setup (i.e., not shipped flat) boxes made from purchased paperboard

Cross-References. Establishments primarily engaged in--

- Manufacturing sanitary food containers of solely plastics materials--are classified in Industry Group 3261, Plastics Product Manufacturing;
- Manufacturing paperboard and converting paperboard into containers--are classified in Industry 322130, Paperboard Mills;
- Manufacturing corrugated and solid fiber boxes--are classified in U.S. Industry 322211, Corrugated and Solid Fiber Box Manufacturing;
- Manufacturing folding paperboard boxes (except corrugated or laminated solid fiber boxes)--are classified in U.S. Industry 322212, Folding Paperboard Box Manufacturing; and
- Manufacturing egg cartons, food trays, and other food containers from molded pulp--are classified in U.S. Industry 322299, All Other Converted Paper Product Manufacturing.

32222 Paper Bag and Coated and Treated Paper Manufacturing[T] See industry description for 322220.

322220 Paper Bag and Coated and Treated Paper Manufacturing

This industry comprises establishments primarily engaged in one or more of the following: (1) cutting and coating paper and paperboard; (2) cutting and laminating paper, paperboard, and other flexible materials (except plastics film to plastics film); (3) manufacturing bags, multiwall bags, sacks of paper, metal foil, coated paper, laminates, or coated combinations of paper and foil with plastics film; (4) manufacturing laminated aluminum and other converted metal foils from purchased foils; and (5) surface coating paper or paperboard.

Cross-References. Establishments primarily engaged in--

- Manufacturing paper from pulp--are classified in Industry 32212, Paper Mills;
- Manufacturing textile bags--are classified in Industry 314910, Textile Bag and Canvas Mills;
- Manufacturing single wall and multiwall plastics bags--are classified in U.S. Industry 326111, Plastics Bag and Pouch Manufacturing;

T—Canadian, Mexican, and United States industries are comparable.

- Manufacturing plastics to plastics packaging laminations--are classified in U.S. Industry 326112, Plastics Packaging Film and Sheet (including Laminated) Manufacturing;
- Manufacturing unsupported plastic film--are classified in U.S. Industry 326113, Unlaminated Plastics Film and Sheet (except Packaging) Manufacturing;
- Manufacturing photographic sensitized paper from purchased paper--are classified in U.S. Industry 325992, Photographic Film, Paper, Plate, and Chemical Manufacturing;
- Printing on purchased packaging materials--are classified in Industry 32311, Printing, based on the printing process used;
- Manufacturing foil cookware, dinnerware, and other semi-rigid metal containers--are classified in U.S. Industry 332999, All Other Miscellaneous Fabricated Metal Product Manufacturing;
- Making aluminum and aluminum foil--are classified in Industry 33131, Alumina and Aluminum Production and Processing; and
- Cutting purchased aluminum foil into smaller lengths and widths--are classified in U.S. Industry 332999, All Other Miscellaneous Fabricated Metal Product Manufacturing.

32223 Stationery Product Manufacturing[T] See industry description for 322230.

322230 Stationery Product Manufacturing

This industry comprises establishments primarily engaged in converting paper or paperboard into products used for writing, filing, art work, and similar applications.

Illustrative Examples:

Computer paper, die-cut, made from purchased paper
Die-cut paper products for office use made from purchased paper or paperboard
Envelopes (i.e., mailing, stationery) made from any material
Tablets (e.g., memo, note, writing) made from purchased paper
Tapes (e.g., adding machine, calculator, cash register) made from purchased paper

Cross-References.
Stationery made from purchased paper

Establishments primarily engaged in manufacturing die-cut paper and paperboard products other than office supplies are classified in U.S. Industry 322299, All Other Converted Paper Product Manufacturing.

32229 Other Converted Paper Product Manufacturing[T]

This industry comprises establishments primarily engaged in (1) converting paper and paperboard into products (except containers, bags, coated and treated paper and paperboard, and stationery products) or (2) converting pulp into pulp products, such as disposable diapers, or molded pulp egg cartons, food trays, and dishes. Processes used include laminating or lining purchased paper or paperboard.

Illustrative Examples:

Crepe paper made from purchased paper
Die-cut paper products (except for office use) made from purchased paper or paperboard
Paper novelties made from purchased paper
Molded pulp products (e.g., egg cartons, food containers, food trays) manufacturing
Sanitary products made from purchased sanitary paper stock

Cross-References. Establishments primarily engaged in--

- Manufacturing pulp from wood or from other materials--are classified in Industry 32211, Pulp Mills;
- Manufacturing paper from pulp or making pulp and manufacturing paper--are classified in Industry 32212, Paper Mills;

T—Canadian, Mexican, and United States industries are comparable.

- Manufacturing paperboard from pulp or making pulp and manufacturing paperboard--are classified in Industry 32213, Paperboard Mills;
- Manufacturing paperboard containers--are classified in Industry 32221, Paperboard Container Manufacturing;
- Manufacturing bags of coated, laminated, or uncoated paper, of metal foil, or combinations thereof--are classified in Industry 32222, Paper Bag and Coated and Treated Paper Manufacturing; and
- Manufacturing stationery and other related office supplies--are classified in Industry 32223, Stationery Product Manufacturing.

322291 Sanitary Paper Product Manufacturing

This U.S. industry comprises establishments primarily engaged in converting purchased sanitary paper stock or wadding into sanitary paper products, such as facial tissues, handkerchiefs, table napkins, toilet paper, towels, disposable diapers, sanitary napkins, and tampons.

322299 All Other Converted Paper Product Manufacturing

This U.S. industry comprises establishments primarily engaged in converting paper or paperboard into products (except containers, bags, coated and treated paper, stationery products, and sanitary paper products) or converting pulp into pulp products, such as egg cartons, food trays, and other food containers from molded pulp.

Illustrative Examples:

Crepe paper made from purchased paper
Die-cut paper products (except for office use) made from purchased paper or paperboard
Molded pulp products (e.g., egg cartons, food containers, food trays) manufacturing
Paper novelties made from purchased paper

Cross-References. Establishments primarily engaged in--

- Manufacturing pulp from wood or from other materials--are classified in Industry 322110, Pulp Mills;
- Manufacturing paper from pulp or making pulp and manufacturing paper--are classified in Industry 32212, Paper Mills;
- Manufacturing paperboard from pulp or making pulp and manufacturing paperboard--are classified in Industry 322130, Paperboard Mills;
- Manufacturing paperboard containers--are classified in Industry 32221, Paperboard Container Manufacturing;
- Manufacturing bags of coated, laminated, or uncoated paper, of metal foil, or combinations thereof--are classified in Industry 322220, Paper Bag and Coated and Treated Paper Manufacturing; and
- Manufacturing stationery and other related office supplies--are classified in Industry 322230, Stationery Product Manufacturing.

323 Printing and Related Support Activities[T]

Industries in the Printing and Related Support Activities subsector print products, such as newspapers, books, labels, business cards, stationery, business forms, and other materials, and perform support activities, such as data imaging, platemaking services, and bookbinding. The support activities included here are an integral part of the printing industry, and a product (a printing plate, a bound book, or a computer disk or file) that is an integral part of the printing industry is almost always provided by these operations.

Processes used in printing include a variety of methods used to transfer an image from a plate, screen, film, or computer file to some medium, such as paper, plastics, metal, textile articles, or wood. The printing processes employed include, but are not limited to, lithographic, gravure, screen, flexographic, digital, and letterpress. In contrast to many other classification systems that locate publishing of printed materials in manufacturing, NAICS classifies the publishing of printed products in Subsector 511, Publishing Industries (except Internet). Though printing and publishing are often carried out by the same enterprise (a newspaper, for example), it is less and less the case that these distinct activities are carried out in the same establishment. When publishing and

T—Canadian, Mexican, and United States industries are comparable.

printing are done in the same establishment, the establishment is classified in Sector 51, Information, in the appropriate NAICS industry even if the receipts for printing exceed those for publishing.

This subsector includes printing on clothing because the production process for that activity is printing, not clothing manufacturing. For instance, the printing of T-shirts is included in this subsector. In contrast, printing on fabric (or grey goods) is not included. This activity is part of the process of finishing the fabric and is included in the Textile Mills subsector in Industry 31331, Textile and Fabric Finishing Mills.

3231 Printing and Related Support Activities[T]

32311 Printing[T]

This industry comprises establishments primarily engaged in printing on apparel and textile products, paper, metal, glass, plastics, and other materials, except fabric (grey goods). The printing processes employed include, but are not limited to, lithographic, gravure, screen, flexographic, digital, and letterpress. Establishments in this industry do not manufacture the stock that they print, but may perform postprinting activities, such as folding, cutting, or laminating the materials they print, and mailing.

Cross-References. Establishments primarily engaged in--

- Providing photocopying service on photocopy equipment without performing traditional printing activities--are classified in Industry 56143, Business Service Centers;
- Printing on grey goods--are classified in Industry 31331, Textile and Fabric Finishing Mills;
- Printing and publishing, known as publishers--are classified in Subsector 511, Publishing Industries (except Internet);
- Performing prepress or postpress services without performing traditional printing activities--are classified in Industry 32312, Support Activities for Printing; and
- Manufacturing and printing advertising specialties--are classified in the Manufacturing sector according to the products made.

323111 Commercial Printing (except Screen and Books)

This U.S. industry comprises establishments primarily engaged in commercial printing (except screen printing, books printing) without publishing (except grey goods printing). The printing processes used in this industry include, but are not limited to, lithographic, gravure, flexographic, letterpress, engraving, and various digital printing technologies. This industry includes establishments engaged in commercial printing on purchased stock materials, such as stationery, invitations, labels, and similar items, on a job-order basis. Establishments primarily engaged in traditional printing activities combined with document photocopying services (i.e., quick printers) or primarily engaged in printing graphical materials using digital printing equipment are included in this industry.

Cross-References. Establishments primarily engaged in--

- Screen printing on purchased stock materials (except books, grey goods, and manifold business forms)--are classified in U.S. Industry 323113, Commercial Screen Printing;
- Printing on grey goods--are classified in Industry 313310, Textile and Fabric Finishing Mills;
- Printing books and pamphlets--are classified in U.S. Industry 323117, Books Printing;
- Manufacturing printed stationery, invitations, labels, and similar items--are classified in Subsector 322, Paper Manufacturing;
- Manufacturing and printing advertising specialties--are classified in the Manufacturing sector according to the products made;
- Providing photocopying service on photocopy equipment without performing traditional printing activities--are classified in U.S. Industry 561439, Other Business Service Centers (including Copy Shops); and
- Printing and publishing, known as publishers--are classified in Subsector 511, Publishing Industries (except Internet).

T—Canadian, Mexican, and United States industries are comparable.

323113 Commercial Screen Printing

This U.S. industry comprises establishments primarily engaged in screen printing without publishing (except books, grey goods, and manifold business forms). This industry includes establishments engaged in screen printing on purchased stock materials, such as stationery, invitations, labels, and similar items, on a job-order basis. Establishments primarily engaged in printing on apparel and textile products, such as T-shirts, caps, jackets, towels, and napkins, are included in this industry.

Cross-References. Establishments primarily engaged in--

- Printing on grey goods--are classified in Industry 313310, Textile and Fabric Finishing Mills;
- Printing books and pamphlets--are classified in U.S. Industry 323117, Books Printing;
- Printing manifold business forms including checkbooks--are classified in U.S. Industry 323111, Commercial Printing (except Screen and Books);
- Manufacturing printed stationery, invitations, labels, and similar items--are classified in Subsector 322, Paper Manufacturing;
- Manufacturing and printing advertising specialties--are classified in the Manufacturing sector according to the products made; and
- Printing and publishing, known as publishers--are classified in Subsector 511, Publishing Industries (except Internet).

323117 Books Printing

This U.S. industry comprises establishments primarily engaged in printing or printing and binding books and pamphlets without publishing.

Cross-References. Establishments primarily engaged in--

- Printing and publishing, known as publishers--are classified in Subsector 511, Publishing Industries (except Internet); and
- Binding books without printing in the same establishment--are classified in Industry 323120, Support Activities for Printing.

32312 Support Activities for Printing[T] See industry description for 323120.

323120 Support Activities for Printing

This industry comprises establishments primarily engaged in performing prepress and postpress services in support of printing activities. Prepress services may include such things as platemaking, typesetting, trade binding, and sample mounting. Postpress services include such things as book or paper bronzing, die cutting, edging, embossing, folding, gilding, gluing, and indexing.

Cross-References. Establishments primarily engaged in--

- Engraving on metal--are classified in U.S. Industry 332812, Metal Coating, Engraving (except Jewelry and Silverware), and Allied Services to Manufacturers;
- Manufacturing photosensitive plates for printing--are classified in U.S. Industry 325992, Photographic Film, Paper, Plate, and Chemical Manufacturing;
- Manufacturing blank plates (except photosensitive plates) for printing--are classified in U.S. Industry 333244, Printing Machinery and Equipment Manufacturing; and
- Printing books or printing and binding books--are classified in U.S. Industry 323117, Books Printing.

T—Canadian, Mexican, and United States industries are comparable.

324 Petroleum and Coal Products Manufacturing[T]

The Petroleum and Coal Products Manufacturing subsector is based on the transformation of crude petroleum and coal into usable products. The dominant process is petroleum refining that involves the separation of crude petroleum into component products through such techniques as cracking and distillation.

In addition, this subsector includes establishments that primarily further process refined petroleum and coal products and produce products, such as asphalt coatings and petroleum lubricating oils. However, establishments that manufacture petrochemicals from refined petroleum are classified in Industry 32511, Petrochemical Manufacturing.

3241 Petroleum and Coal Products Manufacturing[T]

32411 Petroleum Refineries[T] See industry description for 324110.

324110 Petroleum Refineries

This industry comprises establishments primarily engaged in refining crude petroleum into refined petroleum. Petroleum refining involves one or more of the following activities: (1) fractionation; (2) straight distillation of crude oil; and (3) cracking.

Cross-References. Establishments primarily engaged in--

- Manufacturing asphalt paving, roofing, and saturated materials from refined petroleum--are classified in Industry 32412, Asphalt Paving, Roofing, and Saturated Materials Manufacturing;
- Manufacturing paper mats and felts and saturating them with asphalt or tar into rolls and sheets--are classified in U.S. Industry 322121, Paper (except Newsprint) Mills;
- Blending or compounding refined petroleum to make lubricating oils and greases and/or re-refining used petroleum lubricating oils--are classified in U.S. Industry 324191, Petroleum Lubricating Oil and Grease Manufacturing;
- Blending purchased biodiesel fuels and purchased refined petroleum--are classified in U.S. Industry 324199, All Other Petroleum and Coal Products Manufacturing;
- Converting nonpetroleum materials into biodiesel fuels--are classified in U.S. Industry 325199, All Other Basic Organic Chemical Manufacturing;
- Manufacturing synthetic lubricating oils and greases--are classified in U.S. Industry 325998, All Other Miscellaneous Chemical Product and Preparation Manufacturing;
- Recovering natural gasoline and/or liquid hydrocarbons from oil and gas field gases--are classified in Industry 211130, Natural Gas Extraction;
- Manufacturing acyclic and cyclic aromatic hydrocarbons (i.e., petrochemicals) from refined petroleum or liquid hydrocarbons--are classified in Industry 325110, Petrochemical Manufacturing;
- Manufacturing cyclic and acyclic chemicals (except petrochemicals)--are classified in Industry 32519, Other Basic Organic Chemical Manufacturing;
- Manufacturing coke oven products in steel mills--are classified in Industry 331110, Iron and Steel Mills and Ferroalloy Manufacturing; and
- Manufacturing coke oven products in coke oven establishments--are classified in U.S. Industry 324199, All Other Petroleum and Coal Products Manufacturing.

32412 Asphalt Paving, Roofing, and Saturated Materials Manufacturing[T]

This industry comprises establishments primarily engaged in (1) manufacturing asphalt and tar paving mixtures and blocks and roofing cements and coatings from purchased asphaltic materials and/or (2) saturating purchased mats and felts with asphalt or tar from purchased asphaltic materials.

T—Canadian, Mexican, and United States industries are comparable.

Cross-References. Establishments primarily engaged in--

- Refining crude petroleum and manufacturing asphalt and tar paving, roofing, and saturated materials--are classified in Industry 32411, Petroleum Refineries; and
- Manufacturing paper mats and felts and saturating them with asphalt or tar--are classified in Industry 32212, Paper Mills.

324121 Asphalt Paving Mixture and Block Manufacturing

This U.S. industry comprises establishments primarily engaged in manufacturing asphalt and tar paving mixtures and blocks from purchased asphaltic materials.

Cross-References.

Establishments primarily engaged in refining crude petroleum and manufacturing asphalt and tar paving mixtures and blocks are classified in Industry 324110, Petroleum Refineries.

324122 Asphalt Shingle and Coating Materials Manufacturing

This U.S. industry comprises establishments primarily engaged in (1) saturating purchased mats and felts with asphalt or tar from purchased asphaltic materials and (2) manufacturing asphalt and tar and roofing cements and coatings from purchased asphaltic materials.

Cross-References. Establishments primarily engaged in--

- Refining crude petroleum and saturating purchased mats and felts with asphalt or tar into rolls and sheets and/or refining crude petroleum and manufacturing asphalt and tar roofing cements and coatings--are classified in Industry 324110, Petroleum Refineries; and
- Manufacturing paper mats and felts and saturating them with asphalt or tar into rolls and sheets--are classified in U.S. Industry 322121, Paper (except Newsprint) Mills.

32419 Other Petroleum and Coal Products Manufacturing[T]

This industry comprises establishments primarily engaged in manufacturing petroleum products (except asphalt paving, roofing, and saturated materials) from refined petroleum or coal products made in coke ovens not integrated with a steel mill.

Illustrative Examples:

Biodiesel fuels not made in petroleum refineries and blended with purchased refined petroleum
Coke oven products (e.g., coke, gases, tars) made in coke oven establishments
Petroleum brake fluids made from refined petroleum
Petroleum briquettes made from refined petroleum
Petroleum jelly made from refined petroleum
Petroleum lubricating oils and greases made from refined petroleum
Petroleum waxes made from refined petroleum
Re-refining used petroleum lubricating oils

Cross-References. Establishments primarily engaged in--

- Manufacturing petroleum products by refining crude petroleum--are classified in Industry 32411, Petroleum Refineries;
- Converting nonpetroleum materials into biodiesel fuels--are classified in Industry 32519, Other Basic Organic Chemical Manufacturing;
- Manufacturing asphalt and tar paving, roofing, and saturated materials from refined petroleum--are classified in Industry 32412, Asphalt Paving, Roofing, and Saturated Materials Manufacturing;

T—Canadian, Mexican, and United States industries are comparable.

- Manufacturing coke oven products in steel mills--are classified in Industry 33111, Iron and Steel Mills and Ferroalloy Manufacturing;
- Manufacturing acyclic and cyclic aromatic hydrocarbons (i.e., petrochemicals) from refined petroleum or liquid hydrocarbons--are classified in Industry 32511, Petrochemical Manufacturing;
- Manufacturing cyclic and acyclic organic chemicals (except petrochemicals)--are classified in Industry 32519, Other Basic Organic Chemical Manufacturing; and
- Manufacturing synthetic lubricating oils and greases--are classified in Industry 32599, All Other Chemical Product and Preparation Manufacturing.

324191 Petroleum Lubricating Oil and Grease Manufacturing

This U.S. industry comprises establishments primarily engaged in blending or compounding refined petroleum to make lubricating oils and greases and/or re-refining used petroleum lubricating oils.

Cross-References. Establishments primarily engaged in--

- Refining crude petroleum and manufacturing lubricating oils and greases--are classified in Industry 324110, Petroleum Refineries; and
- Manufacturing synthetic lubricating oils and greases--are classified in U.S. Industry 325998, All Other Miscellaneous Chemical Product and Preparation Manufacturing.

324199 All Other Petroleum and Coal Products Manufacturing

This U.S. industry comprises establishments primarily engaged in manufacturing petroleum products (except asphalt paving, roofing, and saturated materials and lubricating oils and greases) from refined petroleum and coal products made in coke ovens not integrated with a steel mill.

Illustrative Examples:

Biodiesel fuels not made in petroleum refineries and blended with purchased refined petroleum
Coke oven products (e.g., coke, gases, tars) made in coke oven establishments
Petroleum briquettes made from refined petroleum
Petroleum jelly made from refined petroleum
Petroleum waxes made from refined petroleum

Cross-References. Establishments primarily engaged in--

- Manufacturing petroleum products by refining crude petroleum--are classified in Industry 324110, Petroleum Refineries;
- Converting nonpetroleum materials into biodiesel fuels--are classified in U.S. Industry 325199, All Other Basic Organic Chemical Manufacturing;
- Manufacturing asphalt paving and roofing materials from refined petroleum--are classified in Industry 32412, Asphalt Paving, Roofing, and Saturated Materials Manufacturing;
- Blending and compounding petroleum lubricating oils and greases and/or re-refining used petroleum lubrication oils and greases--are classified in U.S. Industry 324191, Petroleum Lubricating Oil and Grease Manufacturing;
- Manufacturing coke oven products in steel mills--are classified in Industry 331110, Iron and Steel Mills and Ferroalloy Manufacturing;
- Manufacturing acyclic and cyclic aromatic hydrocarbons (i.e., petrochemicals) from refined petroleum or liquid hydrocarbons--are classified in Industry 325110, Petrochemical Manufacturing; and
- Manufacturing cyclic and acyclic organic chemicals (except petrochemicals)--are classified in Industry 32519, Other Basic Organic Chemical Manufacturing.

T—Canadian, Mexican, and United States industries are comparable.

325 Chemical Manufacturing[T]

The Chemical Manufacturing subsector is based on the transformation of organic and inorganic raw materials by a chemical process and the formulation of products. This subsector distinguishes the production of basic chemicals that comprise the first industry group from the production of intermediate and end products produced by further processing of basic chemicals that make up the remaining industry groups.

This subsector does not include all industries transforming raw materials by a chemical process. It is common for some chemical processing to occur during mining operations. These beneficiating operations, such as copper concentrating, are classified in Sector 21, Mining, Quarrying, and Oil and Gas Extraction. Furthermore, the refining of crude petroleum is included in Subsector 324, Petroleum and Coal Products Manufacturing. In addition, the manufacturing of aluminum oxide is included in Subsector 331, Primary Metal Manufacturing; and beverage distilleries are classified in Subsector 312, Beverage and Tobacco Product Manufacturing. As is the case of these two activities, the grouping of industries into subsectors may take into account the association of the activities performed with other activities in the subsector.

3251 Basic Chemical Manufacturing[T]

This industry group comprises establishments primarily engaged in manufacturing chemicals using basic processes, such as thermal cracking and distillation. Chemicals manufactured in this industry group are usually separate chemical elements or separate chemically-defined compounds.

32511 Petrochemical Manufacturing[T] See industry description for 325110.

325110 Petrochemical Manufacturing

This industry comprises establishments primarily engaged in (1) manufacturing acyclic (i.e., aliphatic) hydrocarbons such as ethylene, propylene, and butylene made from refined petroleum or liquid hydrocarbons and/or (2) manufacturing cyclic aromatic hydrocarbons such as benzene, toluene, styrene, xylene, ethyl benzene, and cumene made from refined petroleum or liquid hydrocarbons.

Cross-References. Establishments primarily engaged in--

- Manufacturing petrochemicals by refining crude petroleum--are classified in Industry 324110, Petroleum Refineries;
- Manufacturing acetylene--are classified in Industry 325120, Industrial Gas Manufacturing;
- Manufacturing basic organic chemicals (except petrochemicals)--are classified in Industry 32519, Other Basic Organic Chemical Manufacturing; and
- Recovering liquid hydrocarbons from oil and gas field gases--are classified in Industry 211130, Natural Gas Extraction.

32512 Industrial Gas Manufacturing[T] See industry description for 325120.

325120 Industrial Gas Manufacturing

This industry comprises establishments primarily engaged in manufacturing industrial organic and inorganic gases in compressed, liquid, and solid forms.

Cross-References. Establishments primarily engaged in--

- Manufacturing chlorine gas--are classified in Industry 325180, Other Basic Inorganic Chemical Manufacturing; and
- Manufacturing ethane and butane gases made from refined petroleum or liquid hydrocarbons--are classified in Industry 325110, Petrochemical Manufacturing.

T—Canadian, Mexican, and United States industries are comparable.

32513 Synthetic Dye and Pigment Manufacturing[T] See industry description for 325130.

325130 Synthetic Dye and Pigment Manufacturing

This industry comprises establishments primarily engaged in manufacturing synthetic organic and inorganic dyes and pigments, such as lakes and toners (except electrostatic and photographic).

Cross-References. Establishments primarily engaged in--

- Manufacturing natural food colorings--are classified in U.S. Industry 311942, Spice and Extract Manufacturing;
- Manufacturing natural organic colorings for nonfood uses (except wood byproducts)--are classified in U.S. Industry 325199, All Other Basic Organic Chemical Manufacturing;
- Manufacturing electrostatic and photographic toners--are classified in U.S. Industry 325992, Photographic Film, Paper, Plate, and Chemical Manufacturing;
- Manufacturing wood byproducts used as dyeing materials--are classified in U.S. Industry 325194, Cyclic Crude, Intermediate, and Gum and Wood Chemical Manufacturing; and
- Manufacturing carbon, bone, and lamp black--are classified in Industry 325180, Other Basic Inorganic Chemical Manufacturing.

32518 Other Basic Inorganic Chemical Manufacturing[T] See industry description for 325180.

325180 Other Basic Inorganic Chemical Manufacturing

This industry comprises establishments primarily engaged in manufacturing basic inorganic chemicals (except industrial gases and synthetic dyes and pigments).

Illustrative Examples:

Alkalies manufacturing
Aluminum compounds, not specified elsewhere by process, manufacturing
Carbides (e.g., baron, calcium, silicon, tungsten) manufacturing
Carbon black manufacturing
Chlorine manufacturing
Hydrochloric acid manufacturing
Potassium inorganic compounds, not specified elsewhere by process, manufacturing
Radioactive isotopes manufacturing
Sulfides and sulfites manufacturing
Sulfuric acid manufacturing

Cross-References. Establishments primarily engaged in--

- Manufacturing industrial gases--are classified in Industry 325120, Industrial Gas Manufacturing;
- Manufacturing inorganic dyes and pigments--are classified in Industry 325130, Synthetic Dye and Pigment Manufacturing;
- Manufacturing household bleaches--are classified in U.S. Industry 325612, Polish and Other Sanitation Good Manufacturing;
- Mining and/or beneficiating alkalies--are classified in U.S. Industry 212391, Potash, Soda, and Borate Mineral Mining;
- Manufacturing chlorine preparations (e.g., for swimming pools)--are classified in U.S. Industry 325998, All Other Miscellaneous Chemical Product and Preparation Manufacturing;
- Manufacturing nitrogenous and phosphoric fertilizers and fertilizer materials--are classified in Industry 32531, Fertilizer Manufacturing;
- Manufacturing pharmaceuticals, medicines, and dietary supplements--are classified in Industry Group 3254, Pharmaceutical and Medicine Manufacturing;

T—Canadian, Mexican, and United States industries are comparable.

- Manufacturing aluminum oxide (alumina)--are classified in U.S. Industry 331313, Alumina Refining and Primary Aluminum Production;
- Manufacturing inorganic insecticidal, herbicidal, fungicidal and pesticidal preparations--are classified in Industry 325320, Pesticide and Other Agricultural Chemical Manufacturing; and
- Manufacturing photographic chemicals--are classified in U.S. Industry 325992, Photographic Film, Paper, Plate, and Chemical Manufacturing.

32519 Other Basic Organic Chemical Manufacturing[T]

This industry comprises establishments primarily engaged in manufacturing basic organic chemicals (except petrochemicals, industrial gases, and synthetic dyes and pigments).

Illustrative Examples:

Biodiesel fuels not made in petroleum refineries and not blended with petroleum
Carbon organic compounds, not specified elsewhere by process, manufacturing
Cyclic intermediates made from refined petroleum or natural gas (except aromatic petrochemicals)
Enzyme proteins (i.e., basic synthetic chemicals) (except pharmaceutical use) manufacturing
Gum and wood chemicals manufacturing
Fatty acids (e.g., margaric, oleic, stearic) manufacturing
Organo-inorganic compound manufacturing
Plasticizers (i.e., basic synthetic chemical) manufacturing
Silicone (except resins) manufacturing
Synthetic sweeteners (i.e., sweetening agents) manufacturing

Cross-References. Establishments primarily engaged in--

- Manufacturing petrochemicals from refined petroleum or liquid hydrocarbons--are classified in Industry 32511, Petrochemical Manufacturing;
- Manufacturing petrochemicals by refining crude petroleum--are classified in Industry 32411, Petroleum Refineries;
- Blending purchased biodiesel fuels and purchased refined petroleum--are classified in Industry 32419, Other Petroleum and Coal Products Manufacturing;
- Manufacturing organic industrial gases--are classified in Industry 32512, Industrial Gas Manufacturing;
- Manufacturing synthetic organic dyes and pigments--are classified in Industry 32513, Synthetic Dye and Pigment Manufacturing;
- Manufacturing natural glycerin--are classified in Industry 32561, Soap and Cleaning Compound Manufacturing;
- Manufacturing activated charcoal--are classified in Industry 32599, All Other Chemical Product and Preparation Manufacturing;
- Manufacturing organic insecticidal, herbicidal, fungicidal, and pesticidal preparations--are classified in Industry 32532, Pesticide and Other Agricultural Chemical Manufacturing;
- Manufacturing elastomers--are classified in Industry 32521, Resin and Synthetic Rubber Manufacturing;
- Manufacturing urea--are classified in Industry 32531, Fertilizer Manufacturing;
- Manufacturing pharmaceuticals, medicines, and dietary supplements--are classified in Industry Group 3254, Pharmaceutical and Medicine Manufacturing;
- Manufacturing coal tar crudes in integrated steel mills with coke ovens--are classified in Industry 33111, Iron and Steel Mills and Ferroalloy Manufacturing;
- Manufacturing coal tar crudes in coke ovens not integrated with steel mills and fuel briquettes from refined petroleum--are classified in Industry 32419, Other Petroleum and Coal Products Manufacturing; and
- Manufacturing natural food colorings--are classified in Industry 31194, Seasoning and Dressing Manufacturing.

325193 Ethyl Alcohol Manufacturing

This U.S. industry comprises establishments primarily engaged in manufacturing nonpotable ethyl alcohol.

T Canadian, Mexican, and United States industries are comparable.

Cross-References. Establishments primarily engaged in--

- Distilling liquors (except brandy)--are classified in Industry 312140, Distilleries; and
- Manufacturing brandies--are classified in Industry 312130, Wineries.

325194 Cyclic Crude, Intermediate, and Gum and Wood Chemical Manufacturing

This U.S. industry comprises establishments primarily engaged in one or more of the following: (1) distilling wood or gum into products, such as tall oil and wood distillates; (2) distilling coal tars; (3) manufacturing wood or gum chemicals, such as naval stores, natural tanning materials, charcoal briquettes, and charcoal (except activated); and (4) manufacturing cyclic crudes or cyclic intermediates (i.e., hydrocarbons, except aromatic petrochemicals) from refined petroleum or natural gas.

Cross-references. Establishments primarily engaged in--

- Manufacturing cyclic chemicals (except aromatic and intermediates)--are classified in U.S. Industry 325199, All Other Basic Organic Chemical Manufacturing;
- Manufacturing aromatic petrochemicals from refined petroleum or natural gas--are classified in Industry 325110, Petrochemical Manufacturing;
- Manufacturing aromatic petrochemicals by refining crude petroleum--are classified in Industry 324110, Petroleum Refineries;
- Manufacturing coal tar crudes in steel mills with coke ovens--are classified in Industry 331110, Iron and Steel Mills and Ferroalloy Manufacturing;
- Manufacturing fuel briquettes from refined petroleum--are classified in U.S. Industry 324199, All Other Petroleum and Coal Products Manufacturing; and
- Manufacturing activated charcoal--are classified in U.S. Industry 325998, All Other Miscellaneous Chemical Product and Preparation Manufacturing.

325199 All Other Basic Organic Chemical Manufacturing

This U.S. industry comprises establishments primarily engaged in manufacturing basic organic chemical products (except aromatic petrochemicals, industrial gases, synthetic organic dyes and pigments, gum and wood chemicals, cyclic crudes and intermediates, and ethyl alcohol).

Illustrative Examples:

Biodiesel fuels not made in petroleum refineries and not blended with petroleum
Calcium organic compounds, not specified elsewhere by process, manufacturing
Carbon organic compounds, not specified elsewhere by process, manufacturing
Enzyme proteins (i.e., basic synthetic chemicals) (except pharmaceutical use) manufacturing
Fatty acids (e.g., margaric, oleic, stearic) manufacturing
Organo-inorganic compound manufacturing
Plasticizers (i.e., basic synthetic chemicals) manufacturing
Silicone (except resins) manufacturing
Synthetic sweeteners (i.e., sweetening agents) manufacturing

Cross-References. Establishments primarily engaged in--

- Manufacturing aromatic petrochemicals from refined petroleum or natural gas--are classified in Industry 325110, Petrochemical Manufacturing;
- Manufacturing aromatic petrochemicals or biodiesel fuels by refining crude petroleum--are classified in Industry 324110, Petroleum Refineries;
- Blending purchased biodiesel fuels and purchased refined petroleum--are classified in U.S. Industry 324199, All Other Petroleum and Coal Products Manufacturing;
- Manufacturing organic industrial gases--are classified in Industry 325120, Industrial Gas Manufacturing;

T—Canadian, Mexican, and United States industries are comparable.

- Manufacturing synthetic organic dyes and pigments--are classified in Industry 325130, Synthetic Dye and Pigment Manufacturing;
- Manufacturing ethyl alcohol--are classified in U.S. Industry 325193, Ethyl Alcohol Manufacturing;
- Manufacturing organic insecticidal, herbicidal, fungicidal, and pesticidal preparations--are classified in Industry 325320, Pesticide and Other Agricultural Chemical Manufacturing;
- Manufacturing elastomers--are classified in Industry 32521, Resin and Synthetic Rubber Manufacturing;
- Manufacturing urea--are classified in U.S. Industry 325311, Nitrogenous Fertilizer Manufacturing;
- Manufacturing pharmaceuticals, medicines, and dietary supplements--are classified in Industry Group 3254, Pharmaceutical and Medicine Manufacturing;
- Manufacturing natural glycerin--are classified in U.S. Industry 325611, Soap and Other Detergent Manufacturing; and
- Manufacturing natural food colorings--are classified in U.S. Industry 311942, Spice and Extract Manufacturing.

3252 Resin, Synthetic Rubber, and Artificial and Synthetic Fibers and Filaments Manufacturing[T]

This industry group comprises establishments primarily engaged in one of the following: (1) manufacturing synthetic resins, plastics materials, and nonvulcanizable elastomers and mixing and blending resins on a custom basis; (2) manufacturing noncustomized synthetic resins; (3) manufacturing synthetic rubber; (4) manufacturing cellulosic (e.g., rayon, acetate) and noncellulosic (e.g., nylon, polyolefin, polyester) fibers and filaments in the form of monofilament, filament yarn, staple, or tow; or (5) manufacturing and texturizing cellulosic and noncellulosic fibers and filaments.

32521 Resin and Synthetic Rubber Manufacturing[T]

This industry comprises establishments primarily engaged in one or more of the following: (1) manufacturing synthetic resins, plastics materials, and nonvulcanizable elastomers and mixing and blending resins on a custom basis; (2) manufacturing noncustomized synthetic resins; and (3) manufacturing synthetic rubber.

Cross-References. Establishments primarily engaged in--

- Manufacturing plastics resins and converting resins into plastics products--are classified in Industry Group 3261, Plastics Product Manufacturing;
- Processing natural, synthetic, or reclaimed rubber into intermediate or final products--are classified in Industry Group 3262, Rubber Product Manufacturing;
- Custom compounding resins made elsewhere--are classified in Industry 32599, All Other Chemical Product and Preparation Manufacturing; and
- Manufacturing resin adhesives--are classified in Industry 32552, Adhesive Manufacturing.

325211 Plastics Material and Resin Manufacturing

This U.S. industry comprises establishments primarily engaged in (1) manufacturing resins, plastics materials, and nonvulcanizable thermoplastic elastomers and mixing and blending resins on a custom basis and/or (2) manufacturing noncustomized synthetic resins.

Cross-References. Establishments primarily engaged in--

- Manufacturing plastics resins and converting resins into plastics products--are classified in Industry Group 3261, Plastics Product Manufacturing;
- Custom compounding resins made elsewhere--are classified in U.S. Industry 325991, Custom Compounding of Purchased Resins; and
- Manufacturing plastics adhesives--are classified in Industry 325520, Adhesive Manufacturing.

T—Canadian, Mexican, and United States industries are comparable.

325212 Synthetic Rubber Manufacturing

This U.S. industry comprises establishments primarily engaged in manufacturing synthetic rubber.

Cross-References. Establishments primarily engaged in--

- Processing natural, synthetic, or reclaimed rubber into intermediate or final products (except adhesives)--are classified in Industry Group 3262, Rubber Product Manufacturing; and
- Manufacturing rubber adhesives--are classified in Industry 325520, Adhesive Manufacturing.

32522 Artificial and Synthetic Fibers and Filaments Manufacturing[T] See industry description for 325220.

325220 Artificial and Synthetic Fibers and Filaments Manufacturing

This industry comprises establishments primarily engaged in (1) manufacturing cellulosic (e.g., rayon, acetate) and noncellulosic (e.g., nylon, polyolefin, polyester) fibers and filaments in the form of monofilament, filament yarn, staple, or tow or (2) manufacturing and texturizing cellulosic and noncellulosic fibers and filaments.

Cross-References. Establishments primarily engaged in--

- Texturizing cellulosic and noncellulosic fibers and filaments made elsewhere--are classified in Industry 313110, Fiber, Yarn, and Thread Mills; and
- Manufacturing textile glass fibers--are classified in U.S. Industry 327212, Other Pressed and Blown Glass and Glassware Manufacturing.

3253 Pesticide, Fertilizer, and Other Agricultural Chemical Manufacturing[T]

This industry group comprises establishments primarily engaged in one or more of the following: (1) manufacturing nitrogenous or phosphatic fertilizer materials; (2) manufacturing fertilizers from sewage or animal waste; (3) manufacturing nitrogenous or phosphatic materials and mixing with other ingredients into fertilizers; (4) mixing ingredients made elsewhere into fertilizers; and (5) formulating and preparing pesticides and other agricultural chemicals.

32531 Fertilizer Manufacturing[T]

This industry comprises establishments primarily engaged in one or more of the following: (1) manufacturing nitrogenous or phosphatic fertilizer materials; (2) manufacturing fertilizers from sewage or animal waste; (3) manufacturing nitrogenous or phosphatic materials and mixing with other ingredients into fertilizers; and (4) mixing ingredients made elsewhere into fertilizers.

325311 Nitrogenous Fertilizer Manufacturing

This U.S. industry comprises establishments primarily engaged in one or more of the following: (1) manufacturing nitrogenous fertilizer materials and mixing ingredients into fertilizers; (2) manufacturing fertilizers from sewage or animal waste; and (3) manufacturing nitrogenous materials and mixing them into fertilizers.

Cross-References.

Establishments primarily engaged in mixing ingredients made elsewhere into nitrogenous fertilizers are classified in U.S. Industry 325314, Fertilizer (Mixing Only) Manufacturing.

T—Canadian, Mexican, and United States industries are comparable.

325312 Phosphatic Fertilizer Manufacturing

This U.S. industry comprises establishments primarily engaged in (1) manufacturing phosphatic fertilizer materials or (2) manufacturing phosphatic materials and mixing them into fertilizers.

Cross-References.

Establishments primarily engaged in mixing ingredients made elsewhere into phosphatic fertilizers are classified in U.S. Industry 325314, Fertilizer (Mixing Only) Manufacturing.

325314 Fertilizer (Mixing Only) Manufacturing

This U.S. industry comprises establishments primarily engaged in mixing ingredients made elsewhere into fertilizers.

Cross-References. Establishments primarily engaged in--

- Manufacturing nitrogenous fertilizer materials or fertilizer materials from sewage or animal waste and mixing these ingredients into nitrogenous fertilizers--are classified in U.S. Industry 325311, Nitrogenous Fertilizer Manufacturing; and
- Manufacturing phosphatic fertilizer materials and mixing these ingredients into phosphatic fertilizers--are classified in U.S. Industry 325312, Phosphatic Fertilizer Manufacturing.

32532 Pesticide and Other Agricultural Chemical Manufacturing^{T} See industry description for 325320.

325320 Pesticide and Other Agricultural Chemical Manufacturing

This industry comprises establishments primarily engaged in the formulation and preparation of agricultural and household pest control chemicals (except fertilizers).

Cross-References. Establishments primarily engaged in--

- Manufacturing basic chemicals requiring further processing before use as agriculture chemicals--are classified in Industry Group 3251, Basic Chemical Manufacturing;
- Manufacturing fertilizers--are classified in Industry 32531, Fertilizer Manufacturing; and
- Manufacturing agricultural lime products--are classified in Industry 327410, Lime Manufacturing.

3254 Pharmaceutical and Medicine Manufacturing^{T}

32541 Pharmaceutical and Medicine Manufacturing^{T}

This industry comprises establishments primarily engaged in one or more of the following: (1) manufacturing biological and medicinal products; (2) processing (i.e., grading, grinding, and milling) botanical drugs and herbs; (3) isolating active medicinal principals from botanical drugs and herbs; and (4) manufacturing pharmaceutical products intended for internal and external consumption in such forms as ampoules, tablets, capsules, vials, ointments, powders, solutions, and suspensions.

325411 Medicinal and Botanical Manufacturing

This U.S. industry comprises establishments primarily engaged in (1) manufacturing uncompounded medicinal chemicals and their derivatives (i.e., generally for use by pharmaceutical preparation manufacturers) and/or (2) grading, grinding, and milling uncompounded botanicals.

T—Canadian, Mexican, and United States industries are comparable.

Cross-References. Establishments primarily engaged in--

- Manufacturing packaged compounded medicinals and botanicals--are classified in U.S. Industry 325412, Pharmaceutical Preparation Manufacturing; and
- Manufacturing vaccines, toxoids, blood fractions, and culture media of plant or animal origin (except for diagnostic use)--are classified in U.S. Industry 325414, Biological Product (except Diagnostic) Manufacturing.

325412 Pharmaceutical Preparation Manufacturing

This U.S. industry comprises establishments primarily engaged in manufacturing in-vivo diagnostic substances and pharmaceutical preparations (except biological) intended for internal and external consumption in dose forms, such as ampoules, tablets, capsules, vials, ointments, powders, solutions, and suspensions.

Cross-References. Establishments primarily engaged in--

- Manufacturing uncompounded medicinal chemicals and their derivatives--are classified in U.S. Industry 325411, Medicinal and Botanical Manufacturing;
- Manufacturing in-vitro diagnostic substances--are classified in U.S. Industry 325413, In-Vitro Diagnostic Substance Manufacturing; and
- Manufacturing vaccines, toxoids, blood fractions, and culture media of plant or animal origin (except for diagnostic use)--are classified in U.S. Industry 325414, Biological Product (except Diagnostic) Manufacturing.

325413 In-Vitro Diagnostic Substance Manufacturing

This U.S. industry comprises establishments primarily engaged in manufacturing in-vitro (i.e., not taken internally) diagnostic substances, such as chemical, biological, or radioactive substances. The substances are used for diagnostic tests that are performed in test tubes, petri dishes, machines, and other diagnostic test-type devices.

Cross-References.

Establishments primarily engaged in manufacturing in-vivo diagnostic substances are classified in U.S. Industry 325412, Pharmaceutical Preparation Manufacturing.

325414 Biological Product (except Diagnostic) Manufacturing

This U.S. industry comprises establishments primarily engaged in manufacturing vaccines, toxoids, blood fractions, and culture media of plant or animal origin (except diagnostic).

Cross-References. Establishments primarily engaged in--

- Manufacturing in-vitro diagnostic substances--are classified in U.S. Industry 325413, In-Vitro Diagnostic Substance Manufacturing; and
- Manufacturing pharmaceutical preparations (except biological and in-vitro diagnostic substances)--are classified in U.S. Industry 325412, Pharmaceutical Preparation Manufacturing.

3255 Paint, Coating, and Adhesive Manufacturing[T]

This industry group comprises establishments primarily engaged in one or more of the following: (1) mixing pigments, solvents, and binders into paints and other coatings; (2) manufacturing allied paint products; and (3) manufacturing adhesives, glues, and caulking compounds.

32551 Paint and Coating Manufacturing[T] See industry description for 325510.

T—Canadian, Mexican, and United States industries are comparable.

325510 Paint and Coating Manufacturing

This industry comprises establishments primarily engaged in (1) mixing pigments, solvents, and binders into paints and other coatings, such as stains, varnishes, lacquers, enamels, shellacs, and water-repellent coatings for concrete and masonry, and/or (2) manufacturing allied paint products, such as putties, paint and varnish removers, paint brush cleaners, and frit.

Cross-References. Establishments primarily engaged in--

- Manufacturing creosote or turpentine--are classified in U.S. Industry 325194, Cyclic Crude, Intermediate, and Gum and Wood Chemical Manufacturing;
- Manufacturing caulking compounds and sealants--are classified in Industry 325520, Adhesive Manufacturing; and
- Manufacturing artists' paints--are classified in Industry 339940, Office Supplies (except Paper) Manufacturing.

32552 Adhesive Manufacturing[T] See industry description for 325520.

325520 Adhesive Manufacturing

This industry comprises establishments primarily engaged in manufacturing adhesives, glues, and caulking compounds.

Cross-References. Establishments primarily engaged in--

- Manufacturing asphalt and tar roofing cements from purchased asphaltic materials--are classified in U.S. Industry 324122, Asphalt Shingle and Coating Materials Manufacturing; and
- Manufacturing gypsum based caulking compounds--are classified in Industry 327420, Gypsum Product Manufacturing.

3256 Soap, Cleaning Compound, and Toilet Preparation Manufacturing[T]

This industry group comprises establishments primarily engaged in (1) manufacturing and packaging soaps, detergents, polishes, surface active agents, textile and leather finishing agents, and other sanitation goods or (2) preparing, blending, compounding, and packaging toilet preparations.

32561 Soap and Cleaning Compound Manufacturing[T]

This industry comprises establishments primarily engaged in manufacturing and packaging soaps and other cleaning compounds, surface active agents, and textile and leather finishing agents used to reduce tension or speed the drying process.

Cross-References. Establishments primarily engaged in--

- Manufacturing synthetic glycerin--are classified in Industry 32519, Other Basic Organic Chemical Manufacturing;
- Manufacturing industrial bleaches--are classified in Industry 32518, Other Basic Inorganic Chemical Manufacturing; and
- Manufacturing shampoos and shaving preparations--are classified in Industry 32562, Toilet Preparation Manufacturing.

T—Canadian, Mexican, and United States industries are comparable.

325611 Soap and Other Detergent Manufacturing

This U.S. industry comprises establishments primarily engaged in manufacturing and packaging soaps and other detergents, such as laundry and dishwashing detergents; toothpaste gels and tooth powders; and natural glycerin.

Cross-References. Establishments primarily engaged in--

- Manufacturing synthetic glycerin--are classified in U.S. Industry 325199, All Other Basic Organic Chemical Manufacturing; and
- Manufacturing shampoos and shaving preparations--are classified in Industry 325620, Toilet Preparation Manufacturing.

325612 Polish and Other Sanitation Good Manufacturing

This U.S. industry comprises establishments primarily engaged in manufacturing and packaging polishes and specialty cleaning preparations.

Cross-References.

Establishments primarily engaged in manufacturing chlorine dioxide (i.e., industrial bleaching agent) are classified in Industry 325180, Other Basic Inorganic Chemical Manufacturing.

325613 Surface Active Agent Manufacturing

This U.S. industry comprises establishments primarily engaged in (1) manufacturing bulk surface active agents for use as wetting agents, emulsifiers, and penetrants and/or (2) manufacturing textile and leather finishing agents used to reduce tension or speed the drying process.

32562 Toilet Preparation Manufacturing[T] See industry description for 325620.

325620 Toilet Preparation Manufacturing

This industry comprises establishments primarily engaged in preparing, blending, compounding, and packaging toilet preparations, such as perfumes, shaving preparations, hair preparations, face creams, lotions (including sunscreens), and other cosmetic preparations.

Cross-References.

Establishments primarily engaged in manufacturing toothpaste are classified in U.S. Industry 325611, Soap and Other Detergent Manufacturing.

3259 Other Chemical Product and Preparation Manufacturing[T]

This industry group comprises establishments primarily engaged in manufacturing chemical products (except basic chemicals; resins, synthetic rubber, cellulosic and noncellulosic fibers and filaments; pesticides, fertilizers, and other agricultural chemicals; pharmaceuticals and medicines; paints, coatings, and adhesives; soaps and cleaning compounds; and toilet preparations).

32591 Printing Ink Manufacturing[T] See industry description for 325910.

T—Canadian, Mexican, and United States industries are comparable.

325910 Printing Ink Manufacturing

This industry comprises establishments primarily engaged in manufacturing printing and inkjet inks and inkjet cartridges.

Cross-References. Establishments primarily engaged in--

- Recycling inkjet cartridges--are classified in U.S. Industry 811212, Computer and Office Machine Repair and Maintenance;
- Manufacturing writing, drawing, and stamping inks--are classified in U.S. Industry 325998, All Other Miscellaneous Chemical Product and Preparation Manufacturing; and
- Manufacturing toners and toner cartridges for photocopiers, fax machines, computer printers, and similar office machines--are classified in U.S. Industry 325992, Photographic Film, Paper, Plate, and Chemical Manufacturing.

32592 Explosives Manufacturing[T] See industry description for 325920.

325920 Explosives Manufacturing

This industry comprises establishments primarily engaged in manufacturing explosives.

Cross-References. Establishments primarily engaged in--

- Manufacturing ammunition, ammunition detonators, and percussion caps--are classified in U.S. Industry 332992, Small Arms Ammunition Manufacturing; and
- Manufacturing pyrotechnics--are classified in U.S. Industry 325998, All Other Miscellaneous Chemical Product and Preparation Manufacturing.

32599 All Other Chemical Product and Preparation Manufacturing[T]

This industry comprises establishments primarily engaged in manufacturing chemical products (except basic chemicals, resins, and synthetic rubber; cellulosic and noncellulosic fibers and filaments; pesticides, fertilizers, and other agricultural chemicals; pharmaceuticals and medicines; paints, coatings, and adhesives; soaps, cleaning compounds, and toilet preparations; printing inks; and explosives).

Illustrative Examples:

Activated carbon and charcoal manufacturing
Antifreeze preparations manufacturing
Custom compounding (i.e., blending and mixing) of purchased plastics resins
Electronic cigarette vapor refills manufacturing
Industrial salt manufacturing
Matches and matchbook manufacturing
Photographic chemicals manufacturing
Pyrotechnics (e.g., flares, flashlight bombs, signals) manufacturing
Sugar substitutes (i.e., synthetic sweeteners blended with other ingredients) made from purchased synthetic sweeteners
Swimming pool chemical preparations manufacturing
Writing inks manufacturing

Cross-References. Establishments primarily engaged in--

- Manufacturing basic chemicals--are classified in Industry Group 3251, Basic Chemical Manufacturing;
- Manufacturing resins, synthetic rubber, and artificial and synthetic fibers and filaments--are classified in Industry Group 3252, Resin, Synthetic Rubber, and Artificial and Synthetic Fibers and Filaments Manufacturing;
- Manufacturing pesticides, fertilizers, and other agricultural chemicals--are classified in Industry Group 3253, Pesticide, Fertilizer, and Other Agricultural Chemical Manufacturing;

~~T—Canadian, Mexican, and Unit~~ed States industries are comparable.

- Manufacturing pharmaceuticals and medicines including medicinal vegetable gelatin (i.e., agar-agar)--are classified in Industry Group 3254, Pharmaceutical and Medicine Manufacturing;
- Manufacturing paints, coatings, and adhesives--are classified in Industry Group 3255, Paint, Coating, and Adhesive Manufacturing;
- Manufacturing soaps and cleaning compounds--are classified in Industry Group 3256, Soap, Cleaning Compound, and Toilet Preparation Manufacturing;
- Manufacturing printing and inkjet inks--are classified in Industry 32591, Printing Ink Manufacturing;
- Manufacturing explosives--are classified in Industry 32592, Explosives Manufacturing;
- Manufacturing photographic paper stock (i.e., unsensitized) and paper mats, mounts, easels, and folders for photographic use--are classified in Subsector 322, Paper Manufacturing;
- Manufacturing dessert gelatins--are classified in Industry 31199, All Other Food Manufacturing; and
- Manufacturing medicinal gelatins--are classified in Industry 32541, Pharmaceutical and Medicine Manufacturing.

325991 Custom Compounding of Purchased Resins

This U.S. industry comprises establishments primarily engaged in (1) custom mixing and blending plastics resins made elsewhere or (2) reformulating plastics resins from recycled plastics products.

Cross-References.

Establishments primarily engaged in manufacturing synthetic resins and custom mixing and blending resins are classified in U.S. Industry 325211, Plastics Material and Resin Manufacturing.

325992 Photographic Film, Paper, Plate, and Chemical Manufacturing

This U.S. industry comprises establishments primarily engaged in manufacturing sensitized film, sensitized paper, sensitized cloth, sensitized plates, toners (i.e., for photocopiers, laser printers, and similar electrostatic printing devices), toner cartridges, and photographic chemicals.

Cross-References.

Establishments primarily engaged in manufacturing photographic paper stock (i.e., unsensitized) and paper mats, mounts, easels, and folders for photographic use are classified in Subsector 322, Paper Manufacturing.

325998 All Other Miscellaneous Chemical Product and Preparation Manufacturing

This U.S. industry comprises establishments primarily engaged in manufacturing chemical products (except basic chemicals, resins, and synthetic rubber; cellulosic and noncellulosic fibers and filaments; pesticides, fertilizers, and other agricultural chemicals; pharmaceuticals and medicines; paints, coatings and adhesives; soaps, cleaning compounds, and toilet preparations; printing inks; explosives; custom compounding of purchased resins; and photographic films, papers, plates, and chemicals).

Illustrative Examples:

Activated carbon and charcoal manufacturing
Antifreeze preparations manufacturing
Electronic cigarette vapor refills manufacturing
Industrial salt manufacturing
Lighter fluids (e.g., charcoal, cigarette) manufacturing
Matches and matchbook manufacturing
Pyrotechnics (e.g., flares, flashlight bombs, signals) manufacturing
Sugar substitutes (i.e., synthetic sweeteners blended with other ingredients) made from purchased synthetic sweeteners
Swimming pool chemical preparations manufacturing
Writing inks manufacturing

T—Canadian, Mexican, and United States industries are comparable.

Cross-References. Establishments primarily engaged in--

- Manufacturing basic chemicals--are classified in Industry Group 3251, Basic Chemical Manufacturing;
- Manufacturing resins, synthetic rubber, and artificial and synthetic fibers and filaments--are classified in Industry Group 3252, Resin, Synthetic Rubber, and Artificial and Synthetic Fibers and Filaments Manufacturing;
- Manufacturing pesticides, fertilizers, and other agricultural chemicals--are classified in Industry Group 3253, Pesticide, Fertilizer, and Other Agricultural Chemical Manufacturing;
- Manufacturing pharmaceuticals and medicines including medicinal vegetable gelatin (i.e., agar-agar)--are classified in Industry Group 3254, Pharmaceutical and Medicine Manufacturing;
- Manufacturing paints, coatings, and adhesives--are classified in Industry Group 3255, Paint, Coating, and Adhesive Manufacturing;
- Manufacturing soaps and cleaning compounds--are classified in Industry 32561, Soap and Cleaning Compound Manufacturing;
- Manufacturing printing and inkjet inks--are classified in Industry 325910, Printing Ink Manufacturing;
- Manufacturing explosives--are classified in Industry 325920, Explosives Manufacturing;
- Custom compounding purchased plastics resins--are classified in U.S. Industry 325991, Custom Compounding of Purchased Resins;
- Manufacturing photographic films, papers, plates, and chemicals--are classified in U.S. Industry 325992, Photographic Film, Paper, Plate, and Chemical Manufacturing; and
- Manufacturing dessert gelatin--are classified in U.S. Industry 311999, All Other Miscellaneous Food Manufacturing.

326 Plastics and Rubber Products Manufacturing[T]

Industries in the Plastics and Rubber Products Manufacturing subsector make goods by processing plastics materials and raw rubber. The core technology employed by establishments in this subsector is that of plastics or rubber product production. Plastics and rubber are combined in the same subsector because plastics are increasingly being used as a substitute for rubber; however the subsector is generally restricted to the production of products made of just one material, either solely plastics or rubber.

Many manufacturing activities use plastics or rubber, for example the manufacture of footwear or furniture. Typically, the production process of these products involves more than one material. In these cases, technologies that allow disparate materials to be formed and combined are of central importance in describing the manufacturing activity. In NAICS, such activities (footwear and furniture manufacturing) are not classified in the Plastics and Rubber Products Manufacturing subsector because the core technologies for these activities are diverse and involve multiple materials.

Within the Plastics and Rubber Products Manufacturing subsector, a distinction is made between plastics and rubber products at the industry group level, although it is not a rigid distinction, as can be seen from the definition of Industry 32622, Rubber and Plastics Hoses and Belting Manufacturing. As materials technology progresses, plastics are increasingly being used as a substitute for rubber; and eventually, the distinction may disappear as a basis for establishment classification.

In keeping with the core technology focus of plastics, lamination of plastics film to plastics film as well as the production of bags from plastics only is classified in this subsector. Lamination and bag production involving plastics and materials other than plastics are classified in Subsector 322, Paper Manufacturing.

3261 Plastics Product Manufacturing[T]

This industry group comprises establishments primarily engaged in processing new or spent (i.e., recycled) plastics resins into intermediate or final products, using such processes as compression molding; extrusion molding; injection molding; blow molding; and casting. Within most of these industries, the production process is such that a wide variety of products can be made.

T—Canadian, Mexican, and United States industries are comparable.

32611 Plastics Packaging Materials and Unlaminated Film and Sheet Manufacturing[T]

This industry comprises establishments primarily engaged in (1) converting plastics resins into unsupported plastics film and sheet and/or (2) forming, coating, or laminating plastics film and sheet into plastics bags.

Cross-References. Establishments primarily engaged in--

- Laminating plastics sheet (except for packaging)--are classified in Industry 32613, Laminated Plastics Plate, Sheet (except Packaging), and Shape Manufacturing;
- Manufacturing plastics blister and bubble packaging--are classified in Industry 32619, Other Plastics Product Manufacturing; and
- Coating or laminating combinations of plastics, foils and paper (except plastics film to plastics film) into film, sheet or bags--are classified in Industry 32222, Paper Bag and Coated and Treated Paper Manufacturing.

326111 Plastics Bag and Pouch Manufacturing

This U.S. industry comprises establishments primarily engaged in (1) converting plastics resins into plastics bags or pouches and/or (2) forming, coating, or laminating plastics film or sheet into single-web or multiweb plastics bags or pouches. Establishments in this industry may print on the bags or pouches they manufacture.

Cross-References. Establishments primarily engaged in--

- Manufacturing laminated or coated combinations of plastics, foils, and paper (except plastics film to plastics film) materials into single wall or multiwall bags--are classified in Industry 322220, Paper Bag and Coated and Treated Paper Manufacturing; and
- Printing on purchased packaging materials--are classified in Industry Group 3231, Printing and Related Support Activities, based on the printing process used.

326112 Plastics Packaging Film and Sheet (including Laminated) Manufacturing

This U.S. industry comprises establishments primarily engaged in converting plastics resins into plastics packaging (flexible) film and packaging sheet.

Cross-References. Establishments primarily engaged in--

- Converting plastics resins into plastics film and unlaminated sheet (except packaging)--are classified in U.S. Industry 326113, Unlaminated Plastics Film and Sheet (except Packaging) Manufacturing;
- Laminating or coating combinations of plastics, foils, and paper (except plastics film to plastics film) film and sheet, packaging or nonpackaging--are classified in Industry 322220, Paper Bag and Coated and Treated Paper Manufacturing;
- Laminating plastics sheet (except for packaging)--are classified in Industry 326130, Laminated Plastics Plate, Sheet (except Packaging), and Shape Manufacturing; and
- Manufacturing plastics bags--are classified in U.S. Industry 326111, Plastics Bag and Pouch Manufacturing.

326113 Unlaminated Plastics Film and Sheet (except Packaging) Manufacturing

This U.S. industry comprises establishments primarily engaged in converting plastics resins into plastics film and unlaminated sheet (except packaging).

Cross-References. Establishments primarily engaged in--

- Converting plastics resins into plastics packaging film and unlaminated packaging sheet--are classified in U.S. Industry 326112, Plastics Packaging Film and Sheet (including Laminated) Manufacturing;

T—Canadian, Mexican, and United States industries are comparable.

- Laminating plastics sheet (except for packaging)--are classified in Industry 326130, Laminated Plastics Plate, Sheet (except Packaging), and Shape Manufacturing;
- Laminating or coating combinations of plastics, foils, and paper (except plastics film to plastics film) film and sheet, packaging or nonpackaging--are classified in Industry 322220, Paper Bag and Coated and Treated Paper Manufacturing; and
- Manufacturing plastics bags--are classified in U.S. Industry 326111, Plastics Bag and Pouch Manufacturing.

32612 Plastics Pipe, Pipe Fitting, and Unlaminated Profile Shape Manufacturing[T]

This industry comprises establishments primarily engaged in manufacturing plastics pipes and pipe fittings, and plastics profile shapes such as rod, tube, and sausage casings.

Cross-References. Establishments primarily engaged in--

- Manufacturing plastics hose--are classified in Industry 32622, Rubber and Plastics Hoses and Belting Manufacturing;
- Manufacturing noncurrent-carrying plastics conduit--are classified in Industry 33593, Wiring Device Manufacturing;
- Manufacturing plastics plumbing fixtures--are classified in Industry 32619, Other Plastics Product Manufacturing; and
- Manufacturing plastics film, plastics unlaminated sheet, and plastics bags--are classified in Industry 32611, Plastics Packaging Materials and Unlaminated Film and Sheet Manufacturing.

326121 Unlaminated Plastics Profile Shape Manufacturing

This U.S. industry comprises establishments primarily engaged in converting plastics resins into nonrigid plastics profile shapes (except film, sheet, and bags), such as rod, tube, and sausage casings.

Cross-References. Establishments primarily engaged in--

- Manufacturing plastics film, plastics unlaminated sheet, and plastics bags--are classified in Industry 32611, Plastics Packaging Materials and Unlaminated Film and Sheet Manufacturing; and
- Manufacturing plastics hoses--are classified in Industry 326220, Rubber and Plastics Hoses and Belting Manufacturing.

326122 Plastics Pipe and Pipe Fitting Manufacturing

This U.S. industry comprises establishments primarily engaged in converting plastics resins into rigid plastics pipes and pipe fittings.

Cross-References. Establishments primarily engaged in--

- Manufacturing plastics hose--are classified in Industry 326220, Rubber and Plastics Hoses and Belting Manufacturing;
- Manufacturing noncurrent-carrying plastics conduit--are classified in U.S. Industry 335932, Noncurrent-Carrying Wiring Device Manufacturing; and
- Manufacturing plastics plumbing fixtures--are classified in U.S. Industry 326191, Plastics Plumbing Fixture Manufacturing.

32613 Laminated Plastics Plate, Sheet (except Packaging), and Shape Manufacturing[T] See industry description for 326130.

T—Canadian, Mexican, and United States industries are comparable.

326130 Laminated Plastics Plate, Sheet (except Packaging), and Shape Manufacturing

This industry comprises establishments primarily engaged in laminating plastics profile shapes such as plate, sheet (except packaging), and rod. The lamination process generally involves bonding or impregnating profiles with plastics resins and compressing them under heat.

Cross-References. Establishments primarily engaged in--

- Manufacturing plastics film, plastics unlaminated sheet, and plastics bags--are classified in Industry 32611, Plastics Packaging Materials and Unlaminated Film and Sheet Manufacturing; and
- Coating or laminating nonplastics film, sheet, or bags with plastics--are classified in Industry 322220, Paper Bag and Coated and Treated Paper Manufacturing.

32614 Polystyrene Foam Product Manufacturing[T] See industry description for 326140.

326140 Polystyrene Foam Product Manufacturing

This industry comprises establishments primarily engaged in manufacturing polystyrene foam products.

Cross-References.

Establishments primarily engaged in manufacturing plastics foam products (except polystyrene) are classified in Industry 326150, Urethane and Other Foam Product (except Polystyrene) Manufacturing.

32615 Urethane and Other Foam Product (except Polystyrene) Manufacturing[T] See industry description for 326150.

326150 Urethane and Other Foam Product (except Polystyrene) Manufacturing

This industry comprises establishments primarily engaged in manufacturing plastics foam products (except polystyrene).

Cross-References.

Establishments primarily engaged in manufacturing polystyrene foam products are classified in Industry 326140, Polystyrene Foam Product Manufacturing.

32616 Plastics Bottle Manufacturing[T] See industry description for 326160.

326160 Plastics Bottle Manufacturing

This industry comprises establishments primarily engaged in manufacturing plastics bottles.

Cross-References.

Establishments primarily engaged in manufacturing plastics containers (except bottles) and plastics bottle caps are classified in U.S. Industry 326199, All Other Plastics Product Manufacturing.

32619 Other Plastics Product Manufacturing[T]

This industry comprises establishments primarily engaged in manufacturing plastics plumbing fixtures and other plastics products (except film, sheet, bags, profile shapes, pipes, pipe fittings, laminates, foam products, and bottles).

T—Canadian, Mexican, and United States industries are comparable.

Illustrative Examples:

Inflatable plastics swimming pool rafts and similar flotation devices manufacturing Plastics air mattresses manufacturing
Plastics bottle caps and lids manufacturing
Plastics bowls and bowl covers manufacturing
Plastics clothes hangers manufacturing
Plastics cups (except foam) manufacturing
Plastics dinnerware (except foam) manufacturing
Plastics gloves manufacturing
Plastics hardware manufacturing
Plastics ice chests or coolers (except plastics foam) manufacturing
Plastics or fiberglass plumbing fixtures (e.g., toilets, shower stalls, urinals) manufacturing Plastics prefabricated buildings manufacturing Plastics siding manufacturing
Plastics trash containers manufacturing
Resilient floor coverings (e.g., sheet, tiles) manufacturing

Cross-References. Establishments primarily engaged in--

- Manufacturing plastics film, plastics unlaminated sheet, and plastics bags--are classified in Industry 32611, Plastics Packaging Materials and Unlaminated Film and Sheet Manufacturing;
- Manufacturing plastics pipes, pipe fittings, and plastics profile shapes (except film, sheet, bags)--are classified in Industry 32612, Plastics Pipe, Pipe Fitting, and Unlaminated Profile Shape Manufacturing;
- Laminating plastics profile shapes, such as plate, sheet, and rod--are classified in Industry 32613, Laminated Plastics Plate, Sheet (except Packaging), and Shape Manufacturing;
- Manufacturing polystyrene foam products--are classified in Industry 32614, Polystyrene Foam Product Manufacturing;
- Manufacturing foam products (except polystyrene)--are classified in Industry 32615, Urethane and Other Foam Product (except Polystyrene) Manufacturing;
- Manufacturing plastics bottles--are classified in Industry 32616, Plastics Bottle Manufacturing;
- Manufacturing plastics furniture parts--are classified in Industry 33721, Office Furniture (including Fixtures) Manufacturing;
- Assembling plastics components into plumbing fixture fittings, such as faucets--are classified in Industry 33291, Metal Valve Manufacturing; and
- Manufacturing rubber floor mats and rubber treads--are classified in Industry 32629, Other Rubber Product Manufacturing.

326191 Plastics Plumbing Fixture Manufacturing

This U.S. industry comprises establishments primarily engaged in manufacturing plastics or fiberglass plumbing fixtures. Examples of products made by these establishments are plastics or fiberglass bathtubs, hot tubs, portable toilets, and shower stalls.

Cross-References. Establishments primarily engaged in--

- Assembling plastics components into plumbing fixture fittings, such as faucets--are classified in U.S. Industry 332913, Plumbing Fixture Fitting and Trim Manufacturing; and
- Manufacturing plastics pipe and pipe fittings--are classified in U.S. Industry 326122, Plastics Pipe and Pipe Fitting Manufacturing.

326199 All Other Plastics Product Manufacturing

This U.S. industry comprises establishments primarily engaged in manufacturing plastics products (except film, sheet, bags, profile shapes, pipes, pipe fittings, laminates, foam products, bottles, and plumbing fixtures).

Illustrative Examples:

Inflatable plastics swimming pool rafts and similar flotation devices manufacturing
Plastics air mattresses manufacturing

T—Canadian, Mexican, and United States industries are comparable.

Plastics bowls and bowl covers manufacturing
Plastics clothes hangers manufacturing
Plastics cups (except foam) manufacturing
Plastics dinnerware (except foam) manufacturing
Plastics gloves manufacturing
Plastics hardware manufacturing
Plastics siding manufacturing
Plastics trash containers manufacturing
Resilient floor coverings (e.g., sheet, tiles) manufacturing

Cross-References. Establishments primarily engaged in--

- Manufacturing plastics film, plastics unlaminated sheet, and plastics bags--are classified in Industry 32611, Plastics Packaging Materials and Unlaminated Film and Sheet Manufacturing;
- Manufacturing plastics pipes, pipe fittings, and plastics profile shapes (except film, sheet, bags)--are classified in Industry 32612, Plastics Pipe, Pipe Fitting, and Unlaminated Profile Shape Manufacturing;
- Laminating plastics profile shapes, such as plate, sheet, and rod--are classified in Industry 326130, Laminated Plastics Plate, Sheet (except Packaging), and Shape Manufacturing;
- Manufacturing polystyrene foam products--are classified in Industry 326140, Polystyrene Foam Product Manufacturing;
- Manufacturing foam (except polystyrene) products--are classified in Industry 326150, Urethane and Other Foam Product (except Polystyrene) Manufacturing;
- Manufacturing plastics bottles--are classified in Industry 326160, Plastics Bottle Manufacturing;
- Manufacturing heavy-duty inflatable plastics boats--are classified in U.S. Industry 336612, Boat Building;
- Manufacturing plastics furniture parts and components--are classified in U.S. Industry 337215, Showcase, Partition, Shelving, and Locker Manufacturing;
- Manufacturing rubber floor mats and rubber treads--are classified in U.S. Industry 326299, All Other Rubber Product Manufacturing;
- Manufacturing plastics plumbing fixtures--are classified in U.S. Industry 326191, Plastics Plumbing Fixture Manufacturing; and
- Assembling plastics components into plumbing fixture fittings, such as faucets--are classified in U.S. Industry 332913, Plumbing Fixture Fitting and Trim Manufacturing.

3262 Rubber Product Manufacturing[T]

This industry group comprises establishments primarily engaged in processing natural, synthetic, or reclaimed rubber materials into intermediate or final products using processes, such as vulcanizing, cementing, molding, extruding, and lathe-cutting.

32621 Tire Manufacturing[T]

This industry comprises establishments primarily engaged in manufacturing tires and inner tubes from natural and synthetic rubber and retreading or rebuilding tires.

Cross-References. Establishments primarily engaged in--

- Repairing tires, such as plugging--are classified in Industry 81119, Other Automotive Repair and Maintenance; and
- Retailing tires--are classified in Industry 44132, Tire Dealers.

326211 Tire Manufacturing (except Retreading)

This U.S. industry comprises establishments primarily engaged in manufacturing tires and inner tubes from natural and synthetic rubber.

Cross-References.

Establishments primarily engaged in retreading or rebuilding tires are classified in U.S. Industry 326212, Tire Retreading.

T—Canadian, Mexican, and United States industries are comparable.

326212 Tire Retreading

This U.S. industry comprises establishments primarily engaged in retreading or rebuilding tires.

Cross-References. Establishments primarily engaged in--

- Repairing tires, such as plugging--are classified in U.S. Industry 811198, All Other Automotive Repair and Maintenance;
- Retailing tires--are classified in Industry 441320, Tire Dealers; and
- Manufacturing tires and inner tubes from natural and synthetic rubber--are classified in U.S. Industry 326211, Tire Manufacturing (except Retreading).

32622 Rubber and Plastics Hoses and Belting Manufacturing[T] See industry description for 326220.

326220 Rubber and Plastics Hoses and Belting Manufacturing

This industry comprises establishments primarily engaged in manufacturing rubber hose and/or plastics (reinforced) hose and belting from natural and synthetic rubber and/or plastics resins. Establishments manufacturing garden hoses from purchased hose are included in this industry.

Cross-References. Establishments primarily engaged in--

- Manufacturing rubber tubing--are classified in U.S. Industry 326299, All Other Rubber Product Manufacturing;
- Manufacturing plastics tubing--are classified in U.S. Industry 326121, Unlaminated Plastics Profile Shape Manufacturing;
- Manufacturing extruded, lathe-cut, or molded rubber goods (except tubing) for mechanical applications--are classified in U.S. Industry 326291, Rubber Product Manufacturing for Mechanical Use; and
- Manufacturing fluid power hose assemblies--are classified in U.S. Industry 332912, Fluid Power Valve and Hose Fitting Manufacturing.

32629 Other Rubber Product Manufacturing[T]

This industry comprises establishments primarily engaged in manufacturing rubber products (except tires, hoses, and belting) from natural and synthetic rubber.

Illustrative Examples:

Birth control devices (e.g., diaphragms, prophylactics) manufacturing
Latex foam rubber manufacturing
Mechanical rubber goods (i.e., molded, extruded, lathe-cut) manufacturing
Reclaiming rubber from waste and scrap
Rubber balloons manufacturing
Rubber bands manufacturing
Rubber floor mats (e.g., door, bath) manufacturing
Rubber hair care products (e.g., combs, curlers) manufacturing
Rubber tubing manufacturing

Cross-References. Establishments primarily engaged in--

- Manufacturing tires and inner tubes--are classified in Industry 32621, Tire Manufacturing;
- Manufacturing rubber hoses and belting--are classified in Industry 32622, Rubber and Plastics Hoses and Belting Manufacturing;
- Rubberizing fabric--are classified in Industry 31332, Fabric Coating Mills;
- Manufacturing rubber gaskets, packing, and sealing devices--are classified in Industry 33999, All Other Miscellaneous Manufacturing;

T—Canadian, Mexican, and United States industries are comparable.

- Manufacturing rubber gloves--are classified in Industry 33911, Medical Equipment and Supplies Manufacturing;
- Manufacturing rubber clothing accessories (e.g., bathing caps)--are classified in Industry 31599, Apparel Accessories and Other Apparel Manufacturing; and
- Manufacturing rubber toys--are classified in Industry 33993, Doll, Toy, and Game Manufacturing.

326291 Rubber Product Manufacturing for Mechanical Use

This U.S. industry comprises establishments primarily engaged in manufacturing rubber goods (except tubing) for mechanical applications, using the processes of molding, extruding or lathe-cutting. Products of this industry are generally parts for motor vehicles, machinery, and equipment.

Cross-References.

Establishments primarily engaged in manufacturing rubber tubing from natural and synthetic rubber or in manufacturing rubber products for mechanical applications using processes other than molding, extruding or lathe-cutting are classified in U.S. Industry 326299, All Other Rubber Product Manufacturing.

326299 All Other Rubber Product Manufacturing

This U.S. industry comprises establishments primarily engaged in manufacturing rubber products (except tires; hoses and belting; and molded, extruded, and lathe-cut rubber goods for mechanical applications (except rubber tubing)) from natural and synthetic rubber. Establishments manufacturing rubber tubing made from natural and synthetic rubber, regardless of process used, are included in this industry.

Illustrative Examples:

Birth control devices (i.e., diaphragms, prophylactics) manufacturing
Latex foam rubber manufacturing
Reclaiming rubber from waste and scrap
Rubber balloons manufacturing
Rubber bands manufacturing
Rubber floor mats (e.g., door, bath) manufacturing
Rubber hair care products (e.g., combs, curlers) manufacturing
Rubber tubing manufacturing

Cross-References. Establishments primarily engaged in--

- Manufacturing tires and inner tubes and rebuilding tires--are classified in Industry 32621, Tire Manufacturing;
- Manufacturing rubber hoses and belting--are classified in Industry 326220, Rubber and Plastics Hoses and Belting Manufacturing;
- Manufacturing heavy-duty inflatable rubber boats--are classified in U.S. Industry 336612, Boat Building;
- Molding, extruding, and lathe-cutting rubber to manufacture rubber goods (except tubing) for mechanical applications--are classified in U.S. Industry 326291, Rubber Product Manufacturing for Mechanical Use;
- Rubberizing fabrics--are classified in Industry 313320, Fabric Coating Mills;
- Manufacturing rubber gasket, packing, and sealing devices--are classified in U.S. Industry 339991, Gasket, Packing, and Sealing Device Manufacturing;
- Manufacturing rubber toys--are classified in Industry 339930, Doll, Toy, and Game Manufacturing;
- Manufacturing rubber gloves--are classified in U.S. Industry 339113, Surgical Appliance and Supplies Manufacturing; and
- Manufacturing rubber clothing accessories (e.g., bathing caps)--are classified in Industry 315990, Apparel Accessories and Other Apparel Manufacturing.

327 Nonmetallic Mineral Product Manufacturing[T]

The Nonmetallic Mineral Product Manufacturing subsector transforms mined or quarried nonmetallic minerals, such as sand, gravel, stone, clay, and refractory materials, into products for intermediate or final consumption.

Processes used include grinding, mixing, cutting, shaping, and honing. Heat often is used in the process and chemicals are frequently mixed to change the composition, purity, and chemical properties for the intended product. For example, glass is produced by heating silica sand to the melting point (sometimes combined with cullet or recycled glass) and then drawn, floated, or blow molded to the desired shape or thickness. Refractory materials are heated and then formed into bricks or other shapes for use in industrial applications.

The Nonmetallic Mineral Product Manufacturing subsector includes establishments that manufacture bricks, refractories, ceramic products, and glass and glass products, such as plate glass and containers. Also included are cement and concrete products, lime, gypsum and other nonmetallic mineral products including abrasive products, ceramic plumbing fixtures, statuary, cut stone products, and mineral wool. The products are used in a wide range of activities from construction and heavy and light manufacturing to articles for personal use.

Mining, beneficiating, and manufacturing activities often occur in a single location. Separate receipts will be collected for these activities whenever possible. When receipts cannot be broken out between mining and manufacturing, establishments that mine or quarry nonmetallic minerals, beneficiate the nonmetallic minerals, and further process the nonmetallic minerals into a more finished manufactured product are classified based on the primary activity of the establishment. A mine that manufactures a small amount of finished products is classified in Sector 21, Mining, Quarrying, and Oil and Gas Extraction. An establishment that mines whose primary output is a more finished manufactured product is classified in the Manufacturing sector.

Excluded from the Nonmetallic Mineral Product Manufacturing subsector are establishments that primarily beneficiate mined nonmetallic minerals. Beneficiation is the process whereby the extracted material is reduced to particles that can be separated into mineral and waste, the former suitable for further processing or direct use. Beneficiation establishments are included in Sector 21, Mining, Quarrying, and Oil and Gas Extraction.

3271 Clay Product and Refractory Manufacturing[T]

This industry group comprises establishments primarily engaged in (1) shaping, molding, glazing, and firing pottery, ceramics, and plumbing fixtures, and electrical supplies made entirely or partly of clay or other ceramic materials or (2) shaping, molding, baking, burning, or hardening clay refractories, nonclay refractories, ceramic tile, structural clay tile, brick, and other structural clay building materials.

32711 Pottery, Ceramics, and Plumbing Fixture Manufacturing[T] See industry description for 327110.

327110 Pottery, Ceramics, and Plumbing Fixture Manufacturing

This industry comprises establishments primarily engaged in shaping, molding, glazing, and firing pottery, ceramics, plumbing fixtures, and electrical supplies made entirely or partly of clay or other ceramic materials.

Illustrative Examples:

Bathroom accessories, vitreous china and earthenware, manufacturing
Ceramic or ferrite permanent magnets manufacturing
Chemical stoneware (i.e., pottery products) manufacturing
Clay and ceramic statuary manufacturing
Earthenware table and kitchen articles, coarse, manufacturing
Porcelain electrical insulators manufacturing
Vitreous china plumbing fixtures manufacturing

Cross-References. Establishments primarily engaged in--

- Manufacturing enameled iron and steel plumbing fixtures--are classified in U.S. Industry 332999, All Other Miscellaneous Fabricated Metal Product Manufacturing;
- Manufacturing metal bathroom accessories--are classified in Subsector 332, Fabricated Metal Product Manufacturing;
- Manufacturing cultured marble and other plastics plumbing fixtures--are classified in U.S. Industry 326191, Plastics Plumbing Fixture Manufacturing;
- Manufacturing clay building materials, such as ceramic tile, bricks, and clay roofing tiles, and refractories--are classified in Industry 327120, Clay Building Material and Refractories Manufacturing;

~~T—Canadian, Mexican, and United~~ States industries are comparable.

- Manufacturing ferrite microwave devices and electronic components--are classified in Subsector 334, Computer and Electronic Product Manufacturing; and
- Manufacturing plastics bathroom accessories--are classified in U.S. Industry 326199, All Other Plastics Product Manufacturing.

32712 Clay Building Material and Refractories Manufacturing[T] See industry description for 327120.

327120 Clay Building Material and Refractories Manufacturing

This industry comprises establishments primarily engaged in shaping, molding, baking, burning, or hardening clay refractories, nonclay refractories, ceramic tile, structural clay tile, brick, and other structural clay building materials. A refractory is a material that will retain its shape and chemical identity when subjected to high temperatures and is used in applications that require extreme resistance to heat, such as furnace linings.

Cross-References. Establishments primarily engaged in--

- Manufacturing resilient flooring and asphalt floor tiles--are classified in U.S. Industry 326199, All Other Plastics Product Manufacturing;
- Manufacturing concrete bricks--are classified in U.S. Industry 327331, Concrete Block and Brick Manufacturing; and
- Manufacturing glass bricks and blocks--are classified in Industry 32721, Glass and Glass Product Manufacturing.

3272 Glass and Glass Product Manufacturing[T]

32721 Glass and Glass Product Manufacturing[T]

This industry comprises establishments primarily engaged in manufacturing glass and/or glass products. Establishments in this industry may manufacture glass and/or glass products by melting silica sand or cullet, or from purchased glass.

Cross-References. Establishments primarily engaged in--

- Manufacturing glass wool (i.e., fiberglass) insulation products--are classified in Industry 32799, All Other Nonmetallic Mineral Product Manufacturing;
- Manufacturing optical lenses (except ophthalmic), such as magnifying, photographic, and projection lenses--are classified in Industry 33331, Commercial and Service Industry Machinery Manufacturing;
- Grinding ophthalmic (i.e., eyeglass) lenses for the trade--are classified in Industry 33911, Medical Equipment and Supplies Manufacturing; and
- Manufacturing fiber optic cable from purchased fiber optic strand--are classified in Industry 33592, Communication and Energy Wire and Cable Manufacturing.

327211 Flat Glass Manufacturing

This U.S. industry comprises establishments primarily engaged in (1) manufacturing flat glass by melting silica sand or cullet or (2) manufacturing both flat glass and laminated glass by melting silica sand or cullet.

Cross-References.

Establishments primarily engaged in manufacturing laminated glass from purchased flat glass are classified in U.S. Industry 327215, Glass Product Manufacturing Made of Purchased Glass.

T—Canadian, Mexican, and United States industries are comparable.

327212 Other Pressed and Blown Glass and Glassware Manufacturing

This U.S. industry comprises establishments primarily engaged in manufacturing glass by melting silica sand or cullet and making pressed, blown, or shaped glass or glassware (except glass packaging containers).

Cross-References. Establishments primarily engaged in--

- Manufacturing flat glass--are classified in U.S. Industry 327211, Flat Glass Manufacturing;
- Manufacturing glass packaging containers in glassmaking operations--are classified in U.S. Industry 327213, Glass Container Manufacturing;
- Manufacturing glass wool (i.e., fiberglass) insulation--are classified in U.S. Industry 327993, Mineral Wool Manufacturing;
- Manufacturing glassware from purchased glass--are classified in U.S. Industry 327215, Glass Product Manufacturing Made of Purchased Glass; and
- Manufacturing fiber optic cable from purchased fiber optic strand--are classified in U.S. Industry 335921, Fiber Optic Cable Manufacturing.

327213 Glass Container Manufacturing

This U.S. industry comprises establishments primarily engaged in manufacturing glass packaging containers.

327215 Glass Product Manufacturing Made of Purchased Glass

This U.S. industry comprises establishments primarily engaged in coating, laminating, tempering, or shaping purchased glass.

Cross-References. Establishments primarily engaged in--

- Manufacturing optical lenses (except ophthalmic), such as magnifying, photographic, and projection lenses--are classified in U.S. Industry 333314, Optical Instrument and Lens Manufacturing;
- Manufacturing ophthalmic (i.e., eyeglass) lenses--are classified in U.S. Industry 339115, Ophthalmic Goods Manufacturing; and
- Manufacturing fiber optic cable from purchased fiber optic strand--are classified in U.S. Industry 335921, Fiber Optic Cable Manufacturing.

3273 Cement and Concrete Product Manufacturing[T]

This industry group comprises establishments primarily engaged in one of the following: (1) manufacturing portland, natural, masonry, pozzolanic, and other hydraulic cements; (2) acting as batch or mixing plants, manufacturing concrete delivered to a purchaser in a plastic and unhardened state; (3) manufacturing concrete pipe, brick, and block; or (4) manufacturing other concrete products (except block, brick, and pipe).

32731 Cement Manufacturing[T] See industry description for 327310.

327310 Cement Manufacturing

This industry comprises establishments primarily engaged in manufacturing portland, natural, masonry, pozzolanic, and other hydraulic cements. Cement manufacturing establishments may calcine earths or mine, quarry, manufacture, or purchase lime.

Cross-References. Establishments primarily engaged in--

- Mining or quarrying limestone--are classified in U.S. Industry 212312, Crushed and Broken Limestone Mining and Quarrying;

T—Canadian, Mexican, and United States industries are comparable.

- Manufacturing lime--are classified in Industry 327410, Lime Manufacturing;
- Manufacturing ready-mix concrete--are classified in Industry 327320, Ready-Mix Concrete Manufacturing; and
- Manufacturing dry mix concrete--are classified in U.S. Industry 327999, All Other Miscellaneous Nonmetallic Mineral Product Manufacturing.

32732 Ready-Mix Concrete Manufacturing[T] See industry description for 327320.

327320 Ready-Mix Concrete Manufacturing

This industry comprises establishments, such as batch plants or mix plants, primarily engaged in manufacturing concrete delivered to a purchaser in a plastic and unhardened state. Ready-mix concrete manufacturing establishments may mine, quarry, or purchase sand and gravel.

Cross-References. Establishments primarily engaged in--

- Operating sand or gravel pits--are classified in U.S. Industry 212321, Construction Sand and Gravel Mining; and
- Manufacturing dry mix concrete--are classified in U.S. Industry 327999, All Other Miscellaneous Nonmetallic Mineral Product Manufacturing.

32733 Concrete Pipe, Brick, and Block Manufacturing[T]

This industry comprises establishments primarily engaged in manufacturing concrete pipe, brick, and block.

Cross-References.

Establishments primarily engaged in manufacturing concrete products (except block, brick, and pipe) are classified in Industry 32739, Other Concrete Product Manufacturing.

327331 Concrete Block and Brick Manufacturing

This U.S. industry comprises establishments primarily engaged in manufacturing concrete block and brick.

327332 Concrete Pipe Manufacturing

This U.S. industry comprises establishments primarily engaged in manufacturing concrete pipe.

32739 Other Concrete Product Manufacturing[T] See industry description for 327390.

327390 Other Concrete Product Manufacturing

This industry comprises establishments primarily engaged in manufacturing concrete products (except block, brick, and pipe).

Cross-References. Establishments primarily engaged in--

- Manufacturing concrete block and brick--are classified in U.S. Industry 327331, Concrete Block and Brick Manufacturing; and
- Manufacturing concrete pipe--are classified in U.S. Industry 327332, Concrete Pipe Manufacturing.

T—Canadian, Mexican, and United States industries are comparable.

3274 Lime and Gypsum Product Manufacturing[T]

This industry group comprises establishments primarily engaged in (1) manufacturing lime from calcitic limestone, dolomitic limestone, or other calcareous materials or (2) manufacturing gypsum products.

32741 Lime Manufacturing[T] See industry description for 327410.

327410 Lime Manufacturing

This industry comprises establishments primarily engaged in manufacturing lime from calcitic limestone, dolomitic limestone, or other calcareous materials, such as coral, chalk, and shells. Lime manufacturing establishments may mine, quarry, collect, or purchase the sources of calcium carbonate.

Cross-References.

Establishments primarily engaged in manufacturing dolomite refractories are classified in Industry 327120, Clay Building Material and Refractories Manufacturing.

32742 Gypsum Product Manufacturing[T] See industry description for 327420.

327420 Gypsum Product Manufacturing

This industry comprises establishments primarily engaged in manufacturing gypsum products, such as wallboard, plaster, plasterboard, molding, ornamental moldings, statuary, and architectural plaster work. Gypsum product manufacturing establishments may mine, quarry, or purchase gypsum.

Cross-References.

Establishments primarily engaged in operating gypsum mines or quarries are classified in U.S. Industry 212399, All Other Nonmetallic Mineral Mining.

3279 Other Nonmetallic Mineral Product Manufacturing[T]

This industry group comprises establishments manufacturing nonmetallic mineral products (except clay products, refractory products, glass products, cement and concrete products, lime, and gypsum products).

32791 Abrasive Product Manufacturing[T] See industry description for 327910.

327910 Abrasive Product Manufacturing

This industry comprises establishments primarily engaged in manufacturing abrasive grinding wheels of natural or synthetic materials, abrasive-coated products, and other abrasive products.

Illustrative Examples:

Aluminum oxide (fused) abrasives manufacturing
Buffing and polishing wheels, abrasive and nonabrasive, manufacturing
Diamond dressing wheels manufacturing
Sandpaper manufacturing
Silicon carbide abrasives manufacturing
Whetstones manufacturing

T—Canadian, Mexican, and United States industries are comparable.

Cross-References. Establishments primarily engaged in--

- Mining and cutting grindstones, pulpstones, and whetstones--are classified in U.S. Industry 212399, All Other Nonmetallic Mineral Mining;
- Manufacturing plastic scouring pads--are classified in U.S. Industry 326199, All Other Plastics Product Manufacturing; and
- Manufacturing metallic scouring pads and steel wool--are classified in U.S. Industry 332999, All Other Miscellaneous Fabricated Metal Product Manufacturing.

32799 All Other Nonmetallic Mineral Product Manufacturing[T]

This industry comprises establishments primarily engaged in manufacturing nonmetallic mineral products (except pottery and plumbing fixtures; clay building materials and refractories; glass and glass products; cement; ready-mix concrete; concrete products; lime; gypsum products; and abrasive products).

Cross-References. Establishments primarily engaged in--

- Manufacturing pottery, ceramics, and plumbing fixtures--are classified in Industry 32711, Pottery, Ceramics, and Plumbing Fixture Manufacturing;
- Mining or quarrying stone, earth, or other nonmetallic minerals--are classified in Industry Group 2123, Nonmetallic Mineral Mining and Quarrying;
- Buying and selling semi-finished monuments and tombstones with no work other than polishing, lettering, or shaping to custom order--are classified in Sector 42, Wholesale Trade, or Sector 44-45, Retail Trade;
- Manufacturing clay building materials and refractories--are classified in Industry 32712, Clay Building Material and Refractories Manufacturing;
- Manufacturing glass and glass products--are classified in Industry 32721, Glass and Glass Product Manufacturing;
- Manufacturing cement--are classified in Industry 32731, Cement Manufacturing;
- Mixing and delivering ready-mix concrete--are classified in Industry 32732, Ready-Mix Concrete Manufacturing;
- Manufacturing concrete pipe, brick, and block--are classified in Industry 32733, Concrete Pipe, Brick, and Block Manufacturing;
- Manufacturing concrete products (except pipe, brick, and block)--are classified in Industry 32739, Other Concrete Product Manufacturing;
- Manufacturing lime--are classified in Industry 32741, Lime Manufacturing;
- Manufacturing gypsum products--are classified in Industry 32742, Gypsum Product Manufacturing;
- Manufacturing abrasive products--are classified in Industry 32791, Abrasive Product Manufacturing; and
- Manufacturing metallic scouring pads and steel wool--are classified in Industry 33299, All Other Fabricated Metal Product Manufacturing.

327991 Cut Stone and Stone Product Manufacturing

This U.S. industry comprises establishments primarily engaged in cutting, shaping, and finishing granite, marble, limestone, slate, and other stone for building and miscellaneous uses. Stone product manufacturing establishments may mine, quarry, or purchase stone.

Cross-References. Establishments primarily engaged in--

- Mining or quarrying stone--are classified in Industry Group 2123, Nonmetallic Mineral Mining and Quarrying; and
- Buying and selling semi-finished monuments and tombstones with no work other than polishing, lettering, or shaping to custom order--are classified in Sector 42, Wholesale Trade, or Sector 44-45, Retail Trade.

T—Canadian, Mexican, and United States industries are comparable.

327992 Ground or Treated Mineral and Earth Manufacturing

This U.S. industry comprises establishments primarily engaged in calcining, dead burning, or otherwise processing beyond beneficiation, clays, ceramic and refractory minerals, barite, and miscellaneous nonmetallic minerals.

Cross-References.

Establishments primarily engaged in crushing, grinding, pulverizing, washing, screening, sizing, or otherwise beneficiating mined clays, ceramics and refractory, and other miscellaneous nonmetallic minerals are classified in Industry Group 2123, Nonmetallic Mineral Mining and Quarrying.

327993 Mineral Wool Manufacturing

This U.S. industry comprises establishments primarily engaged in manufacturing mineral wool and mineral wool (i.e., fiberglass) insulation products made of such siliceous materials as rock, slag, and glass or combinations thereof.

Cross-References.

Establishments primarily engaged in manufacturing metallic scouring pads and steel wool are classified in U.S. Industry 332999, All Other Miscellaneous Fabricated Metal Product Manufacturing.

327999 All Other Miscellaneous Nonmetallic Mineral Product Manufacturing

This U.S. industry comprises establishments primarily engaged in manufacturing nonmetallic mineral products (except pottery, ceramics, and plumbing fixtures; clay building materials and refractories; glass and glass products; cement; ready-mix concrete; concrete products; lime; gypsum products; abrasive products; cut stone and stone products; ground and treated minerals and earth; and mineral wool).

Illustrative Examples:

Dry mix concrete manufacturing
Mica products manufacturing
Manmade and engineered proppants (e.g., resin-coated sand, ceramic materials) manufacturing
Stucco and stucco products manufacturing
Synthetic stones, for gem stones and industrial use, manufac-

Cross-References. Establishments primarily engaged in--

- Manufacturing pottery, ceramics, and plumbing fixtures--are classified in Industry 327110, Pottery, Ceramics, and Plumbing Fixture Manufacturing;
- Manufacturing clay building materials and refractories--are classified in Industry 327120, Clay Building Material and Refractories Manufacturing;
- Manufacturing glass and glass products--are classified in Industry 32721, Glass and Glass Product Manufacturing;
- Manufacturing cement--are classified in Industry 327310, Cement Manufacturing;
- Mixing and delivering ready-mix concrete--are classified in Industry 327320, Ready-Mix Concrete Manufacturing;
- Manufacturing concrete pipe, brick, and block--are classified in Industry 32733, Concrete Pipe, Brick, and Block Manufacturing;
- Manufacturing concrete products (except pipe, brick, and block)--are classified in Industry 327390, Other Concrete Product Manufacturing;
- Manufacturing lime--are classified in Industry 327410, Lime Manufacturing;
- Manufacturing gypsum products--are classified in Industry 327420, Gypsum Product Manufacturing;
- Manufacturing abrasives and abrasive products--are classified in Industry 327910, Abrasive Product Manufacturing;

T—Canadian, Mexican, and United States industries are comparable.

- Manufacturing cut stone and stone products--are classified in U.S. Industry 327991, Cut Stone and Stone Product Manufacturing;
- Manufacturing ground and treated minerals and earth (i.e., not at the mine site)--are classified in U.S. Industry 327992, Ground or Treated Mineral and Earth Manufacturing; and
- Manufacturing mineral wool and fiberglass insulation products--are classified in U.S. Industry 327993, Mineral Wool Manufacturing.

331 Primary Metal Manufacturing[T]

Industries in the Primary Metal Manufacturing subsector smelt and/or refine ferrous and nonferrous metals from ore, pig or scrap, using electrometallurgical and other process metallurgical techniques. Establishments in this subsector also manufacture metal alloys and superalloys by introducing other chemical elements to pure metals. The output of smelting and refining, usually in ingot form, is used in rolling, drawing, and extruding operations to make sheet, strip, bar, rod, or wire, and in molten form to make castings and other basic metal products.

Primary manufacturing of ferrous and nonferrous metals begins with ore or concentrate as the primary input. Establishments manufacturing primary metals from ore and/or concentrate remain classified in the primary smelting, primary refining, or iron and steel mill industries regardless of the form of their output. Establishments primarily engaged in secondary smelting and/or secondary refining recover ferrous and nonferrous metals from scrap and/or dross. The output of the secondary smelting and/or secondary refining industries is limited to shapes such as ingot or billet that will be further processed. Recovery of metals from scrap often occurs in establishments that are primarily engaged in activities, such as rolling, drawing, extruding, or similar processes.

Excluded from the Primary Metal Manufacturing subsector are establishments primarily engaged in manufacturing ferrous and nonferrous forgings (except ferrous forgings made in steel mills) and stampings. Although forging, stamping, and casting are all methods used to make metal shapes, forging and stamping do not use molten metals and are included in Subsector 332, Fabricated Metal Product Manufacturing. Establishments primarily engaged in operating coke ovens are classified in Industry 32419, Other Petroleum and Coal Products Manufacturing.

3311 Iron and Steel Mills and Ferroalloy Manufacturing[T]

33111 Iron and Steel Mills and Ferroalloy Manufacturing[T]

See industry description for 331110.

331110 Iron and Steel Mills and Ferroalloy Manufacturing

This industry comprises establishments primarily engaged in one or more of the following: (1) direct reduction of iron ore; (2) manufacturing pig iron in molten or solid form; (3) converting pig iron into steel; (4) making steel; (5) making steel and manufacturing shapes (e.g., bar, plate, rod, sheet, strip, wire); (6) making steel and forming pipe and tube; and (7) manufacturing electrometallurgical ferroalloys. Ferroalloys add critical elements, such as silicon and manganese for carbon steel and chromium, vanadium, tungsten, titanium, and molybdenum for low- and high-alloy metals. Ferroalloys include iron-rich alloys and more pure forms of elements added during the steel manufacturing process that alter or improve the characteristics of the metal.

Cross-References. Establishments primarily engaged in--

- Operating coke ovens--are classified in U.S. Industry 324199, All Other Petroleum and Coal Products Manufacturing;
- Manufacturing nonferrous superalloys, such as cobalt or nickel-based superalloys--are classified in U.S. Industry 331492, Secondary Smelting, Refining, and Alloying of Nonferrous Metal (except Copper and Aluminum);
- Manufacturing concrete reinforcing bar by rolling and drawing steel from purchased steel--are classified in U.S. Industry 331221, Rolled Steel Shape Manufacturing; and
- Manufacturing fabricated structural metal products from concrete reinforcing bars and fabricated bar joists--are classified in U.S. Industry 332312, Fabricated Structural Metal Manufacturing.

T—Canadian, Mexican, and United States industries are comparable.

3312 Steel Product Manufacturing from Purchased Steel[T]

This industry group comprises establishments primarily engaged in manufacturing iron and steel tube and pipe, drawing steel wire, and rolling or drawing shapes from purchased iron or steel.

33121 Iron and Steel Pipe and Tube Manufacturing from Purchased Steel[T] See industry description for 331210.

331210 Iron and Steel Pipe and Tube Manufacturing from Purchased Steel

This industry comprises establishments primarily engaged in manufacturing welded, riveted, or seamless pipe and tube from purchased iron or steel.

Cross-References.

Establishments primarily engaged in making steel and further processing the steel into steel pipe and tube are classified in Industry 331110, Iron and Steel Mills and Ferroalloy Manufacturing.

33122 Rolling and Drawing of Purchased Steel[T]

This industry comprises establishments primarily engaged in rolling and/or drawing steel shapes, such as plate, sheet, strip, rod, and bar, from purchased steel.

Cross-References. Establishments primarily engaged in--

- Making steel and rolling and/or drawing steel--are classified in Industry 33111, Iron and Steel Mills and Ferroalloy Manufacturing; and
- Manufacturing wire products from purchased wire--are classified in Industry 33261, Spring and Wire Product Manufacturing.

331221 Rolled Steel Shape Manufacturing

This U.S. industry comprises establishments primarily engaged in rolling or drawing shapes (except wire), such as plate, sheet, strip, rod, and bar, from purchased steel.

Cross-References. Establishments primarily engaged in--

- Making steel and rolling or drawing steel shapes, or manufacturing concrete reinforcing bars in an iron and steel mill--are classified in Industry 331110, Iron and Steel Mills and Ferroalloy Manufacturing;
- Drawing wire from purchased steel--are classified in U.S. Industry 331222, Steel Wire Drawing; and
- Manufacturing fabricated structural metal products from concrete reinforcing bars and fabricated bar joists--are classified in U.S. Industry 332312, Fabricated Structural Metal Manufacturing.

331222 Steel Wire Drawing

This U.S. industry comprises establishments primarily engaged in drawing wire from purchased steel.

Cross-References. Establishments primarily engaged in--

- Making steel and drawing steel wire--are classified in Industry 331110, Iron and Steel Mills and Ferroalloy Manufacturing; and
- Manufacturing wire products, such as nails, spikes, and paper clips, from purchased steel wire--are classified in Industry 33261, Spring and Wire Product Manufacturing.

T—Canadian, Mexican, and United States industries are comparable.

3313 Alumina and Aluminum Production and Processing[T]

33131 Alumina and Aluminum Production and Processing[T]

This industry comprises establishments primarily engaged in one or more of the following: (1) refining alumina; (2) making (i.e., the primary production) aluminum from alumina; (3) recovering aluminum from scrap or dross; (4) alloying purchased aluminum; and (5) manufacturing aluminum primary forms (e.g., bar, foil, pipe, plate, rod, sheet, tube, wire).

Cross-References. Establishments primarily engaged in--

- Manufacturing aluminum oxide abrasives and refractories--are classified in Subsector 327, Nonmetallic Mineral Product Manufacturing;
- Sorting, breaking up, and wholesaling scrap aluminum metal without also smelting or refining--are classified in Industry 42393, Recyclable Material Merchant Wholesalers; and
- Operating facilities where commingled recyclable materials, such as paper, plastics, used beverage cans, and metals, are sorted into distinct categories without also smelting or refining--are classified in Industry 56292, Materials Recovery Facilities.

331313 Alumina Refining and Primary Aluminum Production

This U.S. industry comprises establishments primarily engaged in one or more of the following: (1) refining alumina (i.e., aluminum oxide) generally from bauxite; (2) making aluminum from alumina; and/or (3) making aluminum from alumina and rolling, drawing, extruding, or casting the aluminum they make into primary forms. Establishments in this industry may make primary aluminum or aluminum-based alloys from alumina.

Cross-references. Establishments primarily engaged in--

- Manufacturing aluminum oxide abrasives and refractories--are classified in Subsector 327, Nonmetallic Mineral Product Manufacturing; and
- Recovering aluminum from scrap or alloying purchased aluminum--are classified in U.S. Industry 331314, Secondary Smelting and Alloying of Aluminum.

331314 Secondary Smelting and Alloying of Aluminum

This U.S. industry comprises establishments primarily engaged in (1) recovering aluminum and aluminum alloys from scrap and/or dross (i.e., secondary smelting) and making billet or ingot (except by rolling) and/or (2) manufacturing alloys, powder, paste, or flake from purchased aluminum.

Cross-References. Establishments primarily engaged in--

- Refining alumina or making aluminum and/or aluminum alloys from alumina--are classified in U.S. Industry 331313, Alumina Refining and Primary Aluminum Production;
- Manufacturing aluminum sheet, plate, and foil from purchased aluminum or by recovering aluminum from scrap and flat rolling or continuous casting--are classified in U.S. Industry 331315, Aluminum Sheet, Plate, and Foil Manufacturing;
- Manufacturing aluminum extruded products or rolled ingot or billet from purchased aluminum or by recovering aluminum from scrap and extruding, rolling, or drawing--are classified in U.S. Industry 331318, Other Aluminum Rolling, Drawing, and Extruding;
- Sorting, breaking up, and wholesaling scrap metal without also smelting or refining--are classified in Industry 423930, Recyclable Material Merchant Wholesalers; and
- Operating facilities where commingled recyclable materials, such as paper, plastics, used beverage cans, and metals, are sorted into distinct categories without also smelting or refining--are classified in Industry 562920, Materials Recovery Facilities.

T—Canadian, Mexican, and United States industries are comparable.

331315 Aluminum Sheet, Plate, and Foil Manufacturing

This U.S. industry comprises establishments primarily engaged in (1) flat rolling or continuous casting sheet, plate, foil and welded tube from purchased aluminum and/or (2) recovering aluminum from scrap and flat rolling or continuous casting sheet, plate, foil, and welded tube in integrated mills.

Cross-References.

Establishments primarily engaged in making aluminum from alumina and flat rolling or continuous casting aluminum sheet, plate, foil, and welded tube are classified in U.S. Industry 331313, Alumina Refining and Primary Aluminum Production.

331318 Other Aluminum Rolling, Drawing, and Extruding

This U.S. industry comprises establishments primarily engaged in (1) rolling, drawing, or extruding shapes (except flat rolled sheet, plate, foil, and welded tube) from purchased aluminum and/or (2) recovering aluminum from scrap and rolling, drawing, or extruding shapes (except flat rolled sheet, plate, foil, and welded tube) in integrated mills.

Illustrative Examples:

Aluminum bar made by extruding purchased aluminum
Nails, aluminum, made in wire drawing plants
Rod made by extruding purchased aluminum
Wire, bare, made in aluminum wire drawing plants
Structural shapes made by rolling purchased aluminum
Tube made by drawing or extruding purchased aluminum

Cross-References. Establishments primarily engaged in--

- Flat rolling sheet, plate, foil, and welded tube from either purchased aluminum or by recovering aluminum from scrap and flat rolling or continuous casting--are classified in U.S. Industry 331315, Aluminum Sheet, Plate, and Foil Manufacturing; and
- Making aluminum from alumina and making aluminum shapes--are classified in U.S. Industry 331313, Alumina Refining and Primary Aluminum Production.

3314 Nonferrous Metal (except Aluminum) Production and Processing[T]

This industry group comprises establishments primarily engaged in nonferrous metal (except aluminum) smelting, refining, rolling, drawing, extruding, and alloying.

33141 Nonferrous Metal (except Aluminum) Smelting and Refining[T] See industry description for 331410.

331410 Nonferrous Metal (except Aluminum) Smelting and Refining

This industry comprises establishments primarily engaged in (1) smelting ores into nonferrous metals and/or (2) the primary refining of nonferrous metals (except aluminum) by electrolytic methods or other processes.

Cross-References. Establishments primarily engaged in--

- Mining and making copper and other nonferrous concentrates (including gold and silver bullion), by processes, such as solvent extraction or electrowinning--are classified in Industry Group 2122, Metal Ore Mining;
- Recovering copper or copper alloys from scrap or dross and/or alloying, rolling, drawing, and extruding purchased copper--are classified in Industry 331420, Copper Rolling, Drawing, Extruding, and Alloying;

T—Canadian, Mexican, and United States industries are comparable.

- Rolling, drawing, and/or extruding nonferrous metal shapes (except copper and aluminum) from purchased nonferrous metals (except copper and aluminum) or by recovering nonferrous metals (except copper and aluminum) and rolling, drawing, or extruding--are classified in U.S. Industry 331491, Nonferrous Metal (except Copper and Aluminum) Rolling, Drawing, and Extruding;
- Recovering nonferrous metals (except copper and aluminum) from scrap and making primary forms and/or alloying purchased nonferrous metals (except copper and aluminum)--are classified in U.S. Industry 331492, Secondary Smelting, Refining, and Alloying of Nonferrous Metal (except Copper and Aluminum);
- Making aluminum from alumina--are classified in U.S. Industry 331313, Alumina Refining and Primary Aluminum Production;
- Operating facilities where commingled recyclable materials, such as paper, plastics, used beverage cans, and metals, are sorted into distinct categories without also smelting or refining--are classified in Industry 562920, Materials Recovery Facilities; and
- Sorting, breaking up, and wholesaling scrap metal without also smelting or refining--are classified in Industry 423930, Recyclable Material Merchant Wholesalers.

33142 Copper Rolling, Drawing, Extruding, and Alloying[T] See industry description for 331420.

331420 Copper Rolling, Drawing, Extruding, and Alloying

This industry comprises establishments primarily engaged in one or more of the following: (1) recovering copper or copper alloys from scraps; (2) alloying purchased copper; (3) rolling, drawing, or extruding shapes (e.g., bar, plate, sheet, strip, tube, wire) from purchased copper; and (4) recovering copper or copper alloys from scrap and rolling, drawing, or extruding shapes (e.g., bar, plate, sheet, strip, tube, wire).

Cross-References. Establishments primarily engaged in--

- Smelting copper ore, primary copper refining, and/or rolling, drawing, or extruding primary copper made in the same establishment--are classified in Industry 331410, Nonferrous Metal (except Aluminum) Smelting and Refining;
- Manufacturing wire products from purchased copper wire--are classified in Industry 33261, Spring and Wire Product Manufacturing;
- Die-casting purchased copper--are classified in U.S. Industry 331523, Nonferrous Metal Die-Casting Foundries;
- Rolling, drawing, or extruding shapes from purchased nonferrous metals (except copper and aluminum) or recovering nonferrous metals (except copper and aluminum) from scrap and rolling, drawing, or extruding--are classified in U.S. Industry 331491, Nonferrous Metal (except Copper and Aluminum) Rolling, Drawing, and Extruding;
- Recovering nonferrous metals (except copper, aluminum) from scrap and making primary forms and/or alloying purchased nonferrous metals (except copper and aluminum)--are classified in U.S. Industry 331492, Secondary Smelting, Refining, and Alloying of Nonferrous Metal (except Copper and Aluminum);
- Insulating purchased copper wire--are classified in U.S. Industry 335929, Other Communication and Energy Wire Manufacturing;
- Operating facilities where commingled recyclable materials, such as paper, plastics, used beverage cans, and metals, are sorted into distinct categories without also smelting or refining--are classified in Industry 562920, Materials Recovery Facilities; and
- Sorting, breaking up, and wholesaling scrap metal without also smelting or refining--are classified in Industry 423930, Recyclable Material Merchant Wholesalers.

33149 Nonferrous Metal (except Copper and Aluminum) Rolling, Drawing, Extruding, and Alloying[T]

This industry comprises establishments primarily engaged in one or more of the following: (1) recovering nonferrous metals (except copper and aluminum) and nonferrous metal alloys from scrap; (2) alloying purchased nonferrous metals (except copper and aluminum); (3) rolling, drawing, and extruding shapes from purchased

T—Canadian, Mexican, and United States industries are comparable.

nonferrous metals (except copper and aluminum); and (4) recovering nonferrous metals from scrap (except copper and aluminum) and rolling, drawing, or extruding shapes in integrated facilities.

Cross-References. Establishments primarily engaged in--

- Rolling, drawing, and/or extruding aluminum or secondary smelting and alloying of aluminum--are classified in Industry 33131, Alumina and Aluminum Production and Processing;
- Recovering copper and copper alloys from scrap, alloying purchased copper, rolling, drawing, or extruding shapes from purchased copper, and recovering copper or copper alloys from scrap and rolling, drawing, or extruding shapes in integrated mills--are classified in Industry 33142, Copper Rolling, Drawing, Extruding, and Alloying;
- Insulating purchased nonferrous wire--are classified in Industry 33592, Communication and Energy Wire and Cable Manufacturing;
- Making primary nonferrous metals and rolling, drawing, or extruding nonferrous metal shapes--are classified in Industry 33141, Nonferrous Metal (except Aluminum) Smelting and Refining;
- Manufacturing products from purchased wire--are classified in Industry 33261, Spring and Wire Product Manufacturing;
- Sorting, breaking up, and wholesaling scrap metal without also smelting or refining--are classified in Industry 42393, Recyclable Material Merchant Wholesalers; and
- Operating facilities where commingled recyclable materials, such as paper, plastics, used beverage cans, and metals, are sorted into distinct categories without also smelting or refining--are classified in Industry 56292, Materials Recovery Facilities.

331491 Nonferrous Metal (except Copper and Aluminum) Rolling, Drawing, and Extruding

This U.S. industry comprises establishments primarily engaged in (1) rolling, drawing, or extruding shapes (e.g., bar, plate, sheet, strip, tube) from purchased nonferrous metals and/or (2) recovering nonferrous metals from scrap and rolling, drawing, and/or extruding shapes (e.g., bar, plate, sheet, strip, tube) in integrated mills.

Cross-References. Establishments primarily engaged in--

- Rolling, drawing, and/or extruding shapes from purchased copper or recovering copper from scrap and rolling, drawing, or extruding shapes--are classified in Industry 331420, Copper Rolling, Drawing, Extruding, and Alloying;
- Recovering nonferrous metals (except copper and aluminum) from scrap and making primary forms and/or alloying purchased nonferrous metals--are classified in U.S. Industry 331492, Secondary Smelting, Refining, and Alloying of Nonferrous Metal (except Copper and Aluminum);
- Rolling, drawing, and/or extruding aluminum--are classified in Industry 33131, Alumina and Aluminum Production and Processing;
- Making primary nonferrous metals and rolling, drawing, or extruding nonferrous metal shapes--are classified in Industry 331410, Nonferrous Metal (except Aluminum) Smelting and Refining; and
- Insulating purchased nonferrous wire--are classified in U.S. Industry 335929, Other Communication and Energy Wire Manufacturing.

331492 Secondary Smelting, Refining, and Alloying of Nonferrous Metal (except Copper and Aluminum)

This U.S. industry comprises establishments primarily engaged in (1) alloying purchased nonferrous metals and/or (2) recovering nonferrous metals from scrap. Establishments in this industry make primary forms (e.g., bar, billet, bloom, cake, ingot, slab, slug, wire) using smelting or refining processes.

Cross-References. Establishments primarily engaged in--

- Recovering aluminum and aluminum alloys from scrap and/or alloying purchased aluminum--are classified in U.S. Industry 331314, Secondary Smelting and Alloying of Aluminum;

T—Canadian, Mexican, and United States industries are comparable.

- Sorting, breaking up, and wholesaling scrap metal without also smelting or refining--are classified in Industry 423930, Recyclable Material Merchant Wholesalers;
- Recovering nonferrous metals from scrap and rolling, drawing, or extruding shapes in integrated facilities--are classified in U.S. Industry 331491, Nonferrous Metal (except Copper and Aluminum) Rolling, Drawing, and Extruding;
- Operating facilities where commingled recyclable materials, such as paper, plastics, used beverage cans, and metals, are sorted into distinct categories without also smelting or refining--are classified in Industry 562920, Materials Recovery Facilities; and
- Recovering copper and copper alloys from scrap and making primary forms, and/or alloying purchased copper--are classified in Industry 331420, Copper Rolling, Drawing, Extruding, and Alloying.

3315 Foundries[T]

This industry group comprises establishments primarily engaged in pouring molten metal into molds or dies to form castings. Establishments making castings and further manufacturing, such as machining or assembling, a specific manufactured product are classified in the industry of the finished product. Foundries may perform operations, such as cleaning and deburring, on the castings they manufacture. More involved processes, such as tapping, threading, milling, or machining to tight tolerances, that transform castings into more finished products are classified elsewhere in the Manufacturing sector based on the product made.

Establishments in this industry group make castings from purchased metals or in integrated secondary smelting and casting facilities. When the production of primary metals is combined with making castings, the establishment is classified in Subsector 331, Primary Metal Manufacturing, with the primary metal made.

33151 Ferrous Metal Foundries[T]

This industry comprises establishments primarily engaged in pouring molten iron and steel into molds of a desired shape to make castings. Establishments in this industry purchase iron and steel made in other establishments.

Cross-References.

Establishments primarily engaged in manufacturing iron or steel castings and further manufacturing them into finished products are classified based on the specific finished product.

331511 Iron Foundries

This U.S. industry comprises establishments primarily engaged in pouring molten pig iron or iron alloys into molds to manufacture castings (e.g., cast iron manhole covers, cast iron pipe, cast iron skillets). Establishments in this industry purchase iron made in other establishments.

Cross-References.

Establishments primarily engaged in manufacturing iron castings and further manufacturing them into finished products are classified based on the specific finished product.

331512 Steel Investment Foundries

This U.S. industry comprises establishments primarily engaged in manufacturing steel investment castings. Investment molds are formed by covering a wax shape with a refractory slurry. After the refractory slurry hardens, the wax is melted, leaving a seamless mold. Investment molds provide highly detailed, consistent castings. Establishments in this industry purchase steel made in other establishments.

Cross-References. Establishments primarily engaged in--

- Manufacturing steel castings (except steel investment castings)--are classified in U.S. Industry 331513, Steel Foundries (except Investment); and

---

T—Canadian, Mexican, and United States industries are comparable.

- Manufacturing steel investment castings and further manufacturing them into finished products--are classified based on the specific finished product.

331513 Steel Foundries (except Investment)

This U.S. industry comprises establishments primarily engaged in manufacturing steel castings (except steel investment castings). Establishments in this industry purchase steel made in other establishments.

Cross-References. Establishments primarily engaged in--

- Manufacturing steel investment castings--are classified in U.S. Industry 331512, Steel Investment Foundries; and
- Manufacturing steel castings and further manufacturing them into finished products--are classified based on the specific finished product.

33152 Nonferrous Metal Foundries[T]

This industry comprises establishments primarily engaged in pouring and/or introducing molten nonferrous metal, under high pressure, into metal molds or dies to manufacture castings. Establishments in this industry purchase nonferrous metals made in other establishments.

Cross-References. Establishments primarily engaged in--

- Manufacturing iron or steel castings--are classified in Industry 33151, Ferrous Metal Foundries; and
- Manufacturing nonferrous metal castings and further manufacturing them into finished products--are classified based on the specific finished product.

331523 Nonferrous Metal Die-Casting Foundries

This U.S. industry comprises establishments primarily engaged in introducing molten nonferrous metal, under high pressure, into molds or dies to make nonferrous metal die-castings. Establishments in this industry purchase nonferrous metals made in other establishments.

Cross-references. Establishments primarily engaged in--

- Pouring molten aluminum into molds to manufacture aluminum castings--are classified in U.S. Industry 331524, Aluminum Foundries (except Die-Casting);
- Pouring molten nonferrous metal (except aluminum) into molds to manufacture nonferrous (except aluminum) castings--are classified in U.S. Industry 331529, Other Nonferrous Metal Foundries (except Die-Casting); and
- Manufacturing nonferrous die-castings and further manufacturing them into finished products--are classified based on the specific finished product.

331524 Aluminum Foundries (except Die-Casting)

This U.S. industry comprises establishments primarily engaged in pouring molten aluminum into molds to manufacture aluminum castings (except nonferrous die-castings). Establishments in this industry purchase aluminum made in other establishments.

Cross-References. Establishments primarily engaged in--

- Manufacturing aluminum die-castings--are classified in U.S. Industry 331523, Nonferrous Metal Die-Casting Foundries; and
- Manufacturing aluminum or aluminum alloy castings and further manufacturing them into finished products--are classified based on the specific finished product.

T—Canadian, Mexican, and United States industries are comparable.

331529 Other Nonferrous Metal Foundries (except Die-Casting)

This U.S. industry comprises establishments primarily engaged in pouring molten nonferrous metals (except aluminum) into molds to manufacture nonferrous castings (except nonferrous die-castings and aluminum castings). Establishments in this industry purchase nonferrous metals, such as copper, nickel, lead, and zinc, made in other establishments.

Cross-references. Establishments primarily engaged in--

- Manufacturing nonferrous die-castings--are classified in U.S. Industry 331523, Nonferrous Metal Die-Casting Foundries;
- Pouring molten aluminum into molds to manufacture aluminum castings--are classified in U.S. Industry 331524, Aluminum Foundries (except Die-Casting); and
- Manufacturing nonferrous castings and further manufacturing them into finished products--are classified based on the specific finished product.

332 Fabricated Metal Product Manufacturing[T]

Industries in the Fabricated Metal Product Manufacturing subsector transform metal into intermediate or end products, other than machinery, computers and electronics, and metal furniture, or treat metals and metal formed products fabricated elsewhere. Important fabricated metal processes are forging, stamping, bending, forming, and machining, used to shape individual pieces of metal; and other processes, such as welding and assembling, used to join separate parts together. Establishments in this subsector may use one of these processes or a combination of these processes.

The NAICS structure for this subsector distinguishes the forging and stamping processes in a single industry. The remaining industries in the subsector group establishments based on similar combinations of processes used to make products.

The manufacturing performed in the Fabricated Metal Product Manufacturing subsector begins with manufactured metal shapes. The establishments in this subsector further fabricate the purchased metal shapes into a product. For instance, the Spring and Wire Product Manufacturing industry starts with wire and fabricates such items. Within manufacturing there are other establishments that make the same products made by this subsector; only these establishments begin production further back in the production process. These establishments have a more integrated operation. For instance, one establishment may manufacture steel, draw it into wire, and make wire products in the same establishment. Such operations are classified in the Primary Metal Manufacturing subsector.

3321 Forging and Stamping[T]

33211 Forging and Stamping[T]

This industry comprises establishments primarily engaged in one or more of the following: (1) manufacturing forgings from purchased metals; (2) manufacturing metal custom roll forming products; (3) manufacturing metal stamped and spun products (except automotive, cans, coins); and (4) manufacturing powder metallurgy products. Establishments making metal forgings, metal stampings, and metal spun products and further manufacturing (e.g., machining, assembling) a specific manufactured product are classified in the industry of the finished product. Metal forging, metal stamping, and metal spun products establishments may perform surface finishing operations, such as cleaning and deburring, on the products they manufacture.

Cross-References. Establishments primarily engaged in--

- Manufacturing metal forgings in integrated primary metal establishments--are classified in Subsector 331, Primary Metal Manufacturing;
- Manufacturing automotive stampings--are classified in Industry 33637, Motor Vehicle Metal Stamping;
- Manufacturing and installing roll formed seamless gutters at construction sites--are classified in Industry 23817, Siding Contractors; and
- Stamping coins--are classified in Industry 33991, Jewelry and Silverware Manufacturing.

T—Canadian, Mexican, and United States industries are comparable.

332111 Iron and Steel Forging

This U.S. industry comprises establishments primarily engaged in manufacturing iron and steel forgings from purchased iron and steel by hammering mill shapes. Establishments making iron and steel forgings and further manufacturing (e.g., machining, assembling) a specific manufactured product are classified in the industry of the finished product. Iron and steel forging establishments may perform surface finishing operations, such as cleaning and deburring, on the forgings they manufacture.

Cross-References. Establishments primarily engaged in--

- Manufacturing iron and steel forgings in integrated iron and steel mills--are classified in Industry 331110, Iron and Steel Mills and Ferroalloy Manufacturing; and
- Manufacturing nonferrous forgings--are classified in U.S. Industry 332112, Nonferrous Forging.

332112 Nonferrous Forging

This U.S. industry comprises establishments primarily engaged in manufacturing nonferrous forgings from purchased nonferrous metals by hammering mill shapes. Establishments making nonferrous forgings and further manufacturing (e.g., machining, assembling) a specific manufactured product are classified in the industry of the finished product. Nonferrous forging establishments may perform surface finishing operations, such as cleaning and deburring, on the forgings they manufacture.

Cross-References. Establishments primarily engaged in--

- Manufacturing iron and steel forgings--are classified in U.S. Industry 332111, Iron and Steel Forging; and
- Manufacturing nonferrous forgings in integrated primary or secondary nonferrous metal production facilities--are classified in Subsector 331, Primary Metal Manufacturing.

332114 Custom Roll Forming

This U.S. industry comprises establishments primarily engaged in custom roll forming metal products by use of rotary motion of rolls with various contours to bend or shape the products.

Cross-References.

Establishments primarily engaged in manufacturing and installing roll formed seamless gutters at construction sites are classified in Industry 238170, Siding Contractors.

332117 Powder Metallurgy Part Manufacturing

This U.S. industry comprises establishments primarily engaged in manufacturing powder metallurgy products using any of the various powder metallurgy processing techniques, such as pressing and sintering or metal injection molding. Establishments in this industry generally make a wide range of parts on a job or order basis.

332119 Metal Crown, Closure, and Other Metal Stamping (except Automotive)

This U.S. industry comprises establishments primarily engaged in (1) stamping metal crowns and closures, such as bottle caps and home canning lids and rings, and/or (2) manufacturing other unfinished metal stampings and spinning unfinished metal products (except automotive, cans, and coins). Establishments making metal stampings and metal spun products and further manufacturing (e.g., machining, assembling) a specific product are classified in the industry of the finished product. Metal stamping and metal spun products establishments may perform surface finishing operations, such as cleaning and deburring, on the products they manufacture.
T—Canadian, Mexican, and United States industries are comparable.

Cross-References. Establishments primarily engaged in--

- Manufacturing automotive stampings--are classified in Industry 336370, Motor Vehicle Metal Stamping;
- Manufacturing metal cans--are classified in U.S. Industry 332431, Metal Can Manufacturing; and
- Stamping coins--are classified in Industry 339910, Jewelry and Silverware Manufacturing.

3322 Cutlery and Handtool Manufacturing[T]

33221 Cutlery and Handtool Manufacturing[T]

This industry comprises establishments primarily engaged in one or more of the following: (1) manufacturing metal kitchen cookware (except by casting (e.g., cast iron skillets) or stamped without further fabrication), utensils, and/or nonprecious and precious plated metal cutlery and flatware; (2) manufacturing saw blades, all types (including those for power sawing machines); and (3) manufacturing nonpowered handtools and edge tools.

Cross-References. Establishments primarily engaged in--

- Manufacturing precious (except precious plated) metal cutlery and flatware--are classified in Industry 33991, Jewelry and Silverware Manufacturing;
- Manufacturing electric razors and hair clippers for use on humans--are classified in Industry 33521, Small Electrical Appliance Manufacturing;
- Manufacturing power hedge shears and trimmers and electric hair clippers for use on animals--are classified in Industry 33311, Agricultural Implement Manufacturing;
- Manufacturing metal cutting dies, attachments, and accessories for machine tools--are classified in Industry 33351, Metalworking Machinery Manufacturing;
- Manufacturing power-driven handtools--are classified in Industry 33399, All Other General Purpose Machinery Manufacturing; and
- Manufacturing finished cast iron kitchen utensils and cookware (i.e., cast iron skillets) and castings for kitchen utensils and cookware--are classified in Industry Group 3315, Foundries.

332215 Metal Kitchen Cookware, Utensil, Cutlery, and Flatware (except Precious) Manufacturing

This U.S. industry comprises establishments primarily engaged in manufacturing metal kitchen cookware (except by casting (e.g., cast iron skillets) or stamped without further fabrication), utensils, and/or nonprecious and precious plated metal cutlery and flatware.

Cross-References. Establishments primarily engaged in--

- Manufacturing precious (except precious plated) metal cutlery and flatware--are classified in Industry 339910, Jewelry and Silverware Manufacturing;
- Manufacturing electric razors and hair clippers for use on humans--are classified in Industry 335210, Small Electrical Appliance Manufacturing;
- Manufacturing power hedge shears and trimmers--are classified in U.S. Industry 333112, Lawn and Garden Tractor and Home Lawn and Garden Equipment Manufacturing;
- Manufacturing nonelectric hair clippers for use on animals--are classified in U.S. Industry 332216, Saw Blade and Handtool Manufacturing;
- Manufacturing finished cast iron kitchen utensils and cookware (i.e., cast iron skillets) and castings for kitchen utensils and cookware--are classified in Industry Group 3315, Foundries; and
- Manufacturing stampings for kitchen utensils, pots, and pans--are classified in U.S. Industry 332119, Metal Crown, Closure, and Other Metal Stamping (except Automotive).

332216 Saw Blade and Handtool Manufacturing

This U.S. industry comprises establishments primarily engaged in (1) manufacturing saw blades, all types (including those for power sawing machines) and/or (2) manufacturing nonpowered handtools and edge tools.

T—Canadian, Mexican, and United States industries are comparable.

Cross-References. Establishments primarily engaged in--

- Manufacturing metal cutting dies, attachments, and accessories for machine tools--are classified in Industry 33351, Metalworking Machinery Manufacturing;
- Manufacturing power-driven handtools--are classified in U.S. Industry 333991, Power-Driven Handtool Manufacturing;
- Manufacturing electric razors and hair clippers for use on humans--are classified in Industry 335210, Small Electrical Appliance Manufacturing;
- Manufacturing electric hair clippers for use on animals--are classified in U.S. Industry 333111, Farm Machinery and Equipment Manufacturing; and
- Manufacturing nonelectric household-type scissors and shears--are classified in U.S. Industry 332215, Metal Kitchen Cookware, Utensil, Cutlery, and Flatware (except Precious) Manufacturing.

3323 Architectural and Structural Metals Manufacturing[T]

This industry group comprises establishments primarily engaged in manufacturing one or more of the following: (1) prefabricated metal buildings, panels and sections; (2) structural metal products; (3) metal plate work products; (4) metal framed windows (i.e., typically using purchased glass) and metal doors; (5) sheet metal work; and (6) ornamental and architectural metal products.

33231 Plate Work and Fabricated Structural Product Manufacturing[T]

This industry comprises establishments primarily engaged in manufacturing one or more of the following: (1) prefabricated metal buildings, panels and sections; (2) structural metal products; and (3) metal plate work products.

Cross-References. Establishments primarily engaged in--

- Making manufactured homes (i.e., mobile homes) and prefabricated wood buildings--are classified in Industry 32199, All Other Wood Product Manufacturing;
- Constructing buildings, bridges, and other heavy construction projects on site--are classified in Sector 23, Construction;
- Building ships, boats, and barges--are classified in Industry 33661, Ship and Boat Building;
- Manufacturing power boilers and heat exchangers--are classified in Industry 33241, Power Boiler and Heat Exchanger Manufacturing;
- Manufacturing heavy gauge tanks--are classified in Industry 33242, Metal Tank (Heavy Gauge) Manufacturing;
- Manufacturing metal plate cooling towers--are classified in Industry 33341, Ventilation, Heating, Air-Conditioning, and Commercial Refrigeration Equipment Manufacturing; and
- Manufacturing metal windows, doors, and studs--are classified in Industry 33232, Ornamental and Architectural Metal Products Manufacturing.

332311 Prefabricated Metal Building and Component Manufacturing

This U.S. industry comprises establishments primarily engaged in manufacturing prefabricated metal buildings, panels, and sections.

Cross-References. Establishments primarily engaged in--

- Making manufactured homes (i.e., mobile homes) and prefabricated wood buildings--are classified in Industry 32199, All Other Wood Product Manufacturing;
- Constructing prefabricated buildings on site--are classified in Subsector 236, Construction of Buildings; and
- Manufacturing metal windows and doors--are classified in U.S. Industry 332321, Metal Window and Door Manufacturing.

T—Canadian, Mexican, and United States industries are comparable.

332312 Fabricated Structural Metal Manufacturing

This U.S. industry comprises establishments primarily engaged in fabricating structural metal products, such as assemblies of concrete reinforcing bars and fabricated bar joists.

Cross-References. Establishments primarily engaged in--

- Manufacturing concrete reinforcing bars in an iron and steel mill--are classified in Industry 331110, Iron and Steel Mills and Ferroalloy Manufacturing;
- Manufacturing metal windows and doors--are classified in U.S. Industry 332321, Metal Window and Door Manufacturing;
- Manufacturing metal studs--are classified in U.S. Industry 332322, Sheet Metal Work Manufacturing;
- Constructing buildings, bridges, and other heavy construction projects on site--are classified in Sector 23, Construction;
- Manufacturing concrete reinforcing bar by rolling and drawing steel from purchased steel--are classified in U.S. Industry 331221, Rolled Steel Shape Manufacturing;
- Building ships, boats, and barges--are classified in Industry 33661, Ship and Boat Building; and
- Prefabricating metal buildings, panels, and sections--are classified in U.S. Industry 332311, Prefabricated Metal Building and Component Manufacturing.

332313 Plate Work Manufacturing

This U.S. industry comprises establishments primarily engaged in manufacturing fabricated metal plate work by cutting, punching, bending, shaping, and welding purchased metal plate.

Cross-References. Establishments primarily engaged in--

- Manufacturing power boilers and heat exchangers--are classified in Industry 332410, Power Boiler and Heat Exchanger Manufacturing;
- Manufacturing heavy gauge tanks--are classified in Industry 332420, Metal Tank (Heavy Gauge) Manufacturing; and
- Manufacturing metal plate cooling towers--are classified in U.S. Industry 333415, Air-Conditioning and Warm Air Heating Equipment and Commercial and Industrial Refrigeration Equipment Manufacturing.

33232 Ornamental and Architectural Metal Products Manufacturing[T]

This industry comprises establishments primarily engaged in manufacturing one or more of the following: (1) metal framed windows (i.e., typically using purchased glass) and metal doors; (2) sheet metal work; and (3) ornamental and architectural metal products.

Cross-References. Establishments primarily engaged in--

- Manufacturing metal covered (i.e., clad) wood windows and doors--are classified in Industry 32191, Millwork;
- Manufacturing bins, cans, vats, and light tanks of sheet metal--are classified in Industry 33243, Metal Can, Box, and Other Metal Container (Light Gauge) Manufacturing;
- Manufacturing prefabricated metal buildings, panels, and sections--are classified in Industry 33231, Plate Work and Fabricated Structural Product Manufacturing;
- Fabricating sheet metal work on site--are classified in Subsector 238, Specialty Trade Contractors;
- Manufacturing metal stampings (except automotive, coins) and custom roll forming products--are classified in Industry 33211, Forging and Stamping;
- Manufacturing automotive stampings--are classified in Industry 33637, Motor Vehicle Metal Stamping; and
- Stamping coins--are classified in Industry 33991, Jewelry and Silverware Manufacturing.

T—Canadian, Mexican, and United States industries are comparable.

332321 Metal Window and Door Manufacturing

This U.S. industry comprises establishments primarily engaged in manufacturing metal framed windows (i.e., typically using purchased glass) and metal doors. Examples of products made by these establishments are metal door frames; metal framed window and door screens; and metal molding and trim (except automotive).

Cross-References. Establishments primarily engaged in--

- Manufacturing wood or metal covered (i.e., clad) wood framed windows and doors--are classified in U.S. Industry 321911, Wood Window and Door Manufacturing; and
- Manufacturing metal automotive molding and trim--are classified in Industry 336370, Motor Vehicle Metal Stamping.

332322 Sheet Metal Work Manufacturing

This U.S. industry comprises establishments primarily engaged in manufacturing sheet metal work (except stampings).

Cross-References. Establishments primarily engaged in--

- Manufacturing sheet metal bins, vats, and light tanks of sheet metal--are classified in U.S. Industry 332439, Other Metal Container Manufacturing;
- Manufacturing metal cans, lids, and ends--are classified in U.S. Industry 332431, Metal Can Manufacturing;
- Fabricating sheet metal work on site--are classified in Subsector 238, Specialty Trade Contractors;
- Manufacturing metal stampings (except automotive, coins) and custom roll forming products--are classified in Industry 33211, Forging and Stamping;
- Manufacturing automotive stampings--are classified in Industry 336370, Motor Vehicle Metal Stamping; and
- Stamping coins--are classified in Industry 339910, Jewelry and Silverware Manufacturing.

332323 Ornamental and Architectural Metal Work Manufacturing

This U.S. industry comprises establishments primarily engaged in manufacturing ornamental and architectural metal work, such as staircases, metal open steel flooring, fire escapes, railings, and scaffolding.

Cross-References.

Establishments primarily engaged in manufacturing prefabricated metal buildings, panels, and sections are classified in U.S. Industry 332311, Prefabricated Metal Building and Component Manufacturing.

3324 Boiler, Tank, and Shipping Container Manufacturing[T]

This industry group comprises establishments primarily engaged in one of the following: (1) manufacturing power boilers and heat exchangers; (2) cutting, forming, and joining heavy gauge metal to manufacture tanks, vessels, and other containers; or (3) forming light gauge metal containers.

33241 Power Boiler and Heat Exchanger Manufacturing[T] See industry description for 332410.

332410 Power Boiler and Heat Exchanger Manufacturing

This industry comprises establishments primarily engaged in manufacturing power boilers and heat exchangers. Establishments in this industry may perform installation in addition to manufacturing power boilers and heat exchangers.

T—Canadian, Mexican, and United States industries are comparable.

Cross-References. Establishments primarily engaged in--

- Manufacturing heavy gauge metal tanks--are classified in Industry 332420, Metal Tank (Heavy Gauge) Manufacturing;
- Manufacturing steam or hot water low pressure heating boilers--are classified in U.S. Industry 333414, Heating Equipment (except Warm Air Furnaces) Manufacturing; and
- Installing power boilers and heat exchangers without manufacturing--are classified in Industry 238220, Plumbing, Heating, and Air-Conditioning Contractors.

33242 Metal Tank (Heavy Gauge) Manufacturing[T] See industry description for 332420.

332420 Metal Tank (Heavy Gauge) Manufacturing

This industry comprises establishments primarily engaged in cutting, forming, and joining heavy gauge metal to manufacture tanks, vessels, and other containers.

Cross-References. Establishments primarily engaged in--

- Manufacturing power boilers--are classified in Industry 332410, Power Boiler and Heat Exchanger Manufacturing;
- Manufacturing light gauge metal containers--are classified in Industry 33243, Metal Can, Box, and Other Metal Container (Light Gauge) Manufacturing; and
- Installing heavy gauge metal tanks without manufacturing--are classified in Industry 238120, Structural Steel and Precast Concrete Contractors.

33243 Metal Can, Box, and Other Metal Container (Light Gauge) Manufacturing[T] This industry comprises establishments primarily engaged in forming light gauge metal containers.

Cross-References. Establishments primarily engaged in--

- Manufacturing foil containers--are classified in Industry 33299, All Other Fabricated Metal Product Manufacturing;
- Reconditioning barrels and drums--are classified in Industry 81131, Commercial and Industrial Machinery and Equipment (except Automotive and Electronic) Repair and Maintenance; and
- Manufacturing heavy gauge metal containers--are classified in Industry 33242, Metal Tank (Heavy Gauge) Manufacturing.

332431 Metal Can Manufacturing

This U.S. industry comprises establishments primarily engaged in manufacturing metal cans, lids, and ends.

Cross-References. Establishments primarily engaged in--

- Manufacturing foil containers--are classified in U.S. Industry 332999, All Other Miscellaneous Fabricated Metal Product Manufacturing; and
- Manufacturing light gauge metal containers (except cans)--are classified in U.S. Industry 332439, Other Metal Container Manufacturing.

332439 Other Metal Container Manufacturing

This U.S. industry comprises establishments primarily engaged in manufacturing metal (light gauge) containers (except cans).

T—Canadian, Mexican, and United States industries are comparable.

Illustrative Examples:

Light gauge metal bins manufacturing
Light gauge metal drums manufacturing

Light gauge metal garbage cans manufacturing

Light gauge metal lunch boxes manufacturing

Light gauge metal mailboxes manufacturing

Light gauge metal tool boxes manufacturing
Light gauge metal vats manufacturing

Metal air cargo containers manufacturing

Metal barrels manufacturing

Vacuum bottles and jugs manufacturing

Cross-References. Establishments primarily engaged in--

- Manufacturing foil containers--are classified in U.S. Industry 332999, All Other Miscellaneous Fabricated Metal Product Manufacturing;
- Manufacturing metal cans--are classified in U.S. Industry 332431, Metal Can Manufacturing;
- Reconditioning barrels and drums--are classified in Industry 811310, Commercial and Industrial Machinery and Equipment (except Automotive and Electronic) Repair and Maintenance; and
- Manufacturing heavy gauge metal containers--are classified in Industry 332420, Metal Tank (Heavy Gauge) Manufacturing.

3325 Hardware Manufacturing[T]

33251 Hardware Manufacturing[T] See industry description for 332510.

332510 Hardware Manufacturing

This industry comprises establishments primarily engaged in manufacturing metal hardware, such as metal hinges, metal handles, keys, and locks (except coin-operated, time locks).

Cross-References. Establishments primarily engaged in--

- Manufacturing bolts, nuts, screws, rivets, washers, hose clamps, and turnbuckles--are classified in U.S. Industry 332722, Bolt, Nut, Screw, Rivet, and Washer Manufacturing;
- Manufacturing nails and spikes from wire drawn elsewhere--are classified in U.S. Industry 332618, Other Fabricated Wire Product Manufacturing;
- Manufacturing metal furniture parts (except hardware)--are classified in U.S. Industry 337215, Showcase, Partition, Shelving, and Locker Manufacturing;
- Drawing wire and manufacturing nails and spikes--are classified in Subsector 331, Primary Metal Manufacturing;
- Manufacturing pole line and transmission hardware--are classified in U.S. Industry 335932, Noncurrent-Carrying Wiring Device Manufacturing;
- Manufacturing coin-operated locking mechanisms--are classified in U.S. Industry 333318, Other Commercial and Service Industry Machinery Manufacturing;
- Manufacturing time locks--are classified in U.S. Industry 334519, Other Measuring and Controlling Device Manufacturing;
- Manufacturing fireplace fixtures and equipment, traps, handcuffs and leg irons, ladder jacks, and other like metal products--are classified in U.S. Industry 332999, All Other Miscellaneous Fabricated Metal Product Manufacturing;
- Manufacturing fire hose nozzles and metal hose couplings (except fluid power)--are classified in U.S. Industry 332919, Other Metal Valve and Pipe Fitting Manufacturing; and
- Manufacturing luggage and utility racks--are classified in Industry 336390, Other Motor Vehicle Parts Manufacturing.

3326 Spring and Wire Product Manufacturing[T]

33261 Spring and Wire Product Manufacturing[T]

This industry comprises establishments primarily engaged in (1) manufacturing steel springs by forming, such as cutting, bending, and heat winding, metal rod or strip stock and/or (2) manufacturing wire springs and fabricated wire products from wire drawn elsewhere (except watch and clock springs).

Cross-References. Establishments primarily engaged in--

- Manufacturing watch and clock springs from purchased wire--are classified in Industry 33451, Navigational, Measuring, Electromedical, and Control Instruments Manufacturing;
- Drawing wire and manufacturing wire products--are classified in Subsector 331, Primary Metal Manufacturing; and
- Manufacturing nonferrous insulated wire from wire drawn elsewhere--are classified in Industry 33592, Communication and Energy Wire and Cable Manufacturing.

332613 Spring Manufacturing

This U.S. industry comprises establishments primarily engaged in manufacturing springs from purchased wire, strip, or rod.

Cross-References. Establishments primarily engaged in--

- Manufacturing watch and clock springs--are classified in U.S. Industry 334519, Other Measuring and Controlling Device Manufacturing; and
- Producing wire, strip, or rod and further fabricating springs--are classified in Subsector 331, Primary Metal Manufacturing.

332618 Other Fabricated Wire Product Manufacturing

This U.S. industry comprises establishments primarily engaged in manufacturing fabricated wire products (except springs) made from purchased wire.

Illustrative Examples:

Barbed wire made from purchased wire
Chain link fencing and fence gates made from purchased wire
Metal baskets made from purchased wire
Nails, brads, and staples made from purchased wire
Noninsulated wire cable made from purchased wire
Paper clips made from purchased wire
Woven wire cloth made from purchased wire

Cross-References. Establishments primarily engaged in--

- Drawing wire and manufacturing wire products--are classified in Subsector 331, Primary Metal Manufacturing;
- Manufacturing springs from purchased wire, strip, or rod--are classified in U.S. Industry 332613, Spring Manufacturing; and
- Insulating nonferrous wire from wire drawn elsewhere--are classified in U.S. Industry 335929, Other Communication and Energy Wire Manufacturing.

3327 Machine Shops; Turned Product; and Screw, Nut, and Bolt Manufacturing[T]

This industry group comprises establishments primarily engaged in one of the following: (1) operating machine shops primarily engaged in machining metal and plastic parts and parts of other composite materials on a job or order basis; (2) machining precision turned products; or (3) manufacturing metal bolts, nuts, screws, rivets, and other industrial fasteners.

T—Canadian, Mexican, and United States industries are comparable.

33271 Machine Shops[T] See industry description for 332710.

332710 Machine Shops

This industry comprises establishments known as machine shops primarily engaged in machining metal and plastic parts and parts of other composite materials on a job or order basis. Generally machine shop jobs are low volume using machine tools, such as lathes (including computer numerically controlled); automatic screw machines; and machines for boring, grinding, milling, and additive manufacturing.

Cross-References. Establishments primarily engaged in--

- Repairing industrial machinery and equipment--are classified in Industry 811310, Commercial and Industrial Machinery and Equipment (except Automotive and Electronic) Repair and Maintenance; and
- Manufacturing parts (except on a job or order basis) for machinery and equipment--are generally classified in the same manufacturing industry that makes complete machinery and equipment.

33272 Turned Product and Screw, Nut, and Bolt Manufacturing[T]

This industry comprises establishments primarily engaged in (1) machining precision turned products or (2) manufacturing metal bolts, nuts, screws, rivets, and other industrial fasteners. Included in this industry are establishments primarily engaged in manufacturing parts for machinery and equipment on a custom basis.

Cross-References.

Establishments primarily engaged in manufacturing plastics fasteners are classified in Industry 32619, Other Plastics Product Manufacturing.

332721 Precision Turned Product Manufacturing

This U.S. industry comprises establishments known as precision turned manufacturers primarily engaged in machining precision products of all materials on a job or order basis. Generally precision turned product jobs are large volume using machines, such as automatic screw machines, rotary transfer machines, computer numerically controlled (CNC) lathes, or turning centers.

Cross-References.

Establishments primarily engaged in manufacturing metal bolts, nuts, screws, rivets, washers, and other industrial fasteners using machines, such as headers, threaders, and nut forming machines, are classified in U.S. Industry 332722, Bolt, Nut, Screw, Rivet, and Washer Manufacturing.

332722 Bolt, Nut, Screw, Rivet, and Washer Manufacturing

This U.S. industry comprises establishments primarily engaged in manufacturing metal bolts, nuts, screws, rivets, washers, and other industrial fasteners using machines, such as headers, threaders, and nut forming machines.

Cross-References. Establishments primarily engaged in--

- Manufacturing precision turned products--are classified in U.S. Industry 332721, Precision Turned Product Manufacturing; and
- Manufacturing plastics fasteners--are classified in U.S. Industry 326199, All Other Plastics Product Manufacturing.

T—Canadian, Mexican, and United States industries are comparable.

3328 Coating, Engraving, Heat Treating, and Allied Activities[T]

33281 Coating, Engraving, Heat Treating, and Allied Activities[T]

This industry comprises establishments primarily engaged in one or more of the following: (1) heat treating metals and metal products; (2) enameling, lacquering, and varnishing metals and metal products; (3) hot dip galvanizing metals and metal products; (4) engraving, chasing, or etching metals and metal products (except jewelry; personal goods carried on or about the person, such as compacts and cigarette cases; precious metal products (except precious plated flatware and other plated ware); and printing plates); (5) powder coating metals and metal products; (6) electroplating, plating, anodizing, coloring, and finishing metals and metal products; and (7) providing other metal surfacing services for the trade. Establishments in this industry coat, engrave, and heat treat metals and metal formed products fabricated elsewhere.

Cross-References. Establishments primarily engaged in--

- Engraving, chasing, or etching jewelry, metal personal goods, or precious metal products (except precious plated flatware and other plated ware)--are classified in Industry 33991, Jewelry and Silverware Manufacturing;
- Engraving, chasing, or etching printing plates--are classified in Industry 32312, Support Activities for Printing; and
- Both fabricating and coating, engraving, and heat treating metals and metal products--are classified in the Manufacturing sector according to the product made.

332811 Metal Heat Treating

This U.S. industry comprises establishments primarily engaged in heat treating, such as annealing, tempering, and brazing, and cryogenically treating metals and metal products for the trade.

Cross-References.

Establishments primarily engaged in both fabricating and heat treating metal products are classified in the Manufacturing sector according to the product made.

332812 Metal Coating, Engraving (except Jewelry and Silverware), and Allied Services to Manufacturers

This U.S. industry comprises establishments primarily engaged in one or more of the following: (1) enameling, lacquering, and varnishing metals and metal products; (2) hot dip galvanizing metals and metal products; (3) engraving, chasing, or etching metals and metal products (except jewelry; personal goods carried on or about the person, such as compacts and cigarette cases; precious metal products (except precious plated flatware and other plated ware); and printing plates); (4) powder coating metals and metal products; and (5) providing other metal surfacing services for the trade. Included in this industry are establishments that perform these processes on other materials, such as plastics, in addition to metals.

Cross-References. Establishments primarily engaged in--

- Both fabricating and coating and engraving products--are classified in the Manufacturing sector according to the product made;
- Engraving, chasing, or etching jewelry, metal personal goods, or precious metal products (except precious plated flatware and other plated ware)--are classified in Industry 339910, Jewelry and Silverware Manufacturing; and
- Engraving, chasing, or etching printing plates--are classified in Industry 323120, Support Activities for Printing.

T—Canadian, Mexican, and United States industries are comparable.

332813 Electroplating, Plating, Polishing, Anodizing, and Coloring

This U.S. industry comprises establishments primarily engaged in electroplating, plating, anodizing, coloring, buffing, polishing, cleaning, and sandblasting metals and metal products for the trade. Included in this industry are establishments that perform these processes on other materials, such as plastics, in addition to metals.

Cross-References.

Establishments primarily engaged in both fabricating and electroplating, plating, polishing, anodizing, and coloring products are classified in the Manufacturing sector according to the product made.

3329 Other Fabricated Metal Product Manufacturing[T]

This industry group comprises establishments primarily engaged in manufacturing fabricated metal products (except forgings and stampings, cutlery and handtools, architectural and structural metals, boilers, tanks, shipping containers, hardware, spring and wire products, machine shop products, turned products, screws, and nuts and bolts).

33291 Metal Valve Manufacturing[T]

This industry comprises establishments primarily engaged in manufacturing one or more of the following metal valves: (1) industrial valves; (2) fluid power valves and hose fittings; (3) plumbing fixture fittings and trim; and (4) other metal valves and pipe fittings.

Cross-References. Establishments primarily engaged in--

- Manufacturing fluid power cylinders and pumps--are classified in Industry 33399, All Other General Purpose Machinery Manufacturing;
- Manufacturing intake and exhaust valves for internal combustion engines--are classified in Industry 33631, Motor Vehicle Gasoline Engine and Engine Parts Manufacturing;
- Manufacturing metal shower rods and metal couplings from purchased metal pipe--are classified in Industry 33299, All Other Fabricated Metal Product Manufacturing;
- Manufacturing plastics aerosol spray nozzles--are classified in Industry 32619, Other Plastics Product Manufacturing;
- Casting iron pipe fittings and couplings without machining--are classified in Industry 33151, Ferrous Metal Foundries; and
- Manufacturing plastics pipe fittings and couplings--are classified in Industry 32612, Plastics Pipe, Pipe Fitting, and Unlaminated Profile Shape Manufacturing.

332911 Industrial Valve Manufacturing

This U.S. industry comprises establishments primarily engaged in manufacturing industrial valves and valves for water works and municipal water systems.

Illustrative Examples:

Complete fire hydrants manufacturing
Industrial-type ball valves manufacturing
Industrial-type butterfly valves manufacturing
Industrial-type check valves manufacturing
Industrial-type gate valves manufacturing
Industrial-type globe valves manufacturing
Industrial-type plug valves manufacturing
Industrial-type solenoid valves (except fluid power) manufacturing
Industrial-type steam traps manufacturing
Valves for nuclear applications manufacturing

T—Canadian, Mexican, and United States industries are comparable.

Cross-References. Establishments primarily engaged in--

- Manufacturing fluid power valves--are classified in U.S. Industry 332912, Fluid Power Valve and Hose Fitting Manufacturing; and
- Manufacturing plumbing and heating inline valves--are classified in U.S. Industry 332919, Other Metal Valve and Pipe Fitting Manufacturing.

332912 Fluid Power Valve and Hose Fitting Manufacturing

This U.S. industry comprises establishments primarily engaged in manufacturing fluid power valves and hose fittings.

Illustrative Examples:

Fluid power aircraft subassemblies manufacturing
Hose assemblies for fluid power systems manufacturing
Hydraulic and pneumatic hose and tube fittings manufacturing
Hydraulic and pneumatic valves manufacturing

Cross-References. Establishments primarily engaged in--

- Manufacturing fluid power cylinders--are classified in U.S. Industry 333995, Fluid Power Cylinder and Actuator Manufacturing;
- Manufacturing fluid power pumps--are classified in U.S. Industry 333996, Fluid Power Pump and Motor Manufacturing;
- Manufacturing intake and exhaust valves for internal combustion engines--are classified in Industry 336310, Motor Vehicle Gasoline Engine and Engine Parts Manufacturing;
- Manufacturing industrial-type valves--are classified in U.S. Industry 332911, Industrial Valve Manufacturing; and
- Manufacturing plumbing and heating inline valves--are classified in U.S. Industry 332919, Other Metal Valve and Pipe Fitting Manufacturing.

332913 Plumbing Fixture Fitting and Trim Manufacturing

This U.S. industry comprises establishments primarily engaged in manufacturing metal and plastics plumbing fixture fittings and trim, such as faucets, flush valves, and shower heads.

Cross-References. Establishments primarily engaged in--

- Manufacturing metal shower rods--are classified in U.S. Industry 332999, All Other Miscellaneous Fabricated Metal Product Manufacturing; and
- Manufacturing fire hose nozzles, lawn hose nozzles, water traps, metal hose couplings (except fluid power), and plumbing and heating inline valves--are classified in U.S. Industry 332919, Other Metal Valve and Pipe Fitting Manufacturing.

332919 Other Metal Valve and Pipe Fitting Manufacturing

This U.S. industry comprises establishments primarily engaged in manufacturing metal valves (except industrial valves, fluid power valves, fluid power hose fittings, and plumbing fixture fittings and trim).

Illustrative Examples:

Aerosol valves manufacturing
Firefighting nozzles manufacturing
Lawn hose nozzles manufacturing
Lawn sprinklers manufacturing
Metal hose couplings (except fluid power) manufacturing

T—Canadian, Mexican, and United States industries are comparable.

Metal pipe flanges and flange unions manufacturing
Water traps manufacturing
Plumbing and heating inline valves (e.g., check,

Cross-References. Establishments primarily engaged in--

- Manufacturing fluid power valves and hose fittings--are classified in U.S. Industry 332912, Fluid Power Valve and Hose Fitting Manufacturing;
- Manufacturing industrial valves--are classified in U.S. Industry 332911, Industrial Valve Manufacturing;
- Manufacturing plumbing fixture fittings and trim--are classified in U.S. Industry 332913, Plumbing Fixture Fitting and Trim Manufacturing;
- Manufacturing plastics aerosol spray nozzles--are classified in U.S. Industry 326199, All Other Plastics Product Manufacturing;
- Casting iron pipe fittings and couplings without machining--are classified in U.S. Industry 331511, Iron Foundries;
- Manufacturing metal couplings from purchased metal pipe--are classified in U.S. Industry 332996, Fabricated Pipe and Pipe Fitting Manufacturing; and
- Manufacturing plastics pipe fittings and couplings--are classified in U.S. Industry 326122, Plastics Pipe and Pipe Fitting Manufacturing.

33299 All Other Fabricated Metal Product Manufacturing[T]

This industry comprises establishments primarily engaged in manufacturing fabricated metal products (except forgings and stampings, cutlery and handtools, architectural and structural metal products, boilers, tanks, shipping containers, hardware, spring and wire products, machine shop products, turned products, screws, nuts and bolts, and metal valves).

Illustrative Examples:

Ammunition manufacturing
Ball and roller bearing manufacturing
Enameled iron and metal sanitary ware manufacturing
Fabricated pipe and pipe fittings made from purchased metal pipe
Foil containers (except bags) manufacturing
Industrial pattern manufacturing
Metal safes manufacturing
Portable metal ladders manufacturing
Small arms and other ordnance manufacturing
Steel wool manufacturing

Cross-References. Establishments primarily engaged in--

- Manufacturing forgings, stampings, and powder metallurgy parts--are classified in Industry 33211, Forging and Stamping;
- Manufacturing cutlery and handtools--are classified in Industry 33221, Cutlery and Handtool Manufacturing;
- Manufacturing architectural and structural metals--are classified in Industry Group 3323, Architectural and Structural Metals Manufacturing;
- Manufacturing boilers, tanks, and shipping containers--are classified in Industry Group 3324, Boiler, Tank, and Shipping Container Manufacturing;
- Manufacturing hardware and safe and vault locks--are classified in Industry 33251, Hardware Manufacturing;
- Manufacturing spring and wire products--are classified in Industry 33261, Spring and Wire Product Manufacturing;
- Manufacturing machine shop products, turned products, screws, and nuts and bolts--are classified in Industry Group 3327, Machine Shops; Turned Product; and Screw, Nut, and Bolt Manufacturing;
- Coating, engraving, heat treating, and allied activities--are classified in Industry 33281, Coating, Engraving, Heat Treating, and Allied Activities;
- Manufacturing plain bearings--are classified in Industry 33361, Engine, Turbine, and Power Transmission Equipment Manufacturing;

T—Canadian, Mexican, and United States industries are comparable.

- Manufacturing military tanks--are classified in Industry 33699, Other Transportation Equipment Manufacturing;
- Manufacturing guided missiles--are classified in Industry 33641, Aerospace Product and Parts Manufacturing;
- Manufacturing cast iron pipe and fittings--are classified in Industry 33151, Ferrous Metal Foundries;
- Manufacturing pipe system fittings (except cast iron couplings and couplings made from purchased pipe) and metal aerosol spray nozzles--are classified in Industry 33291, Metal Valve Manufacturing;
- Manufacturing welded and seamless steel pipes from purchased steel--are classified in Industry 33121, Iron and Steel Pipe and Tube Manufacturing from Purchased Steel;
- Manufacturing plastics plumbing fixtures and plastics portable chemical toilets--are classified in Industry 32619, Other Plastics Product Manufacturing;
- Manufacturing vitreous and semivitreous pottery sanitary ware--are classified in Industry 32711, Pottery, Ceramics, and Plumbing Fixture Manufacturing;
- Manufacturing blasting caps, detonating caps, and safety fuses--are classified in Industry 32592, Explosives Manufacturing;
- Manufacturing fireworks--are classified in Industry 32599, All Other Chemical Product and Preparation Manufacturing;
- Manufacturing metal furniture frames--are classified in Industry 33721, Office Furniture (including Fixtures) Manufacturing;
- Manufacturing metal mechanically refrigerated drinking fountains--are classified in Industry 33341, Ventilation, Heating, Air-Conditioning, and Commercial Refrigeration Equipment Manufacturing;
- Manufacturing metal foil bags--are classified in Industry 32222, Paper Bag and Coated and Treated Paper Manufacturing;
- Manufacturing aluminum foil--are classified in Industry 33131, Alumina and Aluminum Production and Processing;
- Manufacturing metal foil (except aluminum)--are classified in Industry Group 3314, Nonferrous Metal (except Aluminum) Production and Processing; and
- Manufacturing metal burial vaults--are classified in Industry 33999, All Other Miscellaneous Manufacturing.

332991 Ball and Roller Bearing Manufacturing

This U.S. industry comprises establishments primarily engaged in manufacturing ball and roller bearings of all materials.

Cross-References.

Establishments primarily engaged in manufacturing plain bearings are classified in U.S. Industry 333613, Mechanical Power Transmission Equipment Manufacturing.

332992 Small Arms Ammunition Manufacturing

This U.S. industry comprises establishments primarily engaged in manufacturing small arms ammunition.

Cross-References. Establishments primarily engaged in--

- Manufacturing ammunition (except small arms)--are classified in U.S. Industry 332993, Ammunition (except Small Arms) Manufacturing;
- Manufacturing blasting and detonating caps and safety fuses--are classified in Industry 325920, Explosives Manufacturing; and
- Manufacturing fireworks--are classified in U.S. Industry 325998, All Other Miscellaneous Chemical Product and Preparation Manufacturing.

T—Canadian, Mexican, and United States industries are comparable.

332993 Ammunition (except Small Arms) Manufacturing

This U.S. industry comprises establishments primarily engaged in manufacturing ammunition (except small arms). Examples of products made by these establishments are bombs, depth charges, rockets (except guided missiles), grenades, mines, and torpedoes.

Cross-References. Establishments primarily engaged in--

- Manufacturing small arms ammunition--are classified in U.S. Industry 332992, Small Arms Ammunition Manufacturing;
- Manufacturing blasting and detonating caps and safety fuses--are classified in Industry 325920, Explosives Manufacturing;
- Manufacturing fireworks--are classified in U.S. Industry 325998, All Other Miscellaneous Chemical Product and Preparation Manufacturing; and
- Manufacturing guided missiles--are classified in U.S. Industry 336414, Guided Missile and Space Vehicle Manufacturing.

332994 Small Arms, Ordnance, and Ordnance Accessories Manufacturing

This U.S. industry comprises establishments primarily engaged in manufacturing small arms, other ordnance, and/or ordnance accessories.

Cross-References. Establishments primarily engaged in--

- Manufacturing military tanks--are classified in U.S. Industry 336992, Military Armored Vehicle, Tank, and Tank Component Manufacturing; and
- Manufacturing guided missiles--are classified in U.S. Industry 336414, Guided Missile and Space Vehicle Manufacturing.

332996 Fabricated Pipe and Pipe Fitting Manufacturing

This U.S. industry comprises establishments primarily engaged in fabricating, such as cutting, threading, and bending, metal pipes and pipe fittings made from purchased metal pipe.

Cross-References. Establishments primarily engaged in--

- Manufacturing cast iron pipe and fittings--are classified in U.S. Industry 331511, Iron Foundries;
- Manufacturing pipe system fittings (except cast iron couplings and couplings made from purchased pipe)--are classified in U.S. Industry 332919, Other Metal Valve and Pipe Fitting Manufacturing; and
- Manufacturing welded and seamless steel pipes from purchased steel--are classified in Industry 331210, Iron and Steel Pipe and Tube Manufacturing from Purchased Steel.

332999 All Other Miscellaneous Fabricated Metal Product Manufacturing

This U.S. industry comprises establishments primarily engaged in manufacturing fabricated metal products (except forgings and stampings, cutlery and handtools, architectural and structural metals, boilers, tanks, shipping containers, hardware, spring and wire products, machine shop products, turned products, screws, nuts and bolts, metal valves, ball and roller bearings, ammunition, small arms and other ordnances and accessories, and fabricated pipes and pipe fittings).

Illustrative Examples:

Foil containers (except bags) manufacturing
Industrial pattern manufacturing
Metal hair curlers manufacturing
Metal ironing boards manufacturing
Metal pallets manufacturing
Metal pipe hangers and supports manufacturing

T—Canadian, Mexican, and United States industries are comparable.

Metal safes manufacturing
Metal vaults (except burial) manufacturing
Permanent metallic magnets manufacturing
Portable metal ladders manufacturing
Sanitary ware (e.g., bathtubs, lavatories, sinks), metal and enameled metal, manufacturing
Steel wool manufacturing

Cross-References. Establishments primarily engaged in--

- Manufacturing forgings and stampings--are classified in Industry 33211, Forging and Stamping;
- Manufacturing cutlery and handtools--are classified in Industry 33221, Cutlery and Handtool Manufacturing;
- Manufacturing architectural and structural metals--are classified in Industry Group 3323, Architectural and Structural Metals Manufacturing;
- Manufacturing boilers, tanks, and shipping containers--are classified in Industry Group 3324, Boiler, Tank, and Shipping Container Manufacturing;
- Manufacturing hardware and safe and vault locks--are classified in Industry 332510, Hardware Manufacturing;
- Manufacturing spring and wire products--are classified in Industry 33261, Spring and Wire Product Manufacturing;
- Manufacturing machine shop products, turned products, screws, and nuts and bolts--are classified in Industry Group 3327, Machine Shops; Turned Product; and Screw, Nut, and Bolt Manufacturing;
- Coating, engraving, heat treating, and allied activities--are classified in Industry 33281, Coating, Engraving, Heat Treating, and Allied Activities;
- Manufacturing ball and roller bearings--are classified in U.S. Industry 332991, Ball and Roller Bearing Manufacturing;
- Manufacturing small arms ammunition--are classified in U.S. Industry 332992, Small Arms Ammunition Manufacturing;
- Manufacturing ammunition (except small arms)--are classified in U.S. Industry 332993, Ammunition (except Small Arms) Manufacturing;
- Manufacturing small firearms that are carried and fired by the individual and/or other ordnance and accessories--are classified in U.S. Industry 332994, Small Arms, Ordnance, and Ordnance Accessories Manufacturing;
- Manufacturing metal pipes and pipe fittings from metal pipe produced elsewhere--are classified in U.S. Industry 332996, Fabricated Pipe and Pipe Fitting Manufacturing;
- Manufacturing cast iron pipe and fittings--are classified in U.S. Industry 331511, Iron Foundries;
- Manufacturing welded and seamless steel pipes from purchased steel--are classified in Industry 331210, Iron and Steel Pipe and Tube Manufacturing from Purchased Steel;
- Manufacturing metal furniture frames--are classified in U.S. Industry 337215, Showcase, Partition, Shelving, and Locker Manufacturing;
- Manufacturing powder metallurgy parts--are classified in U.S. Industry 332117, Powder Metallurgy Part Manufacturing;
- Manufacturing metal boxes--are classified in U.S. Industry 332439, Other Metal Container Manufacturing;
- Manufacturing metal nozzles, hose couplings, and aerosol valves--are classified in U.S. Industry 332919, Other Metal Valve and Pipe Fitting Manufacturing;
- Manufacturing metal foil bags--are classified in Industry 322220, Paper Bag and Coated and Treated Paper Manufacturing;
- Manufacturing aluminum foil--are classified in Industry 33131, Alumina and Aluminum Production and Processing;
- Manufacturing metal foil (except aluminum)--are classified in Industry Group 3314, Nonferrous Metal (except Aluminum) Production and Processing;
- Manufacturing metal burial vaults--are classified in U.S. Industry 339995, Burial Casket Manufacturing;
- Manufacturing plastics plumbing fixtures--are classified in U.S. Industry 326191, Plastics Plumbing Fixture Manufacturing;
- Manufacturing vitreous and semivitreous pottery sanitary ware--are classified in Industry 327110, Pottery, Ceramics, and Plumbing Fixture Manufacturing;

T—Canadian, Mexican, and United States industries are comparable.

- Manufacturing plastics portable chemical toilets--are classified in U.S. Industry 326199, All Other Plastics Product Manufacturing; and
- Manufacturing metal mechanically refrigerated drinking fountains--are classified in U.S. Industry 333415, Air-Conditioning and Warm Air Heating Equipment and Commercial and Industrial Refrigeration Equipment Manufacturing.

333 Machinery Manufacturing[T]

Industries in the Machinery Manufacturing subsector create end products that apply mechanical force, for example, the application of gears and levers, to perform work. Some important processes for the manufacture of machinery are forging, stamping, bending, forming, and machining that are used to shape individual pieces of metal. Processes, such as welding and assembling are used to join separate parts together. Although these processes are similar to those used in metal fabricating establishments, machinery manufacturing is different because it typically employs multiple metal forming processes in manufacturing the various parts of the machine. Moreover, complex assembly operations are an inherent part of the production process.

In general, design considerations are very important in machinery production. Establishments specialize in making machinery designed for particular applications. Thus, design is considered to be part of the production process for the purpose of implementing NAICS. The NAICS structure reflects this by defining industries and industry groups that make machinery for different applications. A broad distinction exists between machinery that is generally used in a variety of industrial applications (i.e., general purpose machinery) and machinery that is designed to be used in a particular industry (i.e., special purpose machinery). Three industry groups consist of special purpose machinery--Agricultural, Construction, and Mining Machinery Manufacturing; Industrial Machinery Manufacturing; and Commercial and Service Industry Machinery Manufacturing. The other industry groups make general purpose machinery: Ventilation, Heating, Air-Conditioning, and Commercial Refrigeration Equipment Manufacturing; Metalworking Machinery Manufacturing; Engine, Turbine, and Power Transmission Equipment Manufacturing; and Other General Purpose Machinery Manufacturing.

3331 Agriculture, Construction, and Mining Machinery Manufacturing[T]

This industry group comprises establishments primarily engaged in manufacturing one or more of the following: (1) farm machinery and equipment, power mowing equipment, and other powered home lawn and garden equipment; (2) construction machinery, surface mining machinery, and logging equipment; and (3) oil and gas field and underground mining machinery and equipment.

33311 Agricultural Implement Manufacturing[T]

This industry comprises establishments primarily engaged in manufacturing farm machinery and equipment, powered mowing equipment, and other powered home lawn and garden equipment.

Illustrative Examples:

Combines (i.e., harvester-threshers) manufacturing
Cotton ginning machinery manufacturing
Fertilizing machinery, farm-type, manufacturing
Haying machines manufacturing
Milking machines manufacturing
Planting machines, farm-type, manufacturing
Plows, farm-type, manufacturing
Poultry brooders, feeders, and waterers manufacturing
Powered lawnmowers manufacturing
Snowblowers and throwers, residential-type, manufacturing
Tractors and attachments, lawn and garden-type and farm-type, manufacturing

Cross-References. Establishments primarily engaged in--

- Manufacturing agricultural handtools and nonpowered lawnmowers--are classified in Industry 33221, Cutlery and Handtool Manufacturing;
- Manufacturing farm conveyors--are classified in Industry 33392, Material Handling Equipment Manufacturing; and

T—Canadian, Mexican, and United States industries are comparable.

- Manufacturing forestry machinery and equipment, such as brush, limb, and log chippers; log splitters; and construction equipment--are classified in Industry 33312, Construction Machinery Manufacturing.

333111 Farm Machinery and Equipment Manufacturing

This U.S. industry comprises establishments primarily engaged in manufacturing agricultural and farm machinery and equipment, and other turf and grounds care equipment, including planting, harvesting, and grass mowing equipment (except lawn and garden-type).

Illustrative Examples:

Combines (i.e., harvester-threshers) manufacturing
Cotton ginning machinery manufacturing
Feed processing equipment, farm-type, manufacturing
Fertilizing machinery, farm-type, manufacturing
Grass mowing equipment (except lawn and garden) manufacturing
Haying machines manufacturing
Milking machines manufacturing
Planting machines, farm-type, manufacturing
Plows, farm-type, manufacturing
Poultry brooders, feeders, and waterers manufacturing
Tractors and attachments, farm-type, manufacturing

Cross-References. Establishments primarily engaged in--

- Manufacturing farm conveyors--are classified in U.S. Industry 333922, Conveyor and Conveying Equipment Manufacturing;
- Manufacturing tractors and lawnmowers for home lawn and garden care--are classified in U.S. Industry 333112, Lawn and Garden Tractor and Home Lawn and Garden Equipment Manufacturing; and
- Manufacturing construction-type tractors--are classified in Industry 333120, Construction Machinery Manufacturing.

333112 Lawn and Garden Tractor and Home Lawn and Garden Equipment Manufacturing

This U.S. industry comprises establishments primarily engaged in manufacturing powered lawnmowers, lawn and garden tractors, and other home lawn and garden equipment, such as tillers, shredders, yard vacuums, and leaf blowers.

Cross-References. Establishments primarily engaged in--

- Manufacturing commercial mowing and other turf and grounds care equipment--are classified in U.S. Industry 333111, Farm Machinery and Equipment Manufacturing; and
- Manufacturing nonpowered lawn and garden shears, edgers, pruners, and lawnmowers--are classified in U.S. Industry 332216, Saw Blade and Handtool Manufacturing.

33312 Construction Machinery Manufacturing[T] See industry description for 333120.

333120 Construction Machinery Manufacturing

This industry comprises establishments primarily engaged in manufacturing construction machinery, surface mining machinery, and logging equipment.

Illustrative Examples:

Backhoes manufacturing
Bulldozers manufacturing
Construction and surface mining-type rock drill bits manufacturing
Construction-type tractors and attachments manufacturing
Off-highway trucks manufacturing
Pile-driving equipment manufacturing

T—Canadian, Mexican, and United States industries are comparable.

Portable crushing, pulverizing, and screening machinery manufacturing
Powered post hole diggers manufacturing
Road graders manufacturing
Surface mining machinery (except drilling) manufacturing

Cross-References. Establishments primarily engaged in--

- Manufacturing drilling and underground mining machinery and equipment--are classified in Industry 33313, Mining and Oil and Gas Field Machinery Manufacturing;
- Manufacturing industrial plant overhead traveling cranes and hoists, truck-type cranes and hoists, winches, aerial work platforms, and automotive wrecker hoists--are classified in Industry 33392, Material Handling Equipment Manufacturing; and
- Manufacturing rail layers, ballast distributors and other railroad track-laying equipment--are classified in Industry 336510, Railroad Rolling Stock Manufacturing.

33313 Mining and Oil and Gas Field Machinery Manufacturing[T]

This industry comprises establishments primarily engaged in manufacturing oil and gas field and underground mining machinery and equipment.

Illustrative Examples:

Coal breakers, cutters, and pulverizers manufacturing
Core drills, underground mining-type, manufacturing
Mineral processing and beneficiating machinery manufacturing
Mining cars manufacturing
Oil and gas field-type derricks manufacturing
Oil and gas field-type drilling machinery and equipment (except offshore floating platforms) manufacturing
Stationary rock crushing machinery manufacturing
Water well drilling machinery manufacturing

Cross-References. Establishments primarily engaged in--

- Manufacturing offshore oil and gas well drilling and production floating platforms--are classified in Industry 33661, Ship and Boat Building;
- Manufacturing surface mining machinery and equipment--are classified in Industry 33312, Construction Machinery Manufacturing;
- Manufacturing coal and ore conveyors--are classified in Industry 33392, Material Handling Equipment Manufacturing;
- Manufacturing underground mining locomotives--are classified in Industry 33651, Railroad Rolling Stock Manufacturing; and
- Manufacturing pumps and pumping equipment--are classified in Industry 33391, Pump and Compressor Manufacturing.

333131 Mining Machinery and Equipment Manufacturing

This U.S. industry comprises establishments primarily engaged in (1) manufacturing underground mining machinery and equipment, such as coal breakers, mining cars, core drills, coal cutters, and rock drills, and (2) manufacturing mineral beneficiating machinery and equipment used in surface or underground mines.

Cross-References. Establishments primarily engaged in--

- Manufacturing surface mining machinery and equipment--are classified in Industry 333120, Construction Machinery Manufacturing;
- Manufacturing well drilling machinery--are classified in U.S. Industry 333132, Oil and Gas Field Machinery and Equipment Manufacturing;
- Manufacturing coal and ore conveyors--are classified in U.S. Industry 333922, Conveyor and Conveying Equipment Manufacturing; and

T—Canadian, Mexican, and United States industries are comparable.

- Manufacturing underground mining locomotives--are classified in Industry 336510, Railroad Rolling Stock Manufacturing.

333132 Oil and Gas Field Machinery and Equipment Manufacturing

This U.S. industry comprises establishments primarily engaged in (1) manufacturing oil and gas field machinery and equipment, such as oil and gas field drilling machinery and equipment; oil and gas field production machinery and equipment; and oil and gas field derricks, and (2) manufacturing water well drilling machinery.

Cross-References. Establishments primarily engaged in--

- Manufacturing offshore oil and gas well drilling and production floating platforms--are classified in U.S. Industry 336611, Ship Building and Repairing;
- Manufacturing underground mining drills--are classified in U.S. Industry 333131, Mining Machinery and Equipment Manufacturing; and
- Manufacturing pumps and pumping equipment--are classified in U.S. Industry 333914, Measuring, Dispensing, and Other Pumping Equipment Manufacturing.

3332 Industrial Machinery Manufacturing[T]

33324 Industrial Machinery Manufacturing[T]

This industry comprises establishments primarily engaged in manufacturing industrial machinery, such as food and beverage manufacturing machinery, semiconductor manufacturing machinery, sawmill and woodworking machinery (except handheld), machinery for making paper and paper products, printing and binding machinery and equipment, textile making machinery, and machinery for making plastics and rubber products.

Cross-References. Establishments primarily engaged in--

- Manufacturing agricultural and farm-type, construction, and mining machinery--are classified in Industry Group 3331, Agriculture, Construction, and Mining Machinery Manufacturing;
- Manufacturing food and beverage packaging machinery or power-driven handtools--are classified in Industry 33399, All Other General Purpose Machinery Manufacturing;
- Manufacturing commercial and industrial refrigeration and freezer equipment--are classified in Industry 33341, Ventilation, Heating, Air-Conditioning, and Commercial Refrigeration Equipment Manufacturing;
- Manufacturing commercial-type cooking and food warming equipment, automotive maintenance equipment (except mechanics' handtools), or photocopiers--are classified in Industry 33331, Commercial and Service Industry Machinery Manufacturing; and
- Manufacturing mechanics' handtools and other nonpowered handtools--are classified in Industry 33221, Cutlery and Handtool Manufacturing.

333241 Food Product Machinery Manufacturing

This U.S. industry comprises establishments primarily engaged in manufacturing food and beverage manufacturing-type machinery and equipment, such as dairy product plant machinery and equipment (e.g., homogenizers, pasteurizers, ice cream freezers), bakery machinery and equipment (e.g., dough mixers, bake ovens, pastry rolling machines), meat and poultry processing and preparation machinery, and other commercial food products machinery (e.g., slicers, choppers, and mixers).

Cross-References. Establishments primarily engaged in--

- Manufacturing food and beverage packaging machinery--are classified in U.S. Industry 333993, Packaging Machinery Manufacturing;

T—Canadian, Mexican, and United States industries are comparable.

- Manufacturing commercial and industrial refrigeration and freezer equipment--are classified in U.S. Industry 333415, Air-Conditioning and Warm Air Heating Equipment and Commercial and Industrial Refrigeration Equipment Manufacturing; and
- Manufacturing commercial-type cooking and food warming equipment--are classified in U.S. Industry 333318, Other Commercial and Service Industry Machinery Manufacturing.

333242 Semiconductor Machinery Manufacturing

This U.S. industry comprises establishments primarily engaged in manufacturing wafer processing equipment, semiconductor assembly and packaging equipment, and other semiconductor making machinery.

Cross-References. Establishments primarily engaged in--

- Manufacturing printed circuit board manufacturing machinery--are classified in U.S. Industry 333249, Other Industrial Machinery Manufacturing; and
- Manufacturing semiconductor testing instruments--are classified in U.S. Industry 334515, Instrument Manufacturing for Measuring and Testing Electricity and Electrical Signals.

333243 Sawmill, Woodworking, and Paper Machinery Manufacturing

This U.S. industry comprises establishments primarily engaged in (1) manufacturing sawmill and woodworking machinery (except handheld), such as circular and band sawing equipment, planing machinery, and sanding machinery, and/or (2) manufacturing paper industry machinery for making paper and paper products, such as pulp making machinery, paper and paperboard making machinery, and paper and paperboard converting machinery.

Cross-References. Establishments primarily engaged in--

- Manufacturing planes, axes, drawknives, and handsaws--are classified in U.S. Industry 332216, Saw Blade and Handtool Manufacturing;
- Manufacturing power-driven handtools--are classified in U.S. Industry 333991, Power-Driven Handtool Manufacturing; and
- Manufacturing printing machinery--are classified in U.S. Industry 333244, Printing Machinery and Equipment Manufacturing.

333244 Printing Machinery and Equipment Manufacturing

This U.S. industry comprises establishments primarily engaged in manufacturing printing and bookbinding machinery and equipment, such as printing presses, typesetting machinery, and bindery machinery.

Cross-References. Establishments primarily engaged in--

- Manufacturing textile printing machinery--are classified in U.S. Industry 333249, Other Industrial Machinery Manufacturing; and
- Manufacturing photocopiers--are classified in U.S. Industry 333316, Photographic and Photocopying Equipment Manufacturing.

333249 Other Industrial Machinery Manufacturing

This U.S. industry comprises establishments primarily engaged in manufacturing industrial machinery (except agricultural and farm-type; construction and mining machinery; food manufacturing-type machinery; semiconductor making machinery; sawmill, woodworking, and paper making machinery; and printing machinery and equipment).
T—Canadian, Mexican, and United States industries are comparable.

Illustrative Examples:

Additive manufacturing machinery manufacturing
Chemical processing machinery and equipment manufacturing
Cigarette making machinery manufacturing
Glass making machinery (e.g., blowing, forming, molding) manufacturing
Petroleum refining machinery manufacturing
Plastics working machinery manufacturing
Rubber working machinery manufacturing
Sewing machines (including household-type) manufacturing
Shoe making and repairing machinery manufacturing
Tannery machinery manufacturing
Textile making machinery manufacturing

Cross-References. Establishments primarily engaged in--

- Manufacturing agricultural and farm-type, construction, and mining machinery--are classified in Industry Group 3331, Agriculture, Construction, and Mining Machinery Manufacturing;
- Manufacturing food and beverage manufacturing-type machinery--are classified in U.S. Industry 333241, Food Product Machinery Manufacturing;
- Manufacturing semiconductor making machinery--are classified in U.S. Industry 333242, Semiconductor Machinery Manufacturing;
- Manufacturing sawmill, woodworking, and paper and paperboard making machinery--are classified in U.S. Industry 333243, Sawmill, Woodworking, and Paper Machinery Manufacturing;
- Manufacturing printing and bookbinding machinery and equipment--are classified in U.S. Industry 333244, Printing Machinery and Equipment Manufacturing;
- Manufacturing automotive maintenance equipment (except mechanics' handtools)--are classified in U.S. Industry 333318, Other Commercial and Service Industry Machinery Manufacturing;
- Manufacturing mechanics' handtools--are classified in U.S. Industry 332216, Saw Blade and Handtool Manufacturing; and
- Manufacturing industrial metal molds for plastics and rubber products making machinery--are classified in U.S. Industry 333511, Industrial Mold Manufacturing.

3333 Commercial and Service Industry Machinery Manufacturing[T]

33331 Commercial and Service Industry Machinery Manufacturing[T]

This industry comprises establishments primarily engaged in manufacturing commercial and service industry machinery, such as optical instruments, photographic and photocopying equipment, automatic vending machinery, commercial laundry and drycleaning machinery, office machinery, automotive maintenance equipment (except mechanics' handtools), and commercial-type cooking equipment.

Cross-References. Establishments primarily engaged in--

- Manufacturing household-type appliances--are classified in Industry Group 3352, Household Appliance Manufacturing;
- Manufacturing computer and peripheral equipment (including point-of-sale terminals and automatic teller machines (ATMs))--are classified in Industry 33411, Computer and Peripheral Equipment Manufacturing;
- Manufacturing facsimile equipment--are classified in Industry 33421, Telephone Apparatus Manufacturing;
- Manufacturing time clocks, time stamps, and electron and proton microscopes--are classified in Industry 33451, Navigational, Measuring, Electromedical, and Control Instruments Manufacturing;
- Manufacturing pencil sharpeners and staplers--are classified in Industry 33994, Office Supplies (except Paper) Manufacturing;
- Manufacturing sensitized film, paper, cloth, and plates, and prepared photographic chemicals--are classified in Industry 32599, All Other Chemical Product and Preparation Manufacturing;
- Manufacturing ophthalmic focus lenses--are classified in Industry 33911, Medical Equipment and Supplies Manufacturing;
- Manufacturing television and video cameras--are classified in Subsector 334, Computer and Electronic Product Manufacturing;

T—Canadian, Mexican, and United States industries are comparable.

- Manufacturing coin-operated arcade games--are classified in Industry 33999, All Other Miscellaneous Manufacturing;
- Manufacturing mechanics' handtools--are classified in Industry 33221, Cutlery and Handtool Manufacturing;
- Manufacturing molded plastics lens blanks--are classified in Industry 32619, Other Plastics Product Manufacturing; and
- Manufacturing molded glass lens blanks--are classified in Industry 32721, Glass and Glass Product Manufacturing.

333314 Optical Instrument and Lens Manufacturing

This U.S. industry comprises establishments primarily engaged in one or more of the following: (1) manufacturing optical instruments and lenses, such as binoculars, microscopes (except electron, proton), telescopes, prisms, and lenses (except ophthalmic); (2) coating or polishing lenses (except ophthalmic); and (3) mounting lenses (except ophthalmic).

Cross-References. Establishments primarily engaged in--

- Manufacturing ophthalmic focus lenses--are classified in U.S. Industry 339115, Ophthalmic Goods Manufacturing;
- Manufacturing electron and proton microscopes--are classified in U.S. Industry 334516, Analytical Laboratory Instrument Manufacturing;
- Manufacturing molded plastics lens blanks--are classified in U.S. Industry 326199, All Other Plastics Product Manufacturing; and
- Manufacturing molded glass lens blanks--are classified in U.S. Industry 327212, Other Pressed and Blown Glass and Glassware Manufacturing.

333316 Photographic and Photocopying Equipment Manufacturing

This U.S. industry comprises establishments primarily engaged in manufacturing photographic and photocopying equipment, such as cameras (except television and video), projectors, film developing equipment, photocopying equipment, and microfilm equipment.

Cross-References. Establishments primarily engaged in--

- Manufacturing sensitized film, paper, cloth, and plates, and prepared photographic chemicals--are classified in U.S. Industry 325992, Photographic Film, Paper, Plate, and Chemical Manufacturing;
- Manufacturing photographic lenses--are classified in U.S. Industry 333314, Optical Instrument and Lens Manufacturing; and
- Manufacturing television and video cameras--are classified in Subsector 334, Computer and Electronic Product Manufacturing.

333318 Other Commercial and Service Industry Machinery Manufacturing

This U.S. industry comprises establishments primarily engaged in manufacturing commercial and service industry equipment (except optical instruments and lenses, and photographic and photocopying equipment).

Illustrative Examples:

Calculators manufacturing
Carnival and amusement park rides manufacturing
Car washing machinery manufacturing
Commercial-type coffee makers and urns manufacturing
Mechanical carpet sweepers manufacturing
Commercial-type cooking equipment (i.e., fryers, microwave ovens, ovens, ranges) manufacturing
Industrial and commercial-type vacuum cleaners manufacturing
Laundry machinery and equipment (except household-type) manufacturing

T—Canadian, Mexican, and United States industries are comparable.

Motor vehicle alignment equipment manufacturing
Power washer cleaning equipment manufacturing
Vending machines manufacturing
Teaching machines (e.g., flight simulators) manufacturing
Water treatment equipment manufacturing

Cross-References. Establishments primarily engaged in--

- Manufacturing optical instruments and lenses--are classified in U.S. Industry 333314, Optical Instrument and Lens Manufacturing;
- Manufacturing photographic and photocopying equipment--are classified in U.S. Industry 333316, Photographic and Photocopying Equipment Manufacturing;
- Manufacturing household-type appliances--are classified in Industry Group 3352, Household Appliance Manufacturing;
- Manufacturing mechanics' handtools--are classified in U.S. Industry 332216, Saw Blade and Handtool Manufacturing;
- Manufacturing coin-operated arcade games--are classified in U.S. Industry 339999, All Other Miscellaneous Manufacturing;
- Manufacturing computers and peripheral equipment (including point-of-sale terminals and automatic teller machines (ATMs))--are classified in Industry 33411, Computer and Peripheral Equipment Manufacturing;
- Manufacturing facsimile equipment--are classified in Industry 334210, Telephone Apparatus Manufacturing;
- Manufacturing time clocks and time stamps--are classified in U.S. Industry 334519, Other Measuring and Controlling Device Manufacturing; and
- Manufacturing pencil sharpeners, staplers, staple removers, hand paper punches, cutters, trimmers, and other hand office equipment--are classified in Industry 339940, Office Supplies (except Paper) Manufacturing.

3334 Ventilation, Heating, Air-Conditioning, and Commercial Refrigeration Equipment Manufacturing[T]

33341 Ventilation, Heating, Air-Conditioning, and Commercial Refrigeration Equipment Manufacturing[T]

This industry comprises establishments primarily engaged in manufacturing ventilating, heating, air-conditioning, and commercial and industrial refrigeration and freezer equipment.

Illustrative Examples:

Air-conditioner filters manufacturing
Air-conditioning and warm air heating combination units manufacturing
Attic fans manufacturing
Dust and fume collecting equipment manufacturing
Gas fireplaces manufacturing
Heating boilers manufacturing
Industrial and commercial-type fans manufacturing
Refrigerated counter and display cases manufacturing
Refrigerated drinking fountains manufacturing
Space heaters (except portable electric) manufacturing

Cross-References. Establishments primarily engaged in--

- Manufacturing household-type fans (except attic), portable electric space heaters, humidifiers, dehumidifiers, and air purification equipment--are classified in Industry 33521, Small Electrical Appliance Manufacturing;
- Manufacturing household-type appliances, such as cooking stoves, ranges, refrigerators, and freezers--are classified in Industry 33522, Major Household Appliance Manufacturing;
- Manufacturing commercial-type cooking equipment--are classified in Industry 33331, Commercial and Service Industry Machinery Manufacturing;
- Manufacturing industrial, power, and marine boilers--are classified in Industry 33241, Power Boiler and Heat Exchanger Manufacturing;
- Manufacturing industrial process furnaces and ovens--are classified in Industry 33399, All Other General Purpose Machinery Manufacturing; and

T—Canadian, Mexican, and United States industries are comparable.

- Manufacturing motor vehicle air-conditioning systems and compressors--are classified in Industry 33639, Other Motor Vehicle Parts Manufacturing.

333413 Industrial and Commercial Fan and Blower and Air Purification Equipment Manufacturing

This U.S. industry comprises establishments primarily engaged in (1) manufacturing stationary air purification equipment, such as industrial dust and fume collection equipment, electrostatic precipitation equipment, warm air furnace filters, air washers, and other dust collection equipment, and/or (2) manufacturing attic fans and industrial and commercial fans and blowers, such as commercial exhaust fans and commercial ventilating fans.

Cross-References. Establishments primarily engaged in--

- Manufacturing air-conditioning equipment (except motor vehicle)--are classified in U.S. Industry 333415, Air-Conditioning and Warm Air Heating Equipment and Commercial and Industrial Refrigeration Equipment Manufacturing;
- Manufacturing motor vehicle air-conditioning systems and compressors--are classified in Industry 336390, Other Motor Vehicle Parts Manufacturing; and
- Manufacturing household-type fans (except attic) and portable air purification equipment--are classified in Industry 335210, Small Electrical Appliance Manufacturing.

333414 Heating Equipment (except Warm Air Furnaces) Manufacturing

This U.S. industry comprises establishments primarily engaged in manufacturing heating equipment (except electric and warm air furnaces), such as heating boilers, heating stoves, floor and wall furnaces, and wall and baseboard heating units.

Cross-References. Establishments primarily engaged in--

- Manufacturing warm air furnaces--are classified in U.S. Industry 333415, Air-Conditioning and Warm Air Heating Equipment and Commercial and Industrial Refrigeration Equipment Manufacturing;
- Manufacturing electric space heaters--are classified in Industry 335210, Small Electrical Appliance Manufacturing;
- Manufacturing household-type cooking stoves and ranges--are classified in Industry 335220, Major Household Appliance Manufacturing;
- Manufacturing industrial, power, and marine boilers--are classified in Industry 332410, Power Boiler and Heat Exchanger Manufacturing;
- Manufacturing industrial process furnaces and ovens--are classified in U.S. Industry 333994, Industrial Process Furnace and Oven Manufacturing; and
- Manufacturing commercial-type cooking equipment--are classified in U.S. Industry 333318, Other Commercial and Service Industry Machinery Manufacturing.

333415 Air-Conditioning and Warm Air Heating Equipment and Commercial and Industrial Refrigeration Equipment Manufacturing

This U.S. industry comprises establishments primarily engaged in (1) manufacturing air-conditioning (except motor vehicle) and warm air furnace equipment and/or (2) manufacturing commercial and industrial refrigeration and freezer equipment.

Illustrative Examples:

Air-conditioning and warm air heating combination units manufacturing
Air-conditioning compressors (except motor vehicle) manufacturing
Heat pumps manufacturing
Air-conditioning condensers and condensing units manufacturing
Dehumidifiers (except portable electric) manufacturing
Refrigerated counter and display cases manufacturing

T—Canadian, Mexican, and United States industries are comparable.

Humidifying equipment (except portable) manufacturing
Refrigerated drinking fountains manufacturing
Snow making machinery manufacturing
Soda fountain cooling and dispensing equipment manufacturing

Cross-References. Establishments primarily engaged in--

- Manufacturing motor vehicle air-conditioning systems and compressors--are classified in Industry 336390, Other Motor Vehicle Parts Manufacturing;
- Manufacturing household-type refrigerators and freezers--are classified in Industry 335220, Major Household Appliance Manufacturing;
- Manufacturing portable electric space heaters, humidifiers, and dehumidifiers--are classified in Industry 335210, Small Electrical Appliance Manufacturing;
- Manufacturing heating boilers, heating stoves, floor and wall mount furnaces, and electric wall and baseboard heating units--are classified in U.S. Industry 333414, Heating Equipment (except Warm Air Furnaces) Manufacturing; and
- Manufacturing furnace air filters--are classified in U.S. Industry 333413, Industrial and Commercial Fan and Blower and Air Purification Equipment Manufacturing.

3335 Metalworking Machinery Manufacturing[T]

33351 Metalworking Machinery Manufacturing[T]

This industry comprises establishments primarily engaged in manufacturing metalworking machinery, such as metal cutting and metal forming machine tools; cutting tools; accessories for metalworking machinery; special dies, tools, jigs, and fixtures; industrial molds; rolling mill machinery; assembly machinery; coil handling, conversion, or straightening equipment; and wire drawing and fabricating machines.

Cross-References. Establishments primarily engaged in--

- Manufacturing handtools (except power-driven), cutting dies (except metal cutting), saw blades, and handsaws--are classified in Industry 33221, Cutlery and Handtool Manufacturing;
- Manufacturing casting molds for heavy steel ingots--are classified in Industry 33151, Ferrous Metal Foundries; and
- Manufacturing power-driven handtools and welding and soldering equipment--are classified in Industry 33399, All Other General Purpose Machinery Manufacturing.

333511 Industrial Mold Manufacturing

This U.S. industry comprises establishments primarily engaged in manufacturing industrial molds for casting metals or forming other materials, such as plastics, glass, or rubber.

Cross-References.

Establishments primarily engaged in manufacturing casting molds for steel ingots are classified in U.S. Industry 331511, Iron Foundries.

333514 Special Die and Tool, Die Set, Jig, and Fixture Manufacturing

This U.S. industry comprises establishments, known as tool and die shops, primarily engaged in manufacturing special tools and fixtures, such as cutting dies and jigs.

T—Canadian, Mexican, and United States industries are comparable.

Cross-References. Establishments primarily engaged in--

- Manufacturing molds for die-casting and foundry casting; and metal molds for plaster working, rubber working, plastics working, and glass working machinery--are classified in U.S. Industry 333511, Industrial Mold Manufacturing;
- Manufacturing molds for heavy steel ingots--are classified in U.S. Industry 331511, Iron Foundries; and
- Manufacturing cutting dies for materials other than metal--are classified in U.S. Industry 332216, Saw Blade and Handtool Manufacturing.

333515 Cutting Tool and Machine Tool Accessory Manufacturing

This U.S. industry comprises establishments primarily engaged in manufacturing accessories and attachments for metal cutting and metal forming machine tools.

Illustrative Examples:

Knives and bits for metalworking lathes, planers, and shapers manufacturing
Measuring attachments (e.g., sine bars) for machine tool manufacturing
Metalworking drill bits manufacturing
Taps and dies (i.e., machine tool accessories) manufacturing

Cross-References.

Establishments primarily engaged in manufacturing saw blades, handsaws, and accessories and attachments for saw blades and for nonpowered metal cutting and forming handtools are classified in U.S. Industry 332216, Saw Blade and Handtool Manufacturing.

333517 Machine Tool Manufacturing

This U.S. industry comprises establishments primarily engaged in (1) manufacturing metal cutting machine tools (except handtools) and/or (2) manufacturing metal forming machine tools (except handtools), such as punching, sheering, bending, forming, pressing, forging and die-casting machines.

Illustrative Examples:

Bending and forming machines, metalworking, manufacturing
Buffing and polishing machines, metalworking, manufacturing
Drilling machines, metalworking, manufacturing
Grinding machines, metalworking, manufacturing
Home workshop metal cutting machine tools (except handtools, welding equipment) manufacturing
Metalworking lathes manufacturing
Milling machines, metalworking, manufacturing
Stamping machines, metalworking, manufacturing

Cross-References. Establishments primarily engaged in--

- Manufacturing welding and soldering equipment--are classified in U.S. Industry 333992, Welding and Soldering Equipment Manufacturing;
- Manufacturing power-driven handtools--are classified in U.S. Industry 333991, Power-Driven Handtool Manufacturing;
- Manufacturing rolling mill machinery and equipment--are classified in U.S. Industry 333519, Rolling Mill and Other Metalworking Machinery Manufacturing; and
- Manufacturing accessories and attachments for metal cutting and forming machine tools (except saw blades)--are classified in U.S. Industry 333515, Cutting Tool and Machine Tool Accessory Manufacturing.

T—Canadian, Mexican, and United States industries are comparable.

333519 Rolling Mill and Other Metalworking Machinery Manufacturing

This U.S. industry comprises establishments primarily engaged in manufacturing rolling mill machinery and equipment and/or other metalworking machinery (except industrial molds; special dies and tools, die sets, jigs, and fixtures; cutting tools and machine tool accessories; and machine tools).

Illustrative Examples:

Assembly machines manufacturing
Cradle assemblies machinery (i.e., wire making equipment) manufacturing
Metalworking coil winding and cutting machinery manufacturing
Rolling mill roll machines, metalworking, manufacturing
Wire drawing and fabricating machinery and equipment (except dies) manufacturing

Cross-References. Establishments primarily engaged in--

- Manufacturing industrial molds--are classified in U.S. Industry 333511, Industrial Mold Manufacturing;
- Manufacturing metal cutting and metal forming machine tools--are classified in U.S. Industry 333517, Machine Tool Manufacturing;
- Manufacturing special dies and tools, die sets, jigs, and fixtures--are classified in U.S. Industry 333514, Special Die and Tool, Die Set, Jig, and Fixture Manufacturing; and
- Manufacturing accessories and attachments for metal cutting and forming machine tools (except saw blades)--are classified in U.S. Industry 333515, Cutting Tool and Machine Tool Accessory Manufacturing.

3336 Engine, Turbine, and Power Transmission Equipment Manufacturing[T]

33361 Engine, Turbine, and Power Transmission Equipment Manufacturing[T]

This industry comprises establishments primarily engaged in manufacturing turbines, power transmission equipment, and internal combustion engines (except automotive gasoline and aircraft).

Illustrative Examples:

Clutches and brakes (except electromagnetic industrial controls, motor vehicle) manufacturing
Diesel and semidiesel engines manufacturing
Electric outboard motors manufacturing
Internal combustion engines for hybrid drive systems (except automotive) manufacturing
Plain bearings (except internal combustion engine) manufacturing
Power transmission pulleys manufacturing
Plain bushings (except internal combustion engine) manufacturing
Speed changers (i.e., power transmission equipment) manufacturing
Speed reducers (i.e., power transmission equipment) manufacturing
Turbine generator set units manufacturing
Universal joints (except aircraft, motor vehicle) manufacturing

Cross-References. Establishments primarily engaged in--

- Manufacturing motor vehicle power transmission equipment--are classified in Industry 33635, Motor Vehicle Transmission and Power Train Parts Manufacturing;
- Manufacturing aircraft engines and aircraft power transmission equipment--are classified in Industry 33641, Aerospace Product and Parts Manufacturing;
- Manufacturing ball and roller bearings--are classified in Industry 33299, All Other Fabricated Metal Product Manufacturing;
- Manufacturing gasoline automotive engines--are classified in Industry 33631, Motor Vehicle Gasoline Engine and Engine Parts Manufacturing; and

T—Canadian, Mexican, and United States industries are comparable.

- Manufacturing electric power transmission, electric power distribution equipment, generators, or prime mover generator sets (except turbines)--are classified in Industry 33531, Electrical Equipment Manufacturing.

333611 Turbine and Turbine Generator Set Units Manufacturing

This U.S. industry comprises establishments primarily engaged in manufacturing turbines (except aircraft); and complete turbine generator set units, such as steam, hydraulic, gas, and wind.

Cross-References. Establishments primarily engaged in--

- Manufacturing aircraft turbines--are classified in U.S. Industry 336412, Aircraft Engine and Engine Parts Manufacturing; and
- Manufacturing generators or prime mover generator sets (except turbines)--are classified in U.S. Industry 335312, Motor and Generator Manufacturing.

333612 Speed Changer, Industrial High-Speed Drive, and Gear Manufacturing

This U.S. industry comprises establishments primarily engaged in manufacturing gears, speed changers, and industrial high-speed drives (except hydrostatic).

Cross-References. Establishments primarily engaged in--

- Manufacturing motor vehicle power transmission equipment--are classified in Industry 336350, Motor Vehicle Transmission and Power Train Parts Manufacturing;
- Manufacturing aircraft power transmission equipment--are classified in U.S. Industry 336413, Other Aircraft Parts and Auxiliary Equipment Manufacturing; and
- Manufacturing industrial hydrostatic transmissions--are classified in U.S. Industry 333996, Fluid Power Pump and Motor Manufacturing.

333613 Mechanical Power Transmission Equipment Manufacturing

This U.S. industry comprises establishments primarily engaged in manufacturing mechanical power transmission equipment (except motor vehicle and aircraft), such as plain bearings, clutches (except motor vehicle and electromagnetic industrial control), couplings, joints, and drive chains.

Cross-References. Establishments primarily engaged in--

- Manufacturing motor vehicle power transmission equipment--are classified in Industry 336350, Motor Vehicle Transmission and Power Train Parts Manufacturing;
- Manufacturing aircraft power transmission equipment--are classified in U.S. Industry 336413, Other Aircraft Parts and Auxiliary Equipment Manufacturing;
- Manufacturing ball and roller bearings--are classified in U.S. Industry 332991, Ball and Roller Bearing Manufacturing; and
- Manufacturing gears, speed changers, and industrial high-speed drives (except hydrostatic)--are classified in U.S. Industry 333612, Speed Changer, Industrial High-Speed Drive, and Gear Manufacturing.

333618 Other Engine Equipment Manufacturing

This U.S. industry comprises establishments primarily engaged in manufacturing internal combustion engines (except automotive gasoline and aircraft).
T—Canadian, Mexican, and United States industries are comparable.

Cross-References. Establishments primarily engaged in--

- Manufacturing gasoline motor vehicle engines and motor vehicle transmissions--are classified in Industry Group 3363, Motor Vehicle Parts Manufacturing;
- Manufacturing gasoline aircraft engines and aircraft transmissions--are classified in Industry 33641, Aerospace Product and Parts Manufacturing;
- Manufacturing turbine and turbine generator set units--are classified in U.S. Industry 333611, Turbine and Turbine Generator Set Units Manufacturing;
- Manufacturing speed changers and industrial high-speed drives and gears--are classified in U.S. Industry 333612, Speed Changer, Industrial High-Speed Drive, and Gear Manufacturing; and
- Manufacturing mechanical power transmission equipment (except motor vehicle and aircraft)--are classified in U.S. Industry 333613, Mechanical Power Transmission Equipment Manufacturing.

3339 Other General Purpose Machinery Manufacturing[T]

This industry group comprises establishments primarily engaged in manufacturing pumps and compressors, material handling equipment, and all other general purpose machinery (except ventilation, heating, air-conditioning, and commercial refrigeration equipment; metalworking machinery; and engines, turbines, and power transmission equipment).

33391 Pump and Compressor Manufacturing[T]

This industry comprises establishments primarily engaged in manufacturing pumps and compressors, such as general purpose air and gas compressors, nonagricultural spraying and dusting equipment, general purpose pumps and pumping equipment (except fluid power pumps and motors), and measuring and dispensing pumps.

Cross-References. Establishments primarily engaged in--

- Manufacturing fluid power pumps and motors and handheld pneumatic spray guns--are classified in Industry 33399, All Other General Purpose Machinery Manufacturing;
- Manufacturing agricultural spraying and dusting equipment--are classified in Industry 33311, Agricultural Implement Manufacturing;
- Manufacturing laboratory vacuum pumps--are classified in Industry 33911, Medical Equipment and Supplies Manufacturing;
- Manufacturing pumps and air-conditioning systems and compressors for motor vehicles--are classified in Industry Group 3363, Motor Vehicle Parts Manufacturing; and
- Manufacturing air-conditioning systems and compressors (except motor vehicle)--are classified in Industry 33341, Ventilation, Heating, Air-Conditioning, and Commercial Refrigeration Equipment Manufacturing.

333912 Air and Gas Compressor Manufacturing

This U.S. industry comprises establishments primarily engaged in manufacturing general purpose air and gas compressors, such as reciprocating compressors, centrifugal compressors, vacuum pumps (except laboratory), and nonagricultural spraying and dusting compressors and spray gun units.

Cross-References. Establishments primarily engaged in--

- Manufacturing refrigeration and air-conditioning (except motor vehicle) systems and compressors--are classified in U.S. Industry 333415, Air-Conditioning and Warm Air Heating Equipment and Commercial and Industrial Refrigeration Equipment Manufacturing;
- Manufacturing motor vehicle air-conditioning systems and compressors--are classified in Industry 336390, Other Motor Vehicle Parts Manufacturing;
- Manufacturing fluid power pumps and motors--are classified in U.S. Industry 333996, Fluid Power Pump and Motor Manufacturing;

T—Canadian, Mexican, and United States industries are comparable.

- Manufacturing agricultural spraying and dusting equipment--are classified in U.S. Industry 333111, Farm Machinery and Equipment Manufacturing;
- Manufacturing laboratory vacuum pumps--are classified in U.S. Industry 339113, Surgical Appliance and Supplies Manufacturing; and
- Manufacturing handheld pneumatic spray guns--are classified in U.S. Industry 333991, Power-Driven Hand-tool Manufacturing.

333914 Measuring, Dispensing, and Other Pumping Equipment Manufacturing

This U.S. industry comprises establishments primarily engaged in (1) manufacturing measuring and dispensing pumps, such as gasoline pumps and lubricating oil measuring and dispensing pumps and/or (2) manufacturing general purpose pumps and pumping equipment (except fluid power pumps and motors), such as reciprocating pumps, turbine pumps, centrifugal pumps, rotary pumps, diaphragm pumps, domestic water system pumps, oil well and oil field pumps, and sump pumps.

Cross-References. Establishments primarily engaged in--

- Manufacturing fluid power pumps and motors--are classified in U.S. Industry 333996, Fluid Power Pump and Motor Manufacturing;
- Manufacturing vacuum pumps (except laboratory)--are classified in U.S. Industry 333912, Air and Gas Compressor Manufacturing;
- Manufacturing laboratory vacuum pumps--are classified in U.S. Industry 339113, Surgical Appliance and Supplies Manufacturing; and
- Manufacturing fluid pumps for motor vehicles, such as oil pumps, water pumps, and power steering pumps--are classified in Industry Group 3363, Motor Vehicle Parts Manufacturing.

33392 Material Handling Equipment Manufacturing[T]

This industry comprises establishments primarily engaged in manufacturing material handling equipment, such as elevators and moving stairs; conveyors and conveying equipment; overhead traveling cranes, hoists, and monorail systems; and industrial trucks, tractors, trailers, and stacker machinery.

Cross-References. Establishments primarily engaged in--

- Manufacturing motor vehicle-type trailers--are classified in Industry 33621, Motor Vehicle Body and Trailer Manufacturing;
- Manufacturing farm-type tractors--are classified in Industry 33311, Agricultural Implement Manufacturing;
- Manufacturing construction-type tractors and cranes--are classified in Industry 33312, Construction Machinery Manufacturing; and
- Manufacturing power transmission pulleys--are classified in Industry 33361, Engine, Turbine, and Power Transmission Equipment Manufacturing.

333921 Elevator and Moving Stairway Manufacturing

This U.S. industry comprises establishments primarily engaged in manufacturing elevators and moving stairways.

Illustrative Examples:

Automobile lifts (i.e., garage-type, service station) manufacturing
Escalators manufacturing
Moving walkways manufacturing
Passenger and freight elevators manufacturing

T—Canadian, Mexican, and United States industries are comparable.

Cross-References.

Establishments primarily engaged in manufacturing commercial conveyor systems and equipment are classified in U.S. Industry 333922, Conveyor and Conveying Equipment Manufacturing.

333922 Conveyor and Conveying Equipment Manufacturing

This U.S. industry comprises establishments primarily engaged in manufacturing conveyors and conveying equipment, such as gravity conveyors, trolley conveyors, tow conveyors, pneumatic tube conveyors, carousel conveyors, farm conveyors, and belt conveyors.

Cross-References. Establishments primarily engaged in--

- Manufacturing passenger or freight elevators, dumbwaiters, and moving stairways--are classified in U.S. Industry 333921, Elevator and Moving Stairway Manufacturing; and
- Manufacturing overhead traveling cranes and monorail systems--are classified in U.S. Industry 333923, Overhead Traveling Crane, Hoist, and Monorail System Manufacturing.

333923 Overhead Traveling Crane, Hoist, and Monorail System Manufacturing

This U.S. industry comprises establishments primarily engaged in manufacturing overhead traveling cranes, hoists, and monorail systems.

Illustrative Examples:

Aerial work platforms manufacturing
Automobile wrecker (i.e., tow truck) hoists manufacturing
Block and tackle manufacturing
Metal pulleys (except power transmission) manufacturing
Winches manufacturing

Cross-References. Establishments primarily engaged in--

- Manufacturing construction-type cranes--are classified in Industry 333120, Construction Machinery Manufacturing;
- Manufacturing aircraft loading hoists--are classified in U.S. Industry 333924, Industrial Truck, Tractor, Trailer, and Stacker Machinery Manufacturing; and
- Manufacturing power transmission pulleys--are classified in U.S. Industry 333613, Mechanical Power Transmission Equipment Manufacturing.

333924 Industrial Truck, Tractor, Trailer, and Stacker Machinery Manufacturing

This U.S. industry comprises establishments primarily engaged in manufacturing industrial trucks, tractors, trailers, and stackers (i.e., truck-type) such as forklifts, pallet loaders and unloaders, and portable loading docks.

Cross-References. Establishments primarily engaged in--

- Manufacturing motor vehicle-type trailers--are classified in Industry 33621, Motor Vehicle Body and Trailer Manufacturing;
- Manufacturing farm-type tractors--are classified in U.S. Industry 333111, Farm Machinery and Equipment Manufacturing; and
- Manufacturing construction-type tractors--are classified in Industry 333120, Construction Machinery Manufacturing.

T—Canadian, Mexican, and United States industries are comparable.

33399 All Other General Purpose Machinery Manufacturing[T]

This industry comprises establishments primarily engaged in manufacturing general purpose machinery (except ventilation, heating, air-conditioning, and commercial refrigeration equipment; metalworking machinery; engines, turbines, and power transmission equipment; pumps and compressors; and material handling equipment).

Illustrative Examples:

Automatic fire sprinkler systems manufacturing
Bridge and gate lifting machinery manufacturing
Fluid power cylinders manufacturing
Fluid power pumps manufacturing
Hydraulic and pneumatic jacks manufacturing
Industrial-type furnaces manufacturing
Packaging machinery manufacturing
Power-driven handtools manufacturing
Scales manufacturing
Welding equipment manufacturing

Cross-References. Establishments primarily engaged in--

- Manufacturing ventilating, heating, air-conditioning (except motor vehicle), commercial refrigeration, and furnace filters--are classified in Industry 33341, Ventilation, Heating, Air-Conditioning, and Commercial Refrigeration Equipment Manufacturing;
- Manufacturing engine, turbine, and power transmission equipment--are classified in Industry Group 3336, Engine, Turbine, and Power Transmission Equipment Manufacturing;
- Manufacturing pumps and compressors--are classified in Industry 33391, Pump and Compressor Manufacturing;
- Manufacturing material handling equipment--are classified in Industry 33392, Material Handling Equipment Manufacturing;
- Manufacturing motor vehicle air-conditioning systems and compressors, engine filters, and pumps--are classified in Industry Group 3363, Motor Vehicle Parts Manufacturing;
- Manufacturing metal cutting, metal forming, and other metalworking machinery--are classified in Industry 33351, Metalworking Machinery Manufacturing;
- Manufacturing power-driven heavy construction or mining hand operated tools, such as tampers, jackhammers, and augers--are classified in Industry 33312, Construction Machinery Manufacturing, or Industry 33313, Mining and Oil and Gas Field Machinery Manufacturing;
- Manufacturing bakery ovens and industrial kilns, such as cement, wood, and chemical--are classified in Industry 33324, Industrial Machinery Manufacturing;
- Manufacturing mechanical jacks, handheld soldering irons, countersink bits, drill bits, router bits, milling cutters, and other machine tools for woodcutting--are classified in Industry 33221, Cutlery and Handtool Manufacturing;
- Manufacturing carnival and amusement park equipment, automotive maintenance equipment, and coin-operated vending machines--are classified in Industry 33331, Commercial and Service Industry Machinery Manufacturing; and
- Manufacturing arc-welding transformers--are classified in Industry 33531, Electrical Equipment Manufacturing.

333991 Power-Driven Handtool Manufacturing

This U.S. industry comprises establishments primarily engaged in manufacturing power-driven (e.g., battery, corded, pneumatic) handtools, such as drills, screwguns, circular saws, chain saws, staplers, and nailers.

Cross-References. Establishments primarily engaged in--

- Manufacturing metal cutting and metal forming machines (including home workshop)--are classified in Industry 33351, Metalworking Machinery Manufacturing;
- Manufacturing countersink bits, drill bits, router bits, milling cutters, and other machine tools for woodcutting--are classified in U.S. Industry 332216, Saw Blade and Handtool Manufacturing;

T—Canadian, Mexican, and United States industries are comparable.

- Manufacturing power-driven heavy construction or mining hand operated tools, such as tampers, jackhammers, and augers--are classified in Industry 333120, Construction Machinery Manufacturing, or Industry 33313, Mining and Oil and Gas Field Machinery Manufacturing; and
- Manufacturing powered home lawn and garden equipment--are classified in U.S. Industry 333112, Lawn and Garden Tractor and Home Lawn and Garden Equipment Manufacturing.

333992 Welding and Soldering Equipment Manufacturing

This U.S. industry comprises establishments primarily engaged in manufacturing welding and soldering equipment and accessories (except transformers), such as arc, resistance, gas, plasma, laser, electron beam, and ultrasonic welding equipment; welding electrodes; coated or cored welding wire; and soldering equipment (except handheld).

Cross-References. Establishments primarily engaged in--

- Manufacturing handheld soldering irons--are classified in U.S. Industry 332216, Saw Blade and Handtool Manufacturing; and
- Manufacturing arc-welding transformers--are classified in U.S. Industry 335311, Power, Distribution, and Specialty Transformer Manufacturing.

333993 Packaging Machinery Manufacturing

This U.S. industry comprises establishments primarily engaged in manufacturing packaging machinery, such as wrapping, bottling, canning, and labeling machinery.

333994 Industrial Process Furnace and Oven Manufacturing

This U.S. industry comprises establishments primarily engaged in manufacturing industrial process ovens, induction and dielectric heating equipment, and kilns (except cement, chemical, wood). Included in this industry are establishments manufacturing laboratory furnaces and ovens.

Cross-References. Establishments primarily engaged in--

- Manufacturing bakery ovens--are classified in U.S. Industry 333241, Food Product Machinery Manufacturing;
- Manufacturing cement, wood, and chemical kilns--are classified in U.S. Industry 333249, Other Industrial Machinery Manufacturing; and
- Manufacturing cremating ovens--are classified in U.S. Industry 333999, All Other Miscellaneous General Purpose Machinery Manufacturing.

333995 Fluid Power Cylinder and Actuator Manufacturing

This U.S. industry comprises establishments primarily engaged in manufacturing fluid power (i.e., hydraulic and pneumatic) cylinders and actuators.

333996 Fluid Power Pump and Motor Manufacturing

This U.S. industry comprises establishments primarily engaged in manufacturing fluid power (i.e., hydraulic and pneumatic) pumps and motors.

Cross-References. Establishments primarily engaged in--

- Manufacturing fluid pumps for motor vehicles, such as oil pumps, water pumps, and power steering pumps--are classified in Industry Group 3363, Motor Vehicle Parts Manufacturing;
- Manufacturing general purpose pumps (except fluid power)--are classified in U.S. Industry 333914, Measuring, Dispensing, and Other Pumping Equipment Manufacturing; and

T—Canadian, Mexican, and United States industries are comparable.

- Manufacturing air compressors--are classified in U.S. Industry 333912, Air and Gas Compressor Manufacturing.

333997 Scale and Balance Manufacturing

This U.S. industry comprises establishments primarily engaged in manufacturing scales and balances, including those used in laboratories.

333999 All Other Miscellaneous General Purpose Machinery Manufacturing

This U.S. industry comprises establishments primarily engaged in manufacturing general purpose machinery (except ventilating, heating, air-conditioning, and commercial refrigeration equipment; metalworking machinery; engines, turbines, and power transmission equipment; pumps and compressors; material handling equipment; power-driven handtools; welding and soldering equipment; packaging machinery; industrial process furnaces and ovens; fluid power cylinders and actuators; fluid power pumps and motors; and scales and balances).

Illustrative Examples:

Automatic fire sprinkler systems manufacturing
Baling machinery (e.g., paper, scrap metal) manufacturing
Bridge and gate lifting machinery manufacturing
Centrifuges, industrial and laboratory-type, manufacturing
Cremating ovens manufacturing
General purpose-type sieves and screening equipment manufacturing
Hydraulic and pneumatic jacks manufacturing
Industrial and general purpose-type filters (except internal combustion engine, warm air furnace) manufacturing

Cross-References. Establishments primarily engaged in--

- Manufacturing ventilating, heating, air-conditioning (except motor vehicle), and commercial refrigeration--are classified in Industry 33341, Ventilation, Heating, Air-Conditioning, and Commercial Refrigeration Equipment Manufacturing;
- Manufacturing motor vehicle air-conditioning systems and compressors--are classified in Industry 336390, Other Motor Vehicle Parts Manufacturing;
- Manufacturing material handling equipment--are classified in Industry 33392, Material Handling Equipment Manufacturing;
- Manufacturing power-driven handtools--are classified in U.S. Industry 333991, Power-Driven Handtool Manufacturing;
- Manufacturing welding and soldering equipment (except handheld soldering irons)--are classified in U.S. Industry 333992, Welding and Soldering Equipment Manufacturing;
- Manufacturing packaging machinery--are classified in U.S. Industry 333993, Packaging Machinery Manufacturing;
- Manufacturing bakery ovens--are classified in U.S. Industry 333241, Food Product Machinery Manufacturing;
- Manufacturing cement, wood, and chemical kilns--are classified in U.S. Industry 333249, Other Industrial Machinery Manufacturing;
- Manufacturing industrial process furnaces and ovens (except bakery)--are classified in U.S. Industry 333994, Industrial Process Furnace and Oven Manufacturing;
- Manufacturing fluid power cylinders and actuators--are classified in U.S. Industry 333995, Fluid Power Cylinder and Actuator Manufacturing;
- Manufacturing fluid power pumps and motors--are classified in U.S. Industry 333996, Fluid Power Pump and Motor Manufacturing;
- Manufacturing scales and balances--are classified in U.S. Industry 333997, Scale and Balance Manufacturing;

T—Canadian, Mexican, and United States industries are comparable.

- Manufacturing carnival and amusement park equipment, automotive maintenance equipment, and coin-operated vending machines--are classified in Industry 33331, Commercial and Service Industry Machinery Manufacturing;
- Manufacturing motor vehicle engine filters and pumps--are classified in Industry Group 3363, Motor Vehicle Parts Manufacturing; and
- Manufacturing mechanical jacks--are classified in U.S. Industry 332216, Saw Blade and Handtool Manufacturing.

334 Computer and Electronic Product Manufacturing[T]

Industries in the Computer and Electronic Product Manufacturing subsector group establishments that manufacture computers, computer peripherals, communications equipment, and similar electronic products, and establishments that manufacture components for such products. The Computer and Electronic Product Manufacturing industries have been combined in the hierarchy of NAICS because of the economic significance they have attained. Their rapid growth suggests that they will become even more important to the economies of all three North American countries in the future, and in addition their manufacturing processes are fundamentally different from the manufacturing processes of other machinery and equipment. The design and use of integrated circuits and the application of highly specialized miniaturization technologies are common elements in the production technologies of the Computer and Electronic Product Manufacturing subsector. Convergence of technology motivates this NAICS subsector. Digitalization of sound recording, for example, causes both the medium (the compact disc) and the equipment to resemble the technologies for recording, storing, transmitting, and manipulating data. Communications technology and equipment have been converging with computer technology. When technologically-related components are in the same sector, it makes it easier to adjust the classification for future changes, without needing to redefine its basic structure. The creation of the Computer and Electronic Product Manufacturing subsector assists in delineating new and emerging industries because the activities that will serve as the probable sources of new industries, such as computer manufacturing and communications equipment manufacturing, or computers and audio equipment, are brought together. As new activities emerge, they are less likely to cross the subsector boundaries of the classification.

3341 Computer and Peripheral Equipment Manufacturing[T]

33411 Computer and Peripheral Equipment Manufacturing[T]

This industry comprises establishments primarily engaged in manufacturing and/or assembling electronic computers, such as mainframes, personal computers, workstations, laptops, and computer servers; and computer peripheral equipment, such as storage devices, printers, monitors, and input/output devices and terminals.
Computers can be analog, digital, or hybrid. Digital computers, the most common type, are devices that do all of the following: (1) store the processing program or programs and the data immediately necessary for the execution of the program; (2) can be freely programmed in accordance with the requirements of the user; (3) perform arithmetical computations specified by the user; and (4) execute, without human intervention, a processing program that requires the computer to modify its execution by logical decision during the processing run. Analog computers are capable of simulating mathematical models and comprise at least analog, control, and programming elements.

Cross-References. Establishments primarily engaged in--

- Manufacturing digital telecommunications switches, and local area network and wide area network communications equipment, such as bridges, routers, and gateways--are classified in Industry 33421, Telephone Apparatus Manufacturing;
- Manufacturing blank magnetic and optical recording media--are classified in Industry 33461, Manufacturing and Reproducing Magnetic and Optical Media;
- Manufacturing machinery or equipment that incorporates electronic computers for operation or control purposes and embedded control applications--are classified in the Manufacturing sector based on the classification of the complete machinery or equipment;
- Manufacturing external audio speakers for computer use--are classified in Industry 33431, Audio and Video Equipment Manufacturing;

T—Canadian, Mexican, and United States industries are comparable.

- Manufacturing internal loaded printed circuit board devices, such as sound, video, controller, and network interface cards; internal and external computer modems; and semiconductor storage devices--are classified in Industry 33441, Semiconductor and Other Electronic Component Manufacturing; and
- Manufacturing other parts, such as casings, stampings, cable sets, and switches, for computers, storage devices and other peripheral equipment--are classified in the Manufacturing sector based on their associated production processes.

334111 Electronic Computer Manufacturing

This U.S. industry comprises establishments primarily engaged in manufacturing and/or assembling electronic computers, such as mainframes, personal computers, workstations, laptops, and computer servers. Computers can be analog, digital, or hybrid. Digital computers, the most common type, are devices that do all of the following: (1) store the processing program or programs and the data immediately necessary for the execution of the program; (2) can be freely programmed in accordance with the requirements of the user; (3) perform arithmetical computations specified by the user; and (4) execute, without human intervention, a processing program that requires the computer to modify its execution by logical decision during the processing run. Analog computers are capable of simulating mathematical models and contain at least analog, control, and programming elements. The manufacture of computers includes the assembly or integration of processors, coprocessors, memory, storage, and input/output devices into a user-programmable final product.

Cross-References. Establishments primarily engaged in--

- Manufacturing digital telecommunications switches, and local area network and wide area network communication equipment, such as bridges, routers, and gateways--are classified in Industry 334210, Telephone Apparatus Manufacturing;
- Manufacturing blank magnetic and optical recording media--are classified in U.S. Industry 334613, Blank Magnetic and Optical Recording Media Manufacturing;
- Manufacturing machinery or equipment that incorporates electronic computers for operation or control purposes and embedded control applications--are classified in the Manufacturing sector based on the classification of the complete machinery or equipment;
- Manufacturing internal, loaded, printed circuit board devices, such as sound, video, controller, and network interface cards; internal and external computer modems; and solid-state storage devices for computers--are classified in Industry 33441, Semiconductor and Other Electronic Component Manufacturing;
- Manufacturing other parts, such as casings, stampings, cable sets, and switches, for computers--are classified in the Manufacturing sector based on their associated production processes; and
- Retailing computers with on-site assembly--are classified in U.S. Industry 443142, Electronics Stores.

334112 Computer Storage Device Manufacturing

This U.S. industry comprises establishments primarily engaged in manufacturing computer storage devices that allow the storage and retrieval of data from a phase change, magnetic, optical, or magnetic/optical media. Examples of products made by these establishments are CD-ROM drives, floppy disk drives, hard disk drives, and tape storage and backup units.

Cross-References. Establishments primarily engaged in--

- Manufacturing blank magnetic and optical recording media--are classified in U.S. Industry 334613, Blank Magnetic and Optical Recording Media Manufacturing;
- Manufacturing semiconductor storage devices, such as memory chips--are classified in U.S. Industry 334413, Semiconductor and Related Device Manufacturing;
- Manufacturing drive controller cards, internal or external to the storage device--are classified in U.S. Industry 334418, Printed Circuit Assembly (Electronic Assembly) Manufacturing; and
- Manufacturing other parts, such as casings, stampings, cable sets, and switches, for computer storage devices--are classified in the Manufacturing sector based on their associated production processes.

T—Canadian, Mexican, and United States industries are comparable.

334118 Computer Terminal and Other Computer Peripheral Equipment Manufacturing

This U.S. industry comprises establishments primarily engaged in manufacturing computer terminals and other computer peripheral equipment (except storage devices).

Illustrative Examples:

Automatic teller machines (ATM) manufacturing
Computer terminals manufacturing
Joystick devices manufacturing
Keyboards, computer peripheral equipment, manufacturing
Monitors, computer peripheral equipment, manufacturing
Mouse devices, computer peripheral equipment, manufacturing
Optical readers and scanners manufacturing
Plotters, computer, manufacturing
Point-of-sale terminals manufacturing
Printers, computer, manufacturing

Cross-References. Establishments primarily engaged in--

- Manufacturing local area network and wide area network communications equipment, such as bridges, routers, and gateways--are classified in Industry 334210, Telephone Apparatus Manufacturing;
- Manufacturing computer storage devices--are classified in U.S. Industry 334112, Computer Storage Device Manufacturing;
- Manufacturing external audio speakers for computer use--are classified in Industry 334310, Audio and Video Equipment Manufacturing;
- Manufacturing internal, loaded, printed circuit board devices, such as sound, video, controller, and network interface cards; and internal and external computer modems used as computer peripherals--are classified in U.S. Industry 334418, Printed Circuit Assembly (Electronic Assembly) Manufacturing;
- Manufacturing digital cameras--are classified in U.S. Industry 333316, Photographic and Photocopying Equipment Manufacturing; and
- Manufacturing other parts, such as casings, stampings, cable sets, and switches, for computer peripheral equipment--are classified in the Manufacturing sector based on their associated production processes.

3342 Communications Equipment Manufacturing[T]

This industry group comprises establishments primarily engaged in manufacturing wire telephone and data communications equipment, radio and television broadcast and wireless communications equipment, and all other communications equipment.

33421 Telephone Apparatus Manufacturing[T] See industry description for 334210.

334210 Telephone Apparatus Manufacturing

This industry comprises establishments primarily engaged in manufacturing wire telephone and data communications equipment. These products may be stand-alone or board-level components of a larger system. Examples of products made by these establishments are central office switching equipment, cordless and wire telephones (except cellular), PBX equipment, telephone answering machines, LAN modems, multi-user modems, and other data communications equipment, such as bridges, routers, and gateways.

Cross-References. Establishments primarily engaged in--

- Manufacturing internal and external computer modems, single-user fax/modems and electronic components used in telephone apparatus--are classified in Industry 33441, Semiconductor and Other Electronic Component Manufacturing; and
- Manufacturing cellular telephones--are classified in Industry 334220, Radio and Television Broadcasting and Wireless Communications Equipment Manufacturing.

T—Canadian, Mexican, and United States industries are comparable.

33422 Radio and Television Broadcasting and Wireless Communications Equipment Manufacturing[T] See industry description for 334220.

334220 Radio and Television Broadcasting and Wireless Communications Equipment Manufacturing

This industry comprises establishments primarily engaged in manufacturing radio and television broadcast and wireless communications equipment. Examples of products made by these establishments are transmitting and receiving antennas, cable television equipment, GPS equipment, pagers, cellular phones, mobile communications equipment, and radio and television studio and broadcasting equipment.

Cross-References. Establishments primarily engaged in--

- Manufacturing household-type audio and video equipment, such as televisions and radio sets--are classified in Industry 334310, Audio and Video Equipment Manufacturing;
- Manufacturing wired and wireless intercommunications equipment (i.e., intercoms)--are classified in Industry 334290, Other Communications Equipment Manufacturing; and
- Manufacturing equipment for measuring and testing communications signals--are classified in U.S. Industry 334515, Instrument Manufacturing for Measuring and Testing Electricity and Electrical Signals.

33429 Other Communications Equipment Manufacturing[T] See industry description for 334290.

334290 Other Communications Equipment Manufacturing

This industry comprises establishments primarily engaged in manufacturing communications equipment (except telephone apparatus, radio and television broadcast equipment, and wireless communications equipment).

Illustrative Examples:

Fire detection and alarm systems manufacturing
Intercom systems and equipment manufacturing
Video-based stadium displays manufacturing
Signals (e.g., highway, pedestrian, railway, traffic)

Cross-References. Establishments primarily engaged in--

- Manufacturing telephone apparatus--are classified in Industry 334210, Telephone Apparatus Manufacturing;
- Manufacturing radio and television broadcast and wireless communications equipment (except wireless intercoms)--are classified in Industry 334220, Radio and Television Broadcasting and Wireless Communications Equipment Manufacturing; and
- Manufacturing automobile audio and related equipment--are classified in Industry 334310, Audio and Video Equipment Manufacturing.

3343 Audio and Video Equipment Manufacturing[T]

33431 Audio and Video Equipment Manufacturing[T] See industry description for 334310.

334310 Audio and Video Equipment Manufacturing

This industry comprises establishments primarily engaged in manufacturing electronic audio and video equipment for home entertainment, motor vehicles, and public address and musical instrument amplification. Examples of products made by these establishments are digital video recorders, televisions, stereo equipment, speaker systems, household-type video cameras, jukeboxes, and amplifiers for musical instruments and public address systems.

T—Canadian, Mexican, and United States industries are comparable.

Cross-References. Establishments primarily engaged in--

- Manufacturing photographic (i.e., still and motion picture) equipment--are classified in U.S. Industry 333316, Photographic and Photocopying Equipment Manufacturing;
- Manufacturing phonograph needles and cartridges--are classified in Industry 33441, Semiconductor and Other Electronic Component Manufacturing;
- Manufacturing auto theft alarms or video-based stadium displays--are classified in Industry 334290, Other Communications Equipment Manufacturing; and
- Manufacturing mobile radios, such as citizens band and FM transceivers for household or motor vehicle uses; studio and broadcast video cameras; and cable decoders and satellite television equipment--are classified in Industry 334220, Radio and Television Broadcasting and Wireless Communications Equipment Manufacturing.

3344 Semiconductor and Other Electronic Component Manufacturing[T]

33441 Semiconductor and Other Electronic Component Manufacturing[T]

This industry comprises establishments primarily engaged in manufacturing semiconductors and other components for electronic applications. Examples of products made by these establishments are capacitors, resistors, microprocessors, bare and loaded printed circuit boards, electron tubes, electronic connectors, and computer modems.

Cross-References. Establishments primarily engaged in--

- Manufacturing X-ray tubes--are classified in Industry 33451, Navigational, Measuring, Electromedical, and Control Instruments Manufacturing;
- Manufacturing glass blanks for electron tubes--are classified in Industry 32721, Glass and Glass Product Manufacturing;
- Manufacturing telephone system components or modules--are classified in Industry 33421, Telephone Apparatus Manufacturing;
- Manufacturing finished products that incorporate loaded printed circuit boards--are classified in the Manufacturing sector based on the production process of making the final product;
- Manufacturing communications antennas--are classified in Industry 33422, Radio and Television Broadcasting and Wireless Communications Equipment Manufacturing; and
- Manufacturing coils, switches, transformers, connectors, capacitors, rheostats, and similar devices for electrical applications--are classified in Subsector 335, Electrical Equipment, Appliance, and Component Manufacturing.

334412 Bare Printed Circuit Board Manufacturing

This U.S. industry comprises establishments primarily engaged in manufacturing bare (i.e., rigid or flexible) printed circuit boards without mounted electronic components. These establishments print, perforate, plate, screen, etch, or photoprint interconnecting pathways for electric current on laminates.

Cross-References. Establishments primarily engaged in--

- Loading components onto printed circuit boards or manufacturing loaded printed circuit boards--are classified in U.S. Industry 334418, Printed Circuit Assembly (Electronic Assembly) Manufacturing; and
- Manufacturing printed circuit laminates--are classified in U.S. Industry 334419, Other Electronic Component Manufacturing.

T—Canadian, Mexican, and United States industries are comparable.

334413 Semiconductor and Related Device Manufacturing

This U.S. industry comprises establishments primarily engaged in manufacturing semiconductors and related solid-state devices. Examples of products made by these establishments are integrated circuits, memory chips, microprocessors, diodes, transistors, solar cells and other optoelectronic devices.

334416 Capacitor, Resistor, Coil, Transformer, and Other Inductor Manufacturing

This U.S. industry comprises establishments primarily engaged in one or more of the following: (1) manufacturing electronic fixed and variable capacitors and condensers; (2) manufacturing electronic resistors, such as fixed and variable resistors, resistor networks, thermistors, and varistors; and (3) manufacturing electronic inductors, such as coils and transformers.

Cross-References. Establishments primarily engaged in--

- Manufacturing electrical capacitors for power generation and distribution, heavy industrial equipment, induction heating and melting, and similar industrial applications--are classified in U.S. Industry 335999, All Other Miscellaneous Electrical Equipment and Component Manufacturing;
- Manufacturing electronic rheostats--are classified in U.S. Industry 334419, Other Electronic Component Manufacturing; and
- Manufacturing electrical transformers used in the generation, storage, transmission, transformation, distribution, and utilization of electrical energy--are classified in U.S. Industry 335311, Power, Distribution, and Specialty Transformer Manufacturing.

334417 Electronic Connector Manufacturing

This U.S. industry comprises establishments primarily engaged in manufacturing electronic connectors, such as coaxial, cylindrical, rack and panel, pin and sleeve, printed circuit and fiber optic.

Cross-References.

Establishments primarily engaged in manufacturing electrical connectors, such as plugs, bus bars, twist on wire connectors and terminals, are classified in U.S. Industry 335931, Current-Carrying Wiring Device Manufacturing.

334418 Printed Circuit Assembly (Electronic Assembly) Manufacturing

This U.S. industry comprises establishments primarily engaged in loading components onto printed circuit boards or who manufacture and ship loaded printed circuit boards. Also known as printed circuit assemblies, electronics assemblies, or modules, these products are printed circuit boards that have some or all of the semiconductor and electronic components inserted or mounted and are inputs to a wide variety of electronic systems and devices.

Cross-References. Establishments primarily engaged in--

- Manufacturing printed circuit laminates--are classified in U.S. Industry 334419, Other Electronic Component Manufacturing;
- Manufacturing bare printed circuit boards--are classified in U.S. Industry 334412, Bare Printed Circuit Board Manufacturing;
- Manufacturing telephone system components or modules--are classified in Industry 334210, Telephone Apparatus Manufacturing; and
- Manufacturing finished products that incorporate loaded printed circuit boards--are classified in the Manufacturing sector based on the production process of making the final product.

T—Canadian, Mexican, and United States industries are comparable.

334419 Other Electronic Component Manufacturing

This U.S. industry comprises establishments primarily engaged in manufacturing electronic components (except bare printed circuit boards; semiconductors and related devices; electronic capacitors; electronic resistors; coils, transformers and other inductors; connectors; and loaded printed circuit boards).

Illustrative Examples:

Crystals and crystal assemblies, electronic, manufacturing
Electron tubes manufacturing
LCD (liquid crystal display) unit screens manufacturing
Microwave components manufacturing
Piezoelectric devices manufacturing
Printed circuit laminates manufacturing
Switches for electronic applications manufacturing
Transducers (except pressure) manufacturing

Cross-References. Establishments primarily engaged in--

- Manufacturing bare printed circuit boards--are classified in U.S. Industry 334412, Bare Printed Circuit Board Manufacturing;
- Manufacturing semiconductors, photonic integrated circuits, and/or silicon wave guides--are classified in U.S. Industry 334413, Semiconductor and Related Device Manufacturing;
- Manufacturing electronic capacitors, electronic resistors, and electronic inductors--are classified in U.S. Industry 334416, Capacitor, Resistor, Coil, Transformer, and Other Inductor Manufacturing;
- Manufacturing electronic connectors--are classified in U.S. Industry 334417, Electronic Connector Manufacturing;
- Loading components onto printed circuit boards or manufacturing loaded printed circuit boards--are classified in U.S. Industry 334418, Printed Circuit Assembly (Electronic Assembly) Manufacturing;
- Manufacturing communications antennas--are classified in Industry 334220, Radio and Television Broadcasting and Wireless Communications Equipment Manufacturing;
- Manufacturing X-ray tubes--are classified in U.S. Industry 334517, Irradiation Apparatus Manufacturing; and
- Manufacturing glass blanks for electron tubes--are classified in Industry 32721, Glass and Glass Product Manufacturing.

3345 Navigational, Measuring, Electromedical, and Control Instruments Manufacturing[T]

33451 Navigational, Measuring, Electromedical, and Control Instruments Manufacturing[T]

This industry comprises establishments primarily engaged in manufacturing navigational, measuring, electromedical, and control instruments. Examples of products made by these establishments are aeronautical instruments, appliance regulators and controls (except switches), laboratory analytical instruments, navigation and guidance systems, and physical properties testing equipment.

Cross-References. Establishments primarily engaged in--

- Manufacturing global positioning system (GPS) equipment--are classified in Industry 33422, Radio and Television Broadcasting and Wireless Communications Equipment Manufacturing;
- Manufacturing motor control switches and relays (including timing relays)--are classified in Industry 33531, Electrical Equipment Manufacturing;
- Manufacturing switches for appliances--are classified in Industry 33593, Wiring Device Manufacturing;
- Manufacturing optical instruments--are classified in Industry 33331, Commercial and Service Industry Machinery Manufacturing;
- Manufacturing glass watch and clock crystals--are classified in Industry 32721, Glass and Glass Product Manufacturing;
- Manufacturing plastics watch and clock crystals--are classified in Industry 32619, Other Plastics Product Manufacturing; and

T—Canadian, Mexican, and United States industries are comparable.

- Manufacturing medical thermometers and other nonelectrical medical apparatus--are classified in Industry 33911, Medical Equipment and Supplies Manufacturing.

334510 Electromedical and Electrotherapeutic Apparatus Manufacturing

This U.S. industry comprises establishments primarily engaged in manufacturing electromedical and electrotherapeutic apparatus, such as magnetic resonance imaging equipment, medical ultrasound equipment, pacemakers, hearing aids, electrocardiographs, and electromedical endoscopic equipment.

Cross-References. Establishments primarily engaged in--

- Manufacturing medical irradiation apparatus--are classified in U.S. Industry 334517, Irradiation Apparatus Manufacturing; and
- Manufacturing nonelectrical medical and therapeutic apparatus--are classified in Industry 33911, Medical Equipment and Supplies Manufacturing.

334511 Search, Detection, Navigation, Guidance, Aeronautical, and Nautical System and Instrument Manufacturing

This U.S. industry comprises establishments primarily engaged in manufacturing search, detection, navigation, guidance, aeronautical, and nautical systems and instruments. Examples of products made by these establishments are aircraft instruments (except engine), flight recorders, navigational instruments and systems, radar systems and equipment, and sonar systems and equipment.

Cross-References. Establishments primarily engaged in--

- Manufacturing global positioning system (GPS) equipment--are classified in Industry 334220, Radio and Television Broadcasting and Wireless Communications Equipment Manufacturing; and
- Manufacturing aircraft engine instruments and meteorological systems and equipment--are classified in U.S. Industry 334519, Other Measuring and Controlling Device Manufacturing.

334512 Automatic Environmental Control Manufacturing for Residential, Commercial, and Appliance Use

This U.S. industry comprises establishments primarily engaged in manufacturing automatic controls and regulators for applications, such as heating, air-conditioning, refrigeration and appliances.

Cross-References. Establishments primarily engaged in--

- Manufacturing industrial process controls--are classified in U.S. Industry 334513, Instruments and Related Products Manufacturing for Measuring, Displaying, and Controlling Industrial Process Variables;
- Manufacturing motor control switches and relays--are classified in U.S. Industry 335314, Relay and Industrial Control Manufacturing;
- Manufacturing switches for appliances--are classified in U.S. Industry 335931, Current-Carrying Wiring Device Manufacturing; and
- Manufacturing appliance timers--are classified in U.S. Industry 334519, Other Measuring and Controlling Device Manufacturing.

334513 Instruments and Related Products Manufacturing for Measuring, Displaying, and Controlling Industrial Process Variables

This U.S. industry comprises establishments primarily engaged in manufacturing instruments and related devices for measuring, displaying, indicating, recording, transmitting, and controlling industrial process variables. These instruments measure, display or control (monitor, analyze, and so forth) industrial process variables, such as temperature, humidity, pressure, vacuum, combustion, flow, level, viscosity, density, acidity, concentration, and rotation. T—Canadian, Mexican, and United States industries are comparable.

Cross-References. Establishments primarily engaged in--

- Manufacturing instruments for measuring or testing electricity and electrical signals--are classified in U.S. Industry 334515, Instrument Manufacturing for Measuring and Testing Electricity and Electrical Signals;
- Manufacturing medical thermometers--are classified in U.S. Industry 339112, Surgical and Medical Instrument Manufacturing;
- Manufacturing glass hydrometers and thermometers for other non-medical uses--are classified in U.S. Industry 334519, Other Measuring and Controlling Device Manufacturing;
- Manufacturing instruments and instrumentation systems for laboratory analysis of samples--are classified in U.S. Industry 334516, Analytical Laboratory Instrument Manufacturing; and
- Manufacturing optical alignment and display instruments, optical comparators, and optical test and inspection equipment--are classified in U.S. Industry 333314, Optical Instrument and Lens Manufacturing.

334514 Totalizing Fluid Meter and Counting Device Manufacturing

This U.S. industry comprises establishments primarily engaged in manufacturing totalizing (i.e., registering) fluid meters and counting devices. Examples of products made by these establishments are gas consumption meters, water consumption meters, parking meters, taxi meters, motor vehicle gauges, and fare collection equipment.

Cross-References. Establishments primarily engaged in--

- Manufacturing integrating meters and counters for measuring the characteristics of electricity and electrical signals--are classified in U.S. Industry 334515, Instrument Manufacturing for Measuring and Testing Electricity and Electrical Signals; and
- Manufacturing instruments and devices that measure, display, or control (i.e., monitor or analyze) related industrial process variables--are classified in U.S. Industry 334513, Instruments and Related Products Manufacturing for Measuring, Displaying, and Controlling Industrial Process Variables.

334515 Instrument Manufacturing for Measuring and Testing Electricity and Electrical Signals

This U.S. industry comprises establishments primarily engaged in manufacturing instruments for measuring and testing the characteristics of electricity and electrical signals. Examples of products made by these establishments are circuit and continuity testers, voltmeters, ohm meters, wattmeters, multimeters, and semiconductor test equipment.

Cross-References.

Establishments primarily engaged in manufacturing electronic monitoring, evaluating, and other electronic support equipment for navigational, radar, and sonar systems are classified in U.S. Industry 334511, Search, Detection, Navigation, Guidance, Aeronautical, and Nautical System and Instrument Manufacturing.

334516 Analytical Laboratory Instrument Manufacturing

This U.S. industry comprises establishments primarily engaged in manufacturing instruments and instrumentation systems for laboratory analysis of the chemical or physical composition or concentration of samples of solid, fluid, gaseous, or composite material.

Cross-References. Establishments primarily engaged in--

- Manufacturing instruments for monitoring and analyzing continuous samples from medical patients--are classified in U.S. Industry 334510, Electromedical and Electrotherapeutic Apparatus Manufacturing; and
- Manufacturing instruments and related devices that measure, display, or control (i.e., monitor or analyze) industrial process variables--are classified in U.S. Industry 334513, Instruments and Related Products Manufacturing for Measuring, Displaying, and Controlling Industrial Process Variables.

T—Canadian, Mexican, and United States industries are comparable.

334517 Irradiation Apparatus Manufacturing

This U.S. industry comprises establishments primarily engaged in manufacturing irradiation apparatus and tubes for applications, such as medical diagnostic, medical therapeutic, industrial, research and scientific evaluation. Irradiation can take the form of beta-rays, gamma-rays, X-rays, or other ionizing radiation.

334519 Other Measuring and Controlling Device Manufacturing

This U.S. industry comprises establishments primarily engaged in manufacturing measuring and controlling devices (except search, detection, navigation, guidance, aeronautical, and nautical instruments and systems; automatic environmental controls for residential, commercial, and appliance use; instruments for measurement, display, and control of industrial process variables; totalizing fluid meters and counting devices; instruments for measuring and testing electricity and electrical signals; analytical laboratory instruments; irradiation equipment; and electromedical and electrotherapeutic apparatus).

Illustrative Examples:

Aircraft engine instruments manufacturing
Automotive emissions testing equipment manufacturing
Clocks assembling
Meteorological instruments manufacturing
Physical properties testing and inspection equipment manufacturing
Polygraph machines manufacturing
Radiation detection and monitoring instruments manufacturing
Surveying instruments manufacturing
Thermometers, liquid-in-glass and bimetal types (except medical), manufacturing
Watches and parts (except crystals) manufacturing

Cross-References. Establishments primarily engaged in--

- Manufacturing medical thermometers--are classified in U.S. Industry 339112, Surgical and Medical Instrument Manufacturing;
- Manufacturing search, detection, navigation, guidance, aeronautical, and nautical systems and instruments--are classified in U.S. Industry 334511, Search, Detection, Navigation, Guidance, Aeronautical, and Nautical System and Instrument Manufacturing;
- Manufacturing automatic controls and regulators for applications, such as heating, air-conditioning, refrigeration and appliances--are classified in U.S. Industry 334512, Automatic Environmental Control Manufacturing for Residential, Commercial, and Appliance Use;
- Manufacturing instruments and related devices that measure, display, or control (i.e., monitor or analyze) industrial process variables--are classified in U.S. Industry 334513, Instruments and Related Products Manufacturing for Measuring, Displaying, and Controlling Industrial Process Variables;
- Manufacturing totalizing (i.e., registering) fluid meters and counting devices, including motor vehicle gauges--are classified in U.S. Industry 334514, Totalizing Fluid Meter and Counting Device Manufacturing;
- Manufacturing instruments for measuring and testing the characteristics of electricity and electrical signals--are classified in U.S. Industry 334515, Instrument Manufacturing for Measuring and Testing Electricity and Electrical Signals;
- Manufacturing instruments for laboratory analysis of the physical composition or concentration of samples of solid, fluid, gaseous, or composite materials--are classified in U.S. Industry 334516, Analytical Laboratory Instrument Manufacturing;
- Manufacturing X-ray apparatus, tubes, or related irradiation apparatus--are classified in U.S. Industry 334517, Irradiation Apparatus Manufacturing;
- Manufacturing electromedical and electrotherapeutic apparatus--are classified in U.S. Industry 334510, Electromedical and Electrotherapeutic Apparatus Manufacturing;
- Manufacturing glass watch and clock crystals--are classified in Industry 32721, Glass and Glass Product Manufacturing;
- Manufacturing plastics watch and clock crystals--are classified in U.S. Industry 326199, All Other Plastics Product Manufacturing; and

T—Canadian, Mexican, and United States industries are comparable.

- Manufacturing timing relays--are classified in U.S. Industry 335314, Relay and Industrial Control Manufacturing.

3346 Manufacturing and Reproducing Magnetic and Optical Media[T]

33461 Manufacturing and Reproducing Magnetic and Optical Media[T]

This industry comprises establishments primarily engaged in (1) manufacturing optical and magnetic media, such as blank audio tapes, blank video tapes, and blank diskettes, and/or (2) mass duplicating (i.e., making copies) audio, video, software, and other data on magnetic, optical, and similar media.

Cross-References. Establishments primarily engaged in--

- Designing, developing, and publishing prepackaged software--are classified in Industry 51121, Software Publishers; and
- Audio, motion picture, and/or video production and/or distribution--are classified in Subsector 512, Motion Picture and Sound Recording Industries.

334613 Blank Magnetic and Optical Recording Media Manufacturing

This U.S. industry comprises establishments primarily engaged in manufacturing blank magnetic and optical recording media, such as blank magnetic tape, blank diskettes, blank optical discs, hard drive media, and blank magnetic tape cassettes.

Cross-References.

Establishments primarily engaged in mass reproducing computer software and other audio and video material are classified in U.S. Industry 334614, Software and Other Prerecorded Compact Disc, Tape, and Record Reproducing.

334614 Software and Other Prerecorded Compact Disc, Tape, and Record Reproducing

This U.S. industry comprises establishments primarily engaged in mass reproducing computer software or other prerecorded audio and video material on magnetic or optical media, such as CD-ROMs, DVDs, tapes, or cartridges. These establishments do not generally develop any software or produce any audio or video content. This industry includes establishments that mass reproduce game CDs and cartridges.

Cross-References. Establishments primarily engaged in--

- Designing, developing, and publishing prepackaged software--are classified in Industry 511210, Software Publishers;
- Audio, motion picture, and/or video production and/or distribution--are classified in Subsector 512, Motion Picture and Sound Recording Industries; and
- Manufacturing blank audio and video tapes, blank diskettes, and blank optical discs--are classified in U.S. Industry 334613, Blank Magnetic and Optical Recording Media Manufacturing.

335 Electrical Equipment, Appliance, and Component Manufacturing[T]

Industries in the Electrical Equipment, Appliance, and Component Manufacturing subsector manufacture products that generate, distribute and use electrical power. Electric Lighting Equipment Manufacturing establishments produce electric lamp bulbs, lighting fixtures, and parts. Household Appliance Manufacturing establishments make both small and major electrical appliances and parts. Electrical Equipment Manufacturing establishments make goods, such as electric motors, generators, transformers, and switchgear apparatus. Other Electrical Equipment and Component Manufacturing establishments make devices for storing electrical power (e.g., batteries), for transmitting electricity (e.g., insulated wire), and wiring devices (e.g., electrical outlets, fuse boxes, and light switches).

T—Canadian, Mexican, and United States industries are comparable.

3351 Electric Lighting Equipment Manufacturing[T]

This industry group comprises establishments primarily engaged in (1) manufacturing electric light bulbs and tubes, and parts and components (except glass blanks for electric light bulbs) or (2) manufacturing electric lighting fixtures (except vehicular), nonelectric lighting equipment, lamp shades (except glass and plastics), and lighting fixture components (except current-carrying wiring devices).

33511 Electric Lamp Bulb and Part Manufacturing[T] See industry description for 335110.

335110 Electric Lamp Bulb and Part Manufacturing

This industry comprises establishments primarily engaged in manufacturing electric light bulbs and tubes, and parts and components (except glass blanks for electric light bulbs).

Cross-References. Establishments primarily engaged in--

- Manufacturing glass blanks for electric light bulbs--are classified in U.S. Industry 327212, Other Pressed and Blown Glass and Glassware Manufacturing;
- Manufacturing vehicular lighting fixtures--are classified in Industry 336320, Motor Vehicle Electrical and Electronic Equipment Manufacturing;
- Manufacturing light emitting diodes (LEDs)--are classified in U.S. Industry 334413, Semiconductor and Related Device Manufacturing; and
- Manufacturing other lighting fixtures (except vehicular)--are classified in Industry 33512, Lighting Fixture Manufacturing.

33512 Lighting Fixture Manufacturing[T]

This industry comprises establishments primarily engaged in manufacturing electric lighting fixtures (except vehicular), nonelectric lighting equipment, lamp shades (except glass and plastics), and lighting fixture components (except current-carrying wiring devices).

Cross-References. Establishments primarily engaged in--

- Manufacturing vehicular lighting fixtures--are classified in Industry 33632, Motor Vehicle Electrical and Electronic Equipment Manufacturing;
- Manufacturing electric light bulbs, tubes, and parts--are classified in Industry 33511, Electric Lamp Bulb and Part Manufacturing;
- Manufacturing current-carrying wiring devices for lighting fixtures--are classified in Industry 33593, Wiring Device Manufacturing;
- Manufacturing ceiling fans or bath fans with integrated lighting fixtures--are classified in Industry 33521, Small Electrical Appliance Manufacturing;
- Manufacturing plastics lamp shades--are classified in Industry 32619, Other Plastics Product Manufacturing;
- Manufacturing glassware and glass parts for lighting fixtures--are classified in Industry 32721, Glass and Glass Product Manufacturing; and
- Manufacturing signaling devices that incorporate electric light bulbs, such as traffic and railway signals--are classified in Industry 33429, Other Communications Equipment Manufacturing.

335121 Residential Electric Lighting Fixture Manufacturing

This U.S. industry comprises establishments primarily engaged in manufacturing fixed or portable residential electric lighting fixtures and lamp shades of metal, paper, or textiles. Residential electric lighting fixtures include those for use both inside and outside the residence.

T—Canadian, Mexican, and United States industries are comparable.

Illustrative Examples:

Ceiling lighting fixtures, residential, manufacturing
Chandeliers, residential, manufacturing
Table lamps (i.e., lighting fixtures) manufacturing

Cross-References. Establishments primarily engaged in--

- Manufacturing glassware for residential lighting fixtures--are classified in Industry 32721, Glass and Glass Product Manufacturing;
- Manufacturing plastics lamp shades--are classified in U.S. Industry 326199, All Other Plastics Product Manufacturing;
- Manufacturing electric light bulbs, tubes, and parts--are classified in Industry 335110, Electric Lamp Bulb and Part Manufacturing;
- Manufacturing ceiling fans or bath fans with integrated lighting fixtures--are classified in Industry 335210, Small Electrical Appliance Manufacturing;
- Manufacturing current-carrying wiring devices for lighting fixtures--are classified in U.S. Industry 335931, Current-Carrying Wiring Device Manufacturing;
- Manufacturing commercial, industrial, and institutional electric lighting fixtures--are classified in U.S. Industry 335122, Commercial, Industrial, and Institutional Electric Lighting Fixture Manufacturing; and
- Manufacturing other lighting fixtures, such as street lights (except traffic signals), flashlights, and nonelectric lighting fixtures--are classified in U.S. Industry 335129, Other Lighting Equipment Manufacturing.

335122 Commercial, Industrial, and Institutional Electric Lighting Fixture Manufacturing

This U.S. industry comprises establishments primarily engaged in manufacturing commercial, industrial, and institutional electric lighting fixtures.

Cross-References. Establishments primarily engaged in--

- Manufacturing glassware for commercial, industrial, and institutional electric lighting fixtures--are classified in Industry 32721, Glass and Glass Product Manufacturing;
- Manufacturing residential electric lighting fixtures--are classified in U.S. Industry 335121, Residential Electric Lighting Fixture Manufacturing;
- Manufacturing current-carrying wiring devices for lighting fixtures--are classified in U.S. Industry 335931, Current-Carrying Wiring Device Manufacturing;
- Manufacturing vehicular lighting fixtures--are classified in Industry 336320, Motor Vehicle Electrical and Electronic Equipment Manufacturing;
- Manufacturing electric light bulbs, tubes, and parts--are classified in Industry 335110, Electric Lamp Bulb and Part Manufacturing;
- Manufacturing other lighting fixtures, such as street lights (except traffic signals), flashlights, and nonelectric lighting equipment--are classified in U.S. Industry 335129, Other Lighting Equipment Manufacturing; and
- Manufacturing signaling devices that incorporate electric light bulbs, such as traffic and railway signals--are classified in Industry 334290, Other Communications Equipment Manufacturing.

335129 Other Lighting Equipment Manufacturing

This U.S. industry comprises establishments primarily engaged in manufacturing electric lighting fixtures (except residential, commercial, industrial, institutional, and vehicular electric lighting fixtures) and nonelectric lighting equipment.

Illustrative Examples:

Christmas tree lighting sets, electric, manufacturing
Fireplace logs, electric, manufacturing

T—Canadian, Mexican, and United States industries are comparable.

Flashlights manufacturing
Insect lamps, electric, manufacturing
Lanterns (e.g., carbide, electric, gas, gasoline, kerosene) manufacturing
Spotlights (except vehicular) manufacturing
Street lighting fixtures (except traffic signals) manufacturing

Cross-References. Establishments primarily engaged in--

- Manufacturing glassware for lighting fixtures--are classified in Industry 32721, Glass and Glass Product Manufacturing;
- Manufacturing electric light bulbs, tubes, and parts--are classified in Industry 335110, Electric Lamp Bulb and Part Manufacturing;
- Manufacturing current-carrying wiring devices for lighting fixtures--are classified in U.S. Industry 335931, Current-Carrying Wiring Device Manufacturing;
- Manufacturing residential electric lighting fixtures--are classified in U.S. Industry 335121, Residential Electric Lighting Fixture Manufacturing;
- Manufacturing commercial, industrial, and institutional electric lighting fixtures--are classified in U.S. Industry 335122, Commercial, Industrial, and Institutional Electric Lighting Fixture Manufacturing;
- Manufacturing vehicular lighting fixtures--are classified in Industry 336320, Motor Vehicle Electrical and Electronic Equipment Manufacturing; and
- Manufacturing signaling devices that incorporate electric light bulbs, such as traffic and railway signals--are classified in Industry 334290, Other Communications Equipment Manufacturing.

3352 Household Appliance Manufacturing[T]

This industry group comprises establishments primarily engaged in manufacturing small electric appliances, electric housewares, and major household appliances.

33521 Small Electrical Appliance Manufacturing[T] See industry description for 335210.

335210 Small Electrical Appliance Manufacturing

This industry comprises establishments primarily engaged in manufacturing small electric appliances and electric housewares, household-type fans (except attic fans), household-type vacuum cleaners, and other electric household-type floor care machines.

Illustrative Examples:

Bath fans, residential, manufacturing
Carpet and floor cleaning equipment, household-type electric, manufacturing
Ceiling fans, residential, manufacturing
Curling irons, household-type electric, manufacturing
Electric blankets manufacturing
Portable electric space heaters manufacturing
Portable hair dryers, electric, manufacturing
Portable cooking appliances (except microwave, convection ovens), household-type electric, manufacturing
Portable humidifiers and dehumidifiers manufacturing
Scissors, electric, manufacturing
Ventilating and exhaust fans (except attic fans), household-type, manufacturing

Cross-References. Establishments primarily engaged in--

- Manufacturing attic fans--are classified in U.S. Industry 333413, Industrial and Commercial Fan and Blower and Air Purification Equipment Manufacturing;
- Manufacturing wall and baseboard heating units for permanent installation--are classified in U.S. Industry 333414, Heating Equipment (except Warm Air Furnaces) Manufacturing;
- Manufacturing room air-conditioners--are classified in U.S. Industry 333415, Air-Conditioning and Warm Air Heating Equipment and Commercial and Industrial Refrigeration Equipment Manufacturing;

T—Canadian, Mexican, and United States industries are comparable.

- Manufacturing microwave and convection ovens--are classified in Industry 335220, Major Household Appliance Manufacturing;
- Manufacturing electric vacuum cleaners for commercial, industrial, and institutional uses, and mechanical carpet sweepers--are classified in U.S. Industry 333318, Other Commercial and Service Industry Machinery Manufacturing; and
- Installing central vacuum cleaning systems--are classified in Industry 238290, Other Building Equipment Contractors.

33522 Major Household Appliance Manufacturing[T] See industry description for 335220.

335220 Major Household Appliance Manufacturing

This industry comprises establishments primarily engaged in manufacturing household-type cooking appliances, household-type laundry equipment, household-type refrigerators, upright and chest freezers, and other electrical and nonelectrical major household-type appliances, such as dishwashers, water heaters, and garbage disposal units.

Cross-References. Establishments primarily engaged in--

- Manufacturing small electric appliances and electric housewares, such as hot plates, griddles, toasters, and electric irons--are classified in Industry 335210, Small Electrical Appliance Manufacturing;
- Manufacturing commercial and industrial refrigerators and freezers--are classified in U.S. Industry 333415, Air-Conditioning and Warm Air Heating Equipment and Commercial and Industrial Refrigeration Equipment Manufacturing;
- Manufacturing commercial-type cooking equipment and commercial-type laundry, drycleaning, and pressing equipment--are classified in U.S. Industry 333318, Other Commercial and Service Industry Machinery Manufacturing; and
- Manufacturing household-type sewing machines--are classified in U.S. Industry 333249, Other Industrial Machinery Manufacturing.

3353 Electrical Equipment Manufacturing[T]

33531 Electrical Equipment Manufacturing[T]

This industry comprises establishments primarily engaged in manufacturing power, distribution, and specialty transformers; electric motors, generators, and motor generator sets; switchgear and switchboard apparatus; relays; and industrial controls.

Cross-References. Establishments primarily engaged in--

- Manufacturing turbine generator set units and electric outboard motors--are classified in Industry 33361, Engine, Turbine, and Power Transmission Equipment Manufacturing;
- Manufacturing electronic component-type transformers and switches--are classified in Industry 33441, Semiconductor and Other Electronic Component Manufacturing;
- Manufacturing environmental controls and industrial process control instruments--are classified in Industry 33451, Navigational, Measuring, Electromedical, and Control Instruments Manufacturing;
- Manufacturing switches for electrical circuits, such as pushbutton and snap switches--are classified in Industry 33593, Wiring Device Manufacturing;
- Manufacturing welding and soldering equipment (except handheld soldering irons)--are classified in Industry 33399, All Other General Purpose Machinery Manufacturing; and
- Manufacturing starting motors and generators for internal combustion engines--are classified in Industry 33632, Motor Vehicle Electrical and Electronic Equipment Manufacturing.

T—Canadian, Mexican, and United States industries are comparable.

335311 Power, Distribution, and Specialty Transformer Manufacturing

This U.S. industry comprises establishments primarily engaged in manufacturing power, distribution, and specialty transformers (except electronic components). Industrial-type and consumer-type transformers in this industry vary (e.g., step up or step down) voltage but do not convert alternating to direct or direct to alternating current.

Illustrative Examples:

Fluorescent ballasts (i.e., transformers) manufacturing
Substation transformers, electric power distribution, manufacturing
Distribution transformers, electric, manufacturing
Transmission and distribution voltage regulators manufacturing

Cross-References.

Establishments primarily engaged in manufacturing electronic component-type transformers are classified in U.S. Industry 334416, Capacitor, Resistor, Coil, Transformer, and Other Inductor Manufacturing.

335312 Motor and Generator Manufacturing

This U.S. industry comprises establishments primarily engaged in manufacturing electric motors (except internal combustion engine starting motors), power generators (except battery charging alternators for internal combustion engines), and motor generator sets (except turbine generator set units). This industry includes establishments rewinding armatures on a factory basis.

Cross-References. Establishments primarily engaged in--

- Manufacturing electric outboard motors--are classified in U.S. Industry 333618, Other Engine Equipment Manufacturing;
- Manufacturing gas, steam, or hydraulic turbine generator set units--are classified in U.S. Industry 333611, Turbine and Turbine Generator Set Units Manufacturing;
- Manufacturing starting motors and battery charging alternators for internal combustion engines--are classified in Industry 336320, Motor Vehicle Electrical and Electronic Equipment Manufacturing;
- Rewinding armatures, not on a factory basis--are classified in Industry 811310, Commercial and Industrial Machinery and Equipment (except Automotive and Electronic) Repair and Maintenance; and
- Manufacturing welding and soldering equipment (except handheld soldering irons)--are classified in U.S. Industry 333992, Welding and Soldering Equipment Manufacturing.

335313 Switchgear and Switchboard Apparatus Manufacturing

This U.S. industry comprises establishments primarily engaged in manufacturing switchgear and switchboard apparatus.

Illustrative Examples:

Circuit breakers, power, manufacturing
Control panels, electric power distribution, manufacturing
Ducts for electrical switchboard apparatus manufacturing
Fuses, electric, manufacturing
Power switching equipment manufacturing
Switches, electric power (except pushbutton, snap, solenoid, tumbler), manufacturing

Cross-References. Establishments primarily engaged in--

- Manufacturing relays--are classified in U.S. Industry 335314, Relay and Industrial Control Manufacturing;

T—Canadian, Mexican, and United States industries are comparable.

- Manufacturing switches for electronic applications--are classified in U.S. Industry 334419, Other Electronic Component Manufacturing; and
- Manufacturing snap, pushbutton, and similar switches for electrical circuits--are classified in U.S. Industry 335931, Current-Carrying Wiring Device Manufacturing.

335314 Relay and Industrial Control Manufacturing

This U.S. industry comprises establishments primarily engaged in manufacturing relays, motor starters and controllers, and other industrial controls and control accessories.

Cross-References. Establishments primarily engaged in--

- Manufacturing environmental and appliance control equipment--are classified in U.S. Industry 334512, Automatic Environmental Control Manufacturing for Residential, Commercial, and Appliance Use; and
- Manufacturing instruments for controlling industrial process variables--are classified in U.S. Industry 334513, Instruments and Related Products Manufacturing for Measuring, Displaying, and Controlling Industrial Process Variables.

3359 Other Electrical Equipment and Component Manufacturing[T]

This industry group comprises establishments manufacturing electrical equipment and components (except electric lighting equipment, household-type appliances, transformers, switchgear, relays, motors, and generators).

33591 Battery Manufacturing[T]

This industry comprises establishments primarily engaged in manufacturing primary and storage batteries.

335911 Storage Battery Manufacturing

This U.S. industry comprises establishments primarily engaged in manufacturing storage batteries.

Illustrative Examples:

Lead acid storage batteries manufacturing
Lithium storage batteries manufacturing
Rechargeable nickel-cadmium (NICAD) batteries

Cross-References.

Establishments primarily engaged in manufacturing primary batteries are classified in U.S. Industry 335912, Primary Battery Manufacturing.

335912 Primary Battery Manufacturing

This U.S. industry comprises establishments primarily engaged in manufacturing wet or dry primary batteries.

Illustrative Examples:

Disposable flashlight batteries manufacturing
Dry cells, primary (e.g., AAA, AA, C, D, 9V), manufacturing
Lithium batteries, primary, manufacturing

Cross-References.

Establishments primarily engaged in manufacturing storage batteries are classified in U.S. Industry 335911, Storage Battery Manufacturing.

T—Canadian, Mexican, and United States industries are comparable.

33592 Communication and Energy Wire and Cable Manufacturing[T]

This industry comprises establishments insulating fiber optic cable, and manufacturing insulated nonferrous wire and cable from nonferrous wire drawn in other establishments.

Cross-References. Establishments primarily engaged in--

- Drawing nonferrous wire--are classified in Subsector 331, Primary Metal Manufacturing;
- Manufacturing cable sets consisting of insulated wire and various connectors for electronic applications--are classified in Industry 33441, Semiconductor and Other Electronic Component Manufacturing;
- Manufacturing extension cords, appliance cords, and similar electrical cord sets from purchased, insulated wire or cable--are classified in Industry 33599, All Other Electrical Equipment and Component Manufacturing; and
- Manufacturing unsheathed fiber optic materials--are classified in Industry 32721, Glass and Glass Product Manufacturing.

335921 Fiber Optic Cable Manufacturing

This U.S. industry comprises establishments primarily engaged in manufacturing insulated fiber optic cable from purchased fiber optic strand.

Cross-References. Establishments primarily engaged in--

- Manufacturing unsheathed fiber optic materials--are classified in Industry 32721, Glass and Glass Product Manufacturing; and
- Manufacturing insulated nonferrous wire and cable from purchased wire--are classified in U.S. Industry 335929, Other Communication and Energy Wire Manufacturing.

335929 Other Communication and Energy Wire Manufacturing

This U.S. industry comprises establishments primarily engaged in manufacturing insulated wire and cable of nonferrous metals from purchased wire.

Cross-References. Establishments primarily engaged in--

- Manufacturing cable sets consisting of insulated wire and various connectors for electronic applications--are classified in U.S. Industry 334419, Other Electronic Component Manufacturing;
- Manufacturing extension cords, appliance cords, and similar electrical cord sets from purchased insulated wire--are classified in U.S. Industry 335999, All Other Miscellaneous Electrical Equipment and Component Manufacturing;
- Drawing and insulating copper wire in the same establishment--are classified in Industry 331420, Copper Rolling, Drawing, Extruding, and Alloying;
- Drawing and insulating aluminum wire in the same establishment--are classified in U.S. Industry 331318, Other Aluminum Rolling, Drawing, and Extruding; and
- Drawing nonferrous wire (except copper and aluminum)--are classified in U.S. Industry 331491, Nonferrous Metal (except Copper and Aluminum) Rolling, Drawing, and Extruding.

33593 Wiring Device Manufacturing[T]

This industry comprises establishments primarily engaged in manufacturing current-carrying wiring devices and noncurrent-carrying wiring devices for wiring electrical circuits.

T—Canadian, Mexican, and United States industries are comparable.

Cross-References. Establishments primarily engaged in--

- Manufacturing ceramic and glass insulators--are classified in Subsector 327, Nonmetallic Mineral Product Manufacturing; and
- Manufacturing electronic component-type connectors, sockets, and switches--are classified in Industry 33441, Semiconductor and Other Electronic Component Manufacturing.

335931 Current-Carrying Wiring Device Manufacturing

This U.S. industry comprises establishments primarily engaged in manufacturing current-carrying wiring devices.

Illustrative Examples:

Bus bars, electrical conductors (except switchgear-type), manufacturing
GFCI (ground fault circuit interrupters) manufacturing
Lamp holders manufacturing
Lightning arrestors and coils manufacturing
Receptacles (i.e., outlets), electrical, manufacturing
Switches for electrical wiring (e.g., pressure, push-button, snap, tumbler) manufacturing

Cross-References. Establishments primarily engaged in--

- Manufacturing electronic component-type connectors--are classified in U.S. Industry 334417, Electronic Connector Manufacturing;
- Manufacturing noncurrent-carrying wiring devices--are classified in U.S. Industry 335932, Noncurrent-Carrying Wiring Device Manufacturing; and
- Manufacturing electronic component-type sockets and switches--are classified in U.S. Industry 334419, Other Electronic Component Manufacturing.

335932 Noncurrent-Carrying Wiring Device Manufacturing

This U.S. industry comprises establishments primarily engaged in manufacturing noncurrent-carrying wiring devices.

Illustrative Examples:

Boxes, electrical wiring (e.g., junction, outlet, switch), manufacturing
Conduits and fittings, electrical, manufacturing
Face plates (i.e., outlet or switch covers) manufacturing
Transmission pole and line hardware manufacturing

Cross-References. Establishments primarily engaged in--

- Manufacturing porcelain and ceramic insulators--are classified in Industry 327110, Pottery, Ceramics, and Plumbing Fixture Manufacturing;
- Manufacturing current-carrying wiring devices--are classified in U.S. Industry 335931, Current-Carrying Wiring Device Manufacturing; and
- Manufacturing glass insulators--are classified in Industry 32721, Glass and Glass Product Manufacturing.

33599 All Other Electrical Equipment and Component Manufacturing[T]

This industry comprises establishments primarily engaged in manufacturing electrical equipment (except electric lighting equipment, household-type appliances, transformers, motors, generators, switchgear, relays, industrial controls, batteries, communication and energy wire and cable, and wiring devices).

T—Canadian, Mexican, and United States industries are comparable.

Illustrative Examples:

Carbon and graphite electrodes and brushes manufacturing
Extension cords made from purchased insulated wire
Door opening and closing devices, electrical, manufacturing
Surge suppressors manufacturing

Cross-References. Establishments primarily engaged in--

- Manufacturing lighting equipment--are classified in Industry Group 3351, Electric Lighting Equipment Manufacturing;
- Manufacturing household-type appliances--are classified in Industry Group 3352, Household Appliance Manufacturing;
- Manufacturing transformers, motors, generators, switchgear, relays, and industrial controls--are classified in Industry 33531, Electrical Equipment Manufacturing;
- Manufacturing batteries--are classified in Industry 33591, Battery Manufacturing;
- Manufacturing communication and energy wire--are classified in Industry 33592, Communication and Energy Wire and Cable Manufacturing;
- Manufacturing current-carrying and noncurrent-carrying wiring devices--are classified in Industry 33593, Wiring Device Manufacturing;
- Manufacturing carbon or graphite gaskets--are classified in Industry 33999, All Other Miscellaneous Manufacturing;
- Manufacturing electronic component-type rectifiers, voltage regulating integrated circuits, power converting integrated circuits, electronic capacitors, electronic resistors, and similar devices--are classified in Industry 33441, Semiconductor and Other Electronic Component Manufacturing; and
- Manufacturing equipment incorporating lasers--are classified in the Manufacturing sector based on the associated production process of the finished equipment.

335991 Carbon and Graphite Product Manufacturing

This U.S. industry comprises establishments primarily engaged in manufacturing carbon, graphite, and metal-graphite brushes and brush stock; carbon or graphite electrodes for thermal and electrolytic uses; carbon and graphite fibers; and other carbon, graphite, and metal-graphite products.

Cross-References.

Establishments primarily engaged in manufacturing carbon or graphite gaskets are classified in U.S. Industry 339991, Gasket, Packing, and Sealing Device Manufacturing.

335999 All Other Miscellaneous Electrical Equipment and Component Manufacturing

This U.S. industry comprises establishments primarily engaged in manufacturing industrial and commercial electric apparatus and other equipment (except lighting equipment, household appliances, transformers, motors, generators, switchgear, relays, industrial controls, batteries, communication and energy wire and cable, wiring devices, and carbon and graphite products). This industry includes power converters (i.e., AC to DC and DC to AC), power supplies, surge suppressors, and similar equipment for industrial-type and consumer-type equipment.

Illustrative Examples:

Appliance cords made from purchased insulated wire
Battery chargers, solid-state, manufacturing
Door opening and closing devices, electrical, manufacturing
Electric bells manufacturing
Extension cords made from purchased insulated wire
Inverters manufacturing
Surge suppressers manufacturing
Uninterruptible power supplies (UPS) manufacturing

T—Canadian, Mexican, and United States industries are comparable.

Cross-References. Establishments primarily engaged in--

- Manufacturing lighting equipment--are classified in Industry Group 3351, Electric Lighting Equipment Manufacturing;
- Manufacturing household-type appliances--are classified in Industry Group 3352, Household Appliance Manufacturing;
- Manufacturing transformers, motors, generators, switchgear, relays, and industrial controls--are classified in Industry 33531, Electrical Equipment Manufacturing;
- Manufacturing primary and storage batteries--are classified in Industry 33591, Battery Manufacturing;
- Manufacturing communication and energy wire and cable from purchased wire or fiber optic strand--are classified in Industry 33592, Communication and Energy Wire and Cable Manufacturing;
- Manufacturing current-carrying and noncurrent-carrying wiring devices--are classified in Industry 33593, Wiring Device Manufacturing;
- Manufacturing electronic component-type rectifiers (except semiconductor)--are classified in U.S. Industry 334419, Other Electronic Component Manufacturing;
- Manufacturing semiconductor rectifiers, voltage regulating integrated circuits, power converting integrated circuits, and similar semiconductor devices--are classified in U.S. Industry 334413, Semiconductor and Related Device Manufacturing;
- Manufacturing electronic component-type capacitors and condensers--are classified in U.S. Industry 334416, Capacitor, Resistor, Coil, Transformer, and Other Inductor Manufacturing;
- Manufacturing carbon and graphite products--are classified in U.S. Industry 335991, Carbon and Graphite Product Manufacturing; and
- Manufacturing equipment incorporating lasers--are classified in the Manufacturing sector based on the associated production process of the finished equipment.

336 Transportation Equipment Manufacturing[T]

Industries in the Transportation Equipment Manufacturing subsector produce equipment for transporting people and goods. Transportation equipment is a type of machinery. An entire subsector is devoted to this activity because of the significance of its economic size in all three North American countries.

Establishments in this subsector utilize production processes similar to those of other machinery manufacturing establishments—bending, forming, welding, machining, and assembling metal or plastic parts into components and finished products. However, the assembly of components and subassemblies and their further assembly into finished vehicles tends to be a more common production process in this subsector than in the Machinery Manufacturing subsector.

NAICS has industry groups for the manufacture of equipment for each mode of transport—road, rail, air and water. Parts for motor vehicles warrant a separate industry group because of their importance and because they require less assembly than complete vehicles.

Land use motor vehicle equipment not designed for highway operation (e.g., agricultural equipment, construction equipment, and material handling equipment) is classified in the appropriate NAICS subsector based on the type and use of the equipment.

3361 Motor Vehicle Manufacturing[T]

This industry group comprises establishments primarily engaged in (1) manufacturing complete automobiles, light duty motor vehicles, and heavy duty trucks (i.e., body and chassis or unibody) or (2) manufacturing motor vehicle chassis only.

33611 Automobile and Light Duty Motor Vehicle Manufacturing[T]

This industry comprises establishments primarily engaged in (1) manufacturing complete automobile and light duty motor vehicles (i.e., body and chassis or unibody) or (2) manufacturing automobile and light duty motor vehicle chassis only.

T—Canadian, Mexican, and United States industries are comparable.

Cross-References.

Establishments primarily engaged in manufacturing car, truck, and bus bodies and assembling vehicles on purchased chassis and manufacturing kit cars for highway use are classified in Industry 33621, Motor Vehicle Body and Trailer Manufacturing.

336111 Automobile Manufacturing

This U.S. industry comprises establishments primarily engaged in (1) manufacturing complete automobiles (i.e., body and chassis or unibody) or (2) manufacturing automobile chassis only.

Cross-References.

Establishments primarily engaged in manufacturing car bodies and assembling vehicles on purchased chassis and manufacturing kit cars for highway use are classified in U.S. Industry 336211, Motor Vehicle Body Manufacturing.

336112 Light Truck and Utility Vehicle Manufacturing

This U.S. industry comprises establishments primarily engaged in (1) manufacturing complete light trucks and utility vehicles (i.e., body and chassis) or (2) manufacturing light truck and utility vehicle chassis only. Vehicles made include light duty vans, pick-up trucks, minivans, and sport utility vehicles.

Cross-References.

Establishments primarily engaged in manufacturing truck and bus bodies and assembling vehicles on purchased chassis are classified in U.S. Industry 336211, Motor Vehicle Body Manufacturing.

33612 Heavy Duty Truck Manufacturing[T] See industry description for 336120.

336120 Heavy Duty Truck Manufacturing

This industry comprises establishments primarily engaged in (1) manufacturing heavy duty truck chassis and assembling complete heavy duty trucks, buses, heavy duty motor homes, and other special purpose heavy duty motor vehicles for highway use or (2) manufacturing heavy duty truck chassis only.

Cross-References. Establishments primarily engaged in--

- Manufacturing truck and bus bodies and assembling vehicles on purchased chassis--are classified in U.S. Industry 336211, Motor Vehicle Body Manufacturing;
- Manufacturing motor homes on purchased chassis--are classified in U.S. Industry 336213, Motor Home Manufacturing;
- Manufacturing vans, minivans, and light trucks--are classified in U.S. Industry 336112, Light Truck and Utility Vehicle Manufacturing;
- Manufacturing military armored vehicles--are classified in U.S. Industry 336992, Military Armored Vehicle, Tank, and Tank Component Manufacturing; and
- Manufacturing off-highway construction equipment--are classified in Industry 333120, Construction Machinery Manufacturing.

3362 Motor Vehicle Body and Trailer Manufacturing[T]

33621 Motor Vehicle Body and Trailer Manufacturing[T]

This industry comprises establishments primarily engaged in (1) manufacturing motor vehicle bodies and cabs or (2) manufacturing truck, automobile and utility trailers, truck trailer chassis, detachable trailer bodies, and

T—Canadian, Mexican, and United States industries are comparable.

detachable trailer chassis. The products made may be sold separately or may be assembled on purchased chassis and sold as complete vehicles.

Motor homes are units where the motor and the living quarters are contained in the same integrated unit, while travel trailers are designed to be towed by a motor unit, such as an automobile or a light truck.

Illustrative Examples:

Bodies and cabs, truck, manufacturing
Camper units, slide-in, for pick-up trucks, manufacturing
Pick-up canopies, caps, or covers manufacturing
Motor homes, self-contained, assembling on purchased chassis
Semi-trailers manufacturing
Travel trailers, recreational, manufacturing

Cross-References. Establishments primarily engaged in--

- Making manufactured homes (i.e., mobile homes)--are classified in Industry 32199, All Other Wood Product Manufacturing;
- Customizing automotive vehicle and trailer interiors (i.e., van conversions) on an individual basis--are classified in Industry 81112, Automotive Body, Paint, Interior, and Glass Repair;
- Manufacturing light duty motor home chassis and assembling complete motor homes--are classified in Industry 33611, Automobile and Light Duty Motor Vehicle Manufacturing; and
- Manufacturing heavy duty truck chassis and assembling heavy duty trucks, buses, motor homes, and other special purpose heavy duty motor vehicles for highway use--are classified in Industry 33612, Heavy Duty Truck Manufacturing.

336211 Motor Vehicle Body Manufacturing

This U.S. industry comprises establishments primarily engaged in manufacturing truck and bus bodies and cabs and automobile bodies. The products made may be sold separately or may be assembled on purchased chassis and sold as complete vehicles.

Cross-References.

Establishments primarily engaged in manufacturing heavy duty chassis and assembling heavy duty trucks, buses, motor homes, and other special purpose heavy duty motor vehicles for highway use are classified in Industry 336120, Heavy Duty Truck Manufacturing.

336212 Truck Trailer Manufacturing

This U.S. industry comprises establishments primarily engaged in manufacturing truck trailers, truck trailer chassis, cargo container chassis, detachable trailer bodies, and detachable trailer chassis for sale separately.

Cross-References.

Establishments primarily engaged in manufacturing utility trailers, light-truck trailers, and travel trailers are classified in U.S. Industry 336214, Travel Trailer and Camper Manufacturing.

336213 Motor Home Manufacturing

This U.S. industry comprises establishments primarily engaged in (1) manufacturing motor homes on purchased chassis and/or (2) manufacturing conversion vans on an assembly line basis. Motor homes are units where the motor and the living quarters are integrated in the same unit.

T—Canadian, Mexican, and United States industries are comparable.

Cross-References. Establishments primarily engaged in--

- Manufacturing light duty motor home chassis and assembling complete motor homes--are classified in U.S. Industry 336112, Light Truck and Utility Vehicle Manufacturing;
- Customizing automotive vehicle and trailer interiors (i.e., van conversions) on an individual basis--are classified in U.S. Industry 811121, Automotive Body, Paint, and Interior Repair and Maintenance; and
- Producing manufactured homes (i.e., mobile homes)--are classified in U.S. Industry 321991, Manufactured Home (Mobile Home) Manufacturing.

336214 Travel Trailer and Camper Manufacturing

This U.S. industry comprises establishments primarily engaged in one or more of the following: (1) manufacturing travel trailers and campers designed to attach to motor vehicles; (2) manufacturing pick-up coaches (i.e., campers) and caps (i.e., covers) for mounting on pick-up trucks; and (3) manufacturing automobile, utility and light-truck trailers. Travel trailers do not have their own motor but are designed to be towed by a motor unit, such as an automobile or a light truck.

Illustrative Examples:

Automobile transporter trailers, single car, manufacturing
Camper units, slide-in, for pick-up trucks, manufacturing
Camping trailers and chassis manufacturing
Horse trailers (except fifth-wheel-type) manufacturing
Pick-up canopies, caps, or covers manufacturing
Travel trailers, recreational, manufacturing
Utility trailers manufacturing

Cross-References.

Establishments primarily engaged in making manufactured homes (i.e., mobile homes) designed to accept permanent water, sewer, and utility connections and equipped with wheels, but not intended for regular highway use, are classified in U.S. Industry 321991, Manufactured Home (Mobile Home) Manufacturing.

3363 Motor Vehicle Parts Manufacturing[T]

This industry group comprises establishments primarily engaged in manufacturing motor vehicle gasoline engines and engine parts, motor vehicle electrical and electronic equipment, motor vehicle steering and suspension components (except springs), motor vehicle brake systems, motor vehicle transmission and power train parts, motor vehicle seating and interior trim, motor vehicle metal stampings, and other motor vehicle parts and accessories. This industry group includes establishments that rebuild motor vehicle parts.

33631 Motor Vehicle Gasoline Engine and Engine Parts Manufacturing[T] See industry description for 336310.

336310 Motor Vehicle Gasoline Engine and Engine Parts Manufacturing

This industry comprises establishments primarily engaged in (1) manufacturing and/or rebuilding motor vehicle gasoline engines and engine parts and/or (2) manufacturing and/or rebuilding carburetors, pistons, piston rings, and engine valves, whether or not for vehicular use.

Illustrative Examples:

Carburetors, all types, manufacturing
Crankshaft assemblies, automotive and truck gasoline engine, manufacturing
Cylinder heads, automotive and truck gasoline engine, manufacturing
Fuel injection systems and parts, automotive and truck gasoline engine, manufacturing
Gasoline engines for hybrid automotive vehicles manufacturing
Pistons and piston rings manufacturing

T—Canadian, Mexican, and United States industries are comparable.

Manifolds (i.e., intake and exhaust), automotive and truck gasoline engine, manufacturing Timing gears and chains, automotive and truck gasoline engine, manufacturing
Pumps (e.g., fuel, oil, water), mechanical, automotive and truck gasoline engine (except power steering), manufacturing
Valves, engine, intake and exhaust, manufacturing

Cross-References. Establishments primarily engaged in--

- Manufacturing wiring harnesses and other vehicular electrical and electronic equipment--are classified in Industry 336320, Motor Vehicle Electrical and Electronic Equipment Manufacturing;
- Manufacturing transmission and power train equipment--are classified in Industry 336350, Motor Vehicle Transmission and Power Train Parts Manufacturing;
- Manufacturing radiators--are classified in Industry 336390, Other Motor Vehicle Parts Manufacturing;
- Manufacturing steering and suspension components--are classified in Industry 336330, Motor Vehicle Steering and Suspension Components (except Spring) Manufacturing;
- Manufacturing parts for machine repair and equipment parts (except electric) on a job or shop basis--are classified in Industry 332710, Machine Shops;
- Manufacturing rubber and plastic belts and hoses without fittings--are classified in Industry 326220, Rubber and Plastics Hoses and Belting Manufacturing; and
- Manufacturing stationary and diesel engines--are classified in U.S. Industry 333618, Other Engine Equipment Manufacturing.

33632 Motor Vehicle Electrical and Electronic Equipment Manufacturing[T] See industry description for 336320.

336320 Motor Vehicle Electrical and Electronic Equipment Manufacturing

This industry comprises establishments primarily engaged in manufacturing and/or rebuilding electrical and electronic equipment for motor vehicles and internal combustion engines. The products made can be used for all types of transportation equipment (i.e., aircraft, automobiles, trucks, trains, ships) or stationary internal combustion engine applications.

Illustrative Examples:

Alternators and generators for internal combustion engines manufacturing
Automotive lighting fixtures manufacturing
Coils, ignition, internal combustion engines, manufacturing
Distributors for internal combustion engines manufacturing
Electrical control chips (modules), motor vehicle, manufacturing
Electrical ignition cable sets for internal combustion engines manufacturing
Generators for internal combustion engines manufacturing
Ignition wiring harness for internal combustion engines manufacturing
Instrument control panels (i.e., assembling purchased gauges), automotive, truck, and bus, manufacturing
Spark plugs for internal combustion engines manufacturing
Windshield washer pumps, automotive, truck, and bus, manufacturing

Cross-References. Establishments primarily engaged in--

- Manufacturing automotive lamps (i.e., bulbs)--are classified in Industry 335110, Electric Lamp Bulb and Part Manufacturing;
- Manufacturing automotive batteries--are classified in U.S. Industry 335911, Storage Battery Manufacturing;
- Manufacturing electric motors for electric vehicles--are classified in U.S. Industry 335312, Motor and Generator Manufacturing;
- Manufacturing railway traffic control signals and passenger car alarms--are classified in Industry 334290, Other Communications Equipment Manufacturing; and

T—Canadian, Mexican, and United States industries are comparable.

- Manufacturing car stereos--are classified in Industry 334310, Audio and Video Equipment Manufacturing.

33633 Motor Vehicle Steering and Suspension Components (except Spring) Manufacturing[T] See industry description for 336330.

336330 Motor Vehicle Steering and Suspension Components (except Spring) Manufacturing

This industry comprises establishments primarily engaged in manufacturing and/or rebuilding motor vehicle steering mechanisms and suspension components (except springs).

Illustrative Examples:

Power steering pumps manufacturing
Rack and pinion steering assemblies manufacturing
Shock absorbers, automotive, truck, and bus, manufacturing
Struts, automotive, truck, and bus, manufacturing
Steering columns, automotive, truck, and bus, manufacturing
Steering wheels, automotive, truck, and bus, manufacturing

Cross-References.

Establishments primarily engaged in manufacturing springs are classified in Industry 33261, Spring and Wire Product Manufacturing.

33634 Motor Vehicle Brake System Manufacturing[T] See industry description for 336340.

336340 Motor Vehicle Brake System Manufacturing

This industry comprises establishments primarily engaged in manufacturing and/or rebuilding motor vehicle brake systems and related components.

Illustrative Examples:

Brake cylinders, master and wheel, automotive, truck, and bus, manufacturing Brake drums, automotive, truck, and bus, manufacturing
Brake hose assemblies manufacturing
bus, manufacturing
Calipers, brake, automotive, truck, and bus, manufacturing

Cross-References.
Brake pads and shoes, automotive, truck, and

Establishments primarily engaged in manufacturing rubber and plastics belts and hoses without fittings are classified in Industry 326220, Rubber and Plastics Hoses and Belting Manufacturing.

33635 Motor Vehicle Transmission and Power Train Parts Manufacturing[T] See industry description for 336350.

336350 Motor Vehicle Transmission and Power Train Parts Manufacturing

This industry comprises establishments primarily engaged in manufacturing and/or rebuilding motor vehicle transmissions and power train parts.

T—Canadian, Mexican, and United States industries are comparable.

Illustrative Examples:

Automatic transmissions, automotive, truck, and bus, manufacturing
Axle bearings, automotive, truck, and bus, manufacturing
Constant velocity joints, automotive, truck, and bus, manufacturing
Differential and rear axle assemblies, automotive, truck, and bus, manufacturing
Torque converters, automotive, truck, and bus, manufacturing
Universal joints, automotive, truck, and bus, manufacturing

33636 Motor Vehicle Seating and Interior Trim Manufacturing[T] See industry description for 336360.

336360 Motor Vehicle Seating and Interior Trim Manufacturing

This industry comprises establishments primarily engaged in manufacturing motor vehicle seating, seats, seat frames, seat belts, and interior trimmings.

Cross-References.

Establishments primarily engaged in manufacturing convertible tops for vehicles and those manufacturing air bags are classified in Industry 336390, Other Motor Vehicle Parts Manufacturing.

33637 Motor Vehicle Metal Stamping[T] See industry description for 336370.

336370 Motor Vehicle Metal Stamping

This industry comprises establishments primarily engaged in manufacturing motor vehicle stampings, such as fenders, tops, body parts, trim, and molding.

Cross-References. Establishments primarily engaged in--

- Manufacturing stampings and further processing the stampings--are classified according to the process of the specific product made; and
- Manufacturing stampings (except motor vehicle)--are classified in U.S. Industry 332119, Metal Crown, Closure, and Other Metal Stamping (except Automotive).

33639 Other Motor Vehicle Parts Manufacturing[T] See industry description for 336390.

336390 Other Motor Vehicle Parts Manufacturing

This industry comprises establishments primarily engaged in manufacturing and/or rebuilding motor vehicle parts and accessories (except motor vehicle gasoline engines and engine parts, motor vehicle electrical and electronic equipment, motor vehicle steering and suspension components, motor vehicle brake systems, motor vehicle transmissions and power train parts, motor vehicle seating and interior trim, and motor vehicle stampings).

Illustrative Examples:

Air bag assemblies manufacturing
Air-conditioners, motor vehicle, manufacturing
Air filters, automotive, truck, and bus, manufacturing
Radiators and cores manufacturing
Catalytic converters, engine exhaust, automotive, truck, and bus, manufacturing
Compressors, motor vehicle air-conditioning, manufacturing
Mufflers and resonators, motor vehicle, manufacturing
Wheels (i.e., rims), automotive, truck, and bus, manufacturing

T—Canadian, Mexican, and United States industries are comparable.

Cross-References. Establishments primarily engaged in--

- Manufacturing motor vehicle gasoline engines and engine parts--are classified in Industry 336310, Motor Vehicle Gasoline Engine and Engine Parts Manufacturing;
- Manufacturing motor vehicle electrical and electronic equipment--are classified in Industry 336320, Motor Vehicle Electrical and Electronic Equipment Manufacturing;
- Manufacturing motor vehicle steering and suspension components--are classified in Industry 336330, Motor Vehicle Steering and Suspension Components (except Spring) Manufacturing;
- Manufacturing motor vehicle brake systems--are classified in Industry 336340, Motor Vehicle Brake System Manufacturing;
- Manufacturing motor vehicle transmissions and power train parts--are classified in Industry 336350, Motor Vehicle Transmission and Power Train Parts Manufacturing;
- Manufacturing motor vehicle seating and interior trim--are classified in Industry 336360, Motor Vehicle Seating and Interior Trim Manufacturing;
- Manufacturing motor vehicle stampings--are classified in Industry 336370, Motor Vehicle Metal Stamping; and
- Manufacturing air-conditioning systems and compressors (except motor vehicle air-conditioning systems)--are classified in U.S. Industry 333415, Air-Conditioning and Warm Air Heating Equipment and Commercial and Industrial Refrigeration Equipment Manufacturing.

3364 Aerospace Product and Parts Manufacturing[T]

33641 Aerospace Product and Parts Manufacturing[T]

This industry comprises establishments primarily engaged in one or more of the following: (1) manufacturing complete aircraft, missiles, or space vehicles; (2) manufacturing aerospace engines, propulsion units, auxiliary equipment or parts; (3) developing and making prototypes of aerospace products; (4) aircraft conversion (i.e., major modifications to systems); and (5) complete aircraft or propulsion systems overhaul and rebuilding (i.e., periodic restoration of aircraft to original design specifications).

Cross-References.

- Establishments primarily engaged in manufacturing space satellites are classified in Industry 33422, Radio and Television Broadcasting and Wireless Communications Equipment Manufacturing;
- Establishments primarily engaged in manufacturing flight simulators are classified in Industry 33331, Commercial and Service Industry Machinery Manufacturing;
- Establishments primarily engaged in the repair of aircraft or aircraft engines (except overhauling, conversion, and rebuilding) are classified in Industry 48819, Other Support Activities for Air Transportation;
- Research and development establishments primarily engaged in aerospace R&D (except prototype production) are classified in Industry 54171, Research and Development in the Physical, Engineering, and Life Sciences;
- Establishments primarily engaged in manufacturing aircraft engine intake and exhaust valves, pistons, or engine filters are classified in Industry 33631, Motor Vehicle Gasoline Engine and Engine Parts Manufacturing;
- Establishments primarily engaged in manufacturing aircraft seating are classified in Industry 33636, Motor Vehicle Seating and Interior Trim Manufacturing;
- Establishments primarily engaged in manufacturing aeronautical, navigational, and guidance systems and instruments are classified in Industry 33451, Navigational, Measuring, Electromedical, and Control Instruments Manufacturing;
- Establishment primarily engaged in manufacturing aircraft engine electrical (aeronautical electrical) equipment or aircraft lighting fixtures are classified in Industry 33632, Motor Vehicle Electrical and Electronic Equipment Manufacturing; and
- Establishments primarily engaged in manufacturing aircraft fluid power subassemblies are classified in Industry 33291, Metal Valve Manufacturing.

T—Canadian, Mexican, and United States industries are comparable.

336411 Aircraft Manufacturing

This U.S. industry comprises establishments primarily engaged in one or more of the following: (1) manufacturing or assembling complete aircraft; (2) developing and making aircraft prototypes; (3) aircraft conversion (i.e., major modifications to systems); and (4) complete aircraft overhaul and rebuilding (i.e., periodic restoration of aircraft to original design specifications).

Cross-References.

- Establishments primarily engaged in manufacturing guided missiles and space vehicles are classified in U.S. Industry 336414, Guided Missile and Space Vehicle Manufacturing;
- Establishments primarily engaged in manufacturing flight simulators are classified in U.S. Industry 333318, Other Commercial and Service Industry Machinery Manufacturing;
- Establishments primarily engaged in the repair of aircraft (except overhauling, conversion, and rebuilding) are classified in Industry 488190, Other Support Activities for Air Transportation; and
- Research and development establishments primarily engaged in aircraft R&D (except prototype production) are classified in U.S. Industry 541715, Research and Development in the Physical, Engineering, and Life Sciences (except Nanotechnology and Biotechnology).

336412 Aircraft Engine and Engine Parts Manufacturing

This U.S. industry comprises establishments primarily engaged in one or more of the following: (1) manufacturing aircraft engines and engine parts; (2) developing and making prototypes of aircraft engines and engine parts; (3) aircraft propulsion system conversion (i.e., major modifications to systems); and (4) aircraft propulsion systems overhaul and rebuilding (i.e., periodic restoration of aircraft propulsion system to original design specifications).

Cross-References.

- Establishments primarily engaged in manufacturing guided missile and space vehicle propulsion units and parts are classified in U.S. Industry 336415, Guided Missile and Space Vehicle Propulsion Unit and Propulsion Unit Parts Manufacturing;
- Establishments primarily engaged in manufacturing aircraft intake and exhaust valves and pistons and aircraft internal combustion engine filters are classified in Industry 336310, Motor Vehicle Gasoline Engine and Engine Parts Manufacturing;
- Establishments primarily engaged in the repair of aircraft engines (except overhauling, conversion, and rebuilding) are classified in Industry 488190, Other Support Activities for Air Transportation;
- Research and development establishments primarily engaged in aircraft engine and engine parts R&D (except prototype production) are classified in U.S. Industry 541715, Research and Development in the Physical, Engineering, and Life Sciences (except Nanotechnology and Biotechnology); and
- Establishments primarily engaged in manufacturing aeronautical instruments are classified in U.S. Industry 334511, Search, Detection, Navigation, Guidance, Aeronautical, and Nautical System and Instrument Manufacturing.

336413 Other Aircraft Parts and Auxiliary Equipment Manufacturing

This U.S. industry comprises establishments primarily engaged in (1) manufacturing aircraft parts or auxiliary equipment (except engines and aircraft fluid power subassemblies) and/or (2) developing and making prototypes of aircraft parts and auxiliary equipment. Auxiliary equipment includes such items as crop dusting apparatus, armament racks, inflight refueling equipment, and external fuel tanks.

Cross-References.

- Establishments primarily engaged in manufacturing aircraft engines and engine parts are classified in U.S. Industry 336412, Aircraft Engine and Engine Parts Manufacturing;

T—Canadian, Mexican, and United States industries are comparable.

- Establishments primarily engaged in manufacturing aeronautical instruments are classified in U.S. Industry 334511, Search, Detection, Navigation, Guidance, Aeronautical, and Nautical System and Instrument Manufacturing;
- Establishments primarily engaged in manufacturing aircraft lighting fixtures and aircraft engine electrical (aeronautical electrical) equipment are classified in Industry 336320, Motor Vehicle Electrical and Electronic Equipment Manufacturing;
- Establishments primarily engaged in manufacturing guided missile and space vehicle parts and auxiliary equipment are classified in U.S. Industry 336419, Other Guided Missile and Space Vehicle Parts and Auxiliary Equipment Manufacturing;
- Establishments primarily engaged in manufacturing of aircraft fluid power subassemblies are classified in U.S. Industry 332912, Fluid Power Valve and Hose Fitting Manufacturing;
- Establishments primarily engaged in manufacturing aircraft seating are classified in Industry 336360, Motor Vehicle Seating and Interior Trim Manufacturing; and
- Research and development establishments primarily engaged in aircraft parts and auxiliary equipment R&D (except prototype production) are classified in U.S. Industry 541715, Research and Development in the Physical, Engineering, and Life Sciences (except Nanotechnology and Biotechnology).

336414 Guided Missile and Space Vehicle Manufacturing

This U.S. industry comprises establishments primarily engaged in (1) manufacturing complete guided missiles and space vehicles and/or (2) developing and making prototypes of guided missiles or space vehicles.

Cross-References.

- Establishments primarily engaged in manufacturing space satellites are classified in Industry 334220, Radio and Television Broadcasting and Wireless Communications Equipment Manufacturing; and
- Research and development establishments primarily engaged in guided missile and space vehicle R&D (except prototype production) are classified in U.S. Industry 541715, Research and Development in the Physical, Engineering, and Life Sciences (except Nanotechnology and Biotechnology).

336415 Guided Missile and Space Vehicle Propulsion Unit and Propulsion Unit Parts Manufacturing

This U.S. industry comprises establishments primarily engaged in (1) manufacturing guided missile and/or space vehicle propulsion units and propulsion unit parts and/or (2) developing and making prototypes of guided missile and space vehicle propulsion units and propulsion unit parts.

Cross-References.

Research and development establishments primarily engaged in guided missile and space propulsion unit and propulsion unit parts R&D (except prototype production) are classified in U.S. Industry 541715, Research and Development in the Physical, Engineering, and Life Sciences (except Nanotechnology and Biotechnology).

336419 Other Guided Missile and Space Vehicle Parts and Auxiliary Equipment Manufacturing

This U.S. industry comprises establishments primarily engaged in (1) manufacturing guided missile and space vehicle parts and auxiliary equipment (except guided missile and space vehicle propulsion units and propulsion unit parts) and/or (2) developing and making prototypes of guided missile and space vehicle parts and auxiliary equipment.

Cross-References.

- Establishments primarily engaged in manufacturing navigational and guidance systems are classified in U.S. Industry 334511, Search, Detection, Navigation, Guidance, Aeronautical, and Nautical System and Instrument Manufacturing;

T—Canadian, Mexican, and United States industries are comparable.

- Establishments primarily engaged in manufacturing guided missile and space vehicle propulsion units and propulsion unit parts are classified in U.S. Industry 336415, Guided Missile and Space Vehicle Propulsion Unit and Propulsion Unit Parts Manufacturing; and
- Research and development establishments primarily engaged in guided missile and space vehicle parts and auxiliary equipment R&D (except prototype production) are classified in U.S. Industry 541715, Research and Development in the Physical, Engineering, and Life Sciences (except Nanotechnology and Biotechnology).

3365 Railroad Rolling Stock Manufacturing[T]

33651 Railroad Rolling Stock Manufacturing[T] See industry description for 336510.

336510 Railroad Rolling Stock Manufacturing

This industry comprises establishments primarily engaged in one or more of the following: (1) manufacturing and/or rebuilding locomotives, locomotive frames and parts; (2) manufacturing railroad, street, and rapid transit cars and car equipment for operation on rails for freight and passenger service; and (3) manufacturing rail layers, ballast distributors, rail tamping equipment and other railway track maintenance equipment.

Cross-References.

- Establishments primarily engaged in manufacturing mining rail cars are classified in U.S. Industry 333131, Mining Machinery and Equipment Manufacturing;
- Establishments primarily engaged in manufacturing locomotive fuel lubricating or cooling medium pumps are classified in U.S. Industry 333914, Measuring, Dispensing, and Other Pumping Equipment Manufacturing;
- Repair establishments of railroad and local transit companies primarily engaged in repairing railroad and transit cars are classified in Industry 488210, Support Activities for Rail Transportation; and
- Establishments not owned by railroad or local transit companies engaged in repairing railroad cars and locomotive engines are classified in Industry 811310, Commercial and Industrial Machinery and Equipment (except Automotive and Electronic) Repair and Maintenance.

3366 Ship and Boat Building[T]

33661 Ship and Boat Building[T]

This industry comprises establishments primarily engaged in operating shipyards or boat yards (i.e., ship or boat manufacturing facilities). Shipyards are fixed facilities with drydocks and fabrication equipment capable of building a ship, defined as watercraft typically suitable or intended for other than personal or recreational use. Boats are defined as watercraft typically suitable or intended for personal use. Activities of shipyards include the construction of ships, their repair, conversion and alteration, production of prefabricated ship and barge sections, and specialized services, such as ship scaling.

Illustrative Examples:

Barge building
Boat yards (i.e., boat manufacturing facilities)
Cargo ship building
Drilling and production platforms, floating, oil and gas, building
Inflatable plastic boats, heavy-duty, manufacturing
Inflatable rubber boats, heavy-duty, manufacturing
Passenger ship building
Rigid inflatable boats (RIBs) manufacturing
Rowboats manufacturing

T—Canadian, Mexican, and United States industries are comparable.

Cross-References. Establishments primarily engaged in--

- Manufacturing inflatable rubber swimming pool rafts and similar flotation devices--are classified in Industry 32629, Other Rubber Product Manufacturing;
- Manufacturing inflatable plastic swimming pool rafts and similar flotation devices--are classified in Industry 32619, Other Plastics Product Manufacturing;
- Fabricating structural assemblies or components for ships, or subcontractors engaged in ship painting, joinery, carpentry work, and electrical wiring installation--are classified based on the production process used; and
- Ship repairs performed in floating drydocks--are classified in Industry 48839, Other Support Activities for Water Transportation.

336611 Ship Building and Repairing

This U.S. industry comprises establishments primarily engaged in operating shipyards. Shipyards are fixed facilities with drydocks and fabrication equipment capable of building a ship, defined as watercraft typically suitable or intended for other than personal or recreational use. Activities of shipyards include the construction of ships, their repair, conversion and alteration, the production of prefabricated ship and barge sections, and specialized services, such as ship scaling.

Illustrative Examples:

Barge building
Cargo ship building
Passenger ship building
Drilling and production platforms, floating, oil and gas, building
Submarine building

Cross-References. Establishments primarily engaged in--

- Fabricating structural assemblies or components for ships, or subcontractors engaged in ship painting, joinery, carpentry work, and electrical wiring installation--are classified based on the production process used; and
- Ship repairs performed in floating drydocks--are classified in Industry 488390, Other Support Activities for Water Transportation.

336612 Boat Building

This U.S. industry comprises establishments primarily engaged in building boats. Boats are defined as watercraft not built in shipyards and typically of the type suitable or intended for personal use. Included in this industry are establishments that manufacture heavy-duty inflatable rubber or inflatable plastic boats (RIBs).

Illustrative Examples:

Dinghy (except inflatable rubber) manufacturing
Inflatable plastic boats, heavy-duty, manufacturing
Inflatable rubber boats, heavy-duty, manufacturing
Motorboats, inboard or outboard, building
Rigid inflatable boats (RIBs) manufacturing
Rowboats manufacturing
Sailboat building, not done in shipyards
Yacht building, not done in shipyards

Cross-References. Establishments primarily engaged in--

- Ship building or ship repairs performed in a shipyard--are classified in U.S. Industry 336611, Ship Building and Repairing;
- Manufacturing inflatable rubber swimming pool rafts and similar flotation devices--are classified in U.S. Industry 326299, All Other Rubber Product Manufacturing; and
- Manufacturing inflatable plastic swimming pool rafts and similar flotation devices--are classified in U.S. Industry 326199, All Other Plastics Product Manufacturing.

~~T—Canadian, Mexican, and Unit~~ed States industries are comparable.

3369 Other Transportation Equipment Manufacturing[T]

33699 Other Transportation Equipment Manufacturing[T]

This industry comprises establishments primarily engaged in manufacturing motorcycles, bicycles, metal tricycles, complete military armored vehicles, tanks, self-propelled weapons, vehicles pulled by draft animals, and other transportation equipment (except motor vehicles, boats, ships, railroad rolling stock, and aerospace products), including parts thereof.

Cross-References. Establishments primarily engaged in--

- Manufacturing ships and boats--are classified in Industry 33661, Ship and Boat Building;
- Manufacturing aerospace products and parts--are classified in Industry 33641, Aerospace Product and Parts Manufacturing;
- Manufacturing motor vehicle parts--are classified in Industry Group 3363, Motor Vehicle Parts Manufacturing;
- Manufacturing children's vehicles (except bicycles and metal tricycles)--are classified in Industry 33993, Doll, Toy, and Game Manufacturing;
- Manufacturing railroad rolling stock--are classified in Industry 33651, Railroad Rolling Stock Manufacturing; and
- Manufacturing motor vehicles--are classified in Industry Group 3361, Motor Vehicle Manufacturing.

336991 Motorcycle, Bicycle, and Parts Manufacturing

This U.S. industry comprises establishments primarily engaged in manufacturing motorcycles, bicycles, tricycles and similar equipment, and parts.

Cross-References. Establishments primarily engaged in--

- Manufacturing children's vehicles (except bicycles and metal tricycles)--are classified in Industry 339930, Doll, Toy, and Game Manufacturing; and
- Manufacturing powered golf carts and other similar motorized personnel carriers--are classified in U.S. Industry 336999, All Other Transportation Equipment Manufacturing.

336992 Military Armored Vehicle, Tank, and Tank Component Manufacturing

This U.S. industry comprises establishments primarily engaged in manufacturing complete military armored vehicles, combat tanks, specialized components for combat tanks, and self-propelled weapons.

Cross-References.

Establishments primarily engaged in manufacturing nonarmored military universal carriers are classified in U.S. Industry 336112, Light Truck and Utility Vehicle Manufacturing.

336999 All Other Transportation Equipment Manufacturing

This U.S. industry comprises establishments primarily engaged in manufacturing transportation equipment (except motor vehicles, motor vehicle parts, boats, ships, railroad rolling stock, aerospace products, motorcycles, bicycles, armored vehicles and tanks).

Illustrative Examples:

All-terrain vehicles (ATVs), wheeled or tracked, manufacturing

T—Canadian, Mexican, and United States industries are comparable.

Animal-drawn vehicles and parts manufacturing
Gocarts (except children's) manufacturing
Race cars manufacturing
Snowmobiles and parts manufacturing

Cross-References. Establishments primarily engaged in--

- Manufacturing motorcycles, bicycles, and parts--are classified in U.S. Industry 336991, Motorcycle, Bicycle, and Parts Manufacturing;
- Manufacturing military armored vehicles, tanks, and tank components--are classified in U.S. Industry 336992, Military Armored Vehicle, Tank, and Tank Component Manufacturing;
- Manufacturing ships and boats--are classified in Industry 33661, Ship and Boat Building;
- Manufacturing aerospace products and parts--are classified in Industry 33641, Aerospace Product and Parts Manufacturing;
- Manufacturing motor vehicle parts--are classified in Industry Group 3363, Motor Vehicle Parts Manufacturing;
- Manufacturing railroad rolling stock--are classified in Industry 336510, Railroad Rolling Stock Manufacturing; and
- Manufacturing motor vehicles--are classified in Industry Group 3361, Motor Vehicle Manufacturing.

337 Furniture and Related Product Manufacturing[T]

Industries in the Furniture and Related Product Manufacturing subsector make furniture and related articles, such as mattresses, window blinds, cabinets, and fixtures. The processes used in the manufacture of furniture include the cutting, bending, molding, laminating, and assembly of such materials as wood, metal, glass, plastics, and rattan. However, the production process for furniture is not solely bending metal, cutting and shaping wood, or extruding and molding plastics. Design and fashion trends play an important part in the production of furniture. The integrated design of the article for both esthetic and functional qualities is also a major part of the process of manufacturing furniture. Design services may be performed by the furniture establishment's work force or may be purchased from industrial designers.

Furniture may be made of any material, but the most common ones used in North America are metal and wood. Furniture manufacturing establishments may specialize in making articles primarily from one material. Some of the equipment required to make a wooden table, for example, is different from that used to make a metal one. However, furniture is usually made from several materials. A wooden table might have metal brackets, and a wooden chair a fabric or plastics seat. Therefore, in NAICS, furniture initially is classified based on the type of furniture (application for which it is designed) rather than the material used. For example, an upholstered sofa is treated as household furniture, although it may also be used in hotels or offices.

When classifying furniture according to the component material from which it is made, furniture made from more than one material is classified based on the material used in the frame, or if there is no frame, the predominant component material. Upholstered household furniture (excluding kitchen and dining room chairs with upholstered seats) is classified without regard to the frame material. Kitchen or dining room chairs with upholstered seats are classified according to the frame material.

Furniture may be made on a stock or custom basis and may be shipped assembled or unassembled (i.e., knockdown). The manufacture of furniture parts and frames is included in this subsector.

Some of the processes used in furniture manufacturing are similar to processes that are used in other segments of manufacturing. For example, cutting and assembly occurs in the production of wood trusses that are classified in Subsector 321, Wood Product Manufacturing. However, the multiple processes that distinguish wood furniture manufacturing from wood product manufacturing warrant inclusion of wooden furniture manufacturing in the Furniture and Related Product Manufacturing subsector. Metal furniture manufacturing uses techniques that are also employed in the manufacturing of roll formed products classified in Subsector 332, Fabricated Metal Product Manufacturing. The molding process for plastics furniture is similar to the molding of other plastics products.
However, plastics furniture producing establishments tend to specialize in furniture.

NAICS attempts to keep furniture manufacturing together, but there are two notable exceptions: seating for transportation equipment and specialized hospital furniture (e.g., hospital beds and operating tables). These exceptions are related to the fact that some of the aspects of the production process for these products, primarily the design, are highly integrated with the other manufactured goods, namely motor vehicles and medical equipment.

T—Canadian, Mexican, and United States industries are comparable.

3371 Household and Institutional Furniture and Kitchen Cabinet Manufacturing[T]

This industry group comprises establishments manufacturing household-type furniture, such as living room, kitchen and bedroom furniture and institutional (i.e., public building) furniture, such as furniture for schools, theaters, and churches.

33711 Wood Kitchen Cabinet and Countertop Manufacturing[T] See industry description for 337110.

337110 Wood Kitchen Cabinet and Countertop Manufacturing

This industry comprises establishments primarily engaged in manufacturing wood or plastics laminated on wood kitchen cabinets, bathroom vanities, and countertops (except freestanding). The cabinets and counters may be made on a stock or custom basis.

Cross-References. Establishments primarily engaged in--

- Manufacturing metal kitchen and bathroom cabinets (except freestanding)--are classified in U.S. Industry 337124, Metal Household Furniture Manufacturing;
- Manufacturing plastics countertops--are classified in U.S. Industry 326199, All Other Plastics Product Manufacturing;
- Manufacturing stone countertops--are classified in U.S. Industry 327991, Cut Stone and Stone Product Manufacturing; and
- Manufacturing wood or plastics laminated on wood countertops (except kitchen and bathroom)--are classified in U.S. Industry 337215, Showcase, Partition, Shelving, and Locker Manufacturing.

33712 Household and Institutional Furniture Manufacturing[T]

This industry comprises establishments primarily engaged in manufacturing household-type and public building furniture (i.e., library, school, theater, and church furniture). This industry includes establishments that manufacture general purpose hospital, laboratory and/or dental furniture (e.g., stools, tables, benches). The furniture may be made on a stock or custom basis and may be assembled or unassembled (i.e., knockdown).

Cross-References. Establishments primarily engaged in--

- Manufacturing specialized hospital and/or dental furniture (e.g., hospital beds, operating tables, dental chairs)--are classified in Industry 33911, Medical Equipment and Supplies Manufacturing;
- Manufacturing wood or plastics laminated on wood kitchen cabinets, bathroom vanities, and countertops (except freestanding)--are classified in Industry 33711, Wood Kitchen Cabinet and Countertop Manufacturing;
- Manufacturing office-type furniture and/or office or store fixtures--are classified in Industry 33721, Office Furniture (including Fixtures) Manufacturing; and
- Repairing or refinishing furniture--are classified in Industry 81142, Reupholstery and Furniture Repair.

337121 Upholstered Household Furniture Manufacturing

This U.S. industry comprises establishments primarily engaged in manufacturing upholstered household-type furniture. The furniture may be made on a stock or custom basis.

Cross-References. Establishments primarily engaged in--

- Reupholstering furniture or upholstering frames to individual order--are classified in Industry 811420, Reupholstery and Furniture Repair;
- Manufacturing wood kitchen and dining room chairs with upholstered seats or backs--are classified in U.S. Industry 337122, Nonupholstered Wood Household Furniture Manufacturing;

T—Canadian, Mexican, and United States industries are comparable.

- Manufacturing metal kitchen and dining room chairs with upholstered seats or backs--are classified in U.S. Industry 337124, Metal Household Furniture Manufacturing; and
- Manufacturing kitchen and dining room chairs (except wood and metal) with upholstered seats or backs--are classified in U.S. Industry 337125, Household Furniture (except Wood and Metal) Manufacturing.

337122 Nonupholstered Wood Household Furniture Manufacturing

This U.S. industry comprises establishments primarily engaged in manufacturing nonupholstered wood household-type furniture and freestanding cabinets (except television, stereo, and sewing machine cabinets). The furniture may be made on a stock or custom basis and may be assembled or unassembled (i.e., knockdown).

Cross-References. Establishments primarily engaged in--

- Manufacturing reed, rattan, plastics and similar furniture--are classified in U.S. Industry 337125, Household Furniture (except Wood and Metal) Manufacturing;
- Manufacturing wood television, stereo, and sewing machine cabinets (i.e., housings)--are classified in U.S. Industry 321999, All Other Miscellaneous Wood Product Manufacturing;
- Manufacturing wood or plastics laminated on wood kitchen cabinets, bathroom vanities, and countertops (except freestanding)--are classified in Industry 337110, Wood Kitchen Cabinet and Countertop Manufacturing; and
- Repairing or refinishing furniture--are classified in Industry 811420, Reupholstery and Furniture Repair.

337124 Metal Household Furniture Manufacturing

This U.S. industry comprises establishments primarily engaged in manufacturing metal household-type furniture and freestanding cabinets. The furniture may be made on a stock or custom basis and may be assembled or unassembled (i.e., knockdown).

Cross-References.

Establishments primarily engaged in manufacturing specialized metal dental and hospital furniture (e.g., dental chairs, hospital beds, operating tables) are classified in Industry 33911, Medical Equipment and Supplies Manufacturing.

337125 Household Furniture (except Wood and Metal) Manufacturing

This U.S. industry comprises establishments primarily engaged in manufacturing household-type furniture of materials other than wood or metal, such as plastics, reed, rattan, wicker, and fiberglass. The furniture may be made on a stock or custom basis and may be assembled or unassembled (i.e., knockdown).

Cross-References. Establishments primarily engaged in--

- Manufacturing concrete, ceramic, or stone furniture--are classified in Subsector 327, Nonmetallic Mineral Product Manufacturing, according to the materials used;
- Manufacturing upholstered household-type furniture--are classified in U.S. Industry 337121, Upholstered Household Furniture Manufacturing;
- Manufacturing metal household-type furniture--are classified in U.S. Industry 337124, Metal Household Furniture Manufacturing; and
- Manufacturing nonupholstered wood household-type furniture--are classified in U.S. Industry 337122, Nonupholstered Wood Household Furniture Manufacturing.

337127 Institutional Furniture Manufacturing

This U.S. industry comprises establishments primarily engaged in manufacturing institutional-type furniture (e.g., library, school, theater, and church furniture). Included in this industry are establishments primarily engaged in T—Canadian, Mexican, and United States industries are comparable.

manufacturing general purpose hospital, laboratory, and dental furniture (e.g., tables, stools, and benches). The furniture may be made on a stock or custom basis and may be assembled or unassembled (i.e., knockdown).

Cross-References. Establishments primarily engaged in--

- Manufacturing specialized hospital furniture (e.g., hospital beds, operating tables)--are classified in U.S. Industry 339113, Surgical Appliance and Supplies Manufacturing;
- Manufacturing specialized dental furniture (e.g., dental chairs)--are classified in U.S. Industry 339114, Dental Equipment and Supplies Manufacturing;
- Manufacturing wood or plastics laminated on wood kitchen cabinets, bathroom vanities, and countertops (except freestanding)--are classified in Industry 337110, Wood Kitchen Cabinet and Countertop Manufacturing;
- Manufacturing office-type furniture and/or office or store fixtures--are classified in Industry 33721, Office Furniture (including Fixtures) Manufacturing; and
- Repairing or refinishing furniture--are classified in Industry 811420, Reupholstery and Furniture Repair.

3372 Office Furniture (including Fixtures) Manufacturing[T]

33721 Office Furniture (including Fixtures) Manufacturing[T]

This industry comprises establishments primarily engaged in manufacturing office furniture and/or office and store fixtures. The furniture may be made on a stock or custom basis and may be assembled or unassembled (i.e., knockdown).

Cross-References. Establishments primarily engaged in--

- Manufacturing millwork on a factory basis--are classified in Industry 32191, Millwork;
- Manufacturing household-type and institutional-type furniture--are classified in Industry 33712, Household and Institutional Furniture Manufacturing;
- Manufacturing refrigerated cabinets, showcases, and display cases--are classified in Industry 33341, Ventilation, Heating, Air-Conditioning, and Commercial Refrigeration Equipment Manufacturing; and
- Manufacturing metal safes and vaults--are classified in Industry 33299, All Other Fabricated Metal Product Manufacturing.

337211 Wood Office Furniture Manufacturing

This U.S. industry comprises establishments primarily engaged in manufacturing wood office-type furniture. The furniture may be made on a stock or custom basis and may be assembled or unassembled (i.e., knockdown).

337212 Custom Architectural Woodwork and Millwork Manufacturing

This U.S. industry comprises establishments primarily engaged in manufacturing custom designed interiors consisting of architectural woodwork and fixtures utilizing wood, wood products, and plastics laminates. All of the industry output is made to individual order on a job shop basis and requires skilled craftsmen as a labor input. A job might include custom manufacturing of display fixtures, gondolas, wall shelving units, entrance and window architectural detail, sales and reception counters, wall paneling, and matching furniture.

Cross-References. Establishments primarily engaged in--

- Manufacturing millwork on a factory basis--are classified in U.S. Industry 321918, Other Millwork (including Flooring);
- Manufacturing wood office-type furniture on a stock or custom basis--are classified in U.S. Industry 337211, Wood Office Furniture Manufacturing; and
- Manufacturing wood office-type and store fixtures on a stock or custom basis--are classified in U.S. Industry 337215, Showcase, Partition, Shelving, and Locker Manufacturing.

T—Canadian, Mexican, and United States industries are comparable.

337214 Office Furniture (except Wood) Manufacturing

This U.S. industry comprises establishments primarily engaged in manufacturing nonwood office-type furniture. The furniture may be made on a stock or custom basis and may be assembled or unassembled (i.e., knockdown).

337215 Showcase, Partition, Shelving, and Locker Manufacturing

This U.S. industry comprises establishments primarily engaged in manufacturing wood and nonwood office and store fixtures, shelving, lockers, frames, partitions, and related fabricated products of wood and nonwood materials, including plastics laminated fixture tops. The products are made on a stock or custom basis and may be assembled or unassembled (i.e., knockdown). Establishments exclusively making furniture parts (e.g., frames) are included in this industry.

Cross-References. Establishments primarily engaged in--

- Manufacturing refrigerated cabinets, showcases, and display cases--are classified in U.S. Industry 333415, Air-Conditioning and Warm Air Heating Equipment and Commercial and Industrial Refrigeration Equipment Manufacturing;
- Manufacturing metal safes and vaults--are classified in U.S. Industry 332999, All Other Miscellaneous Fabricated Metal Product Manufacturing; and
- Manufacturing wood or plastics laminated kitchen and bathroom countertops--are classified in Industry 337110, Wood Kitchen Cabinet and Countertop Manufacturing.

3379 Other Furniture Related Product Manufacturing[T]

This industry group comprises establishments manufacturing furniture related products, such as mattresses, blinds, and shades.

33791 Mattress Manufacturing[T] See industry description for 337910.

337910 Mattress Manufacturing

This industry comprises establishments primarily engaged in manufacturing innerspring, box spring, and non-innerspring mattresses, including mattresses for waterbeds.

Cross-References. Establishments primarily engaged in--

- Manufacturing individual wire springs--are classified in Industry 33261, Spring and Wire Product Manufacturing; and
- Manufacturing inflatable mattresses--are classified in Subsector 326, Plastics and Rubber Products Manufacturing.

33792 Blind and Shade Manufacturing[T] See industry description for 337920.

337920 Blind and Shade Manufacturing

This industry comprises establishments primarily engaged in manufacturing one or more of the following: venetian blinds, other window blinds, and shades; curtain and drapery rods and poles; and/or curtain and drapery fixtures. The blinds and shades may be made on a stock or custom basis and may be made of any material.

Cross-References. Establishments primarily engaged in--

- Manufacturing canvas awnings--are classified in Industry 314910, Textile Bag and Canvas Mills; and

T—Canadian, Mexican, and United States industries are comparable.

- Manufacturing curtains and draperies--are classified in Industry 314120, Curtain and Linen Mills.

339 Miscellaneous Manufacturing[T]

Industries in the Miscellaneous Manufacturing subsector make a wide range of products that cannot readily be classified in specific NAICS subsectors in manufacturing. Processes used by these establishments vary significantly, both among and within industries. For example, a variety of manufacturing processes are used in manufacturing sporting and athletic goods that include products such as tennis racquets and golf balls. The processes for these products differ from each other, and the processes differ significantly from the fabrication processes used in making dolls or toys, the melting and shaping of precious metals to make jewelry, and the bending, forming, and assembly used in making medical products.

The industries in this subsector are defined by what is made rather than how it is made. Although individual establishments might be appropriately classified elsewhere in the NAICS structure, for historical continuity, these product-based industries were maintained. In most cases, no one process or material predominates for an industry. Establishments in this subsector manufacture products as diverse as medical equipment and supplies, jewelry, sporting goods, toys, and office supplies.

3391 Medical Equipment and Supplies Manufacturing[T]

33911 Medical Equipment and Supplies Manufacturing[T]

This industry comprises establishments primarily engaged in manufacturing medical equipment and supplies. Examples of products made by these establishments are surgical and medical instruments, surgical appliances and supplies, dental equipment and supplies, orthodontic goods, ophthalmic goods, dentures, and orthodontic appliances.

Cross-References. Establishments primarily engaged in--

- Manufacturing laboratory instruments, X-ray apparatus, electromedical apparatus (including electronic hearing aids), and thermometers (except medical)--are classified in Industry 33451, Navigational, Measuring, Electromedical, and Control Instruments Manufacturing;
- Manufacturing molded glass lens blanks--are classified in Industry 32721, Glass and Glass Product Manufacturing;
- Manufacturing molded plastics lens blanks--are classified in Industry 32619, Other Plastics Product Manufacturing;
- Retailing and grinding prescription eyeglasses--are classified in Industry 44613, Optical Goods Stores;
- Manufacturing sporting goods helmets and protective equipment--are classified in Industry 33992, Sporting and Athletic Goods Manufacturing;
- Manufacturing general purpose hospital, laboratory, and/or dental furniture (e.g., stools, tables, benches)--are classified in Industry 33712, Household and Institutional Furniture Manufacturing;
- Manufacturing laboratory scales and balances, laboratory furnaces and ovens, and/or laboratory centrifuges--are classified in Industry 33399, All Other General Purpose Machinery Manufacturing;
- Manufacturing laboratory distilling equipment--are classified in Industry 33324, Industrial Machinery Manufacturing; and
- Manufacturing laboratory freezers--are classified in Industry 33341, Ventilation, Heating, Air-Conditioning, and Commercial Refrigeration Equipment Manufacturing.

339112 Surgical and Medical Instrument Manufacturing

This U.S. industry comprises establishments primarily engaged in manufacturing medical, surgical, ophthalmic, and veterinary instruments and apparatus (except electrotherapeutic, electromedical and irradiation apparatus). Examples of products made by these establishments are syringes, hypodermic needles, anesthesia apparatus, blood transfusion equipment, catheters, surgical clamps, and medical thermometers.

T—Canadian, Mexican, and United States industries are comparable.

Cross-References. Establishments primarily engaged in--

- Manufacturing electromedical and electrotherapeutic apparatus--are classified in U.S. Industry 334510, Electromedical and Electrotherapeutic Apparatus Manufacturing;
- Manufacturing irradiation apparatus--are classified in U.S. Industry 334517, Irradiation Apparatus Manufacturing;
- Manufacturing surgical (except dental) and orthopedic appliances or specialized hospital furniture (e.g., hospital beds, operating tables)--are classified in U.S. Industry 339113, Surgical Appliance and Supplies Manufacturing;
- Manufacturing dental equipment, dental supplies, dental laboratory apparatus, and dental laboratory furniture--are classified in U.S. Industry 339114, Dental Equipment and Supplies Manufacturing;
- Manufacturing general purpose hospital, laboratory, and/or dental furniture (e.g., stools, tables, benches)--are classified in U.S. Industry 337127, Institutional Furniture Manufacturing;
- Manufacturing thermometers (except medical)--are classified in U.S. Industry 334519, Other Measuring and Controlling Device Manufacturing; and
- Manufacturing ophthalmic goods--are classified in U.S. Industry 339115, Ophthalmic Goods Manufacturing.

339113 Surgical Appliance and Supplies Manufacturing

This U.S. industry comprises establishments primarily engaged in manufacturing surgical appliances and supplies. Examples of products made by these establishments are orthopedic devices, prosthetic appliances, surgical dressings, crutches, surgical sutures, personal industrial safety devices (except protective eyewear), hospital beds, and operating room tables.

Cross-References. Establishments primarily engaged in--

- Manufacturing dental equipment, dental supplies, dental laboratory apparatus, and specialized dental laboratory furniture (e.g., dental chairs)--are classified in U.S. Industry 339114, Dental Equipment and Supplies Manufacturing;
- Manufacturing general purpose hospital, laboratory, and/or dental furniture (e.g., stools, tables, benches)--are classified in U.S. Industry 337127, Institutional Furniture Manufacturing;
- Manufacturing electronic hearing aids--are classified in U.S. Industry 334510, Electromedical and Electrotherapeutic Apparatus Manufacturing;
- Manufacturing industrial protective eyewear--are classified in U.S. Industry 339115, Ophthalmic Goods Manufacturing; and
- Manufacturing sporting goods helmets and protective equipment--are classified in Industry 339920, Sporting and Athletic Goods Manufacturing.

339114 Dental Equipment and Supplies Manufacturing

This U.S. industry comprises establishments primarily engaged in manufacturing dental equipment and supplies used by dental laboratories and offices of dentists, such as dental chairs, dental instrument delivery systems, dental hand instruments, dental impression material, and dental cements.

Cross-References.

Establishments primarily engaged in manufacturing dentures, crowns, bridges, and orthodontic appliances customized for individual application are classified in U.S. Industry 339116, Dental Laboratories.

339115 Ophthalmic Goods Manufacturing

This U.S. industry comprises establishments primarily engaged in manufacturing ophthalmic goods. Examples of products made by these establishments are prescription eyeglasses (except manufactured in a retail setting), contact lenses, sunglasses, eyeglass frames, reading glasses made to standard powers, and protective eyewear.
T—Canadian, Mexican, and United States industries are comparable.

Cross-References. Establishments primarily engaged in--

- Manufacturing molded glass lens blanks--are classified in U.S. Industry 327212, Other Pressed and Blown Glass and Glassware Manufacturing;
- Manufacturing molded plastics lens blanks--are classified in U.S. Industry 326199, All Other Plastics Product Manufacturing; and
- Retailing and grinding prescription eyeglasses--are classified in Industry 446130, Optical Goods Stores.

339116 Dental Laboratories

This U.S. industry comprises establishments primarily engaged in manufacturing dentures, crowns, bridges, and orthodontic appliances customized for individual application.

Cross-References.

Establishments primarily engaged in manufacturing dental equipment and supplies are classified in U.S. Industry 339114, Dental Equipment and Supplies Manufacturing.

3399 Other Miscellaneous Manufacturing[T]

This industry group comprises establishments primarily engaged in miscellaneous manufacturing, such as jewelry and silverware manufacturing, sporting and athletic goods manufacturing, doll, toy, and game manufacturing, office supplies (except paper) manufacturing, sign manufacturing, and all other miscellaneous manufacturing.

33991 Jewelry and Silverware Manufacturing[T] See industry description for 339910.

339910 Jewelry and Silverware Manufacturing

This industry comprises establishments primarily engaged in one or more of the following: (1) manufacturing, engraving, chasing, or etching jewelry; (2) manufacturing, engraving, chasing, or etching metal personal goods (i.e., small articles carried on or about the person, such as compacts or cigarette cases); (3) manufacturing, engraving, chasing, or etching precious metal solid, precious metal clad, or pewter flatware and other hollowware; (4) stamping coins; (5) manufacturing unassembled jewelry parts and stock shop products, such as sheet, wire, and tubing; (6) cutting, slabbing, tumbling, carving, engraving, polishing, or faceting precious or semiprecious stones and gems; (7) recutting, repolishing, and setting gem stones; and (8) drilling, sawing, and peeling cultured and costume pearls. This industry includes establishments primarily engaged in manufacturing precious solid, precious clad, and precious plated jewelry and personal goods.

Cross-References. Establishments primarily engaged in--

- Manufacturing nonprecious and precious plated metal cutlery and flatware--are classified in U.S. Industry 332215, Metal Kitchen Cookware, Utensil, Cutlery, and Flatware (except Precious) Manufacturing;
- Manufacturing nonprecious metal plated ware (except cutlery and flatware)--are classified in U.S. Industry 332999, All Other Miscellaneous Fabricated Metal Product Manufacturing;
- Engraving, chasing, or etching nonprecious and precious plated metal cutlery, flatware and other plated ware--are classified in U.S. Industry 332812, Metal Coating, Engraving (except Jewelry and Silverware), and Allied Services to Manufacturers;
- Plating jewelry--are classified in U.S. Industry 332813, Electroplating, Plating, Polishing, Anodizing, and Coloring;
- Manufacturing synthetic stones--are classified in U.S. Industry 327999, All Other Miscellaneous Nonmetallic Mineral Product Manufacturing; and
- Manufacturing personal goods (except metal) carried on or about the person, such as compacts and cigarette cases--are classified in U.S. Industry 316998, All Other Leather Good and Allied Product Manufacturing.

T—Canadian, Mexican, and United States industries are comparable.

33992 Sporting and Athletic Goods Manufacturing[T] See industry description for 339920.

339920 Sporting and Athletic Goods Manufacturing

This industry comprises establishments primarily engaged in manufacturing sporting and athletic goods (except apparel and footwear).

Cross-References. Establishments primarily engaged in--

- Manufacturing athletic apparel--are classified in Subsector 315, Apparel Manufacturing;
- Manufacturing athletic footwear--are classified in Industry 316210, Footwear Manufacturing; and
- Manufacturing small arms and small arms ammunition--are classified in Industry 33299, All Other Fabricated Metal Product Manufacturing.

33993 Doll, Toy, and Game Manufacturing[T] See industry description for 339930.

339930 Doll, Toy, and Game Manufacturing

This industry comprises establishments primarily engaged in manufacturing complete dolls, doll parts, doll clothes, action figures, toys, games (including electronic), hobby kits, and children's vehicles (except metal bicycles and tricycles).

Cross-References. Establishments primarily engaged in--

- Manufacturing metal tricycles and bicycles--are classified in U.S. Industry 336991, Motorcycle, Bicycle, and Parts Manufacturing;
- Manufacturing sporting and athletic goods--are classified in Industry 339920, Sporting and Athletic Goods Manufacturing;
- Manufacturing coin-operated game machines--are classified in U.S. Industry 339999, All Other Miscellaneous Manufacturing;
- Manufacturing electronic video game cartridges and reproducing video game software--are classified in U.S. Industry 334614, Software and Other Prerecorded Compact Disc, Tape, and Record Reproducing; and
- Publishing or publishing and reproducing game software--are classified in Industry 511210, Software Publishers.

33994 Office Supplies (except Paper) Manufacturing[T] See industry description for 339940.

339940 Office Supplies (except Paper) Manufacturing

This industry comprises establishments primarily engaged in manufacturing office supplies. Examples of products made by these establishments are pens, pencils, felt tip markers, crayons, chalk, pencil sharpeners, staplers, modeling clay, hand operated stamps, stamp pads, stencils, carbon paper, and inked ribbons.

Cross-References. Establishments primarily engaged in--

- Manufacturing writing, drawing, and india inks--are classified in U.S. Industry 325998, All Other Miscellaneous Chemical Product and Preparation Manufacturing;
- Manufacturing rubber erasers--are classified in U.S. Industry 326299, All Other Rubber Product Manufacturing;
- Manufacturing paper office supplies--are classified in Subsector 322, Paper Manufacturing;
- Printing manifold business forms and manufacturing blankbooks, looseleaf binders, and looseleaf devices--are classified in U.S. Industry 323111, Commercial Printing (except Screen and Books);

T—Canadian, Mexican, and United States industries are comparable.

- Manufacturing drafting tables and boards--are classified in U.S. Industry 337127, Institutional Furniture Manufacturing; and
- Manufacturing inkjet and toner cartridges--are classified in Industry Group 3259, Other Chemical Product and Preparation Manufacturing.

33995 Sign Manufacturing[T] See industry description for 339950.

339950 Sign Manufacturing

This industry comprises establishments primarily engaged in manufacturing signs and related displays of all materials (except printing paper and paperboard signs, notices, displays).

Cross-References. Establishments primarily engaged in--

- Printing advertising specialties or printing paper and paperboard signs, notices, and displays--are classified in Industry 32311, Printing;
- Manufacturing and printing advertising specialties--are classified in the Manufacturing sector according to the products made;
- Manufacturing die-cut paperboard displays--are classified in U.S. Industry 322299, All Other Converted Paper Product Manufacturing; and
- Sign lettering and painting--are classified in Industry 541890, Other Services Related to Advertising.

33999 All Other Miscellaneous Manufacturing[T]

This industry comprises establishments primarily engaged in miscellaneous manufacturing (except medical equipment and supplies, jewelry and flatware, sporting and athletic goods, dolls, toys, games, office supplies (except paper), and signs).

Illustrative Examples:

Artificial Christmas trees manufacturing
Burial caskets and cases manufacturing
Candles manufacturing
Coin-operated amusement machines (except jukebox) manufacturing
Electronic cigarettes manufacturing
Floor and dust mops manufacturing
Fasteners, buttons, needles, and pins (except precious metals or precious and semiprecious stones and gems) manufacturing
Gasket, packing, and sealing devices manufacturing
Musical instruments (except toy) manufacturing
Portable fire extinguishers manufacturing
Umbrellas manufacturing

Cross-References. Establishments primarily engaged in--

- Manufacturing medical equipment and supplies--are classified in Industry Group 3391, Medical Equipment and Supplies Manufacturing;
- Manufacturing jewelry and flatware--are classified in Industry 33991, Jewelry and Silverware Manufacturing;
- Manufacturing sporting and athletic goods--are classified in Industry 33992, Sporting and Athletic Goods Manufacturing;
- Manufacturing dolls, toys, and games--are classified in Industry 33993, Doll, Toy, and Game Manufacturing;
- Manufacturing office supplies (except paper)--are classified in Industry 33994, Office Supplies (except Paper) Manufacturing;
- Manufacturing signs--are classified in Industry 33995, Sign Manufacturing;
- Manufacturing concrete burial vaults--are classified in Industry 32739, Other Concrete Product Manufacturing;

T—Canadian, Mexican, and United States industries are comparable.

- Manufacturing Christmas tree glass ornaments and glass lamp shades--are classified in Industry 32721, Glass and Glass Product Manufacturing;
- Manufacturing Christmas tree lighting sets--are classified in Industry 33512, Lighting Fixture Manufacturing;
- Manufacturing beauty and barber chairs--are classified in Industry 33712, Household and Institutional Furniture Manufacturing;
- Manufacturing burnt wood articles--are classified in Industry 32199, All Other Wood Product Manufacturing;
- Dressing and bleaching furs--are classified in Industry 31611, Leather and Hide Tanning and Finishing;
- Manufacturing paper, textile, and metal lamp shades--are classified in Industry 33512, Lighting Fixture Manufacturing;
- Manufacturing plastics lamp shades--are classified in Industry 32619, Other Plastics Product Manufacturing;
- Manufacturing matches and electronic cigarette vapor refills--are classified in Industry 32599, All Other Chemical Product and Preparation Manufacturing;
- Manufacturing metal products, such as metal combs and hair curlers--are classified in Industry 33299, All Other Fabricated Metal Product Manufacturing;
- Manufacturing plastics products, such as plastics combs and hair curlers--are classified in Industry 32619, Other Plastics Product Manufacturing; and
- Manufacturing electric hair clippers for use on humans--are classified in Industry 33521, Small Electrical Appliance Manufacturing.

339991 Gasket, Packing, and Sealing Device Manufacturing

This U.S. industry comprises establishments primarily engaged in manufacturing gaskets, packing, and sealing devices of all materials.

339992 Musical Instrument Manufacturing

This U.S. industry comprises establishments primarily engaged in manufacturing musical instruments (except toys).

Cross-References.

Establishments primarily engaged in manufacturing toy musical instruments are classified in Industry 339930, Doll, Toy, and Game Manufacturing.

339993 Fastener, Button, Needle, and Pin Manufacturing

This U.S. industry comprises establishments primarily engaged in manufacturing fasteners, buttons, needles, pins, and buckles (except made of precious metals or precious and semiprecious stones and gems).

Cross-References. Establishments primarily engaged in--

- Manufacturing buttons, pins, and buckles made of precious metals or precious and semiprecious stones and gems--are classified in Industry 339910, Jewelry and Silverware Manufacturing;
- Manufacturing hypodermic and suture needles--are classified in U.S. Industry 339112, Surgical and Medical Instrument Manufacturing; and
- Manufacturing phonograph and styli needles--are classified in U.S. Industry 334419, Other Electronic Component Manufacturing.

339994 Broom, Brush, and Mop Manufacturing

This U.S. industry comprises establishments primarily engaged in manufacturing brooms, mops, and brushes. T—Canadian, Mexican, and United States industries are comparable.

339995 Burial Casket Manufacturing

This U.S. industry comprises establishments primarily engaged in manufacturing burial caskets, cases, and vaults (except concrete).

Cross-References.

Establishments primarily engaged in manufacturing concrete burial vaults are classified in Industry 327390, Other Concrete Product Manufacturing.

339999 All Other Miscellaneous Manufacturing

This U.S. industry comprises establishments primarily engaged in miscellaneous manufacturing (except medical equipment and supplies, jewelry and flatware, sporting and athletic goods, dolls, toys, games, office supplies (except paper), musical instruments, fasteners, buttons, needles, pins, brooms, brushes, mops, and burial caskets).

Illustrative Examples:

Artificial Christmas trees manufacturing
Candles manufacturing
Christmas tree ornaments (except glass and electric) manufacturing
Cigarette lighters (except precious metal) manufacturing
Coin-operated amusement machines (except jukebox) manufacturing
Electronic cigarettes manufacturing
Hairpieces (e.g., wigs, toupees, wiglets) manufacturing
Portable fire extinguishers manufacturing
Potpourri manufacturing
Tobacco pipes manufacturing
Umbrellas manufacturing

Cross-References. Establishments primarily engaged in--

- Manufacturing medical equipment and supplies--are classified in Industry Group 3391, Medical Equipment and Supplies Manufacturing;
- Manufacturing jewelry and flatware--are classified in Industry 339910, Jewelry and Silverware Manufacturing;
- Manufacturing sporting and athletic goods--are classified in Industry 339920, Sporting and Athletic Goods Manufacturing;
- Manufacturing dolls, toys, and games--are classified in Industry 339930, Doll, Toy, and Game Manufacturing;
- Manufacturing office supplies (except paper)--are classified in Industry 339940, Office Supplies (except Paper) Manufacturing;
- Manufacturing signs--are classified in Industry 339950, Sign Manufacturing;
- Manufacturing gasket, packing, and sealing devices--are classified in U.S. Industry 339991, Gasket, Packing, and Sealing Device Manufacturing;
- Manufacturing musical instruments--are classified in U.S. Industry 339992, Musical Instrument Manufacturing;
- Manufacturing fasteners, buttons, needles, and pins--are classified in U.S. Industry 339993, Fastener, Button, Needle, and Pin Manufacturing;
- Manufacturing brooms, brushes, and mops--are classified in U.S. Industry 339994, Broom, Brush, and Mop Manufacturing;
- Manufacturing burial caskets--are classified in U.S. Industry 339995, Burial Casket Manufacturing;
- Manufacturing Christmas tree glass ornaments and glass lamp shades--are classified in U.S. Industry 327215, Glass Product Manufacturing Made of Purchased Glass;
- Manufacturing Christmas tree lighting sets--are classified in U.S. Industry 335129, Other Lighting Equipment Manufacturing;
- Manufacturing beauty and barber chairs--are classified in U.S. Industry 337127, Institutional Furniture Manufacturing;

T—Canadian, Mexican, and United States industries are comparable.

- Manufacturing burnt wood articles--are classified in U.S. Industry 321999, All Other Miscellaneous Wood Product Manufacturing;
- Dressing and bleaching furs--are classified in Industry 316110, Leather and Hide Tanning and Finishing;
- Manufacturing paper, textile, and metal lamp shades--are classified in U.S. Industry 335121, Residential Electric Lighting Fixture Manufacturing;
- Manufacturing plastics lamp shades--are classified in U.S. Industry 326199, All Other Plastics Product Manufacturing;
- Manufacturing matches and electronic cigarette vapor refills--are classified in U.S. Industry 325998, All Other Miscellaneous Chemical Product and Preparation Manufacturing;
- Manufacturing metal products, such as metal combs and hair curlers--are classified in U.S. Industry 332999, All Other Miscellaneous Fabricated Metal Product Manufacturing;
- Manufacturing plastics products, such as plastics combs and hair curlers--are classified in U.S. Industry 326199, All Other Plastics Product Manufacturing; and
- Manufacturing electric hair clippers for use on humans--are classified in Industry 335210, Small Electrical Appliance Manufacturing.

T—Canadian, Mexican, and United States industries are comparable.

Sector 42--Wholesale Trade[T]

The Sector as a Whole

The Wholesale Trade sector comprises establishments engaged in wholesaling merchandise, generally without transformation, and rendering services incidental to the sale of merchandise. The merchandise described in this sector includes the outputs of agriculture, mining, manufacturing, and certain information industries, such as publishing.

The wholesaling process is an intermediate step in the distribution of merchandise. Wholesalers are organized to sell or arrange the purchase or sale of (a) goods for resale (i.e., goods sold to other wholesalers or retailers), (b) capital or durable nonconsumer goods, and (c) raw and intermediate materials and supplies used in production. Wholesalers sell merchandise to other businesses and normally operate from a warehouse or office. These warehouses and offices are characterized by having little or no display of merchandise. In addition, neither the design nor the location of the premises is intended to solicit walk-in traffic. Wholesalers do not normally use advertising directed to the general public. Customers are generally reached initially via telephone, in-person marketing, or by specialized advertising that may include Internet and other electronic means. Follow-up orders are either vendor-initiated or client-initiated, generally based on previous sales, and typically exhibit strong ties between sellers and buyers. In fact, transactions are often conducted between wholesalers and clients that have long-standing business relationships.

This sector comprises two main types of wholesalers: merchant wholesalers that sell goods on their own account and business-to-business electronic markets, agents, and brokers that arrange sales and purchases for others generally for a commission or fee.

(1) Establishments that sell goods on their own account are known as wholesale merchants, distributors, jobbers, drop shippers, and import/export merchants. Also included as wholesale merchants are sales offices and sales branches (but not retail stores) maintained by manufacturing, refining, or mining enterprises apart from their plants or mines for the purpose of marketing their products and group purchasing organizations (e.g., purchasing and selling goods on their own account). Merchant wholesale establishments typically maintain their own warehouse, where they receive and handle goods for their customers. Goods are generally sold without transformation, but may include integral functions, such as sorting, packaging, labeling, and other marketing services.

(2) Establishments arranging for the purchase or sale of goods owned by others or purchasing goods, generally on a commission basis are known as business-to-business electronic markets, agents and brokers, commission merchants, import/export agents and brokers, auction companies, group purchasing organizations (e.g., purchasing or arranging for the purchases of goods owned by others), and manufacturers' representatives. These establishments operate from offices and generally do not own or handle the goods they sell.

Some wholesale establishments may be connected with a single manufacturer and promote and sell the particular manufacturer's products to a wide range of other wholesalers or retailers. Other wholesalers may be connected to a retail chain, or limited number of retail chains, and only provide a variety of products needed by that particular retail operation(s). These wholesalers may obtain the products from a wide range of manufacturers. Still other wholesalers may not take title to the goods, but act as agents and brokers for a commission.

Although, in general, wholesaling normally denotes sales in large volumes, durable nonconsumer goods may be sold in single units. Sales of capital or durable nonconsumer goods used in the production of goods and services, such as farm machinery, medium- and heavy-duty trucks, and industrial machinery, are always included in wholesale trade.

423 Merchant Wholesalers, Durable Goods

Industries in the Merchant Wholesalers, Durable Goods subsector sell capital or durable goods to other businesses. Merchant wholesalers generally take title to the goods that they sell; in other words, they buy and sell goods on their own account. Durable goods are new or used items generally with a normal life expectancy of three years or more. Durable goods merchant wholesale trade establishments are engaged in wholesaling products, such as motor vehicles, furniture, construction materials, machinery and equipment (including household-type appliances), metals and minerals (except petroleum), sporting goods, toys and hobby goods, recyclable materials, and parts.

T—Canadian, Mexican, and United States industries are comparable.

Business-to-business electronic markets, agents, and brokers primarily engaged in wholesaling durable goods, generally on a commission or fee basis, are classified in Subsector 425, Wholesale Electronic Markets and Agents and Brokers.

4231 Motor Vehicle and Motor Vehicle Parts and Supplies Merchant Wholesalers

This industry group comprises establishments primarily engaged in the merchant wholesale distribution of automobiles and other motor vehicles, motor vehicle supplies, tires, and new and used parts.

42311 Automobile and Other Motor Vehicle Merchant Wholesalers
See industry description for 423110.

423110 Automobile and Other Motor Vehicle Merchant Wholesalers

This industry comprises establishments primarily engaged in the merchant wholesale distribution of new and used passenger automobiles, trucks, trailers, and other motor vehicles, such as motorcycles, motor homes, and snowmobiles.

42312 Motor Vehicle Supplies and New Parts Merchant Wholesalers
See industry description for 423120.

423120 Motor Vehicle Supplies and New Parts Merchant Wholesalers

This industry comprises establishments primarily engaged in the merchant wholesale distribution of motor vehicle supplies, accessories, tools, and equipment; and new motor vehicle parts (except new tires and tubes).

Cross-References. Establishments primarily engaged in--

- Merchant wholesale distribution of new and/or used tires and tubes--are classified in Industry 423130, Tire and Tube Merchant Wholesalers;
- Merchant wholesale distribution of automotive chemicals (except lubricating oils and greases)--are classified in Industry 424690, Other Chemical and Allied Products Merchant Wholesalers;
- Merchant wholesale distribution of lubricating oils and greases--are classified in Industry 424720, Petroleum and Petroleum Products Merchant Wholesalers (except Bulk Stations and Terminals); and
- Merchant wholesale distribution of used motor vehicle parts--are classified in Industry 423140, Motor Vehicle Parts (Used) Merchant Wholesalers.

42313 Tire and Tube Merchant Wholesalers See industry description for 423130.

423130 Tire and Tube Merchant Wholesalers

This industry comprises establishments primarily engaged in the merchant wholesale distribution of new and/or used tires and tubes for passenger and commercial vehicles.

Cross-References. Establishments primarily engaged in--

- Merchant wholesale distribution of other new automobile parts and accessories--are classified in Industry 423120, Motor Vehicle Supplies and New Parts Merchant Wholesalers; and
- Merchant wholesale distribution of other used automobile parts and accessories--are classified in Industry 423140, Motor Vehicle Parts (Used) Merchant Wholesalers.

42314 Motor Vehicle Parts (Used) Merchant Wholesalers
See industry description for 423140.

T—Canadian, Mexican, and United States industries are comparable.

423140 Motor Vehicle Parts (Used) Merchant Wholesalers

This industry comprises establishments primarily engaged in the merchant wholesale distribution of used motor vehicle parts (except used tires and tubes) and establishments primarily engaged in dismantling motor vehicles for the purpose of selling the parts.

Cross-References. Establishments primarily engaged in--

- Dismantling motor vehicles for the purpose of selling scrap--are classified in Industry 423930, Recyclable Material Merchant Wholesalers; and
- Merchant wholesale distribution of new and/or used tires and tubes--are classified in Industry 423130, Tire and Tube Merchant Wholesalers.

4232 Furniture and Home Furnishing Merchant Wholesalers

This industry group comprises establishments primarily engaged in the merchant wholesale distribution of furniture (except hospital beds, medical furniture, and drafting tables), home furnishings, and/or housewares.

42321 Furniture Merchant Wholesalers
See industry description for 423210.

423210 Furniture Merchant Wholesalers

This industry comprises establishments primarily engaged in the merchant wholesale distribution of furniture (except hospital beds, medical furniture, and drafting tables).

Illustrative Examples:

Household-type furniture merchant wholesalers
Outdoor furniture merchant wholesalers
Mattresses merchant wholesalers
Public building furniture merchant wholesalers
Office furniture merchant wholesalers
Religious furniture merchant wholesalers

Cross-References. Establishments primarily engaged in--

- Merchant wholesale distribution of partitions, shelving, lockers, and store fixtures--are classified in Industry 423440, Other Commercial Equipment Merchant Wholesalers;
- Merchant wholesale distribution of hospital beds and medical furniture--are classified in Industry 423450, Medical, Dental, and Hospital Equipment and Supplies Merchant Wholesalers; and
- Merchant wholesale distribution of drafting tables--are classified in Industry 423490, Other Professional Equipment and Supplies Merchant Wholesalers.

42322 Home Furnishing Merchant Wholesalers
See industry description for 423220.

423220 Home Furnishing Merchant Wholesalers

This industry comprises establishments primarily engaged in the merchant wholesale distribution of home furnishings and/or housewares.

Illustrative Examples:

Carpet merchant wholesalers
Glassware, household-type, merchant wholesalers
Chinaware, household-type, merchant wholesalers
Curtains merchant wholesalers
Household-type cooking utensils merchant wholesalers
Lamps (i.e., lighting fixtures) merchant wholesalers
Draperies merchant wholesalers

T—Canadian, Mexican, and United States industries are comparable.

Linens (e.g., bath, bed, table) merchant wholesalers
Floor coverings merchant wholesalers
Window shades and blinds merchant wholesalers

Cross-References. Establishments primarily engaged in--

- Merchant wholesale distribution of household-type gas and electric appliances (except water heaters and heating stoves (i.e., noncooking))--are classified in Industry 423620, Household Appliances, Electric Housewares, and Consumer Electronics Merchant Wholesalers; and
- Merchant wholesale distribution of precious metal flatware--are classified in Industry 423940, Jewelry, Watch, Precious Stone, and Precious Metal Merchant Wholesalers.

4233 Lumber and Other Construction Materials Merchant Wholesalers

This industry group comprises establishments primarily engaged in the merchant wholesale distribution of lumber, plywood, millwork, and wood panels; brick, stone, and related construction materials; roofing, siding, and insulation materials; and other construction materials, including manufactured homes (i.e., mobile homes) and/or prefabricated buildings.

42331 Lumber, Plywood, Millwork, and Wood Panel Merchant Wholesalers
See industry description for 423310.

423310 Lumber, Plywood, Millwork, and Wood Panel Merchant Wholesalers

This industry comprises establishments primarily engaged in the merchant wholesale distribution of lumber; plywood; reconstituted wood fiber products; wood fencing; doors and windows and their frames (all materials); wood roofing and siding; and/or other wood or metal millwork.

Cross-References. Establishments primarily engaged in--

- Merchant wholesale distribution of nonwood roofing and siding materials--are classified in Industry 423330, Roofing, Siding, and Insulation Material Merchant Wholesalers; and
- Merchant wholesale distribution of timber and timber products, such as railroad ties, logs, firewood, and pulpwood--are classified in Industry 423990, Other Miscellaneous Durable Goods Merchant Wholesalers.

42332 Brick, Stone, and Related Construction Material Merchant Wholesalers
See industry description for 423320.

423320 Brick, Stone, and Related Construction Material Merchant Wholesalers

This industry comprises establishments primarily engaged in the merchant wholesale distribution of stone, cement, lime, construction sand, and gravel; brick; asphalt and concrete mixtures; and/or concrete, stone, and structural clay products.

Cross-References. Establishments primarily engaged in--

- Merchant wholesale distribution of refractory brick and other refractory products--are classified in Industry 423840, Industrial Supplies Merchant Wholesalers; and
- Selling ready-mix concrete--are classified in Industry 327320, Ready-Mix Concrete Manufacturing.

42333 Roofing, Siding, and Insulation Material Merchant Wholesalers
See industry description for 423330.

T—Canadian, Mexican, and United States industries are comparable.

423330 Roofing, Siding, and Insulation Material Merchant Wholesalers

This industry comprises establishments primarily engaged in the merchant wholesale distribution of nonwood roofing and nonwood siding and insulation materials.

Cross-References.

Establishments primarily engaged in the merchant wholesale distribution of wood roofing and wood siding are classified in Industry 423310, Lumber, Plywood, Millwork, and Wood Panel Merchant Wholesalers.

42339 Other Construction Material Merchant Wholesalers
See industry description for 423390.

423390 Other Construction Material Merchant Wholesalers

This industry comprises (1) establishments primarily engaged in the merchant wholesale distribution of manufactured homes (i.e., mobile homes) and/or prefabricated buildings and (2) establishments primarily engaged in the merchant wholesale distribution of construction materials (except lumber, plywood, millwork, wood panels, brick, stone, roofing, siding, electrical and wiring supplies, and insulation materials).

Illustrative Examples:

Flat glass merchant wholesalers
Prefabricated buildings (except wood) merchant wholesalers
Ornamental ironwork merchant wholesalers
Wire fencing and fencing accessories merchant wholesalers
Plate glass merchant wholesalers

Cross-References. Establishments primarily engaged in--

- Merchant wholesale distribution of products of the primary metals industries--are classified in Industry 423510, Metal Service Centers and Other Metal Merchant Wholesalers;
- Merchant wholesale distribution of lumber; plywood; reconstituted wood fiber products; wood fencing; doors, windows, and their frames; wood roofing and wood siding; and other wood or metal millwork--are classified in Industry 423310, Lumber, Plywood, Millwork, and Wood Panel Merchant Wholesalers;
- Merchant wholesale distribution of stone, cement, lime, construction sand and gravel; brick; asphalt and concrete mixtures (except ready-mix concrete); and/or concrete, stone, and structural clay products--are classified in Industry 423320, Brick, Stone, and Related Construction Material Merchant Wholesalers;
- Merchant wholesale distribution of nonwood roofing and nonwood siding and insulation materials--are classified in Industry 423330, Roofing, Siding, and Insulation Material Merchant Wholesalers;
- Merchant wholesale distribution of electrical supplies and wiring supplies--are classified in Industry 423610, Electrical Apparatus and Equipment, Wiring Supplies, and Related Equipment Merchant Wholesalers; and
- Selling ready-mix concrete--are classified in Industry 327320, Ready-Mix Concrete Manufacturing.

4234 Professional and Commercial Equipment and Supplies Merchant Wholesalers

This industry group comprises establishments primarily engaged in the merchant wholesale distribution of photographic equipment and supplies; office, computer, and computer peripheral equipment; and medical, dental, hospital, ophthalmic, and other commercial and professional equipment and supplies.

42341 Photographic Equipment and Supplies Merchant Wholesalers
See industry description for 423410.

T—Canadian, Mexican, and United States industries are comparable.

423410 Photographic Equipment and Supplies Merchant Wholesalers

This industry comprises establishments primarily engaged in the merchant wholesale distribution of photographic equipment and supplies (except office equipment).

Illustrative Examples:

Photofinishing equipment merchant wholesalers
Television cameras merchant wholesalers
Photographic camera equipment and supplies merchant wholesalers
Video cameras (except household-type) merchant wholesalers
Photographic film and plates merchant wholesalers

Cross-References. Establishments primarily engaged in--

- Merchant wholesale distribution of household-type video cameras--are classified in Industry 423620, Household Appliances, Electric Housewares, and Consumer Electronics Merchant Wholesalers;

and

- Merchant wholesale distribution of office equipment, such as photocopy and microfilm equipment--are classified in Industry 423420, Office Equipment Merchant Wholesalers.

42342 Office Equipment Merchant Wholesalers
See industry description for 423420.

423420 Office Equipment Merchant Wholesalers

This industry comprises establishments primarily engaged in the merchant wholesale distribution of office machines and related equipment (except computers and computer peripheral equipment).

Accounting machines merchant wholesalers
Mailing machines merchant wholesalers
Calculators and calculating machines merchant wholesalers
Cash registers merchant wholesalers
Security safes merchant wholesalers
Copying machines merchant wholesalers
Microfilm equipment and supplies merchant wholesalers

Cross-References. Establishments primarily engaged in--

- Merchant wholesale distribution of office furniture--are classified in Industry 423210, Furniture Merchant Wholesalers;
- Merchant wholesale distribution of computers and computer peripheral equipment--are classified in Industry 423430, Computer and Computer Peripheral Equipment and Software Merchant Wholesalers; and
- Merchant wholesale distribution of office supplies--are classified in Industry 424120, Stationery and Office Supplies Merchant Wholesalers.

42343 Computer and Computer Peripheral Equipment and Software Merchant Wholesalers
See industry description for 423430.

423430 Computer and Computer Peripheral Equipment and Software Merchant Wholesalers

This industry comprises establishments primarily engaged in the merchant wholesale distribution of computers, computer peripheral equipment, loaded computer boards, and/or computer software.

T—Canadian, Mexican, and United States industries are comparable.

Cross-References. Establishments primarily engaged in--

- Merchant wholesale distribution of modems and other electronic communications equipment--are classified in Industry 423690, Other Electronic Parts and Equipment Merchant Wholesalers; and
- Selling, planning, and designing computer systems that integrate computer hardware, software, and communication technologies--are classified in U.S. Industry 541512, Computer Systems Design Services.

42344 Other Commercial Equipment Merchant Wholesalers
See industry description for 423440.

423440 Other Commercial Equipment Merchant Wholesalers

This industry comprises establishments primarily engaged in the merchant wholesale distribution of commercial and related machines and equipment (except photographic equipment and supplies; office equipment; and computers and computer peripheral equipment and software) generally used in restaurants and stores.

Illustrative Examples:

Balances and scales (except laboratory) merchant wholesalers
Commercial shelving merchant wholesalers
Coin-operated merchandising machine merchant wholesalers
Electrical signs merchant wholesalers
Commercial chinaware merchant wholesalers
Partitions merchant wholesalers
Commercial cooking equipment merchant wholesalers
Store fixtures (except refrigerated) merchant wholesalers

Cross-References. Establishments primarily engaged in--

- Merchant wholesale distribution of photographic equipment and supplies--are classified in Industry 423410, Photographic Equipment and Supplies Merchant Wholesalers;
- Merchant wholesale distribution of office machines and related equipment--are classified in Industry 423420, Office Equipment Merchant Wholesalers;
- Merchant wholesale distribution of computers, computer peripheral equipment, and computer software--are classified in Industry 423430, Computer and Computer Peripheral Equipment and Software Merchant Wholesalers;
- Merchant wholesale distribution of laboratory scales and balances (except medical and dental)--are classified in Industry 423490, Other Professional Equipment and Supplies Merchant Wholesalers; and
- Merchant wholesale distribution of refrigerated store fixtures--are classified in Industry 423740, Refrigeration Equipment and Supplies Merchant Wholesalers.

42345 Medical, Dental, and Hospital Equipment and Supplies Merchant Wholesalers
See industry description for 423450.

423450 Medical, Dental, and Hospital Equipment and Supplies Merchant Wholesalers

This industry comprises establishments primarily engaged in the merchant wholesale distribution of professional medical equipment, instruments, and supplies (except ophthalmic equipment and instruments and goods used by ophthalmologists, optometrists, and opticians).

Illustrative Examples:

Dental equipment and supplies merchant wholesalers
Surgical dressings merchant wholesalers
Electromedical equipment merchant wholesalers
Patient monitoring equipment merchant wholesalers
Hospital beds merchant wholesalers
Prosthetic appliances and supplies merchant wholesalers
Hospital furniture merchant wholesalers

T—Canadian, Mexican, and United States industries are comparable.

Surgical instruments and apparatus merchant wholesalers
Medical and dental X-ray machines and parts

Cross-References.

Establishments primarily engaged in the merchant wholesale distribution of professional equipment, instruments, and/or goods sold, prescribed, or used by ophthalmologists, optometrists, and opticians are classified in Industry 423460, Ophthalmic Goods Merchant Wholesalers.

42346 Ophthalmic Goods Merchant Wholesalers
See industry description for 423460.

423460 Ophthalmic Goods Merchant Wholesalers

This industry comprises establishments primarily engaged in the merchant wholesale distribution of professional equipment, instruments, and/or goods sold, prescribed, or used by ophthalmologists, optometrists, and opticians.

Illustrative Examples:

Binoculars merchant wholesalers
Optometric equipment and supplies merchant wholesalers
Ophthalmic frames merchant wholesalers
Sunglasses merchant wholesalers
Ophthalmic lenses merchant wholesalers

42349 Other Professional Equipment and Supplies Merchant Wholesalers
See industry description for 423490.

423490 Other Professional Equipment and Supplies Merchant Wholesalers

This industry comprises establishments primarily engaged in the merchant wholesale distribution of professional equipment and supplies (except ophthalmic goods and medical, dental, and hospital equipment and supplies).

Illustrative Examples:

Church supplies (except silverware, plated ware) merchant wholesalers
School equipment and supplies (except books, furniture) merchant wholesalers
Drafting tables and instruments merchant wholesalers
Scientific instruments merchant wholesalers
Laboratory equipment (except medical, dental) merchant wholesalers
Surveying equipment and supplies merchant wholesalers

Cross-References. Establishments primarily engaged in--

- Merchant wholesale distribution of professional equipment, instruments, and/or goods sold, prescribed, or used by ophthalmologists, optometrists, and opticians, such as ophthalmic frames and lenses, and sunglasses--are classified in Industry 423460, Ophthalmic Goods Merchant Wholesalers;
- Merchant wholesale distribution of professional medical equipment, instruments, and supplies used by medical and dental practitioners (except ophthalmic equipment, instruments, and goods used by ophthalmologists, optometrists, and opticians) and medical facilities--are classified in Industry 423450, Medical, Dental, and Hospital Equipment and Supplies Merchant Wholesalers;
- Merchant wholesale distribution of silverware and plated flatware--are classified in Industry 423940, Jewelry, Watch, Precious Stone, and Precious Metal Merchant Wholesalers;
- Merchant wholesale distribution of books--are classified in Industry 424920, Book, Periodical, and Newspaper Merchant Wholesalers; and
- Merchant wholesale distribution of school furniture--are classified in Industry 423210, Furniture Merchant Wholesalers.

T—Canadian, Mexican, and United States industries are comparable.

4235 Metal and Mineral (except Petroleum) Merchant Wholesalers

This industry group comprises establishments primarily engaged in the merchant wholesale distribution of products of the primary metals industries (including metal service centers) and coal, coke, metal ores, and/or non-metallic minerals (except precious and semiprecious stones and minerals used in construction).

42351 Metal Service Centers and Other Metal Merchant Wholesalers

See industry description for 423510.

423510 Metal Service Centers and Other Metal Merchant Wholesalers

This industry comprises establishments primarily engaged in the merchant wholesale distribution of products of the primary metals industries. Service centers maintain inventory and may perform functions, such as sawing, shearing, bending, leveling, cleaning, or edging, on a custom basis as part of sales transactions.

Illustrative Examples:

Cast iron pipe merchant wholesalers
Metal rods merchant wholesalers
Metal bars (except precious) merchant wholesalers
Metal sheets merchant wholesalers
Metal ingots (except precious) merchant wholesalers
Metal spikes merchant wholesalers
Metal pipe merchant wholesalers
Nails merchant wholesalers
Metal plates merchant wholesalers
Noninsulated wire merchant wholesalers

Cross-References. Establishments primarily engaged in--

- Merchant wholesale distribution of gold, silver, and platinum--are classified in Industry 423940, Jewelry, Watch, Precious Stone, and Precious Metal Merchant Wholesalers;
- Merchant wholesale distribution of automotive, industrial, and other recyclable metal scrap--are classified in Industry 423930, Recyclable Material Merchant Wholesalers; and
- Merchant wholesale distribution of insulated wire--are classified in Industry 423610, Electrical Apparatus and Equipment, Wiring Supplies, and Related Equipment Merchant Wholesalers.

42352 Coal and Other Mineral and Ore Merchant Wholesalers

See industry description for 423520.

423520 Coal and Other Mineral and Ore Merchant Wholesalers

This industry comprises establishments primarily engaged in the merchant wholesale distribution of coal, coke, metal ores, and/or nonmetallic minerals (except precious and semiprecious stones and minerals used in construction, such as sand and gravel).

Cross-References. Establishments primarily engaged in--

- Merchant wholesale distribution of nonmetallic minerals used in construction, such as sand and gravel--are classified in Industry 423320, Brick, Stone, and Related Construction Material Merchant Wholesalers;
- Merchant wholesale distribution of crude petroleum--are classified in Industry Group 4247, Petroleum and Petroleum Products Merchant Wholesalers; and
- Merchant wholesale distribution of precious and semiprecious stones and metals--are classified in Industry 423940, Jewelry, Watch, Precious Stone, and Precious Metal Merchant Wholesalers.

4236 Household Appliances and Electrical and Electronic Goods Merchant Wholesalers

This industry group comprises establishments primarily engaged in the merchant wholesale distribution of electrical apparatus and equipment, wiring supplies, and related equipment; household appliances, electric housewares, and consumer electronics; and other electronic parts and equipment.

T—Canadian, Mexican, and United States industries are comparable.

42361 Electrical Apparatus and Equipment, Wiring Supplies, and Related Equipment Merchant Wholesalers
See industry description for 423610.

423610 Electrical Apparatus and Equipment, Wiring Supplies, and Related Equipment Merchant Wholesalers

This industry comprises establishments primarily engaged in the merchant wholesale distribution of electrical construction materials; wiring supplies; electric light fixtures; light bulbs; and/or electrical power equipment for the generation, transmission, distribution, or control of electric energy.

42362 Household Appliances, Electric Housewares, and Consumer Electronics Merchant Wholesalers
See industry description for 423620.

423620 Household Appliances, Electric Housewares, and Consumer Electronics Merchant Wholesalers

This industry comprises establishments primarily engaged in the merchant wholesale distribution of household-type gas and electric appliances (except water heaters and heating stoves (i.e., noncooking)), room air-conditioners, and/or household-type audio or video equipment.

Illustrative Examples:

Household-type sewing machines merchant wholesalers
Household-type radios (including automotive) merchant wholesalers
Household-type video cameras merchant wholesalers
Household-type refrigerators merchant wholesalers
Television sets merchant wholesalers
Toothbrushes, electric, merchant wholesalers
Curling irons, electric, merchant wholesalers

Cross-References. Establishments primarily engaged in--

- Merchant wholesale distribution of gas and electric water heaters and heating stoves (i.e., noncooking)--are classified in Industry 423720, Plumbing and Heating Equipment and Supplies (Hydronics) Merchant Wholesalers; and
- Merchant wholesale distribution of nonhousehold-type video cameras--are classified in Industry 423410, Photographic Equipment and Supplies Merchant Wholesalers.

42369 Other Electronic Parts and Equipment Merchant Wholesalers
See industry description for 423690.

423690 Other Electronic Parts and Equipment Merchant Wholesalers

This industry comprises establishments primarily engaged in the merchant wholesale distribution of electronic parts and equipment (except electrical apparatus and equipment, wiring supplies, and construction materials; electrical and electronic appliances; and television sets and radios).

Illustrative Examples:

Blank audio and video tapes merchant wholesalers
Communications equipment merchant wholesalers
Blank compact discs (CDs) merchant wholesalers
Radar equipment merchant wholesalers
Blank digital video discs (DVDs) merchant wholesalers
Telegraph equipment merchant wholesalers
Blank diskettes merchant wholesalers
Telephone equipment merchant wholesalers
Broadcasting equipment merchant wholesalers
Unloaded computer boards merchant wholesalers

T—Canadian, Mexican, and United States industries are comparable.

Cross-References. Establishments primarily engaged in--

- Merchant wholesale distribution of household-type gas and electric appliances (except water heaters and heating stoves (i.e., noncooking)), room air-conditioners, clothes dryers, and/or household-type audio or video equipment--are classified in Industry 423620, Household Appliances, Electric Housewares, and Consumer Electronics Merchant Wholesalers;
- Merchant wholesale distribution of computers, computer peripheral equipment, and loaded computer boards--are classified in Industry 423430, Computer and Computer Peripheral Equipment and Software Merchant Wholesalers; and
- Merchant wholesale distribution of electrical construction materials, wiring supplies, electric light fixtures, light bulbs, and/or electrical power equipment for generation, transmission, distribution, or control of electric energy--are classified in Industry 423610, Electrical Apparatus and Equipment, Wiring Supplies, and Related Equipment Merchant Wholesalers.

4237 Hardware, and Plumbing and Heating Equipment and Supplies Merchant Wholesalers

This industry group comprises establishments primarily engaged in the merchant wholesale distribution of hardware; plumbing and heating equipment and supplies (hydronics); warm air heating and air-conditioning equipment and supplies; and refrigeration equipment and supplies.

42371 Hardware Merchant Wholesalers

See industry description for 423710.

423710 Hardware Merchant Wholesalers

This industry comprises establishments primarily engaged in the merchant wholesale distribution of hardware, knives, or handtools.

Illustrative Examples:

Brads merchant wholesalers
Cutlery merchant wholesalers
Knives (except disposable plastics) merchant wholesalers
Power handtools (e.g., drills, saws, sanders) merchant wholesalers
Fasteners (e.g., bolts, nuts, rivets, screws) merchant wholesalers
Staples merchant wholesalers
Handtools (except motor vehicle, machinists' precision) merchant wholesalers
Tacks merchant wholesalers

Cross-References. Establishments primarily engaged in--

- Merchant wholesale distribution of nails, noninsulated wire, and screening--are classified in Industry 423510, Metal Service Centers and Other Metal Merchant Wholesalers;
- Merchant wholesale distribution of motor vehicle handtools and equipment--are classified in Industry 423120, Motor Vehicle Supplies and New Parts Merchant Wholesalers;
- Merchant wholesale distribution of machinists' precision handtools--are classified in Industry 423830, Industrial Machinery and Equipment Merchant Wholesalers; and
- Merchant wholesale distribution of disposable plastics knives and eating utensils--are classified in Industry 424130, Industrial and Personal Service Paper Merchant Wholesalers.

42372 Plumbing and Heating Equipment and Supplies (Hydronics) Merchant Wholesalers

See industry description for 423720.

423720 Plumbing and Heating Equipment and Supplies (Hydronics) Merchant Wholesalers

This industry comprises establishments primarily engaged in the merchant wholesale distribution of plumbing equipment, hydronic heating equipment, household-type water heaters, and/or supplies.

T—Canadian, Mexican, and United States industries are comparable.

Cross-References. Establishments primarily engaged in--

- Selling and installing plumbing, heating and air-conditioning equipment--are classified in Industry 238220, Plumbing, Heating, and Air-Conditioning Contractors;
- Merchant wholesale distribution of warm air heating and air-conditioning equipment--are classified in Industry 423730, Warm Air Heating and Air-Conditioning Equipment and Supplies Merchant Wholesalers; and
- Merchant wholesale distribution of household-type gas and electric appliances (except water heaters and heating stoves (i.e., noncooking)), room air-conditioners, clothes dryers, and/or household-type audio or video equipment--are classified in Industry 423620, Household Appliances, Electric Housewares, and Consumer Electronics Merchant Wholesalers.

42373 Warm Air Heating and Air-Conditioning Equipment and Supplies Merchant Wholesalers
See industry description for 423730.

423730 Warm Air Heating and Air-Conditioning Equipment and Supplies Merchant Wholesalers

This industry comprises establishments primarily engaged in the merchant wholesale distribution of warm air heating and air-conditioning equipment and supplies.

Illustrative Examples:

Air pollution control equipment and supplies merchant wholesalers
Automotive air-conditioners merchant wholesalers
Non-portable electric baseboard heaters merchant wholesalers
Air-conditioning equipment (except room units) merchant wholesalers
Warm air central heating equipment merchant wholesalers

Cross-References. Establishments primarily engaged in--

- Merchant wholesale distribution of household-type gas and electric appliances (except water heaters and heating stoves (i.e., noncooking)) and room air-conditioners--are classified in Industry 423620, Household Appliances, Electric Housewares, and Consumer Electronics Merchant Wholesalers;
- Merchant wholesale distribution of hydronic heating equipment--are classified in Industry 423720, Plumbing and Heating Equipment and Supplies (Hydronics) Merchant Wholesalers; and
- Selling and installing warm air heating and air-conditioning equipment--are classified in Industry 238220, Plumbing, Heating, and Air-Conditioning Contractors.

42374 Refrigeration Equipment and Supplies Merchant Wholesalers
See industry description for 423740.

423740 Refrigeration Equipment and Supplies Merchant Wholesalers

This industry comprises establishments primarily engaged in the merchant wholesale distribution of refrigeration equipment (except household-type refrigerators, freezers, and air-conditioners).

Illustrative Examples:

Cold storage machinery merchant wholesalers
Refrigerated display cases merchant wholesalers
Commercial refrigerators merchant wholesalers

T—Canadian, Mexican, and United States industries are comparable.

Cross-References. Establishments primarily engaged in--

- Merchant wholesale distribution of household-type refrigerators, freezers, and room air-conditioners--are classified in Industry 423620, Household Appliances, Electric Housewares, and Consumer Electronics Merchant Wholesalers; and
- Merchant wholesale distribution of air-conditioning equipment (except room units)--are classified in Industry 423730, Warm Air Heating and Air-Conditioning Equipment and Supplies Merchant Wholesalers.

4238 Machinery, Equipment, and Supplies Merchant Wholesalers

This industry group comprises establishments primarily engaged in the merchant wholesale distribution of construction, mining, farm, garden, industrial, service establishment, and transportation machinery, equipment, and supplies.

42381 Construction and Mining (except Oil Well) Machinery and Equipment Merchant Wholesalers

See industry description for 423810.

423810 Construction and Mining (except Oil Well) Machinery and Equipment Merchant Wholesalers

This industry comprises establishments primarily engaged in the merchant wholesale distribution of specialized machinery, equipment, and related parts generally used in construction, mining (except oil well), and logging activities.

Illustrative Examples:

Excavating machinery and equipment merchant wholesalers
Road construction and maintenance machinery merchant wholesalers
Forestry machinery and equipment merchant wholesalers
Scaffolding merchant wholesalers
Mining cranes merchant wholesalers

Cross-References.

Establishments primarily engaged in the merchant wholesale distribution of oil well machinery and equipment are classified in Industry 423830, Industrial Machinery and Equipment Merchant Wholesalers.

42382 Farm and Garden Machinery and Equipment Merchant Wholesalers

See industry description for 423820.

423820 Farm and Garden Machinery and Equipment Merchant Wholesalers

This industry comprises establishments primarily engaged in the merchant wholesale distribution of specialized machinery, equipment, and related parts generally used in agricultural, farm, and lawn and garden activities.

Illustrative Examples:

Animal feeders merchant wholesalers
Milking machinery and equipment merchant wholesalers
Lawnmowers merchant wholesalers
Harvesting machinery and equipment merchant wholesalers
Planting machinery and equipment merchant wholesalers

42383 Industrial Machinery and Equipment Merchant Wholesalers

See industry description for 423830.

T—Canadian, Mexican, and United States industries are comparable.

423830 Industrial Machinery and Equipment Merchant Wholesalers

This industry comprises establishments primarily engaged in the merchant wholesale distribution of specialized machinery, equipment, and related parts generally used in manufacturing, oil well, and warehousing activities.

Illustrative Examples:

Fluid power transmission equipment merchant wholesalers
Metalworking machinery and equipment merchant wholesalers
Food processing machinery and equipment merchant wholesalers
Oil well machinery and equipment merchant wholesalers
Material handling machinery and equipment merchant wholesalers

Cross-References. Establishments primarily engaged in--

- Merchant wholesale distribution of specialized machinery, equipment, and related parts generally used in construction, mining (except oil well), and logging activities--are classified in Industry 423810, Construction and Mining (except Oil Well) Machinery and Equipment Merchant Wholesalers; and
- Merchant wholesale distribution of supplies used in machinery and equipment generally used in manufacturing, oil well, and warehousing activities--are classified in Industry 423840, Industrial Supplies Merchant Wholesalers.

42384 Industrial Supplies Merchant Wholesalers
See industry description for 423840.

423840 Industrial Supplies Merchant Wholesalers

This industry comprises establishments primarily engaged in the merchant wholesale distribution of supplies for machinery and equipment generally used in manufacturing, oil well, and warehousing activities.

Illustrative Examples:

Industrial containers merchant wholesalers
Refractory materials (e.g., brick, blocks, shapes) merchant wholesalers
Industrial diamonds merchant wholesalers
Welding supplies (except welding gases) merchant wholesalers
Printing inks merchant wholesalers

Cross-References. Establishments primarily engaged in--

- Merchant wholesale distribution of hydraulic and pneumatic (fluid power) pumps, motors, pistons, and valves--are classified in Industry 423830, Industrial Machinery and Equipment Merchant Wholesalers; and
- Merchant wholesale distribution of welding gases--are classified in Industry 424690, Other Chemical and Allied Products Merchant Wholesalers.

42385 Service Establishment Equipment and Supplies Merchant Wholesalers
See industry description for 423850.

423850 Service Establishment Equipment and Supplies Merchant Wholesalers

This industry comprises establishments primarily engaged in the merchant wholesale distribution of specialized equipment and supplies of the type used by service establishments (except specialized equipment and supplies used in offices, stores, hotels, restaurants, schools, health and medical facilities, photographic facilities, and specialized

T—Canadian, Mexican, and United States industries are comparable.

Illustrative Examples:

Amusement park equipment merchant wholesalers
Janitorial equipment and supplies merchant wholesalers
Beauty parlor equipment and supplies merchant wholesalers
Undertakers' equipment and supplies merchant wholesalers
Car wash equipment and supplies merchant wholesalers
Upholsterers' equipment and supplies (except fabrics) merchant wholesalers
Drycleaning equipment and supplies merchant wholesalers

Cross-References. Establishments primarily engaged in--

- Merchant wholesale distribution of janitorial and automotive chemicals--are classified in Industry 424690, Other Chemical and Allied Products Merchant Wholesalers;
- Merchant wholesale distribution of piece goods, fabrics, knitting yarns (except industrial), thread and other notions--are classified in Industry 424310, Piece Goods, Notions, and Other Dry Goods Merchant Wholesalers; and
- Merchant wholesale distribution of industrial yarns--are classified in Industry 424990, Other Miscellaneous Nondurable Goods Merchant Wholesalers.

42386 Transportation Equipment and Supplies (except Motor Vehicle) Merchant Wholesalers
See industry description for 423860.

423860 Transportation Equipment and Supplies (except Motor Vehicle) Merchant Wholesalers

This industry comprises establishments primarily engaged in the merchant wholesale distribution of transportation equipment and supplies (except marine pleasure craft and motor vehicles).

Illustrative Examples:

Aircraft merchant wholesalers
Railroad cars merchant wholesalers
Motorized passenger golf carts merchant wholesalers

Cross-References. Establishments primarily engaged in--

- Merchant wholesale distribution of motor vehicles and motor vehicle parts--are classified in Industry Group 4231, Motor Vehicle and Motor Vehicle Parts and Supplies Merchant Wholesalers; and
- Merchant wholesale distribution of marine pleasure craft--are classified in Industry 423910, Sporting and Recreational Goods and Supplies Merchant Wholesalers.

4239 Miscellaneous Durable Goods Merchant Wholesalers

This industry group comprises establishments primarily engaged in the merchant wholesale distribution of sporting, recreational, toy, hobby, and jewelry goods and supplies, and precious stones and metals.

42391 Sporting and Recreational Goods and Supplies Merchant Wholesalers
See industry description for 423910.

423910 Sporting and Recreational Goods and Supplies Merchant Wholesalers

This industry comprises establishments primarily engaged in the merchant wholesale distribution of sporting goods and accessories; billiard and pool supplies; sporting firearms and ammunition; and/or marine pleasure craft, equipment, and supplies.

T—Canadian, Mexican, and United States industries are comparable.

Cross-References. Establishments primarily engaged in--

- Merchant wholesale distribution of motor vehicles and trailers--are classified in Industry 423110, Automobile and Other Motor Vehicle Merchant Wholesalers;
- Merchant wholesale distribution of motorized passenger golf carts--are classified in Industry 423860, Transportation Equipment and Supplies (except Motor Vehicle) Merchant Wholesalers; and
- Merchant wholesale distribution of athletic apparel and athletic footwear--are classified in Industry Group 4243, Apparel, Piece Goods, and Notions Merchant Wholesalers.

42392 Toy and Hobby Goods and Supplies Merchant Wholesalers
See industry description for 423920.

423920 Toy and Hobby Goods and Supplies Merchant Wholesalers

This industry comprises establishments primarily engaged in the merchant wholesale distribution of games, toys, fireworks, playing cards, hobby goods and supplies, and/or related goods.

42393 Recyclable Material Merchant Wholesalers
See industry description for 423930.

423930 Recyclable Material Merchant Wholesalers

This industry comprises establishments primarily engaged in the merchant wholesale distribution of automotive scrap, industrial scrap, and other recyclable materials. Included in this industry are auto wreckers primarily engaged in dismantling motor vehicles for the purpose of wholesaling scrap.

Cross-References. Establishments primarily engaged in--

- Dismantling motor vehicles for the purpose of selling used parts--are classified in Industry 423140, Motor Vehicle Parts (Used) Merchant Wholesalers; and
- Operating facilities where commingled recyclable materials, such as paper, plastics, used beverage cans, and metals, are sorted into distinct categories--are classified in Industry 562920, Materials Recovery Facilities.

42394 Jewelry, Watch, Precious Stone, and Precious Metal Merchant Wholesalers
See industry description for 423940.

423940 Jewelry, Watch, Precious Stone, and Precious Metal Merchant Wholesalers

This industry comprises establishments primarily engaged in the merchant wholesale distribution of jewelry, precious and semiprecious stones, precious metals and metal flatware, costume jewelry, watches, clocks, silverware, and/or jewelers' findings.

Cross-References. Establishments primarily engaged in--

- Merchant wholesale distribution of precious metal ores or concentrates--are classified in Industry 423520, Coal and Other Mineral and Ore Merchant Wholesalers; and
- Merchant wholesale distribution of nonprecious flatware--are classified in Industry 423220, Home Furnishing Merchant Wholesalers.

42399 Other Miscellaneous Durable Goods Merchant Wholesalers
See industry description for 423990.

T—Canadian, Mexican, and United States industries are comparable.

423990 Other Miscellaneous Durable Goods Merchant Wholesalers

This industry comprises establishments primarily engaged in the merchant wholesale distribution of durable goods (except motor vehicles and motor vehicle parts and supplies; furniture and home furnishings; lumber and other construction materials; professional and commercial equipment and supplies; metals and minerals (except petroleum); electrical goods; hardware, and plumbing and heating equipment and supplies; machinery, equipment and supplies; sporting and recreational goods and supplies; toy and hobby goods and supplies; recyclable materials; and jewelry, watches, precious stones and precious metals).

Illustrative Examples:

Firearms (except sporting) merchant wholesalers
Musical instruments merchant wholesalers
Prerecorded audio and video tapes and discs merchant wholesalers
Phonograph records merchant wholesalers
Prerecorded compact discs (CDs) and digital video discs (DVDs) merchant wholesalers
Timber and timber products (except lumber) merchant wholesalers

Cross-References. Establishments primarily engaged in--

- Merchant wholesale distribution of automobiles and other motor vehicles, motor vehicle supplies, tires, and new and used parts--are classified in Industry Group 4231, Motor Vehicle and Motor Vehicle Parts and Supplies Merchant Wholesalers;
- Merchant wholesale distribution of furniture and home furnishings--are classified in Industry Group 4232, Furniture and Home Furnishing Merchant Wholesalers;
- Merchant wholesale distribution of lumber, plywood, millwork, wood panels, brick, stone, roofing, siding, and other nonelectrical construction materials--are classified in Industry Group 4233, Lumber and Other Construction Materials Merchant Wholesalers;
- Merchant wholesale distribution of photographic, office, computer and computer peripheral, medical, dental, hospital, ophthalmic, and other commercial and professional equipment and supplies--are classified in Industry Group 4234, Professional and Commercial Equipment and Supplies Merchant Wholesalers;
- Merchant wholesale distribution of coal and other minerals and ores and semi-finished metal products--are classified in Industry Group 4235, Metal and Mineral (except Petroleum) Merchant Wholesalers;
- Merchant wholesale distribution of household appliances and electrical goods--are classified in Industry Group 4236, Household Appliances and Electrical and Electronic Goods Merchant Wholesalers;
- Merchant wholesale distribution of hardware; and plumbing, heating, air-conditioning, and refrigeration equipment and supplies--are classified in Industry Group 4237, Hardware, and Plumbing and Heating Equipment and Supplies Merchant Wholesalers;
- Merchant wholesale distribution of construction, mining, farm, garden, industrial, service establishment, and transportation machinery, equipment and supplies--are classified in Industry Group 4238, Machinery, Equipment, and Supplies Merchant Wholesalers;
- Merchant wholesale distribution of sporting goods and accessories; billiard and pool supplies; sporting firearms and ammunition; and/or marine pleasure craft, equipment, and supplies--are classified in Industry 423910, Sporting and Recreational Goods and Supplies Merchant Wholesalers;
- Merchant wholesale distribution of toys, fireworks, playing cards, hobby goods and supplies and/or related goods--are classified in Industry 423920, Toy and Hobby Goods and Supplies Merchant Wholesalers;
- Merchant wholesale distribution of automotive, industrial, and other recyclable materials--are classified in Industry 423930, Recyclable Material Merchant Wholesalers;
- Merchant wholesale distribution of jewelry, precious and semiprecious stones, precious metals and metal flatware, costume jewelry, watches, clocks, silverware, and/or jewelers' findings--are classified in Industry 423940, Jewelry, Watch, Precious Stone, and Precious Metal Merchant Wholesalers; and
- Selling and installing fire suppression systems and fire extinguishers--are classified in Industry 238220, Plumbing, Heating, and Air-Conditioning Contractors.

T—Canadian, Mexican, and United States industries are comparable.

424 Merchant Wholesalers, Nondurable Goods

Industries in the Merchant Wholesalers, Nondurable Goods subsector sell nondurable goods to other businesses. Nondurable goods are items generally with a normal life expectancy of less than three years. Nondurable goods merchant wholesale trade establishments are engaged in wholesaling products, such as paper and paper products, chemicals and chemical products, drugs, textiles and textile products, apparel, footwear, groceries, farm products, petroleum and petroleum products, alcoholic beverages, books, magazines, newspapers, flowers and nursery stock, and tobacco products.

The detailed industries within the subsector are organized in the classification structure based on the products sold.

Business-to-business electronic markets, agents, and brokers primarily engaged in wholesaling nondurable goods, generally on a commission or fee basis, are classified in Subsector 425, Wholesale Electronic Markets and Agents and Brokers.

4241 Paper and Paper Product Merchant Wholesalers

This industry group comprises establishments primarily engaged in the merchant wholesale distribution of bulk printing and writing paper; stationery and office supplies; and industrial and personal service paper.

42411 Printing and Writing Paper Merchant Wholesalers

See industry description for 424110.

424110 Printing and Writing Paper Merchant Wholesalers

This industry comprises establishments primarily engaged in the merchant wholesale distribution of bulk printing and/or writing paper generally on rolls for further processing.

Illustrative Examples:

Bulk envelope paper merchant wholesalers
Bulk paper (e.g., fine, printing, writing) merchant wholesalers
Bulk groundwood paper merchant wholesalers

Cross-References.

Establishments primarily engaged in the merchant wholesale distribution of stationery and office paper (e.g., carbon, computer, copier, typewriter) are classified in Industry 424120, Stationery and Office Supplies Merchant Wholesalers.

42412 Stationery and Office Supplies Merchant Wholesalers

See industry description for 424120.

424120 Stationery and Office Supplies Merchant Wholesalers

This industry comprises establishments primarily engaged in the merchant wholesale distribution of stationery, office supplies, and/or gift wrap.

Illustrative Examples:

Photocopy supplies merchant wholesalers
Envelope merchant wholesalers
Social stationery merchant wholesalers
File cards and folders merchant wholesalers
Greeting cards merchant wholesalers
Office paper (e.g., carbon, computer, copier, typewriter) merchant wholesalers Writing pens merchant wholesalers
Pencils merchant wholesalers

T—Canadian, Mexican, and United States industries are comparable.

Cross-References.

Establishments primarily engaged in the merchant wholesale distribution of bulk printing and/or writing paper are classified in Industry 424110, Printing and Writing Paper Merchant Wholesalers.

42413 Industrial and Personal Service Paper Merchant Wholesalers
See industry description for 424130.

424130 Industrial and Personal Service Paper Merchant Wholesalers

This industry comprises establishments primarily engaged in the merchant wholesale distribution of kraft wrapping and other coarse paper, paperboard, converted paper (except stationery and office supplies), and/or related disposable plastics products.

Illustrative Examples:

Corrugated paper merchant wholesalers
Disposable plastics eating utensils merchant wholesalers
Paper napkins merchant wholesalers
Paper and disposable plastics dishes merchant wholesalers
Paperboard and disposable plastics boxes merchant wholesalers
Paper towels merchant wholesalers
Paper and disposable plastics shipping supplies merchant wholesalers Plastics bags merchant wholesalers
Paper bags merchant wholesalers
Sanitary paper products merchant wholesalers
Wrapping paper (except gift wrap) merchant wholesalers
Waxed paper merchant wholesalers

Cross-References.

Establishments primarily engaged in the merchant wholesale distribution of stationery, office supplies, and/or gift wrap are classified in Industry 424120, Stationery and Office Supplies Merchant Wholesalers.

4242 Drugs and Druggists' Sundries Merchant Wholesalers

42421 Drugs and Druggists' Sundries Merchant Wholesalers
See industry description for 424210.

424210 Drugs and Druggists' Sundries Merchant Wholesalers

This industry comprises establishments primarily engaged in the merchant wholesale distribution of biological and medical products; botanical drugs and herbs; and pharmaceutical products intended for internal and/or external consumption in such forms as ampoules, tablets, capsules, vials, ointments, powders, solutions, and suspensions.

Illustrative Examples:

Antibiotics merchant wholesalers
Endocrine substances merchant wholesalers
Blood derivatives merchant wholesalers
In-vitro and in-vivo diagnostics merchant wholesalers
Botanicals merchant wholesalers
Vaccines merchant wholesalers
Cosmetics merchant wholesalers
Vitamins merchant wholesalers

Cross-References.

Establishments primarily engaged in the merchant wholesale distribution of surgical, dental, and hospital equipment are classified in Industry 423450, Medical, Dental, and Hospital Equipment and Supplies Merchant Wholesalers.

T—Canadian, Mexican, and United States industries are comparable.

4243 Apparel, Piece Goods, and Notions Merchant Wholesalers

This industry group comprises establishments primarily engaged in the merchant wholesale distribution of piece goods, notions, and other dry goods; men's and boys' clothing and furnishings; women's, children's, and infants' clothing and accessories; and footwear.

42431 Piece Goods, Notions, and Other Dry Goods Merchant Wholesalers
See industry description for 424310.

424310 Piece Goods, Notions, and Other Dry Goods Merchant Wholesalers

This industry comprises establishments primarily engaged in the merchant wholesale distribution of piece goods, fabrics, knitting yarns (except industrial), thread and other notions, and/or hair accessories.

Cross-References.

- Establishments primarily engaged as converters who buy fabric goods in the grey, have them finished on a contract basis, and sell at wholesale are classified in Industry 313310, Textile and Fabric Finishing Mills; and
- Establishments primarily engaged in merchant wholesale distribution of industrial yarns are classified in Industry 424990, Other Miscellaneous Nondurable Goods Merchant Wholesalers.

42432 Men's and Boys' Clothing and Furnishings Merchant Wholesalers
See industry description for 424320.

424320 Men's and Boys' Clothing and Furnishings Merchant Wholesalers

This industry comprises establishments primarily engaged in the merchant wholesale distribution of men's and/or boys' clothing and furnishings.

Illustrative Examples:

Men's and boys' hosiery merchant wholesalers
Men's and boys' suits merchant wholesalers
Men's and boys' nightwear merchant wholesalers
Men's and boys' underwear merchant wholesalers
Men's and boys' sportswear merchant wholesalers
Men's and boys' work clothing merchant wholesalers

Cross-References.

Establishments primarily engaged in the merchant wholesale distribution of unisex clothing and men's fur clothing are classified in Industry 424330, Women's, Children's, and Infants' Clothing and Accessories Merchant Wholesalers.

42433 Women's, Children's, and Infants' Clothing and Accessories Merchant Wholesalers
See industry description for 424330.

424330 Women's, Children's, and Infants' Clothing and Accessories Merchant Wholesalers

This industry comprises establishments primarily engaged in the merchant wholesale distribution of (1) women's, children's, infants', and/or unisex clothing and accessories and/or (2) fur clothing.

Illustrative Examples:

Dresses merchant wholesalers
Millinery merchant wholesalers
Fur clothing merchant wholesalers
Women's, children's, and infants' hosiery merchant wholesalers
Lingerie merchant wholesalers

T—Canadian, Mexican, and United States industries are comparable.

42434 Footwear Merchant Wholesalers
See industry description for 424340.

424340 Footwear Merchant Wholesalers

This industry comprises establishments primarily engaged in the merchant wholesale distribution of footwear (including athletic) of leather, rubber, and other materials.

4244 Grocery and Related Product Merchant Wholesalers

This industry group comprises establishments primarily engaged in the merchant wholesale distribution of (1) a general line of groceries; (2) packaged frozen food; (3) dairy products; (4) poultry and poultry products; (5) confectioneries; (6) fish and seafood; (7) meats and meat products; (8) fresh fruits and vegetables; and (9) other grocery and related products.

42441 General Line Grocery Merchant Wholesalers
See industry description for 424410.

424410 General Line Grocery Merchant Wholesalers

This industry comprises establishments primarily engaged in the merchant wholesale distribution of a general line (wide range) of groceries.

Cross-References.

Establishments primarily engaged in the merchant wholesale distribution of a specialized line of groceries are classified elsewhere in Sector 42, Wholesale Trade, according to the product sold.

42442 Packaged Frozen Food Merchant Wholesalers
See industry description for 424420.

424420 Packaged Frozen Food Merchant Wholesalers

This industry comprises establishments primarily engaged in the merchant wholesale distribution of packaged frozen foods (except dairy products).

Illustrative Examples:

Frozen bakery products merchant wholesalers
Packaged frozen fish merchant wholesalers
Frozen juices merchant wholesalers
Packaged frozen meats merchant wholesalers
Frozen vegetables merchant wholesalers
Packaged frozen poultry merchant wholesalers

Cross-References.

Establishments primarily engaged in the merchant wholesale distribution of frozen dairy products are classified in Industry 424430, Dairy Product (except Dried or Canned) Merchant Wholesalers.

42443 Dairy Product (except Dried or Canned) Merchant Wholesalers
See industry description for 424430.

424430 Dairy Product (except Dried or Canned) Merchant Wholesalers

This industry comprises establishments primarily engaged in the merchant wholesale distribution of dairy products (except dried or canned).

T—Canadian, Mexican, and United States industries are comparable.

Illustrative Examples:

Butter merchant wholesalers
Fluid milk (except canned) merchant wholesalers
Cheese merchant wholesalers
Ice cream and ices merchant wholesalers
Cream merchant wholesalers
Yogurt merchant wholesalers

Cross-References. Establishments primarily engaged in--

- Merchant wholesale distribution of dried or canned dairy products and dairy substitutes--are classified in Industry 424490, Other Grocery and Related Products Merchant Wholesalers; and
- Pasteurizing and bottling milk--are classified in U.S. Industry 311511, Fluid Milk Manufacturing.

42444 Poultry and Poultry Product Merchant Wholesalers
See industry description for 424440.

424440 Poultry and Poultry Product Merchant Wholesalers

This industry comprises establishments primarily engaged in the merchant wholesale distribution of poultry and/or poultry products (except canned and packaged frozen).

Cross-References. Establishments primarily engaged in--

- Merchant wholesale distribution of packaged frozen poultry--are classified in Industry 424420, Packaged Frozen Food Merchant Wholesalers;
- Merchant wholesale distribution of canned poultry--are classified in Industry 424490, Other Grocery and Related Products Merchant Wholesalers; and
- Slaughtering and dressing poultry--are classified in U.S. Industry 311615, Poultry Processing.

42445 Confectionery Merchant Wholesalers
See industry description for 424450.

424450 Confectionery Merchant Wholesalers

This industry comprises establishments primarily engaged in the merchant wholesale distribution of confectioneries; salted or roasted nuts; popcorn; potato, corn, and similar chips; and/or fountain fruits and syrups.

Cross-References. Establishments primarily engaged in--

- Merchant wholesale distribution of frozen pretzels--are classified in Industry 424420, Packaged Frozen Food Merchant Wholesalers; and
- Merchant wholesale distribution of pretzels (except frozen)--are classified in Industry 424490, Other Grocery and Related Products Merchant Wholesalers.

42446 Fish and Seafood Merchant Wholesalers
See industry description for 424460.

424460 Fish and Seafood Merchant Wholesalers

This industry comprises establishments primarily engaged in the merchant wholesale distribution of fish and seafood (except canned or packaged frozen).

Cross-References. Establishments primarily engaged in--

- Merchant wholesale distribution of packaged frozen fish and seafood--are classified in Industry 424420, Packaged Frozen Food Merchant Wholesalers;

T—Canadian, Mexican, and United States industries are comparable.

- Merchant wholesale distribution of canned fish and seafood--are classified in Industry 424490, Other Grocery and Related Products Merchant Wholesalers; and
- Canning, smoking, salting, drying, or freezing seafood and shucking and packing fresh shellfish--are classified in Industry 311710, Seafood Product Preparation and Packaging.

42447 Meat and Meat Product Merchant Wholesalers
See industry description for 424470.

424470 Meat and Meat Product Merchant Wholesalers

This industry comprises establishments primarily engaged in the merchant wholesale distribution of meats and meat products (except canned and packaged frozen) and/or lard.

Cross-References. Establishments primarily engaged in--

- Merchant wholesale distribution of packaged frozen meats--are classified in Industry 424420, Packaged Frozen Food Merchant Wholesalers;
- Merchant wholesale distribution of canned meats--are classified in Industry 424490, Other Grocery and Related Products Merchant Wholesalers; and
- Preparing boxed beef from purchased carcasses--are classified in U.S. Industry 311612, Meat Processed from Carcasses.

42448 Fresh Fruit and Vegetable Merchant Wholesalers
See industry description for 424480.

424480 Fresh Fruit and Vegetable Merchant Wholesalers

This industry comprises establishments primarily engaged in the merchant wholesale distribution of fresh fruits and vegetables.

42449 Other Grocery and Related Products Merchant Wholesalers
See industry description for 424490.

424490 Other Grocery and Related Products Merchant Wholesalers

This industry comprises establishments primarily engaged in the merchant wholesale distribution of groceries and related products (except a general line of groceries; packaged frozen food; dairy products (except dried and canned); poultry products (except canned); confectioneries; fish and seafood (except canned); meat products (except canned); and fresh fruits and vegetables). Included in this industry are establishments primarily engaged in the bottling and merchant wholesale distribution of spring and mineral waters processed by others.

Illustrative Examples:

Bakery products (except frozen) merchant wholesalers
Canned seafood merchant wholesalers
Canned fish merchant wholesalers
Canned vegetables merchant wholesalers
Canned fruits merchant wholesalers
Dried milk merchant wholesalers
Canned meats merchant wholesalers
Soft drinks merchant wholesalers
Canned milk merchant wholesalers

Cross-References. Establishments primarily engaged in--

- Merchant wholesale distribution of grains, field beans, livestock, and other farm product raw materials--are classified in Industry Group 4245, Farm Product Raw Material Merchant Wholesalers;
- Merchant wholesale distribution of beer, wine, and distilled alcoholic beverages--are classified in Industry Group 4248, Beer, Wine, and Distilled Alcoholic Beverage Merchant Wholesalers;

T—Canadian, Mexican, and United States industries are comparable.

- Bottling soft drinks--are classified in Industry 31211, Soft Drink and Ice Manufacturing;
- Merchant wholesale distribution of a general line of groceries--are classified in Industry 424410, General Line Grocery Merchant Wholesalers;
- Merchant wholesale distribution of packaged frozen foods (except dairy)--are classified in Industry 424420, Packaged Frozen Food Merchant Wholesalers;
- Merchant wholesale distribution of dairy products--are classified in Industry 424430, Dairy Product (except Dried or Canned) Merchant Wholesalers;
- Merchant wholesale distribution of poultry and poultry products (except canned and packaged frozen)--are classified in Industry 424440, Poultry and Poultry Product Merchant Wholesalers;
- Merchant wholesale distribution of confectioneries; salted or roasted nuts; popcorn; potato, corn, and similar chips; and/or fountain fruits and syrups--are classified in Industry 424450, Confectionery Merchant Wholesalers;
- Merchant wholesale distribution of fish and seafood (except canned and packaged frozen)--are classified in Industry 424460, Fish and Seafood Merchant Wholesalers;
- Merchant wholesale distribution of meats (except canned and packaged frozen)--are classified in Industry 424470, Meat and Meat Product Merchant Wholesalers;
- Merchant wholesale distribution of fresh fruits and vegetables--are classified in Industry 424480, Fresh Fruit and Vegetable Merchant Wholesalers;
- Purifying and bottling water--are classified in U.S. Industry 312112, Bottled Water Manufacturing; and
- Roasting coffee--are classified in Industry 311920, Coffee and Tea Manufacturing.

4245 Farm Product Raw Material Merchant Wholesalers

This industry group comprises establishments primarily engaged in the merchant wholesale distribution of agricultural products (except raw milk, live poultry, and fresh fruits and vegetables), such as grains, field beans, livestock, and other farm product raw materials (excluding seeds).

42451 Grain and Field Bean Merchant Wholesalers

See industry description for 424510.

424510 Grain and Field Bean Merchant Wholesalers

This industry comprises establishments primarily engaged in the merchant wholesale distribution of grains, such as corn, wheat, oats, barley, and unpolished rice; dry beans; and soybeans and other inedible beans. Included in this industry are establishments primarily engaged in operating country or terminal grain elevators primarily for the purpose of wholesaling.

Cross-References. Establishments primarily engaged in--

- Merchant wholesale distribution of field and garden seeds--are classified in Industry 424910, Farm Supplies Merchant Wholesalers; and
- Operating grain elevators for storage only--are classified in Industry 493130, Farm Product Warehousing and Storage.

42452 Livestock Merchant Wholesalers

See industry description for 424520.

424520 Livestock Merchant Wholesalers

This industry comprises establishments primarily engaged in the merchant wholesale distribution of livestock (except horses and mules).

T—Canadian, Mexican, and United States industries are comparable.

Illustrative Examples:

Cattle merchant wholesalers
Hogs merchant wholesalers
Goats merchant wholesalers
Sheep merchant wholesalers

Cross-References.

Establishments primarily engaged in the merchant wholesale distribution of horses and mules are classified in Industry 424590, Other Farm Product Raw Material Merchant Wholesalers.

42459 Other Farm Product Raw Material Merchant Wholesalers
See industry description for 424590.

424590 Other Farm Product Raw Material Merchant Wholesalers

This industry comprises establishments primarily engaged in the merchant wholesale distribution of farm products (except grain and field beans, livestock, raw milk, live poultry, and fresh fruits and vegetables).

Illustrative Examples:

Chicks, live, merchant wholesalers
Mules merchant wholesalers
Hides merchant wholesalers
Raw cotton merchant wholesalers
Horses merchant wholesalers
Raw pelts merchant wholesalers
Leaf tobacco merchant wholesalers
Sod merchant wholesalers

Cross-References. Establishments primarily engaged in--

- Merchant wholesale distribution of raw milk--are classified in Industry 424430, Dairy Product (except Dried or Canned) Merchant Wholesalers;
- Merchant wholesale distribution of live poultry (except chicks)--are classified in Industry 424440, Poultry and Poultry Product Merchant Wholesalers;
- Merchant wholesale distribution of grain, dry beans, and soybeans and other inedible beans--are classified in Industry 424510, Grain and Field Bean Merchant Wholesalers;
- Merchant wholesale distribution of livestock (except horses and mules), such as cattle, hogs, sheep, and goats--are classified in Industry 424520, Livestock Merchant Wholesalers; and
- Merchant wholesale distribution of fresh fruits and vegetables--are classified in Industry 424480, Fresh Fruit and Vegetable Merchant Wholesalers.

4246 Chemical and Allied Products Merchant Wholesalers

This industry group comprises establishments primarily engaged in the merchant wholesale distribution of chemicals, plastics materials and basic forms and shapes, and allied products.

42461 Plastics Materials and Basic Forms and Shapes Merchant Wholesalers
See industry description for 424610.

424610 Plastics Materials and Basic Forms and Shapes Merchant Wholesalers

This industry comprises establishments primarily engaged in the merchant wholesale distribution of plastics materials and resins, and unsupported plastics film, sheet, sheeting, rod, tube, and other basic forms and shapes.

42469 Other Chemical and Allied Products Merchant Wholesalers
See industry description for 424690.

T—Canadian, Mexican, and United States industries are comparable.

424690 Other Chemical and Allied Products Merchant Wholesalers

This industry comprises establishments primarily engaged in the merchant wholesale distribution of chemicals and allied products (except agricultural and medicinal chemicals, paints and varnishes, fireworks, and plastics materials and basic forms and shapes).

Illustrative Examples:

Acids merchant wholesalers
Industrial chemicals merchant wholesalers
Automotive chemicals (except lubricating oils and greases) merchant wholesalers
Industrial salts merchant wholesalers
Dyestuffs merchant wholesalers
Rosins merchant wholesalers
Explosives (except ammunition and fireworks) merchant wholesalers
Turpentine merchant wholesalers

Cross-References. Establishments primarily engaged in--

- Merchant wholesale distribution of ammunition--are classified in Industry Group 4239, Miscellaneous Durable Goods Merchant Wholesalers;
- Merchant wholesale distribution of biological and medical products; botanical drugs and herbs; and pharmaceutical products intended for internal and external consumption in such forms as ampoules, tablets, capsules, vials, ointments, powders, solutions, and suspensions--are classified in Industry 424210, Drugs and Druggists' Sundries Merchant Wholesalers;
- Merchant wholesale distribution of farm supplies, such as animal feeds, fertilizers, agricultural chemicals, pesticides, seeds, and plant bulbs--are classified in Industry 424910, Farm Supplies Merchant Wholesalers;
- Merchant wholesale distribution of paints, varnishes, and similar coatings, pigments, wallpaper, and supplies, such as paintbrushes and rollers--are classified in Industry 424950, Paint, Varnish, and Supplies Merchant Wholesalers;
- Merchant wholesale distribution of lubricating oils and greases--are classified in Industry 424720, Petroleum and Petroleum Products Merchant Wholesalers (except Bulk Stations and Terminals);
- Merchant wholesale distribution of fireworks--are classified in Industry 423920, Toy and Hobby Goods and Supplies Merchant Wholesalers; and
- Merchant wholesale distribution of plastics materials and resins, and unsupported plastics film, sheet, sheeting, rod, tube, and other basic forms and shapes--are classified in Industry 424610, Plastics Materials and Basic Forms and Shapes Merchant Wholesalers.

4247 Petroleum and Petroleum Products Merchant Wholesalers

This industry group comprises establishments primarily engaged in the merchant wholesale distribution of petroleum and petroleum products, including liquefied petroleum gas.

42471 Petroleum Bulk Stations and Terminals
See industry description for 424710.

424710 Petroleum Bulk Stations and Terminals

This industry comprises establishments with bulk liquid storage facilities primarily engaged in the merchant wholesale distribution of crude petroleum and petroleum products, including liquefied petroleum gas.

Cross-References.

Establishments primarily engaged in bulk storage of petroleum are classified in Industry 493190, Other Warehousing and Storage.

42472 Petroleum and Petroleum Products Merchant Wholesalers (except Bulk Stations and Terminals)
See industry description for 424720.

T—Canadian, Mexican, and United States industries are comparable.

424720 Petroleum and Petroleum Products Merchant Wholesalers (except Bulk Stations and Terminals)

This industry comprises establishments primarily engaged in the merchant wholesale distribution of petroleum and petroleum products (except from bulk liquid storage facilities).

Illustrative Examples:

Gasoline merchant wholesalers (except bulk stations, terminals)
Lubricating oil and grease merchant wholesalers (except bulk stations, terminals)
Bottled liquid petroleum gas merchant wholesalers
Fuel oil merchant wholesalers (except bulk stations, terminals)

Cross-References.

Establishments primarily engaged in the merchant wholesale distribution of crude petroleum and petroleum products from bulk liquid storage facilities are classified in Industry 424710, Petroleum Bulk Stations and Terminals.

4248 Beer, Wine, and Distilled Alcoholic Beverage Merchant Wholesalers

This industry group comprises establishments primarily engaged in the merchant wholesale distribution of beer, ale, wine, and/or distilled alcoholic beverages.

42481 Beer and Ale Merchant Wholesalers
See industry description for 424810.

424810 Beer and Ale Merchant Wholesalers

This industry comprises establishments primarily engaged in the merchant wholesale distribution of beer, ale, porter, and other fermented malt beverages.

42482 Wine and Distilled Alcoholic Beverage Merchant Wholesalers
See industry description for 424820.

424820 Wine and Distilled Alcoholic Beverage Merchant Wholesalers

This industry comprises establishments primarily engaged in the merchant wholesale distribution of wine, distilled alcoholic beverages, and/or neutral spirits and ethyl alcohol used in blended wines and distilled liquors.

4249 Miscellaneous Nondurable Goods Merchant Wholesalers

This industry group comprises establishments primarily engaged in the merchant wholesale distribution of nondurable goods, such as farm supplies; books, periodicals and newspapers; flowers; nursery stock; paints; varnishes; tobacco and tobacco products; and other miscellaneous nondurable goods, such as cut Christmas trees and pet supplies.

42491 Farm Supplies Merchant Wholesalers
See industry description for 424910.

424910 Farm Supplies Merchant Wholesalers

This industry comprises establishments primarily engaged in the merchant wholesale distribution of farm supplies, such as animal feeds, fertilizers, agricultural chemicals, pesticides, plant seeds, and plant bulbs.

T—Canadian, Mexican, and United States industries are comparable.

Cross-References. Establishments primarily engaged in--

- Merchant wholesale distribution of pet food--are classified in Industry 424490, Other Grocery and Related Products Merchant Wholesalers;
- Merchant wholesale distribution of grains--are classified in Industry 424510, Grain and Field Bean Merchant Wholesalers;
- Merchant wholesale distribution of pet supplies--are classified in Industry 424990, Other Miscellaneous Nondurable Goods Merchant Wholesalers; and
- Merchant wholesale distribution of nursery stock (except seeds and plant bulbs)--are classified in Industry 424930, Flower, Nursery Stock, and Florists' Supplies Merchant Wholesalers.

42492 Book, Periodical, and Newspaper Merchant Wholesalers
See industry description for 424920.

424920 Book, Periodical, and Newspaper Merchant Wholesalers

This industry comprises establishments primarily engaged in the merchant wholesale distribution of books, periodicals, and newspapers.

42493 Flower, Nursery Stock, and Florists' Supplies Merchant Wholesalers
See industry description for 424930.

424930 Flower, Nursery Stock, and Florists' Supplies Merchant Wholesalers

This industry comprises establishments primarily engaged in the merchant wholesale distribution of flowers, florists' supplies, and/or nursery stock (except plant seeds and plant bulbs).

Cross-References. Establishments primarily engaged in--

- Merchant wholesale distribution of cut Christmas trees--are classified in Industry 424990, Other Miscellaneous Nondurable Goods Merchant Wholesalers; and
- Merchant wholesale distribution of plant seeds and plant bulbs--are classified in Industry 424910, Farm Supplies Merchant Wholesalers.

42494 Tobacco and Tobacco Product Merchant Wholesalers
See industry description for 424940.

424940 Tobacco and Tobacco Product Merchant Wholesalers

This industry comprises establishments primarily engaged in the merchant wholesale distribution of tobacco products, such as cigarettes, snuff, cigars, and pipe tobacco.

Cross-References.

Establishments primarily engaged in the merchant wholesale distribution of leaf tobacco are classified in Industry 424590, Other Farm Product Raw Material Merchant Wholesalers.

42495 Paint, Varnish, and Supplies Merchant Wholesalers
See industry description for 424950.

424950 Paint, Varnish, and Supplies Merchant Wholesalers

This industry comprises establishments primarily engaged in the merchant wholesale distribution of paints, varnishes, and similar coatings; pigments; wallpaper; and supplies, such as paintbrushes and rollers.

T—Canadian, Mexican, and United States industries are comparable.

Cross-References.

Establishments primarily engaged in the merchant wholesale distribution of artists' paints are classified in Industry 424990, Other Miscellaneous Nondurable Goods Merchant Wholesalers.

42499 Other Miscellaneous Nondurable Goods Merchant Wholesalers

See industry description for 424990.

424990 Other Miscellaneous Nondurable Goods Merchant Wholesalers

This industry comprises establishments primarily engaged in the merchant wholesale distribution of nondurable goods (except printing and writing paper; stationery and office supplies; industrial and personal service paper; drugs and druggists' sundries; apparel, piece goods, and notions; grocery and related products; farm product raw materials; chemical and allied products; petroleum and petroleum products; beer, wine, and distilled alcoholic beverages; farm supplies; books, periodicals, and newspapers; flowers, nursery stock, and florists' supplies; tobacco and tobacco products; and paint, varnishes, wallpaper, and supplies).

Illustrative Examples:

Artists' supplies merchant wholesalers
Pet supplies (except pet food) merchant wholesalers
Burlap merchant wholesalers
Statuary (except religious) merchant wholesalers
Christmas trees (e.g., artificial, cut) merchant wholesalers
Textile bags merchant wholesalers
Industrial yarns merchant wholesalers

Cross-References. Establishments primarily engaged in--

- Distribution of advertising specialties--are classified in Industry 541890, Other Services Related to Advertising;
- Merchant wholesale distribution of farm supplies--are classified in Industry 424910, Farm Supplies Merchant Wholesalers;
- Merchant wholesale distribution of books, periodicals, and newspapers--are classified in Industry 424920, Book, Periodical, and Newspaper Merchant Wholesalers;
- Merchant wholesale distribution of flowers, nursery stock, and florists' supplies--are classified in Industry 424930, Flower, Nursery Stock, and Florists' Supplies Merchant Wholesalers;
- Merchant wholesale distribution of tobacco and its products--are classified in Industry 424940, Tobacco and Tobacco Product Merchant Wholesalers;
- Merchant wholesale distribution of paints, varnishes, and similar coatings; pigments; wallpaper; and supplies--are classified in Industry 424950, Paint, Varnish, and Supplies Merchant Wholesalers;
- Merchant wholesale distribution of bulk printing and/or writing paper--are classified in Industry 424110, Printing and Writing Paper Merchant Wholesalers;
- Merchant wholesale distribution of stationery, office supplies, and/or gift wrap--are classified in Industry 424120, Stationery and Office Supplies Merchant Wholesalers;
- Merchant wholesale distribution of kraft wrapping and other coarse paper, paperboard, converted paper (except stationery and office supplies), and related disposable plastics products--are classified in Industry 424130, Industrial and Personal Service Paper Merchant Wholesalers;
- Merchant wholesale distribution of biological and medical products; botanical drugs and herbs; and pharmaceutical products intended for internal and external consumption--are classified in Industry 424210, Drugs and Druggists' Sundries Merchant Wholesalers;
- Merchant wholesale distribution of clothing and accessories, footwear, piece goods, yard goods, notions, and/or hair accessories--are classified in Industry Group 4243, Apparel, Piece Goods, and Notions Merchant Wholesalers;
- Merchant wholesale distribution of meat, poultry, seafood, confectioneries, fruits and vegetables; and other groceries and related products--are classified in Industry Group 4244, Grocery and Related Product Merchant Wholesalers;

T—Canadian, Mexican, and United States industries are comparable.

- Merchant wholesale distribution of grains, field beans, livestock, and other farm product raw materials--are classified in Industry Group 4245, Farm Product Raw Material Merchant Wholesalers;
- Merchant wholesale distribution of chemicals; plastics materials and basic forms and shapes; and allied products--are classified in Industry Group 4246, Chemical and Allied Products Merchant Wholesalers;
- Merchant wholesale distribution of petroleum and petroleum products--are classified in Industry Group 4247, Petroleum and Petroleum Products Merchant Wholesalers;
- Merchant wholesale distribution of beer, ale, wine, and distilled alcoholic beverages--are classified in Industry Group 4248, Beer, Wine, and Distilled Alcoholic Beverage Merchant Wholesalers;
- Merchant wholesale distribution of pet foods--are classified in Industry 424490, Other Grocery and Related Products Merchant Wholesalers;
- Merchant wholesale distribution of religious statuary--are classified in Industry 423490, Other Professional Equipment and Supplies Merchant Wholesalers; and
- Merchant wholesale distribution of knitting yarns (except industrial)--are classified in Industry 424310, Piece Goods, Notions, and Other Dry Goods Merchant Wholesalers.

425 Wholesale Electronic Markets and Agents and Brokers

Industries in the Wholesale Electronic Markets and Agents and Brokers subsector arrange for the sale of goods owned by others, generally on a fee or commission basis. They act on behalf of the buyers and sellers of goods. This subsector contains agents and brokers as well as business-to-business electronic markets that facilitate wholesale trade.

4251 Wholesale Electronic Markets and Agents and Brokers

42511 Business to Business Electronic Markets
See industry description for 425110.

425110 Business to Business Electronic Markets

This industry comprises business-to-business electronic markets bringing together buyers and sellers of goods using the Internet or other electronic means and generally receiving a commission or fee for the service. Business-to-business electronic markets for durable and nondurable goods are included in this industry.

Cross-References.

Establishments primarily engaged in bringing together buyers and sellers of goods using the Internet in a business-to-consumer or consumer-to-consumer environment are classified in Industry 454110, Electronic Shopping and Mail-Order Houses.

42512 Wholesale Trade Agents and Brokers
See industry description for 425120.

425120 Wholesale Trade Agents and Brokers

This industry comprises wholesale trade agents and brokers acting on behalf of buyers or sellers in the wholesale distribution of goods. Agents and brokers do not take title to the goods being sold but rather receive a commission or fee for their service. Agents and brokers for all durable and nondurable goods are included in this industry.

Illustrative Examples:

Independent sales representatives Manufacturers' sales representatives

T—Canadian, Mexican, and United States industries are comparable.

Cross-References.

Establishments acting in the capacity of agents or brokers that operate using the Internet or other electronic means instead of a sales force are classified in Industry 425110, Business to Business Electronic Markets.

T—Canadian, Mexican, and United States industries are comparable.

Sector 44-45--Retail Trade[T]

The Sector as a Whole

The Retail Trade sector comprises establishments engaged in retailing merchandise, generally without transformation, and rendering services incidental to the sale of merchandise.

The retailing process is the final step in the distribution of merchandise; retailers are, therefore, organized to sell merchandise in small quantities to the general public. This sector comprises two main types of retailers: store and nonstore retailers.

1. Store retailers operate fixed point-of-sale locations, located and designed to attract a high volume of walk-in customers. In general, retail stores have extensive displays of merchandise and use mass-media advertising to attract customers. They typically sell merchandise to the general public for personal or household consumption, but some also serve business and institutional clients. These include office supply stores, computer and software stores, building materials dealers, plumbing supply stores, and electrical supply stores. Catalog showrooms, gasoline stations, automotive dealers, and mobile home dealers are treated as store retailers.

In addition to retailing merchandise, some types of store retailers are also engaged in the provision of after-sales services, such as repair and installation. For example, new automobile dealers, electronics and appliance stores, and musical instrument and supplies stores often provide repair services. As a general rule, establishments engaged in retailing merchandise and providing after-sales services are classified in this sector.

The first eleven subsectors of retail trade are store retailers. The establishments are grouped into industries and industry groups typically based on one or more of the following criteria:

(a) The merchandise line or lines carried by the store; for example, specialty stores are distinguished from general-line stores.

(b) The usual trade designation of the establishments. This criterion applies in cases where a store type is well recognized by the industry and the public, but difficult to define strictly in terms of merchandise lines carried; for example, pharmacies, hardware stores, and department stores.

(c) Capital requirements in terms of display equipment; for example, food stores have equipment requirements not found in other retail industries.

(d) Human resource requirements in terms of expertise; for example, the staff of an automobile dealer requires knowledge in financing, registering, and licensing issues that are not necessary in other retail industries.

1. Nonstore retailers, like store retailers, are organized to serve the general public, but their retailing methods differ. The establishments of this subsector reach customers and market merchandise with methods, such as the broadcasting of "infomercials," the broadcasting and publishing of direct-response advertising, the publishing of paper and electronic catalogs, door-to-door solicitation, in-home demonstration, selling from portable stalls (street vendors, except food), and distribution through vending machines. Establishments engaged in the direct sale (nonstore) of products, such as home heating oil dealers and home delivery newspaper routes, are included here.

The buying of goods for resale is a characteristic of retail trade establishments that particularly distinguishes them from establishments in the agriculture, manufacturing, and construction industries. For example, farms that sell their products at or from the point of production are not classified in retail, but rather in agriculture. Similarly, establishments that both manufacture and sell their products to the general public are not classified in retail, but rather in manufacturing. However, establishments that engage in processing activities incidental to retailing are classified in retail. This includes optical goods stores that do in-store grinding of lenses, and meat and seafood markets.

Wholesalers also engage in the buying of goods for resale, but they are not usually organized to serve the general public. They typically operate from a warehouse or office, and neither the design nor the location of these premises is intended to solicit a high volume of walk-in traffic. Wholesalers supply institutional, industrial, wholesale, and retail clients; their operations are, therefore, generally organized to purchase, sell, and deliver merchandise in larger

T—Canadian, Mexican, and United States industries are comparable.

quantities. However, dealers of durable nonconsumer goods, such as farm machinery and heavy-duty trucks, are included in wholesale trade even if they often sell these products in single units.

441 Motor Vehicle and Parts Dealers

Industries in the Motor Vehicle and Parts Dealers subsector retail motor vehicles and parts from fixed point-of-sale locations. Establishments in this subsector typically operate from a showroom and/or an open lot where the vehicles are on display. The display of vehicles and the related parts require little by way of display equipment. The personnel generally include both the sales and sales support staff familiar with the requirements for registering and financing a vehicle as well as a staff of parts experts and mechanics trained to provide repair and maintenance services for the vehicles. Specific industries included in this subsector identify the type of vehicle being retailed. Sales of capital or durable nonconsumer goods, such as medium- and heavy-duty trucks, are always included in wholesale trade. These goods are virtually never sold through retail methods.

4411 Automobile Dealers

This industry group comprises establishments primarily engaged in retailing new and used automobiles and light trucks, such as sport utility vehicles, and passenger and cargo vans.

44111 New Car Dealers See industry description for 441110.

441110 New Car Dealers

This industry comprises establishments primarily engaged in retailing new automobiles and light trucks, such as sport utility vehicles, and passenger and cargo vans, or retailing these new vehicles in combination with activities, such as repair services, retailing used cars, and selling replacement parts and accessories.

Illustrative Examples:

Automobile dealers, new only, or new and used Light utility truck dealers, new only, or new and used *Cross-References.* Establishments primarily engaged in--

- Retailing used automobiles and light trucks without retailing new automobiles and light trucks--are classified in Industry 441120, Used Car Dealers;
- Providing automotive repair services without retailing new automotive vehicles--are classified in Industry Group 8111, Automotive Repair and Maintenance; and
- Merchant wholesale distribution of new medium- and heavy-duty trucks, buses, and other motor vehicles--are classified in Industry 423110, Automobile and Other Motor Vehicle Merchant Wholesalers.

44112 Used Car Dealers
See industry description for 441120.

441120 Used Car Dealers

This industry comprises establishments primarily engaged in retailing used automobiles and light trucks, such as sport utility vehicles, and passenger and cargo vans.

Illustrative Examples:

Antique auto dealers
Automobile dealers, used only
Light truck dealers, used only

T—Canadian, Mexican, and United States industries are comparable.

Cross-References. Establishments primarily engaged in--

- Retailing new automobiles and light trucks--are classified in Industry 441110, New Car Dealers; and
- Merchant wholesale distribution of used medium- and heavy-duty trucks, buses, and other motor vehicles--are classified in Industry 423110, Automobile and Other Motor Vehicle Merchant Wholesalers.

4412 Other Motor Vehicle Dealers

This industry group comprises establishments primarily engaged in retailing new and used vehicles (except automobiles, light trucks, such as sport utility vehicles, and passenger and cargo vans).

44121 Recreational Vehicle Dealers

See industry description for 441210.

441210 Recreational Vehicle Dealers

This industry comprises establishments primarily engaged in retailing new and/or used recreational vehicles commonly referred to as RVs or retailing these new vehicles in combination with activities, such as repair services and selling replacement parts and accessories.

Illustrative Examples:

Motor home dealers
Recreational vehicle (RV) parts and accessories stores
Recreational vehicle (RV) dealers
Travel trailer dealers

Cross-References. Establishments primarily engaged in--

- Retailing new or used boat trailers and utility trailers--are classified in Industry 44122, Motorcycle, Boat, and Other Motor Vehicle Dealers; and
- Retailing manufactured homes (i.e., mobile homes), parts, and equipment--are classified in Industry 453930, Manufactured (Mobile) Home Dealers.

44122 Motorcycle, Boat, and Other Motor Vehicle Dealers

This industry comprises establishments primarily engaged in retailing new and used motorcycles, boats, and other vehicles (except automobiles, light trucks, and recreational vehicles), or retailing these new vehicles in combination with activities, such as repair services and selling replacement parts and accessories.

Illustrative Examples:

Aircraft dealers
Motorcycle dealers
All-terrain vehicle (ATV) dealers
Utility trailer dealers
Boat dealers, new and used

Cross-References. Establishments primarily engaged in--

- Retailing new nonmotorized bicycles, surfboards, or wind sailboards--are classified in Industry 45111, Sporting Goods Stores;
- Retailing used nonmotorized bicycles, surfboards, or wind sailboards--are classified in Industry 45331, Used Merchandise Stores;
- Retailing new or used automobiles and light trucks--are classified in Industry Group 4411, Automobile Dealers;
- Retailing new or used recreational vehicles, such as travel trailers--are classified in Industry 44121, Recreational Vehicle Dealers;

T—Canadian, Mexican, and United States industries are comparable.

- Providing repair services for vehicles without retailing new vehicles--are classified in the appropriate industry for the repair services; and
- Retailing fuel and marine supplies at a marina--are classified in Industry 71393, Marinas.

441222 Boat Dealers

This U.S. industry comprises establishments primarily engaged in (1) retailing new and/or used boats or retailing new boats in combination with activities, such as repair services and selling replacement parts and accessories, and/or (2) retailing new and/or used outboard motors, boat trailers, marine supplies, parts, and accessories.

Illustrative Examples:

Boat dealers (e.g., power boats, rowboats, sailboats)
Outboard motor dealers
Marine supply dealers

Cross-References. Establishments primarily engaged in--

- Retailing new surfboards or wind sailboards--are classified in Industry 451110, Sporting Goods Stores;
- Retailing used surfboards or wind sailboards--are classified in Industry 453310, Used Merchandise Stores;
- Providing boat repair services without retailing new boats--are classified in Industry 811490, Other Personal and Household Goods Repair and Maintenance;
- Retailing new or used personal watercraft--are classified in U.S. Industry 441228, Motorcycle, ATV, and All Other Motor Vehicle Dealers; and
- Operating docking and/or storage facilities for pleasure craft owners--are classified in Industry 713930, Marinas.

441228 Motorcycle, ATV, and All Other Motor Vehicle Dealers

This U.S. industry comprises establishments primarily engaged in retailing new and/or used motorcycles, motor scooters, motorbikes, mopeds, off-road all-terrain vehicles (ATV), personal watercraft, utility trailers, and other motor vehicles (except automobiles, light trucks, recreational vehicles, and boats) or retailing these new vehicles in combination with activities, such as repair services and selling replacement parts and accessories.

All-terrain vehicle (ATV) dealers
Motorcycle dealers
Moped dealers
Motorcycle parts and accessories dealers
Personal watercraft dealers
Aircraft dealers
Snowmobile dealers
Powered golf cart dealers
Utility trailer dealers

Cross-References. Establishments primarily engaged in--

- Retailing new automobiles and light trucks--are classified in Industry 441110, New Car Dealers;
- Retailing used automobiles and light trucks--are classified in Industry 441120, Used Car Dealers;
- Retailing new or used recreational vehicles, such as travel trailers--are classified in Industry 441210, Recreational Vehicle Dealers;
- Retailing new or used boats, outboard motors, boat trailers, and marine supplies--are classified in U.S. Industry 441222, Boat Dealers;
- Retailing new nonmotorized bicycles--are classified in Industry 451110, Sporting Goods Stores;
- Retailing used nonmotorized bicycles--are classified in Industry 453310, Used Merchandise Stores; and
- Providing vehicle repair services without retailing new vehicles--are classified in the appropriate industry

T—Canadian, Mexican, and United States industries are comparable.

4413 Automotive Parts, Accessories, and Tire Stores

This industry group comprises establishments primarily engaged in retailing new, used, and/or rebuilt automotive parts and accessories, including tires and tubes. Included in this industry group are establishments primarily engaged in retailing automotive parts and accessories in combination with automotive repair services.

44131 Automotive Parts and Accessories Stores
See industry description for 441310.

441310 Automotive Parts and Accessories Stores

This industry comprises one or more of the following: (1) establishments known as automotive supply stores primarily engaged in retailing new, used, and/or rebuilt automotive parts and accessories; (2) automotive supply stores that are primarily engaged in both retailing automotive parts and accessories and repairing automobiles; and (3) establishments primarily engaged in retailing and installing automotive accessories.

Illustrative Examples:

Automotive parts and supply stores
Truck cap stores
Automotive stereo stores
Used automotive parts stores
Speed shops

Cross-References. Establishments primarily engaged in--

- Retailing automotive parts and accessories via electronic home shopping, mail-order, or direct sale--are classified in Subsector 454, Nonstore Retailers;
- Retailing new or used tires--are classified in Industry 441320, Tire Dealers; and
- Repairing and replacing automotive parts, such as transmissions, mufflers, and brake linings (except establishments known as automotive supply stores)--are classified in Industry 81111, Automotive Mechanical and Electrical Repair and Maintenance.

44132 Tire Dealers
See industry description for 441320.

441320 Tire Dealers

This industry comprises establishments primarily engaged in retailing new and/or used tires and tubes or retailing new tires in combination with automotive repair services.

Cross-References. Establishments primarily engaged in--

- Retailing tires via electronic home shopping, mail-order, or direct sale--are classified in Subsector 454, Nonstore Retailers;
- Tire retreading or recapping--are classified in U.S. Industry 326212, Tire Retreading; and
- Merchant wholesale distribution of new/used tires for medium- and heavy-duty trucks, buses, and other motor vehicles--are classified in Industry 423130, Tire and Tube Merchant Wholesalers.

442 Furniture and Home Furnishings Stores

Industries in the Furniture and Home Furnishings Stores subsector retail new furniture and home furnishings from fixed point-of-sale locations. Establishments in this subsector usually operate from showrooms and have substantial areas for the presentation of their products. Many offer interior decorating services in addition to the sale of products.

T—Canadian, Mexican, and United States industries are comparable.

4421 Furniture Stores

44211 Furniture Stores
See industry description for 442110.

442110 Furniture Stores

This industry comprises establishments primarily engaged in retailing new furniture, such as household furniture (e.g., baby furniture, box springs, and mattresses) and outdoor furniture; office furniture (except sold in combination with office supplies and equipment); and/or furniture sold in combination with major appliances, home electronics, home furnishings, or floor coverings.

Cross-References. Establishments primarily engaged in--

- Retailing furniture via electronic home shopping, mail-order, or direct sale--are classified in Subsector 454, Nonstore Retailers;
- Retailing used furniture--are classified in Industry 453310, Used Merchandise Stores;
- Retailing custom furniture made on the premises--are classified in Subsector 337, Furniture and Related Product Manufacturing; and
- Retailing new office furniture and a range of new office equipment and supplies--are classified in Industry 453210, Office Supplies and Stationery Stores.

4422 Home Furnishings Stores

This industry group comprises establishments primarily engaged in retailing new home furnishings (except furniture).

44221 Floor Covering Stores
See industry description for 442210.

442210 Floor Covering Stores

This industry comprises establishments primarily engaged in retailing new floor coverings, such as rugs and carpets, vinyl floor coverings, and floor tile (except ceramic or wood only); or retailing new floor coverings in combination with installation and repair services.

Cross-References. Establishments primarily engaged in--

- Retailing floor coverings via electronic home shopping, mail-order, or direct sale--are classified in Subsector 454, Nonstore Retailers;
- Installing floor coverings without retailing new floor coverings--are classified in Industry 238330, Flooring Contractors;
- Retailing ceramic floor tile or wood floor coverings only--are classified in Industry 444190, Other Building Material Dealers; and
- Retailing used rugs and carpets--are classified in Industry 453310, Used Merchandise Stores.

44229 Other Home Furnishings Stores

This industry comprises establishments primarily engaged in retailing new home furnishings (except furniture and floor coverings).

Illustrative Examples:

Bath shops Kitchenware stores

T—Canadian, Mexican, and United States industries are comparable.

Chinaware stores
Window treatment stores
Glassware stores

Cross-References. Establishments primarily engaged in--

- Retailing home furnishings via electronic home shopping, mail-order, or direct sale--are classified in Subsector 454, Nonstore Retailers;
- Retailing custom curtains and draperies made on the premises--are classified in Industry 31412, Curtain and Linen Mills;
- Retailing new mirrored glass, lighting fixtures, and new ceramic floor tile or wood floor coverings only--are classified in Industry 44419, Other Building Material Dealers;
- Retailing new furniture--are classified in Industry 44211, Furniture Stores;
- Retailing new floor coverings (except ceramic or wood only)--are classified in Industry 44221, Floor Covering Stores; and
- Retailing used home furnishings--are classified in Industry 45331, Used Merchandise Stores.

442291 Window Treatment Stores

This U.S. industry comprises establishments primarily engaged in retailing new window treatments, such as curtains, drapes, blinds, and shades.

Cross-References. Establishments primarily engaged in--

- Retailing window treatments via electronic home shopping, mail-order, or direct sale--are classified in Subsector 454, Nonstore Retailers; and
- Retailing custom curtains and draperies made on the premises--are classified in Industry 314120, Curtain and Linen Mills.

442299 All Other Home Furnishings Stores

This U.S. industry comprises establishments primarily engaged in retailing new home furnishings (except floor coverings, furniture, and window treatments).

Illustrative Examples:

Bath shops
Kitchenware stores
Chinaware stores
Linen stores
Electric lamp shops
Picture frame shops, custom
Glassware stores
Wood-burning stove stores
Housewares stores

Cross-References. Establishments primarily engaged in--

- Retailing home furnishings via electronic home shopping, mail-order, or direct sale--are classified in Subsector 454, Nonstore Retailers;
- Retailing new mirrored glass or lighting fixtures--are classified in Industry 444190, Other Building Material Dealers;
- Retailing new furniture--are classified in Industry 442110, Furniture Stores;
- Retailing new floor coverings--are classified in Industry 442210, Floor Covering Stores;
- Retailing new window treatments--are classified in U.S. Industry 442291, Window Treatment Stores; and

T—Canadian, Mexican, and United States industries are comparable.

443 Electronics and Appliance Stores

Industries in the Electronics and Appliance Stores subsector retail new electronics and appliances from point-of-sale locations. Establishments in this subsector often operate from locations that have special provisions for floor displays requiring special electrical capacity to accommodate the proper demonstration of the products. The staff includes sales personnel knowledgeable in the characteristics and warranties of the line of goods retailed and may also include trained repair persons to handle the maintenance and repair of the electronic equipment and appliances. The classifications within this subsector are made principally on the type of product and knowledge required to operate each type of store.

4431 Electronics and Appliance Stores

44314 Electronics and Appliance Stores

This industry comprises establishments primarily engaged in one of the following: (1) retailing an array of new household-type appliances and consumer-type electronic products, such as televisions, computers, and cameras; (2) specializing in retailing a single line of new consumer-type electronic products; (3) retailing these new products in combination with repair and support services; (4) retailing new prepackaged computer software; and/or (5) retailing prerecorded audio and video media, such as CDs, DVDs, and tapes.

Illustrative Examples:

Appliance stores, household type
Cellular telephone accessories stores
Consumer-type electronic stores (e.g., televisions,

Cross-References. Establishments primarily engaged in--

- Retailing new appliance and electronic products via electronic home shopping, mail-order, or direct sale--are classified in Subsector 454, Nonstore Retailers;
- Retailing new computers, computer peripherals, and prepackaged software in combination with retailing new office equipment, office furniture, and office supplies--are classified in Industry 45321, Office Supplies and Stationery Stores;
- Retailing new sewing machines in combination with selling new sewing supplies, fabrics, patterns, yarns, and other needlework accessories--are classified in Industry 45113, Sewing, Needlework, and Piece Goods Stores;
- Retailing new electronic toys, such as dedicated game consoles and handheld electronic games--are classified in Industry 45112, Hobby, Toy, and Game Stores;
- Providing television or other electronic equipment repair services without retailing new televisions or electronic equipment--are classified in Industry 81121, Electronic and Precision Equipment Repair and Maintenance;
- Providing household-type appliance repair services without retailing new appliances--are classified in Industry 81141, Home and Garden Equipment and Appliance Repair and Maintenance;
- Developing film and/or making photographic slides, prints, and enlargements without retailing a range of new photographic equipment and supplies--are classified in Industry 81292, Photofinishing;
- Retailing used appliance and electronic products--are classified in Industry 45331, Used Merchandise Stores; and
- Retailing automotive electronic sound systems--are classified in Industry 44131, Automotive Parts and Accessories Stores.

443141 Household Appliance Stores

This U.S. industry comprises establishments known as appliance stores primarily engaged in retailing an array of new household appliances, such as refrigerators, dishwashers, ovens, irons, coffee makers, hair dryers, electric razors, room air-conditioners, microwave ovens, sewing machines, and vacuum cleaners, or retailing new appliances in combination with appliance repair services.

T—Canadian, Mexican, and United States industries are comparable.

Cross-References. Establishments primarily engaged in--

- Retailing household appliances via electronic home shopping, mail-order, or direct sale--are classified in Subsector 454, Nonstore Retailers;
- Retailing new sewing machines in combination with selling new sewing supplies, fabrics, patterns, yarns, and other needlework accessories--are classified in Industry 451130, Sewing, Needlework, and Piece Goods Stores;
- Providing household-type appliance repair services without retailing new appliances--are classified in U.S. Industry 811412, Appliance Repair and Maintenance; and
- Retailing used appliances--are classified in Industry 453310, Used Merchandise Stores.

443142 Electronics Stores

This U.S. industry comprises: (1) establishments known as consumer electronics stores primarily engaged in retailing a general line of new consumer-type electronic products such as televisions, computers, and cameras; (2) establishments specializing in retailing a single line of consumer-type electronic products; (3) establishments primarily engaged in retailing these new electronic products in combination with repair and support services; (4) establishments primarily engaged in retailing new prepackaged computer software; and/or (5) establishments primarily engaged in retailing prerecorded audio and video media, such as CDs, DVDs, and tapes.

Illustrative Examples:

Cellular telephone accessories stores
Consumer-type electronic stores (e.g., televisions, computers, cameras)
Stereo stores (except automotive)
Radio and television stores
Computer stores

Cross-References. Establishments primarily engaged in--

- Retailing electronic goods via electronic home shopping, mail-order, or direct sale--are classified in Subsector 454, Nonstore Retailers;
- Retailing automotive electronic sound systems--are classified in Industry 441310, Automotive Parts and Accessories Stores;
- Retailing new computers, computer peripherals, and prepackaged software in combination with retailing new office equipment, office furniture, and office supplies--are classified in Industry 453210, Office Supplies and Stationery Stores;
- Retailing new cellular telephones and communication service plans--are classified in U.S. Industry 517312, Wireless Telecommunications Carriers (except Satellite);
- Providing television or other electronic equipment repair services without retailing new televisions or electronic products--are classified in Industry 81121, Electronic and Precision Equipment Repair and Maintenance;
- Developing film and/or making photographic slides, prints, and enlargements without retailing a range of new photographic equipment and supplies--are classified in Industry 81292, Photofinishing;
- Retailing new electronic toys, such as dedicated video game consoles and handheld electronic games--are classified in Industry 451120, Hobby, Toy, and Game Stores; and
- Retailing used electronics--are classified in Industry 453310, Used Merchandise Stores.

444 Building Material and Garden Equipment and Supplies Dealers

Industries in the Building Material and Garden Equipment and Supplies Dealers subsector retail new building material and garden equipment and supplies from fixed point-of-sale locations. Establishments in this subsector have display equipment designed to handle lumber and related products and garden equipment and supplies that may be kept either indoors or outdoors under covered areas. The staff is usually knowledgeable in the use of the specific products being retailed in the construction, repair, and maintenance of the home and associated grounds.

T—Canadian, Mexican, and United States industries are comparable.

4441 Building Material and Supplies Dealers

This industry group comprises establishments primarily engaged in retailing new building materials and supplies.

44411 Home Centers
See industry description for 444110.

444110 Home Centers

This industry comprises establishments known as home centers primarily engaged in retailing a general line of new home repair and improvement materials and supplies, such as lumber, plumbing goods, electrical goods, tools, housewares, hardware, and lawn and garden supplies, with no one merchandise line predominating. The merchandise lines are normally arranged in separate departments.

Cross-References.

Establishments primarily engaged in retailing a general line of new hardware items, such as tools and builders' hardware, are classified in Industry 444130, Hardware Stores.

44412 Paint and Wallpaper Stores See industry description for 444120.

444120 Paint and Wallpaper Stores

This industry comprises establishments known as paint and wallpaper stores primarily engaged in retailing paint, wallpaper, and related supplies.

Cross-References.

Establishments primarily engaged in retailing automotive paints are classified in Industry 441310, Automotive Parts and Accessories Stores.

44413 Hardware Stores
See industry description for 444130.

444130 Hardware Stores

This industry comprises establishments known as hardware stores primarily engaged in retailing a general line of new hardware items, such as tools and builders' hardware.

Cross-References. Establishments primarily engaged in--

- Retailing hardware items via electronic home shopping, mail-order, or direct sale--are classified in Subsector 454, Nonstore Retailers;
- Retailing a general line of home repair and improvement materials and supplies, known as home centers--are classified in Industry 444110, Home Centers; and
- Retailing used hardware items--are classified in Industry 453310, Used Merchandise Stores.

44419 Other Building Material Dealers
See industry description for 444190.

444190 Other Building Material Dealers

This industry comprises establishments (except those known as home centers, paint and wallpaper stores, and hardware stores) primarily engaged in retailing specialized lines of new building materials, such as lumber, fencing,

T—Canadian, Mexican, and United States industries are comparable.

glass, doors, plumbing fixtures and supplies, electrical supplies, prefabricated buildings and kits, and kitchen and bath cabinets and countertops to be installed.

Illustrative Examples:

Electrical supply stores
Kitchen cabinet (except custom) stores
Fencing dealers
Lumber yards, retail
Floor covering stores, wood or ceramic tile only
Plumbing supply stores
Garage door dealers
Prefabricated building dealers
Glass stores

Cross-References. Establishments primarily engaged in--

- Retailing building materials via electronic home shopping, mail-order, or direct sale--are classified in Subsector 454, Nonstore Retailers;
- Retailing used building materials--are classified in Industry 453310, Used Merchandise Stores;
- Providing carpentry/installation services for products--are classified in Industry 238350, Finish Carpentry Contractors;
- Installing plumbing fixtures and supplies--are classified in Industry 238220, Plumbing, Heating, and Air-Conditioning Contractors;
- Installing electrical supplies, such as lighting fixtures and ceiling fans--are classified in Industry 238210, Electrical Contractors and Other Wiring Installation Contractors;
- Making custom furniture (e.g., kitchen cabinets)--are classified in Subsector 337, Furniture and Related Product Manufacturing;
- Retailing a general line of new hardware items, known as hardware stores--are classified in Industry 444130, Hardware Stores;
- Retailing paint and wallpaper, known as paint and wallpaper stores--are classified in Industry 444120, Paint and Wallpaper Stores; and
- Retailing a general line of home repair and improvement materials and supplies, known as home centers--are classified in Industry 444110, Home Centers.

4442 Lawn and Garden Equipment and Supplies Stores

This industry group comprises establishments primarily engaged in retailing new lawn and garden equipment and supplies.

44421 Outdoor Power Equipment Stores
See industry description for 444210.

444210 Outdoor Power Equipment Stores

This industry comprises establishments primarily engaged in retailing new outdoor power equipment or retailing new outdoor power equipment in combination with activities, such as repair services and selling replacement parts.

Cross-References. Establishments primarily engaged in--

- Retailing outdoor power equipment via electronic home shopping, mail-order, or direct sale--are classified in Subsector 454, Nonstore Retailers;
- Providing outdoor power equipment repair services without retailing new outdoor power equipment--are classified in U.S. Industry 811411, Home and Garden Equipment Repair and Maintenance; and
- Retailing used outdoor power equipment--are classified in Industry 453310, Used Merchandise Stores.

44422 Nursery, Garden Center, and Farm Supply Stores
See industry description for 444220.

T—Canadian, Mexican, and United States industries are comparable.

444220 Nursery, Garden Center, and Farm Supply Stores

This industry comprises establishments primarily engaged in retailing nursery and garden products, such as trees, shrubs, plants, seeds, bulbs, and sod, that are predominantly grown elsewhere. These establishments may sell a limited amount of a product they grow themselves. Also included in this industry are establishments primarily engaged in retailing farm supplies, such as animal (except pet) feed.

Cross-References. Establishments primarily engaged in--

- Retailing nursery and garden products via electronic home shopping, mail-order, or direct sale--are classified in Subsector 454, Nonstore Retailers;
- Providing landscaping services--are classified in Industry 561730, Landscaping Services; and
- Growing and retailing nursery stock--are classified in U.S. Industry 111421, Nursery and Tree Production.

445 Food and Beverage Stores

Industries in the Food and Beverage Stores subsector usually retail food and beverage merchandise from fixed point-of-sale locations. Establishments in this subsector have special equipment (e.g., freezers, refrigerated display cases, refrigerators) for displaying food and beverage goods. They have staff trained in the processing of food products to guarantee the proper storage and sanitary conditions required by regulatory authority.

4451 Grocery Stores

This industry group comprises establishments primarily engaged in retailing a general line of food products.

44511 Supermarkets and Other Grocery (except Convenience) Stores
See industry description for 445110.

445110 Supermarkets and Other Grocery (except Convenience) Stores

This industry comprises establishments generally known as supermarkets and grocery stores primarily engaged in retailing a general line of food, such as canned and frozen foods; fresh fruits and vegetables; and fresh and prepared meats, fish, and poultry. Included in this industry are delicatessen-type establishments primarily engaged in retailing a general line of food.

Cross-References. Establishments primarily engaged in--

- Retailing automotive fuels in combination with a convenience store or food mart--are classified in Industry 447110, Gasoline Stations with Convenience Stores;
- Retailing a limited line of goods, known as convenience stores or food marts (except those with fuel pumps)--are classified in Industry 445120, Convenience Stores;
- Retailing frozen food and freezer meal plans via direct sales to residential customers--are classified in Industry 454390, Other Direct Selling Establishments;
- Providing food services in delicatessen-type establishments--are classified in U.S. Industry 722513, Limited-Service Restaurants; and
- Retailing fresh meat in delicatessen-type establishments--are classified in Industry 445210, Meat Markets.

44512 Convenience Stores
See industry description for 445120.

445120 Convenience Stores

This industry comprises establishments known as convenience stores or food marts (except those with fuel pumps) primarily engaged in retailing a limited line of goods that generally includes milk, bread, soda, and snacks.

T—Canadian, Mexican, and United States industries are comparable.

Cross-References. Establishments primarily engaged in--

- Retailing a general line of food, known as supermarkets and grocery stores--are classified in Industry 445110, Supermarkets and Other Grocery (except Convenience) Stores; and
- Retailing automotive fuels in combination with a convenience store or food mart--are classified in Industry 447110, Gasoline Stations with Convenience Stores.

4452 Specialty Food Stores

This industry group comprises establishments primarily engaged in retailing specialized lines of food.

44521 Meat Markets
See industry description for 445210.

445210 Meat Markets

This industry comprises establishments primarily engaged in retailing fresh, frozen, or cured meats and poultry. Delicatessen-type establishments primarily engaged in retailing fresh meat are included in this industry.

Illustrative Examples:

Baked ham stores
Meat markets
Butcher shops
Poultry dealers
Frozen meat shops

Cross-References. Establishments primarily engaged in--

- Retailing meat and poultry via electronic home shopping, mail-order, or direct sale--are classified in Subsector 454, Nonstore Retailers;
- Retailing a general line of food, known as supermarkets and grocery stores--are classified in Industry 445110, Supermarkets and Other Grocery (except Convenience) Stores; and
- Providing food services in delicatessen-type establishments--are classified in U.S. Industry 722513, Limited-Service Restaurants.

44522 Fish and Seafood Markets See industry description for 445220.

445220 Fish and Seafood Markets

This industry comprises establishments primarily engaged in retailing fresh, frozen, or cured fish and seafood products.

Cross-References.

Establishments primarily engaged in retailing fish and seafood products via electronic home shopping, mail-order, or direct sale are classified in Subsector 454, Nonstore Retailers.

44523 Fruit and Vegetable Markets
See industry description for 445230.

445230 Fruit and Vegetable Markets

This industry comprises establishments primarily engaged in retailing fresh fruits and vegetables.

T—Canadian, Mexican, and United States industries are comparable.

Cross-References. Establishments primarily engaged in--

- Retailing fruits and vegetables via electronic home shopping, mail-order, or direct sale--are classified in Subsector 454, Nonstore Retailers; and
- Growing and selling vegetables and/or fruits at roadside stands--are classified in Subsector 111, Crop Production.

44529 Other Specialty Food Stores

This industry comprises establishments primarily engaged in retailing specialty foods (except meat, fish, seafood, and fruits and vegetables) not for immediate consumption and not made on the premises.

Illustrative Examples:

Baked goods stores (except immediate consumption)
Dairy product stores
Coffee and tea (i.e., packaged) stores
Gourmet food stores
Confectionery (i.e., packaged) stores
Nut (i.e., packaged) stores

Cross-References. Establishments primarily engaged in--

- Retailing specialty foods via electronic home shopping, mail-order, or direct sale--are classified in Subsector 454, Nonstore Retailers;
- Retailing baked goods made on the premises but not for immediate consumption--are classified in Industry 31181, Bread and Bakery Product Manufacturing;
- Retailing fresh, frozen, or cured meats and poultry--are classified in Industry 44521, Meat Markets;
- Retailing fresh, frozen, or cured fish and seafood products--are classified in Industry 44522, Fish and Seafood Markets;
- Retailing fresh fruits and vegetables--are classified in Industry 44523, Fruit and Vegetable Markets;
- Retailing candy and confectionery products not for immediate consumption and made on the premises--are classified in Industry Group 3113, Sugar and Confectionery Product Manufacturing; and
- Selling snack foods (e.g., doughnuts, bagels, ice cream, popcorn) for immediate consumption--are classified in Industry 72251, Restaurants and Other Eating Places.

445291 Baked Goods Stores

This U.S. industry comprises establishments primarily engaged in retailing baked goods not for immediate consumption and not made on the premises.

Cross-References. Establishments primarily engaged in--

- Retailing baked goods via electronic home shopping, mail-order, or direct sale--are classified in Subsector 454, Nonstore Retailers;
- Selling snack foods (e.g., doughnuts, bagels, ice cream, popcorn) for immediate consumption--are classified in U.S. Industry 722515, Snack and Nonalcoholic Beverage Bars; and
- Retailing baked goods made on the premises but not for immediate consumption--are classified in U.S. Industry 311811, Retail Bakeries.

445292 Confectionery and Nut Stores

This U.S. industry comprises establishments primarily engaged in retailing candy and other confections, nuts, and popcorn not for immediate consumption and not made on the premises.

T—Canadian, Mexican, and United States industries are comparable.

Cross-References. Establishments primarily engaged in--

- Retailing confectionery goods and nuts via electronic home shopping, mail-order, or direct sale--are classified in Subsector 454, Nonstore Retailers;
- Retailing confectionery goods and nuts made on the premises and not packaged for immediate consumption--are classified in Industry Group 3113, Sugar and Confectionery Product Manufacturing;
- Selling snack foods (e.g., doughnuts, bagels, ice cream, popcorn) for immediate consumption--are classified in U.S. Industry 722515, Snack and Nonalcoholic Beverage Bars; and
- Retailing baked goods made on the premises but not for immediate consumption--are classified in U.S. Industry 311811, Retail Bakeries.

445299 All Other Specialty Food Stores

This U.S. industry comprises establishments primarily engaged in retailing miscellaneous specialty foods (except meat, fish, seafood, fruit and vegetables, confections, nuts, popcorn, and baked goods) not for immediate consumption and not made on the premises.

Illustrative Examples:

Coffee and tea (i.e., packaged) stores
Soft drink (i.e., bottled) stores
Dairy product stores
Spice stores
Gourmet food stores
Water (i.e., bottled) stores

Cross-References. Establishments primarily engaged in--

- Retailing specialty foods via electronic home shopping, mail-order, or direct sale--are classified in Subsector 454, Nonstore Retailers;
- Selling snack foods (e.g., doughnuts, bagels, ice cream, popcorn) for immediate consumption--are classified in U.S. Industry 722515, Snack and Nonalcoholic Beverage Bars;
- Retailing fresh, frozen, or cured meats and poultry--are classified in Industry 445210, Meat Markets;
- Retailing fresh, frozen, or cured fish and seafood products--are classified in Industry 445220, Fish and Seafood Markets;
- Retailing fresh fruits and vegetables--are classified in Industry 445230, Fruit and Vegetable Markets;
- Retailing candy and other confections, nuts, and popcorn not for immediate consumption and not made on the premises--are classified in U.S. Industry 445292, Confectionery and Nut Stores; and
- Retailing baked goods not for immediate consumption and not made on the premises--are classified in U.S. Industry 445291, Baked Goods Stores.

4453 Beer, Wine, and Liquor Stores

44531 Beer, Wine, and Liquor Stores
See industry description for 445310.

445310 Beer, Wine, and Liquor Stores

This industry comprises establishments primarily engaged in retailing packaged alcoholic beverages, such as ale, beer, wine, and liquor.

Cross-References.

Establishments primarily engaged in retailing packaged liquor in combination with providing prepared drinks for immediate consumption on the premises are classified in Industry 722410, Drinking Places (Alcoholic Beverages).

T—Canadian, Mexican, and United States industries are comparable.

446 Health and Personal Care Stores

Industries in the Health and Personal Care Stores subsector retail health and personal care merchandise from fixed point-of-sale locations. Establishments in this subsector are characterized principally by the products they retail, and some health and personal care stores may have specialized staff trained in dealing with the products. Staff may include pharmacists, opticians, and other professionals engaged in retailing, advising customers, and/or fitting the product sold to the customer's needs.

4461 Health and Personal Care Stores

44611 Pharmacies and Drug Stores
See industry description for 446110.

446110 Pharmacies and Drug Stores

This industry comprises establishments known as pharmacies and drug stores engaged in retailing prescription or nonprescription drugs and medicines.

Cross-References. Establishments primarily engaged in--

- Retailing food supplement products, such as vitamins, nutrition supplements, and body enhancing supplements--are classified in U.S. Industry 446191, Food (Health) Supplement Stores; and
- Retailing prescription and nonprescription drugs via electronic home shopping, mail-order, or direct sale--are classified in Subsector 454, Nonstore Retailers.

44612 Cosmetics, Beauty Supplies, and Perfume Stores
See industry description for 446120.

446120 Cosmetics, Beauty Supplies, and Perfume Stores

This industry comprises establishments known as cosmetic or perfume stores or beauty supply shops primarily engaged in retailing cosmetics, perfumes, toiletries, and personal grooming products.

Cross-References. Establishments primarily engaged in--

- Providing beauty salon services--are classified in U.S. Industry 812112, Beauty Salons; and
- Retailing perfumes, cosmetics, and beauty supplies via electronic home shopping, mail-order, or direct sale--are classified in Subsector 454, Nonstore Retailers.

44613 Optical Goods Stores
See industry description for 446130.

446130 Optical Goods Stores

This industry comprises establishments primarily engaged in one or more of the following: (1) retailing and fitting prescription eyeglasses and contact lenses; (2) retailing prescription eyeglasses in combination with the grinding of lenses to order on the premises; and (3) selling nonprescription eyeglasses.

Cross-References. Establishments primarily engaged in--

- Grinding ophthalmic lenses without retailing lenses--are classified in U.S. Industry 339115, Ophthalmic Goods Manufacturing;
- The private or group practice of optometry, even though glasses and contact lenses are sold at these establishments--are classified in Industry 621320, Offices of Optometrists; and

T—Canadian, Mexican, and United States industries are comparable.

- Retailing eyeglasses and contact lenses via electronic home shopping or mail-order--are classified in Industry 454110, Electronic Shopping and Mail-Order Houses.

44619 Other Health and Personal Care Stores

This industry comprises establishments primarily engaged in retailing health and personal care items (except drugs, medicines, optical goods, perfumes, cosmetics, and beauty supplies).

Illustrative Examples:

Convalescent supply stores
Prosthetic stores
Food (i.e., health) supplement stores
Sick room supply stores
Hearing aid stores

Cross-References. Establishments primarily engaged in--

- Retailing health and personal care items via electronic home shopping, mail-order, or direct sale--are classified in Subsector 454, Nonstore Retailers;
- Retailing orthopedic shoes--are classified in Industry 44821, Shoe Stores;
- Retailing orthopedic and prosthetic appliances that are made on the premises--are classified in Industry 33911, Medical Equipment and Supplies Manufacturing;
- Retailing prescription and nonprescription drugs and medicines--are classified in Industry 44611, Pharmacies and Drug Stores;
- Retailing eyeglasses and contact lenses--are classified in Industry 44613, Optical Goods Stores;
- Retailing perfumes, cosmetics, and beauty supplies--are classified in Industry 44612, Cosmetics, Beauty Supplies, and Perfume Stores; and
- Retailing naturally organic foods, such as fruits and vegetables, dairy products, and cereals and grains--are classified in Subsector 445, Food and Beverage Stores.

446191 Food (Health) Supplement Stores

This U.S. industry comprises establishments primarily engaged in retailing food supplement products, such as vitamins, nutrition supplements, and body enhancing supplements.

Cross-References. Establishments primarily engaged in--

- Retailing food supplement products via electronic home shopping, mail-order, or direct sale--are classified in Subsector 454, Nonstore Retailers;
- Retailing prescription and nonprescription drugs and medicines--are classified in Industry 446110, Pharmacies and Drug Stores; and
- Retailing naturally organic foods, such as fruits and vegetables, dairy products, and cereals and grains--are classified in Subsector 445, Food and Beverage Stores.

446199 All Other Health and Personal Care Stores

This U.S. industry comprises establishments primarily engaged in retailing specialized lines of health and personal care merchandise (except drugs, medicines, optical goods, cosmetics, beauty supplies, perfume, and food supplement products).

Illustrative Examples:

Convalescent supply stores
Prosthetic stores
Hearing aid stores
Sick room supply stores

T—Canadian, Mexican, and United States industries are comparable.

Cross-References. Establishments primarily engaged in--

- Retailing specialized health and personal care merchandise via electronic home shopping, mail-order, or direct sale--are classified in Subsector 454, Nonstore Retailers;
- Retailing food supplement products--are classified in U.S. Industry 446191, Food (Health) Supplement Stores;
- Retailing prescription or nonprescription drugs and medicines--are classified in Industry 446110, Pharmacies and Drug Stores;
- Retailing eyeglasses and contact lenses--are classified in Industry 446130, Optical Goods Stores;
- Retailing perfumes, cosmetics, and beauty supplies--are classified in Industry 446120, Cosmetics, Beauty Supplies, and Perfume Stores;
- Retailing orthopedic shoes--are classified in Industry 448210, Shoe Stores; and
- Retailing orthopedic and prosthetic appliances that are made on the premises--are classified in U.S. Industry 339113, Surgical Appliance and Supplies Manufacturing.

447 Gasoline Stations

Industries in the Gasoline Stations subsector retail automotive fuels (e.g., gasoline, diesel fuel, gasohol, alternative fuels) and automotive oils or retail these products in combination with convenience store items. These establishments have specialized equipment for storing and dispensing automotive fuels.

4471 Gasoline Stations

44711 Gasoline Stations with Convenience Stores
See industry description for 447110.

447110 Gasoline Stations with Convenience Stores

This industry comprises establishments engaged in retailing automotive fuels (e.g., diesel fuel, gasohol, gasoline) in combination with convenience store or food mart items. These establishments can either be in a convenience store (i.e., food mart) setting or a gasoline station setting. These establishments may also provide automotive repair services.

Cross-References. Establishments primarily engaged in--

- Retailing automotive fuels without a convenience store--are classified in Industry 447190, Other Gasoline Stations; and
- Retailing a limited line of goods, known as convenience stores or food marts (except those with fuel pumps)--are classified in Industry 445120, Convenience Stores.

44719 Other Gasoline Stations
See industry description for 447190.

447190 Other Gasoline Stations

This industry comprises establishments known as gasoline stations (except those with convenience stores) primarily engaged in (1) retailing automotive fuels (e.g., diesel fuel, gasohol, gasoline, alternative fuels) or (2) retailing these fuels in combination with activities, such as providing repair services; selling automotive oils, replacement parts, and accessories; and/or providing food services.

Illustrative Examples:

Gasoline stations without convenience stores
Truck stops
Marine service stations

T—Canadian, Mexican, and United States industries are comparable.

Cross-References. Establishments primarily engaged in--

- Repairing motor vehicles without retailing automotive fuels--are classified in Industry Group 8111, Automotive Repair and Maintenance; and
- Retailing automotive fuels in combination with a convenience store or food mart--are classified in Industry 447110, Gasoline Stations with Convenience Stores.

448 Clothing and Clothing Accessories Stores

Industries in the Clothing and Clothing Accessories Stores subsector retail new clothing and clothing accessories from fixed point-of-sale locations. Establishments in this subsector have similar display equipment and staff that is knowledgeable regarding fashion trends and the proper match of styles, colors, and combinations of clothing and accessories to the characteristics and tastes of the customer.

4481 Clothing Stores

This industry group comprises establishments primarily engaged in retailing new clothing.

44811 Men's Clothing Stores
See industry description for 448110.

448110 Men's Clothing Stores

This industry comprises establishments primarily engaged in retailing a general line of new men's and boys' clothing. These establishments may provide basic alterations, such as hemming, taking in or letting out seams, or lengthening or shortening sleeves.

Cross-References. Establishments primarily engaged in--

- Retailing men's and boys' clothing via electronic home shopping, mail-order, or direct sale--are classified in Subsector 454, Nonstore Retailers;
- Retailing custom men's clothing made on the premises--are classified in Industry Group 3152, Cut and Sew Apparel Manufacturing;
- Retailing new men's and boys' accessories--are classified in Industry 448150, Clothing Accessories Stores;
- Retailing specialized new apparel, such as raincoats, leather coats, fur apparel, and swimwear--are classified in Industry 448190, Other Clothing Stores;
- Retailing new clothing for all genders and age groups--are classified in Industry 448140, Family Clothing Stores;
- Retailing secondhand clothes--are classified in Industry 453310, Used Merchandise Stores; and
- Providing clothing alterations and repair--are classified in Industry 811490, Other Personal and Household Goods Repair and Maintenance.

44812 Women's Clothing Stores
See industry description for 448120.

448120 Women's Clothing Stores

This industry comprises establishments primarily engaged in retailing a general line of new women's, misses', and juniors' clothing, including maternity wear. These establishments may provide basic alterations, such as hemming, taking in or letting out seams, or lengthening or shortening sleeves.

Cross-References. Establishments primarily engaged in--

- Retailing women's clothing via electronic home shopping, mail-order, or direct sale--are classified in Subsector 454, Nonstore Retailers;

T—Canadian, Mexican, and United States industries are comparable.

- Retailing custom women's clothing made on the premises--are classified in Industry Group 3152, Cut and Sew Apparel Manufacturing;
- Retailing new women's accessories--are classified in Industry 448150, Clothing Accessories Stores;
- Retailing new clothing for all genders and age groups--are classified in Industry 448140, Family Clothing Stores;
- Retailing specialized new apparel, such as bridal gowns, raincoats, leather coats, fur apparel, and swimwear--are classified in Industry 448190, Other Clothing Stores;
- Retailing secondhand clothes--are classified in Industry 453310, Used Merchandise Stores; and
- Providing clothing alterations and repair--are classified in Industry 811490, Other Personal and Household Goods Repair and Maintenance.

44813 Children's and Infants' Clothing Stores
See industry description for 448130.

448130 Children's and Infants' Clothing Stores

This industry comprises establishments primarily engaged in retailing a general line of new children's and infants' clothing. These establishments may provide basic alterations, such as hemming, taking in or letting out seams, or lengthening or shortening sleeves.

Cross-References. Establishments primarily engaged in--

- Retailing children's and infants' clothing via electronic home shopping, mail-order, or direct sale--are classified in Subsector 454, Nonstore Retailers;
- Retailing new children's and infants' accessories--are classified in Industry 448150, Clothing Accessories Stores;
- Retailing new clothing for all genders or age groups--are classified in Industry 448140, Family Clothing Stores;
- Retailing secondhand clothes--are classified in Industry 453310, Used Merchandise Stores; and
- Providing clothing alterations and repair--are classified in Industry 811490, Other Personal and Household Goods Repair and Maintenance.

44814 Family Clothing Stores
See industry description for 448140.

448140 Family Clothing Stores

This industry comprises establishments primarily engaged in retailing a general line of new clothing for men, women, and children, without specializing in sales for an individual gender or age group. These establishments may provide basic alterations, such as hemming, taking in or letting out seams, or lengthening or shortening sleeves.

Cross-References. Establishments primarily engaged in--

- Retailing clothing for all genders via electronic home shopping, mail-order, or direct sale--are classified in Subsector 454, Nonstore Retailers;
- Retailing new men's and boys' clothing--are classified in Industry 448110, Men's Clothing Stores;
- Retailing new women's, misses', and juniors' clothing--are classified in Industry 448120, Women's Clothing Stores;
- Retailing new children's and infants' clothing--are classified in Industry 448130, Children's and Infants' Clothing Stores;
- Retailing specialized new apparel, such as raincoats, bridal gowns, leather coats, fur apparel, and swimwear--are classified in Industry 448190, Other Clothing Stores;
- Providing clothing alterations and repair--are classified in Industry 811490, Other Personal and Household Goods Repair and Maintenance; and
- Retailing secondhand clothes--are classified in Industry 453310, Used Merchandise Stores.

T—Canadian, Mexican, and United States industries are comparable.

44815 Clothing Accessories Stores
See industry description for 448150.

448150 Clothing Accessories Stores

This industry comprises establishments primarily engaged in retailing single or combination lines of new clothing accessories, such as hats and caps, costume jewelry, gloves, handbags, ties, wigs, toupees, and belts.

Illustrative Examples:

Costume jewelry stores
Wig and hairpiece stores
Neckwear stores

Cross-References. Establishments primarily engaged in--

- Retailing specialized lines of clothing via electronic home shopping, mail-order, or direct sale--are classified in Subsector 454, Nonstore Retailers;
- Retailing precious jewelry and watches--are classified in Industry 448310, Jewelry Stores;
- Retailing used clothing accessories--are classified in Industry 453310, Used Merchandise Stores;
- Retailing luggage, briefcases, trunks, or these products in combination with a general line of leather items (except leather apparel), known as luggage and leather goods stores--are classified in Industry 448320, Luggage and Leather Goods Stores; and
- Retailing leather apparel--are classified in Industry 448190, Other Clothing Stores.

44819 Other Clothing Stores
See industry description for 448190.

448190 Other Clothing Stores

This industry comprises establishments primarily engaged in retailing specialized lines of new clothing (except general lines of men's, women's, children's, infants', and family clothing). These establishments may provide basic alterations, such as hemming, taking in or letting out seams, or lengthening or shortening sleeves.

Illustrative Examples:

Bridal gown (except custom) shops
Leather coat stores
Costume shops
Lingerie stores
Fur apparel stores
Swimwear stores
Hosiery stores
Uniform (except athletic) stores

Cross-References. Establishments primarily engaged in--

- Retailing specialized apparel via electronic home shopping, mail-order, or direct sale--are classified in Subsector 454, Nonstore Retailers;
- Retailing custom apparel and accessories made on the premises--are classified in Subsector 315, Apparel Manufacturing;
- Retailing new men's and boys' clothing--are classified in Industry 448110, Men's Clothing Stores;
- Retailing new women's, misses', and juniors' clothing, including maternity wear--are classified in Industry 448120, Women's Clothing Stores;
- Retailing new children's and infants' clothing--are classified in Industry 448130, Children's and Infants' Clothing Stores;
- Retailing new clothing for all genders or age groups--are classified in Industry 448140, Family Clothing Stores;
- Retailing athletic uniforms--are classified in Industry 451110, Sporting Goods Stores;
- Retailing secondhand clothes--are classified in Industry 453310, Used Merchandise Stores;

T—Canadian, Mexican, and United States industries are comparable.

- Retailing luggage, briefcases, trunks, or these products in combination with a general line of leather items (except leather apparel), known as luggage and leather goods stores--are classified in Industry 448320, Luggage and Leather Goods Stores; and
- Providing clothing alterations and repair--are classified in Industry 811490, Other Personal and Household Goods Repair and Maintenance.

4482 Shoe Stores

44821 Shoe Stores
See industry description for 448210.

448210 Shoe Stores

This industry comprises establishments primarily engaged in retailing all types of new footwear (except hosiery and specialty sports footwear, such as golf shoes, bowling shoes, and spiked shoes). Establishments primarily engaged in retailing new tennis shoes or sneakers are included in this industry.

Cross-References. Establishments primarily engaged in--

- Retailing footwear via electronic home shopping, mail-order, or direct sale--are classified in Subsector 454, Nonstore Retailers;
- Retailing hosiery--are classified in Industry 448190, Other Clothing Stores;
- Retailing new specialty sports footwear (e.g., bowling shoes, golf shoes, spiked shoes)--are classified in Industry 451110, Sporting Goods Stores; and
- Retailing used footwear--are classified in Industry 453310, Used Merchandise Stores.

4483 Jewelry, Luggage, and Leather Goods Stores

This industry group comprises establishments primarily engaged in retailing new jewelry (except costume jewelry); new sterling and plated silverware; new watches and clocks; and new luggage with or without a general line of new leather goods and accessories, such as hats, gloves, handbags, ties, and belts.

44831 Jewelry Stores
See industry description for 448310.

448310 Jewelry Stores

This industry comprises establishments primarily engaged in retailing one or more of the following items: (1) new jewelry (except costume jewelry); (2) new sterling and plated silverware; and (3) new watches and clocks. Also included are establishments retailing these new products in combination with lapidary work and/or repair services.

Cross-References. Establishments primarily engaged in--

- Retailing new costume jewelry--are classified in Industry 448150, Clothing Accessories Stores;
- Retailing jewelry via electronic home shopping, mail-order, or direct sale--are classified in Subsector 454, Nonstore Retailers;
- Retailing antique or used jewelry, silverware, and watches and clocks--are classified in Industry 453310, Used Merchandise Stores;
- Providing jewelry or watch and clock repair without retailing new jewelry or watches and clocks--are classified in Industry 811490, Other Personal and Household Goods Repair and Maintenance; and
- Cutting and setting gem stones--are classified in Industry 339910, Jewelry and Silverware Manufacturing.

44832 Luggage and Leather Goods Stores
See industry description for 448320.

T—Canadian, Mexican, and United States industries are comparable.

448320 Luggage and Leather Goods Stores

This industry comprises establishments known as luggage and leather goods stores primarily engaged in retailing new luggage, briefcases, and trunks, or retailing these new products in combination with a general line of leather items (except leather apparel), such as belts, gloves, and handbags.

Cross-References. Establishments primarily engaged in--

- Retailing luggage and leather goods via electronic home shopping, mail-order, or direct sale--are classified in Subsector 454, Nonstore Retailers;
- Retailing used luggage and leather goods--are classified in Industry 453310, Used Merchandise Stores;
- Retailing single or combination lines of new clothing accessories (e.g., gloves, handbags, or leather belts)--are classified in Industry 448150, Clothing Accessories Stores; and
- Retailing new leather coats--are classified in Industry 448190, Other Clothing Stores.

451 Sporting Goods, Hobby, Musical Instrument, and Book Stores

Industries in the Sporting Goods, Hobby, Musical Instrument, and Book Stores subsector are engaged in retailing and providing expertise on the use of sporting equipment or supplies for other specific leisure activities, such as needlework and musical instruments. Book stores are also included in this subsector.

4511 Sporting Goods, Hobby, and Musical Instrument Stores

This industry group comprises establishments primarily engaged in retailing new sporting goods, games and toys, and musical instruments.

45111 Sporting Goods Stores
See industry description for 451110.

451110 Sporting Goods Stores

This industry comprises establishments primarily engaged in retailing new sporting goods, such as bicycles and bicycle parts; camping equipment; exercise and fitness equipment; athletic uniforms; specialty sports footwear; and other sporting goods, equipment, and accessories.

Illustrative Examples:

Athletic uniform supply stores
Fishing supply stores
Bicycle (except motorized) shops
Golf pro shops
Bowling equipment and supply stores
Saddlery stores
Diving equipment stores
Sporting goods (e.g., scuba, skiing, outdoor) stores
Exercise equipment stores
Sporting gun shops

Cross-References. Establishments primarily engaged in--

- Retailing sporting goods via electronic home shopping, mail-order, or direct sale--are classified in Subsector 454, Nonstore Retailers;
- Retailing new or used campers (pick-up coaches) and camping trailers--are classified in Industry 441210, Recreational Vehicle Dealers;
- Retailing new or used snowmobiles, motorized bicycles, and motorized golf carts--are classified in U.S. Industry 441228, Motorcycle, ATV, and All Other Motor Vehicle Dealers;
- Retailing new shoes (except specialty sports footwear, such as golf shoes, bowling shoes, and spiked shoes)--are classified in Industry 448210, Shoe Stores;
- Repairing or servicing sporting goods, without retailing new sporting goods--are classified in Industry 811490, Other Personal and Household Goods Repair and Maintenance; and

~~T—Canadian, Mexican, and Unit~~ed States industries are comparable.

- Retailing used sporting goods and used bicycles--are classified in Industry 453310, Used Merchandise Stores.

45112 Hobby, Toy, and Game Stores
See industry description for 451120.

451120 Hobby, Toy, and Game Stores

This industry comprises establishments primarily engaged in retailing new toys, games, and hobby and craft supplies (except needlecraft).

Cross-References. Establishments primarily engaged in--

- Retailing toys, games, and hobby and craft supplies via electronic home shopping, mail-order, or direct sale--are classified in Subsector 454, Nonstore Retailers;
- Retailing artists' supplies or collectors' items, such as coins, stamps, autographs, and cards--are classified in U.S. Industry 453998, All Other Miscellaneous Store Retailers (except Tobacco Stores);
- Retailing new computer software (e.g., game software)--are classified in U.S. Industry 443142, Electronics Stores;
- Retailing used toys, games, and hobby supplies--are classified in Industry 453310, Used Merchandise Stores; and
- Retailing new sewing supplies, fabrics, and needlework accessories--are classified in Industry 451130, Sewing, Needlework, and Piece Goods Stores.

45113 Sewing, Needlework, and Piece Goods Stores
See industry description for 451130.

451130 Sewing, Needlework, and Piece Goods Stores

This industry comprises establishments primarily engaged in retailing new sewing supplies, fabrics, patterns, yarns, and other needlework accessories or retailing these products in combination with selling new sewing machines.

Illustrative Examples:

Fabric shops
Sewing supply stores
Needlecraft sewing supply stores
Upholstery materials stores

Cross-References. Establishments primarily engaged in--

- Retailing sewing supplies via electronic home shopping, mail-order, or direct sale--are classified in Subsector 454, Nonstore Retailers;
- Retailing new sewing machines only and in combination with retailing other new appliances--are classified in U.S. Industry 443141, Household Appliance Stores; and
- Retailing used sewing, needlework, and piece goods--are classified in Industry 453310, Used Merchandise Stores.

45114 Musical Instrument and Supplies Stores
See industry description for 451140.

451140 Musical Instrument and Supplies Stores

This industry comprises establishments primarily engaged in retailing new musical instruments, sheet music, and related supplies; or retailing these new products in combination with musical instrument repair, rental, or music instruction.

~~T—Canadian, Mexican, and Unit~~ed States industries are comparable.

Illustrative Examples:

Musical instrument stores
Sheet music stores
Piano stores

Cross-References. Establishments primarily engaged in--

- Retailing musical instruments, sheet music, and related supplies via electronic home shopping, mail-order, or direct sale--are classified in Subsector 454, Nonstore Retailers;
- Retailing new musical recordings--are classified in U.S. Industry 443142, Electronics Stores; and
- Retailing used musical instruments (including used rare musical instruments), sheet music, and related supplies--are classified in Industry 453310, Used Merchandise Stores.

4512 Book Stores and News Dealers 45121

Book Stores and News Dealers

This industry comprises establishments primarily engaged in retailing new books, newspapers, magazines, and other periodicals.

Cross-References. Establishments primarily engaged in--

- Retailing newspapers, magazines, and other periodicals via electronic home shopping, mail-order, or direct sale--are classified in Subsector 454, Nonstore Retailers;
- Home delivery of newspapers--are classified in Industry 45439, Other Direct Selling Establishments; and
- Retailing used books, newspapers, magazines, and other periodicals--are classified in Industry 45331, Used Merchandise Stores.

451211 Book Stores

This U.S. industry comprises establishments primarily engaged in retailing new books.

Cross-References. Establishments primarily engaged in--

- Retailing books via electronic home shopping, mail-order, or direct sale--are classified in Subsector 454, Non-store Retailers; and
- Retailing used books (including used rare books)--are classified in Industry 453310, Used Merchandise Stores.

451212 News Dealers and Newsstands

This U.S. industry comprises establishments primarily engaged in retailing current newspapers, magazines, and other periodicals.

Cross-References. Establishments primarily engaged in--

- Home delivery of newspapers--are classified in Industry 454390, Other Direct Selling Establishments;
- Retailing newspapers and periodicals by mail-order--are classified in Industry 454110, Electronic Shopping and Mail-Order Houses; and
- Retailing used newspapers, magazines, and other periodicals--are classified in Industry 453310, Used Merchandise Stores.

T—Canadian, Mexican, and United States industries are comparable.

452 General Merchandise Stores

Industries in the General Merchandise Stores subsector retail new general merchandise from fixed point-of-sale locations. Establishments in this subsector are unique in that they have the equipment and staff capable of retailing a large variety of goods from a single location. This includes a variety of display equipment and staff trained to provide information on many lines of products.

4522 Department Stores

45221 Department Stores

See industry description for 452210.

452210 Department Stores

This industry comprises establishments known as department stores that have separate departments for general lines of new merchandise, such as apparel, jewelry, home furnishings, and toys, with no one merchandise line predominating. Department stores may sell perishable groceries, such as fresh fruits, vegetables, and dairy products, but such sales are insignificant. Department stores may have separate customer checkout areas in each department, central customer checkout areas, or both.

Cross-References. Establishments primarily engaged in--

- Retailing a general line of merchandise via electronic home shopping, mail-order, or direct sale--are classified in Subsector 454, Nonstore Retailers;
- Retailing apparel without a significant amount of housewares or general merchandise--are classified in Subsector 448, Clothing and Clothing Accessories Stores;
- Retailing a general line of merchandise in combination with a general line of perishable groceries, known as warehouse clubs, superstores, or supercenters--are classified in U.S. Industry 452311, Warehouse Clubs and Supercenters; and
- Retailing used merchandise--are classified in Industry 453310, Used Merchandise Stores.

4523 General Merchandise Stores, including Warehouse Clubs and Supercenters

45231 General Merchandise Stores, including Warehouse Clubs and Supercenters

This industry comprises establishments primarily engaged in retailing new goods in general merchandise stores (except department stores). These establishments retail a general line of new merchandise, such as apparel, automotive parts, dry goods, hardware, groceries, housewares, and home furnishings, with no one merchandise line predominating. Establishments known as warehouse clubs, superstores, or supercenters are included in this industry.

Illustrative Examples:

Dollar stores
General merchandise catalog showrooms (except catalog mail-order)
General merchandise trading posts
General stores
Home and auto supply stores
Superstores (i.e., food and general merchandise)
Variety stores
Warehouse clubs (i.e., food and general merchandise)

Cross-References. Establishments primarily engaged in--

- Retailing a general line of merchandise via electronic home shopping, mail-order, or direct sale--are classified in Subsector 454, Nonstore Retailers;
- Retailing a general line of food, known as supermarkets and grocery stores--are classified in Industry 44511, Supermarkets and Other Grocery (except Convenience) Stores;

T—Canadian, Mexican, and United States industries are comparable.

- Retailing automotive parts--are classified in Industry 44131, Automotive Parts and Accessories Stores;
- Retailing a general line of new merchandise, known as department stores--are classified in Industry 45221, Department Stores;
- Retailing merchandise in catalog showrooms of mail-order houses--are classified in Industry 45411, Electronic Shopping and Mail-Order Houses;
- Retailing a general line of new hardware items, known as hardware stores--are classified in Industry 44413, Hardware Stores;
- Retailing a general line of new home repair and improvement materials and supplies, known as home centers--are classified in Industry 44411, Home Centers; and
- Retailing used merchandise--are classified in Industry 45331, Used Merchandise Stores.

452311 Warehouse Clubs and Supercenters

This U.S. industry comprises establishments known as warehouse clubs, superstores, or supercenters, primarily engaged in retailing a general line of groceries, including a significant amount and variety of fresh fruits, vegetables, dairy products, meats, and other perishable groceries, in combination with a general line of new merchandise, such as apparel, furniture, and appliances.

Cross-References. Establishments primarily engaged in--

- Retailing a general line of merchandise via electronic home shopping, mail-order, or direct sale--are classified in Subsector 454, Nonstore Retailers;
- Retailing a general line of food, known as supermarkets and grocery stores--are classified in Industry 445110, Supermarkets and Other Grocery (except Convenience) Stores;
- Retailing a general line of new merchandise, known as department stores--are classified in Industry 452210, Department Stores;
- Retailing a general line of new merchandise, except department stores, warehouse clubs, superstores, and supercenters--are classified in U.S. Industry 452319, All Other General Merchandise Stores; and
- Retailing used merchandise--are classified in Industry 453310, Used Merchandise Stores.

452319 All Other General Merchandise Stores

This U.S. industry comprises establishments primarily engaged in retailing new goods in general merchandise stores (except department stores, warehouse clubs, superstores, and supercenters). These establishments retail a general line of new merchandise, such as apparel, automotive parts, dry goods, hardware, housewares or home furnishings, and other lines in limited amounts, with none of the lines predominating.

Illustrative Examples:

Dollar stores
General merchandise catalog showrooms (except catalog mail-order)
General merchandise trading posts
General stores
Home and auto supply stores
Variety stores

Cross-References. Establishments primarily engaged in--

- Retailing a general line of merchandise via electronic home shopping, mail-order, or direct sale--are classified in Subsector 454, Nonstore Retailers;
- Retailing automotive parts--are classified in Industry 441310, Automotive Parts and Accessories Stores;
- Retailing a general line of new merchandise, known as department stores--are classified in Industry 452210, Department Stores;
- Retailing a general line of merchandise in combination with a general line of perishable groceries, known as warehouse clubs, superstores, or supercenters--are classified in U.S. Industry 452311, Warehouse Clubs and Supercenters;

T—Canadian, Mexican, and United States industries are comparable.

- Retailing merchandise in catalog showrooms of mail-order houses--are classified in Industry 454110, Electronic Shopping and Mail-Order Houses;
- Retailing a general line of new hardware items, known as hardware stores--are classified in Industry 444130, Hardware Stores;
- Retailing a general line of new home repair and improvement materials and supplies, known as home centers--are classified in Industry 444110, Home Centers; and
- Retailing used merchandise--are classified in Industry 453310, Used Merchandise Stores.

453 Miscellaneous Store Retailers

Industries in the Miscellaneous Store Retailers subsector retail merchandise from fixed point-of-sale locations (except new or used motor vehicles and parts; new furniture and home furnishings; new appliances and electronic products; new building materials and garden equipment and supplies; food and beverages; health and personal care goods; gasoline; new clothing and accessories; and new sporting goods, hobby goods, books, and music). Establishments in this subsector include stores with unique characteristics, such as florists, used merchandise stores, and pet and pet supply stores.

4531 Florists

45311 Florists
See industry description for 453110.

453110 Florists

This industry comprises establishments known as florists primarily engaged in retailing cut flowers, floral arrangements, and potted plants purchased from others. These establishments usually prepare the arrangements they sell.

Cross-References. Establishments primarily engaged in--

- Retailing flowers or nursery stock grown on premises--are classified in Industry 11142, Nursery and Floriculture Production;
- Retailing trees, shrubs, plants, seeds, bulbs, and sod grown elsewhere--are classified in Industry 444220, Nursery, Garden Center, and Farm Supply Stores; and
- Retailing flowers via electronic home shopping, mail-order, or direct sale--are classified in Subsector 454, Nonstore Retailers.

4532 Office Supplies, Stationery, and Gift Stores

This industry group comprises establishments primarily engaged in retailing new office supplies, stationery, gifts, novelty merchandise, and souvenirs.

45321 Office Supplies and Stationery Stores
See industry description for 453210.

453210 Office Supplies and Stationery Stores

This industry comprises establishments primarily engaged in one or more of the following: (1) retailing new stationery, school supplies, and office supplies; (2) retailing a combination of new office equipment, furniture, and supplies; and (3) retailing new office equipment, furniture, and supplies in combination with selling new computers.

Cross-References. Establishments primarily engaged in--

- Retailing stationery, school supplies, and office supplies via electronic shopping, mail-order, or direct sale--are classified in Subsector 454, Nonstore Retailers;

T—Canadian, Mexican, and United States industries are comparable.

- Retailing greeting cards--are classified in Industry 453220, Gift, Novelty, and Souvenir Stores;
- Retailing new computers without retailing other consumer-type electronic products or office equipment, furniture, and supplies--are classified in U.S. Industry 443142, Electronics Stores;
- Printing business forms--are classified in Industry 32311, Printing;
- Retailing new office furniture--are classified in Industry 442110, Furniture Stores; and
- Retailing used office supplies--are classified in Industry 453310, Used Merchandise Stores.

45322 Gift, Novelty, and Souvenir Stores
See industry description for 453220.

453220 Gift, Novelty, and Souvenir Stores

This industry comprises establishments primarily engaged in retailing new gifts, novelty merchandise, souvenirs, greeting cards, seasonal and holiday decorations, and curios.

Illustrative Examples:

Balloon shops
Greeting card shops
Christmas stores
Novelty shops
Curio shops
Souvenir shops
Gift shops
Fruit basket or fruit bouquet stores

Cross-References. Establishments primarily engaged in--

- Retailing gifts and novelties via electronic home shopping, mail-order, or direct sale--are classified in Subsector 454, Nonstore Retailers;
- Retailing stationery--are classified in Industry 453210, Office Supplies and Stationery Stores; and
- Retailing used curios and novelties--are classified in Industry 453310, Used Merchandise Stores.

4533 Used Merchandise Stores

45331 Used Merchandise Stores
See industry description for 453310.

453310 Used Merchandise Stores

This industry comprises establishments primarily engaged in retailing used merchandise, antiques, and secondhand goods (except motor vehicles, such as automobiles, RVs, motorcycles, and boats; motor vehicle parts; tires; and mobile homes).

Illustrative Examples:

Antique shops
Used household-type appliance stores
Used book stores
Used merchandise thrift shops
Used clothing stores
Used sporting goods stores

Cross-References. Establishments primarily engaged in--

- Retailing used merchandise via electronic home shopping, mail-order, or direct sale--are classified in Subsector 454, Nonstore Retailers;
- Operating pawnshops--are classified in U.S. Industry 522298, All Other Nondepository Credit Intermediation;
- Retailing used automobiles--are classified in Industry 441120, Used Car Dealers;
- Retailing used automobile parts (except tires and tubes)--are classified in Industry 441310, Automotive Parts and Accessories Stores;

T—Canadian, Mexican, and United States industries are comparable.

- Retailing used tires--are classified in Industry 441320, Tire Dealers;
- Retailing used mobile homes--are classified in Industry 453930, Manufactured (Mobile) Home Dealers;
- Retailing used recreational vehicles--are classified in Industry 441210, Recreational Vehicle Dealers;
- Retailing used boats--are classified in U.S. Industry 441222, Boat Dealers;
- Retailing used motorcycles, aircraft, snowmobiles, and utility trailers--are classified in U.S. Industry 441228, Motorcycle, ATV, and All Other Motor Vehicle Dealers; and
- Retailing a general line of used merchandise on an auction basis (except electronic auctions)--are classified in U.S. Industry 453998, All Other Miscellaneous Store Retailers (except Tobacco Stores).

4539 Other Miscellaneous Store Retailers

This industry group comprises establishments primarily engaged in retailing new miscellaneous specialty store merchandise (except motor vehicle and parts dealers; furniture and home furnishings stores; consumer-type electronics and appliance stores; building material and garden equipment and supplies dealers; food and beverage stores; health and personal care stores; gasoline stations; clothing and clothing accessories stores; sporting goods, hobby, book, and music stores; general merchandise stores; florists; office supplies, stationery, and gift stores; and used merchandise stores). This industry group also includes establishments primarily engaged in retailing a general line of new and used merchandise on an auction basis (except electronic auctions).

45391 Pet and Pet Supplies Stores
See industry description for 453910.

453910 Pet and Pet Supplies Stores

This industry comprises establishments primarily engaged in retailing pets, pet foods, and pet supplies.

Cross-References. Establishments primarily engaged in--

- Retailing pets, pet foods, and pet supplies via electronic home shopping, mail-order, or direct sale--are classified in Subsector 454, Nonstore Retailers;
- Providing pet grooming and boarding services--are classified in Industry 812910, Pet Care (except Veterinary) Services; and
- Providing veterinary services--are classified in Industry 541940, Veterinary Services.

45392 Art Dealers
See industry description for 453920.

453920 Art Dealers

This industry comprises establishments primarily engaged in retailing original and limited edition art works. Included in this industry are establishments primarily engaged in displaying works of art for retail sale in art galleries.

Cross-References. Establishments primarily engaged in--

- Retailing original and limited edition art works via electronic home shopping, mail-order, or direct sale--are classified in Subsector 454, Nonstore Retailers;
- Retailing art reproductions (except limited editions)--are classified in U.S. Industry 442299, All Other Home Furnishings Stores;
- Retailing artists' supplies--are classified in U.S. Industry 453998, All Other Miscellaneous Store Retailers (except Tobacco Stores); and
- Displaying works of art not for retail sale in art galleries--are classified in Industry 712110, Museums.

45393 Manufactured (Mobile) Home Dealers
See industry description for 453930.

T—Canadian, Mexican, and United States industries are comparable.

453930 Manufactured (Mobile) Home Dealers

This industry comprises establishments primarily engaged in retailing new and/or used manufactured homes (i.e., mobile homes), parts, and equipment.

Cross-References. Establishments primarily engaged in--

- Retailing new or used motor homes, campers, and travel trailers--are classified in Industry 441210, Recreational Vehicle Dealers; and
- Retailing prefabricated buildings and kits without construction--are classified in Industry 444190, Other Building Material Dealers.

45399 All Other Miscellaneous Store Retailers

This industry comprises establishments primarily engaged in retailing specialized lines of merchandise (except motor vehicle and parts dealers; furniture and home furnishings stores; electronics and appliance stores; building material and garden equipment and supplies dealers; food and beverage stores; health and personal care stores; gasoline stations; clothing and clothing accessories stores; sporting goods, hobby, book, and music stores; general merchandise stores; florists; office supplies, stationery, and gift stores; used merchandise stores; pet and pet supplies stores; art dealers; and manufactured home (i.e., mobile home) dealers). This industry also includes establishments primarily engaged in retailing a general line of new and used merchandise on an auction basis (except electronic auctions).

Illustrative Examples:

Art supply stores
Swimming pool supply stores, new
Tobacco stores
Cemetery memorial (e.g., markers, headstones, vaults) dealers Cigar stores

Cross-References. Establishments primarily engaged in--

- Retailing merchandise via electronic home shopping, mail-order, or direct sale--are classified in Subsector 454, Nonstore Retailers;
- Retailing merchandise via electronic auctions--are classified in Industry 45411, Electronic Shopping and Mail-Order Houses;
- Auctioning on the location of others as independent auctioneers--are classified in Industry 56199, All Other Support Services;
- Retailing pets and pet supplies--are classified in Industry 45391, Pet and Pet Supplies Stores;
- Retailing original and limited edition art works--are classified in Industry 45392, Art Dealers;
- Retailing manufactured homes (i.e., mobile homes)--are classified in Industry 45393, Manufactured (Mobile) Home Dealers;
- Retailing new books--are classified in Industry 45121, Book Stores and News Dealers;
- Retailing new jewelry (except costume jewelry)--are classified in Industry 44831, Jewelry Stores;
- Retailing new costume jewelry--are classified in Industry 44815, Clothing Accessories Stores;
- Operating pawnshops--are classified in Industry 52229, Other Nondepository Credit Intermediation; and
- Retailing used merchandise (except automobiles, RVs, mobile homes, motorcycles, boats, motor vehicle parts, tires, aircraft, snowmobiles, and utility trailers)--are classified in Industry 45331, Used Merchandise Stores.

453991 Tobacco Stores

This U.S. industry comprises establishments primarily engaged in retailing cigarettes, cigars, tobacco, pipes, and other smokers' supplies.

T—Canadian, Mexican, and United States industries are comparable.

Illustrative Examples:

Cigar stores
Smokers' supply stores
Cigarette stands (i.e., permanent)
Tobacco stores

Cross-References. Establishments primarily engaged in--

- Retailing tobacco products and smokers' supplies via electronic home shopping, mail-order, or direct sale--are classified in Subsector 454, Nonstore Retailers; and
- Retailing electronic cigarettes--are classified in U.S. Industry 453998, All Other Miscellaneous Store Retailers (except Tobacco Stores).

453998 All Other Miscellaneous Store Retailers (except Tobacco Stores)

This U.S. industry comprises establishments primarily engaged in retailing specialized lines of merchandise (except motor vehicle and parts dealers; furniture and home furnishings stores; electronics and appliance stores; building material and garden equipment and supplies dealers; food and beverage stores; health and personal care stores; gasoline stations; clothing and clothing accessories stores; sporting goods, hobby, book and music stores; general merchandise stores; florists; office supplies, stationery, and gift stores; used merchandise stores; pet and pet supplies stores; art dealers; manufactured home (i.e., mobile home) dealers; and tobacco stores). This industry also includes establishments primarily engaged in retailing a general line of new and used merchandise on an auction basis (except electronic auctions).

Illustrative Examples:

Art supply stores
General merchandise auction houses
Candle shops
Home security equipment stores
Cemetery memorial (e.g., headstones, markers, vaults) dealers
Hot tub stores
Collectors' items (e.g., autograph, coin, card, stamp) shops (except used rare items)
Swimming pool supply stores
Fireworks shops (permanent location)
Trophy (e.g., awards and plaques) shops
Flower shops, artificial or dried

Cross-References. Establishments primarily engaged in--

- Retailing specialized lines of merchandise via electronic home shopping, mail-order, or direct sale--are classified in Subsector 454, Nonstore Retailers;
- Retailing merchandise via electronic auctions--are classified in Industry 454110, Electronic Shopping and Mail-Order Houses;
- Auctioning on the location of others as independent auctioneers--are classified in Industry 561990, All Other Support Services;
- Retailing pets and pet supplies--are classified in Industry 453910, Pet and Pet Supplies Stores;
- Retailing original and limited edition art works--are classified in Industry 453920, Art Dealers;
- Retailing manufactured homes (i.e., mobile homes)--are classified in Industry 453930, Manufactured (Mobile) Home Dealers;
- Retailing cigarettes, cigars, tobacco, pipes, and other smokers' supplies--are classified in U.S. Industry 453991, Tobacco Stores;
- Retailing antiques--are classified in Industry 453310, Used Merchandise Stores;
- Retailing new books--are classified in U.S. Industry 451211, Book Stores;
- Retailing new jewelry (except costume jewelry)--are classified in Industry 448310, Jewelry Stores; and
- Retailing new costume jewelry--are classified in Industry 448150, Clothing Accessories Stores.

T—Canadian, Mexican, and United States industries are comparable.

454 Nonstore Retailers

Industries in the Nonstore Retailers subsector retail merchandise using methods, such as the broadcasting of infomercials, the broadcasting and publishing of direct-response advertising, the publishing of paper and electronic catalogs, door-to-door solicitation, in-home demonstration, selling from portable stalls, and distribution through vending machines. Establishments in this subsector include mail-order houses, vending machine operators, home delivery sales, door-to-door sales, party plan sales, electronic shopping, and sales through portable stalls (e.g., street vendors, except food). Establishments engaged in the direct sale (i.e., nonstore) of products, such as home heating oil dealers and newspaper delivery service providers, are included in this subsector.

4541 Electronic Shopping and Mail-Order Houses

45411 Electronic Shopping and Mail-Order Houses

See industry description for 454110.

454110 Electronic Shopping and Mail-Order Houses

This industry comprises establishments primarily engaged in retailing all types of merchandise using nonstore means, such as catalogs, toll free telephone numbers, or electronic media, such as interactive television or the Internet. Included in this industry are establishments primarily engaged in retailing from catalog showrooms of mail-order houses.

Illustrative Examples:

Catalog (i.e., order-taking) offices of mail-order houses
Collectors' items, mail-order houses
Computer software, mail-order houses
Home shopping television orders
Internet auction sites, retail
Mail-order book clubs (not publishing)
Mail-order houses
Web retailers

Cross-References. Establishments primarily engaged in--

- Store retailing or a combination of store retailing and nonstore retailing in the same establishment--are classified in Sector 44-45, Retail Trade, based on the classification of the store portion of the activity;
- Retailing a general line of new and used merchandise on an auction basis from physical auction sites--are classified in U.S. Industry 453998, All Other Miscellaneous Store Retailers (except Tobacco Stores);
- Facilitating business-to-business electronic sales of new and used merchandise on an auction basis using the Internet--are classified in Industry 425110, Business to Business Electronic Markets;
- Providing telemarketing (e.g., telephone marketing) services for others--are classified in U.S. Industry 561422, Telemarketing Bureaus and Other Contact Centers;
- Providing Internet publishing of classified ads--are classified in Industry 519130, Internet Publishing and Broadcasting and Web Search Portals; and
- Hosting Internet retail sites without performing associated activities such as payment processing or fulfillment--are classified in Industry 518210, Data Processing, Hosting, and Related Services.

4542 Vending Machine Operators

45421 Vending Machine Operators

See industry description for 454210.

454210 Vending Machine Operators

This industry comprises establishments primarily engaged in retailing merchandise through vending machines that they service.

T—Canadian, Mexican, and United States industries are comparable.

Cross-References. Establishments primarily engaged in--

- Supplying and servicing coin-operated photobooths, rest rooms, and lockers--are classified in Industry 812990, All Other Personal Services; and
- Supplying and servicing coin-operated amusement and gambling devices in places of business operated by others--are classified in Subsector 713, Amusement, Gambling, and Recreation Industries.

4543 Direct Selling Establishments

This industry group comprises establishments primarily engaged in nonstore retailing (except electronic, mail-order, or vending machine sales). These establishments typically go to the customers' location rather than the customer coming to them (e.g., door-to-door sales, home parties). Examples of establishments in this industry are home delivery newspaper routes; home delivery of heating oil, liquefied petroleum (LP) gas, and other fuels; locker meat provisioners; frozen food and freezer meal plan providers; coffee-break supplies providers; and bottled water or water softener services.

45431 Fuel Dealers
See industry description for 454310.

454310 Fuel Dealers

This industry comprises establishments primarily engaged in retailing heating oil, liquefied petroleum (LP) gas, and other fuels via direct selling.

Cross-References. Establishments primarily engaged in--

- Providing oil burner repair services--are classified in U.S. Industry 811411, Home and Garden Equipment Repair and Maintenance; and
- Installing oil burners--are classified in Industry 238220, Plumbing, Heating, and Air-Conditioning Contractors.

45439 Other Direct Selling Establishments See industry description for 454390.

454390 Other Direct Selling Establishments

This industry comprises establishments primarily engaged in retailing merchandise (except food for immediate consumption and fuel) via direct sale to the customer by means, such as in-house sales (i.e., party plan merchandising), truck or wagon sales, and portable stalls (i.e., street vendors).

Illustrative Examples:

Direct selling bottled water providers
Direct selling home delivery newspaper routes
Direct selling coffee-break supplies providers
Direct selling locker meat provisioners
Direct selling frozen food and freezer meal plan providers
Direct selling party plan merchandisers

Cross-References. Establishments primarily engaged in--

- Preparing and selling meals and snacks for immediate consumption from motorized vehicles or nonmotorized carts, catering a route--are classified in Industry 722330, Mobile Food Services; and
- Retailing heating oil, liquefied petroleum (LP) gas, and other fuels via direct sale--are classified in Industry 454310, Fuel Dealers.

T—Canadian, Mexican, and United States industries are comparable.

Sector 48-49--Transportation and Warehousing[T]

The Sector as a Whole

The Transportation and Warehousing sector includes industries providing transportation of passengers and cargo, warehousing and storage for goods, scenic and sightseeing transportation, and support activities related to modes of transportation. Establishments in these industries use transportation equipment or transportation related facilities as a productive asset. The type of equipment depends on the mode of transportation. The modes of transportation are air, rail, water, road, and pipeline.

The Transportation and Warehousing sector distinguishes three basic types of activities: subsectors for each mode of transportation, a subsector for warehousing and storage, and a subsector for establishments providing support activities for transportation. In addition, there are subsectors for establishments that provide passenger transportation for scenic and sightseeing purposes, postal services, and courier services.

A separate subsector for support activities is established in the sector because, first, support activities for transportation are inherently multimodal, such as freight transportation arrangement, or have multimodal aspects. Secondly, there are production process similarities among the support activity industries.

One of the support activities identified in the Support Activities for Transportation subsector is the routine repair and maintenance of transportation equipment (e.g., aircraft at an airport, railroad rolling stock at a railroad terminal, or ships at a harbor or port facility). Such establishments do not perform complete overhauling or rebuilding of transportation equipment (i.e., periodic restoration of transportation equipment to original design specifications) or transportation equipment conversion (i.e., major modification to systems). An establishment that primarily performs factory (or shipyard) overhauls, rebuilding, or conversions of aircraft, railroad rolling stock, or ships is classified in Subsector 336, Transportation Equipment Manufacturing, according to the type of equipment.

Many of the establishments in this sector often operate on networks, with physical facilities, labor forces, and equipment spread over an extensive geographic area.

Warehousing establishments in this sector are distinguished from merchant wholesaling in that the warehouse establishments do not sell the goods.

Excluded from this sector are establishments primarily engaged in providing travel agent services that support transportation and other establishments, such as hotels, businesses, and government agencies. These establishments are classified in Sector 56, Administrative and Support and Waste Management and Remediation Services. Also, establishments primarily engaged in providing rental and leasing of transportation equipment without operator are classified in Subsector 532, Rental and Leasing Services.

481 Air Transportation[T]

Industries in the Air Transportation subsector provide air transportation of passengers and/or cargo using aircraft, such as airplanes and helicopters. The subsector distinguishes scheduled from nonscheduled air transportation. Scheduled air carriers fly regular routes on regular schedules and operate even if flights are only partially loaded. Nonscheduled carriers often operate during nonpeak time slots at busy airports. These establishments have more flexibility with respect to choice of airport, hours of operation, load factors, and similar operational characteristics. Nonscheduled carriers provide chartered air transportation of passengers, cargo, or specialty flying services. Specialty flying services establishments use general purpose aircraft to provide a variety of specialized flying services.

Scenic and sightseeing air transportation and air courier services are not included in this subsector but are included in Subsector 487, Scenic and Sightseeing Transportation, and in Subsector 492, Couriers and Messengers, respectively. Although these activities may use aircraft, they are different from the activities included in air transportation. Air sightseeing does not usually involve place-to-place transportation; the passenger's flight (e.g., balloon ride, aerial sightseeing) typically starts and ends at the same location. Courier services (individual package or cargo delivery) include more than air transportation; road transportation is usually required to deliver the cargo to the intended recipient.

T—Canadian, Mexican, and United States industries are comparable.

4811 Scheduled Air Transportation[T]

48111 Scheduled Air Transportation[T]

This industry comprises establishments primarily engaged in providing air transportation of passengers and/or cargo over regular routes and on regular schedules. Establishments in this industry operate flights even if partially loaded. Establishments primarily engaged in providing scheduled air transportation of mail on a contract basis are included in this industry.

Illustrative Examples:

Air commuter carriers, scheduled
Scheduled air passenger carriers
Scheduled air cargo carriers (except air couriers)

Cross-References. Establishments primarily engaged in--

- Providing air courier services--are classified in Industry 49211, Couriers and Express Delivery Services;
- Providing air transportation of passengers, cargo, or specialty flying services with no regular routes and regular schedules--are classified in Industry 48121, Nonscheduled Air Transportation; and
- Providing helicopter rides for scenic and sightseeing transportation--are classified in Industry 48799, Scenic and Sightseeing Transportation, Other.

481111 Scheduled Passenger Air Transportation

This U.S. industry comprises establishments primarily engaged in providing air transportation of passengers or passengers and freight over regular routes and on regular schedules. Establishments in this industry operate flights even if partially loaded. Scheduled air passenger carriers including commuter and helicopter carriers (except scenic and sightseeing) are included in this industry.

Cross-References. Establishments primarily engaged in--

- Providing air transportation of passengers or passengers and cargo with no regular routes and regular schedules--are classified in U.S. Industry 481211, Nonscheduled Chartered Passenger Air Transportation;
- Providing helicopter rides for scenic and sightseeing transportation--are classified in Industry 487990, Scenic and Sightseeing Transportation, Other; and
- Providing air transportation of cargo (without transporting passengers) over regular routes and on regular schedules--are classified in U.S. Industry 481112, Scheduled Freight Air Transportation.

481112 Scheduled Freight Air Transportation

This U.S. industry comprises establishments primarily engaged in providing air transportation of cargo without transporting passengers over regular routes and on regular schedules. Establishments in this industry operate flights even if partially loaded. Establishments primarily engaged in providing scheduled air transportation of mail on a contract basis are included in this industry.

Cross-References. Establishments primarily engaged in--

- Providing air courier services--are classified in Industry 492110, Couriers and Express Delivery Services;
- Providing air transportation of cargo with no regular routes and regular schedules--are classified in U.S. Industry 481212, Nonscheduled Chartered Freight Air Transportation; and
- Providing air transportation of passengers or passengers and cargo over regular routes and on regular schedules--are classified in U.S. Industry 481111, Scheduled Passenger Air Transportation.

T—Canadian, Mexican, and United States industries are comparable.

4812 Nonscheduled Air Transportation[T]

48121 Nonscheduled Air Transportation[T]

This industry comprises establishments primarily engaged in (1) providing air transportation of passengers and/or cargo with no regular routes and regular schedules or (2) providing specialty flying services with no regular routes and regular schedules using general purpose aircraft. These establishments have more flexibility with respect to choice of airports, hours of operation, load factors, and similar operational characteristics.

Illustrative Examples:

Air taxi services
Nonscheduled air freight transportation services
Aircraft charter services
Nonscheduled air passenger transportation services

Cross-References. Establishments primarily engaged in--

- Crop dusting using specialized aircraft--are classified in Industry 11511, Support Activities for Crop Production;
- Fighting forest fires using specialized water bombers--are classified in Industry 11531, Support Activities for Forestry;
- Providing air transportation of passengers and/or cargo over regular routes and on regular schedules--are classified in Industry 48111, Scheduled Air Transportation;
- Providing specialized air sightseeing services--are classified in Industry 48799, Scenic and Sightseeing Transportation, Other;
- Aerial gathering of geophysical data--are classified in Industry 54136, Geophysical Surveying and Mapping Services;
- Providing aerial and/or other surveying and mapping services--are classified in Industry 54137, Surveying and Mapping (except Geophysical) Services;
- Providing air ambulance services using specialized equipment--are classified in Industry 62191, Ambulance Services;
- Operating specialized flying schools, including all training for commercial pilots--are classified in Industry 61151, Technical and Trade Schools;
- Operating recreation aviation clubs--are classified in Industry 71399, All Other Amusement and Recreation Industries;
- Operating advocacy aviation clubs--are classified in Industry 81331, Social Advocacy Organizations; and
- Providing air courier services--are classified in Industry 49211, Couriers and Express Delivery Services.

481211 Nonscheduled Chartered Passenger Air Transportation

This U.S. industry comprises establishments primarily engaged in providing air transportation of passengers or passengers and cargo with no regular routes and regular schedules.

Cross-References. Establishments primarily engaged in--

- Providing specialty air transportation or flying services with no regular routes and regular schedules using general purpose aircraft--are classified in U.S. Industry 481219, Other Nonscheduled Air Transportation;
- Providing specialized air sightseeing services--are classified in Industry 487990, Scenic and Sightseeing Transportation, Other;
- Providing air transportation of passengers or passengers and cargo over regular routes and on regular schedules--are classified in U.S. Industry 481111, Scheduled Passenger Air Transportation; and
- Providing air transportation of cargo (without transporting passengers) with no regular routes and schedules--are classified in U.S. Industry 481212, Nonscheduled Chartered Freight Air Transportation.

T—Canadian, Mexican, and United States industries are comparable.

481212 Nonscheduled Chartered Freight Air Transportation

This U.S. industry comprises establishments primarily engaged in providing air transportation of cargo without transporting passengers with no regular routes and regular schedules.

Cross-References. Establishments primarily engaged in--

- Providing specialty air transportation or flying services with no regular routes and regular schedules using general purpose aircraft--are classified in U.S. Industry 481219, Other Nonscheduled Air Transportation;
- Providing air courier services--are classified in Industry 492110, Couriers and Express Delivery Services;
- Providing air transportation of cargo without transporting passengers over regular routes and on regular schedules--are classified in U.S. Industry 481112, Scheduled Freight Air Transportation; and
- Providing air transportation of cargo and passengers with no regular routes and schedules--are classified in U.S. Industry 481211, Nonscheduled Chartered Passenger Air Transportation.

481219 Other Nonscheduled Air Transportation

This U.S. industry comprises establishments primarily engaged in providing air transportation with no regular routes and regular schedules (except nonscheduled chartered passenger and/or cargo air transportation). These establishments provide a variety of specialty air transportation or flying services based on individual customer needs using general purpose aircraft.

Illustrative Examples:

Aircraft charter services (i.e., general purpose aircraft used for a variety of specialty air and flying

Cross-References. Establishments primarily engaged in--

- Providing air transportation of passengers or passengers and cargo with no regular routes and regular schedules--are classified in U.S. Industry 481211, Nonscheduled Chartered Passenger Air Transportation;
- Providing air transportation of cargo without transporting passengers with no regular routes and regular schedules--are classified in U.S. Industry 481212, Nonscheduled Chartered Freight Air Transportation;
- Crop dusting using specialized aircraft--are classified in U.S. Industry 115112, Soil Preparation, Planting, and Cultivating;
- Fighting forest fires using specialized water bombers--are classified in Industry 115310, Support Activities for Forestry;
- Providing specialized air sightseeing services--are classified in Industry 487990, Scenic and Sightseeing Transportation, Other;
- Operating specialized flying schools, including all training for commercial pilots--are classified in U.S. Industry 611512, Flight Training;
- Providing specialized air ambulance services using specialized equipment--are classified in Industry 621910, Ambulance Services;
- Operating recreation aviation clubs--are classified in Industry 713990, All Other Amusement and Recreation Industries;
- Operating advocacy aviation clubs--are classified in U.S. Industry 813319, Other Social Advocacy Organizations;
- Aerial gathering of geophysical data for surveying and mapping--are classified in Industry 541360, Geophysical Surveying and Mapping Services; and
- Providing aerial and/or other surveying and mapping services--are classified in Industry 541370, Surveying and Mapping (except Geophysical) Services.

T—Canadian, Mexican, and United States industries are comparable.

482 Rail Transportation[T]

Industries in the Rail Transportation subsector provide rail transportation of passengers and/or cargo using railroad rolling stock. The railroads in this subsector primarily either operate on networks, with physical facilities, labor force, and equipment spread over an extensive geographic area, or operate over a short distance on a local rail line. Scenic and sightseeing rail transportation and street railroads, commuter rail, and rapid transit are not included in this subsector but are included in Subsector 487, Scenic and Sightseeing Transportation, and Subsector 485, Transit and Ground Passenger Transportation, respectively. Although these activities use railroad rolling stock, they are different from the activities included in rail transportation. Sightseeing and scenic railroads do not usually involve place-to-place transportation; the passenger's trip typically starts and ends at the same location. Commuter railroads operate in a manner more consistent with local and urban transit and are often part of integrated transit systems.

4821 Rail Transportation[T]

48211 Rail Transportation[T]

This industry comprises establishments primarily engaged in operating railroads (except street railroads, commuter rail, urban rapid transit, and scenic and sightseeing trains). Line-haul railroads and short-line railroads are included in this industry.

Cross-References. Establishments primarily engaged in--

- Operating street railroads, commuter rail, and urban rapid transit systems--are classified in Industry Group 4851, Urban Transit Systems;
- Operating scenic and sightseeing trains--are classified in Industry 48711, Scenic and Sightseeing Transportation, Land; and
- Operating switching and terminal facilities as separate establishments--are classified in Industry 48821, Support Activities for Rail Transportation.

482111 Line-Haul Railroads

This U.S. industry comprises establishments known as line-haul railroads primarily engaged in operating railroads for the transport of passengers and/or cargo over a long distance within a rail network. These establishments provide for the intercity movement of trains between the terminals and stations on main and branch lines of a line-haul rail network (except for local switching services).

Cross-References. Establishments primarily engaged in--

- Operating switching and terminal facilities as separate establishments--are classified in Industry 488210, Support Activities for Rail Transportation;
- Operating railroads over a short distance on local rail lines--are classified in U.S. Industry 482112, Short Line Railroads; and
- Operating commuter rail systems--are classified in U.S. Industry 485112, Commuter Rail Systems.

482112 Short Line Railroads

This U.S. industry comprises establishments known as short-line railroads primarily engaged in operating railroads for the transport of cargo over a short distance on local rail lines not part of a rail network.

Cross-References. Establishments primarily engaged in--

- Operating street railroads, commuter rail, and urban rapid transit systems--are classified in Industry Group 4851, Urban Transit Systems;
- Operating scenic and sightseeing trains--are classified in Industry 487110, Scenic and Sightseeing Transportation, Land;

T—Canadian, Mexican, and United States industries are comparable.

- Operating switching and terminal facilities as separate establishments--are classified in Industry 488210, Support Activities for Rail Transportation; and
- Operating railroads for the transport of passengers and/or cargo over a long distance--are classified in U.S. Industry 482111, Line-Haul Railroads.

483 Water Transportation[T]

Industries in the Water Transportation subsector provide water transportation of passengers and cargo using watercraft, such as ships, barges, and boats.

The subsector is composed of two industry groups: (1) one for deep sea, coastal, and Great Lakes; and (2) one for inland water transportation. This split typically reflects the difference in equipment used.

Scenic and sightseeing water transportation services are not included in this subsector but are included in Subsector 487, Scenic and Sightseeing Transportation. Although these activities use watercraft, they are different from the activities included in water transportation. Water sightseeing does not usually involve place-to-place transportation; the passenger's trip starts and ends at the same location.

4831 Deep Sea, Coastal, and Great Lakes Water Transportation[T]

48311 Deep Sea, Coastal, and Great Lakes Water Transportation[T]

This industry comprises establishments primarily engaged in providing deep sea, coastal, Great Lakes, and St. Lawrence Seaway water transportation. Marine transportation establishments using the facilities of the St. Lawrence Seaway Authority Commission are considered to be using the Great Lakes Water Transportation System.

Cross-References. Establishments primarily engaged in--

- Providing inland water transportation on lakes, rivers, or intracoastal waterways (except on the Great Lakes System)--are classified in Industry 48321, Inland Water Transportation;
- Providing scenic and sightseeing water transportation, such as harbor cruises--are classified in Industry 48721, Scenic and Sightseeing Transportation, Water; and
- Operating floating casinos (i.e., gambling cruises, riverboat gambling casinos)--are classified in Industry 71321, Casinos (except Casino Hotels).

483111 Deep Sea Freight Transportation

This U.S. industry comprises establishments primarily engaged in providing deep sea transportation of cargo to or from foreign ports.

Cross-References.

Establishments primarily engaged in providing deep sea transportation of cargo to and from domestic ports are classified in U.S. Industry 483113, Coastal and Great Lakes Freight Transportation.

483112 Deep Sea Passenger Transportation

This U.S. industry comprises establishments primarily engaged in providing deep sea transportation of passengers to or from foreign ports.

Cross-References. Establishments primarily engaged in--

- Providing deep sea transportation of passengers to and from domestic ports--are classified in U.S. Industry 483114, Coastal and Great Lakes Passenger Transportation; and
- Operating floating casinos (i.e., gambling cruises)--are classified in Industry 713210, Casinos (except Casino Hotels).

T—Canadian, Mexican, and United States industries are comparable.

483113 Coastal and Great Lakes Freight Transportation

This U.S. industry comprises establishments primarily engaged in providing water transportation of cargo in coastal waters, on the Great Lakes System, or deep seas between ports of the United States, Puerto Rico, and United States island possessions or protectorates. Marine transportation establishments using the facilities of the St. Lawrence Seaway Authority Commission are considered to be using the Great Lakes Water Transportation System. Establishments primarily engaged in providing coastal and/or Great Lakes barge transportation services are included in this industry.

Cross-References. Establishments primarily engaged in--

- Providing deep sea transportation of cargo to or from foreign ports--are classified in U.S. Industry 483111, Deep Sea Freight Transportation; and
- Providing inland water transportation of cargo on lakes, rivers, or intracoastal waterways (except on the Great Lakes System)--are classified in U.S. Industry 483211, Inland Water Freight Transportation.

483114 Coastal and Great Lakes Passenger Transportation

This U.S. industry comprises establishments primarily engaged in providing water transportation of passengers in coastal waters, the Great Lakes System, or deep seas between ports of the United States, Puerto Rico, and United States island possessions and protectorates. Marine transportation establishments using the facilities of the St. Lawrence Seaway Authority Commission are considered to be using the Great Lakes Water Transportation System.

Cross-References. Establishments primarily engaged in--

- Providing inland water transportation of passengers on lakes, rivers, or intracoastal waterways (except on the Great Lakes System)--are classified in U.S. Industry 483212, Inland Water Passenger Transportation;
- Providing scenic and sightseeing water transportation, such as harbor cruises--are classified in Industry 487210, Scenic and Sightseeing Transportation, Water; and
- Operating floating casinos (i.e., gambling cruises)--are classified in Industry 713210, Casinos (except Casino Hotels).

4832 Inland Water Transportation[T]

48321 Inland Water Transportation[T]

This industry comprises establishments primarily engaged in providing inland water transportation of passengers and/or cargo on lakes, rivers, or intracoastal waterways (except on the Great Lakes System).

Cross-References. Establishments primarily engaged in--

- Providing water transportation in deep sea, coastal, or on the Great Lakes System--are classified in Industry Group 4831, Deep Sea, Coastal, and Great Lakes Water Transportation;
- Providing scenic and sightseeing water transportation, such as harbor cruises--are classified in Industry 48721, Scenic and Sightseeing Transportation, Water; and
- Operating floating casinos (i.e., gambling cruises, riverboat gambling casinos)--are classified in Industry 71321, Casinos (except Casino Hotels).

483211 Inland Water Freight Transportation

This U.S. industry comprises establishments primarily engaged in providing inland water transportation of cargo on lakes, rivers, or intracoastal waterways (except on the Great Lakes System).

T—Canadian, Mexican, and United States industries are comparable.

Cross-References. Establishments primarily engaged in--

- Providing deep sea transportation of cargo to and from foreign ports--are classified in U.S. Industry 483111, Deep Sea Freight Transportation; and
- Providing water transportation of cargo in coastal waters or on the Great Lakes System--are classified in U.S. Industry 483113, Coastal and Great Lakes Freight Transportation.

483212 Inland Water Passenger Transportation

This U.S. industry comprises establishments primarily engaged in providing inland water transportation of passengers on lakes, rivers, or intracoastal waterways (except on the Great Lakes System).

Cross-References. Establishments primarily engaged in--

- Providing deep sea transportation of passengers to and from foreign ports--are classified in U.S. Industry 483112, Deep Sea Passenger Transportation;
- Operating floating casinos (i.e., gambling cruises, riverboat gambling casinos)--are classified in Industry 713210, Casinos (except Casino Hotels);
- Operating cruise ships or ferries in coastal waters or on the Great Lakes System--are classified in U.S. Industry 483114, Coastal and Great Lakes Passenger Transportation; and
- Providing scenic and sightseeing water transportation, such as harbor cruises--are classified in Industry 487210, Scenic and Sightseeing Transportation, Water.

484 Truck Transportation[T]

Industries in the Truck Transportation subsector provide over-the-road transportation of cargo using motor vehicles, such as trucks and tractor trailers. The subsector is subdivided into general freight trucking and specialized freight trucking. This distinction reflects differences in equipment used, type of load carried, scheduling, terminal, and other networking services. General freight transportation establishments handle a wide variety of general commodities, generally palletized, and transported in a container or van trailer. Specialized freight transportation is the transportation of cargo that, because of size, weight, shape, or other inherent characteristics, requires specialized equipment for transportation.

Each of these industry groups is further subdivided based on distance traveled. Local trucking establishments primarily carry goods within a single metropolitan area and its adjacent nonurban areas. Long-distance trucking establishments carry goods between metropolitan areas.

The Specialized Freight Trucking industry group includes a separate industry for Used Household and Office Goods Moving. The household and office goods movers are separated because of the substantial network of establishments that has developed to deal with local and long-distance moving and the associated storage. In this area, the same establishment provides both local and long-distance services, while other specialized freight establishments generally limit their services to either local or long-distance hauling.

4841 General Freight Trucking[T]

This industry group comprises establishments primarily engaged in providing general freight trucking. General freight trucking establishments handle a wide variety of commodities, generally palletized, and transported in a container or van trailer. The establishments of this industry group provide a combination of the following network activities: local pick-up, local sorting and terminal operations, line-haul, destination sorting and terminal operations, and local delivery.

48411 General Freight Trucking, Local[T] See industry description for 484110.

T—Canadian, Mexican, and United States industries are comparable.

484110 General Freight Trucking, Local

This industry comprises establishments primarily engaged in providing local general freight trucking. General freight trucking establishments handle a wide variety of commodities, generally palletized and transported in a container or van trailer. Local general freight trucking establishments usually provide trucking within a metropolitan area which may cross state lines. Generally the trips are same-day return.

Cross-References. Establishments primarily engaged in--

- Operating independent trucking terminals--are classified in Industry 488490, Other Support Activities for Road Transportation; and
- Providing general freight long-distance trucking including all North American international travel--are classified in Industry 48412, General Freight Trucking, Long-Distance.

48412 General Freight Trucking, Long-Distance[T]

This industry comprises establishments primarily engaged in providing long-distance general freight trucking. General freight trucking establishments handle a wide variety of commodities, generally palletized and transported in a container or van trailer. Long-distance general freight trucking establishments usually provide trucking between metropolitan areas which may cross North American country borders. Included in this industry are establishments operating as truckload (TL) or less than truckload (LTL) carriers.

Cross-References. Establishments primarily engaged in--

- Providing courier services--are classified in Industry 49211, Couriers and Express Delivery Services;
- Providing warehousing services of general freight--are classified in Industry 49311, General Warehousing and Storage;
- Providing specialized freight trucking--are classified in Industry Group 4842, Specialized Freight Trucking;
- Operating independent trucking terminals--are classified in Industry 48849, Other Support Activities for Road Transportation; and
- Providing local general freight trucking services--are classified in Industry 48411, General Freight Trucking, Local.

484121 General Freight Trucking, Long-Distance, Truckload

This U.S. industry comprises establishments primarily engaged in providing long-distance general freight truckload (TL) trucking. These long-distance general freight truckload carrier establishments provide full truck movement of freight from origin to destination. The shipment of freight on a truck is characterized as a full single load not combined with other shipments.

Cross-References. Establishments primarily engaged in--

- Providing general freight long-distance, less than truckload trucking--are classified in U.S. Industry 484122, General Freight Trucking, Long-Distance, Less Than Truckload;
- Providing specialized freight trucking--are classified in Industry Group 4842, Specialized Freight Trucking;
- Operating independent trucking terminals--are classified in Industry 488490, Other Support Activities for Road Transportation; and
- Providing local general freight trucking services--are classified in Industry 484110, General Freight Trucking, Local.

484122 General Freight Trucking, Long-Distance, Less Than Truckload

This U.S. industry comprises establishments primarily engaged in providing long-distance, general freight, less than truckload (LTL) trucking. LTL carriage is characterized as multiple shipments combined onto a single truck for multiple deliveries within a network. These establishments are generally characterized by the following network

T—Canadian, Mexican, and United States industries are comparable.

activities: local pick-up, local sorting and terminal operations, line-haul, destination sorting and terminal operations, and local delivery.

Cross-References. Establishments primarily engaged in--

- Providing courier services--are classified in Industry 492110, Couriers and Express Delivery Services;
- Providing warehousing services of general freight--are classified in Industry 493110, General Warehousing and Storage;
- Providing specialized freight trucking--are classified in Industry Group 4842, Specialized Freight Trucking;
- Operating independent trucking terminals--are classified in Industry 488490, Other Support Activities for Road Transportation;
- Providing general freight long-distance truckload trucking--are classified in U.S. Industry 484121, General Freight Trucking, Long-Distance, Truckload; and
- Providing local general freight trucking services--are classified in Industry 484110, General Freight Trucking, Local.

4842 Specialized Freight Trucking[T]

This industry group comprises establishments primarily engaged in providing local or long-distance specialized freight trucking. The establishments of this industry are primarily engaged in the transportation of freight which, because of size, weight, shape, or other inherent characteristics, requires specialized equipment, such as flatbeds, tankers, or refrigerated trailers. This industry includes the transportation of used household, institutional, and commercial furniture and equipment.

48421 Used Household and Office Goods Moving[T] See industry description for 484210.

484210 Used Household and Office Goods Moving

This industry comprises establishments primarily engaged in providing local or long-distance trucking of used household, used institutional, or used commercial furniture and equipment. Incidental packing and storage activities are often provided by these establishments.

48422 Specialized Freight (except Used Goods) Trucking, Local[T] See industry description for 484220.

484220 Specialized Freight (except Used Goods) Trucking, Local

This industry comprises establishments primarily engaged in providing local, specialized trucking. Local trucking establishments provide trucking within a metropolitan area that may cross state lines. Generally the trips are same-day return.

Illustrative Examples:

Local agricultural products trucking
Local dump trucking (e.g., gravel, sand, top-soil)
Local boat hauling
Local livestock trucking
Local bulk liquids trucking

Cross-References. Establishments primarily engaged in--

- Providing long-distance specialized freight (except used goods) trucking including all North American international travel--are classified in Industry 484230, Specialized Freight (except Used Goods) Trucking, Long-Distance;
- Providing local general freight trucking--are classified in Industry 484110, General Freight Trucking, Local;

T—Canadian, Mexican, and United States industries are comparable.

- Providing trucking of used household and office goods--are classified in Industry 484210, Used Household and Office Goods Moving; and
- Providing waste collection--are classified in Industry Group 5621, Waste Collection.

48423 Specialized Freight (except Used Goods) Trucking, Long-Distance[T] See industry description for 484230.

484230 Specialized Freight (except Used Goods) Trucking, Long-Distance

This industry comprises establishments primarily engaged in providing long-distance specialized trucking. These establishments provide trucking between metropolitan areas that may cross North American country borders.

Illustrative Examples:

Long-distance automobile carrier trucking
Long-distance refrigerated product trucking
Long-distance bulk liquid trucking
Long-distance trucking of waste
Long-distance hazardous material trucking

Cross-References. Establishments primarily engaged in--

- Providing local specialized freight trucking (except used goods)--are classified in Industry 484220, Specialized Freight (except Used Goods) Trucking, Local;
- Providing long-distance general freight trucking including all North American international travel--are classified in Industry 48412, General Freight Trucking, Long-Distance;
- Providing trucking of used household and office goods--are classified in Industry 484210, Used Household and Office Goods Moving; and
- Collecting and/or hauling hazardous waste, nonhazardous waste, and/or recyclable materials within a local area--are classified in Industry 56211, Waste Collection.

485 Transit and Ground Passenger Transportation[T]

Industries in the Transit and Ground Passenger Transportation subsector include a variety of passenger transportation activities, such as urban transit systems; chartered bus, school bus, and interurban bus transportation; and taxis. These activities are distinguished based primarily on such production process factors as vehicle types, routes, and schedules.

In this subsector, the principal splits identify scheduled transportation as separate from nonscheduled transportation. The scheduled transportation industry groups are Urban Transit Systems, Interurban and Rural Bus Transportation, and School and Employee Bus Transportation. The nonscheduled industry groups are the Charter Bus Industry and Taxi and Limousine Service. The Other Transit and Ground Passenger Transportation industry group includes both scheduled and nonscheduled transportation.

Scenic and sightseeing ground transportation services are not included in this subsector but are included in Subsector 487, Scenic and Sightseeing Transportation. Sightseeing does not usually involve place-to-place transportation; the passenger's trip starts and ends at the same location.

4851 Urban Transit Systems[T]

48511 Urban Transit Systems[T]

This industry comprises establishments primarily engaged in operating local and suburban passenger transit systems over regular routes and on regular schedules within a metropolitan area and its adjacent nonurban areas. Such transportation systems involve the use of one or more modes of transport including light rail, commuter rail, subways, and streetcars, as well as buses and other motor vehicles.

T—Canadian, Mexican, and United States industries are comparable.

Cross-References. Establishments primarily engaged in--

- Providing scenic and sightseeing transportation on land--are classified in Industry 48711, Scenic and Sightseeing Transportation, Land;
- Providing support services to transit and ground transportation--are classified in Industry Group 4884, Support Activities for Road Transportation; and
- Providing interurban and rural bus transportation--are classified in Industry 48521, Interurban and Rural Bus Transportation.

485111 Mixed Mode Transit Systems

This U.S. industry comprises establishments primarily engaged in operating local and suburban ground passenger transit systems using more than one mode of transport over regular routes and on regular schedules within a metropolitan area and its adjacent nonurban areas.

Cross-References. Establishments primarily engaged in--

- Operating local and suburban passenger transit systems using only one mode of transportation--are classified according to the mode of transport; and
- Providing support services to transit and ground passenger transportation--are classified in Industry Group 4884, Support Activities for Road Transportation.

485112 Commuter Rail Systems

This U.S. industry comprises establishments primarily engaged in operating local and suburban commuter rail systems over regular routes and on a regular schedule within a metropolitan area and its adjacent nonurban areas. Commuter rail is usually characterized by reduced fares, multiple ride and commutation tickets, and mostly used by passengers during the morning and evening peak periods.

Cross-References. Establishments primarily engaged in--

- Operating local and suburban mass passenger transit systems using both commuter rail and another mode of transport--are classified in U.S. Industry 485111, Mixed Mode Transit Systems;
- Operating a subway system--are classified in U.S. Industry 485119, Other Urban Transit Systems; and
- Providing scenic and sightseeing transportation on land--are classified in Industry 487110, Scenic and Sightseeing Transportation, Land.

485113 Bus and Other Motor Vehicle Transit Systems

This U.S. industry comprises establishments primarily engaged in operating local and suburban passenger transportation systems using buses or other motor vehicles over regular routes and on regular schedules within a metropolitan area and its adjacent nonurban areas.

Cross-References. Establishments primarily engaged in--

- Operating local and suburban passenger transportation systems using both a bus or other motor vehicle and another mode of transport--are classified in U.S. Industry 485111, Mixed Mode Transit Systems;
- Providing interurban and rural bus transportation--are classified in Industry 485210, Interurban and Rural Bus Transportation; and
- Providing scenic and sightseeing transportation using buses or other motor vehicles--are classified in Industry 487110, Scenic and Sightseeing Transportation, Land.

T—Canadian, Mexican, and United States industries are comparable.

485119 Other Urban Transit Systems

This U.S. industry comprises establishments primarily engaged in operating local and suburban ground passenger transit systems (except mixed mode transit systems, commuter rail systems, and buses and other motor vehicles) over regular routes and on regular schedules within a metropolitan area and its adjacent nonurban areas.

Illustrative Examples:

Commuter cable car systems (i.e., stand-alone)
Light rail systems (i.e., stand-alone)
Commuter tramway systems (i.e., stand-alone)
Monorail transit systems (i.e., stand-alone)
Commuter trolley systems (i.e., stand-alone)

Cross-References. Establishments primarily engaged in--

- Operating local and suburban ground passenger transit systems using more than one mode of transport--are classified in U.S. Industry 485111, Mixed Mode Transit Systems;
- Providing local and suburban passenger transportation using commuter rail systems--are classified in U.S. Industry 485112, Commuter Rail Systems; and
- Operating local and suburban bus transit systems--are classified in U.S. Industry 485113, Bus and Other Motor Vehicle Transit Systems.

4852 Interurban and Rural Bus Transportation[T]

48521 Interurban and Rural Bus Transportation[T] See industry description for 485210.

485210 Interurban and Rural Bus Transportation

This industry comprises establishments primarily engaged in providing bus passenger transportation over regular routes and on regular schedules, principally outside a single metropolitan area and its adjacent nonurban areas.

Cross-References. Establishments primarily engaged in--

- Providing scenic and sightseeing transportation using buses--are classified in Industry 487110, Scenic and Sightseeing Transportation, Land;
- Providing buses for charter--are classified in Industry 485510, Charter Bus Industry;
- Operating local and suburban bus transit systems--are classified in U.S. Industry 485113, Bus and Other Motor Vehicle Transit Systems; and
- Operating independent bus terminals--are classified in Industry 488490, Other Support Activities for Road Transportation.

4853 Taxi and Limousine Service[T]

This industry group comprises establishments primarily engaged in providing passenger transportation by automobile or van or providing an array of specialty and luxury passenger transportation services via limousine or luxury sedan generally on a reserved basis. These establishments do not operate over regular routes and on regular schedules.

48531 Taxi Service[T] See industry description for 485310.

T—Canadian, Mexican, and United States industries are comparable.

485310 Taxi Service

This industry comprises establishments primarily engaged in providing passenger transportation by automobile or van, not operated over regular routes and on regular schedules. Establishments of taxicab owner/operators, taxicab fleet operators, or taxicab organizations are included in this industry.

Cross-References. Establishments primarily engaged in--

- Providing special needs transportation services (except to and from school or work) for the infirm, elderly, or handicapped--are classified in U.S. Industry 485991, Special Needs Transportation;
- Providing limousine services--are classified in Industry 485320, Limousine Service; and
- Providing scheduled shuttle services between hotels, airports, or other destination points--are classified in U.S. Industry 485999, All Other Transit and Ground Passenger Transportation.

48532 Limousine Service[T] See industry description for 485320.

485320 Limousine Service

This industry comprises establishments primarily engaged in providing an array of specialty and luxury passenger transportation services via limousine or luxury sedan generally on a reserved basis. These establishments do not operate over regular routes and on regular schedules.

Cross-References. Establishments primarily engaged in--

- Providing taxi services--are classified in Industry 485310, Taxi Service; and
- Providing scheduled shuttle services between hotels, airports, or other destination points--are classified in U.S. Industry 485999, All Other Transit and Ground Passenger Transportation.

4854 School and Employee Bus Transportation[T]

48541 School and Employee Bus Transportation[T] See industry description for 485410.

485410 School and Employee Bus Transportation

This industry comprises establishments primarily engaged in providing buses and other motor vehicles to transport pupils to and from school or employees to and from work.

Cross-References. Establishments primarily engaged in--

- Operating local and suburban bus transit systems--are classified in U.S. Industry 485113, Bus and Other Motor Vehicle Transit Systems;
- Providing interurban and rural bus transportation--are classified in Industry 485210, Interurban and Rural Bus Transportation; and
- Providing buses for charter--are classified in Industry 485510, Charter Bus Industry.

4855 Charter Bus Industry[T]

48551 Charter Bus Industry[T] See industry description for 485510.

T—Canadian, Mexican, and United States industries are comparable.

485510 Charter Bus Industry

This industry comprises establishments primarily engaged in providing buses for charter. These establishments provide bus services to meet customers' road transportation needs and generally do not operate over fixed routes and on regular schedules.

Cross-References. Establishments primarily engaged in--

- Providing scenic and local sightseeing transportation using buses--are classified in Industry 487110, Scenic and Sightseeing Transportation, Land; and
- Providing interurban and rural bus transportation--are classified in Industry 485210, Interurban and Rural Bus Transportation.

4859 Other Transit and Ground Passenger Transportation[T]

48599 Other Transit and Ground Passenger Transportation[T]

This industry comprises establishments primarily engaged in providing other transit and ground passenger transportation (except urban transit systems, interurban and rural bus transportation, taxi services, school and employee bus transportation, charter bus services, and limousine services (except shuttle services)). Shuttle services (except employee bus) and special needs transportation services are included in this industry. Shuttle services establishments generally travel within a metropolitan area and its adjacent nonurban areas on regular routes, on regular schedules and provide services between hotels, airports, or other destination points. Establishments in the Special Needs Transportation industry provide passenger transportation to the infirm, elderly, or handicapped. These establishments may use specially equipped vehicles to provide passenger transportation.

Cross-References. Establishments primarily engaged in--

- Providing school or employee bus transportation for the infirm, elderly, or handicapped--are classified in Industry 48541, School and Employee Bus Transportation;
- Providing ambulance services for emergency and medical purposes--are classified in Industry 62191, Ambulance Services;
- Operating urban transit systems--are classified in Industry Group 4851, Urban Transit Systems;
- Providing interurban and rural bus transportation--are classified in Industry 48521, Interurban and Rural Bus Transportation;
- Providing taxi services and/or limousine services (except shuttle services)--are classified in Industry Group 4853, Taxi and Limousine Service; and
- Providing buses for charter--are classified in Industry 48551, Charter Bus Industry.

485991 Special Needs Transportation

This U.S. industry comprises establishments primarily engaged in providing special needs transportation (except to and from school or work) to the infirm, elderly, or handicapped. These establishments may use specially equipped vehicles to provide passenger transportation.

Cross-References. Establishments primarily engaged in--

- Providing school or employee bus transportation for the infirm, elderly, or handicapped--are classified in Industry 485410, School and Employee Bus Transportation; and
- Providing ambulance services for emergency and medical purposes--are classified in Industry 621910, Ambulance Services.

T—Canadian, Mexican, and United States industries are comparable.

485999 All Other Transit and Ground Passenger Transportation

This U.S. industry comprises establishments primarily engaged in providing ground passenger transportation (except urban transit systems; interurban and rural bus transportation, taxi and/or limousine services (except shuttle services), school and employee bus transportation, charter bus services, and special needs transportation). Establishments primarily engaged in operating shuttle services and vanpools are included in this industry. Shuttle services establishments generally provide travel on regular routes and on regular schedules between hotels, airports, or other destination points.

Cross-References. Establishments primarily engaged in--

- Operating urban transit systems--are classified in Industry Group 4851, Urban Transit Systems;
- Providing interurban and rural bus transportation--are classified in Industry 485210, Interurban and Rural Bus Transportation;
- Providing taxi and/or limousine services (except shuttle services)--are classified in Industry Group 4853, Taxi and Limousine Service;
- Providing school and employee bus transportation (including for the infirm, elderly, or handicapped)--are classified in Industry 485410, School and Employee Bus Transportation;
- Providing buses for charter--are classified in Industry 485510, Charter Bus Industry;
- Providing special needs transportation (except to and from school or work) for the infirm, elderly, or handicapped--are classified in U.S. Industry 485991, Special Needs Transportation; and
- Providing ambulance services for emergency and medical purposes--are classified in Industry 621910, Ambulance Services.

486 Pipeline Transportation[T]

Industries in the Pipeline Transportation subsector use transmission pipelines to transport products, such as crude oil, natural gas, refined petroleum products, and slurry. Industries are identified based on the products transported (i.e., pipeline transportation of crude oil, natural gas, refined petroleum products, and other products).

The Pipeline Transportation of Natural Gas industry includes the storage of natural gas because the storage is usually done by the pipeline establishment and because a pipeline is inherently a network in which all the nodes are interdependent.

4861 Pipeline Transportation of Crude Oil[T]

48611 Pipeline Transportation of Crude Oil[T] See industry description for 486110.

486110 Pipeline Transportation of Crude Oil

This industry comprises establishments primarily engaged in the pipeline transportation of crude oil.

Cross-References. Establishments primarily engaged in--

- Providing the pipeline transportation of natural gas--are classified in Industry 486210, Pipeline Transportation of Natural Gas;
- Providing the pipeline transportation of refined petroleum products--are classified in Industry 486910, Pipeline Transportation of Refined Petroleum Products; and
- Operating oil and gas field gathering lines--are classified in Sector 21, Mining, Quarrying, and Oil and Gas Extraction.

4862 Pipeline Transportation of Natural Gas[T]

48621 Pipeline Transportation of Natural Gas[T] See industry description for 486210.

T—Canadian, Mexican, and United States industries are comparable.

486210 Pipeline Transportation of Natural Gas

This industry comprises establishments primarily engaged in the pipeline transportation of natural gas from processing plants to local distribution systems. This industry includes the storage of natural gas because the storage is usually done by the pipeline establishment and because a pipeline is inherently a network in which all the nodes are interdependent.

Cross-References. Establishments primarily engaged in--

- Operating oil and gas field gathering lines--are classified in Sector 21, Mining, Quarrying, and Oil and Gas Extraction; and
- Providing natural gas to the end consumer--are classified in Industry 221210, Natural Gas Distribution.

4869 Other Pipeline Transportation[T]

This industry group comprises establishments primarily engaged in the pipeline transportation of products (except crude oil and natural gas).

48691 Pipeline Transportation of Refined Petroleum Products[T] See industry description for 486910.

486910 Pipeline Transportation of Refined Petroleum Products

This industry comprises establishments primarily engaged in the pipeline transportation of refined petroleum products.

48699 All Other Pipeline Transportation[T] See industry description for 486990.

486990 All Other Pipeline Transportation

This industry comprises establishments primarily engaged in the pipeline transportation of products (except crude oil, natural gas, and refined petroleum products).

Cross-References. Establishments primarily engaged in--

- Providing pipeline transportation of crude oil--are classified in Industry 486110, Pipeline Transportation of Crude Oil;
- Providing pipeline transportation of natural gas--are classified in Industry 486210, Pipeline Transportation of Natural Gas;
- Providing pipeline transportation of refined petroleum products--are classified in Industry 486910, Pipeline Transportation of Refined Petroleum Products; and
- Operating water distribution systems--are classified in Industry 221310, Water Supply and Irrigation Systems.

487 Scenic and Sightseeing Transportation[T]

Industries in the Scenic and Sightseeing Transportation subsector utilize transportation equipment to provide recreation and entertainment. These activities have a production process distinct from passenger transportation carried out for the purpose of other types of for-hire transportation. This process does not emphasize efficient transportation; in fact, such activities often use obsolete vehicles, such as steam trains, to provide some extra ambience. The activity is local in nature, usually involving a same-day return to the point of departure.

The Scenic and Sightseeing Transportation subsector is separated into three industries based on the mode: land, water, and other.

T—Canadian, Mexican, and United States industries are comparable.

Activities that are recreational in nature and involve participation by the customer, such as white water rafting, are generally excluded from this subsector, unless they impose an impact on part of the transportation system. Charter boat fishing, for example, is included in the Scenic and Sightseeing Transportation, Water industry.

4871 Scenic and Sightseeing Transportation, Land^T

48711 Scenic and Sightseeing Transportation, Land^T See industry description for 487110.

487110 Scenic and Sightseeing Transportation, Land

This industry comprises establishments primarily engaged in providing scenic and sightseeing transportation on land, such as sightseeing buses and trolleys, steam train excursions, and horse-drawn sightseeing rides. The services provided are usually local and involve same-day return to place of origin.

Cross-References. Establishments primarily engaged in--

- Operating aerial trams or aerial cable cars--are classified in Industry 487990, Scenic and Sightseeing Transportation, Other;
- Providing sporting services, such as pack trains--are classified in Industry 713990, All Other Amusement and Recreation Industries;
- Providing intercity and rural bus transportation--are classified in Industry 485210, Interurban and Rural Bus Transportation;
- Providing buses for charter--are classified in Industry 485510, Charter Bus Industry;
- Operating local and suburban passenger transit systems--are classified in Industry 48511, Urban Transit Systems; and
- Providing passenger travel arrangements and tours--are classified in Industry Group 5615, Travel Arrangement and Reservation Services.

4872 Scenic and Sightseeing Transportation, Water^T

48721 Scenic and Sightseeing Transportation, Water^T See industry description for 487210.

487210 Scenic and Sightseeing Transportation, Water

This industry comprises establishments primarily engaged in providing scenic and sightseeing transportation on water. The services provided are usually local and involve same-day return to place of origin.

Illustrative Examples:

Airboat (i.e., swamp buggy) operation
Excursion boat operation
Charter fishing boat services
Harbor sightseeing tours
Dinner cruises

Cross-References. Establishments primarily engaged in--

- Providing recreation services, such as fishing guides, white water rafting, parasailing, and water skiing--are classified in Industry 713990, All Other Amusement and Recreation Industries;
- Providing water taxi services--are classified in Industry 48321, Inland Water Transportation;
- Providing water transportation of passengers--are classified in Subsector 483, Water Transportation;
- Operating floating casinos (i.e., gambling cruises or riverboat casinos)--are classified in Industry 713210, Casinos (except Casino Hotels); and
- Providing boat rental without operators--are classified in U.S. Industry 532284, Recreational Goods Rental.

T—Canadian, Mexican, and United States industries are comparable.

4879 Scenic and Sightseeing Transportation, Other[T]

48799 Scenic and Sightseeing Transportation, Other[T] See industry description for 487990.

487990 Scenic and Sightseeing Transportation, Other

This industry comprises establishments primarily engaged in providing scenic and sightseeing transportation (except on land and water). The services provided are usually local and involve same-day return to place of departure.

Illustrative Examples:

Aerial cable cars, scenic and sightseeing operation
Helicopter rides, scenic and sightseeing operation
Aerial tramways, scenic and sightseeing operation
Hot air balloon rides, scenic and sightseeing operation
Glider excursions

Cross-References. Establishments primarily engaged in--

- Providing recreational activities, such as hang gliding--are classified in Industry 713990, All Other Amusement and Recreation Industries; and
- Providing scheduled or nonscheduled air transportation of passengers or specialty flying services--are classified in Subsector 481, Air Transportation.

488 Support Activities for Transportation[T]

Industries in the Support Activities for Transportation subsector provide services which support transportation. These services may be provided to transportation carrier establishments or to the general public. This subsector includes a wide array of establishments, including air traffic control services, marine cargo handling, and motor vehicle towing.

The Support Activities for Transportation subsector includes services to transportation but is separated by type of mode serviced. The Support Activities for Rail Transportation industry includes services to the rail industry (e.g., railroad switching and terminal establishments).

Ship repair and maintenance not done in a shipyard are included in the Other Support Activities for Water Transportation industry. An example would be floating drydock services in a harbor.

Excluded from this subsector are establishments primarily engaged in providing factory conversion and overhaul of transportation equipment, which are classified in Subsector 336, Transportation Equipment Manufacturing. Also, establishments primarily engaged in providing rental and leasing of transportation equipment without operator are classified in Subsector 532, Rental and Leasing Services.

4881 Support Activities for Air Transportation[T]

This industry group comprises establishments primarily engaged in providing services to the air transportation industry. These services include airport operation, servicing, repairing (except factory conversion and overhaul of aircraft), maintaining and storing aircraft, and ferrying aircraft.

48811 Airport Operations[T]

This industry comprises establishments primarily engaged in (1) operating international, national, or civil airports or public flying fields or (2) supporting airport operations (except special food services contractors), such as rental of hangar space, air traffic control services, baggage handling services, and cargo handling services.

T—Canadian, Mexican, and United States industries are comparable.

Cross-References. Establishments primarily engaged in--

- Providing factory conversion, overhaul, and rebuilding of aircraft--are classified in Industry 33641, Aerospace Product and Parts Manufacturing;
- Wholesaling fuel at airports--are classified in Industry 42472, Petroleum and Petroleum Products Merchant Wholesalers (except Bulk Stations and Terminals);
- Providing airport janitorial services--are classified in Industry 56172, Janitorial Services; and
- Providing food services at airports on a contractual arrangement (i.e., food service contractors)--are classified in Industry 72231, Food Service Contractors.

488111 Air Traffic Control

This U.S. industry comprises establishments primarily engaged in providing air traffic control services to regulate the flow of air traffic.

488119 Other Airport Operations

This U.S. industry comprises establishments primarily engaged in (1) operating international, national, or civil airports, or public flying fields or (2) supporting airport operations, such as rental of hangar space, and providing baggage handling and/or cargo handling services.

Cross-References. Establishments primarily engaged in--

- Providing air traffic control services--are classified in U.S. Industry 488111, Air Traffic Control;
- Providing factory conversion, overhaul, and rebuilding of aircraft--are classified in Industry 33641, Aerospace Product and Parts Manufacturing;
- Wholesaling fuel at airports--are classified in Industry 424720, Petroleum and Petroleum Products Merchant Wholesalers (except Bulk Stations and Terminals);
- Providing airport janitorial services--are classified in Industry 561720, Janitorial Services; and
- Providing food services at airports on a contractual arrangement (i.e., food service contractors)--are classified in Industry 722310, Food Service Contractors.

48819 Other Support Activities for Air Transportation[T] See industry description for 488190.

488190 Other Support Activities for Air Transportation

This industry comprises establishments primarily engaged in providing specialized services for air transportation (except air traffic control and other airport operations).

Illustrative Examples:

Aircraft maintenance and repair services (except factory conversions, overhauls, rebuilding)

Cross-References. Establishments primarily engaged in--

- Wholesaling fuel at airports--are classified in Industry 424720, Petroleum and Petroleum Products Merchant Wholesalers (except Bulk Stations and Terminals);
- Providing aircraft janitorial services--are classified in Industry 561720, Janitorial Services;
- Providing air traffic control services--are classified in U.S. Industry 488111, Air Traffic Control;
- Providing airport operations (except air traffic control)--are classified in U.S. Industry 488119, Other Airport Operations;
- Providing factory conversion, overhaul, and rebuilding of aircraft--are classified in Industry 33641, Aerospace Product and Parts Manufacturing; and

T—Canadian, Mexican, and United States industries are comparable.

- Providing food services to airlines on a contractual arrangement (i.e., food service contractors)--are classified in Industry 722310, Food Service Contractors.

4882 Support Activities for Rail Transportation[T]

48821 Support Activities for Rail Transportation[T]
See industry description for 488210.

488210 Support Activities for Rail Transportation

This industry comprises establishments primarily engaged in providing specialized services for railroad transportation including servicing, routine repairing (except factory conversion, overhaul, or rebuilding of rolling stock), and maintaining rail cars; loading and unloading rail cars; and operating independent terminals.

Cross-References. Establishments primarily engaged in--

- Providing railroad car rental--are classified in U.S. Industry 532411, Commercial Air, Rail, and Water Transportation Equipment Rental and Leasing;
- Factory conversion, overhaul, or rebuilding of railroad rolling stock--are classified in Industry 336510, Railroad Rolling Stock Manufacturing; and
- Providing rail car janitorial services--are classified in Industry 561720, Janitorial Services.

4883 Support Activities for Water Transportation[T]

This industry group comprises establishments primarily engaged in one of the following: (1) operating ports, harbors (including docking and pier facilities), or canals; (2) providing stevedoring and other marine cargo handling services (except warehousing); (3) providing navigational services to shipping; or (4) providing other services to water transportation.

48831 Port and Harbor Operations[T] See industry description for 488310.

488310 Port and Harbor Operations

This industry comprises establishments primarily engaged in operating ports, harbors (including docking and pier facilities), or canals.

Cross-References. Establishments primarily engaged in--

- Providing stevedoring and other marine cargo handling services--are classified in Industry 488320, Marine Cargo Handling;
- Providing navigational services to shipping--are classified in Industry 488330, Navigational Services to Shipping; and
- Operating docking and/or storage facilities, known as marinas--are classified in Industry 713930, Marinas.

48832 Marine Cargo Handling[T] See industry description for 488320.

488320 Marine Cargo Handling

This industry comprises establishments primarily engaged in providing stevedoring and other marine cargo handling services (except warehousing).

T—Canadian, Mexican, and United States industries are comparable.

Cross-References. Establishments primarily engaged in--

- Preparing freight for transportation--are classified in U.S. Industry 488991, Packing and Crating;
- Operating general merchandise, refrigerated, or other warehousing and storage facilities--are classified in Subsector 493, Warehousing and Storage; and
- Operating docking and pier facilities--are classified in Industry 488310, Port and Harbor Operations.

48833 Navigational Services to Shipping[T] See industry description for 488330.

488330 Navigational Services to Shipping

This industry comprises establishments primarily engaged in providing navigational services to shipping. Marine salvage establishments are included in this industry.

Illustrative Examples:

Docking and undocking marine vessel services
Piloting services, water transportation
Marine vessel traffic reporting services
Tugboat services, harbor operation

Cross-References. Establishments primarily engaged in--

- Providing water transportation of barges (except coastal or Great Lakes barge transportation services)--are classified in U.S. Industry 483211, Inland Water Freight Transportation; and
- Providing coastal and/or Great Lakes barge transportation services--are classified in U.S. Industry 483113, Coastal and Great Lakes Freight Transportation.

48839 Other Support Activities for Water Transportation[T] See industry description for 488390.

488390 Other Support Activities for Water Transportation

This industry comprises establishments primarily engaged in providing services to water transportation (except port and harbor operations; marine cargo handling services; and navigational services to shipping).

Illustrative Examples:

Floating drydocks (i.e., routine repair and maintenance of ships)
Ship scaling services

Cross-References. Establishments primarily engaged in--

- Ship painting--are classified in Industry 238320, Painting and Wall Covering Contractors;
- Providing ship janitorial services--are classified in Industry 561720, Janitorial Services;
- Operating port, harbor, or canal facilities--are classified in Industry 488310, Port and Harbor Operations;
- Providing dredging services--are classified in Industry 237990, Other Heavy and Civil Engineering Construction;
- Providing stevedoring and other marine cargo handling services--are classified in Industry 488320, Marine Cargo Handling;
- Providing navigational services to shipping--are classified in Industry 488330, Navigational Services to Shipping; and
- Providing ship overhauling or repairs in a shipyard--are classified in U.S. Industry 336611, Ship Building

T—Canadian, Mexican, and United States industries are comparable.

4884 Support Activities for Road Transportation[T]

This industry group comprises establishments primarily engaged in (1) towing light or heavy motor vehicles, both local and long-distance, or (2) providing other services to road network users.

48841 Motor Vehicle Towing[T] See industry description for 488410.

488410 Motor Vehicle Towing

This industry comprises establishments primarily engaged in towing light or heavy motor vehicles, both local and long-distance. These establishments may provide incidental services, such as storage and emergency road repair services.

Cross-References. Establishments primarily engaged in--

- Operating gasoline stations--are classified in Industry Group 4471, Gasoline Stations;
- Providing automotive repair and maintenance--are classified in Industry Group 8111, Automotive Repair and Maintenance; and
- Both retailing automotive parts and accessories, and repairing automobiles, known as automotive supply stores--are classified in Industry 441310, Automotive Parts and Accessories Stores.

48849 Other Support Activities for Road Transportation[T] See industry description for 488490.

488490 Other Support Activities for Road Transportation

This industry comprises establishments primarily engaged in providing services (except motor vehicle towing) to road network users.

Illustrative Examples:

Bridge, tunnel, and highway operations
Pilot car services (i.e., wide load warning services)
Driving services (e.g., automobile, truck delivery)

Cross-References. Establishments primarily engaged in--

- Providing automotive repair and maintenance--are classified in Industry Group 8111, Automotive Repair and Maintenance;
- Providing towing services to motor vehicles--are classified in Industry 488410, Motor Vehicle Towing;
- Providing a network for busing in combination with providing terminal services--are classified in Industry 485210, Interurban and Rural Bus Transportation; and
- Providing a network for trucking in combination with providing terminal services--are classified in Subsector 484, Truck Transportation.

4885 Freight Transportation Arrangement[T]

48851 Freight Transportation Arrangement[T] See industry description for 488510.

488510 Freight Transportation Arrangement

This industry comprises establishments primarily engaged in arranging transportation of freight between shippers and carriers. These establishments are usually known as freight forwarders, marine shipping agents, or customs brokers and offer a combination of services spanning transportation modes.

T—Canadian, Mexican, and United States industries are comparable.

Cross-References.

Establishments primarily engaged in tariff and freight rate consulting services are classified in U.S. Industry 541614, Process, Physical Distribution, and Logistics Consulting Services.

4889 Other Support Activities for Transportation[T]

48899 Other Support Activities for Transportation[T]

This industry comprises establishments primarily engaged in providing support activities to transportation (except for air transportation; rail transportation; water transportation; road transportation; and freight transportation arrangement).

Illustrative Examples:

Arrangement of vanpools or carpools
Independent pipeline terminal facilities
Stockyards (i.e., not for fattening or selling livestock)

Cross-References. Establishments primarily engaged in--

- Providing support activities for air transportation--are classified in Industry Group 4881, Support Activities for Air Transportation;
- Providing support activities for rail transportation--are classified in Industry Group 4882, Support Activities for Rail Transportation;
- Providing support activities for water transportation--are classified in Industry Group 4883, Support Activities for Water Transportation;
- Providing support activities for road transportation--are classified in Industry Group 4884, Support Activities for Road Transportation;
- Arranging transportation of freight between shippers and carriers--are classified in Industry 48851, Freight Transportation Arrangement;
- Providing tariff and freight rate consulting services--are classified in Industry 54161, Management Consulting Services;
- Operating stockyards for fattening livestock--are classified in Subsector 112, Animal Production and Aquaculture; and
- Providing packaging and labeling services--are classified in Industry 56191, Packaging and Labeling Services.

488991 Packing and Crating

This U.S. industry comprises establishments primarily engaged in packing, crating, and otherwise preparing goods for transportation.

Cross-References.

Establishments primarily engaged in providing packaging and labeling services are classified in Industry 561910, Packaging and Labeling Services.

488999 All Other Support Activities for Transportation

This U.S. industry comprises establishments primarily engaged in providing support activities to transportation (except for air transportation; rail transportation; water transportation; road transportation; freight transportation arrangement; and packing and crating).

T—Canadian, Mexican, and United States industries are comparable.

Illustrative Examples:

Arrangement of vanpools or carpools

Stockyards (i.e., not for fattening or selling livestock)

Independent pipeline terminal facilities

Cross-References. Establishments primarily engaged in--

- Operating stockyards for fattening livestock--are classified in Subsector 112, Animal Production and Aquaculture;
- Providing tariff and freight rate consulting services--are classified in U.S. Industry 541614, Process, Physical Distribution, and Logistics Consulting Services;
- Providing packing and crating services for transportation--are classified in U.S. Industry 488991, Packing and Crating;
- Providing support activities for air transportation--are classified in Industry Group 4881, Support Activities for Air Transportation;
- Providing support activities for rail transportation--are classified in Industry 488210, Support Activities for Rail Transportation;
- Providing support activities for water transportation--are classified in Industry Group 4883, Support Activities for Water Transportation;
- Providing support activities for road transportation--are classified in Industry Group 4884, Support Activities for Road Transportation; and
- Arranging transportation of freight between shippers and carriers--are classified in Industry 488510, Freight Transportation Arrangement.

491 Postal Service[T]

The Postal Service subsector includes the activities of the National Post Office and its subcontractors operating under a universal service obligation to provide mail services, and using the infrastructure required to fulfill that obligation. These services include delivering letters and small parcels. These articles can be described as those that can be handled by one person without using special equipment. This allows the collection, pick-up, and delivery operations to be done with limited labor costs and minimal equipment. Sorting and transportation activities, where necessary, are generally mechanized. The restriction to small parcels distinguishes these establishments from those in the transportation industries. These establishments may also provide express delivery services using the infrastructure established for provision of basic mail services.

The traditional activity of the National Postal Service is described in this subsector. Subcontractors include rural post offices on contract to the Postal Service.

Bulk transportation of mail on contract to the Postal Service is not included here, because it is usually done by transportation establishments that carry other customers' cargo as well. Establishments that provide courier and express delivery services without operating under a universal service obligation are classified in Subsector 492, Couriers and Messengers.

4911 Postal Service[T]

49111 Postal Service[T] See industry description for 491110.

491110 Postal Service

This industry comprises establishments primarily engaged in providing mail services under a universal service obligation. Mail services include the carriage of letters, printed matter, or mailable packages, including acceptance, collection, processing, and delivery. Due to the infrastructure requirements of providing mail service under a universal service obligation, postal service establishments often provide parcel and express delivery services in addition to the mail service. Establishments primarily engaged in performing one or more parts of the basic mail service, such as sorting, routing and/or delivery (except bulk transportation of mail) are included in this industry.

T—Canadian, Mexican, and United States industries are comparable.

Cross-References. Establishments primarily engaged in--

- Providing bulk transportation of mail on a contract basis to and from postal service establishments--are classified in Industry Group 4841, General Freight Trucking;
- Providing services outside of the basic mail service, such as mail presort, mail consolidation, or address bar coding services, on a contract or fee basis--are classified in U.S. Industry 561499, All Other Business Support Services;
- Providing courier services--are classified in Industry 492110, Couriers and Express Delivery Services;
- Providing mailbox services along with other business services--are classified in U.S. Industry 561431, Private Mail Centers; and
- Providing local messenger and delivery services--are classified in Industry 492210, Local Messengers and Local Delivery.

492 Couriers and Messengers[T]

Industries in the Couriers and Messengers subsector provide intercity, local, and/or international delivery of parcels and documents (including express delivery services) without operating under a universal service obligation. These articles may originate in the U.S. but be delivered to another country and can be described as those that may be handled by one person without using special equipment. This allows the collection, pick-up, and delivery operations to be done with limited labor costs and minimal equipment. Sorting and transportation activities, where necessary, are generally mechanized. The restriction to small parcels partly distinguishes these establishments from those in the transportation industries. The complete network of courier services establishments also distinguishes these transportation services from local messenger and delivery establishments in this subsector. This includes the establishments that perform intercity transportation as well as establishments that, under contract to them, perform local pick-up and delivery. Messengers, which usually deliver within a metropolitan or single urban area, may use bicycle, foot, small truck, or van.

4921 Couriers and Express Delivery Services[T]

49211 Couriers and Express Delivery Services[T]

See industry description for 492110.

492110 Couriers and Express Delivery Services

This industry comprises establishments primarily engaged in providing air, surface, or combined mode courier and express delivery services of parcels, but not operating under a universal service obligation. These parcels can include goods and documents, but the express delivery services are not part of the normal mail service. These services are generally between metropolitan areas, urban centers, or international, but the establishments of this industry form a network that includes local pick-up and delivery to serve their customers' needs.

Illustrative Examples:

Air courier services, except establishments operating under a universal service obligation

Express delivery services, except establishments operating under a universal service obligation

Courier services (i.e., intercity network), except establishments operating under a universal service obligation

Cross-References. Establishments primarily engaged in--

- Providing parcel and express delivery services in addition to mail services under a universal service obligation--are classified in Industry 491110, Postal Service;
- Providing messenger and delivery services within a metropolitan area or within an urban center--are classified in Industry 492210, Local Messengers and Local Delivery; and
- Providing the truck transportation of palletized general freight--are classified in Industry Group 4841, General Freight Trucking.

T—Canadian, Mexican, and United States industries are comparable.

4922 Local Messengers and Local Delivery[T]

49221 Local Messengers and Local Delivery[T] See industry description for 492210.

492210 Local Messengers and Local Delivery

This industry comprises establishments primarily engaged in providing local messenger and delivery services of small items within a single metropolitan area or within an urban center. These establishments generally provide point-to-point pick-up and delivery and do not operate as part of an intercity courier network.

Illustrative Examples:

Letters, documents, or small parcels local delivery services
Grocery delivery services (i.e., independent service from grocery store)
Alcoholic beverages delivery services
Restaurant meals delivery services (i.e., independent service from restaurant)

Cross-References. Establishments primarily engaged in--

- Providing local letter and parcel delivery services as part of an intercity courier network--are classified in Industry 492110, Couriers and Express Delivery Services;
- Operating the National Postal Service or providing postal services on a contract basis (except the bulk transportation of mail)--are classified in Industry 491110, Postal Service; and
- Providing the bulk transportation of mail on a contract basis to and from Postal Service establishments--are classified in Industry Group 4841, General Freight Trucking.

493 Warehousing and Storage[T]

Industries in the Warehousing and Storage subsector are primarily engaged in operating warehousing and storage facilities for general merchandise, refrigerated goods, and other warehouse products. These establishments provide facilities to store goods. They do not sell the goods they handle. These establishments take responsibility for storing the goods and keeping them secure. They may also provide a range of services, often referred to as logistics services, related to the distribution of goods. Logistics services can include labeling, breaking bulk, inventory control and management, light assembly, order entry and fulfillment, packaging, pick and pack, price marking and ticketing, and transportation arrangement. However, establishments in this industry group always provide warehousing or storage services in addition to any logistic services. Furthermore, the warehousing or storage of goods must be more than incidental to the performance of services, such as price marking.

Bonded warehousing and storage services and warehouses located in free trade zones are included in the industries of this subsector.

4931 Warehousing and Storage[T]

49311 General Warehousing and Storage[T] See industry description for 493110.

493110 General Warehousing and Storage

This industry comprises establishments primarily engaged in operating merchandise warehousing and storage facilities. These establishments generally handle goods in containers, such as boxes, barrels, and/or drums, using equipment, such as forklifts, pallets, and racks. They are not specialized in handling bulk products of any particular type, size, or quantity of goods or products.

T—Canadian, Mexican, and United States industries are comparable.

Cross-References. Establishments primarily engaged in--

- Renting or leasing space for self-storage--are classified in Industry 531130, Lessors of Miniwarehouses and Self-Storage Units; and
- Selling in combination with handling and/or distributing goods to other wholesale or retail establishments--are classified in Sector 42, Wholesale Trade.

49312 Refrigerated Warehousing and Storage[T] See industry description for 493120.

493120 Refrigerated Warehousing and Storage

This industry comprises establishments primarily engaged in operating refrigerated warehousing and storage facilities. Establishments primarily engaged in the storage of furs for the trade are included in this industry. The services provided by these establishments include blast freezing, tempering, and modified atmosphere storage services.

Cross-References.

Establishments primarily engaged in storing furs (except for the trade) and garments are classified in Industry 812320, Drycleaning and Laundry Services (except Coin-Operated).

49313 Farm Product Warehousing and Storage[T] See industry description for 493130.

493130 Farm Product Warehousing and Storage

This industry comprises establishments primarily engaged in operating bulk farm product warehousing and storage facilities (except refrigerated). Grain elevators primarily engaged in storage are included in this industry.

Cross-References. Establishments primarily engaged in--

- Operating refrigerated warehousing and storage facilities--are classified in Industry 493120, Refrigerated Warehousing and Storage; and
- Storing grains and field beans (i.e., grain elevators) as an incidental activity to sales--are classified in Industry 424510, Grain and Field Bean Merchant Wholesalers.

49319 Other Warehousing and Storage[T] See industry description for 493190.

493190 Other Warehousing and Storage

This industry comprises establishments primarily engaged in operating warehousing and storage facilities (except general merchandise, refrigerated, and farm product warehousing and storage).

Illustrative Examples:

Bulk petroleum storage
Lumber storage terminals
Document storage and warehousing
Whiskey warehousing

Cross-References. Establishments primarily engaged in--

- Renting or leasing space for self-storage--are classified in Industry 531130, Lessors of Miniwarehouses and Self-Storage Units;

T—Canadian, Mexican, and United States industries are comparable.

- Storing hazardous materials for treatment and disposal--are classified in U.S. Industry 562211, Hazardous Waste Treatment and Disposal;
- Operating general warehousing and storage facilities--are classified in Industry 493110, General Warehousing and Storage;
- Wholesaling crude petroleum and petroleum products from bulk liquid storage facilities--are classified in Industry 424710, Petroleum Bulk Stations and Terminals;
- Operating refrigerated warehousing and storage facilities--are classified in Industry 493120, Refrigerated Warehousing and Storage; and
- Operating farm product warehousing and storage facilities--are classified in Industry 493130, Farm Product Warehousing and Storage.

T—Canadian, Mexican, and United States industries are comparable.

Sector 51--Information[T]

The Sector as a Whole

The Information sector comprises establishments engaged in the following processes: (a) producing and distributing information and cultural products, (b) providing the means to transmit or distribute these products as well as data or communications, and (c) processing data.

The main components of this sector are the publishing industries, including software publishing, and both traditional publishing and publishing exclusively on the Internet; the motion picture and sound recording industries; the broadcasting industries, including traditional broadcasting and broadcasting exclusively over the Internet; the telecommunications industries; and Web search portals, data processing industries, and the information services industries.

The expressions ''information age'' and ''global information economy'' are used with considerable frequency today. The general idea of an ''information economy'' includes both the notion of industries primarily producing, processing, and distributing information, as well as the idea that every industry is using available information and information technology to reorganize and make themselves more productive. For the purposes of NAICS, it is the transformation of information into a commodity that is produced and distributed by a number of growing industries that is at issue.

Cultural products are those that directly express attitudes, opinions, ideas, values, and artistic creativity; provide entertainment; or offer information and analysis concerning the past and present. Included in this definition are popular, mass-produced products as well as cultural products that normally have a more limited audience, such as poetry books, literary magazines, or classical records.

The unique characteristics of information and cultural products, and of the processes involved in their production and distribution, distinguish the Information sector from the goods-producing and service-producing sectors. Some of these characteristics are:

1. Unlike traditional goods, an ''information or cultural product,'' such as an on-line newspaper or a television program, does not necessarily have tangible qualities, nor is it necessarily associated with a particular form. A movie can be shown at a movie theater, on a television broadcast, through video-on-demand or rented at a local video store. A sound recording can be aired on radio, embedded in multimedia products, or sold at a record store.

2. Unlike traditional services, the delivery of these products does not require direct contact between the supplier and the consumer.

3. The value of these products to the consumer lies in their informational, educational, cultural, or entertainment content, not in the format in which they are distributed. Most of these products are protected from unlawful reproduction by copyright laws.

4. The intangible property aspect of information and cultural products makes the processes involved in their production and distribution very different from goods and services. Only those possessing the rights to these works are authorized to reproduce, alter, improve, and distribute them. Acquiring and using these rights often involves significant costs. In addition, technology is revolutionizing the distribution of these products. It is possible to distribute them in a physical form, via broadcast, or on-line.

5. Distributors of information and cultural products can easily add value to the products they distribute. For instance, broadcasters add advertising not contained in the original product. This capacity means that unlike traditional distributors, they derive revenue not from sale of the distributed product to the final consumer, but from those who pay for the privilege of adding information to the original product. Similarly, a directory and mailing list publisher can acquire the rights to thousands of previously published newspaper and periodical articles and add new value by providing search and software and organizing the information in a way that facilitates research and retrieval. These products often command a much higher price than the original information.

The distribution modes for information commodities may either eliminate the necessity for traditional manufacture, or reverse the conventional order of manufacture-distribute: A newspaper distributed on-line, for

T—Canadian, Mexican, and United States industries are comparable.

example, can be printed locally or by the final consumer. Similarly, packaged software is available mainly on-line. The NAICS Information sector is designed to make such economic changes transparent as they occur, or to facilitate designing surveys that will monitor the new phenomena and provide data to analyze the changes.

Many of the industries in the NAICS Information sector are engaged in producing products protected by copyright law, or in distributing them (other than distribution by traditional wholesale and retail methods). Examples are traditional publishing industries, software and directory and mailing list publishing industries, and film and sound industries. Broadcasting and telecommunications industries and information providers and processors are also included in the Information sector, because their technologies are so closely linked to other industries in the Information sector.

511 Publishing Industries (except Internet)[T]

Industries in the Publishing Industries (except Internet) subsector group establishments engaged in the publishing of newspapers, magazines, other periodicals, and books, as well as directory and mailing list and software publishing. In general, these establishments, which are known as publishers, issue copies of works for which they usually possess copyright. Works may be in one or more formats including traditional print form, CD-ROM, or proprietary electronic networks. Publishers may publish works originally created by others for which they have obtained the rights and/or works that they have created in-house. Software publishing is included here because the activity, creation of a copyrighted product and bringing it to market, is equivalent to the creation process for other types of intellectual products.

In NAICS, publishing--the reporting, writing, editing, and other processes that are required to create an edition of a newspaper--is treated as a major economic activity in its own right, rather than as a subsidiary activity to a manufacturing activity, printing. Thus, publishing is classified in the Information sector; whereas, printing remains in the Manufacturing sector. In part, the NAICS classification reflects the fact that publishing increasingly takes place in establishments that are physically separate from the associated printing establishments. More crucially, the NAICS classification of book and newspaper publishing is intended to portray their roles in a modern economy, in which they do not resemble manufacturing activities.

Music publishers are not included in the Publishing Industries (except Internet) subsector, but are included in the Motion Picture and Sound Recording Industries subsector. Reproduction of prepackaged software is treated in NAICS as a manufacturing activity; on-line distribution of software products is in the Information sector; and custom design of software to client specifications is included in the Professional, Scientific, and Technical Services sector. These distinctions arise because of the different ways that software is created, reproduced, and distributed. The Publishing Industries (except Internet) subsector includes establishments that publish software exclusively on the Internet but excludes establishments that publish other content exclusively on the Internet. Establishments publishing content other than software exclusively on the Internet are included in Subsector 519, Other Information Services. The Publishing Industries (except Internet) subsector also excludes products, such as manifold business forms and appointment books. Information is not the essential component of these items. Establishments producing these items are included in Subsector 323, Printing and Related Support Activities.

5111 Newspaper, Periodical, Book, and Directory Publishers[T]

This industry group comprises establishments primarily engaged in publishing newspapers, magazines, other periodicals, books, directories and mailing lists, and other works, such as calendars, greeting cards, and maps. These works are characterized by the intellectual creativity required in their development and are usually protected by copyright. Publishers distribute or arrange for the distribution of these works.

Publishing establishments may create the works in-house, or contract for, purchase, or compile works that were originally created by others. These works may be published in one or more formats, such as print and/or electronic form, including proprietary electronic networks. Establishments in this industry may print, reproduce, or offer direct access to the works themselves or may arrange with others to carry out such functions.

Establishments that both print and publish may fill excess capacity with commercial or job printing. However, the publishing activity is still considered to be the primary activity of these establishments.

51111 Newspaper Publishers[T] See industry description for 511110.

T—Canadian, Mexican, and United States industries are comparable.

511110 Newspaper Publishers

This industry comprises establishments known as newspaper publishers. Establishments in this industry carry out operations necessary for producing and distributing newspapers, including gathering news; writing news columns, feature stories, and editorials; and selling and preparing advertisements. These establishments may publish newspapers in print or electronic form.

Cross-References.

- Establishments publishing newspapers exclusively on the Internet are classified in Industry 519130, Internet Publishing and Broadcasting and Web Search Portals;
- Establishments primarily engaged in printing newspapers without publishing are classified in Industry 32311, Printing;
- Establishments, such as trade associations, schools and universities, and social welfare organizations, that publish newsletters for distribution to their membership, but that are not commonly known as newspaper publishers, are classified according to their primary activity designation;
- Establishments primarily engaged in supplying the news media with information, such as news, reports, and pictures, are classified in Industry 519110, News Syndicates; and
- Establishments of independent representatives primarily engaged in selling advertising space are classified in Industry 541840, Media Representatives.

51112 Periodical Publishers[T] See industry description for 511120.

511120 Periodical Publishers

This industry comprises establishments known either as magazine publishers or periodical publishers. These establishments carry out the operations necessary for producing and distributing magazines and other periodicals, such as gathering, writing, and editing articles, and selling and preparing advertisements. These establishments may publish magazines and other periodicals in print or electronic form.

Illustrative Examples:

Comic book publishers (except exclusive Internet publishing)
Radio and television guide publishers (except exclusive Internet publishing)
Magazine publishers (except exclusive Internet publishing)
Scholarly journal publishers (except exclusive Internet publishing)
Newsletter publishers (except exclusive Internet publishing)
Trade journal publishers (except exclusive Internet publishing)

Cross-References.

- Establishments publishing periodicals exclusively on the Internet are classified in Industry 519130, Internet Publishing and Broadcasting and Web Search Portals;
- Establishments primarily engaged in printing periodicals without publishing are classified in Industry 32311, Printing;
- Establishments, such as trade associations, schools and universities, and social welfare organizations, that publish magazines and periodicals for distribution to their membership, but that are not commonly known as periodical publishers, are classified according to their primary activity designation;
- Establishments primarily engaged in publishing directories and mailing lists are classified in Industry 511140, Directory and Mailing List Publishers; and
- Establishments of independent representatives primarily engaged in selling advertising space are classified in Industry 541840, Media Representatives.

T—Canadian, Mexican, and United States industries are comparable.

51113 Book Publishers[T] See industry description for 511130.

511130 Book Publishers

This industry comprises establishments known as book publishers. Establishments in this industry carry out design, editing, and marketing activities necessary for producing and distributing books. These establishments may publish books in print, electronic, or audio form.

Illustrative Examples:

Atlas publishers (except exclusive Internet publishing)
Religious book publishers (except exclusive Internet publishing)
Book publishers (except exclusive Internet publishing)
School textbook publishers (except exclusive Internet publishing)
Encyclopedia publishers (except exclusive Internet publishing)
Technical manual publishers (except exclusive Internet publishing)
Map publishers (except exclusive Internet publishing) Travel guide book publishers (except exclusive Internet publishing)

Cross-References.

- Establishments publishing books on the Internet exclusively are classified in Industry 519130, Internet Publishing and Broadcasting and Web Search Portals;
- Establishments primarily engaged in printing books without publishing are classified in U.S. Industry 323117, Books Printing;
- Establishments known as music publishers are classified in Industry 512230, Music Publishers;
- Establishments, such as trade associations, schools and universities, and social welfare organizations, that publish books for distribution to their membership, that are not commonly known as book publishers, are classified according to their primary activity designation; and
- Book clubs primarily engaged in direct sales activities without publishing are classified in Industry 454390, Other Direct Selling Establishments.

51114 Directory and Mailing List Publishers[T] See industry description for 511140.

511140 Directory and Mailing List Publishers

This industry comprises establishments primarily engaged in publishing directories, mailing lists, and collections or compilations of fact. The products are typically protected in their selection, arrangement and/or presentation. Examples are lists of mailing addresses, telephone directories, directories of businesses, collections or compilations of proprietary drugs or legal case results, compilations of public records, etc. These establishments may publish directories and mailing lists in print or electronic form.

Illustrative Examples:

Business directory publishers (except exclusive Internet publishing)
Mailing list publishers (except exclusive Internet publishing)
Directory publishers (except exclusive Internet publishing)
Telephone directory publishers (except exclusive Internet publishing)

T—Canadian, Mexican, and United States industries are comparable.

Cross-References. Establishments primarily engaged in--

- Operating Web search portals or developing and publishing, exclusively on the Internet, collections or compilations of creative works or facts--are classified in Industry 519130, Internet Publishing and Broadcasting and Web Search Portals;
- Compiling mailing lists in conjunction with providing direct mail advertising services--are classified in Industry 541860, Direct Mail Advertising;
- Printing without publishing directories and mailing lists--are classified in Industry 32311, Printing;
- Publishing computer software--are classified in Industry 511210, Software Publishers;
- Creating and publishing encyclopedias and similar collections of creative works in print and/or electronic media--are classified in Industry 511130, Book Publishers; and
- Creating and publishing collections of creative works that are periodically updated--are classified in Industry 511120, Periodical Publishers.

51119 Other Publishers[T]

This industry comprises establishments known as publishers (except newspaper, magazine, book, directory, mailing list, and music publishers). These establishments may publish works in print or electronic form.

Illustrative Examples:

Art print publishers (except exclusive Internet publishing)
Greeting card publishers (except exclusive Internet publishing)
Calendar publishers (except exclusive Internet

Cross-References.

- Establishments publishing exclusively on the Internet are classified in Industry 51913, Internet Publishing and Broadcasting and Web Search Portals;
- Establishments known as newspaper publishers are classified in Industry 51111, Newspaper Publishers;
- Establishments known as magazine and other periodical publishers are classified in Industry 51112, Periodical Publishers;
- Establishments known as book publishers are classified in Industry 51113, Book Publishers;
- Establishments primarily engaged in publishing directories and mailing lists are classified in Industry 51114, Directory and Mailing List Publishers;
- Establishments known as music publishers are classified in Industry 51223, Music Publishers; and
- Establishments primarily engaged in manufacturing appointment books and/or manifold business forms are classified in Industry 32311, Printing.

511191 Greeting Card Publishers

This U.S. industry comprises establishments primarily engaged in publishing greeting cards.

Cross-References. Establishments primarily engaged in--

- Publishing greeting cards exclusively on the Internet--are classified in Industry 519130, Internet Publishing and Broadcasting and Web Search Portals; and
- Printing greeting cards without publishing--are classified in Industry 32311, Printing.

511199 All Other Publishers

This U.S. industry comprises establishments generally known as publishers (except newspaper, magazine, book, directory, database, music, and greeting card publishers). These establishments may publish works in print or electronic form.

T—Canadian, Mexican, and United States industries are comparable.

Illustrative Examples:

Art print publishers (except exclusive Internet publishing)

Calendar publishers (except exclusive Internet

Cross-References.

- Establishments publishing exclusively on the Internet are classified in Industry 519130, Internet Publishing and Broadcasting and Web Search Portals;
- Establishments known as newspaper publishers are classified in Industry 511110, Newspaper Publishers;
- Establishments known as magazine or other periodical publishers are classified in Industry 511120, Periodical Publishers;
- Establishments known as book publishers are classified in Industry 511130, Book Publishers;
- Establishments primarily engaged in publishing directories and mailing lists are classified in Industry 511140, Directory and Mailing List Publishers;
- Establishments primarily engaged in greeting card publishing are classified in U.S. Industry 511191, Greeting Card Publishers;
- Establishments known as music publishers are classified in Industry 512230, Music Publishers; and
- Establishments primarily engaged in manufacturing appointment books and/or manifold business forms are classified in U.S. Industry 323111, Commercial Printing (except Screen and Books).

5112 Software Publishers[T]

51121 Software Publishers[T] See industry description for 511210.

511210 Software Publishers

This industry comprises establishments primarily engaged in computer software publishing or publishing and reproduction. Establishments in this industry carry out operations necessary for producing and distributing computer software, such as designing, providing documentation, assisting in installation, and providing support services to software purchasers. These establishments may design, develop, and publish, or publish only. These establishments may publish and distribute software remotely through subscriptions and downloads.

Cross-References. Establishments primarily engaged in--

- Reselling packaged software--are classified in Sector 42, Wholesale Trade, or Sector 44-45, Retail Trade;
- Providing access for clients to software published by others from a central host site--are classified in Industry 518210, Data Processing, Hosting, and Related Services;
- Designing software to meet the needs of specific users--are classified in U.S. Industry 541511, Custom Computer Programming Services; and
- Mass duplication of software--are classified in U.S. Industry 334614, Software and Other Prerecorded Compact Disc, Tape, and Record Reproducing.

512 Motion Picture and Sound Recording Industries[T]

Industries in the Motion Picture and Sound Recording Industries subsector group establishments involved in the production and distribution of motion pictures and sound recordings. While producers and distributors of motion pictures and sound recordings issue works for sale as traditional publishers do, the processes are sufficiently different to warrant placing establishments engaged in these activities in a separate subsector. Production is typically a complex process that involves several distinct types of establishments that are engaged in activities, such as contracting with performers, creating the film or sound content, and providing technical postproduction services. Film distribution is often to exhibitors, such as theaters and broadcasters, rather than through the wholesale and retail distribution chain. When the product is in a mass-produced form, NAICS treats production and distribution as

T—Canadian, Mexican, and United States industries are comparable.

the major economic activity as it does in the Publishing Industries (except Internet) subsector, rather than as a subsidiary activity to the manufacture of such products.

This subsector does not include establishments primarily engaged in the wholesale distribution of video and sound recordings, such as compact discs and audio tapes; these establishments are included in the Wholesale Trade sector. Reproduction of video and sound recordings that is carried out separately from establishments engaged in production and distribution is treated in NAICS as a manufacturing activity.

5121 Motion Picture and Video Industries[T]

This industry group comprises establishments primarily engaged in the production and/or distribution of motion pictures, videos, television programs, or commercials; in the exhibition of motion pictures; or in the provision of postproduction and related services.

51211 Motion Picture and Video Production[T] See industry description for 512110.

512110 Motion Picture and Video Production

This industry comprises establishments primarily engaged in producing, or producing and distributing motion pictures, videos, television programs, or television commercials.

Cross-References. Establishments primarily engaged in--

- Producing motion pictures and videos on contract as independent producers--are classified in Industry 711510, Independent Artists, Writers, and Performers;
- Providing teleproduction and other postproduction services--are classified in U.S. Industry 512191, Teleproduction and Other Postproduction Services;
- Providing video taping of weddings, special events, and/or business inventories--are classified in Industry 54192, Photographic Services;
- Providing motion picture laboratory services--are classified in U.S. Industry 512199, Other Motion Picture and Video Industries;
- Providing mass duplication and packaging of video discs, tapes, and film--are classified in U.S. Industry 334614, Software and Other Prerecorded Compact Disc, Tape, and Record Reproducing; and
- Acquiring distribution rights and distributing motion pictures and videos--are classified in Industry 512120, Motion Picture and Video Distribution.

51212 Motion Picture and Video Distribution[T] See industry description for 512120.

512120 Motion Picture and Video Distribution

This industry comprises establishments primarily engaged in acquiring distribution rights and distributing film and video productions to motion picture theaters, television networks and stations, and exhibitors.

Cross-References. Establishments primarily engaged in--

- Producing and distributing motion pictures and videos--are classified in Industry 512110, Motion Picture and Video Production;
- Merchant wholesale distribution of blank video cassette tapes and discs--are classified in Industry 423690, Other Electronic Parts and Equipment Merchant Wholesalers;
- Merchant wholesale distribution of prerecorded video cassette tapes and discs--are classified in Industry 423990, Other Miscellaneous Durable Goods Merchant Wholesalers;
- Providing mass duplication and packaging of video tapes and discs--are classified in U.S. Industry 334614, Software and Other Prerecorded Compact Disc, Tape, and Record Reproducing;

T—Canadian, Mexican, and United States industries are comparable.

- Providing motion picture footage (via film libraries) to producers--are classified in U.S. Industry 512199, Other Motion Picture and Video Industries;
- Renting video tapes and discs to the general public--are classified in U.S. Industry 532282, Video Tape and Disc Rental; and
- Selling video cassettes and discs to the general public--are classified in U.S. Industry 443142, Electronics Stores.

51213 Motion Picture and Video Exhibition[T]

This industry comprises establishments primarily engaged in operating motion picture theaters and/or exhibiting motion pictures or videos at film festivals, and so forth.

512131 Motion Picture Theaters (except Drive-Ins)

This U.S. industry comprises establishments primarily engaged in operating motion picture theaters (except drive-ins) and/or exhibiting motion pictures or videos at film festivals, and so forth.

512132 Drive-In Motion Picture Theaters

This U.S. industry comprises establishments primarily engaged in operating drive-in motion picture theaters.

51219 Postproduction Services and Other Motion Picture and Video Industries[T]

This industry comprises establishments primarily engaged in providing postproduction services and other services to the motion picture industry, including specialized motion picture or video postproduction services, such as editing, film/tape transfers, titling, subtitling, credits, closed captioning, and computer-produced graphics, animation and special effects, as well as developing and processing motion picture film.

Illustrative Examples:

Motion picture film laboratories
Stock footage film libraries
Postproduction facilities
Teleproduction services

Cross-References. Establishments primarily engaged in--

- Mass duplicating video discs, tapes, and film--are classified in Industry 33461, Manufacturing and Reproducing Magnetic and Optical Media;
- Providing audio services for film, television, and video productions--are classified in Industry 51224, Sound Recording Studios;
- Renting wardrobes and costumes for motion picture production--are classified in Industry 53228, Other Consumer Goods Rental;
- Renting studio equipment--are classified in Industry 53249, Other Commercial and Industrial Machinery and Equipment Rental and Leasing; and
- Casting actors and actresses with production companies--are classified in Industry 56131, Employment Placement Agencies and Executive Search Services.

512191 Teleproduction and Other Postproduction Services

This U.S. industry comprises establishments primarily engaged in providing specialized motion picture or video postproduction services, such as editing, film/tape transfers, subtitling, credits, closed captioning, and animation and special effects.

T—Canadian, Mexican, and United States industries are comparable.

Cross-References. Establishments primarily engaged in--

- Mass duplicating video discs, tapes, and film--are classified in U.S. Industry 334614, Software and Other Prerecorded Compact Disc, Tape, and Record Reproducing;
- Developing and processing motion picture film--are classified in U.S. Industry 512199, Other Motion Picture and Video Industries;
- Providing audio services for film, television, and video productions--are classified in Industry 512240, Sound Recording Studios; and
- Acquiring distribution rights and distributing film and video productions to motion picture theaters, television networks and stations, and exhibitors--are classified in Industry 512120, Motion Picture and Video Distribution.

512199 Other Motion Picture and Video Industries

This U.S. industry comprises establishments primarily engaged in providing motion picture and video services (except motion picture and video production, distribution, exhibition, and teleproduction and other postproduction services).

Illustrative Examples:

Motion picture film laboratories
Stock footage film libraries
Film preservation services

Cross-References. Establishments primarily engaged in--

- Renting wardrobes and costumes for motion picture production--are classified in U.S. Industry 532281, Formal Wear and Costume Rental;
- Renting studio equipment--are classified in Industry 532490, Other Commercial and Industrial Machinery and Equipment Rental and Leasing;
- Casting actors and actresses with production companies--are classified in U.S. Industry 561311, Employment Placement Agencies;
- Motion picture and video production--are classified in Industry 512110, Motion Picture and Video Production;
- Motion picture and video distribution--are classified in Industry 512120, Motion Picture and Video Distribution;
- Teleproduction and other postproduction services--are classified in U.S. Industry 512191, Teleproduction and Other Postproduction Services; and
- Motion picture and video exhibition--are classified in Industry 51213, Motion Picture and Video Exhibition.

5122 Sound Recording Industries[T]

This industry group comprises establishments primarily engaged in producing and distributing musical recordings, publishing music, or providing sound recording and related services.

51223 Music Publishers[T] See industry description for 512230.

512230 Music Publishers

This industry comprises establishments primarily engaged in acquiring and registering copyrights for musical compositions in accordance with law and promoting and authorizing the use of these compositions in recordings, radio, television, motion pictures, live performances, print, or other media. Establishments in this industry represent the interests of the songwriter or other owners of musical compositions to produce revenues from the use of such works, generally through licensing agreements. These establishments may own the copyright or act as administrator

T—Canadian, Mexican, and United States industries are comparable.

of the music copyrights on behalf of copyright owners. Publishers of music books and sheet music are included in this industry.

Cross-References.

Establishments primarily engaged as independent songwriters who act as their own publishers are classified in Industry 711510, Independent Artists, Writers, and Performers.

51224 Sound Recording Studios[T] See industry description for 512240.

512240 Sound Recording Studios

This industry comprises establishments primarily engaged in providing the facilities and technical expertise for sound recording in a studio. This industry includes establishments that provide audio production and postproduction services to produce master recordings. These establishments may provide audio services for film, television, and video productions.

Cross-References. Establishments primarily engaged in--

- Record production and/or releasing, promoting, and distributing sound recordings--are classified in Industry 512250, Record Production and Distribution; and
- Providing mass duplication of recorded products--are classified in U.S. Industry 334614, Software and Other Prerecorded Compact Disc, Tape, and Record Reproducing.

51225 Record Production and Distribution[T] See industry description for 512250.

512250 Record Production and Distribution

This industry comprises establishments primarily engaged in record production (e.g., tapes, CDs) and/or releasing, promoting, and distributing sound recordings to wholesalers, retailers, or directly to the public. These establishments contract with artists, arrange and finance the production of original master recordings, and/or produce master recordings themselves, such as audio tapes/cassettes and compact discs. Establishments in this industry hold the copyright to the master recording, or obtain reproduction and distribution rights to master recordings produced by others, and derive most of their revenues from the sales, leasing, licensing, or distribution of master recordings.

Cross-References. Establishments primarily engaged in--

- Promoting and authorizing the use of musical works in various media--are classified in Industry 512230, Music Publishers;
- Providing facilities and technical expertise for recording musical performances--are classified in Industry 512240, Sound Recording Studios;
- Mass duplication of recorded products--are classified in U.S. Industry 334614, Software and Other Prerecorded Compact Disc, Tape, and Record Reproducing;
- Merchant wholesale distribution of blank audio cassettes, tapes, and discs--are classified in Industry 423690, Other Electronic Parts and Equipment Merchant Wholesalers;
- Merchant wholesale distribution of prerecorded audio cassettes, tapes, and discs--are classified in Industry 423990, Other Miscellaneous Durable Goods Merchant Wholesalers;
- Retailing records, tapes, and compact discs without producing recordings--are classified in Sector 44-45, Retail Trade;
- Managing the careers of artists--are classified in Industry 711410, Agents and Managers for Artists, Athletes, Entertainers, and Other Public Figures; and

T—Canadian, Mexican, and United States industries are comparable.

- Producing albums on contract as independent producers--are classified in Industry 711510, Independent Artists, Writers, and Performers.

51229 Other Sound Recording Industries[T] See industry description for 512290.

512290 Other Sound Recording Industries

This industry comprises establishments primarily engaged in providing sound recording services (except record production, distribution, music publishing, and sound recording in a studio). Establishments in this industry provide services, such as the audio recording of meetings and conferences.

Cross-References. Establishments primarily engaged in--

- Promoting and authorizing the use of musical works in various media--are classified in Industry 512230, Music Publishers;
- Providing facilities and expertise for recording musical performances--are classified in Industry 512240, Sound Recording Studios;
- Record production and/or releasing, promoting, and distributing sound recordings--are classified in Industry 512250, Record Production and Distribution;
- Providing mass duplication of recorded products--are classified in U.S. Industry 334614, Software and Other Prerecorded Compact Disc, Tape, and Record Reproducing; and
- Organizing and promoting the presentation of performing arts productions--are classified in Industry Group 7113, Promoters of Performing Arts, Sports, and Similar Events.

515 Broadcasting (except Internet)[T]

Industries in the Broadcasting (except Internet) subsector include establishments that create content or acquire the right to distribute content and subsequently broadcast the content. The industry groups (Radio and Television Broadcasting and Cable and Other Subscription Programming) are based on differences in the methods of communication and the nature of services provided. The Radio and Television Broadcasting industry group includes establishments that operate broadcasting studios and facilities for over-the-air or satellite delivery of radio and television programs of entertainment, news, talk, and the like. These establishments are often engaged in the production and purchase of programs and generating revenues from the sale of air time to advertisers and from donations, subsidies, and/or the sale of programs. The Cable and Other Subscription Programming industry group includes establishments operating studios and facilities for the broadcasting of programs that are typically narrowcast in nature (limited format, such as news, sports, education, and youth-oriented programming) on a subscription or fee basis.

The distribution of cable and other subscription programming is included in Subsector 517, Telecommunications. Establishments that broadcast exclusively on the Internet are included in Subsector 519, Other Information Services.

5151 Radio and Television Broadcasting[T]

This industry group comprises establishments primarily engaged in operating broadcast studios and facilities for over-the-air or satellite delivery of radio and television programs. These establishments are often engaged in the production or purchase of programs or generate revenues from the sale of air time to advertisers, from donations and subsidies, or from the sale of programs.

51511 Radio Broadcasting[T]

This industry comprises establishments primarily engaged in broadcasting audio signals. These establishments operate radio broadcasting studios and facilities for the transmission of aural programming to the public, to affiliates, or to subscribers. The radio programs may include entertainment, news, talk shows, business data, or religious services.

T—Canadian, Mexican, and United States industries are comparable.

Cross-References. Establishments primarily engaged in--

- Broadcasting exclusively on the Internet--are classified in Industry 51913, Internet Publishing and Broadcasting and Web Search Portals; and
- Producing taped radio programming--are classified in Industry 51229, Other Sound Recording Industries.

515111 Radio Networks

This U.S. industry comprises establishments primarily engaged in assembling and transmitting aural programming to their affiliates or subscribers via over-the-air broadcasts, cable, or satellite. The programming covers a wide variety of material, such as news services, religious programming, weather, sports, or music.

Cross-References. Establishments primarily engaged in--

- Broadcasting exclusively on the Internet--are classified in Industry 519130, Internet Publishing and Broadcasting and Web Search Portals; and
- Producing taped radio programming--are classified in Industry 512290, Other Sound Recording Industries.

515112 Radio Stations

This U.S. industry comprises establishments primarily engaged in broadcasting aural programs by radio to the public. Programming may originate in their own studio, from an affiliated network, or from external sources.

51512 Television Broadcasting[T] See industry description for 515120.

515120 Television Broadcasting

This industry comprises establishments primarily engaged in broadcasting images together with sound. These establishments operate television broadcasting studios and facilities for the programming and transmission of programs to the public. These establishments also produce or transmit visual programming to affiliated broadcast television stations, which in turn broadcast the programs to the public on a predetermined schedule. Programming may originate in their own studio, from an affiliated network, or from external sources.

Cross-References. Establishments primarily engaged in--

- Broadcasting exclusively on the Internet--are classified in Industry 519130, Internet Publishing and Broadcasting and Web Search Portals;
- Producing taped television program materials--are classified in Industry 512110, Motion Picture and Video Production;
- Furnishing cable and other pay television services--are classified in U.S. Industry 517311, Wired Telecommunications Carriers; and
- Producing and broadcasting television programs for cable and satellite television systems--are classified in Industry 515210, Cable and Other Subscription Programming.

5152 Cable and Other Subscription Programming[T]

51521 Cable and Other Subscription Programming[T] See industry description for 515210.

515210 Cable and Other Subscription Programming

This industry comprises establishments primarily engaged in operating studios and facilities for the broadcasting of programs on a subscription or fee basis. The broadcast programming is typically narrowcast in nature (e.g., limited format, such as news, sports, education, or youth-oriented). These establishments produce programming in

---

T—Canadian, Mexican, and United States industries are comparable.

their own facilities or acquire programming from external sources. The programming material is usually delivered to a third party, such as cable systems or direct-to-home satellite systems, for transmission to viewers.

Cross-References. Establishments primarily engaged in--

- Producing taped television program materials--are classified in Industry 512110, Motion Picture and Video Production;
- Producing and transmitting television programs to affiliated stations--are classified in Industry 515120, Television Broadcasting;
- Furnishing cable and other pay television services--are classified in U.S. Industry 517311, Wired Telecommunications Carriers; and
- Retailing merchandise by electronic media, such as television--are classified in Industry 454110, Electronic Shopping and Mail-Order Houses.

517 Telecommunications[T]

Industries in the Telecommunications subsector group establishments that provide telecommunications and the services related to that activity (e.g., telephony, including Voice over Internet Protocol (VoIP); cable and satellite television distribution services; Internet access; telecommunications reselling services). The Telecommunications subsector is primarily engaged in operating and/or providing access to facilities for the transmission of voice, data, text, sound, and video. Transmission facilities may be based on a single technology or a combination of technologies. Establishments in the Telecommunications subsector are grouped into three industry groups. The first two are comprised of establishments that operate transmission facilities and infrastructure that they own and/or lease, and provide telecommunications services using those facilities. The distinction between the first two industry groups is the type of infrastructure operated (i.e., wired and/or wireless or satellite). The third industry group is comprised of establishments that provide support activities, telecommunications reselling services, or many of the same services provided by establishments in the first two industry groups, but do not operate as telecommunications carriers. Establishments primarily engaged as independent contractors in the installation and maintenance of broadcasting and telecommunications systems are classified in Sector 23, Construction. Establishments known as Internet cafes, primarily engaged in offering limited Internet connectivity in combination with other services such as facsimile services, training, rental of on-site personal computers, game rooms, or food services are classified in Subsector 561, Administrative and Support Services, or Subsector 722, Food Services and Drinking Places, depending on the primary activity.

5173 Wired and Wireless Telecommunications Carriers[T]

51731 Wired and Wireless Telecommunications Carriers[T]

This industry comprises establishments primarily engaged in operating, maintaining, and/or providing access to switching and transmission facilities and infrastructure that they own and/or lease for the transmission of voice, data, text, sound, and video using wired and wireless telecommunications networks. Transmission facilities may be based on a single technology or a combination of technologies. By exception, establishments providing satellite television distribution services using facilities and infrastructure that they operate are included in this industry.

Illustrative Examples:

Broadband Internet service providers, wired (e.g., cable, DSL)
Cable television distribution services
Cellular telephone services
Direct-to-home satellite system (DTH) services
Satellite television distribution systems
Telecommunications carriers, wired
VoIP service providers, using own operated wired telecommunications infrastructure
Wireless Internet service providers, except satellite
Wireless telecommunications carriers, except satellite
Wireless telephone communications carriers, except satellite

T—Canadian, Mexican, and United States industries are comparable.

Cross-References. Establishments primarily engaged in--

- Producing and distributing a channel of television programming for cable or satellite television systems--are classified in Industry 51521, Cable and Other Subscription Programming;
- Producing and distributing radio programs for cable or satellite radio systems--are classified in Industry 51511, Radio Broadcasting;
- Reselling telecommunications services (except satellite telecommunications), without operating a network, and/or operating as mobile virtual network operations (MVNO)--are classified in Industry 51791, Other Telecommunications;
- Operating and maintaining satellite networks and/or reselling satellite telecommunications services--are classified in Industry 51741, Satellite Telecommunications;
- Providing Internet access services via client-supplied telecommunications connections (e.g., dial-up ISPs)--are classified in Industry 51791, Other Telecommunications;
- Providing voice over Internet protocol (VoIP) services via client-supplied telecommunications connections--are classified in Industry 51791, Other Telecommunications;
- Providing limited Internet connectivity at locations known as Internet cafes, in combination with other services such as facsimile services, training, rental of on-site personal computers, game rooms, or food services--are classified in Industry 56143, Business Service Centers, or Subsector 722, Food Services and Drinking Places, depending on the primary activity; and
- Operating coin-operated pay telephones--are classified in Industry 81299, All Other Personal Services.

517311 Wired Telecommunications Carriers

This U.S. industry comprises establishments primarily engaged in operating and/or providing access to transmission facilities and infrastructure that they own and/or lease for the transmission of voice, data, text, sound, and video using wired telecommunications networks. Transmission facilities may be based on a single technology or a combination of technologies. Establishments in this industry use the wired telecommunications network facilities that they operate to provide a variety of services, such as wired telephony services, including VoIP services; wired (cable) audio and video programming distribution; and wired broadband Internet services. By exception, establishments providing satellite television distribution services using facilities and infrastructure that they operate are included in this industry.

Illustrative Examples:

Broadband Internet service providers, wired (e.g., cable, DSL)
Cable television distribution services
Closed-circuit television (CCTV) services
Direct-to-home satellite system (DTH) services
Local telephone carriers, wired
Long-distance telephone carriers, wired
Multichannel multipoint distribution services (MMDS)
Satellite television distribution systems
Telecommunications carriers, wired
VoIP service providers, using own operated wired telecommunications infrastructure

Cross-References. Establishments primarily engaged in--

- Producing and distributing a channel of television programming for cable or satellite television systems--are classified in Industry 515210, Cable and Other Subscription Programming;
- Operating and maintaining wireless telecommunications networks--are classified in U.S. Industry 517312, Wireless Telecommunications Carriers (except Satellite);
- Producing and distributing radio programs for cable or satellite radio systems--are classified in U.S. Industry 515111, Radio Networks;
- Reselling telecommunications services (except satellite telecommunications), without operating a network--are classified in U.S. Industry 517911, Telecommunications Resellers;
- Reselling satellite telecommunications services--are classified in Industry 517410, Satellite Telecommunications;

T—Canadian, Mexican, and United States industries are comparable.

- Providing Internet access services via client-supplied telecommunications connections (e.g., dial-up ISPs)--are classified in U.S. Industry 517919, All Other Telecommunications;
- Providing voice over Internet protocol (VoIP) services via client-supplied telecommunications connections--are classified in U.S. Industry 517919, All Other Telecommunications;
- Providing limited Internet connectivity at locations known as Internet cafes, in combination with other services such as facsimile services, training, rental of on-site personal computers, game rooms, or food services--are classified in U.S. Industry 561439, Other Business Service Centers (including Copy Shops), or Subsector 722, Food Services and Drinking Places, depending on the primary activity; and
- Operating coin-operated pay telephones--are classified in Industry 812990, All Other Personal Services.

517312 Wireless Telecommunications Carriers (except Satellite)

This U.S. industry comprises establishments primarily engaged in operating and maintaining switching and transmission facilities to provide communications via the airwaves. Establishments in this industry have spectrum licenses and provide services using that spectrum, such as cellular phone services, paging services, wireless Internet access, and wireless video services.

Illustrative Examples:

Cellular telephone services
Paging services, except satellite
Wireless Internet service providers, except satellite
Wireless telephone communications carriers, except

Cross-References. Establishments primarily engaged in--

- Operating and maintaining wired telecommunications networks--are classified in U.S. Industry 517311, Wired Telecommunications Carriers;
- Operating and maintaining satellite networks--are classified in Industry 517410, Satellite Telecommunications;
- Providing satellite television distribution services--are classified in U.S. Industry 517311, Wired Telecommunications Carriers; and
- Operating as mobile virtual network operations (MVNO)--are classified in U.S. Industry 517911, Telecommunications Resellers.

5174 Satellite Telecommunications[T]

51741 Satellite Telecommunications[T] See industry description for 517410.

517410 Satellite Telecommunications

This industry comprises establishments primarily engaged in providing telecommunications services to other establishments in the telecommunications and broadcasting industries by forwarding and receiving communications signals via a system of satellites or reselling satellite telecommunications.

Cross-References.

Establishments primarily engaged in providing direct-to-home satellite television services to individual households or consumers are classified in U.S. Industry 517311, Wired Telecommunications Carriers.

T—Canadian, Mexican, and United States industries are comparable.

5179 Other Telecommunications[T]

51791 Other Telecommunications[T]

This industry comprises establishments primarily engaged in (1) purchasing access and network capacity from owners and operators of telecommunications networks and reselling wired and wireless telecommunications services (except satellite) to businesses and households; (2) providing specialized telecommunications services, such as satellite tracking, communications telemetry, and radar station operation; (3) providing satellite terminal stations and associated facilities connected with one or more terrestrial systems and capable of transmitting telecommunications to, and receiving telecommunications from, satellite systems; or (4) providing Internet access services or Voice over Internet protocol (VoIP) services via client-supplied telecommunications connections. Establishments in this industry do not operate as telecommunications carriers. Mobile virtual network operators (MVNOs) are included in this industry.

517911 Telecommunications Resellers

This U.S. industry comprises establishments engaged in purchasing access and network capacity from owners and operators of telecommunications networks and reselling wired and wireless telecommunications services (except satellite) to businesses and households. Establishments in this industry resell telecommunications; they do not operate transmission facilities and infrastructure. Mobile virtual network operators (MVNOs) are included in this industry.

Cross-References. Establishments primarily engaged in--

- Operating and maintaining wired telecommunications networks--are classified in U.S. Industry 517311, Wired Telecommunications Carriers;
- Operating and maintaining wireless telecommunications networks--are classified in U.S. Industry 517312, Wireless Telecommunications Carriers (except Satellite); and
- Reselling satellite telecommunications services--are classified in Industry 517410, Satellite Telecommunications.

517919 All Other Telecommunications

This U.S. industry comprises establishments primarily engaged in providing specialized telecommunications services, such as satellite tracking, communications telemetry, and radar station operation. This industry also includes establishments primarily engaged in providing satellite terminal stations and associated facilities connected with one or more terrestrial systems and capable of transmitting telecommunications to, and receiving telecommunications from, satellite systems. Establishments providing Internet services or Voice over Internet protocol (VoIP) services via client-supplied telecommunications connections are also included in this industry.

Illustrative Examples:

Dial-up Internet service providers
VoIP service providers, using client-supplied telecommunications connections
Internet service providers using client-supplied telecommunications connections (e.g., dial-up ISPs)
Satellite tracking stations

Cross-References. Establishments primarily engaged in--

- Providing wired broadband Internet services or wired VoIP services via own operated telecommunications infrastructure--are classified in U.S. Industry 517311, Wired Telecommunications Carriers;
- Providing expert advice in the field of information technology or in integrating communication and computer systems--are classified in Industry 54151, Computer Systems Design and Related Services; and
- Providing satellite telecommunications services--are classified in Industry 517410, Satellite Telecommunications.

T—Canadian, Mexican, and United States industries are comparable.

518 Data Processing, Hosting, and Related Services[T]

Industries in the Data Processing, Hosting, and Related Services subsector group establishments that provide the infrastructure for hosting and/or data processing services.

5182 Data Processing, Hosting, and Related Services[T]

51821 Data Processing, Hosting, and Related Services[T] See industry description for 518210.

518210 Data Processing, Hosting, and Related Services

This industry comprises establishments primarily engaged in providing infrastructure for hosting or data processing services. These establishments may provide specialized hosting activities, such as Web hosting, streaming services, or application hosting (except software publishing), or they may provide general time-share mainframe facilities to clients. Data processing establishments provide complete processing and specialized reports from data supplied by clients or provide automated data processing and data entry services.

Illustrative Examples:

Application hosting
Optical scanning services
Web hosting
Computer data storage services
Video and audio streaming services
Computer input preparation services
Microfilm imaging services
Computer time rental

Cross-References. Establishments primarily engaged in--

- Providing text processing and related document preparation activities--are classified in Industry 561410, Document Preparation Services;
- Providing on-site management and operation of a client's data processing facilities--are classified in U.S. Industry 541513, Computer Facilities Management Services;
- Software design, development, and publishing, or software publishing only--are classified in Industry 511210, Software Publishers;
- Providing wired broadband Internet access services using own operated telecommunications infrastructure, in combination with Web hosting--are classified in U.S. Industry 517311, Wired Telecommunications Carriers;
- Providing Internet access via client-supplied telecommunications connections in combination with Web hosting--are classified in U.S. Industry 517919, All Other Telecommunications;
- Operating Web search portals--are classified in Industry 519130, Internet Publishing and Broadcasting and Web Search Portals;
- Providing access to computers and office equipment, as well as other office support services--are classified in Industry 56143, Business Service Centers;
- Processing financial transactions, such as credit card transactions--are classified in Industry 522320, Financial Transactions Processing, Reserve, and Clearinghouse Activities; and
- Providing payroll processing services--are classified in U.S. Industry 541214, Payroll Services.

519 Other Information Services[T]

Industries in the Other Information Services subsector group establishments supplying information, storing and providing access to information, searching and retrieving information, operating Web sites that use search engines to allow for searching information on the Internet, or publishing and/or broadcasting content exclusively on the Internet. The main components of the subsector are news syndicates, libraries, archives, exclusive Internet publishing and/or broadcasting, and Web search portals.

T—Canadian, Mexican, and United States industries are comparable.

5191 Other Information Services[T]

51911 News Syndicates[T] See industry description for 519110.

519110 News Syndicates

This industry comprises establishments primarily engaged in supplying information, such as news reports, articles, pictures, and features, to the news media.

Cross-References.

Independent writers and journalists (including photojournalists) are classified in Industry 711510, Independent Artists, Writers, and Performers.

51912 Libraries and Archives[T] See industry description for 519120.

519120 Libraries and Archives

This industry comprises establishments primarily engaged in providing library or archive services. These establishments are engaged in maintaining collections of documents (e.g., books, journals, newspapers, and music) and facilitating the use of such documents (recorded information regardless of its physical form and characteristics) as required to meet the informational, research, educational, or recreational needs of their user. These establishments may also acquire, research, store, preserve, and generally make accessible to the public historical documents, photographs, maps, audio material, audiovisual material, and other archival material of historical interest. All or portions of these collections may be accessible electronically.

Cross-References. Establishments primarily engaged in--

- Providing stock footage (via motion picture and video tape libraries) to the media, multimedia, and advertising industries--are classified in U.S. Industry 512199, Other Motion Picture and Video Industries;
- Providing stock music to the media, multimedia, and advertising industries--are classified in Industry 512290, Other Sound Recording Industries;
- Providing stock photos to the media, multimedia, and advertising industries--are classified in Industry 519190, All Other Information Services; and
- Distributing film and video productions to motion picture theaters, television networks and stations, and exhibitors--are classified in Industry 512120, Motion Picture and Video Distribution.

51913 Internet Publishing and Broadcasting and Web Search Portals[T] See industry description for 519130.

519130 Internet Publishing and Broadcasting and Web Search Portals

This industry comprises establishments primarily engaged in (1) publishing and/or broadcasting content on the Internet exclusively or (2) operating Web sites that use a search engine to generate and maintain extensive databases of Internet addresses and content in an easily searchable format (and known as Web search portals). The publishing and broadcasting establishments in this industry do not provide traditional (non-Internet) versions of the content that they publish or broadcast. They provide textual, audio, and/or video content of general or specific interest on the Internet exclusively. Establishments known as Web search portals often provide additional Internet services, such as email, connections to other Web sites, auctions, news, and other limited content, and serve as a home base for Internet users.

T—Canadian, Mexican, and United States industries are comparable.

Illustrative Examples:

Internet book publishers
Internet sports sites
Internet entertainment sites
Internet video broadcast sites
Internet news publishers
Internet periodical publishers
Internet radio stations
Internet search portals
Web search portals
Internet search Web sites
Internet social networking sites

Cross-References. Establishments primarily engaged in--

- Providing wired broadband Internet access using own operated telecommunications infrastructure--are classified in U.S. Industry 517311, Wired Telecommunications Carriers;
- Providing both Internet publishing and other print or electronic (e.g., CD-ROM, diskette) editions in the same establishment or using proprietary networks to distribute content--are classified in Subsector 511, Publishing Industries (except Internet), based on the materials produced;
- Providing Internet access via client-supplied telecommunications connections--are classified in U.S. Industry 517919, All Other Telecommunications;
- Providing streaming services on content owned by others--are classified in Industry 518210, Data Processing, Hosting, and Related Services;
- Wholesaling goods on the Internet--are classified in Sector 42, Wholesale Trade;
- Retailing goods on the Internet--are classified in Sector 44-45, Retail Trade; and
- Operating stock brokerages, travel reservation systems, purchasing services, and similar activities using the Internet rather than traditional methods--are classified with the more traditional establishments providing these services.

51919 All Other Information Services[T] See industry description for 519190.

519190 All Other Information Services

This industry comprises establishments primarily engaged in providing other information services (except news syndicates, libraries, archives, Internet publishing and broadcasting, and Web search portals).

Illustrative Examples:

News clipping services
Telephone-based recorded information services
Stock photo agencies

Cross-References. Establishments primarily engaged in--

- Providing wired broadband Internet access services using own operated telecommunications infrastructure--are classified in U.S. Industry 517311, Wired Telecommunications Carriers;
- Providing Internet access via client-supplied telecommunications connections--are classified in U.S. Industry 517919, All Other Telecommunications;
- Publishing (except exclusively on the Internet)--are classified in Subsector 511, Publishing Industries (except Internet);
- Publishing or broadcasting exclusively on the Internet--are classified in Industry 519130, Internet Publishing and Broadcasting and Web Search Portals;
- Operating Web search portals--are classified in Industry 519130, Internet Publishing and Broadcasting and Web Search Portals;
- Operating news syndicates--are classified in Industry 519110, News Syndicates; and
- Operating libraries and archives--are classified in Industry 519120, Libraries and Archives.

T—Canadian, Mexican, and United States industries are comparable.

Sector 52--Finance and Insurance[T]

The Sector as a Whole

The Finance and Insurance sector comprises establishments primarily engaged in financial transactions (transactions involving the creation, liquidation, or change in ownership of financial assets) and/or in facilitating financial transactions. Three principal types of activities are identified:

1. 1. Raising funds by taking deposits and/or issuing securities and, in the process, incurring liabilities. Establishments engaged in this activity use raised funds to acquire financial assets by making loans and/or purchasing securities. Putting themselves at risk, they channel funds from lenders to borrowers and transform or repackage the funds with respect to maturity, scale, and risk. This activity is known as financial intermediation.

2. 2. Pooling of risk by underwriting insurance and annuities. Establishments engaged in this activity collect fees, insurance premiums, or annuity considerations; build up reserves; invest those reserves; and make contractual payments. Fees are based on the expected incidence of the insured risk and the expected return on investment.

3. 3. Providing specialized services facilitating or supporting financial intermediation, insurance, and employee benefit programs.

In addition, monetary authorities charged with monetary control are included in this sector.

The subsectors, industry groups, and industries within the Finance and Insurance sector are defined on the basis of their unique production processes. As with all industries, the production processes are distinguished by their use of specialized human resources and specialized physical capital. In addition, the way in which these establishments acquire and allocate financial capital, their source of funds, and the use of those funds provides a third basis for distinguishing characteristics of the production process. For instance, the production process in raising funds through deposit-taking is different from the process of raising funds in bond or money markets. The process of making loans to individuals also requires different production processes than does the creation of investment pools or the underwriting of securities.

Most of the Finance and Insurance subsectors contain one or more industry groups of (1) intermediaries with similar patterns of raising and using funds and (2) establishments engaged in activities that facilitate, or are otherwise related to, that type of financial or insurance intermediation. Industries within this sector are defined in terms of activities for which a production process can be specified, and many of these activities are not exclusive to a particular type of financial institution. To deal with the varied activities taking place within existing financial institutions, the approach is to split these institutions into components performing specialized services. This requires defining the units engaged in providing those services and developing procedures that allow for their delineation. These units are the equivalents for finance and insurance of the establishments defined for other industries. The output of many financial services, as well as the inputs and the processes by which they are combined, cannot be observed at a single location and can only be defined at a higher level of the organizational structure of the enterprise. Additionally, a number of independent activities that represent separate and distinct production processes may take place at a single location belonging to a multilocation financial firm. Activities are more likely to be homogeneous with respect to production characteristics than are locations, at least in financial services. The classification defines activities broadly enough that it can be used both by those classifying by location and by those employing a more top-down approach to the delineation of the establishment.

Establishments engaged in activities that facilitate, or are otherwise related to, the various types of intermediation are included in multiple subsectors, rather than in a separate subsector dedicated to services alone, because these services are performed by intermediaries, as well as by specialist establishments, and the extent to which the activity of the intermediaries can be separately identified is not clear.

Financial industries are extensive users of electronic means for facilitating the verification of financial balances, authorizing transactions, transferring funds to and from transactors' accounts, notifying banks (or credit card issuers) of the individual transactions, and providing daily summaries. Since these transaction processing activities are integral to the production of finance and insurance services, establishments that principally provide a financial transaction processing service are classified in this sector, rather than in the data processing industry in the Information sector.

T—Canadian, Mexican, and United States industries are comparable.

Legal entities that hold portfolios of assets on behalf of others are significant and data on them are required for a variety of purposes. Thus for NAICS, these funds, trusts, and other financial vehicles are the fifth subsector of the Finance and Insurance sector. These entities earn interest, dividends, and other property income, but have little or no employment and no revenue from the sale of services. Separate establishments and employees devoted to the management of funds are classified in Industry Group 5239, Other Financial Investment Activities.

521 Monetary Authorities-Central Bank[T]

The Monetary Authorities-Central Bank subsector groups establishments that engage in performing central banking functions, such as issuing currency, managing the Nation's money supply and international reserves, holding deposits that represent the reserves of other banks and other central banks, and acting as a fiscal agent for the central government.

5211 Monetary Authorities-Central Bank[T]

52111 Monetary Authorities-Central Bank[T] See industry description for 521110.

521110 Monetary Authorities-Central Bank

This industry comprises establishments primarily engaged in performing central banking functions, such as issuing currency, managing the Nation's money supply and international reserves, holding deposits that represent the reserves of other banks and other central banks, and acting as a fiscal agent for the central government.

Cross-References.

Establishments of the Board of Governors of the Federal Reserve System are classified in Industry 921130, Public Finance Activities.

522 Credit Intermediation and Related Activities[T]

Industries in the Credit Intermediation and Related Activities subsector group establishments that (1) lend funds raised from depositors; (2) lend funds raised from credit market borrowing; or (3) facilitate the lending of funds or issuance of credit by engaging in such activities as mortgage and loan brokerage, clearinghouse and reserve services, and check cashing services.

5221 Depository Credit Intermediation

This industry group comprises establishments primarily engaged in accepting deposits (or share deposits) and in lending funds from these deposits. Within this group, industries are defined on the basis of differences in the types of deposit liabilities assumed and in the nature of the credit extended.

52211 Commercial Banking
See industry description for 522110.

522110 Commercial Banking

This industry comprises establishments primarily engaged in accepting demand and other deposits and making commercial, industrial, and consumer loans. Commercial banks and branches of foreign banks are included in this industry.

Cross-References.

- Establishments primarily engaged in credit card banking are classified in Industry 522210, Credit Card Issuing;

T—Canadian, Mexican, and United States industries are comparable.

- Establishments known as industrial banks and primarily engaged in accepting deposits are classified in Industry 522190, Other Depository Credit Intermediation; and
- Establishments of depository institutions primarily engaged in trust activities are classified in U.S. Industry 523991, Trust, Fiduciary, and Custody Activities.

52212 Savings Institutions

See industry description for 522120.

522120 Savings Institutions

This industry comprises establishments primarily engaged in accepting time deposits, making mortgage and real estate loans, and investing in high-grade securities. Savings and loan associations and savings banks are included in this industry.

Cross-References.

Establishments primarily engaged in accepting demand and other deposits and making all types of loans are classified in Industry 522110, Commercial Banking.

52213 Credit Unions

See industry description for 522130.

522130 Credit Unions

This industry comprises establishments primarily engaged in accepting members' share deposits in cooperatives that are organized to offer consumer loans to their members.

52219 Other Depository Credit Intermediation

See industry description for 522190.

522190 Other Depository Credit Intermediation

This industry comprises establishments primarily engaged in accepting deposits and lending funds (except commercial banking, savings institutions, and credit unions). Establishments known as industrial banks or Morris Plans and primarily engaged in accepting deposits, and private banks (i.e., unincorporated banks) are included in this industry.

Cross-References.

- Establishments primarily engaged in accepting demand and other deposits and making all types of loans are classified in Industry 522110, Commercial Banking;
- Establishments primarily engaged in accepting time deposits are classified in Industry 522120, Savings Institutions;
- Establishments primarily engaged in accepting members' share deposits in cooperatives are classified in Industry 522130, Credit Unions; and
- Establishments known as industrial banks and Morris Plans and primarily engaged in providing nondepository credit are classified in U.S. Industry 522298, All Other Nondepository Credit Intermediation.

5222 Nondepository Credit Intermediation

This industry group comprises establishments, both public (government-sponsored enterprises) and private, primarily engaged in extending credit or lending funds raised by credit market borrowing, such as issuing commercial paper or other debt instruments or by borrowing from other financial intermediaries. Within this group, industries are defined on the basis of the type of credit being extended.
T—Canadian, Mexican, and United States industries are comparable.

52221 Credit Card Issuing
See industry description for 522210.

522210 Credit Card Issuing

This industry comprises establishments primarily engaged in providing credit by issuing credit cards. Credit card issuance provides the funds required to purchase goods and services in return for payment of the full balance or payments on an installment basis. Credit card banks are included in this industry.

Cross-References.

Establishments primarily engaged in issuing cards that contain a stored pre-paid value are classified with the industry providing the service represented by the cards, such as transit fare cards in Subsector 482, Rail Transportation, and long-distance telephone cards in Subsector 517, Telecommunications.

52222 Sales Financing
See industry description for 522220.

522220 Sales Financing

This industry comprises establishments primarily engaged in sales financing or sales financing in combination with leasing. Sales financing establishments are primarily engaged in lending money for the purpose of providing collateralized goods through a contractual installment sales agreement, either directly from or through arrangements with dealers.

Cross-References.

Establishments not engaged in sales financing, but primarily engaged in providing leases for equipment and other assets are classified in Subsector 532, Rental and Leasing Services.

52229 Other Nondepository Credit Intermediation

This industry comprises establishments primarily engaged in making cash loans or extending credit through credit instruments (except credit cards and sales finance agreements).

Illustrative Examples:

Consumer finance companies (i.e., unsecured cash loans)
Mortgage companies
International trade financing
Secondary market financing

Cross-References. Establishments primarily engaged in--

- Providing credit sales by issuing credit cards--are classified in Industry 52221, Credit Card Issuing;
- Providing leases for equipment and other assets without sales financing--are classified in Subsector 532, Rental and Leasing Services;
- Accepting deposits and lending funds from these deposits--are classified in Industry Group 5221, Depository Credit Intermediation;
- Arranging loans for others on a commission or fee basis--are classified in Industry 52231, Mortgage and Nonmortgage Loan Brokers; and
- Guaranteeing international trade loans--are classified in Industry 52412, Direct Insurance (except Life, Health, and Medical) Carriers.

T—Canadian, Mexican, and United States industries are comparable.

522291 Consumer Lending

This U.S. industry comprises establishments primarily engaged in making unsecured cash loans to consumers.

Illustrative Examples:

Finance companies (i.e., unsecured cash loans)
Personal credit institutions (i.e., unsecured cash loans)
Loan companies (i.e., consumer, personal, student, small)
Student loan companies

Cross-References. Establishments primarily engaged in--

- Accepting deposits and lending funds from these deposits--are classified in Industry Group 5221, Depository Credit Intermediation; and
- Arranging loans for others on a commission or fee basis--are classified in Industry 522310, Mortgage and Nonmortgage Loan Brokers.

522292 Real Estate Credit

This U.S. industry comprises establishments primarily engaged in lending funds with real estate as collateral.

Illustrative Examples:

Home equity credit lending
Mortgage companies
Mortgage banking (i.e., nondepository mortgage

Cross-References. Establishments primarily engaged in--

- Servicing loans--are classified in Industry 522390, Other Activities Related to Credit Intermediation;
- Arranging loans for others on a commission or fee basis--are classified in Industry 522310, Mortgage and Nonmortgage Loan Brokers; and
- Accepting deposits and lending funds secured by real estate--are classified in Industry Group 5221, Depository Credit Intermediation.

522293 International Trade Financing

This U.S. industry comprises establishments primarily engaged in providing one or more of the following: (1) working capital funds to U.S. exporters; (2) lending funds to foreign buyers of U.S. goods; and/or (3) lending funds to domestic buyers of imported goods.

Illustrative Examples:

Agreement corporations (i.e., international trade financing)
Export-Import banks
Edge Act corporations (i.e., international trade financing)
Trade banks (i.e., international trade financing)

Cross-References. Establishments primarily engaged in--

- Guaranteeing international trade loans--are classified in U.S. Industry 524126, Direct Property and Casualty Insurance Carriers;
- Brokering international trade loans--are classified in Industry 522310, Mortgage and Nonmortgage Loan Brokers; and
- Accepting deposits and lending funds from these deposits--are classified in Industry Group 5221, Depository Credit Intermediation.

T—Canadian, Mexican, and United States industries are comparable.

522294 Secondary Market Financing

This U.S. industry comprises establishments primarily engaged in buying, pooling, and repackaging loans for sale to others on the secondary market.

Illustrative Examples:

Federal Home Loan Mortgage Corporation (FHLMC)
Government National Mortgage Association (GNMA)
Federal National Mortgage Association (FNMA)
Student Loan Marketing Association (SLMA)

522298 All Other Nondepository Credit Intermediation

This U.S. industry comprises establishments primarily engaged in providing nondepository credit (except credit card issuing, sales financing, consumer lending, real estate credit, international trade financing, and secondary market financing). Examples of types of lending in this industry are short-term inventory credit, agricultural lending (except real estate and sales financing), and consumer cash lending secured by personal property.

Illustrative Examples:

Commodity Credit Corporation
Morris Plans (i.e., known as), nondepository
Factoring accounts receivable
Pawnshops
Industrial banks (i.e., known as), nondepository

Cross-References.

- Establishments primarily engaged in providing credit sales funding are classified in Industry 522210, Credit Card Issuing;
- Establishments primarily engaged in sales financing or sales financing in combination with leasing are classified in Industry 522220, Sales Financing;
- Establishments primarily engaged in making unsecured cash loans to consumers are classified in U.S. Industry 522291, Consumer Lending;
- Establishments primarily engaged in lending funds with real estate as collateral are classified in U.S. Industry 522292, Real Estate Credit;
- Establishments primarily engaged in international trade financing are classified in U.S. Industry 522293, International Trade Financing;
- Establishments primarily engaged in buying, pooling, and repackaging loans for sale to others on the secondary market are classified in U.S. Industry 522294, Secondary Market Financing; and
- Establishments known as industrial banks or Morris Plans and primarily engaged in accepting deposits are classified in Industry 522190, Other Depository Credit Intermediation.

5223 Activities Related to Credit Intermediation

This industry group comprises establishments primarily engaged in facilitating credit intermediation by performing activities, such as arranging loans by bringing borrowers and lenders together and clearing checks and credit card transactions.

52231 Mortgage and Nonmortgage Loan Brokers
See industry description for 522310.

522310 Mortgage and Nonmortgage Loan Brokers

This industry comprises establishments primarily engaged in arranging loans by bringing borrowers and lenders together on a commission or fee basis.

T—Canadian, Mexican, and United States industries are comparable.

Cross-References. Establishments primarily engaged in--

- Lending funds with real estate as collateral--are classified in U.S. Industry 522292, Real Estate Credit; and
- Servicing loans--are classified in Industry 522390, Other Activities Related to Credit Intermediation.

52232 Financial Transactions Processing, Reserve, and Clearinghouse Activities
See industry description for 522320.

522320 Financial Transactions Processing, Reserve, and Clearinghouse Activities

This industry comprises establishments primarily engaged in providing one or more of the following: (1) financial transaction processing (except central bank); (2) reserve and liquidity services (except central bank); and/or (3) check or other financial instrument clearinghouse services (except central bank).

Illustrative Examples:

Automated clearinghouses, bank or check (except central bank)
Credit card processing services
Check clearing services (except central bank)

Cross-References.

- Establishments primarily engaged in nonfinancial data and electronic transaction processing are classified in Industry 518210, Data Processing, Hosting, and Related Services; and
- Establishments of the central bank primarily engaged in check clearing and other financial transaction processing are classified in Industry 521110, Monetary Authorities-Central Bank.

52239 Other Activities Related to Credit Intermediation
See industry description for 522390.

522390 Other Activities Related to Credit Intermediation

This industry comprises establishments primarily engaged in facilitating credit intermediation (except mortgage and loan brokerage; and financial transactions processing, reserve, and clearinghouse activities).

Illustrative Examples:

Check cashing services
Money order issuance services
Loan servicing
Travelers' check issuance services
Money transmission services
Payday lending services

Cross-References. Establishments primarily engaged in--

- Arranging loans for others on a commission or fee basis--are classified in Industry 522310, Mortgage and Nonmortgage Loan Brokers;
- Providing financial transactions processing, reserve, and clearinghouse activities--are classified in Industry 522320, Financial Transactions Processing, Reserve, and Clearinghouse Activities;
- Foreign currency exchange dealing--are classified in Industry 523130, Commodity Contracts Dealing; and
- Providing escrow services (except real estate)--are classified in U.S. Industry 523991, Trust, Fiduciary, and Custody Activities.

523 Securities, Commodity Contracts, and Other Financial Investments and Related Activities[T]

Industries in the Securities, Commodity Contracts, and Other Financial Investments and Related Activities subsector group establishments that are primarily engaged in one of the following: (1) underwriting securities issues

T—Canadian, Mexican, and United States industries are comparable.

and/or making markets for securities and commodities; (2) acting as agents (i.e., brokers) between buyers and sellers of securities and commodities; (3) providing securities and commodity exchange services; and (4) providing other services, such as managing portfolios of assets; providing investment advice; and trust, fiduciary, and custody services.

5231 Securities and Commodity Contracts Intermediation and Brokerage[T]

This industry group comprises establishments primarily engaged in putting capital at risk in the process of underwriting securities issues or in making markets for securities and commodities; and those acting as agents and/or brokers between buyers and sellers of securities and commodities, usually charging a commission.

52311 Investment Banking and Securities Dealing
See industry description for 523110.

523110 Investment Banking and Securities Dealing

This industry comprises establishments primarily engaged in underwriting, originating, and/or maintaining markets for issues of securities. Investment bankers act as principals (i.e., investors who buy or sell on their own account) in firm commitment transactions or act as agents in best effort and standby commitments. This industry also includes establishments acting as principals in buying or selling securities generally on a spread basis, such as securities dealers or stock option dealers.

Illustrative Examples:

Bond dealing (i.e., acting as a principal in dealing securities to investors)
Stock options dealing
Securities underwriting

Cross-References.

- Establishments primarily engaged in acting as agents (i.e., brokers) in buying or selling securities on a commission or transaction fee basis are classified in Industry 523120, Securities Brokerage; and
- Investment clubs or individual investors primarily engaged in buying or selling financial contracts (e.g., securities) on their own account are classified in Industry 523910, Miscellaneous Intermediation.

52312 Securities Brokerage
See industry description for 523120.

523120 Securities Brokerage

This industry comprises establishments primarily engaged in acting as agents (i.e., brokers) between buyers and sellers in buying or selling securities on a commission or transaction fee basis.

Illustrative Examples:

Mutual fund agencies (i.e., brokerages)
Stock brokerages
Securities brokerages

Cross-References.

Establishments primarily engaged in investment banking and securities dealing (i.e., buying or selling securities on their own account) are classified in Industry 523110, Investment Banking and Securities Dealing.

52313 Commodity Contracts Dealing
See industry description for 523130.

T—Canadian, Mexican, and United States industries are comparable.

523130 Commodity Contracts Dealing

This industry comprises establishments primarily engaged in acting as principals (i.e., investors who buy or sell for their own account) in buying or selling spot or futures commodity contracts or options, such as precious metals, foreign currency, oil, or agricultural products, generally on a spread basis.

Cross-References. Establishments primarily engaged in--

- Acting as agents (i.e., brokers) in buying or selling spot or futures commodity contracts on a commission or transaction fee basis--are classified in Industry 523140, Commodity Contracts Brokerage; and
- Buying and selling physical commodities for resale to other than the general public--are classified in Sector 42, Wholesale Trade.

52314 Commodity Contracts Brokerage
See industry description for 523140.

523140 Commodity Contracts Brokerage

This industry comprises establishments primarily engaged in acting as agents (i.e., brokers) in buying or selling spot or futures commodity contracts or options on a commission or transaction fee basis.

Illustrative Examples:

Commodity contracts brokerages
Financial futures brokerages
Commodity futures brokerages

Cross-References. Establishments primarily engaged in--

- Acting as principals in buying or selling spot or futures commodity contracts generally on a spread basis--are classified in Industry 523130, Commodity Contracts Dealing; and
- Buying and selling physical commodities for resale to other than the general public--are classified in Sector 42, Wholesale Trade.

5232 Securities and Commodity Exchanges[T]

52321 Securities and Commodity Exchanges[T] See industry description for 523210.

523210 Securities and Commodity Exchanges

This industry comprises establishments primarily engaged in furnishing physical or electronic marketplaces for the purpose of facilitating the buying and selling of stocks, stock options, bonds, or commodity contracts.

Cross-References.

Establishments primarily engaged in investment banking, securities dealing, securities brokering, commodity contracts dealing, or commodity contracts brokering are classified in Industry Group 5231, Securities and Commodity Contracts Intermediation and Brokerage.

5239 Other Financial Investment Activities[T]

This industry group comprises establishments primarily engaged in one of the following: (1) acting as principals in buying or selling financial contracts (except investment bankers, securities dealers, and commodity contracts dealers); (2) acting as agents (i.e., brokers) (except securities brokerages and commodity contracts brokerages) in

T—Canadian, Mexican, and United States industries are comparable.

buying or selling financial contracts; or (3) providing other investment services (except securities and commodity exchanges), such as portfolio management; investment advice; and trust, fiduciary, and custody services.

52391 Miscellaneous Intermediation

See industry description for 523910.

523910 Miscellaneous Intermediation

This industry comprises establishments primarily engaged in acting as principals (except investment bankers, securities dealers, and commodity contracts dealers) in buying or selling financial contracts generally on a spread basis. Principals are investors that buy or sell for their own account.

Illustrative Examples:

Investment clubs
Tax liens dealing (i.e., acting as a principal in dealing tax liens to investors)
Mineral royalties or leases dealing (i.e., acting as a principal in dealing royalties or leases to investors)

Cross-References.

Establishments primarily engaged in investment banking, securities dealing, securities brokering, commodity contracts dealing, or commodity contracts brokering are classified in Industry Group 5231, Securities and Commodity Contracts Intermediation and Brokerage.

52392 Portfolio Management

See industry description for 523920.

523920 Portfolio Management

This industry comprises establishments primarily engaged in managing the portfolio assets (i.e., funds) of others on a fee or commission basis. Establishments in this industry have the authority to make investment decisions, and they derive fees based on the size and/or overall performance of the portfolio.

Illustrative Examples:

Managing trusts
Pension fund managing
Mutual fund managing
Portfolio fund managing

Cross-References.

Establishments primarily engaged in investment banking, securities dealing, securities brokering, commodity contracts dealing, or commodity contracts brokering are classified in Industry Group 5231, Securities and Commodity Contracts Intermediation and Brokerage.

52393 Investment Advice

See industry description for 523930.

523930 Investment Advice

This industry comprises establishments primarily engaged in providing customized investment advice to clients on a fee basis, but do not have the authority to execute trades. Primary activities performed by establishments in this industry are providing financial planning advice and investment counseling to meet the goals and needs of specific clients.

T—Canadian, Mexican, and United States industries are comparable.

Illustrative Examples:

Financial investment advice services, customized, fees paid by client
Investment advisory services, customized, fees paid by client
Financial planning services, customized, fees paid by

Cross-References.

- Establishments providing investment advice in conjunction with their primary activity, such as portfolio management, or the sale of stocks, bonds, annuities, and real estate, are classified according to their primary activity; and
- Establishments known as publishers providing generalized investment information to subscribers are classified in Subsector 511, Publishing Industries (except Internet), or Industry 519130, Internet Publishing and Broadcasting and Web Search Portals.

52399 All Other Financial Investment Activities

This industry comprises establishments primarily engaged in acting as agents or brokers (except securities brokerages and commodity contracts brokerages) in buying and selling financial contracts and those providing financial investment services (except securities and commodity exchanges, portfolio management, and investment advice).

Illustrative Examples:

Bank trust offices
Fiduciary agencies (except real estate)
Escrow agencies (except real estate)
Stock quotation services

Cross-References. Establishments primarily engaged in--

- Investment banking, securities dealing, securities brokerage, commodity contracts dealing, or commodity contracts brokering--are classified in Industry Group 5231, Securities and Commodity Contracts Intermediation and Brokerage;
- Acting as principals (except investment bankers, securities dealers, and commodity contracts dealers) in buying or selling financial contracts (except securities or commodity contracts)--are classified in Industry 52391, Miscellaneous Intermediation;
- Furnishing physical or electronic marketplaces for the purpose of facilitating the buying and selling of securities and commodities--are classified in Industry 52321, Securities and Commodity Exchanges;
- Managing the portfolio assets (i.e., funds) of others--are classified in Industry 52392, Portfolio Management;
- Providing customized investment advice--are classified in Industry 52393, Investment Advice;
- Awarding grants from trust funds--are classified in Industry 81321, Grantmaking and Giving Services;
- Performing real estate escrow or real estate fiduciary activities--are classified in Industry 53139, Other Activities Related to Real Estate; and
- Financial transactions processing, reserve, and clearinghouse activities--are classified in Industry 52232, Financial Transactions Processing, Reserve, and Clearinghouse Activities.

523991 Trust, Fiduciary, and Custody Activities

This U.S. industry comprises establishments primarily engaged in providing trust, fiduciary, and custody services to others, as instructed, on a fee or contract basis, such as bank trust offices and escrow agencies (except real estate).

T—Canadian, Mexican, and United States industries are comparable.

Cross-References. Establishments primarily engaged in--

- Managing the portfolio assets (i.e., funds) of others--are classified in Industry 523920, Portfolio Management;
- Performing real estate escrow or real estate fiduciary activities--are classified in Industry 531390, Other Activities Related to Real Estate; and
- Awarding grants from trust funds--are classified in Industry 81321, Grantmaking and Giving Services.

523999 Miscellaneous Financial Investment Activities

This U.S. industry comprises establishments primarily engaged in acting as agents and/or brokers (except securities brokerages and commodity contracts brokerages) in buying or selling financial contracts and those providing financial investment services (except securities and commodity exchanges; portfolio management; investment advice; and trust, fiduciary, and custody services) on a fee or commission basis.

Illustrative Examples:

Exchange clearinghouses, commodities or securities
Stock quotation services
Gas lease brokers' offices

Cross-References. Establishments primarily engaged in--

- Investment banking, securities dealing, securities brokering, commodity contracts dealing, or commodity contracts brokering--are classified in Industry Group 5231, Securities and Commodity Contracts Intermediation and Brokerage;
- Acting as principals (except investment bankers, securities dealers, and commodity contracts dealers) in buying or selling financial contracts--are classified in Industry 523910, Miscellaneous Intermediation;
- Furnishing physical or electronic marketplaces for the purpose of facilitating the buying and selling of securities and commodities--are classified in Industry 523210, Securities and Commodity Exchanges;
- Managing the portfolio assets (i.e., funds) of others--are classified in Industry 523920, Portfolio Management;
- Providing customized investment advice--are classified in Industry 523930, Investment Advice;
- Providing trust, fiduciary, and custody services to others--are classified in U.S. Industry 523991, Trust, Fiduciary, and Custody Activities; and
- Financial transactions processing, reserve, and clearinghouse activities--are classified in Industry 522320, Financial Transactions Processing, Reserve, and Clearinghouse Activities.

524 Insurance Carriers and Related Activities[T]

Industries in the Insurance Carriers and Related Activities subsector group establishments that are primarily engaged in one of the following: (1) underwriting (assuming the risk, assigning premiums, and so forth) annuities and insurance policies or (2) facilitating such underwriting by selling insurance policies and by providing other insurance and employee benefit related services.

5241 Insurance Carriers[T]

This industry group comprises establishments primarily engaged in underwriting (assuming the risk, assigning premiums, and so forth) annuities and insurance policies and investing premiums to build up a portfolio of financial assets to be used against future claims. Direct insurance carriers are establishments that are primarily engaged in initially underwriting and assuming the risk of annuities and insurance policies. Reinsurance carriers are establishments that are primarily engaged in assuming all or part of the risk associated with an existing insurance policy (or set of policies) originally underwritten by another insurance carrier.

Industries are defined in terms of the type of risk being insured against, such as death, loss of employment because of age or disability, and/or property damage. Contributions and premiums are set on the basis of actuarial

T—Canadian, Mexican, and United States industries are comparable.

calculations of probable payouts based on risk factors from experience tables and expected investment returns on reserves.

52411 Direct Life, Health, and Medical Insurance Carriers

This industry comprises establishments primarily engaged in initially underwriting (i.e., assuming the risk and assigning premiums) annuities and life insurance policies, disability income insurance policies, accidental death and dismemberment insurance policies, and health and medical insurance policies.

Cross-References.

- Establishments primarily engaged in reinsuring insurance policies are classified in Industry 52413, Reinsurance Carriers;
- Legal entities (i.e., funds, plans, and/or programs) organized to provide insurance and employee benefits exclusively for the sponsor, firm, or its employees or members are classified in Industry Group 5251, Insurance and Employee Benefit Funds; and
- HMO establishments providing health care services are classified in Industry 62149, Other Outpatient Care Centers.

524113 Direct Life Insurance Carriers

This U.S. industry comprises establishments primarily engaged in initially underwriting (i.e., assuming the risk and assigning premiums) annuities and life insurance policies, disability income insurance policies, and accidental death and dismemberment insurance policies.

Cross-References.

- Establishments primarily engaged in reinsuring life insurance policies, disability income insurance policies, and accidental death and dismemberment insurance policies are classified in Industry 524130, Reinsurance Carriers; and
- Legal entities (i.e., funds, plans, and/or programs) organized to provide insurance and employee benefits exclusively for the sponsor, firm, or its employees or members are classified in Industry Group 5251, Insurance and Employee Benefit Funds.

524114 Direct Health and Medical Insurance Carriers

This U.S. industry comprises establishments primarily engaged in initially underwriting (i.e., assuming the risk and assigning premiums) health and medical insurance policies. Group hospitalization plans and HMO establishments that provide health and medical insurance policies without providing health care services are included in this industry.

Cross-References.

- HMO establishments that provide both health care services and underwrite health and medical insurance are classified in U.S. Industry 621491, HMO Medical Centers;
- Establishments primarily engaged in reinsuring health insurance policies are classified in Industry 524130, Reinsurance Carriers; and
- Legal entities (i.e., funds, plans, and/or programs) organized to provide health- and welfare-related employee benefits exclusively for the sponsor's employees or members are classified in Industry 525120, Health and Welfare Funds.

T—Canadian, Mexican, and United States industries are comparable.

52412 Direct Insurance (except Life, Health, and Medical) Carriers

This industry comprises establishments primarily engaged in initially underwriting (i.e., assuming the risk and assigning premiums) various types of insurance policies (except life, disability income, accidental death and dismemberment, and health and medical insurance policies).

Illustrative Examples:

Automobile insurance carriers, direct
Property and casualty insurance carriers, direct
Bank deposit insurance carriers, direct
Title insurance carriers, real estate, direct
Mortgage guaranty insurance carriers, direct
Warranty insurance carriers (e.g., appliance, automobile, homeowners', product), direct

Cross-References.

- Establishments primarily engaged in reinsuring insurance policies are classified in Industry 52413, Reinsurance Carriers;
- Legal entities (i.e., funds, plans, and/or programs) organized to provide insurance and employee benefits exclusively for the sponsor, firm, or its employees or members are classified in Industry Group 5251, Insurance and Employee Benefit Funds; and
- Establishments primarily engaged in initially underwriting annuities and life insurance policies, disability income insurance policies, accidental death and dismemberment insurance policies, and health and medical insurance policies are classified in Industry 52411, Direct Life, Health, and Medical Insurance Carriers.

524126 Direct Property and Casualty Insurance Carriers

This U.S. industry comprises establishments primarily engaged in initially underwriting (i.e., assuming the risk and assigning premiums) insurance policies that protect policyholders against losses that may occur as a result of property damage or liability.

Illustrative Examples:

Automobile insurance carriers, direct
Malpractice insurance carriers, direct
Fidelity insurance carriers, direct
Mortgage guaranty insurance carriers, direct
Homeowners' insurance carriers, direct
Surety insurance carriers, direct
Liability insurance carriers, direct

Cross-References.

Establishments primarily engaged in reinsuring property and casualty insurance policies are classified in Industry 524130, Reinsurance Carriers.

524127 Direct Title Insurance Carriers

This U.S. industry comprises establishments primarily engaged in initially underwriting (i.e., assuming the risk and assigning premiums) insurance policies to protect the owners of real estate or real estate creditors against loss sustained by reason of any title defect to real property.

Cross-References.

Establishments primarily engaged in reinsuring title insurance policies are classified in Industry 524130, Reinsurance Carriers.

T—Canadian, Mexican, and United States industries are comparable.

524128 Other Direct Insurance (except Life, Health, and Medical) Carriers

This U.S. industry comprises establishments primarily engaged in initially underwriting (e.g., assuming the risk, assigning premiums) insurance policies (except life, disability income, accidental death and dismemberment, health and medical, property and casualty, and title insurance policies).

Illustrative Examples:

Bank deposit insurance carriers, direct
Product warranty insurance carriers, direct
Deposit or share insurance carriers, direct
Warranty insurance carriers (e.g., appliance, automobile, homeowners', product), direct

Cross-References. Establishments primarily engaged in--

- Reinsuring insurance policies--are classified in Industry 524130, Reinsurance Carriers;
- Initially underwriting annuities and life insurance policies, disability income insurance policies, and accidental death and dismemberment insurance policies--are classified in U.S. Industry 524113, Direct Life Insurance Carriers;
- Initially underwriting health and medical insurance policies--are classified in U.S. Industry 524114, Direct Health and Medical Insurance Carriers;
- Initially underwriting property and casualty insurance policies--are classified in U.S. Industry 524126, Direct Property and Casualty Insurance Carriers; and
- Initially underwriting title insurance policies--are classified in U.S. Industry 524127, Direct Title Insurance Carriers.

52413 Reinsurance Carriers
See industry description for 524130.

524130 Reinsurance Carriers

This industry comprises establishments primarily engaged in assuming all or part of the risk associated with existing insurance policies originally underwritten by other insurance carriers.

Cross-References. Establishments primarily engaged in--

- Initially underwriting annuities and life insurance policies, disability income insurance policies, accidental death and dismemberment insurance policies, and health and medical insurance policies--are classified in Industry 52411, Direct Life, Health, and Medical Insurance Carriers; and
- Initially underwriting various types of insurance policies (except life, disability income, accidental death and dismemberment, and health and medical insurance policies)--are classified in Industry 52412, Direct Insurance (except Life, Health, and Medical) Carriers.

5242 Agencies, Brokerages, and Other Insurance Related Activities[T]

This industry group comprises establishments primarily engaged in (1) acting as agents (i.e., brokers) in selling annuities and insurance policies or (2) providing other employee benefits and insurance related services, such as claims adjustment and third party administration.

52421 Insurance Agencies and Brokerages
See industry description for 524210.

524210 Insurance Agencies and Brokerages

This industry comprises establishments primarily engaged in acting as agents (i.e., brokers) in selling annuities and insurance policies.

T—Canadian, Mexican, and United States industries are comparable.

Cross-References.

Establishments primarily engaged in underwriting annuities and insurance policies are classified in Industry Group 5241, Insurance Carriers.

52429 Other Insurance Related Activities

This industry comprises establishments primarily engaged in providing services related to insurance (except insurance agencies and brokerages).

Illustrative Examples:

Claims adjusting, insurance
Insurance plan administrative services, third party
Insurance actuarial services
Insurance claims adjusting

Cross-References. Establishments primarily engaged in--

- Managing the portfolio assets (i.e., funds) of others--are classified in Industry 52392, Portfolio Management;
- Acting as agents (i.e., brokers) in selling annuities and insurance policies--are classified in Industry 52421, Insurance Agencies and Brokerages; and
- Providing actuarial consulting services--are classified in Industry 54161, Management Consulting Services.

524291 Claims Adjusting

This U.S. industry comprises establishments primarily engaged in investigating, appraising, and settling insurance claims.

524292 Third Party Administration of Insurance and Pension Funds

This U.S. industry comprises establishments primarily engaged in providing third party administration services of insurance and pension funds, such as claims processing and other administrative services to insurance carriers, employee benefit plans, and self-insurance funds.

Cross-References. Establishments primarily engaged in--

- Managing the portfolio assets (i.e., funds) of others--are classified in Industry 523920, Portfolio Management; and
- Providing actuarial consulting services--are classified in U.S. Industry 541612, Human Resources Consulting Services.

524298 All Other Insurance Related Activities

This U.S. industry comprises establishments primarily engaged in providing insurance services on a contract or fee basis (except insurance agencies and brokerages, claims adjusting, and third party administration). Insurance advisory services, insurance actuarial services, and insurance ratemaking services are included in this industry.

Cross-References. Establishments primarily engaged in--

- Providing actuarial consulting services--are classified in U.S. Industry 541612, Human Resources Consulting Services;
- Acting as agents (i.e., brokers) in selling annuities and insurance policies--are classified in Industry 524210, Insurance Agencies and Brokerages;
- Insurance claims adjusting--are classified in U.S. Industry 524291, Claims Adjusting; and

T—Canadian, Mexican, and United States industries are comparable.

- Third party administration services of insurance and pension funds--are classified in U.S. Industry 524292, Third Party Administration of Insurance and Pension Funds.

525 Funds, Trusts, and Other Financial Vehicles

Industries in the Funds, Trusts, and Other Financial Vehicles subsector group legal entities (i.e., funds, plans, and/or programs) organized to pool securities or other assets on behalf of shareholders or beneficiaries of employee benefit or other trust funds. The portfolios are customized to achieve specific investment characteristics, such as diversification, risk, rate of return, and price volatility. These entities earn interest, dividends, and other investment income, but have little or no employment and no revenue from the sale of services. Establishments with employees devoted to the management of funds are classified in Industry Group 5239, Other Financial Investment Activities. Establishments primarily engaged in holding the securities of (or other equity interests in) other firms are classified in Sector 55, Management of Companies and Enterprises. Equity real estate investment trusts (REITs) that are primarily engaged in leasing buildings, dwellings, or other real estate property to others are classified in Subsector 531, Real Estate.

5251 Insurance and Employee Benefit Funds

This industry group comprises legal entities (i.e., funds, plans, and/or programs) organized to provide insurance and employee benefits exclusively for the sponsor, firm, or its employees or members.

52511 Pension Funds

See industry description for 525110.

525110 Pension Funds

This industry comprises legal entities (i.e., funds, plans, and/or programs) organized to provide retirement income benefits exclusively for the sponsor's employees or members.

Illustrative Examples:

Employee benefit plans
Retirement plans
Pension funds and plans

Cross-References. Establishments primarily engaged in--

- Managing portfolios of pension funds--are classified in Industry 523920, Portfolio Management; and
- Initially underwriting annuities--are classified in U.S. Industry 524113, Direct Life Insurance Carriers.

52512 Health and Welfare Funds

See industry description for 525120.

525120 Health and Welfare Funds

This industry comprises legal entities (i.e., funds, plans, and/or programs) organized to provide medical, surgical, hospital, vacation, training, and other health- and welfare-related employee benefits exclusively for the sponsor's employees or members.

Cross-References. Establishments primarily engaged in--

- Managing portfolios of health and welfare funds--are classified in Industry 523920, Portfolio Management; and
- Third party claims administration of health and welfare plans--are classified in U.S. Industry 524292, Third Party Administration of Insurance and Pension Funds.

T—Canadian, Mexican, and United States industries are comparable.

52519 Other Insurance Funds
See industry description for 525190.

525190 Other Insurance Funds

This industry comprises legal entities (i.e., funds (except pension, and health- and welfare-related employee benefit funds)) organized to provide insurance exclusively for the sponsor, firm, or its employees or members. Self-insurance funds (except employee benefit funds) and workers' compensation insurance funds are included in this industry.

Cross-References.

- Legal entities (i.e., funds, plans, and/or programs) organized to provide retirement income benefits exclusively for the sponsor's employees or members are classified in Industry 525110, Pension Funds;
- Legal entities (i.e., funds, plans, and/or programs) organized to provide health- and welfare-related employee benefits exclusively for the sponsor's employees or members are classified in Industry 525120, Health and Welfare Funds;
- Establishments primarily engaged in managing portfolios of insurance funds are classified in Industry 523920, Portfolio Management;
- Establishments primarily engaged in third party claims administration of insurance and other employee benefit funds are classified in U.S. Industry 524292, Third Party Administration of Insurance and Pension Funds; and
- Establishments primarily engaged in providing insurance on a fee or contract basis are classified in Industry Group 5241, Insurance Carriers.

5259 Other Investment Pools and Funds

This industry group comprises legal entities (i.e., investment pools and/or funds) organized to pool securities or other assets (except insurance and employee benefit funds) on behalf of shareholders, unitholders, or beneficiaries.

52591 Open-End Investment Funds
See industry description for 525910.

525910 Open-End Investment Funds

This industry comprises legal entities (i.e., open-end investment funds) organized to pool assets that consist of securities or other financial instruments. Shares in these pools are offered to the public in an initial offering with additional shares offered continuously and perpetually and redeemed at a specific price determined by the net asset value.

Illustrative Examples:

Investment funds, open-ended Money market mutual funds, open-ended

52592 Trusts, Estates, and Agency Accounts See industry description for 525920.

525920 Trusts, Estates, and Agency Accounts

This industry comprises legal entities, trusts, estates, or agency accounts, administered on behalf of the beneficiaries under the terms of a trust agreement, will, or agency agreement.

T—Canadian, Mexican, and United States industries are comparable.

Illustrative Examples:

Bankruptcy estates
Private estates (i.e., administering on behalf of beneficiaries)
Personal investment trusts
Testamentary trusts

Cross-References. Establishments primarily engaged in--

- Managing portfolios of trusts--are classified in Industry 523920, Portfolio Management;
- Administering personal estates--are classified in U.S. Industry 523991, Trust, Fiduciary, and Custody Activities; and
- Operating businesses of trusts and bankruptcy estates--are classified according to the kind of business operated.

52599 Other Financial Vehicles

See industry description for 525990.

525990 Other Financial Vehicles

This industry comprises legal entities (i.e., funds (except insurance and employee benefit funds; open-end investment funds; trusts, estates, and agency accounts)). Included in this industry are mortgage real estate investment trusts (REITs).

Illustrative Examples:

Closed-end investment funds
Special purpose financial vehicles
Collateralized mortgage obligations (CMOs)
Unit investment trust funds
Face-amount certificate funds
Mortgage real estate investment trusts (REITs)
Real estate mortgage investment conduits (REMICs)

Cross-References.

- Legal entities (i.e., funds, plans, and programs) that provide insurance and employee benefits exclusively for the sponsor, firm, or its employees or members are classified in Industry Group 5251, Insurance and Employee Benefit Funds;
- Legal entities (i.e., open-end investment funds) organized to pool assets that consist of securities or other financial instruments, where the pools are offered to the public in an initial offering with additional shares offered continuously and perpetually at a specific price determined by the net asset value, are classified in Industry 525910, Open-End Investment Funds;
- Legal entities (i.e., trusts, estates, or agency accounts) administered on behalf of the beneficiaries under the terms of a trust agreement, will, or agency agreement are classified in Industry 525920, Trusts, Estates, and Agency Accounts; and
- Equity real estate investment trusts (REITs) that are primarily engaged in leasing buildings, dwellings, or other real estate property to others are classified in Industry Group 5311, Lessors of Real Estate, based on primary type of real estate property leased.

T—Canadian, Mexican, and United States industries are comparable.

Sector 53--Real Estate and Rental and Leasing[T]

The Sector as a Whole

The Real Estate and Rental and Leasing sector comprises establishments primarily engaged in renting, leasing, or otherwise allowing the use of tangible or intangible assets, and establishments providing related services. The major portion of this sector comprises establishments that rent, lease, or otherwise allow the use of their own assets by others. The assets may be tangible, as is the case of real estate and equipment, or intangible, as is the case with patents and trademarks.

This sector also includes establishments primarily engaged in managing real estate for others, selling, renting and/or buying real estate for others, and appraising real estate. These activities are closely related to this sector's main activity, and from a production basis they are included here. In addition, a substantial proportion of property management is self-performed by lessors.

The main components of this sector are the real estate lessors industries (including equity real estate investment trusts (REITs)); equipment lessors industries (including motor vehicles, computers, and consumer goods); and lessors of nonfinancial intangible assets (except copyrighted works).

Excluded from this sector are establishments primarily engaged in renting or leasing equipment with operators. Establishments renting or leasing equipment with operators are classified in various subsectors of NAICS depending on the nature of the services provided (e.g., transportation, construction, agriculture). These activities are excluded from this sector because the client is paying for the expertise and knowledge of the equipment operator, in addition to the rental of the equipment. In many cases, such as the rental of heavy construction equipment, the operator is essential to operate the equipment.

531 Real Estate[T]

Industries in the Real Estate subsector group establishments primarily engaged in renting or leasing real estate to others; managing real estate for others; selling, buying, or renting real estate for others; and providing other real estate related services, such as appraisal services.

This subsector includes equity real estate investment trusts (REITs) primarily engaged in leasing buildings, dwellings, or other real estate property to others. Mortgage REITs are classified in Subsector 525, Funds, Trusts, and Other Financial Vehicles.

Establishments primarily engaged in subdividing and developing unimproved real estate and constructing buildings for sale are classified in Subsector 236, Construction of Buildings. Establishments primarily engaged in subdividing and improving raw land for subsequent sale to builders are classified in Subsector 237, Heavy and Civil Engineering Construction.

5311 Lessors of Real Estate[T]

This industry group comprises establishments primarily engaged in acting as lessors of (1) residential buildings and dwellings; (2) nonresidential buildings (except miniwarehouses); (3) miniwarehouses and self-storage units; and (4) other real estate property.

53111 Lessors of Residential Buildings and Dwellings
See industry description for 531110.

531110 Lessors of Residential Buildings and Dwellings

This industry comprises establishments primarily engaged in acting as lessors of buildings used as residences or dwellings, such as single-family homes, apartment buildings, and town homes. Included in this industry are owner-lessors and establishments renting real estate and then acting as lessors in subleasing it to others. The establishments in this industry may manage the property themselves or have another establishment manage it for them.

T—Canadian, Mexican, and United States industries are comparable.

Cross-References.

Establishments primarily engaged in managing residential real estate for others are classified in U.S. Industry 531311, Residential Property Managers.

53112 Lessors of Nonresidential Buildings (except Miniwarehouses)
See industry description for 531120.

531120 Lessors of Nonresidential Buildings (except Miniwarehouses)

This industry comprises establishments primarily engaged in acting as lessors of buildings (except miniwarehouses and self-storage units) that are not used as residences or dwellings. Included in this industry are: (1) owner-lessors of nonresidential buildings; (2) establishments renting real estate and then acting as lessors in subleasing it to others; and (3) establishments providing full service office space, whether on a lease or service contract basis. The establishments in this industry may manage the property themselves or have another establishment manage it for them.

Cross-References. Establishments primarily engaged in--

- Acting as lessors of buildings used as residences or dwellings--are classified in Industry 531110, Lessors of Residential Buildings and Dwellings;
- Renting or leasing space for self-storage--are classified in Industry 531130, Lessors of Miniwarehouses and Self-Storage Units;
- Managing nonresidential real estate for others--are classified in U.S. Industry 531312, Nonresidential Property Managers;
- Providing a range of office support services, such as mailbox rental, other postal and mailing (except direct mail advertising) services, document copying services, facsimile services, word processing services or on-site personal computer rental, that are not providing office space--are classified in Industry 56143, Business Service Centers;
- Managing and operating arenas, stadiums, theaters, or other related facilities and promoting and organizing performing arts productions, sports events, and similar events at those facilities--are classified in Industry 711310, Promoters of Performing Arts, Sports, and Similar Events with Facilities; and
- Operating public and contract general merchandise warehousing and storage facilities--are classified in Industry 493110, General Warehousing and Storage.

53113 Lessors of Miniwarehouses and Self-Storage Units
See industry description for 531130.

531130 Lessors of Miniwarehouses and Self-Storage Units

This industry comprises establishments primarily engaged in renting or leasing space for self-storage. These establishments provide secure space (i.e., rooms, compartments, lockers, containers, or outdoor space) where clients can store and retrieve their goods.

Cross-References. Establishments primarily engaged in--

- Operating public and contract general merchandise warehousing and storage facilities--are classified in Industry 493110, General Warehousing and Storage; and
- Operating coin-operated lockers--are classified in Industry 812990, All Other Personal Services.

53119 Lessors of Other Real Estate Property
See industry description for 531190.

T—Canadian, Mexican, and United States industries are comparable.

531190 Lessors of Other Real Estate Property

This industry comprises establishments primarily engaged in acting as lessors of real estate (except buildings), such as manufactured home (i.e., mobile home) sites, vacant lots, and grazing land.

Cross-References. Establishments primarily engaged in--

- Acting as lessors of buildings used as residences or dwellings, including on-site manufactured (mobile) homes--are classified in Industry 531110, Lessors of Residential Buildings and Dwellings;
- Acting as lessors of buildings (except miniwarehouses and self-storage units) that are not used as residences or dwellings--are classified in Industry 531120, Lessors of Nonresidential Buildings (except Miniwarehouses); and
- Renting or leasing space for self-storage--are classified in Industry 531130, Lessors of Miniwarehouses and Self-Storage Units.

5312 Offices of Real Estate Agents and Brokers[T]

53121 Offices of Real Estate Agents and Brokers[T]
See industry description for 531210.

531210 Offices of Real Estate Agents and Brokers

This industry comprises establishments primarily engaged in acting as agents and/or brokers in one or more of the following: (1) selling real estate for others; (2) buying real estate for others; and (3) renting real estate for others.

5313 Activities Related to Real Estate[T]

This industry group comprises establishments primarily engaged in providing real estate services (except lessors of real estate and offices of real estate agents and brokers). Included in this industry group are establishments primarily engaged in managing real estate for others and appraising real estate.

53131 Real Estate Property Managers

This industry comprises establishments primarily engaged in managing real property for others. Management includes ensuring that various activities associated with the overall operation of the property are performed, such as collecting rents and overseeing other services (e.g., maintenance, security, trash removal.)

Cross-References.

- Establishments primarily engaged in acting as lessors of real estate are classified in Industry Group 5311, Lessors of Real Estate; and
- Establishments formed on behalf of individual condominium owners or homeowners are classified in Industry 81399, Other Similar Organizations (except Business, Professional, Labor, and Political Organizations).

531311 Residential Property Managers

This U.S. industry comprises establishments primarily engaged in managing residential real estate for others.

Cross-References.

- Establishments primarily engaged in managing nonresidential real estate for others are classified in U.S. Industry 531312, Nonresidential Property Managers;
- Establishments primarily engaged in acting as lessors of buildings used as residences or dwellings are classified in Industry 531110, Lessors of Residential Buildings and Dwellings; and

T—Canadian, Mexican, and United States industries are comparable.

- Establishments formed on behalf of individual residential condominium owners or homeowners are classified in Industry 813990, Other Similar Organizations (except Business, Professional, Labor, and Political Organizations).

531312 Nonresidential Property Managers

This U.S. industry comprises establishments primarily engaged in managing nonresidential real estate for others.

Cross-References.

- Establishments primarily engaged in managing residential real estate for others are classified in U.S. Industry 531311, Residential Property Managers;
- Establishments primarily engaged in acting as lessors of buildings (except miniwarehouses and self-storage units) that are not used as residences or dwellings are classified in Industry 531120, Lessors of Nonresidential Buildings (except Miniwarehouses);
- Establishments primarily engaged in renting or leasing space for self-storage are classified in Industry 531130, Lessors of Miniwarehouses and Self-Storage Units; and
- Establishments formed on behalf of individual nonresidential condominium owners are classified in Industry 813990, Other Similar Organizations (except Business, Professional, Labor, and Political Organizations).

53132 Offices of Real Estate Appraisers
See industry description for 531320.

531320 Offices of Real Estate Appraisers

This industry comprises establishments primarily engaged in estimating the fair market value of real estate.

53139 Other Activities Related to Real Estate
See industry description for 531390.

531390 Other Activities Related to Real Estate

This industry comprises establishments primarily engaged in performing real estate related services (except lessors of real estate, offices of real estate agents and brokers, real estate property managers, and offices of real estate appraisers).

Illustrative Examples:

Real estate escrow agencies
Real estate fiduciaries' offices
Real estate listing services

Cross-References. Establishments primarily engaged in--

- Acting as lessors of real estate--are classified in Industry Group 5311, Lessors of Real Estate;
- Selling, buying, and/or renting real estate for others--are classified in Industry 531210, Offices of Real Estate Agents and Brokers;
- Managing real estate for others--are classified in Industry 53131, Real Estate Property Managers;
- Estimating fair market value of real estate--are classified in Industry 531320, Offices of Real Estate Appraisers; and
- Researching public land records for ownership of titles and/or conveying real estate titles--are classified in U.S. Industry 541191, Title Abstract and Settlement Offices.

T—Canadian, Mexican, and United States industries are comparable.

532 Rental and Leasing Services[T]

Industries in the Rental and Leasing Services subsector include establishments that provide a wide array of tangible goods, such as automobiles, computers, consumer goods, and industrial machinery and equipment, to customers in return for a periodic rental or lease payment.

The subsector includes two main types of establishments: (1) those that are engaged in renting consumer goods and equipment and (2) those that are engaged in leasing machinery and equipment often used for business operations. The first type typically operates from a retail-like or storefront facility and maintains inventories of goods that are rented for short periods of time. The latter type typically does not operate from retail-like locations or maintain inventories, and offers longer-term leases. These establishments work directly with clients to enable them to acquire the use of equipment on a lease basis, or they work with equipment vendors or dealers to support the marketing of equipment to their customers under lease arrangements. Equipment lessors generally structure lease contracts to meet the specialized needs of their clients and use their remarketing expertise to find other users for previously leased equipment. Establishments that provide operating and capital (i.e., finance) leases are included in this subsector.

Establishments primarily engaged in leasing in combination with providing loans are classified in Sector 52, Finance and Insurance. Establishments primarily engaged in leasing real property are classified in Subsector 531, Real Estate. Establishments primarily engaged in renting or leasing equipment with operators are classified in various subsectors of NAICS depending on the nature of the services provided (e.g., transportation, construction, agriculture). These activities are excluded from this subsector since the client is paying for the expertise and knowledge of the equipment operator, in addition to the rental of the equipment. In many cases, such as the rental of heavy construction equipment, the operator is essential to operate the equipment. Likewise, since the provision of crop harvesting services includes both the equipment and operator, it is included in Subsector 115, Support Activities for Agriculture and Forestry. The rental or leasing of copyrighted works is classified in Sector 51, Information, and the rental or leasing of assets, such as patents, trademarks, and/or licensing agreements, is classified in Subsector 533, Lessors of Nonfinancial Intangible Assets (except Copyrighted Works).

5321 Automotive Equipment Rental and Leasing[T]

This industry group comprises establishments primarily engaged in renting or leasing passenger cars and trucks without drivers and utility trailers. These establishments generally operate from a retail-like facility. Some establishments offer only short-term rental, others only longer-term leases, and some provide both types of services.

53211 Passenger Car Rental and Leasing[T]

This industry comprises establishments primarily engaged in renting or leasing passenger cars without drivers.

Cross-References. Establishments primarily engaged in--

- Renting or leasing passenger cars with drivers (e.g., limousines, hearses, taxis)--are classified in Industry Group 4853, Taxi and Limousine Service;
- Retailing passenger cars through sales or lease arrangements--are classified in Industry Group 4411, Automobile Dealers; and
- Leasing passenger cars in combination with providing loans to buyers of such vehicles--are classified in Sector 52, Finance and Insurance.

532111 Passenger Car Rental

This U.S. industry comprises establishments primarily engaged in renting passenger cars without drivers, generally for short periods of time.

Cross-References. Establishments primarily engaged in--

- Leasing passenger cars without drivers, generally for long periods of time--are classified in U.S. Industry 532112, Passenger Car Leasing; and

T—Canadian, Mexican, and United States industries are comparable.

- Renting or leasing passenger cars with drivers (e.g., limousines, hearses, taxis)--are classified in Industry Group 4853, Taxi and Limousine Service.

532112 Passenger Car Leasing

This U.S. industry comprises establishments primarily engaged in leasing passenger cars without drivers, generally for long periods of time.

Cross-References. Establishments primarily engaged in--

- Renting passenger cars without drivers, generally for short periods of time--are classified in U.S. Industry 532111, Passenger Car Rental;
- Renting or leasing passenger cars with drivers (e.g., limousines, hearses, taxis)--are classified in Industry Group 4853, Taxi and Limousine Service;
- Retailing passenger cars through sales or lease arrangements--are classified in Industry Group 4411, Automobile Dealers; and
- Leasing passenger cars in combination with providing loans to buyers of such vehicles--are classified in Sector 52, Finance and Insurance.

53212 Truck, Utility Trailer, and RV (Recreational Vehicle) Rental and Leasing[T] See industry description for 532120.

532120 Truck, Utility Trailer, and RV (Recreational Vehicle) Rental and Leasing

This industry comprises establishments primarily engaged in renting or leasing, without drivers, one or more of the following: trucks, truck tractors, buses, semi-trailers, utility trailers, or RVs (recreational vehicles).

Cross-References. Establishments primarily engaged in--

- Renting recreational goods, such as pleasure boats, canoes, motorcycles, mopeds, or bicycles--are classified in U.S. Industry 532284, Recreational Goods Rental;
- Renting or leasing farm tractors, industrial equipment, and industrial trucks, such as forklifts and other material handling equipment--are classified in Industry 532490, Other Commercial and Industrial Machinery and Equipment Rental and Leasing;
- Renting or leasing mobile home sites--are classified in Industry 531190, Lessors of Other Real Estate Property;
- Retailing vehicles commonly referred to as RVs through sales or lease arrangements--are classified in Industry 441210, Recreational Vehicle Dealers; and
- Leasing trucks, utility trailers, and RVs in combination with providing loans to buyers of such vehicles--are classified in Sector 52, Finance and Insurance.

5322 Consumer Goods Rental[T]

This industry group comprises establishments primarily engaged in renting personal and household-type goods. Establishments classified in this industry group generally provide short-term rental although in some instances, the goods may be leased for longer periods of time. These establishments often operate from a retail-like or storefront facility.

53221 Consumer Electronics and Appliances Rental[T] See industry description for 532210.

532210 Consumer Electronics and Appliances Rental

This industry comprises establishments primarily engaged in renting consumer electronics equipment and appliances, such as televisions, stereos, and refrigerators. Included in this industry are appliance rental centers.

T—Canadian, Mexican, and United States industries are comparable.

Cross-References. Establishments primarily engaged in--

- Renting or leasing computers--are classified in Industry 532420, Office Machinery and Equipment Rental and Leasing; and
- Renting a range of consumer, commercial, and industrial equipment, such as lawn and garden equipment, home repair tools, and party and banquet equipment--are classified in Industry 532310, General Rental Centers.

53228 Other Consumer Goods Rental[T]

This industry comprises establishments primarily engaged in renting consumer goods (except consumer electronics and appliances).

Illustrative Examples:

Costume rental
Formal wear rental
Furniture (i.e., residential) rental centers
Hospital bed rental and leasing (i.e., home use)
Party rental supply centers
Sporting goods rental
Video disc rental for home electronic equipment (e.g., DVD)

Cross-References. Establishments primarily engaged in--

- Renting consumer electronics and appliances--are classified in Industry 53221, Consumer Electronics and Appliances Rental;
- Renting a general line of products, such as lawn and garden equipment, home repair tools, and party and banquet equipment--are classified in Industry 53231, General Rental Centers;
- Renting medical equipment (except home health equipment), such as electromedical and electrotherapeutic apparatus--are classified in Industry 53249, Other Commercial and Industrial Machinery and Equipment Rental and Leasing;
- Retailing and renting musical instruments--are classified in Industry 45114, Musical Instrument and Supplies Stores;
- Providing home health care services and home health equipment--are classified in Industry 62161, Home Health Care Services; and
- Laundering and supplying uniforms and other work apparel--are classified in Industry 81233, Linen and Uniform Supply.

532281 Formal Wear and Costume Rental

This U.S. industry comprises establishments primarily engaged in renting clothing, such as formal wear, costumes (e.g., theatrical), or other clothing (except laundered uniforms and work apparel).

Cross-References.

Establishments primarily engaged in laundering and supplying uniforms and other work apparel are classified in U.S. Industry 812332, Industrial Launderers.

532282 Video Tape and Disc Rental

This U.S. industry comprises establishments primarily engaged in renting prerecorded video tapes and discs for home electronic equipment.

Cross-References. Establishments primarily engaged in--

- Renting video recorders and players--are classified in Industry 532210, Consumer Electronics and Appliances Rental;

T—Canadian, Mexican, and United States industries are comparable.

- Retailing prerecorded video tapes and discs--are classified in U.S. Industry 443142, Electronics Stores; and
- Theatrical distribution of motion pictures and videos--are classified in Subsector 512, Motion Picture and Sound Recording Industries.

532283 Home Health Equipment Rental

This U.S. industry comprises establishments primarily engaged in renting home-type health and invalid equipment, such as wheel chairs, hospital beds, oxygen tanks, walkers, and crutches.

Cross-References. Establishments primarily engaged in--

- Renting medical equipment (except home health equipment), such as electromedical and electrotherapeutic apparatus--are classified in Industry 532490, Other Commercial and Industrial Machinery and Equipment Rental and Leasing; and
- Providing home health care services and home health equipment--are classified in Industry 621610, Home Health Care Services.

532284 Recreational Goods Rental

This U.S. industry comprises establishments primarily engaged in renting recreational goods, such as bicycles, canoes, motorcycles, skis, sailboats, beach chairs, and beach umbrellas.

532289 All Other Consumer Goods Rental

This U.S. industry comprises establishments primarily engaged in renting consumer goods and products (except consumer electronics and appliances; formal wear and costumes; prerecorded video tapes and discs for home electronic equipment; home health furniture and equipment; and recreational goods). Included in this industry are furniture rental centers and party rental supply centers.

Cross-References. Establishments primarily engaged in--

- Renting consumer electronics and appliances--are classified in Industry 532210, Consumer Electronics and Appliances Rental;
- Renting formal wear and costumes--are classified in U.S. Industry 532281, Formal Wear and Costume Rental;
- Renting video tapes and discs--are classified in U.S. Industry 532282, Video Tape and Disc Rental;
- Renting home health furniture and equipment--are classified in U.S. Industry 532283, Home Health Equipment Rental;
- Renting recreational goods--are classified in U.S. Industry 532284, Recreational Goods Rental;
- Renting a range of consumer, commercial, and industrial equipment, such as lawn and garden equipment, home repair tools, and party and banquet equipment--are classified in Industry 532310, General Rental Centers; and
- Retailing and renting musical instruments--are classified in Industry 451140, Musical Instrument and Supplies Stores.

5323 General Rental Centers[T]

53231 General Rental Centers[T] See industry description for 532310.

532310 General Rental Centers

This industry comprises establishments primarily engaged in renting a range of consumer, commercial, and industrial equipment. Establishments in this industry typically operate from conveniently located facilities where they maintain inventories of goods and equipment that they rent for short periods of time. The type of equipment

T—Canadian, Mexican, and United States industries are comparable.

that establishments in this industry provide often includes, but is not limited to: audio visual equipment, contractors' and builders' tools and equipment, home repair tools, lawn and garden equipment, moving equipment and supplies, and party and banquet equipment and supplies.

Cross-References. Establishments primarily engaged in--

- Renting trucks and trailers without drivers--are classified in Industry 532120, Truck, Utility Trailer, and RV (Recreational Vehicle) Rental and Leasing;
- Renting party and banquet equipment--are classified in U.S. Industry 532289, All Other Consumer Goods Rental;
- Renting heavy construction equipment without operators--are classified in U.S. Industry 532412, Construction, Mining, and Forestry Machinery and Equipment Rental and Leasing; and
- Renting specialized types of commercial and industrial equipment, such as garden tractors or public address systems--are classified in Industry 532490, Other Commercial and Industrial Machinery and Equipment Rental and Leasing.

5324 Commercial and Industrial Machinery and Equipment Rental and Leasing[T]

This industry group comprises establishments primarily engaged in renting or leasing commercial-type and industrial-type machinery and equipment. Establishments included in this industry group are generally involved in providing capital or investment-type equipment that clients use in their business operations. These establishments typically cater to a business clientele and do not generally operate a retail-like or storefront facility.

53241 Construction, Transportation, Mining, and Forestry Machinery and Equipment Rental and Leasing[T]

This industry comprises establishments primarily engaged in renting or leasing one or more of the following without operators: heavy construction, off-highway transportation, mining, and forestry machinery and equipment. Establishments in this industry may rent or lease products, such as aircraft, railroad cars, steamships, tugboats, bulldozers, earthmoving equipment, well drilling machinery and equipment, or cranes.

Cross-References. Establishments primarily engaged in--

- Renting or leasing automobiles or trucks without operators--are classified in Industry Group 5321, Automotive Equipment Rental and Leasing;
- Renting or leasing air, rail, highway, and water transportation equipment with operators--are classified in Sector 48-49, Transportation and Warehousing, based on their primary activity;
- Renting or leasing heavy construction equipment with operators--are classified in Industry Group 2389, Other Specialty Trade Contractors;
- Renting or leasing heavy equipment for mining with operators--are classified in Industry 21311, Support Activities for Mining;
- Renting or leasing heavy equipment for forestry with operators--are classified in Industry 11531, Support Activities for Forestry; and
- Leasing heavy equipment in combination with providing loans to buyers of such equipment--are classified in Sector 52, Finance and Insurance.

532411 Commercial Air, Rail, and Water Transportation Equipment Rental and Leasing

This U.S. industry comprises establishments primarily engaged in renting or leasing off-highway transportation equipment without operators, such as aircraft, railroad cars, steamships, or tugboats.

Cross-References. Establishments primarily engaged in--

- Renting or leasing air, rail, highway, and water transportation equipment with operators--are classified in Sector 48-49, Transportation and Warehousing, based on their primary activity;
- Renting pleasure boats--are classified in U.S. Industry 532284, Recreational Goods Rental; and

T—Canadian, Mexican, and United States industries are comparable.

- Renting or leasing automobiles or trucks without drivers--are classified in Industry Group 5321, Automotive Equipment Rental and Leasing.

532412 Construction, Mining, and Forestry Machinery and Equipment Rental and Leasing

This U.S. industry comprises establishments primarily engaged in renting or leasing heavy equipment without operators that may be used for construction, mining, or forestry, such as bulldozers, earthmoving equipment, well drilling machinery and equipment, or cranes.

Cross-References. Establishments primarily engaged in--

- Renting or leasing cranes with operators--are classified in Industry 238990, All Other Specialty Trade Contractors;
- Renting or leasing construction equipment with operators (except cranes)--are classified in Industry 238910, Site Preparation Contractors;
- Renting or leasing heavy equipment for mining with operators--are classified in Industry 21311, Support Activities for Mining;
- Renting or leasing heavy equipment for forestry with operators--are classified in Industry 115310, Support Activities for Forestry; and
- Leasing heavy equipment in combination with providing loans to buyers of such equipment--are classified in Sector 52, Finance and Insurance.

53242 Office Machinery and Equipment Rental and Leasing[T] See industry description for 532420.

532420 Office Machinery and Equipment Rental and Leasing

This industry comprises establishments primarily engaged in renting or leasing office machinery and equipment, such as computers, office furniture, duplicating machines (i.e., copiers), or facsimile machines.

Cross-References. Establishments primarily engaged in--

- Renting or leasing residential furniture--are classified in U.S. Industry 532289, All Other Consumer Goods Rental; and
- Leasing office machinery and equipment in combination with providing loans to buyers of such equipment--are classified in Sector 52, Finance and Insurance.

53249 Other Commercial and Industrial Machinery and Equipment Rental and Leasing[T] See industry description for 532490.

532490 Other Commercial and Industrial Machinery and Equipment Rental and Leasing

This industry comprises establishments primarily engaged in renting or leasing nonconsumer-type machinery and equipment (except heavy construction, transportation, mining, and forestry machinery and equipment without operators; and office machinery and equipment). Establishments in this industry rent or lease products, such as manufacturing equipment; metalworking, telecommunications, motion picture, theatrical machinery and equipment, or service industry machinery; institutional (i.e., public building) furniture, such as furniture for schools, theaters, or buildings; or agricultural equipment without operators.

Cross-References. Establishments primarily engaged in--

- Renting or leasing heavy construction, off-highway transportation, mining, and forestry machinery and equipment without operators--are classified in Industry 53241, Construction, Transportation, Mining, and Forestry Machinery and Equipment Rental and Leasing;

T—Canadian, Mexican, and United States industries are comparable.

- Renting or leasing office machinery and equipment--are classified in Industry 532420, Office Machinery and Equipment Rental and Leasing;
- Renting or leasing agricultural machinery and equipment with operators--are classified in Subsector 115, Support Activities for Agriculture and Forestry;
- Renting or leasing dump trucks without operator--are classified in Industry 532120, Truck, Utility Trailer, and RV (Recreational Vehicle) Rental and Leasing;
- Renting home furniture or medical equipment for home use--are classified in Industry 53228, Other Consumer Goods Rental; and
- Leasing nonconsumer machinery and equipment in combination with providing loans to buyers of such equipment--are classified in Sector 52, Finance and Insurance.

533 Lessors of Nonfinancial Intangible Assets (except Copyrighted Works)[T]

Industries in the Lessors of Nonfinancial Intangible Assets (except Copyrighted Works) subsector include establishments primarily engaged in assigning rights to assets, such as patents, trademarks, brand names, and/or franchise agreements, for which a royalty payment or licensing fee is paid to the asset holder. Establishments in this subsector own the patents, trademarks, and/or franchise agreements that they allow others to use or reproduce for a fee and may or may not have created those assets.

Establishments that allow franchisees the use of the franchise name, contingent on the franchisee buying products or services from the franchisor, are classified elsewhere.

Excluded from this subsector are establishments primarily engaged in leasing real property and establishments primarily engaged in leasing tangible assets, such as automobiles, computers, consumer goods, and industrial machinery and equipment. These establishments are classified in Subsector 531, Real Estate, and Subsector 532, Rental and Leasing Services, respectively.

5331 Lessors of Nonfinancial Intangible Assets (except Copyrighted Works)[T]

53311 Lessors of Nonfinancial Intangible Assets (except Copyrighted Works)[T] See industry description for 533110.

533110 Lessors of Nonfinancial Intangible Assets (except Copyrighted Works)

This industry comprises establishments primarily engaged in assigning rights to assets, such as patents, trademarks, brand names, and/or franchise agreements, for which a royalty payment or licensing fee is paid to the asset holder.

Cross-References.

- Establishments primarily engaged in producing, reproducing, and/or distributing copyrighted works are classified in Sector 51, Information;
- Independent artists, writers, and performers primarily engaged in creating copyrighted works are classified in Industry 711510, Independent Artists, Writers, and Performers;
- Establishments primarily engaged in leasing real property are classified in Subsector 531, Real Estate;
- Establishments primarily engaged in leasing tangible assets, such as automobiles, computers, consumer goods, and industrial machinery and equipment, are classified in Subsector 532, Rental and Leasing Services; and
- Establishments that allow franchisees the use of the franchise name, contingent on the franchisee buying products or services from the franchisor, are classified elsewhere.

T—Canadian, Mexican, and United States industries are comparable.

Sector 54--Professional, Scientific, and Technical Services[T]

The Sector as a Whole

The Professional, Scientific, and Technical Services sector comprises establishments that specialize in performing professional, scientific, and technical activities for others. These activities require a high degree of expertise and training. The establishments in this sector specialize according to expertise and provide these services to clients in a variety of industries and, in some cases, to households. Activities performed include: legal advice and representation; accounting, bookkeeping, and payroll services; architectural, engineering, and specialized design services; computer services; consulting services; research services; advertising services; photographic services; translation and interpretation services; veterinary services; and other professional, scientific, and technical services. This sector excludes establishments primarily engaged in providing a range of day-to-day office administrative services, such as financial planning, billing and recordkeeping, personnel supply, and physical distribution and logistics. These establishments are classified in Sector 56, Administrative and Support and Waste Management and Remediation Services.

541 Professional, Scientific, and Technical Services[T]

Industries in the Professional, Scientific, and Technical Services subsector group establishments engaged in processes where human capital is the major input. These establishments make available the knowledge and skills of their employees, often on an assignment basis, where an individual or team is responsible for the delivery of services to the client. The individual industries of this subsector are defined on the basis of the particular expertise and training of the services provider.

The distinguishing feature of the Professional, Scientific, and Technical Services subsector is the fact that most of the industries grouped in it have production processes that are almost wholly dependent on worker skills. In most of these industries, equipment and materials are not of major importance, unlike health care, for example, where "high-tech" machines and materials are important collaborating inputs to labor skills in the production of health care. Thus, the establishments classified in this subsector sell expertise. Much of the expertise requires degrees, though not in every case.

5411 Legal Services[T]

This industry group comprises establishments primarily engaged in offering legal services, such as those offered by offices of lawyers, offices of notaries, and title abstract and settlement offices, and paralegal services.

54111 Offices of Lawyers[T] See industry description for 541110.

541110 Offices of Lawyers

This industry comprises offices of legal practitioners known as lawyers or attorneys (i.e., counselors-at-law) primarily engaged in the practice of law. Establishments in this industry may provide expertise in a range or in specific areas of law, such as criminal law, corporate law, family and estate law, patent law, real estate law, or tax law.

Cross-References.

Establishments of legal practitioners (except lawyers or attorneys) primarily engaged in providing specialized legal or paralegal services are classified in Industry 54119, Other Legal Services.

54112 Offices of Notaries[T] See industry description for 541120.

T—Canadian, Mexican, and United States industries are comparable.

541120 Offices of Notaries

This industry comprises establishments (except offices of lawyers and attorneys) primarily engaged in drafting, approving, and executing legal documents, such as real estate transactions, wills, and contracts; and in receiving, indexing, and storing such documents.

Cross-References.

- Establishments of lawyers and attorneys primarily engaged in the practice of law are classified in Industry 541110, Offices of Lawyers; and
- Establishments of notaries public engaged in activities, such as administering oaths and taking affidavits and depositions, witnessing and certifying signatures on documents, but not empowered to draw and approve legal documents and contracts, are classified in U.S. Industry 541199, All Other Legal Services.

54119 Other Legal Services[T]

This industry comprises establishments of legal practitioners (except lawyers and attorneys) primarily engaged in providing specialized legal or paralegal services.

Illustrative Examples:

Notary public services
Process serving services
Paralegal services
Real estate settlement offices
Patent agent services (i.e., patent filing and searching services)
Real estate title abstract companies

Cross-References.

- Establishments of lawyers and attorneys primarily engaged in the practice of law are classified in Industry 54111, Offices of Lawyers; and
- Establishments (except offices of lawyers, attorneys, and paralegals) primarily engaged in providing arbitration and conciliation services are classified in Industry 54199, All Other Professional, Scientific, and Technical Services.

541191 Title Abstract and Settlement Offices

This U.S. industry comprises establishments (except offices of lawyers and attorneys) primarily engaged in one or more of the following activities: (1) researching public land records to gather information relating to real estate titles; (2) preparing documents necessary for the transfer of the title, financing, and settlement; (3) conducting final real estate settlements and closings; and (4) filing legal and other documents relating to the sale of real estate. Real estate settlement offices, title abstract companies, and title search companies are included in this industry.

Cross-References.

Establishments of lawyers and attorneys primarily engaged in the practice of law are classified in Industry 541110, Offices of Lawyers.

541199 All Other Legal Services

This U.S. industry comprises establishments of legal practitioners (except offices of lawyers and attorneys, settlement offices, and title abstract offices). These establishments are primarily engaged in providing specialized legal or paralegal services.

T—Canadian, Mexican, and United States industries are comparable.

Illustrative Examples:

Notary public services
Patent agent services (i.e., patent filing and searching services)
Paralegal services
Process serving services

Cross-References.

- Establishments of lawyers and attorneys primarily engaged in the practice of law are classified in Industry 541110, Offices of Lawyers;
- Establishments (except offices of lawyers and attorneys) primarily engaged in researching public land records for ownership or title; preparing documents necessary for the transfer of the title, financing, and settlement; conducting final real estate settlements and closings; and/or filing legal and other documents relating to the sale of real estate are classified in U.S. Industry 541191, Title Abstract and Settlement Offices; and
- Establishments (except offices of lawyers, attorneys, and paralegals) primarily engaged in providing arbitration and conciliation services are classified in Industry 541990, All Other Professional, Scientific, and Technical Services.

5412 Accounting, Tax Preparation, Bookkeeping, and Payroll Services[T]

54121 Accounting, Tax Preparation, Bookkeeping, and Payroll Services[T]

This industry comprises establishments primarily engaged in providing services, such as auditing of accounting records, designing accounting systems, preparing financial statements, developing budgets, preparing tax returns, processing payrolls, bookkeeping, and billing.

Illustrative Examples:

Accountants' offices
Payroll processing services
Bookkeeping services
Tax return preparation services

Cross-References.

Establishments providing computer data processing services at their own facility for others are classified in Industry 51821, Data Processing, Hosting, and Related Services.

541211 Offices of Certified Public Accountants

This U.S. industry comprises establishments of accountants that are certified to audit the accounting records of public and private organizations and to attest to compliance with generally accepted accounting practices. Offices of certified public accountants (CPAs) may provide one or more of the following accounting services: (1) auditing financial statements; (2) designing accounting systems; (3) preparing financial statements; (4) developing budgets; and (5) providing advice on matters related to accounting. These establishments may also provide related services, such as bookkeeping, tax return preparation, and payroll processing.

Cross-References. Establishments primarily engaged in--

- Providing tax return preparation services only--are classified in U.S. Industry 541213, Tax Preparation Services;
- Providing payroll processing services only--are classified in U.S. Industry 541214, Payroll Services; and
- Providing accounting, bookkeeping, and billing services--are classified in U.S. Industry 541219, Other Accounting Services.

T—Canadian, Mexican, and United States industries are comparable.

541213 Tax Preparation Services

This U.S. industry comprises establishments (except offices of CPAs) engaged in providing tax return preparation services without also providing accounting, bookkeeping, billing, or payroll processing services. Basic knowledge of tax law and filing requirements is required.

Cross-References.

- Establishments of CPAs are classified in U.S. Industry 541211, Offices of Certified Public Accountants;
- Establishments of non-CPAs providing payroll services along with tax return preparation services are classified in U.S. Industry 541214, Payroll Services;
- Establishments of non-CPAs providing accounting, bookkeeping, or billing services along with tax return preparation services are classified in U.S. Industry 541219, Other Accounting Services; and
- Establishments providing computer data processing services at their own facility for others are classified in Industry 518210, Data Processing, Hosting, and Related Services.

541214 Payroll Services

This U.S. industry comprises establishments (except offices of CPAs) engaged in the following without also providing accounting, bookkeeping, or billing services: (1) collecting information on hours worked, pay rates, deductions, and other payroll-related data from their clients and (2) using that information to generate paychecks, payroll reports, and tax filings. These establishments may use data processing and tabulating techniques as part of providing their services.

Cross-References.

- Establishments of CPAs are classified in U.S. Industry 541211, Offices of Certified Public Accountants;
- Establishments of non-CPAs providing tax return preparation services only are classified in U.S. Industry 541213, Tax Preparation Services; and
- Establishments of non-CPAs providing accounting, bookkeeping, or billing services along with payroll services are classified in U.S. Industry 541219, Other Accounting Services.

541219 Other Accounting Services

This U.S. industry comprises establishments (except offices of CPAs) engaged in providing accounting services (except tax return preparation services only or payroll services only). These establishments may also provide tax return preparation or payroll services. Accountant (except CPA) offices, bookkeeper offices, and billing offices are included in this industry.

Cross-References.

- Establishments of CPAs are classified in U.S. Industry 541211, Offices of Certified Public Accountants;
- Establishments of non-CPAs engaged in providing tax return preparation services only are classified in U.S. Industry 541213, Tax Preparation Services; and
- Establishments of non-CPAs engaged in providing payroll services only are classified in U.S. Industry 541214, Payroll Services.

5413 Architectural, Engineering, and Related Services[T]

This industry group comprises establishments primarily engaged in architectural, engineering, and related services, such as drafting services, building inspection services, geophysical surveying and mapping services, surveying and mapping (except geophysical) services, and testing services.

54131 Architectural Services[T] See industry description for 541310.

T—Canadian, Mexican, and United States industries are comparable.

541310 Architectural Services

This industry comprises establishments primarily engaged in planning and designing residential, institutional, leisure, commercial, and industrial buildings and structures by applying knowledge of design, construction procedures, zoning regulations, building codes, and building materials.

Cross-References. Establishments primarily engaged in--

- Planning and designing the development of land areas--are classified in Industry 541320, Landscape Architectural Services; and
- Both the design and construction of buildings, highways, or other structures or in managing construction projects--are classified in Sector 23, Construction, according to the type of project.

54132 Landscape Architectural Services[T] See industry description for 541320.

541320 Landscape Architectural Services

This industry comprises establishments primarily engaged in planning and designing the development of land areas for projects, such as parks and other recreational areas; airports; highways; hospitals; schools; land subdivisions; and commercial, industrial, and residential areas, by applying knowledge of land characteristics, location of buildings and structures, use of land areas, and design of landscape projects.

Illustrative Examples:

Garden planning services
Landscape architects' offices
Golf course or ski area design services
Landscape consulting services
Industrial land use planning services
Landscape design services

Cross-References.

Establishments primarily engaged in providing landscape care and maintenance services and/or installing trees, shrubs, plants, lawns, or gardens along with the design of landscape plans are classified in Industry 561730, Landscaping Services.

54133 Engineering Services[T] See industry description for 541330.

541330 Engineering Services

This industry comprises establishments primarily engaged in applying physical laws and principles of engineering in the design, development, and utilization of machines, materials, instruments, structures, processes, and systems. The assignments undertaken by these establishments may involve any of the following activities: provision of advice, preparation of feasibility studies, preparation of preliminary and final plans and designs, provision of technical services during the construction or installation phase, inspection and evaluation of engineering projects, and related services.

Illustrative Examples:

Civil engineering services
Environmental engineering services
Construction engineering services
Mechanical engineering services
Engineers' offices

T—Canadian, Mexican, and United States industries are comparable.

Cross-References. Establishments primarily engaged in--

- Planning and designing computer systems that integrate computer hardware, software, and communication technologies--are classified in U.S. Industry 541512, Computer Systems Design Services;
- Performing surveying and mapping services of the surface of the earth, including the sea floor--are classified in Industry 541370, Surveying and Mapping (except Geophysical) Services;
- Gathering, interpreting, and mapping geophysical data--are classified in Industry 541360, Geophysical Surveying and Mapping Services;
- Creating and developing designs and specifications that optimize the use, value, and appearance of products--are classified in Industry 541420, Industrial Design Services;
- Providing advice and assistance to others on environmental issues, such as the control of environmental contamination from pollutants, toxic substances, and hazardous materials--are classified in Industry 541620, Environmental Consulting Services; and
- Both the design and construction of buildings, highways, and other structures or in managing construction projects--are classified in Sector 23, Construction, according to the type of project.

54134 Drafting Services[T] See industry description for 541340.

541340 Drafting Services

This industry comprises establishments primarily engaged in drawing detailed layouts, plans, and illustrations of buildings, structures, systems, or components from engineering and architectural specifications.

54135 Building Inspection Services[T] See industry description for 541350.

541350 Building Inspection Services

This industry comprises establishments primarily engaged in providing building inspection services. These establishments typically evaluate all aspects of the building structure and component systems and prepare a report on the physical condition of the property, generally for buyers or others involved in real estate transactions. Building inspection bureaus and establishments providing home inspection services are included in this industry.

Cross-References. Establishments primarily engaged in--

- Inspecting buildings for termites and other pests--are classified in Industry 561710, Exterminating and Pest Control Services;
- Inspecting buildings for hazardous materials--are classified in Industry 541620, Environmental Consulting Services; and
- Conducting building inspections and enforcing building codes and standards--are classified in Industry 926150, Regulation, Licensing, and Inspection of Miscellaneous Commercial Sectors.

54136 Geophysical Surveying and Mapping Services[T] See industry description for 541360.

541360 Geophysical Surveying and Mapping Services

This industry comprises establishments primarily engaged in gathering, interpreting, and mapping geophysical data. Establishments in this industry often specialize in locating and measuring the extent of subsurface resources, such as oil, gas, and minerals, but they may also conduct surveys for engineering purposes. Establishments in this industry use a variety of surveying techniques depending on the purpose of the survey, including magnetic surveys, gravity surveys, seismic surveys, or electrical and electromagnetic surveys.

T—Canadian, Mexican, and United States industries are comparable.

Cross-References.

Establishments primarily engaged in taking core samples, drilling test wells, or other mine development activities (except geophysical surveying and mapping) on a contract basis for others are classified in Industry 21311, Support Activities for Mining.

54137 Surveying and Mapping (except Geophysical) ServicesT See industry description for 541370.

541370 Surveying and Mapping (except Geophysical) Services

This industry comprises establishments primarily engaged in performing surveying and mapping services of the surface of the earth, including the sea floor. These services may include surveying and mapping of areas above or below the surface of the earth, such as the creation of view easements or segregating rights in parcels of land by creating underground utility easements.

Illustrative Examples:

Cadastral surveying services
Mapping (except geophysical) services
Cartographic surveying services
Topographic surveying services
Geodetic surveying services

Cross-References. Establishments primarily engaged in--

- Providing geophysical surveying and mapping services--are classified in Industry 541360, Geophysical Surveying and Mapping Services;
- Publishing atlases and maps, except for exclusive Internet publishing--are classified in Industry 511130, Book Publishers; and
- Publishing atlases and maps exclusively on the Internet--are classified in Industry 519130, Internet Publishing and Broadcasting and Web Search Portals.

54138 Testing LaboratoriesT See industry description for 541380.

541380 Testing Laboratories

This industry comprises establishments primarily engaged in performing physical, chemical, and other analytical testing services, such as acoustics or vibration testing, assaying, biological testing (except medical and veterinary), calibration testing, electrical and electronic testing, geotechnical testing, mechanical testing, nondestructive testing, or thermal testing. The testing may occur in a laboratory or on-site.

Cross-References. Establishments primarily engaged in--

- Laboratory testing for the medical profession--are classified in Industry 62151, Medical and Diagnostic Laboratories;
- Veterinary testing services--are classified in Industry 541940, Veterinary Services; and
- Auto emissions testing--are classified in U.S. Industry 811198, All Other Automotive Repair and Maintenance.

5414 Specialized Design ServicesT

This industry group comprises establishments providing specialized design services (except architectural, engineering, and computer systems design).

T—Canadian, Mexican, and United States industries are comparable.

54141 Interior Design Services[T] See industry description for 541410.

541410 Interior Design Services

This industry comprises establishments primarily engaged in planning, designing, and administering projects in interior spaces to meet the physical and aesthetic needs of people using them, taking into consideration building codes, health and safety regulations, traffic patterns and floor planning, mechanical and electrical needs, and interior fittings and furniture. Interior designers and interior design consultants work in areas, such as hospitality design, health care design, institutional design, commercial and corporate design, and residential design. This industry also includes interior decorating consultants engaged exclusively in providing aesthetic services associated with interior spaces.

54142 Industrial Design Services[T] See industry description for 541420.

541420 Industrial Design Services

This industry comprises establishments primarily engaged in creating and developing designs and specifications that optimize the use, value, and appearance of their products. These services can include the determination of the materials, construction, mechanisms, shape, color, and surface finishes of the product, taking into consideration human characteristics and needs, safety, market appeal, and efficiency in production, distribution, use, and maintenance. Establishments providing automobile or furniture industrial design services or industrial design consulting services are included in this industry.

Cross-References. Establishments primarily engaged in--

- Applying physical laws and principles of engineering in the design, development, and utilization of machines, materials, instruments, structures, processes, and systems--are classified in Industry 541330, Engineering Services; and
- Designing clothing, shoes, or jewelry--are classified in Industry 541490, Other Specialized Design Services.

54143 Graphic Design Services[T] See industry description for 541430.

541430 Graphic Design Services

This industry comprises establishments primarily engaged in planning, designing, and managing the production of visual communication in order to convey specific messages or concepts, clarify complex information, or project visual identities. These services can include the design of printed materials, packaging, advertising, signage systems, and corporate identification (logos). This industry also includes commercial artists engaged exclusively in generating drawings and illustrations requiring technical accuracy or interpretative skills.

Illustrative Examples:

Commercial art studios
Independent commercial or graphic artists
Corporate identification (i.e., logo) design services
Medical art or illustration services
Graphic design consulting services

Cross-References.

- Establishments primarily engaged in creating and/or placing public display advertising material are classified in Industry 541850, Outdoor Advertising; and

T—Canadian, Mexican, and United States industries are comparable.

- Independent artists primarily engaged in creating and selling visual artwork for noncommercial use and independent cartoonists are classified in Industry 711510, Independent Artists, Writers, and Performers.

54149 Other Specialized Design Services[T] See industry description for 541490.

541490 Other Specialized Design Services

This industry comprises establishments primarily engaged in providing professional design services (except architectural, landscape architecture, engineering, interior, industrial, graphic, and computer systems design).

Illustrative Examples:

Costume design services (except independent theatrical costume designers)
Jewelry design services
Fashion design services
Float design services
Shoe design services
Fur design services
Textile design services

Cross-References. Establishments primarily engaged in--

- Providing architectural design services--are classified in Industry 541310, Architectural Services;
- Providing landscape architecture design services--are classified in Industry 541320, Landscape Architectural Services;
- Providing engineering design services--are classified in Industry 541330, Engineering Services;
- Providing interior design services--are classified in Industry 541410, Interior Design Services;
- Providing industrial design services--are classified in Industry 541420, Industrial Design Services;
- Providing graphic design services--are classified in Industry 541430, Graphic Design Services;
- Providing computer systems design services--are classified in U.S. Industry 541512, Computer Systems Design Services; and
- Operating as independent theatrical costume or set designers--are classified in Industry 711510, Independent Artists, Writers, and Performers.

5415 Computer Systems Design and Related Services[T]

54151 Computer Systems Design and Related Services[T]

This industry comprises establishments primarily engaged in providing expertise in the field of information technologies through one or more of the following activities: (1) writing, modifying, testing, and supporting software to meet the needs of a particular customer; (2) planning and designing computer systems that integrate computer hardware, software, and communication technologies; (3) on-site management and operation of clients' computer systems and/or data processing facilities; and (4) other professional and technical computer related advice and services.

Illustrative Examples:

Computer facilities management services
Custom computer programming services
Computer hardware or software consulting services
Software installation services
Computer systems integration design services

Cross-References. Establishments primarily engaged in--

- Selling computer hardware or software products from retail-like locations and providing supporting services, such as customized assembly of personal computers--are classified in Industry 44314, Electronics and Appliance Stores;

T—Canadian, Mexican, and United States industries are comparable.

- Merchant wholesaling computer hardware or software products and providing supporting services, such as customized assembly of personal computers--are classified in Industry 42343, Computer and Computer Peripheral Equipment and Software Merchant Wholesalers;
- Software design, development, and publishing, or software publishing only--are classified in Industry 51121, Software Publishers; and
- Providing computer data processing services at their own facility for others--are classified in Industry 51821, Data Processing, Hosting, and Related Services.

541511 Custom Computer Programming Services

This U.S. industry comprises establishments primarily engaged in writing, modifying, testing, and supporting software to meet the needs of a particular customer.

Cross-References. Establishments primarily engaged in--

- Software design, development, and publishing, or software publishing only--are classified in Industry 511210, Software Publishers; and
- Planning and designing computer systems that integrate computer hardware, software, and communication technologies, even though such establishments may provide custom software as an integral part of their services--are classified in U.S. Industry 541512, Computer Systems Design Services.

541512 Computer Systems Design Services

This U.S. industry comprises establishments primarily engaged in planning and designing computer systems that integrate computer hardware, software, and communication technologies. The hardware and software components of the system may be provided by this establishment or company as part of integrated services or may be provided by third parties or vendors. These establishments often install the system and train and support users of the system.

Illustrative Examples:

Computer systems integration design consulting services
Local area network (LAN) computer systems integration design services
Information management computer systems integration design services
Office automation computer systems integration design services

Cross-References. Establishments primarily engaged in--

- Selling computer hardware or software products and systems from retail-like locations, and providing supporting services, such as customized assembly of personal computers--are classified in U.S. Industry 443142, Electronics Stores; and
- Merchant wholesaling computer hardware or software products and providing supporting services, such as customized assembly of personal computers--are classified in Industry 423430, Computer and Computer Peripheral Equipment and Software Merchant Wholesalers.

541513 Computer Facilities Management Services

This U.S. industry comprises establishments primarily engaged in providing on-site management and operation of clients' computer systems and/or data processing facilities. Establishments providing computer systems or data processing facilities support services are included in this industry.

Cross-References.

Establishments primarily engaged in providing computer data processing services at their own facility for others are classified in Industry 518210, Data Processing, Hosting, and Related Services.

T—Canadian, Mexican, and United States industries are comparable.

541519 Other Computer Related Services

This U.S. industry comprises establishments primarily engaged in providing computer related services (except custom programming, systems integration design, and facilities management services). Establishments providing computer disaster recovery services or software installation services are included in this industry.

Cross-References. Establishments primarily engaged in--

- Providing custom computer programming services--are classified in U.S. Industry 541511, Custom Computer Programming Services;
- Providing computer systems integration design services--are classified in U.S. Industry 541512, Computer Systems Design Services; and
- Providing computer systems and/or data processing facilities management services--are classified in U.S. Industry 541513, Computer Facilities Management Services.

5416 Management, Scientific, and Technical Consulting Services[T]

This industry group comprises establishments primarily engaged in providing advice and assistance to businesses and other organizations on management, environmental, scientific, and technical issues.

54161 Management Consulting Services[T]

This industry comprises establishments primarily engaged in providing advice and assistance to businesses and other organizations on management issues, such as strategic and organizational planning; financial planning and budgeting; marketing objectives and policies; human resource policies, practices, and planning; production scheduling; and control planning.

Illustrative Examples:

Actuarial, benefit, and compensation consulting services
Marketing consulting services
Human resources consulting services
Administrative and general management consulting services
Process, physical distribution, and logistics consulting services

Cross-References.

- Establishments primarily engaged in providing a range of day-to-day office administrative services, such as financial planning, billing and recordkeeping, personnel, and physical distribution and logistics, are classified in Industry 56111, Office Administrative Services;
- Establishments primarily engaged in providing executive search, recruitment, and placement services are classified in Industry 56131, Employment Placement Agencies and Executive Search Services;
- Establishments primarily engaged in administering, overseeing, and managing other establishments of the company or enterprise (except government establishments) are classified in Industry 55111, Management of Companies and Enterprises;
- Government establishments primarily engaged in administering, overseeing, and managing governmental programs are classified in Sector 92, Public Administration;
- Establishments primarily engaged in professional and management development training are classified in Industry 61143, Professional and Management Development Training;
- Establishments primarily engaged in listing employment vacancies and in selecting, referring, and placing applicants in employment are classified in Industry 56131, Employment Placement Agencies and Executive Search Services;
- Establishments primarily engaged in developing and implementing public relations plans are classified in Industry 54182, Public Relations Agencies;
- Establishments primarily engaged in developing and conducting marketing research or public opinion polling are classified in Industry 54191, Marketing Research and Public Opinion Polling;

T—Canadian, Mexican, and United States industries are comparable.

- Establishments primarily engaged in planning and designing industrial processes and systems are classified in Industry 54133, Engineering Services;
- Establishments primarily engaged in planning and designing computer systems are classified in Industry 54151, Computer Systems Design and Related Services; and
- Establishments primarily engaged in providing financial investment advice services are classified in Industry 52393, Investment Advice.

541611 Administrative Management and General Management Consulting Services

This U.S. industry comprises establishments primarily engaged in providing operating advice and assistance to businesses and other organizations on administrative management issues, such as financial planning and budgeting, equity and asset management, records management, office planning, strategic and organizational planning, site selection, new business start-up, and business process improvement. This industry also includes establishments of general management consultants that provide a full range of administrative, human resource, marketing, process, physical distribution, logistics, or other management consulting services to clients.

Illustrative Examples:

Administrative management consulting services
Site selection consulting services
Strategic planning consulting services
Financial management (except investment advice) consulting services
General management consulting services

Cross-References.

- Establishments primarily engaged in providing a range of day-to-day office administrative services, such as financial planning, billing and recordkeeping, personnel, and physical distribution and logistics, are classified in Industry 561110, Office Administrative Services;
- Establishments providing operations consulting services are classified in U.S. Industry 541614, Process, Physical Distribution, and Logistics Consulting Services;
- Establishments primarily engaged in administering, overseeing, and managing other establishments of the company or enterprise (except government establishments) are classified in U.S. Industry 551114, Corporate, Subsidiary, and Regional Managing Offices;
- Government establishments primarily engaged in administering, overseeing, and managing governmental programs are classified in Sector 92, Public Administration;
- Establishments primarily engaged in providing investment advice are classified in Industry 523930, Investment Advice;
- Establishments primarily engaged in providing professional and management development training are classified in Industry 611430, Professional and Management Development Training; and
- Establishments primarily engaged in providing executive search, recruitment, and placement services are classified in U.S. Industry 561312, Executive Search Services.

541612 Human Resources Consulting Services

This U.S. industry comprises establishments primarily engaged in providing advice and assistance to businesses and other organizations in one or more of the following areas: (1) human resource and personnel policies, practices, and procedures; (2) employee benefits planning, communication, and administration; (3) compensation systems planning; and (4) wage and salary administration.

Illustrative Examples:

Benefit or compensation consulting services
Employee assessment consulting services
Personnel management consulting services

T—Canadian, Mexican, and United States industries are comparable.

Cross-References. Establishments primarily engaged in--

- Providing professional and management development training--are classified in Industry 611430, Professional and Management Development Training;
- Listing employment vacancies and selecting, referring, and placing applicants in employment--are classified in U.S. Industry 561311, Employment Placement Agencies; and
- Providing executive search, recruitment, and placement services--are classified in U.S. Industry 561312, Executive Search Services.

541613 Marketing Consulting Services

This U.S. industry comprises establishments primarily engaged in providing operating advice and assistance to businesses and other organizations on marketing issues, such as developing marketing objectives and policies, sales forecasting, new product developing and pricing, licensing and franchise planning, and marketing planning and strategy.

Illustrative Examples:

Customer services management consulting services
New product development consulting services
Marketing management consulting services

Cross-References. Establishments primarily engaged in--

- Developing and implementing public relations plans--are classified in Industry 541820, Public Relations Agencies; and
- Developing and conducting marketing research or public opinion polling--are classified in Industry 541910, Marketing Research and Public Opinion Polling.

541614 Process, Physical Distribution, and Logistics Consulting Services

This U.S. industry comprises establishments primarily engaged in providing operating advice and assistance to businesses and other organizations in: (1) manufacturing operations improvement; (2) productivity improvement; (3) production planning and control; (4) quality assurance and quality control; (5) inventory management; (6) distribution networks; (7) warehouse use, operations, and utilization; (8) transportation and shipment of goods and materials; and (9) materials management and handling.

Illustrative Examples:

Freight rate or tariff rate consulting services
Productivity improvement consulting services
Transportation management consulting services
Inventory planning and control management consulting services
Manufacturing management consulting services

Cross-References. Establishments primarily engaged in--

- Planning and designing industrial processes and systems--are classified in Industry 541330, Engineering Services; and
- Providing computer systems integration design services--are classified in U.S. Industry 541512, Computer Systems Design Services.

541618 Other Management Consulting Services

This U.S. industry comprises establishments primarily engaged in providing management consulting services (except administrative and general management consulting; human resources consulting; marketing consulting; or process, physical distribution, and logistics consulting). Establishments providing telecommunications or utilities management consulting services are included in this industry.

~~T Canadian, Mexican, and Unit~~ed States industries are comparable.

Cross-References. Establishments primarily engaged in--

- Providing administrative and general management consulting services--are classified in U.S. Industry 541611, Administrative Management and General Management Consulting Services;
- Providing human resources consulting services--are classified in U.S. Industry 541612, Human Resources Consulting Services;
- Providing marketing consulting services--are classified in U.S. Industry 541613, Marketing Consulting Services; and
- Providing process, physical distribution, and logistics consulting services--are classified in U.S. Industry 541614, Process, Physical Distribution, and Logistics Consulting Services.

54162 Environmental Consulting Services[T] See industry description for 541620.

541620 Environmental Consulting Services

This industry comprises establishments primarily engaged in providing advice and assistance to businesses and other organizations on environmental issues, such as the control of environmental contamination from pollutants, toxic substances, and hazardous materials. These establishments identify problems (e.g., inspect buildings for hazardous materials), measure and evaluate risks, and recommend solutions. They employ a multidisciplined staff of scientists, engineers, and other technicians with expertise in areas, such as air and water quality, asbestos contamination, remediation, ecological restoration, and environmental law. Establishments providing sanitation or site remediation consulting services are included in this industry.

Cross-References.

- Establishments primarily engaged in environmental remediation are classified in Industry 562910, Remediation Services;
- Establishments primarily engaged in providing environmental engineering services are classified in Industry 541330, Engineering Services;
- Establishments primarily engaged in individual activities as part of an ecological restoration project are classified according to the primary activity; and
- Government establishments primarily engaged in administering, overseeing, and managing governmental ecological restoration programs are classified in Industry 924110, Administration of Air and Water Resource and Solid Waste Management Programs.

54169 Other Scientific and Technical Consulting Services[T] See industry description for 541690.

541690 Other Scientific and Technical Consulting Services

This industry comprises establishments primarily engaged in providing advice and assistance to businesses and other organizations on scientific and technical issues (except environmental).

Illustrative Examples:

Agricultural consulting services
Motion picture consulting services
Biological consulting services
Physics consulting services
Chemical consulting services
Radio consulting services
Economic consulting services
Safety consulting services
Energy consulting services
Security consulting services

T—Canadian, Mexican, and United States industries are comparable.

Cross-References.

Establishments primarily engaged in environmental consulting are classified in Industry 541620, Environmental Consulting Services.

5417 Scientific Research and Development Services[T]

This industry group comprises establishments engaged in conducting original investigation undertaken on a systematic basis to gain new knowledge (research) and/or the application of research findings or other scientific knowledge for the creation of new or significantly improved products or processes (experimental development). Techniques may include modeling and simulation. The industries within this industry group are defined on the basis of the domain of research; that is, on the scientific expertise of the establishment.

54171 Research and Development in the Physical, Engineering, and Life Sciences[T]

This industry comprises establishments primarily engaged in conducting research and experimental development in the physical, engineering, and life sciences, such as agriculture, electronics, environmental, biology, botany, biotechnology, computers, chemistry, food, fisheries, forests, geology, health, mathematics, medicine, nanotechnology, oceanography, pharmacy, physics, veterinary, and other allied subjects.

Cross-References. Establishments primarily engaged in--

- Providing veterinary testing services--are classified in Industry 54194, Veterinary Services;
- Providing medical laboratory testing for humans--are classified in Industry 62151, Medical and Diagnostic Laboratories;
- Providing physical, chemical, or other analytical testing services (except medical or veterinary), such as acoustics or vibration testing, calibration testing, electrical and electronic testing, geotechnical testing, mechanical testing, nondestructive testing, or thermal testing--are classified in Industry 54138, Testing Laboratories;
- Manufacturing products (e.g., apparel, electronic equipment, automotive equipment) using nanomaterials--are classified in Sector 31-33, Manufacturing, according to the process of the specific product made; and
- Manufacturing vaccines, toxoids, blood fractions, and culture media of plant or animal origin (except diagnostic use) and/or uncompounded medicinal chemicals and their derivatives (i.e., enzyme proteins and antibiotics for pharmaceutical use)--are classified in Industry 32541, Pharmaceutical and Medicine Manufacturing.

541713 Research and Development in Nanotechnology

This U.S. industry comprises establishments primarily engaged in conducting nanotechnology research and experimental development. Nanotechnology research and experimental development involves the study of matter at the nanoscale (i.e., a scale of about 1 to 100 nanometers). This research and development in nanotechnology may result in development of new nanotechnology processes or in prototypes of new or altered materials and/or products that may be reproduced, utilized, or implemented by various industries.

Cross-References. Establishments primarily engaged in--

- Conducting research and experimental development in biotechnology (except nanobiotechnology)--are classified in U.S. Industry 541714, Research and Development in Biotechnology (except Nanobiotechnology);
- Conducting research and experimental development in the physical, engineering, and life sciences (except nanotechnology and biotechnology)--are classified in U.S. Industry 541715, Research and Development in the Physical, Engineering, and Life Sciences (except Nanotechnology and Biotechnology);
- Providing veterinary testing services--are classified in Industry 541940, Veterinary Services;
- Providing physical, chemical, or other analytical testing services (except medical or veterinary), such as acoustics or vibration testing, calibration testing, electrical and electronic testing, geotechnical testing,

T—Canadian, Mexican, and United States industries are comparable.

mechanical testing, nondestructive testing, or thermal testing--are classified in Industry 541380, Testing Laboratories;

- Providing medical laboratory testing for humans--are classified in U.S. Industry 621511, Medical Laboratories; and
- Manufacturing products (e.g., apparel, electronic equipment, automotive equipment) using nanomaterials--are classified in Sector 31-33, Manufacturing, according to the process of the specific product made.

541714 Research and Development in Biotechnology (except Nanobiotechnology)

This U.S. industry comprises establishments primarily engaged in conducting biotechnology (except nanobiotechnology) research and experimental development. Biotechnology (except nanobiotechnology) research and experimental development involves the study of the use of microorganisms and cellular and biomolecular processes to develop or alter living or non-living materials. This research and development in biotechnology (except nanobiotechnology) may result in development of new biotechnology (except nanobiotechnology) processes or in prototypes of new or genetically-altered products that may be reproduced, utilized, or implemented by various industries.

Illustrative Examples:

Cloning research and experimental development laboratories
DNA technologies (e.g., microarrays) research and experimental development laboratories
Nucleic acid chemistry research and experimental development laboratories
Protein engineering research and experimental development laboratories
Recombinant DNA research and experimental development laboratories

Cross-References. Establishments primarily engaged in--

- Conducting research and experimental development in nanotechnology (e.g., nanobiotechnology)--are classified in U.S. Industry 541713, Research and Development in Nanotechnology;
- Conducting research and experimental development in the physical, engineering, and life sciences (except nanotechnology and biotechnology)--are classified in U.S. Industry 541715, Research and Development in the Physical, Engineering, and Life Sciences (except Nanotechnology and Biotechnology);
- Providing physical, chemical, or other analytical testing services (except medical or veterinary), such as acoustics or vibration testing, calibration testing, electrical and electronic testing, geotechnical testing, mechanical testing, nondestructive testing, or thermal testing--are classified in Industry 541380, Testing Laboratories;
- Providing veterinary testing services--are classified in Industry 541940, Veterinary Services;
- Providing medical laboratory testing for humans--are classified in U.S. Industry 621511, Medical Laboratories;
- Manufacturing vaccines, toxoids, blood fractions, and culture media of plant or animal origin (except diagnostic use)--are classified in U.S. Industry 325414, Biological Product (except Diagnostic) Manufacturing; and
- Manufacturing uncompounded medicinal chemicals and their derivatives (i.e., enzyme proteins and antibiotics for pharmaceutical use)--are classified in U.S. Industry 325411, Medicinal and Botanical Manufacturing.

541715 Research and Development in the Physical, Engineering, and Life Sciences (except Nanotechnology and Biotechnology)

This U.S. industry comprises establishments primarily engaged in conducting research and experimental development (except nanotechnology and biotechnology research and experimental development) in the physical, engineering, and life sciences, such as agriculture, electronics, environmental, biology, botany, computers, chemistry, food, fisheries, forests, geology, health, mathematics, medicine, oceanography, pharmacy, physics, veterinary and other allied subjects.

T—Canadian, Mexican, and United States industries are comparable.

Cross-References. Establishments primarily engaged in--

- Conducting research and experimental development in nanotechnology--are classified in U.S. Industry 541713, Research and Development in Nanotechnology;
- Conducting research and experimental development in biotechnology (except nanobiotechnology)--are classified in U.S. Industry 541714, Research and Development in Biotechnology (except Nanobiotechnology);
- Providing physical, chemical, or other analytical testing services (except medical or veterinary), such as acoustics or vibration testing, calibration testing, electrical and electronic testing, geotechnical testing, mechanical testing, nondestructive testing, or thermal testing--are classified in Industry 541380, Testing Laboratories;
- Providing veterinary testing services--are classified in Industry 541940, Veterinary Services; and
- Providing medical laboratory testing for humans--are classified in U.S. Industry 621511, Medical Laboratories.

54172 Research and Development in the Social Sciences and Humanities[T] See industry description for 541720.

541720 Research and Development in the Social Sciences and Humanities

This industry comprises establishments primarily engaged in conducting research and analyses in cognitive development, sociology, psychology, language, behavior, economic, and other social science and humanities research.

Cross-References.

Establishments primarily engaged in marketing research are classified in Industry 541910, Marketing Research and Public Opinion Polling.

5418 Advertising, Public Relations, and Related Services[T]

This industry group comprises establishments primarily engaged in advertising, public relations, and related services, such as media buying, independent media representation, outdoor advertising, direct mail advertising, advertising material distribution services, and other services related to advertising.

54181 Advertising Agencies[T] See industry description for 541810.

541810 Advertising Agencies

This industry comprises establishments primarily engaged in creating advertising campaigns and placing such advertising in periodicals, newspapers, radio and television, or other media. These establishments are organized to provide a full range of services (i.e., through in-house capabilities or subcontracting), including advice, creative services, account management, production of advertising material, media planning, and buying (i.e., placing advertising).

Cross-References. Establishments primarily engaged in--

- Purchasing advertising space from media outlets and reselling it directly to advertising agencies or individual companies--are classified in Industry 541830, Media Buying Agencies;
- Conceptualizing and producing artwork or graphic designs without providing other advertising agency services--are classified in Industry 541430, Graphic Design Services;
- Creating direct mail advertising campaigns--are classified in Industry 541860, Direct Mail Advertising;
- Providing marketing consulting services--are classified in U.S. Industry 541613, Marketing Consulting Services; and

T—Canadian, Mexican, and United States industries are comparable.

- Selling media time or space for media owners as independent representatives--are classified in Industry 541840, Media Representatives.

54182 Public Relations Agencies[T] See industry description for 541820.

541820 Public Relations Agencies

This industry comprises establishments primarily engaged in designing and implementing public relations campaigns. These campaigns are designed to promote the interests and image of their clients. Establishments providing lobbying, political consulting, or public relations consulting are included in this industry.

54183 Media Buying Agencies[T] See industry description for 541830.

541830 Media Buying Agencies

This industry comprises establishments primarily engaged in purchasing advertising time or space from media outlets and reselling it to advertising agencies or individual companies directly.

Cross-References. Establishments primarily engaged in--

- Selling time and space to advertisers for media owners as independent representatives--are classified in Industry 541840, Media Representatives; and
- Creating advertising campaigns and placing such advertising in media--are classified in Industry 541810, Advertising Agencies.

54184 Media Representatives[T] See industry description for 541840.

541840 Media Representatives

This industry comprises establishments of independent representatives primarily engaged in selling media time or space for media owners.

Illustrative Examples:

Newspaper advertising representatives (i.e., independent of media owners)
Radio advertising representatives (i.e., independent of media owners)
Publishers' advertising representatives (i.e., independent of media owners)
Television advertising representatives (i.e., independent of media owners)

Cross-References. Establishments primarily engaged in--

- Purchasing advertising time or space from media outlets and reselling it directly to advertising agencies or individual companies--are classified in Industry 541830, Media Buying Agencies; and
- Creating advertising campaigns and placing such advertising in media--are classified in Industry 541810, Advertising Agencies.

54185 Outdoor Advertising[T] See industry description for 541850.

T—Canadian, Mexican, and United States industries are comparable.

541850 Outdoor Advertising

This industry comprises establishments primarily engaged in creating and designing public display advertising campaign materials, such as printed, painted, or electronic displays; and/or placing such displays on indoor or outdoor billboards and panels, or on or within transit vehicles or facilities, shopping malls, retail (in-store) displays, and other display structures or sites.

Cross-References. Establishments primarily engaged in--

- Providing sign lettering and painting services--are classified in Industry 541890, Other Services Related to Advertising;
- Printing paper or paperboard signs--are classified in Industry 32311, Printing;
- Erecting display boards--are classified in Industry 238990, All Other Specialty Trade Contractors; and
- Manufacturing electrical, mechanical, or plate signs and point-of-sale advertising displays--are classified in Industry 339950, Sign Manufacturing.

54186 Direct Mail Advertising[T] See industry description for 541860.

541860 Direct Mail Advertising

This industry comprises establishments primarily engaged in (1) creating and designing advertising campaigns for the purpose of distributing advertising materials (e.g., coupons, flyers, samples) or specialties (e.g., keychains, magnets, pens with customized messages imprinted) by mail or other direct distribution and/or (2) preparing advertising materials or specialties for mailing or other direct distribution. These establishments may also compile, maintain, sell, and rent mailing lists.

Cross-References. Establishments primarily engaged in--

- The direct distribution or delivery (e.g., door-to-door, windshield placement) of advertisements or samples--are classified in Industry 541870, Advertising Material Distribution Services;
- Distributing advertising specialties for clients who wish to use such materials for promotional purposes--are classified in Industry 541890, Other Services Related to Advertising;
- Creating advertising campaigns and placing such advertising in media--are classified in Industry 541810, Advertising Agencies;
- Compiling and selling mailing lists without providing direct mail advertising services--are classified in Industry 511140, Directory and Mailing List Publishers; and
- Publishing or broadcasting exclusively on the Internet--are classified in Industry 519130, Internet Publishing and Broadcasting and Web Search Portals.

54187 Advertising Material Distribution Services[T] See industry description for 541870.

541870 Advertising Material Distribution Services

This industry comprises establishments primarily engaged in the direct distribution or delivery of advertisements (e.g., circulars, coupons, handbills) or samples. Establishments in this industry use methods, such as delivering advertisements or samples door-to-door, placing flyers or coupons on car windshields in parking lots, or handing out samples in retail stores.

Cross-References. Establishments primarily engaged in--

- Creating and designing advertising campaigns for the purpose of distributing advertising materials or samples through the mail--are classified in Industry 541860, Direct Mail Advertising;

T—Canadian, Mexican, and United States industries are comparable.

- Publishing newspapers or operating television stations or on-line information services--are classified in Sector 51, Information; and
- Distributing advertising specialties (e.g., keychains, magnets, or pens with customized messages imprinted) to clients who wish to use such materials for promotional purposes--are classified in Industry 541890, Other Services Related to Advertising.

54189 Other Services Related to Advertising[T] See industry description for 541890.

541890 Other Services Related to Advertising

This industry comprises establishments primarily engaged in providing advertising services (except advertising agency services, public relations agency services, media buying agency services, media representative services, display advertising services, direct mail advertising services, advertising material distribution services, and marketing consulting services).

Illustrative Examples:

Advertising specialties (e.g., keychains, magnets, pens) distribution services (except direct mail)
Sign lettering and painting services
Display lettering services
Store window dressing or trimming services
Mannequin decorating services
Welcoming services (i.e., advertising services)
Merchandise demonstration services

Cross-References. Establishments primarily engaged in--

- Creating advertising campaigns and placing such advertising in newspapers, television, or other media--are classified in Industry 541810, Advertising Agencies;
- Designing and implementing public relations campaigns--are classified in Industry 541820, Public Relations Agencies;
- Purchasing advertising time or space from media outlets and reselling it directly to advertising agencies or individual companies--are classified in Industry 541830, Media Buying Agencies;
- Selling media time or space for media owners as independent representatives--are classified in Industry 541840, Media Representatives;
- Providing display advertising services (except aerial)--are classified in Industry 541850, Outdoor Advertising;
- Providing direct distribution or delivery (e.g., door-to-door, windshield placement) of advertisements or samples--are classified in Industry 541870, Advertising Material Distribution Services;
- Providing direct mail advertising services--are classified in Industry 541860, Direct Mail Advertising;
- Publishing newspapers or operating television stations or on-line information services--are classified in Sector 51, Information; and
- Providing marketing consulting services--are classified in U.S. Industry 541613, Marketing Consulting Services.

5419 Other Professional, Scientific, and Technical Services[T]

This industry group comprises establishments engaged in professional, scientific, and technical services (except legal services; accounting, tax preparation, bookkeeping, and related services; architectural, engineering, and related services; specialized design services; computer systems design and related services; management, scientific, and technical consulting services; scientific research and development services; and advertising, public relations, and related services).

54191 Marketing Research and Public Opinion Polling[T] See industry description for 541910.

T—Canadian, Mexican, and United States industries are comparable.

541910 Marketing Research and Public Opinion Polling

This industry comprises establishments primarily engaged in systematically gathering, recording, tabulating, and presenting marketing and public opinion data.

Illustrative Examples:

Broadcast media rating services
Political opinion polling services
Marketing analysis or research services
Statistical sampling services
Opinion research services

Cross-References. Establishments primarily engaged in--

- Providing research and analysis in economics, sociology, and related fields--are classified in Industry 541720, Research and Development in the Social Sciences and Humanities; and
- Providing advice and counsel on marketing strategies--are classified in U.S. Industry 541613, Marketing Consulting Services.

54192 Photographic Services[T]

This industry comprises establishments primarily engaged in providing still, video, or digital photography services. These establishments may specialize in a particular field of photography, such as commercial and industrial photography, portrait photography, and special events photography. Commercial or portrait photography studios are included in this industry.

Cross-References. Establishments primarily engaged in--

- Producing film and videotape for commercial exhibition or sale--are classified in Industry 51211, Motion Picture and Video Production;
- Developing still photographs--are classified in Industry 81292, Photofinishing;
- Developing motion picture film--are classified in Industry 51219, Postproduction Services and Other Motion Picture and Video Industries;
- Taking, developing, and selling artistic, news, or other types of photographs on a freelance basis, such as photojournalists--are classified in Industry 71151, Independent Artists, Writers, and Performers; and
- Supplying and servicing automatic photography machines in places of business operated by others--are classified in Industry 81299, All Other Personal Services.

541921 Photography Studios, Portrait

This U.S. industry comprises establishments known as portrait studios primarily engaged in providing still, video, or digital portrait photography services.

Illustrative Examples:

Home photography services
School photography services
Passport photography services
Videotaping services for special events (e.g.,

Cross-References. Establishments primarily engaged in--

- Producing film and videotape for commercial exhibition or sale--are classified in Industry 512110, Motion Picture and Video Production;
- Developing still photographs--are classified in Industry 81292, Photofinishing;
- Developing motion picture film--are classified in U.S. Industry 512199, Other Motion Picture and Video Industries;

T—Canadian, Mexican, and United States industries are comparable.

- Taking, developing, and selling artistic, news, or other types of photographs on a freelance basis, such as photojournalists--are classified in Industry 711510, Independent Artists, Writers, and Performers; and
- Supplying and servicing automatic photography machines in places of business operated by others--are classified in Industry 812990, All Other Personal Services.

541922 Commercial Photography

This U.S. industry comprises establishments primarily engaged in providing commercial photography services, generally for advertising agencies, publishers, and other business and industrial users.

Cross-References. Establishments primarily engaged in--

- Producing film and videotape for commercial exhibition or sale--are classified in Industry 512110, Motion Picture and Video Production;
- Developing still photographs--are classified in Industry 81292, Photofinishing;
- Developing motion picture film--are classified in U.S. Industry 512199, Other Motion Picture and Video Industries;
- Taking, developing, and selling artistic, news, or other types of photographs on a freelance basis, such as photojournalists--are classified in Industry 711510, Independent Artists, Writers, and Performers; and
- Supplying and servicing automatic photography machines in places of business operated by others--are classified in Industry 812990, All Other Personal Services.

54193 Translation and Interpretation Services[T] See industry description for 541930.

541930 Translation and Interpretation Services

This industry comprises establishments primarily engaged in translating written material and interpreting speech from one language to another and establishments primarily engaged in providing sign language services.

Cross-References. Establishments primarily engaged in--

- Providing transcription services--are classified in Industry 561410, Document Preparation Services;
- Providing real-time (i.e., simultaneous) closed captioning services for live television performances, at meetings and conferences--are classified in U.S. Industry 561492, Court Reporting and Stenotype Services;
- Providing film or tape closed captioning services--are classified in U.S. Industry 512191, Teleproduction and Other Postproduction Services; and
- Analyzing handwriting--are classified in Industry 541990, All Other Professional, Scientific, and Technical Services.

54194 Veterinary Services[T] See industry description for 541940.

541940 Veterinary Services

This industry comprises establishments of licensed veterinary practitioners primarily engaged in the practice of veterinary medicine, dentistry, or surgery for animals; and establishments primarily engaged in providing testing services for licensed veterinary practitioners.

Illustrative Examples:

Animal hospitals
Veterinary clinics
Veterinarians' offices
Veterinary testing laboratories

T—Canadian, Mexican, and United States industries are comparable.

Cross-References. Establishments primarily engaged in--

- Providing veterinary research and development services--are classified in Industry 54171, Research and Development in the Physical, Engineering, and Life Sciences;
- Providing nonveterinary pet care services, such as boarding or grooming pets--are classified in Industry 812910, Pet Care (except Veterinary) Services;
- Providing animal breeding services or boarding horses--are classified in Industry 115210, Support Activities for Animal Production; and
- Transporting pets--are classified in U.S. Industry 485991, Special Needs Transportation.

54199 All Other Professional, Scientific, and Technical Services[T] See industry description for 541990.

541990 All Other Professional, Scientific, and Technical Services

This industry comprises establishments primarily engaged in the provision of professional, scientific, or technical services (except legal services; accounting, tax preparation, bookkeeping, and related services; architectural, engineering, and related services; specialized design services; computer systems design and related services; management, scientific, and technical consulting services; scientific research and development services; advertising, public relations, and related services; market research and public opinion polling; photographic services; translation and interpretation services; and veterinary services).

Illustrative Examples:

Appraisal (except real estate) services
Marine surveyor (i.e., appraiser) services
Arbitration and conciliation services (except by lawyer, attorney, or paralegal offices)
Patent broker services (i.e., patent marketing services)
Commodity inspector services
Pipeline or power line inspection (i.e., visual) services
Consumer credit counseling services
Weather forecasting services
Handwriting analysis services

Cross-References. Establishments primarily engaged in--

- Providing legal services--are classified in Industry Group 5411, Legal Services;
- Providing accounting, tax preparation, bookkeeping, and payroll services--are classified in Industry Group 5412, Accounting, Tax Preparation, Bookkeeping, and Payroll Services;
- Providing architectural, engineering, and related services--are classified in Industry Group 5413, Architectural, Engineering, and Related Services;
- Providing specialized design services--are classified in Industry Group 5414, Specialized Design Services;
- Providing computer systems design and related services--are classified in Industry Group 5415, Computer Systems Design and Related Services;
- Providing management, scientific, and technical consulting services--are classified in Industry Group 5416, Management, Scientific, and Technical Consulting Services;
- Providing scientific research and development services--are classified in Industry Group 5417, Scientific Research and Development Services;
- Providing advertising and related services--are classified in Industry Group 5418, Advertising, Public Relations, and Related Services;
- Providing marketing research and public opinion polling--are classified in Industry 541910, Marketing Research and Public Opinion Polling;
- Providing photographic services--are classified in Industry 54192, Photographic Services;
- Providing translation and interpretation services--are classified in Industry 541930, Translation and Interpretation Services;
- Providing veterinary services--are classified in Industry 541940, Veterinary Services; and
- Providing real estate appraisal services--are classified in Industry 531320, Offices of Real Estate Appraisers.

T—Canadian, Mexican, and United States industries are comparable.

Sector 55--Management of Companies and Enterprises[T]

The Sector as a Whole

The Management of Companies and Enterprises sector comprises (1) establishments that hold the securities of (or other equity interests in) companies and enterprises for the purpose of owning a controlling interest or influencing management decisions or (2) establishments (except government establishments) that administer, oversee, and manage establishments of the company or enterprise and that normally undertake the strategic or organizational planning and decision-making role of the company or enterprise. Establishments that administer, oversee, and manage may hold the securities of the company or enterprise.

Establishments in this sector perform essential activities that are often undertaken in-house by establishments in many sectors of the economy. By consolidating the performance of these activities of the enterprise at one establishment, economies of scale are achieved.

Government establishments primarily engaged in administering, overseeing, and managing governmental programs are classified in Sector 92, Public Administration. Establishments primarily engaged in providing a range of day-to-day office administrative services, such as financial planning, billing and recordkeeping, personnel, and physical distribution and logistics, are classified in Industry 56111, Office Administrative Services.

551 Management of Companies and Enterprises[T]

Industries in the Management of Companies and Enterprises subsector include three main types of establishments: (1) those that hold the securities of (or other equity interests in) companies and enterprises; (2) those (except government establishments) that administer, oversee, and manage other establishments of the company or enterprise but do not hold the securities of these establishments; and (3) those that both administer, oversee, and manage other establishments of the company or enterprise and hold the securities of (or other equity interests in) these establishments. Those establishments that administer, oversee, and manage normally undertake the strategic or organizational planning and decision-making role of the company or enterprise.

5511 Management of Companies and Enterprises[T]

55111 Management of Companies and Enterprises[T]

This industry comprises (1) establishments primarily engaged in holding the securities of (or other equity interests in) companies and enterprises for the purpose of owning a controlling interest or influencing management decisions or (2) establishments (except government establishments) that administer, oversee, and manage other establishments of the company or enterprise and that normally undertake the strategic or organizational planning and decision-making role of the company or enterprise. Establishments that administer, oversee, and manage may hold the securities of the company or enterprise.

Cross-References.

- Establishments primarily engaged in holding the securities of companies or enterprises and operating these entities are classified according to the business operated;
- Establishments primarily engaged in holding the securities of depository banks and operating these entities are classified in Industry Group 5221, Depository Credit Intermediation;
- Establishments primarily engaged in providing a single service to other establishments of the company or enterprise, such as trucking, warehousing, research and development, and data processing, are classified according to the service provided; and
- Government establishments primarily engaged in administering, overseeing, and managing governmental programs are classified in Sector 92, Public Administration.

T—Canadian, Mexican, and United States industries are comparable.

551111 Offices of Bank Holding Companies

This U.S. industry comprises legal entities known as bank holding companies primarily engaged in holding the securities of (or other equity interests in) companies and enterprises for the purpose of owning a controlling interest or influencing the management decisions of these firms. The holding companies in this industry do not administer, oversee, and manage other establishments of the company or enterprise whose securities they hold.

Cross-References. Establishments primarily engaged in--

- Holding the securities of (or other equity interests in) a company or enterprise and administering, overseeing, and managing establishments of the company or enterprise whose securities they hold--are classified in U.S. Industry 551114, Corporate, Subsidiary, and Regional Managing Offices; and
- Holding the securities of depository banks and operating these entities--are classified in Industry Group 5221, Depository Credit Intermediation.

551112 Offices of Other Holding Companies

This U.S. industry comprises legal entities known as holding companies (except bank holding) primarily engaged in holding the securities of (or other equity interests in) companies and enterprises for the purpose of owning a controlling interest or influencing the management decisions of these firms. The holding companies in this industry do not administer, oversee, and manage other establishments of the company or enterprise whose securities they hold.

Cross-References. Establishments primarily engaged in--

- Holding the securities of (or other equity interests in) depository banks for the purpose of owning a controlling interest or influencing the management decisions of these firms--are classified in U.S. Industry 551111, Offices of Bank Holding Companies;
- Holding the securities of (or other equity interests in) a company or enterprise and administering, overseeing, and managing establishments of the company or enterprise whose securities they hold--are classified in U.S. Industry 551114, Corporate, Subsidiary, and Regional Managing Offices; and
- Holding the securities of companies or enterprises and operating these entities--are classified according to the business operated.

551114 Corporate, Subsidiary, and Regional Managing Offices

This U.S. industry comprises establishments (except government establishments) primarily engaged in administering, overseeing, and managing other establishments of the company or enterprise. These establishments normally undertake the strategic or organizational planning and decision-making role of the company or enterprise. Establishments in this industry may hold the securities of the company or enterprise.

Illustrative Examples:

Centralized administrative offices
Head offices
Corporate offices
Holding companies that manage
District and regional offices
Subsidiary management offices

Cross-References.

- Government establishments primarily engaged in administering, overseeing, and managing governmental programs are classified in Sector 92, Public Administration;
- Legal entities known as bank holding companies that do not administer, oversee, and manage other establishments of the companies or enterprises whose securities they hold are classified in U.S. Industry 551111, Offices of Bank Holding Companies; and

T—Canadian, Mexican, and United States industries are comparable.

- Legal entities known as holding companies (except bank holding) that do not administer, oversee, and manage other establishments of the companies or enterprises whose securities they hold are classified in U.S. Industry 551112, Offices of Other Holding Companies.

T—Canadian, Mexican, and United States industries are comparable.

Sector 56--Administrative and Support and Waste Management and Remediation Services[T]

The Sector as a Whole

The Administrative and Support and Waste Management and Remediation Services sector comprises establishments performing routine support activities for the day-to-day operations of other organizations. These essential activities are often undertaken in-house by establishments in many sectors of the economy. The establishments in this sector specialize in one or more of these support activities and provide these services to clients in a variety of industries and, in some cases, to households. Activities performed include: office administration, hiring and placing of personnel, document preparation and similar clerical services, solicitation, collection, security and surveillance services, cleaning, and waste disposal services.

The administrative and management activities performed by establishments in this sector are typically on a contract or fee basis. These activities may also be performed by establishments that are part of the company or enterprise. However, establishments involved in administering, overseeing, and managing other establishments of the company or enterprise are classified in Sector 55, Management of Companies and Enterprises. Establishments in Sector 55, Management of Companies and Enterprises, normally undertake the strategic and organizational planning and decision-making role of the company or enterprise. Government establishments engaged in administering, overseeing, and managing governmental programs are classified in Sector 92, Public Administration.

561 Administrative and Support Services[T]

Industries in the Administrative and Support Services subsector group establishments engaged in activities that support the day-to-day operations of other organizations. The processes employed in this sector (e.g., general management, personnel administration, clerical activities, cleaning activities) are often integral parts of the activities of establishments found in all sectors of the economy. The establishments classified in this subsector have specialization in one or more of these activities and can, therefore, provide services to clients in a variety of industries and, in some cases, to households. The individual industries of this subsector are defined on the basis of the particular process that they are engaged in and the particular services they provide.

Many of the activities performed in this subsector are ongoing routine support functions that all businesses and organizations must do and that they have traditionally done for themselves. Recent trends, however, are to contract or purchase such services from businesses that specialize in such activities and can, therefore, provide the services more efficiently.

The industries in this subsector cannot be viewed as strictly "support." The Travel Arrangement and Reservation Services industry group includes travel agents, tour operators, and providers of other travel arrangement services, such as hotel and restaurant reservations and arranging the purchase of tickets, serving many types of clients, including individual consumers. This group was placed in this subsector because the services are often of the "support" nature (e.g., travel arrangement), and businesses and other organizations increasingly purchase such services.

The administrative and management activities performed by establishments in this sector are typically on a contract or fee basis. These activities may also be performed by establishments that are part of the company or enterprise. However, establishments involved in administering, overseeing, and managing other establishments of the company or enterprise are classified in Sector 55, Management of Companies and Enterprises. Establishments in Sector 55, Management of Companies and Enterprises, normally undertake the strategic and organizational planning and decision-making role of the company or enterprise. Government establishments engaged in administering, overseeing, and managing governmental programs are classified in Sector 92, Public Administration.

5611 Office Administrative Services[T]

56111 Office Administrative Services[T] See industry description for 561110.

T—Canadian, Mexican, and United States industries are comparable.

561110 Office Administrative Services

This industry comprises establishments primarily engaged in providing a range of day-to-day office administrative services, such as financial planning; billing and recordkeeping; personnel; and physical distribution and logistics, for others on a contract or fee basis. These establishments do not provide operating staff to carry out the complete operations of a business.

Cross-References. Establishments primarily engaged in--

- Holding the securities or financial assets of companies and enterprises for the purpose of controlling them and influencing their management decisions--are classified in U.S. Industry 551111, Offices of Bank Holding Companies, or U.S. Industry 551112, Offices of Other Holding Companies;
- Administering, overseeing, and managing other establishments of the company or enterprise (except government establishments)--are classified in U.S. Industry 551114, Corporate, Subsidiary, and Regional Managing Offices;
- Providing computer facilities management--are classified in U.S. Industry 541513, Computer Facilities Management Services;
- Providing construction management--are classified in Sector 23, Construction, by type of construction project managed;
- Providing farm management--are classified in U.S. Industry 115116, Farm Management Services;
- Managing real property for others--are classified in Industry 53131, Real Estate Property Managers;
- Providing food services management at institutional, governmental, commercial, or industrial locations--are classified in Industry 722310, Food Service Contractors;
- Providing management advice without day-to-day management--are classified in Industry 54161, Management Consulting Services;
- Providing both management and operating staff for the complete operation of a client's business, such as a hotel, restaurant, mine site, or hospital--are classified according to the industry of the establishment operated; and
- Providing only one of the support services (e.g., accounting services) that establishments in this industry provide--are classified in the appropriate industry according to the service provided.

5612 Facilities Support Services[T]

56121 Facilities Support Services[T] See industry description for 561210.

561210 Facilities Support Services

This industry comprises establishments primarily engaged in providing operating staff to perform a combination of support services within a client's facilities. Establishments in this industry typically provide a combination of services, such as janitorial, maintenance, trash disposal, guard and security, mail routing, reception, laundry, and related services to support operations within facilities. These establishments provide operating staff to carry out these support activities, but are not involved with or responsible for the core business or activities of the client. Establishments providing facilities (except computer and/or data processing) operation support services and establishments providing private jail services or operating correctional facilities (i.e., jails) on a contract or fee basis are included in this industry.

Cross-References.

- Establishments primarily engaged in providing only one of the support services (e.g., janitorial services) that establishments in this industry provide are classified in the appropriate industry according to the service provided;
- Establishments primarily engaged in providing management and operating staff for the complete operation of a client's establishment, such as a hotel, restaurant, mine, or hospital, are classified according to the industry of the establishment operated;

T—Canadian, Mexican, and United States industries are comparable.

- Establishments primarily engaged in providing on-site management and operation of a client's computer systems and/or data processing facilities are classified in U.S. Industry 541513, Computer Facilities Management Services; and
- Governmental correctional institutions are classified in Industry 922140, Correctional Institutions.

5613 Employment Services[T]

This industry group comprises establishments primarily engaged in one of the following: (1) listing employment vacancies and referring or placing applicants for employment; (2) providing executive search, recruitment, and placement services; (3) supplying workers to clients' businesses for limited periods of time to supplement the working force of the client; or (4) providing human resources and human resource management services to client businesses and households.

56131 Employment Placement Agencies and Executive Search Services[T]

This industry comprises establishments primarily engaged in one of the following: 1) listing employment vacancies and referring or placing applicants for employment; or 2) providing executive search, recruitment, and placement services.

Illustrative Examples:

Employment agencies
Executive placement agencies or services
Executive search services

Cross-References. Establishments primarily engaged in--

- Supplying their own employees for limited periods of time to supplement the working force of a client's business--are classified in Industry 56132, Temporary Help Services;
- Providing human resources and human resource management services to client businesses and households--are classified in Industry 56133, Professional Employer Organizations;
- Providing advice and assistance on human resource and personnel policies, practices, and procedures; and employee benefits and compensation systems--are classified in Industry 54161, Management Consulting Services; and
- Representing models, entertainers, athletes, and other public figures as their agent or manager--are classified in Industry 71141, Agents and Managers for Artists, Athletes, Entertainers, and Other Public Figures.

561311 Employment Placement Agencies

This U.S. industry comprises establishments primarily engaged in listing employment vacancies and in referring or placing applicants for employment. The individuals referred or placed are not employees of the employment agencies.

Illustrative Examples:

Babysitting bureaus (i.e., registries)
Employment registries
Model registries
Casting agencies or bureaus (i.e., motion picture, theatrical, video) Employment agencies

Cross-References. Establishments primarily engaged in--

- Providing executive search, recruitment, and placement services--are classified in U.S. Industry 561312, Executive Search Services;
- Supplying their own employees for limited periods of time to supplement the working force of a client's business--are classified in Industry 561320, Temporary Help Services;

T—Canadian, Mexican, and United States industries are comparable.

- Providing human resources and human resource management services to client businesses and households--are classified in Industry 561330, Professional Employer Organizations; and
- Representing models, entertainers, athletes, and other public figures as their agent or manager--are classified in Industry 711410, Agents and Managers for Artists, Athletes, Entertainers, and Other Public Figures.

561312 Executive Search Services

This U.S. industry comprises establishments primarily engaged in providing executive search, recruitment, and placement services for clients with specific executive and senior management position requirements. The range of services provided by these establishments may include developing a search strategy and position specification based on the culture and needs of the client; researching, identifying, screening, and interviewing candidates; verifying candidate qualifications; and assisting in final offer negotiations and assimilation of the selected candidate. The individuals identified, recruited, or placed are not employees of the executive search services establishments.

Illustrative Examples:

Senior executive search services
Executive placement services
Executive search services

Cross-References. Establishments primarily engaged in--

- Listing employment vacancies and in referring or placing applicants for employment--are classified in U.S. Industry 561311, Employment Placement Agencies;
- Supplying their own employees for limited periods of time to supplement the working force of a client's business--are classified in Industry 561320, Temporary Help Services;
- Providing human resources and human resource management services to client businesses and households--are classified in Industry 561330, Professional Employer Organizations;
- Providing administrative and general management consulting services--are classified in U.S. Industry 541611, Administrative Management and General Management Consulting Services;
- Providing advice and assistance on human resource and personnel policies, practices, and procedures; and employee benefits and compensation systems--are classified in U.S. Industry 541612, Human Resources Consulting Services;
- Providing professional and management development training--are classified in Industry 611430, Professional and Management Development Training; and
- Representing models, entertainers, athletes, and other public figures as their agent or manager--are classified in Industry 711410, Agents and Managers for Artists, Athletes, Entertainers, and Other Public Figures.

56132 Temporary Help Services[T] See industry description for 561320.

561320 Temporary Help Services

This industry comprises establishments primarily engaged in supplying workers to clients' businesses for limited periods of time to supplement the working force of the client. The individuals provided are employees of the temporary help services establishment. However, these establishments do not provide direct supervision of their employees at the clients' work sites.

Illustrative Examples:

Help supply services
Model supply services
Labor (except farm) contractors (i.e., personnel suppliers)
Temporary employment or temporary staffing services
Manpower pools

T—Canadian, Mexican, and United States industries are comparable.

Cross-References. Establishments primarily engaged in--

- Providing human resources and human resource management services to client businesses and households--are classified in Industry 561330, Professional Employer Organizations;
- Supplying farm labor--are classified in U.S. Industry 115115, Farm Labor Contractors and Crew Leaders;
- Providing operating staff to perform a combination of services to support operations within a client's facilities--are classified in Industry 561210, Facilities Support Services;
- Providing executive search, recruitment, and placement services--are classified in U.S. Industry 561312, Executive Search Services;
- Listing employment vacancies and referring or placing applicants for employment--are classified in U.S. Industry 561311, Employment Placement Agencies; and
- Representing models, entertainers, athletes, and other public figures as their agent or manager--are classified in Industry 711410, Agents and Managers for Artists, Athletes, Entertainers, and Other Public Figures.

56133 Professional Employer OrganizationsT See industry description for 561330.

561330 Professional Employer Organizations

This industry comprises establishments primarily engaged in providing human resources and human resource management services to client businesses and households. Establishments in this industry operate in a co-employment relationship with client businesses or organizations and are specialized in performing a wide range of human resource and personnel management duties, such as payroll, payroll tax, benefits administration, workers' compensation, unemployment, and human resource administration. Professional employer organizations (PEOs) are responsible for payroll, including withholding and remitting employment-related taxes, for some or all of the employees of their clients, and also serve as the employer of those employees for benefits and related purposes.

Cross-References. Establishments primarily engaged in--

- Supplying their own employees for limited periods of time to supplement the working force of a client's business--are classified in Industry 561320, Temporary Help Services; and
- Listing employment vacancies and referring or placing applicants for employment--are classified in U.S. Industry 561311, Employment Placement Agencies.

5614 Business Support ServicesT

This industry group comprises establishments engaged in performing activities that are ongoing routine business support functions that businesses and organizations traditionally do for themselves.

56141 Document Preparation ServicesT See industry description for 561410.

561410 Document Preparation Services

This industry comprises establishments primarily engaged in one or more of the following: (1) letter or resume writing; (2) document editing or proofreading; (3) typing, word processing, or desktop publishing; and (4) stenography (except court reporting or stenotype recording), transcription, and other secretarial services.

Cross-References. Establishments primarily engaged in--

- Providing verbatim reporting and stenotype recording of live legal proceedings and transcribing subsequent recorded materials--are classified in U.S. Industry 561492, Court Reporting and Stenotype Services;
- Performing prepress and postpress services in support of printing activities--are classified in Industry 323120, Support Activities for Printing;

T—Canadian, Mexican, and United States industries are comparable.

- Providing document translation services--are classified in Industry 541930, Translation and Interpretation Services;
- Photocopying, duplicating, and other document copying services, with or without a range of other office support services (except printing)--are classified in U.S. Industry 561439, Other Business Service Centers (including Copy Shops); and
- Providing document copying services in combination with printing services, with or without a range of other office support services, and establishments known as quick or digital printers--are classified in U.S. Industry 323111, Commercial Printing (except Screen and Books).

56142 Telephone Call Centers[T]

This industry comprises (1) establishments primarily engaged in answering telephone calls and relaying messages to clients and (2) establishments primarily engaged in providing telemarketing services on a contract or fee basis for others, such as promoting clients' products or services by telephone; taking orders for clients by telephone; and soliciting contributions or providing information for clients by telephone. Telemarketing establishments never own the product or provide the service that they are representing and generally originate and/or receive calls for others.

Cross-References. Establishments primarily engaged in--

- Providing paging and beeper transmission services--are classified in Industry 51731, Wired and Wireless Telecommunications Carriers;
- Organizing and conducting fundraising campaigns on a contract or fee basis, that may include telephone solicitation services--are classified in Industry 56149, Other Business Support Services; and
- Gathering, recording, tabulating, and presenting marketing and public opinion data, that may include telephone canvassing services--are classified in Industry 54191, Marketing Research and Public Opinion Polling.

561421 Telephone Answering Services

This U.S. industry comprises establishments primarily engaged in answering telephone calls and relaying messages to clients.

Cross-References.

Establishments primarily engaged in providing paging or beeper transmission services are classified in U.S. Industry 517312, Wireless Telecommunications Carriers (except Satellite).

561422 Telemarketing Bureaus and Other Contact Centers

This U.S. industry comprises establishments primarily engaged in operating call centers that initiate or receive communications for others via telephone, facsimile, email, or other communication modes for purposes such as: (1) promoting clients' products or services, (2) taking orders for clients, (3) soliciting contributions for a client, and (4) providing information or assistance regarding a client's products or services. These establishments do not own the product or provide the services they are representing on behalf of clients.

Cross-References. Establishments primarily engaged in--

- Answering telephone calls and relaying messages to clients--are classified in U.S. Industry 561421, Telephone Answering Services;
- Organizing and conducting fundraising campaigns on a contract or fee basis, that may include telephone solicitation services--are classified in U.S. Industry 561499, All Other Business Support Services; and
- Gathering, recording, tabulating, and presenting marketing and public opinion data, that may include telephone canvassing services--are classified in Industry 541910, Marketing Research and Public Opinion Polling.

T—Canadian, Mexican, and United States industries are comparable.

56143 Business Service Centers[T]

This industry comprises (1) establishments primarily engaged in providing mailbox rental and other postal and mailing services (except direct mail advertising); (2) establishments, generally known as copy centers or shops, primarily engaged in providing photocopying, duplicating, blueprinting, and other document copying services without also providing printing services (i.e., offset printing, quick printing, digital printing, prepress services); and (3) establishments that provide a range of office support services (except printing services), such as mailing services, document copying services, facsimile services, word processing services, on-site PC rental services, and office product sales.

Cross-References. Establishments primarily engaged in--

- Operating contract post offices--are classified in Industry 49111, Postal Service;
- Delivering letters and parcels (except under a universal service obligation)--are classified in Subsector 492, Couriers and Messengers;
- Providing voice mailbox services--are classified in Industry 56142, Telephone Call Centers;
- Providing direct mail advertising services--are classified in Industry 54186, Direct Mail Advertising;
- Providing full service office space, whether on a lease or service contract basis--are classified in Industry 53112, Lessors of Nonresidential Buildings (except Miniwarehouses);
- Providing document copying services in combination with printing services, with or without a range of other office support services, and establishments known as quick or digital printers--are classified in Industry 32311, Printing; and
- Providing only one of the support services (e.g., word processing services) that establishments in this industry provide--are classified in the appropriate industry according to the service provided.

561431 Private Mail Centers

This U.S. industry comprises (1) establishments primarily engaged in providing mailbox rental and other postal and mailing (except direct mail advertising) services or (2) establishments engaged in providing these mailing services along with one or more other office support services, such as facsimile services, word processing services, on-site PC rental services, and office product sales.

Cross-References. Establishments primarily engaged in--

- Operating contract post offices--are classified in Industry 491110, Postal Service;
- Delivering letters and parcels (except under a universal service obligation)--are classified in Subsector 492, Couriers and Messengers;
- Providing voice mailbox services--are classified in U.S. Industry 561421, Telephone Answering Services;
- Providing direct mail advertising services--are classified in Industry 541860, Direct Mail Advertising;
- Providing only one of the support services (e.g., word processing services) that establishments in this industry provide--are classified in the appropriate industry according to the service provided; and
- Providing full service office space, whether on a lease or service contract basis--are classified in Industry 531120, Lessors of Nonresidential Buildings (except Miniwarehouses).

561439 Other Business Service Centers (including Copy Shops)

This U.S. industry comprises (1) establishments generally known as copy centers or shops primarily engaged in providing photocopying, duplicating, blueprinting, and other document copying services, without also providing printing services (e.g., offset printing, quick printing, digital printing, prepress services) and (2) establishments (except private mail centers) engaged in providing a range of office support services (except printing services), such as document copying services, facsimile services, word processing services, on-site PC rental services, and office product sales.

T—Canadian, Mexican, and United States industries are comparable.

Cross-References.

- Establishments primarily engaged in providing document copying services in combination with printing services, with or without a range of other office support services, and establishments known as quick or digital printers are classified in U.S. Industry 323111, Commercial Printing (except Screen and Books);
- Establishments primarily engaged in providing mailbox rental and other postal and mailing services, with or without one or more other office support services (except printing), are classified in U.S. Industry 561431, Private Mail Centers;
- Establishments exclusively engaged in providing a single office support service (except document copying) to clients, but not the range of office support services that establishments in this industry may provide, are classified according to the service provided; and
- Establishments primarily engaged in providing full service office space, whether on a lease or service contract basis, are classified in Industry 531120, Lessors of Nonresidential Buildings (except Miniwarehouses).

56144 Collection Agencies[T] See industry description for 561440.

561440 Collection Agencies

This industry comprises establishments primarily engaged in collecting payments for claims and remitting payments collected to their clients.

Illustrative Examples:

Account or delinquent account collection services
Tax collection services on a contract or fee basis
Bill or debt collection services

Cross-References. Establishments primarily engaged in--

- Repossessing tangible assets--are classified in U.S. Industry 561491, Repossession Services; and
- Providing financing to others by factoring accounts receivables (i.e., assuming the risk of collection and credit losses)--are classified in U.S. Industry 522298, All Other Nondepository Credit Intermediation.

56145 Credit Bureaus[T] See industry description for 561450.

561450 Credit Bureaus

This industry comprises establishments primarily engaged in compiling information, such as credit and employment histories, and providing the information to financial institutions, retailers, and others who have a need to evaluate the creditworthiness of individuals and businesses.

Illustrative Examples:

Credit agencies
Credit rating services
Credit investigation services
Credit reporting bureaus

56149 Other Business Support Services[T]

This industry comprises establishments primarily engaged in providing business support services (except secretarial and other document preparation services; telephone answering or telemarketing services; private mail services or document copying services conducted as separate activities or in conjunction with other office support services; monetary debt collection services; and credit reporting services).

T—Canadian, Mexican, and United States industries are comparable.

Illustrative Examples:

Address bar coding services
Mail presorting services
Bar code imprinting services
Real-time (i.e., simultaneous) closed captioning of live television performances, meetings, conferences
Court reporting services
Repossession services
Fundraising organization services on a contract or fee basis

Cross-References. Establishments primarily engaged in--

- Providing secretarial and other document preparation services--are classified in Industry 56141, Document Preparation Services;
- Providing telephone answering or telemarketing services--are classified in Industry 56142, Telephone Call Centers;
- Providing private mail services; document copying services (except printing services); and/or a range of office support services (except printing)--are classified in Industry 56143, Business Service Centers;
- Providing document copying services in combination with printing services, with or without a range of other office support services, and establishments known as quick or digital printers--are classified in Industry 32311, Printing;
- Providing monetary debt collection services--are classified in Industry 56144, Collection Agencies;
- Providing credit reporting services--are classified in Industry 56145, Credit Bureaus; and
- Providing film or tape captioning or subtitling services--are classified in Industry 51219, Postproduction Services and Other Motion Picture and Video Industries.

561491 Repossession Services

This U.S. industry comprises establishments primarily engaged in repossessing tangible assets (e.g., automobiles, boats, equipment, planes, furniture, appliances) for the creditor as a result of delinquent debts.

Cross-References.

Establishments primarily engaged in providing monetary debt collection services are classified in Industry 561440, Collection Agencies.

561492 Court Reporting and Stenotype Services

This U.S. industry comprises establishments primarily engaged in providing verbatim reporting and stenotype recording of live legal proceedings and transcribing subsequent recorded materials.

Illustrative Examples:

Real-time (i.e., simultaneous) closed captioning of live television performances, meetings, confer-

Cross-References. Establishments primarily engaged in--

- Providing stenotype recording of correspondence, reports, and other documents or in providing document transcription services--are classified in Industry 561410, Document Preparation Services; and
- Providing film or tape captioning or subtitling services--are classified in U.S. Industry 512191, Teleproduction and Other Postproduction Services.

561499 All Other Business Support Services

This U.S. industry comprises establishments primarily engaged in providing business support services (except secretarial and other document preparation services; telephone answering and telemarketing services; private mail

~~T—Canadian, Mexican, and Unit~~ed States industries are comparable.

services or document copying services conducted as separate activities or in conjunction with other office support services; monetary debt collection services; credit reporting services; repossession services; and court reporting and stenotype recording services).

Illustrative Examples:

Address bar coding services
Fundraising organization services on a contract or fee basis
Bar code imprinting services
Mail presorting services

Cross-References. Establishments primarily engaged in--

- Providing secretarial and other document preparation services--are classified in Industry 561410, Document Preparation Services;
- Providing telephone answering or telemarketing services--are classified in Industry 56142, Telephone Call Centers;
- Providing private mail services, document copying services without printing services, and/or a range of office support services--are classified in Industry 56143, Business Service Centers;
- Providing document copying services in combination with printing services, with or without one or more other office support services, and establishments known as quick or digital printers--are classified in U.S. Industry 323111, Commercial Printing (except Screen and Books);
- Providing monetary debt collection services--are classified in Industry 561440, Collection Agencies;
- Providing credit reporting services--are classified in Industry 561450, Credit Bureaus;
- Providing repossession services--are classified in U.S. Industry 561491, Repossession Services; and
- Providing court reporting and stenotype services--are classified in U.S. Industry 561492, Court Reporting and Stenotype Services.

5615 Travel Arrangement and Reservation Services[T]

This industry group comprises establishments primarily engaged in one of the following: (1) travel agency services; (2) arranging and assembling tours; or (3) other travel arrangement and reservation services.

56151 Travel Agencies[T] See industry description for 561510.

561510 Travel Agencies

This industry comprises establishments primarily engaged in acting as agents in selling travel, tour, and accommodation services to the general public and commercial clients.

Cross-References. Establishments primarily engaged in--

- Arranging and assembling tours that they generally sell through travel agencies or on their own account--are classified in Industry 561520, Tour Operators;
- Providing guide services, such as archeological, museum, tourist, hunting, or fishing--are classified in Industry 713990, All Other Amusement and Recreation Industries; and
- Providing reservation services (e.g., accommodations, entertainment events, travel)--are classified in U.S. Industry 561599, All Other Travel Arrangement and Reservation Services.

56152 Tour Operators[T] See industry description for 561520.

T—Canadian, Mexican, and United States industries are comparable.

561520 Tour Operators

This industry comprises establishments primarily engaged in arranging and assembling tours. The tours are sold through travel agencies or tour operators. Travel or wholesale tour operators are included in this industry.

Cross-References. Establishments primarily engaged in--

- Acting as agents in selling travel, tour, and accommodation services to the general public and commercial clients--are classified in Industry 561510, Travel Agencies;
- Conducting scenic and sightseeing tours--are classified in Subsector 487, Scenic and Sightseeing Transportation; and
- Providing guide services, such as archeological, museum, tourist, hunting, or fishing--are classified in Industry 713990, All Other Amusement and Recreation Industries.

56159 Other Travel Arrangement and Reservation Services[T]

This industry comprises establishments (except travel agencies and tour operators) primarily engaged in providing travel arrangement and reservation services.

Illustrative Examples:

Condominium time-share exchange services
Road and travel services automobile clubs
Convention or visitors bureaus
Ticket (e.g., amusement, sports, theatrical) agencies
Ticket (e.g., airline, bus, cruise ship, sports, theatrical) offices
Reservation (e.g., airline, car rental, hotel, restaurant) services

Cross-References.

- Establishments primarily engaged in arranging the rental of vacation properties are classified in Industry 53121, Offices of Real Estate Agents and Brokers;
- Travel agencies are classified in Industry 56151, Travel Agencies;
- Tour operators are classified in Industry 56152, Tour Operators;
- Automobile clubs (i.e., enthusiasts' clubs, except road and travel services) are classified in Industry 81341, Civic and Social Organizations; and
- Establishments primarily engaged in organizing, promoting, and/or managing events, such as business and trade shows, conventions, conferences, and meetings (whether or not they manage and provide the staff to operate the facilities in which these events take place), are classified in Industry 56192, Convention and Trade Show Organizers.

561591 Convention and Visitors Bureaus

This U.S. industry comprises establishments primarily engaged in marketing and promoting communities and facilities to businesses and leisure travelers through a range of activities, such as assisting organizations in locating meeting and convention sites; providing travel information on area attractions, lodging accommodations, restaurants; providing maps; and organizing group tours of local historical, recreational, and cultural attractions.

Cross-References.

Establishments primarily engaged in organizing, promoting, and/or managing events, such as business and trade shows, conventions, conferences, and meetings (whether or not they manage and provide the staff to operate the facilities in which these events take place), are classified in Industry 561920, Convention and Trade Show Organizers.

T—Canadian, Mexican, and United States industries are comparable.

561599 All Other Travel Arrangement and Reservation Services

This U.S. industry comprises establishments (except travel agencies, tour operators, and convention and visitors bureaus) primarily engaged in providing travel arrangement and reservation services.

Illustrative Examples:

Condominium time-share exchange services
Ticket (e.g., airline, bus, cruise ship, sports, theatrical) offices
Road and travel services automobile clubs
Reservation (e.g., airline, car rental, hotel, restaurant) services
Ticket (e.g., amusement, sports, theatrical) agencies

Cross-References.

- Establishments primarily engaged in arranging the rental of vacation properties are classified in Industry 531210, Offices of Real Estate Agents and Brokers;
- Travel agencies are classified in Industry 561510, Travel Agencies;
- Tour operators are classified in Industry 561520, Tour Operators;
- Convention and visitors bureaus are classified in U.S. Industry 561591, Convention and Visitors Bureaus;
- Establishments primarily engaged in organizing, promoting, and/or managing events, such as business and trade shows, conventions, conferences, and meetings (whether or not they manage and provide the staff to operate the facilities in which these events take place), are classified in Industry 561920, Convention and Trade Show Organizers; and
- Automobile clubs (i.e., enthusiasts' clubs, except road and travel services) are classified in Industry 813410, Civic and Social Organizations.

5616 Investigation and Security Services[T]

This industry group comprises establishments primarily engaged in one of the following: (1) investigation, guard, and armored car services; (2) selling security systems, such as burglar and fire alarms and locking devices, along with installation, repair, or monitoring services; or (3) remote monitoring of electronic security alarm systems.

56161 Investigation, Guard, and Armored Car Services[T]

This industry comprises establishments primarily engaged in providing one or more of the following: (1) investigation and detective services; (2) guard and patrol services; and (3) picking up and delivering money, receipts, or other valuable items with personnel and equipment to protect such properties while in transit.

Illustrative Examples:

Armored car services
Private detective services
Bodyguard services
Security guard services
Polygraph services

Cross-References. Establishments primarily engaged in--

- Providing credit checks--are classified in Industry 56145, Credit Bureaus; and
- Selling, installing, monitoring, and maintaining security systems and devices (e.g., burglar and fire alarm systems)--are classified in Industry 56162, Security Systems Services.

561611 Investigation Services

This U.S. industry comprises establishments primarily engaged in providing investigation and detective services.

T—Canadian, Mexican, and United States industries are comparable.

Illustrative Examples:

Fingerprinting services
Private detective services
Polygraph services
Private investigative services

Cross-References.

Establishments primarily engaged in providing credit checks are classified in Industry 561450, Credit Bureaus.

561612 Security Guards and Patrol Services

This U.S. industry comprises establishments primarily engaged in providing guard and patrol services, such as bodyguard, guard dog, and parking security services.

Cross-References.

Establishments primarily engaged in selling, installing, monitoring, and maintaining security systems and devices, such as burglar and fire alarms and locking devices, are classified in Industry 56162, Security Systems Services.

561613 Armored Car Services

This U.S. industry comprises establishments primarily engaged in picking up and delivering money, receipts, or other valuable items. These establishments maintain personnel and equipment to protect such properties while in transit.

56162 Security Systems Services[T]

This industry comprises establishments engaged in (1) selling security systems, such as burglar and fire alarms and locking devices, along with installation, repair, or monitoring services or (2) remote monitoring of electronic security alarm systems.

Cross-References. Establishments primarily engaged in--

- Selling security systems for buildings without installation, repair, or monitoring services--are classified in Sector 42, Wholesale Trade, or Sector 44-45, Retail Trade;
- Retailing motor vehicle security systems, with or without installation or repair services--are classified in Industry 44131, Automotive Parts and Accessories Stores; and
- Providing key duplication services--are classified in Industry 81149, Other Personal and Household Goods Repair and Maintenance.

561621 Security Systems Services (except Locksmiths)

This U.S. industry comprises establishments primarily engaged in (1) selling security alarm systems, such as burglar and fire alarms, along with installation, repair, or monitoring services or (2) remote monitoring of electronic security alarm systems.

Cross-References. Establishments primarily engaged in--

- Selling security alarm systems for buildings, without installation, repair, or monitoring services--are classified in Sector 42, Wholesale Trade, or Sector 44-45, Retail Trade; and
- Retailing motor vehicle security systems, with or without installation or repair services--are classified in Industry 441310, Automotive Parts and Accessories Stores.

T—Canadian, Mexican, and United States industries are comparable.

561622 Locksmiths

This U.S. industry comprises establishments primarily engaged in (1) selling mechanical or electronic locking devices, safes, and security vaults, along with installation, repair, rebuilding, or adjusting services or (2) installing, repairing, rebuilding, and adjusting mechanical or electronic locking devices, safes, and security vaults.

Cross-References. Establishments primarily engaged in--

- Selling security systems, such as locking devices, safes, and vaults, without installation or maintenance services--are classified in Sector 42, Wholesale Trade, or Sector 44-45, Retail Trade; and
- Providing key duplication services--are classified in Industry 811490, Other Personal and Household Goods Repair and Maintenance.

5617 Services to Buildings and Dwellings[T]

This industry group comprises establishments primarily engaged in one of the following: (1) exterminating and pest control services; (2) janitorial services; (3) landscaping services; (4) carpet and upholstery cleaning services; or (5) other services to buildings and dwellings.

56171 Exterminating and Pest Control Services[T] See industry description for 561710.

561710 Exterminating and Pest Control Services

This industry comprises establishments primarily engaged in exterminating and controlling birds, mosquitoes, rodents, termites, and other insects and pests (except for crop production and forestry production). Establishments providing fumigation services are included in this industry.

Cross-References.

Establishments primarily engaged in providing pest control for crop or forestry production are classified in Subsector 115, Support Activities for Agriculture and Forestry.

56172 Janitorial Services[T] See industry description for 561720.

561720 Janitorial Services

This industry comprises establishments primarily engaged in cleaning building interiors, interiors of transportation equipment (e.g., aircraft, rail cars, ships), and/or windows.

Illustrative Examples:

Custodial services
Service station cleaning and degreasing services
Housekeeping (i.e., cleaning) services
Washroom sanitation services
Maid (i.e., cleaning) services

Cross-References. Establishments primarily engaged in--

- Cleaning building exteriors (except sandblasting and window cleaning) or chimneys--are classified in Industry 561790, Other Services to Buildings and Dwellings; and
- Sandblasting building exteriors--are classified in Industry 238990, All Other Specialty Trade Contractors.

56173 Landscaping Services[T] See industry description for 561730.

~~T—Canadian, Mexican, and Unite~~d States industries are comparable.

561730 Landscaping Services

This industry comprises (1) establishments primarily engaged in providing landscape care and maintenance services and/or installing trees, shrubs, plants, lawns, or gardens and (2) establishments primarily engaged in providing these services along with the design of landscape plans and/or the construction (i.e., installation) of walkways, retaining walls, decks, fences, ponds, and similar structures.

Cross-References. Establishments primarily engaged in--

- Installing artificial turf or constructing (i.e., installing) walkways, retaining walls, decks, fences, ponds, or similar structures--are classified in Sector 23, Construction;
- Planning and designing the development of land areas for projects, such as parks and other recreational areas; airports; highways; hospitals; schools; land subdivisions; and commercial, industrial, and residential areas (without also installing trees, shrubs, plants, lawns/gardens, walkways, retaining walls, decks, and similar items or structures)--are classified in Industry 541320, Landscape Architectural Services; and
- Retailing landscaping materials and providing the installation and maintenance of these materials--are classified in Industry 444220, Nursery, Garden Center, and Farm Supply Stores.

56174 Carpet and Upholstery Cleaning Services[T] See industry description for 561740.

561740 Carpet and Upholstery Cleaning Services

This industry comprises establishments primarily engaged in cleaning and dyeing used rugs, carpets, and upholstery.

Cross-References. Establishments primarily engaged in--

- Rug repair not associated with rug cleaning--are classified in Industry 811490, Other Personal and Household Goods Repair and Maintenance; and
- Reupholstering and repairing furniture--are classified in Industry 811420, Reupholstery and Furniture Repair.

56179 Other Services to Buildings and Dwellings[T]
See industry description for 561790.

561790 Other Services to Buildings and Dwellings

This industry comprises establishments primarily engaged in providing services to buildings and dwellings (except exterminating and pest control; janitorial; landscaping care and maintenance; and carpet and upholstery cleaning).

Illustrative Examples:

Building exterior cleaning services (except sandblasting, window cleaning)
Swimming pool cleaning and maintenance services
Chimney cleaning services
Ventilation duct cleaning services
Drain or gutter cleaning services

Cross-References. Establishments primarily engaged in--

- Providing exterminating and pest control services--are classified in Industry 561710, Exterminating and Pest Control Services;
- Providing janitorial services--are classified in Industry 561720, Janitorial Services;
- Providing landscaping care and maintenance--are classified in Industry 561730, Landscaping Services;
- Providing carpet and upholstery cleaning services--are classified in Industry 561740, Carpet and Upholstery Cleaning Services; and

- Sandblasting building exteriors--are classified in Industry 238990, All Other Specialty Trade Contractors.

5619 Other Support Services[T]

This industry group comprises establishments primarily engaged in providing day-to-day business and other organizational support services (except office administrative services; facilities support services; employment services; business support services; travel arrangement and reservation services; security and investigation services; and services to buildings and dwellings).

56191 Packaging and Labeling Services[T] See industry description for 561910.

561910 Packaging and Labeling Services

This industry comprises establishments primarily engaged in packaging client-owned materials. The services may include labeling and/or imprinting the package.

Illustrative Examples:

Apparel and textile folding and packaging services
Kit assembling and packaging services
Blister packaging services
Shrink wrapping services
Gift wrapping services

Cross-References. Establishments primarily engaged in--

- Processing client-owned materials into a different product, such as mixing water and concentrate to produce soft drinks--are classified in Sector 31-33, Manufacturing;
- Providing aerosol packaging services--are classified in U.S. Industry 325998, All Other Miscellaneous Chemical Product and Preparation Manufacturing;
- Providing packing and crating services incidental to transportation--are classified in U.S. Industry 488991, Packing and Crating;
- Providing warehousing services, as well as packaging or other logistics services--are classified in Industry Group 4931, Warehousing and Storage; and
- Providing packing and crating services for agricultural products--are classified in U.S. Industry 115114, Postharvest Crop Activities (except Cotton Ginning).

56192 Convention and Trade Show Organizers[T] See industry description for 561920.

561920 Convention and Trade Show Organizers

This industry comprises establishments primarily engaged in organizing, promoting, and/or managing events, such as business and trade shows, conventions, conferences, and meetings (whether or not they manage and provide the staff to operate the facilities in which these events take place).

Cross-References.

Establishments primarily engaged in organizing, promoting, and/or managing live performing arts productions, sports events, and similar events, such as festivals (whether or not they manage and provide the staff to operate the facilities in which these events take place), are classified in Industry Group 7113, Promoters of Performing Arts, Sports, and Similar Events.

56199 All Other Support Services[T] See industry description for 561990.

T—Canadian, Mexican, and United States industries are comparable.

561990 All Other Support Services

This industry comprises establishments primarily engaged in providing day-to-day business and other organizational support services (except office administrative services, facilities support services, employment services, business support services, travel arrangement and reservation services, security and investigation services, services to buildings and other structures, packaging and labeling services, and convention and trade show organizing services).

Illustrative Examples:

Bartering services
Flagging (i.e., traffic control) services
Bottle exchanges
Float decorating services
Cloth cutting, bolting, or winding for the trade
Inventory taking services
Contract meter reading services
Lumber grading services
Diving services on a contract or fee basis

Cross-References. Establishments primarily engaged in--

- Providing office administrative services--are classified in Industry 561110, Office Administrative Services;
- Providing facilities support services--are classified in Industry 561210, Facilities Support Services;
- Providing employment services--are classified in Industry Group 5613, Employment Services;
- Providing business support services--are classified in Industry Group 5614, Business Support Services;
- Providing travel arrangement and reservation services--are classified in Industry Group 5615, Travel Arrangement and Reservation Services;
- Providing security and investigation services--are classified in Industry Group 5616, Investigation and Security Services;
- Providing services to buildings and other structures--are classified in Industry Group 5617, Services to Buildings and Dwellings;
- Providing packaging and labeling services--are classified in Industry 561910, Packaging and Labeling Services; and
- Organizing, promoting, and/or managing conferences, conventions, and trade shows (whether or not they manage and provide the staff to operate the facilities in which these events take place)--are classified in Industry 561920, Convention and Trade Show Organizers.

562 Waste Management and Remediation Services[T]

Industries in the Waste Management and Remediation Services subsector group establishments engaged in the collection, treatment, and disposal of waste materials. This includes establishments engaged in local hauling of waste materials; operating materials recovery facilities (i.e., those that sort recyclable materials from the trash stream); providing remediation services (i.e., those that provide for the cleanup of contaminated buildings, mine sites, soil, or ground water); and providing septic pumping and other miscellaneous waste management services. There are three industry groups within the subsector that separate these activities into waste collection, waste treatment and disposal, and remediation and other waste management.

Excluded from this subsector are establishments primarily engaged in collecting, treating, and disposing waste through sewer systems or sewage treatment facilities that are classified in Industry 22132, Sewage Treatment Facilities, and establishments primarily engaged in long-distance hauling of waste materials that are classified in Industry 48423, Specialized Freight (except Used Goods) Trucking, Long-Distance. Also, there are some activities that appear to be related to waste management, but that are not included in this subsector. For example, establishments primarily engaged in providing waste management consulting services are classified in Industry 54162, Environmental Consulting Services.

T—Canadian, Mexican, and United States industries are comparable.

5621 Waste Collection

56211 Waste Collection

This industry comprises establishments primarily engaged in (1) collecting and/or hauling hazardous waste, nonhazardous waste, and/or recyclable materials within a local area and/or (2) operating hazardous or nonhazardous waste transfer stations. Hazardous waste collection establishments may be responsible for the identification, treatment, packaging, and labeling of waste for the purposes of transport.

Cross-References. Establishments primarily engaged in--

- Long-distance trucking of waste--are classified in Industry 48423, Specialized Freight (except Used Goods) Trucking, Long-Distance;
- Operating facilities for separating and sorting recyclable materials from nonhazardous waste streams (i.e., garbage) and/or for sorting commingled recyclable materials, such as paper, plastics, and metal cans, into distinct categories--are classified in Industry 56292, Materials Recovery Facilities; and
- Collecting and/or hauling in combination with disposal of waste materials--are classified in Industry 56221, Waste Treatment and Disposal.

562111 Solid Waste Collection

This U.S. industry comprises establishments primarily engaged in one or more of the following: (1) collecting and/or hauling nonhazardous solid waste (i.e., garbage) within a local area; (2) operating nonhazardous solid waste transfer stations; and (3) collecting and/or hauling mixed recyclable materials within a local area.

Cross-References. Establishments primarily engaged in--

- Long-distance trucking of waste--are classified in Industry 484230, Specialized Freight (except Used Goods) Trucking, Long-Distance;
- Collecting and/or hauling in combination with disposal of nonhazardous waste materials--are classified in Industry 56221, Waste Treatment and Disposal;
- Collecting and/or hauling hazardous waste within a local area and/or operating hazardous waste transfer stations--are classified in U.S. Industry 562112, Hazardous Waste Collection;
- Collecting and removing debris, such as brush or rubble, within a local area--are classified in U.S. Industry 562119, Other Waste Collection; and
- Operating facilities for separating and sorting recyclable materials from nonhazardous waste streams (i.e., garbage) and/or for sorting commingled recyclable materials, such as paper, plastics, and metal cans, into distinct categories--are classified in Industry 562920, Materials Recovery Facilities.

562112 Hazardous Waste Collection

This U.S. industry comprises establishments primarily engaged in collecting and/or hauling hazardous waste within a local area and/or operating hazardous waste transfer stations. Hazardous waste collection establishments may be responsible for the identification, treatment, packaging, and labeling of waste for the purposes of transport.

Cross-References. Establishments primarily engaged in--

- Long-distance trucking of waste--are classified in Industry 484230, Specialized Freight (except Used Goods) Trucking, Long-Distance;
- Collecting and/or hauling in combination with disposal of hazardous waste materials--are classified in U.S. Industry 562211, Hazardous Waste Treatment and Disposal;
- Collecting and/or hauling nonhazardous solid waste (i.e., garbage) and/or recyclable materials within a local area and/or operating nonhazardous solid waste transfer stations--are classified in U.S. Industry 562111, Solid Waste Collection; and

---

T—Canadian, Mexican, and United States industries are comparable.

- Collecting and removing debris, such as brush or rubble, within a local area--are classified in U.S. Industry 562119, Other Waste Collection.

562119 Other Waste Collection

This U.S. industry comprises establishments primarily engaged in collecting and/or hauling waste (except nonhazardous solid waste and hazardous waste) within a local area. Establishments engaged in brush or rubble removal services are included in this industry.

Cross-References. Establishments primarily engaged in--

- Long-distance trucking of waste--are classified in Industry 484230, Specialized Freight (except Used Goods) Trucking, Long-Distance;
- Collecting and/or hauling in combination with disposal of waste materials--are classified in Industry Group 5622, Waste Treatment and Disposal;
- Collecting and/or hauling nonhazardous solid waste (i.e., garbage) or mixed recyclable materials within a local area or operating nonhazardous solid waste transfer stations--are classified in U.S. Industry 562111, Solid Waste Collection;
- Collecting and/or hauling hazardous waste within a local area or operating hazardous waste transfer stations--are classified in U.S. Industry 562112, Hazardous Waste Collection; and
- Operating facilities for separating and sorting recyclable materials from nonhazardous waste streams (i.e., garbage) and/or for sorting commingled recyclable materials, such as paper, plastics, and metal cans, into distinct categories--are classified in Industry 562920, Materials Recovery Facilities.

5622 Waste Treatment and Disposal 56221

Waste Treatment and Disposal

This industry comprises establishments primarily engaged in (1) operating waste treatment or disposal facilities (except sewer systems or sewage treatment facilities) or (2) the combined activity of collecting and/or hauling of waste materials within a local area and operating waste treatment or disposal facilities. Waste combustors or incinerators (including those that may produce byproducts, such as electricity), solid waste landfills, and compost dumps are included in this industry.

Cross-References. Establishments primarily engaged in--

- Collecting, treating, and disposing waste through sewer systems or sewage treatment facilities--are classified in Industry 22132, Sewage Treatment Facilities; and
- Manufacturing compost--are classified in Industry 32531, Fertilizer Manufacturing.

562211 Hazardous Waste Treatment and Disposal

This U.S. industry comprises establishments primarily engaged in (1) operating treatment and/or disposal facilities for hazardous waste or (2) the combined activity of collecting and/or hauling of hazardous waste materials within a local area and operating treatment or disposal facilities for hazardous waste.

Cross-References. Establishments primarily engaged in--

- Operating landfills for the disposal of nonhazardous solid waste--are classified in U.S. Industry 562212, Solid Waste Landfill;
- Operating combustors and incinerators for the disposal of nonhazardous solid waste--are classified in U.S. Industry 562213, Solid Waste Combustors and Incinerators;
- Collecting, treating, and disposing waste through sewer systems or sewage treatment facilities--are classified in Industry 221320, Sewage Treatment Facilities; and

T—Canadian, Mexican, and United States industries are comparable.

- Operating nonhazardous waste treatment and disposal facilities (except landfills, combustors, incinerators, and sewer systems or sewage treatment facilities)--are classified in U.S. Industry 562219, Other Nonhazardous Waste Treatment and Disposal.

562212 Solid Waste Landfill

This U.S. industry comprises establishments primarily engaged in (1) operating landfills for the disposal of nonhazardous solid waste or (2) the combined activity of collecting and/or hauling nonhazardous waste materials within a local area and operating landfills for the disposal of nonhazardous solid waste. These establishments may produce byproducts, such as methane.

Cross-References. Establishments primarily engaged in--

- Operating treatment and/or disposal facilities for hazardous waste--are classified in U.S. Industry 562211, Hazardous Waste Treatment and Disposal;
- Operating combustors and incinerators for the disposal of nonhazardous solid waste--are classified in U.S. Industry 562213, Solid Waste Combustors and Incinerators;
- Collecting, treating, and disposing waste through sewer systems or sewage treatment facilities--are classified in Industry 221320, Sewage Treatment Facilities;
- Operating nonhazardous waste treatment and disposal facilities (except landfills, combustors, incinerators, and sewer systems or sewage treatment facilities)--are classified in U.S. Industry 562219, Other Nonhazardous Waste Treatment and Disposal; and
- Manufacturing compost--are classified in U.S. Industry 325314, Fertilizer (Mixing Only) Manufacturing.

562213 Solid Waste Combustors and Incinerators

This U.S. industry comprises establishments primarily engaged in operating combustors and incinerators for the disposal of nonhazardous solid waste. These establishments may produce byproducts, such as electricity and steam.

Cross-References. Establishments primarily engaged in--

- Operating treatment and/or disposal facilities for hazardous waste--are classified in U.S. Industry 562211, Hazardous Waste Treatment and Disposal;
- Operating landfills for the disposal of nonhazardous solid waste--are classified in U.S. Industry 562212, Solid Waste Landfill;
- Collecting, treating, and disposing waste through sewer systems or sewage treatment facilities--are classified in Industry 221320, Sewage Treatment Facilities; and
- Operating nonhazardous waste treatment and disposal facilities (except landfills, combustors, incinerators, and sewer systems or sewage treatment facilities)--are classified in U.S. Industry 562219, Other Nonhazardous Waste Treatment and Disposal.

562219 Other Nonhazardous Waste Treatment and Disposal

This U.S. industry comprises establishments primarily engaged in (1) operating nonhazardous waste treatment and disposal facilities (except landfills, combustors, incinerators and sewer systems or sewage treatment facilities) or (2) the combined activity of collecting and/or hauling of nonhazardous waste materials within a local area and operating waste treatment or disposal facilities (except landfills, combustors, incinerators and sewer systems, or sewage treatment facilities). Compost dumps are included in this industry.

Cross-References. Establishments primarily engaged in--

- Operating landfills for the disposal of nonhazardous solid waste--are classified in U.S. Industry 562212, Solid Waste Landfill;
- Operating combustors and incinerators for the disposal of nonhazardous solid waste--are classified in U.S. Industry 562213, Solid Waste Combustors and Incinerators;

T—Canadian, Mexican, and United States industries are comparable.

- Collecting, treating, and disposing waste through sewer systems or sewage treatment facilities--are classified in Industry 221320, Sewage Treatment Facilities; and
- Manufacturing compost--are classified in U.S. Industry 325314, Fertilizer (Mixing Only) Manufacturing.

5629 Remediation and Other Waste Management Services

This industry group comprises establishments primarily engaged in remediation and other waste management services (except waste collection, waste treatment and disposal, and waste management consulting services).

56291 Remediation Services

See industry description for 562910.

562910 Remediation Services

This industry comprises establishments primarily engaged in one or more of the following: (1) remediation and cleanup of contaminated buildings, mine sites, soil, or ground water; (2) integrated mine reclamation activities, including demolition, soil remediation, waste water treatment, hazardous material removal, contouring land, and revegetation; and (3) asbestos, lead paint, and other toxic material abatement.

Cross-References. Establishments primarily engaged in--

- Environmental engineering services--are classified in Industry 541330, Engineering Services;
- Developing remedial action plans--are classified in Industry 541620, Environmental Consulting Services;
- Excavating soil--are classified in Industry 238910, Site Preparation Contractors;
- Individual activities as part of a reclamation, remediation, or restoration project--are classified according to the primary activity;
- Building modifications to alleviate radon gas--are classified in Industry 238990, All Other Specialty Trade Contractors; and
- Collecting, treating, and disposing waste water through sewer systems or sewage treatment facilities--are classified in Industry 221320, Sewage Treatment Facilities.

56292 Materials Recovery Facilities

See industry description for 562920.

562920 Materials Recovery Facilities

This industry comprises establishments primarily engaged in (1) operating facilities for separating and sorting recyclable materials from nonhazardous waste streams (i.e., garbage) and/or (2) operating facilities where commingled recyclable materials, such as paper, plastics, used beverage cans, and metals, are sorted into distinct categories.

Cross-References.

Establishments primarily engaged in merchant wholesaling automotive, industrial, and other recyclable materials are classified in Industry 423930, Recyclable Material Merchant Wholesalers.

56299 All Other Waste Management Services

This industry comprises establishments primarily engaged in waste management services (except waste collection, waste treatment and disposal, remediation, operation of materials recovery facilities, and waste management consulting services).
T—Canadian, Mexican, and United States industries are comparable.

Illustrative Examples:

Beach cleaning and maintenance services
Pumping (i.e., cleaning) cesspools, portable toilets, or septic tanks
Cesspool cleaning services
Sewer cleaning and rodding services
Portable toilet renting and/or servicing
Sewer or storm basin cleanout services

Cross-References. Establishments primarily engaged in--

- Collecting and/or hauling waste within a local area--are classified in Industry 56211, Waste Collection;
- Long-distance trucking of waste--are classified in Industry 48423, Specialized Freight (except Used Goods) Trucking, Long-Distance;
- Operating treatment or disposal facilities (except sewer systems or sewage treatment facilities) for waste--are classified in Industry 56221, Waste Treatment and Disposal;
- Collecting, treating, and disposing waste through sewer systems or sewage treatment facilities--are classified in Industry 22132, Sewage Treatment Facilities;
- Remediation and cleanup of contaminated buildings, mine sites, soil, or ground water--are classified in Industry 56291, Remediation Services;
- Operating facilities for separating and sorting recyclable materials from nonhazardous waste streams (i.e., garbage) or where commingled recyclable materials, such as paper, plastics, and metal cans, are sorted into distinct categories--are classified in Industry 56292, Materials Recovery Facilities;
- Installing septic tanks--are classified in Industry 23891, Site Preparation Contractors; and
- Providing waste management consulting services, such as developing remedial action plans--are classified in Industry 54162, Environmental Consulting Services.

562991 Septic Tank and Related Services

This U.S. industry comprises establishments primarily engaged in (1) pumping (i.e., cleaning) septic tanks and cesspools and/or (2) renting and/or servicing portable toilets.

Cross-References. Establishments primarily engaged in--

- Installing septic tanks--are classified in Industry 238910, Site Preparation Contractors; and
- Cleaning and rodding sewers and catch basins--are classified in U.S. Industry 562998, All Other Miscellaneous Waste Management Services.

562998 All Other Miscellaneous Waste Management Services

This U.S. industry comprises establishments primarily engaged in providing waste management services (except waste collection, waste treatment and disposal, remediation, operation of materials recovery facilities, septic tank pumping and related services, and waste management consulting services).

Illustrative Examples:

Beach cleaning and maintenance services
Sewer or storm basin cleanout services
Catch basin cleaning services
Tank cleaning and disposal services, commercial or industrial
Sewer cleaning and rodding services

Cross-References. Establishments primarily engaged in--

- Collecting and/or hauling waste within a local area--are classified in Industry 56211, Waste Collection;
- Long-distance trucking of waste--are classified in Industry 484230, Specialized Freight (except Used Goods) Trucking, Long-Distance;
- Operating treatment or disposal facilities (except sewer systems or sewage treatment facilities) for waste--are classified in Industry 56221, Waste Treatment and Disposal;

~~T—Canadian, Mexican, and Unit~~ed States industries are comparable.

- Collecting, treating, and disposing waste through sewer systems or sewage treatment facilities--are classified in Industry 221320, Sewage Treatment Facilities;
- Remediation and cleanup of contaminated buildings, mine sites, soil, or ground water--are classified in Industry 562910, Remediation Services;
- Operating facilities for separating and sorting recyclable materials from nonhazardous waste streams (i.e., garbage) or for sorting commingled recyclable materials, such as paper, plastics, and metal cans, into distinct categories--are classified in Industry 562920, Materials Recovery Facilities;
- Pumping (i.e., cleaning) cesspools, portable toilets, and septic tanks or renting portable toilets--are classified in U.S. Industry 562991, Septic Tank and Related Services; and
- Providing waste management consulting services, such as developing remedial action plans--are classified in Industry 541620, Environmental Consulting Services.

T—Canadian, Mexican, and United States industries are comparable.

Sector 61--Educational Services[T]

The Sector as a Whole

The Educational Services sector comprises establishments that provide instruction and training in a wide variety of subjects. This instruction and training is provided by specialized establishments, such as schools, colleges, universities, and training centers. These establishments may be privately owned and operated for profit or not for profit, or they may be publicly owned and operated. They may also offer food and/or accommodation services to their students.

Educational services are usually delivered by teachers or instructors that explain, tell, demonstrate, supervise, and direct learning. Instruction is imparted in diverse settings, such as educational institutions, the workplace, or the home, and through diverse means, such as correspondence, television, the Internet, or other electronic and distance-learning methods. The training provided by these establishments may include the use of simulators and simulation methods. It can be adapted to the particular needs of the students, for example sign language can replace verbal language for teaching students with hearing impairments. All industries in the sector share this commonality of process, namely, labor inputs of instructors with the requisite subject matter expertise and teaching ability.

611 Educational Services[T]

Industries in the Educational Services subsector provide instruction and training in a wide variety of subjects. The instruction and training is provided by specialized establishments, such as schools, colleges, universities, and training centers.

The subsector is structured according to level and type of educational services. Elementary and secondary schools, junior colleges and colleges, universities, and professional schools correspond to a recognized series of formal levels of education designated by diplomas, associate degrees (including equivalent certificates), and degrees. The remaining industry groups are based more on the type of instruction or training offered, and the levels are not always as formally defined. The establishments are often highly specialized, many offering instruction in a very limited subject matter, for example ski lessons or one specific computer software package. Within the subsector, the level and types of training that are required of the instructors and teachers vary depending on the industry.

Establishments that manage schools and other educational establishments on a contractual basis are classified in this subsector if they both manage the operation and provide the operating staff. Such establishments are classified in the Educational Services subsector based on the type of facility managed and operated.

6111 Elementary and Secondary Schools[T]

61111 Elementary and Secondary Schools

See industry description for 611110.

611110 Elementary and Secondary Schools

This industry comprises establishments primarily engaged in furnishing academic courses and associated course work that comprise a basic preparatory education. A basic preparatory education ordinarily constitutes kindergarten through 12th grade. This industry includes school boards and school districts.

Illustrative Examples:

Elementary schools
Parochial schools, elementary or secondary
High schools
Primary schools
Kindergartens
Schools for the physically disabled, elementary or secondary
Military academies, elementary or secondary

T—Canadian, Mexican, and United States industries are comparable.

Cross-References.

- Establishments primarily engaged in providing preschool or pre-kindergarten education are classified in Industry 624410, Child Day Care Services; and
- College level military academies are classified in Industry 611310, Colleges, Universities, and Professional Schools.

6112 Junior Colleges[T]

61121 Junior Colleges[T] See industry description for 611210.

611210 Junior Colleges

This industry comprises establishments primarily engaged in furnishing academic, or academic and technical, courses and granting associate degrees, certificates, or diplomas below the baccalaureate level. The requirement for admission to an associate or equivalent degree program is at least a high school diploma or equivalent general academic training. Instruction may be provided in diverse settings, such as the establishment's or client's training facilities, educational institutions, the workplace, or the home, and through diverse means, such as correspondence, television, the Internet, or other electronic and distance-learning methods. The training provided by these establishments may include the use of simulators and simulation methods.

6113 Colleges, Universities, and Professional Schools[T]

61131 Colleges, Universities, and Professional Schools[T] See industry description for 611310.

611310 Colleges, Universities, and Professional Schools

This industry comprises establishments primarily engaged in furnishing academic courses and granting degrees at baccalaureate or graduate levels. The requirement for admission is at least a high school diploma or equivalent general academic training. Instruction may be provided in diverse settings, such as the establishment's or client's training facilities, educational institutions, the workplace, or the home, and through diverse means, such as correspondence, television, the Internet, or other electronic and distance-learning methods. The training provided by these establishments may include the use of simulators and simulation methods.

Illustrative Examples:

Colleges (except junior colleges)
Theological seminaries offering baccalaureate or graduate degrees
Military academies, college level
Universities
Professional schools (e.g., business administration, dental, law, medical)

Cross-References.

Establishments primarily engaged in furnishing academic, or academic and technical, courses and granting associate degrees, certificates, or diplomas below the baccalaureate level are classified in Industry 611210, Junior Colleges.

6114 Business Schools and Computer and Management Training[T]

This industry group comprises establishments primarily engaged in one of the following: (1) offering courses in office procedures and secretarial and stenographic skills and may offer courses in basic office skills, such as word processing; (2) conducting computer training (except computer repair); or (3) offering an array of short duration courses and seminars for management and professional development. Instruction may be provided in diverse

~~T—Canadian, Mexican, and Unite~~d States industries are comparable.

settings, such as the establishment's or client's training facilities, educational institutions, the workplace, or the home, and through diverse means, such as correspondence, television, the Internet, or other electronic and distance-learning methods. The training provided by these establishments may include the use of simulators and simulation methods.

61141 Business and Secretarial Schools[T] See industry description for 611410.

611410 Business and Secretarial Schools

This industry comprises establishments primarily engaged in offering courses in office procedures and secretarial and stenographic skills and may offer courses in basic office skills, such as word processing. In addition, these establishments may offer such classes as office machine operation, reception, communications, and other skills designed for individuals pursuing a clerical or secretarial career. Instruction may be provided in diverse settings, such as the establishment's or client's training facilities, educational institutions, the workplace, or the home, and through diverse means, such as correspondence, television, the Internet, or other electronic and distance-learning methods. The training provided by these establishments may include the use of simulators and simulation methods.

Cross-References. Establishments primarily engaged in--

- Offering computer training (except computer repair)--are classified in Industry 611420, Computer Training;
- Offering academic degrees (e.g., baccalaureate, graduate level) in business education--are classified in Industry 611310, Colleges, Universities, and Professional Schools; and
- Offering training in the maintenance and repair of computers--are classified in U.S. Industry 611519, Other Technical and Trade Schools.

61142 Computer Training[T] See industry description for 611420.

611420 Computer Training

This industry comprises establishments primarily engaged in conducting computer training (except computer repair), such as computer programming, software packages, computerized business systems, computer electronics technology, computer operations, and local area network management. Instruction may be provided in diverse settings, such as the establishment's or client's training facilities, educational institutions, the workplace, or the home, and through diverse means, such as correspondence, television, the Internet, or other electronic and distance-learning methods. The training provided by these establishments may include the use of simulators and simulation methods.

Cross-References. Establishments primarily engaged in--

- Offering training in the maintenance and repair of computers--are classified in U.S. Industry 611519, Other Technical and Trade Schools; and
- Computer retailing, wholesaling, or computer system designing that may also provide computer training--are classified in their appropriate industries.

61143 Professional and Management Development Training[T] See industry description for 611430.

611430 Professional and Management Development Training

This industry comprises establishments primarily engaged in offering an array of short duration courses and seminars for management and professional development. Training for career development may be provided directly to individuals or through employers' training programs, and courses may be customized or modified to meet the

T—Canadian, Mexican, and United States industries are comparable.

special needs of customers. Instruction may be provided in diverse settings, such as the establishment's or client's training facilities, educational institutions, the workplace, or the home, and through diverse means, such as correspondence, television, the Internet, or other electronic and distance-learning methods. The training provided by these establishments may include the use of simulators and simulation methods.

Cross-References. Establishments primarily engaged in--

- Advising clients on human resource and training issues without providing the training--are classified in U.S. Industry 541612, Human Resources Consulting Services; and
- Offering academic degrees (e.g., baccalaureate, graduate level)--are classified in Industry 611310, Colleges, Universities, and Professional Schools.

6115 Technical and Trade Schools[T]

61151 Technical and Trade Schools[T]

This industry comprises establishments primarily engaged in offering vocational and technical training in a variety of technical subjects and trades. The training often leads to job-specific certification. Instruction may be provided in diverse settings, such as the establishment's or client's training facilities, educational institutions, the workplace, or the home, and through diverse means, such as correspondence, television, the Internet, or other electronic and distance-learning methods. The training provided by these establishments may include the use of simulators and simulation methods.

Illustrative Examples:

Apprenticeship training programs
Graphic arts schools
Aviation and flight training schools
Modeling schools
Computer repair training
Nursing schools (except academic)
Cosmetology schools
Real estate schools
Electronic equipment repair training
Truck driving schools

Cross-References. Establishments primarily engaged in--

- Offering courses in office procedures and secretarial and stenographic skills--are classified in Industry 61141, Business and Secretarial Schools;
- Offering computer training (except computer repair)--are classified in Industry 61142, Computer Training;
- Offering professional and management development training--are classified in Industry 61143, Professional and Management Development Training;
- Offering academic courses that may also offer technical and trade courses--are classified according to the type of school;
- Specialty air transportation services that may also provide flight training--are classified in Industry 48121, Nonscheduled Air Transportation; and
- Offering registered nursing training with academic degrees (e.g., associate, baccalaureate)--are classified in Industry 61121, Junior Colleges, or Industry 61131, Colleges, Universities, and Professional Schools.

611511 Cosmetology and Barber Schools

This U.S. industry comprises establishments primarily engaged in offering training in barbering, hair styling, or the cosmetic arts, such as makeup or skin care. These schools provide job-specific certification.

611512 Flight Training

This U.S. industry comprises establishments primarily engaged in offering aviation and flight training. These establishments may offer vocational training, recreational training, or both.

T—Canadian, Mexican, and United States industries are comparable.

Cross-References. Establishments primarily engaged in--

- Offering specialized military training (except flight instruction, academies, and basic training)--are classified in U.S. Industry 611519, Other Technical and Trade Schools;
- Operating college level military academies--are classified in Industry 611310, Colleges, Universities, and Professional Schools;
- National security and military basic training (except academies)--are classified in Industry 928110, National Security; and
- Providing specialty air transportation services that may also provide flight training--are classified in U.S. Industry 481219, Other Nonscheduled Air Transportation.

611513 Apprenticeship Training

This U.S. industry comprises establishments primarily engaged in offering apprenticeship training programs. These programs involve applied training as well as course work.

611519 Other Technical and Trade Schools

This U.S. industry comprises establishments primarily engaged in offering job or career vocational or technical courses (except cosmetology and barber training, aviation and flight training, and apprenticeship training). The curriculums offered by these schools are highly structured and specialized and lead to job-specific certification.

Illustrative Examples:

Bartending schools
Modeling schools
Broadcasting schools
Real estate schools
Computer repair training
Truck driving schools
Graphic arts schools
Specialized military training (except flight instruction, academies, and basic training)

Cross-References. Establishments primarily engaged in--

- Offering courses in office procedures and secretarial and stenographic skills--are classified in Industry 611410, Business and Secretarial Schools;
- Offering computer training (except computer repair)--are classified in Industry 611420, Computer Training;
- Offering professional and management development training--are classified in Industry 611430, Professional and Management Development Training;
- Offering registered nursing training with academic degrees (e.g., associate, baccalaureate)--are classified in Industry 611210, Junior Colleges, or Industry 611310, College, Universities, and Professional Schools;
- Offering aviation and flight training, including military flight instruction--are classified in U.S. Industry 611512, Flight Training;
- Operating college level military academies--are classified in Industry 611310, Colleges, Universities, and Professional Schools;
- National security and military basic training (except academies)--are classified in Industry 928110, National Security;
- Offering cosmetology and barber training--are classified in U.S. Industry 611511, Cosmetology and Barber Schools;
- Offering academic courses that may also offer technical and trade courses--are classified according to the type of school; and
- Offering apprenticeship training programs--are classified in U.S. Industry 611513, Apprenticeship Training.

T—Canadian, Mexican, and United States industries are comparable.

6116 Other Schools and Instruction[T]

This industry group comprises establishments primarily engaged in offering or providing instruction (except academic schools, colleges, and universities; and business, computer, management, technical, or trade instruction). Instruction may be provided in diverse settings, such as the establishment's or client's training facilities, educational institutions, the workplace, or the home, and through diverse means, such as correspondence, television, the Internet, or other electronic and distance-learning methods. The training provided by these establishments may include the use of simulators and simulation methods.

61161 Fine Arts Schools[T] See industry description for 611610.

611610 Fine Arts Schools

This industry comprises establishments primarily engaged in offering instruction in the arts, including dance, art, drama, and music.

Illustrative Examples:

Art (except commercial and graphic) instruction
Music instruction (e.g., piano, guitar)
Dancc instruction
Music schools (except academic)
Dance studios
Performing arts schools (except academic)
Drama schools (except academic)
Photography schools (except commercial photography)
Fine arts schools (except academic)

Cross-References.

- Establishments offering high school diplomas or academic degrees (i.e., even if they specialize in fine arts) are classified elsewhere in this subsector according to the type of school; and
- Establishments primarily engaged in offering courses in commercial and graphic arts and commercial photography are classified in U.S. Industry 611519, Other Technical and Trade Schools.

61162 Sports and Recreation Instruction[T] See industry description for 611620.

611620 Sports and Recreation Instruction

This industry comprises establishments, such as camps and schools, primarily engaged in offering instruction in athletic activities to groups of individuals. Overnight and day sports instruction camps are included in this industry.

Illustrative Examples:

Camps, sports instruction
Professional sports instructors (i.e., not participating in sporting events) Cheerleading instruction
Riding instruction academies or schools
Sports (e.g., baseball, basketball, football, golf) instruction
Martial arts instruction, camps or schools
Swimming instruction

Cross-References.
Gymnastics instruction

- Establishments primarily engaged in operating overnight recreational camps that may offer some athletic instruction in addition to other activities are classified in U.S. Industry 721214, Recreational and Vacation Camps (except Campgrounds);
- Establishments primarily engaged in operating sports and recreation establishments that also offer athletic instruction are classified in Sector 71, Arts, Entertainment, and Recreation;

T—Canadian, Mexican, and United States industries are comparable.

- Independent (i.e., freelance) athletes engaged in providing sports instruction and participating in spectator sporting events are classified in U.S. Industry 711219, Other Spectator Sports; and
- Establishments primarily engaged in offering academic courses that may also offer athletic instruction are classified according to the type of school.

61163 Language Schools[T] See industry description for 611630.

611630 Language Schools

This industry comprises establishments primarily engaged in offering foreign language instruction (including sign language). These establishments are designed to offer language instruction ranging from conversational skills for personal enrichment to intensive training courses for career or educational opportunities.

Cross-References. Establishments primarily engaged in--

- Offering academic courses that may also offer language instruction--are classified according to type of school; and
- Providing translation and interpretation services--are classified in Industry 541930, Translation and Interpretation Services.

61169 All Other Schools and Instruction[T]

This industry comprises establishments primarily engaged in offering instruction (except business, computer, management, technical, trade, fine arts, athletic, and language instruction). Also excluded from this industry are academic schools, colleges, and universities.

Illustrative Examples:

Academic tutoring services
Public speaking training
Automobile driving schools
Speed reading instruction
Exam preparation services

Cross-References. Establishments primarily engaged in--

- Offering elementary and secondary school instruction--are classified in Industry 61111, Elementary and Secondary Schools;
- Offering junior college instruction--are classified in Industry 61121, Junior Colleges;
- Offering college, university, and professional school instruction with academic degrees (e.g., baccalaureate, graduate)--are classified in Industry 61131, Colleges, Universities, and Professional Schools;
- Offering business, computer (except computer repair), and management training--are classified in Industry Group 6114, Business Schools and Computer and Management Training;
- Offering vocational and technical instruction (e.g., computer repair and maintenance)--are classified in Industry 61151, Technical and Trade Schools;
- Offering fine arts instruction--are classified in Industry 61161, Fine Arts Schools;
- Offering sports and recreation instruction--are classified in Industry 61162, Sports and Recreation Instruction; and
- Offering language instruction--are classified in Industry 61163, Language Schools.

611691 Exam Preparation and Tutoring

This U.S. industry comprises establishments primarily engaged in offering preparation for standardized examinations and/or academic tutoring services.

T—Canadian, Mexican, and United States industries are comparable.

Illustrative Examples:

Academic tutoring services
Learning centers offering remedial courses
College board preparation centers
Professional examination review instruction

611692 Automobile Driving Schools

This U.S. industry comprises establishments primarily engaged in offering automobile driving instruction.

Cross-References.

Establishments primarily engaged in offering truck and bus driving instruction are classified in U.S. Industry 611519, Other Technical and Trade Schools.

611699 All Other Miscellaneous Schools and Instruction

This U.S. industry comprises establishments primarily engaged in offering instruction (except business, computer, management, technical, trade, fine arts, athletic, language instruction, tutoring, and automobile driving instruction). Also excluded from this industry are academic schools, colleges, and universities.

Illustrative Examples:

Public speaking training
Survival training
Speed reading instruction
Yoga instruction, camps, or schools

Cross-References. Establishments primarily engaged in--

- Offering elementary and secondary school instruction--are classified in Industry 611110, Elementary and Secondary Schools;
- Offering junior college instruction--are classified in Industry 611210, Junior Colleges;
- Offering college, university, and professional school instruction with academic degrees (e.g., baccalaureate, graduate)--are classified in Industry 611310, Colleges, Universities, and Professional Schools;
- Offering business, computer (except computer repair), and management training--are classified in Industry Group 6114, Business Schools and Computer and Management Training;
- Offering vocational and technical instruction (e.g., computer repair and maintenance)--are classified in Industry 61151, Technical and Trade Schools;
- Offering fine arts instruction--are classified in Industry 611610, Fine Arts Schools;
- Offering sports and recreation instruction--are classified in Industry 611620, Sports and Recreation Instruction;
- Offering language instruction--are classified in Industry 611630, Language Schools;
- Offering exam preparation and tutoring services--are classified in U.S. Industry 611691, Exam Preparation and Tutoring; and
- Offering automobile driving instruction--are classified in U.S. Industry 611692, Automobile Driving Schools.

6117 Educational Support Services[T]

61171 Educational Support Services[T] See industry description for 611710.

611710 Educational Support Services

This industry comprises establishments primarily engaged in providing non-instructional services that support educational processes or systems.

T—Canadian, Mexican, and United States industries are comparable.

Illustrative Examples:

Educational consultants
Educational testing services
Educational guidance counseling services
Student exchange programs
Educational testing evaluation services

Cross-References. Establishments primarily engaged in--

- Providing job training for the unemployed, underemployed, physically disabled, and persons who have a job market disadvantage because of lack of education or job skills--are classified in Industry 624310, Vocational Rehabilitation Services; and
- Conducting research and analyses in cognitive development--are classified in Industry 541720, Research and Development in the Social Sciences and Humanities.

T—Canadian, Mexican, and United States industries are comparable.

Sector 62--Health Care and Social Assistance[T]

The Sector as a Whole

The Health Care and Social Assistance sector comprises establishments providing health care and social assistance for individuals. The sector includes both health care and social assistance because it is sometimes difficult to distinguish between the boundaries of these two activities. The industries in this sector are arranged on a continuum starting with establishments providing medical care exclusively, continuing with those providing health care and social assistance, and finally finishing with those providing only social assistance. Establishments in this sector deliver services by trained professionals. All industries in the sector share this commonality of process, namely, labor inputs of health practitioners or social workers with the requisite expertise. Many of the industries in the sector are defined based on the educational degree held by the practitioners included in the industry.

Excluded from this sector are aerobic classes in Subsector 713, Amusement, Gambling, and Recreation Industries, and non-medical diet and weight reducing centers in Subsector 812, Personal and Laundry Services. Although these can be viewed as health services, these services are not typically delivered by health practitioners.

621 Ambulatory Health Care Services[T]

Industries in the Ambulatory Health Care Services subsector provide health care services directly or indirectly to ambulatory patients and do not usually provide inpatient services. Health practitioners in this subsector provide outpatient services, with the facilities and equipment not usually being the most significant part of the production process.

6211 Offices of Physicians[T]

62111 Offices of Physicians[T]

This industry comprises establishments of health practitioners having the degree of M.D. (Doctor of Medicine) or D.O. (Doctor of Osteopathy) primarily engaged in the independent practice of general or specialized medicine (e.g., anesthesiology, oncology, ophthalmology, psychiatry) or surgery. These practitioners operate private or group practices in their own offices (e.g., centers, clinics) or in the facilities of others, such as hospitals or HMO medical centers.

Cross-References.

- Medical centers primarily engaged in providing emergency medical care for accident or trauma victims and ambulatory surgical centers primarily engaged in providing surgery on an outpatient basis are classified in Industry 62149, Other Outpatient Care Centers;
- Establishments of oral pathologists are classified in Industry 62121, Offices of Dentists; and
- Establishments of speech or voice pathologists are classified in Industry 62134, Offices of Physical, Occupational and Speech Therapists, and Audiologists.

621111 Offices of Physicians (except Mental Health Specialists)

This U.S. industry comprises establishments of health practitioners having the degree of M.D. (Doctor of Medicine) or D.O. (Doctor of Osteopathy) primarily engaged in the independent practice of general or specialized medicine (except psychiatry or psychoanalysis) or surgery. These practitioners operate private or group practices in their own offices (e.g., centers, clinics) or in the facilities of others, such as hospitals or HMO medical centers.

Cross-References.

- Establishments of physicians primarily engaged in the independent practice of psychiatry or psychoanalysis are classified in U.S. Industry 621112, Offices of Physicians, Mental Health Specialists;

T—Canadian, Mexican, and United States industries are comparable.

- Freestanding medical centers primarily engaged in providing emergency medical care for accident or catastrophe victims and freestanding ambulatory surgical centers primarily engaged in providing surgery on an outpatient basis are classified in U.S. Industry 621493, Freestanding Ambulatory Surgical and Emergency Centers;
- Establishments of oral pathologists are classified in Industry 621210, Offices of Dentists; and
- Establishments of speech or voice pathologists are classified in Industry 621340, Offices of Physical, Occupational and Speech Therapists, and Audiologists.

621112 Offices of Physicians, Mental Health Specialists

This U.S. industry comprises establishments of health practitioners having the degree of M.D. (Doctor of Medicine) or D.O. (Doctor of Osteopathy) primarily engaged in the independent practice of psychiatry or psychoanalysis. These practitioners operate private or group practices in their own offices (e.g., centers, clinics) or in the facilities of others, such as hospitals or HMO medical centers.

6212 Offices of Dentists[T]

62121 Offices of Dentists[T] See industry description for 621210.

621210 Offices of Dentists

This industry comprises establishments of health practitioners having the degree of D.M.D. (Doctor of Dental Medicine), D.D.S. (Doctor of Dental Surgery), or D.D.Sc. (Doctor of Dental Science) primarily engaged in the independent practice of general or specialized dentistry or dental surgery. These practitioners operate private or group practices in their own offices (e.g., centers, clinics) or in the facilities of others, such as hospitals or HMO medical centers. They can provide either comprehensive preventive, cosmetic, or emergency care, or specialize in a single field of dentistry.

Cross-References.

- Establishments known as dental laboratories primarily engaged in making dentures, artificial teeth, and orthodontic appliances to order for dentists are classified in U.S. Industry 339116, Dental Laboratories; and
- Establishments of dental hygienists primarily engaged in cleaning teeth and gums or establishments of denturists primarily engaged in taking impressions for and fitting dentures are classified in U.S. Industry 621399, Offices of All Other Miscellaneous Health Practitioners.

6213 Offices of Other Health Practitioners[T]

This industry group comprises establishments of independent health practitioners (except physicians and dentists).

62131 Offices of Chiropractors[T] See industry description for 621310.

621310 Offices of Chiropractors

This industry comprises establishments of health practitioners having the degree of D.C. (Doctor of Chiropractic) primarily engaged in the independent practice of chiropractic. These practitioners provide diagnostic and therapeutic treatment of neuromusculoskeletal and related disorders through the manipulation and adjustment of the spinal column and extremities, and operate private or group practices in their own offices (e.g., centers, clinics) or in the facilities of others, such as hospitals or HMO medical centers.

62132 Offices of Optometrists[T] See industry description for 621320.

T—Canadian, Mexican, and United States industries are comparable.

621320 Offices of Optometrists

This industry comprises establishments of health practitioners having the degree of O.D. (Doctor of Optometry) primarily engaged in the independent practice of optometry. These practitioners examine, diagnose, treat, and manage diseases and disorders of the visual system, the eye, and associated structures as well as diagnose related systemic conditions. Offices of optometrists prescribe and/or provide eyeglasses, contact lenses, low vision aids, and vision therapy. They operate private or group practices in their own offices (e.g., centers, clinics) or in the facilities of others, such as hospitals or HMO medical centers, and may also provide the same services as opticians, such as selling and fitting prescription eyeglasses and contact lenses.

Cross-References.

- Offices of opticians primarily engaged in selling and fitting prescription eyeglasses and contact lenses are classified in Industry 446130, Optical Goods Stores; and
- Offices of physicians primarily engaged in the independent practice of ophthalmology are classified in U.S. Industry 621111, Offices of Physicians (except Mental Health Specialists).

62133 Offices of Mental Health Practitioners (except Physicians)[T] See industry description for 621330.

621330 Offices of Mental Health Practitioners (except Physicians)

This industry comprises establishments of independent mental health practitioners (except physicians) primarily engaged in (1) the diagnosis and treatment of mental, emotional, and behavioral disorders and/or (2) the diagnosis and treatment of individual or group social dysfunction brought about by such causes as mental illness, alcohol and substance abuse, physical and emotional trauma, or stress. These practitioners operate private or group practices in their own offices (e.g., centers, clinics) or in the facilities of others, such as hospitals or HMO medical centers.

Cross-References.

Establishments of psychiatrists, psychoanalysts, and psychotherapists having the degree of M.D. (Doctor of Medicine) or D.O. (Doctor of Osteopathy) are classified in U.S. Industry 621112, Offices of Physicians, Mental Health Specialists.

62134 Offices of Physical, Occupational and Speech Therapists, and Audiologists[T] See industry description for 621340.

621340 Offices of Physical, Occupational and Speech Therapists, and Audiologists

This industry comprises establishments of independent health practitioners primarily engaged in one of the following: (1) providing physical therapy services to patients who have impairments, functional limitations, disabilities, or changes in physical functions and health status resulting from injury, disease or other causes, or who require prevention, wellness or fitness services; (2) planning and administering educational, recreational, and social activities designed to help patients or individuals with disabilities regain physical or mental functioning or adapt to their disabilities; and (3) diagnosing and treating speech, language, or hearing problems. These practitioners operate private or group practices in their own offices (e.g., centers, clinics) or in the facilities of others, such as hospitals or HMO medical centers.

Illustrative Examples:

Audiologists' offices
Recreational (e.g., art, dance, music) therapists' offices
Industrial therapists' offices
Speech pathologists' offices
Occupational therapists' offices
Physical therapists' offices

T—Canadian, Mexican, and United States industries are comparable.

62139 Offices of All Other Health Practitioners[T]

This industry comprises establishments of independent health practitioners (except physicians; dentists; chiropractors; optometrists; mental health specialists; physical, occupational, and speech therapists; and audiologists). These practitioners operate private or group practices in their own offices (e.g., centers, clinics) or in the facilities of others, such as hospitals or HMO medical centers.

Illustrative Examples:

Acupuncturists' (except MDs or DOs) offices
Inhalation or respiratory therapists' offices
Dental hygienists' offices
Midwives' offices
Denturists' offices
Naturopaths' offices
Dietitians' offices
Podiatrists' offices
Homeopaths' offices
Registered or licensed practical nurses' offices

Cross-References. Establishments primarily engaged in--

- The independent practice of medicine (i.e., physicians)--are classified in Industry 62111, Offices of Physicians;
- The independent practice of dentistry--are classified in Industry 62121, Offices of Dentists;
- The independent practice of chiropractic--are classified in Industry 62131, Offices of Chiropractors;
- The independent practice of optometry--are classified in Industry 62132, Offices of Optometrists;
- The independent practice of mental health (except physicians)--are classified in Industry 62133, Offices of Mental Health Practitioners (except Physicians); and
- The independent practice of physical, occupational, and speech therapy, and audiology--are classified in Industry 62134, Offices of Physical, Occupational and Speech Therapists, and Audiologists.

621391 Offices of Podiatrists

This U.S. industry comprises establishments of health practitioners having the degree of D.P.M. (Doctor of Podiatric Medicine) primarily engaged in the independent practice of podiatry. These practitioners diagnose and treat diseases and deformities of the foot and operate private or group practices in their own offices (e.g., centers, clinics) or in the facilities of others, such as hospitals or HMO medical centers.

621399 Offices of All Other Miscellaneous Health Practitioners

This U.S. industry comprises establishments of independent health practitioners (except physicians; dentists; chiropractors; optometrists; mental health specialists; physical, occupational, and speech therapists; audiologists; and podiatrists). These practitioners operate private or group practices in their own offices (e.g., centers, clinics) or in the facilities of others, such as hospitals or HMO medical centers.

Illustrative Examples:

Acupuncturists' (except MDs or DOs) offices
Hypnotherapists' offices
Dental hygienists' offices
Inhalation or respiratory therapists' offices
Denturists' offices
Midwives' offices
Dietitians' offices
Naturopaths' offices
Homeopaths' offices
Registered or licensed practical nurses' offices

Cross-References. Establishments primarily engaged in--

- The independent practice of medicine (i.e., physicians)--are classified in Industry 62111, Offices of Physicians;
- The independent practice of dentistry--are classified in Industry 621210, Offices of Dentists;
- The independent practice of chiropractic--are classified in Industry 621310, Offices of Chiropractors;

T—Canadian, Mexican, and United States industries are comparable.

- The independent practice of optometry--are classified in Industry 621320, Offices of Optometrists;
- The independent practice of mental health (except physicians)--are classified in Industry 621330, Offices of Mental Health Practitioners (except Physicians);
- The independent practice of physical, occupational, and speech therapy, and audiology--are classified in Industry 621340, Offices of Physical, Occupational and Speech Therapists, and Audiologists; and
- The independent practice of podiatry--are classified in U.S. Industry 621391, Offices of Podiatrists.

6214 Outpatient Care Centers[T]

This industry group comprises establishments with medical staff primarily engaged in providing a range of outpatient services, such as family planning, diagnosis and treatment of mental health disorders and alcohol and other substance abuse, and other general or specialized outpatient care.

62141 Family Planning Centers[T] See industry description for 621410.

621410 Family Planning Centers

This industry comprises establishments with medical staff primarily engaged in providing a range of family planning services on an outpatient basis, such as contraceptive services, genetic and prenatal counseling, voluntary sterilization, and therapeutic and medically induced termination of pregnancy.

Illustrative Examples:

Birth control clinics
Fertility clinics
Childbirth preparation classes
Pregnancy counseling centers

62142 Outpatient Mental Health and Substance Abuse Centers[T] See industry description for 621420.

621420 Outpatient Mental Health and Substance Abuse Centers

This industry comprises establishments with medical staff primarily engaged in providing outpatient services related to the diagnosis and treatment of mental health disorders and alcohol and other substance abuse. These establishments generally treat patients who do not require inpatient treatment. They may provide a counseling staff and information regarding a wide range of mental health and substance abuse issues and/or refer patients to more extensive treatment programs, if necessary.

Illustrative Examples:

Outpatient alcoholism treatment centers and clinics (except hospitals)
Outpatient mental health centers and clinics (except hospitals)
Outpatient detoxification centers and clinics (except hospitals)
Outpatient substance abuse treatment centers and clinics (except hospitals)
Outpatient drug addiction treatment centers and clinics (except hospitals)

Cross-References.

- Establishments known and licensed as hospitals primarily engaged in the inpatient treatment of mental health and substance abuse illnesses with an emphasis on medical treatment and monitoring are classified in Industry 622210, Psychiatric and Substance Abuse Hospitals; and
- Establishments primarily engaged in the inpatient treatment of mental health and substance abuse illnesses with an emphasis on residential care and counseling rather than medical treatment are classified in Industry 623220, Residential Mental Health and Substance Abuse Facilities.

T—Canadian, Mexican, and United States industries are comparable.

62149 Other Outpatient Care Centers[T]

This industry comprises establishments with medical staff primarily engaged in providing general or specialized outpatient care (except family planning centers and outpatient mental health and substance abuse centers). Centers or clinics of health practitioners with different degrees from more than one industry practicing within the same establishment (i.e., Doctor of Medicine and Doctor of Dental Medicine) are included in this industry.

Illustrative Examples:

Dialysis centers and clinics
Outpatient biofeedback centers and clinics
Freestanding ambulatory surgical centers and clinics
Outpatient community health centers and clinics
Freestanding emergency medical centers and clinics
Outpatient sleep disorder centers and clinics Health maintenance organization (HMO) medical centers and clinics

Cross-References.

- Physician walk-in centers are classified in Industry 62111, Offices of Physicians;
- Centers and clinics of health practitioners from the same industry primarily engaged in the independent practice of their profession are classified in Industry 62111, Offices of Physicians; Industry 62121, Offices of Dentists; and Industry Group 6213, Offices of Other Health Practitioners;
- Family planning centers are classified in Industry 62141, Family Planning Centers;
- Outpatient mental health and substance abuse centers are classified in Industry 62142, Outpatient Mental Health and Substance Abuse Centers;
- HMO establishments (except those providing health care services) primarily engaged in underwriting health and medical insurance policies are classified in Industry 52411, Direct Life, Health, and Medical Insurance Carriers; and
- Establishments known and licensed as hospitals that also perform ambulatory surgery and emergency room services are classified in Subsector 622, Hospitals.

621491 HMO Medical Centers

This U.S. industry comprises establishments with physicians and other medical staff primarily engaged in providing a range of outpatient medical services to the health maintenance organization (HMO) subscribers with a focus generally on primary health care. These establishments are owned by the HMO. Included in this industry are HMO establishments that both provide health care services and underwrite health and medical insurance policies.

Cross-References.

- Health practitioners or health practitioner groups contracting to provide their services to subscribers of prepaid health plans are classified in Industry 62111, Offices of Physicians; Industry 621210, Offices of Dentists; and Industry Group 6213, Offices of Other Health Practitioners; and
- HMO establishments (except those providing health care services) primarily engaged in underwriting and administering health and medical insurance policies are classified in U.S. Industry 524114, Direct Health and Medical Insurance Carriers.

621492 Kidney Dialysis Centers

This U.S. industry comprises establishments with medical staff primarily engaged in providing outpatient kidney or renal dialysis services.

621493 Freestanding Ambulatory Surgical and Emergency Centers

This U.S. industry comprises establishments with physicians and other medical staff primarily engaged in (1) providing surgical services (e.g., orthoscopic and cataract surgery) on an outpatient basis or (2) providing emergency care services (e.g., setting broken bones, treating lacerations, or tending to patients suffering injuries as a

T—Canadian, Mexican, and United States industries are comparable.

result of accidents, trauma, or medical conditions necessitating immediate medical care) on an outpatient basis. Outpatient surgical establishments have specialized facilities, such as operating and recovery rooms, and specialized equipment, such as anesthetic or X-ray equipment.

Illustrative Examples:

Freestanding ambulatory surgical centers and clinics
Freestanding trauma centers (except hospitals)
Freestanding emergency medical centers and clinics
Urgent medical care centers and clinics (except

Cross-References.

- Physician walk-in centers are classified in U.S. Industry 621111, Offices of Physicians (except Mental Health Specialists); and
- Establishments known and licensed as hospitals that also perform ambulatory surgery and emergency room services are classified in Subsector 622, Hospitals.

621498 All Other Outpatient Care Centers

This U.S. industry comprises establishments with medical staff primarily engaged in providing general or specialized outpatient care (except family planning centers, outpatient mental health and substance abuse centers, HMO medical centers, kidney dialysis centers, and freestanding ambulatory surgical and emergency centers). Centers or clinics of health practitioners with different degrees from more than one industry practicing within the same establishment (i.e., Doctor of Medicine and Doctor of Dental Medicine) are included in this industry.

Illustrative Examples:

Outpatient biofeedback centers and clinics
Outpatient pain therapy centers and clinics
Outpatient community health centers and clinics

Cross-References.

- Physician walk-in centers are classified in U.S. Industry 621111, Offices of Physicians (except Mental Health Specialists);
- Centers and clinics of health practitioners from the same industry primarily engaged in the independent practice of their profession are classified in Industry 62111, Offices of Physicians; Industry 621210, Offices of Dentists; and Industry Group 6213, Offices of Other Health Practitioners;
- Family planning centers are classified in Industry 621410, Family Planning Centers;
- Outpatient mental health and substance abuse centers are classified in Industry 621420, Outpatient Mental Health and Substance Abuse Centers;
- HMO medical centers are classified in U.S. Industry 621491, HMO Medical Centers;
- Dialysis centers are classified in U.S. Industry 621492, Kidney Dialysis Centers; and
- Freestanding ambulatory surgical and emergency centers are classified in U.S. Industry 621493, Freestanding Ambulatory Surgical and Emergency Centers.

6215 Medical and Diagnostic Laboratories[T]

62151 Medical and Diagnostic Laboratories[T]

This industry comprises establishments known as medical and diagnostic laboratories primarily engaged in providing analytic or diagnostic services, including body fluid analysis and diagnostic imaging, generally to the medical profession or to the patient on referral from a health practitioner.

T—Canadian, Mexican, and United States industries are comparable.

Illustrative Examples:

Dental or medical X-ray laboratories
Medical pathology laboratories
Diagnostic imaging centers
Medical testing laboratories
Medical forensic laboratories

Cross-References.

Establishments, such as dental, optical, and orthopedic laboratories, primarily engaged in providing the following activities to the medical profession, respectively: making dentures, artificial teeth, and orthodontic appliances to prescription; grinding lenses to prescription; and making orthopedic or prosthetic appliances to prescription are classified in Industry 33911, Medical Equipment and Supplies Manufacturing.

621511 Medical Laboratories

This U.S. industry comprises establishments known as medical laboratories primarily engaged in providing analytic or diagnostic services, including body fluid analysis, generally to the medical profession or to the patient on referral from a health practitioner.

Illustrative Examples:

Blood analysis laboratories
Medical pathology laboratories
Medical bacteriological laboratories
Medical testing laboratories
Medical forensic laboratories

Cross-References.

- Establishments known as dental laboratories primarily engaged in making dentures, artificial teeth, and orthodontic appliances to prescription are classified in U.S. Industry 339116, Dental Laboratories;
- Establishments known as optical laboratories primarily engaged in grinding lenses to prescription are classified in U.S. Industry 339115, Ophthalmic Goods Manufacturing; and
- Establishments known as orthopedic laboratories primarily engaged in making orthopedic or prosthetic appliances to prescription are classified in U.S. Industry 339113, Surgical Appliance and Supplies Manufacturing.

621512 Diagnostic Imaging Centers

This U.S. industry comprises establishments known as diagnostic imaging centers primarily engaged in producing images of the patient generally on referral from a health practitioner.

Illustrative Examples:

Computer tomography (CT-scan) centers
Medical radiological laboratories
Dental or medical X-ray laboratories
Ultrasound imaging centers
Magnetic resonance imaging (MRI) centers

6216 Home Health Care Services[T]

62161 Home Health Care Services[T] See industry description for 621610.

621610 Home Health Care Services

This industry comprises establishments primarily engaged in providing skilled nursing services in the home, along with a range of the following: personal care services; homemaker and companion services; physical therapy;

T—Canadian, Mexican, and United States industries are comparable.

medical social services; medications; medical equipment and supplies; counseling; 24-hour home care; occupation and vocational therapy; dietary and nutritional services; speech therapy; audiology; and high-tech care, such as intravenous therapy.

Illustrative Examples:

Home health care agencies
Visiting nurse associations
Home infusion therapy services
In-home hospice care services

Cross-References.

- In-home health services provided by establishments of health practitioners and others primarily engaged in the independent practice of their profession are classified in Industry 62111, Offices of Physicians; Industry 621210, Offices of Dentists; Industry Group 6213, Offices of Other Health Practitioners; and U.S. Industry 621999, All Other Miscellaneous Ambulatory Health Care Services; and
- Establishments primarily engaged in renting or leasing products for home health care are classified in U.S. Industry 532283, Home Health Equipment Rental.

6219 Other Ambulatory Health Care Services[T]

This industry group comprises establishments primarily engaged in providing ambulatory health care services (except offices of physicians, dentists, and other health practitioners; outpatient care centers; medical laboratories and diagnostic imaging centers; and home health care providers).

62191 Ambulance Services[T] See industry description for 621910.

621910 Ambulance Services

This industry comprises establishments primarily engaged in providing transportation of patients by ground or air, along with medical care. These services are often provided during a medical emergency but are not restricted to emergencies. The vehicles are equipped with lifesaving equipment operated by medically trained personnel.

Cross-References.

Establishments primarily engaged in providing transportation of the disabled or elderly (without medical care) are classified in U.S. Industry 485991, Special Needs Transportation.

62199 All Other Ambulatory Health Care Services[T]

This industry comprises establishments primarily engaged in providing ambulatory health care services (except offices of physicians, dentists, and other health practitioners; outpatient care centers; medical and diagnostic laboratories; home health care providers; and ambulances).

Illustrative Examples:

Blood donor stations
Pacemaker monitoring services
Blood or body organ banks
Physical fitness evaluation services (except by offices of health practitioners)
Health screening services (except by offices of health practitioners)
Smoking cessation programs
Hearing testing services (except by offices of audiologists)

T—Canadian, Mexican, and United States industries are comparable.

Cross-References.

□ Establishments primarily engaged in the independent practice of medicine are classified in Industry 62111, Offices of Physicians;
□ Establishments primarily engaged in the independent practice of dentistry are classified in Industry 62121, Offices of Dentists;
□ Establishments primarily engaged in the independent practice of health care (except offices of physicians and dentists) are classified in Industry Group 6213, Offices of Other Health Practitioners; □ Establishments primarily engaged in providing general or specialized outpatient care services are classified in Industry Group 6214, Outpatient Care Centers;
□ Establishments primarily engaged in providing home health care services are classified in Industry 62161, Home Health Care Services;
□ Establishments primarily engaged in transportation of patients by ground or air, along with medical care are classified in Industry 62191, Ambulance Services; and
□ Establishments known as medical and diagnostic laboratories primarily engaged in providing analytic or diagnostic services are classified in Industry 62151, Medical and Diagnostic Laboratories.

621991 Blood and Organ Banks

This U.S. industry comprises establishments primarily engaged in collecting, storing, and distributing blood and blood products and storing and distributing body organs.

621999 All Other Miscellaneous Ambulatory Health Care Services

This U.S. industry comprises establishments primarily engaged in providing ambulatory health care services (except offices of physicians, dentists, and other health practitioners; outpatient care centers; medical and diagnostic laboratories; home health care providers; ambulances; and blood and organ banks).

Illustrative Examples:

Health screening services (except by offices of health practitioners)
Physical fitness evaluation services (except by offices of health practitioners)
Hearing testing services (except by offices of audiologists)
Smoking cessation programs
Pacemaker monitoring services

Cross-References.

□ Establishments primarily engaged in the independent practice of medicine are classified in Industry 62111, Offices of Physicians;
□ Establishments primarily engaged in the independent practice of dentistry are classified in Industry 621210, Offices of Dentists;
□ Establishments primarily engaged in the independent practice of health care (except offices of physicians and dentists) are classified in Industry Group 6213, Offices of Other Health Practitioners; □ Establishments primarily engaged in providing general or specialized outpatient care services are classified in Industry Group 6214, Outpatient Care Centers;
□ Establishments primarily engaged in providing home health care services are classified in Industry 621610, Home Health Care Services;
□ Establishments primarily engaged in the transportation of patients by ground or air, along with medical care are classified in Industry 621910, Ambulance Services;
□ Establishments known as medical and diagnostic laboratories primarily engaged in providing analytic or diagnostic services are classified in Industry 62151, Medical and Diagnostic Laboratories; and □
Blood and organ banks are classified in U.S. Industry 621991, Blood and Organ Banks.

T—Canadian, Mexican, and United States industries are comparable.

622 Hospitals[T]

Industries in the Hospitals subsector provide medical, diagnostic, and treatment services that include physician, nursing, and other health services to inpatients and the specialized accommodation services required by inpatients. Hospitals may also provide outpatient services as a secondary activity. Establishments in the Hospitals subsector provide inpatient health services, many of which can only be provided using the specialized facilities and equipment that form a significant and integral part of the production process.

6221 General Medical and Surgical Hospitals[T]

62211 General Medical and Surgical Hospitals[T] See industry description for 622110.

622110 General Medical and Surgical Hospitals

This industry comprises establishments known and licensed as general medical and surgical hospitals primarily engaged in providing diagnostic and medical treatment (both surgical and nonsurgical) to inpatients with any of a wide variety of medical conditions. These establishments maintain inpatient beds and provide patients with food services that meet their nutritional requirements. These hospitals have an organized staff of physicians and other medical staff to provide patient care services. These establishments usually provide other services, such as outpatient services, anatomical pathology services, diagnostic X-ray services, clinical laboratory services, operating room services for a variety of procedures, and pharmacy services.

6222 Psychiatric and Substance Abuse Hospitals[T]

62221 Psychiatric and Substance Abuse Hospitals[T] See industry description for 622210.

622210 Psychiatric and Substance Abuse Hospitals

This industry comprises establishments known and licensed as psychiatric and substance abuse hospitals primarily engaged in providing diagnostic, medical treatment, and monitoring services for inpatients who suffer from mental illness or substance abuse disorders. The treatment often requires an extended stay in the hospital. These establishments maintain inpatient beds and provide patients with food services that meet their nutritional requirements. They have an organized staff of physicians and other medical staff to provide patient care services. Psychiatric, psychological, and social work services are available at the facility. These hospitals usually provide other services, such as outpatient services, clinical laboratory services, diagnostic X-ray services, and electroencephalograph services.

Cross-References.

- Establishments primarily engaged in providing treatment of mental health and substance abuse illnesses on an exclusively outpatient basis are classified in Industry 621420, Outpatient Mental Health and Substance Abuse Centers;
- Establishments referred to as hospitals but primarily engaged in providing inpatient treatment of mental health and substance abuse illnesses with the emphasis on counseling rather than medical treatment are classified in Industry 623220, Residential Mental Health and Substance Abuse Facilities; and
- Establishments referred to as hospitals but primarily engaged in providing residential care for persons diagnosed with intellectual and developmental disabilities are classified in Industry 623210, Residential Intellectual and Developmental Disability Facilities.

6223 Specialty (except Psychiatric and Substance Abuse) Hospitals[T]

62231 Specialty (except Psychiatric and Substance Abuse) Hospitals[T] See industry description for 622310.

T—Canadian, Mexican, and United States industries are comparable.

622310 Specialty (except Psychiatric and Substance Abuse) Hospitals

This industry comprises establishments known and licensed as specialty hospitals primarily engaged in providing diagnostic and medical treatment to inpatients with a specific type of disease or medical condition (except psychiatric or substance abuse). Hospitals providing long-term care for the chronically ill and hospitals providing rehabilitation, restorative, and adjustive services to physically challenged or disabled people are included in this industry. These establishments maintain inpatient beds and provide patients with food services that meet their nutritional requirements. They have an organized staff of physicians and other medical staff to provide patient care services. These hospitals may provide other services, such as outpatient services, diagnostic X-ray services, clinical laboratory services, operating room services, physical therapy services, educational and vocational services, and psychological and social work services.

Cross-References.

- Establishments known and licensed as hospitals primarily engaged in providing diagnostic and therapeutic inpatient services for a variety of medical conditions, both surgical and nonsurgical, are classified in Industry 622110, General Medical and Surgical Hospitals;
- Establishments known and licensed as hospitals primarily engaged in providing diagnostic and treatment services for inpatients with psychiatric or substance abuse illnesses are classified in Industry 622210, Psychiatric and Substance Abuse Hospitals;
- Establishments referred to as hospitals but primarily engaged in providing inpatient nursing and rehabilitative services to persons requiring convalescence are classified in Industry 623110, Nursing Care Facilities (Skilled Nursing Facilities);
- Establishments referred to as hospitals but primarily engaged in providing residential care of persons diagnosed with intellectual and developmental disabilities are classified in Industry 623210, Residential Intellectual and Developmental Disability Facilities; and
- Establishments referred to as hospitals but primarily engaged in providing inpatient treatment for mental health and substance abuse illnesses with the emphasis on counseling rather than medical treatment are classified in Industry 623220, Residential Mental Health and Substance Abuse Facilities.

623 Nursing and Residential Care Facilities[T]

Industries in the Nursing and Residential Care Facilities subsector provide residential care combined with either nursing, supervisory, or other types of care as required by the residents. In this subsector, the facilities are a significant part of the production process, and the care provided is a mix of health and social services with the health services being largely some level of nursing services.

6231 Nursing Care Facilities (Skilled Nursing Facilities)[T]

62311 Nursing Care Facilities (Skilled Nursing Facilities)[T] See industry description for 623110.

623110 Nursing Care Facilities (Skilled Nursing Facilities)

This industry comprises establishments primarily engaged in providing inpatient nursing and rehabilitative services. The care is generally provided for an extended period of time to individuals requiring nursing care. These establishments have a permanent core staff of registered or licensed practical nurses who, along with other staff, provide nursing and continuous personal care services.

Illustrative Examples:

Convalescent homes or convalescent hospitals (except psychiatric)
Nursing homes
Rest homes with nursing care
Assisted living facilities for the elderly with nursing care
Inpatient care hospices

T—Canadian, Mexican, and United States industries are comparable.

Cross-References.

- Assisted living facilities with on-site nursing care facilities are classified in U.S. Industry 623311, Continuing Care Retirement Communities; and
- Psychiatric convalescent homes are classified in Industry 623220, Residential Mental Health and Substance Abuse Facilities.

6232 Residential Intellectual and Developmental Disability, Mental Health, and Substance Abuse Facilities[T]

This industry group comprises establishments primarily engaged in providing residential care (but not licensed hospital care) to people with intellectual and developmental disabilities, mental illness, or substance abuse problems.

62321 Residential Intellectual and Developmental Disability Facilities[T] See industry description for 623210.

623210 Residential Intellectual and Developmental Disability Facilities

This industry comprises establishments (e.g., group homes, hospitals, intermediate care facilities) primarily engaged in providing residential care services for persons diagnosed with intellectual and developmental disabilities. These facilities may provide some health care, though the focus is room, board, protective supervision, and counseling.

Cross-References.

- Establishments primarily engaged in providing inpatient treatment of mental health and substance abuse illnesses with an emphasis on counseling rather than medical treatment are classified in Industry 623220, Residential Mental Health and Substance Abuse Facilities;
- Establishments primarily engaged in providing treatment of mental health and substance abuse illnesses on an exclusively outpatient basis are classified in Industry 621420, Outpatient Mental Health and Substance Abuse Centers; and
- Establishments known and licensed as hospitals primarily engaged in providing inpatient treatment of mental health and substance abuse illnesses with an emphasis on medical treatment and monitoring are classified in Industry 622210, Psychiatric and Substance Abuse Hospitals.

62322 Residential Mental Health and Substance Abuse Facilities[T] See industry description for 623220.

623220 Residential Mental Health and Substance Abuse Facilities

This industry comprises establishments primarily engaged in providing residential care and treatment for patients with mental health and substance abuse illnesses. These establishments provide room, board, supervision, and counseling services. Although medical services may be available at these establishments, they are incidental to the counseling, mental rehabilitation, and support services offered. These establishments generally provide a wide range of social services in addition to counseling.

Illustrative Examples:

Alcoholism or drug addiction rehabilitation facilities (except licensed hospitals)
Psychiatric convalescent homes or hospitals
Mental health halfway houses
Residential group homes for the emotionally disturbed

T—Canadian, Mexican, and United States industries are comparable.

Cross-References.

- Establishments primarily engaged in providing treatment of mental health and substance abuse illnesses on an exclusively outpatient basis are classified in Industry 621420, Outpatient Mental Health and Substance Abuse Centers;
- Establishments primarily engaged in providing residential care for persons diagnosed with intellectual and developmental disabilities are classified in Industry 623210, Residential Intellectual and Developmental Disability Facilities; and
- Establishments known and licensed as hospitals primarily engaged in providing inpatient treatment of mental health and substance abuse illnesses with an emphasis on medical treatment and monitoring are classified in Industry 622210, Psychiatric and Substance Abuse Hospitals.

6233 Continuing Care Retirement Communities and Assisted Living Facilities for the Elderly[T]

62331 Continuing Care Retirement Communities and Assisted Living Facilities for the Elderly[T]

This industry comprises establishments primarily engaged in providing residential and personal care services for (1) the elderly and other persons who are unable to fully care for themselves and/or (2) the elderly and other persons who do not desire to live independently. The care typically includes room, board, supervision, and assistance in daily living, such as housekeeping services. In some instances these establishments provide skilled nursing care for residents in separate on-site facilities.

Illustrative Examples:

Assisted living facilities
Assisted living facilities for the elderly without nursing care
Continuing care retirement communities
Rest homes without nursing care

Cross-References.

- Establishments primarily engaged in providing inpatient nursing and rehabilitative services are classified in Industry 62311, Nursing Care Facilities (Skilled Nursing Facilities); and
- Apartment or condominium complexes where people live independently in rented housing units are classified in Industry 53111, Lessors of Residential Buildings and Dwellings.

623311 Continuing Care Retirement Communities

This U.S. industry comprises establishments primarily engaged in providing a range of residential and personal care services with on-site nursing care facilities for (1) the elderly and other persons who are unable to fully care for themselves and/or (2) the elderly and other persons who do not desire to live independently. Individuals live in a variety of residential settings with meals, housekeeping, social, leisure, and other services available to assist residents in daily living. Assisted living facilities with on-site nursing care facilities are included in this industry.

Cross-References.

- Establishments primarily engaged in providing inpatient nursing and rehabilitative services are classified in Industry 623110, Nursing Care Facilities (Skilled Nursing Facilities);
- Assisted living facilities without on-site nursing care facilities are classified in U.S. Industry 623312, Assisted Living Facilities for the Elderly; and
- Apartment or condominium complexes where people live independently in rented housing units are classified in Industry 531110, Lessors of Residential Buildings and Dwellings.

T—Canadian, Mexican, and United States industries are comparable.

623312 Assisted Living Facilities for the Elderly

This U.S. industry comprises establishments primarily engaged in providing residential and personal care services (i.e., without on-site nursing care facilities) for (1) the elderly or other persons who are unable to fully care for themselves and/or (2) the elderly or other persons who do not desire to live independently. The care typically includes room, board, supervision, and assistance in daily living, such as housekeeping services.

Illustrative Examples:

Assisted living facilities without on-site nursing care facilities
Rest homes without nursing care
Assisted living facilities for the elderly without

Cross-References.

- Assisted living facilities with on-site nursing care facilities are classified in U.S. Industry 623311, Continuing Care Retirement Communities;
- Assisted living facilities for the elderly with nursing care or rest homes with nursing care are classified in Industry 623110, Nursing Care Facilities (Skilled Nursing Facilities); and
- Apartment or condominium complexes where people live independently in rented or owned housing units are classified in Industry 531110, Lessors of Residential Buildings and Dwellings.

6239 Other Residential Care Facilities[T]

62399 Other Residential Care Facilities[T] See industry description for 623990.

623990 Other Residential Care Facilities

This industry comprises establishments primarily engaged in providing residential care (except residential intellectual and developmental disability facilities, residential mental health and substance abuse facilities, continuing care retirement communities, and assisted living facilities for the elderly). These establishments also provide supervision and personal care services.

Illustrative Examples:

Boot or disciplinary camps (except correctional) for delinquent youth
Group homes for the hearing or visually impaired
Child group foster homes
Halfway group homes for delinquents or ex-offenders
Delinquent youth halfway group homes
Homes for unwed mothers
Group homes for the disabled without nursing care
Orphanages

Cross-References.

- Residential intellectual and developmental disability facilities are classified in Industry 623210, Residential Intellectual and Developmental Disability Facilities;
- Continuing care retirement communities are classified in U.S. Industry 623311, Continuing Care Retirement Communities;
- Residential mental health and substance abuse facilities are classified in Industry 623220, Residential Mental Health and Substance Abuse Facilities;
- Assisted living facilities for the elderly without nursing care are classified in U.S. Industry 623312, Assisted Living Facilities for the Elderly;
- Establishments primarily engaged in providing inpatient nursing and rehabilitative services are classified in Industry 623110, Nursing Care Facilities (Skilled Nursing Facilities);

T—Canadian, Mexican, and United States industries are comparable.

- Establishments primarily engaged in providing temporary shelter are classified in U.S. Industry 624221, Temporary Shelters; and
- Correctional camps are classified in Industry 922140, Correctional Institutions.

624 Social Assistance[T]

Industries in the Social Assistance subsector provide a wide variety of social assistance services directly to their clients. These services do not include residential or accommodation services, except on a short-stay basis.

6241 Individual and Family Services[T]

This industry group comprises establishments primarily engaged in providing nonresidential social assistance to children and youth, the elderly, persons with disabilities, and all other individuals and families.

62411 Child and Youth Services[T] See industry description for 624110.

624110 Child and Youth Services

This industry comprises establishments primarily engaged in providing nonresidential social assistance services for children and youth. These establishments provide for the welfare of children in such areas as adoption and foster care, drug prevention, life skills training, and positive social development.

Illustrative Examples:

Adoption agencies
Youth centers (except recreational only)
Child guidance organizations
Youth self-help organizations
Foster care placement services

Cross-References.

- Youth recreational centers are classified in Industry 713940, Fitness and Recreational Sports Centers;
- Youth recreational sports teams and leagues are classified in Industry 713990, All Other Amusement and Recreation Industries;
- Scouting organizations are classified in Industry 813410, Civic and Social Organizations; and
- Establishments primarily engaged in providing day care services for children are classified in Industry 624410, Child Day Care Services.

62412 Services for the Elderly and Persons with Disabilities[T] See industry description for 624120.

624120 Services for the Elderly and Persons with Disabilities

This industry comprises establishments primarily engaged in providing nonresidential social assistance services to improve the quality of life for the elderly, persons diagnosed with intellectual and developmental disabilities, or persons with disabilities. These establishments provide for the welfare of these individuals in such areas as day care, non-medical home care or homemaker services, social activities, group support, and companionship.

Cross-References. Establishments primarily engaged in--

- Providing job training for persons diagnosed with intellectual and developmental disabilities or persons with disabilities--are classified in Industry 624310, Vocational Rehabilitation Services;
- Providing residential care for the elderly, persons diagnosed with intellectual and developmental disabilities, or persons with disabilities--are classified in Subsector 623, Nursing and Residential Care Facilities; and

T—Canadian, Mexican, and United States industries are comparable.

- Providing in-home health care services--are classified in Subsector 621, Ambulatory Health Care Services.

62419 Other Individual and Family Services[T] See industry description for 624190.

624190 Other Individual and Family Services

This industry comprises establishments primarily engaged in providing nonresidential individual and family social assistance services (except those specifically directed toward children, the elderly, persons diagnosed with intellectual and developmental disabilities, or persons with disabilities).

Illustrative Examples:

Community action services agencies
Marriage counseling services (except by offices of mental health practitioners)
Crisis intervention centers
Multi-purpose social services centers
Family social services agencies
Family welfare services
Self-help organizations (except for disabled persons, the elderly, persons diagnosed with intellectual and developmental disabilities)
Suicide crisis centers
Hotline centers
Telephone counseling services

Cross-References. Establishments primarily engaged in--

- Providing clinical psychological and psychiatric social counseling services--are classified in Industry 621330, Offices of Mental Health Practitioners (except Physicians);
- Providing child and youth social assistance services (except day care)--are classified in Industry 624110, Child and Youth Services;
- Providing child day care services--are classified in Industry 624410, Child Day Care Services;
- Providing social assistance services for the elderly, persons diagnosed with intellectual and developmental disabilities, and persons with disabilities--are classified in Industry 624120, Services for the Elderly and Persons with Disabilities;
- Community action advocacy--are classified in U.S. Industry 813319, Other Social Advocacy Organizations; and
- Providing in-home health care services--are classified in Subsector 621, Ambulatory Health Care Services.

6242 Community Food and Housing, and Emergency and Other Relief Services[T]

This industry group comprises establishments primarily engaged in one of the following: (1) collecting, preparing, and delivering food for the needy; (2) providing short-term emergency shelter, temporary residential shelter, transitional housing, volunteer construction or repair of low-cost housing, and/or repair of homes for individuals or families in need; or (3) providing food, shelter, clothing, medical relief, resettlement, and counseling to victims of domestic or international disasters or conflicts (e.g., wars).

62421 Community Food Services[T] See industry description for 624210.

624210 Community Food Services

This industry comprises establishments primarily engaged in the collection, preparation, and delivery of food for the needy. Establishments in this industry may also distribute clothing and blankets to the poor. These establishments may prepare and deliver meals to persons who by reason of age, disability, or illness are unable to prepare meals for themselves; collect and distribute salvageable or donated food; or prepare and provide meals at fixed or mobile locations. Food banks, meal delivery programs, and soup kitchens are included in this industry.

T—Canadian, Mexican, and United States industries are comparable.

62422 Community Housing Services[T]

This industry comprises establishments primarily engaged in providing one or more of the following community housing services: (1) short-term emergency shelter for victims of domestic violence, sexual assault, or child abuse; (2) temporary residential shelter for the homeless, runaway youths, and patients and families caught in medical crises; (3) transitional housing for low-income individuals and families; (4) volunteer construction or repair of low-cost housing, in partnership with the homeowner who may assist in construction or repair work; and (5) repair of homes for elderly or disabled homeowners. These establishments may operate their own shelter, they may subsidize housing using existing homes, apartments, hotels, or motels, or they may require a low-cost mortgage or work (sweat) equity.

Cross-References.

Central offices of government housing programs are classified in Industry 92511, Administration of Housing Programs.

624221 Temporary Shelters

This U.S. industry comprises establishments primarily engaged in providing (1) short-term emergency shelter for victims of domestic violence, sexual assault, or child abuse and/or (2) temporary residential shelter for homeless individuals or families, runaway youth, and patients and families caught in medical crises. These establishments may operate their own shelters or may subsidize housing using existing homes, apartments, hotels, or motels.

Cross-References.

Establishments primarily engaged in providing emergency shelter for victims of domestic or international disasters or conflicts are classified in Industry 624230, Emergency and Other Relief Services.

624229 Other Community Housing Services

This U.S. industry comprises establishments primarily engaged in providing one or more of the following community housing services: (1) transitional housing to low-income individuals and families; (2) volunteer construction or repair of low-cost housing, in partnership with the homeowner who may assist in the construction or repair work; and (3) the repair of homes for elderly or disabled homeowners. These establishments may subsidize housing using existing homes, apartments, hotels, or motels or may require a low-cost mortgage or sweat equity. These establishments may also provide low-income families with furniture and household supplies.

Cross-References.

Central offices of government housing programs are classified in Industry 925110, Administration of Housing Programs.

62423 Emergency and Other Relief Services[T] See industry description for 624230.

624230 Emergency and Other Relief Services

This industry comprises establishments primarily engaged in providing food, shelter, clothing, medical relief, resettlement, and counseling to victims of domestic or international disasters or conflicts (e.g., wars).

6243 Vocational Rehabilitation Services[T]

62431 Vocational Rehabilitation Services[T] See industry description for 624310.

T—Canadian, Mexican, and United States industries are comparable.

624310 Vocational Rehabilitation Services

This industry comprises (1) establishments primarily engaged in providing vocational rehabilitation or habilitation services, such as job counseling, job training, and work experience, to unemployed and underemployed persons, persons with disabilities, and persons who have a job market disadvantage because of lack of education, job skill, or experience and (2) establishments primarily engaged in providing training and employment to persons with disabilities. Vocational rehabilitation job training facilities (except schools) and sheltered workshops (i.e., work experience centers) are included in this industry.

Cross-References.

- Schools (except high schools) primarily engaged in providing vocational training are classified in Industry 61151, Technical and Trade Schools;
- Vocational high schools are classified in Industry 611110, Elementary and Secondary Schools; and
- Establishments primarily engaged in providing career and vocational counseling (except rehabilitative) are classified in Industry 611710, Educational Support Services.

6244 Child Day Care Services[T]

62441 Child Day Care Services[T] See industry description for 624410.

624410 Child Day Care Services

This industry comprises establishments primarily engaged in providing day care of infants or children. These establishments generally care for preschool children, but may care for older children when they are not in school and may also offer pre-kindergarten and/or kindergarten educational programs.

Illustrative Examples:

Child day care babysitting services
Nursery schools
Child or infant day care centers
Preschool centers

Cross-References.

Establishments primarily engaged in offering kindergarten educational programs are classified in Industry 611110, Elementary and Secondary Schools.

T—Canadian, Mexican, and United States industries are comparable.

Sector 71--Arts, Entertainment, and Recreation[T]

The Sector as a Whole

The Arts, Entertainment, and Recreation sector includes a wide range of establishments that operate facilities or provide services to meet varied cultural, entertainment, and recreational interests of their patrons. This sector comprises (1) establishments that are involved in producing, promoting, or participating in live performances, events, or exhibits intended for public viewing; (2) establishments that preserve and exhibit objects and sites of historical, cultural, or educational interest; and (3) establishments that operate facilities or provide services that enable patrons to participate in recreational activities or pursue amusement, hobby, and leisure-time interests. Some establishments that provide cultural, entertainment, or recreational facilities and services are classified in other sectors. Excluded from this sector are: (1) establishments that provide both accommodations and recreational facilities, such as hunting and fishing camps and resort and casino hotels are classified in Subsector 721, Accommodation; (2) restaurants and night clubs that provide live entertainment in addition to the sale of food and beverages are classified in Subsector 722, Food Services and Drinking Places; (3) motion picture theaters, libraries and archives, and publishers of newspapers, magazines, books, periodicals, and computer software are classified in Sector 51, Information; and (4) establishments using transportation equipment to provide recreational and entertainment services, such as those operating sightseeing buses, dinner cruises, or helicopter rides, are classified in Subsector 487, Scenic and Sightseeing Transportation.

711 Performing Arts, Spectator Sports, and Related Industries[T]

Industries in the Performing Arts, Spectator Sports, and Related Industries subsector group establishments that produce or organize and promote live presentations involving the performances of actors and actresses, singers, dancers, musical groups and artists, athletes, and other entertainers, including independent (i.e., freelance) entertainers and the establishments that manage their careers. The classification recognizes four basic processes: (1) producing (i.e., presenting) events; (2) organizing, managing, and/or promoting events; (3) managing and representing entertainers; and (4) providing the artistic, creative and technical skills necessary to the production of these live events. Also, this subsector contains four industries for performing arts companies. Each is defined on the basis of the particular skills of the entertainers involved in the presentations.

The industry structure for this subsector makes a clear distinction between performing arts companies and performing artists (i.e., independent or freelance). Although not unique to arts and entertainment, freelancing is a particularly important phenomenon in this Performing Arts, Spectator Sports, and Related Industries subsector. Distinguishing this activity from the production activity is a meaningful process differentiation. This approach, however, is difficult to implement in the case of musical groups (i.e., companies) and artists, especially pop groups. These establishments tend to be more loosely organized and it can be difficult to distinguish companies from freelancers. For this reason, NAICS includes one industry that covers both musical groups and musical artists. This subsector contains two industries for Industry Group 7113, Promoters of Performing Arts, Sports, and Similar Events, one for those that operate facilities and another for those that do not. This is because there are significant differences in cost structures between those promoters that manage and provide the staff to operate facilities and those that do not. In addition to promoters without facilities, other industries in this subsector include establishments that may operate without permanent facilities. These types of establishments include performing arts companies; musical groups and artists; spectator sports; and independent (i.e., freelance) artists, writers, and performers.

Excluded from this subsector are nightclubs. Some nightclubs promote live entertainment on a regular basis and it can be argued that they could be classified in Industry Group 7113, Promoters of Performing Arts, Sports, and Similar Events. However, since most of these establishments function as any other drinking place when they do not promote entertainment and because most of their revenue is derived from sale of food and beverages, they are classified in Subsector 722, Food Services and Drinking Places.

7111 Performing Arts Companies[T]

This industry group comprises establishments primarily engaged in producing live presentations involving the performances of actors and actresses, singers, dancers, musical groups and artists, and other performing artists.

T—Canadian, Mexican, and United States industries are comparable.

71111 Theater Companies and Dinner Theaters[T] See industry description for 711110.

711110 Theater Companies and Dinner Theaters

This industry comprises (1) companies, groups, or theaters primarily engaged in producing the following live theatrical presentations: musicals; operas; plays; and comedy, improvisational, mime, and puppet shows and (2) establishments, commonly known as dinner theaters, engaged in producing live theatrical productions and in providing food and beverages for consumption on the premises. Theater groups or companies may or may not operate their own theater or other facility for staging their shows.

Illustrative Examples:

Comedy troupes
Opera companies
Live theatrical productions (except dance)
Theatrical stock or repertory companies
Musical theater companies

Cross-References.

- Establishments, such as nightclubs, primarily engaged in providing food and beverages for consumption on the premises and that also present live nontheatrical entertainment are classified in Subsector 722, Food Services and Drinking Places;
- Establishments primarily engaged in organizing, managing, and/or promoting performing arts productions without producing their own shows are classified in Industry Group 7113, Promoters of Performing Arts, Sports, and Similar Events;
- Companies, groups, or theaters primarily engaged in producing all types of live theatrical dance presentations are classified in Industry 711120, Dance Companies;
- Freelance producers and performing artists (except musicians and vocalists) primarily engaged in theatrical activities independent of a company or group are classified in Industry 711510, Independent Artists, Writers, and Performers; and
- Musicians and vocalists are classified in Industry 711130, Musical Groups and Artists.

71112 Dance Companies[T] See industry description for 711120.

711120 Dance Companies

This industry comprises companies, groups, or theaters primarily engaged in producing all types of live theatrical dance (e.g., ballet, contemporary dance, folk dance) presentations. Dance companies or groups may or may not operate their own theater or other facility for staging their shows.

Cross-References.

- Establishments, such as exotic dance clubs, primarily engaged in providing food and beverages for consumption on the premises and that also present live dance entertainment are classified in Subsector 722, Food Services and Drinking Places;
- Establishments primarily engaged in organizing, promoting, and/or managing dance productions without producing their own shows are classified in Industry Group 7113, Promoters of Performing Arts, Sports, and Similar Events; and
- Freelance producers and dancers primarily engaged in theatrical activities independent of a company or group are classified in Industry 711510, Independent Artists, Writers, and Performers.

71113 Musical Groups and Artists[T] See industry description for 711130.

T—Canadian, Mexican, and United States industries are comparable.

711130 Musical Groups and Artists

This industry comprises (1) groups primarily engaged in producing live musical entertainment (except theatrical musical or opera productions) and (2) independent (i.e., freelance) artists primarily engaged in providing live musical entertainment. Musical groups and artists may perform in front of a live audience or in a studio, and may or may not operate their own facilities for staging their shows.

Illustrative Examples:

Bands
Musical groups (except theatrical musical groups)
Drum and bugle corps (i.e., drill teams)
Orchestras
Independent musicians or vocalists

Cross-References.

- Establishments primarily engaged in organizing, promoting, and/or managing concerts and other musical performances without producing their own shows are classified in Industry Group 7113, Promoters of Performing Arts, Sports, and Similar Events;
- Companies, groups, or theaters primarily engaged in producing theatrical musicals and opera productions are classified in Industry 711110, Theater Companies and Dinner Theaters; and
- Freelance producers (except musical groups and artists) primarily engaged in musical activities independent of a company or group are classified in Industry 711510, Independent Artists, Writers, and Performers.

71119 Other Performing Arts Companies[T] See industry description for 711190.

711190 Other Performing Arts Companies

This industry comprises companies or groups (except theater companies, dance companies, and musical groups and artists) primarily engaged in producing live theatrical presentations.

Illustrative Examples:

Carnival traveling shows
Ice skating companies
Circuses
Magic shows

Cross-References.

- Establishments, such as nightclubs, primarily engaged in providing food and beverages for consumption on the premises and that also present live nontheatrical entertainment are classified in Subsector 722, Food Services and Drinking Places;
- Establishments primarily engaged in organizing, promoting, and/or managing ice skating shows, circuses, and other live performing arts presentations without producing their own shows are classified in Industry Group 7113, Promoters of Performing Arts, Sports, and Similar Events;
- Theater companies and groups (except dance) or dinner theaters engaged in producing musicals; plays; operas; and comedy, improvisational, mime, and puppet shows are classified in Industry 711110, Theater Companies and Dinner Theaters;
- Dance companies or groups are classified in Industry 711120, Dance Companies;
- Freelance producers and performing artists (except musicians and vocalists) are classified in Industry 711510, Independent Artists, Writers, and Performers; and
- Musical groups and independent musicians and vocalists are classified in Industry 711130, Musical Groups and Artists.

T—Canadian, Mexican, and United States industries are comparable.

7112 Spectator Sports[T]

71121 Spectator Sports[T]

This industry comprises (1) sports teams or clubs primarily participating in live sporting events before a paying audience; (2) establishments primarily engaged in operating racetracks; (3) independent athletes engaged in participating in live sporting or racing events before a paying audience; (4) owners of racing participants, such as cars, dogs, and horses, primarily engaged in entering them in racing events or other spectator sports events; and (5) establishments, such as sports trainers, primarily engaged in providing specialized services to support participants in sports events or competitions. The sports teams and clubs included in this industry may or may not operate their own arena, stadium, or other facility for presenting their games or other spectator sports events.

Cross-References.

- Establishments primarily engaged in promoting sporting events without participating in sporting events are classified in Industry Group 7113, Promoters of Performing Arts, Sports, and Similar Events;
- Establishments, such as youth league baseball teams, primarily engaged in participating in sporting events for recreational purposes without playing before a paying audience are classified in Industry 71399, All Other Amusement and Recreation Industries;
- Amateur, semiprofessional, or professional athletic associations or leagues are classified in Industry 81399, Other Similar Organizations (except Business, Professional, Labor, and Political Organizations);
- Establishments primarily engaged in representing or managing the careers of sports figures are classified in Industry 71141, Agents and Managers for Artists, Athletes, Entertainers, and Other Public Figures;
- Independent athletes engaged in providing sports instruction without participating in sporting events before a paying audience are classified in Industry 61162, Sports and Recreation Instruction;
- Independent athletes exclusively engaged in endorsing products or making speeches are classified in Industry 71151, Independent Artists, Writers, and Performers; and
- Establishments primarily engaged in raising horses, mules, donkeys, and other equines are classified in Industry 11292, Horses and Other Equine Production.

711211 Sports Teams and Clubs

This U.S. industry comprises professional or semiprofessional sports teams or clubs primarily engaged in participating in live sporting events, such as baseball, basketball, football, hockey, soccer, and jai alai games, before a paying audience. These establishments may or may not operate their own arena, stadium, or other facility for presenting these events.

Cross-References.

- Establishments primarily engaged in promoting sporting events without participating in sporting events are classified in Industry Group 7113, Promoters of Performing Arts, Sports, and Similar Events;
- Establishments, such as youth league baseball teams, primarily engaged in participating in sporting events for recreational purposes without playing before a paying audience are classified in Industry 713990, All Other Amusement and Recreation Industries; and
- Amateur, semiprofessional, or professional athletic associations or leagues are classified in Industry 813990, Other Similar Organizations (except Business, Professional, Labor, and Political Organizations).

711212 Racetracks

This U.S. industry comprises establishments primarily engaged in operating racetracks. These establishments may also present and/or promote the events, such as auto, dog, and horse races, held in these facilities.

T—Canadian, Mexican, and United States industries are comparable.

Cross-References.

- Owners of racing participants, such as cars, dogs, and horses, primarily engaged in entering them in racing events; trainers of racing participants; and independent athletes, such as jockeys and race car drivers, primarily engaged in participating in racing events are classified in U.S. Industry 711219, Other Spectator Sports; and
- Establishments primarily engaged in operating stand-alone casinos are classified in Industry 713210, Casinos (except Casino Hotels).

711219 Other Spectator Sports

This U.S. industry comprises (1) independent athletes, such as professional or semiprofessional golfers, boxers, and race car drivers, primarily engaged in participating in live sporting or racing events before a paying audience; (2) owners of racing participants, such as cars, dogs, and horses, primarily engaged in entering them in racing events or other spectator events; and (3) establishments, such as sports trainers, primarily engaged in providing specialized services required to support participants in sports events or competitions.

Cross-References.

- Establishments primarily engaged in operating racetracks are classified in U.S. Industry 711212, Racetracks;
- Establishments primarily engaged in representing or managing the careers of sports figures are classified in Industry 711410, Agents and Managers for Artists, Athletes, Entertainers, and Other Public Figures;
- Independent athletes engaged in providing sports instruction without participating in sporting events before a paying audience are classified in Industry 611620, Sports and Recreation Instruction;
- Independent athletes exclusively engaged in endorsing products or making speeches are classified in Industry 711510, Independent Artists, Writers, and Performers; and
- Establishments primarily engaged in raising horses, mules, donkeys, and other equines are classified in Industry 112920, Horses and Other Equine Production.

7113 Promoters of Performing Arts, Sports, and Similar Events[T]

This industry group comprises establishments primarily engaged in organizing, promoting, and/or managing live performing arts productions, sports events, and similar events, held in facilities that they manage and operate or in facilities that are managed and operated by others.

71131 Promoters of Performing Arts, Sports, and Similar Events with Facilities[T] See industry description for 711310.

711310 Promoters of Performing Arts, Sports, and Similar Events with Facilities

This industry comprises establishments primarily engaged in (1) organizing, promoting, and/or managing live performing arts productions, sports events, and similar events, such as state fairs, county fairs, agricultural fairs, concerts, and festivals, held in facilities that they manage and operate and/or (2) managing and providing the staff to operate arenas, stadiums, theaters, or other related facilities for rent to other promoters.

Cross-References. Establishments primarily engaged in--

- Producing live performances (but may also promote the performances and/or operate the facilities where the performances take place)--are classified in Industry Group 7111, Performing Arts Companies;
- Operating racetracks (but may also promote the events held in these facilities)--are classified in U.S. Industry 711212, Racetracks;
- Presenting sporting events (but may also promote the sporting events and/or operate the stadiums or arenas where the sporting events take place)--are classified in U.S. Industry 711211, Sports Teams and Clubs;

T—Canadian, Mexican, and United States industries are comparable.

- Organizing, promoting, and/or managing conventions, conferences, and trade shows (but may also operate the facilities where these events take place)--are classified in Industry 561920, Convention and Trade Show Organizers;
- Organizing, promoting, and/or managing performing arts productions, sports events, and similar events in facilities managed and operated by others--are classified in Industry 711320, Promoters of Performing Arts, Sports, and Similar Events without Facilities; and
- Leasing stadiums, arenas, theaters, and other related facilities to others without operating the facilities--are classified in Industry 531120, Lessors of Nonresidential Buildings (except Miniwarehouses).

71132 Promoters of Performing Arts, Sports, and Similar Events without Facilities[T] See industry description for 711320.

711320 Promoters of Performing Arts, Sports, and Similar Events without Facilities

This industry comprises promoters primarily engaged in organizing, promoting, and/or managing live performing arts productions, sports events, and similar events, such as state fairs, county fairs, agricultural fairs, concerts, and festivals, in facilities that are managed and operated by others. Theatrical (except motion picture) booking agencies are included in this industry.

Cross-References. Establishments primarily engaged in--

- Booking motion pictures or videos--are classified in U.S. Industry 512199, Other Motion Picture and Video Industries;
- Producing live performances (but may also promote the performances)--are classified in Industry Group 7111, Performing Arts Companies;
- Operating racetracks (but may also promote the events held in these facilities)--are classified in U.S. Industry 711212, Racetracks;
- Presenting sporting events (but may also promote the sporting events)--are classified in U.S. Industry 711211, Sports Teams and Clubs;
- Organizing, promoting, and/or managing conventions, conferences, and trade shows (but may also operate the facilities where these events take place)--are classified in Industry 561920, Convention and Trade Show Organizers;
- Organizing, promoting, and/or managing performing arts, sports, and similar events in facilities they manage or operate--are classified in Industry 711310, Promoters of Performing Arts, Sports, and Similar Events with Facilities; and
- Operating amateur, semiprofessional, or professional athletic associations or leagues--are classified in Industry 813990, Other Similar Organizations (except Business, Professional, Labor, and Political Organizations).

7114 Agents and Managers for Artists, Athletes, Entertainers, and Other Public Figures[T]

71141 Agents and Managers for Artists, Athletes, Entertainers, and Other Public Figures[T] See industry description for 711410.

711410 Agents and Managers for Artists, Athletes, Entertainers, and Other Public Figures

This industry comprises establishments of agents and managers primarily engaged in representing and/or managing creative and performing artists, sports figures, entertainers, and other public figures. The representation and management includes activities, such as representing clients in contract negotiations; managing or organizing clients' financial affairs; and generally promoting the careers of their clients.

Illustrative Examples:

Celebrities' agents or managers Sports figures' agents or managers

T—Canadian, Mexican, and United States industries are comparable.

Literary agents
Talent agents
Modeling agents

Cross-References.

- Establishments primarily engaged in supplying models to clients are classified in Industry 561320, Temporary Help Services; and
- Establishments known as model registries primarily engaged in recruiting and placing models for clients are classified in U.S. Industry 561311, Employment Placement Agencies.

7115 Independent Artists, Writers, and Performers[T]

71151 Independent Artists, Writers, and Performers[T] See industry description for 711510.

711510 Independent Artists, Writers, and Performers

This industry comprises independent (i.e., freelance) individuals primarily engaged in performing in artistic productions, in creating artistic and cultural works or productions, or in providing technical expertise necessary for these productions. This industry also includes athletes and other celebrities exclusively engaged in endorsing products and making speeches or public appearances for which they receive a fee.

Illustrative Examples:

Independent actors or actresses
Independent producers
Independent art restorers
Independent recording technicians
Independent artists (except musical, commercial, or medical)
Independent speakers
Independent cartoonists
Independent theatrical costume designers
Independent dancers
Independent theatrical lighting technicians
Independent journalists
Independent technical writers

Cross-References.

- Freelance musicians and vocalists are classified in Industry 711130, Musical Groups and Artists;
- Independent commercial artists and graphic designers are classified in Industry 541430, Graphic Design Services; and
- Artisans and craftspersons are classified in Sector 31-33, Manufacturing.

712 Museums, Historical Sites, and Similar Institutions[T]

Industries in the Museums, Historical Sites, and Similar Institutions subsector engage in the preservation and exhibition of objects, sites, and natural wonders of historical, cultural, and/or educational value.

7121 Museums, Historical Sites, and Similar Institutions[T]

71211 Museums[T] See industry description for 712110.

712110 Museums

This industry comprises establishments primarily engaged in the preservation and exhibition of objects of historical, cultural, and/or educational value.

T—Canadian, Mexican, and United States industries are comparable.

Illustrative Examples:

Art galleries (except retail)
Planetariums
Art museums
Science or technology museums
Halls of fame
Wax museums

Cross-References.

Commercial art galleries primarily engaged in selling art objects are classified in Industry 453920, Art Dealers.

71212 Historical Sites[T] See industry description for 712120.

712120 Historical Sites

This industry comprises establishments primarily engaged in the preservation and exhibition of sites, buildings, forts, or communities that describe events or persons of particular historical interest. Archeological sites, battlefields, historical ships, and pioneer villages are included in this industry.

71213 Zoos and Botanical Gardens[T] See industry description for 712130.

712130 Zoos and Botanical Gardens

This industry comprises establishments primarily engaged in the preservation and exhibition of live plant and animal life displays.

Illustrative Examples:

Aquariums
Wild animal parks
Arboreta
Zoological gardens
Aviaries

71219 Nature Parks and Other Similar Institutions[T] See industry description for 712190.

712190 Nature Parks and Other Similar Institutions

This industry comprises establishments primarily engaged in the preservation and exhibition of natural areas or settings.

Bird or wildlife sanctuaries
Natural wonder tourist attractions (e.g., caverns, waterfalls)
Conservation areas
Nature centers or preserves
National parks

Cross-References.

Establishments primarily engaged in operating commercial hunting or fishing preserves (e.g., game farms) are

T—Canadian, Mexican, and United States industries are comparable.

713 Amusement, Gambling, and Recreation Industries[T]

Industries in the Amusement, Gambling, and Recreation Industries subsector (1) operate facilities where patrons can primarily engage in sports, recreation, amusement, or gambling activities and/or (2) provide other amusement and recreation services, such as supplying and servicing amusement devices in places of business operated by others; operating sports teams, clubs, or leagues engaged in playing games for recreational purposes; and guiding tours without using transportation equipment.

This subsector does not cover all establishments providing recreational services. Other sectors of NAICS also provide recreational services. Providers of recreational services are often engaged in processes classified in other sectors of NAICS. For example, operators of resorts and hunting and fishing camps provide both accommodation and recreational facilities and services. These establishments are classified in Subsector 721, Accommodation, partly to reflect the significant costs associated with the provision of accommodation services and partly to ensure consistency with international standards. Likewise, establishments using transportation equipment to provide recreational and entertainment services, such as those operating sightseeing buses, dinner cruises, or helicopter rides, are classified in Sector 48-49, Transportation and Warehousing.

The industry groups in this subsector highlight particular types of activities: amusement parks and arcades, gambling industries, and other amusement and recreation industries. The groups, however, are not all-inclusive of the activity. The Gambling Industries industry group does not provide for full coverage of gambling activities. For example, casino hotels are classified in Subsector 721, Accommodation; and horse and dog racing tracks are classified in Industry Group 7112, Spectator Sports.

7131 Amusement Parks and Arcades[T]

This industry group comprises establishments primarily engaged in operating amusement parks and amusement arcades and parlors.

71311 Amusement and Theme Parks[T] See industry description for 713110.

713110 Amusement and Theme Parks

This industry comprises establishments, known as amusement or theme parks, primarily engaged in operating a variety of attractions, such as mechanical rides, water rides, games, shows, theme exhibits, refreshment stands, and picnic grounds. These establishments may lease space to others on a concession basis.

Cross-References. Establishments primarily engaged in--

- Operating mechanical or water rides on a concession basis in amusement parks, fairs, and carnivals or operating a single attraction, such as a waterslide--are classified in Industry 713990, All Other Amusement and Recreation Industries;
- Operating refreshment stands on a concession basis--are classified in Industry 72251, Restaurants and Other Eating Places;
- Supplying and servicing coin-operated amusement (except gambling) devices in places of business operated by others--are classified in Industry 713990, All Other Amusement and Recreation Industries;
- Supplying and servicing coin-operated gambling devices (e.g., slot machines or video gambling terminals) in places of business operated by others--are classified in Industry 713290, Other Gambling Industries; and
- Organizing, promoting, and/or managing events, such as carnivals and fairs, with or without facilities--are classified in Industry Group 7113, Promoters of Performing Arts, Sports, and Similar Events.

71312 Amusement Arcades[T] See industry description for 713120.

T—Canadian, Mexican, and United States industries are comparable.

713120 Amusement Arcades

This industry comprises establishments primarily engaged in operating amusement (except gambling, billiard, or pool) arcades and parlors.

Cross-References. Establishments primarily engaged in--

- Supplying and servicing coin-operated amusement (except gambling) devices in places of business operated by others or in operating billiard or pool parlors--are classified in Industry 713990, All Other Amusement and Recreation Industries;
- Operating bingo, off-track betting, or slot machine parlors or in supplying and servicing coin-operated gambling devices (e.g., slot machines or video gambling terminals) in places of business operated by others--are classified in Industry 713290, Other Gambling Industries;
- Operating casinos (except casino hotels)--are classified in Industry 713210, Casinos (except Casino Hotels); and
- Operating casino hotels--are classified in Industry 721120, Casino Hotels.

7132 Gambling Industries[T]

This industry group comprises establishments (except casino hotels) primarily engaged in operating gambling facilities, such as casinos, bingo halls, and video gaming terminals, or in the provision of gambling services, such as lotteries and off-track betting. Casino hotels are classified in Industry 72112, Casino Hotels.

71321 Casinos (except Casino Hotels)[T] See industry description for 713210.

713210 Casinos (except Casino Hotels)

This industry comprises establishments primarily engaged in operating gambling facilities that offer table wagering games along with other gambling activities, such as slot machines and sports betting. These establishments often provide food and beverage services. Included in this industry are floating casinos (i.e., gambling cruises, riverboat casinos).

Cross-References. Establishments primarily engaged in--

- Operating bingo, off-track betting, or slot machine parlors or in supplying and servicing coin-operated gambling devices, such as slot machines and video gaming terminals, in places of business operated by others--are classified in Industry 713290, Other Gambling Industries; and
- Operating casino hotels--are classified in Industry 721120, Casino Hotels.

71329 Other Gambling Industries[T] See industry description for 713290.

713290 Other Gambling Industries

This industry comprises establishments primarily engaged in operating gambling facilities (except casinos or casino hotels) or providing gambling services.

Illustrative Examples:

Bingo, off-track betting, or slot machine parlors
Coin-operated gambling device concession operators (i.e., supplying and servicing in others' facilities)
Bookmakers
Lottery ticket sales agents (except retail stores)
Card rooms (e.g., poker rooms)

T—Canadian, Mexican, and United States industries are comparable.

Cross-References. Establishments primarily engaged in--

- Operating casinos--are classified in Industry 713210, Casinos (except Casino Hotels);
- Operating casino hotels--are classified in Industry 721120, Casino Hotels;
- Operating facilities with coin-operated amusement (except gambling) devices--are classified in Industry 713120, Amusement Arcades;
- Supplying and servicing coin-operated amusement (except gambling) devices in places of business operated by others--are classified in Industry 713990, All Other Amusement and Recreation Industries; and
- Operating racetracks or presenting live racing or sporting events--are classified in Industry 71121, Spectator Sports.

7139 Other Amusement and Recreation Industries[T]

This industry group comprises establishments primarily engaged in operating golf courses and country clubs; skiing facilities; marinas; fitness and recreational sports centers; bowling centers; and providing other amusement and recreation services.

71391 Golf Courses and Country Clubs[T] See industry description for 713910.

713910 Golf Courses and Country Clubs

This industry comprises (1) establishments primarily engaged in operating golf courses (except miniature) and (2) establishments primarily engaged in operating golf courses, along with dining facilities and other recreational facilities that are known as country clubs. These establishments often provide food and beverage services, equipment rental services, and golf instruction services.

Cross-References. Establishments primarily engaged in--

- Operating driving ranges and miniature golf courses--are classified in Industry 713990, All Other Amusement and Recreation Industries; and
- Operating resorts where golf facilities are combined with accommodations--are classified in Industry Group 7211, Traveler Accommodation.

71392 Skiing Facilities[T] See industry description for 713920.

713920 Skiing Facilities

This industry comprises establishments engaged in (1) operating downhill, cross country, or related skiing areas and/or (2) operating equipment, such as ski lifts and tows. These establishments often provide food and beverage services, equipment rental services, and ski instruction services. Four season resorts without accommodations are included in this industry.

Cross-References.

Establishments primarily engaged in operating resorts where skiing facilities are combined with accommodations are classified in Industry Group 7211, Traveler Accommodation.

71393 Marinas[T] See industry description for 713930.

T—Canadian, Mexican, and United States industries are comparable.

713930 Marinas

This industry comprises establishments, commonly known as marinas, engaged in operating docking and/or storage facilities for pleasure craft owners, with or without one or more related activities, such as retailing fuel and marine supplies; and repairing, maintaining, or renting pleasure boats.

Cross-References. Establishments primarily engaged in--

- Building ships--are classified in U.S. Industry 336611, Ship Building and Repairing;
- Building boats--are classified in U.S. Industry 336612, Boat Building;
- Renting pleasure boats--are classified in U.S. Industry 532284, Recreational Goods Rental;
- Repairing pleasure boats--are classified in Industry 811490, Other Personal and Household Goods Repair and Maintenance;
- Retailing marine supplies--are classified in U.S. Industry 441222, Boat Dealers; and
- Retailing fuel for boats--are classified in Industry 447190, Other Gasoline Stations.

71394 Fitness and Recreational Sports Centers[T] See industry description for 713940.

713940 Fitness and Recreational Sports Centers

This industry comprises establishments primarily engaged in operating fitness and recreational sports facilities featuring exercise and other active physical fitness conditioning or recreational sports activities, such as swimming, skating, or racquet sports.

Illustrative Examples:

Aerobic dance or exercise centers
Ice or roller skating rinks
Gymnasiums
Physical fitness centers
Handball, racquetball, or tennis club facilities
Swimming or wave pools

Cross-References.

- Establishments primarily engaged in providing non-medical services to assist clients in attaining or maintaining a desired weight are classified in U.S. Industry 812191, Diet and Weight Reducing Centers;
- Establishments primarily engaged in providing personal fitness training services are classified in Industry 812990, All Other Personal Services;
- Establishments primarily engaged in operating health resorts and spas where recreational facilities are combined with accommodations are classified in Industry 721110, Hotels (except Casino Hotels) and Motels; and
- Recreational sports clubs (i.e., sports teams) not operating sports facilities are classified in Industry 713990, All Other Amusement and Recreation Industries.

71395 Bowling Centers[T] See industry description for 713950.

713950 Bowling Centers

This industry comprises establishments engaged in operating bowling centers. These establishments often provide food and beverage services.

71399 All Other Amusement and Recreation Industries[T] See industry description for 713990.

T—Canadian, Mexican, and United States industries are comparable.

713990 All Other Amusement and Recreation Industries

This industry comprises establishments (except amusement parks and arcades; gambling industries; golf courses and country clubs; skiing facilities; marinas; fitness and recreational sports centers; and bowling centers) primarily engaged in providing recreational and amusement services.

Illustrative Examples:

Amusement ride or coin-operated nongambling amusement device concession operators (i.e., supplying and servicing in others' facilities)
Miniature golf courses
Archery or shooting ranges
Recreational day camps (except instructional)
Billiard or pool parlors
Recreational or youth sports teams
Boating clubs (without marinas)
Recreational sports clubs (i.e., sports teams) not operating sports facilities Dance halls
Riding stables

Cross-References.

- Establishments primarily engaged in operating amusement parks and arcades are classified in Industry Group 7131, Amusement Parks and Arcades;
- Establishments primarily engaged in operating gambling facilities (except casino hotels) or providing gambling services are classified in Industry Group 7132, Gambling Industries;
- Establishments primarily engaged in operating casino hotels are classified in Industry 721120, Casino Hotels;
- Establishments primarily engaged in operating golf courses (except miniature) and country clubs are classified in Industry 713910, Golf Courses and Country Clubs;
- Establishments primarily engaged in operating skiing facilities without hotel accommodation are classified in Industry 713920, Skiing Facilities;
- Establishments primarily engaged in operating resorts where recreational facilities are combined with lodging are classified in Industry Group 7211, Traveler Accommodation;
- Establishments primarily engaged in operating marinas are classified in Industry 713930, Marinas;
- Establishments primarily engaged in operating fitness and recreational sports centers are classified in Industry 713940, Fitness and Recreational Sports Centers;
- Establishments primarily engaged in operating bowling centers are classified in Industry 713950, Bowling Centers;
- Establishments primarily engaged in operating instructional camps, such as sports camps, fine arts camps, and computer camps, are classified in Sector 61, Educational Services, based on the nature of instruction;
- Independent athletes engaged in participating in sporting events before a paying audience are classified in U.S. Industry 711219, Other Spectator Sports;
- Independent athletes engaged in providing sports instruction without participating in sporting events before a paying audience are classified in Industry 611620, Sports and Recreation Instruction;
- Independent athletes exclusively engaged in endorsing products or making speeches are classified in Industry 711510, Independent Artists, Writers, and Performers;
- Establishments primarily engaged in providing scenic and sightseeing transportation are classified in Subsector 487, Scenic and Sightseeing Transportation;
- Aviation clubs primarily engaged in providing specialty air and flying services are classified in U.S. Industry 481219, Other Nonscheduled Air Transportation;
- Aviation clubs primarily engaged in advocating social and political causes are classified in U.S. Industry 813319, Other Social Advocacy Organizations; and
- Amateur, semiprofessional, or professional athletic associations or leagues are classified in Industry 813990, Other Similar Organizations (except Business, Professional, Labor, and Political Organizations).

T—Canadian, Mexican, and United States industries are comparable.

Sector 72--Accommodation and Food Services[T]

The Sector as a Whole

The Accommodation and Food Services sector comprises establishments providing customers with lodging and/ or preparing meals, snacks, and beverages for immediate consumption. The sector includes both accommodation and food services establishments because the two activities are often combined at the same establishment.
Excluded from this sector are civic and social organizations; amusement and recreation parks; theaters; and other recreation or entertainment facilities providing food and beverage services.

721 Accommodation[T]

Industries in the Accommodation subsector provide lodging or short-term accommodations for travelers, vacationers, and others. There is a wide range of establishments in these industries. Some provide lodging only, while others provide meals, laundry services, and recreational facilities, as well as lodging. Lodging establishments are classified in this subsector even if the provision of complementary services generates more revenue. The types of complementary services provided vary from establishment to establishment.
The subsector is organized into three groups: (1) traveler accommodation, (2) recreational accommodation, and (3) rooming and boarding houses, dormitories, and workers' camps. The Traveler Accommodation industry group includes establishments that primarily provide traditional types of lodging services. This group includes hotels, motels, and bed-and-breakfast inns. In addition to lodging, these establishments may provide a range of other services to their guests. The RV (Recreational Vehicle) Parks and Recreational Camps industry group includes establishments that operate lodging facilities primarily designed to accommodate outdoor enthusiasts. Included are travel trailer campsites, recreational vehicle parks, and outdoor adventure retreats. The Rooming and Boarding Houses, Dormitories, and Workers' Camps industry group includes establishments providing temporary or longer-term accommodations, that for the period of occupancy, may serve as a principal residence. Board (i.e., meals) may be provided but is not essential.
Establishments that manage short-stay accommodation establishments (e.g., hotels and motels) on a contractual basis are classified in this subsector if they both manage the operation and provide the operating staff. Such establishments are classified based on the type of facility managed and operated.

7211 Traveler Accommodation[T]

This industry group comprises establishments primarily engaged in providing short-term lodging in facilities, such as hotels, motels, casino hotels, and bed-and-breakfast inns. In addition to lodging, these establishments may provide a range of other services to their guests.

72111 Hotels (except Casino Hotels) and Motels[T] See industry description for 721110.

721110 Hotels (except Casino Hotels) and Motels

This industry comprises establishments primarily engaged in providing short-term lodging in facilities known as hotels, motor hotels, resort hotels, and motels. The establishments in this industry may offer food and beverage services, recreational services, conference rooms, convention services, laundry services, parking, and other services.

Cross-References. Establishments primarily engaged in--

- Providing short-term lodging with a casino on the premises--are classified in Industry 721120, Casino Hotels; and
- Providing short-term lodging in facilities known as bed-and-breakfast inns, youth hostels, housekeeping cabins and cottages, and tourist homes--are classified in Industry 72119, Other Traveler Accommodation.

T—Canadian, Mexican, and United States industries are comparable.

72112 Casino Hotels[T] See industry description for 721120.

721120 Casino Hotels

This industry comprises establishments primarily engaged in providing short-term lodging in hotel facilities with a casino on the premises. The casino on premises includes table wagering games and may include other gambling activities, such as slot machines and sports betting. These establishments generally offer a range of services and amenities, such as food and beverage services, entertainment, valet parking, swimming pools, and conference and convention facilities.

Cross-References. Establishments primarily engaged in--

- Providing short-term lodging in facilities known as hotels and motels that provide limited gambling activities, such as slot machines, without a casino on the premises--are classified in Industry 721110, Hotels (except Casino Hotels) and Motels; and
- Operating stand-alone casinos--are classified in Industry 713210, Casinos (except Casino Hotels).

72119 Other Traveler Accommodation[T]

This industry comprises establishments primarily engaged in providing short-term lodging (except hotels, motels, and casino hotels).

Illustrative Examples:

Bed-and-breakfast inns
Tourist homes
Guest houses
Youth hostels
Housekeeping cabins and cottages

Cross-References. Establishments primarily engaged in--

- Providing short-term lodging in facilities known as hotels without a casino on the premises--are classified in Industry 72111, Hotels (except Casino Hotels) and Motels; and
- Providing short-term lodging in facilities known as hotels with a casino on the premises--are classified in Industry 72112, Casino Hotels.

721191 Bed-and-Breakfast Inns

This U.S. industry comprises establishments primarily engaged in providing short-term lodging in facilities known as bed-and-breakfast inns. These establishments provide short-term lodging in private homes or small buildings converted for this purpose. Bed-and-breakfast inns are characterized by a highly personalized service and inclusion of a full breakfast in the room rate.

721199 All Other Traveler Accommodation

This U.S. industry comprises establishments primarily engaged in providing short-term lodging (except hotels, motels, casino hotels, and bed-and-breakfast inns).

Illustrative Examples:

Guest houses
Tourist homes
Housekeeping cabins and cottages
Youth hostels

T—Canadian, Mexican, and United States industries are comparable.

Cross-References. Establishments primarily engaged in--

- Providing short-term lodging in facilities known as hotels without a casino on the premises--are classified in Industry 721110, Hotels (except Casino Hotels) and Motels;
- Providing short-term lodging in facilities known as hotels with a casino on the premises--are classified in Industry 721120, Casino Hotels; and
- Providing short-term lodging in establishments known as bed-and-breakfast inns--are classified in U.S. Industry 721191, Bed-and-Breakfast Inns.

7212 RV (Recreational Vehicle) Parks and Recreational Camps[T]

72121 RV (Recreational Vehicle) Parks and Recreational Camps[T]

This industry comprises establishments primarily engaged in operating recreational vehicle parks and campgrounds and recreational and vacation camps. These establishments cater to outdoor enthusiasts and are characterized by the type of accommodation and by the nature and the range of recreational facilities and activities provided to their clients.

Illustrative Examples:

Campgrounds
Fishing and hunting camps
Travel trailer campsites
Outdoor adventure retreats
Vacation camps (except instructional, day)
Recreational vehicle parks

Cross-References. Establishments primarily engaged in--

- Operating recreational facilities without accommodations--are classified in Subsector 713, Amusement, Gambling, and Recreation Industries;
- Operating instructional camps, such as sports camps, fine arts camps, and computer camps--are classified in Sector 61, Educational Services, based on the nature of instruction;
- Operating children's day camps (except instructional)--are classified in Industry 71399, All Other Amusement and Recreation Industries; and
- Acting as lessors of residential mobile home sites (i.e., trailer parks)--are classified in Industry 53119, Lessors of Other Real Estate Property.

721211 RV (Recreational Vehicle) Parks and Campgrounds

This U.S. industry comprises establishments primarily engaged in operating sites to accommodate campers and their equipment, including tents, tent trailers, travel trailers, and RVs (recreational vehicles). These establishments may provide access to facilities, such as washrooms, laundry rooms, recreation halls, playgrounds, stores, and snack bars.

Cross-References. Establishments primarily engaged in--

- Operating recreational facilities without accommodations--are classified in Subsector 713, Amusement, Gambling, and Recreation Industries; and
- Acting as lessors of residential mobile home sites (i.e., trailer parks)--are classified in Industry 531190, Lessors of Other Real Estate Property.

721214 Recreational and Vacation Camps (except Campgrounds)

This U.S. industry comprises establishments primarily engaged in operating overnight recreational camps, such as children's camps, family vacation camps, hunting and fishing camps, and outdoor adventure retreats, that offer trail riding, white water rafting, hiking, and similar activities. These establishments provide accommodation facilities,

T—Canadian, Mexican, and United States industries are comparable.

such as cabins and fixed campsites, and other amenities, such as food services, recreational facilities and equipment, and organized recreational activities.

Illustrative Examples:

Fishing camps with accommodation facilities
Dude ranches
Vacation camps (except campgrounds, day, instructional)
Hunting camps with accommodation facilities
Wilderness camps
Outdoor adventure retreats with accommodation facilities

Cross-References. Establishments primarily engaged in--

- Operating instructional camps, such as sports camps, fine arts camps, and computer camps--are classified in Sector 61, Educational Services, based on the nature of instruction; and
- Operating children's day camps (except instructional)--are classified in Industry 713990, All Other Amusement and Recreation Industries.

7213 Rooming and Boarding Houses, Dormitories, and Workers' Camps[T]

72131 Rooming and Boarding Houses, Dormitories, and Workers' Camps[T] See industry description for 721310.

721310 Rooming and Boarding Houses, Dormitories, and Workers' Camps

This industry comprises establishments primarily engaged in operating rooming and boarding houses and similar facilities, such as fraternity houses, sorority houses, off campus dormitories, residential clubs, and workers' camps. These establishments provide temporary or longer-term accommodations, which, for the period of occupancy, may serve as a principal residence. These establishments also may provide complementary services, such as housekeeping, meals, and laundry services.

Illustrative Examples:

Dormitories (off campus)
Sorority houses
Fraternity houses
Workers' camps
Rooming houses

722 Food Services and Drinking Places[T]

Industries in the Food Services and Drinking Places subsector prepare meals, snacks, and beverages to customer order for immediate on-premises and off-premises consumption. There is a wide range of establishments in these industries. Some provide food and drink only, while others provide various combinations of seating space, waiter/ waitress services, and incidental amenities, such as limited entertainment. The industries in the subsector are grouped based on the type and level of services provided. The industry groups are Special Food Services, such as food service contractors, caterers, and mobile food services; Drinking Places (Alcoholic Beverages); and Restaurants and Other Eating Places.

Food and beverage services at hotels and motels, amusement parks, theaters, casinos, country clubs, similar recreational facilities, and civic and social organizations are included in this subsector only if these services are provided by a separate establishment primarily engaged in providing food and beverage services.

Excluded from this subsector are establishments operating dinner cruises. These establishments are classified in Subsector 487, Scenic and Sightseeing Transportation, because they utilize transportation equipment to provide scenic recreational entertainment.

T—Canadian, Mexican, and United States industries are comparable.

7223 Special Food Services[T]

This industry group comprises establishments primarily engaged in providing food services at one or more of the following locations: (1) the customer's location; (2) a location designated by the customer; or (3) from motorized vehicles or nonmotorized carts.

72231 Food Service Contractors[T] See industry description for 722310.

722310 Food Service Contractors

This industry comprises establishments primarily engaged in providing food services at institutional, governmental, commercial, or industrial locations of others based on contractual arrangements with these types of organizations for a specified period of time. The establishments of this industry provide food services for the convenience of the contracting organization or the contracting organization's customers. The contractual arrangement of these establishments with contracting organizations may vary by type of facility operated (e.g., cafeteria, restaurant, fast-food eating place), revenue sharing, cost structure, and personnel provided. Management staff is always provided by food service contractors.

Illustrative Examples:

Airline food service contractors
Food concession contractors (e.g., at sporting, entertainment, convention facilities)
Cafeteria food service contractors (e.g., at schools,

Cross-References. Establishments primarily engaged in--

- Providing food services on a single-event basis--are classified in Industry 722320, Caterers; and
- Supplying and servicing food vending machines--are classified in Industry 454210, Vending Machine Operators.

72232 Caterers[T] See industry description for 722320.

722320 Caterers

This industry comprises establishments primarily engaged in providing single event-based food services. These establishments generally have equipment and vehicles to transport meals and snacks to events and/or prepare food at an off-premise site. Banquet halls with catering staff are included in this industry. Examples of events catered by establishments in this industry are graduation parties, wedding receptions, business or retirement luncheons, and trade shows.

Cross-References. Establishments primarily engaged in--

- Preparing and serving meals and snacks for immediate consumption from motorized vehicles or nonmotorized carts--are classified in Industry 722330, Mobile Food Services;
- Providing food services at institutional, governmental, commercial, or industrial locations of others (e.g., airline contractors, industrial caterers) based on contractual arrangements for a specified period of time--are classified in Industry 722310, Food Service Contractors; and
- Renting out facilities without providing catering staff--are classified in Industry 531120, Lessors of Nonresidential Buildings (except Miniwarehouses).

72233 Mobile Food Services[T] See industry description for 722330.

T—Canadian, Mexican, and United States industries are comparable.

722330 Mobile Food Services

This industry comprises establishments primarily engaged in preparing and serving meals and snacks for immediate consumption from motorized vehicles or nonmotorized carts. The establishment is the central location from which the caterer route is serviced, not each vehicle or cart. Included in this industry are establishments primarily engaged in providing food services from vehicles, such as hot dog carts and ice cream trucks.

Illustrative Examples:

Ice cream truck vendors
Mobile food concession stands
Mobile canteens
Mobile refreshment stands
Mobile food carts
Mobile snack stands

Cross-References. Establishments primarily engaged in--

- Selling a specialty snack (e.g., ice cream, frozen yogurt, cookies, popcorn) or nonalcoholic beverages, except from mobile vehicles, for consumption on or near the premises--are classified in U.S. Industry 722515, Snack and Nonalcoholic Beverage Bars;
- Selling unprepared foods, such as vegetables, nuts, or fruit, from carts--are classified in Industry 454390, Other Direct Selling Establishments;
- Providing food services or selling food specialties, such as hamburgers, hot dogs, chicken, pizza, or specialty cuisines, except from mobile vehicles--are classified based on the type of food service provided to patrons; and
- Operating as street vendors (except food)--are classified in Industry 454390, Other Direct Selling Establishments.

7224 Drinking Places (Alcoholic Beverages)[T]

72241 Drinking Places (Alcoholic Beverages)[T] See industry description for 722410.

722410 Drinking Places (Alcoholic Beverages)

This industry comprises establishments known as bars, taverns, nightclubs, or drinking places primarily engaged in preparing and serving alcoholic beverages for immediate consumption. These establishments may also provide limited food services.

Cross-References. Establishments primarily engaged in--

- Preparing and serving alcoholic beverages (i.e., not known as bars or taverns) and providing food services to patrons--are classified in Industry 72251, Restaurants and Other Eating Places;
- Operating a civic or social association with a bar for the association members--are classified in Industry 813410, Civic and Social Organizations;
- Retailing packaged alcoholic beverages not for immediate consumption on the premises--are classified in Industry 445310, Beer, Wine, and Liquor Stores; and
- Operating discotheques or dance clubs without selling alcoholic beverages--are classified in Industry 713990, All Other Amusement and Recreation Industries.

7225 Restaurants and Other Eating Places[T]

72251 Restaurants and Other Eating Places[T]

This industry comprises establishments primarily engaged in one of the following: (1) providing food services to patrons who order and are served while seated (i.e., waiter/waitress service) and pay after eating; (2) providing food services to patrons who generally order or select items (e.g., at a counter, in a buffet line) and pay before eating; or

T—Canadian, Mexican, and United States industries are comparable.

(3) preparing and/or serving a specialty snack (e.g., ice cream, frozen yogurt, cookies) and/or nonalcoholic beverages (e.g., coffee, juices, sodas) for consumption on or near the premises.

Cross-References. Establishments primarily engaged in--

- Preparing and serving alcoholic beverages and known as bars, taverns, or nightclubs--are classified in Industry 72241, Drinking Places (Alcoholic Beverages);
- Preparing and serving snacks and nonalcoholic beverages from mobile vehicles--are classified in Industry 72233, Mobile Food Services;
- Presenting live theatrical productions and providing food and beverages for consumption on the premises--are classified in Industry 71111, Theater Companies and Dinner Theaters;
- Retailing confectionery goods and nuts not packaged for immediate consumption--are classified in Industry 44529, Other Specialty Food Stores; and
- Retailing baked goods (e.g., pretzels, doughnuts, cookies, and bagels) not baked on the premises and not for immediate consumption--are classified in Industry 44529, Other Specialty Food Stores.

722511 Full-Service Restaurants

This U.S. industry comprises establishments primarily engaged in providing food services to patrons who order and are served while seated (i.e., waiter/waitress service) and pay after eating. These establishments may provide this type of food service to patrons in combination with selling alcoholic beverages, providing carryout services, or presenting live nontheatrical entertainment.

Cross-References. Establishments primarily engaged in--

- Providing food services where patrons generally order or select items and pay before eating, other than mobile food services, cafeterias, grill buffets, buffets, and snack and nonalcoholic beverage bars--are classified in U.S. Industry 722513, Limited-Service Restaurants;
- Preparing and serving meals for immediate consumption using cafeteria-style or buffet serving equipment, known as cafeterias, grill buffets, or buffets--are classified in U.S. Industry 722514, Cafeterias, Grill Buffets, and Buffets;
- Selling a specialty snack (e.g., ice cream, frozen yogurt, cookies, popcorn) or nonalcoholic beverage, except from mobile vehicles, for consumption on or near the premises--are classified in U.S. Industry 722515, Snack and Nonalcoholic Beverage Bars;
- Preparing and serving alcoholic beverages and known as bars, taverns, or nightclubs--are classified in Industry 722410, Drinking Places (Alcoholic Beverages); and
- Presenting live theatrical productions and providing food and beverages for consumption on the premises--are classified in Industry 711110, Theater Companies and Dinner Theaters.

722513 Limited-Service Restaurants

This U.S. industry comprises establishments primarily engaged in providing food services (except snack and nonalcoholic beverage bars) where patrons generally order or select items and pay before eating. Food and drink may be consumed on premises, taken out, or delivered to the customer's location. Some establishments in this industry may provide these food services in combination with selling alcoholic beverages.

Illustrative Examples:

Delicatessen restaurants
Pizza delivery shops
Family restaurants, limited-service
Takeout eating places
Fast-food restaurants
Fast casual restaurants
Takeout sandwich shops
Limited-service pizza parlors

T—Canadian, Mexican, and United States industries are comparable.

Cross-References. Establishments primarily engaged in--

- Preparing and serving meals for immediate consumption using cafeteria-style serving equipment, known as cafeterias--are classified in U.S. Industry 722514, Cafeterias, Grill Buffets, and Buffets;
- Providing food services to patrons who order and are served while seated and pay after eating--are classified in U.S. Industry 722511, Full-Service Restaurants;
- Selling a specialty snack (e.g., ice cream, frozen yogurt, candy, cookies) or nonalcoholic beverages, except from mobile vehicles, for consumption on or near the premises--are classified in U.S. Industry 722515, Snack and Nonalcoholic Beverage Bars;
- Retailing confectionery goods and nuts not packaged for immediate consumption--are classified in U.S. Industry 445292, Confectionery and Nut Stores;
- Retailing baked goods (e.g., pretzels, doughnuts, cookies, and bagels) not baked on the premises and not for immediate consumption--are classified in U.S. Industry 445291, Baked Goods Stores; and
- Preparing and serving alcoholic beverages, known as bars, taverns, or nightclubs--are classified in Industry 722410, Drinking Places (Alcoholic Beverages).

722514 Cafeterias, Grill Buffets, and Buffets

This U.S. industry comprises establishments, known as cafeterias, grill buffets, or buffets, primarily engaged in preparing and serving meals for immediate consumption using cafeteria-style or buffet serving equipment, such as steam tables, refrigerated areas, display grills, and self-service nonalcoholic beverage dispensing equipment. Patrons select from food and drink items on display in a continuous cafeteria line or from buffet stations.

Cross-References. Establishments primarily engaged in--

- Providing food services to patrons who order and are served while seated and pay after eating--are classified in U.S. Industry 722511, Full-Service Restaurants;
- Providing food services where patrons generally order or select items and pay before eating, other than mobile food services, cafeterias, grill buffets, buffets, and snack and nonalcoholic beverage bars--are classified in U.S. Industry 722513, Limited-Service Restaurants; and
- Selling a specialty snack (e.g., ice cream, frozen yogurt, cookies, popcorn) or nonalcoholic beverage, except from mobile vehicles, for consumption on or near the premises--are classified in U.S. Industry 722515, Snack and Nonalcoholic Beverage Bars.

722515 Snack and Nonalcoholic Beverage Bars

This U.S. industry comprises establishments primarily engaged in (1) preparing and/or serving a specialty snack, such as ice cream, frozen yogurt, cookies, or popcorn, or (2) serving nonalcoholic beverages, such as coffee, juices, or sodas for consumption on or near the premises. These establishments may carry and sell a combination of snack, nonalcoholic beverage, and other related products (e.g., coffee beans, mugs, coffee makers) but generally promote and sell a unique snack or nonalcoholic beverage.

Illustrative Examples:

Beverage bars
Carryout service doughnut shops with on-premises baking
Carryout service bagel shops with on-premises baking
Coffee shops, on-premises brewing
Carryout service pretzel shops with on-premises baking
Carryout service cookie shops with on-premises baking
Ice cream parlors

Cross-References. Establishments primarily engaged in--

- Selling one or more of the following food specialties (except from mobile vehicles): hamburgers, hot dogs, pizza, chicken, specialty cuisines--are classified based on the type of food service provided to patrons;

T—Canadian, Mexican, and United States industries are comparable.

- Preparing and serving snacks and nonalcoholic beverages from mobile vehicles--are classified in Industry 722330, Mobile Food Services;
- Retailing confectionery goods and nuts not packaged for immediate consumption--are classified in U.S. Industry 445292, Confectionery and Nut Stores; and
- Retailing baked goods (e.g., pretzels, doughnuts, cookies, and bagels) not baked on the premises and not for immediate consumption--are classified in U.S. Industry 445291, Baked Goods Stores.

T—Canadian, Mexican, and United States industries are comparable.

Sector 81--Other Services (except Public Administration)[T]

The Sector as a Whole

The Other Services (except Public Administration) sector comprises establishments engaged in providing services not specifically provided for elsewhere in the classification system. Establishments in this sector are primarily engaged in activities such as equipment and machinery repairing, promoting or administering religious activities, grantmaking, advocacy, and providing drycleaning and laundry services, personal care services, death care services, pet care services, photofinishing services, temporary parking services, and dating services.

Private households that engage in employing workers on or about the premises in activities primarily concerned with the operation of the household are included in this sector.

Excluded from this sector are establishments primarily engaged in retailing new equipment and also performing repairs and general maintenance on equipment. These establishments are classified in Sector 44-45, Retail Trade.

811 Repair and Maintenance[T]

Industries in the Repair and Maintenance subsector restore machinery, equipment, and other products to working order. These establishments also typically provide general or routine maintenance (i.e., servicing) on such products to ensure they work efficiently and to prevent breakdown and unnecessary repairs.

The NAICS structure for this subsector brings together most types of repair and maintenance establishments and categorizes them based on production processes (i.e., on the type of repair and maintenance activity performed, and the necessary skills, expertise, and processes that are found in different repair and maintenance establishments). This NAICS classification does not delineate between repair services provided to businesses versus those that serve households. Although some industries primarily serve either businesses or households, separation by class of customer is limited by the fact that many establishments serve both. Establishments repairing computers and consumer electronics products are two examples of such overlap.

The Repair and Maintenance subsector does not include all establishments that do repair and maintenance. For example, a substantial amount of repair is done by establishments that also manufacture machinery, equipment, and other goods. These establishments are included in the Manufacturing sector in NAICS. In addition, repair of transportation equipment is often provided by or based at transportation facilities, such as airports and seaports, and these activities are included in the Transportation and Warehousing sector. A particularly unique situation exists with repair of buildings. Plumbing, electrical installation and repair, painting and decorating, and other construction-related establishments are often involved in performing installation or other work on new construction as well as providing repair services on existing structures. While some specialize in repair, it is difficult to distinguish between the two types and all are included in the Construction sector.

Excluded from this subsector are establishments primarily engaged in rebuilding or remanufacturing machinery and equipment. These are classified in Sector 31-33, Manufacturing. Also excluded are retail establishments that provide after-sale services and repair. These are classified in Sector 44-45, Retail Trade.

8111 Automotive Repair and Maintenance[T]

This industry group comprises establishments involved in providing repair and maintenance services for automotive vehicles, such as passenger cars, trucks, and vans, and all trailers. Establishments in this industry group employ mechanics with specialized technical skills to diagnose and repair the mechanical and electrical systems for automotive vehicles, repair automotive interiors, and paint or repair automotive exteriors.

81111 Automotive Mechanical and Electrical Repair and Maintenance[T]

This industry comprises establishments primarily engaged in providing mechanical or electrical repair and maintenance services for automotive vehicles, such as passenger cars, trucks, and vans, and all trailers. These establishments may specialize in a single service or may provide a wide range of these services.

T—Canadian, Mexican, and United States industries are comparable.

Cross-References. Establishments primarily engaged in--

- Retailing automotive vehicles and automotive parts and accessories and also providing automotive vehicle repair services--are classified in Subsector 441, Motor Vehicle and Parts Dealers;
- Retailing motor fuels and also providing automotive vehicle repair services--are classified in Industry Group 4471, Gasoline Stations;
- Changing motor oil and lubricating the chassis of automotive vehicles--are classified in Industry 81119, Other Automotive Repair and Maintenance;
- Providing automotive vehicle air-conditioning repair--are classified in Industry 81119, Other Automotive Repair and Maintenance; and
- Motorcycle repair and maintenance services--are classified in Industry 81149, Other Personal and Household Goods Repair and Maintenance.

811111 General Automotive Repair

This U.S. industry comprises establishments primarily engaged in providing (1) a wide range of mechanical and electrical repair and maintenance services for automotive vehicles, such as passenger cars, trucks, and vans, and all trailers or (2) engine repair and replacement.

Illustrative Examples:

Automobile repair garages (except gasoline service stations)
General automotive repair shops

Cross-References. Establishments primarily engaged in--

- Retailing new automotive parts and accessories and also providing automotive vehicle repair services--are classified in Industry 441310, Automotive Parts and Accessories Stores;
- Changing motor oil and lubricating the chassis of automotive vehicles--are classified in U.S. Industry 811191, Automotive Oil Change and Lubrication Shops;
- Replacing and repairing automotive vehicle exhaust systems--are classified in U.S. Industry 811112, Automotive Exhaust System Repair;
- Replacing and repairing automotive vehicle transmissions--are classified in U.S. Industry 811113, Automotive Transmission Repair;
- Retailing motor fuels and also providing automotive vehicle repair services--are classified in Industry Group 4471, Gasoline Stations;
- Retailing automobiles and light trucks for highway use and also providing automotive vehicle repair services--are classified in Industry Group 4411, Automobile Dealers; and
- Motorcycle repair and maintenance services--are classified in Industry 811490, Other Personal and Household Goods Repair and Maintenance.

811112 Automotive Exhaust System Repair

This U.S. industry comprises establishments primarily engaged in replacing or repairing exhaust systems of automotive vehicles, such as passenger cars, trucks, and vans.

Illustrative Examples:

Automotive exhaust system replacement and repair shops

Cross-References.

Establishments primarily engaged in motorcycle repair and maintenance services are classified in Industry 811490, Other Personal and Household Goods Repair and Maintenance.

T—Canadian, Mexican, and United States industries are comparable.

811113 Automotive Transmission Repair

This U.S. industry comprises establishments primarily engaged in replacing or repairing transmissions of automotive vehicles, such as passenger cars, trucks, and vans.

Cross-References.

Establishments primarily engaged in motorcycle repair and maintenance services are classified in Industry 811490, Other Personal and Household Goods Repair and Maintenance.

811118 Other Automotive Mechanical and Electrical Repair and Maintenance

This U.S. industry comprises establishments primarily engaged in providing specialized mechanical or electrical repair and maintenance services (except engine repair and replacement, exhaust systems repair, and transmission repair) for automotive vehicles, such as passenger cars, trucks, and vans, and all trailers.

Illustrative Examples:

Automotive brake repair shops
Automotive radiator repair shops
Automotive electrical repair shops
Automotive tune-up shops

Cross-References. Establishments primarily engaged in--

- Providing a wide range of mechanical and electrical automotive vehicle repair or specializing in engine repair or replacement--are classified in U.S. Industry 811111, General Automotive Repair;
- Replacing and repairing automotive vehicle exhaust systems--are classified in U.S. Industry 811112, Automotive Exhaust System Repair;
- Replacing and repairing automotive vehicle transmissions--are classified in U.S. Industry 811113, Automotive Transmission Repair;
- Providing automotive vehicle air-conditioning repair--are classified in U.S. Industry 811198, All Other Automotive Repair and Maintenance; and
- Motorcycle repair and maintenance services--are classified in Industry 811490, Other Personal and Household Goods Repair and Maintenance.

81112 Automotive Body, Paint, Interior, and Glass Repair[T]

This industry comprises establishments primarily engaged in providing one or more of the following: (1) repairing or customizing automotive vehicles, such as passenger cars, trucks, and vans, and all trailer bodies and interiors; (2) painting automotive vehicle and trailer bodies; (3) replacing, repairing, and/or tinting automotive vehicle glass; and (4) customizing automobile, truck, and van interiors for the physically disabled or other customers with special requirements.

Illustrative Examples:

Automotive body shops
Automotive paint shops
Automotive glass shops
Automotive windshield repair shops

Cross-References. Establishments primarily engaged in--

- Manufacturing automotive vehicles and trailers or customizing these vehicles on an assembly line basis--are classified in Subsector 336, Transportation Equipment Manufacturing; and
- Motorcycle repair and maintenance services--are classified in Industry 81149, Other Personal and Household Goods Repair and Maintenance.

T—Canadian, Mexican, and United States industries are comparable.

811121 Automotive Body, Paint, and Interior Repair and Maintenance

This U.S. industry comprises establishments primarily engaged in repairing or customizing automotive vehicles, such as passenger cars, trucks, and vans, and all trailer bodies and interiors; and/or painting automotive vehicles and trailer bodies.

Illustrative Examples:

Automotive body shops
Automotive body conversion services
Automotive upholstery shops
Automotive paint shops

Cross-References. Establishments primarily engaged in--

- Automotive glass replacement, repair and/or tinting--are classified in U.S. Industry 811122, Automotive Glass Replacement Shops;
- Manufacturing automotive vehicles and trailers or customizing these vehicles on an assembly line basis--are classified in Subsector 336, Transportation Equipment Manufacturing; and
- Motorcycle repair and maintenance services--are classified in Industry 811490, Other Personal and Household Goods Repair and Maintenance.

811122 Automotive Glass Replacement Shops

This U.S. industry comprises establishments primarily engaged in replacing, repairing, and/or tinting automotive vehicle glass, such as passenger car, truck, and van glass.

Cross-References.

Establishments primarily engaged in motorcycle repair and maintenance services are classified in Industry 811490, Other Personal and Household Goods Repair and Maintenance.

81119 Other Automotive Repair and Maintenance[T]

This industry comprises establishments primarily engaged in providing automotive repair and maintenance services (except mechanical and electrical repair and maintenance; transmission repair; and body, paint, interior, and glass repair) for automotive vehicles, such as passenger cars, trucks, and vans, and all trailers.

Illustrative Examples:

Automotive air-conditioning repair shops
Automotive tire repair (except retreading) shops
Automotive oil change and lubrication shops
Car washes
Automotive rustproofing and undercoating shops

Cross-References. Establishments primarily engaged in--

- Tire retreading or recapping--are classified in Industry 32621, Tire Manufacturing;
- Automotive vehicle mechanical and electrical repair and maintenance--are classified in Industry 81111, Automotive Mechanical and Electrical Repair and Maintenance;
- Automotive body, paint, interior, and glass repair--are classified in Industry 81112, Automotive Body, Paint, Interior, and Glass Repair; and
- Motorcycle repair and maintenance services--are classified in Industry 81149, Other Personal and Household Goods Repair and Maintenance.

T—Canadian, Mexican, and United States industries are comparable.

811191 Automotive Oil Change and Lubrication Shops

This U.S. industry comprises establishments primarily engaged in changing motor oil and lubricating the chassis of automotive vehicles, such as passenger cars, trucks, and vans.

Cross-References.

Establishments primarily engaged in motorcycle repair and maintenance services are classified in Industry 811490, Other Personal and Household Goods Repair and Maintenance.

811192 Car Washes

This U.S. industry comprises establishments primarily engaged in cleaning, washing, and/or waxing automotive vehicles, such as passenger cars, trucks, and vans, and trailers.

Illustrative Examples:

Automotive detail shops
Mobile car and truck washes
Car washes

811198 All Other Automotive Repair and Maintenance

This U.S. industry comprises establishments primarily engaged in providing automotive repair and maintenance services (except mechanical and electrical repair and maintenance; body, paint, interior, and glass repair; motor oil change and lubrication; and car washing) for automotive vehicles, such as passenger cars, trucks, and vans, and all trailers.

Illustrative Examples:

Automotive air-conditioning repair shops
Automotive tire repair (except retreading) shops
Automotive rustproofing and undercoating shops

Cross-References. Establishments primarily engaged in--

- Tire retreading or recapping--are classified in U.S. Industry 326212, Tire Retreading;
- Providing a range of mechanical and electrical automotive vehicle repair or specializing in engine repair or replacement--are classified in U.S. Industry 811111, General Automotive Repair;
- Replacing and repairing automotive vehicle exhaust systems--are classified in U.S. Industry 811112, Automotive Exhaust System Repair;
- Replacing and repairing automotive vehicle transmissions--are classified in U.S. Industry 811113, Automotive Transmission Repair;
- Repairing or customizing automotive vehicle bodies and interiors--are classified in U.S. Industry 811121, Automotive Body, Paint, and Interior Repair and Maintenance;
- Replacing, repairing, and/or tinting automotive glass--are classified in U.S. Industry 811122, Automotive Glass Replacement Shops;
- Changing motor oil and lubricating the chassis of automotive vehicles--are classified in U.S. Industry 811191, Automotive Oil Change and Lubrication Shops;
- Cleaning, washing, and/or waxing automotive vehicles and trailers--are classified in U.S. Industry 811192, Car Washes;
- Motorcycle repair and maintenance services--are classified in Industry 811490, Other Personal and Household Goods Repair and Maintenance; and
- Retailing and installing automotive audio equipment--are classified in Industry 441310, Automotive Parts and Accessories Stores.

T—Canadian, Mexican, and United States industries are comparable.

8112 Electronic and Precision Equipment Repair and Maintenance[T]

81121 Electronic and Precision Equipment Repair and Maintenance[T]

This industry comprises establishments primarily engaged in repairing and maintaining one or more of the following: (1) consumer electronic equipment; (2) computers; (3) office machines; (4) communication equipment; and (5) other electronic and precision equipment and instruments, without retailing these products as new. Establishments in this industry repair items, such as microscopes, radar and sonar equipment, televisions, stereos, video recorders, computers, fax machines, photocopying machines, two-way radios and other communications equipment, scientific instruments, and medical equipment.

Cross-References. Establishments primarily engaged in--

- Installing and monitoring home security systems--are classified in Industry 56162, Security Systems Services;
- Retailing new radios, televisions, and other consumer electronics and also providing repair services--are classified in Industry 44314, Electronics and Appliance Stores;
- Retailing new computers and computer peripherals and also providing repair services--are classified in Industry 44314, Electronics and Appliance Stores;
- Retailing new cellular telephones and communication service plans, and also providing repair services--are classified in Industry 51731, Wired and Wireless Telecommunications Carriers;
- Rewinding armatures and rebuilding electric motors on a factory basis--are classified in Industry 33531, Electrical Equipment Manufacturing; and
- Factory rebuilding or overhauling of electronic and precision equipment--are classified in the Manufacturing sector by type of equipment.

811211 Consumer Electronics Repair and Maintenance

This U.S. industry comprises establishments primarily engaged in repairing and maintaining consumer electronics, such as televisions, stereos, speakers, video recorders, CD and DVD players, radios, and cameras, without retailing new consumer electronics.

Cross-References. Establishments primarily engaged in--

- Repairing computers and peripheral equipment--are classified in U.S. Industry 811212, Computer and Office Machine Repair and Maintenance;
- Installing and monitoring home security systems--are classified in U.S. Industry 561621, Security Systems Services (except Locksmiths);
- Retailing new radios, televisions, and other consumer electronics and also providing repair services--are classified in U.S. Industry 443142, Electronics Stores; and
- Repairing telephones, fax machines, and two-way radios--are classified in U.S. Industry 811213, Communication Equipment Repair and Maintenance.

811212 Computer and Office Machine Repair and Maintenance

This U.S. industry comprises establishments primarily engaged in repairing and maintaining computers and office machines without retailing new computers and office machines, such as photocopying machines; computer terminals, storage devices, and printers; and CD-ROM drives.

Cross-References. Establishments primarily engaged in--

- Retailing new computers and computer peripherals and also providing repair services--are classified in U.S. Industry 443142, Electronics Stores; and
- Repairing and servicing fax machines--are classified in U.S. Industry 811213, Communication Equipment Repair and Maintenance.

T—Canadian, Mexican, and United States industries are comparable.

811213 Communication Equipment Repair and Maintenance

This U.S. industry comprises establishments primarily engaged in repairing and maintaining communication equipment without retailing new communication equipment, such as telephones, fax machines, communications transmission equipment, and two-way radios.

Cross-References. Establishments primarily engaged in--

- Retailing new cellular telephones and communication service plans, and also providing repair services--are classified in U.S. Industry 517312, Wireless Telecommunications Carriers (except Satellite); and
- Repairing stereo and other consumer electronic equipment--are classified in U.S. Industry 811211, Consumer Electronics Repair and Maintenance.

811219 Other Electronic and Precision Equipment Repair and Maintenance

This U.S. industry comprises establishments primarily engaged in repairing and maintaining (without retailing) electronic and precision equipment (except consumer electronics, computers and office machines, and communications equipment). Establishments in this industry repair and maintain equipment, such as medical diagnostic imaging equipment, measuring and surveying instruments, laboratory instruments, and radar and sonar equipment.

Cross-References. Establishments primarily engaged in--

- Rewinding armatures and rebuilding electric motors on a factory basis--are classified in U.S. Industry 335312, Motor and Generator Manufacturing;
- Repairing stereo and other consumer electronic equipment--are classified in U.S. Industry 811211, Consumer Electronics Repair and Maintenance;
- Repairing computers and office machines--are classified in U.S. Industry 811212, Computer and Office Machine Repair and Maintenance;
- Repairing communication equipment--are classified in U.S. Industry 811213, Communication Equipment Repair and Maintenance; and
- Factory rebuilding or overhauling of electronic and precision equipment--are classified in the Manufacturing sector by type of equipment.

8113 Commercial and Industrial Machinery and Equipment (except Automotive and Electronic) Repair and Maintenance[T]

81131 Commercial and Industrial Machinery and Equipment (except Automotive and Electronic) Repair and Maintenance[T]

See industry description for 811310.

811310 Commercial and Industrial Machinery and Equipment (except Automotive and Electronic) Repair and Maintenance

This industry comprises establishments primarily engaged in the repair and maintenance of commercial and industrial machinery and equipment. Establishments in this industry either sharpen/install commercial and industrial machinery blades and saws or provide welding (e.g., automotive, general) repair services; or repair agricultural and other heavy and industrial machinery and equipment (e.g., forklifts and other material handling equipment, machine tools, commercial refrigeration equipment, construction equipment, and mining machinery).

Cross-References. Establishments primarily engaged in--

- Automotive repair (except welding) and maintenance--are classified in Industry Group 8111, Automotive Repair and Maintenance;

T—Canadian, Mexican, and United States industries are comparable.

- Repairing and maintaining electronic and precision equipment--are classified in Industry 81121, Electronic and Precision Equipment Repair and Maintenance;
- Oil well rig building, repairing, and dismantling, on a contract basis--are classified in U.S. Industry 213112, Support Activities for Oil and Gas Operations;
- Oil and gas pipeline and related structures construction and repair--are classified in Industry 237120, Oil and Gas Pipeline and Related Structures Construction;
- Repairing and servicing aircraft--are classified in Industry 488190, Other Support Activities for Air Transportation;
- Converting, rebuilding, and overhauling aircraft--are classified in Industry 33641, Aerospace Product and Parts Manufacturing;
- Repairing and servicing railroad cars and engines--are classified in Industry 488210, Support Activities for Rail Transportation;
- Rebuilding or remanufacturing railroad engines and cars--are classified in Industry 336510, Railroad Rolling Stock Manufacturing;
- Repairing and overhauling ships at floating drydocks--are classified in Industry 488390, Other Support Activities for Water Transportation;
- Repairing and overhauling ships at shipyards--are classified in U.S. Industry 336611, Ship Building and Repairing;
- Rewinding armatures or rebuilding electric motors on a factory basis--are classified in U.S. Industry 335312, Motor and Generator Manufacturing; and
- Repairing and maintaining home and garden equipment (e.g., sharpening or installing blades and saws)--are classified in U.S. Industry 811411, Home and Garden Equipment Repair and Maintenance.

8114 Personal and Household Goods Repair and Maintenance[T]

This industry group comprises establishments primarily engaged in home and garden equipment and appliance repair and maintenance; reupholstery and furniture repair; footwear and leather goods repair; and other personal and household goods repair and maintenance.

81141 Home and Garden Equipment and Appliance Repair and Maintenance[T]

This industry comprises establishments primarily engaged in repairing and servicing home and garden equipment and/or household-type appliances without retailing new equipment or appliances. Establishments in this industry repair and maintain items, such as lawnmowers, edgers, snowblowers, leaf blowers, washing machines, clothes dryers, and refrigerators.

Cross-References. Establishments primarily engaged in--

- Retailing outdoor power equipment and also providing repair services--are classified in Industry 44421, Outdoor Power Equipment Stores;
- Retailing an array of new appliances and also providing repair services--are classified in Industry 44314, Electronics and Appliance Stores;
- Repairing, servicing, or installing central heating and air-conditioning equipment--are classified in Industry 23822, Plumbing, Heating, and Air-Conditioning Contractors; and
- Repairing commercial refrigeration equipment--are classified in Industry 81131, Commercial and Industrial Machinery and Equipment (except Automotive and Electronic) Repair and Maintenance.

811411 Home and Garden Equipment Repair and Maintenance

This U.S. industry comprises establishments primarily engaged in repairing and servicing home and garden equipment without retailing new home and garden equipment, such as lawnmowers, handheld power tools, edgers, snowblowers, leaf blowers, and trimmers.

T—Canadian, Mexican, and United States industries are comparable.

Cross-References.

Establishments primarily engaged in retailing new outdoor power equipment and also providing repair services are classified in Industry 444210, Outdoor Power Equipment Stores.

811412 Appliance Repair and Maintenance

This U.S. industry comprises establishments primarily engaged in repairing and servicing household appliances without retailing new appliances, such as refrigerators, stoves, washing machines, clothes dryers, and room air-conditioners.

Cross-References. Establishments primarily engaged in--

- Installing central heating and air-conditioning equipment--are classified in Industry 238220, Plumbing, Heating, and Air-Conditioning Contractors;
- Repairing commercial refrigeration equipment--are classified in Industry 811310, Commercial and Industrial Machinery and Equipment (except Automotive and Electronic) Repair and Maintenance; and
- Retailing an array of new appliances and also providing repair services--are classified in U.S. Industry 443141, Household Appliance Stores.

81142 Reupholstery and Furniture Repair[T] See industry description for 811420.

811420 Reupholstery and Furniture Repair

This industry comprises establishments primarily engaged in one or more of the following: (1) reupholstering furniture; (2) refinishing furniture; (3) repairing furniture; and (4) repairing and restoring furniture.

Cross-References. Establishments primarily engaged in--

- Automotive vehicle and trailer upholstery repair--are classified in U.S. Industry 811121, Automotive Body, Paint, and Interior Repair and Maintenance; and
- The restoration of museum pieces--are classified in Industry 711510, Independent Artists, Writers, and Performers.

81143 Footwear and Leather Goods Repair[T] See industry description for 811430.

811430 Footwear and Leather Goods Repair

This industry comprises establishments primarily engaged in repairing footwear and/or repairing other leather or leather-like goods without retailing new footwear and leather or leather-like goods, such as handbags and briefcases.

Cross-References. Establishments primarily engaged in--

- Retailing new luggage and leather goods and also providing repair services--are classified in Industry 448320, Luggage and Leather Goods Stores;
- Shining shoes--are classified in Industry 812990, All Other Personal Services; and
- Repairing leather clothing--are classified in Industry 811490, Other Personal and Household Goods Repair and Maintenance.

81149 Other Personal and Household Goods Repair and Maintenance[T] See industry description for 811490.

T—Canadian, Mexican, and United States industries are comparable.

811490 Other Personal and Household Goods Repair and Maintenance

This industry comprises establishments primarily engaged in repairing and servicing personal or household-type goods without retailing new personal or household-type goods (except home and garden equipment, appliances, furniture, and footwear and leather goods). Establishments in this industry repair items, such as garments; watches; jewelry; musical instruments; bicycles and motorcycles; and motorboats, canoes, sailboats, and other recreational boats.

Cross-References. Establishments primarily engaged in--

- Repairing home and garden equipment--are classified in U.S. Industry 811411, Home and Garden Equipment Repair and Maintenance;
- Repairing appliances--are classified in U.S. Industry 811412, Appliance Repair and Maintenance;
- Reupholstering and repairing furniture--are classified in Industry 811420, Reupholstery and Furniture Repair;
- Repairing footwear and leather goods--are classified in Industry 811430, Footwear and Leather Goods Repair;
- Operating marinas and providing a range of other services including boat cleaning and repair--are classified in Industry 713930, Marinas; and
- Drycleaning garments--are classified in Industry Group 8123, Drycleaning and Laundry Services.

812 Personal and Laundry Services[T]

Industries in the Personal and Laundry Services subsector group establishments that provide personal and laundry services to individuals, households, and businesses. Services performed include: personal care services; death care services; laundry and drycleaning services; and a wide range of other personal services, such as pet care (except veterinary) services, photofinishing services, temporary parking services, and dating services.

The Personal and Laundry Services subsector is by no means all-inclusive of the services that could be termed personal services (i.e., those provided to individuals rather than businesses). There are many other subsectors, as well as sectors, that provide services to persons. Establishments providing legal, accounting, tax preparation, architectural, portrait photography, and similar professional services are classified in Sector 54, Professional, Scientific, and Technical Services; those providing job placement, travel arrangement, home security, interior and exterior house cleaning, exterminating, lawn and garden care, and similar support services are classified in Sector 56, Administrative and Support and Waste Management and Remediation Services; those providing health and social services are classified in Sector 62, Health Care and Social Assistance; those providing amusement and recreation services are classified in Sector 71, Arts, Entertainment, and Recreation; those providing educational instruction are classified in Sector 61, Educational Services; those providing repair services are classified in Subsector 811, Repair and Maintenance; and those providing spiritual, civic, and advocacy services are classified in Subsector 813, Religious, Grantmaking, Civic, Professional, and Similar Organizations.

8121 Personal Care Services

This industry group comprises establishments, such as barber and beauty shops, that provide appearance care services to individual consumers.

81211 Hair, Nail, and Skin Care Services

This industry comprises establishments primarily engaged in one or more of the following: (1) providing hair care services; (2) providing nail care services; and (3) providing facials or applying makeup (except permanent makeup).

Illustrative Examples:

Barber shops
Hair stylist shops
Beauty salons
Nail salons
Cosmetology salons

T—Canadian, Mexican, and United States industries are comparable.

Cross-References. Establishments primarily engaged in--

- Offering training in barbering, hair styling, or the cosmetic arts--are classified in Industry 61151, Technical and Trade Schools;
- Providing massage, electrolysis (i.e., hair removal), permanent makeup, or tanning services--are classified in Industry 81219, Other Personal Care Services; and
- Providing medical skin care services (e.g., cosmetic surgery, dermatology)--are classified in Sector 62, Health Care and Social Assistance.

812111 Barber Shops

This U.S. industry comprises establishments known as barber shops or men's hair stylist shops primarily engaged in cutting, trimming, and styling men's and boys' hair; and/or shaving and trimming men's beards.

Cross-References. Establishments primarily engaged in--

- Offering training in barbering--are classified in U.S. Industry 611511, Cosmetology and Barber Schools; and
- Providing hair care services (except establishments known as barber shops or men's hair stylists)--are classified in U.S. Industry 812112, Beauty Salons.

812112 Beauty Salons

This U.S. industry comprises establishments (except those known as barber shops or men's hair stylist shops) primarily engaged in one or more of the following: (1) cutting, trimming, shampooing, coloring, waving, or styling hair; (2) providing facials; and (3) applying makeup (except permanent makeup).

Illustrative Examples:

Beauty parlors or shops
Facial salons or shops
Combined beauty and barber shops
Hairdressing salons or shops
Cosmetology salons or shops
Unisex or women's hair stylist shops

Cross-References. Establishments primarily engaged in--

- Cutting, trimming, and styling men's and boys' hair (known as barber shops or men's hair stylist shops)--are classified in U.S. Industry 812111, Barber Shops;
- Offering training in hair styling or the cosmetic arts--are classified in U.S. Industry 611511, Cosmetology and Barber Schools;
- Providing nail care services--are classified in U.S. Industry 812113, Nail Salons;
- Providing massage, electrolysis (i.e., hair removal), permanent makeup, or tanning services--are classified in U.S. Industry 812199, Other Personal Care Services; and
- Providing medical skin care services (e.g., cosmetic surgery, dermatology)--are classified in Sector 62, Health Care and Social Assistance.

812113 Nail Salons

This U.S. industry comprises establishments primarily engaged in providing nail care services, such as manicures, pedicures, and nail extensions.

81219 Other Personal Care Services

This industry comprises establishments primarily engaged in providing personal care services (except hair, nail, facial, or nonpermanent makeup services).

T—Canadian, Mexican, and United States industries are comparable.

Illustrative Examples:

Day spas
Depilatory or electrolysis (i.e., hair removal) salons
Permanent makeup salons
Ear piercing services
Steam or turkish baths
Tanning salons
Hair replacement (except by offices of physicians) or weaving services Massage parlors
Tattoo parlors
Non-medical diet and weight reducing centers

Cross-References. Establishments primarily engaged in--

- Providing hair, nail, facial, or nonpermanent makeup services--are classified in Industry 81211, Hair, Nail, and Skin Care Services;
- Operating physical fitness facilities--are classified in Industry 71394, Fitness and Recreational Sports Centers;
- Providing personal fitness training services--are classified in Industry 81299, All Other Personal Services;
- Operating health resorts and spas that provide lodging--are classified in Industry 72111, Hotels (except Casino Hotels) and Motels; and
- Providing medical or surgical hair replacement or weight reduction services--are classified in Sector 62, Health Care and Social Assistance.

812191 Diet and Weight Reducing Centers

This U.S. industry comprises establishments primarily engaged in providing non-medical services to assist clients in attaining or maintaining a desired weight. The sale of weight reduction products, such as food supplements, may be an integral component of the program. These services typically include individual or group counseling, menu and exercise planning, and weight and body measurement monitoring.

Cross-References. Establishments primarily engaged in--

- Operating physical fitness facilities--are classified in Industry 713940, Fitness and Recreational Sports Centers;
- Providing personal fitness training services--are classified in Industry 812990, All Other Personal Services;
- Operating health resorts and spas that provide lodging--are classified in Industry 721110, Hotels (except Casino Hotels) and Motels; and
- Providing medical or surgical weight reduction--are classified in Sector 62, Health Care and Social Assistance.

812199 Other Personal Care Services

This U.S. industry comprises establishments primarily engaged in providing personal care services (except hair, nail, facial, nonpermanent makeup, or non-medical diet and weight reducing services).

Illustrative Examples:

Day spas
Depilatory or electrolysis (i.e., hair removal) salons
Saunas
Ear piercing services
Steam or turkish baths
Tanning salons
Hair replacement (except by offices of physicians) or weaving services Massage parlors
Tattoo parlors
Permanent makeup salons

T—Canadian, Mexican, and United States industries are comparable.

Cross-References. Establishments primarily engaged in--

- Cutting, trimming, and styling men's and boys' hair (known as barber shops or men's hair stylist shops)--are classified in U.S. Industry 812111, Barber Shops;
- Providing hair, facial, or nonpermanent makeup services (except establishments known as barber shops or men's hair stylist shops)--are classified in U.S. Industry 812112, Beauty Salons;
- Nail care services--are classified in U.S. Industry 812113, Nail Salons;
- Providing non-medical diet and weight reducing services--are classified in U.S. Industry 812191, Diet and Weight Reducing Centers;
- Operating health resorts and spas that provide lodging--are classified in Industry 721110, Hotels (except Casino Hotels) and Motels; and
- Providing medical or surgical hair replacement or weight reduction services--are classified in Sector 62, Health Care and Social Assistance.

8122 Death Care Services

This industry group comprises establishments primarily engaged in preparing the dead for burial or interment, conducting funerals, operating sites or structures reserved for the interment of human or animals remains, and/or cremating the dead.

81221 Funeral Homes and Funeral Services
See industry description for 812210.

812210 Funeral Homes and Funeral Services

This industry comprises establishments primarily engaged in preparing the dead for burial or interment and conducting funerals (i.e., providing facilities for wakes, arranging transportation for the dead, selling caskets and related merchandise). Funeral homes combined with crematories are included in this industry.

Cross-References.

Establishments (except funeral homes) primarily engaged in cremating the dead are classified in Industry 812220, Cemeteries and Crematories.

81222 Cemeteries and Crematories
See industry description for 812220.

812220 Cemeteries and Crematories

This industry comprises establishments primarily engaged in operating sites or structures reserved for the interment of human or animal remains and/or cremating the dead.

Illustrative Examples:

Cemetery associations (i.e., operators of cemeteries)
Memorial gardens (i.e., burial places)
Crematories (except combined with funeral homes)
Pet cemeteries
Mausoleums

Cross-References.

Crematories combined with funeral homes are classified in Industry 812210, Funeral Homes and Funeral Services.

T—Canadian, Mexican, and United States industries are comparable.

8123 Drycleaning and Laundry Services

This industry group comprises establishments primarily engaged in operating coin-operated or similar self-service laundries and drycleaners; providing drycleaning and laundry services (except coin-operated); and supplying, on a rental or contract basis, laundered items (e.g., uniforms, gowns, shop towels, etc.). Included in this industry group are establishments primarily engaged in supplying and servicing coin-operated laundry and drycleaning equipment in places of business operated by others, such as apartments and dormitories.

81231 Coin-Operated Laundries and Drycleaners
See industry description for 812310.

812310 Coin-Operated Laundries and Drycleaners

This industry comprises establishments primarily engaged in (1) operating facilities with coin-operated or similar self-service laundry and drycleaning equipment for customer use on the premises and/or (2) supplying and servicing coin-operated or similar self-service laundry and drycleaning equipment for customer use in places of business operated by others, such as apartments and dormitories.

81232 Drycleaning and Laundry Services (except Coin-Operated)
See industry description for 812320.

812320 Drycleaning and Laundry Services (except Coin-Operated)

This industry comprises establishments primarily engaged in one or more of the following: (1) providing drycleaning services (except coin-operated); (2) providing laundering services (except linen and uniform supply or coin-operated); (3) providing drop-off and pick-up sites for laundries and/or drycleaners; and (4) providing specialty cleaning services for specific types of garments and other textile items (except carpets and upholstery), such as fur, leather, or suede garments; wedding gowns; hats; draperies; and pillows. These establishments may provide all, a combination of, or none of the cleaning services on the premises.

Cross-References. Establishments primarily engaged in--

- Supplying laundered linens and uniforms on a rental or contract basis--are classified in Industry 81233, Linen and Uniform Supply;
- Operating coin-operated or similar self-service laundry or drycleaning facilities--are classified in Industry 812310, Coin-Operated Laundries and Drycleaners; and
- Cleaning used carpets and upholstery--are classified in Industry 561740, Carpet and Upholstery Cleaning Services.

81233 Linen and Uniform Supply

This industry comprises establishments primarily engaged in supplying, on a rental or contract basis, laundered items, such as uniforms, gowns and coats, table linens, bed linens, towels, clean room apparel, and treated mops or shop towels.

812331 Linen Supply

This U.S. industry comprises establishments primarily engaged in supplying, on a rental or contract basis, laundered items, such as table and bed linens; towels; diapers; and uniforms, gowns, or coats of the type used by doctors, nurses, barbers, beauticians, and waitresses.

Cross-References.

Establishments primarily engaged in supplying, on a rental or contract basis, laundered industrial work uniforms and related work clothing are classified in U.S. Industry 812332, Industrial Launderers.

T—Canadian, Mexican, and United States industries are comparable.

812332 Industrial Launderers

This U.S. industry comprises establishments primarily engaged in supplying, on a rental or contract basis, laundered industrial work uniforms and related work clothing, such as protective apparel (flame and heat resistant) and clean room apparel; dust control items, such as treated mops, rugs, mats, dust tool covers, cloths, and shop or wiping towels.

Cross-References.

Establishments primarily engaged in supplying, on a rental or contract basis, laundered uniforms, gowns or coats of the type used by doctors, nurses, barbers, beauticians, and waitresses are classified in U.S. Industry 812331, Linen Supply.

8129 Other Personal Services

This industry group comprises establishments primarily engaged in providing personal services (except personal care services, death care services, or drycleaning and laundry services).

81291 Pet Care (except Veterinary) Services
See industry description for 812910.

812910 Pet Care (except Veterinary) Services

This industry comprises establishments primarily engaged in providing pet care services (except veterinary), such as boarding, grooming, sitting, and training pets.

Cross-References. Establishments primarily engaged in--

- Practicing veterinary medicine--are classified in Industry 541940, Veterinary Services;
- Boarding horses--are classified in Industry 115210, Support Activities for Animal Production; and
- Transporting pets--are classified in U.S. Industry 485991, Special Needs Transportation.

81292 Photofinishing

This industry comprises establishments primarily engaged in developing film and/or making photographic slides, prints, and enlargements.

Cross-References.

Establishments primarily engaged in processing motion picture film for the motion picture and television industries are classified in Industry 51219, Postproduction Services and Other Motion Picture and Video Industries.

812921 Photofinishing Laboratories (except One-Hour)

This U.S. industry comprises establishments (except those known as "one-hour" photofinishing labs) primarily engaged in developing film and/or making photographic slides, prints, and enlargements.

Cross-References.

- Establishments primarily engaged in processing motion picture film for the motion picture and television industries are classified in U.S. Industry 512199, Other Motion Picture and Video Industries; and
- Establishments known as "one-hour" photofinishing labs are classified in U.S. Industry 812922, One-Hour Photofinishing.

T—Canadian, Mexican, and United States industries are comparable.

812922 One-Hour Photofinishing

This U.S. industry comprises establishments known as "one-hour" photofinishing labs primarily engaged in developing film and/or making photographic slides, prints, and enlargements on a short turnaround or while-you-wait basis.

Cross-References.

Photofinishing laboratories (except those known as "one-hour" photofinishing labs) are classified in U.S. Industry 812921, Photofinishing Laboratories (except One-Hour).

81293 Parking Lots and Garages
See industry description for 812930.

812930 Parking Lots and Garages

This industry comprises establishments primarily engaged in providing parking space for motor vehicles, usually on an hourly, daily, or monthly basis and/or valet parking services.

Cross-References.

Establishments primarily engaged in providing extended or dead storage of motor vehicles are classified in Industry 493190, Other Warehousing and Storage.

81299 All Other Personal Services
See industry description for 812990.

812990 All Other Personal Services

This industry comprises establishments primarily engaged in providing personal services (except personal care services, death care services, drycleaning and laundry services, pet care services, photofinishing services, or parking space and/or valet parking services).

Illustrative Examples:

Bail bonding or bondsperson services
Shoeshine services
Coin-operated personal services machine (e.g., blood pressure, locker, photographic, scale, shoeshine) concession operators
Social escort services
Consumer buying services
Wedding planning services
Dating services
Personal fitness training services

Cross-References. Establishments primarily engaged in--

- Providing personal care services--are classified in Industry Group 8121, Personal Care Services;
- Providing death care services--are classified in Industry Group 8122, Death Care Services;
- Providing drycleaning and laundry services--are classified in Industry Group 8123, Drycleaning and Laundry Services;
- Providing pet care (except veterinary) services--are classified in Industry 812910, Pet Care (except Veterinary) Services;
- Practicing veterinary medicine--are classified in Industry 541940, Veterinary Services;
- Providing photofinishing services--are classified in Industry 81292, Photofinishing; and
- Providing parking space for motor vehicles and/or valet parking services--are classified in Industry 812930, Parking Lots and Garages.

T—Canadian, Mexican, and United States industries are comparable.

813 Religious, Grantmaking, Civic, Professional, and Similar Organizations[T]

Industries in the Religious, Grantmaking, Civic, Professional, and Similar Organizations subsector group establishments that organize and promote religious activities; support various causes through grantmaking; advocate various social and political causes; and promote and defend the interests of their members.

The industry groups within the subsector are defined in terms of their activities, such as establishments that provide funding for specific causes or for a variety of charitable causes; establishments that advocate and actively promote causes and beliefs for the public good; and establishments that have an active membership structure to promote causes and represent the interests of their members. Establishments in this subsector may publish newsletters, books, and periodicals for distribution to their members.

8131 Religious Organizations

81311 Religious Organizations

See industry description for 813110.

813110 Religious Organizations

This industry comprises (1) establishments primarily engaged in operating religious organizations, such as churches, religious temples, and monasteries, and/or (2) establishments primarily engaged in administering an organized religion or promoting religious activities.

Illustrative Examples:

Churches
Shrines, religious
Monasteries (except schools)
Synagogues
Mosques, religious
Temples, religious

Cross-References.

- Schools, colleges, or universities operated by religious organizations are classified in Sector 61, Educational Services;
- Radio and television stations operated by religious organizations are classified in Subsector 515, Broadcasting (except Internet);
- Publishing houses operated by religious organizations are classified in Subsector 511, Publishing Industries (except Internet);
- Establishments operated by religious organizations primarily engaged in health and social assistance for individuals are classified in Sector 62, Health Care and Social Assistance; and
- Used merchandise stores operated by religious organizations are classified in Industry 453310, Used Merchandise Stores.

8132 Grantmaking and Giving Services 81321

Grantmaking and Giving Services

This industry comprises (1) establishments known as grantmaking foundations or charitable trusts and (2) establishments primarily engaged in raising funds for a wide range of social welfare activities, such as health, educational, scientific, and cultural activities.

Cross-References. Establishments primarily engaged in--

- Providing trust management services for others--are classified in Industry 52392, Portfolio Management;
- Organizing and conducting fundraising campaigns on a contract or fee basis--are classified in Industry 56149, Other Business Support Services;
- Providing telemarketing services for others--are classified in Industry 56142, Telephone Call Centers;

T—Canadian, Mexican, and United States industries are comparable.

- Raising funds for political purposes--are classified in Industry 81394, Political Organizations;
- Advocating social causes or issues--are classified in Industry 81331, Social Advocacy Organizations; and
- Conducting health research--are classified in Industry 54171, Research and Development in the Physical, Engineering, and Life Sciences.

813211 Grantmaking Foundations

This U.S. industry comprises establishments known as grantmaking foundations or charitable trusts. Establishments in this industry award grants from trust funds based on a competitive selection process or the preferences of the foundation managers and grantors; or fund a single entity, such as a museum or university.

Community foundations
Philanthropic trusts
Corporate foundations, awarding grants
Scholarship trusts
Grantmaking foundations

Cross-References.

Establishments primarily engaged in providing trust management services for others are classified in Industry 523920, Portfolio Management.

813212 Voluntary Health Organizations

This U.S. industry comprises establishments primarily engaged in raising funds for health related research, such as disease (e.g., heart, cancer, diabetes) prevention, health education, and patient services.

Illustrative Examples:

Disease awareness fundraising organizations
Health research fundraising organizations
Voluntary health organizations
Disease research (e.g., heart, cancer) fundraising

Cross-References.

- Establishments primarily engaged in raising funds for a wide range of social welfare activities, such as educational, scientific, cultural, or health, are classified in U.S. Industry 813219, Other Grantmaking and Giving Services;
- Establishments primarily engaged in organizing and conducting fundraising campaigns on a contract or fee basis are classified in U.S. Industry 561499, All Other Business Support Services;
- Establishments primarily engaged in providing telemarketing services for others are classified in U.S. Industry 561422, Telemarketing Bureaus and Other Contact Centers;
- Establishments known as grantmaking foundations or charitable trusts are classified in U.S. Industry 813211, Grantmaking Foundations; and
- Establishments primarily engaged in conducting health research are classified in Industry 54171, Research and Development in the Physical, Engineering, and Life Sciences.

813219 Other Grantmaking and Giving Services

This U.S. industry comprises establishments (except voluntary health organizations) primarily engaged in raising funds for a wide range of social welfare activities, such as educational, scientific, cultural, and health.

T—Canadian, Mexican, and United States industries are comparable.

Illustrative Examples:

Community chests
United fund councils
Federated charities
United funds for colleges

Cross-References.

- Establishments primarily engaged in raising funds for health related research are classified in U.S. Industry 813212, Voluntary Health Organizations;
- Establishments known as grantmaking foundations or charitable trusts are classified in U.S. Industry 813211, Grantmaking Foundations;
- Establishments primarily engaged in organizing and conducting fundraising campaigns on a contract or fee basis are classified in U.S. Industry 561499, All Other Business Support Services;
- Establishments primarily engaged in providing telemarketing services for others are classified in U.S. Industry 561422, Telemarketing Bureaus and Other Contact Centers;
- Establishments primarily engaged in raising funds for political purposes are classified in Industry 813940, Political Organizations; and
- Establishments primarily engaged in advocating social causes or issues are classified in Industry 81331, Social Advocacy Organizations.

8133 Social Advocacy Organizations 81331

Social Advocacy Organizations

This industry comprises establishments primarily engaged in promoting a particular cause or working for the realization of a specific social or political goal to benefit a broad or specific constituency. These organizations may solicit contributions and offer memberships to support these goals.

Illustrative Examples:

Community action advocacy organizations
Firearms advocacy organizations
Conservation advocacy organizations
Human rights advocacy organizations
Environmental advocacy organizations
Wildlife preservation organizations

Cross-References.

- Establishments primarily engaged in promoting the civic and social interests of their members are classified in Industry 81341, Civic and Social Organizations;
- Establishments primarily engaged in promoting the interests of organized labor and union employees are classified in Industry 81393, Labor Unions and Similar Labor Organizations;
- Establishments primarily engaged in providing legal services for social advocacy organizations are classified in Industry Group 5411, Legal Services;
- Establishments primarily engaged in providing community action services, such as community action services agencies, are classified in Industry 62419, Other Individual and Family Services; and
- Government establishments primarily engaged in administering, overseeing, and managing governmental ecological restoration programs are classified in Industry 92411, Administration of Air and Water Resource and Solid Waste Management Programs.

813311 Human Rights Organizations

This U.S. industry comprises establishments primarily engaged in promoting causes associated with human rights either for a broad or specific constituency. Establishments in this industry address issues, such as protecting and promoting the broad constitutional rights and civil liberties of individuals and those suffering from neglect, abuse, or exploitation; promoting the interests of specific groups, such as children, women, senior citizens, or persons with

T—Canadian, Mexican, and United States industries are comparable.

disabilities; improving relations between racial, ethnic, and cultural groups; and promoting voter education and registration. These organizations may solicit contributions and offer memberships to support these causes.

Illustrative Examples:

Civil liberties organizations
Senior citizens' advocacy organizations
Human rights advocacy organizations
Veterans' rights organizations

Cross-References. Establishments primarily engaged in--

- Promoting the interests of organized labor and union employees--are classified in Industry 813930, Labor Unions and Similar Labor Organizations; and
- Providing legal services for human rights organizations--are classified in Industry Group 5411, Legal Services.

813312 Environment, Conservation and Wildlife Organizations

This U.S. industry comprises establishments primarily engaged in promoting the preservation and protection of the environment and wildlife. Establishments in this industry address issues, such as clean air and water; global warming; conserving and developing natural resources, including land, plant, water, and energy resources; and protecting and preserving wildlife and endangered species. These organizations may solicit contributions and offer memberships to support these causes.

Illustrative Examples:

Animal rights organizations
Natural resource preservation organizations
Conservation advocacy organizations
Wildlife preservation organizations
Humane societies

Cross-References.

- Establishments primarily engaged in providing legal services for environment, conservation, and wildlife organizations are classified in Industry Group 5411, Legal Services; and
- Government establishments primarily engaged in administering, overseeing, and managing governmental ecological restoration programs are classified in Industry 924110, Administration of Air and Water Resource and Solid Waste Management Programs.

813319 Other Social Advocacy Organizations

This U.S. industry comprises establishments primarily engaged in social advocacy (except human rights and environmental protection, conservation, and wildlife preservation). Establishments in this industry address issues, such as peace and international understanding; community action (excluding civic organizations); or advancing social causes, such as firearms safety, drunk driving prevention, or drug abuse awareness. These organizations may solicit contributions and offer memberships to support these causes.

Illustrative Examples:

Community action advocacy organizations
Substance abuse prevention advocacy organizations
Firearms advocacy organizations
Taxpayers' advocacy organizations
Peace advocacy organizations

Cross-References. Establishments primarily engaged in--

- Advocating human rights issues--are classified in U.S. Industry 813311, Human Rights Organizations;

T—Canadian, Mexican, and United States industries are comparable.

- Promoting the preservation and protection of the environment and wildlife--are classified in U.S. Industry 813312, Environment, Conservation and Wildlife Organizations;
- Promoting the civic and social interests of their members--are classified in Industry 813410, Civic and Social Organizations;
- Providing legal services for social advocacy organizations--are classified in Industry Group 5411, Legal Services; and
- Providing community action services, such as community action service agencies--are classified in Industry 624190, Other Individual and Family Services.

8134 Civic and Social Organizations

81341 Civic and Social Organizations
See industry description for 813410.

813410 Civic and Social Organizations

This industry comprises establishments primarily engaged in promoting the civic and social interests of their members. Establishments in this industry may operate bars and restaurants for their members.

Illustrative Examples:

Alumni associations
Granges
Automobile clubs (except travel)
Parent-teacher associations
Booster clubs
Scouting organizations
Ethnic associations
Social clubs
Fraternal lodges
Veterans' membership organizations

Cross-References.

- Establishments of insurance offices operated by fraternal benefit organizations are classified in Subsector 524, Insurance Carriers and Related Activities;
- Establishments primarily engaged in operating residential fraternity and sorority houses are classified in Industry 721310, Rooming and Boarding Houses, Dormitories, and Workers' Camps; and
- Establishments primarily engaged in providing travel arrangements and reservation services, such as automobile travel clubs or motor travel clubs, are classified in U.S. Industry 561599, All Other Travel Arrangement and Reservation Services.

8139 Business, Professional, Labor, Political, and Similar Organizations

This industry group comprises establishments primarily engaged in promoting the interests of their members (except religious organizations, social advocacy organizations, and civic and social organizations). Examples of establishments in this industry are business associations, professional organizations, labor unions, and political organizations.

81391 Business Associations
See industry description for 813910.

813910 Business Associations

This industry comprises establishments primarily engaged in promoting the business interests of their members. These establishments may conduct research on new products and services; develop market statistics; sponsor quality and certification standards; lobby public officials; or publish newsletters, books, or periodicals for distribution to their members.

T—Canadian, Mexican, and United States industries are comparable.

Illustrative Examples:

Agricultural organizations (except youth farming organizations, farm granges)
Real estate boards
Chambers of commerce
Trade associations
Manufacturers' associations

Cross-References.

- Establishments owned by their members but organized to perform a specific business function, such as common marketing of crops, joint advertising, or buying cooperatives, are classified according to their primary activity;
- Establishments primarily engaged in promoting the professional interests of their members and the profession as a whole are classified in Industry 813920, Professional Organizations;
- Establishments primarily engaged in promoting the interests of organized labor and union employees, such as trade unions, are classified in Industry 813930, Labor Unions and Similar Labor Organizations; and
- Establishments primarily engaged in lobbying public officials (i.e., lobbyists) are classified in Industry 541820, Public Relations Agencies.

81392 Professional Organizations
See industry description for 813920.

813920 Professional Organizations

This industry comprises establishments primarily engaged in promoting the professional interests of their members and the profession as a whole. These establishments may conduct research; develop statistics; sponsor quality and certification standards; lobby public officials; or publish newsletters, books, or periodicals for distribution to their members.

Illustrative Examples:

Bar associations
Learned societies
Dentists' associations
Peer review boards
Engineers' associations
Professional standards review boards
Health professionals' associations
Scientists' associations

Cross-References. Establishments primarily engaged in--

- Promoting the business interests of their members--are classified in Industry 813910, Business Associations; and
- Lobbying public officials (i.e., lobbyists)--are classified in Industry 541820, Public Relations Agencies.

81393 Labor Unions and Similar Labor Organizations
See industry description for 813930.

813930 Labor Unions and Similar Labor Organizations

This industry comprises establishments primarily engaged in promoting the interests of organized labor and union employees.

81394 Political Organizations
See industry description for 813940.

T—Canadian, Mexican, and United States industries are comparable.

813940 Political Organizations

This industry comprises establishments primarily engaged in promoting the interests of national, state, or local political parties or candidates. Included are political groups organized to raise funds for a political party or individual candidates.

Illustrative Examples:

Campaign organizations, political
Political organizations or clubs
Political action committees (PACs)
Political parties
Political campaign organizations

Cross-References. Establishments primarily engaged in--

- Organizing and conducting fundraising campaigns on a contract or fee basis--are classified in U.S. Industry 561499, All Other Business Support Services; and
- Providing telemarketing services for others--are classified in U.S. Industry 561422, Telemarketing Bureaus and Other Contact Centers.

81399 Other Similar Organizations (except Business, Professional, Labor, and Political Organizations)
See industry description for 813990.

813990 Other Similar Organizations (except Business, Professional, Labor, and Political Organizations)

This industry comprises establishments (except religious organizations, social advocacy organizations, civic and social organizations, business associations, professional organizations, labor unions, and political organizations) primarily engaged in promoting the interests of their members.

Illustrative Examples:

Athletic associations and leagues, regulatory
Property owners' associations
Condominium and homeowners' associations
Tenants' associations (except advocacy)
Cooperative owners' associations

Cross-References. Establishments primarily engaged in--

- Operating religious organizations, such as churches, religious temples, and monasteries--are classified in Industry 813110, Religious Organizations;
- Raising funds for a wide range of social welfare activities and establishments known as grantmaking foundations or charitable trusts--are classified in Industry 81321, Grantmaking and Giving Services;
- Advocating social causes or issues--are classified in Industry 81331, Social Advocacy Organizations;
- Promoting the civic and social interests of their members--are classified in Industry 813410, Civic and Social Organizations;
- Promoting the business interests of their members--are classified in Industry 813910, Business Associations;
- Promoting the professional interests of their members and the profession as a whole--are classified in Industry 813920, Professional Organizations;
- Promoting the interests of organized labor and union employees--are classified in Industry 813930, Labor Unions and Similar Labor Organizations;
- Promoting the interests of national, state, or local political parties or candidates--are classified in Industry 813940, Political Organizations; and
- Providing recreational and amusement services, such as recreational or youth sports league teams--are

T—Canadian, Mexican, and United States industries are comparable.

814 Private Households[T]

Industries in the Private Households subsector include private households that engage in employing workers on or about the premises in activities primarily concerned with the operation of the household. These private households may employ individuals, such as cooks, maids, butlers, and outside workers, such as gardeners, caretakers, and other maintenance workers.

8141 Private Households[T]

81411 Private Households[T] See industry description for 814110.

814110 Private Households

This industry comprises private households primarily engaged in employing workers on or about the premises in activities primarily concerned with the operation of the household. These private households may employ individuals, such as cooks, maids, nannies, butlers, and outside workers, such as gardeners, caretakers, and other maintenance workers.

T—Canadian, Mexican, and United States industries are comparable.

Sector 92--Public Administration[T]

The Sector as a Whole

The Public Administration sector consists of establishments of federal, state, and local government agencies that administer, oversee, and manage public programs and have executive, legislative, or judicial authority over other institutions within a given area. These agencies also set policy, create laws, adjudicate civil and criminal legal cases, and provide for public safety and for national defense. In general, government establishments in the Public Administration sector oversee governmental programs and activities that are not performed by private establishments. Establishments in this sector typically are engaged in the organization and financing of the production of public goods and services, most of which are provided for free or at prices that are not economically significant.

Government establishments also engage in a wide range of productive activities covering not only public goods and services but also individual goods and services similar to those produced in sectors typically identified with private-sector establishments. In general, ownership is not a criterion for classification in NAICS. Therefore, government establishments engaged in the production of private-sector-like goods and services should be classified in the same industry as private-sector establishments engaged in similar activities.

As a practical matter, it is difficult to identify separate establishment detail for many government agencies. To the extent that separate establishment records are available, the administration of governmental programs is classified in Sector 92, Public Administration, while the operation of governmental programs is classified elsewhere in NAICS based on the activities performed. For example, the governmental administrative authority for an airport is classified in Industry 92612, Regulation and Administration of Transportation Programs, while operating the airport is classified in Industry 48811, Airport Operations. When separate records for multi-establishment companies are not available to distinguish between the administration of a governmental program and the operation of it, the establishment is classified in Sector 92, Public Administration.

Examples of government-provided goods and services that are classified in sectors other than Public Administration include: schools, classified in Sector 61, Educational Services; hospitals, classified in Subsector 622, Hospitals; establishments operating transportation facilities, classified in Sector 48-49, Transportation and Warehousing; the operation of utilities, classified in Sector 22, Utilities; and the Government Printing Office, classified in Subsector 323, Printing and Related Support Activities.

921 Executive, Legislative, and Other General Government Support

The Executive, Legislative, and Other General Government Support subsector groups offices of government executives, legislative bodies, public finance, and general government support.

9211 Executive, Legislative, and Other General Government Support

92111 Executive Offices

See industry description for 921110.

921110 Executive Offices

This industry comprises government establishments serving as offices of chief executives and their advisory committees and commissions. This industry includes offices of the president, governors, and mayors, in addition to executive advisory commissions.

92112 Legislative Bodies

See industry description for 921120.

T—Canadian, Mexican, and United States industries are comparable.

921120 Legislative Bodies

This industry comprises government establishments serving as legislative bodies and their advisory committees and commissions. Included in this industry are legislative bodies, such as Congress, state legislatures, and advisory and study legislative commissions.

92113 Public Finance Activities
See industry description for 921130.

921130 Public Finance Activities

This industry comprises government establishments primarily engaged in public finance, taxation, and monetary policy. Included are financial administration activities, such as monetary policy; tax administration and collection; custody and disbursement of funds; debt and investment administration; auditing activities; and government employee retirement trust fund administration.

Cross-References. Establishments primarily engaged in--

- Administering income maintenance programs--are classified in Industry 923130, Administration of Human Resource Programs (except Education, Public Health, and Veterans' Affairs Programs);
- Regulating insurance and banking institutions--are classified in Industry 926150, Regulation, Licensing, and Inspection of Miscellaneous Commercial Sectors; and
- Performing central banking functions, such as issuing currency and acting as the fiscal agent for the central government--are classified in Industry 521110, Monetary Authorities-Central Bank.

92114 Executive and Legislative Offices, Combined
See industry description for 921140.

921140 Executive and Legislative Offices, Combined

This industry comprises government establishments serving as councils and boards of commissioners or supervisors and such bodies where the chief executive (e.g., county executive or city mayor) is a member of the legislative body (e.g., county or city council) itself.

Cross-References. Establishments primarily engaged in--

- Serving as offices of chief executives--are classified in Industry 921110, Executive Offices; and
- Serving as legislative bodies--are classified in Industry 921120, Legislative Bodies.

92115 American Indian and Alaska Native Tribal Governments
See industry description for 921150.

921150 American Indian and Alaska Native Tribal Governments

This industry comprises American Indian and Alaska Native governing bodies. Establishments in this industry perform legislative, judicial, and administrative functions for their American Indian and Alaska Native lands. Included in this industry are American Indian and Alaska Native councils, courts, and law enforcement bodies.

Cross-References.

- Establishments primarily engaged in providing funding for American Indian and Alaska Native tribal programs through commercial activities, such as gaming, are classified in the industry of the commercial activity; and
- Government establishments providing public administration of American Indian and Alaska Native affairs are classified in Industry 921190, Other General Government Support.

T—Canadian, Mexican, and United States industries are comparable.

92119 Other General Government Support
See industry description for 921190.

921190 Other General Government Support

This industry comprises government establishments primarily engaged in providing general support for government. Such support services include personnel services, election boards, and other general government support establishments that are not classified elsewhere in public administration.

Illustrative Examples:

Civil rights commissions
Personnel offices, government
Civil service commissions
Supply agencies, government
General services departments, government

Cross-References.

- Government establishments primarily engaged in serving as offices of chief executives and their advisory committees and commissions are classified in Industry 921110, Executive Offices;
- Government establishments primarily engaged in serving as legislative bodies and their advisory committees and commissions are classified in Industry 921120, Legislative Bodies;
- Government establishments primarily engaged in providing administration of public finance, tax collection, and monetary policy programs are classified in Industry 921130, Public Finance Activities;
- Government establishments primarily engaged in serving as combined executive and legislative offices are classified in Industry 921140, Executive and Legislative Offices, Combined; and
- Establishments primarily engaged in serving as American Indian or Alaska Native tribal leadership are classified in Industry 921150, American Indian and Alaska Native Tribal Governments.

922 Justice, Public Order, and Safety Activities

The Justice, Public Order, and Safety Activities subsector groups government establishments engaged in the administration of justice, public order, and safety programs.

9221 Justice, Public Order, and Safety Activities

92211 Courts
See industry description for 922110.

922110 Courts

This industry comprises civilian courts of law (except American Indian and Alaska Native tribal courts). Included in this industry are civilian courts, courts of law, and sheriffs' offices conducting court functions only.

Cross-References.

- Government establishments primarily engaged in operating military courts are classified in Industry 928110, National Security; and
- Establishments primarily engaged in operating American Indian or Alaska Native tribal courts are classified in Industry 921150, American Indian and Alaska Native Tribal Governments.

92212 Police Protection
See industry description for 922120.

T—Canadian, Mexican, and United States industries are comparable.

922120 Police Protection

This industry comprises government establishments primarily engaged in criminal and civil law enforcement, police, traffic safety, and other activities related to the enforcement of the law and preservation of order. Combined police and fire departments are included in this industry.

Cross-References.

- Government establishments primarily engaged in prosecution are classified in Industry 922130, Legal Counsel and Prosecution;
- Government establishments primarily engaged in collection of law enforcement statistics are classified in Industry 922190, Other Justice, Public Order, and Safety Activities;
- Government establishments primarily engaged in providing police service for the military or National Guard are classified in Industry 928110, National Security;
- Government establishments primarily engaged in providing police service for tribal governments are classified in Industry 921150, American Indian and Alaska Native Tribal Governments;
- Government establishments primarily engaged in enforcing immigration laws are classified in Industry 928120, International Affairs;
- Sheriffs' offices conducting court functions only are classified in Industry 922110, Courts; and
- Private establishments primarily engaged in providing security and investigation services are classified in Industry 56161, Investigation, Guard, and Armored Car Services.

92213 Legal Counsel and Prosecution
See industry description for 922130.

922130 Legal Counsel and Prosecution

This industry comprises government establishments primarily engaged in providing legal counsel or prosecution services for the government.

Illustrative Examples:

Attorney generals' offices
Public defenders' offices
District attorneys' offices
Public prosecutors' offices

Cross-References.

Government establishments primarily engaged in collecting criminal justice statistics are classified in Industry 922190, Other Justice, Public Order, and Safety Activities.

92214 Correctional Institutions
See industry description for 922140.

922140 Correctional Institutions

This industry comprises government establishments primarily engaged in managing and operating correctional institutions. The facility is generally designed for the confinement, correction, and rehabilitation of adult and/or juvenile offenders sentenced by a court.

Illustrative Examples:

Correctional institutions, public administration
Penitentiaries, public administration
Detention centers, public administration
Prisons, public administration
Jails, public administration

T—Canadian, Mexican, and United States industries are comparable.

Cross-References.

- Government establishments primarily engaged in operating halfway houses for ex-criminal offenders and delinquent youths are classified in Industry 623990, Other Residential Care Facilities; and
- Establishments primarily engaged in managing or operating correctional facilities owned by others are classified in Industry 561210, Facilities Support Services.

92215 Parole Offices and Probation Offices
See industry description for 922150.

922150 Parole Offices and Probation Offices

This industry comprises government establishments primarily engaged in judicially administering probation offices, parole offices and boards, and pardon boards.

Cross-References.

- Private establishments primarily engaged in providing parole or probation services are classified in Industry 624190, Other Individual and Family Services; and
- Government establishments primarily engaged in providing probation, parole, and pardon activities as an integral part of a central administrative corrections' office are classified in Industry 922140, Correctional Institutions.

92216 Fire Protection
See industry description for 922160.

922160 Fire Protection

This industry comprises government establishments primarily engaged in firefighting and other related fire protection activities. Government establishments providing combined fire protection and ambulance or rescue services are classified in this industry.

Cross-References. Establishments primarily engaged in--

- Forest firefighting--are classified in Industry 115310, Support Activities for Forestry;
- Providing combined police and fire protection services--are classified in Industry 922120, Police Protection;
- Providing firefighting services as a commercial activity--are classified in Industry 561990, All Other Support Services; and
- Providing ambulance services without fire protection service--are classified in Industry 621910, Ambulance Services.

92219 Other Justice, Public Order, and Safety Activities
See industry description for 922190.

922190 Other Justice, Public Order, and Safety Activities

This industry comprises government establishments primarily engaged in public order and safety (except courts, police protection, legal counsel and prosecution, correctional institutions, parole offices, probation offices, pardon boards, and fire protection). These establishments include the general administration of public order and safety programs. Government establishments responsible for the collection of statistics on public safety are included in this industry.
T—Canadian, Mexican, and United States industries are comparable.

Illustrative Examples:

Consumer product safety commissions, public administration
Emergency planning and management offices, government
Disaster preparedness and management offices, government
Public safety bureaus and statistics centers, government

Cross-References. Government establishments primarily engaged in--

- Serving as civilian courts of law (except American Indian and Alaska Native tribal courts)--are classified in Industry 922110, Courts;
- Criminal and civil law enforcement, police, traffic safety, and similar activities related to the enforcement of law--are classified in Industry 922120, Police Protection;
- Providing legal counsel to or prosecution services for their governments--are classified in Industry 922130, Legal Counsel and Prosecution;
- The confinement, correction, and rehabilitation of adult and juvenile offenders sentenced by a court--are classified in Industry 922140, Correctional Institutions;
- Judicially administering probation offices, parole offices and boards, and pardon boards--are classified in Industry 922150, Parole Offices and Probation Offices; and
- Firefighting and other related fire protection activities--are classified in Industry 922160, Fire Protection.

923 Administration of Human Resource Programs

The Administration of Human Resource Programs subsector groups government establishments primarily engaged in the administration of human resource programs.

9231 Administration of Human Resource Programs

92311 Administration of Education Programs
See industry description for 923110.

923110 Administration of Education Programs

This industry comprises government establishments primarily engaged in the central coordination, planning, supervision, and administration of funds, policies, intergovernmental activities, statistical reports and data collection, and centralized programs for educational administration. Government scholarship programs are included in this industry.

Illustrative Examples:

Education offices, nonoperating, public administration
State education departments
Education statistics centers, government
University regents or boards, government

Cross-References.

Schools and local school boards are classified in Subsector 611, Educational Services.

92312 Administration of Public Health Programs
See industry description for 923120.

923120 Administration of Public Health Programs

This industry comprises government establishments primarily engaged in the planning, administration, and coordination of public health programs and services, including environmental health activities, mental health,

T—Canadian, Mexican, and United States industries are comparable.

categorical health programs, health statistics, and immunization services. Government establishments primarily engaged in conducting public health-related inspections are included in this industry.

Illustrative Examples:

Communicable disease program administration, public administration
Mental health program administration, public administration
Coroners' offices, public administration
Public health program administration, nonoperating, public administration
Health program administration, public administration

Cross-References. Government establishments primarily engaged in--

- Operating hospitals (i.e., government or military)--are classified in Subsector 622, Hospitals;
- Providing health care in a clinical setting (i.e., military or government clinics)--are classified in Subsector 621, Ambulatory Health Care Services; and
- Inspecting food, plants, animals, and other agriculture products--are classified in Industry 926140, Regulation of Agricultural Marketing and Commodities.

92313 Administration of Human Resource Programs (except Education, Public Health, and Veterans' Affairs Programs)
See industry description for 923130.

923130 Administration of Human Resource Programs (except Education, Public Health, and Veterans' Affairs Programs)

This industry comprises government establishments primarily engaged in the planning, administration, and coordination of programs for public assistance, social work, and welfare activities. The administration of Social Security, disability insurance, Medicare, unemployment insurance, and workers' compensation programs are included in this industry.

Cross-References. Government establishments primarily engaged in--

- Administering veterans' programs--are classified in Industry 923140, Administration of Veterans' Affairs;
- Operating state employment job service offices--are classified in U.S. Industry 561311, Employment Placement Agencies; and
- Operating programs for public assistance, social work, and welfare--are classified in Subsector 624, Social Assistance.

92314 Administration of Veterans' Affairs
See industry description for 923140.

923140 Administration of Veterans' Affairs

This industry comprises government establishments primarily engaged in the administration of programs of assistance, training, counseling, and other services to veterans and their dependents, heirs, or survivors. Included in this industry are Veterans' Affairs offices that maintain liaison and coordinate activities with other service organizations and governmental agencies.

Cross-References.

- Government establishments operating veterans' hospitals are classified in Subsector 622, Hospitals;
- Establishments providing veterans' insurance are classified in Subsector 524, Insurance Carriers and Related Activities; and
- Establishments operating civic and social organizations for veterans are classified in Industry 813410, Civic and Social Organizations.

T—Canadian, Mexican, and United States industries are comparable.

924 Administration of Environmental Quality Programs

The Administration of Environmental Quality Programs subsector groups government establishments primarily engaged in the administration of environmental quality.

9241 Administration of Environmental Quality Programs

92411 Administration of Air and Water Resource and Solid Waste Management Programs
See industry description for 924110.

924110 Administration of Air and Water Resource and Solid Waste Management Programs

This industry comprises government establishments primarily engaged in one or more of the following: (1) the administration, regulation, and enforcement of air and water resource programs; (2) the administration and regulation of solid waste management programs; (3) the administration and regulation of water and air pollution control and prevention programs; (4) the administration and regulation of flood control programs; (5) the administration and regulation of drainage development and water resource consumption programs; (6) the administration and regulation of toxic waste removal and cleanup programs; and (7) coordination of these activities at intergovernmental levels.

Illustrative Examples:

Environmental protection program administration, public administration
Waste management program (except sanitation districts) administration, public administration
Pollution control program administration, public administration
Water control and quality program administration, public administration

Cross-References. Government establishments primarily engaged in--

- Operating water and irrigation systems--are classified in Industry 221310, Water Supply and Irrigation Systems;
- Administering sanitation districts--are classified in Industry 926130, Regulation and Administration of Communications, Electric, Gas, and Other Utilities;
- Operating sewage treatment facilities--are classified in Industry 221320, Sewage Treatment Facilities; and
- Providing waste collection, treatment, disposal, and/or remediation--are classified in Subsector 562, Waste Management and Remediation Services.

92412 Administration of Conservation Programs
See industry description for 924120.

924120 Administration of Conservation Programs

This industry comprises government establishments primarily engaged in the administration, regulation, supervision, and control of land use, including recreational areas; conservation and preservation of natural resources; erosion control; geological survey program administration; weather forecasting program administration; and the administration and protection of publicly and privately owned forest lands. Government establishments responsible for planning, management, regulation, and conservation of game, fish, and wildlife populations, including wildlife management areas and field stations; and other administrative matters relating to the protection of fish, game, and wildlife are included in this industry.

Cross-References. Government establishments primarily engaged in--

- Operating parks--are classified in Industry 712190, Nature Parks and Other Similar Institutions;
- Operating forest property--are classified in Subsector 113, Forestry and Logging;

T—Canadian, Mexican, and United States industries are comparable.

- Geophysical surveying and/or mapping--are classified in Industry 541360, Geophysical Surveying and Mapping Services;
- Surveying and/or mapping (except geophysical)--are classified in Industry 541370, Surveying and Mapping (except Geophysical) Services;
- Weather forecasting--are classified in Industry 541990, All Other Professional, Scientific, and Technical Services;
- Operating fish and game preserves--are classified in Industry 712130, Zoos and Botanical Gardens; and
- Serving as urban planning commissions--are classified in Industry 925120, Administration of Urban Planning and Community and Rural Development.

925 Administration of Housing Programs, Urban Planning, and Community Development

The Administration of Housing Programs, Urban Planning, and Community Development subsector groups government establishments primarily engaged in the administration of housing, urban planning, and community development.

9251 Administration of Housing Programs, Urban Planning, and Community Development

92511 Administration of Housing Programs
See industry description for 925110.

925110 Administration of Housing Programs

This industry comprises government establishments primarily engaged in the administration and planning of housing programs.

Cross-References. Government establishments primarily engaged in--

- Operating government rental housing--are classified in Subsector 531, Real Estate;
- Conducting building inspections and enforcing building codes and standards--are classified in Industry 926150, Regulation, Licensing, and Inspection of Miscellaneous Commercial Sectors; and
- Buying, pooling, and repackaging mortgages or home loans for sale to others on the secondary market--are classified in U.S. Industry 522294, Secondary Market Financing.

92512 Administration of Urban Planning and Community and Rural Development
See industry description for 925120.

925120 Administration of Urban Planning and Community and Rural Development

This industry comprises government establishments primarily engaged in the administration and planning of the development of urban and rural areas. Included in this industry are government zoning boards and commissions.

Illustrative Examples:

Land redevelopment agencies, government
Regional planning and development program administration, public administration
Urban planning commissions, government
Zoning boards and commissions, public administration

926 Administration of Economic Programs

This subsector comprises government establishments primarily engaged in the administration of economic

T—Canadian, Mexican, and United States industries are comparable.

9261 Administration of Economic Programs

92611 Administration of General Economic Programs
See industry description for 926110.

926110 Administration of General Economic Programs

This industry comprises government establishments primarily engaged in the administration, promotion, and development of economic resources, including business, industry, and tourism. Included in this industry are government establishments responsible for the development of general statistical data and analyses and promotion of the general economic well-being of the governed area.

Illustrative Examples:

Consumer protection offices, public administration
Small business development agencies, public administration
Economic development agencies, government
Trade commissions, government
General economics statistical agencies, public administration

92612 Regulation and Administration of Transportation Programs
See industry description for 926120.

926120 Regulation and Administration of Transportation Programs

This industry comprises government establishments primarily engaged in the administration, regulation, licensing, planning, inspection, and investigation of transportation services and facilities. Included in this industry are government establishments responsible for motor vehicle and operator licensing, the Coast Guard (except the Coast Guard Academy), and parking authorities.

Cross-References. Government establishments primarily engaged in--

- Operating airports, railroads, depots, ports, toll roads and bridges, and other transportation facilities and systems--are classified in Sector 48-49, Transportation and Warehousing;
- Operating parking lots and parking garages--are classified in Industry 812930, Parking Lots and Garages;
- Operating automobile safety inspection and emission testing facilities--are classified in Industry Group 8111, Automotive Repair and Maintenance;
- Building and/or maintaining roads and highways--are classified in Industry 237310, Highway, Street, and Bridge Construction;
- Providing air traffic control services--are classified in U.S. Industry 488111, Air Traffic Control; and
- Operating weigh stations--are classified in Industry 488490, Other Support Activities for Road Transportation.

92613 Regulation and Administration of Communications, Electric, Gas, and Other Utilities
See industry description for 926130.

926130 Regulation and Administration of Communications, Electric, Gas, and Other Utilities

This industry comprises government establishments primarily engaged in the administration, regulation, licensing, and inspection of utilities, such as communications, electric power (including fossil, nuclear, solar, water, and wind), gas and water supply, and sewerage.

Cross-References.

Government establishments primarily engaged in operating utilities are classified in Subsector 221, Utilities.

T—Canadian, Mexican, and United States industries are comparable.

92614 Regulation of Agricultural Marketing and Commodities
See industry description for 926140.

926140 Regulation of Agricultural Marketing and Commodities

This industry comprises government establishments primarily engaged in the planning, administration, and coordination of agricultural programs for production, marketing, and utilization, including educational and promotional activities. Included in this industry are government establishments responsible for regulating and controlling the grading and inspection of food, plants, animals, and other agricultural products.

Cross-References. Government establishments primarily engaged in--

- Administering programs for developing economic data about agriculture and trade in agricultural products--are classified in Industry 926110, Administration of General Economic Programs;
- Administering programs for the conservation of natural resources--are classified in Industry Group 9241, Administration of Environmental Quality Programs; and
- Administering food stamp programs--are classified in Industry 923130, Administration of Human Resource Programs (except Education, Public Health, and Veterans' Affairs Programs).

92615 Regulation, Licensing, and Inspection of Miscellaneous Commercial Sectors
See industry description for 926150.

926150 Regulation, Licensing, and Inspection of Miscellaneous Commercial Sectors

This industry comprises government establishments primarily engaged in the regulation, licensing, and inspection of commercial sectors, such as retail trade, professional occupations, manufacturing, mining, construction, and services. Included in this industry are government establishments maintaining physical standards, regulating hazardous conditions not elsewhere classified, and enforcing alcoholic beverage control regulations.

Illustrative Examples:

Alcoholic beverage control boards, public administration
Labor management negotiations boards, government
Banking regulatory agencies, public administration
Licensing and permit issuance for business operations, government
Building inspections, government
Licensing and permit issuance for professional occupations, government
Insurance commissions, government
Securities regulation commissions, public administration

Cross-References. Government establishments primarily engaged in--

- Regulating, administering, and inspecting transportation services and facilities--are classified in Industry 926120, Regulation and Administration of Transportation Programs; and
- Regulating, administering, and inspecting communications, electric, gas, and other utilities--are classified in Industry 926130, Regulation and Administration of Communications, Electric, Gas, and Other Utilities.

927 Space Research and Technology

This subsector comprises government establishments that conduct space research.

9271 Space Research and Technology

92711 Space Research and Technology
See industry description for 927110.

T—Canadian, Mexican, and United States industries are comparable.

927110 Space Research and Technology

This industry comprises government establishments primarily engaged in the administration and operations of space flights, space research, and space exploration. Included in this industry are government establishments operating space flight centers.

Cross-References.

- Private establishments primarily engaged in providing space freight transportation are classified in U.S. Industry 481212, Nonscheduled Chartered Freight Air Transportation;
- Government establishments primarily engaged in manufacturing aerospace vehicles and parts are classified in Industry 33641, Aerospace Product and Parts Manufacturing; and
- Government establishments primarily engaged in manufacturing space satellites are classified in Industry 334220, Radio and Television Broadcasting and Wireless Communications Equipment Manufacturing.

928 National Security and International Affairs

This subsector comprises government establishments primarily engaged in national security and international affairs.

9281 National Security and International Affairs

92811 National Security
See industry description for 928110.

928110 National Security

This industry comprises government establishments of the Armed Forces, including the National Guard, primarily engaged in national security and related activities.

Illustrative Examples:

Air Force
Military police
Army
Military training schools (except military service academies)
Marine Corps
National Guard
Military courts
Navy

Cross-References. Government establishments primarily engaged in--

- Operating college level military service academies--are classified in Industry 611310, Colleges, Universities, and Professional Schools; and
- Regulating and administering water transportation, such as the U.S. Coast Guard and the Merchant Marine--are classified in Industry 926120, Regulation and Administration of Transportation Programs.

92812 International Affairs
See industry description for 928120.

928120 International Affairs

This industry comprises establishments of U.S. and foreign governments primarily engaged in international affairs and programs relating to other nations and peoples.

T—Canadian, Mexican, and United States industries are comparable.

Cross-References.

- Private-sector trade associations and councils are classified in Industry 813910, Business Associations; and
- Government establishments administering international trade, such as trade commissions and councils, are classified in Industry 926110, Administration of General Economic Programs.

T—Canadian, Mexican, and United States industries are comparable.

Part II

List of Short Titles

List of Short Titles

Standard Short Titles for 2017 NAICS United States are shown below. They have been created for the use of those who find that space limitations preclude the use of the full title for the dissemination of data classified to NAICS. The adoption of these titles is recommended in all cases when the full title cannot be used.

The standard short titles are limited to 45 spaces. If the official full title falls within 45 spaces, it remains unchanged.

Note: For definitions of abbreviations and acronyms see page 639.

Code	Short title
11	**AGRICULTURE, FORESTRY, FISHING AND HUNTING**
111	**Crop production**
1111	Oilseed and grain farming
11111	Soybean farming
111110	Soybean farming
11112	Oilseed, except soybean, farming
111120	Oilseed, except soybean, farming
11113	Dry pea and bean farming
111130	Dry pea and bean farming
11114	Wheat farming
111140	Wheat farming
11115	Corn farming
111150	Corn farming
11116	Rice farming
111160	Rice farming
11119	Other grain farming
111191	Oilseed and grain combination farming
111199	All other grain farming
1112	Vegetable and melon farming
11121	Vegetable and melon farming
111211	Potato farming
111219	Other vegetable and melon farming
1113	Fruit and tree nut farming
11131	Orange groves
111310	Orange groves
11132	Citrus, except orange, groves
111320	Citrus, except orange, groves
11133	Noncitrus fruit and tree nut farming
111331	Apple orchards
111332	Grape vineyards
111333	Strawberry farming
111334	Berry, except strawberry, farming
111335	Tree nut farming
111336	Fruit and tree nut combination farming
111339	Other noncitrus fruit farming
1114	Greenhouse and nursery production
11141	Food crops grown under cover
111411	Mushroom production
111419	Other food crops grown under cover
11142	Nursery and floriculture production
111421	Nursery and tree production
111422	Floriculture production
1119	Other crop farming
11191	Tobacco farming
111910	Tobacco farming
11192	Cotton farming
111920	Cotton farming
11193	Sugarcane farming
111930	Sugarcane farming
11194	Hay farming
111940	Hay farming
11199	All other crop farming
111991	Sugar beet farming
111992	Peanut farming
111998	All other miscellaneous crop farming
112	**Animal production and aquaculture**
1121	Cattle ranching and farming 11211
Beef cattle ranching, farming, and feedlots	
112111	Beef cattle ranching and farming
112112	Cattle feedlots
11212	Dairy cattle and milk production
112120	Dairy cattle and milk production
11213	Dual-purpose cattle ranching and farming
112130	Dual-purpose cattle ranching and farming
1122	Hog and pig farming
11221	Hog and pig farming
112210	Hog and pig farming
1123	Poultry and egg production
11231	Chicken egg production
112310	Chicken egg production
11232	Broilers and meat type chicken production
112320	Broilers and meat type chicken production
11233	Turkey production
112330	Turkey production
11234	Poultry hatcheries
112340	Poultry hatcheries
11239	Other poultry production
112390	Other poultry production
1124	Sheep and goat farming
11241	Sheep farming
112410	Sheep farming
11242	Goat farming
112420	Goat farming
1125	Aquaculture
11251	Aquaculture
112511	Finfish farming and fish hatcheries
112512	Shellfish farming
112519	Other aquaculture

Note: For definitions of abbreviations and acronyms see page 639.

1129 Other animal production
11291 Apiculture
112910 Apiculture
11292 Horses and other equine production
112920 Horses and other equine production
11293 Fur-bearing animal and rabbit production
112930 Fur-bearing animal and rabbit production
11299 All other animal production
112990 All other animal production

113 Forestry and logging

1131 Timber tract operations
11311 Timber tract operations
113110 Timber tract operations
1132 Forest nursery and gathering forest products
11321 Forest nursery and gathering forest products
113210 Forest nursery and gathering forest products
1133 Logging
11331 Logging
113310 Logging

114 Fishing, hunting and trapping

1141 Fishing
11411 Fishing
114111 Finfish fishing
114112 Shellfish fishing
114119 Other marine fishing
1142 Hunting and trapping
11421 Hunting and trapping
114210 Hunting and trapping

115 Agriculture and forestry support activities

1151 Support activities for crop production
11511 Support activities for crop production
115111 Cotton ginning
115112 Soil preparation, planting, and cultivating
115113 Crop harvesting, primarily by machine
115114 Other postharvest crop activities
115115 Farm labor contractors and crew leaders
115116 Farm management services
1152 Support activities for animal production
11521 Support activities for animal production
115210 Support activities for animal production
1153 Support activities for forestry
11531 Support activities for forestry
115310 Support activities for forestry

21 MINING, QUARRYING, AND OIL AND GAS EXTRACTION

211 Oil and gas extraction

2111 Oil and gas extraction
21112 Crude petroleum extraction
211120 Crude petroleum extraction
21113 Natural gas extraction
211130 Natural gas extraction

212 Mining, except oil and gas

2121 Coal mining
21211 Coal mining
212111 Bituminous coal and lignite surface mining
212112 Bituminous coal underground mining
212113 Anthracite mining
2122 Metal ore mining
21221 Iron ore mining
212210 Iron ore mining
21222 Gold ore and silver ore mining
212221 Gold ore mining
212222 Silver ore mining
21223 Copper, nickel, lead, and zinc mining
212230 Copper, nickel, lead, and zinc mining
21229 Other metal ore mining
212291 Uranium-radium-vanadium ore mining
212299 All other metal ore mining
2123 Nonmetallic mineral mining and quarrying
21231 Stone mining and quarrying
212311 Dimension stone mining and quarrying
212312 Crushed and broken limestone mining
212313 Crushed and broken granite mining
212319 Other crushed and broken stone mining
21232 Sand, gravel, clay, and refractory mining
212321 Construction sand and gravel mining
212322 Industrial sand mining

Note: For definitions of abbreviations and acronyms see page 639.

212324 Kaolin and ball clay mining 212325 Clay, ceramic, and refractory minerals mining
21239 Other nonmetallic mineral mining
212391 Potash, soda, and borate mineral mining
212392 Phosphate rock mining 212393 Other chemical and fertilizer mineral mining
212399 All other nonmetallic mineral mining

213 Support activities for mining

2131 Support activities for mining
21311 Support activities for mining
213111 Drilling oil and gas wells
213112 Support activities for oil and gas operations
213113 Support activities for coal mining
213114 Support activities for metal mining
213115 Support activities for nonmetallic minerals

22 UTILITIES

221 Utilities

2211 Power generation and supply
22111 Electric power generation
221111 Hydroelectric power generation
221112 Fossil fuel electric power generation
221113 Nuclear electric power generation
221114 Solar electric power generation
221115 Wind electric power generation
221116 Geothermal electric power generation
221117 Biomass electric power generation
221118 Other electric power generation
22112 Electric power transmission and distribution
221121 Electric bulk power transmission and control
221122 Electric power distribution
2212 Natural gas distribution
22121 Natural gas distribution
221210 Natural gas distribution
2213 Water, sewage and other systems
22131 Water supply and irrigation systems
221310 Water supply and irrigation systems
22132 Sewage treatment facilities
221320 Sewage treatment facilities
22133 Steam and air-conditioning supply
221330 Steam and air-conditioning supply

23 CONSTRUCTION

236 Construction of buildings

2361 Residential building construction
23611 Residential building construction
236115 New single-family general contractors
236116 New multifamily general contractors
236117 New housing for-sale builders
236118 Residential remodelers
2362 Nonresidential building construction
23621 Industrial building construction
236210 Industrial building construction
23622 Commercial building construction
236220 Commercial building construction

237 Heavy and civil engineering construction

2371 Utility system construction
23711 Water and sewer system construction
237110 Water and sewer system construction
23712 Oil and gas pipeline construction
237120 Oil and gas pipeline construction
23713 Power and communication system construction
237130 Power and communication system construction
2372 Land subdivision
23721 Land subdivision
237210 Land subdivision
2373 Highway, street, and bridge construction
23731 Highway, street, and bridge construction
237310 Highway, street, and bridge construction
2379 Other heavy construction
23799 Other heavy construction
237990 Other heavy construction

238 Specialty trade contractors

2381 Building foundation and exterior contractors
23811 Poured concrete structure contractors
238110 Poured concrete structure contractors
23812 Steel and precast concrete contractors
238120 Steel and precast concrete contractors

Note: For definitions of abbreviations and acronyms see page 639.

23813 Framing contractors
238130 Framing contractors
23814 Masonry contractors
238140 Masonry contractors
23815 Glass and glazing contractors
238150 Glass and glazing contractors
23816 Roofing contractors
238160 Roofing contractors
23817 Siding contractors
238170 Siding contractors
23819 Other building exterior contractors
238190 Other building exterior contractors
2382 Building equipment contractors
23821 Electrical and wiring contractors
238210 Electrical and wiring contractors
23822 Plumbing and HVAC contractors
238220 Plumbing and HVAC contractors
23829 Other building equipment contractors
238290 Other building equipment contractors
2383 Building finishing contractors
23831 Drywall and insulation contractors
238310 Drywall and insulation contractors
23832 Painting and wall covering contractors
238320 Painting and wall covering contractors
23833 Flooring contractors
238330 Flooring contractors
23834 Tile and terrazzo contractors
238340 Tile and terrazzo contractors
23835 Finish carpentry contractors
238350 Finish carpentry contractors
23839 Other building finishing contractors
238390 Other building finishing contractors
2389 Other specialty trade contractors
23891 Site preparation contractors
238910 Site preparation contractors
23899 All other specialty trade contractors
238990 All other specialty trade contractors

31-33 MANUFACTURING

311 Food manufacturing

3111 Animal food manufacturing
31111 Animal food manufacturing
311111 Dog and cat food manufacturing
311119 Other animal food manufacturing
3112 Grain and oilseed milling
31121 Flour milling and malt manufacturing
311211 Flour milling
311212 Rice milling
311213 Malt manufacturing
31122 Starch and vegetable oil manufacturing
311221 Wet corn milling
311224 Soybean and other oilseed processing
311225 Fats and oils refining and blending
31123 Breakfast cereal manufacturing
311230 Breakfast cereal manufacturing
3113 Sugar and confectionery product manufacturing
31131 Sugar manufacturing
311313 Beet sugar manufacturing
311314 Cane sugar manufacturing
31134 Nonchocolate confectionery manufacturing
311340 Nonchocolate confectionery manufacturing
31135 Chocolate and confectionery manufacturing
311351 Chocolate and confectionery mfg. from cacao
311352 Confectionery mfg. from purchased chocolate
3114 Fruit and vegetable preserving and specialty
31141 Frozen food manufacturing
311411 Frozen fruit and vegetable manufacturing
311412 Frozen specialty food manufacturing
31142 Fruit and vegetable canning and drying
311421 Fruit and vegetable canning
311422 Specialty canning
311423 Dried and dehydrated food manufacturing
3115 Dairy product manufacturing
31151 Dairy product, except frozen, manufacturing
311511 Fluid milk manufacturing
311512 Creamery butter manufacturing
311513 Cheese manufacturing
311514 Dry, condensed, and evaporated dairy products
31152 Ice cream and frozen dessert manufacturing
311520 Ice cream and frozen dessert manufacturing
3116 Animal slaughtering and processing
31161 Animal slaughtering and processing
311611 Animal, except poultry, slaughtering
311612 Meat processed from carcasses
311613 Rendering and meat byproduct processing
311615 Poultry processing

Note: For definitions of abbreviations and acronyms see page 639.

3117 Seafood product preparation and packaging
31171 Seafood product preparation and packaging
311710 Seafood product preparation and packaging
3118 Bakeries and tortilla manufacturing
31181 Bread and bakery product manufacturing
311811 Retail bakeries
311812 Commercial bakeries
311813 Frozen cakes and other pastries manufacturing
31182 Cookie, cracker, and pasta manufacturing
311821 Cookie and cracker manufacturing
311824 Pasta, dough and mixes from purchased flour
31183 Tortilla manufacturing
311830 Tortilla manufacturing
3119 Other food manufacturing
31191 Snack food manufacturing
311911 Roasted nuts and peanut butter manufacturing
311919 Other snack food manufacturing
31192 Coffee and tea manufacturing
311920 Coffee and tea manufacturing
31193 Flavoring syrup and concentrate manufacturing
311930 Flavoring syrup and concentrate manufacturing
31194 Seasoning and dressing manufacturing
311941 Mayonnaise, dressing, and sauce manufacturing
311942 Spice and extract manufacturing
31199 All other food manufacturing
311991 Perishable prepared food manufacturing
311999 All other miscellaneous food manufacturing

312 Beverage and tobacco product manufacturing

3121 Beverage manufacturing
31211 Soft drink and ice manufacturing
312111 Soft drink manufacturing
312112 Bottled water manufacturing
312113 Ice manufacturing
31212 Breweries
312120 Breweries
31213 Wineries
312130 Wineries
31214 Distilleries
312140 Distilleries
3122 Tobacco manufacturing
31223 Tobacco manufacturing
312230 Tobacco manufacturing

313 Textile mills

3131 Fiber, yarn, and thread mills
31311 Fiber, yarn, and thread mills
313110 Fiber, yarn, and thread mills
3132 Fabric mills
31321 Broadwoven fabric mills
313210 Broadwoven fabric mills
31322 Narrow fabric mills and schiffli embroidery
313220 Narrow fabric mills and schiffli embroidery
31323 Nonwoven fabric mills
313230 Nonwoven fabric mills
31324 Knit fabric mills
313240 Knit fabric mills
3133 Textile and fabric finishing mills
31331 Textile and fabric finishing mills
313310 Textile and fabric finishing mills
31332 Fabric coating mills
313320 Fabric coating mills

314 Textile product mills

3141 Textile furnishings mills
31411 Carpet and rug mills
314110 Carpet and rug mills
31412 Curtain and linen mills
314120 Curtain and linen mills
3149 Other textile product mills
31491 Textile bag and canvas mills
314910 Textile bag and canvas mills
31499 All other textile product mills
314994 Rope, twine, tire cord and tire fabric mills
314999 All other miscellaneous textile product mills

315 Apparel manufacturing

3151 Apparel knitting mills
31511 Hosiery and sock mills
315110 Hosiery and sock mills

Note: For definitions of abbreviations and acronyms see page 639.

31519 Other apparel knitting mills
315190 Other apparel knitting mills
3152 Cut and sew apparel manufacturing
31521 Cut and sew apparel contractors
315210 Cut and sew apparel contractors
31522 Men's and boys' cut and sew apparel mfg
315220 Men's and boys' cut and sew apparel mfg
31524 Women's, girls', infants' cut-sew apparel mfg
315240 Women's, girls', infants' cut-sew apparel mfg
31528 Other cut and sew apparel manufacturing
315280 Other cut and sew apparel manufacturing
3159 Accessories and other apparel manufacturing
31599 Accessories and other apparel manufacturing
315990 Accessories and other apparel manufacturing

316 Leather and allied product manufacturing

3161 Leather and hide tanning and finishing
31611 Leather and hide tanning and finishing
316110 Leather and hide tanning and finishing
3162 Footwear manufacturing
31621 Footwear manufacturing
316210 Footwear manufacturing
3169 Other leather product manufacturing
31699 Other leather product manufacturing
316992 Women's handbag and purse manufacturing
316998 All other leather and allied good mfg.

321 Wood product manufacturing

3211 Sawmills and wood preservation
32111 Sawmills and wood preservation
321113 Sawmills
321114 Wood preservation 3212 Plywood and engineered wood product mfg.
32121 Plywood and engineered wood product mfg.
321211 Hardwood veneer and plywood manufacturing
321212 Softwood veneer and plywood manufacturing
321213 Engineered wood member manufacturing
321214 Truss manufacturing 321219 Reconstituted wood product manufacturing
3219 Other wood product manufacturing
32191 Millwork
321911 Wood window and door manufacturing
321912 Cut stock, resawing lumber, and planing
321918 Other millwork, including flooring
32192 Wood container and pallet manufacturing
321920 Wood container and pallet manufacturing
32199 All other wood product manufacturing
321991 Manufactured home, mobile home, manufacturing
321992 Prefabricated wood building manufacturing
321999 Miscellaneous wood product manufacturing

322 Paper manufacturing

3221 Pulp, paper, and paperboard mills
32211 Pulp mills
322110 Pulp mills
32212 Paper mills
322121 Paper, except newsprint, mills
322122 Newsprint mills
32213 Paperboard mills
322130 Paperboard mills
3222 Converted paper product manufacturing
32221 Paperboard container manufacturing
322211 Corrugated and solid fiber box manufacturing
322212 Folding paperboard box manufacturing
322219 Other paperboard container manufacturing
32222 Paper bag and coated and treated paper mfg.
322220 Paper bag and coated and treated paper mfg.
32223 Stationery product manufacturing
322230 Stationery product manufacturing
32229 Other converted paper product manufacturing

Note: For definitions of abbreviations and acronyms see page 639.

322291 Sanitary paper product manufacturing
322299 All other converted paper product mfg.

323 Printing and related support activities

3231 Printing and related support activities
32311 Printing
323111 Commercial printing, except screen and books
323113 Commercial screen printing
323117 Books printing
32312 Support activities for printing
323120 Support activities for printing

324 Petroleum and coal products manufacturing

3241 Petroleum and coal products manufacturing
32411 Petroleum refineries
324110 Petroleum refineries
32412 Asphalt paving and roofing materials mfg.
324121 Asphalt paving mixture and block mfg.
324122 Asphalt shingle and coating materials mfg.
32419 Other petroleum and coal products mfg.
324191 Petroleum lubricating oil and grease mfg.
324199 All other petroleum and coal products mfg.

325 Chemical manufacturing

3251 Basic chemical manufacturing
32511 Petrochemical manufacturing
325110 Petrochemical manufacturing
32512 Industrial gas manufacturing
325120 Industrial gas manufacturing
32513 Synthetic dye and pigment manufacturing
325130 Synthetic dye and pigment manufacturing
32518 Other basic inorganic chemical manufacturing
325180 Other basic inorganic chemical manufacturing
32519 Other basic organic chemical manufacturing
325193 Ethyl alcohol manufacturing 325194 Cyclic crude, intermediate, wood chemical mfg
325199 All other basic organic chemical mfg.
3252 Resin, rubber, and artificial fibers mfg.
32521 Resin and synthetic rubber manufacturing
325211 Plastics material and resin manufacturing
325212 Synthetic rubber manufacturing
32522 Artificial fibers and filaments manufacturing
325220 Artificial fibers and filaments manufacturing
3253 Agricultural chemical manufacturing
32531 Fertilizer manufacturing
325311 Nitrogenous fertilizer manufacturing
325312 Phosphatic fertilizer manufacturing
325314 Fertilizer, mixing only, manufacturing
32532 Pesticide and other ag. chemical mfg.
325320 Pesticide and other ag. chemical mfg.
3254 Pharmaceutical and medicine manufacturing
32541 Pharmaceutical and medicine manufacturing
325411 Medicinal and botanical manufacturing 325412 Pharmaceutical preparation manufacturing
325413 In-vitro diagnostic substance manufacturing
325414 Other biological product manufacturing
3255 Paint, coating, and adhesive manufacturing
32551 Paint and coating manufacturing
325510 Paint and coating manufacturing
32552 Adhesive manufacturing
325520 Adhesive manufacturing
3256 Soap, cleaning compound, and toiletry mfg.
32561 Soap and cleaning compound manufacturing
325611 Soap and other detergent manufacturing
325612 Polish and other sanitation good mfg.
325613 Surface active agent manufacturing
32562 Toilet preparation manufacturing
325620 Toilet preparation manufacturing
3259 Other chemical product and preparation mfg.
32591 Printing ink manufacturing

Note: For definitions of abbreviations and acronyms see page 639.

325910 Printing ink manufacturing
32592 Explosives manufacturing
325920 Explosives manufacturing
32599 All other chemical preparation manufacturing
325991 Custom compounding of purchased resins
325992 Photographic film and chemical manufacturing
325998 Other miscellaneous chemical product mfg.

326 Plastics and rubber products manufacturing

3261 Plastics product manufacturing
32611 Plastics packaging materials, film and sheet
326111 Plastics bag and pouch manufacturing
326112 Plastics packaging film and sheet mfg.
326113 Nonpackaging plastics film and sheet mfg.
32612 Plastics pipe, fittings, and profile shapes
326121 Unlaminated plastics profile shape mfg.
326122 Plastics pipe and pipe fitting manufacturing
32613 Laminated plastics plate, sheet, and shapes
326130 Laminated plastics plate, sheet, and shapes
32614 Polystyrene foam product manufacturing
326140 Polystyrene foam product manufacturing
32615 Urethane and other foam product manufacturing
326150 Urethane and other foam product manufacturing
32616 Plastics bottle manufacturing
326160 Plastics bottle manufacturing
32619 Other plastics product manufacturing
326191 Plastics plumbing fixture manufacturing
326199 All other plastics product manufacturing
3262 Rubber product manufacturing
32621 Tire manufacturing
326211 Tire manufacturing, except retreading
326212 Tire retreading
32622 Rubber and plastics hose and belting mfg.
326220 Rubber and plastics hose and belting mfg.
32629 Other rubber product manufacturing
326291 Rubber product mfg. for mechanical use
326299 All other rubber product manufacturing

327 Nonmetallic mineral product manufacturing

3271 Clay product and refractory manufacturing
32711 Pottery, ceramics, and plumbing fixture mfg.
327110 Pottery, ceramics, and plumbing fixture mfg.
32712 Clay building material and refractories mfg.
327120 Clay building material and refractories mfg.
3272 Glass and glass product manufacturing
32721 Glass and glass product manufacturing
327211 Flat glass manufacturing
327212 Other pressed and blown glass and glassware
327213 Glass container manufacturing
327215 Glass product mfg. made of purchased glass
3273 Cement and concrete product manufacturing
32731 Cement manufacturing
327310 Cement manufacturing
32732 Ready-mix concrete manufacturing
327320 Ready-mix concrete manufacturing
32733 Concrete pipe, brick, and block manufacturing
327331 Concrete block and brick manufacturing
327332 Concrete pipe manufacturing
32739 Other concrete product manufacturing
327390 Other concrete product manufacturing
3274 Lime and gypsum product manufacturing
32741 Lime manufacturing
327410 Lime manufacturing
32742 Gypsum product manufacturing
327420 Gypsum product manufacturing
3279 Other nonmetallic mineral products
32791 Abrasive product manufacturing

Note: For definitions of abbreviations and acronyms see page 639.

327910 Abrasive product manufacturing 32799 All other nonmetallic mineral products mfg.
327991 Cut stone and stone product manufacturing
327992 Ground or treated minerals and earths mfg.
327993 Mineral wool manufacturing 327999 Miscellaneous nonmetallic mineral products

331 Primary metal manufacturing

3311 Iron and steel mills and ferroalloy mfg.
33111 Iron and steel mills and ferroalloy mfg.
331110 Iron and steel mills and ferroalloy mfg.
3312 Steel product mfg. from purchased steel
33121 Iron, steel pipe and tube from purchase steel
331210 Iron, steel pipe and tube from purchase steel
33122 Rolling and drawing of purchased steel
331221 Rolled steel shape manufacturing
331222 Steel wire drawing
3313 Alumina and aluminum production
33131 Alumina and aluminum production
331313 Alumina refining, primary aluminum production
331314 Secondary smelting and alloying of aluminum
331315 Aluminum sheet, plate, and foil manufacturing
331318 Other aluminum rolling, drawing and extruding
3314 Other nonferrous metal production
33141 Other nonferrous metal production
331410 Other nonferrous metal production
33142 Rolled, drawn, extruded, and alloyed copper
331420 Rolled, drawn, extruded, and alloyed copper
33149 Nonferrous metal, except Cu and Al, shaping
331491 Nonferrous metal, except Cu and Al, shaping
331492 Secondary processing of other nonferrous
3315 Foundries
33151 Ferrous metal foundries
331511 Iron foundries
331512 Steel investment foundries
331513 Steel foundries, except investment
33152 Nonferrous metal foundries
331523 Nonferrous metal die-casting foundries
331524 Aluminum foundries, except die-casting
331529 Other nonferrous foundries, exc. die-casting

332 Fabricated metal product manufacturing

3321 Forging and stamping
33211 Forging and stamping
332111 Iron and steel forging
332112 Nonferrous forging
332114 Custom roll forming
332117 Powder metallurgy part manufacturing
332119 Other metal stamping, except automotive
3322 Cutlery and handtool manufacturing
33221 Cutlery and handtool manufacturing
332215 Metal cookware, cutlery and flatware mfg.
332216 Saw blade and handtool manufacturing 3323 Architectural and structural metals mfg.
33231 Plate work and fabricated structural products
332311 Prefabricated metal buildings and components
332312 Fabricated structural metal manufacturing
332313 Plate work manufacturing 33232 Ornamental and architectural metal products
332321 Metal window and door manufacturing
332322 Sheet metal work manufacturing
332323 Ornamental and architectural metal work mfg.
3324 Boiler, tank, and shipping container mfg.
33241 Power boiler and heat exchanger manufacturing
332410 Power boiler and heat exchanger manufacturing
33242 Metal tank, heavy gauge, manufacturing
332420 Metal tank, heavy gauge, manufacturing

Note: For definitions of abbreviations and acronyms see page 639.

33243 Metal can, box, and other container mfg.
332431 Metal can manufacturing
332439 Other metal container manufacturing
3325 Hardware manufacturing
33251 Hardware manufacturing
332510 Hardware manufacturing
3326 Spring and wire product manufacturing
33261 Spring and wire product manufacturing
332613 Spring manufacturing
332618 Other fabricated wire product manufacturing
3327 Machine shops and threaded product mfg.
33271 Machine shops
332710 Machine shops
33272 Turned product and screw, nut, and bolt mfg.
332721 Precision turned product manufacturing
332722 Bolt, nut, screw, rivet, and washer mfg.
3328 Coating, engraving, and heat treating metals
33281 Coating, engraving, and heat treating metals
332811 Metal heat treating
332812 Metal coating and nonprecious engraving
332813 Electroplating, anodizing, and coloring metal
3329 Other fabricated metal product manufacturing
33291 Metal valve manufacturing
332911 Industrial valve manufacturing
332912 Fluid power valve and hose fitting mfg.
332913 Plumbing fixture fitting and trim mfg.
332919 Other metal valve and pipe fitting mfg.
33299 All other fabricated metal product mfg.
332991 Ball and roller bearing manufacturing
332992 Small arms ammunition manufacturing
332993 Ammunition, except small arms, manufacturing
332994 Small arms and ordnance manufacturing
332996 Fabricated pipe and pipe fitting mfg.
332999 Miscellaneous fabricated metal product mfg.

333 Machinery manufacturing
3331 Ag., construction, and mining machinery mfg.
33311 Agricultural implement manufacturing
333111 Farm machinery and equipment manufacturing
333112 Lawn and garden equipment manufacturing
33312 Construction machinery manufacturing
333120 Construction machinery manufacturing
33313 Mining and oil and gas field machinery mfg.
333131 Mining machinery and equipment manufacturing
333132 Oil and gas field machinery and equipment
3332 Industrial machinery manufacturing
33324 Industrial machinery manufacturing
333241 Food product machinery manufacturing
333242 Semiconductor machinery manufacturing
333243 Sawmill, woodworking, and paper machinery mfg
333244 Printing machinery and equipment mfg.
333249 Other industrial machinery manufacturing
3333 Commercial and service industry machinery
33331 Commercial and service industry machinery
333314 Optical instrument and lens manufacturing
333316 Photographic and photocopying equipment mfg.
333318 Other commercial and service machinery mfg.
3334 HVAC and commercial refrigeration equipment
33341 HVAC and commercial refrigeration equipment
333413 Fan, blower, air purification equipment mfg.
333414 Heating equipment, except warm air furnaces
333415 AC, refrigeration, and forced air heating
3335 Metalworking machinery manufacturing
33351 Metalworking machinery manufacturing

Note: For definitions of abbreviations and acronyms see page 639.

333511 Industrial mold manufacturing
333514 Special tool, die, jig, and fixture mfg.
333515 Cutting tool and machine tool accessory mfg.
333517 Machine tool manufacturing
333519 Other metalworking machinery manufacturing
3336 Turbine and power transmission equipment mfg.
33361 Turbine and power transmission equipment mfg.
333611 Turbine and turbine generator set units mfg.
333612 Speed changer, drive, and gear manufacturing
333613 Mechanical power transmission equipment mfg.
333618 Other engine equipment manufacturing
3339 Other general purpose machinery manufacturing
33391 Pump and compressor manufacturing
333912 Air and gas compressor manufacturing
333914 Measuring, dispensing, and pumping equip. mfg
33392 Material handling equipment manufacturing
333921 Elevator and moving stairway manufacturing
333922 Conveyor and conveying equipment mfg.
333923 Overhead cranes, hoists, and monorail systems
333924 Industrial truck, trailer, and stacker mfg.
33399 All other general purpose machinery mfg.
333991 Power-driven handtool manufacturing
333992 Welding and soldering equipment manufacturing
333993 Packaging machinery manufacturing
333994 Industrial process furnace and oven mfg.
333995 Fluid power cylinder and actuator mfg.
333996 Fluid power pump and motor manufacturing
333997 Scale and balance manufacturing
333999 Miscellaneous general purpose machinery mfg.

334 Computer and electronic product manufacturing

3341 Computer and peripheral equipment mfg.
33411 Computer and peripheral equipment mfg.
334111 Electronic computer manufacturing
334112 Computer storage device manufacturing
334118 Other computer peripheral equipment mfg.
3342 Communications equipment manufacturing
33421 Telephone apparatus manufacturing
334210 Telephone apparatus manufacturing
33422 Broadcast and wireless communications equip.
334220 Broadcast and wireless communications equip.
33429 Other communications equipment manufacturing
334290 Other communications equipment manufacturing
3343 Audio and video equipment manufacturing
33431 Audio and video equipment manufacturing
334310 Audio and video equipment manufacturing
3344 Semiconductor and electronic component mfg.
33441 Semiconductor and electronic component mfg.
334412 Bare printed circuit board manufacturing
334413 Semiconductors and related device mfg.
334416 Capacitor, resistor, and inductor mfg.
334417 Electronic connector manufacturing
334418 Printed circuit assembly manufacturing
334419 Other electronic component manufacturing
3345 Electronic instrument manufacturing
33451 Electronic instrument manufacturing
334510 Electromedical apparatus manufacturing
334511 Search, detection, and navigation instruments
334512 Automatic environmental control manufacturing
334513 Industrial process variable instruments
334514 Totalizing fluid meters and counting devices

Note: For definitions of abbreviations and acronyms see page 639.

334515 Electricity and signal testing instruments
334516 Analytical laboratory instrument mfg.
334517 Irradiation apparatus manufacturing
334519 Other measuring and controlling device mfg.
3346 Magnetic media manufacturing and reproducing
33461 Magnetic media manufacturing and reproducing
334613 Blank magnetic and optical media mfg
334614 Software and prerecorded media reproducing

335 Electrical equipment and appliance mfg.

3351 Electric lighting equipment manufacturing
33511 Electric lamp bulb and part manufacturing
335110 Electric lamp bulb and part manufacturing
33512 Lighting fixture manufacturing
335121 Residential electric lighting fixture mfg.
335122 Nonresidential electric lighting fixture mfg.
335129 Other lighting equipment manufacturing
3352 Household appliance manufacturing
33521 Small electrical appliance manufacturing
335210 Small electrical appliance manufacturing
33522 Major household appliance manufacturing
335220 Major household appliance manufacturing
3353 Electrical equipment manufacturing
33531 Electrical equipment manufacturing
335311 Electric power and specialty transformer mfg.
335312 Motor and generator manufacturing
335313 Switchgear and switchboard apparatus mfg.
335314 Relay and industrial control manufacturing
3359 Other electrical equipment and component mfg.
33591 Battery manufacturing
335911 Storage battery manufacturing
335912 Primary battery manufacturing
33592 Communication and energy wire and cable mfg.
335921 Fiber optic cable manufacturing
335929 Other communication and energy wire mfg.
33593 Wiring device manufacturing
335931 Current-carrying wiring device manufacturing
335932 Noncurrent-carrying wiring device mfg.
33599 Other electrical equipment and component mfg.
335991 Carbon and graphite product manufacturing
335999 Miscellaneous electrical equipment mfg.

336 Transportation equipment manufacturing

3361 Motor vehicle manufacturing
33611 Automobile and light truck manufacturing
336111 Automobile manufacturing
336112 Light truck and utility vehicle manufacturing
33612 Heavy duty truck manufacturing
336120 Heavy duty truck manufacturing
3362 Motor vehicle body and trailer manufacturing
33621 Motor vehicle body and trailer manufacturing
336211 Motor vehicle body manufacturing
336212 Truck trailer manufacturing
336213 Motor home manufacturing
336214 Travel trailer and camper manufacturing
3363 Motor vehicle parts manufacturing
33631 Motor vehicle gasoline engine and parts mfg.
336310 Motor vehicle gasoline engine and parts mfg.
33632 Motor vehicle electric equipment mfg.
336320 Motor vehicle electric equipment mfg.
33633 Motor vehicle steering and suspension parts
336330 Motor vehicle steering and suspension parts

Note: For definitions of abbreviations and acronyms see page 639.

33634 Motor vehicle brake system manufacturing
336340 Motor vehicle brake system manufacturing
33635 Motor vehicle power train components mfg.
336350 Motor vehicle power train components mfg.
33636 Motor vehicle seating and interior trim mfg.
336360 Motor vehicle seating and interior trim mfg.
33637 Motor vehicle metal stamping
336370 Motor vehicle metal stamping
33639 Other motor vehicle parts manufacturing
336390 Other motor vehicle parts manufacturing
3364 Aerospace product and parts manufacturing
33641 Aerospace product and parts manufacturing
336411 Aircraft manufacturing
336412 Aircraft engine and engine parts mfg.
336413 Other aircraft parts and equipment
336414 Guided missile and space vehicle mfg.
336415 Space vehicle propulsion units and parts mfg.
336419 Other guided missile and space vehicle parts
3365 Railroad rolling stock manufacturing
33651 Railroad rolling stock manufacturing
336510 Railroad rolling stock manufacturing
3366 Ship and boat building
33661 Ship and boat building
336611 Ship building and repairing
336612 Boat building
3369 Other transportation equipment manufacturing
33699 Other transportation equipment manufacturing
336991 Motorcycle, bicycle, and parts manufacturing
336992 Military armored vehicles and tank parts mfg.
336999 All other transportation equipment mfg.

337 Furniture and related product manufacturing

3371 Household and institutional furniture mfg.
33711 Wood kitchen cabinet and countertop mfg.
337110 Wood kitchen cabinet and countertop mfg.
33712 Other household and institutional furniture
337121 Upholstered household furniture manufacturing
337122 Nonupholstered wood household furniture mfg.
337124 Metal household furniture manufacturing
337125 Household furniture, exc. wood or metal, mfg.
337127 Institutional furniture manufacturing
3372 Office furniture and fixtures manufacturing
33721 Office furniture and fixtures manufacturing
337211 Wood office furniture manufacturing
337212 Custom architectural woodwork and millwork
337214 Office furniture, except wood, manufacturing
337215 Showcases, partitions, shelving, and lockers
3379 Other furniture related product manufacturing
33791 Mattress manufacturing
337910 Mattress manufacturing
33792 Blind and shade manufacturing
337920 Blind and shade manufacturing

339 Miscellaneous manufacturing

3391 Medical equipment and supplies manufacturing
33911 Medical equipment and supplies manufacturing
339112 Surgical and medical instrument manufacturing
339113 Surgical appliance and supplies manufacturing
339114 Dental equipment and supplies manufacturing
339115 Ophthalmic goods manufacturing
339116 Dental laboratories
3399 Other miscellaneous manufacturing
33991 Jewelry and silverware manufacturing

Note: For definitions of abbreviations and acronyms see page 639.

339910 Jewelry and silverware manufacturing
33992 Sporting and athletic goods manufacturing
339920 Sporting and athletic goods manufacturing
33993 Doll, toy, and game manufacturing
339930 Doll, toy, and game manufacturing
33994 Office supplies, except paper, manufacturing
339940 Office supplies, except paper, manufacturing
33995 Sign manufacturing
339950 Sign manufacturing
33999 All other miscellaneous manufacturing
339991 Gasket, packing, and sealing device mfg.
339992 Musical instrument manufacturing
339993 Fastener, button, needle, and pin mfg.
339994 Broom, brush, and mop manufacturing
339995 Burial casket manufacturing
339999 All other miscellaneous manufacturing

42 WHOLESALE TRADE

423 Merchant wholesalers, durable goods

4231 Motor vehicle and parts merchant wholesalers
42311 Motor vehicle merchant wholesalers
423110 Motor vehicle merchant wholesalers
42312 New motor vehicle parts merchant wholesalers
423120 New motor vehicle parts merchant wholesalers
42313 Tire and tube merchant wholesalers
423130 Tire and tube merchant wholesalers
42314 Used motor vehicle parts merchant wholesalers
423140 Used motor vehicle parts merchant wholesalers
4232 Furniture and furnishing merchant wholesalers
42321 Furniture merchant wholesalers
423210 Furniture merchant wholesalers
42322 Home furnishing merchant wholesalers
423220 Home furnishing merchant wholesalers
4233 Lumber and const. supply merchant wholesalers
42331 Lumber and wood merchant wholesalers
423310 Lumber and wood merchant wholesalers
42332 Masonry material merchant wholesalers
423320 Masonry material merchant wholesalers
42333 Roofing and siding merchant wholesalers
423330 Roofing and siding merchant wholesalers
42339 Other const. material merchant wholesalers
423390 Other const. material merchant wholesalers
4234 Commercial equip. merchant wholesalers
42341 Photographic equip. merchant wholesalers
423410 Photographic equip. merchant wholesalers
42342 Office equipment merchant wholesalers
423420 Office equipment merchant wholesalers
42343 Computer and software merchant wholesalers
423430 Computer and software merchant wholesalers
42344 Other commercial equip. merchant wholesalers
423440 Other commercial equip. merchant wholesalers
42345 Medical equipment merchant wholesalers
423450 Medical equipment merchant wholesalers
42346 Ophthalmic goods merchant wholesalers
423460 Ophthalmic goods merchant wholesalers
42349 Other professional equip. merchant wholesaler
423490 Other professional equip. merchant wholesaler
4235 Metal and mineral merchant wholesalers
42351 Metal merchant wholesalers
423510 Metal merchant wholesalers
42352 Coal and other mineral merchant wholesalers

Note: For definitions of abbreviations and acronyms see page 639.

423520 Coal and other mineral merchant wholesalers
4236 Appliance and electric goods merchant whls.
42361 Elec. equip. and wiring merchant wholesalers
423610 Elec. equip. and wiring merchant wholesalers
42362 Appliance and electronics merchant whls.
423620 Appliance and electronics merchant whls.
42369 Other electronic parts merchant wholesalers
423690 Other electronic parts merchant wholesalers
4237 Hardware and plumbing merchant wholesalers
42371 Hardware merchant wholesalers
423710 Hardware merchant wholesalers
42372 Plumbing equip. merchant wholesalers
423720 Plumbing equip. merchant wholesalers
42373 HVAC equip. merchant wholesalers
423730 HVAC equip. merchant wholesalers
42374 Refrigeration equip. merchant wholesalers
423740 Refrigeration equip. merchant wholesalers
4238 Machinery and supply merchant wholesalers
42381 Construction equipment merchant wholesalers
423810 Construction equipment merchant wholesalers
42382 Farm and garden equip. merchant wholesalers
423820 Farm and garden equip. merchant wholesalers
42383 Industrial machinery merchant wholesalers
423830 Industrial machinery merchant wholesalers
42384 Industrial supplies merchant wholesalers
423840 Industrial supplies merchant wholesalers
42385 Service estab. equip. merchant wholesalers
423850 Service estab. equip. merchant wholesalers
42386 Transport. goods merchant wholesalers
423860 Transport. goods merchant wholesalers
4239 Misc. durable goods merchant wholesalers
42391 Sporting goods merchant wholesalers
423910 Sporting goods merchant wholesalers
42392 Toy and hobby goods merchant wholesalers
423920 Toy and hobby goods merchant wholesalers
42393 Recyclable material merchant wholesalers
423930 Recyclable material merchant wholesalers
42394 Jewelry merchant wholesalers
423940 Jewelry merchant wholesalers
42399 Other durable goods merchant wholesalers
423990 Other durable goods merchant wholesalers

424 Merchant wholesalers, nondurable goods

4241 Paper and paper product merchant wholesalers
42411 Printing and writing paper merch. whls.
424110 Printing and writing paper merch. whls.
42412 Office supplies merchant wholesalers
424120 Office supplies merchant wholesalers
42413 Industrial paper merchant wholesalers
424130 Industrial paper merchant wholesalers
4242 Druggists' goods merchant wholesalers
42421 Druggists' goods merchant wholesalers
424210 Druggists' goods merchant wholesalers
4243 Apparel and piece goods merchant wholesalers
42431 Piece goods merchant wholesalers
424310 Piece goods merchant wholesalers
42432 Men's and boys' clothing merchant wholesalers
424320 Men's and boys' clothing merchant wholesalers
42433 Women's and children's clothing merch. whls.
424330 Women's and children's clothing merch. whls.
42434 Footwear merchant wholesalers
424340 Footwear merchant wholesalers

Note: For definitions of abbreviations and acronyms see page 639.

4244 Grocery and related product wholesalers
42441 General line grocery merchant wholesalers
424410 General line grocery merchant wholesalers
42442 Packaged frozen food merchant wholesalers
424420 Packaged frozen food merchant wholesalers
42443 Dairy product merchant wholesalers
424430 Dairy product merchant wholesalers
42444 Poultry product merchant wholesalers
424440 Poultry product merchant wholesalers
42445 Confectionery merchant wholesalers
424450 Confectionery merchant wholesalers
42446 Fish and seafood merchant wholesalers
424460 Fish and seafood merchant wholesalers
42447 Meat and meat product merchant wholesalers
424470 Meat and meat product merchant wholesalers
42448 Fruit and vegetable merchant wholesalers
424480 Fruit and vegetable merchant wholesalers
42449 Other grocery product merchant wholesalers
424490 Other grocery product merchant wholesalers
4245 Farm product raw material merch. whls.
42451 Grain and field bean merchant wholesalers
424510 Grain and field bean merchant wholesalers
42452 Livestock merchant wholesalers
424520 Livestock merchant wholesalers
42459 Other farm product raw material merch. whls.
424590 Other farm product raw material merch. whls.
4246 Chemical merchant wholesalers
42461 Plastics materials merchant wholesalers
424610 Plastics materials merchant wholesalers
42469 Other chemicals merchant wholesalers
424690 Other chemicals merchant wholesalers
4247 Petroleum merchant wholesalers
42471 Petroleum bulk stations and terminals
424710 Petroleum bulk stations and terminals
42472 Other petroleum merchant wholesalers
424720 Other petroleum merchant wholesalers
4248 Alcoholic beverage merchant wholesalers
42481 Beer and ale merchant wholesalers
424810 Beer and ale merchant wholesalers
42482 Wine and spirit merchant wholesalers
424820 Wine and spirit merchant wholesalers
4249 Misc. nondurable goods merchant wholesalers
42491 Farm supplies merchant wholesalers
424910 Farm supplies merchant wholesalers
42492 Book and periodical merchant wholesalers
424920 Book and periodical merchant wholesalers
42493 Nursery and florist merchant wholesalers
424930 Nursery and florist merchant wholesalers
42494 Tobacco and tobacco product merch. whls.
424940 Tobacco and tobacco product merch. whls.
42495 Paint and supplies merchant wholesalers
424950 Paint and supplies merchant wholesalers
42499 Other nondurable goods merchant wholesalers
424990 Other nondurable goods merchant wholesalers

425 Electronic markets and agents and brokers

4251 Electronic markets and agents and brokers
42511 Business to business electronic markets
425110 Business to business electronic markets
42512 Wholesale trade agents and brokers
425120 Wholesale trade agents and brokers

44-45 RETAIL TRADE

441 Motor vehicle and parts dealers

4411 Automobile dealers
44111 New car dealers
441110 New car dealers

Note: For definitions of abbreviations and acronyms see page 639.

44112 Used car dealers
441120 Used car dealers
4412 Other motor vehicle dealers
44121 Recreational vehicle dealers
441210 Recreational vehicle dealers
44122 Motorcycle, boat, and other vehicle dealers
441222 Boat dealers
441228 Motorcycle, ATV, and other vehicle dealers
4413 Auto parts, accessories, and tire stores
44131 Automotive parts and accessories stores
441310 Automotive parts and accessories stores
44132 Tire dealers
441320 Tire dealers

442 Furniture and home furnishings stores

4421 Furniture stores
44211 Furniture stores
442110 Furniture stores
4422 Home furnishings stores
44221 Floor covering stores
442210 Floor covering stores
44229 Other home furnishings stores
442291 Window treatment stores
442299 All other home furnishings stores

443 Electronics and appliance stores

4431 Electronics and appliance stores
44314 Electronics and appliance stores
443141 Household appliance stores
443142 Electronics stores

444 Building material and garden supply stores

4441 Building material and supplies dealers
44411 Home centers
444110 Home centers
44412 Paint and wallpaper stores
444120 Paint and wallpaper stores
44413 Hardware stores
444130 Hardware stores
44419 Other building material dealers
444190 Other building material dealers
4442 Lawn and garden equipment and supplies stores
44421 Outdoor power equipment stores
444210 Outdoor power equipment stores
44422 Nursery, garden, and farm supply stores
444220 Nursery, garden, and farm supply stores

445 Food and beverage stores

4451 Grocery stores
44511 Supermarkets and other grocery stores
445110 Supermarkets and other grocery stores
44512 Convenience stores
445120 Convenience stores
4452 Specialty food stores
44521 Meat markets
445210 Meat markets
44522 Fish and seafood markets
445220 Fish and seafood markets
44523 Fruit and vegetable markets
445230 Fruit and vegetable markets
44529 Other specialty food stores
445291 Baked goods stores
445292 Confectionery and nut stores
445299 All other specialty food stores
4453 Beer, wine, and liquor stores
44531 Beer, wine, and liquor stores
445310 Beer, wine, and liquor stores

446 Health and personal care stores

4461 Health and personal care stores
44611 Pharmacies and drug stores
446110 Pharmacies and drug stores
44612 Cosmetic and beauty supply stores
446120 Cosmetic and beauty supply stores
44613 Optical goods stores
446130 Optical goods stores
44619 Other health and personal care stores
446191 Food, health, supplement stores
446199 All other health and personal care stores

447 Gasoline stations

4471 Gasoline stations 44711 Gasoline stations with convenience stores

Note: For definitions of abbreviations and acronyms see page 639.

447110 Gasoline stations with convenience stores
44719 Other gasoline stations
447190 Other gasoline stations

448 Clothing and clothing accessories stores

4481 Clothing stores
44811 Men's clothing stores
448110 Men's clothing stores
44812 Women's clothing stores
448120 Women's clothing stores
44813 Children's and infants' clothing stores
448130 Children's and infants' clothing stores
44814 Family clothing stores
448140 Family clothing stores
44815 Clothing accessories stores
448150 Clothing accessories stores
44819 Other clothing stores
448190 Other clothing stores
4482 Shoe stores
44821 Shoe stores
448210 Shoe stores
4483 Jewelry, luggage, and leather goods stores
44831 Jewelry stores
448310 Jewelry stores
44832 Luggage and leather goods stores
448320 Luggage and leather goods stores

451 Sports, hobby, music instrument, book stores

4511 Sporting goods and musical instrument stores
45111 Sporting goods stores
451110 Sporting goods stores
45112 Hobby, toy, and game stores
451120 Hobby, toy, and game stores
45113 Sewing, needlework, and piece goods stores
451130 Sewing, needlework, and piece goods stores
45114 Musical instrument and supplies stores
451140 Musical instrument and supplies stores
4512 Book stores and news dealers
45121 Book stores and news dealers
451211 Book stores
451212 News dealers and newsstands

452 General merchandise stores

4522 Department stores
45221 Department stores
452210 Department stores
4523 Other general merchandise stores
45231 Other general merchandise stores
452311 Warehouse clubs and supercenters
452319 All other general merchandise stores

453 Miscellaneous store retailers

4531 Florists
45311 Florists
453110 Florists
4532 Office supplies, stationery, and gift stores
45321 Office supplies and stationery stores
453210 Office supplies and stationery stores
45322 Gift, novelty, and souvenir stores
453220 Gift, novelty, and souvenir stores
4533 Used merchandise stores
45331 Used merchandise stores
453310 Used merchandise stores
4539 Other miscellaneous store retailers
45391 Pet and pet supplies stores
453910 Pet and pet supplies stores
45392 Art dealers
453920 Art dealers
45393 Manufactured, mobile, home dealers
453930 Manufactured, mobile, home dealers
45399 All other miscellaneous store retailers
453991 Tobacco stores
453998 Store retailers not specified elsewhere

454 Nonstore retailers

4541 Electronic shopping and mail-order houses
45411 Electronic shopping and mail-order houses
454110 Electronic shopping and mail-order houses
4542 Vending machine operators
45421 Vending machine operators
454210 Vending machine operators
4543 Direct selling establishments
45431 Fuel dealers
454310 Fuel dealers
45439 Other direct selling establishments
454390 Other direct selling establishments

Note: For definitions of abbreviations and acronyms see page 639.

48-49 TRANSPORTATION AND WAREHOUSING

481 Air transportation

4811 Scheduled air transportation
48111 Scheduled air transportation
481111 Scheduled passenger air transportation
481112 Scheduled freight air transportation
4812 Nonscheduled air transportation
48121 Nonscheduled air transportation
481211 Nonscheduled air passenger chartering
481212 Nonscheduled air freight chartering
481219 Other nonscheduled air transportation

482 Rail transportation

4821 Rail transportation
48211 Rail transportation
482111 Line-haul railroads
482112 Short line railroads

483 Water transportation

4831 Sea, coastal, and Great Lakes transportation
48311 Sea, coastal, and Great Lakes transportation
483111 Deep sea freight transportation
483112 Deep sea passenger transportation
483113 Coastal and Great Lakes freight transport.
483114 Coastal and Great Lakes passenger transport.
4832 Inland water transportation
48321 Inland water transportation
483211 Inland water freight transportation
483212 Inland water passenger transportation

484 Truck transportation

4841 General freight trucking
48411 General freight trucking, local
484110 General freight trucking, local
48412 General freight trucking, long-distance
484121 General freight trucking, long-distance TL
484122 General freight trucking, long-distance LTL
4842 Specialized freight trucking
48421 Used household and office goods moving
484210 Used household and office goods moving
48422 Other specialized trucking, local
484220 Other specialized trucking, local
48423 Other specialized trucking, long-distance
484230 Other specialized trucking, long-distance

485 Transit and ground passenger transportation

4851 Urban transit systems
48511 Urban transit systems
485111 Mixed mode transit systems
485112 Commuter rail systems
485113 Bus and other motor vehicle transit systems
485119 Other urban transit systems
4852 Interurban and rural bus transportation
48521 Interurban and rural bus transportation
485210 Interurban and rural bus transportation
4853 Taxi and limousine service
48531 Taxi service
485310 Taxi service
48532 Limousine service
485320 Limousine service
4854 School and employee bus transportation
48541 School and employee bus transportation
485410 School and employee bus transportation
4855 Charter bus industry
48551 Charter bus industry
485510 Charter bus industry
4859 Other ground passenger transportation
48599 Other ground passenger transportation
485991 Special needs transportation
485999 All other ground passenger transportation

486 Pipeline transportation

4861 Pipeline transportation of crude oil
48611 Pipeline transportation of crude oil
486110 Pipeline transportation of crude oil
4862 Pipeline transportation of natural gas

Note: For definitions of abbreviations and acronyms see page 639.

48621 Pipeline transportation of natural gas
486210 Pipeline transportation of natural gas
4869 Other pipeline transportation
48691 Refined petroleum product pipeline transport.
486910 Refined petroleum product pipeline transport.
48699 All other pipeline transportation
486990 All other pipeline transportation

487 Scenic and sightseeing transportation

4871 Scenic and sightseeing transportation, land
48711 Scenic and sightseeing transportation, land
487110 Scenic and sightseeing transportation, land
4872 Scenic and sightseeing transportation, water
48721 Scenic and sightseeing transportation, water
487210 Scenic and sightseeing transportation, water
4879 Scenic and sightseeing transportation, other
48799 Scenic and sightseeing transportation, other
487990 Scenic and sightseeing transportation, other

488 Support activities for transportation

4881 Support activities for air transportation
48811 Airport operations
488111 Air traffic control
488119 Other airport operations
48819 Other support activities for air transport.
488190 Other support activities for air transport.
4882 Support activities for rail transportation
48821 Support activities for rail transportation
488210 Support activities for rail transportation
4883 Support activities for water transportation
48831 Port and harbor operations
488310 Port and harbor operations
48832 Marine cargo handling
488320 Marine cargo handling
48833 Navigational services to shipping
488330 Navigational services to shipping
48839 Other support activities for water transport.
488390 Other support activities for water transport.
4884 Support activities for road transportation
48841 Motor vehicle towing
488410 Motor vehicle towing
48849 Other support activities for road transport.
488490 Other support activities for road transport.
4885 Freight transportation arrangement
48851 Freight transportation arrangement
488510 Freight transportation arrangement
4889 Other support activities for transportation
48899 Other support activities for transportation
488991 Packing and crating
488999 All other support activities for transport.

491 Postal service

4911 Postal service
49111 Postal service
491110 Postal service

492 Couriers and messengers

4921 Couriers and express delivery services
49211 Couriers and express delivery services
492110 Couriers and express delivery services
4922 Local messengers and local delivery
49221 Local messengers and local delivery
492210 Local messengers and local delivery

493 Warehousing and storage

4931 Warehousing and storage
49311 General warehousing and storage
493110 General warehousing and storage
49312 Refrigerated warehousing and storage
493120 Refrigerated warehousing and storage
49313 Farm product warehousing and storage
493130 Farm product warehousing and storage
49319 Other warehousing and storage
493190 Other warehousing and storage

Note: For definitions of abbreviations and acronyms see page 639.

51 INFORMATION

511 Publishing industries, except Internet

5111 Newspaper, book, and directory publishers
51111 Newspaper publishers
511110 Newspaper publishers
51112 Periodical publishers
511120 Periodical publishers
51113 Book publishers
511130 Book publishers
51114 Directory and mailing list publishers
511140 Directory and mailing list publishers
51119 Other publishers
511191 Greeting card publishers
511199 All other publishers
5112 Software publishers
51121 Software publishers
511210 Software publishers

512 Motion picture and sound recording industries

5121 Motion picture and video industries
51211 Motion picture and video production
512110 Motion picture and video production
51212 Motion picture and video distribution
512120 Motion picture and video distribution
51213 Motion picture and video exhibition
512131 Motion picture theaters, except drive-ins
512132 Drive-in motion picture theaters
51219 Postproduction and other related industries
512191 Teleproduction and postproduction services
512199 Other motion picture and video industries
5122 Sound recording industries
51223 Music publishers
512230 Music publishers
51224 Sound recording studios
512240 Sound recording studios
51225 Record production and distribution
512250 Record production and distribution
51229 Other sound recording industries
512290 Other sound recording industries

515 Broadcasting, except Internet
5151 Radio and television broadcasting
51511 Radio broadcasting
515111 Radio networks
515112 Radio stations
51512 Television broadcasting
515120 Television broadcasting
5152 Cable and other subscription programming
51521 Cable and other subscription programming
515210 Cable and other subscription programming

517 Telecommunications

5173 Wired and wireless carriers
51731 Wired and wireless carriers
517311 Wired telecommunications carriers
517312 Wireless telecommunications carriers
5174 Satellite telecommunications
51741 Satellite telecommunications
517410 Satellite telecommunications
5179 Other telecommunications
51791 Other telecommunications
517911 Telecommunications resellers
517919 All other telecommunications

518 Data processing, hosting and related services

5182 Data processing, hosting and related services
51821 Data processing, hosting and related services
518210 Data processing, hosting and related services

519 Other information services

5191 Other information services
51911 News syndicates
519110 News syndicates
51912 Libraries and archives
519120 Libraries and archives
51913 Internet publishing and web search portals
519130 Internet publishing and web search portals
51919 All other information services
519190 All other information services

Note: For definitions of abbreviations and acronyms see page 639.

52 FINANCE AND INSURANCE

521 Monetary authorities-central bank

5211 Monetary authorities-central bank
52111 Monetary authorities-central bank
521110 Monetary authorities-central bank

522 Credit intermediation and related activities

5221 Depository credit intermediation
52211 Commercial banking
522110 Commercial banking
52212 Savings institutions
522120 Savings institutions
52213 Credit unions
522130 Credit unions
52219 Other depository credit intermediation
522190 Other depository credit intermediation
5222 Nondepository credit intermediation
52221 Credit card issuing
522210 Credit card issuing
52222 Sales financing
522220 Sales financing
52229 Other nondepository credit intermediation
522291 Consumer lending
522292 Real estate credit
522293 International trade financing
522294 Secondary market financing
522298 All other nondepository credit intermediation
5223 Activities related to credit intermediation
52231 Mortgage and nonmortgage loan brokers
522310 Mortgage and nonmortgage loan brokers
52232 Financial transaction processing and clearing
522320 Financial transaction processing and clearing
52239 Other credit intermediation activities
522390 Other credit intermediation activities

523 Securities, commodity contracts, investments

5231 Securities and commodity contracts brokerage
52311 Investment banking and securities dealing
523110 Investment banking and securities dealing
52312 Securities brokerage
523120 Securities brokerage
52313 Commodity contracts dealing
523130 Commodity contracts dealing
52314 Commodity contracts brokerage
523140 Commodity contracts brokerage
5232 Securities and commodity exchanges
52321 Securities and commodity exchanges
523210 Securities and commodity exchanges
5239 Other financial investment activities
52391 Miscellaneous intermediation
523910 Miscellaneous intermediation
52392 Portfolio management
523920 Portfolio management
52393 Investment advice
523930 Investment advice
52399 All other financial investment activities
523991 Trust, fiduciary, and custody activities
523999 Miscellaneous financial investment activities

524 Insurance carriers and related activities

5241 Insurance carriers
52411 Direct life and health insurance carriers
524113 Direct life insurance carriers
524114 Direct health and medical insurance carriers
52412 Direct insurers, except life and health
524126 Direct property and casualty insurers
524127 Direct title insurance carriers
524128 Other direct insurance carriers
52413 Reinsurance carriers
524130 Reinsurance carriers
5242 Insurance agencies and brokerages
52421 Insurance agencies and brokerages
524210 Insurance agencies and brokerages
52429 Other insurance related activities
524291 Claims adjusting
524292 Third party administration of insurance funds
524298 All other insurance related activities

525 Funds, trusts, and other financial vehicles

Note: For definitions of abbreviations and acronyms see page 639.

5251 Insurance and employee benefit funds
52511 Pension funds
525110 Pension funds
52512 Health and welfare funds
525120 Health and welfare funds
52519 Other insurance funds
525190 Other insurance funds
5259 Other investment pools and funds
52591 Open-end investment funds
525910 Open-end investment funds
52592 Trusts, estates, and agency accounts
525920 Trusts, estates, and agency accounts
52599 Other financial vehicles
525990 Other financial vehicles

53 REAL ESTATE AND RENTAL AND LEASING

531 Real estate

5311 Lessors of real estate
53111 Lessors of residential buildings
531110 Lessors of residential buildings
53112 Lessors of nonresidential buildings
531120 Lessors of nonresidential buildings
53113 Miniwarehouse and self-storage unit operators
531130 Miniwarehouse and self-storage unit operators
53119 Lessors of other real estate property
531190 Lessors of other real estate property
5312 Offices of real estate agents and brokers
53121 Offices of real estate agents and brokers
531210 Offices of real estate agents and brokers
5313 Activities related to real estate
53131 Real estate property managers
531311 Residential property managers
531312 Nonresidential property managers
53132 Offices of real estate appraisers
531320 Offices of real estate appraisers
53139 Other activities related to real estate
531390 Other activities related to real estate

532 Rental and leasing services

5321 Automotive equipment rental and leasing
53211 Passenger car rental and leasing
532111 Passenger car rental
532112 Passenger car leasing
53212 Truck, trailer, and RV rental and leasing
532120 Truck, trailer, and RV rental and leasing
5322 Consumer goods rental 53221
Consumer electronics and appliances rental
532210 Consumer electronics and applianc-es rental
53228 Other consumer goods rental
532281 Formal wear and costume rental
532282 Video tape and disc rental
532283 Home health equipment rental
532284 Recreational goods rental
532289 All other consumer goods rental
5323 General rental centers
53231 General rental centers
532310 General rental centers
5324 Machinery and equipment rental and leasing
53241 Heavy machinery rental and leasing
532411 Transportation equipment rental and leasing
532412 Other heavy machinery rental and leasing
53242 Office equipment rental and leasing
532420 Office equipment rental and leasing
53249 Other machinery rental and leasing
532490 Other machinery rental and leasing

533 Lessors of nonfinancial intangible assets

5331 Lessors of nonfinancial intangible assets
53311 Lessors of nonfinancial intangible assets
533110 Lessors of nonfinancial intangible assets

54 PROFESSIONAL AND TECHNICAL SERVICES

541 Professional and technical services

5411 Legal services
54111 Offices of lawyers
541110 Offices of lawyers
54112 Offices of notaries

Note: For definitions of abbreviations and acronyms see page 639.

541120 Offices of notaries
54119 Other legal services
541191 Title abstract and settlement offices
541199 All other legal services
5412 Accounting and bookkeeping services
54121 Accounting and bookkeeping services
541211 Offices of certified public accountants
541213 Tax preparation services
541214 Payroll services
541219 Other accounting services
5413 Architectural and engineering services
54131 Architectural services
541310 Architectural services
54132 Landscape architectural services
541320 Landscape architectural services
54133 Engineering services
541330 Engineering services
54134 Drafting services
541340 Drafting services
54135 Building inspection services
541350 Building inspection services
54136 Geophysical surveying and mapping services
541360 Geophysical surveying and mapping services
54137 Other surveying and mapping services
541370 Other surveying and mapping services
54138 Testing laboratories
541380 Testing laboratories
5414 Specialized design services
54141 Interior design services
541410 Interior design services
54142 Industrial design services
541420 Industrial design services
54143 Graphic design services
541430 Graphic design services
54149 Other specialized design services
541490 Other specialized design services
5415 Computer systems design and related services
54151 Computer systems design and related services
541511 Custom computer programming services
541512 Computer systems design services
541513 Computer facilities management services
541519 Other computer related services
5416 Management and technical consulting services
54161 Management consulting services
541611 Administrative management consulting services
541612 Human resources consulting services
541613 Marketing consulting services
541614 Process and logistics consulting services
541618 Other management consulting services
54162 Environmental consulting services
541620 Environmental consulting services
54169 Other technical consulting services
541690 Other technical consulting services
5417 Scientific research and development services
54171 Physical, engineering and biological research
541713 Research and development in nanotechnology
541714 Research and development in biotechnology
541715 Other physical and biological research
54172 Social science and humanities research
541720 Social science and humanities research
5418 Advertising, PR, and related services
54181 Advertising agencies
541810 Advertising agencies
54182 Public relations agencies
541820 Public relations agencies
54183 Media buying agencies
541830 Media buying agencies
54184 Media representatives
541840 Media representatives
54185 Outdoor advertising
541850 Outdoor advertising
54186 Direct mail advertising
541860 Direct mail advertising
54187 Advertising material distribution services
541870 Advertising material distribution services
54189 Other services related to advertising
541890 Other services related to advertising
5419 Other professional and technical services
54191 Marketing research and public opinion polling
541910 Marketing research and public opinion polling
54192 Photographic services
541921 Photography studios, portrait
541922 Commercial photography
54193 Translation and interpretation services

Note: For definitions of abbreviations and acronyms see page 639.

541930 Translation and interpretation services
54194 Veterinary services
541940 Veterinary services
54199 All other professional and technical services
541990 All other professional and technical services

55 MANAGEMENT OF COMPANIES AND ENTERPRISES

551 Management of companies and enterprises

5511 Management of companies and enterprises
55111 Management of companies and enterprises
551111 Offices of bank holding companies
551112 Offices of other holding companies
551114 Managing offices

56 ADMINISTRATIVE AND WASTE SERVICES

561 Administrative and support services

5611 Office administrative services
56111 Office administrative services
561110 Office administrative services
5612 Facilities support services
56121 Facilities support services
561210 Facilities support services
5613 Employment services
56131 Employment placement and executive search
561311 Employment placement agencies
561312 Executive search services
56132 Temporary help services
561320 Temporary help services
56133 Professional employer organizations
561330 Professional employer organizations
5614 Business support services
56141 Document preparation services
561410 Document preparation services
56142 Telephone call centers
561421 Telephone answering services
561422 Telemarketing and other contact centers
56143 Business service centers
561431 Private mail centers
561439 Other business service centers
56144 Collection agencies
561440 Collection agencies
56145 Credit bureaus
561450 Credit bureaus
56149 Other business support services
561491 Repossession services
561492 Court reporting and stenotype services
561499 All other business support services
5615 Travel arrangement and reservation services
56151 Travel agencies
561510 Travel agencies
56152 Tour operators
561520 Tour operators
56159 Other travel arrangement services
561591 Convention and visitors bureaus
561599 All other travel arrangement services
5616 Investigation and security services
56161 Security and armored car services
561611 Investigation services
561612 Security guards and patrol services
561613 Armored car services
56162 Security systems services
561621 Security systems services, except locksmiths
561622 Locksmiths
5617 Services to buildings and dwellings
56171 Exterminating and pest control services
561710 Exterminating and pest control services
56172 Janitorial services
561720 Janitorial services
56173 Landscaping services
561730 Landscaping services
56174 Carpet and upholstery cleaning services
561740 Carpet and upholstery cleaning services
56179 Other services to buildings and dwellings
561790 Other services to buildings and dwellings
5619 Other support services
56191 Packaging and labeling services
561910 Packaging and labeling services
56192 Convention and trade show organizers
561920 Convention and trade show organizers
56199 All other support services
561990 All other support services

Note: For definitions of abbreviations and acronyms see page 639.

562 Waste management and remediation services

5621 Waste collection
56211 Waste collection
562111 Solid waste collection
562112 Hazardous waste collection
562119 Other waste collection
5622 Waste treatment and disposal
56221 Waste treatment and disposal
562211 Hazardous waste treatment and disposal
562212 Solid waste landfill 562213
Solid waste combustors and incinerators
562219 Other nonhazardous waste disposal
5629 Remediation and other waste services
56291 Remediation services
562910 Remediation services
56292 Materials recovery facilities
562920 Materials recovery facilities
56299 All other waste management services
562991 Septic tank and related services
562998 Miscellaneous waste management services

61 EDUCATIONAL SERVICES

611 Educational services

6111 Elementary and secondary schools
61111 Elementary and secondary schools
611110 Elementary and secondary schools
6112 Junior colleges
61121 Junior colleges
611210 Junior colleges
6113 Colleges and universities
61131 Colleges and universities
611310 Colleges and universities
6114 Business, computer and management training
61141 Business and secretarial schools
611410 Business and secretarial schools
61142 Computer training
611420 Computer training
61143 Management training
611430 Management training
6115 Technical and trade schools
61151 Technical and trade schools
611511 Cosmetology and barber schools
611512 Flight training
611513 Apprenticeship training
611519 Other technical and trade schools
6116 Other schools and instruction
61161 Fine arts schools
611610 Fine arts schools
61162 Sports and recreation instruction
611620 Sports and recreation instruction
61163 Language schools
611630 Language schools
61169 All other schools and instruction
611691 Exam preparation and tutoring
611692 Automobile driving schools
611699 Miscellaneous schools and instruction
6117 Educational support services
61171 Educational support services
611710 Educational support services

62 HEALTH CARE AND SOCIAL ASSISTANCE

621 Ambulatory health care services

6211 Offices of physicians
62111 Offices of physicians
621111 Offices of physicians, except mental health
621112 Offices of mental health physicians
6212 Offices of dentists
62121 Offices of dentists
621210 Offices of dentists
6213 Offices of other health practitioners
62131 Offices of chiropractors
621310 Offices of chiropractors
62132 Offices of optometrists
621320 Offices of optometrists
62133 Offices of mental health practitioners
621330 Offices of mental health practitioners
62134 Offices of specialty therapists
621340 Offices of specialty therapists
62139 Offices of all other health practitioners
621391 Offices of podiatrists
621399 Offices of miscellaneous health practitioners
6214 Outpatient care centers
62141 Family planning centers
621410 Family planning centers
62142 Outpatient mental health centers
621420 Outpatient mental health centers
62149 Other outpatient care centers
621491 HMO medical centers
621492 Kidney dialysis centers

Note: For definitions of abbreviations and acronyms see page 639.

621493 Freestanding emergency medical centers
621498 All other outpatient care centers
6215 Medical and diagnostic laboratories
62151 Medical and diagnostic laboratories
621511 Medical laboratories
621512 Diagnostic imaging centers
6216 Home health care services
62161 Home health care services
621610 Home health care services
6219 Other ambulatory health care services
62191 Ambulance services
621910 Ambulance services
62199 All other ambulatory health care services
621991 Blood and organ banks
621999 Miscellaneous ambulatory health care services

622 Hospitals

6221 General medical and surgical hospitals
62211 General medical and surgical hospitals
622110 General medical and surgical hospitals
6222 Psychiatric and substance abuse hospitals
62221 Psychiatric and substance abuse hospitals
622210 Psychiatric and substance abuse hospitals
6223 Other hospitals
62231 Other hospitals
622310 Other hospitals

623 Nursing and residential care facilities

6231 Nursing care facilities, skilled nursing
62311 Nursing care facilities, skilled nursing
623110 Nursing care facilities, skilled nursing
6232 Residential mental health facilities
62321 Residential developmental disability homes
623210 Residential developmental disability homes
62322 Residential mental and substance abuse care
623220 Residential mental and substance abuse care
6233 Continuing care, assisted living facilities
62331 Continuing care, assisted living facilities
623311 Continuing care retirement communities
623312 Assisted living facilities for the elderly
6239 Other residential care facilities
62399 Other residential care facilities
623990 Other residential care facilities

624 Social assistance

6241 Individual and family services
62411 Child and youth services
624110 Child and youth services
62412 Services for the elderly and disabled
624120 Services for the elderly and disabled
62419 Other individual and family services
624190 Other individual and family services
6242 Emergency and other relief services
62421 Community food services
624210 Community food services
62422 Community housing services
624221 Temporary shelters
624229 Other community housing services
62423 Emergency and other relief services
624230 Emergency and other relief services
6243 Vocational rehabilitation services
62431 Vocational rehabilitation services
624310 Vocational rehabilitation services
6244 Child day care services
62441 Child day care services
624410 Child day care services

71 ARTS, ENTERTAINMENT, AND RECREATION

711 Performing arts and spectator sports

7111 Performing arts companies
71111 Theater companies and dinner theaters
711110 Theater companies and dinner theaters
71112 Dance companies
711120 Dance companies
71113 Musical groups and artists
711130 Musical groups and artists
71119 Other performing arts companies
711190 Other performing arts companies
7112 Spectator sports
71121 Spectator sports
711211 Sports teams and clubs
711212 Racetracks

Note: For definitions of abbreviations and acronyms see page 639.

711219 Other spectator sports 7113 Promoters of performing arts and sports
71131 Promoters with facilities
711310 Promoters with facilities
71132 Promoters without facilities
711320 Promoters without facilities
7114 Agents and managers for public figures
71141 Agents and managers for public figures
711410 Agents and managers for public figures
7115 Independent artists, writers, and performers
71151 Independent artists, writers, and performers
711510 Independent artists, writers, and performers

712 Museums, historical sites, zoos, and parks

7121 Museums, historical sites, zoos, and parks
71211 Museums
712110 Museums
71212 Historical sites
712120 Historical sites
71213 Zoos and botanical gardens
712130 Zoos and botanical gardens
71219 Nature parks and other similar institutions
712190 Nature parks and other similar institutions

713 Amusements, gambling, and recreation

7131 Amusement parks and arcades
71311 Amusement and theme parks
713110 Amusement and theme parks
71312 Amusement arcades
713120 Amusement arcades
7132 Gambling industries
71321 Casinos, except casino hotels
713210 Casinos, except casino hotels
71329 Other gambling industries
713290 Other gambling industries
7139 Other amusement and recreation industries
71391 Golf courses and country clubs
713910 Golf courses and country clubs
71392 Skiing facilities
713920 Skiing facilities
71393 Marinas
713930 Marinas
71394 Fitness and recreational sports centers
713940 Fitness and recreational sports centers
71395 Bowling centers
713950 Bowling centers
71399 All other amusement and recreation industries
713990 All other amusement and recreation industries

72 ACCOMMODATION AND FOOD SERVICES

721 Accommodation

7211 Traveler accommodation
72111 Hotels and motels, except casino hotels
721110 Hotels and motels, except casino hotels
72112 Casino hotels
721120 Casino hotels
72119 Other traveler accommodation
721191 Bed-and-breakfast inns
721199 All other traveler accommodation
7212 RV parks and recreational camps
72121 RV parks and recreational camps
721211 RV parks and campgrounds
721214 Recreational and vacation camps
7213 Rooming and boarding houses and dorms
72131 Rooming and boarding houses and dorms
721310 Rooming and boarding houses and dorms

722 Food services and drinking places

7223 Special food services
72231 Food service contractors
722310 Food service contractors
72232 Caterers
722320 Caterers
72233 Mobile food services
722330 Mobile food services
7224 Drinking places, alcoholic beverages
72241 Drinking places, alcoholic beverages
722410 Drinking places, alcoholic beverages
7225 Restaurants and other eating places
72251 Restaurants and other eating places
722511 Full-service restaurants

Note: For definitions of abbreviations and acronyms see page 639.

722513 Limited-service restaurants
722514 Cafeterias, grill buffets, and buffets
722515 Snack and nonalcoholic beverage bars

81 OTHER SERVICES, EXCEPT PUBLIC ADMINISTRATION

811 Repair and maintenance

8111 Automotive repair and maintenance
81111 Automotive mechanical and electrical repair
811111 General automotive repair
811112 Automotive exhaust system repair
811113 Automotive transmission repair
811118 Other automotive mechanical and elec. repair
81112 Automotive body, interior, and glass repair
811121 Automotive body and interior repair
811122 Automotive glass replacement shops
81119 Other automotive repair and maintenance
811191 Automotive oil change and lubrication shops
811192 Car washes
811198 All other automotive repair and maintenance
8112 Electronic equipment repair and maintenance
81121 Electronic equipment repair and maintenance
811211 Consumer electronics repair and maintenance
811212 Computer and office machine repair
811213 Communication equipment repair
811219 Other electronic equipment repair
8113 Commercial machinery repair and maintenance
81131 Commercial machinery repair and maintenance
811310 Commercial machinery repair and maintenance
8114 Household goods repair and maintenance
81141 Home and garden equip. and appliance repair
811411 Home and garden equipment repair
811412 Appliance repair and maintenance
81142 Reupholstery and furniture repair
811420 Reupholstery and furniture repair
81143 Footwear and leather goods repair
811430 Footwear and leather goods repair
81149 Other household goods repair and maintenance
811490 Other household goods repair and maintenance

812 Personal and laundry services

8121 Personal care services
81211 Hair, nail, and skin care services
812111 Barber shops
812112 Beauty salons
812113 Nail salons
81219 Other personal care services
812191 Diet and weight reducing centers
812199 Other personal care services
8122 Death care services
81221 Funeral homes and funeral services
812210 Funeral homes and funeral services
81222 Cemeteries and crematories
812220 Cemeteries and crematories
8123 Drycleaning and laundry services
81231 Coin-operated laundries and drycleaners
812310 Coin-operated laundries and drycleaners
81232 Drycleaning and laundry services
812320 Drycleaning and laundry services
81233 Linen and uniform supply
812331 Linen supply
812332 Industrial launderers
8129 Other personal services
81291 Pet care, except veterinary, services
812910 Pet care, except veterinary, services
81292 Photofinishing
812921 Photofinishing laboratories, except one-hour
812922 One-hour photofinishing
81293 Parking lots and garages
812930 Parking lots and garages
81299 All other personal services
812990 All other personal services

813 Membership associations and organizations

8131 Religious organizations
81311 Religious organizations
813110 Religious organizations
8132 Grantmaking and giving services

Note: For definitions of abbreviations and acronyms see page 639.

81321 Grantmaking and giving services
813211 Grantmaking foundations
813212 Voluntary health organizations
813219 Other grantmaking and giving services
8133 Social advocacy organizations
81331 Social advocacy organizations
813311 Human rights organizations
813312 Environment and conservation organizations
813319 Other social advocacy organizations
8134 Civic and social organizations
81341 Civic and social organizations
813410 Civic and social organizations
8139 Professional and similar organizations
81391 Business associations
813910 Business associations
81392 Professional organizations
813920 Professional organizations
81393 Labor unions and similar labor organizations
813930 Labor unions and similar labor organizations
81394 Political organizations
813940 Political organizations
81399 Other similar organizations
813990 Other similar organizations

814 Private households

8141 Private households
81411 Private households
814110 Private households

92 PUBLIC ADMINISTRATION

921 Executive, legislative and general government

9211 Executive, legislative and general government
92111 Executive offices
921110 Executive offices
92112 Legislative bodies
921120 Legislative bodies
92113 Public finance activities
921130 Public finance activities
92114 Executive and legislative offices, combined
921140 Executive and legislative offices, combined
92115 Tribal governments
921150 Tribal governments
92119 Other general government support
921190 Other general government support

922 Justice, public order, and safety activities

9221 Justice, public order, and safety activities
92211 Courts
922110 Courts
92212 Police protection
922120 Police protection
92213 Legal counsel and prosecution
922130 Legal counsel and prosecution
92214 Correctional institutions
922140 Correctional institutions
92215 Parole offices and probation offices
922150 Parole offices and probation offices
92216 Fire protection
922160 Fire protection
92219 Other justice and safety activities
922190 Other justice and safety activities

923 Administration of human resource programs

9231 Administration of human resource programs
92311 Administration of education programs
923110 Administration of education programs
92312 Administration of public health programs
923120 Administration of public health programs
92313 Other human resource programs administration
923130 Other human resource programs administration
92314 Administration of veterans' affairs
923140 Administration of veterans' affairs

924 Administration of environmental programs

9241 Administration of environmental programs
92411 Air, water, and waste program administration
924110 Air, water, and waste program administration

Note: For definitions of abbreviations and acronyms see page 639.

92412 Administration of conservation programs
924120 Administration of conservation programs

925 Community and housing program administration

9251 Community and housing program administration
92511 Administration of housing programs
925110 Administration of housing programs
92512 Urban and rural development administration
925120 Urban and rural development administration

926 Administration of economic programs

9261 Administration of economic programs
92611 Administration of general economic programs
926110 Administration of general economic programs
92612 Transportation program administration
926120 Transportation program administration
92613 Utility regulation and administration
926130 Utility regulation and administration
92614 Agricultural market and commodity regulation
926140 Agricultural market and commodity regulation
92615 Licensing and regulating commercial sectors
926150 Licensing and regulating commercial sectors

927 Space research and technology

9271 Space research and technology
92711 Space research and technology
927110 Space research and technology

928 National security and international affairs

9281 National security and international affairs
92811 National security
928110 National security
92812 International affairs
928120 International affairs

Note: For definitions of abbreviations and acronyms see page 639.

Abbreviations and Acronyms Used in Short Titles

Abbreviation/Acronym	Word
AC	air-conditioning agriculture aluminum
ag.	all-terrain vehicle construction
Al	copper electrical equipment establish-
ATV	ment
const.	except health maintenance organization
Cu	heating, ventilation, and air-conditioning
elec.	less than truckload merchant manufac-
equip.	turing miscellaneous public relations
estab.	recreational vehicle truckload transpor-
exc.	tation wholesalers
HMO	
HVAC	
LTL	
merch.	
mfg. or mfg	
misc.	
PR	
RV	
TL	
transport.	
whls.	

Part III

Appendixes

Appendixes A and B map the changes for 2017 NAICS to the 2012 NAICS in 2017 NAICS sequence (Appendix A) and 2012 NAICS sequence (Appendix B). The tables do not provide a comprehensive guide to all economic activities, but rather provide a map for the largest and most important changes from 2012 to 2017.

A full concordance for 2012 NAICS to 2017 NAICS is available on the Census Bureau's Web site at census.gov/naics.

Appendix A

2017 NAICS U.S. Matched to 2012 NAICS U.S.

2017 NAICS Code	2017 NAICS	Status Code	2012 NAICS Code	2012 NAICS
21112	Crude Petroleum Extraction			
211120	Crude Petroleum Extraction	N	*211111	Crude Petroleum and Natural Gas Extraction - *crude petroleum extraction*
21113	Natural Gas Extraction			
211130	Natural Gas Extraction	N	*211111	Crude Petroleum and Natural Gas Extraction - *natural gas extraction*
			211112	Natural Gas Liquid Extraction
212230	Copper, Nickel, Lead, and Zinc Mining	N	212231	Lead Ore and Zinc Ore Mining
			212234	Copper Ore and Nickel Ore Mining
333914	Measuring, Dispensing, and Other Pumping Equipment Manufacturing	N	333911	Pump and Pumping Equipment Manufacturing
			333913	Measuring and Dispensing Pump Manufacturing
33522	Major Household Appliance Manufacturing			
335220	Major Household Appliance Manufacturing	N	335221	Household Cooking Appliance Manufacturing
			335222	Household Refrigerator and Home Freezer Manufacturing
			335224	Household Laundry Equipment Manufacturing
			335228	Other Major Household Appliance Manufacturing

*—Part of 2012 NAICS United States industry; N—New NAICS industry for 2017

2017 NAICS Code	2017 NAICS U.S. Description	Status Code	2012 NAICS Code	2012 NAICS U.S. Description
4522	Department Stores			
45221	Department Stores			
452210	Department Stores	N	452111	Department Stores (except Discount Department Stores)
			*452112	Discount Department Stores - *insignificant perishable grocery sales*
4523	General Merchandise Stores, including Warehouse Clubs and Supercenters			
45231	General Merchandise Stores, including Warehouse Clubs and Supercenters			
452311	Warehouse Clubs and Supercenters	N	452910	Warehouse Clubs and Supercenters
			*452112	Discount Department Stores - *significant perishable grocery sales*
452319	All Other General Merchandise Stores	N	452990	All Other General Merchandise Stores
454110	Electronic Shopping and Mail-Order Houses	N	454111	Electronic Shopping
			454112	Electronic Auctions
			454113	Mail-Order Houses
51225	Record Production and Distribution			
512250	Record Production and Distribution	N	512210	Record Production
			512220	Integrated Record Production/Distribution
5173	Wired and Wireless Telecommunications Carriers			
51731	Wired and Wireless Telecommunications Carriers			
517311	Wired Telecommunications Carriers	N	517110	Wired Telecommunications Carriers

*—Part of 2012 NAICS United States industry; N—New NAICS industry for 2017

2017 NAICS Code	2017 NAICS	Status Code	2012 NAICS Code	2012 NAICS
517312	Wireless Telecommunications Carriers (except Satellite)	N	517210	Wireless Telecommunications Carriers (except Satellite)
53228	Other Consumer Goods Rental			
532281	Formal Wear and Costume Rental	N	532220	Formal Wear and Costume Rental
532282	Video Tape and Disc Rental	N	532230	Video Tape and Disc Rental
532283	Home Health Equipment Rental	N	532291	Home Health Equipment Rental
532284	Recreational Goods Rental	N	532292	Recreational Goods Rental
532289	All Other Consumer Goods Rental	N	532299	All Other Consumer Goods Rental
541713	Research and Development in Nanotechnology	N	*541711	Research and Development in Biotechnology - *nanobiotechnologies research and experimental development laboratories*
			*541712	Research and Development in the Physical, Engineering, and Life Sciences (except Biotechnology) - *nanotechnology research and experimental development laboratories*
541714	Research and Development in Biotechnology (except Nanobiotechnology)	N	*541711	Research and Development in Biotechnology - *except nanobiotechnologies research and experimental development laboratories*
541715	Research and Development in the Physical, Engineering, and Life Sciences (except Nanotechnology and Biotechnology)	N	*541712	Research and Development in the Physical, Engineering, and Life Sciences (except Biotechnology) - *except nanotechnology research and experimental development laboratories*

*—Part of 2012 NAICS United States industry; N—New NAICS industry for 2017

Appendix B

2012 NAICS U.S. Matched to 2017 NAICS U.S.

2012 NAICS Code	2012 NAICS	Status Code	2017 NAICS Code	2017 NAICS
211111	Crude Petroleum and Natural Gas Extraction			
	crude petroleum extraction	pt.	211120	Crude Petroleum Extraction
	natural gas extraction		211130	Natural Gas Extraction
211112	Natural Gas Liquid Extraction	pt.	211130	Natural Gas Extraction
212231	Lead Ore and Zinc Ore Mining	pt.	212230	Copper, Nickel, Lead, and Zinc Mining
212234	Copper Ore and Nickel Ore Mining	pt.	212230	Copper, Nickel, Lead, and Zinc Mining
333911	Pump and Pumping Equipment Manufacturing	pt.	333914	Measuring, Dispensing, and Other Pumping Equipment Manufacturing
333913	Measuring and Dispensing Pump Manufacturing	pt.	333914	Measuring, Dispensing, and Other Pumping Equipment Manufacturing
335221	Household Cooking Appliance Manufacturing	pt.	335220	Major Household Appliance Manufacturing
335222	Household Refrigerator and Home Freezer Manufacturing	pt.	335220	Major Household Appliance Manufacturing
335224	Household Laundry Equipment Manufacturing	pt.	335220	Major Household Appliance Manufacturing
335228	Other Major Household Appliance Manufacturing	pt.	335220	Major Household Appliance Manufacturing
452111	Department Stores (except Discount Department Stores)	pt.	452210	Department Stores

pt.—Part of 2017 NAICS United States industry

2012 NAICS Code	2012 NAICS	Status Code	2017 NAICS Code	2017 NAICS
452112	Discount Department Stores *insignificant perishable grocery sales*	pt.	452210	Department Stores
	significant perishable grocery sales	pt.	452311	Warehouse Clubs and Supercenters
452910	Warehouse Clubs and Supercenters	pt.	452311	Warehouse Clubs and Supercenters
452990	All Other General Merchandise Stores		452319	All Other General Merchandise Stores
454111	Electronic Shopping	pt.	454110	Electronic Shopping and Mail-Order Houses
454112	Electronic Auctions	pt.	454110	Electronic Shopping and Mail-Order Houses
454113	Mail-Order Houses	pt.	454110	Electronic Shopping and Mail-Order Houses
512210	Record Production	pt.	512250	Record Production and Distribution
512220	Integrated Record Produc-	pt.	512250	Record Production and Distribution
517110	Wired Telecommunications Carriers		517311	Wired Telecommunications Carriers
517210	Wireless Telecommunications Car- riers (except Satellite)		517312	Wireless Telecommunications Carriers
532220	Formal Wear and Costume Rental		532281	Formal Wear and Costume Rental
532230	Video Tape and Disc Rental		532282	Video Tape and Disc Rental
532291	Home Health Equipment Rental		532283	Home Health Equipment Rental
532292	Recreational Goods Rental		532284	Recreational Goods Rental
532299	All Other Consumer Goods Rental		532289	All Other Consumer Goods Rental

pt.—Part of 2017 NAICS United States industry

2012 NAICS Code	2012 NAICS	Status Code	2017 NAICS Code	2017 NAICS
541711	Research and Development in Biotechnology			
	nanobiotechnologies research and experimental development laboratories	pt.	541713	Research and Development in Nanotechnology
	except nanobiotechnologies research and experimental development laboratories		541714	Research and Development in Biotechnology (except Nanobiotechnology)
541712	Research and Development in the Physical, Engineering, and Life Sciences (except Biotechnology)			
	nanotechnology research and experimental development laboratories	pt.	541713	Research and Development in Nanotechnology
	except nanotechnology research and experimental development laboratories		541715	Research and Development in the Physical, Engineering, and Life Sciences (except Nanotechnology and Biotechnology)

pt.—Part of 2017 NAICS United States industry

Part IV

Alphabetic Index

Alphabetic Index

311611 Abattoirs 621410
Abortion clinics
334519 Abrasion testing machines manufacturing
339114 Abrasive points, wheels, and disks, dental, manufacturing
327910 Abrasive products manufacturing
212322 Abrasive sand quarrying and/or beneficiating
212399 Abrasive stones (e.g., emery, grindstones, hones, pumice) mining and/or beneficiating
423840 Abrasives merchant wholesalers
212399 Abrasives, natural, mining and/or beneficiating
322121 Absorbent paper stock manufacturing
332420 Absorbers, gas, heavy gauge metal, manufacturing
334513 Absorption analyzers, industrial process type (e.g., infrared), manufacturing
237310 Abutment construction
611691 Academic tutoring services
611310 Academies, college or university
611110 Academies, elementary or secondary
611210 Academies, junior college
611310 Academies, military service (college)
611620 Academies, riding instruction
334511 Acceleration indicators and systems components, aerospace type, manufacturing
325199 Accelerators (i.e., basic synthetic chemical) manufacturing
334519 Accelerometers (except aerospace type) manufacturing
238330 Access flooring installation 424320 Accessories, clothing, men's and boy's, merchant wholesalers
813319 Accident prevention associations
524130 Accidental and health reinsurance carriers
524113 Accidental death and dismemberment insurance carriers, direct
524113 Accidental death and dismemberment insurance underwriting, direct
339992 Accordions and parts manufacturing
561440 Account collection services
541219 Accountants' (except CPAs) offices
541219 Accountants' (except CPAs) private practices
541211 Accountants' (i.e., CPAs) offices, certified public
541211 Accountants' (i.e., CPAs) private practices, certified public
813920 Accountants' associations 541211 Accounting (i.e., CPAs) services, certified public
423420 Accounting machines merchant wholesalers
541219 Accounting services (except CPAs)
332420 Accumulators, industrial pressure vessels, heavy gauge metal, manufacturing 325211
Acetal resins manufacturing 325199 Acetaldehyde manufacturing 325220 Acetate fibers and filaments manufacturing 325194 Acetate of lime, natural, made by distillation of wood
313110 Acetate spun yarns made from purchased fiber
325199 Acetates, not specified elsewhere by process, manufacturing
325199 Acetic acid manufacturing
325199 Acetic anhydride manufacturing
325199 Acetin manufacturing
325194 Acetone, natural, manufacturing
325199 Acetone, synthetic, manufacturing
332420 Acetylene cylinders, heavy gauge metal, manufacturing
325120 Acetylene manufacturing
325411 Acetylsalicylic acid manufacturing
325130 Acid dyes, synthetic organic, manufacturing
325199 Acid esters, not specified elsewhere by process, manufacturing
324110 Acid oils made in petroleum refineries
236210 Acid plant construction
562211 Acid waste disposal facilities
562211 Acid waste treatment facilities
334513 Acidity (i.e., pH) instruments, industrial process type, manufacturing
334516 Acidity (i.e., pH) measuring equipment, laboratory analysis-type, manufacturing

213112 Acidizing oil and gas field wells on a contract basis
311511 Acidophilus milk manufacturing
424690 Acids merchant wholesalers 325199 Acids, organic, not specified elsewhere by process, manufacturing
111219 Acorn squash farming, field, bedding plant and seed production
238310 Acoustical ceiling tile and panel installation
541330 Acoustical engineering consulting services
238310 Acoustical foam (i.e., sound barrier) installation
332323 Acoustical suspension systems, metal, manufacturing
541330 Acoustical system engineering design services
541380 Acoustics testing laboratories or services
325199 Acrolein manufacturing 325212 Acrylate rubber manufacturing 325212 Acrylate-butadiene rubber manufacturing 313110 Acrylic and modacrylic filament yarn throwing, twisting, texturizing, or winding purchased yarn
325220 Acrylic fibers and filaments manufacturing
326113 Acrylic film and unlaminated sheet (except packaging) manufacturing
325211 Acrylic resins manufacturing
325212 Acrylic rubber manufacturing 313110 Acrylic spun yarns made from purchased fiber
325220 Acrylonitrile fibers and filaments manufacturing
325199 Acrylonitrile manufacturing 325211 Acrylonitrile-butadiene-styrene (ABS) resins manufacturing
334519 Actinometers, meteorological, manufacturing
339930 Action figures manufacturing
325998 Activated carbon or charcoal manufacturing
624120 Activity centers for disabled persons, the elderly, and persons diagnosed with intellectual and developmental disabilities
711510 Actors, independent
711510 Actresses, independent 541612 Actuarial consulting services (except insurance actuarial services)
524298 Actuarial services, insurance
333995 Actuators, fluid power, manufacturing
423830 Actuators, fluid power, merchant wholesalers
611519 Acupuncture training
621399 Acupuncturists' (except MDs or DOs) offices (e.g., centers, clinics)
621111 Acupuncturists' (MDs or DOs) offices (e.g., centers, clinics)
325110 Acyclic hydrocarbons (e.g., butene, ethylene, propene) (except acetylene) made from refined petroleum or liquid hydrocarbons
332993 Adapters, bombcluster, manufacturing
333318 Adding machines manufacturing 236118 Addition, alteration and renovation (i.e., construction), multifamily building
236118 Addition, alteration and renovation (i.e., construction), residential building
236118 Addition, alteration and renovation of single-family dwellings
236220 Addition, alteration and renovation, commercial and institutional building
236220 Addition, alteration and renovation, commercial warehouse
236220 Addition, alteration and renovation, for-sale builders, commercial and institutional building
236220 Addition, alteration and renovation, for-sale builders, commercial warehouse
236220 Addition, alteration and renovation, for-sale builders, hotel and motel
236210 Addition, alteration and renovation, for-sale builders, industrial building (except warehouses)
236220 Addition, alteration and renovation, for-sale builders, industrial warehouse
236220 Addition, alteration and renovation, general contractors, commercial and institutional building
236220 Addition, alteration and renovation, general contractors, commercial warehouse
236220 Addition, alteration and renovation, general contractors, hotel and motel
236210 Addition, alteration and renovation, general contractors, industrial building (except warehouses)
236220 Addition, alteration and renovation, general contractors, industrial warehouse
236220 Addition, alteration and renovation, hotel and motel
236210 Addition, alteration and renovation, industrial building (except warehouses)
236220 Addition, alteration and renovation, industrial warehouse
236118 Addition, alteration and renovation, multifamily building, for-sale builders

236118 Addition, alteration and renovation, multi-family building, general contractors
236118 Addition, alteration and renovation, residential building, for-sale builders
236118 Addition, alteration and renovation, residential building, general contractors
236118 Addition, alteration and renovation, single-family housing, for-sale builders
236118 Addition, alteration and renovation, single-family housing, general contractors
333249 Additive manufacturing machinery manufacturing
325998 Additive preparations for gasoline (e.g., anti-knock preparations, detergents, gum inhibitors) manufacturing
561499 Address bar coding services
511140 Address list publishers (except exclusive Internet publishing)
511140 Address list publishers and printing combined
323111 Address lists commercial printing (except screen) without publishing
323113 Address lists screen printing without publishing
423420 Addressing machines merchant wholesalers
322220 Adhesive tape (except medical) made from purchased materials
339113 Adhesive tape, medical, manufacturing
325520 Adhesives (except asphalt, dental, gypsum base) manufacturing
424690 Adhesives and sealants merchant wholesalers
325199 Adipic acid esters or amines manufacturing
325199 Adipic acid manufacturing
325199 Adiponitrile manufacturing
561440 Adjustment agencies (except insurance)
236220 Administration building construction
922110 Administrative courts
541611 Administrative management consulting services
561110 Administrative management services
523991 Administrators of private estates
327120 Adobe bricks manufacturing
624110 Adoption agencies
624110 Adoption services, child
325411 Adrenal derivatives, uncompounded, manufacturing
325412 Adrenal medicinal preparations manufacturing
624120 Adult day care centers 611691
Adult literacy instruction
327110 Advanced and technical ceramic products manufacturing
621399 Advanced practicing registered nurses' (APRNs) offices (e.g., centers, clinics)
541810 Advertising agencies
541810 Advertising agency consulting services
541870 Advertising material (e.g., coupons, flyers, samples) direct distribution services
541860 Advertising material preparation services for mailing or other direct distribution
323111 Advertising materials (e.g., coupons, flyers) commercial printing (except screen) without publishing
541840 Advertising media representatives (i.e., independent of media owners)
511120 Advertising periodical publishers (except exclusive Internet publishing)
511120 Advertising periodical publishers and printing combined
519130 Advertising periodical publishers, exclusively on Internet
515112 Advertising sales offices of independent and public radio broadcast stations
541850 Advertising services, indoor or outdoor display
541890 Advertising specialty (e.g., keychain, magnet, pen) distribution services
541850 Advertising, aerial
921110 Advisory commissions, executive government
921120 Advisory commissions, legislative
487990 Aerial cable car, scenic and sightseeing, operation
333316 Aerial cameras manufacturing
115112 Aerial crop dusting or spraying (i.e., using specialized or dedicated aircraft)
115310 Aerial forest mulching or seeding
541360 Aerial geophysical surveying services
238910 Aerial or picker truck, construction, rental with operator
541370 Aerial surveying (except geophysical) services
487990 Aerial tramway, scenic and sightseeing, operation
333923 Aerial work platforms manufacturing
713940 Aerobic dance and exercise centers
611620 Aerobic dance and exercise instruction
423860 Aeronautical equipment and supplies merchant wholesalers

334511 Aeronautical systems and instruments manufacturing
334511 Aeronautical systems and instruments overhauling, conversion, or rebuilding
325998 Aerosol can filling on a job-order or contract basis
332431 Aerosol cans, light gauge metal, manufacturing
325998 Aerosol packaging services
332919 Aerosol valves manufacturing 423860
Aerospace equipment and supplies merchant wholesalers
541715 Aerospace research and development (except prototype production)
332410 Aftercoolers (i.e., heat exchangers) manufacturing
423120 Aftermarket parts, automotive, merchant wholesalers
325620 After-shave preparations manufacturing
325414 Agar culture media manufacturing
325411 Agar-agar manufacturing
212399 Agate mining and/or beneficiating
111998 Agave farming
522293 Agencies of foreign banks (i.e., trade financing)
524210 Agencies, insurance
522310 Agencies, loan
531210 Agencies, real estate
531390 Agencies, real estate escrow
425120 Agents and brokers, durable goods, wholesale trade
425120 Agents and brokers, nondurable goods, wholesale trade
531390 Agents' offices, real estate escrow
711410 Agents, artists'
711410 Agents, authors'
711410 Agents, celebrities'
711410 Agents, entertainers'
812320 Agents, laundry and drycleaning
711410 Agents, modeling
711410 Agents, public figures'
531210 Agents, real estate
488510 Agents, shipping
711410 Agents, sports figures'
711410 Agents, talent
711410 Agents, theatrical talent
212210 Agglomerates, iron ore, beneficiating
333120 Aggregate spreaders manufacturing
325414 Aggressins (except in-vitro) manufacturing 551112 Agreement corporation (except international trade financing)
522293 Agreement corporations (i.e., international trade financing)
524126 Agricultural (i.e., crop, livestock) insurance carriers, direct
424910 Agricultural chemicals merchant wholesalers
541690 Agricultural consulting services
926140 Agricultural cooperative extension program administration
522298 Agricultural credit institutions, making loans or extending credit (except real estate, sales financing)
711320 Agricultural fair managers without facilities
711320 Agricultural fair organizers without facilities
711320 Agricultural fair promoters without facilities
332216 Agricultural handtools (e.g., hay forks, hoes, rakes, spades), nonpowered, manufacturing
423820 Agricultural implements merchant wholesalers
522298 Agricultural lending (except real estate, sales financing)
327410 Agricultural lime manufacturing
424910 Agricultural limestone merchant wholesalers
212312 Agricultural limestone mining and/or beneficiating
423820 Agricultural machinery and equipment merchant wholesalers
532490 Agricultural machinery and equipment rental or leasing
811310 Agricultural machinery and equipment repair and maintenance services
511120 Agricultural magazine and periodical publishers (except exclusive Internet publishing)
511120 Agricultural magazine and periodical publishers and printing combined
519130 Agricultural magazine and periodical publishers, exclusively on Internet
323111 Agricultural magazines and periodicals commercial printing (except screen) without publishing
323113 Agricultural magazines and periodicals screen printing without publishing
926140 Agricultural marketing services government

813910 Agricultural organizations (except youth farming organizations, farm granges)
926140 Agricultural pest and weed regulation, government
484220 Agricultural products trucking, local
531190 Agricultural property rental or leasing
926140 Agriculture fair boards administration
115115 Agriculture production or harvesting crews
541715 Agriculture research and development laboratories or services (except biotechnology and nanotechnology research and development)
541690 Agrology consulting services
541690 Agronomy consulting services 624110 Aid to families with dependent children (AFDC)
621910 Air ambulance services
336390 Air bag assemblies manufacturing
336390 Air bag initiators manufacturing
336612 Air boat building
336340 Air brake systems and parts, automotive, truck, and bus, manufacturing
481212 Air cargo carriers (except air couriers), nonscheduled
481112 Air cargo carriers (except air couriers), scheduled
332439 Air cargo containers, light gauge metal, manufacturing
335313 Air circuit breakers manufacturing
481111 Air commuter carriers, scheduled 333912 Air compressors (except air-conditioning, refrigeration) manufacturing
423830 Air compressors (except air-conditioning, refrigeration) merchant wholesalers
492110 Air courier services (except establishments operating under a universal service obligation)
332322 Air cowls, sheet metal (except stampings), manufacturing
336390 Air filters, automotive, truck, and bus, manufacturing
334512 Air flow controllers (except valves), air-conditioning and refrigeration, manufacturing
928110 Air Force
325612 Air fresheners manufacturing
313230 Air laid nonwoven fabrics manufacturing
481211 Air passenger carriers, nonscheduled
481111 Air passenger carriers, scheduled
423730 Air pollution control equipment and supplies merchant wholesalers
335210 Air purification equipment, portable, manufacturing
333413 Air purification equipment, stationary, manufacturing
332420 Air receiver tanks, heavy gauge metal, manufacturing
333413 Air scrubbing systems manufacturing
711310 Air show managers with facilities
711320 Air show managers without facilities
711310 Air show organizers with facilities
711320 Air show organizers without facilities
711310 Air show promoters with facilities
711320 Air show promoters without facilities
238220 Air system balancing and testing
481211 Air taxi services
334511 Air traffic control radar systems and equipment manufacturing
611519 Air traffic control schools 488111 Air traffic control services (except military)
928110 Air traffic control, military
238220 Air vent installation
333413 Air washers (i.e., air scrubbers) manufacturing
487210 Airboat (i.e., swamp buggy) operation
334511 Airborne navigational systems manufacturing
334220 Airborne radio communications equipment manufacturing
532210 Air-conditioner rental
811412 Air-conditioner, window, repair and maintenance services
336390 Air-conditioners, motor vehicle, manufacturing
423620 Air-conditioners, room, merchant wholesalers
333415 Air-conditioners, unit (e.g., motor home, travel trailer, window), manufacturing
333415 Air-conditioning and warm air heating combination units manufacturing
333415 Air-conditioning compressors (except motor vehicle) manufacturing
333415 Air-conditioning condensers and condensing units manufacturing
333415 Air-conditioning equipment (except motor vehicle) manufacturing
423730 Air-conditioning equipment (except room units) merchant wholesalers

221330 Air-conditioning supply 238220 Air-conditioning system (except window) installation
331491 Aircraft and automotive wire and cable (except aluminum, copper) made from purchased nonferrous metals (except aluminum, copper) in wire drawing plants
331420 Aircraft and automotive wire or cable made from purchased copper in wire drawing plants
332994 Aircraft artillery manufacturing
336413 Aircraft assemblies, subassemblies, and parts (except engines) manufacturing
336413 Aircraft auxiliary parts (e.g., crop dusting, external fuel tanks, inflight refueling equipment) manufacturing
336413 Aircraft brakes manufacturing
333999 Aircraft carrier catapults manufacturing
481219 Aircraft charter services (i.e., general purpose aircraft used for a variety of specialty air and flying services)
481211 Aircraft charter services, passenger
336413 Aircraft control surface assemblies manufacturing
336411 Aircraft conversions (i.e., major modifications to system)
441228 Aircraft dealers
336412 Aircraft engine and engine parts (except carburetors, pistons, piston rings, valves) manufacturing
333924 Aircraft engine cradles manufacturing
334519 Aircraft engine instruments manufacturing
336412 Aircraft engine overhauling
336412 Aircraft engine rebuilding
423860 Aircraft engines and parts merchant wholesalers
423860 Aircraft equipment and supplies merchant wholesalers
488190 Aircraft ferrying services
334511 Aircraft flight instruments (except engine instruments) manufacturing
336413 Aircraft fuselage wing tail and similar assemblies manufacturing
488119 Aircraft hangar rental
332510 Aircraft hardware, metal, manufacturing
488190 Aircraft inspection services
926120 Aircraft inspection, government
561720 Aircraft janitorial services
336320 Aircraft lighting fixtures manufacturing
333924 Aircraft loading hoists manufacturing
488190 Aircraft maintenance and repair services (except factory conversion, factory overhaul, factory rebuilding)
336411 Aircraft manufacturing
423860 Aircraft merchant wholesalers
336411 Aircraft overhauling
488119 Aircraft parking service
336413 Aircraft propellers and parts manufacturing
336411 Aircraft rebuilding (i.e., restoration to original design specifications)
532411 Aircraft rental or leasing without operator
336360 Aircraft seats manufacturing
488190 Aircraft testing services
314999 Aircraft tie-down strap assemblies (except leather) manufacturing
326211 Aircraft tire manufacturing
336412 Aircraft turbines manufacturing
811420 Aircraft upholstery repair
336413 Aircraft wheels manufacturing
333413 Aircurtains manufacturing
336413 Airframe assemblies (except for guided missiles) manufacturing
336419 Airframe assemblies for guided missiles manufacturing
334511 Airframe equipment instruments manufacturing
722310 Airline food services contractors
561599 Airline reservation services
561599 Airline ticket offices
332313 Airlocks, fabricated metal plate work, manufacturing
481112 Airmail carriers, scheduled
532411 Airplane rental or leasing without operator
488119 Airport baggage handling services
236220 Airport building construction
488119 Airport cargo handling services
531190 Airport leasing, not operating airport, rental or leasing
335311 Airport lighting transformers manufacturing
485999 Airport limousine services (i.e., shuttle)
488119 Airport operators (e.g., civil, international, national)
488190 Airport passenger screening security services
237310 Airport runway construction
238210 Airport runway lighting contractors

237310 Airport runway line painting (e.g., striping)
488119 Airport runway maintenance services
485999 Airport shuttle services
236220 Airport terminal construction
488119 Airports, civil, operation and maintenance
334511 Airspeed instruments (aeronautical) manufacturing
212399 Alabaster mining and/or beneficiating
423610 Alarm apparatus, electric, merchant wholesalers
334519 Alarm clocks manufacturing
238210 Alarm system (e.g., fire, burglar), electric, installation only
334290 Alarm system central monitoring equipment manufacturing
561621 Alarm system monitoring services
334290 Alarm systems and equipment manufacturing
561621 Alarm systems sales combined with installation, repair, or monitoring services
323111 Albums (e.g., photo, scrap) and refills manufacturing
424120 Albums, photo, merchant wholesalers
424690 Alcohol, industrial, merchant wholesalers
922120 Alcohol, tobacco, and firearms control
926150 Alcoholic beverage control boards
492210 Alcoholic beverage delivery service
722410 Alcoholic beverage drinking places
312140 Alcoholic beverages (except brandy) distilling
424810 Alcoholic beverages (except distilled spirits, wine) merchant wholesalers
312130 Alcoholic beverages, brandy, distilling
424820 Alcoholic beverages, wine, and distilled spirits merchant wholesalers
624190 Alcoholism and drug addiction self-help organizations
624190 Alcoholism counseling (except medical treatment), nonresidential
623220 Alcoholism rehabilitation facilities (except licensed hospitals), residential
622210 Alcoholism rehabilitation hospitals
624190 Alcoholism self-help organizations 621420
Alcoholism treatment centers and clinics (except hospitals), outpatient
325199 Aldehydes manufacturing
312120 Ale brewing
424810 Ale merchant wholesalers
111940 Alfalfa hay farming
311119 Alfalfa meal, dehydrated, manufacturing
424910 Alfalfa merchant wholesalers
311119 Alfalfa prepared as feed for animals
111998 Alfalfa seed farming
111419 Alfalfa sprout farming, grown under cover
311119 Alfalfa, cubed, manufacturing
112519 Algae farming
325199 Alginates (e.g., calcium, potassium, sodium) manufacturing
325199 Alginic acid manufacturing
334519 Alidades, surveying, manufacturing 333318
Alignment equipment, motor vehicle, manufacturing
325110 Aliphatic (e.g., hydrocarbons) (except acetylene) made from refined petroleum or liquid hydrocarbons
324110 Aliphatic chemicals (i.e., acyclic) made in petroleum refineries
325180 Alkalies manufacturing
424690 Alkalies merchant wholesalers
335912 Alkaline cell primary batteries manufacturing
335911 Alkaline cell storage batteries (i.e., nickel-cadmium, nickel-iron, silver oxide-zinc) manufacturing
335912 Alkaline manganese primary batteries manufacturing
325211 Alkyd resins manufacturing
324110 Alkylates made in petroleum refineries
325414 Allergenic extracts (except diagnostic substances) manufacturing 325414 Allergens manufacturing 621111 Allergists' offices (e.g., centers, clinics) 112519 Alligator production, farm raising 331513 Alloy steel castings (except investment),
unfinished, manufacturing
331314 Alloying purchased aluminum metals
331420 Alloying purchased copper
331420 Alloying purchased copper metals
331492 Alloying purchased nonferrous metals (except aluminum, copper)
441228 All-terrain vehicle (ATV) dealers
423110 All-terrain vehicles (ATVs) merchant wholesalers
336999 All-terrain vehicles (ATVs), wheeled or tracked, manufacturing
325211 Allyl resins manufacturing
323120 Almanac binding without printing

511130 Almanac publishers (except exclusive Internet publishing)
511130 Almanac publishers and printing combined
519130 Almanac publishers, exclusively on Internet
323117 Almanacs printing and binding without publishing
323117 Almanacs printing without publishing
111335 Almond farming
115114 Almond hulling and shelling
311999 Almond pastes manufacturing
111998 Aloe farming
112990 Alpaca production
721110 Alpine skiing facilities with accommodations (i.e., ski resorts)
713920 Alpine skiing facilities without accommodations
237130 Alternative energy (e.g., geothermal, ocean wave, solar, wind) structure construction
454310 Alternative fuels, direct selling
334515 Alternator and generator testers manufacturing
336320 Alternators and generators for internal combustion engines manufacturing 334511
Altimeters, aeronautical, manufacturing 212391
Alum, natural, mining and/or beneficiating 327120
Alumina fused refractories manufacturing 327110
Alumina porcelain insulators manufacturing
331313 Alumina refining 327120 Aluminous refractory cement manufacturing
331313 Aluminum alloys made from bauxite or alumina producing primary aluminum and manufacturing
331314 Aluminum alloys made from scrap or dross
423510 Aluminum and aluminum alloy primary forms merchant wholesalers
331318 Aluminum bar made by extruding purchased aluminum
331318 Aluminum bar made in integrated secondary smelting and extruding mills
331314 Aluminum billet made from purchased aluminum
331314 Aluminum billet made in integrated secondary smelting and rolling mills
332431 Aluminum cans, light gauge metal, manufacturing
331524 Aluminum castings (except die-castings), unfinished, manufacturing
325180 Aluminum chloride manufacturing 332812

Aluminum coating of metal products for the trade
325180 Aluminum compounds, not specified elsewhere by process, manufacturing 331523 Aluminum die-casting foundries 331523 Aluminum die-castings, unfinished, manufacturing
238350 Aluminum door and window, residential-type, installation
331314 Aluminum extrusion ingot (i.e., billet), secondary
331314 Aluminum flakes made from purchased aluminum
331315 Aluminum foil made by flat rolling purchased aluminum
331315 Aluminum foil made in integrated secondary smelting and flat rolling mills
423510 Aluminum foil, plate, sheet, coil, and roll products merchant wholesalers
332112 Aluminum forgings made from purchased metals, unfinished
331524 Aluminum foundries (except die-casting)
332999 Aluminum freezer foil not made in rolling mills
325180 Aluminum hydroxide (i.e., alumina trihydrate) manufacturing
331313 Aluminum ingot and other primary aluminum production shapes made from bauxite or alumina
331314 Aluminum ingot made from purchased aluminum
331314 Aluminum ingot, secondary smelting of aluminum and manufacturing
331314 Aluminum ingot, secondary, manufacturing
332999 Aluminum ladders manufacturing
327910 Aluminum oxide (fused) abrasives manufacturing
331313 Aluminum oxide refining
331318 Aluminum pipe made by extruding purchased aluminum
331318 Aluminum pipe made in integrated secondary smelting and extruding mills
236210 Aluminum plant construction 331315 Aluminum plate made by continuous casting purchased aluminum
331315 Aluminum plate made by flat rolling purchased aluminum
331315 Aluminum plate made in integrated secondary smelting and continuous casting mills

331315 Aluminum plate made in integrated secondary smelting and flat rolling mills
331313 Aluminum producing from alumina
331314 Aluminum recovering from scrap and making ingot and billet (except by rolling)
331318 Aluminum rod made by extruding purchased aluminum
331318 Aluminum rod made in integrated secondary smelting and extruding mills
331313 Aluminum shapes (e.g., bar, ingot, rod, sheet) made by producing primary aluminum and manufacturing
331315 Aluminum sheet made by flat rolling purchased aluminum
331315 Aluminum sheet made in integrated secondary smelting and flat rolling mills
238170 Aluminum siding installation
331314 Aluminum smelting, secondary, and making ingot and billet (except by rolling)
325180 Aluminum sulfate manufacturing
331318 Aluminum tube blooms made by extruding purchased aluminum
331318 Aluminum tube blooms made in integrated secondary smelting and extruding mills
331318 Aluminum tube made by drawing or extruding purchased aluminum
331318 Aluminum tube made in integrated secondary smelting and drawing plants
331318 Aluminum tube made in integrated secondary smelting and extruding mills
331315 Aluminum welded tube made by flat rolling purchased aluminum
331315 Aluminum welded tube made in integrated secondary smelting and flat rolling mills
813410 Alumni associations
813410 Alumni clubs
325180 Alums (e.g., aluminum ammonium sulfate, aluminum potassium sulfate) manufacturing
212393 Alunite mining and/or beneficiating
515112 AM radio stations
333131 Amalgamators (i.e., metallurgical and mining machinery) manufacturing
339114 Amalgams, dental, manufacturing
111998 Amaranth farming
713990 Amateur sports teams, recreational
325920 Amatols manufacturing
212393 Amblygonite mining and/or beneficiating
922160 Ambulance and fire service combined
336211 Ambulance bodies manufacturing
423110 Ambulance merchant wholesalers
621910 Ambulance services, air or ground
336211 Ambulances assembling on purchased chassis
621493 Ambulatory surgical centers and clinics, freestanding
921150 American Indian or Alaska Native tribal councils
921150 American Indian or Alaska Native tribal courts
921150 American Indian or Alaska Native, tribal chief's or chairman's office
212399 Amethyst mining and/or beneficiating
334516 Amino acid analyzers, laboratory-type, manufacturing
325211 Amino resins manufacturing
325211 Amino-aldehyde resins manufacturing
325194 Aminoanthraquinone manufacturing
325194 Aminoazobenzene manufacturing
325194 Aminoazotoluene manufacturing
325194 Aminophenol manufacturing
424690 Ammonia (except fertilizer material) merchant wholesalers
325311 Ammonia, anhydrous and aqueous, manufacturing
424910 Ammonia, fertilizer material, merchant wholesalers
325612 Ammonia, household-type, manufacturing
325180 Ammonium chloride manufacturing
325180 Ammonium compounds, not specified elsewhere by process, manufacturing
325180 Ammonium hydroxide manufacturing
325180 Ammonium molybdate manufacturing
325311 Ammonium nitrate manufacturing
325180 Ammonium perchlorate manufacturing
325312 Ammonium phosphates manufacturing
236210 Ammonium plant construction
325311 Ammonium sulfate manufacturing
325180 Ammonium thiosulfate manufacturing
423990 Ammunition (except sporting) merchant wholesalers
332993 Ammunition (i.e., more than 30 mm., more than 1.18 inch) manufacturing
332439 Ammunition boxes, light gauge metal, manufacturing
321920 Ammunition boxes, wood, manufacturing
332994 Ammunition carts manufacturing
332993 Ammunition loading and assembling plants

332992 Ammunition, small arms (i.e., 30 mm. or less, 1.18 inch or less), manufacturing
423910 Ammunition, sporting, merchant wholesalers
334515 Ampere-hour meters manufacturing
325411 Amphetamines, uncompounded, manufacturing
334310 Amplifiers (e.g., auto, home, musical instrument, public address) manufacturing
334220 Amplifiers (e.g., RF power and IF), broadcast and studio equipment, manufacturing
423690 Amplifiers, audio (except household-type), merchant wholesalers
335999 Amplifiers, magnetic, pulse, and maser, manufacturing
713120 Amusement arcades
713990 Amusement device (except gambling) concession operators (i.e., supplying and servicing in others' facilities)
713120 Amusement device (except gambling) parlors, coin-operated
713120 Amusement devices (except gambling) operated in own facilities
236220 Amusement facility construction
531120 Amusement facility rental or leasing
339999 Amusement machines, coin-operated, manufacturing
423850 Amusement park equipment merchant wholesalers
713110 Amusement parks (e.g., theme, water)
713990 Amusement ride concession operators (i.e., supplying and servicing in others' facilities)

325199 Amyl acetate manufacturing 325412 Analgesic preparations manufacturing 334111 Analog computers manufacturing 423490 Analytical instruments (e.g., chromatographic, photometers, spectrographs) merchant wholesalers

334515 Analyzers for testing electrical characteristics manufacturing
334513 Analyzers, industrial process control type, manufacturing
237990 Anchored earth retention contractors
114111 Anchovy fishing
212325 Andalusite mining and/or beneficiating
332999 Andirons manufacturing
339112 Anesthesia apparatus manufacturing
621111 Anesthesiologists' offices (e.g., centers, clinics)
325412 Anesthetic preparations manufacturing
325411 Anesthetics, uncompounded, manufacturing
325412 Angiourographic diagnostic preparations manufacturing
332999 Angle irons, metal, manufacturing
333515 Angle rings (i.e., a machine tool accessory) manufacturing
332911 Angle valves, industrial-type, manufacturing
334511 Angle-of-attack instrumentation manufacturing
334511 Angle-of-yaw instrumentation manufacturing
112420 Angora goat farming
325311 Anhydrous ammonia manufacturing
311512 Anhydrous butterfat manufacturing
325220 Anidex fibers and filaments manufacturing
325194 Aniline manufacturing
112519 Animal aquaculture (except finfish, shellfish)
325180 Animal black manufacturing
813910 Animal breeders' associations
812220 Animal cemeteries
712130 Animal exhibits, live
311611 Animal fats (except poultry and small game) produced in slaughtering plants
311613 Animal fats rendering
311119 Animal feed mills (except dog and cat) manufacturing
311111 Animal feed mills, dog and cat, manufacturing
424910 Animal feeds (except pet food) merchant wholesalers
311119 Animal feeds, prepared (except dog and cat), manufacturing
311111 Animal feeds, prepared, dog and cat, manufacturing
313110 Animal fiber yarn twisting or winding of purchased yarn
812910 Animal grooming services
424590 Animal hair, wool, or mohair merchant wholesalers
541940 Animal hospitals
311613 Animal oil rendering
926140 Animal quarantine service, government
813312 Animal rights organizations
712130 Animal safari parks
115210 Animal semen banks
236220 Animal shelter and clinic construction

812910 Animal shelters
114210 Animal trapping, commercial
332999 Animal traps, metal (except wire), manufacturing
813312 Animal welfare associations or leagues
336999 Animal-drawn vehicles and parts manufacturing
711510 Animated cartoon artists, independent
512120 Animated cartoon distribution
512110 Animated cartoon production
512110 Animated cartoon production and distribution
325998 Anise oil manufacturing
315110 Anklets, sheer hosiery or socks, knitting or knitting and finishing
325194 Annatto extract manufacturing
332811 Annealing metals and metal products for the trade
332420 Annealing vats, heavy gauge metal, manufacturing
711510 Announcers, independent radio and television
524113 Annuities underwriting
332991 Annular ball bearings manufacturing
334513 Annunciators, relay and solid-state types, industrial display, manufacturing
333249 Anodizing equipment manufacturing
332813 Anodizing metals and metal products for the trade
561421 Answering services, telephone
325320 Ant poisons manufacturing
325412 Antacid preparations manufacturing
238290 Antenna, household-type, installation
423690 Antennas merchant wholesalers
334220 Antennas, satellite, manufacturing
334220 Antennas, transmitting and receiving, manufacturing
325412 Anthelmintic preparations manufacturing
325194 Anthracene manufacturing 212113 Anthracite beneficiating (e.g., crushing, screening, washing, cleaning, sizing)
213113 Anthracite mine tunneling on a contract basis
212113 Anthracite mining and/or beneficiating
213113 Anthracite mining services (except site preparation and related construction contractor activities) on a contract basis
325130 Anthraquinone dyes manufacturing
332994 Antiaircraft artillery manufacturing
325412 Antibacterial preparations manufacturing
325412 Antibiotic preparations manufacturing
424210 Antibiotics merchant wholesalers
325411 Antibiotics, uncompounded, manufacturing
325411 Anticholinergics, uncompounded, manufacturing
325411 Anticonvulsants, uncompounded, manufacturing
325412 Antidepressant preparations manufacturing
325411 Antidepressants, uncompounded, manufacturing
424690 Antifreeze merchant wholesalers
325998 Antifreeze preparations manufacturing
325414 Antigens manufacturing
325412 Antihistamine preparations manufacturing
325130 Antimony based pigments manufacturing
212299 Antimony concentrates mining and/or beneficiating
212299 Antimony ores mining and/or beneficiating
325180 Antimony oxide (except pigments) manufacturing
331410 Antimony refining, primary
325412 Antineoplastic preparations manufacturing
325620 Antiperspirants, personal, manufacturing
813319 Antipoverty advocacy organizations
325412 Antipyretic preparations manufacturing
811121 Antique and classic automotive restoration
441120 Antique auto dealers
424920 Antique book merchant wholesalers
453310 Antique dealers (except motor vehicles)
423210 Antique furniture merchant wholesalers
811420 Antique furniture repair and restoration shops
423220 Antique home furnishings merchant wholesalers
423220 Antique houseware merchant wholesalers
423940 Antique jewelry merchant wholesalers
453310 Antique shops
332913 Antiscald bath and shower valves, plumbing, manufacturing
325998 Antiscaling compounds manufacturing
325412 Antiseptic preparations manufacturing
424210 Antiseptics merchant wholesalers
325414 Antiserums manufacturing
325412 Antispasmodic preparations manufacturing

332994 Antisubmarine projectors manufacturing
332994 Antitank rocket launchers manufacturing
325414 Antitoxins manufacturing
325414 Antivenoms manufacturing
236116 Apartment building construction general contractors
236117 Apartment building for-sale builders
531110 Apartment building rental or leasing
531110 Apartment hotel rental or leasing
531311 Apartment managers' offices
531110 Apartment rental or leasing
212392 Apatite mining and/or beneficiating
212325 Aplite mining and/or beneficiating
446110 Apothecaries
331491 Apparatus wire and cord (except aluminum, copper) made from purchased nonferrous metals (except aluminum, copper) in wire drawing plants
331420 Apparatus wire or cord made from purchased copper in wire drawing plants
331318 Apparatus wire or cord made in aluminum wire drawing plants
448150 Apparel accessory stores
315210 Apparel cut and sew contractors
314999 Apparel fillings (e.g., cotton mill waste, kapok) manufacturing
315990 Apparel findings and trimmings cut and sewn from purchased fabric (except apparel contractors)
561910 Apparel folding and packaging services
812320 Apparel pressing services 448130 Apparel stores, children's and infants' clothing
448110 Apparel stores, men's and boys' clothing
453310 Apparel stores, used clothing
448120 Apparel stores, women's and girls' clothing
315210 Apparel trimmings and findings cut and sew apparel contractors
424310 Apparel trimmings merchant wholesalers
313220 Apparel webbings manufacturing 315280 Apparel, fur (except apparel contractors), manufacturing
315210 Apparel, fur, cut and sew apparel contractors
111331 Apple orchards
312130 Applejack distilling
334512 Appliance controls manufacturing
335999 Appliance cords made from purchased insulated wire
423710 Appliance hardware merchant wholesalers
332510 Appliance hardware, metal, manufacturing
334512 Appliance regulators (except switches) manufacturing
532210 Appliance rental
443141 Appliance stores, household-type 453310 Appliance stores, household-type, used 334519 Appliance timers manufacturing 811412 Appliance, household-type, repair and maintenance services without retailing new appliances
423620 Appliances, household-type (except water heaters, heating stoves (i.e., noncooking)), gas and electric, merchant wholesalers
423450 Appliances, surgical, merchant wholesalers
518210 Application hosting
511210 Applications development and publishing, except on a custom basis
541511 Applications software programming services, custom computer
511210 Applications software, computer, packaged
321999 Applicators, wood, manufacturing
315210 Appliqueing on apparel
314999 Appliqueing on textile products (except apparel)
323111 Appointment books and refills manufacturing
541990 Appraisal (except real estate) services
531320 Appraisal services, real estate
531320 Appraisers' offices, real estate
611513 Apprenticeship training programs
111339 Apricot farming
812331 Apron supply services
316998 Aprons for textile machinery, leather, manufacturing
316998 Aprons, leather (e.g., blacksmith's, welder's), manufacturing
315990 Aprons, waterproof (e.g., plastics, rubberized fabric), rubberizing fabric and manufacturing aprons
315210 Aprons, waterproof (including rubberized fabric, plastics), cut and sew apparel contractors
315990 Aprons, waterproof (including rubberized fabric, plastics), cut and sewn from purchased fabric (except apparel contractors)
315210 Aprons, work (except leather), cut and sew apparel contractors

315220 Aprons, work (except leather, waterproof), men's and boys', cut and sewn from purchased fabric (except apparel contractors)

315240 Aprons, work (except waterproof, leather), women's and girls', cut and sewn from purchased fabric (except apparel contractors)

332999 Aquarium accessories, metal, manufacturing

424990 Aquarium fish and supplies merchant wholesalers

712130 Aquariums

327215 Aquariums made from purchased glass

237110 Aqueduct construction

541990 Arbitration and conciliation services (except by attorney, paralegal)

333517 Arbor presses, metalworking, manufacturing

712130 Arboreta

712130 Arboretums 561730

Arborist services

333515 Arbors (i.e., a machine tool accessory) manufacturing

334510 Arc lamp units, electrotherapeutic (except infrared, ultraviolet), manufacturing

335129 Arc lighting fixtures (except electrotherapeutic), electric, manufacturing

713120 Arcades, amusement

339113 Arch supports, orthopedic, manufacturing

541720 Archeological research and development services

712120 Archeological sites (i.e., public display)

339920 Archery equipment manufacturing

423910 Archery equipment merchant wholesalers

713990 Archery ranges

321213 Arches, glue laminated or pre-engineered wood, manufacturing

541310 Architects' (except landscape) offices

541310 Architects' (except landscape) private practices

813920 Architects' associations 423490 Architects' equipment and supplies merchant wholesalers

541320 Architects' offices, landscape

541320 Architects' private practices, landscape

541310 Architectural (except landscape) consultants' offices

541310 Architectural (except landscape) design services

541310 Architectural (except landscape) services

327331 Architectural block, concrete (e.g., fluted, ground face, screen, slump, split), manufacturing

325510 Architectural coatings (i.e., paint) manufacturing

332323 Architectural metalwork manufacturing

423390 Architectural metalwork merchant wholesalers

453310 Architectural salvage dealers

327110 Architectural sculptures, clay, manufacturing

327991 Architectural sculptures, stone, manufacturing

541320 Architectural services, landscape

453998 Architectural supply stores

327120 Architectural terra cotta manufacturing

327390 Architectural wall panels, precast concrete, manufacturing

337212 Architectural woodwork and fixtures (i.e., custom designed interiors) manufacturing

519120 Archives

316210 Arctics, plastics or plastics soled fabric upper, manufacturing

316210 Arctics, rubber or rubber soled fabric, manufacturing

333992 Arc-welding equipment manufacturing

335311 Arc-welding transformers, separate solid-state, manufacturing

335129 Area and sports luminaries (e.g., stadium lighting fixtures), electric, manufacturing

236220 Arena construction

711310 Arena operators

531120 Arena, no promotion of events, rental or leasing

212311 Argillite mining or quarrying

325120 Argon manufacturing

315210 Arm bands cut and sew apparel contractors

315990 Arm bands, elastic, cut and sewn from purchased fabric (except apparel contractors)

335314 Armature relays manufacturing

335312 Armature rewinding on a factory basis

811310 Armature rewinding services (except on an assembly line or factory basis)

335312 Armatures, industrial, manufacturing

928110 Armed forces

332993 Arming and fusing devices, missile, manufacturing

331110 Armor plate made in iron and steel mills

331420 Armored cable made from purchased copper in wire drawing plants

331420 Armored cable, copper, made in integrated secondary smelting and drawing plants

561613 Armored car services 336992 Armored military vehicles (except tanks) and parts manufacturing

236220 Armory construction

928110 Army

424690 Aromatic chemicals merchant wholesalers

325110 Aromatic petrochemicals made from refined petroleum or liquid hydrocarbons

113210 Aromatic wood gathering

488999 Arrangement of car pools and vanpools

335931 Arrestors and coils, lighting, manufacturing

325320 Arsenate insecticides manufacturing

325180 Arsenates (except insecticides) manufacturing

325130 Arsenic based pigments manufacturing

325180 Arsenic compounds, not specified elsewhere by process, manufacturing

212393 Arsenic mineral mining and/or beneficiating

325320 Arsenite insecticides manufacturing

325180 Arsenites (except insecticides) manufacturing

611610 Art (except commercial or graphic) instruction

453920 Art auctions

453920 Art dealers

712110 Art galleries (except retail)

453920 Art galleries retailing art

327420 Art goods (e.g., gypsum, plaster of paris) manufacturing

424990 Art goods merchant wholesalers

712110 Art museums

314999 Art needlework contractors on apparel

314999 Art needlework on clothing for the trade

511199 Art print (except exclusive Internet publishing) publishers

511199 Art print publishers and printing combined

323111 Art prints commercial printing (except screen) without publishing

323113 Art prints screen printing without publishing

511199 Art publishers (except exclusive Internet publishing)

519130 Art publishers, exclusively on Internet

711510 Art restorers, independent

611610 Art schools (except academic), fine

611519 Art schools, commercial or graphic

541430 Art services, commercial

541430 Art services, graphic

541430 Art studios, commercial

453998 Art supply stores

621340 Art therapists' offices (e.g., centers, clinics)

237110 Artesian well construction

111219 Artichoke farming, field, bedding plant and seed production

311421 Artichokes, canned, manufacturing

424990 Artificial Christmas trees merchant wholesalers

339999 Artificial flower arrangements assembled from purchased components

424930 Artificial flowers and plants merchant wholesalers

334511 Artificial horizon instrumentation manufacturing

115210 Artificial insemination services for livestock

115210 Artificial insemination services for pets

339113 Artificial limbs manufacturing

423450 Artificial limbs merchant wholesalers

238990 Artificial turf installation

312111 Artificially carbonated waters manufacturing

332993 Artillery ammunition (i.e., more than 30 mm., more than 1.18 inch) manufacturing

711510 Artists (except commercial, musical), independent

711510 Artists (i.e., painters), independent

711410 Artists' agents or managers

339940 Artist's paint manufacturing

339940 Artist's supplies (except paper) manufacturing

424990 Artists' supplies merchant wholesalers

541430 Artists, independent commercial

541430 Artists, independent graphic

541430 Artists, independent medical

926110 Arts and cultural program administration, government

711310 Arts event managers with facilities

711320 Arts event managers without facilities

711310 Arts event organizers with facilities

711320 Arts event organizers without facilities

711310 Arts event promoters with facilities
711320 Arts event promoters without facilities
711310 Arts festival managers with facilities
711320 Arts festival managers without facilities
711310 Arts festival organizers with facilities
711320 Arts festival organizers without facilities
711310 Arts festival promoters with facilities
711320 Arts festival promoters without facilities
562910 Asbestos abatement services
212399 Asbestos mining and/or beneficiating
327999 Asbestos products (except brake shoes and clutches) manufacturing
562910 Asbestos removal contractors
325411 Ascorbic acid (i.e., vitamin C), uncompounded, manufacturing
315210 Ascots cut and sew apparel contractors
315990 Ascots, men's and boys', cut and sewn from purchased fabric (except apparel contractors)
562111 Ash collection services
562111 Ash hauling, local
484220 Ash, garbage, recyclable material, refuse, rubbish, trash, or waste hauling (except collection or disposal)
212399 Ash, volcanic, mining and/or beneficiating
327215 Ashtrays made from purchased glass 327212
Ashtrays, glass, made in glass making plants
327110 Ashtrays, pottery, manufacturing
111219 Asparagus farming, field, bedding plant and seed production
324110 Asphalt and asphaltic materials made in petroleum refineries
423320 Asphalt and concrete mixtures merchant wholesalers
424710 Asphalt binder bulk stations and terminals, merchant wholesalers
424720 Asphalt binder merchant wholesalers (except bulk stations, terminals)
238990 Asphalt coating and sealing, residential and commercial parking lot and driveway
327999 Asphalt concrete crushing and grinding (except at construction site)
423330 Asphalt felts and coatings merchant wholesalers
238330 Asphalt flooring, installation only
322121 Asphalt paper made in paper mills 237310
Asphalt paving (i.e., highway, road, street, public sidewalk)
324121 Asphalt paving blocks made from purchased asphaltic materials
324121 Asphalt paving mixtures made from purchased asphaltic materials
324110 Asphalt paving mixtures made in petroleum refineries
324121 Asphalt road compounds made from purchased asphaltic materials
212399 Asphalt rock mining and/or beneficiating
238160 Asphalt roof shingle installation 324122
Asphalt roofing cements made from purchased asphaltic materials
324122 Asphalt roofing coatings made from purchased asphaltic materials
333120 Asphalt roofing construction machinery manufacturing
423330 Asphalt roofing shingles merchant wholesalers
324122 Asphalt saturated boards made from purchased asphaltic materials
324122 Asphalt saturated mats and felts made from purchased asphaltic materials and paper
324122 Asphalt shingles made from purchased asphaltic materials
424710 Asphalt, liquid, bulk stations and terminals, merchant wholesalers
424720 Asphalt, liquid, merchant wholesalers (except bulk stations, terminals)
212399 Asphalt, native, mining and/or beneficiating
238990 Asphalting, residential and commercial driveway and parking area
541380 Assaying services
336213 Assembly line conversions of purchased vans and minivans
336310 Assembly line rebuilding of automotive and truck gasoline engines
336350 Assembly line rebuilding of automotive, truck, and bus transmissions
333519 Assembly machines manufacturing
236210 Assembly plant construction 336120 Assembly plants, heavy trucks, and buses on chassis of own manufacture
336112 Assembly plants, light trucks on chassis of own manufacture
336112 Assembly plants, minivans on chassis of own manufacture
336111 Assembly plants, passenger car, on chassis of own manufacture
336112 Assembly plants, sport utility vehicles on chassis of own manufacture
921130 Assessor's offices, tax

325613 Assistants, textile and leather finishing, manufacturing
623311 Assisted living facilities with on-site nursing facilities
623312 Assisted living facilities without on-site nursing care facilities
813311 Associations for retired persons, advocacy
522120 Associations, savings and loan
325412 Astringent preparations manufacturing
812990 Astrology services
711219 Athletes, amateur, independent
711219 Athletes, independent (i.e., participating in live sports events)
813990 Athletic associations, regulatory
315220 Athletic clothing (except team athletic uniforms), men's, boys' and unisex (i.e., sized without regard to gender), cut and sewn from purchased fabric (except apparel contractors)
315240 Athletic clothing (except team athletic uniforms), women's and girls', cut and sewn from purchased fabric (except apparel contractors)
315210 Athletic clothing cut and sew apparel contractors
315190 Athletic clothing made in apparel knitting mills
713940 Athletic club facilities, physical fitness
713990 Athletic clubs (i.e., sports teams) not operating sports facilities, recreational
236220 Athletic court, indoor, construction
451110 Athletic equipment and supply stores (including uniforms)
237990 Athletic field (except stadium) construction
424340 Athletic footwear merchant wholesalers
339920 Athletic goods (except ammunition, clothing, footwear, small arms) manufacturing
423910 Athletic goods (except apparel, footwear, nonspecialty) merchant wholesalers 813990 Athletic leagues (i.e., regulating bodies) 448210 Athletic shoe (except bowling, golf, spiked) stores
316210 Athletic shoes manufacturing 316210 Athletic shoes, plastics or plastics soled fabric upper, manufacturing
316210 Athletic shoes, rubber or rubber soled fabric upper, manufacturing
315110 Athletic socks knitting or knitting and finishing
423910 Athletic uniforms merchant wholesalers
315210 Athletic uniforms, team, cut and sew apparel contractors
315280 Athletic uniforms, team, cut and sewn from purchased fabric (except apparel contractors)
511130 Atlas publishers (except exclusive Internet publishing)
511130 Atlas publishers and printing combined
519130 Atlas publishers, exclusively on Internet
323111 Atlases commercial printing (except screen) without publishing
424920 Atlases merchant wholesalers
323113 Atlases screen printing without publishing
238290 ATMs (automatic teller machines) installation
334118 ATMs (automatic teller machines) manufacturing
335999 Atom smashers (i.e., particle accelerators) manufacturing
334516 Atomic force microscopes manufacturing
339999 Atomizers (e.g., perfumes) manufacturing
325411 Atropine and derivatives manufacturing
316998 Attache cases, all materials, manufacturing
333112 Attachments, powered lawn and garden equipment, manufacturing
333413 Attic fans manufacturing
238310 Attic space insulating
922130 Attorney generals' offices
541110 Attorneys' offices
541110 Attorneys' private practices
453998 Auction houses (general merchandise)
424520 Auction markets, livestock (except horses, mules), merchant wholesalers
424590 Auction markets, tobacco, horses, mules, merchant wholesalers
561990 Auctioneers, independent
531210 Auctioning real estate for others (i.e., agents, brokers)
454110 Auctions, Internet retail 454110 Audio and video content downloading retail sales sites
423990 Audio and video tapes and disks, prerecorded, merchant wholesalers
321999 Audio cabinets (i.e., housings), wood, manufacturing
238210 Audio equipment installation (except automotive) contractors
443142 Audio equipment stores (except automotive)
423620 Audio equipment, household-type, merchant wholesalers

512290 Audio recording of meetings or conferences
512240 Audio recording postproduction services
512240 Audio recording restoration services
532490 Audio visual equipment rental or leasing
334515 Audiofrequency oscillators manufacturing
334510 Audiological equipment, electromedical, manufacturing
621340 Audiologists' offices (e.g., centers, clinics)
334515 Audiometers (except medical) manufacturing
334613 Audiotape, blank, manufacturing
423690 Audiotapes, blank, merchant wholesalers
541211 Auditing accountants' (i.e., CPAs) offices
541211 Auditing accountants' (i.e., CPAs) private practices
541211 Auditing services (i.e., CPA services), accounts
236220 Auditorium construction
531120 Auditorium rental or leasing
541211 Auditors' (i.e., CPAs) offices, accounts
541211 Auditors' (i.e., CPAs) private practices, accounts
921190 Auditor's offices, government
213113 Auger coal mining services (except site preparation and related construction contractor activities) on a contract basis
333120 Augers (except mining-type) manufacturing
333131 Augers, mining-type, manufacturing
332216 Augers, nonpowered, manufacturing
711410 Authors' agents or managers
711510 Authors, independent
423120 Auto body shop supplies merchant wholesalers
721110 Auto courts, lodging
441310 Auto supply stores
339114 Autoclaves, dental, manufacturing
332420 Autoclaves, industrial-type, heavy gauge metal, manufacturing
339113 Autoclaves, laboratory-type (except dental), manufacturing
336411 Autogiros manufacturing
238290 Automated and revolving door installation
334510 Automated blood and body fluid analyzers (except laboratory) manufacturing
522320 Automated clearinghouses, bank or check (except central bank)
518210 Automated data processing services 522320

Automated Teller Machine (ATM) or Automated Loan Machine (ALM) network operation
332911 Automatic (i.e., controlling-type, regulating) valves, industrial-type, manufacturing
423690 Automatic call distributors merchant wholesalers
334516 Automatic chemical analyzers, laboratory-type, manufacturing
238290 Automatic gate (e.g., garage, parking lot) installation
812310 Automatic laundries, coin-operated
454210 Automatic merchandising machine operators
333517 Automatic screw machines, metal cutting type, manufacturing
334118 Automatic teller machines (ATM) manufacturing
423420 Automatic teller machines (ATM) merchant wholesalers
336350 Automatic transmissions, automotive, truck, and bus, manufacturing
423120 Automobile accessories (except tires, tubes) merchant wholesalers
334220 Automobile antennas manufacturing
423110 Automobile auction merchant wholesalers
425120 Automobile auctions, wholesale
336211 Automobile bodies, passenger car, manufacturing
484220 Automobile carrier trucking, local
484230 Automobile carrier trucking, long-distance
813410 Automobile clubs (except road and travel services)
561599 Automobile clubs, road and travel services
721110 Automobile courts, lodging
493190 Automobile dead storage
441110 Automobile dealers, new only or new and used
441120 Automobile dealers, used only
611692 Automobile driving schools
522220 Automobile finance leasing companies
522220 Automobile financing
423120 Automobile glass merchant wholesalers
332510 Automobile hardware, metal, manufacturing
541420 Automobile industrial design services
524126 Automobile insurance carriers, direct

532112 Automobile leasing

333921 Automobile lifts (i.e., garage-type, service station) manufacturing

423110 Automobile merchant wholesalers

812930 Automobile parking garages or lots

441310 Automobile parts dealers

325612 Automobile polishes and cleaners manufacturing

541380 Automobile proving and testing grounds

711212 Automobile racetracks

611620 Automobile racing schools

711219 Automobile racing teams

334310 Automobile radio receivers manufacturing

532111 Automobile rental

485320 Automobile rental with driver (except shuttle service, taxis)

561491 Automobile repossession services

336360 Automobile seat covers manufacturing

336360 Automobile seat frames, metal, manufacturing

423120 Automobile service station equipment merchant wholesalers

561920 Automobile show managers

561920 Automobile show organizers

561920 Automobile show promoters

332618 Automobile skid chains made from purchased wire

335911 Automobile storage batteries manufacturing

332613 Automobile suspension springs, heavy gauge metal, manufacturing

336212 Automobile transporter trailers, multi-car, manufacturing

336214 Automobile transporter trailers, single car, manufacturing

336360 Automobile trimmings, textile, manufacturing

333923 Automobile wrecker (i.e., tow truck) hoists manufacturing

336211 Automobile wrecker truck bodies manufacturing

336211 Automobile wreckers assembling on purchased chassis

336111 Automobiles assembling on chassis of own manufacture

339930 Automobiles, children's, manufacturing

423730 Automotive air-conditioners merchant wholesalers

811198 Automotive air-conditioning repair shops

334515 Automotive ammeters and voltmeters manufacturing

441310 Automotive audio equipment stores

811121 Automotive body shops

811118 Automotive brake repair shops

423120 Automotive brakes merchant wholesalers

424690 Automotive chemicals (except lubricating greases, lubrication oils) merchant wholesalers

811192 Automotive detail shops

811192 Automotive detailing services (i.e., cleaning, polishing)

334515 Automotive electrical engine diagnostic equipment manufacturing

811118 Automotive electrical repair shops

335931 Automotive electrical switches manufacturing

334519 Automotive emissions testing equipment manufacturing

811198 Automotive emissions testing services

811111 Automotive engine repair and replacement shops

811112 Automotive exhaust system repair and replacement shops

424310 Automotive fabrics merchant wholesalers

811111 Automotive fleet repair and maintenance services

811118 Automotive front end alignment shops

811122 Automotive glass shops 336320 Automotive harness and ignition sets manufacturing

335110 Automotive light bulbs manufacturing

336320 Automotive lighting fixtures manufacturing

332710 Automotive machine shops

336390 Automotive mirrors, framed, manufacturing

811191 Automotive oil change and lubrication shops

331318 Automotive or aircraft wire and cable made in aluminum wire drawing plants

811121 Automotive paint shops

424950 Automotive paints merchant wholesalers

441310 Automotive parts and supply stores

441310 Automotive parts dealers, used

423120 Automotive parts, new, merchant wholesalers

423140 Automotive parts, used, merchant wholesalers

811118 Automotive radiator repair shops
423620 Automotive radios merchant wholesalers
811111 Automotive repair and replacement shops, general
811198 Automotive rustproofing and undercoating shops
811198 Automotive safety inspection services
423120 Automotive stampings merchant wholesalers
334290 Automotive theft alarm systems manufacturing
441320 Automotive tire dealers
811198 Automotive tire repair (except retreading) shops
811113 Automotive transmission repair shops
811118 Automotive tune-up shops
811121 Automotive upholstery shops
811192 Automotive washing and polishing
336330 Automotive, truck and bus steering assemblies and parts manufacturing
336330 Automotive, truck and bus suspension assemblies and parts (except springs) manufacturing
339992 Autophones (organs with perforated music rolls) manufacturing
335311 Autotransformers for switchboards (except telephone switchboards) manufacturing
335311 Autotransformers manufacturing 237990
Avalanche, rockslide, mudslide, or roadside protection construction
712130 Aviaries
112990 Aviaries (i.e., raising birds for sale) 813319
Aviation advocacy organizations 481219 Aviation clubs providing a variety of air transportation activities to the general
public
488119 Aviation clubs, primarily providing flying field services to the general public
713990 Aviation clubs, recreational
324110 Aviation fuels manufacturing
611512 Aviation schools
111339 Avocado farming
332216 Awls manufacturing
238190 Awning installation
423390 Awnings (except canvas) merchant wholesalers
314910 Awnings and canopies, outdoor, made from purchased fabrics
424990 Awnings, canvas, merchant wholesalers
326199 Awnings, rigid plastics or fiberglass, manufacturing
332322 Awnings, sheet metal (except stampings), manufacturing
332216 Axes manufacturing
336350 Axle bearings, automotive, truck, and bus, manufacturing
331110 Axles, rolled or forged, made in iron and steel mills
111421 Azalea farming
325920 Azides explosive materials manufacturing
325130 Azine dyes manufacturing
325130 Azo dyes manufacturing
325194 Azobenzene manufacturing
424330 Baby and infant car seats merchant wholesalers
424330 Baby and infant high chairs merchant wholesalers
424330 Baby bottles merchant wholesalers
424330 Baby clothing merchant wholesalers
448130 Baby clothing shops
311422 Baby foods (including meats) canning
424490 Baby foods, canned, merchant wholesalers
311514 Baby formula, fresh, processed, and bottled, manufacturing
423210 Baby furniture merchant wholesalers
325620 Baby powder and baby oil manufacturing
333997 Baby scales manufacturing
812990 Baby shoe bronzing services
561311 Babysitting bureaus (i.e., registries)
624410 Babysitting services in provider's own home, child day care
624410 Babysitting services, child day care
238910 Backfilling, construction 332913
Backflow preventers, plumbing, manufacturing
561611 Background check services
112111 Backgrounding, cattle
238910 Backhoe rental with operator
333120 Backhoes manufacturing
424990 Backpacks, textile, merchant wholesalers
311612 Bacon, slab and sliced, made from purchased carcasses
311611 Bacon, slab and sliced, produced in slaughtering plants
325414 Bacterial vaccines manufacturing
325414 Bacterins (i.e., bacterial vaccines) manufacturing

621511 Bacteriological laboratories, diagnostic
621511 Bacteriological laboratories, medical
424210 Bacteriological medicines merchant wholesalers
541715 Bacteriological research and development laboratories or services (except biotechnology and nanotechnology research and development)
314999 Badges, fabric, manufacturing
332999 Badges, metal, manufacturing
326199 Badges, plastics, manufacturing
339920 Badminton equipment manufacturing
332313 Baffles, fabricated metal plate work, manufacturing
316110 Bag leather manufacturing
332993 Bag loading plants, ammunition, manufacturing
333993 Bag opening, filling, and closing machines manufacturing
722511 Bagel shops, full service
722515 Bagel shops, on premise baking and carryout service
311812 Bagels made in commercial bakeries
322220 Bags (except plastics only) made by laminating or coating combinations of purchased plastics, foil and paper
316998 Bags (i.e., luggage), all materials, manufacturing
313240 Bags and bagging fabrics made in warp or weft knitting mills
316998 Bags, athletic, manufacturing
322220 Bags, coated paper, made from purchased paper
322220 Bags, foil, made from purchased foil
339920 Bags, golf, manufacturing
313110 Bags, hemp, made from purchased fiber
322220 Bags, multiwall, made from purchased uncoated paper
424130 Bags, paper and disposable plastics, merchant wholesalers
322220 Bags, paper, uncoated, made from purchased paper
326111 Bags, plastics film, single wall or multiwall, manufacturing
314910 Bags, plastics, made from purchased woven plastics
339920 Bags, punching, manufacturing
423930 Bags, reclaimed, merchant wholesalers
314910 Bags, rubberized fabric, manufacturing
314999 Bags, sleeping, manufacturing
314910 Bags, textile, made from purchased woven or knitted materials
424990 Bags, textile, merchant wholesalers
322220 Bags, uncoated paper, made from purchased paper
812990 Bail bonding services
423390 Bailey bridges merchant wholesalers
339920 Bait, artificial, fishing, manufacturing
423910 Bait, artificial, merchant wholesalers
424990 Bait, live, merchant wholesalers
112511 Baitfish production, farm raising
311422 Baked beans canning
311813 Baked goods (except bread, bread-type rolls), frozen, manufacturing
445291 Baked goods stores, retailing only (except immediate consumption)
445210 Baked ham stores
311811 Bakeries with baking from flour on the premises, retailing not for immediate consumption
315210 Bakers' service apparel, washable, cut and sew apparel contractors
315220 Bakers' service apparel, washable, men's and boys', cut and sewn from purchased fabric (except apparel contractors)
315240 Bakers' service apparel, washable, women's and girls', cut and sewn from purchased fabric (except apparel contractors)
722515 Bakery cafes, on premise baking and selling for immediate consumption
333241 Bakery machinery and equipment manufacturing
423830 Bakery machinery and equipment merchant wholesalers
333241 Bakery ovens manufacturing
424490 Bakery products (except frozen) merchant wholesalers
311821 Bakery products, dry (e.g., biscuits, cookies, crackers), manufacturing
311812 Bakery products, fresh (i.e., bread, cakes, doughnuts, pastries), made in commercial bakeries
424420 Bakery products, frozen, merchant wholesalers
311351 Baking chocolate made from cacao beans
311352 Baking chocolate made from purchased chocolate
311999 Baking powder manufacturing
423440 Balances and scales (except laboratory) merchant wholesalers
423490 Balances and scales, laboratory (except dental, medical), merchant wholesalers

333997 Balances, including laboratory-type, manufacturing
333318 Balancing equipment, motor vehicle, manufacturing
423120 Balancing equipment, motor vehicle, merchant wholesalers
423830 Balancing machines (except automotive) merchant wholesalers
332323 Balcony railings, metal, manufacturing
238190 Balcony, metal, installation
238120 Balcony, precast concrete, installation
333111 Bale throwers manufacturing
332618 Bale ties made from purchased wire
333111 Balers, farm-type (e.g., cotton, hay, straw), manufacturing
333999 Baling machinery (e.g., paper, scrap metal) manufacturing
332991 Ball bearings manufacturing
212324 Ball clay mining and/or beneficiating
333613 Ball joints (except aircraft, motor vehicle) manufacturing
339940 Ball point pens manufacturing
332911 Ball valves, industrial-type, manufacturing
335311 Ballasts (i.e., transformers) manufacturing
711120 Ballet companies
711510 Ballet dancers, independent
711120 Ballet productions, live theatrical
611610 Ballet schools (except academic)
316210 Ballet slippers manufacturing
453220 Balloon shops
812990 Balloon-o-gram services
326199 Balloons, plastics, manufacturing
326299 Balloons, rubber, manufacturing
713990 Ballrooms
339920 Balls, baseball, basketball, football, golf, tennis, pool, and bowling, manufacturing
339930 Balls, rubber (except athletic equipment), manufacturing
331110 Balls, steel, made in iron and steel mills
113210 Balsam needles gathering
111339 Banana farming
115114 Banana ripening
315210 Band uniforms cut and sew apparel contractors
315280 Band uniforms cut and sewn from purchased fabric (except apparel contractors)
424210 Bandages (except surgical) merchant wholesalers
339113 Bandages and dressings, surgical and orthopedic, manufacturing
315210 Bandeaux cut and sew apparel contractors
315240 Bandeaux, women's and girls', cut and sewn from purchased fabric (except apparel contractors)
711130 Bands
711130 Bands, dance 711130
Bands, musical
333243 Bandsaws, woodworking-type, manufacturing
339992 Banjos and parts manufacturing
334511 Bank and turn indicators and components (aeronautical instruments) manufacturing
236220 Bank building construction
531120 Bank building rental or leasing
332999 Bank chests, metal, manufacturing
522320 Bank clearinghouse associations
524128 Bank deposit insurance carriers, direct
423420 Bank equipment merchant wholesalers
332323 Bank fixtures, ornamental metal, manufacturing
551111 Bank holding companies (except managing)
523991 Bank trust offices
813910 Bankers' associations
926150 Banking regulatory agencies
611519 Banking schools (training in banking)
521110 Banking, central
523110 Banking, investment
525920 Bankruptcy estates
522110 Banks, commercial
522210 Banks, credit card
521110 Banks, Federal Reserve
522190 Banks, industrial (i.e., known as), depository
522298 Banks, industrial (i.e., known as), nondepository
522190 Banks, private (i.e., unincorporated)
522120 Banks, savings
522293 Banks, trade (i.e., international trade financing)
314999 Banners made from purchased fabrics (except banner printing)
332323 Bannisters, metal, manufacturing

531120 Banquet hall rental or leasing
722320 Banquet halls with catering staff
327991 Baptismal fonts, cut stone, manufacturing
813920 Bar associations
561499 Bar code imprinting services
423440 Bar equipment merchant wholesalers
331318 Bar made by extruding purchased aluminum
331318 Bar made by rolling purchased aluminum
333519 Bar mill machinery, metalworking, manufacturing
325611 Bar soaps manufacturing 331318 Bar, aluminum, made in integrated secondary smelting and extruding mills
331318 Bar, aluminum, made in integrated secondary smelting and rolling mills
331420 Bar, copper and copper alloy, made from purchased copper or in integrated secondary smelting and rolling, drawing or extruding plants
331491 Bar, nonferrous metals (except aluminum, copper), made from purchased metals in wire drawing plants or in integrated secondary smelting and rolling, drawing, or extruding plants
311421 Barbecue sauce manufacturing
335220 Barbecues, grills, and braziers manufacturing
331222 Barbed and twisted wire made in wire drawing plants
332618 Barbed wire made from purchased wire
611511 Barber colleges
236220 Barber shop construction
423850 Barber shop equipment and supplies merchant wholesalers
812111 Barber shops
332215 Barber's scissors, manufacturing 315210 Barbers' service apparel, washable, cut and sew apparel contractors
315220 Barbers' service apparel, washable, men's and boys', cut and sewn from purchased fabric (except apparel contractors)
325412 Barbiturate preparations manufacturing
325411 Barbiturates, uncompounded, manufacturing
325411 Barbituric acid manufacturing
336611 Barge building
532411 Barge rental or leasing without crew
332312 Barge sections, prefabricated metal, manufacturing
483211 Barge transportation, canal (freight) 483113 Barge transportation, coastal or Great Lakes (including St. Lawrence Seaway)
212393 Barite mining and/or beneficiating
327992 Barite processing beyond beneficiation
325180 Barium compounds, not specified elsewhere by process, manufacturing
325180 Barium hydroxide manufacturing 325412 Barium in-vivo diagnostic substances manufacturing
212393 Barium ores mining and/or beneficiating
327992 Barium processing beyond beneficiation
113210 Bark gathering
111199 Barley farming, field and seed production
311119 Barley feed, chopped, crushed or ground, manufacturing
311211 Barley flour manufacturing
311213 Barley, malt, manufacturing 332323 Barn stanchions and standards manufacturing
334519 Barographs manufacturing
334519 Barometers manufacturing
423490 Barometers merchant wholesalers
332410 Barometric condensers manufacturing
236220 Barrack construction
321920 Barrel heading and staves manufacturing
332994 Barrels, gun, manufacturing
332439 Barrels, light gauge metal, manufacturing
423840 Barrels, new and reconditioned, merchant wholesalers
321920 Barrels, wood, coopered, manufacturing
332999 Barricades, metal, manufacturing
541110 Barristers' offices
541110 Barristers' private practices
722410 Bars (i.e., drinking places), alcoholic beverage
331410 Bars made in primary copper smelting and refining mills
331110 Bars, concrete reinforcing (rebar) made in steel mills
331221 Bars, concrete reinforcing (rebar), made from purchased steel in steel rolling mills
332312 Bars, concrete reinforcing, manufacturing
331110 Bars, iron, made in iron and steel mills
423510 Bars, metal (except precious), merchant wholesalers
331221 Bars, steel, made from purchased steel in cold rolling mills

331110 Bars, steel, made in iron and steel mills
611519 Bartending schools
561990 Bartering services
325130 Barytes based pigments manufacturing
212393 Barytes mining and/or beneficiating
212319 Basalt crushed and broken stone mining and/or beneficiating
212311 Basalt mining or quarrying
561210 Base facilities operation support services
315210 Baseball caps (except plastics) cut and sew apparel contractors
315990 Baseball caps cut and sewn from purchased fabric (except apparel contractors)
711211 Baseball clubs, professional or semiprofessional
713990 Baseball clubs, recreational
339920 Baseball equipment and supplies (except footwear, uniforms) manufacturing
423910 Baseball equipment and supplies merchant wholesalers
611620 Baseball instruction, camps, or schools
711211 Baseball teams, professional or semiprofessional
315210 Baseball uniforms cut and sew apparel contractors
315280 Baseball uniforms cut and sewn from purchased fabric (except apparel contractors)
423730 Baseboard heaters, electric, non-portable, merchant wholesalers
333414 Baseboard heating equipment manufacturing
321918 Baseboards, floor, wood, manufacturing
332321 Baseboards, metal, manufacturing
711211 Basketball clubs, professional or semiprofessional
713990 Basketball clubs, recreational
339920 Basketball equipment and supplies (except footwear, uniforms) manufacturing
611620 Basketball instruction, camps, or schools
711211 Basketball teams, professional or semiprofessional
315210 Basketball uniforms cut and sew apparel contractors
315280 Basketball uniforms cut and sewn from purchased fabric (except apparel contractors)
424990 Baskets merchant wholesalers
331222 Baskets, iron or steel, made in wire drawing plants
332618 Baskets, metal, made from purchased wire
321920 Baskets, wood (e.g., round stave, veneer), manufacturing
337125 Bassinets, reed and rattan, manufacturing
339992 Bassoons manufacturing
212299 Bastnaesite mining and/or beneficiating
335210 Bath fans with integral lighting fixture, residential, manufacturing
335210 Bath fans, residential, manufacturing 314110
Bath mats and bath sets made in carpet mills
326299 Bath mats, rubber, manufacturing
325620 Bath salts manufacturing
442299 Bath shops
713990 Bathing beaches
315990 Bathing caps, rubber, manufacturing
315210 Bathing suits cut and sew apparel contractors
315190 Bathing suits made in apparel knitting mills
315220 Bathing suits, men's and boys', cut and sewn from purchased fabric (except apparel contractors)
315240 Bathing suits, women's, girls', and infants', cut and sewn from purchased fabric (except apparel contractors)
315210 Bathrobes cut and sew apparel contractors
315190 Bathrobes made in apparel knitting mills
315220 Bathrobes, men's and boys', cut and sewn from purchased fabric (except apparel contractors)
315240 Bathrobes, women's, girls', and infants', cut and sewn from purchased fabric (except apparel contractors)
423220 Bathroom accessories merchant wholesalers
327110 Bathroom accessories, vitreous china and earthenware, manufacturing
326199 Bathroom and toilet accessories, plastics, manufacturing
332999 Bathroom fixtures, metal, manufacturing
238220 Bathroom plumbing fixture and sanitary ware installation
333997 Bathroom scales manufacturing
337110 Bathroom vanities (except freestanding), stock or custom wood, manufacturing
812199 Baths, steam or turkish
238390 Bathtub refinishing, on-site
423720 Bathtubs merchant wholesalers
332999 Bathtubs, metal, manufacturing
326191 Bathtubs, plastics, manufacturing

611620 Baton instruction
624221 Battered women's shelters
423610 Batteries (except automotive) merchant wholesalers
441310 Batteries, automotive, dealers
423120 Batteries, automotive, merchant wholesalers
453998 Batteries, except automotive, dealers
335912 Batteries, primary, dry or wet, manufacturing
335911 Batteries, rechargeable, manufacturing
335911 Batteries, storage, manufacturing 311824 Batters, prepared, made from purchased flour
311211 Batters, prepared, made in flour mills
335999 Battery chargers, solid-state, manufacturing
334515 Battery testers, electrical, manufacturing
712120 Battlefields
314999 Batts and batting (except nonwoven fabrics) manufacturing
327120 Bauxite brick manufacturing
423520 Bauxite merchant wholesalers
212299 Bauxite mining and/or beneficiating
325998 Bay oil manufacturing
454390 Bazaars (i.e., temporary stands)
332994 BB guns manufacturing
332992 BB shot manufacturing
532284 Beach chair rental
713990 Beach clubs, recreational
562998 Beach maintenance and cleaning services
316210 Beach sandals, plastics or plastics soled fabric upper, manufacturing
316210 Beach sandals, rubber or rubber soled fabric upper, manufacturing
532284 Beach umbrella rental
339999 Beach umbrellas manufacturing
713990 Beaches, bathing
315210 Beachwear cut and sew apparel contractors
315190 Beachwear made in apparel knitting mills
315220 Beachwear, men's and boys', cut and sewn from purchased fabric (except apparel contractors)
315240 Beachwear, women's, girls', and infants', cut and sewn from purchased fabric (except apparel contractors)
333517 Beader machines, metalworking, manufacturing
314999 Beading on textile products (except apparel) for the trade
333249 Beaming machinery for yarn manufacturing
313110 Beaming yarn
321113 Beams, wood, made from logs or bolts
111219 Bean (except dry) farming, field and seed production
115114 Bean cleaning
111130 Bean farming, dry, field and seed production
111419 Bean sprout farming, grown under cover
311422 Beans, baked, canning 424490 Beans, dry edible, merchant wholesalers 424510 Beans, dry inedible, merchant wholesalers 423510 Bearing piles, metal, merchant wholesalers 332216 Bearing pullers, handtools, manufacturing 336310 Bearings (e.g., camshaft, crankshaft, connecting rod), automotive and truck gasoline engine, manufacturing
423840 Bearings merchant wholesalers
332991 Bearings, ball and roller, manufacturing
333613 Bearings, plain (except internal combustion engine), manufacturing
812112 Beautician services
333318 Beauty and barber shop equipment (except chairs) manufacturing
812112 Beauty and barber shops, combined
711310 Beauty pageant managers with facilities
711320 Beauty pageant managers without facilities
711310 Beauty pageant organizers with facilities
711320 Beauty pageant organizers without facilities
711310 Beauty pageant promoters with facilities
711320 Beauty pageant promoters without facilities
423850 Beauty parlor equipment and supplies merchant wholesalers
812112 Beauty parlors
424210 Beauty preparations merchant wholesalers
236220 Beauty salon construction
812112 Beauty salons
611511 Beauty schools
812112 Beauty shops
424210 Beauty supplies merchant wholesalers
446120 Beauty supply stores
721191 Bed and breakfast inns

337122 Bed frames, wood household-type, manufacturing
812331 Bed linen supply services
442110 Bed stores, retail
335210 Bedcoverings, electric, manufacturing
111422 Bedding plant growing (except vegetable and melon bedding plants)
424930 Bedding plants merchant wholesalers
315210 Bedjackets cut and sew apparel contractors
315240 Bedjackets, women's and girls', cut and sewn from purchased fabric (except apparel contractors)
337122 Bedroom furniture (except upholstered), wood household-type, manufacturing
423210 Beds (except hospital) merchant wholesalers
337122 Beds (except hospital), wood household-type, manufacturing
337124 Beds (including cabinet and folding), metal household-type (except hospital), manufacturing
339113 Beds, hospital, manufacturing
423450 Beds, hospital, merchant wholesalers
337910 Beds, sleep-system ensembles (i.e., flotation, adjustable), manufacturing
337122 Beds, wood dormitory-type, manufacturing
337122 Beds, wood hotel-type, manufacturing
314120 Bedspreads and bed sets made from purchased fabrics
313240 Bedspreads and bed sets made in lace mills
313240 Bedspreads and bed sets made in warp or weft knitting mills
112910 Bee pollen collection
112910 Bee production (i.e., apiculture)
311611 Beef carcasses, half carcasses, primal and sub-primal cuts, produced in slaughtering plants
112112 Beef cattle feedlots (except stockyards for transportation)
112111 Beef cattle ranching or farming
311611 Beef produced in slaughtering plants
311612 Beef stew made from purchased carcasses
311612 Beef, primal and sub-primal cuts, made from purchased carcasses
424910 Beekeeping supplies merchant wholesalers
517312 Beeper (i.e., radio pager) communication carriers
327213 Beer bottles, glass, manufacturing
312120 Beer brewing
332431 Beer cans, light gauge metal, manufacturing
333415 Beer cooling and dispensing equipment manufacturing
332439 Beer kegs, light gauge metal, manufacturing
453998 Beer making supply stores
424810 Beer merchant wholesalers
445310 Beer stores, packaged
424590 Bees merchant wholesalers
325612 Beeswax polishes and waxes manufacturing
112910 Beeswax production
111219 Beet farming (except sugar beets), field, bedding plant and seed production
311313 Beet pulp, dried, manufacturing
311313 Beet sugar refining
541720 Behavioral research and development services
325412 Belladonna preparations manufacturing
332999 Bellows, hand, manufacturing
333999 Bellows, industrial-type, manufacturing
339992 Bells (musical instruments) manufacturing
335999 Bells, electric, manufacturing
424310 Belt and buckle assembly kits merchant wholesalers
333922 Belt conveyor systems manufacturing
316998 Belt laces, leather, manufacturing
316110 Belting butts, curried or rough, manufacturing
313220 Belting fabrics, narrow woven
316998 Belting for machinery, leather, manufacturing
316110 Belting leather, manufacturing
314999 Belting made from purchased fabrics
423840 Belting, industrial, merchant wholesalers
326220 Belting, rubber (e.g., conveyor, elevator, transmission), manufacturing
482112 Beltline railroads
315210 Belts, apparel (e.g., fabric, leather, vinyl), cut and sew apparel contractors
315990 Belts, apparel (e.g., fabric, leather, vinyl), cut and sewn from purchased fabric (except apparel contractors)
332618 Belts, conveyor, made from purchased wire
332618 Belts, drying, made from purchased wire
316998 Belts, leather safety, manufacturing
332994 Belts, machine gun, manufacturing

315210 Belts, money, any material, cut and sew apparel contractors
315990 Belts, money, any material, cut and sewn from purchased fabric (except apparel contractors)
337127 Benches, park-type (except concrete, stone), manufacturing
337127 Benches, public building-type, manufacturing
337127 Benches, work, manufacturing
333517 Bending and forming machines, metalworking, manufacturing
332996 Bends, pipe, made from purchased metal pipe
541612 Benefit consulting services
111998 Bentgrass seed farming
212325 Bentonite mining and/or beneficiating
321999 Bentwood (steam bent) products (except furniture) manufacturing
325194 Benzaldehyde manufacturing
325320 Benzene hexachloride (BHC) insecticides manufacturing
325110 Benzene made from refined petroleum or liquid hydrocarbons
324110 Benzene made in petroleum refineries
325194 Benzoic acid manufacturing
311421 Berries, canned, manufacturing
424480 Berries, fresh, merchant wholesalers
115113 Berries, machine harvesting
111334 Berry (except strawberry) farming
321920 Berry crates, wood, wirebound, manufacturing
321920 Berry cups, veneer and splint, manufacturing
333111 Berry harvesting machines manufacturing
212299 Beryl mining and/or beneficiating
327110 Beryllia porcelain insulators manufacturing
331529 Beryllium castings (except die-castings), unfinished manufacturing
212299 Beryllium concentrates beneficiating
331523 Beryllium die-castings, unfinished, manufacturing
212299 Beryllium ores mining and/or beneficiating
325180 Beryllium oxide manufacturing
331410 Beryllium refining, primary
334517 Beta-ray irradiation equipment manufacturing
335999 Betatrons manufacturing
813910 Better business bureaus
713290 Betting information services
722515 Beverage (e.g., coffee, juice, soft drink) bars, nonalcoholic, fixed location
311930 Beverage bases manufacturing
424490 Beverage bases merchant wholesalers
423830 Beverage bottling machinery merchant wholesalers
424490 Beverage concentrates merchant wholesalers
327213 Beverage containers, glass, manufacturing
423740 Beverage coolers, mechanical, merchant wholesalers
311930 Beverage flavorings (except coffee based) manufacturing
423830 Beverage processing machinery merchant wholesalers
722330 Beverage stands, nonalcoholic, mobile
311930 Beverage syrups (except coffee based) manufacturing
424810 Beverages, alcoholic (except distilled spirits, wine), merchant wholesalers
312120 Beverages, beer, ale, and malt liquors, manufacturing
311514 Beverages, dietary, dairy and nondairy based
312111 Beverages, fruit and vegetable drinks, cocktails, and ades, manufacturing
311421 Beverages, fruit and vegetable juice, manufacturing
312140 Beverages, liquors (except brandies), manufacturing
311511 Beverages, milk based (except dietary), manufacturing
312112 Beverages, naturally carbonated bottled water, manufacturing
312111 Beverages, soft drink (including artificially carbonated waters), manufacturing
424820 Beverages, wine and distilled spirits, merchant wholesalers
312130 Beverages, wines and brandies, manufacturing
314999 Bias bindings made from purchased fabrics
313220 Bias bindings, woven, manufacturing
611699 Bible schools (except degree granting)
813110 Bible societies
315210 Bibs and aprons, waterproof (e.g., plastics, rubber, similar materials), cut and sew apparel contractors
315990 Bibs and aprons, waterproof (e.g., plastics, rubber, similar materials), cut and sewn from purchased fabric (except apparel contractors)

315990 Bibs and aprons, waterproof (e.g., plastics, rubber, similar materials), rubberizing fabric and manufacturing bibs and aprons
451110 Bicycle (except motorized) shops
453310 Bicycle (except motorized) shops, used
492210 Bicycle courier
333912 Bicycle pumps manufacturing
532284 Bicycle rental
811490 Bicycle repair and maintenance shops without retailing new bicycles
441228 Bicycle shops, motorized
423910 Bicycle tires and tubes merchant wholesalers
423110 Bicycle, motorized, merchant wholesalers
423910 Bicycles (except motorized) merchant wholesalers
336991 Bicycles and parts manufacturing
327110 Bidets, vitreous china, manufacturing
561440 Bill collection services
541850 Billboard display advertising services
238990 Billboard erection
339950 Billboards manufacturing
423990 Billboards merchant wholesalers
333519 Billet mill machinery, metalworking, manufacturing
423510 Billets, metal, merchant wholesalers
331110 Billets, steel, made in iron and steel mills
316998 Billfolds, all materials, manufacturing
339920 Billiard equipment and supplies manufacturing
423910 Billiard equipment and supplies merchant wholesalers
713990 Billiard parlors
713990 Billiard rooms
541219 Billing services
322130 Binder's board manufacturing 424120 Binders, looseleaf, merchant wholesalers 333244 Bindery machinery manufacturing 314999 Binding carpets and rugs for the trade 333318 Binding equipment (i.e., plastics or tape binding), office-type, manufacturing 424310 Binding, textile, merchant wholesalers
314999 Bindings, bias, made from purchased fabrics
313220 Bindings, narrow woven, manufacturing
713290 Bingo halls 713290
Bingo parlors
316998 Binocular cases manufacturing
453998 Binocular stores
333314 Binoculars manufacturing
423460 Binoculars merchant wholesalers
332313 Bins, fabricated metal plate work, manufacturing
332439 Bins, light gauge metal, manufacturing
423390 Bins, storage, merchant wholesalers
324110 Biodiesel fuels made in petroleum refineries
324199 Biodiesel fuels not made in petroleum refineries and blended with purchased refined petroleum
325199 Biodiesel fuels not made in petroleum refineries and not blended with petroleum
621498 Biofeedback centers and clinics, outpatient
562910 Biohazard cleanup services 339113
Biohazard protective clothing and accessories manufacturing
541380 Biological (except medical, veterinary) testing laboratories or services
541690 Biological consulting services
621511 Biological laboratories, diagnostic
424210 Biologicals and allied products merchant wholesalers
541715 Biology research and development laboratories or services (except biotechnology and nanotechnology research and development)
221117 Biomass electric power generation 334118
Biometrics system input devices (e.g., retinal scan, iris pattern recognition, hand geometry) manufacturing
541714 Biotechnology research and development laboratories or services (except nanobiotechnology research and development)
541714 Biotechnology research and development laboratories or services in agriculture (except nanobiotechnology research and development)
541714 Biotechnology research and development laboratories or services in bacteriology (except nanobiotechnology research and development)
541714 Biotechnology research and development laboratories or services in biology (except nanobiotechnology research and development)
541714 Biotechnology research and development laboratories or services in botany (except nanobiotechnology research and development)

541714 Biotechnology research and development laboratories or services in chemical sciences (except nanobiotechnology research and development)
541714 Biotechnology research and development laboratories or services in entomology (except nanobiotechnology research and development)
541714 Biotechnology research and development laboratories or services in environmental science (except nanobiotechnology research and development)
541714 Biotechnology research and development laboratories or services in food science (except nanobiotechnology research and development)
541714 Biotechnology research and development laboratories or services in genetics (except nanobiotechnology research and development)
541714 Biotechnology research and development laboratories or services in health sciences (except nanobiotechnology research and development)
541714 Biotechnology research and development laboratories or services in industrial research (except nanobiotechnology research and development)
541714 Biotechnology research and development laboratories or services in the medical sciences (except nanobiotechnology research and development)
541714 Biotechnology research and development laboratories or services in the physical sciences (except nanobiotechnology research and development)
541714 Biotechnology research and development laboratories or services in the veterinary sciences (except nanobiotechnology research and development)
423690 Bipolar transistors merchant wholesalers
311119 Bird feed, prepared, manufacturing 112990 Bird production (e.g., canaries, love birds, parakeets, parrots)
561710 Bird proofing services
712190 Bird sanctuaries
621410 Birth control clinics
326299 Birth control devices (i.e., diaphragms, prophylactics) manufacturing
325412 Birth control pills manufacturing
311812 Biscuits, bread-type, made in commercial bakeries
331410 Bismuth refining, primary
112990 Bison production
333515 Bits and knives for metalworking lathes, planers, and shapers manufacturing
333515 Bits, drill, metalworking, manufacturing
332216 Bits, edge tool, woodworking, manufacturing
333120 Bits, rock drill, construction and surface mining-type, manufacturing
333132 Bits, rock drill, oil and gas field-type, manufacturing
333131 Bits, rock drill, underground mining-type, manufacturing
212111 Bituminous coal and lignite surface mine site development for own account
212111 Bituminous coal cleaning plants
212111 Bituminous coal crushing 213113 Bituminous coal mining services (except site preparation and related construction contractor activities) on a contract basis
212111 Bituminous coal or lignite beneficiating (e.g., cleaning, crushing, screening, washing)
213113 Bituminous coal or lignite surface mine site development (except site preparation and related construction contractor activities) on a contract basis
212111 Bituminous coal screening plants
212111 Bituminous coal stripping (except on a contract, fee, or other basis)
213113 Bituminous coal stripping service on a contract basis
212111 Bituminous coal surface mining and/or beneficiating
212112 Bituminous coal underground mine site development for own account
212112 Bituminous coal underground mining or mining and beneficiating
212111 Bituminous coal washeries 212319 Bituminous limestone mining and/or beneficiating
213113 Bituminous or lignite auger mining service on a contract basis
212319 Bituminous sandstone mining and/or beneficiating
325130 Black pigments (except carbon black, bone black, lamp black) manufacturing
423510 Black plate merchant wholesalers
111334 Blackberry farming
423490 Blackboards merchant wholesalers 339940 Blackboards, framed, manufacturing
327991 Blackboards, unframed, slate, manufacturing

331110 Blackplate made in iron and steel mills
316998 Blacksmith's aprons, leather, manufacturing
311314 Blackstrap molasses manufacturing
238990 Blacktop work, residential and commercial driveway and parking area
811310 Blade sharpening, commercial and industrial machinery and equipment
423710 Blades (e.g., knife, saw) merchant wholesalers
333120 Blades for graders, scrapers, bulldozers, and snowplows manufacturing
332215 Blades, knife and razor, manufacturing
424210 Blades, razor, merchant wholesalers
332216 Blades, saw, all types, manufacturing
325130 Blanc fixe (i.e., barium sulfate, precipitated) manufacturing
332992 Blank cartridges (i.e., 30 mm. or less, 1.18 inch or less) manufacturing
423690 Blank CDs and DVDs merchant wholesalers
423690 Blank diskettes merchant wholesalers
334613 Blank tapes, audio and video, manufacturing
423690 Blank tapes, audio and video, merchant wholesalers
323111 Blankbooks and refills manufacturing
424120 Blankbooks merchant wholesalers
314910 Blanket bags manufacturing
314120 Blankets (except electric) made from purchased fabrics or felts
423220 Blankets (except electric) merchant wholesalers
313210 Blankets and bedspreads made in broadwoven fabric mills
335210 Blankets, electric, manufacturing
423620 Blankets, electric, merchant wholesalers
313230 Blankets, nonwoven fabric, manufacturing
327212 Blanks for electric light bulbs, glass, made in glass making plants
333515 Blanks, cutting tool, manufacturing 327215
Blanks, ophthalmic lens and optical glass, made from purchased glass
327212 Blanks, ophthalmic lens and optical glass, made in glass making plants
423830 Blanks, tips, and inserts merchant wholesalers
321912 Blanks, wood (e.g., bowling pins, handles, textile machinery accessories), manufacturing
311411 Blast freezing on a contract basis
236210 Blast furnace construction
327992 Blast furnace slag processing
331110 Blast furnaces
238910 Blast hole drilling (except mining)
212322 Blast sand quarrying and/or beneficiating
325920 Blasting accessories (e.g., caps, fuses, ignitors, squibbs) manufacturing
325920 Blasting powders manufacturing
213113 Blasting services, coal mining, on a contract basis
213114 Blasting services, metal mining, on a contract basis
213115 Blasting services, nonmetallic minerals mining (except fuels) on a contract basis
238910 Blasting, building demolition
238910 Blasting, construction site
238390 Bleacher installation
337127 Bleacher seating manufacturing
424690 Bleaches merchant wholesalers
325612 Bleaches, formulated for household use, manufacturing
325180 Bleaching agents, inorganic, manufacturing
325199 Bleaching agents, organic, manufacturing
212325 Bleaching clay mining and/or beneficiating
333249 Bleaching machinery for textiles manufacturing
313310 Bleaching textile products, apparel, and fabrics
212230 Blende (zinc) mining and/or beneficiating
311211 Blended flour made in flour mills
335210 Blenders, household-type electric, manufacturing
325620 Blending and compounding perfume bases
311119 Blending animal feed
312130 Blending brandy
312140 Blending distilled beverages (except brandy)
312130 Blending wines
336411 Blimps (i.e., aircraft) manufacturing 337920
Blinds (e.g., mini, venetian, vertical), all materials, manufacturing
423220 Blinds and shades, window, merchant wholesalers
331410 Blister copper manufacturing
561910 Blister packaging services
333923 Block and tackle manufacturing

312113 Block ice manufacturing 324121 Blocks, asphalt paving, made from purchased asphaltic materials

327331 Blocks, concrete and cinder, manufacturing

327120 Blocks, fire clay, manufacturing

327212 Blocks, glass, made in glass making plants

321999 Blocks, tackle, wood, manufacturing

321999 Blocks, tailors' pressing wood, manufacturing

621511 Blood analysis laboratories

334516 Blood bank process equipment manufacturing

621991 Blood banks

325413 Blood derivative in-vitro diagnostic substances manufacturing

325414 Blood derivatives manufacturing

424210 Blood derivatives merchant wholesalers

621991 Blood donor stations

325414 Blood fractions manufacturing

325413 Blood glucose test kits manufacturing

424210 Blood plasma merchant wholesalers

339112 Blood pressure apparatus manufacturing

621999 Blood pressure screening facilities

621999 Blood pressure screening services

812990 Blood pressure testing machine concession operators, coin-operated

339113 Blood testing apparatus, laboratory-type, manufacturing

339112 Blood transfusion equipment manufacturing

333519 Blooming and slabbing mill machinery, metalworking, manufacturing

423510 Blooms, metal, merchant wholesalers

331110 Blooms, steel, made in iron and steel mills

315210 Blouses cut and sew apparel contractors

315190 Blouses made in apparel knitting mills

315240 Blouses, women's, girls', and infants', cut and sewn from purchased fabric (except apparel contractors)

335210 Blow dryers, household-type electric, manufacturing

333249 Blow molding machinery for plastics manufacturing

332216 Blow torches manufacturing

333413 Blower filter units manufacturing

238220 Blower or fan, cooling and dry heating, installation

333111 Blowers, forage, manufacturing

423830 Blowers, industrial, merchant wholesalers

333112 Blowers, leaf, manufacturing

423820 Blowers, snow and leaf, merchant wholesalers

238310 Blown-in insulation (e.g., cellulose, vermiculite) installation

221210 Blue gas, carbureted, distribution

111334 Blueberry farming

114111 Bluefish fishing

111998 Bluegrass-Kentucky seed farming

541340 Blueprint drafting services

333316 Blueprint equipment manufacturing

423420 Blueprinting equipment merchant wholesalers

561439 Blueprinting services

212311 Bluestone mining or quarrying

325620 Blushes, face, manufacturing

423920 Board games merchant wholesalers

921130 Board of Governors, Federal Reserve

321219 Board, bagasse, manufacturing

327420 Board, gypsum, manufacturing

321219 Board, particle, manufacturing

115210 Boarding horses (except racehorses)

721310 Boarding houses

611110 Boarding schools, elementary or secondary

812910 Boarding services, pet

921120 Boards of supervisors, county and local

813910 Boards of trade

324122 Boards, asphalt saturated, made from purchased asphaltic materials

321999 Boards, bulletin, wood and cork, manufacturing

321999 Boards, wood (e.g., clip, ironing, meat, pastry), manufacturing

321113 Boards, wood, made from logs or bolts

321912 Boards, wood, resawing purchased lumber

336320 Boat and ship lighting fixtures manufacturing

441222 Boat dealers, new and used

541330 Boat engineering design services

484220 Boat hauling, truck, local

484230 Boat hauling, truck, long-distance

238990 Boat lift installation

333923 Boat lifts manufacturing

532411 Boat rental (except pleasure) without crew

532411 Boat rental or leasing, commercial
532284 Boat rental, pleasure
332312 Boat sections, prefabricated metal, manufacturing
423910 Boat supplies, pleasure, merchant wholesalers
441222 Boat trailer dealers
336212 Boat transporter trailers, multi-unit, manufacturing
336214 Boat transporter trailers, single-unit, manufacturing
336612 Boat yards (i.e., boat manufacturing facilities)
487210 Boat, fishing charter, operation
811490 Boat, pleasure, repair and maintenance services without retailing new boats
713930 Boating clubs with marinas
713990 Boating clubs without marinas
423860 Boats (except pleasure) merchant wholesalers
336612 Boats (i.e., suitable or intended for personal use) manufacturing
336612 Boats, inflatable plastics (except toy-type), manufacturing
423910 Boats, pleasure (e.g., canoes, motorboats, sailboats), merchant wholesalers
321912 Bobbin blocks and blanks, wood, manufacturing
322219 Bobbins, fiber, made from purchased paperboard
333249 Bobbins, textile machinery, manufacturing
339920 Bobsleds manufacturing
812320 Bobtailers, laundry and drycleaning
713990 Boccie ball courts
423110 Bodies, motor vehicle, merchant wholesalers
713940 Body building studios, physical fitness
811121 Body conversion services, automotive
561612 Body guard services
811121 Body shops, automotive
315210 Body stockings cut and sew apparel contractors
315190 Body stockings made in apparel knitting mills
315240 Body stockings, women's and girls', cut and sewn from purchased fabric (except apparel contractors)
332994 Bofors guns manufacturing
238290 Boiler and pipe insulation installation
332410 Boiler casings manufacturing
238220 Boiler chipping, cleaning and scaling

334513 Boiler controls, industrial, power, and marine-type, manufacturing
332919 Boiler couplings and drains, plumbing and heating-type, manufacturing 238290
Boiler covering installation 332911 Boiler gauge
cocks, industrial-type,
manufacturing
331210 Boiler tubes, wrought, made from purchased iron
238220 Boiler, heating, installation
423720 Boilers (e.g., heating, hot water, power, steam) merchant wholesalers
333414 Boilers, heating, manufacturing
332410 Boilers, power, manufacturing
311612 Bologna made from purchased carcasses
332722 Bolts, metal, manufacturing
326199 Bolts, nuts, and rivets, plastics, manufacturing
423710 Bolts, nuts, rivets, screws, and other fasteners merchant wholesalers
333924 Bomb lifts manufacturing
332993 Bomb loading and assembling plants
332993 Bombcluster adapters manufacturing
332993 Bombs manufacturing
523120 Bond brokerages
523110 Bond dealing (i.e., acting as a principal in dealing securities to investors)
322230 Bond paper made from purchased paper
322121 Bond paper made in paper mills 493190
Bonded warehousing (except farm products,
general merchandise,
refrigerated)
493130 Bonded warehousing, farm products (except refrigerated)
493110 Bonded warehousing, general merchandise
493120 Bonded warehousing, refrigerated
313230 Bonded-fiber fabrics manufacturing
332812 Bonderizing metal and metal products for the trade
524126 Bonding, fidelity or surety insurance, direct
812990 Bondsperson services
325180 Bone black manufacturing
327110 Bone china manufacturing
339112 Bone drills manufacturing
311119 Bone meal prepared as feed for animals and fowls
339999 Bone novelties manufacturing

339112 Bone plates and screws manufacturing
339112 Bone rongeurs manufacturing
311613 Bones, fat, rendering
511130 Book (e.g., hardback, paperback, audio) publishers (except exclusive Internet publishing)
454110 Book clubs, not publishing, mail-order
813410 Book discussion clubs
332999 Book ends, metal, manufacturing
322220 Book paper made by coating purchased paper
322220 Book paper, coated, made from purchased paper
322121 Book paper, coated, made in paper mills
511130 Book publishers and printing combined
519130 Book publishers, exclusively on Internet
511130 Book publishers, university press (except exclusive Internet publishing)
451211 Book stores
453310 Book stores, used
316110 Bookbinder's leather manufacturing
333244 Bookbinding machines manufacturing
323120 Bookbinding shops
323120 Bookbinding without printing
337125 Bookcases (except wood and metal), household-type, manufacturing
337214 Bookcases (except wood), office-type, manufacturing
337124 Bookcases, metal household-type, manufacturing
337122 Bookcases, wood household-type, manufacturing
337211 Bookcases, wood office-type, manufacturing
713290 Bookies
561599 Booking (e.g., airline, car rental, hotel, restaurant) services
512199 Booking agencies, motion picture
512199 Booking agencies, motion picture or video productions
711320 Booking agencies, theatrical (except motion picture)
541219 Bookkeepers' offices
541219 Bookkeepers' private practices 423420
Bookkeeping machines merchant wholesalers
541219 Bookkeeping services
713290 Bookmakers
519120 Bookmobiles
424920 Books merchant wholesalers
323117 Books printing and binding without publishing
323117 Books printing without publishing
424120 Books, sales or receipt, merchant wholesalers
323111 Books, sales, manifold, printing
339920 Boomerangs manufacturing
813410 Booster clubs
486990 Booster pumping station (except natural gas, petroleum)
486110 Booster pumping station, crude oil transportation
486210 Booster pumping station, natural gas transportation
486910 Booster pumping station, refined petroleum products transportation
424330 Booster seats merchant wholesalers
332993 Boosters and bursters, artillery, manufacturing
335311 Boosters, feeder voltage (i.e., electrical transformers), manufacturing
423850 Boot and shoe cut stock and findings merchant wholesalers
316998 Boot and shoe cut stock and findings, leather, manufacturing
321999 Boot and shoe lasts, all materials, manufacturing
623990 Boot camps for delinquent youth
333249 Boot making and repairing machinery manufacturing
811430 Boot repair shops without retailing new boots
812990 Bootblack parlors
424340 Boots (e.g., hiking, western, work) merchant wholesalers
316210 Boots, dress and casual, children's and infants', manufacturing
316210 Boots, dress and casual, men's, manufacturing
316210 Boots, dress and casual, women's, manufacturing
316210 Boots, hiking, children's and infants', manufacturing
316210 Boots, hiking, men's, manufacturing
316210 Boots, hiking, women's, manufacturing
316210 Boots, plastics or plastics soled fabric upper, manufacturing
316210 Boots, rubber or rubber soled fabric upper, manufacturing

212391 Borate, natural, mining and/or beneficiating
325180 Borax (i.e., sodium borate) manufacturing
212391 Borax, crude, ground or pulverized, mining and/or beneficiating
325320 Bordeaux mixture insecticides manufacturing
325180 Boric acid manufacturing 333517 Boring machines, metalworking, manufacturing
213114 Boring test holes for metal mining on a contract basis
213115 Boring test holes for nonmetallic minerals mining (except fuels) on a contract basis
333517 Boring, drilling, and milling machine combinations, metalworking, manufacturing
238910 Boring, for building construction
212391 Boron compounds prepared at beneficiating plants
325180 Boron compounds, not specified elsewhere by process, manufacturing
212391 Boron mineral mining and/or beneficiating
325180 Borosilicate manufacturing 424210 Botanical drugs and herbs merchant wholesalers
325412 Botanical extract preparations (except in-vitro diagnostics) manufacturing
712130 Botanical gardens
325320 Botanical insecticides manufacturing
424210 Botanicals merchant wholesalers 541715 Botany research and development laboratories or services (except biotechnology and nanotechnology research and development)
326199 Bottle caps and lids, plastics, manufacturing
332119 Bottle caps and tops, metal, stamping
321999 Bottle corks manufacturing 321999 Bottle covers, willow, rattan, and reed, manufacturing
561990 Bottle exchanges
335210 Bottle warmers, household-type electric, manufacturing
333993 Bottle washers, packaging machinery, manufacturing
454310 Bottled gas dealers, direct selling 424490 Bottled water (except water treating) merchant wholesalers
454390 Bottled water providers, direct selling
423840 Bottles (except waste) merchant wholesalers
327213 Bottles (i.e., bottling, canning, packaging), glass, manufacturing
326160 Bottles, plastics, manufacturing 332439 Bottles, vacuum, light gauge metal, manufacturing
423930 Bottles, waste, merchant wholesalers
333993 Bottling machinery (e.g., capping, filling, labeling, sterilizing, washing) manufacturing
423830 Bottling machinery and equipment merchant wholesalers
335121 Boudoir lamp fixtures manufacturing
311422 Bouillon canning
311423 Bouillon made in dehydration plants 212319 Boulder crushed and broken mining and/or beneficiating
324199 Boulets (i.e., fuel bricks) made from refined petroleum
561611 Bounty hunting services
424590 Bovine semen merchant wholesalers
315210 Bow ties cut and sew apparel contractors
315990 Bow ties, men's and boys', cut and sewn from purchased fabric (except apparel contractors)
238290 Bowling alley equipment installation
713950 Bowling alleys
337127 Bowling center furniture manufacturing
713950 Bowling centers
423910 Bowling equipment and supplies merchant wholesalers
451110 Bowling equipment and supply stores
611620 Bowling instruction
713990 Bowling leagues or teams, recreational
321912 Bowling pin blanks manufacturing
339920 Bowling pin machines, automatic, manufacturing
326199 Bowls and bowl covers, plastics, manufacturing
321999 Bowls, wood, turned and shaped, manufacturing
314999 Bows made from purchased fabrics
339920 Bows, archery, manufacturing
316998 Bows, shoe, leather, manufacturing
321920 Box cleats, wood, manufacturing
311991 Box lunches (for sale off premises) manufacturing

321920 Box shook manufacturing
423840 Box shooks merchant wholesalers
337215 Box spring frames manufacturing
423210 Box springs merchant wholesalers
337910 Box springs, assembled, made from purchased spring
316998 Box toes (i.e., shoe cut stock), leather, manufacturing
311612 Boxed beef made from purchased carcasses
311611 Boxed beef produced in slaughtering plants
311612 Boxed meat produced from purchased carcasses
311611 Boxed meats produced in slaughtering plants
711219 Boxers, independent professional
423840 Boxes and crates, industrial (except disposable plastics, paperboard, waste), merchant wholesalers
423610 Boxes and fittings, electrical, merchant wholesalers
321920 Boxes, cigar, wood or part wood, manufacturing
322211 Boxes, corrugated and solid fiber, made from purchased paper or paperboard
335932 Boxes, electrical wiring (e.g., junction, outlet, switch), manufacturing
322212 Boxes, folding (except corrugated), made from purchased paperboard
316998 Boxes, hat (except paper or paperboard), manufacturing
321920 Boxes, jewelry, wood or part wood, manufacturing
316998 Boxes, leather, manufacturing
332439 Boxes, light gauge metal, manufacturing
424130 Boxes, paperboard and disposable plastics, merchant wholesalers
322219 Boxes, sanitary food (except folding), made from purchased paper or paperboard
322219 Boxes, setup (i.e., not shipped flat), made from purchased paperboard
322211 Boxes, shipping, laminated paper and paperboard, made from purchased paperboard
336211 Boxes, truck (e.g., cargo, dump, utility, van), assembled on purchased chassis
423930 Boxes, waste, merchant wholesalers
321920 Boxes, wood, manufacturing 321920
Boxes, wood, plain or fabric covered, nailed or lock corner, manufacturing
711211 Boxing clubs, professional or semiprofessional
713990 Boxing clubs, recreational
339920 Boxing equipment manufacturing
711310 Boxing event managers with facilities
711320 Boxing event managers without facilities
711310 Boxing event organizers with facilities
711320 Boxing event organizers without facilities
711310 Boxing event promoters with facilities
711320 Boxing event promoters without facilities
813410 Boy guiding organizations
623990 Boys' and girls' residential facilities (e.g., homes, ranches, villages)
721214 Boys' camps (except day, instructional)
611620 Boys' camps, sports instruction
611620 Boys' camps, sports instructor
713990 Boys' day camps (except instructional)
315110 Boys' socks manufacturing
111334 Boysenberry farming
339910 Bracelets, precious metal, manufacturing
115112 Bracing of orchard trees and vines
332510 Brackets (i.e., builder's hardware-type), metal, manufacturing
332618 Brackets made from purchased wire
321918 Brackets, wood, manufacturing
423710 Brads merchant wholesalers
331222 Brads, iron or steel, wire or cut, made in wire drawing plants
332618 Brads, metal, made from purchased wire
333249 Braiding machinery for textiles manufacturing
313220 Braiding narrow fabrics
336340 Brake and brake parts, automotive, truck, and bus, manufacturing
336340 Brake caliper assemblies, automotive, truck, and bus, manufacturing
336340 Brake cylinders, master and wheel, automotive, truck, and bus, manufacturing
336340 Brake discs (rotor), automotive, truck, and bus, manufacturing
336340 Brake drums, automotive, truck, and bus, manufacturing
325998 Brake fluid, synthetic, manufacturing
324191 Brake fluids, petroleum, made from refined petroleum
336340 Brake hose assemblies manufacturing
336340 Brake linings, automotive, truck, and bus, manufacturing

336340 Brake pads and shoes, automotive, truck, and bus, manufacturing

811118 Brake repair shops, automotive

333318 Brake service equipment (except mechanic's handtools), motor vehicle, manufacturing

336340 Brake shoes and pads, asbestos, manufacturing

335314 Brakes and clutches, electromagnetic, manufacturing

336510 Brakes and parts for railroad rolling stock manufacturing

335314 Brakes, electromagnetic, manufacturing

333517 Brakes, press, metalworking, manufacturing

311212 Bran and other residues of milling rice

522110 Branches of foreign banks

521110 Branches, Federal Reserve Bank

533110 Brand name licensing

115210 Branding

339940 Branding irons (i.e., marking irons) manufacturing

424820 Brandy and brandy spirits merchant wholesalers

312130 Brandy distilling

315210 Bra-slips cut and sew apparel contractors

315240 Bra-slips, women's and girls', cut and sewn from purchased fabric (except apparel contractors)

331523 Brass die-castings, unfinished, manufacturing

331529 Brass foundries (except die-casting)

423720 Brass goods, plumbers', merchant wholesalers

325612 Brass polishes manufacturing

331420 Brass products, rolling, drawing, or extruding, made from purchased copper or in integrated secondary smelting and rolling, drawing or extruding plants

315210 Brassieres cut and sew apparel contractors

315240 Brassieres cut and sewn from purchased fabric (except apparel contractors)

332323 Brasswork, ornamental, manufacturing

335220 Braziers, barbecue, manufacturing

111335 Brazil nut farming

325194 Brazilwood extract manufacturing

332811 Brazing (i.e., hardening) metals and metal products for the trade

311824 Bread and bread-type roll mixes made from purchased flour

311812 Bread and bread-type rolls made in commercial bakeries

311999 Bread crumbs not made in bakeries

335210 Bread machines, household-type electric, manufacturing

333241 Bread slicing machinery manufacturing

333993 Bread wrapping machines manufacturing

424490 Bread, packaged (except frozen), merchant wholesalers

212113 Breakers, anthracite mining and/or beneficiating

333131 Breakers, coal, manufacturing

332919 Breakers, vacuum, plumbing, manufacturing

311340 Breakfast bars, nonchocolate covered, manufacturing

311230 Breakfast cereals manufacturing

424490 Breakfast cereals merchant wholesalers

237990 Breakwater construction

332313 Breechings, fabricated metal plate work, manufacturing

112990 Breeding of pets (e.g., birds, cats, dogs)

115210 Breeding, animal, services

312120 Breweries

311211 Brewers' and distillers' flakes and grits, corn, manufacturing

311213 Brewers' malt manufacturing

325194 Brewers' pitch made by distillation of wood

311212 Brewers' rice manufacturing

424490 Brewers' yeast merchant wholesalers

333241 Brewery machinery manufacturing

238990 Brick driveway contractors

238990 Brick paver (e.g., driveways, patios, sidewalks) installation

238140 Brick veneer, installation

238140 Bricklaying contractors 423320 Bricks (except refractory) merchant wholesalers

327120 Bricks (i.e., common, face, glazed, hollow, vitrified), clay, manufacturing

327120 Bricks, adobe, manufacturing

327120 Bricks, clay refractory, manufacturing

327331 Bricks, concrete, manufacturing

327215 Bricks, glass, made from purchased glass

327212 Bricks, glass, made in glass making plants

327120 Bricks, nonclay refractory, manufacturing

315210 Bridal dresses or gowns cut and sew apparel contractors

315240 Bridal dresses or gowns, custom made
315240 Bridal dresses or gowns, women's and girls', cut and sewn from purchased fabric (except apparel contractors)
448190 Bridal gown shops (except custom)
532281 Bridal wear rental 333999 Bridge and gate lifting machinery manufacturing
611699 Bridge and other card game instruction
321114 Bridge and trestle parts, wood, treating
237310 Bridge approach construction
713990 Bridge clubs, recreational
237310 Bridge construction
237310 Bridge decking construction
238320 Bridge painting
332312 Bridge sections, prefabricated metal, manufacturing
488490 Bridge, tunnel, and highway operations
339116 Bridges, custom made in dental laboratories
334515 Bridges, electrical (e.g., Kelvin, megohm, vacuum tube, Wheatstone), manufacturing
316110 Bridle leather manufacturing
237990 Bridle path construction
423990 Briefcases merchant wholesalers
316998 Briefcases, all materials, manufacturing
315210 Briefs cut and sew apparel contractors
315190 Briefs, underwear, made in apparel knitting mills
315220 Briefs, underwear, men's and boys', cut and sewn from purchased fabric (except apparel contractors)
315240 Briefs, underwear, women's, girls', and infants', cut and sewn from purchased fabric (except apparel contractors)
212393 Brimstone mining and/or beneficiating
311421 Brining of fruits and vegetables
212210 Briquets, iron, mining and/or beneficiating
324199 Briquettes, petroleum, made from refined petroleum
424590 Bristles merchant wholesalers
322130 Bristols board stock manufacturing
322121 Bristols paper stock manufacturing
333515 Broaches (i.e., a machine tool accessory) manufacturing
423830 Broaches (i.e., a machine tool accessory) merchant wholesalers
333517 Broaching machines, metalworking, manufacturing
334220 Broadcast equipment (including studio), for radio and television, manufacturing
811213 Broadcast equipment repair and maintenance services
541910 Broadcast media rating services
423690 Broadcasting equipment merchant wholesalers
519130 Broadcasting exclusively on Internet, audio
519130 Broadcasting exclusively on Internet, video
515111 Broadcasting networks, radio
515120 Broadcasting networks, television
611519 Broadcasting schools
236220 Broadcasting station construction
515112 Broadcasting stations (except exclusively on Internet), radio
515120 Broadcasting stations, television
515112 Broadcasting studio, radio station
711110 Broadway theaters
313210 Broadwoven fabrics (except rugs, tire fabrics) weaving
313310 Broadwoven fabrics finishing
313210 Brocades weaving
111219 Broccoli farming, field, bedding plant and seed production
424920 Brochures merchant wholesalers
112320 Broiler chicken production
523140 Brokerages, commodity contracts
524210 Brokerages, insurance
522310 Brokerages, loan
522310 Brokerages, mortgage
531210 Brokerages, real estate
523120 Brokerages, securities
524210 Brokers' offices, insurance
522310 Brokers' offices, loan
522310 Brokers' offices, mortgage
531210 Brokers' offices, real estate
325180 Bromine manufacturing
325199 Bromochloromethane manufacturing
339112 Bronchoscopes (except electromedical) manufacturing
334510 Bronchoscopes, electromedical, manufacturing
331523 Bronze die-castings, unfinished, manufacturing
331529 Bronze foundries (except die-casting)
325910 Bronze printing inks manufacturing

331420 Bronze products, rolling, drawing, or extruding, made from purchased copper or in integrated secondary smelting and rolling, drawing or extruding plants
111199 Broomcorn farming
424590 Broomcorn merchant wholesalers 423850
Brooms (except household-type) merchant wholesalers
423220 Brooms and brushes, household-type, merchant wholesalers
339994 Brooms, hand and machine, manufacturing
311422 Broth (except seafood) canning
311313 Brown beet sugar refining
212111 Brown coal mining and/or beneficiating
212210 Brown ore mining and/or beneficiating
311313 Brown sugar made from beet sugar
311314 Brown sugar manufacturing
325411 Brucine manufacturing
212325 Brucite mining and/or beneficiating
335991 Brush blocks, carbon or molded graphite, manufacturing
321912 Brush blocks, wood, turned and shaped
562119 Brush collection services
562119 Brush hauling, local
562119 Brush removal services
335991 Brushes and brush stock contacts, electric, carbon and graphite, manufacturing 339940
Brushes, artists', manufacturing 424990 Brushes, artists', merchant wholesalers 339994 Brushes, household-type and industrial, manufacturing
423840 Brushes, industrial, merchant wholesalers
339994 Brushes, paint (except artists'), manufacturing
326299 Brushes, rubber, manufacturing 333517
Brushing machines, metalworking, manufacturing
335991 Brushplates, carbon or graphite, manufacturing
111219 Brussel sprout farming, field, bedding plant and seed production
325620 Bubble bath preparations manufacturing
326199 Bubble packaging materials, plastics, manufacturing
333120 Bucket and scarifier teeth manufacturing
333922 Buckets, elevator or conveyor, manufacturing
333120 Buckets, excavating (e.g., clamshell, concrete, drag scraper, dragline, shovel), manufacturing
321920 Buckets, wood, coopered, manufacturing
339993 Buckles and buckle parts (including shoe) manufacturing
111199 Buckwheat farming
311211 Buckwheat flour manufacturing
921130 Budget agencies, government
112990 Buffalo production
722514 Buffet eating places
337122 Buffets (furniture), wood, manufacturing
333517 Buffing and polishing machines, metalworking, manufacturing
327910 Buffing and polishing wheels, abrasive and nonabrasive, manufacturing
325612 Buffing compounds manufacturing 333991
Buffing machines, handheld power-driven, manufacturing
332813 Buffing metals and metal products for the trade
316110 Buffings, russet, manufacturing
332510 Builder's hardware, metal, manufacturing
541310 Building architectural design services
238210 Building automation system installation contractors
423320 Building blocks (e.g., cinder, concrete) merchant wholesalers
423310 Building board (e.g., fiber, flake, particle) merchant wholesalers
561720 Building cleaning services, interior
561720 Building cleaning services, janitorial
238910 Building demolition
541690 Building envelope consulting services
561790 Building exterior cleaning services (except sandblasting, window cleaning)
238310 Building fireproofing contractors
238390 Building fixture and fitting (except mechanical equipment) installation
238130 Building framing (except structural steel)
561790 Building gas systems conversion (e.g., from manufactured to natural gas) services
541350 Building inspection bureaus
541350 Building inspection services 926150
Building inspections, government 238310 Building insulation contractors 237210 Building lot subdividing 326199 Building materials (e.g., fascia, panels, siding, soffit), plastics, manufacturing
444190 Building materials supply dealers

423390 Building materials, fiberglass (except insulation, roofing, siding), merchant wholesalers
213112 Building oil and gas well foundations on a contract basis
326199 Building panels, corrugated and flat, plastics, manufacturing
423390 Building paper merchant wholesalers
322121 Building paper stock manufacturing
334512 Building services monitoring controls, automatic, manufacturing
925110 Building standards agencies, government
423320 Building stone merchant wholesalers
327120 Building tile, clay, manufacturing 531110
Building, apartment, rental or leasing 213112
Building, erecting, repairing, and dismantling oil and gas field rigs and derricks on a contract basis
531120 Building, nonresidential (except mini-warehouse), rental or leasing
236118 Building, residential, addition, alteration and renovation
531110 Building, residential, rental or leasing
321991 Buildings, mobile, commercial use, manufacturing
332311 Buildings, prefabricated metal, manufacturing
423390 Buildings, prefabricated nonwood, merchant wholesalers
423310 Buildings, prefabricated wood, merchant wholesalers
321992 Buildings, prefabricated, wood, manufacturing
238350 Built-in wood cabinets constructed on site
327999 Built-up mica manufacturing 335110
Bulbs, electric light, complete, manufacturing
311211 Bulgur (flour) manufacturing 424710
Bulk gasoline stations, merchant wholesalers
484220 Bulk liquids trucking, local
484230 Bulk liquids trucking, long-distance 484110
Bulk mail truck transportation, contract, local
484121 Bulk mail truck transportation, contract, long-distance (TL)
493190 Bulk petroleum storage 424710 Bulk stations, petroleum, merchant wholesalers
332420 Bulk storage tanks, heavy gauge metal, manufacturing
237990 Bulkhead wall or embarkment construction
115210 Bull testing stations
532412 Bulldozer rental or leasing without operator
238910 Bulldozer rental with operator
333120 Bulldozers manufacturing 332992 Bullet jackets and cores (i.e., 30 mm. or less, 1.18 inch or less) manufacturing
321999 Bulletin boards, wood and cork, manufacturing
339113 Bulletproof vests manufacturing
423990 Bulletproof vests merchant wholesalers
212221 Bullion, gold, produced at the mine
212222 Bullion, silver, produced at the mine
336390 Bumpers and bumperettes assembled, automotive, truck, and bus, manufacturing
333318 Bundling machinery (e.g., box strapping, mail, newspaper) manufacturing
321999 Bungs, wood, manufacturing
236220 Bunkhouse construction 339113 Bunsen burners manufacturing 315210 Buntings cut and sew apparel contractors 315240 Buntings, infants', cut and sewn from purchased fabric (except apparel contractors)
334513 Buoyancy instruments, industrial process-type, manufacturing
321999 Buoys, cork, manufacturing 332313
Buoys, fabricated plate work metal, manufacturing
561621 Burglar alarm monitoring services
561621 Burglar alarm sales combined with installation, repair, or monitoring services
238210 Burglar alarm system, electric, installation only
334290 Burglar alarm systems and equipment manufacturing
524126 Burglary and theft insurance carriers, direct
339995 Burial caskets and cases manufacturing
423850 Burial caskets merchant wholesalers
315210 Burial garments cut and sew apparel contractors
315280 Burial garments cut and sewn from purchased fabric (except apparel contractors)
524128 Burial insurance carriers, direct
339995 Burial vaults (except concrete, stone) manufacturing

327390 Burial vaults, concrete and precast terrazzo, manufacturing
327991 Burial vaults, stone, manufacturing
424990 Burlap merchant wholesalers
711110 Burlesque companies
212325 Burley mining and/or beneficiating
313310 Burling and mending fabrics
335311 Burner ignition transformers manufacturing
423720 Burners, fuel oil and distillate oil, merchant wholesalers
333414 Burners, heating, manufacturing
423830 Burners, industrial, merchant wholesalers
332811 Burning metals and metal products for the trade
333517 Burnishing machines, metalworking, manufacturing
321999 Burnt wood articles manufacturing
314999 Burnt-out laces manufacturing
112920 Burro production
212399 Burrstones, natural, mining and/or beneficiating
335313 Bus bar structures, switchgear-type, manufacturing
335931 Bus bars, electrical conductors (except switchgear-type), manufacturing
336211 Bus bodies assembling on purchased chassis
336211 Bus bodies manufacturing
541850 Bus card advertising services 485510 Bus charter services (except scenic, sightseeing)
541850 Bus display advertising services
611519 Bus driver training
485210 Bus line operation, intercity
485113 Bus line, local (except mixed mode)
423110 Bus merchant wholesalers
485410 Bus operation, school and employee
532120 Bus rental or leasing
485113 Bus services, urban and suburban (except mixed mode)
236220 Bus shelter construction
236220 Bus terminal construction
488490 Bus terminal operation, independent
561599 Bus ticket offices
485113 Bus transit systems (except mixed mode)
423610 Busbars and trolley ducts merchant wholesalers
336120 Buses (except trackless trolley) assembling on chassis of own manufacture
487110 Buses, scenic and sightseeing operation
336510 Buses, trackless trolley, manufacturing
333613 Bushings, plain (except internal combustion engine), manufacturing
326199 Bushings, plastics, manufacturing
321999 Bushings, wood, manufacturing
813910 Business associations
541990 Business brokers (except real estate brokers)
611410 Business colleges or schools not offering academic degrees
611310 Business colleges or schools offering baccalaureate or graduate degrees
323111 Business directories commercial printing (except screen) without publishing
323113 Business directories screen printing without publishing
511140 Business directory publishers (except exclusive Internet publishing)
511140 Business directory publishers and printing combined
519130 Business directory publishers, exclusively on Internet
323113 Business forms (except manifold) screen printing without publishing
323111 Business forms commercial printing (except screen) without publishing
323111 Business forms, manifold, printing
423420 Business machines and equipment (except computers) merchant wholesalers
541611 Business management consulting services
561110 Business management services 541720 Business research and development services
611410 Business schools not offering academic degrees
561439 Business service centers (except private mail centers)
561439 Business service centers (except private mail centers) providing range of office support services (except printing)
541611 Business start-up consulting services
425110 Business to business electronic markets, durable goods, wholesale trade
425110 Business to business electronic markets, nondurable goods, wholesale trade
454110 Business to Consumer retail sales Internet sites
325211 Butadiene copolymers containing less than 50 percent butadiene manufacturing

325212 Butadiene copolymers containing more than 50 percent butadiene manufacturing
325199 Butadiene made from alcohol
325110 Butadiene made from refined petroleum or liquid hydrocarbons
325212 Butadiene rubber (i.e., polybutadiene) manufacturing
424720 Butane gas merchant wholesalers (except bulk stations, terminals)
325110 Butane made from refined petroleum or liquid hydrocarbons
211130 Butane, natural, mining
445210 Butcher shops
332215 Butcher's knives manufacturing
311512 Butter manufacturing
424430 Butter merchant wholesalers
333241 Butter processing machinery manufacturing
424490 Butter substitutes merchant wholesalers
311512 Butter, creamery and whey, manufacturing
332911 Butterfly valves, industrial-type, manufacturing
311511 Buttermilk manufacturing
424430 Buttermilk merchant wholesalers
111219 Butternut squash farming, field, bedding plant and seed production
335912 Button cells, primary batteries, manufacturing
333249 Buttonhole and eyelet machinery manufacturing
315210 Buttonhole making apparel contractors
315210 Buttonhole making, fur goods, cut and sew apparel contractors
315210 Buttonholing and button covering apparel contractors
339993 Buttons (except precious metal, precious stones, semiprecious stones) manufacturing
424310 Buttons merchant wholesalers
339910 Buttons, precious metal, precious stones, semiprecious stones, manufacturing
325199 Butyl acetate manufacturing
325212 Butyl rubber manufacturing
324110 Butylene (i.e., butene) made in petroleum refineries
325110 Butylene made from refined petroleum or liquid hydrocarbons
531210 Buyers' agents, real estate, offices
531210 Buying agencies, real estate
531210 Buying real estate for others (i.e., agents, brokers)
485310 Cab (i.e., taxi) services
336112 Cab and chassis, light trucks and vans, manufacturing
111219 Cabbage farming, field, bedding plant and seed production
236115 Cabin construction general contractors
336612 Cabin cruiser building
334511 Cabin environment indicators, transmitters, and sensors manufacturing
236117 Cabin for-sale builders
423710 Cabinet hardware and fittings merchant wholesalers
332510 Cabinet hardware, metal, manufacturing
444190 Cabinet stores, kitchen (except custom), to be installed
238350 Cabinet work performed at the construction site
238350 Cabinetry work performed at the construction site
337214 Cabinets (except wood), office-type, freestanding, manufacturing
321999 Cabinets (i.e., housings), wood (e.g., sewing machines, stereo, television), manufacturing
337110 Cabinets, kitchen (except freestanding), stock or custom wood, manufacturing
423310 Cabinets, kitchen, built-in, merchant wholesalers
423210 Cabinets, kitchen, freestanding, merchant wholesalers
337124 Cabinets, metal (i.e., bathroom, kitchen) (except freestanding), manufacturing
337124 Cabinets, metal household-type, freestanding, manufacturing
337124 Cabinets, metal, radio and television, manufacturing
238350 Cabinets, wood built-in, constructed on site
337122 Cabinets, wood household-type, freestanding, manufacturing
337211 Cabinets, wood office-type, freestanding, manufacturing
721199 Cabins, housekeeping
515210 Cable broadcasting networks
485119 Cable car systems (except mixed mode), commuter
487110 Cable car, land, scenic and sightseeing operation
334220 Cable decoders manufacturing
237130 Cable laying (e.g., cable television, electricity, marine, telephone), including underground

517311 Cable program distribution operators 238990
Cable splicing (except electrical or fiber optic)
238210 Cable splicing, electrical or fiber optic
517311 Cable television distribution services
238210 Cable television hookup contractors
515210 Cable television networks
334220 Cable television transmission and receiving equipment manufacturing
517311 Cable TV providers (except networks)
331420 Cable, copper (e.g., armored, bare, insulated), made from purchased copper in wire drawing plants
331420 Cable, copper (e.g., armored, bare, insulated), made in integrated secondary smelting and wire drawing plants
331222 Cable, iron or steel, insulated or armored, made in wire drawing plants
335929 Cable, nonferrous, insulated, or armored, made from purchased nonferrous wire
332618 Cable, noninsulated wire, made from purchased wire
423510 Cable, wire (except insulated), merchant wholesalers
333111 Cabs for agricultural machinery manufacturing
333120 Cabs for construction machinery manufacturing
333924 Cabs for industrial trucks manufacturing
111339 Cactus fruit farming
541512 CAD (computer-aided design) systems integration design services
541370 Cadastral surveying services
339920 Caddy carts manufacturing
331410 Cadmium refining, primary
541512 CAE (computer-aided engineering) systems integration design services
722513 Cafes, limited-service
337215 Cafeteria fixtures manufacturing 722310
Cafeteria food services contractors (e.g., government office cafeterias, hospital cafeterias, school cafeterias)
337127 Cafeteria furniture manufacturing
337127 Cafeteria tables and benches manufacturing
722514 Cafeterias
325411 Caffeine and derivatives (i.e., basic chemicals) manufacturing
315210 Caftans cut and sew apparel contractors
315220 Caftans, men's and boys', cut and sewn from purchased fabric (except apparel contractors)
315240 Caftans, women's, girls', and infants', cut and sewn from purchased fabric (except apparel contractors)
332618 Cages made from purchased wire
238910 Caisson (i.e., drilled building foundations) construction
237990 Caisson (i.e., marine or pneumatic structures) construction
332420 Caissons, underwater work, heavy gauge metal, manufacturing
453998 Cake decorating supply stores
311999 Cake frosting manufacturing
311942 Cake frosting mixes manufacturing
311824 Cake mixes made from purchased flour
311340 Cake ornaments, confectionery, manufacturing
311813 Cake, frozen, manufacturing
311812 Cakes, baking (except frozen), made in commercial bakeries
212230 Calamine mining and/or beneficiating
212221 Calaverite mining and/or beneficiating
212312 Calcareous tufa crushed and broken stone mining and/or beneficiating
212311 Calcareous tufa mining or quarrying
325510 Calcimines manufacturing
424950 Calcimines merchant wholesalers
212392 Calcined phosphate rock mining and/or beneficiating
324199 Calcining petroleum coke from refined petroleum
212399 Calcite mining and/or beneficiating
325180 Calcium carbide, chloride, and hypochlorite manufacturing
325199 Calcium citrate manufacturing
327410 Calcium hydroxide (i.e., hydrated lime) manufacturing
325180 Calcium hypochlorite manufacturing
325180 Calcium inorganic compounds, not specified elsewhere by process, manufacturing
325199 Calcium organic compounds, not specified elsewhere by process, manufacturing
325199 Calcium oxalate manufacturing
327410 Calcium oxide (i.e., quicklime) manufacturing
423420 Calculators and calculating machines merchant wholesalers
333318 Calculators manufacturing 511199 Calendar publishers (except exclusive Internet publishing)

511199 Calendar publishers and printing combined
519130 Calendar publishers, exclusively on Internet
453998 Calendar shops
323111 Calendars commercial printing (except screen) without publishing
323113 Calendars screen printing without publishing
333249 Calendering machinery for plastics manufacturing
333249 Calendering machinery for textiles manufacturing
313310 Calendering textile products, apparel, and fabrics
112111 Calf (e.g., feeder, stocker, veal) production
315110 Calf high sheer hosiery knitting or knitting and finishing
541380 Calibration and certification testing laboratories or services
332216 Calipers and dividers, machinists' precision tools, manufacturing
336340 Calipers, brake, automotive, truck, and bus, manufacturing
339992 Calliopes (steam organs) manufacturing
541512 CAM (computer-aided manufacturing) systems integration design services
532210 Camcorder rental
423410 Camcorders (except household-type) merchant wholesalers
334310 Camcorders manufacturing
326211 Camelback (i.e., retreading material) manufacturing
333249 Camelback (i.e., retreading materials) machinery manufacturing
316998 Camera carrying bags, all materials, manufacturing
423410 Camera equipment and supplies, photographic, merchant wholesalers
333314 Camera lenses manufacturing 811211 Camera repair shops without retailing new cameras
443142 Camera shops, photographic
711510 Cameramen, independent (freelance)
333316 Cameras (except television, video) manufacturing
334220 Cameras, television, manufacturing
423410 Cameras, television, merchant wholesalers
423410 Cameras, video (except household-type), merchant wholesalers
315210 Camisoles cut and sew apparel contractors
315240 Camisoles, women's and girls', cut and sewn from purchased fabric (except apparel contractors)
337124 Camp furniture, metal, manufacturing 337125 Camp furniture, reed and rattan, manufacturing
337122 Camp furniture, wood, manufacturing
813940 Campaign organizations, political
441210 Camper dealers, recreational
441210 Camper parts and accessories stores
532120 Camper rental
336214 Camper units, slide-in, for pick-up trucks, manufacturing
721211 Campgrounds
325194 Camphor, natural, manufacturing
325199 Camphor, synthetic, manufacturing
423910 Camping equipment and supplies merchant wholesalers
423110 Camping trailer merchant wholesalers
336214 Camping trailers and chassis manufacturing
721214 Camps (except day, instructional)
713990 Camps (except instructional), day 623990 Camps, boot or disciplinary (except correctional), for delinquent youth
611620 Camps, sports instruction
721211 Campsites
333515 Cams (i.e., a machine tool accessory) manufacturing
333517 Can forming machines, metalworking, manufacturing
332618 Can keys made from purchased wire
332431 Can lids and ends, light gauge metal, manufacturing
332216 Can openers (except electric) manufacturing
335210 Can openers, household-type electric, manufacturing
483211 Canal barge transportation (freight)
237990 Canal construction
488310 Canal maintenance services (except dredging)
488310 Canal operation
483212 Canal passenger transportation
221310 Canal, irrigation
333318 Canceling machinery, postal office-type, manufacturing
923120 Cancer detection program administration
622310 Cancer hospitals
311340 Candied fruits and fruit peel manufacturing
713950 Candle pin bowling alleys

713950 Candle pin bowling centers
453998 Candle shops
339999 Candles manufacturing
424990 Candles merchant wholesalers
311351 Candy bars, chocolate (including chocolate covered), made from cacao beans
311340 Candy bars, nonchocolate, manufacturing
424450 Candy merchant wholesalers 311352 Candy stores, chocolate, candy made on premises not for immediate consumption
311340 Candy stores, nonchocolate, candy made on premises, not for immediate consumption
445292 Candy stores, packaged, retailing only
311351 Candy, chocolate, made from cacao beans
111930 Cane farming, sugar, field production
311314 Cane sugar manufacturing
424490 Cane sugar, refined, merchant wholesalers
311314 Cane syrup manufacturing
339999 Canes (except orthopedic) manufacturing
332993 Canisters, ammunition, manufacturing
424490 Canned foods (e.g., fish, meat, seafood, soups) merchant wholesalers
311611 Canned meats (except poultry) produced in slaughtering plants
311911 Canned nuts manufacturing
236210 Cannery construction
311710 Cannery, seafood
311421 Canning fruits and vegetables
311421 Canning jams and jellies
333993 Canning machinery manufacturing
311615 Canning poultry (except baby and pet food)
311422 Canning soups (except seafood)
423840 Canning supplies merchant wholesalers
311710 Canning, fish, crustacea, and mollusks
332994 Cannons manufacturing
339112 Cannulae manufacturing
532284 Canoe rental
713990 Canoeing, recreational
311225 Canola (rapeseed) oil, cake and meal, made from purchased oils
311224 Canola (rapeseed) oil, cake and meal, made in crushing mills
111120 Canola farming, field and seed production
332322 Canopies, sheet metal (except stampings), manufacturing
332431 Cans, aluminum, light gauge metal, manufacturing
332431 Cans, light gauge metal, manufacturing
332431 Cans, steel, light gauge metal, manufacturing
111219 Cantaloupe farming, field, bedding plant and seed production
722515 Canteens, fixed location
722330 Canteens, mobile
321912 Cants, resawed (lumber), manufacturing
314910 Canvas bags manufacturing
339940 Canvas board, artist's, manufacturing
314910 Canvas products made from purchased canvas or canvas substitutes
424990 Canvas products merchant wholesalers
316210 Canvas shoes, plastics soled fabric upper, manufacturing
316210 Canvas shoes, rubber soled fabric upper, manufacturing
339940 Canvas, artist's, prepared on frames, manufacturing
313210 Canvases weaving
454390 Canvassers (door-to-door), headquarters for retail sale of merchandise, direct selling
423610 Capacitors (except electronic) merchant wholesalers
335999 Capacitors (except electronic), fixed and variable, manufacturing
334416 Capacitors, electronic, fixed and variable, manufacturing
423690 Capacitors, electronic, merchant wholesalers
315240 Capes (except fur, waterproof), women's and girls', cut and sewn from purchased fabric (except apparel contractors)
315210 Capes cut and sew apparel contractors
315280 Capes, fur (except apparel contractors), manufacturing
315280 Capes, waterproof (e.g., plastics, rubber, similar materials), cut and sewn from purchased fabric (except apparel contractors)
237110 Capping of water wells
333993 Capping, sealing, and lidding packaging machinery manufacturing
325199 Caprolactam manufacturing 315990 Caps (except fur, leather) cut and sewn from purchased fabric (except apparel contractors)
315210 Caps (i.e., apparel accessory) cut and sew apparel contractors

315990 Caps (i.e., apparel accessory) cut and sewn from purchased fabric (except fur, leather, apparel contractors)

315210 Caps and gowns, academic, cut and sew apparel contractors

315280 Caps and gowns, academic, cut and sewn from purchased fabric (except apparel contractors)

335931 Caps and plugs, attachment, electric, manufacturing

332119 Caps and tops, bottle, metal, stamping

336214 Caps for pick-up trucks manufacturing

325998 Caps for toy pistols manufacturing

315190 Caps made in apparel knitting mills

325920 Caps, blasting and detonating, manufacturing

332993 Caps, bomb, manufacturing 315280 Caps, fur (except apparel contractors), manufacturing

316998 Caps, heel and toe, leather, manufacturing

315280 Caps, leather (except apparel contractors), manufacturing

315210 Caps, textiles, straw, fur-felt, and wool-felt, cut and sew apparel contractors

315990 Caps, textiles, straw, fur-felt, and wool-felt, cut and sewn from purchased fabric (except apparel contractors)

325998 Capsules, gelatin, empty, manufacturing

334290 Car alarm manufacturing

336211 Car bodies, kit, manufacturing

811192 Car detailers

532112 Car leasing

483212 Car lighters (i.e., ferries), inland waters (except on Great Lakes system)

485999 Car pool operation

488999 Car pools, arrangement of

532111 Car rental

532111 Car rental agencies

561599 Car rental reservation services

811111 Car repair shops, general

332999 Car seals, metal, manufacturing

337125 Car seats, infant (except metal), manufacturing

334310 Car stereos manufacturing

522298 Car title lending

423850 Car wash equipment and supplies merchant wholesalers

811192 Car washes

333318 Car washing machinery manufacturing

331110 Car wheels, rolled steel, made in iron and steel mills

325180 Carbides (e.g., boron, calcium, silicon, tungsten) manufacturing

332994 Carbines manufacturing

325199 Carbinol manufacturing

325211 Carbohydrate plastics manufacturing

423510 Carbon and alloy steel primary forms merchant wholesalers

334510 Carbon arc lamp units, electrotherapeutic (except infrared and ultraviolet), manufacturing

325180 Carbon black manufacturing

424690 Carbon black merchant wholesalers

327120 Carbon brick manufacturing

325120 Carbon dioxide manufacturing

325180 Carbon disulfide manufacturing

335991 Carbon electrodes and contacts, electric, manufacturing

325180 Carbon inorganic compounds manufacturing

334290 Carbon monoxide detectors manufacturing

423690 Carbon monoxide detectors, electronic, merchant wholesalers

325199 Carbon organic compounds, not specified elsewhere by process, manufacturing

339940 Carbon paper manufacturing

335991 Carbon specialties for aerospace use (except gaskets) manufacturing

335991 Carbon specialties for electrical use manufacturing

335991 Carbon specialties for mechanical use (except gaskets) manufacturing

325199 Carbon tetrachloride manufacturing

325998 Carbon, activated, manufacturing

424490 Carbonated beverages merchant wholesalers

312111 Carbonated soda manufacturing

312111 Carbonated soft drinks manufacturing

325180 Carbonic acid manufacturing

333249 Carbonizing equipment for processing wool manufacturing

313310 Carbonizing textile fibers

335991 Carbons, electric, manufacturing

335991 Carbons, lighting, manufacturing

325998 Carburetor cleaners manufacturing

336310 Carburetors, all types, manufacturing

316998 Card cases (except metal) manufacturing

339910 Card cases, precious metal, manufacturing
423920 Card games merchant wholesalers
713290 Card rooms (e.g., poker rooms)
453220 Card shops, greeting
337122 Card table sets (furniture), wood, manufacturing
337124 Card table sets, metal, manufacturing
424130 Cardboard products merchant wholesalers
322130 Cardboard stock manufacturing
322220 Cardboard, laminated or surface coated, made from purchased paperboard
313230 Carded nonwoven fabrics manufacturing
313110 Carded yarn manufacturing
325412 Cardiac preparations manufacturing
333249 Carding machinery for textiles manufacturing
313310 Carding textile fibers 334510 Cardiodynameter manufacturing 334510 Cardiographs manufacturing 621111 Cardiologists' offices (e.g., centers, clinics) 334510 Cardiophone, electric, manufacturing 334510 Cardioscope manufacturing 334510 Cardiotachometer manufacturing 323111 Cards (e.g., business, greeting, playing, postcards, trading) commercial printing (except screen) without publishing
323113 Cards (e.g., business, greeting, playing, postcards, trading) screen printing without publishing
322299 Cards, die-cut (except office supply) made from purchased paper or paperboard
322230 Cards, die-cut office supply (e.g., index, library, time recording), made from purchased paper or paperboard
424120 Cards, greeting, merchant wholesalers
****** Cards, publishing -- see specific product
611710 Career and vocational counseling services (except rehabilitative)
481112 Cargo carriers, air, scheduled
488390 Cargo checkers, marine 811310 Cargo container repair and maintenance services
488330 Cargo salvaging, marine
336611 Cargo ship building
488390 Cargo surveyors, marine
488490 Cargo surveyors, truck transportation
423110 Cargo van merchant wholesalers
333318 Carnival and amusement park rides manufacturing
333318 Carnival and amusement park shooting gallery machinery manufacturing
423850 Carnival equipment merchant wholesalers
713990 Carnival ride concession operators (i.e., supplying and servicing in others' facilities)
711190 Carnival traveling shows
212291 Carnotite mining and/or beneficiating
333922 Carousel conveyors (e.g., luggage) manufacturing
333318 Carousels (i.e., merry-go-rounds) manufacturing
238350 Carpenters (except framing)
611513 Carpenters' apprenticeship training
332216 Carpenter's handtools, nonelectric, manufacturing
423710 Carpenters' tools merchant wholesalers
532490 Carpentry equipment rental or leasing
238350 Carpentry work (except framing)
238130 Carpentry, framing
333318 Carpet and floor cleaning equipment, electric commercial-type, manufacturing
335210 Carpet and floor cleaning equipment, household-type electric, manufacturing
532490 Carpet and rug cleaning equipment rental or leasing
313110 Carpet and rug yarn spinning
532289 Carpet and rug, residential, rental
423850 Carpet cleaning equipment and supplies merchant wholesalers
561740 Carpet cleaning on customers' premises
561740 Carpet cleaning plants
561740 Carpet cleaning services
314999 Carpet cutting and binding
313210 Carpet linings (except felt) weaving
423220 Carpet merchant wholesalers
313230 Carpet paddings, nonwoven, manufacturing
442210 Carpet stores
333318 Carpet sweepers, mechanical, manufacturing
238330 Carpet, installation only
314110 Carpets and rugs made from textile materials
321999 Carpets, cork, manufacturing
332311 Carports, prefabricated metal, manufacturing
487110 Carriage, horse-drawn, operation

339930 Carriages, baby, manufacturing
339930 Carriages, doll, manufacturing
334210 Carrier equipment (i.e., analog, digital), telephone, manufacturing
111219 Carrot farming, field, bedding plant and seed production
311991 Carrots, cut, peeled or sliced fresh, manufacturing
722513 Carryout restaurants
336111 Cars, electric, for highway use, assembling on chassis of own manufacture
333131 Cars, mining, manufacturing
541370 Cartographic surveying services
333993 Carton filling machinery manufacturing
423840 Cartons (except paper and paperboard) merchant wholesalers
322299 Cartons, egg, molded pulp manufacturing
322212 Cartons, folding (except milk), made from purchased paperboard
322219 Cartons, milk, made from purchased paper or paperboard
424130 Cartons, paper and paperboard, merchant wholesalers
711510 Cartoonists, independent
333991 Cartridge (i.e., powder) handheld power-driven tools manufacturing
332992 Cartridge cases for ammunition (i.e., 30 mm. or less, 1.18 inch or less) manufacturing
331420 Cartridge cups, discs, and sheets, copper and copper alloy, made from purchased copper or in integrated secondary smelting and rolling, drawing or extruding plants
424120 Cartridge toner merchant wholesalers
332992 Cartridges (i.e., 30 mm. or less, 1.18 inch or less) manufacturing
339920 Carts, caddy, manufacturing
423860 Carts, golf, motorized passenger merchant wholesalers
333924 Carts, grocery, made from purchased wire
333112 Carts, lawn and garden-type, manufacturing
332215 Carving sets manufacturing
111219 Casaba melon farming, field, bedding plant and seed production
316110 Case leather manufacturing
325220 Casein fibers and filaments manufacturing
325211 Casein plastics manufacturing
311514 Casein, dry and wet, manufacturing
332321 Casements, metal, manufacturing
316998 Cases, jewelry (except metal), manufacturing
339910 Cases, jewelry, metal, manufacturing
316998 Cases, luggage, manufacturing
316998 Cases, musical instrument, manufacturing
321920 Cases, shipping, wood, wirebound, manufacturing
321920 Cases, wood packing, nailed or lock corner, manufacturing
321920 Cases, wood shipping, nailed or lock corner, manufacturing
332439 Cash boxes, light gauge metal, manufacturing
532420 Cash register rental or leasing 333318
Cash registers (except point of sales terminals) manufacturing
423420 Cash registers merchant wholesalers
111335 Cashew farming
211130 Casing-head butane and propane production
326121 Casings, sausage, nonrigid plastics, manufacturing
332313 Casings, scroll, fabricated metal plate work, manufacturing
332322 Casings, sheet metal (except stampings), manufacturing
236220 Casino construction
721120 Casino hotels
423910 Casino supplies merchant wholesalers
713210 Casinos (except casino hotels)
332510 Casket hardware, metal, manufacturing
339995 Caskets, burial, manufacturing
423850 Caskets, burial, merchant wholesalers
321920 Casks, wood, coopered, manufacturing
111219 Cassava farming, field and seed production
335210 Casseroles, household-type electric, manufacturing
334614 Cassette tapes, prerecorded audio, mass reproducing
532282 Cassette, prerecorded video, rental 423990
Cassettes, prerecorded audio and video, merchant wholesalers
331511 Cast iron brake shoes, railroad, manufacturing
331511 Cast iron pipe and pipe fittings manufacturing
423510 Cast iron pipe merchant wholesalers
331511 Cast iron railroad car wheels manufacturing

331513 Cast steel railroad car wheels, unfinished, manufacturing
327390 Cast stone, concrete (except structural), manufacturing
327120 Castable refractories, clay, manufacturing
327120 Castable refractories, nonclay, manufacturing
332510 Casters, furniture, metal manufacturing
332510 Casters, industrial, metal, manufacturing
561311 Casting agencies (i.e., motion picture, theatrical, video)
561311 Casting agencies, motion picture or video
561311 Casting agencies, theatrical
561311 Casting bureaus (e.g., motion picture, theatrical, video)
561311 Casting bureaus, motion picture or video
561311 Casting bureaus, theatrical
331529 Castings (except die-castings), nonferrous metals (except aluminum), unfinished, manufacturing
331524 Castings (except die-castings), unfinished, aluminum, manufacturing
331511 Castings, compacted graphite iron, unfinished, manufacturing
331511 Castings, malleable iron, unfinished, manufacturing
423510 Castings, metal, merchant wholesalers
331513 Castings, steel (except investment), unfinished, manufacturing
331511 Castings, unfinished iron (e.g., ductile, gray, malleable, semisteel), manufacturing
311224 Castor oil and pomace made in crushing mills
316210 Casual shoes, children's and infants', manufacturing
316210 Casual shoes, men's, manufacturing
316210 Casual shoes, women's, manufacturing
524126 Casualty insurance carriers, direct
621512 CAT (computerized axial tomography) scanner centers
311111 Cat food manufacturing
325998 Cat litter manufacturing
112990 Cat production
511199 Catalog (i.e., mail-order, store merchandise) publishers (except exclusive Internet publishing)
511199 Catalog (i.e., mail-order, store merchandise) publishers and printing combined
454110 Catalog (i.e., order-taking) offices of mail-order houses
511140 Catalog of collections publishers (except exclusive Internet publishing)
511140 Catalog of collections publishers and printing combined
519130 Catalog of collections publishers, exclusively on Internet
452319 Catalog showrooms, general merchandise (except catalog mail-order)
323111 Catalogs commercial printing (except screen) without publishing
323111 Catalogs of collections commercial printing (except screen) without publishing
323113 Catalogs of collections screen printing without publishing
323113 Catalogs screen printing without publishing
336390 Catalytic converters, engine exhaust, automotive, truck, and bus, manufacturing
332994 Catapult guns manufacturing
562998 Catch basin cleaning services
722320 Caterers
722320 Catering services, social
112511 Catfish production, farm raising
325412 Cathartic preparations manufacturing
339112 Catheters manufacturing
334419 Cathode ray tubes (CRT) manufacturing
335999 Cathodic protection equipment manufacturing
238190 Cathodic protection, installation
212399 Catlinite mining and/or beneficiating
424990 Cats merchant wholesalers
311421 Catsup manufacturing
112111 Cattle conditioning operations
112111 Cattle farming or ranching
333111 Cattle feeding and watering equipment manufacturing
112112 Cattle feedlots (except stockyards for transportation)
311119 Cattle feeds, supplements, concentrates, and premixes, manufacturing
424520 Cattle merchant wholesalers
115210 Cattle spraying
111219 Cauliflower farming, field, bedding plant and seed production
238390 Caulking (i.e., waterproofing) contractors
325520 Caulking compounds (except gypsum base) manufacturing
332216 Caulking guns, nonpowered, manufacturing

424690 Caulking materials merchant wholesalers

524291 Cause-of-loss investigators, insurance

237310 Causeway construction

325180 Caustic potash manufacturing

325180 Caustic soda (i.e., sodium hydroxide) manufacturing

424690 Caustic soda merchant wholesalers

712190 Caverns (i.e., natural wonder tourist attractions)

334220 CB (citizens' band) radios manufacturing

332216 C-clamps manufacturing

334112 CD-ROM drives manufacturing

334614 CD-ROM, software, mass reproducing

337122 Cedar chests manufacturing

325998 Cedar oil manufacturing

238130 Ceiling beam, wood, installation

444190 Ceiling fan stores

335210 Ceiling fans with integral lighting fixture, residential, manufacturing

335210 Ceiling fans, residential, manufacturing

335122 Ceiling lighting fixtures, commercial, industrial, and institutional, manufacturing

335121 Ceiling lighting fixtures, residential, manufacturing

321912 Ceiling lumber, dressed, resawing purchased lumber

321113 Ceiling lumber, made from logs or bolts

238310 Ceiling tile installation

423390 Ceiling tile merchant wholesalers

238390 Ceiling, metal, installation

334519 Ceilometers manufacturing

711410 Celebrities' agents or managers

711510 Celebrity spokespersons, independent

111219 Celery farming, field, bedding plant and seed production

212393 Celestite mining and/or beneficiating

325220 Cellophane film or sheet manufacturing

424120 Cellophane tape merchant wholesalers

339992 Cellos and parts manufacturing

237130 Cellular phone tower construction

443142 Cellular telephone accessories stores

517312 Cellular telephone communication carriers

517312 Cellular telephone services

517312 Cellular telephone stores, primarily selling cellular phone service plans

334220 Cellular telephones manufacturing

423690 Cellular telephones merchant wholesalers

325199 Cellulose acetate (except resins) manufacturing

325211 Cellulose acetate resins manufacturing

424610 Cellulose film merchant wholesalers

325211 Cellulose nitrate resins manufacturing

325211 Cellulose propionate resins manufacturing

325211 Cellulose resins manufacturing

325211 Cellulose xanthate (viscose) manufacturing

238310 Cellulosic fiber insulation installation

325220 Cellulosic fibers and filaments manufacturing

325220 Cellulosic filament yarn manufacturing

326113 Cellulosic plastics film and unlaminated sheet (except packaging) manufacturing

325220 Cellulosic staple fibers manufacturing

327310 Cement (e.g., hydraulic, masonry, portland, pozzolana) manufacturing

238140 Cement block laying

327310 Cement clinker manufacturing

333249 Cement kilns manufacturing

423320 Cement merchant wholesalers

236210 Cement plant construction

212312 Cement rock crushed and broken stone mining and/or beneficiating

327120 Cement, clay refractory, manufacturing

327420 Cement, Keene's (i.e., tiling plaster), manufacturing

325520 Cement, rubber, manufacturing 213112 Cementing oil and gas well casings on a contract basis

423830 Cement-making machinery merchant wholesalers

324122 Cements, asphalt roofing, made from purchased asphaltic materials

339114 Cements, dental, manufacturing

812220 Cemeteries

812220 Cemetery associations (i.e., operators)

812220 Cemetery management services 453998 Cemetery memorial dealers (e.g., headstones, markers, vaults)

561730 Cemetery plot care services

812220 Cemetery subdividers 333517 Centering machines, metalworking, manufacturing

519120 Centers for documentation (i.e., archives)

624120 Centers, senior citizens'

238220 Central air-conditioning equipment installation
521110 Central bank, monetary authorities
238220 Central cooling equipment and piping installation
238220 Central heating equipment and piping installation
423730 Central heating equipment, warm air, merchant wholesalers
325412 Central nervous system stimulant preparations manufacturing
334210 Central office and switching equipment, telephone, manufacturing
522320 Central reserve financial institutions (except central bank)
333318 Central vacuuming systems, commercial-type, manufacturing
335210 Central vacuuming systems, household-type, manufacturing
551114 Centralized administrative offices
327320 Central-mixed concrete manufacturing
333914 Centrifugal pumps manufacturing
333999 Centrifuges, industrial and laboratory-type, manufacturing
325411 Cephalosporin, uncompounded, manufacturing
423330 Ceramic and clay roofing materials merchant wholesalers
325130 Ceramic colors manufacturing
423320 Ceramic construction materials (except refractory and ceramic roofing tile) merchant wholesalers
327999 Ceramic fiber manufacturing
333994 Ceramic kilns and furnaces manufacturing
238340 Ceramic tile installation
444190 Ceramic tile stores
327120 Ceramic tiles, floor and wall, manufacturing
423220 Ceramic wall (except structural) and floor tile merchant wholesalers
611610 Ceramics instruction
311211 Cereal grain flour manufacturing
311211 Cereal grain germ manufacturing
424490 Cereal products merchant wholesalers
212299 Cerium concentrates mining and/or beneficiating
212299 Cerium ores mining and/or beneficiating
325180 Cerium salts manufacturing
523120 Certificate of deposit (CD) brokers' offices
923110 Certification of schools and teachers
541211 Certified accountants' offices 523930 Certified financial planners, customized, fees paid by client
541211 Certified public accountants' (CPAs) offices
621399 Certified registered nurse anesthetists' (CRNAs) offices (e.g., centers, clinics)
212230 Cerussite mining and/or beneficiating
339113 Cervical collars manufacturing 325180
Cesium and cesium compounds, not specified elsewhere by process, manufacturing
562991 Cesspool cleaning services
238910 Cesspool construction
325199 Cetyl alcohol manufacturing
335210 Chafing dishes, household-type electric, manufacturing
332999 Chain fittings manufacturing
333923 Chain hoists manufacturing
332323 Chain ladders, metal, manufacturing
238990 Chain link fence installation
332618 Chain link fencing and fence gates made from purchased wire
331222 Chain link fencing, iron or steel, made in wire drawing plants
332618 Chain made from purchased wire
332216 Chain saw blades manufacturing
333991 Chain saws, handheld power-driven, manufacturing
332618 Chain, welded, made from purchased wire
339910 Chains or necklace, precious metal, manufacturing
333613 Chains, power transmission, manufacturing
334519 Chains, surveyor's, manufacturing
423830 Chainsaws merchant wholesalers
337121 Chair and couch springs, assembled, manufacturing
337215 Chair glides manufacturing
337215 Chair seats for furniture manufacturing
337122 Chairs (except upholstered), wood household-type, manufacturing
337214 Chairs (except wood), office-type, manufacturing
337127 Chairs, barber, beauty shop (i.e., hydraulic), manufacturing
337125 Chairs, cane, wood household-type, manufacturing
339114 Chairs, dentist's, manufacturing

423850 Chairs, hydraulic, beauty and barber shop, merchant wholesalers
337124 Chairs, metal household-type (except upholstered), manufacturing
337127 Chairs, portable folding, auditorium-type, manufacturing
337127 Chairs, stacking, auditorium-type, manufacturing
337121 Chairs, upholstered household-type (except dining room, kitchen), manufacturing
337211 Chairs, wood office-type, manufacturing
212230 Chalcocite mining and/or beneficiating
212230 Chalcopyrite mining and/or beneficiating
339940 Chalk (e.g., artist's, blackboard, carpenter's, marking, tailor's), manufacturing
212312 Chalk crushed and broken stone mining and/or beneficiating
212312 Chalk, ground or otherwise treated, mining and/or beneficiating
339940 Chalkboards, framed, manufacturing
711130 Chamber musical groups
711130 Chamber orchestras
813910 Chambers of commerce
313210 Chambrays weaving
333517 Chamfering machines, metalworking, manufacturing
316110 Chamois leather manufacturing
424990 Chamois, leather, merchant wholesalers
312130 Champagne method sparkling wine, manufacturing
335122 Chandeliers, commercial, industrial, and institutional electric, manufacturing
335121 Chandeliers, residential, manufacturing
333318 Change making machines manufacturing
325180 Channel black manufacturing
237990 Channel construction
332323 Channels, furring metal, manufacturing
325194 Charcoal (except activated) manufacturing
325194 Charcoal briquettes, wood, manufacturing
424990 Charcoal merchant wholesalers
325998 Charcoal, activated, manufacturing
522210 Charge card issuing
423410 Charged coupled devices (CCD) merchant wholesalers
813211 Charitable trusts, awarding grants
611699 Charm schools
481212 Charter air freight services
481211 Charter air passenger services 485510
Charter bus services (except scenic, sightseeing)
487210 Charter fishing boat operation
611110 Charter schools
333515 Chasers (i.e., a machine tool accessory) manufacturing
212399 Chasers mining and/or beneficiating 332812
Chasing metals and metal products (except printing plates) for the trade
336111 Chassis, automobile, manufacturing
336120 Chassis, heavy truck, with or without cabs, manufacturing
336112 Chassis, light truck and utility, manufacturing
423110 Chassis, motor vehicle, merchant wholesalers
561311 Chauffeur registries
611519 Chauffeur training 315210 Chauffeurs' hats
and caps cut and sew apparel contractors
315990 Chauffeurs' hats and caps cut and sewn from purchased fabric (except apparel contractors)
522390 Check cashing services
521110 Check clearing activities of the central bank
522320 Check clearing services (except central banks)
522320 Check clearinghouse services (except central banks)
423420 Check handling machines merchant wholesalers
812990 Check room services
522320 Check validation services 332911
Check valves, industrial-type, manufacturing
333318 Check writing machines manufacturing
316998 Checkbook covers (except metal) manufacturing
339910 Checkbook covers, precious metal, manufacturing
323111 Checkbooks and refills printing
339930 Checkers and checkerboards manufacturing
611620 Cheerleading instruction, camps, or schools
311513 Cheese (except cottage cheese) manufacturing
311513 Cheese analogs manufacturing
311941 Cheese based salad dressing manufacturing

424450 Cheese confections (e.g., curls, puffs) merchant wholesalers
311919 Cheese curls and puffs manufacturing
424430 Cheese merchant wholesalers
333241 Cheese processing machinery manufacturing
311513 Cheese products, imitation or substitute, manufacturing
311513 Cheese spreads manufacturing
311511 Cheese, cottage, manufacturing
311513 Cheese, imitation or substitute, manufacturing
311513 Cheese, natural (except cottage cheese), manufacturing
313210 Cheesecloths weaving 236210 Chemical (except petrochemical process-type) plant construction
424690 Chemical additives (e.g., concrete, food, fuel, oil) merchant wholesalers
423490 Chemical and technical pottery products merchant wholesalers
541690 Chemical consulting services
541330 Chemical engineering services 313310 Chemical finishing (e.g., fire, mildew, water resistance) fabrics
424690 Chemical gases merchant wholesalers
423830 Chemical industries machinery and equipment merchant wholesalers
333249 Chemical kilns manufacturing
332710 Chemical milling job shops
333517 Chemical milling machines, metalworking, manufacturing
333249 Chemical processing machinery and equipment manufacturing
541715 Chemical research and development laboratories or services (except biotechnology and nanotechnology research and development)
327110 Chemical stoneware (i.e., pottery products) manufacturing
326191 Chemical toilets, plastics, manufacturing
115112 Chemical treatment of soil for crops
213112 Chemically treating oil and gas wells (e.g., acidizing, bailing, swabbing) on a contract basis
424690 Chemicals (except agriculture) (e.g., automotive, household, industrial, photographic) merchant wholesalers
424910 Chemicals, agricultural, merchant wholesalers
315210 Chemises cut and sew apparel contractors
315190 Chemises made in apparel knitting mills
315240 Chemises, women's and girls', cut and sewn from purchased fabric (except apparel contractors)
111339 Cherry farming
113210 Cherry gum, gathering
339930 Chessmen and chessboards manufacturing
325194 Chestnut extract manufacturing
113210 Chestnut gum, gathering
321920 Chests for tools, wood, manufacturing
332999 Chests, fire or burglary resistive, metal, manufacturing
332999 Chests, money, metal, manufacturing
332999 Chests, safe deposit, metal, manufacturing
311340 Chewing gum base manufacturing 333241 Chewing gum machinery manufacturing 311340 Chewing gum manufacturing 424450 Chewing gum merchant wholesalers 312230 Chewing tobacco manufacturing 424940 Chewing tobacco merchant wholesalers 424440 Chicken and chicken products (except canned and packaged frozen) merchant wholesalers
333111 Chicken brooders manufacturing
321920 Chicken coops (i.e., crates), wood, wire-bound for shipping poultry, manufacturing
321992 Chicken coops, prefabricated, wood, manufacturing
112310 Chicken egg production
112310 Chicken eggs (table, hatching) production
333111 Chicken feeders manufacturing
311119 Chicken feeds, prepared, manufacturing
112340 Chicken hatcheries
332618 Chicken netting made from purchased wire
112320 Chicken production (except egg laying)
311615 Chickens, processing, fresh, frozen, canned, or cooked (except baby and pet food)
311615 Chickens, slaughtering and dressing
424590 Chicks, live, merchant wholesalers
111998 Chicory farming
624410 Child day care centers
624410 Child day care services
624410 Child day care services in provider's own home
624410 Child day care, before or after school, separate from schools

623990 Child group foster homes

624110 Child guidance agencies

624110 Child welfare services

621410 Childbirth preparation classes

721214 Children's camps (except day, instructional)

424330 Children's clothing merchant wholesalers

511199 Children's coloring book publishers (except exclusive Internet publishing)

519130 Children's coloring book publishers, exclusively on Internet

622110 Children's hospitals, general

622210 Children's hospitals, psychiatric or substance abuse

622310 Children's hospitals, specialty (except psychiatric, substance abuse)

448210 Children's shoe stores

316210 Children's shoes (except orthopedic extension) manufacturing

315110 Children's socks manufacturing

423920 Children's vehicles (except bicycles) merchant wholesalers

623990 Children's villages

311422 Chili con carne canning

311942 Chili pepper or powder manufacturing

311421 Chili sauce manufacturing

238220 Chilled water system installation

339992 Chimes and parts (musical instruments) manufacturing

335999 Chimes, electric, manufacturing

327390 Chimney caps, concrete, manufacturing

561790 Chimney cleaning services

238220 Chimney liner installation

561790 Chimney sweep (i.e., cleaning) services

238140 Chimney, brick, block or stone, contractors

238110 Chimney, concrete, construction

212324 China clay mining and/or beneficiating

337122 China closets, wood, manufacturing

327110 China cooking ware manufacturing

811490 China repair services

327110 China tableware, vitreous, manufacturing

442299 Chinaware stores

423440 Chinaware, commercial, merchant wholesalers

423220 Chinaware, household-type, merchant wholesalers

112930 Chinchilla production

311422 Chinese foods canning

311999 Chinese noodles, fried, manufacturing

111219 Chinese pea farming, bedding plant and seed production

313210 Chintzes weaving

333249 Chip placement machinery manufacturing

322130 Chipboard (i.e., paperboard) stock manufacturing

321219 Chipboard (i.e., particle core, wood chip face) manufacturing

322220 Chipboard, laminated or surface coated, made from purchased paperboard

321113 Chipper mills (except portable) 333112

Chippers (i.e., shredders), lawn and garden-type, manufacturing

333120 Chippers, portable, commercial (e.g., brush, limb, log), manufacturing

333243 Chippers, stationary (e.g., log), manufacturing

424450 Chips (e.g., corn, potato) merchant wholesalers

621310 Chiropractors' offices (e.g., centers, clinics)

332216 Chisels manufacturing 333991 Chis-

els, handheld power-driven, manufacturing

111219 Chive farming, field, bedding plant and seed production

325199 Chloral manufacturing

325320 Chlordane insecticides manufacturing

325180 Chloride of lime manufacturing

325212 Chlorinated rubber, synthetic, manufacturing

325180 Chlorine compounds, not specified elsewhere by process, manufacturing

325180 Chlorine dioxide manufacturing

325180 Chlorine manufacturing

424690 Chlorine merchant wholesalers

325199 Chloroacetic acid manufacturing

325194 Chlorobenzene manufacturing

325120 Chlorodifluoromethane manufacturing

325120 Chlorofluorocarbon gases manufacturing

325199 Chloroform manufacturing

325194 Chloronaphthalene manufacturing

325194 Chlorophenol manufacturing

325199 Chloropicrin manufacturing

325212 Chloroprene rubber manufacturing

325212 Chlorosulfonated polyethylenes manufacturing

325180 Chlorosulfonic acid manufacturing

325194 Chlorotoluene manufacturing

311352 Chocolate (coating, instant, liquor, syrups) made from purchased chocolate

311351 Chocolate (e.g., coatings, instant, liquor, syrups) made from cacao beans

424490 Chocolate (except candy) merchant wholesalers

311351 Chocolate bars made from cocoa beans

424450 Chocolate candy merchant wholesalers

311352 Chocolate coatings and syrups made from purchased chocolate

424490 Chocolate coatings merchant wholesalers

311352 Chocolate covered candy bars made from purchased chocolate

311352 Chocolate covered granola bars made from purchased chocolate

311511 Chocolate drink (milk based) manufacturing

311511 Chocolate milk manufacturing 333241

Chocolate processing machinery manufacturing

424490 Chocolate syrups (except fountain) merchant wholesalers

311351 Chocolate, confectionery, made from cacao beans

711130 Choirs

334416 Chokes for electronic circuitry manufacturing

325414 Cholera serums manufacturing

325320 Cholinesterase inhibitors used as insecticides manufacturing

311412 Chop suey, frozen, manufacturing

115113 Chopping and silo filling

711510 Choreographers, independent

311412 Chow mein, frozen, manufacturing

311710 Chowders, seafood, manufacturing

621399 Christian Science practitioners' offices (e.g., centers, clinics)

424990 Christmas ornaments merchant wholesalers

453220 Christmas stores

333132 Christmas tree assemblies, oil and gas field-type, manufacturing 111421 Christmas tree growing 335129 Christmas tree lighting sets, electric, manufacturing

339999 Christmas tree ornaments (except electric, glass) manufacturing

327215 Christmas tree ornaments made from purchased glass

327212 Christmas tree ornaments, glass, made in glass making plants

424990 Christmas trees (e.g., artificial, cut) merchant wholesalers

339999 Christmas trees, artificial, manufacturing

454390 Christmas trees, cut, direct selling 334516

Chromatographic instruments, laboratory-type, manufacturing

334513 Chromatographs, industrial process-type, manufacturing

325130 Chrome pigments (e.g., chrome green, chrome orange, chrome yellow) manufacturing

332813 Chrome plating metals and metal products for the trade

325180 Chromic acid manufacturing

212299 Chromite mining and/or beneficiating

325180 Chromium compounds, not specified elsewhere by process, manufacturing

212299 Chromium concentrates beneficiating

212299 Chromium ore mining and/or beneficiating

325180 Chromium oxide manufacturing

331410 Chromium refining, primary

325180 Chromium salts manufacturing

622310 Chronic disease hospitals

334519 Chronographs manufacturing

334519 Chronometers manufacturing

334516 Chronoscopes manufacturing

333517 Chucking machines, automatic, metalworking, manufacturing

333515 Chucks (i.e., a machine tool accessory) manufacturing

112390 Chukar partridge production

238290 Church bell and tower clock installation

337127 Church furniture (except concrete, stone) manufacturing

423490 Church supplies (except plated ware, silverware) merchant wholesalers

813110 Churches

332313 Chutes, fabricated metal plate work, manufacturing

333241 Cider presses manufacturing

311941 Cider vinegar manufacturing

312130 Cider, alcoholic, manufacturing

311941 Cider, nonalcoholic, manufacturing

326199 Cigar and cigarette holders, plastics, manufacturing

321920 Cigar boxes, wood and part wood, manufacturing

316998 Cigar cases (except metal) manufacturing
339910 Cigar cases, precious metal, manufacturing
312230 Cigar manufacturing
453991 Cigar stores
316998 Cigarette cases (except metal) manufacturing
339910 Cigarette cases, precious metal, manufacturing
339999 Cigarette holders manufacturing
339999 Cigarette lighter flints manufacturing
339999 Cigarette lighters (except precious metal) manufacturing
424990 Cigarette lighters merchant wholesalers
333249 Cigarette making machinery manufacturing
322299 Cigarette paper made from purchased paper
322121 Cigarette paper made in paper mills
322299 Cigarette paper, book, made from purchased paper
453991 Cigarette stands, permanent
454390 Cigarette stands, temporary 325220
Cigarette tow, cellulosic fiber, manufacturing
333318 Cigarette vending machines manufacturing
312230 Cigarettes manufacturing
424940 Cigarettes merchant wholesalers
424940 Cigars merchant wholesalers
325411 Cinchona and derivatives (i.e., basic chemicals) manufacturing
327331 Cinder (clinker) block, concrete, manufacturing
238140 Cinder block installation
236220 Cinema construction
512131 Cinemas
711510 Cinematographers, independent
212299 Cinnabar mining and/or beneficiating
333249 Circuit board making machinery manufacturing
423690 Circuit boards merchant wholesalers
334412 Circuit boards, printed, bare, manufacturing
423610 Circuit breakers merchant wholesalers
335313 Circuit breakers, air, manufacturing
335313 Circuit breakers, power, manufacturing
922110 Circuit courts
334515 Circuit testers manufacturing 423690 Circuits, integrated, merchant wholesalers
313240 Circular (i.e., weft) fabrics knitting
541870 Circular direct distribution services
333249 Circular knitting machinery manufacturing
333991 Circular saws, handheld power-driven, manufacturing
333243 Circular saws, woodworking-type, stationary, manufacturing
519120 Circulating libraries
711190 Circus companies
711190 Circuses
443142 Citizens' band (CB) radio stores
334220 Citizens' band (CB) radios manufacturing
423690 Citizens' band (CB) radios merchant wholesalers
325199 Citral manufacturing
325199 Citrates, not specified elsewhere by process, manufacturing
325199 Citric acid manufacturing
325998 Citronella oil manufacturing
325199 Citronellal manufacturing
115112 Citrus grove cultivation services
111320 Citrus groves (except orange)
311119 Citrus pulp, cattle feed, manufacturing
311411 Citrus pulp, frozen, manufacturing
921120 City and town councils
921110 City and town managers' offices
485113 City bus services (except mixed mode)
922110 City or county courts
541320 City planning services
813410 Civic associations
236220 Civic center construction
541330 Civil engineering services
813311 Civil liberties organizations
921190 Civil rights commissions
921190 Civil service commissions
524291 Claims adjusting, insurance
524292 Claims processing services, insurance, third party
114112 Clam digging
112512 Clam production, farm raising 333515
Clamps (i.e., a machine tool accessory) manufacturing
339112 Clamps, surgical, manufacturing
339992 Clarinets and parts manufacturing
316998 Clasps, shoe (leather), manufacturing

813410 Classic car clubs
711120 Classical dance companies
711130 Classical musical artists, independent
711130 Classical musical groups
212325 Clay (except kaolin, ball) mining and/or beneficiating
327110 Clay and ceramic statuary manufacturing
212325 Clay bleaching
423320 Clay construction materials (except refractory and clay roofing tile) merchant wholesalers
327120 Clay refractories (e.g., mortar, brick, tile, block) manufacturing
212324 Clay, ball, mining and/or beneficiating
212325 Clay, ceramic and refractory minerals, mining and/or beneficiating
212325 Clay, fire, mining and/or beneficiating
339940 Clay, modeling, manufacturing
212324 Clay, natural, mining and/or beneficiating
333249 Clayworking and tempering machinery manufacturing
812332 Clean room apparel supply services
236210 Clean room construction
339113 Clean room suits and accessories manufacturing
812320 Cleaners, drycleaning and laundry service (except coin-operated)
335210 Cleaners, household-type electric vacuum, manufacturing
561790 Cleaning (e.g., power sweeping, washing) driveways and parking lots
332813 Cleaning and descaling metals and metal products for the trade
812320 Cleaning and dyeing plants (except rug cleaning plants)
311212 Cleaning and polishing rice
561790 Cleaning building exteriors (except sandblasting, window cleaning)
238990 Cleaning building interiors during and immediately after construction
561740 Cleaning carpets
424690 Cleaning compounds and preparations merchant wholesalers
335999 Cleaning equipment, ultrasonic (except dental, medical), manufacturing
561720 Cleaning homes
333131 Cleaning machinery, mining-type, manufacturing
238990 Cleaning new building interiors immediately after construction
561720 Cleaning offices
213112 Cleaning oil and gas field lease tanks on a contract basis
213112 Cleaning out (e.g., bailing out, steam cleaning, swabbing) wells on a contract basis
212113 Cleaning plants, anthracite coal
212111 Cleaning plants, bituminous coal
561740 Cleaning plants, carpet and rug
115210 Cleaning poultry houses
561740 Cleaning rugs
561740 Cleaning services, carpet and rug 561720
Cleaning shopping centers 561790 Cleaning swimming pools 213112 Cleaning wells on a contract basis 213112 Cleaning, repairing, and dismantling oil and gas field lease tanks on a contract basis
321918 Clear and finger joint wood moldings manufacturing
522320 Clearinghouses, bank or check
523999 Clearinghouses, commodity exchange or securities exchange
316210 Cleated athletic shoes manufacturing
332215 Cleavers manufacturing
611410 Clerical schools
315210 Clerical vestments cut and sew apparel contractors
315280 Clerical vestments cut and sewn from purchased fabric (except apparel contractors)
315190 Clerical vestments made in apparel knitting mills
316210 Climbing shoes, plastics or plastics soled fabric upper, manufacturing
316210 Climbing shoes, rubber or rubber soled fabric upper, manufacturing
236220 Clinic construction
621399 Clinical nurse specialists' (CNSs) offices (e.g., centers, clinics)
621111 Clinical pathologists' offices (e.g., centers, clinics)
621399 Clinical pharmacists' offices (e.g., centers, clinics)
621330 Clinical psychologists' offices (e.g., centers, clinics)
****** Clinics, medical -- see type
621498 Clinics/centers of health practitioners from more than one industry practicing within the same establishment

621498 Clinics/centers of health practitioners with multi-industry degrees
321999 Clipboards, wood, manufacturing
332216 Clippers for animal use, nonelectric, manufacturing
332215 Clippers, fingernail and toenail, manufacturing
519190 Clipping services, news 332994
Clips, gun, manufacturing
334519 Clock materials and parts (except crystals) manufacturing
334519 Clock or watch springs, precision, made from purchased wire
334310 Clock radios manufacturing
811490 Clock repair shops without retailing new clocks
448310 Clock shops
334519 Clocks assembling 334519 Clocks assembling from purchased components
423940 Clocks merchant wholesalers 541714
Cloning research and experimental development laboratories
561492 Closed captioning services, real-time (i.e., simultaneous)
512191 Closed captioning services, taped material
517311 Closed-circuit television (CCTV) services
334220 Closed-circuit television equipment manufacturing
525990 Closed-end investment funds
423220 Closet accessories merchant wholesalers
453998 Closet organizer stores
238390 Closet organizer system installation
423840 Closures, industrial, merchant wholesalers
332119 Closures, metal, stamping
424130 Closures, paper and disposable plastics, merchant wholesalers
327910 Cloth (e.g., aluminum oxide, garnet, emery, silicon carbide) coated manufacturing
561990 Cloth cutting, bolting, or winding for the trade
333249 Cloth spreading machinery manufacturing
321999 Cloth winding reels, wood, manufacturing
332618 Cloth, woven wire, made from purchased wire
334512 Clothes dryer controls, including dryness controls, manufacturing
811412 Clothes dryer, household-type, repair and maintenance services without retailing new clothes dryers
321999 Clothes dryers (clothes horses), wood, manufacturing
423850 Clothes dryers (except household-type) merchant wholesalers
423620 Clothes dryers merchant wholesalers
424990 Clothes hangers merchant wholesalers
326199 Clothes hangers, plastics, manufacturing
321999 Clothes poles, wood, manufacturing
326199 Clothespins, plastics, manufacturing
321999 Clothespins, wood, manufacturing
448150 Clothing accessories stores
424330 Clothing accessories, women's, children's, and infants', merchant wholesalers
541490 Clothing design services
532281 Clothing rental (except industrial launderer, linen supply)
811490 Clothing repair shops, alterations only
448130 Clothing stores, children's and infants'
448140 Clothing stores, family
448110 Clothing stores, men's and boys'
453310 Clothing stores, used
448120 Clothing stores, women's and girls'
339930 Clothing, doll, manufacturing
315280 Clothing, fur (except apparel contractors), manufacturing
315210 Clothing, fur, cut and sew apparel contractors
315280 Clothing, leather or sheep-lined (except apparel contractors), manufacturing
315210 Clothing, leather or sheep-lined, cut and sew apparel contractors
424320 Clothing, men's and boys', merchant wholesalers
315210 Clothing, water resistant, cut and sew apparel contractors
315220 Clothing, water resistant, men's and boys', cut and sewn from purchased fabric (except apparel contractors)
315240 Clothing, water resistant, women's, girls', and infants', cut and sewn from purchased fabric (except apparel contractors)
315210 Clothing, waterproof, cut and sew apparel contractors
315280 Clothing, waterproof, cut and sewn from purchased fabric (except apparel contractors)
315210 Clothing, water-repellent, cut and sew apparel contractors

315220 Clothing, water-repellent, men's and boys', cut and sewn from purchased fabric (except apparel contractors)
315240 Clothing, water-repellent, women's, girls', and infants', cut and sewn from purchased fabric (except apparel contractors)
424330 Clothing, women's, children's, and infants', merchant wholesalers
339994 Cloths (except chemically treated), dusting and polishing, manufacturing
325612 Cloths, dusting and polishing, chemically treated, manufacturing
325998 Clove oil manufacturing
111940 Clover hay farming
111998 Clover seed farming
721310 Clubs, residential
339920 Clubs, sporting goods (e.g., golf, Indian), manufacturing
336350 Clutches and clutch discs, asbestos, manufacturing
525990 CMOs (collateralized mortgage obligations)
325413 Coagulation in-vitro diagnostic substances manufacturing
325412 Coagulation in-vivo diagnostic substances manufacturing
333922 Coal and ore conveyors manufacturing
212113 Coal beneficiating plants, anthracite 212111
Coal beneficiating plants, bituminous or lignite (surface or underground)
333131 Coal breakers, cutters, and pulverizers manufacturing
332322 Coal chutes, sheet metal (except stampings), manufacturing
454310 Coal dealers, direct selling 423520 Coal
dust merchant wholesalers 211130 Coal gasifica-
tion at mine site 484220 Coal hauling, truck, local
211130 Coal liquefaction at mine site 423520
Coal merchant wholesalers 213113 Coal mining
services (except site preparation and related construction
contractor activities)
213113 Coal mining support services (tunneling, blasting, training, overburden removal)(except site preparation and related construction contractor activities)
486990 Coal pipeline transportation
211130 Coal pyrolysis
424690 Coal tar distillates and resins merchant wholesalers
325194 Coal tar distillates manufacturing 324121
Coal tar paving materials made from purchased coal tar
423320 Coal tar paving materials merchant wholesalers
424690 Coal tar products, primary and intermediate, merchant wholesalers
325211 Coal tar resins manufacturing
212113 Coal, anthracite, mining and/or beneficiating
212111 Coal, bituminous, beneficiating
212112 Coal, bituminous, underground mining or mining and beneficiating
212111 Coal, brown, mining and/or beneficiating
926120 Coast Guard (except academy)
483113 Coastal freight transportation to and from domestic ports
483114 Coastal passenger transportation to and from domestic ports
483113 Coastal shipping of freight to and from domestic ports
812331 Coat (e.g., barber's, beautician's, doctor's, nurse's) supply services
332618 Coat hangers made from purchased wire
315280 Coat linings, fur (except apparel contractors), manufacturing
315210 Coat linings, fur, cut and sew apparel contractors
448190 Coat stores
315990 Coat trimmings fabric cut and sewn from purchased fabric (except apparel contractors)
315210 Coat trimmings, fabric, cut and sew apparel contractors
322220 Coated board made from purchased paperboard
322130 Coated board made in paperboard mills
324122 Coating compounds, tar, made from purchased asphaltic materials
238390 Coating concrete structures with plastics
332812 Coating metals and metal products for the trade
332812 Coating of metal and metal products with plastics for the trade
335110 Coating purchased light bulbs
322220 Coating purchased papers for nonpackaging applications (except photosensitive paper)
322220 Coating purchased papers for packaging applications
311351 Coatings, chocolate, made from cacao beans

315210 Coats (e.g., tailored, fur, artificial leather, leather, sheep-lined), cut and sew apparel contractors

315220 Coats (except fur, leather, waterproof), men's and boys', cut and sewn from purchased fabric (except apparel contractors)

315240 Coats (except fur, leather, waterproof), women's, girls', and infants', cut and sewn from purchased fabric (except apparel contractors)

315280 Coats (including tailored), leather or sheep-lined (except apparel contractors), manufacturing

315280 Coats, artificial leather, cut and sewn from purchased fabric (except apparel contractors)

315280 Coats, fur (except apparel contractors), manufacturing

315280 Coats, leather (except apparel contractors), manufacturing

424320 Coats, men's and boys', merchant wholesalers

315220 Coats, nontailored service apparel (e.g., laboratory, mechanics', medical), men's and boys', cut and sewn from purchased fabric (except apparel contractors)

315210 Coats, nontailored service apparel (e.g., laboratory, medical, mechanics'), cut and sew apparel contractors

315240 Coats, nontailored service apparel (e.g., laboratory, medical, mechanics'), women's and girls', cut and sewn from purchased fabric (except apparel contractors)

315220 Coats, tailored (except fur, leather), men's and boys', cut and sewn from purchased fabric (except apparel contractors)

315240 Coats, tailored (except fur, leather), women's and girls', cut and sewn from purchased fabric

315280 Coats, waterproof (e.g., plastics, rubberized fabric, similar materials), cut and sewn from purchased fabric (except apparel contractors)

315280 Coats, waterproof (e.g., plastics, rubberized fabric, similar materials), rubberizing fabric and manufacturing coats

315210 Coats, waterproof (i.e., plastics, rubberized fabric, similar materials), cut and sew apparel contractors

424330 Coats, women's, children's, and infants', merchant wholesalers

331318 Coaxial cable made in aluminum wire drawing plants

423610 Coaxial cable merchant wholesalers

331420 Coaxial cable, copper, made from purchased copper in wire drawing plants

331491 Coaxial cable, nonferrous metals (except aluminum, copper), made from purchased nonferrous metals (except aluminum, copper) in wire drawing plants

335929 Coaxial cable, nonferrous, made from purchased nonferrous wire

334417 Coaxial connectors manufacturing

339991 Coaxial mechanical face seals manufacturing

325180 Cobalt 60 (i.e., radioactive cobalt) manufacturing

325180 Cobalt chloride manufacturing

325180 Cobalt compounds, not specified elsewhere by process, manufacturing

212299 Cobalt concentrates beneficiating

212299 Cobalt ores mining and/or beneficiating

331410 Cobalt refining, primary

325180 Cobalt sulfate manufacturing

325411 Cocaine and derivatives (i.e., basic chemicals) manufacturing

332913 Cocks, drain, plumbing, manufacturing

722410 Cocktail lounges

311999 Cocktail mixes, dry, manufacturing 424820

Cocktails, alcoholic, premixed, merchant wholesalers

311351 Cocoa (e.g., instant, mix, mixed with other ingredients, powder drink, powdered) made from cacao beans

424590 Cocoa beans merchant wholesalers

311351 Cocoa butter made from cocoa beans 311352

Cocoa, powdered drink, prepared, made from purchased chocolate

311352 Cocoa, powdered, made from purchased chocolate

311352 Cocoa, powdered, mixed with other ingredients, made from purchased chocolate

311225 Coconut oil made from purchased oils

311224 Coconut oil made in crushing mills

111339 Coconut tree farming

311999 Coconut, desiccated and shredded, manufacturing

114111 Cod catching

114111 Cod fishing

311710 Cod liver oil extraction, crude, processing

325411 Cod liver oil, medicinal, uncompounded, manufacturing

325411 Codeine and derivatives (i.e., basic chemicals) manufacturing
333993 Coding, dating, and imprinting packaging machinery manufacturing
561330 Co-employment staffing services
445299 Coffee and tea (i.e., packaged) stores
722330 Coffee carts, mobile
311920 Coffee concentrates (i.e., instant coffee) manufacturing
311920 Coffee extracts manufacturing
111339 Coffee farming
322299 Coffee filters made from purchased paper
311920 Coffee flavoring and syrups (i.e., made from coffee) manufacturing
333318 Coffee makers and urns, commercial-type, manufacturing
423440 Coffee makers, commercial, merchant wholesalers
335210 Coffee makers, household-type electric, manufacturing
423620 Coffee makers, household-type, merchant wholesalers
424490 Coffee merchant wholesalers
311920 Coffee roasting
333241 Coffee roasting and grinding machinery (i.e., food manufacturing-type) manufacturing
722515 Coffee shops, on premise brewing
311920 Coffee substitute manufacturing
337122 Coffee tables, wood, manufacturing
311920 Coffee, blended, manufacturing
312111 Coffee, iced, manufacturing
311920 Coffee, instant and freeze-dried, manufacturing
454390 Coffee-break supplies providers, direct selling
237990 Cofferdam construction
423850 Coffins merchant wholesalers
487110 Cog railway, scenic and sightseeing, operation
237130 Co-generation plant construction
541720 Cognitive research and development services
811310 Coil rewinding (except on an assembly line or factory basis)
333519 Coil winding and cutting machinery, metalworking, manufacturing
423830 Coil winding machines, spring, merchant wholesalers
332613 Coiled springs (except clock, watch), light gauge, made from purchased wire or strip, manufacturing
332613 Coiled springs, heavy gauge metal, manufacturing
335312 Coils for motors and generators manufacturing
423690 Coils, electronic, merchant wholesalers
336320 Coils, ignition, internal combustion engines, manufacturing
332996 Coils, pipe, made from purchased metal pipe
333318 Coin counting machinery manufacturing
561990 Coin pick-up services, parking meter
316998 Coin purses (except metal) manufacturing
339910 Coin purses, precious metal, manufacturing
423420 Coin sorting machines merchant wholesalers
333318 Coin wrapping machines manufacturing
339999 Coin-operated amusement machines (except jukebox) manufacturing
812310 Coin-operated drycleaners and laundries
713290 Coin-operated gambling device concession operators (i.e., supplying and servicing in others' facilities)
339999 Coin-operated gambling devices manufacturing
423990 Coin-operated game machines merchant wholesalers
334310 Coin-operated jukebox manufacturing
812310 Coin-operated laundry and drycleaning routes (i.e., concession operators)
423440 Coin-operated merchandising machine merchant wholesalers
713990 Coin-operated nongambling amusement device concession operators (i.e., supplying and servicing in others' facilities)
812990 Coin-operated personal service machine (e.g., blood pressure, locker, photographic, scale, shoeshine) concession operators
423440 Coin-operated phonographs and vending machines merchant wholesalers
333318 Coin-operated vending machines manufacturing
423940 Coins merchant wholesalers
423520 Coke merchant wholesalers
221210 Coke oven gas distribution
324199 Coke oven products (e.g., coke, gases, tars) made in coke oven establishments
331110 Coke oven products made in iron and steel mills

324110 Coke, petroleum, made in petroleum refineries
335110 Cold cathode fluorescent lamp tubes manufacturing
332111 Cold forgings made from purchased iron or steel, unfinished
332112 Cold forgings made from purchased nonferrous metals, unfinished
325412 Cold remedies manufacturing
333519 Cold rolling mill machinery, metalworking, manufacturing
331221 Cold rolling steel shapes (e.g., bar, plate, rod, sheet, strip) made from purchased steel
493120 Cold storage locker services 423740 Cold storage machinery merchant wholesalers
236220 Cold storage plant construction
493120 Cold storage warehousing
332811 Cold treating metals for the trade
311991 Cole slaw, fresh, manufacturing
212391 Colemanite mining and/or beneficiating
311612 Collagen sausage casings made from purchased hides
332439 Collapsible tubes (e.g., toothpaste, glue), light gauge metal, manufacturing
315210 Collar and cuff sets cut and sew apparel contractors
315190 Collar and cuff sets made in apparel knitting mills
315240 Collar and cuff sets, women's and girls', cut and sewn from purchased fabric (except apparel contractors)
316110 Collar leather, manufacturing 111219 Collard farming, field, bedding plant and seed production
333515 Collars (i.e., a machine tool accessory) manufacturing
316998 Collars and collar pads (i.e., harness) manufacturing
316998 Collars, dog, manufacturing 333613 Collars, shaft for power transmission equipment, manufacturing
522294 Collateralized mortgage obligation (CMO) issuing, private
525990 Collateralized mortgage obligations (CMOs)
333244 Collating machinery for printing and bookbinding manufacturing
333318 Collating machinery, office-type, manufacturing
453220 Collectible gift shops (e.g., crystal, pewter, porcelain)
812320 Collecting and distributing agents, laundry and drycleaning
561440 Collection agencies
561440 Collection agencies, accounts 221320 Collection, treatment, and disposal of waste through a sewer system
813930 Collective bargaining units
335312 Collector rings for motors and generators manufacturing
453998 Collectors' items (e.g., autograph, card, coin, stamp) shops (except used rare items)
454110 Collectors' items, mail-order houses 611691 College board preparation centers 611691 College entrance exam preparation instruction
611710 College selection services
611310 Colleges (except junior colleges)
611511 Colleges, barber and beauty
611210 Colleges, community
611210 Colleges, junior
611310 Colleges, universities, and professional schools
333515 Collets (i.e., a machine tool accessory) manufacturing
325620 Colognes manufacturing
424210 Colognes merchant wholesalers
334510 Colonscopes, electromedical, manufacturing
812199 Color consulting services (i.e., personal care services)
325130 Color pigments, inorganic (except bone black, carbon black, lamp black), manufacturing
325130 Color pigments, organic (except animal black, bone black), manufacturing
323120 Color separation services, for the printing trade
334516 Colorimeters, laboratory-type, manufacturing
423920 Coloring books merchant wholesalers
316110 Coloring leather
332813 Coloring metals and metal products (except coating) for the trade
339113 Colostomy appliances manufacturing
812220 Columbariums
212299 Columbite mining and/or beneficiating
212299 Columbium ores mining and/or beneficiating
327420 Columns, architectural or ornamental plaster work, manufacturing

332420 Columns, fractionating, heavy gauge metal, manufacturing
321918 Columns, porch, wood, manufacturing
316998 Comb cases (except metal) manufacturing
339910 Comb cases, precious metal, manufacturing
334512 Combination limit and fan controls manufacturing
112990 Combination livestock farming (except dairy, poultry)
334512 Combination oil and hydronic controls manufacturing
333111 Combines (i.e., harvester-threshers) manufacturing
423820 Combines merchant wholesalers
313310 Combing and converting top
333249 Combing machinery for textiles manufacturing
313310 Combing textile fibers 115113 Combining, agricultural 332999 Combs, metal, manufacturing
326199 Combs, plastics, manufacturing 326299 Combs, rubber, manufacturing 334513 Combustion control instruments (except commercial, household furnace-type) manufacturing
541330 Combustion engineering consulting services
562211 Combustors, hazardous waste
562213 Combustors, nonhazardous solid waste
711510 Comedians, independent
711110 Comedy troupes
812990 Comfort station operation
314120 Comforters made from purchased fabrics
511120 Comic book publishers (except exclusive Internet publishing)
511120 Comic book publishers and printing combined (except exclusive Internet publishing)
519130 Comic book publishers, exclusively on Internet
451212 Comic book stores
323111 Comic books commercial printing (except screen) without publishing
323113 Comic books screen printing without publishing
811310 Commercial and industrial machinery repair and maintenance services
522220 Commercial and inventory financing (except international trade financing)
541430 Commercial art services
541430 Commercial artists, independent
311812 Commercial bakeries
522110 Commercial banking
522110 Commercial banks
236220 Commercial building construction
236220 Commercial building construction for-sale builders
236220 Commercial building construction general contractors
531120 Commercial building rental or leasing
561450 Commercial credit reporting bureaus
323111 Commercial digital printing (except books)
323111 Commercial engraving printing (except books)
423830 Commercial fishing equipment and supplies (except boats, ships) merchant wholesalers
323111 Commercial flexographic printing (except books)
238220 Commercial freezer installation
811310 Commercial gaming machine repair and maintenance services
323111 Commercial gravure printing (except books)
541430 Commercial illustration services
541430 Commercial illustrators, independent
238290 Commercial kitchen food preparation equipment (e.g., mixers, ovens, stoves) installation
323111 Commercial letterpress printing (except books)
335122 Commercial lighting fixtures, electric, manufacturing
323111 Commercial lithographic (offset) printing (except books)
523120 Commercial note brokers' offices
523110 Commercial paper dealing (i.e., acting as a principal in dealing securities to investors)
541922 Commercial photography services 323111 Commercial printing (except screen, books)
531312 Commercial property managing
323111 Commercial quick printing (except books)
531210 Commercial real estate agencies
531210 Commercial real estate agents' offices
531312 Commercial real estate property managers' offices
811310 Commercial refrigeration equipment repair and maintenance services

238220 Commercial refrigeration system installation
323113 Commercial screen printing (except books, manifold business forms, grey goods)
424120 Commercial stationery supplies merchant wholesalers
334519 Commercial timing mechanisms manufacturing
512110 Commercials, television, production
238290 Commercial-type door installation 445110 Commissaries, primarily groceries 523140 Commodity contract pool operators 523130 Commodity contract trading companies 523140 Commodity contracts brokerages 523140 Commodity contracts brokers' offices 523130 Commodity contracts dealing (i.e., acting as a principal in dealing commodities to investors)
523210 Commodity contracts exchanges
523140 Commodity contracts floor brokers 523130 Commodity contracts floor traders (i.e., acting as a principal in dealing commodities to investors)
523130 Commodity contracts floor trading (i.e., acting as a principal in dealing commodities to investors)
523140 Commodity contracts options brokerages
523130 Commodity contracts options dealing (i.e., acting as a principal in dealing commodities to investors)
523130 Commodity contracts traders (i.e., acting as a principal in dealing commodities to investors)
522298 Commodity Credit Corporation
523140 Commodity futures brokerages
541990 Commodity inspection services
212325 Common clay mining and/or beneficiating
212321 Common sand quarrying and/or beneficiating
212325 Common shale mining and/or beneficiating
923120 Communicable disease program administration
237130 Communication antenna construction
541430 Communication design services, visual
238210 Communication equipment installation
811213 Communication equipment repair and maintenance services
237130 Communication tower construction
926130 Communications commissions
423690 Communications equipment merchant wholesalers
334220 Communications equipment, mobile and microwave, manufacturing
334210 Communications headgear, telephone, manufacturing
926130 Communications licensing commissions and agencies
334515 Communications signal testing and evaluation equipment manufacturing
335929 Communications wire and cable, nonferrous, made from purchased nonferrous wire
331318 Communications wire or cable made in aluminum wire drawing plants
331420 Communications wire or cable, copper, made from purchased copper in wire drawing plants
331491 Communications wire or cable, nonferrous metals (except aluminum, copper), made from purchased nonferrous metals (except aluminum, copper) in wire drawing plants
311812 Communion wafer manufacturing
813319 Community action advocacy organizations
624190 Community action service agencies
624120 Community centers (except recreational only), adult
624110 Community centers (except recreational only), youth
813219 Community chests
611210 Community colleges 611210 Community colleges offering a wide variety of academic and technical training
925120 Community development agencies, government
813211 Community foundations 621498 Community health centers and clinics, outpatient
624190 Community health education services (except health care services)
923120 Community health programs administration
624210 Community meals, social services
712110 Community museums 924120 Community recreation programs, government
923130 Community social service program administration
711110 Community theaters
335312 Commutators, electric motor, manufacturing

481111 Commuter air carriers, scheduled 485113
Commuter bus operation (except mixed mode)
485112 Commuter rail systems (except mixed mode)
485111 Commuter transit systems, mixed mode (e.g., bus, commuter rail, subway combination)
334310 Compact disc players (e.g., automotive, household-type) manufacturing
423620 Compact disc players merchant wholesalers
423990 Compact discs (CDs), prerecorded, merchant wholesalers
334614 Compact discs (i.e., CD-ROM), software, mass reproducing
334614 Compact discs, prerecorded audio, mass reproducing
334613 Compact discs, recordable or rewritable, blank, manufacturing
335110 Compact fluorescent light bulbs manufacturing
423830 Compactors, trash, industrial, merchant wholesalers
339910 Compacts, precious metal, manufacturing
316998 Compacts, solid leather, manufacturing
112990 Companion animals production (e.g., cats, dogs, parakeets, parrots)
624120 Companion services for disabled persons, the elderly, and persons diagnosed with intellectual and developmental disabilities
333314 Comparators, optical, manufacturing
334511 Compasses, gyroscopic and magnetic (except portable), manufacturing
334519 Compasses, portable magnetic-type, manufacturing
541612 Compensation consulting services
541612 Compensation planning services
525190 Compensation, workers, insurance funds
311119 Complete feed, livestock, manufacturing
711510 Composers, independent
322219 Composite cans (i.e., foil-fiber and other combinations) manufacturing
562219 Compost dumps
325314 Compost manufacturing
325120 Compressed and liquefied industrial gas manufacturing
332911 Compressed gas cylinder valves manufacturing
424690 Compressed gases (except LP gas) merchant wholesalers
424710 Compressed liquefied petroleum gas (LPG) bulk stations and terminals, merchant wholesalers
321219 Compression modified wood manufacturing
333249 Compression molding machinery for plastics manufacturing
339991 Compression packings manufacturing
532490 Compressor, air and gas, rental or leasing
237120 Compressor, metering and pumping station, gas and oil pipeline, construction
423830 Compressors (except air-conditioning, refrigeration) merchant wholesalers
333912 Compressors, air and gas, general purpose-type, manufacturing
423730 Compressors, air-conditioning, merchant wholesalers
336390 Compressors, motor vehicle air-conditioning, manufacturing
423740 Compressors, refrigeration, merchant wholesalers
238210 Computer and network cable installation
541715 Computer and related hardware research and development laboratories or services (except nanotechnology research and development)
423430 Computer boards, loaded, merchant wholesalers
423690 Computer boards, unloaded, merchant wholesalers
334419 Computer cable sets (e.g., monitor, printer) manufacturing
423690 Computer chips merchant wholesalers
423430 Computer data storage devices merchant wholesalers
518210 Computer data storage services
541519 Computer disaster recovery services
813410 Computer enthusiasts clubs
811212 Computer equipment repair and maintenance services without retailing new computers
443142 Computer equipment stores
238330 Computer flooring installation 323111 Computer forms (manifold or continuous) printing
337124 Computer furniture, metal household-type, manufacturing
337122 Computer furniture, wood household-type, manufacturing
541512 Computer hardware consulting services or consultants

518210 Computer input preparation services
334118 Computer input/output equipment manufacturing
611420 Computer operator training
424120 Computer paper supplies merchant wholesalers
322230 Computer paper, die-cut, made from purchased paper
423430 Computer peripheral equipment merchant wholesalers
532420 Computer peripheral equipment rental or leasing
811212 Computer peripheral equipment repair and maintenance, without retailing new computer peripheral equipment
325992 Computer printer toner cartridges manufacturing
423430 Computer printers merchant wholesalers
541511 Computer program or software development, custom
611420 Computer programming schools
541511 Computer programming services, custom
532420 Computer rental or leasing
811212 Computer repair and maintenance services, without retailing new computers
611519 Computer repair training
334111 Computer servers manufacturing
541511 Computer software analysis and design services, custom
541512 Computer software consulting services or consultants
541511 Computer software programming services, custom
511210 Computer software publishers, packaged
511210 Computer software publishing and reproduction
541511 Computer software support services, custom
334613 Computer software tapes and disks, blank, rigid and floppy, manufacturing
611420 Computer software training
454110 Computer software, mail-order houses
423430 Computer software, packaged, merchant wholesalers
443142 Computer stores
541513 Computer systems facilities (i.e., clients' facilities) management and operation services
541512 Computer systems integration analysis and design services
541512 Computer systems integration design consulting services
541512 Computer systems integrator services
334118 Computer terminals manufacturing
423430 Computer terminals merchant wholesalers
518210 Computer time leasing
518210 Computer time rental
518210 Computer time sharing services
621512 Computer tomography (CT-SCAN) centers
611420 Computer training (except repair)
532282 Computer video game rental
541340 Computer-aided design drafting (CADD) services
541512 Computer-aided design (CAD) systems integration design services
541512 Computer-aided engineering (CAE) systems integration design services
541512 Computer-aided manufacturing (CAM) systems integration design services
334517 Computerized axial tomography (CT/CAT) scanners manufacturing
334512 Computerized environmental control systems for buildings manufacturing
334111 Computers manufacturing
423430 Computers merchant wholesalers
325411 Concentrated medicinal chemicals, uncompounded, manufacturing
311930 Concentrates, drink (except frozen fruit juice), manufacturing
311930 Concentrates, flavoring (except coffee based), manufacturing
424450 Concentrates, fountain (except soft drink), merchant wholesalers
311411 Concentrates, frozen fruit juice, manufacturing
423520 Concentrates, metallic, merchant wholesalers
333131 Concentration machinery, mining-type, manufacturing
711130 Concert artists, independent
711320 Concert booking agencies
711310 Concert hall operators
531120 Concert hall, no promotion of events, rental or leasing
711310 Concert managers with facilities
711320 Concert managers without facilities
711310 Concert organizers with facilities
711320 Concert organizers without facilities
711310 Concert promoters with facilities

711320 Concert promoters without facilities
561599 Concert ticket offices
713990 Concession operators, amusement device (except gambling) and ride
722330 Concession snack stands, mobile
812990 Concierge services 926150 Conciliation and mediation services, government
325998 Concrete additive preparations (e.g., curing, hardening) manufacturing
424690 Concrete additives merchant wholesalers
327320 Concrete batch plants (including temporary)
238140 Concrete block laying
238910 Concrete breaking and cutting for demolition
423320 Concrete building products merchant wholesalers
238390 Concrete coating, glazing or sealing
327999 Concrete crushing and grinding (except at construction site)
238110 Concrete finishing
333120 Concrete finishing machinery manufacturing
238110 Concrete floor surfacing
238190 Concrete form contractors
332322 Concrete forms, sheet metal (except stampings), manufacturing
327390 Concrete furniture (e.g., benches, tables) manufacturing
333120 Concrete gunning equipment manufacturing
333120 Concrete mixing machinery, portable, manufacturing
423320 Concrete mixtures merchant wholesalers
238990 Concrete patio construction
237310 Concrete paving (i.e., highway, road, street, public sidewalk)
238990 Concrete paving, residential and commercial driveway and parking area
238110 Concrete pouring
423810 Concrete processing equipment merchant wholesalers
238120 Concrete product (e.g., structural precast, structural prestressed) installation
333249 Concrete products forming machinery manufacturing
327390 Concrete products, precast (except block, brick and pipe), manufacturing
238110 Concrete pumping (i.e., placement)
238120 Concrete reinforcement placement
332312 Concrete reinforcing bar (rebar) assemblies, fabrication
331110 Concrete reinforcing bar (rebar) made in iron and steel mills
331221 Concrete reinforcing bar (rebar), made from purchased steel in cold rolling mills
331221 Concrete reinforcing bar (rebar), made from purchased steel in steel rolling mills
423510 Concrete reinforcing bars merchant wholesalers
332618 Concrete reinforcing mesh made from purchased wire
238110 Concrete repair
238110 Concrete resurfacing 238990 Concrete sawing and drilling (except demolition)
327390 Concrete tanks manufacturing
327999 Concrete, dry mixture, manufacturing
211130 Condensate, cycle, natural gas production
333241 Condensed and evaporated milk machinery manufacturing
311514 Condensed milk manufacturing
311514 Condensed, evaporated or powdered whey, manufacturing
332410 Condenser boxes, metal, manufacturing
335999 Condensers (except electronic), fixed and variable, manufacturing
334416 Condensers, electronic, manufacturing
423690 Condensers, electronic, merchant wholesalers
332410 Condensers, steam, manufacturing
335312 Condensers, synchronous, electric, manufacturing
423830 Condensing units (except air-conditioning, refrigeration) merchant wholesalers
423730 Condensing units, air-conditioning, merchant wholesalers
423740 Condensing units, refrigeration, merchant wholesalers
326299 Condom manufacturing
813990 Condominium corporations
236117 Condominium for-sale builders
531312 Condominium managers' offices, commercial
531311 Condominium managers' offices, residential
813990 Condominium owners' associations
561599 Condominium time-share exchange services
236116 Condominium, multifamily, construction general contractors

236115 Condominium, single-family, construction general contractors
335931 Conductor connectors, solderless connectors, sleeves, or soldering lugs, manufacturing
711510 Conductors, independent
423320 Conduit and pipe, concrete, merchant wholesalers
423610 Conduit, electric wire and cable, merchant wholesalers
327120 Conduit, vitrified clay, manufacturing
331210 Conduit, welded and lock joint, made from purchased iron or steel
335932 Conduits and fittings, electrical, manufacturing
423610 Conduits and raceways, electrical, merchant wholesalers
327332 Conduits, concrete, manufacturing
322219 Cones (e.g., winding yarn, string, ribbon, cloth), fiber, made from purchased paperboard
311821 Cones, ice cream, manufacturing
327110 Cones, pyrometric, earthenware, manufacturing
311313 Confectioner's beet sugar manufacturing
311314 Confectioner's powdered sugar manufacturing
311351 Confectionery chocolate made from cacao beans
333241 Confectionery machinery manufacturing
424450 Confectionery merchant wholesalers
722515 Confectionery snack shops, made on premises with carryout services
445292 Confectionery stores, packaged, retailing only
311340 Confectionery, nonchocolate, manufacturing
531120 Conference center, no promotion of events, rental or leasing
322299 Confetti made from purchased paper
921120 Congress of the United States
336310 Connecting rods, automotive and truck gasoline engine, manufacturing
335931 Connectors and terminals for electrical devices manufacturing
335931 Connectors, electric cord, manufacturing
423610 Connectors, electrical, merchant wholesalers
334417 Connectors, electronic (e.g., coaxial, cylindrical, printed circuit, rack and panel), manufacturing
423690 Connectors, electronic, merchant wholesalers
335313 Connectors, power, manufacturing
335931 Connectors, solderless (wiring devices), manufacturing
335931 Connectors, twist on wire (i.e., nuts), manufacturing
813312 Conservation advocacy organizations
924120 Conservation and reclamation agencies
712190 Conservation areas
611310 Conservatories of music (colleges or universities)
712130 Conservatories, botanical
711510 Conservators (i.e., art, artifact restorers), independent
611610 Conservatory of music (except academic)
453310 Consignment shops, used merchandise
336350 Constant velocity joints, automotive, truck, and bus, manufacturing
813940 Constituencies' associations, political party
325520 Construction adhesives (except asphalt, gypsum base) manufacturing
813910 Construction associations
238990 Construction elevator (i.e., temporary use during construction) erection and dismantling
541330 Construction engineering services
238910 Construction equipment (except crane) rental with operator
541990 Construction estimation services
532412 Construction form rental
522292 Construction lending
423810 Construction machinery and equipment merchant wholesalers
532412 Construction machinery and equipment rental or leasing without operator
811310 Construction machinery and equipment repair and maintenance services
333120 Construction machinery manufacturing
236220 Construction management, commercial and institutional building
237990 Construction management, dam
237310 Construction management, highway, road, street and bridge
236210 Construction management, industrial building (except warehouses)
237990 Construction management, marine structure
237990 Construction management, mass transit

236116 Construction management, multifamily building
237120 Construction management, oil and gas pipeline
237120 Construction management, oil refinery and petrochemical complex
237990 Construction management, outdoor recreation facility
237130 Construction management, power and communication transmission line
236118 Construction management, residential remodeling
236115 Construction management, single-family building
237990 Construction management, tunnel
237110 Construction management, water and sewage treatment plant
237110 Construction management, water and sewer line
423610 Construction materials, electrical, merchant wholesalers
322230 Construction paper, school and art, made from purchased paper
322121 Construction paper, school and art, made in paper mills
212321 Construction sand and gravel beneficiating

(e.g., grinding, screening, washing) 212321

Construction sand or gravel dredging 541370

Construction surveying services 333120 Construction-type tractors and attachments manufacturing
928120 Consulates
****** Consultants -- see specific activity
813920 Consultants' associations
531390 Consultants', real estate (except appraisers), offices
541330 Consulting engineers' offices
541330 Consulting engineers' private practices
812990 Consumer buying services
541990 Consumer credit counseling services
561450 Consumer credit reporting bureaus
423620 Consumer electronics merchant wholesalers
532210 Consumer electronics rental
811211 Consumer electronics repair and maintenance services without retailing new consumer electronics
522291 Consumer finance companies (i.e., unsecured cash loans)
522291 Consumer lending
922190 Consumer product safety commissions
926110 Consumer protection offices 443142 Consumer-type electronic stores (e.g., televisions, computers, cameras)
334514 Consumption meters (e.g., gas, water) manufacturing
524128 Contact lens insurance, direct
339115 Contact lenses manufacturing
423460 Contact lenses merchant wholesalers
335931 Contacts, electrical (except carbon and graphite), manufacturing
335991 Contacts, electrical, carbon and graphite, manufacturing
322130 Container board stock manufacturing
336611 Container ship building
484110 Container trucking services, local
484121 Container trucking services, long-distance (TL)
327213 Containers for packaging, bottling, and canning, glass, manufacturing
332439 Containers, air cargo, light gauge metal, manufacturing
332999 Containers, foil (except bags), manufacturing
423220 Containers, household (except paper and disposable plastics), merchant wholesalers
423840 Containers, industrial, merchant wholesalers
332439 Containers, light gauge metal (except cans), manufacturing
424130 Containers, paper and disposable plastics, merchant wholesalers
321920 Containers, wood, manufacturing
712110 Contemporary art museums
711120 Contemporary dance companies
623311 Continuing care retirement communities
611430 Continuing education seminars or conferences
325412 Contraceptive preparations manufacturing
213112 Contract services (except site preparation and related construction contractor activities) for oil and gas fields
561320 Contract staffing services
****** Contractors -- see specific activity
813910 Contractors' associations 315210 Contractors, cut and sew apparel 325412 Contrast media in-vivo diagnostic substances (e.g., iodine, barium) manufacturing
335314 Control circuit devices, magnet and solid-state, manufacturing

335314 Control circuit relays, industrial, manufacturing
335314 Control equipment, electric, manufacturing
335313 Control panels, electric power distribution, manufacturing
238210 Control system (e.g., environmental, humidity, temperature) installation
335311 Control transformers manufacturing
332912 Control valves, fluid power, manufacturing
332911 Control valves, industrial-type, manufacturing
921130 Controllers' and comptrollers' offices, government
334513 Controllers for process variables (e.g., electric, electronic, mechanical, pneumatic operation) manufacturing
334290 Controlling equipment, street light, manufacturing
335314 Controls and control accessories, industrial, manufacturing
335314 Controls for adjustable speed drives manufacturing
334514 Controls, revolution and timing instruments, manufacturing
623110 Convalescent homes or convalescent hospitals (except psychiatric)
623220 Convalescent homes or hospitals for psychiatric patients
446199 Convalescent supply stores
335220 Convection ovens (including portable), household-type, manufacturing
423720 Convectors merchant wholesalers
445120 Convenience food stores
447110 Convenience food with gasoline stations
335931 Convenience outlets, electric, manufacturing
561591 Convention and visitors bureaus
561591 Convention bureaus
531120 Convention center, no promotion of events, rental or leasing
561920 Convention decorators
561920 Convention managers
561920 Convention or trade show event planners
561920 Convention organizers
561920 Convention promoters
561920 Convention services
813110 Convents (except schools)
424130 Converted paper (except stationery and office supplies) merchant wholesalers
316110 Converters, leather
335312 Converters, phase and rotary, electrical equipment, manufacturing
313310 Converters, piece goods
337121 Convertible sofas (except futons) manufacturing
336390 Convertible tops for automotive, truck, and bus, manufacturing
313310 Converting textiles
423830 Conveying equipment (except farm) merchant wholesalers
423820 Conveying equipment, farm, merchant wholesalers
326220 Conveyor belts, rubber, manufacturing
238290 Conveyor system installation
333922 Conveyors and conveying equipment manufacturing
311612 Cooked meats made from purchased carcasses
311824 Cookie dough made from purchased flour
722515 Cookie shops, on premise baking and carryout service
311821 Cookies manufacturing
424490 Cookies merchant wholesalers
311821 Cookies, filled, manufacturing
311225 Cooking and baking oil sprays made from purchased oils
335210 Cooking appliances (except convection, microwave ovens), household-type electric portable, manufacturing
311351 Cooking chocolate made from cacao beans
333318 Cooking equipment (i.e., fryers, microwave ovens, ovens, ranges), commercial-type, manufacturing
423440 Cooking equipment, commercial, merchant wholesalers
423620 Cooking equipment, gas and electric, household-type, merchant wholesalers
424490 Cooking oils merchant wholesalers
611519 Cooking schools
331511 Cooking utensils, cast iron, manufacturing
332215 Cooking utensils, fabricated metal, manufacturing
327212 Cooking utensils, glass and glass ceramic, made in glass making plants
423220 Cooking utensils, household-type, merchant wholesalers
327110 Cooking ware (e.g., stoneware, coarse earthenware, pottery), manufacturing
327215 Cooking ware made from purchased glass

327212 Cooking ware made in glass making plants
327110 Cooking ware, china, manufacturing
327110 Cooking ware, fine earthenware, manufacturing
332215 Cookware, fabricated metal, manufacturing
221330 Cooled air distribution 326199 Coolers or ice chests, plastics (except foam), manufacturing
326140 Coolers or ice chests, polystyrene foam, manufacturing
423740 Coolers, mechanical, merchant wholesalers
333415 Coolers, refrigeration, manufacturing
333415 Coolers, water, manufacturing
423730 Cooling equipment and supplies merchant wholesalers
238220 Cooling tower installation
333415 Cooling towers manufacturing
321920 Cooperage manufacturing
321920 Cooperage stock (e.g., heading, hoops, staves) manufacturing
423840 Cooperage stock merchant wholesalers
321920 Cooperage stock mills
236117 Cooperative apartment for-sale builders
531311 Cooperative apartment managers' offices
236116 Cooperative apartment, construction general contractors
812331 Cooperative hospital laundries (i.e., linen supply services)
524113 Cooperative life insurance organizations
813990 Cooperative owners' associations 321920 Coopered tubs manufacturing 332216 Coordinate and contour measuring machines, machinists' precision tools, manufacturing
532420 Copier rental or leasing
327120 Coping, wall, clay, manufacturing
327390 Copings, concrete, manufacturing
331529 Copper alloy castings (except die-castings), unfinished, manufacturing
331420 Copper alloys (e.g., brass, bronze) made from purchased metal or scrap
331410 Copper alloys made in primary copper smelting and refining mills
423510 Copper and copper alloy primary forms merchant wholesalers
331420 Copper and copper-based shapes (e.g., cake, ingot, slag, wire bar) made from purchased metal or scrap
325130 Copper base pigments manufacturing
212230 Copper beneficiating plants
325180 Copper chloride manufacturing
325612 Copper cleaners manufacturing
325180 Copper compounds, not specified elsewhere by process, manufacturing
331410 Copper concentrate refining
331523 Copper die-casting foundries 331523 Copper die-castings, unfinished, manufacturing
331420 Copper foil made from purchased metal or scrap
332999 Copper foil not made in rolling mills
332112 Copper forgings made from purchased metals, unfinished
331529 Copper foundries (except die-casting)
325180 Copper iodide manufacturing
212230 Copper ore concentrates recovery
212230 Copper ore mine site development for own account
212230 Copper ores mining and/or beneficiating
331420 Copper powder, flakes, and paste made from purchased copper
331420 Copper products made by drawing purchased copper
331420 Copper products made by rolling, drawing, or extruding purchased copper
331420 Copper products made in integrated secondary smelting and extruding mills
331420 Copper products made in integrated secondary smelting mills and drawing plants
238160 Copper roofing installation
331420 Copper secondary smelting and alloying
331420 Copper secondary smelting and refining from purchased metal or scrap
331410 Copper shapes (e.g., bar, billet, ingot, plate, sheet) made in primary copper smelting and refining mills
331410 Copper smelting and refining, primary
325180 Copper sulfate manufacturing
212230 Copper-water precipitates
561439 Copy centers (except combined with printing services)
561439 Copy shops (except combined with printing services)
423420 Copying machines merchant wholesalers
314994 Cord (except wire) manufacturing
335931 Cord connectors, electric, manufacturing

314994 Cord for reinforcing rubber tires, industrial belting, and fuel cells manufacturing
331420 Cord sets, flexible, made from purchased copper in wire drawing plants
331318 Cord sets, flexible, made in aluminum wire drawing plants
331491 Cord sets, flexible, nonferrous metals (except aluminum, copper), made from purchased nonferrous metals (except aluminum, copper) in wire drawing plants
314994 Cordage (except wire) manufacturing
333249 Cordage and rope (except wire) making machines manufacturing
423840 Cordage merchant wholesalers
325920 Cordite explosive materials manufacturing
334210 Cordless telephones (except cellular) manufacturing
313220 Cords and braids, narrow woven, manufacturing
313210 Corduroys weaving
333994 Core baking and mold drying ovens manufacturing
213112 Core cutting in oil and gas wells, on a contract basis
238910 Core drilling and test boring for construction
213112 Core drilling, exploration services, oil and gas field
333131 Core drills, underground mining-type, manufacturing
322219 Cores (i.e., all-fiber, nonfiber ends of any material), fiber, made from purchased paperboard
332992 Cores, bullet (i.e., 30 mm. or less, 1.18 inch or less), manufacturing
332999 Cores, sand foundry, manufacturing
423840 Cork merchant wholesalers
321999 Cork products (except gaskets) manufacturing
321999 Corks, bottle, manufacturing
111421 Corms farming
311230 Corn breakfast foods manufacturing
311919 Corn chips and related corn snacks manufacturing
424450 Corn chips and related corn snacks merchant wholesalers
311340 Corn confections manufacturing
321992 Corn cribs, prefabricated, wood, manufacturing
311221 Corn dextrin manufacturing
115114 Corn drying
111150 Corn farming (except sweet corn), field and seed production
311211 Corn flour manufacturing
311221 Corn gluten feed manufacturing
311221 Corn gluten meal manufacturing
333111 Corn heads for combines manufacturing
311211 Corn meal made in flour mills
424490 Corn milling products (except pet and livestock feeds) merchant wholesalers
311221 Corn oil cake and meal manufacturing
311225 Corn oil made from purchased oils
311221 Corn oil mills
311221 Corn oil, crude and refined, made by wet milling corn
333111 Corn pickers and shellers manufacturing
335210 Corn poppers, household-type electric, manufacturing
333241 Corn popping machinery (i.e., food manufacturing-type) manufacturing
333318 Corn popping machines, commercial-type, manufacturing
339113 Corn remover and bunion pad manufacturing
115114 Corn shelling
311221 Corn starch manufacturing
311221 Corn sweeteners (e.g., dextrose, fructose, glucose) made by wet milling corn
311999 Corn syrups made from purchased sweeteners
311213 Corn, malt, manufacturing
424510 Corn, raw (except seed corn), merchant wholesalers
339112 Corneal microscopes manufacturing
311612 Corned meats made from purchases carcasses
316998 Corners, luggage, leather, manufacturing
339992 Cornets and parts manufacturing 332322
Cornices, sheet metal (except stampings), manufacturing
321918 Cornices, wood, manufacturing
112320 Cornish hen production
424490 Cornmeal, edible, merchant wholesalers
212325 Cornwall stone mining and/or beneficiating
923120 Coroners' offices
522130 Corporate credit unions
813211 Corporate foundations, awarding grants
541430 Corporate identification (i.e., logo) design services

541110 Corporate law offices
551114 Corporate offices
721310 Corporate rooming and boarding houses
115210 Corralling, drovers
332323 Corrals, metal, manufacturing
325998 Correction fluids (i.e., typewriter) manufacturing
922140 Correctional boot camps
561210 Correctional facilities, privately operated
561210 Correctional facility operation on a contract or fee basis
922140 Correctional institutions
237120 Corrosion protection, underground pipeline and oil storage tank
322211 Corrugated and solid fiber boxes made from purchased paper or paperboard
322211 Corrugated and solid fiberboard pads made from purchased paper or paperboard
238160 Corrugated metal roofing installation 322211
Corrugated paper made from purchased paper or paperboard
424130 Corrugated paper merchant wholesalers
331221 Corrugating iron or steel in cold rolling mills made from purchased iron or steel
315210 Corselets cut and sew apparel contractors
315240 Corselets, women's and girls', cut and sewn from purchased fabric (except apparel contractors)
315210 Corsets and allied garments (except surgical) cut and sew apparel contractors
315240 Corsets and allied garments (except surgical), women's and girls', cut and sewn from purchased fabric (except apparel contractors)
339113 Corsets, surgical, manufacturing
325411 Cortisone, uncompounded, manufacturing
212399 Corundum mining and/or beneficiating
611511 Cosmetic art schools (e.g., makeup, skin care)
316998 Cosmetic bags (except metal) manufacturing
339910 Cosmetic bags, precious metal, manufacturing
325620 Cosmetic creams, lotions, and oils manufacturing
561910 Cosmetic kit assembling and packaging services
424210 Cosmetics merchant wholesalers
446120 Cosmetics stores
812112 Cosmetology salons or shops
611511 Cosmetology schools 541490 Costume design services (except independent theatrical costume designers)
711510 Costume designers, independent theatrical
339910 Costume jewelry manufacturing
423940 Costume jewelry merchant wholesalers
448150 Costume jewelry stores
532281 Costume rental
448190 Costume stores (including theatrical)
315210 Costumes (e.g., lodge, masquerade, theatrical) cut and sew apparel contractors
315280 Costumes (e.g., lodge, masquerade, theatrical) cut and sewn from purchased fabric (except apparel contractors)
424320 Costumes, clothing, men's and boys', merchant wholesalers
424330 Costumes, women's, children's, and infants', merchant wholesalers
337121 Cot springs, assembled, manufacturing
337124 Cots, metal household-type, manufacturing
337122 Cots, wood household-type, manufacturing
311511 Cottage cheese manufacturing
236115 Cottage construction general contractors
236117 Cottage for-sale builders
531110 Cottage rental or leasing
721199 Cottages, housekeeping
332722 Cotter pins, metal, manufacturing
424990 Cotton (except raw) merchant wholesalers
339113 Cotton and cotton balls, absorbent, manufacturing
333111 Cotton balers and presses manufacturing
314999 Cotton battings (except nonwoven batting) manufacturing
313110 Cotton cordage spun yarns made from purchased fiber
313210 Cotton fabrics, broadwoven, weaving
313220 Cotton fabrics, narrow woven weaving
111920 Cotton farming, field and seed production
322121 Cotton fiber paper stock manufacturing
115111 Cotton ginning
333111 Cotton ginning machinery manufacturing
333111 Cotton picker and stripper harvesting machinery manufacturing
313110 Cotton spun yarns made from purchased fiber
313110 Cotton thread manufacturing
339113 Cotton tipped applicators manufacturing

115113 Cotton, machine harvesting
424590 Cotton, raw, merchant wholesalers
111920 Cottonseed farming
311225 Cottonseed oil made from purchased oils
311224 Cottonseed oil, cake and meal, made in crushing mills
337121 Couch springs, assembled, manufacturing
337121 Couches, upholstered, manufacturing
311340 Cough drops (except medicated) manufacturing
325412 Cough drops, medicated, manufacturing
325412 Cough medicines manufacturing
334513 Coulometric analyzers, industrial process-type, manufacturing
334516 Coulometric analyzers, laboratory-type, manufacturing
325199 Coumarin manufacturing
325211 Coumarone-indene resins manufacturing
926110 Councils of Economic Advisers 624190
Counseling services (except by psychiatrists, psychoanalysts, or psychotherapists)
621410 Counseling services, family planning
541110 Counselors' at law offices
541110 Counselors' at law private practices
334519 Count rate meters, nuclear radiation, manufacturing
334514 Counter type registers manufacturing
337215 Counter units (except refrigerated) manufacturing
333515 Counterbores (i.e., a machine tool accessory), metalworking, manufacturing
332216 Counterbores and countersinking bits, woodworking, manufacturing
334511 Countermeasure sets (e.g., active countermeasures, jamming equipment) manufacturing
334514 Counters (e.g., electrical, electronic, mechanical), totalizing, manufacturing
316998 Counters (i.e., shoe cut stock), leather, manufacturing
333415 Counters and display cases, refrigerated, manufacturing
334514 Counters, revolution, manufacturing
333515 Countersinks (i.e., a machine tool accessory) manufacturing
238390 Countertop and cabinet, metal (except residential-type), installation
238350 Countertop, residential-type, installation
423310 Countertops (except granite) merchant wholesalers
337215 Countertops (except kitchen and bathroom), wood or plastics laminated on wood, manufacturing
337110 Countertops (i.e., kitchen, bathroom), wood or plastics laminated on wood, manufacturing
326199 Countertops, plastics, manufacturing
327991 Countertops, stone, manufacturing
337110 Countertops, wood, manufacturing
334514 Counting devices manufacturing
713910 Country clubs
711130 Country musical artists, independent
711130 Country musical groups
921120 County commissioners
925120 County development agencies
921110 County supervisors' and executives' offices
923110 County supervisors of education (except school boards)
332919 Couplings, hose, metal (except fluid power), manufacturing
333613 Couplings, mechanical power transmission, manufacturing
332996 Couplings, pipe, made from purchased metal pipe
541870 Coupon direct distribution services
561990 Coupon processing services
561990 Coupon redemption services (i.e., clearinghouse)
492110 Courier services (i.e., intercity network) (except establishments operating under a universal service obligation)
611410 Court reporting schools
561492 Court reporting services 922110 Courts of law, civilian (except American Indian or Alaska Native)
921150 Courts, American Indian or Alaska Native
922110 Courts, civilian (except American Indian or Alaska Native)
928110 Courts, military
922110 Courts, small claims 315210 Coveralls, work, cut and sew apparel contractors
315220 Coveralls, work, men's and boys', cut and sewn from purchased fabric (except apparel contractors)
315240 Coveralls, work, women's and girls', cut and sewn from purchased fabric (except apparel contractors)

314910 Covers (e.g., boat, swimming pool, truck) made from purchased fabrics
332313 Covers, annealing, fabricated metal plate work, manufacturing
321999 Covers, bottle and demijohn, willow, rattan, and reed, manufacturing
332313 Covers, floating, fabricated metal plate work, manufacturing
332322 Cowls, sheet metal (except stampings), manufacturing
111219 Cowpea (except dry) farming, field and seed production
111130 Cowpea farming, dry, field and seed production
541211 CPAs' (certified public accountants) offices
611699 CPR (cardiopulmonary resuscitation) training and certification
332618 Crab traps made from purchased wire
114112 Crabbing
333241 Cracker making machinery manufacturing
311821 Crackers (e.g., graham, soda) manufacturing
424490 Crackers merchant wholesalers 333519
Cradle assembly machinery (i.e., wire making
equipment) manufacturing
337122 Cradles, wood, manufacturing
453220 Craft (except craft supply) stores
339930 Craft and hobby kits and sets manufacturing
561920 Craft fair managers
561920 Craft fair organizers
561920 Craft fair promoters
423920 Craft kits merchant wholesalers
451120 Craft supply stores (except needlecraft)
611513 Craft union apprenticeship training programs
111334 Cranberry farming
335314 Crane and hoist controls, including metal mill, manufacturing
532412 Crane rental or leasing without operator
238990 Crane rental with operator
423810 Cranes (except industrial) merchant wholesalers
333120 Cranes, construction-type, manufacturing
333924 Cranes, industrial truck, manufacturing
423830 Cranes, industrial, merchant wholesalers
423810 Cranes, mining, merchant wholesalers
333923 Cranes, overhead traveling, manufacturing
325998 Crankcase additive preparations manufacturing
336310 Crankshaft assemblies, automotive and truck gasoline engine, manufacturing
333517 Crankshaft grinding machines metal cutting type, manufacturing
321920 Crates (e.g., berry, butter, fruit, vegetable) made of wood, wirebound, manufacturing
424130 Crates, paperboard and disposable plastics, merchant wholesalers
488991 Crating goods for shipping
112512 Crawfish production, farm raising
238910 Crawler tractor rental with operator
114112 Crayfish fishing
339940 Crayons manufacturing
311511 Cream manufacturing
424430 Cream merchant wholesalers
325199 Cream of tartar manufacturing
333111 Cream separators, farm-type, manufacturing
333241 Cream separators, industrial, manufacturing
424430 Cream stations merchant wholesalers
311514 Cream, dried and powdered, manufacturing
311512 Creamery butter manufacturing
424430 Creamery products (except canned) merchant wholesalers
424490 Creamery products, canned, merchant wholesalers
313310 Crease resistant finishing of fabrics
561450 Credit agencies
323111 Credit and identification card imprinting, embossing, and encoding
326199 Credit and identification card stock, plastics, manufacturing
524126 Credit and other financial responsibility insurance carriers, direct
561440 Credit arrears collection services
561450 Credit bureaus
522210 Credit card banks
522210 Credit card issuing
812990 Credit card notification services (i.e., lost or stolen card reporting)
522320 Credit card processing services
561450 Credit clearinghouses
561450 Credit investigation services
524113 Credit life insurance carriers, direct
561450 Credit rating services

541990 Credit repair (i.e., counseling) services, consumer
561450 Credit reporting bureaus
522130 Credit unions
333999 Cremating ovens manufacturing 812220
Crematories (except combined with funeral homes)
111219 Crenshaw melon farming, field, bedding plant and seed production
325194 Creosote made by distillation of coal tar
325194 Creosote made by distillation of wood tar
321114 Creosoting of wood
322299 Crepe paper made from purchased paper
325211 Cresol resins manufacturing
325211 Cresol-furfural resins manufacturing
325194 Cresols made by distillation of coal tar
325194 Cresylic acids made from refined petroleum or natural gas
115115 Crew leaders, farm labor
315110 Crew socks knitting or knitting and finishing
237990 Cribbing (i.e., shore protection), construction
337124 Cribs (i.e., baby beds), metal, manufacturing
337122 Cribs (i.e., baby beds), wood, manufacturing
112990 Cricket production
562910 Crime scene cleanup services
922120 Criminal investigation offices, government
922190 Criminal justice statistics centers, government
541110 Criminal law offices
111998 Crimson cloves seed farming
624190 Crisis intervention centers
114111 Croaker fishing
313110 Crochet spun yarns (e.g., cotton, manmade fiber, silk, wool) made from purchased fiber
314999 Crochet ware made from purchased materials
335210 Crock pots, household-type electric, manufacturing
327110 Crockery manufacturing
311812 Croissants, baking, made in commercial bakeries
115114 Crop cleaning
333111 Crop driers manufacturing
115112 Crop dusting
524126 Crop insurance carrier, direct 423820 Crop
preparation machinery (e.g., cleaning, conditioning, drying) merchant wholesalers
115112 Crop spraying
316998 Crops, riding, manufacturing
339920 Croquet sets manufacturing
713920 Cross country skiing facilities without accommodations
332911 Cross valves, industrial-type, manufacturing
321114 Crossties, treating
311812 Croutons and bread crumbs made in commercial bakeries
423840 Crowns and closures, metal, merchant wholesalers
332119 Crowns, metal (e.g., bottle, can), stamping
334419 CRT (cathode ray tube) manufacturing
327120 Crucibles, fire clay, manufacturing
327120 Crucibles, graphite, magnesite, chrome, silica, or other nonclay materials, manufacturing
311221 Crude corn oil manufacturing
424720 Crude oil merchant wholesalers (except bulk stations, terminals)
486110 Crude oil pipeline transportation
324110 Crude oil refining
424710 Crude oil terminals, merchant wholesalers
211120 Crude petroleum from oil sand
211120 Crude petroleum from oil shale
211120 Crude petroleum lease condensate production
211120 Crude petroleum production
324110 Crude petroleum refineries
424990 Crude rubber merchant wholesalers
336320 Cruise control mechanisms, electronic, automotive, truck, and bus, manufacturing
483114 Cruise lines (i.e., deep sea passenger transportation to and from domestic ports, including Puerto Rico)
483112 Cruise lines (i.e., deep sea passenger transportation to or from foreign ports)
561599 Cruise reservation services
561599 Cruise ship ticket offices
713210 Cruises, gambling
115310 Cruising timber
311812 Crullers (except frozen) made in commercial bakeries

311813 Crullers, frozen, made in a commercial bakery
423320 Crushed stone merchant wholesalers
333120 Crushing machinery, portable, manufacturing
333131 Crushing machinery, stationary, manufacturing
212111 Crushing plants, bituminous coal 423810 Crushing, pulverizing, and screening machinery, construction and mining, merchant wholesalers
423830 Crushing, pulverizing, and screening machinery, industrial, merchant wholesalers
333120 Crushing, pulverizing, and screening machinery, portable, manufacturing 112512 Crustacean production, farm raising 339113 Crutches and walkers manufacturing 423450 Crutches merchant wholesalers 532283 Crutches, invalid, rental
423830 Cryogenic cooling devices merchant wholesalers
332420 Cryogenic tanks, heavy gauge metal, manufacturing
332811 Cryogenic treating metals for the trade
212399 Cryolite mining and/or beneficiating
311340 Crystallized fruits and fruit peel manufacturing
334419 Crystals and crystal assemblies, electronic, manufacturing
334517 CT/CAT (computerized axial tomography) scanners manufacturing
621512 CT-SCAN (computer tomography) centers
335313 Cubicles (i.e., electric switchboard equipment) manufacturing
111219 Cucumber farming (except under cover), field, bedding plant and seed production
111419 Cucumber farming, grown under cover
339993 Cuff links (except precious) manufacturing
339910 Cuff links, precious metal, manufacturing
332999 Cuffs, leg, iron, manufacturing
611519 Culinary arts schools
112310 Cull hen production
212113 Culm bank recovery, anthracite (except on a contract basis)
213113 Culm bank recovery, anthracite, on a contract basis
212111 Culm bank recovery, bituminous coal or lignite (except on a contract basis)
213113 Culm bank recovery, coal, on a contract basis
315210 Culottes cut and sew apparel contractors
315240 Culottes, women's and girls', cut and sewn from purchased fabric (except apparel contractors)
111422 Cultivated florist greens growing
423820 Cultivating machinery and equipment merchant wholesalers
115112 Cultivation services
333111 Cultivators, farm-type, manufacturing
333112 Cultivators, powered, lawn and garden-type, manufacturing
926110 Cultural and arts development support program administration
325414 Culture media manufacturing
326191 Cultured marble plumbing fixtures manufacturing
326199 Cultured marble products (except plumbing fixtures) manufacturing
112512 Cultured pearl production, farm raising
326199 Cultured stone products (except plumbing fixtures) manufacturing
238910 Culvert or bridge removal
327332 Culvert pipe, concrete, manufacturing
238990 Culvert, concrete, residential and commercial paved area
332313 Culverts, fabricated metal plate work, manufacturing
237310 Culverts, highway, road and street, construction
332322 Culverts, sheet metal (except stampings), manufacturing
325110 Cumene made from refined petroleum or liquid hydrocarbons
324110 Cumene made in petroleum refineries
315210 Cummerbunds cut and sew apparel contractors
315990 Cummerbunds cut and sewn from purchased fabric (except apparel contractors)
332313 Cupolas, fabricated metal plate work, manufacturing
212230 Cuprite mining and/or beneficiating
423440 Cups, commercial (except paper and disposable plastics), merchant wholesalers
322299 Cups, molded pulp, manufacturing 424130 Cups, paper and disposable plastics, merchant wholesalers
423220 Cups, plastics (except disposable), merchant wholesalers

326199 Cups, plastics (except foam), manufacturing
326140 Cups, polystyrene foam, manufacturing
238990 Curb and gutter construction, residential and commercial driveway and parking area, concrete
327991 Curbing, granite and stone, manufacturing
237310 Curbs and street gutters, highway, road and street, construction
311513 Curds, cheese, made in a cheese plant, manufacturing
424460 Cured fish merchant wholesalers
311611 Cured hides and skins produced in slaughtering plants
311612 Cured meats (e.g., brined, dried, and salted) made from purchased carcasses
333111 Curers, tobacco, manufacturing
311710 Curing fish and seafood
453220 Curio shops
424990 Curios merchant wholesalers
326299 Curlers, hair, rubber, manufacturing
713990 Curling facilities
423620 Curling irons, electric, merchant wholesalers
335210 Curling irons, household-type electric, manufacturing
111334 Currant farming
333318 Currency counting machinery manufacturing
423420 Currency handling machines merchant wholesalers
335311 Current limiting reactors, electrical, manufacturing
334515 Current measuring equipment manufacturing
335931 Current taps, attachment plug and screw shell types, manufacturing
423610 Current-carrying wiring devices merchant wholesalers
316110 Currying furs
316110 Currying leather
442291 Curtain and drapery stores, packaged
812320 Curtain cleaning services
337920 Curtain or drapery fixtures (e.g., poles, rods, rollers) manufacturing
337920 Curtain rods and fittings manufacturing
321999 Curtain stretchers, wood, manufacturing
238150 Curtain wall, glass, installation
238190 Curtain wall, metal, installation
332323 Curtain wall, metal, manufacturing
238120 Curtain wall, precast concrete, installation
313210 Curtains and draperies made in broadwoven fabric mills
314120 Curtains and draperies, window, made from purchased fabrics
313240 Curtains made in lace mills 313240 Curtains made in warp or weft knitting mills
423220 Curtains merchant wholesalers
337121 Cushion springs, assembled, manufacturing
314120 Cushions (except carpet, springs) made from purchased fabrics
326150 Cushions, carpet and rug, urethane and other foam plastics (except polystrene), manufacturing
311520 Custard, frozen, manufacturing
561720 Custodial services 337212 Custom architectural millwork and fixtures, manufacturing on a job shop basis
236116 Custom builders (except for-sale), multifamily buildings
236115 Custom builders (except for-sale), single-family home
236117 Custom builders, for-sale builders, multifamily buildings
236117 Custom builders, for-sale builders, single-family home
325991 Custom compounding (i.e., blending and mixing) of purchased plastics resins
337212 Custom design interiors (i.e., coordinated furniture, architectural woodwork, fixtures), manufacturing
311119 Custom milling of animal feed
442299 Custom picture frame shops 333517 Custom roll forming machines, metalworking, manufacturing
332114 Custom roll forming metal products
321113 Custom sawmills
311611 Custom slaughtering
315220 Custom tailors, men's and boys' dress shirts, cut and sewn from purchased fabric
315220 Custom tailors, men's and boys' suits, cut and sewn from purchased fabric
315240 Custom tailors, women's and girls' dresses cut and sewn from purchased fabric (except apparel contractors)
561422 Customer service call centers
541613 Customer service management consulting services

488510 Customs brokers
921130 Customs bureaus
541614 Customs consulting services
327215 Cut and engraved glassware made from purchased glass
315210 Cut and sew apparel contractors
111422 Cut flower growing
111422 Cut rose growing
316998 Cut stock for boots and shoes manufacturing
321912 Cut stock manufacturing 327991 Cut stone bases (e.g., desk sets pedestals, lamps, plaques and similar small particles) manufacturing
327991 Cut stone products (e.g., blocks, statuary) manufacturing
811490 Cutlery (e.g., knives, scissors) sharpening, household-type
423710 Cutlery merchant wholesalers
332215 Cutlery, nonprecious and precious plated metal, manufacturing
339910 Cutlery, precious metal (except precious plated), manufacturing
333517 Cut-off machines, metalworking, manufacturing
335931 Cutouts, switch and fuse, manufacturing
333131 Cutters, coal, manufacturing
332216 Cutters, glass, manufacturing
333515 Cutters, metal milling, manufacturing
113310 Cutting and transporting timber
213112 Cutting cores in oil and gas wells on a contract basis
332216 Cutting dies (e.g., paper, leather, textile) manufacturing
332216 Cutting dies (except metal cutting) manufacturing
333514 Cutting dies, metalworking, manufacturing
315210 Cutting fabric owned by others for apparel
339114 Cutting instruments, dental, manufacturing
333517 Cutting machines, metalworking, manufacturing
238910 Cutting new rights of way
316110 Cutting of leather
424470 Cutting of purchased carcasses (except boxed meat cut on an assembly line basis) merchant wholesalers
324191 Cutting oils made from refined petroleum
325998 Cutting oils, synthetic, manufacturing
113310 Cutting timber
327215 Cutting, engraving, etching, painting or polishing purchased glass
111422 Cuttings farming
325180 Cyanides manufacturing 212325 Cyanite mining and/or beneficiating 211130 Cycle condensate production 325110 Cyclic aromatic hydrocarbons made from refined petroleum or liquid hydrocarbons
324110 Cyclic aromatic hydrocarbons made in petroleum refineries
424690 Cyclic crudes and intermediates merchant wholesalers
325194 Cyclic crudes made by distillation of coal tar
325194 Cyclic intermediates made from refined petroleum or natural gas (except aromatic petrochemicals)
325212 Cyclo rubber, synthetic, manufacturing
325194 Cyclohexane manufacturing
332313 Cyclones, industrial, fabricated metal plate work, manufacturing
325194 Cyclopentane made from refined petroleum or natural gas
325194 Cyclopropane made from refined petroleum or natural gas
325412 Cyclopropane medicinal preparations manufacturing
325194 Cycloterpenes manufacturing
335999 Cyclotrons manufacturing
333517 Cylinder boring machines metal cutting type, manufacturing
336310 Cylinder heads, automotive and truck gasoline engine, manufacturing
327332 Cylinder pipe, prestressed concrete, manufacturing
332618 Cylinder wire cloth made from purchased wire
332994 Cylinders and clips, gun, manufacturing
333995 Cylinders, fluid power, manufacturing
336340 Cylinders, master brake (new and rebuilt), manufacturing
332420 Cylinders, pressure, heavy gauge metal, manufacturing
334417 Cylindrical connectors, electronic, manufacturing
332991 Cylindrical roller bearings manufacturing
339992 Cymbals and parts manufacturing
339112 Cystoscopes (except electromedical) manufacturing

334510 Cystoscopes, electromedical, manufacturing
325413 Cytology and histology in-vitro diagnostic substances manufacturing
621511 Cytology health laboratories
112120 Dairy cattle farming
311119 Dairy cattle feeds, supplements, concentrates, and premixes, manufacturing
424430 Dairy depots merchant wholesalers
311514 Dairy food canning
112420 Dairy goat farming
112111 Dairy heifer replacement production
541690 Dairy herd consulting services
115210 Dairy herd improvement associations
333241 Dairy product plant machinery and equipment
445299 Dairy product stores
424430 Dairy products (except canned, dried) merchant wholesalers
424490 Dairy products, dried or canned, merchant wholesalers
424430 Dairy products, frozen, merchant wholesalers
112410 Dairy sheep farming
237990 Dam construction
332312 Dam gates, metal plate, manufacturing
334512 Damper operators (e.g., electric, pneumatic, thermostatic) manufacturing
332322 Dampers, sheet metal (except stampings), manufacturing
238390 Dampproofing contractors
711130 Dance bands
713940 Dance centers, aerobic
711120 Dance companies
711310 Dance festival managers with facilities
711320 Dance festival managers without facilities
711310 Dance festival organizers with facilities
711320 Dance festival organizers without facilities
711310 Dance festival promoters with facilities
711320 Dance festival promoters without facilities
531120 Dance hall rental or leasing
713990 Dance halls
611610 Dance instruction
711120 Dance productions, live theatrical
611610 Dance schools
611610 Dance studios
711120 Dance theaters
621340 Dance therapists' offices (e.g., centers, clinics)
711120 Dance troupes
711510 Dancers, independent 313110 Darning thread (e.g., cotton, manmade fibers, silk, wool) manufacturing
332994 Dart guns manufacturing
339930 Darts and dart games manufacturing
518210 Data capture imaging services
334210 Data communications equipment (e.g., bridges, gateways, routers) manufacturing
518210 Data entry services
423430 Data keying equipment merchant wholesalers
334513 Data loggers, industrial process-type, manufacturing
518210 Data processing computer services
541513 Data processing facilities (i.e., clients' facilities) management and operation services
423430 Data processing machines, computer, merchant wholesalers
518210 Data processing services (except payroll services, financial transaction processing services)
323111 Databases commercial printing (except screen) without publishing
323113 Databases screen printing without publishing
111339 Date farming
339940 Date stamps, hand operated, manufacturing
311423 Dates, dried, made in dehydration plants
311340 Dates, sugared and stuffed, manufacturing
334519 Dating devices and machines (except rubber stamps) manufacturing
812990 Dating services 333923 Davits manufacturing
****** Day camps, instructional -- see type of instruction
624120 Day care centers for disabled persons, the elderly, and persons diagnosed with intellectual and developmental disabilities
624120 Day care centers, adult
624410 Day care centers, child or infant
624410 Day care services, child or infant
812199 Day spas
621310 DCs' (doctors of chiropractic) offices (e.g., centers, clinics)
621210 DDSs' (doctors of dental surgery) offices (e.g., centers, clinics)

325320 DDT (dichlorodiphenyltrichloroethane) insecticides manufacturing
922120 DEA (Drug Enforcement Administration)
332510 Dead bolts, metal, manufacturing
****** Dealers -- see type
562119 Debris removal services
561440 Debt collection services
333517 Deburring machines, metalworking, manufacturing
334515 Decade boxes (i.e., capacitance, inductance, resistance) manufacturing
325199 Decahydronaphthalene manufacturing
327110 Decalcomania on china and glass for the trade
339999 Decalcomania work (except on china, glass)
111339 Deciduous tree fruit (except apples, citrus) farming
238190 Deck and grate (except roof), metal, installation
238350 Deck construction, residential-type
327215 Decorated glassware made from purchased glass
327110 Decorating china (e.g., encrusting gold, silver, other metal on china) for the trade
541410 Decorating consulting services, interior
335129 Decorative area lighting fixtures (except residential) manufacturing
335121 Decorative area lighting fixtures, residential, manufacturing
712110 Decorative art museums
238150 Decorative glass and mirror installation
327212 Decorative glassware made in glass making plants
335110 Decorative lamp bulbs manufacturing
238190 Decorative steel and wrought iron work installation
314999 Decorative stitching contractors on apparel
314999 Decorative stitching on textile articles and apparel
321918 Decorative wood moldings (e.g., base, chair rail, crown, shoe) manufacturing
115114 Decorticating flax
483113 Deep sea freight transportation to or from domestic ports (including Puerto Rico)
483111 Deep sea freight transportation to or from foreign ports
483114 Deep sea passenger transportation to and from domestic ports (including Puerto Rico)
483112 Deep sea passenger transportation to or from foreign ports
333318 Deep-fat fryers, commercial-type, manufacturing
335210 Deep-fat fryers, household-type electric, manufacturing
112990 Deer production
334510 Defibrillators manufacturing
325312 Defluorinated phosphates manufacturing
325998 Defoamers and antifoaming agents manufacturing
325320 Defoliants manufacturing
325998 Degreasing preparations for machinery parts manufacturing
325612 Degreasing preparations, household-type, manufacturing
333415 Dehumidifiers (except portable electric) manufacturing
335210 Dehumidifiers, portable electric, manufacturing
311514 Dehydrated milk manufacturing
311423 Dehydrating fruits and vegetables
311423 Dehydrating potato products (e.g., flakes, granules)
325998 Deicing preparations manufacturing
322110 Deinking plants
322110 Deinking recovered paper
424470 Deli meats merchant wholesalers
722513 Delicatessen restaurants
333997 Delicatessen scales manufacturing
445210 Delicatessens (except grocery store, restaurants)
445110 Delicatessens primarily retailing a range of grocery items and meats
561440 Delinquent account collection services
623990 Delinquent youth halfway group homes
115114 Delinting cottonseed
332618 Delivery cases made from purchased wire
492210 Delivery service (except as part of intercity courier network, U.S. Postal Service)
334515 Demand meters, electric, manufacturing
541720 Demographic research and development services
238910 Demolition contractor
238910 Demolition, building and structure
541890 Demonstration services, merchandise
336212 Demountable cargo containers manufacturing

325193 Denatured alcohol manufacturing
313210 Denims weaving
321219 Densified wood manufacturing 333316
Densitometers (except laboratory analytical) manufacturing
334516 Densitometers, laboratory analytical, manufacturing
334513 Density and specific gravity instruments, industrial process-type, manufacturing
339114 Dental alloys for amalgams manufacturing
424210 Dental care preparations merchant wholesalers
339114 Dental chairs manufacturing
423450 Dental chairs merchant wholesalers
339114 Dental equipment and instruments manufacturing
423450 Dental equipment and supplies merchant wholesalers
811219 Dental equipment repair and maintenance services
325620 Dental floss manufacturing
339114 Dental glues and cements manufacturing
339114 Dental hand instruments (e.g., forceps) manufacturing
611519 Dental hygienist schools
621399 Dental hygienists' offices (e.g., centers, clinics)
339114 Dental impression materials manufacturing
339114 Dental instrument delivery systems manufacturing
524114 Dental insurance carriers, direct
339116 Dental laboratories 339114 Dental
laboratory equipment manufacturing
541715 Dental research and development laboratories or services
611310 Dental schools
621210 Dental surgeons' offices (e.g., centers, clinics)
611519 Dental technician schools
339114 Dental wax manufacturing
621512 Dental X-ray laboratories
325611 Dentifrices manufacturing
424210 Dentifrices merchant wholesalers
813920 Dentists' associations
621210 Dentists' offices (e.g., centers, clinics)
423450 Dentists' professional supplies merchant wholesalers
325620 Denture adhesives manufacturing
325620 Denture cleaners, effervescent, manufacturing
339114 Denture materials manufacturing
339116 Dentures, custom made in dental laboratories
621399 Denturists' offices (e.g., centers, clinics)
561720 Deodorant servicing of rest rooms
325612 Deodorants (except personal) manufacturing
424690 Deodorants (except personal) merchant wholesalers
325620 Deodorants, personal, manufacturing
424210 Deodorants, personal, merchant wholesalers
238290 Deodorization (i.e., air filtration) system installation
561720 Deodorizing services
452210 Department stores
812199 Depilatory (i.e., hair removal) salons
325620 Depilatory preparations manufacturing
332813 Depolishing metals and metal products for the trade
523999 Deposit brokers
524128 Deposit or share insurance carriers, direct
561492 Deposition services
522110 Depository trust companies
339113 Depressors, tongue, manufacturing
332994 Depth charge projectors manufacturing
332993 Depth charges manufacturing
424210 Dermatological medicines merchant wholesalers
325412 Dermatological preparations manufacturing
621111 Dermatologists' offices (e.g., centers, clinics)
213112 Derrick building, repairing, and dismantling at oil and gas fields on a contract basis
333132 Derricks, oil and gas field-type, manufacturing
325998 Desalination kits manufacturing
327992 Desiccants, activated clay, manufacturing
424120 Desk accessories, office, merchant wholesalers
335210 Desk fans, electric, manufacturing
335122 Desk lamps, commercial, electric, manufacturing
335121 Desk lamps, residential, electric, manufacturing
316998 Desk sets, leather, manufacturing

337214 Desks (except wood), office-type, manufacturing
337122 Desks, wood household-type, manufacturing
337211 Desks, wood office-type, manufacturing
561410 Desktop publishing services (i.e., document preparation services)
424490 Dessert powders merchant wholesalers
424430 Desserts, dairy, merchant wholesalers
311520 Desserts, frozen (except bakery), manufacturing
311813 Desserts, frozen bakery, manufacturing
811192 Detailing services (i.e., cleaning and polishing), automotive
115112 Detasseling corn 561611
Detective agencies
334519 Detectors, scintillation, manufacturing
922140 Detention centers
325611 Detergents (e.g., dishwashing, industrial, laundry) manufacturing
424690 Detergents merchant wholesalers
331492 Detinning scrap (e.g., cans)
325920 Detonating caps, cord, fuses, and primers manufacturing
325920 Detonators (except ammunition) manufacturing
424690 Detonators (except ammunition) merchant wholesalers
332993 Detonators, ammunition (i.e., more than 30 mm., more than 1.18 inch), manufacturing
621420 Detoxification centers and clinics (except hospitals), outpatient
622210 Detoxification hospitals
325180 Deuterium oxide (i.e., heavy water) manufacturing
325992 Developers, prepared photographic, manufacturing
336411 Developing and producing prototypes for aircraft
336412 Developing and producing prototypes for aircraft engines and engine parts
336413 Developing and producing prototypes for aircraft parts (except engines) and auxiliary equipment
336414 Developing and producing prototypes for complete guided missiles and space vehicles
336419 Developing and producing prototypes for guided missile and space vehicle components
336415 Developing and producing prototypes for guided missile and space vehicle engines
423410 Developing apparatus, photographic, merchant wholesalers
333316 Developing equipment, film, manufacturing
926110 Development assistance program administration
813311 Developmentally disabled advocacy organizations
238910 Dewatering contractors
111334 Dewberry farming
325520 Dextrin glues manufacturing
311221 Dextrin made by wet milling corn
212319 Diabase crushed and broken stone mining and/or beneficiating
212311 Diabase mining or quarrying
325412 Diagnostic biological preparations (except in-vitro) manufacturing
811198 Diagnostic centers without repair, automotive
334510 Diagnostic equipment, electromedical, manufacturing
423450 Diagnostic equipment, medical, merchant wholesalers
334510 Diagnostic equipment, MRI (magnetic resonance imaging), manufacturing 621512 Diagnostic imaging centers (medical) 811219 Diagnostic imaging equipment repair and maintenance services
424210 Diagnostic reagents merchant wholesalers
325413 Diagnostic substances, in-vitro, manufacturing
424210 Diagnostics, in-vitro and in-vivo, merchant wholesalers
332216 Dial indicators, machinists' precision tools, manufacturing
517919 Dial-up Internet service providers, using client-supplied telecommunications connections
621492 Dialysis centers and clinics
334510 Dialysis equipment, electromedical, manufacturing
325312 Diammonium phosphates manufacturing
332618 Diamond cloths made from purchased wire
339910 Diamond cutting and polishing
333514 Diamond dies, metalworking, manufacturing
327910 Diamond dressing wheels manufacturing
423940 Diamonds (except industrial) merchant wholesalers

423840 Diamonds, industrial, merchant wholesalers
212399 Diamonds, industrial, mining and/or beneficiating
315240 Diaper covers, infants', cut and sewn from purchased fabric (except apparel contractors)
315210 Diaper covers, water resistant and water-proof, cut and sew apparel contractors
812331 Diaper supply services
314999 Diapers (except disposable) made from purchased fabrics
424330 Diapers (except paper) merchant wholesalers
322291 Diapers, disposable, made from purchased paper or textile fiber
322121 Diapers, disposable, made in paper mills
424130 Diapers, paper, merchant wholesalers
326299 Diaphragms (i.e., birth control device), rubber, manufacturing
323111 Diaries manufacturing
511199 Diary and time scheduler publishers (except exclusive Internet publishing)
519130 Diary and time scheduler publishers, exclusively on Internet
212325 Diaspore mining and/or beneficiating
334510 Diathermy apparatus, electromedical, manufacturing
334510 Diathermy units manufacturing
212399 Diatomaceous earth mining and/or beneficitating
327992 Diatomaceous earth processing beyond beneficiation
212399 Diatomite mining and/or beneficiating
325992 Diazo (i.e., whiteprint) paper and cloth, sensitized, manufacturing
325120 Dichlorodifluoromethane manufacturing
325180 Dichromates manufacturing 315210 Dick-eys cut and sew apparel contractors 315240 Dickeys, women's and girls', cut and sewn from purchased fabric (except apparel contractors)
333318 Dictating machines manufacturing
423420 Dictating machines merchant wholesalers
561410 Dictation services
611699 Diction schools
323117 Dictionaries printing and binding without publishing
323117 Dictionaries printing without publishing
323120 Dictionary binding without printing
511130 Dictionary publishers (except exclusive Internet publishing)
511130 Dictionary publishers and printing combined
519130 Dictionary publishers, exclusively on Internet
325211 Dicyandiamine resins manufacturing
333514 Die sets for metal stamping presses manufacturing
333517 Die sinking machines, metalworking, manufacturing
333511 Die-casting dies manufacturing
333517 Die-casting machines, metalworking, manufacturing
331523 Die-castings, aluminum, unfinished, manufacturing
331523 Die-castings, nonferrous metals, unfinished, manufacturing
322299 Die-cut paper products (except for office use) made from purchased paper or paperboard
322230 Die-cut paper products for office use made from purchased paper or paperboard
333994 Dielectric industrial heating equipment manufacturing
333514 Dies and die holders for metal cutting and forming (except threading) manufacturing
333515 Dies and taps (i.e., a machine tool accessory) manufacturing
332216 Dies, cutting (except metal cutting), manufacturing
333514 Dies, metalworking (except threading), manufacturing
423830 Dies, metalworking, merchant wholesalers
333514 Dies, plastics forming, manufacturing
332216 Dies, steel rule (except metal cutting), manufacturing
333514 Dies, steel rule, metal cutting, manufacturing
333618 Diesel and semidiesel engines manufacturing
811111 Diesel engine repair shops, automotive
423830 Diesel engines and parts, industrial, merchant wholesalers
424710 Diesel fuel bulk stations and terminals, merchant wholesalers
424720 Diesel fuel merchant wholesalers (except bulk stations, terminals)
324110 Diesel fuels made in petroleum refineries
812191 Diet centers, non-medical
812191 Diet workshops

311514 Dietary drinks, dairy and nondairy based, manufacturing
424210 Dietary supplements merchant wholesalers
325412 Dietary supplements, compounded, manufacturing
325411 Dietary supplements, uncompounded, manufacturing
325194 Diethylcyclohexane manufacturing
325199 Diethylene glycol manufacturing
813920 Dietitians' associations
621399 Dietitians' offices (e.g., centers, clinics)
336350 Differential and rear axle assemblies, automotive, truck, and bus, manufacturing
334513 Differential pressure instruments, industrial process-type, manufacturing
334516 Differential thermal analysis instruments, laboratory-type, manufacturing
332420 Digesters, industrial-type, heavy gauge metal, manufacturing
325412 Digestive system preparations manufacturing
238910 Digging foundations
333316 Digital cameras manufacturing
334111 Digital computers manufacturing
334513 Digital displays of process variables manufacturing
334515 Digital panel meters, electricity measuring, manufacturing
323111 Digital printing (e.g., billboards, other large format graphic materials, high resolution) (except books)
333244 Digital printing presses manufacturing
334515 Digital test equipment (e.g., electronic and electrical circuits and equipment testing) manufacturing
423620 Digital video disc (DVD) players merchant wholesalers
334310 Digital video disc players manufacturing
423990 Digital video discs (DVDs), prerecorded, merchant wholesalers
325412 Digitalis medicinal preparations manufacturing
423430 Digitizer and light pen tables merchant wholesalers
325411 Digitoxin, uncompounded, manufacturing
325211 Diisocyanate resins manufacturing 237990
Dike and other flood control structure construction
111219 Dill farming, field and seed production
321113 Dimension lumber, hardwood, made from logs or bolts
321912 Dimension lumber, hardwood, resawing purchased lumber
321113 Dimension lumber, made from logs or bolts
321912 Dimension lumber, resawing purchased lumber
321113 Dimension lumber, softwood, made from logs or bolts
321912 Dimension lumber, softwood, resawing purchased lumber
321912 Dimension stock, hardwood, manufacturing
321912 Dimension stock, softwood, manufacturing
321912 Dimension stock, wood, manufacturing
327991 Dimension stone dressing and manufacturing
327991 Dimension stone for buildings manufacturing
212311 Dimension stone mining or quarrying
325199 Dimethyl divinyl acetylene (di-isopropenyl acetylene) manufacturing
325199 Dimethylhydrazine manufacturing 335931
Dimmer switches, outlet box mounting-type, manufacturing
722511 Diners, full service
722513 Diners, limited-service 337124 Dinette
sets, metal household-type, manufacturing
336612 Dinghies manufacturing 337124
Dining room chairs (including upholstered), metal, manufacturing
337125 Dining room chairs (including upholstered), plastics manufacturing
337122 Dining room chairs (including upholstered), wood, manufacturing
337124 Dining room furniture, metal household-type, manufacturing
337122 Dining room furniture, wood household-type, manufacturing
487210 Dinner cruises 711110
Dinner theaters
311412 Dinners, frozen (except seafood-based), manufacturing
311710 Dinners, frozen seafood, manufacturing
424420 Dinners, frozen, merchant wholesalers
326199 Dinnerware, plastics (except polystyrene foam), manufacturing
326140 Dinnerware, polystyrene foam, manufacturing
334515 Diode and transistor testers manufacturing

423690 Diodes merchant wholesalers 334413 Diodes, solid-state (e.g., germanium, silicon), manufacturing
212313 Diorite crushed and broken stone mining and/or beneficiating
212311 Diorite mining or quarrying
325194 Diphenylamine manufacturing
928120 Diplomatic services
311941 Dips (except cheese and sour cream based) manufacturing
325320 Dips (i.e., pesticides), cattle and sheep, manufacturing
311513 Dips, cheese based, manufacturing
311511 Dips, sour cream based, manufacturing
334112 Direct access storage devices manufacturing
517311 Direct broadcast satellite (DBS) services
325130 Direct dyes manufacturing
541860 Direct mail advertising services
541860 Direct mail or other direct distribution advertising campaign services
454110 Direct mailers (i.e., selling own merchandise)
331110 Direct reduction of iron ore
454390 Direct selling of merchandise (door-to-door)
213111 Directional drilling of oil and gas wells on a contract basis
812210 Director services, funeral
323111 Directories commercial printing (except screen) without publishing
323113 Directories screen printing without publishing
711510 Directors (i.e., film, motion picture, music, theatrical), independent
711510 Directors, independent motion picture
711510 Directors, independent music
511140 Directory and mailing list publishers (except exclusive Internet publishing)
511140 Directory and mailing list publishers and printing combined
511140 Directory publishers (except exclusive Internet publishing)
511140 Directory publishers and printing combined
519130 Directory publishers, exclusively on Internet
541870 Directory, telephone, distribution on a contract basis
517311 Direct-to-home satellite system (DTH) services
238910 Dirt moving for construction
524113 Disability insurance carriers, direct
524113 Disability insurance underwriting, direct
624120 Disability support groups
623990 Disabled group homes without nursing care
922190 Disaster preparedness and management offices, government
624230 Disaster relief services
711510 Disc jockeys, independent
623990 Disciplinary camps for delinquent youth
713990 Discotheques (except those serving alcoholic beverages)
722410 Discotheques, alcoholic beverage 812990 Discount buying services, including medical cards and similar negotiated discount plans for individuals
511199 Discount coupon book publishers (except exclusive Internet publishing)
511199 Discount coupon book publishers and printing combined
519130 Discount coupon book publishers, exclusively on Internet
323111 Discount coupon books commercial printing (except screen) without publishing
323113 Discount coupon books screen printing without publishing
813212 Disease awareness fundraising organizations
115112 Disease control for crops
813212 Disease research (e.g., cancer, heart) fundraising organizations
541940 Disease testing services, veterinary
313240 Dishcloths made in warp or weft knitting mills
423440 Dishes, commercial (except paper and disposable plastics), merchant wholesalers
423220 Dishes, household-type (except disposable plastics, paper), merchant wholesalers
424130 Dishes, paper and disposable plastics, merchant wholesalers
327110 Dishes, pottery, manufacturing
339930 Dishes, toy, manufacturing 321999 Dishes, wood, manufacturing 325611 Dishwasher detergents manufacturing 811412 Dishwasher, household-type, repair and maintenance services without retailing new dishwashers
335220 Dishwashers, household-type, manufacturing

423620 Dishwashers, household-type, merchant wholesalers
423440 Dishwashing equipment, commercial-type, merchant wholesalers
333318 Dishwashing machines, commercial-type, manufacturing
335220 Dishwashing machines, household-type, manufacturing
424690 Disinfectants (except agricultural) merchant wholesalers
325612 Disinfectants, household-type and industrial, manufacturing
561720 Disinfecting services
518210 Disk and diskette conversion services
518210 Disk and diskette recertification services
332613 Disk and ring springs, heavy gauge metal, manufacturing
334112 Disk drives, computer, manufacturing
423430 Disk drives, computer, merchant wholesalers
423430 Diskettes, blank computer, merchant wholesalers
334613 Diskettes, blank, manufacturing
423690 Diskettes, blank, merchant wholesalers
238910 Dismantling engineering structures (e.g., oil storage tank)
238290 Dismantling large-scale machinery and equipment
213112 Dismantling of oil well rigs on a contract basis
333914 Dispensing and measuring pumps (e.g., gasoline, lubricants) manufacturing
325130 Disperse dyes manufacturing
325510 Dispersions, pigment, manufacturing
541850 Display advertising services
423440 Display cases (except refrigerated) merchant wholesalers
337215 Display cases and fixtures (except refrigerated) manufacturing
333415 Display cases, refrigerated, manufacturing
423740 Display cases, refrigerated, merchant wholesalers
334513 Display instruments, industrial process control-type, manufacturing
541890 Display lettering services
339950 Displays (e.g., counter, floor, point-of-purchase) manufacturing
335912 Disposable flashlight batteries manufacturing
424130 Disposable plastics products (e.g., boxes, cups, cutlery, dishes, sanitary food containers) merchant wholesalers
334511 Distance measuring equipment (DME), aeronautical, manufacturing
325194 Distillates, wood, manufacturing
333994 Distillation ovens, charcoal and coke, manufacturing
424820 Distilled alcoholic beverages merchant wholesalers
325998 Distilled water manufacturing
312140 Distilleries
311213 Distiller's malt manufacturing
423830 Distillery machinery merchant wholesalers
312140 Distilling alcoholic beverages (except brandy)
312130 Distilling brandy
333249 Distilling equipment (except beverage), including laboratory-type, manufacturing
333241 Distilling equipment, beverage, manufacturing
312140 Distilling potable liquor (except brandy)
334515 Distortion meters and analyzers manufacturing
335313 Distribution boards, electric, manufacturing
335313 Distribution cutouts manufacturing
423610 Distribution equipment, electrical, merchant wholesalers
237120 Distribution line, gas and oil, construction
237110 Distribution line, sewer and water, construction
221330 Distribution of cooled air
221122 Distribution of electric power
221330 Distribution of heated air
221210 Distribution of manufactured gas
221210 Distribution of natural gas
221330 Distribution of steam heat
335311 Distribution transformers, electric, manufacturing
336320 Distributor cap and rotor for internal combustion engines manufacturing
813910 Distributors' associations
336320 Distributors for internal combustion engines manufacturing
551114 District and regional offices
922130 District attorneys' offices
333120 Ditchers and trenchers, self-propelled, manufacturing
325412 Diuretic preparations manufacturing
332216 Dividers, machinists' precision tools, manufacturing
451110 Diving equipment stores

561990 Diving services on a contract or fee basis
621210 DMDs' (doctors of dental medicine) offices (e.g., centers, clinics)
541714 DNA technologies (e.g., microarrays) research and experimental development laboratories
621511 DNA testing laboratories
531120 Dock and associated building rental or leasing
237990 Dock construction
488330 Docking and undocking marine vessel services
488310 Docking facility operations
621310 Doctors of chiropractic (DCs) offices (e.g., centers, clinics)
621210 Doctors of dental medicine (DMDs) offices (e.g., centers, clinics)
621210 Doctors of dental surgery (DDSs) offices (e.g., centers, clinics)
621320 Doctors of optometry (ODs) offices (e.g., centers, clinics)
621112 Doctors of osteopathy (DOs), mental health, offices (e.g., centers, clinics)
621111 Doctors of osteopathy (DOs, except mental health) offices (e.g., centers, clinics)
621391 Doctors of podiatry (DPs) offices (e.g., centers, clinics)
621330 Doctors of psychology offices (e.g., centers, clinics)
561439 Document copying services (except combined with printing services)
561439 Document duplicating services (except combined with printing services) 561410
Document preparation services 561990 Document shredding services 493190 Document storage and warehousing 561410 Document transcription services
325110 Dodecene made from refined petroleum or liquid hydrocarbons
311111 Dog and cat food (e.g., canned, dry, frozen, semimoist), manufacturing
311111 Dog food manufacturing
316998 Dog furnishings (e.g., collars, harnesses, leashes, muzzles) manufacturing
711219 Dog owners, race (i.e., racing dogs)
812910 Dog pounds
112990 Dog production
711212 Dog racetracks
711219 Dog racing kennels
424990 Dogs merchant wholesalers
322299 Doilies, paper, made from purchased paper
339930 Doll carriages and carts manufacturing
339930 Doll clothing manufacturing
452319 Dollar stores
333924 Dollies manufacturing
423920 Dolls merchant wholesalers
339930 Dolls, doll parts, and doll clothing (except wigs) manufacturing
212312 Dolomite crushed and broken stone mining and/or beneficiating
212311 Dolomite mining or quarrying
327410 Dolomite, dead-burned, manufacturing
327410 Dolomitic lime manufacturing
212319 Dolomitic marble crushed and broken stone mining and/or beneficiating
212311 Dolomitic marble mining or quarrying
114111 Dolphin fishing 112920
Donkey production
332321 Door and jamb assemblies, metal, manufacturing
238350 Door and window frame construction
238350 Door and window, prefabricated, installation
332321 Door frames and sash, metal, manufacturing
321911 Door frames and sash, wood and covered wood, manufacturing
332322 Door hoods, sheet metal (except stampings), manufacturing
321911 Door jambs, wood, manufacturing
332510 Door locks, metal, manufacturing 332510
Door opening and closing devices (except electrical), metal, manufacturing
335999 Door opening and closing devices, electrical, manufacturing
321918 Door shutters, wood, manufacturing
444190 Door stores
321918 Door trim, wood molding, manufacturing
321911 Door units, prehung, wood and covered wood, manufacturing
238290 Door, commercial- or industrial-type, installation
238350 Door, folding, installation
314110 Doormats, all materials (except entirely of rubber or plastics), manufacturing
326199 Doormats, plastics, manufacturing
326299 Doormats, rubber, manufacturing
423310 Doors and door frames merchant wholesalers

326199 Doors and door frames, plastics, manufacturing
321911 Doors, combination screen-storm, wood, manufacturing
332321 Doors, metal, manufacturing
332999 Doors, safe and vault, metal, manufacturing
327215 Doors, unframed glass, made from purchased glass
321911 Doors, wood and covered wood, manufacturing
541870 Door-to-door distribution of advertising materials (e.g., coupons, flyers, samples)
454390 Door-to-door retailing of merchandise, direct selling
325510 Dopes, paint, and lacquer manufacturing
336612 Dories building
721310 Dormitories, off campus
236220 Dormitory construction
621112 DOs' (doctors of osteopathy), mental health, offices (e.g., centers, clinics)
621111 DOs' (doctors of osteopathy, except mental health) offices (e.g., centers, clinics)
334519 Dosimetry devices manufacturing
333241 Dough mixing machinery (i.e., food manufacturing-type) manufacturing 722511 Doughnut shops, full service 722515 Doughnut shops, on premise baking and carryout service
311812 Doughnuts (except frozen) made in commercial bakeries
311813 Doughnuts, frozen, manufacturing
424420 Doughs, frozen, merchant wholesalers
311211 Doughs, prepared, made in flour mills
311824 Doughs, refrigerated or frozen, made from purchased flour
812990 Doula services (providing coaching and support during childbirth)
333243 Dovetailing machines, woodworking-type, manufacturing
332722 Dowel pins, metal, manufacturing
321999 Dowels, wood, manufacturing 315210 Down-filled clothing cut and sew apparel contractors
315220 Down-filled clothing, men's and boys', cut and sewn from purchased fabric (except apparel contractors)
315240 Down-filled clothing, women's, girls', and infants', cut and sewn from purchased fabric (except apparel contractors)
713920 Downhill skiing facilities without accommodations
238170 Downspout, gutter, and gutter guard installation
332322 Downspouts, sheet metal (except stampings), manufacturing
621391 DPs' (doctors of podiatry) offices (e.g., centers, clinics)
334513 Draft gauges, industrial process-type, manufacturing
334519 Drafting instruments manufacturing
423490 Drafting instruments merchant wholesalers
339940 Drafting materials (except instruments and tables) manufacturing
541340 Drafting services
337127 Drafting tables and boards manufacturing
423490 Drafting tables merchant wholesalers
541340 Draftsmen's offices
711212 Drag strips
333120 Draglines, crawler, manufacturing
423860 Draglines, ship, merchant wholesalers
325194 Dragon's blood manufacturing
333111 Drags, farm-type equipment, manufacturing
333120 Drags, road construction and road maintenance equipment, manufacturing
212399 Dragstones mining and/or beneficiating
561790 Drain cleaning services
332913 Drain cocks, plumbing, manufacturing
325612 Drain pipe cleaners manufacturing
332999 Drain plugs, magnetic, metal, manufacturing
327120 Drain tile, clay, manufacturing
238220 Drain, waste and vent system installation
237990 Drainage canal and ditch construction
237990 Drainage project construction
238910 Drainage system (e.g., cesspool, septic tank) installation
337110 Drainboards, wood or plastics laminated on wood, manufacturing
213113 Draining or pumping coal mines on a contract basis
213114 Draining or pumping of metal mines on a contract basis
213115 Draining or pumping of nonmetallic mineral mines (except fuels) on a contract basis
611610 Drama schools (except academic)
314120 Draperies made from purchased fabrics or sheet goods

423220 Draperies merchant wholesalers
812320 Drapery cleaning services
238390 Drapery fixture (e.g., hardware, rods, tracks) installation
423710 Drapery hardware merchant wholesalers
424310 Drapery material merchant wholesalers
339113 Drapes, surgical, disposable, manufacturing
333519 Draw bench machines manufacturing
315210 Drawers cut and sew apparel contractors
315190 Drawers, apparel, made in apparel knitting mills
315220 Drawers, men's and boys', cut and sewn from purchased fabric (except apparel contractors)
315240 Drawers, women's and girls', cut and sewn from purchased fabric (except apparel contractors)
325998 Drawing inks manufacturing
331222 Drawing iron or steel wire from purchased iron or steel
331222 Drawing iron or steel wire from purchased iron or steel and fabricating wire products
333249 Drawing machinery for textiles manufacturing
337127 Drawing tables and boards, artist's, manufacturing
332216 Drawknives manufacturing
336611 Dredge building 423810 Dredges (except ships') merchant wholesalers
423860 Dredges, ship, merchant wholesalers
237990 Dredging (e.g., canal, channel, ditch, waterway)
333120 Dredging machinery manufacturing 315210 Dress and semidress gloves cut and sew apparel contractors
315990 Dress and semidress gloves cut and sewn from purchased fabric (except apparel contractors)
315190 Dress and semidress gloves made in apparel knitting mills
316210 Dress shoes, children's and infants', manufacturing
316210 Dress shoes, men's, manufacturing
316210 Dress shoes, women's, manufacturing
448190 Dress shops
532281 Dress suit rental
315210 Dress trimmings cut and sew apparel contractors
315990 Dress trimmings cut and sewn from purchased fabric (except apparel contractors)
424990 Dressed furs and skins merchant wholesalers
337124 Dressers, metal, manufacturing
337122 Dressers, wood, manufacturing 315210 Dresses cut and sew apparel contractors 315190 Dresses made in apparel knitting mills 424330 Dresses merchant wholesalers 315190 Dresses, hand-knit, manufacturing 315240 Dresses, women's, girls', and infants', cut and sewn from purchased fabric (except apparel contractors)
316110 Dressing (i.e., bleaching, blending, currying, scraping, tanning) furs
315210 Dressing gowns cut and sew apparel contractors
315240 Dressing gowns, women's and girls', cut and sewn from purchased fabric (except apparel contractors)
316110 Dressing hides
311615 Dressing small game
337124 Dressing tables, metal, manufacturing
337122 Dressing tables, wood, manufacturing
423450 Dressings, medical, merchant wholesalers
339113 Dressings, surgical, manufacturing
424490 Dried foods (e.g., fruits, milk, vegetables) merchant wholesalers
311612 Dried meats made from purchased carcasses
212392 Dried phosphate rock mining and/or beneficiating
325510 Driers, paint and varnish, manufacturing
325992 Driers, photographic chemical, manufacturing
333316 Driers, photographic, manufacturing
334511 Driftmeters, aeronautical, manufacturing
333515 Drill bits, metalworking, manufacturing
332216 Drill bits, woodworking, manufacturing
333517 Drill presses, metalworking, manufacturing
333243 Drill presses, woodworking-type, manufacturing
332999 Drill stands, metal, manufacturing
238910 Drilled pier (i.e., for building foundations) contractors
238910 Drilled shaft (i.e., drilled building foundations) construction

336611 Drilling and production platforms, floating, oil and gas, building
213111 Drilling directional oil and gas field wells on a contract basis
333132 Drilling equipment, oil and gas field-type, manufacturing
333131 Drilling equipment, underground mining-type, manufacturing
213111 Drilling for gas on a contract basis
213111 Drilling for oil on a contract basis 213111
Drilling gas and oil field wells on a contract basis
333517 Drilling machines, metalworking, manufacturing
325998 Drilling mud compounds, conditioners, and additives (except bentonites) manufacturing
424690 Drilling muds merchant wholesalers
213111 Drilling oil and gas field service wells on a contract basis
339910 Drilling pearls
213112 Drilling rat holes and mouse holes at oil and gas fields on a contract basis
333132 Drilling rigs, oil and gas field-type, manufacturing
213113 Drilling services for coal mining on a contract basis
213114 Drilling services for metal mining on a contract basis
213115 Drilling services for nonmetallic mineral (except fuels) mining on a contract basis
213112 Drilling shot holes at oil and gas fields on a contract basis
213112 Drilling site preparation at oil and gas fields on a contract basis
213111 Drilling water intake wells, oil and gas field on a contract basis
237110 Drilling water wells (except water intake wells in oil and gas fields)
313210 Drills weaving
333131 Drills, core, underground mining-type, manufacturing
339114 Drills, dental, manufacturing
333991 Drills, handheld power-driven (except heavy construction and mining-type), manufacturing
332216 Drills, handheld, nonelectric, manufacturing
333131 Drills, rock, underground mining-type, manufacturing
213112 Drill-stem testing in oil, gas, dry, and service well drilling on a contract basis
311999 Drink powder mixes (except chocolate, coffee, milk based, tea) manufacturing
311351 Drink powdered mixes, cocoa, made from cacao
311352 Drink powdered mixes, cocoa, made from purchased cocoa
311511 Drink, chocolate milk, manufacturing
238220 Drinking fountain installation
332999 Drinking fountains (except mechanically refrigerated), metal, manufacturing
326191 Drinking fountains (except mechanically refrigerated), plastics, manufacturing
423720 Drinking fountains (except refrigerated) merchant wholesalers
333415 Drinking fountains, refrigerated, manufacturing
423740 Drinking fountains, refrigerated, merchant wholesalers
327110 Drinking fountains, vitreous china, non-refrigerated, manufacturing
722410 Drinking places (i.e., bars, lounges, taverns), alcoholic
312111 Drinks, fruit (except juice), manufacturing
333613 Drive chains, bicycle and motorcycle, manufacturing
811118 Drive shaft repair shops, automotive 336350
Drive shafts and half shafts, automotive, truck, and bus, manufacturing
512132 Drive-in motion picture theaters
237990 Drive-in movie facility construction
722513 Drive-in restaurants
611692 Driver education
611692 Driver training schools (except bus, heavy equipment, truck)
711219 Drivers, harness or race car
423840 Drives and gears merchant wholesalers
333612 Drives, high-speed industrial (except hydrostatic), manufacturing
561790 Driveway cleaning (e.g., power sweeping, washing) services
238990 Driveway paving or sealing
713990 Driving ranges, golf
488490 Driving services (e.g., automobile, truck delivery)
238310 Drop ceiling installation
332111 Drop forgings made from purchased iron or steel, unfinished
333517 Drop hammers, metal forging and shaping, manufacturing
812320 Drop-off and pick-up sites for laundries and drycleaners

813319 Drug abuse prevention advocacy organizations
623220 Drug addiction rehabilitation facilities (except licensed hospitals), residential
622210 Drug addiction rehabilitation hospitals
624190 Drug addiction self-help organizations
621420 Drug addiction treatment centers and clinics (except hospitals), outpatient
922120 Drug enforcement agencies and offices
424210 Drug proprietaries merchant wholesalers
446110 Drug stores
424210 Druggists' sundries merchant wholesalers
424210 Drugs merchant wholesalers
711130 Drum and bugle corps (i.e., drill teams)
333924 Drum cradles manufacturing
339992 Drums (musical instruments), parts, and accessories manufacturing
332439 Drums, light gauge metal, manufacturing
423840 Drums, new and reconditioned, merchant wholesalers
326199 Drums, plastics (i.e., containers), manufacturing
321920 Drums, plywood, manufacturing
321920 Drums, shipping, wood, wirebound, manufacturing
813319 Drunk driving prevention advocacy organizations
311422 Dry beans canning
424510 Dry beans, inedible, merchant wholesalers 484230 Dry bulk carrier, truck, long-distance
484220 Dry bulk trucking (except garbage collection, garbage hauling), local
335912 Dry cell primary batteries, single and multiple cell, manufacturing
335912 Dry cells, primary (e.g., AAA, AA, C, D, 9V), manufacturing
238220 Dry heating equipment installation
325120 Dry ice (i.e., solid carbon dioxide) manufacturing
424690 Dry ice merchant wholesalers
311514 Dry milk manufacturing
333241 Dry milk processing machinery manufacturing
311514 Dry milk products and mixture manufacturing
311514 Dry milk products for animal feed manufacturing
327999 Dry mix concrete manufacturing
311824 Dry mixes made from purchased flour
311824 Dry pasta manufacturing 311824 Dry pasta packaged with other ingredients made in dry pasta plants
335210 Dry shavers (i.e., electric razors) manufacturing
238910 Dry well construction
812320 Drycleaner drop-off and pick-up sites
812320 Drycleaners (except coin-operated) 335220
Drycleaning and laundry machines, household-type,
manufacturing
333318 Drycleaning equipment and machinery manufacturing
423850 Drycleaning equipment and supplies merchant wholesalers
812310 Drycleaning machine routes (i.e., concession operators), coin-operated or similar self-service
236220 Drycleaning plant construction
812320 Drycleaning plants (except rug cleaning plants)
325612 Drycleaning preparations manufacturing
812320 Drycleaning services (except coin-operated)
812310 Drycleaning services, coin-operated or similar self-service
424690 Drycleaning solvents and chemicals merchant wholesalers
336611 Drydock, floating, building
488390 Drydocks, floating (i.e., routine repair and maintenance of ships)
532210 Dryer, clothes, rental
335220 Dryers, clothes, household-type, gas and electric, manufacturing
423620 Dryers, clothes, merchant wholesalers
423620 Dryers, hair, merchant wholesalers
335220 Dryers, household-type laundry, manufacturing
339113 Dryers, laboratory-type, manufacturing
333318 Dryers, laundry (except household-type), manufacturing
311710 Drying fish and seafood
333249 Drying kilns, lumber, manufacturing
333249 Drying machinery for textiles manufacturing
423310 Drywall board merchant wholesalers
238310 Drywall contractors
238310 Drywall finishing (e.g., sanding, spackling, stippling, taping, texturing)
238310 Drywall hanging
238310 Drywall installation

423320 Drywall supplies merchant wholesalers
713950 Duck pin bowling alleys
713950 Duck pin bowling centers
112390 Duck production
313210 Ducks weaving
311615 Ducks, processing, fresh, frozen, canned, or cooked
311615 Ducks, slaughtering and dressing
561790 Duct cleaning services 238290 Duct insulation installation 322220 Duct tape made from purchased materials 238220 Duct work (e.g., cooling, dust collection, exhaust, heating, ventilation) installation
331511 Ductile iron castings, unfinished, manufacturing
331511 Ductile iron foundries
332313 Ducting, fabricated metal plate work, manufacturing
335313 Ducts for electrical switchboard apparatus manufacturing
332322 Ducts, sheet metal, manufacturing
721214 Dude ranches
339920 Dumbbells manufacturing
238290 Dumbwaiter installation
333921 Dumbwaiters manufacturing
212325 Dumortierite mining and/or beneficiating
336212 Dump trailers manufacturing
532120 Dump truck rental or leasing without operator
484220 Dump trucking (e.g., gravel, sand, top-soil)
562119 Dump trucking of rubble or brush with collection or disposal
333131 Dumpers, mining car, manufacturing
562219 Dumps, compost
562212 Dumps, nonhazardous solid waste (e.g., trash)
336211 Dump-truck lifting mechanisms manufacturing
315210 Dungarees cut and sew apparel contractors
315220 Dungarees, men's and boys', cut and sewn from purchased fabric (except apparel contractors)
315240 Dungarees, women's, girls', and infants', cut and sewn from purchased fabric (except apparel contractors)
423860 Dunnage, marine supplies, merchant wholesalers
236116 Duplex (i.e., one unit above the other), construction general contractors
236115 Duplex (i.e., side-by-side) construction general contractors
236117 Duplex for-sale builders
531110 Duplex houses (i.e., single-family) rental or leasing
335931 Duplex receptacles, electrical, manufacturing
325910 Duplicating inks manufacturing 532420 Duplicating machine (e.g., copier) rental or leasing
333517 Duplicating machines (e.g., key cutting), metalworking, manufacturing
425120 Durable goods agents and brokers, wholesale trade
425110 Durable goods business to business electronic markets, wholesale trade
311211 Durum flour manufacturing
333413 Dust and fume collecting equipment manufacturing
314999 Dust cloths made from purchased fabrics
238220 Dust collecting and bag house equipment installation
423730 Dust collection equipment merchant wholesalers
812332 Dust control textile item (e.g., cloths, mats, mops, rugs, shop towels) supply services
315210 Dusters (i.e., apparel) cut and sew apparel contractors
315240 Dusters (i.e., apparel), women's and girls', cut and sewn from purchased fabric (except apparel contractors)
333111 Dusters, farm-type, manufacturing
115112 Dusting crops 445310 Duty free liquor shops
334112 DVD (digital video disc) drives, computer peripheral equipment, manufacturing
334310 DVD (digital video disc) players manufacturing
531110 Dwelling rental or leasing
332311 Dwellings, prefabricated metal, manufacturing
325998 Dye preparations, clothing, household-type, manufacturing
316110 Dyeing furs
313310 Dyeing gloves, woven or knit, for the trade
316110 Dyeing leather
333249 Dyeing machinery for textiles manufacturing
423830 Dyeing machinery, textile, merchant wholesalers
313310 Dyeing textile products and fabrics

424690 Dyes, industrial, merchant wholesalers
325130 Dyes, inorganic, manufacturing
325194 Dyes, natural, manufacturing
325130 Dyes, synthetic organic, manufacturing
424690 Dyestuffs merchant wholesalers
325920 Dynamite manufacturing
424690 Dynamite merchant wholesalers
334519 Dynamometers manufacturing
335312 Dynamos, electric (except automotive), manufacturing
335312 Dynamotors manufacturing
812199 Ear piercing services
237990 Earth retention system construction
334220 Earth station communications equipment manufacturing
517919 Earth stations (except satellite telecommunication carriers)
517410 Earth stations for satellite communication carriers
212399 Earth, diatomaceous, mining and/or beneficiating
212325 Earth, fuller's (e.g., all natural bleaching clays), mining and/or beneficiating
327110 Earthenware table and kitchen articles, coarse, manufacturing
327110 Earthenware, commercial and household, semivitreous, manufacturing
237990 Earth-filled dam construction
532412 Earth-moving equipment rental or leasing without operator
311119 Earthworm food and bedding manufacturing
112990 Earthworm hatcheries
339940 Easels, artists', manufacturing
424130 Eating utensils, disposable plastics, merchant wholesalers
332322 Eaves, sheet metal (except stampings), manufacturing
238170 Eavestrough installation
423330 Eavestroughing merchant wholesalers
327110 Ecclesiastical statuary, clay, manufacturing
327420 Ecclesiastical statuary, gypsum, manufacturing
327999 Ecclesiastical statuary, paper mache, manufacturing
327991 Ecclesiastical statuary, stone, manufacturing
332999 Ecclesiastical ware, precious plated metal, manufacturing
541620 Ecological restoration consulting services
541690 Economic consulting services
926110 Economic development agencies, government
928120 Economic development assistance (i.e., international), government
541720 Economic research and development services
332410 Economizers (i.e., power boiler accessory) manufacturing
522298 Edge Act corporations (except international trade financing)
522293 Edge Act corporations (i.e., international trade financing)
332216 Edge tools, woodworking (e.g., augers, bits, countersinks), manufacturing
333316 Editing equipment, motion picture (e.g., rewinders, splicers, titlers, viewers), manufacturing
561410 Editing services
923110 Education offices, nonoperating
923110 Education program administration
923110 Education statistics centers, government
236220 Educational building construction
611710 Educational consultants
611710 Educational curriculum development services
611710 Educational guidance counseling services
611710 Educational support services
611710 Educational testing evaluation services
611710 Educational testing services
813211 Educational trusts, awarding grants
813920 Educators' associations
114111 Eel fishing
325412 Effervescent salts manufacturing
541614 Efficiency management (i.e., efficiency expert) consulting services
424130 Egg cartons, paper and disposable plastics, merchant wholesalers
321920 Egg cases, wood, manufacturing
335210 Egg cookers, household-type electric, manufacturing
112340 Egg hatcheries, poultry
311824 Egg noodles, dry, manufacturing
311991 Egg noodles, fresh, manufacturing
112310 Egg production, chicken
112330 Egg production, turkey
311999 Egg substitutes manufacturing

312140 Eggnog, alcoholic, manufacturing
311514 Eggnog, canned, nonalcoholic, manufacturing
311511 Eggnog, fresh, nonalcoholic, manufacturing
311511 Eggnog, nonalcoholic (except canned), manufacturing
111219 Eggplant farming (except under cover), field, bedding plant and seed production
111419 Eggplant farming, grown under cover
424440 Eggs merchant wholesalers
112310 Eggs, chicken (table, hatching) production
311999 Eggs, processed, manufacturing
334515 Elapsed time meters, electronic, manufacturing
313210 Elastic fabrics, more than 12 inches in width, weaving
313220 Elastic fabrics, narrow woven, manufacturing
339113 Elastic hosiery, orthopedic, manufacturing
325220 Elastomeric fibers and filaments manufacturing
325211 Elastomers (except synthetic rubber) manufacturing
325212 Elastomers, synthetic rubber, manufacturing
332322 Elbows for conductor pipe, hot air ducts, and stovepipe, sheet metal (except stampings), manufacturing
332919 Elbows, pipe, metal (except made from purchased pipe), manufacturing
921190 Election boards
334512 Electric air cleaner controls, automatic, manufacturing
334513 Electric and electronic controllers, industrial process-type, manufacturing
336111 Electric automobiles for highway use manufacturing
335999 Electric bells manufacturing
335210 Electric blankets manufacturing
423620 Electric blankets merchant wholesalers
335210 Electric comfort heating equipment, portable, manufacturing
238210 Electric contracting
335999 Electric fence chargers manufacturing
335311 Electric furnace transformers manufacturing
334512 Electric heat proportioning controls, modulating controls, manufacturing
335110 Electric lamp bulb parts (except glass blanks) manufacturing
335110 Electric lamps (i.e., light bulbs) manufacturing
237130 Electric light and power plant (except hydroelectric) construction
335110 Electric light bulbs, complete, manufacturing
423610 Electric light fixtures merchant wholesalers
811310 Electric motor repair and maintenance services, commercial or industrial
423610 Electric motors, wiring supplies, and lighting fixtures merchant wholesalers
339992 Electric musical instruments manufacturing
333618 Electric outboard motors manufacturing
221122 Electric power brokers
221121 Electric power control
238210 Electric power control panel and outlet installation
221122 Electric power distribution systems
221117 Electric power generation, biomass 221112
Electric power generation, fossil fuel (e.g., coal, oil, gas)
221116 Electric power generation, geothermal
221111 Electric power generation, hydroelectric
221113 Electric power generation, nuclear
221114 Electric power generation, solar
221118 Electric power generation, tidal
221115 Electric power generation, wind
237130 Electric power transmission line and tower construction
221121 Electric power transmission systems
423610 Electric prime movers merchant wholesalers
334512 Electric space heater controls, automatic, manufacturing
335210 Electric space heaters, portable, manufacturing
333415 Electric warm air (i.e., forced air) furnaces manufacturing
423610 Electrical apparatus merchant wholesalers
238210 Electrical contractors 336320 Electrical
control chips (modules), motor vehicle, manufacturing
541330 Electrical engineering services
238210 Electrical equipment and appliance installation
811310 Electrical generating and transmission equipment repair and maintenance services
541360 Electrical geophysical surveying services

336320 Electrical ignition cable sets for internal combustion engines manufacturing
327110 Electrical insulators, ceramic, manufacturing
811219 Electrical measuring instrument repair and maintenance services
335932 Electrical metallic tube (EMTs) manufacturing
561990 Electrical meter reading services, contract
334515 Electrical network analyzers manufacturing
334515 Electrical power measuring equipment manufacturing
811118 Electrical repair shops, automotive
339950 Electrical signs manufacturing
423440 Electrical signs merchant wholesalers
327110 Electrical supplies, ceramic, manufacturing
444190 Electrical supply stores
541380 Electrical testing laboratories or services
238210 Electrical wiring contractors
238210 Electrical work
238210 Electrical, electrical wiring, and low voltage electrical work
335210 Electrically heated bed coverings manufacturing
238210 Electrician
611513 Electricians' apprenticeship training 334515 Electricity and electrical signal measuring instruments manufacturing
334515 Electricity and electrical signal testing equipment manufacturing
237130 Electricity generating plant (except hydroelectric) construction
237990 Electricity generating plant, hydroelectric, construction
334510 Electrocardiographs manufacturing
335999 Electrochemical generators (i.e., fuel cells) manufacturing
333517 Electrochemical milling machines, metalworking, manufacturing
333517 Electrode discharge metal cutting machines manufacturing
333992 Electrode holders, welding, manufacturing
335991 Electrodes for thermal and electrolytic uses, carbon and graphite, manufacturing
334513 Electrodes used in industrial process measurement manufacturing
335110 Electrodes, cold cathode fluorescent lamp, manufacturing
333992 Electrodes, welding, manufacturing
334510 Electroencephalographs manufacturing
334510 Electrogastrograph manufacturing
332912 Electrohydraulic servo valves, fluid power, manufacturing
812199 Electrolysis (i.e., hair removal) salons
325412 Electrolyte in-vivo diagnostic substances manufacturing
334513 Electrolytic conductivity instruments, industrial process-type, manufacturing
334516 Electrolytic conductivity instruments, laboratory-type, manufacturing
333517 Electrolytic metal cutting machines manufacturing
334513 Electromagnetic flowmeters manufacturing
541360 Electromagnetic geophysical surveying services
334514 Electromechanical counters manufacturing
334510 Electromedical diagnostic equipment manufacturing
334510 Electromedical equipment manufacturing
423450 Electromedical equipment merchant wholesalers
334510 Electromedical therapy equipment manufacturing
331110 Electrometallurgical ferroalloy manufacturing
331110 Electrometallurgical steel manufacturing
334510 Electromyographs manufacturing
333992 Electron beam welding equipment manufacturing
335999 Electron linear accelerators manufacturing
334516 Electron microprobes, laboratory-type, manufacturing
334516 Electron microscopes manufacturing
334516 Electron paramagnetic spin-type apparatus manufacturing
333249 Electron tube machinery manufacturing
334419 Electron tube parts (e.g., bases, getters, guns) (except glass blanks) manufacturing
327215 Electron tube parts, glass blanks, made from purchased glass
327212 Electron tube parts, glass blanks, made in glass making plants
334515 Electron tube test equipment manufacturing
334419 Electron tubes manufacturing 333517 Electron-discharge metal cutting machines manufacturing

423690 Electronic aircraft instruments merchant wholesalers
454110 Electronic auctions, retail
453998 Electronic cigarette stores 325998
Electronic cigarette vapor refills manufacturing
339999 Electronic cigarettes manufacturing
424940 Electronic cigarettes merchant wholesalers
541990 Electronic communication content verification services
423690 Electronic communications equipment merchant wholesalers
238210 Electronic containment fencing for pets, installation
238210 Electronic control installation and service
238210 Electronic control system installation
518210 Electronic data processing services
511140 Electronic directory publishers (except exclusive Internet publishing)
519130 Electronic directory publishers, exclusively on Internet
611519 Electronic equipment repair training
522320 Electronic financial payment services
522320 Electronic funds transfer services
713120 Electronic game arcades
423920 Electronic games merchant wholesalers
334511 Electronic guidance systems and equipment manufacturing
541870 Electronic marketing services
425110 Electronic markets, durable goods, business to business, wholesale trade
425110 Electronic markets, nondurable goods, business to business, wholesale trade
443142 Electronic part and component stores
423690 Electronic parts (e.g., condensers, connectors, switches) merchant wholesalers
323120 Electronic prepress services for the printing trade
541715 Electronic research and development laboratories or services (except nanotechnology research and development)
423690 Electronic sound equipment (except household-type and automotive) merchant wholesalers
334515 Electronic test equipment for testing electrical characteristics manufacturing
541380 Electronic testing laboratories or services
334514 Electronic totalizing counters manufacturing
339930 Electronic toys and games manufacturing
423690 Electronic tubes (e.g., industrial, receiving, transmitting) merchant wholesalers
423930 Electronics parts, recyclable, merchant wholesalers
334516 Electrophoresis instruments manufacturing
333249 Electroplating machinery and equipment manufacturing
332813 Electroplating metals and formed products for the trade
238320 Electrostatic painting, on-site, contractors
335999 Electrostatic particle accelerators manufacturing
333413 Electrostatic precipitation equipment manufacturing
334510 Electrotherapeutic apparatus manufacturing
335110 Electrotherapeutic lamp bulbs for ultraviolet and infrared radiation manufacturing
334510 Electrotherapy units manufacturing
323120 Electrotype plate preparation services
333244 Electrotyping machinery manufacturing
334516 Elemental analyzers manufacturing
611110 Elementary and secondary schools
611110 Elementary schools
237310 Elevated highway construction
332323 Elevator guide rails, metal, manufacturing
238290 Elevator installation
423830 Elevators merchant wholesalers
333922 Elevators, farm, manufacturing
333921 Elevators, passenger and freight, manufacturing
112990 Elk production
325998 Embalming fluids manufacturing
812210 Embalming services
237990 Embankment construction
928120 Embassies
316110 Embossing leather
323120 Embossing plate preparation services
339940 Embossing stamps manufacturing
313310 Embossing textile products and fabrics
313220 Embroideries, Schiffli machine, manufacturing
314999 Embroidering contractors on apparel
314999 Embroidering on textile products or apparel for the trade
339930 Embroidery kits manufacturing

333249 Embroidery machinery manufacturing 424310 Embroidery products merchant wholesalers 313110 Embroidery spun yarns (e.g., cotton, manmade fiber, silk, wool) made from purchased fiber

313110 Embroidery thread (e.g., cotton, manmade fibers, silk, wool) manufacturing

335122 Emergency lighting (i.e., battery backup) manufacturing

621493 Emergency medical centers and clinics, freestanding

621910 Emergency medical transportation services, air or ground

922190 Emergency planning and management offices, government

453998 Emergency preparedness supply stores

624230 Emergency relief services 488410 Emergency road services (i.e., tow service) 624221 Emergency shelters (except for victims of domestic or international disasters or conflicts)

624230 Emergency shelters for victims of domestic or international disasters or conflicts

561421 Emergency telephone dispatch (i.e., contractor) services

212399 Emery mining and/or beneficiating

811198 Emissions testing without repair, automotive

541612 Employee assessment consulting services

541612 Employee benefit consulting services 525110 Employee benefit pension plans 525120 Employee benefit plans (except pension) 524292 Employee benefit plans, third party administrative processing services

485410 Employee bus services

541612 Employee compensation consulting services

621999 Employee drug testing services

561330 Employee leasing services 813930 Employees' associations for improvement of wages and working conditions

561311 Employment agencies

561311 Employment agencies, motion picture or video

561311 Employment agencies, radio or television

561311 Employment agencies, theatrical 561311 Employment placement agencies or services

561311 Employment referral agencies or services

561311 Employment registries

335932 EMTs (electrical metallic tube) manufacturing

112390 Emu production

325613 Emulsifiers (i.e., surface active agents) manufacturing

325510 Enamel paints manufacturing

212322 Enamel sand quarrying and/or beneficiating

332215 Enameled metal cutting utensils

332812 Enameling metals and metal products for the trade

333994 Enameling ovens manufacturing

424950 Enamels merchant wholesalers

339114 Enamels, dental, manufacturing

323120 Encyclopedia binding without printing

511130 Encyclopedia publishers (except exclusive Internet publishing)

511130 Encyclopedia publishers and printing combined

519130 Encyclopedia publishers, exclusively on Internet

323117 Encyclopedias printing and binding without publishing

323117 Encyclopedias printing without publishing

337124 End tables, metal, manufacturing

337122 End tables, wood, manufacturing

111219 Endive farming (except under cover), field, bedding plant and seed production

111419 Endive farming, grown under cover

325411 Endocrine products, uncompounded, manufacturing

424210 Endocrine substances merchant wholesalers

621210 Endodontists' offices (e.g., centers, clinics)

334510 Endoscopic equipment, electromedical (e.g., bronchoscopes, colonoscopes, cystoscopes), manufacturing

325320 Endrin insecticides manufacturing

624229 Energy assistance programs

541690 Energy consulting services

334512 Energy cutoff controls, residential and commercial types, manufacturing

926110 Energy development and conservation agencies, nonoperating

926130 Energy development and conservation programs, government

541350 Energy efficiency inspection services

334515 Energy measuring equipment, electrical, manufacturing

926110 Energy program administration 331318 Energy wire or cable made in aluminum wire drawing plants
331420 Energy wire or cable, copper, made from purchased copper in wire drawing plants
331491 Energy wire or cable, nonferrous metals (except aluminum, copper), made from purchased nonferrous metals (except aluminum, copper) in wire drawing plants
924110 Enforcement of environmental and pollution control regulations
336310 Engine block assemblies, automotive and truck gasoline, manufacturing
325998 Engine degreasers manufacturing
336310 Engine intake and exhaust valves manufacturing
811310 Engine repair (except automotive, small engine)
811111 Engine repair and replacement shops, automotive
811411 Engine repair, small
325998 Engine starting fluids manufacturing 423120 Engine testing equipment, motor vehicle, merchant wholesalers
541330 Engineering consulting services
541330 Engineering design services 541715 Engineering research and development laboratories or services (except nanotechnology research and development)
541330 Engineering services
238320 Engineering structure (e.g., oil storage tank, water tower) painting
813920 Engineers' associations
423490 Engineers' equipment and supplies merchant wholesalers
541330 Engineers' offices
541330 Engineers' private practices 336412 Engines and engine parts, aircraft (except carburetors, pistons, piston rings, valves), manufacturing
336310 Engines and parts (except diesel), automotive and truck, manufacturing
423860 Engines and parts, aircraft, merchant wholesalers
423120 Engines and parts, automotive, new, merchant wholesalers
423860 Engines and turbines, marine, merchant wholesalers
333618 Engines, diesel and semidiesel, manufacturing
333618 Engines, diesel locomotive, manufacturing
423830 Engines, internal combustion (except aircraft, automotive), merchant wholesalers
333618 Engines, internal combustion (except aircraft, nondiesel automotive), manufacturing
333618 Engines, natural gas, manufacturing
111219 English pea farming (except under cover), field, bedding plant and seed production
111419 English pea farming, grown under cover
332216 Engraver's handtools, nonpowered, manufacturing
339910 Engraving and etching precious metal flatware
339910 Engraving and etching precious metal jewelry
339910 Engraving and/or etching costume jewelry
423830 Engraving machinery merchant wholesalers
332812 Engraving metals and metal products (except printing plates) for the trade
323120 Engraving printing plate, for the printing trade
333316 Enlargers, photographic, manufacturing
315210 Ensemble dresses cut and sew apparel contractors
315190 Ensemble dresses made in apparel knitting mills
315240 Ensemble dresses, women's and girls', cut and sewn from purchased fabric (except apparel contractors)
711130 Ensembles, musical
926110 Enterprise development program administration
711410 Entertainers' agents or managers
711510 Entertainers, independent
519130 Entertainment sites, Internet
541715 Entomological research and development laboratories or services (except biotechnology and nanotechnology research and development)
115112 Entomological service, agricultural
541690 Entomology consulting services
333243 Envelope making machinery manufacturing
424110 Envelope paper, bulk, merchant wholesalers
333318 Envelope stuffing, sealing, and addressing machinery manufacturing
322230 Envelopes (i.e., mailing, stationery) made from any material
424120 Envelopes merchant wholesalers
813312 Environmental advocacy organizations

541620 Environmental consulting services
238210 Environmental control system installation
423830 Environmental controlling instruments and equipment merchant wholesalers
541330 Environmental engineering services
923120 Environmental health program administration
924110 Environmental protection program administration
541620 Environmental reclamation planning services
562910 Environmental remediation services
541715 Environmental research and development laboratories or services (except biotechnology and nanotechnology research and development)
541380 Environmental testing laboratories or services
325413 Enzyme and isoenzyme in-vitro diagnostic substances manufacturing
325199 Enzyme proteins (i.e., basic synthetic chemicals) (except pharmaceutical use) manufacturing
325411 Enzyme proteins (i.e., basic synthetic chemicals), pharmaceutical use, manufacturing
325130 Eosin dyes manufacturing
325411 Ephedrine and derivatives (i.e., basic chemicals) manufacturing
325211 Epichlorohydrin bisphenol manufacturing
325211 Epichlorohydrin diphenol manufacturing
325212 Epichlorohydrin elastomers manufacturing
325520 Epoxy adhesives manufacturing
238190 Epoxy application contractors
325510 Epoxy coatings made from purchased resins
325211 Epoxy resins manufacturing
923130 Equal employment opportunity offices
621340 Equestrian physical therapists' offices (e.g., centers, clinics)
115210 Equine boarding
522220 Equipment finance leasing 238910
Equipment rental (except crane), construction, with operator
531130 Equity real estate investment trusts (REITs), primarily leasing miniwarehouses and self-storage units
531120 Equity real estate investment trusts (REITs), primarily leasing nonresidential buildings (except miniwarehouses)
531190 Equity real estate investment trusts (REITs), primarily leasing real estate (except residential buildings and dwellings, nonresidential buildings, miniwarehouses, and self-storage units)
531110 Equity real estate investment trusts (REITs), primarily leasing residential buildings and dwellings
326299 Erasers, rubber or rubber and abrasive combined, manufacturing
238120 Erecting structural steel
238190 Erection and dismantling, poured concrete form
325411 Ergot alkaloids (i.e., basic chemicals) manufacturing
541330 Erosion control engineering services
238290 Escalator installation
333921 Escalators manufacturing
423830 Escalators merchant wholesalers
111219 Escarole farming (except under cover), field, bedding plant and seed production
111419 Escarole farming, grown under cover
812990 Escort services, social
523991 Escrow agencies (except real estate)
531390 Escrow agencies, real estate
325998 Essential oils manufacturing
424690 Essential oils merchant wholesalers
325199 Essential oils, synthetic, manufacturing
541990 Estate assessment (i.e., appraisal) services
541110 Estate law offices
325211 Ester gum manufacturing
325199 Esters, not specified elsewhere by process, manufacturing
812112 Esthetician (i.e., skin care) services
115310 Estimating timber
454110 E-tailers
333242 Etching equipment, semiconductor, manufacturing
332812 Etching metals and metal products (except printing plates) for the trade
325110 Ethane made from refined petroleum or liquid hydrocarbons
211130 Ethane recovered from oil and gas field gases
325193 Ethanol, nonpotable, manufacturing
813410 Ethnic associations
711510 Ethnic dancers, independent
711320 Ethnic festival managers without facilities

711320 Ethnic festival organizers without facilities
711310 Ethnic festival promoters with facilities
711320 Ethnic festival promoters without facilities
325194 Ethyl acetate, natural, manufacturing
325199 Ethyl acetate, synthetic, manufacturing
424820 Ethyl alcohol merchant wholesalers
325193 Ethyl alcohol, nonpotable, manufacturing
312140 Ethyl alcohol, potable, manufacturing
325199 Ethyl butyrate manufacturing
325199 Ethyl cellulose (except resins) manufacturing
325199 Ethyl chloride manufacturing
325199 Ethyl ether manufacturing
325199 Ethyl formate manufacturing
325199 Ethyl nitrite manufacturing
325199 Ethyl perhydrophenanthrene manufacturing
325110 Ethylbenzene made from refined petroleum or liquid hydrocarbons
325211 Ethylcellulose plastics manufacturing
325199 Ethylene glycol ether manufacturing
325199 Ethylene glycol manufacturing
325110 Ethylene made from refined petroleum or liquid hydrocarbons
324110 Ethylene made in petroleum refineries
325199 Ethylene oxide manufacturing
325212 Ethylene-propylene rubber manufacturing
325212 Ethylene-propylene-nonconjugated diene (EPDM) rubber manufacturing
325211 Ethylene-vinyl acetate resins manufacturing
325998 Eucalyptus oil manufacturing
311514 Evaporated milk manufacturing
334519 Evaporation meters manufacturing
333415 Evaporative condensers (i.e., heat transfer equipment) manufacturing
561920 Event and meeting planning services
611691 Exam preparation services
423810 Excavating machinery and equipment merchant wholesalers
213112 Excavating mud pits, slush pits, and cellars at oil and gas fields on a contract basis
238910 Excavating, earthmoving or land clearing, mining (except overburden removal at open pit mine sites or quarries)
238910 Excavating, earthmoving, or land clearing contractors
238910 Excavation contractors
333120 Excavators (e.g., power shovels) manufacturing
321999 Excelsior (e.g., pads, wrappers) manufacturing
423840 Excelsior (e.g., pads, wrappers) merchant wholesalers
523999 Exchange clearinghouses, commodities or securities
332410 Exchangers, heat, manufacturing
523210 Exchanges, commodity contracts
523210 Exchanges, securities
335312 Exciter assemblies, motor and generator, manufacturing
531210 Exclusive buyers' agencies
531210 Exclusive buyers' agents, offices of
487210 Excursion boat operation
921140 Executive and legislative office combinations
561110 Executive management services
921110 Executive offices, federal, state, and local (e.g., governor, mayor, president)
561312 Executive placement consulting services
561312 Executive placement services
561312 Executive search consulting services
561312 Executive search services
531120 Executive suites (i.e., full service office space provision)
811490 Exercise and athletic equipment repair and maintenance services without retailing new exercise and athletic equipment
713940 Exercise centers
532284 Exercise equipment rental
451110 Exercise equipment stores
339920 Exercise machines manufacturing
621340 Exercise physiologists' offices (e.g., centers, clinics)
336390 Exhaust and tail pipes, automotive, truck, and bus, manufacturing
333413 Exhaust fans, industrial and commercial-type, manufacturing
238220 Exhaust system (e.g., kitchens, industrial work areas) installation
811112 Exhaust system repair and replacement shops, automotive
336390 Exhaust systems and parts, automotive, truck, and bus, manufacturing
531120 Exhibition hall, no promotion of events, rental or leasing
624190 Ex-offender rehabilitation agencies
624190 Ex-offender self-help organizations

316110 Exotic leathers manufacturing

332312 Expansion joints, metal, manufacturing

541715 Experimental farms

213113 Exploration services for coal (except geophysical surveying and mapping) on a contract basis

213114 Exploration services for metal (except geophysical surveying and mapping) on a contract basis

213115 Exploration services for nonmetallic minerals (except geophysical surveying and mapping) on a contract basis

213112 Exploration services for oil and gas (except geophysical surveying and mapping) on a contract basis

424690 Explosives (except ammunition, fireworks) merchant wholesalers

325920 Explosives manufacturing

522293 Export trading companies (i.e., international trade financing)

522293 Export-Import banks 333316 Exposure meters, photographic, manufacturing

492110 Express delivery services (except establishments operating under a universal service obligation)

622310 Extended care hospitals (except mental, substance abuse)

335999 Extension cords made from purchased insulated wire

321999 Extension ladders, wood, manufacturing

321999 Extension planks, wood, manufacturing

238310 Exterior insulation finish system installation

321918 Exterior wood shutters manufacturing

325320 Exterminating chemical products (e.g., fungicides, insecticides, pesticides) manufacturing

561710 Exterminating services

423990 Extinguishers, fire, merchant wholesalers

333120 Extractors, piling, manufacturing

311920 Extracts, essences and preparations, coffee, manufacturing

311920 Extracts, essences and preparations, tea, manufacturing

311942 Extracts, food (except coffee, meat), manufacturing

311942 Extracts, malt, manufacturing 325194 Extracts, natural dyeing and tanning, manufacturing

326291 Extruded, molded or lathe-cut rubber goods manufacturing

333249 Extruding machinery for plastics and rubber manufacturing

333249 Extruding machinery for yarn manufacturing

333517 Extruding machines, metalworking, manufacturing

331318 Extrusion billet made by rolling purchased aluminum

331318 Extrusion billet, aluminum, made in integrated secondary smelting and rolling mills

333514 Extrusion dies for use with all materials manufacturing

331318 Extrusion ingot made by rolling purchased aluminum

331318 Extrusion ingot, aluminum, made in integrated secondary smelting and rolling mills

331313 Extrusion ingot, primary aluminum, manufacturing

325412 Eye and ear preparations manufacturing

621991 Eye banks

339112 Eye examining instruments and apparatus manufacturing

325620 Eye makeup (e.g., eye shadow, eyebrow pencil, mascara) manufacturing

622310 Eye, ear, nose, and throat hospitals

316998 Eyeglass cases, all materials, manufacturing

339115 Eyeglass frames (i.e., fronts and temples), ophthalmic, manufacturing

423460 Eyeglasses merchant wholesalers

315210 Eyelet making contractors on apparel

339993 Eyelets, metal, manufacturing

339115 Eyes, glass and plastics, manufacturing

313310 Fabric finishing

313310 Fabric mercerizing

451130 Fabric shops

325612 Fabric softeners manufacturing

424690 Fabric softeners merchant wholesalers

238310 Fabric wall system, noise insulating, installation

332312 Fabricated bar joists manufacturing

332996 Fabricated pipe and pipe fittings made from purchased pipe

332313 Fabricated plate work manufacturing

314994 Fabricated rope products (e.g., nets, slings) made in cordage or twine mills

332312 Fabricated structural metal manufacturing

321213 Fabricated structural wood members (except trusses) manufacturing

238390 Fabrication, metal cabinet or countertop, on site
313210 Fabrics (except rug, tire fabrics), broadwoven, weaving
314994 Fabrics for reinforcing rubber tires, industrial belting, and fuel cells manufacturing
313240 Fabrics, knit, made in warp or weft knit fabric mills
313240 Fabrics, lace, made in lace mills
313220 Fabrics, narrow woven, weaving
313230 Fabrics, nonwoven, manufacturing
424310 Fabrics, textile (except burlap, felt), merchant wholesalers
332618 Fabrics, woven wire, made from purchased wire
325620 Face creams (e.g., cleansing, moisturizing) manufacturing
335932 Face plates (i.e., outlet or switch covers) manufacturing
525990 Face-amount certificate funds
812112 Facial salons
424130 Facial tissue merchant wholesalers
322291 Facial tissues made from purchased paper
322121 Facial tissues made in paper mills
561210 Facilities (except computer operation) support services
541513 Facilities (i.e., clients' facilities) management and operation services, computer systems or data processing
541513 Facilities (i.e., clients' facilities) support services, computer systems or data processing
333517 Facing machines, metalworking, manufacturing
334210 Facsimile equipment, stand-alone, manufacturing
532420 Facsimile machine rental or leasing 811213 Facsimile machine repair and maintenance services
423690 Facsimile machines merchant wholesalers
325992 Facsimile toner cartridges manufacturing
522298 Factoring accounts receivable
236210 Factory construction
711310 Fair managers with facilities, agricultural
711320 Fair managers without facilities, agricultural
711310 Fair organizers with facilities, agricultural
711320 Fair organizers without facilities, agricultural
711310 Fair promoters with facilities
711310 Fair promoters with facilities, agricultural
711320 Fair promoters without facilities
711320 Fair promoters without facilities, agricultural
238190 Falsework construction
448140 Family clothing stores 621210 Family dentists' offices (e.g., centers, clinics)
713120 Family fun centers
541110 Family law offices
621111 Family physicians' offices (e.g., centers, clinics)
621410 Family planning centers
621410 Family planning counseling services
722511 Family restaurants, full service
722513 Family restaurants, limited-service
624190 Family social service agencies
624190 Family welfare services
326220 Fan belts, rubber or plastics, manufacturing
813410 Fan clubs
334512 Fan controls, temperature responsive, manufacturing
316110 Fancy leathers manufacturing
335210 Fans (except attic), household-type electric, manufacturing
336320 Fans, electric cooling, automotive, truck, and bus, manufacturing
335210 Fans, household-type kitchen, manufacturing
423620 Fans, household-type, merchant wholesalers
333413 Fans, industrial and commercial-type, manufacturing
423830 Fans, industrial, merchant wholesalers
423850 Fare boxes, public transit vehicle, merchant wholesalers
334514 Fare collection equipment manufacturing
311211 Farina (except breakfast food) made in flour mills
311230 Farina, breakfast cereal, manufacturing
236220 Farm building construction 332311 Farm buildings, prefabricated metal, manufacturing
321992 Farm buildings, prefabricated wood, manufacturing
237990 Farm drainage tile installation
532490 Farm equipment rental or leasing
813410 Farm granges

115115 Farm labor contractors 423820 Farm machinery and equipment merchant wholesalers
811310 Farm machinery and equipment repair and maintenance services
115116 Farm management services
522292 Farm mortgage lending 493130 Farm product warehousing and storage (except refrigerated)
493120 Farm product warehousing and storage, refrigerated
484220 Farm products hauling, local
484230 Farm products trucking, long-distance
332420 Farm storage tanks, heavy gauge metal, manufacturing
424910 Farm supplies merchant wholesalers
444220 Farm supply stores
532490 Farm tractor rental or leasing
333111 Farm tractors and attachments manufacturing
333111 Farm wagons manufacturing
813910 Farmers' associations
813910 Farmers' unions
****** Farming -- see type
531190 Farmland rental or leasing
333922 Farm-type conveyors manufacturing
115210 Farriers
112210 Farrow-to-finish operations
238170 Fascia and soffit installation
423330 Fascia, building (except wood), merchant wholesalers
541490 Fashion design services
541490 Fashion designer services
722513 Fast casual restaurants
423710 Fasteners (e.g., bolts, nuts, rivets, screws) merchant wholesalers
339993 Fasteners (e.g., glove, hook and eye, slide, snap) manufacturing
424310 Fasteners, clothing, merchant wholesalers
423610 Fastening devices, electrical, merchant wholesalers
722513 Fast-food restaurants
334511 Fathometers manufacturing 334519 Fatigue testing machines, industrial, mechanical, manufacturing
311611 Fats, animal (except poultry, small game), produced in slaughtering plants
311613 Fats, animal, rendering
112112 Fattening cattle
325199 Fatty acid esters and amines manufacturing
325199 Fatty acids (e.g., margaric, oleic, stearic) manufacturing
325199 Fatty alcohols manufacturing
327110 Faucet handles, vitreous china and earthenware, manufacturing
332913 Faucets, plumbing, manufacturing
532420 Fax machine rental or leasing
811213 Fax machine repair and maintenance services
339999 Feather dusters manufacturing
315210 Feather-filled clothing cut and sew apparel contractors
315240 Feather-filled clothing, jackets, and vests, women's, girls', and infants', cut and sewn from purchased fabric (except apparel contractors)
315220 Feather-filled clothing, men's and boys', cut and sewn from purchased fabric (except apparel contractors)
424590 Feathers merchant wholesalers
339999 Feathers, preparing (i.e., for use in apparel and textile products)
519110 Feature syndicates (i.e., advice columns, comic, news)
522294 Federal Agricultural Mortgage Corporation
926120 Federal Aviation Administration (except air traffic control)
922120 Federal Bureau of Investigation (FBI)
926130 Federal Communications Commission (FCC)
522130 Federal credit unions
522298 Federal Home Loan Banks (FHLB) 522294 Federal Home Loan Mortgage Corporation (FHLMC)
522294 Federal Intermediate Credit Bank
522292 Federal Land Banks 522294 Federal National Mortgage Association (FNMA)
922120 Federal police services
521110 Federal Reserve Banks or Branches
921130 Federal Reserve Board of Governors
522120 Federal savings and loan associations (S&L)
522120 Federal savings banks
813219 Federated charities
813930 Federation of workers, labor organizations
813930 Federations of labor

424910 Feed additives merchant wholesalers
316998 Feed bags for horses manufacturing
314910 Feed bags made from purchased woven or knitted materials
311119 Feed concentrates, animal, manufacturing
311514 Feed grade dry milk products manufacturing
311119 Feed premixes, animal, manufacturing
333111 Feed processing equipment, farm-type, manufacturing
444220 Feed stores (except pet)
453910 Feed stores, pet
311119 Feed supplements, animal (except cat, dog), manufacturing
311111 Feed supplements, dog and cat, manufacturing
112112 Feed yards (except stockyards for transportation), cattle
112111 Feeder calf production
112210 Feeder pig farming
335311 Feeder voltage regulators and boosters (i.e., electrical transformers) manufacturing
423820 Feeders, animal, merchant wholesalers
333131 Feeders, mineral beneficiating-type, manufacturing
112112 Feedlots (except stockyards for transportation), cattle
112210 Feedlots (except stockyards for transportation), hog
112410 Feedlots (except stockyards for transportation), lamb
424910 Feeds (except pet) merchant wholesalers
311111 Feeds, prepared for dog and cat, manufacturing
311119 Feeds, prepared, for animals (except cat, dog) manufacturing
311119 Feeds, specialty (e.g., guinea pig, mice, mink), manufacturing
212325 Feldspar mining and/or beneficiating 327992 Feldspar processing beyond beneficiation 424990 Felt merchant wholesalers 339940 Felt tip markers manufacturing 322121 Felts, asphalt, made in paper mills 313210 Felts, broadwoven, weaving 313230 Felts, nonwoven, manufacturing 331222 Fence gates, posts, and fittings, iron or steel, made in wire drawing plants
238990 Fence installation (except electronic containment fencing for pets)
331110 Fence posts, iron or steel, made in iron and steel mills
332323 Fences and gates (except wire), metal, manufacturing
423390 Fencing (except wood) merchant wholesalers
332618 Fencing and fence gates made from purchased wire
423390 Fencing and fencing accessories, wire, merchant wholesalers
238990 Fencing contractors (except electronic containment fencing for pets)
444190 Fencing dealers
339920 Fencing equipment (sporting goods) manufacturing
321999 Fencing, prefabricated sections, wood, manufacturing
321999 Fencing, wood (except rough pickets, poles, and rails), manufacturing
423310 Fencing, wood, merchant wholesalers
212299 Ferberite ores and concentrates mining and/or beneficiating
333249 Fermentation equipment, chemical, manufacturing
332420 Fermentation tanks, heavy gauge metal, manufacturing
424810 Fermented malt beverages merchant wholesalers
325180 Ferric chloride manufacturing
325180 Ferric oxide manufacturing
325130 Ferric oxide pigments manufacturing
333318 Ferris wheels manufacturing
212299 Ferroalloy ores (except vanadium) (e.g., chromium, columbium, molybdenum, tungsten) mining and/or beneficiating
331110 Ferroalloys manufacturing
423510 Ferroalloys merchant wholesalers
331110 Ferrochromium manufacturing
325180 Ferrocyanides manufacturing
331110 Ferromanganese manufacturing
331110 Ferromolybdenum manufacturing
331110 Ferrophosphorus manufacturing
331110 Ferrosilicon manufacturing
331110 Ferrotitanium manufacturing
331110 Ferrotungsten manufacturing
332111 Ferrous forgings made from purchased iron or steel, unfinished
331221 Ferrous metal powder, paste, and flake made from purchased iron or steel

423510 Ferrous metals merchant wholesalers

331110 Ferrovanadium manufacturing

483114 Ferry passenger transportation, Great Lakes (including St. Lawrence Seaway)

336611 Ferryboat building

621410 Fertility clinics

424910 Fertilizer and fertilizer materials merchant wholesalers

115112 Fertilizer application for crops

212393 Fertilizer minerals, natural, mining and/or beneficiating

325314 Fertilizers, mixed, made in plants not manufacturing fertilizer materials

325311 Fertilizers, mixed, made in plants producing nitrogenous fertilizer materials

325312 Fertilizers, mixed, made in plants producing phosphatic fertilizer materials

325311 Fertilizers, natural organic (except compost), manufacturing

325311 Fertilizers, of animal waste origin, manufacturing

325311 Fertilizers, of sewage origin, manufacturing

561730 Fertilizing lawns

333111 Fertilizing machinery, farm-type, manufacturing

111998 Fescue seed farming

711310 Festival managers with facilities

711320 Festival managers without facilities

711310 Festival of arts managers with facilities

711320 Festival of arts managers without facilities

711310 Festival of arts organizers with facilities

711320 Festival of arts organizers without facilities

711310 Festival of arts promoters with facilities

711320 Festival of arts promoters without facilities

711310 Festival organizers with facilities

711320 Festival organizers without facilities

711310 Festival promoters with facilities

711320 Festival promoters without facilities

325412 Fever remedy preparations manufacturing

522294 FHLMC (Federal Home Loan Mortgage Corporation)

322219 Fiber cans and drums (i.e., all-fiber, nonfiber ends of any material) made from purchased paperboard

424130 Fiber cans and drums merchant wholesalers

322219 Fiber drums made from purchased paperboard

337125 Fiber furniture (except upholstered), household-type, manufacturing

238210 Fiber optic cable (except transmission lines) installation

335921 Fiber optic cable made from purchased fiber optic strand

237130 Fiber optic cable transmission line construction

334417 Fiber optic connectors manufacturing

322219 Fiber spools, reels, blocks made from purchased paperboard

322219 Fiber tubes made from purchased paperboard

314999 Fiber, textile recovery from textile mill waste and rags

321219 Fiberboard manufacturing

423310 Fiberboard merchant wholesalers

423390 Fiberglass building materials (except insulation, roofing, siding) merchant wholesalers

424310 Fiberglass fabrics merchant wholesalers

313210 Fiberglass fabrics weaving

327993 Fiberglass insulation products manufacturing

313220 Fiberglasses, narrow woven, weaving

325220 Fibers and filaments, cellulosic, manufacturing and texturizing

325220 Fibers and filaments, noncellulosic, manufacturing and texturizing

335991 Fibers, carbon and graphite, manufacturing

327212 Fibers, glass, textile, made in glass making plants

424690 Fibers, manmade, merchant wholesalers

424590 Fibers, vegetable, merchant wholesalers

511130 Fiction book publishers (except exclusive Internet publishing)

511130 Fiction book publishers and printing combined

519130 Fiction book publishers, exclusively on Internet

323120 Fiction bookbinding without printing

323117 Fiction books printing and binding without publishing

323117 Fiction books printing without publishing

524126 Fidelity insurance carriers, direct

531390 Fiduciaries', real estate, offices

523991 Fiduciary agencies (except real estate)

332994 Field artillery manufacturing

315210 Field jackets, military, cut and sew apparel contractors

315220 Field jackets, military, men's and boys', cut and sewn from purchased fabric (except apparel contractors)
111421 Field nurseries (i.e., growing of flowers and shrubbery)
238140 Field stone (i.e., masonry) installation
334515 Field strength and intensity measuring equipment, electrical, manufacturing
336211 Fifth-wheel assemblies manufacturing
111339 Fig farming
711219 Figure skaters, independent
335110 Filaments for electric lamp bulbs manufacturing
111335 Filbert farming
115114 Filbert hulling and shelling 424120
File cards and folders merchant wholesalers
322230 File folders (e.g., accordion, expanding, hanging, manila) made from purchased paper and paperboard
333515 Files (i.e., a machine tool accessory) manufacturing
332216 Files, handheld, manufacturing 337214 Filing cabinets (except wood), office-type, manufacturing
337211 Filing cabinets, wood, office-type, manufacturing
333517 Filing machines, metalworking, manufacturing
212399 Fill dirt pits mining and/or beneficiating
424120 Filler paper, looseleaf, merchant wholesalers
325510 Fillers, wood (e.g., dry, liquid, paste), manufacturing
314999 Filling (except nonwoven textile), upholstery, manufacturing
311999 Fillings, cake or pie (except fruits, meat, vegetables), manufacturing
711510 Film actors, independent
519120 Film archives
541380 Film badge testing (i.e., radiation testing) laboratories or services
812921 Film developing and printing (except motion picture, one-hour)
812922 Film developing and printing, one-hour
333316 Film developing equipment manufacturing
423410 Film developing equipment merchant wholesalers
512120 Film distribution agencies
512120 Film distribution, motion picture and video
512131 Film festivals exhibitors 423410 Film finishing equipment merchant wholesalers
512120 Film libraries, commercial distribution
512199 Film libraries, motion picture or video, stock footage
512191 Film or tape closed captioning
512191 Film or video transfer services
512199 Film processing laboratories, motion picture
711510 Film producers, independent
512199 Film restoration services
512110 Film studios producing films
423410 Film, camera, merchant wholesalers
423410 Film, photographic, merchant wholesalers
326113 Film, plastics (except packaging), manufacturing
326112 Film, plastics, packaging, manufacturing
325992 Film, sensitized (e.g., camera, motion picture, X-ray), manufacturing 512110
Films, motion picture production 512110 Films, motion picture production and distribution
424130 Filter papers merchant wholesalers 327110
Filtering media, pottery, manufacturing 336390 Filters (e.g., air, engine oil, fuel) automotive, truck, and bus, manufacturing
333413 Filters, air-conditioner, manufacturing
334419 Filters, electronic component-type, manufacturing
333413 Filters, furnace, manufacturing
333999 Filters, industrial and general purpose-type (except internal combustion engine, warm air furnace), manufacturing
322299 Filters, paper, made from purchased paper
221310 Filtration plant, water
212322 Filtration sand quarrying and/or beneficiating
332993 Fin assemblies, mortar, manufacturing
332993 Fin assemblies, torpedo and bomb, manufacturing
522291 Finance companies (i.e., unsecured cash loans)
523140 Financial futures brokerages
551112 Financial holding companies
523930 Financial investment advice services, customized, fees paid by client

511120 Financial magazine and periodical publishers (except exclusive Internet publishing)
511120 Financial magazine and periodical publishers and printing combined
519130 Financial magazine and periodical publishers, exclusively on Internet
323111 Financial magazines and periodicals commercial printing (except screen) without publishing
323113 Financial magazines and periodicals screen printing without publishing
541611 Financial management consulting (except investment advice) services
523930 Financial planning services, customized, fees paid by client
522320 Financial transactions processing (except central bank)
521110 Financial transactions processing of the central bank
522220 Financing, sales
522294 Financing, secondary market
316998 Findings, boot and shoe, manufacturing
339910 Findings, jeweler's, manufacturing
315210 Findings, suit and coat (e.g., coat fronts, pockets), cut and sew apparel contractors
315990 Findings, suit and coat (e.g., coat fronts, pockets), cut and sewn from purchased fabric (except apparel contractors)
712110 Fine arts museums
611610 Fine arts schools (except academic)
722511 Fine dining restaurants, full service
424110 Fine paper, bulk, merchant wholesalers
114111 Finfish fishing (e.g., flounder, salmon, trout)
112511 Finfish production, farm raising
112511 Finfish, hatcheries
321213 Finger joint lumber manufacturing
561611 Fingerprint services
238350 Finish carpentry
314110 Finishing (e.g., dyeing) rugs and carpets
325613 Finishing agents, textile and leather, manufacturing
238310 Finishing drywall contractors
316110 Finishing hides and skins on a contract basis
316110 Finishing leather
333249 Finishing machinery for textile manufacturing
611110 Finishing schools, secondary
561621 Fire alarm monitoring services 561621 Fire alarm sales combined with installation, repair, or monitoring services
238210 Fire alarm system, electric, installation only
236220 Fire and flood restoration of commercial and institutional buildings
236118 Fire and flood restoration, multifamily building, general contractors
236118 Fire and flood restoration, single-family housing, general contractors
922160 Fire and rescue service
212325 Fire clay mining and/or beneficiating
922160 Fire departments (e.g., government, volunteer (except private))
334290 Fire detection and alarm systems manufacturing
334519 Fire detector systems, nonelectric, manufacturing
332321 Fire doors, metal, manufacturing
238190 Fire escape installation
332323 Fire escapes, metal, manufacturing
325998 Fire extinguisher chemical preparations manufacturing
238220 Fire extinguisher installation
238220 Fire extinguisher installation and repair
424690 Fire extinguisher preparations merchant wholesalers
811310 Fire extinguisher repair and maintenance, without installation
423990 Fire extinguisher sales combined with rental and/or service, merchant wholesalers
541990 Fire extinguisher testing and/or inspection, without sales, service, or installation
423990 Fire extinguishers merchant wholesalers
339999 Fire extinguishers, portable, manufacturing
611519 Fire fighter training schools
314999 Fire hose, textile, made from purchased materials
237110 Fire hydrant installation
332911 Fire hydrant valves manufacturing
423840 Fire hydrants merchant wholesalers
332911 Fire hydrants, complete, manufacturing
524126 Fire insurance carriers, direct
541380 Fire insurance underwriters' laboratories
524291 Fire investigators
922160 Fire marshals' offices
922160 Fire prevention offices, government

115310 Fire prevention, forest
325998 Fire retardant chemical preparations manufacturing
238220 Fire sprinkler system installation
236220 Fire station construction
423990 Firearms (except sporting) merchant wholesalers
813319 Firearms advocacy organizations
611699 Firearms training
332994 Firearms, small, manufacturing
423910 Firearms, sporting, merchant wholesalers
336611 Fireboat building
327120 Firebrick, clay refractories, manufacturing
315210 Firefighters' dress uniforms cut and sew apparel contractors
315220 Firefighters' dress uniforms, men's, cut and sewn from purchased fabric (except apparel contractors)
315240 Firefighters' dress uniforms, women's, cut and sewn from purchased fabric (except apparel contractors)
922160 Firefighting (except forest), government and volunteer (except private)
423850 Firefighting equipment and supplies merchant wholesalers
922160 Firefighting services (except forest and private)
561990 Firefighting services as a commercial activity
339113 Firefighting suits and accessories manufacturing
115310 Firefighting, forest
332999 Fireplace fixtures and equipment manufacturing
333414 Fireplace inserts (i.e., heat directing) manufacturing
423320 Fireplace linings merchant wholesalers
335129 Fireplace logs, electric, manufacturing
238140 Fireplace, masonry, installation
238220 Fireplace, natural gas, installation
423720 Fireplaces, gas, merchant wholesalers
423220 Fireplaces, prefabricated (except gas), merchant wholesalers
423720 Fireplaces, prefabricated gas, merchant wholesalers
238310 Fireproof flooring installation
238310 Fireproofing buildings
238310 Firestop contractors
321999 Firewood and fuel wood containing fuel binder manufacturing
454310 Firewood dealers, direct selling
423990 Firewood merchant wholesalers
713990 Fireworks display services
325998 Fireworks manufacturing
423920 Fireworks merchant wholesalers
453998 Fireworks shops (i.e., permanent location)
327110 Firing china for the trade
321920 Firkins and kits, wood, coopered, manufacturing
611699 First-aid instruction
424210 First-aid kits (except industrial) merchant wholesalers
423450 First-aid kits, industrial, merchant wholesalers
424210 First-aid supplies merchant wholesalers
339113 First-aid, snake bite, or burn kits manufacturing
424460 Fish (except canned, packaged frozen) merchant wholesalers
924120 Fish and game agencies
311710 Fish and marine animal oils processing
924120 Fish and wildlife conservation program administration
311710 Fish egg bait canning
112511 Fish farms, finfish
112512 Fish farms, shellfish
334511 Fish finders (i.e., sonar) manufacturing
311119 Fish food for feeding fish manufacturing
311710 Fish freezing (e.g., blocks, fillets, ready-to-serve products)
325411 Fish liver oils, medicinal, uncompounded, manufacturing
311710 Fish manufacturing
445220 Fish markets
311710 Fish meal processing
236210 Fish processing plant construction
332216 Fish wire (i.e., electrical wiring tool) manufacturing
424490 Fish, canned, merchant wholesalers
311710 Fish, curing, drying, pickling, salting, and smoking
424420 Fish, packaged frozen, merchant wholesalers
424460 Fish, salted or preserved (except canned), merchant wholesalers
424990 Fish, tropical, merchant wholesalers
541715 Fisheries research and development laboratories or services
114111 Fisheries, finfish

114112 Fisheries, shellfish
487210 Fishing boat charter operation
336611 Fishing boat, commercial, building
721214 Fishing camps with accommodation facilities
713990 Fishing clubs, recreational
423910 Fishing equipment and supplies (except commercial) merchant wholesalers
213112 Fishing for tools at oil and gas fields on a contract basis
713990 Fishing guide services
332215 Fishing knives manufacturing 314999 Fishing nets made from purchased materials
713990 Fishing piers
114210 Fishing preserves 451110 Fishing supply stores (e.g., bait)
339920 Fishing tackle and equipment (except lines, nets, seines) manufacturing
713940 Fitness centers
423910 Fitness equipment and supplies merchant wholesalers
713940 Fitness salons
713940 Fitness spas without accommodations
326122 Fittings and unions, rigid plastics pipe, manufacturing
423720 Fittings and valves, plumbers', merchant wholesalers
423610 Fittings, electrical, merchant wholesalers
423840 Fittings, industrial, merchant wholesalers
326122 Fittings, rigid plastics pipe, manufacturing
331511 Fittings, soil and pressure pipe, cast iron, manufacturing
713950 Five pin bowling centers
445299 Fix-and-freeze meal stores
488119 Fixed base operators
722515 Fixed location refreshment stands
325992 Fixers, prepared photographic, manufacturing
337920 Fixtures (e.g., poles, rods, rollers), curtain and drapery, manufacturing
423610 Fixtures, electric lighting, merchant wholesalers
423740 Fixtures, refrigerated, merchant wholesalers
423440 Fixtures, store (except refrigerated), merchant wholesalers
337215 Fixtures, store display, manufacturing
453998 Flag and banner shops
561990 Flagging (i.e., traffic control) services
238990 Flagpole installation 332323 Flagpoles, metal, manufacturing 321999 Flagpoles, wood, manufacturing 314999 Flags, textile (e.g., banners, bunting, emblems, pennants), made from purchased fabrics
212311 Flagstone mining or quarrying
327991 Flagstones cutting
321219 Flakeboard manufacturing
331221 Flakes made from purchased iron or steel
331314 Flakes, aluminum, made from purchased aluminum
331110 Flakes, iron or steel, made in iron and steel mills
334516 Flame photometers manufacturing
812332 Flame resistant clothing supply services
334512 Flame safety controls for furnaces and boilers manufacturing
332994 Flame throwers manufacturing
333517 Flange facing machines, metalworking, manufacturing
332991 Flange units, ball or roller bearing, manufacturing
332919 Flanges and flange unions, pipe, metal, manufacturing
315210 Flannel shirts cut and sew apparel contractors
315220 Flannel shirts, men's and boys', cut and sewn from purchased fabric (except apparel contractors)
315240 Flannel shirts, women's, girls', and infants', cut and sewn from purchased fabric (except apparel contractors)
313210 Flannels, broadwoven, weaving
325998 Flares manufacturing 333316 Flash apparatus, photographic, manufacturing
335110 Flash bulbs, photographic, manufacturing
238170 Flashing contractors 335912 Flashlight batteries, disposable, manufacturing
335110 Flashlight bulb manufacturing
335129 Flashlights manufacturing
423610 Flashlights merchant wholesalers
313240 Flat (i.e., warp) fabrics knitting
331221 Flat bright steel strip made in cold rolling mills made from purchased steel
327211 Flat glass (e.g., float, plate) manufacturing

423390 Flat glass merchant wholesalers
334118 Flat panel displays (i.e., complete units), computer peripheral equipment, manufacturing
332613 Flat springs (except clock, watch), light gauge, made from purchased wire or strip, manufacturing
332613 Flat springs, heavy gauge metal, manufacturing
336212 Flatbed trailers, commercial, manufacturing
484220 Flatbed trucking, local
484230 Flatbed trucking, long-distance
331110 Flats, iron or steel, made in iron and steel mills
321920 Flats, wood, greenhouse, manufacturing
423220 Flatware (except plated, precious) merchant wholesalers
332215 Flatware, nonprecious and precious plated metal, manufacturing
423940 Flatware, precious and plated, merchant wholesalers
311942 Flavor extracts (except coffee) manufacturing
311511 Flavored milk drinks manufacturing
312111 Flavored water manufacturing
311930 Flavoring concentrates (except coffee based) manufacturing
424490 Flavoring extracts (except for fountain use) merchant wholesalers
325199 Flavoring materials (i.e., basic synthetic chemicals such as coumarin) manufacturing
311930 Flavoring pastes, powders, and syrups for soft drink manufacturing
313110 Flax spun yarns made from purchased fiber
111120 Flaxseed farming, field and seed production
311225 Flaxseed oil made from purchased oils
311224 Flaxseed oil made in crushing mills
531190 Flea market space (except under roof) rental or leasing
531120 Flea market space, under roof, rental or leasing
454390 Flea markets, temporary location, direct selling
453310 Flea markets, used merchandise, permanent
325320 Flea powders or sprays manufacturing
532112 Fleet leasing, passenger vehicle
316110 Fleshers, leather (i.e., flesh side of split leather), manufacturing
334112 Flexible (i.e., floppy) magnetic disk drives manufacturing
332999 Flexible metal hose and tubing manufacturing
322220 Flexible packaging sheet materials made by coating or laminating purchased paper
322220 Flexible packaging sheet materials made by laminating purchased foil
326112 Flexible packaging, plastics film, manufacturing
334412 Flexible wiring boards, bare, manufacturing
325910 Flexographic inks manufacturing
323120 Flexographic plate preparation services
323111 Flexographic printing (except books, grey goods)
333244 Flexographic printing presses manufacturing
339920 Flies, artificial fishing, manufacturing
334511 Flight and navigation sensors, transmitters, and displays manufacturing
611519 Flight attendant schools
334511 Flight recorders (i.e., black boxes) manufacturing
333318 Flight simulation machinery manufacturing
611512 Flight simulation training
611512 Flight training schools
212325 Flint clay mining and/or beneficiating
327992 Flint processing beyond beneficiation
339999 Flints, lighter, manufacturing
321113 Flitches (i.e., veneer stock) made in sawmills
334512 Float controls, residential and commercial types, manufacturing
561990 Float decorating services
541490 Float design services
327120 Floaters, glasshouse, clay, manufacturing
713210 Floating casinos (i.e., gambling cruises, riverboat casinos)
332313 Floating covers, fabricated metal plate work, manufacturing
311710 Floating factory ships, seafood processing
332812 Flocking metals and metal products for the trade
237990 Flood control project construction
332312 Flood gates, metal plate, manufacturing
335129 Floodlights (i.e., lighting fixtures) manufacturing
237990 Floodway canal and ditch construction

321918 Floor baseboards, wood, manufacturing
442210 Floor covering stores (except wood or ceramic tile only)
444190 Floor covering stores, wood or ceramic tile only
423220 Floor coverings merchant wholesalers
326199 Floor coverings, linoleum, manufacturing
326199 Floor coverings, resilient, manufacturing
326199 Floor coverings, rubber, manufacturing
326199 Floor coverings, vinyl, manufacturing
332312 Floor jacks, metal, manufacturing
335121 Floor lamps (i.e., lighting fixtures), residential, manufacturing
238330 Floor laying, scraping, finishing and refinishing
423850 Floor maintenance equipment merchant wholesalers
326299 Floor mats (e.g., bath, door), rubber, manufacturing
325612 Floor polishes and waxes manufacturing
332312 Floor posts, adjustable metal, manufacturing
532490 Floor sanding machine rental or leasing
333318 Floor sanding, washing, and polishing machines, commercial-type, manufacturing
335210 Floor scrubbing and shampooing machines, household-type electric, manufacturing
335210 Floor standing fans, household-type electric, manufacturing
238330 Floor tile and sheets, installation only
327120 Floor tile, ceramic, manufacturing
321214 Floor trusses, wood, manufacturing
335210 Floor waxers and polishers, household-type electric, manufacturing
532490 Floor waxing equipment rental or leasing
332323 Flooring, open steel (i.e., grating), manufacturing
332322 Flooring, sheet metal (except stampings), manufacturing
321114 Flooring, wood block, treating
321918 Flooring, wood, manufacturing
423310 Flooring, wood, merchant wholesalers
334112 Floppy disk drives manufacturing
561422 Floral wire services (i.e., telemarketing services)
453110 Florists
327110 Florists' articles, red earthenware, manufacturing
424930 Florist's supplies merchant wholesalers
333131 Flotation machinery, mining-type, manufacturing
114111 Flounder fishing
314910 Flour bags made from purchased woven or knitted materials
424490 Flour merchant wholesalers
333241 Flour milling machinery manufacturing
311230 Flour mills, breakfast cereal, manufacturing
311211 Flour mills, cereals grains (except breakfast cereals, rice)
311211 Flour mixes made in flour mills
311824 Flour, blended or self-rising, made from purchased flour
311211 Flour, blended, prepared, or self-rising (except rice), made in flour mills
311213 Flour, malt, manufacturing
311212 Flour, rice, manufacturing
321999 Flour, wood, manufacturing
335314 Flow actuated electrical switches manufacturing
334513 Flow instruments, industrial process-type, manufacturing
327420 Flower boxes, plaster of paris, manufacturing
111421 Flower bulb growing
424910 Flower bulbs merchant wholesalers
111422 Flower growing
327110 Flower pots, red earthenware, manufacturing
111422 Flower seed production
453998 Flower shops, artificial or dried
453110 Flower shops, fresh
561920 Flower show managers
561920 Flower show organizers
561920 Flower show promoters
424930 Flowers merchant wholesalers
339999 Flowers, artificial (except glass, plastics), manufacturing
327120 Flue lining, clay, manufacturing
423320 Flue pipe and linings merchant wholesalers
332322 Flues, stove and furnace, sheet metal (except stampings), manufacturing
423830 Fluid meters, industrial, merchant wholesalers
332439 Fluid milk shipping containers, light gauge metal, manufacturing
311511 Fluid milk substitutes processing

333995 Fluid power actuators manufacturing
332912 Fluid power aircraft subassemblies manufacturing
333995 Fluid power cylinders manufacturing
332912 Fluid power hose assemblies manufacturing
333996 Fluid power motors manufacturing
333996 Fluid power pumps manufacturing
423830 Fluid power transmission equipment merchant wholesalers
332912 Fluid power valves and hose fittings manufacturing
334513 Fluidic devices, circuits, and systems for process control, manufacturing
332313 Flumes, fabricated metal plate work, manufacturing
332322 Flumes, sheet metal (except stampings), manufacturing
325180 Fluoboric acid manufacturing 335311 Fluorescent ballasts (i.e., transformers) manufacturing
325130 Fluorescent dyes manufacturing 335110 Fluorescent lamp electrodes, cold cathode, manufacturing
335110 Fluorescent lamp tubes, electric, manufacturing
335122 Fluorescent lighting fixtures, commercial, institutional, and industrial electric, manufacturing
335121 Fluorescent lighting fixtures, residential, manufacturing
335311 Fluorescent lighting transformers manufacturing
325120 Fluorinated hydrocarbon gases manufacturing
325180 Fluorine manufacturing
212393 Fluorite mining and/or beneficiating
325212 Fluoro rubbers manufacturing
325212 Fluorocarbon derivative rubbers manufacturing
325220 Fluorocarbon fibers and filaments manufacturing
325120 Fluorocarbon gases manufacturing
325211 Fluorohydrocarbon resins manufacturing
325211 Fluoro-polymer resins manufacturing
334517 Fluoroscopes manufacturing
334517 Fluoroscopic X-ray apparatus and tubes manufacturing
212393 Fluorspar mining and/or beneficiating
332999 Flush tanks, metal, manufacturing
332913 Flush valves, plumbing, manufacturing
332911 Flushing hydrant manufacturing
339992 Flutes and parts manufacturing
325998 Fluxes (e.g., brazing, galvanizing, soldering, welding) manufacturing
325320 Fly sprays manufacturing
339999 Fly swatters manufacturing 541870 Flyer direct distribution (except direct mail) services
713990 Flying clubs, recreational
488119 Flying field operators
611512 Flying instruction
335129 Flytraps, electrical, manufacturing
336310 Flywheels and ring gears, automotive and truck gasoline engine, manufacturing
515112 FM radio stations
522294 FNMA (Federal National Mortgage Association)
238310 Foam insulation installation
424130 Foam plastic trays merchant wholesalers
326150 Foam plastics products (except polystrene) manufacturing
326140 Foam polystyrene products manufacturing
424990 Foam rubber merchant wholesalers 424610 Foam, plastics, resins and shapes, merchant wholesalers
322220 Foil bags made from purchased foil
332999 Foil containers (except bags) manufacturing
332999 Foil not made in rolling mills 322220 Foil sheet, laminating purchased foil sheets for packaging applications
331315 Foil, aluminum, made by flat rolling purchased aluminum
331315 Foil, aluminum, made in integrated secondary smelting and flat rolling mills
331420 Foil, copper, made from purchased metal or scrap
331491 Foil, gold, made by rolling purchased metals or scrap
331491 Foil, nickel, made by rolling purchased metals or scrap
331491 Foil, silver, made by rolling purchased metals or scrap
424120 Folders, file, merchant wholesalers 561910 Folding and packaging services, textile and apparel

322130 Folding boxboard stock manufacturing
322212 Folding boxes (except corrugated) made from purchased paperboard
322212 Folding paper and paperboard containers (except corrugated) made from purchased paperboard
111422 Foliage growing
711120 Folk dance companies
711510 Folk dancers, independent
423430 Font cartridges merchant wholesalers
445110 Food (i.e., groceries) stores
446191 Food (i.e., health) supplement stores
336999 Food (vendor) carts on wheels manufacturing
424690 Food additives, chemical, merchant wholesalers
624210 Food banks
722330 Food carts, mobile 333241 Food choppers, grinders, mixers, and slicers (i.e., food manufacturing-type) manufacturing
311942 Food coloring, natural, manufacturing
325130 Food coloring, synthetic, manufacturing
722310 Food concession contractors (e.g., convention facilities, entertainment facilities, sporting facilities)
722330 Food concession stands, mobile
322299 Food containers made from molded pulp
326140 Food containers, polystyrene foam, manufacturing
322219 Food containers, sanitary (except folding), made from purchased paper or paperboard
322212 Food containers, sanitary, folding, made from purchased paperboard
333241 Food dehydrating equipment (except household-type) manufacturing
923130 Food distribution program administration, government
311942 Food extracts (except coffee, meat) manufacturing
926140 Food inspection agencies 811310 Food machinery repair and maintenance services
335210 Food mixers, household-type electric, manufacturing
333993 Food packaging machinery manufacturing
327213 Food packaging, glass, manufacturing
624210 Food pantries
423830 Food processing machinery and equipment merchant wholesalers
236210 Food processing plant construction 333241 Food product machinery manufacturing 541715 Food research and development laboratories or services (except biotechnology and nanotechnology research and development)
722310 Food service contractors, airline
722310 Food service contractors, cafeteria 722310 Food service contractors, concession operators (e.g., convention facilities, entertainment facilities, sporting facilities)
722310 Food service contractors, industrial
722310 Food service contractors, institutional
423440 Food service equipment (except refrigerated), commercial, merchant wholesalers
923120 Food service health inspections
326111 Food storage bags, plastics film, single wall or multiwall, manufacturing
541380 Food testing laboratories or services
322299 Food trays, molded pulp, manufacturing
333318 Food warming equipment, commercial-type, manufacturing
335220 Food waste disposal units, household-type, manufacturing
424410 Food, general-line, merchant wholesalers
311991 Food, prepared, perishable, packaged for individual resale
424420 Foods, prepared, packaged frozen, merchant wholesalers
339113 Foot appliances, orthopedic, manufacturing
621391 Foot specialists' (podiatry) offices (e.g., centers, clinics)
711211 Football clubs, professional or semiprofessional
713990 Football clubs, recreational
339920 Football equipment and supplies (except footwear, uniforms) manufacturing
423910 Football equipment and supplies merchant wholesalers
611620 Football instruction, camps, or schools
711211 Football teams, professional or semiprofessional
316210 Footholds, plastics or plastics soled fabric upper, manufacturing
316210 Footholds, rubber or rubber soled fabric upper, manufacturing
315110 Footies, sheer, knitting or knitting and finishing
238110 Footing and foundation concrete contractors

451110 Footwear (e.g., bowling, golf, spiked), specialty sports, stores
333249 Footwear making or repairing machinery manufacturing
424340 Footwear merchant wholesalers 326199
Footwear parts (e.g., heels, soles), plastics, manufacturing
326299 Footwear parts (e.g., heels, soles, soling strips), rubber, manufacturing
316210 Footwear, athletic, manufacturing
316210 Footwear, children's (except orthopedic extension), manufacturing
316210 Footwear, children's, leather or vinyl upper with rubber or plastics soles, manufacturing
316210 Footwear, men's (except orthopedic extension), manufacturing
316210 Footwear, men's leather or vinyl upper with rubber or plastics soles, manufacturing
316210 Footwear, plastics or plastics soled fabric uppers, manufacturing
316210 Footwear, women's (except orthopedic extension), manufacturing
316210 Footwear, women's leather or vinyl upper with rubber or plastics soles, manufacturing
339112 Forceps, surgical, manufacturing
523140 Foreign currency exchange brokering services
523130 Foreign currency exchange dealing (i.e., acting as a principal in dealing commodities to investors)
523130 Foreign currency exchange services (i.e., selling to the public)
928120 Foreign economic and social development services, government
928120 Foreign government service
611630 Foreign language schools
928120 Foreign missions
541380 Forensic (except medical) laboratories or services
621511 Forensic laboratories, medical
621111 Forensic pathologists' offices
531190 Forest land rental or leasing
115310 Forest management plans preparation
113210 Forest nurseries for reforestation, growing trees
423990 Forest products (except lumber) merchant wholesalers
484230 Forest products trucking, long-distance
115310 Forest thinning
423810 Forestry machinery and equipment merchant wholesalers
532412 Forestry machinery and equipment rental or leasing
811310 Forestry machinery and equipment repair and maintenance services
541715 Forestry research and development laboratories or services
115310 Forestry services
333517 Forging machinery and hammers manufacturing
332111 Forgings made from purchased iron or steel, unfinished
331110 Forgings, iron or steel, made in iron and steel mills
423510 Forgings, metal, merchant wholesalers
811310 Forklift repair and maintenance services
423830 Forklift trucks (except log) merchant wholesalers
333924 Forklifts manufacturing
332216 Forks, handtools (e.g., garden, hay, manure), manufacturing
332215 Forks, table, nonprecious and precious plated metal, manufacturing
331222 Form ties made in wire drawing plants
315210 Formal jackets cut and sew apparel contractors
315220 Formal jackets, men's and boys', cut and sewn from purchased fabric (except apparel contractors)
532281 Formal wear rental
325199 Formaldehyde manufacturing
325199 Formalin manufacturing
325199 Formic acid manufacturing
238190 Forming contractor
333517 Forming machines (except drawing), metalworking, manufacturing
327110 Forms for dipped rubber products, pottery, manufacturing
238190 Forms for poured concrete, erecting and dismantling
423420 Forms handling machines merchant wholesalers
332322 Forms, concrete, sheet metal (except stampings), manufacturing
321999 Forms, display, boot and shoe, all materials, manufacturing
424120 Forms, paper (e.g., business, office, sales), merchant wholesalers
236220 For-sale builders (i.e., building on own land, for sale), commercial and institutional building

236210 For-sale builders (i.e., building on own land, for sale), industrial building (except warehouses)
236117 For-sale builders (i.e., building on own land, for sale), residential
236117 For-sale builders (i.e., building on own land, for sale), single-family housing
312130 Fortified wines manufacturing
812990 Fortune-telling services
624110 Foster care placement agencies
624110 Foster home placement services
238140 Foundation (e.g., brick, block, stone), building, contractors
238390 Foundation dampproofing (including installing rigid foam insulation)
238910 Foundation digging (i.e., excavation)
238910 Foundation drilling contractors
315210 Foundation garments cut and sew apparel contractors
315240 Foundation garments, women's and girls', cut and sewn from purchased fabric (except apparel contractors)
238110 Foundation, building, poured concrete, contractors
238130 Foundation, building, wood, contractors
325620 Foundations (i.e., makeup) manufacturing
331529 Foundries (except die-casting), nonferrous metals (except aluminum)
331524 Foundries, aluminum (except die-casting)
331523 Foundries, die-casting, aluminum
331523 Foundries, die-casting, nonferrous metals
331511 Foundries, iron (i.e., ductile, gray, malleable, semisteel)
331513 Foundries, steel (except investment)
331512 Foundries, steel investment
333511 Foundry casting molds manufacturing
236210 Foundry construction
325998 Foundry core oil, wash, and wax manufacturing
332999 Foundry cores manufacturing
423830 Foundry machinery and equipment merchant wholesalers
811310 Foundry machinery and equipment repair and maintenance services
332999 Foundry pattern making
423510 Foundry products merchant wholesalers
212322 Foundry sand quarrying and/or beneficiating
424450 Fountain fruits and syrups (except soft drink) merchant wholesalers
335129 Fountain lighting fixtures manufacturing
339940 Fountain pens manufacturing
424450 Fountain syrups (except soft drink) merchant wholesalers
332999 Fountains (except drinking), metal, manufacturing
332999 Fountains, drinking (except mechanically refrigerated), metal, manufacturing
423720 Fountains, drinking (except refrigerated), merchant wholesalers
423740 Fountains, drinking, refrigerated, merchant wholesalers
327420 Fountains, plaster of paris, manufacturing
333415 Fountains, refrigerated drinking, manufacturing
713920 Four season ski resorts without accommodations
333243 Fourdrinier machinery manufacturing
332618 Fourdrinier wire cloth made from purchased wire
112930 Fox production
335312 Fractional horsepower electric motors manufacturing
333249 Fractionating equipment, chemical, manufacturing
211130 Fractionating natural gas liquids 333318
Frame and body alignment equipment, motor vehicle, manufacturing
332999 Frames and handles, handbag and luggage, metal, manufacturing
423220 Frames and pictures merchant wholesalers
339940 Frames for artist's canvases (i.e., stretchers) manufacturing
333249 Frames for textile making machinery manufacturing
332321 Frames, door and window, metal, manufacturing
321911 Frames, door and window, wood, manufacturing
332999 Frames, metal, lamp shade, manufacturing
332999 Frames, metal, umbrella and parasol, manufacturing
339999 Frames, mirror and picture, all materials, manufacturing
423460 Frames, ophthalmic, merchant wholesalers
238130 Framework, house, contractors
238130 Framing contractors
533110 Franchise agreements, leasing, selling or licensing, without providing other services

813410 Fraternal associations or lodges, social or civic
524113 Fraternal life insurance organizations
813410 Fraternal lodges
813410 Fraternal organizations
813410 Fraternities (except residential)
721310 Fraternity houses
621493 Freestanding ambulatory surgical centers and clinics
621498 Freestanding birth centers, outpatient
621493 Freestanding emergency medical centers and clinics
311423 Freeze-dried, food processing, fruits and vegetables
811310 Freezer, commercial, repair and maintenance services
335220 Freezers, chest and upright household-type, manufacturing
423740 Freezers, commercial-type, merchant wholesalers
423620 Freezers, household-type, merchant wholesalers
333415 Freezing equipment, industrial and commercial-type, manufacturing
311710 Freezing fish (e.g., blocks, fillets, ready-to-serve products)
488210 Freight car cleaning services
481112 Freight carriers (except air couriers), air, scheduled
481212 Freight charter services, air
488510 Freight forwarding
482111 Freight railways, line-haul
482112 Freight railways, short-line or beltline
541614 Freight rate auditor services
541614 Freight rate consulting services
483113 Freight shipping on the Great Lakes system (including St. Lawrence Seaway)
541614 Freight traffic consulting services
481212 Freight transportation, air, charter services
481212 Freight transportation, air, nonscheduled
483113 Freight transportation, deep sea, to and from domestic ports
483111 Freight transportation, deep sea, to or from foreign ports
483211 Freight transportation, inland waters (except on Great Lakes system)
311411 French fries, frozen, pre-cooked, manufacturing
311412 French toast, frozen, manufacturing
335312 Frequency converters (i.e., electric generators) manufacturing
334515 Frequency meters (e.g., electrical, electronic, mechanical) manufacturing
334515 Frequency synthesizers manufacturing
238310 Fresco (i.e., decorative plaster finishing) contractors
424460 Fresh fish merchant wholesalers
424480 Fresh fruits, vegetables, and berries merchant wholesalers
424470 Fresh meats merchant wholesalers
424440 Fresh poultry merchant wholesalers
424460 Fresh seafood merchant wholesalers
339992 Fretted instruments and parts manufacturing
313220 Fringes weaving
325510 Frit manufacturing
114119 Frog fishing
112519 Frog production, farm raising 331110
Frogs, iron or steel, made in iron and steel mills
811118 Front end alignment shops, automotive
423820 Frost protection machinery merchant wholesalers
311999 Frosting, prepared, manufacturing
311411 Frozen ades, drinks and cocktail mixes, manufacturing
311812 Frozen bread and bread-type rolls, made in commercial bakeries
311813 Frozen cake manufacturing
311411 Frozen citrus pulp manufacturing
311520 Frozen custard manufacturing
722515 Frozen custard stands, fixed location
311520 Frozen desserts (except bakery) manufacturing
311412 Frozen dinners (except seafood-based) manufacturing
311824 Frozen doughs made from purchased flour
424460 Frozen fish (except packaged) merchant wholesalers
454390 Frozen food and freezer meal plan providers, direct selling
326111 Frozen food bags, plastics film, single wall or multiwall, manufacturing
311412 Frozen food entrees (except seafood-based), packaged, manufacturing
424420 Frozen foods, packaged (except dairy products), merchant wholesalers
311411 Frozen fruit and vegetable processing

311411 Frozen fruits, fruit juices, and vegetables, manufacturing
311612 Frozen meat pies (i.e., tourtires) made from purchased carcasses
445210 Frozen meat stores
424470 Frozen meats (except packaged) merchant wholesalers
311412 Frozen pizza manufacturing
311412 Frozen pot pies manufacturing
424440 Frozen poultry (except packaged) merchant wholesalers
311412 Frozen rice dishes manufacturing
424460 Frozen seafood (except packaged) merchant wholesalers
311412 Frozen side dishes manufacturing
311412 Frozen soups (except seafood) manufacturing
311412 Frozen waffles manufacturing
424430 Frozen yogurt merchant wholesalers
111336 Fruit and tree nut combination farming
445230 Fruit and vegetable stands, permanent
311423 Fruit and vegetables, dehydrating, manufacturing
453220 Fruit basket or fruit bouquet stores (except exclusively by Internet)
321920 Fruit baskets, veneer and splint, manufacturing
311421 Fruit brining
311421 Fruit butters manufacturing
424450 Fruit concentrates, fountain, merchant wholesalers
321920 Fruit crates, wood, wirebound, manufacturing
312111 Fruit drinks (except juice), manufacturing
311942 Fruit extracts manufacturing
111419 Fruit farming, grown under cover
311211 Fruit flour, meal, and powders, manufacturing
333111 Fruit harvesting machines manufacturing
311421 Fruit juice canning
311411 Fruit juice concentrates, frozen, manufacturing
311421 Fruit juices, fresh, manufacturing
445230 Fruit markets
311340 Fruit peel products (e.g., candied, crystallized, glace, glazed) manufacturing
311421 Fruit pickling
311421 Fruit pie fillings, canning
311520 Fruit pops, frozen, manufacturing
115114 Fruit precooling
115114 Fruit sorting, grading, and packing
445230 Fruit stands, permanent
454390 Fruit stands, temporary
111421 Fruit stock (e.g., plants, seedlings, trees) growing
311930 Fruit syrups, flavoring, manufacturing
311991 Fruit, cut or peeled, fresh, manufacturing
115113 Fruit, machine harvesting
115114 Fruit, sun drying
115114 Fruit, vacuum cooling
311340 Fruits (e.g., candied, crystallized, glazed) manufacturing
326199 Fruits and vegetables, artificial, plastics, manufacturing
311423 Fruits dehydrating (except sun drying)
311421 Fruits pickling
339999 Fruits, artificial (except glass, plastics), manufacturing
327215 Fruits, artificial, made from purchased glass
327212 Fruits, artificial, made in glass making plants
311421 Fruits, canned, manufacturing
424490 Fruits, canned, merchant wholesalers
424480 Fruits, fresh, merchant wholesalers
311411 Fruits, frozen, manufacturing
424420 Fruits, frozen, merchant wholesalers
112320 Fryer chicken production
335210 Fryers, household-type electric, manufacturing
311351 Fudge, chocolate, made from cacao beans
311352 Fudge, chocolate, made from purchased chocolate
311340 Fudge, nonchocolate, manufacturing
424690 Fuel additives merchant wholesalers
326299 Fuel bladders, rubber, manufacturing
324199 Fuel briquettes or boulets made from refined petroleum
335999 Fuel cells, electrochemical generators, manufacturing
334413 Fuel cells, solid-state, manufacturing
334519 Fuel densitometers, aircraft engine, manufacturing
336310 Fuel injection systems and parts, automotive and truck gasoline engine, manufacturing

334519 Fuel mixture indicators, aircraft engine, manufacturing
454310 Fuel oil (i.e., heating) dealers, direct selling
424710 Fuel oil bulk stations and terminals, merchant wholesalers
238220 Fuel oil burner installation
424720 Fuel oil merchant wholesalers (except bulk stations, terminals)
424720 Fuel oil truck jobbers
324110 Fuel oils manufacturing 325180 Fuel propellants, solid inorganic, not specified elsewhere by process, manufacturing
325199 Fuel propellants, solid organic, not specified elsewhere by process, manufacturing
336320 Fuel pumps, electric, automotive, truck, and bus, manufacturing
336310 Fuel pumps, mechanical, automotive and truck gasoline engine, manufacturing
334519 Fuel system instruments, aircraft, manufacturing
334519 Fuel totalizers, aircraft engine, manufacturing
424720 Fuel, aircraft, merchant wholesalers (except bulk stations, terminals)
423520 Fuel, coal and coke, merchant wholesalers
424720 Fueling aircraft (except on contract basis), merchant wholesalers
488190 Fueling aircraft on a contract or fee basis
324110 Fuels, jet, manufacturing
531120 Full service office space provision
722511 Full service restaurants
423520 Fuller's earth merchant wholesalers
212325 Fuller's earth mining and/or beneficiating
327992 Fuller's earth processing beyond beneficiating
332313 Fumigating chambers, fabricated metal plate work, manufacturing
115114 Fumigating grain
561710 Fumigating services (except crop fumigating)
334515 Function generators manufacturing
561499 Fundraising campaign organization services on a contract or fee basis
334118 Funds transfer devices manufacturing
525110 Funds, employee benefit pension
525120 Funds, health and welfare
525990 Funds, mutual, closed-end
525910 Funds, mutual, open-ended
525110 Funds, pension
525190 Funds, self-insurance (except employee benefit funds)
812210 Funeral director services
423850 Funeral home supplies merchant wholesalers
812210 Funeral homes
812210 Funeral homes combined with crematories
524128 Funeral insurance carriers, direct
812210 Funeral parlors
325320 Fungicides manufacturing
424910 Fungicides, agricultural, merchant wholesalers
315280 Fur accessories and trimmings (except apparel contractors) manufacturing
315210 Fur accessories and trimmings cut and sew apparel contractors
315280 Fur apparel (e.g., capes, coats, hats, jackets, neckpieces) (except apparel contractors) manufacturing
315210 Fur apparel (e.g., capes, coats, hats, jackets, neckpieces) cut and sew apparel contractors
448190 Fur apparel stores
315280 Fur clothing (except apparel contractors) manufacturing
315210 Fur clothing cut and sew apparel contractors
424330 Fur clothing merchant wholesalers
423930 Fur cuttings and scraps merchant wholesalers
541490 Fur design services
315210 Fur finishers, liners, and buttonhole makers cut and sew apparel contractors
812320 Fur garment cleaning services
811490 Fur garment repair shops without retailing new fur garments
315280 Fur plates and trimmings (except apparel contractors) manufacturing
315210 Fur plates and trimmings cut and sew apparel contractors
532281 Fur rental
493120 Fur storage warehousing for the trade
316110 Fur stripping
112930 Fur-bearing animal production 236210 Furnace (i.e., industrial plant structure) construction
325180 Furnace black manufacturing

332322 Furnace casings, sheet metal (except stampings), manufacturing
238220 Furnace conversion (i.e., from one fuel to another)
333413 Furnace filters manufacturing
332322 Furnace flues, sheet metal (except stampings), manufacturing
238220 Furnace humidifier installation
238220 Furnace installation
238220 Furnace, forced air, installation
333414 Furnaces (except forced air), heating, manufacturing
423720 Furnaces (except forced air), heating, merchant wholesalers
333994 Furnaces and ovens for drying and redrying, industrial process-type, manufacturing
333994 Furnaces and ovens, semiconductor wafer, manufacturing
339114 Furnaces, dental laboratory, manufacturing
333414 Furnaces, floor and wall, manufacturing
333994 Furnaces, industrial and laboratory-type (except dental), manufacturing
423830 Furnaces, industrial process, merchant wholesalers
333415 Furnaces, warm air (i.e., forced air), manufacturing
423730 Furnaces, warm air (i.e., forced air), merchant wholesalers
424320 Furnishings (except shoes), men's and boys', merchant wholesalers
424330 Furnishings (except shoes), women's, girls', and infants', merchant wholesalers
448150 Furnishings stores, men's and boys'
448150 Furnishings stores, women's and girls'
423210 Furniture (except drafting tables, hospital beds, medical furniture) merchant wholesalers
337124 Furniture (except upholstered), metal household-type, manufacturing
337214 Furniture (except wood), office-type, padded, upholstered, or plain, manufacturing
337125 Furniture (except wood, metal, upholstered) indoor and outdoor household-type, manufacturing
532289 Furniture (i.e., residential) rental centers
442110 Furniture and appliance stores (i.e., primarily retailing furniture)
561740 Furniture cleaning on customers' premises
561740 Furniture cleaning services
423220 Furniture coverings and protectors merchant wholesalers
541420 Furniture design services
321912 Furniture dimension stock, hardwood, unfinished, manufacturing
321912 Furniture dimension stock, softwood, unfinished, manufacturing
321912 Furniture dimension stock, unfinished wood, manufacturing
337215 Furniture frames and parts, metal, manufacturing
337215 Furniture frames, wood, manufacturing
332510 Furniture hardware, metal, manufacturing
321999 Furniture inlays manufacturing
484210 Furniture moving, used
423210 Furniture parts merchant wholesalers
337215 Furniture parts, finished metal, manufacturing
337215 Furniture parts, finished plastics, manufacturing
337215 Furniture parts, finished wood, manufacturing
325612 Furniture polishes and waxes manufacturing
811420 Furniture refinishing shops
811420 Furniture repair shops
811420 Furniture reupholstering shops
332613 Furniture springs, light gauge, unassembled, made from purchased wire or strip
321912 Furniture squares, unfinished hardwood, manufacturing
442110 Furniture stores (e.g., household, office, outdoor)
453310 Furniture stores, used
327215 Furniture tops, glass (e.g., beveled, cut, polished), made from purchased glass
314999 Furniture trimmings made from purchased fabrics
327991 Furniture, cut stone (i.e., benches, tables, church), manufacturing
337127 Furniture, factory-type (e.g., cabinets, stools, tool stands, work benches), manufacturing
532283 Furniture, home health, rental
339113 Furniture, hospital, specialized (e.g., hospital beds, operating room furniture), manufacturing
337121 Furniture, household-type, upholstered on frames of any material, manufacturing
532490 Furniture, institutional (i.e. public building), rental or leasing

337127 Furniture, institutional, manufacturing
337127 Furniture, laboratory-type (e.g., benches, cabinets, stools, tables), manufacturing
532420 Furniture, office, rental or leasing
337211 Furniture, office-type, padded, upholstered, or plain wood, manufacturing
337124 Furniture, outdoor metal household-type (e.g., beach, garden, lawn, porch), manufacturing
337122 Furniture, outdoor wood household-type (e.g., beach, garden, lawn, porch), manufacturing
337127 Furniture, public building (e.g., church, library, school, theater), manufacturing
532289 Furniture, residential, rental or leasing
337127 Furniture, restaurant-type, manufacturing
337122 Furniture, unassembled or knock-down wood household-type, manufacturing
337122 Furniture, unfinished wood household-type, manufacturing
337122 Furniture, wood household-type, not upholstered (except TV and radio housings, and sewing machine cabinets), manufacturing
448190 Furriers
423850 Furriers equipment and supplies merchant wholesalers
332323 Furring channels, sheet metal, manufacturing
316110 Furs, dressed (e.g., bleached, curried, dyed, scraped, tanned), manufacturing
424990 Furs, dressed, merchant wholesalers
424590 Furs, raw, merchant wholesalers
335313 Fuse clips and blocks, electric, manufacturing
335931 Fuse cutouts manufacturing
335313 Fuse mountings, electric power, manufacturing
332993 Fuses ammunition (i.e., more than 30 mm., more than 1.18 inch) manufacturing
423610 Fuses, electric, merchant wholesalers
335313 Fuses, electrical, manufacturing
325194 Fustic wood extract manufacturing
337122 Futon frames manufacturing
337121 Futons with frames manufacturing
523140 Futures commodity contracts brokerages
523140 Futures commodity contracts brokers' offices
523130 Futures commodity contracts dealing (i.e., acting as a principal in dealing commodities to investors)
523210 Futures commodity contracts exchanges
212319 Gabbro crushed and broken stone mining and/or beneficiating
212311 Gabbro mining or quarrying
237990 Gabion construction
316210 Gaiters, plastics or plastics soled fabric upper, manufacturing
316210 Gaiters, rubber or rubber soled fabric upper, manufacturing
212230 Galena mining and/or beneficiating
712110 Galleries, art (except retail)
453920 Galleries, art, retail
713990 Galleries, shooting
316210 Galoshes, plastics or plastics soled fabric upper, manufacturing
316210 Galoshes, rubber, or rubber soled fabric upper, manufacturing
423510 Galvanized iron and steel products merchant wholesalers
238160 Galvanized iron roofing installation
333519 Galvanizing machinery manufacturing
331110 Galvanizing metals and metal formed products made in iron and steel mills
332812 Galvanizing metals and metal products for the trade
334515 Galvanometers (except geophysical) manufacturing
334519 Galvanometers, geophysical, manufacturing
325194 Gambier extract manufacturing
921130 Gambling control boards, nonoperating
713290 Gambling control boards, operating gambling activities
713210 Gambling cruises
713290 Gambling device arcades or parlors, coin-operated
713290 Gambling device concession operators (i.e., supplying and servicing in others' facilities), coin-operated
924120 Game and inland fish agencies
334614 Game cartridge software, mass reproducing
114210 Game preserves, commercial
114210 Game propagation
114210 Game retreats
713120 Game rooms (except gambling)
423430 Game software merchant wholesalers
924120 Game wardens
423920 Games (except coin-operated) merchant wholesalers

339930 Games (except coin-operated), children's and adult, manufacturing
339999 Games, coin-operated, manufacturing
423990 Games, coin-operated, merchant wholesalers
334614 Games, computer software, mass reproducing
511210 Games, computer software, publishing
423920 Gaming consoles merchant wholesalers
334517 Gamma-ray irradiation equipment manufacturing
212319 Ganister crushed and broken stone mining and/or beneficiating
236220 Garage and service station, commercial, construction
444190 Garage door dealers
335999 Garage door openers manufacturing 238290
Garage door, commercial- or industrial-type, installation
238350 Garage door, residential-type, installation
332321 Garage doors, metal, manufacturing
321911 Garage doors, wood, manufacturing
812930 Garages, automobile parking
811198 Garages, do-it-yourself automotive repair
811111 Garages, general automotive repair (except gasoline service stations)
332311 Garages, prefabricated metal, manufacturing
321992 Garages, prefabricated wood, manufacturing
332439 Garbage cans, light gauge metal, manufacturing
562111 Garbage collection services
562213 Garbage disposal combustors or incinerators
562212 Garbage disposal landfills
236210 Garbage disposal plant construction 333318
Garbage disposal units, commercial-type, manufacturing
423440 Garbage disposal units, commercial-type, merchant wholesalers
335220 Garbage disposal units, household-type, manufacturing
423620 Garbage disposal units, household-type, merchant wholesalers
562212 Garbage dumps
562111 Garbage hauling, local 333994 Garbage
incinerators (except precast concrete) manufacturing
327390 Garbage incinerators, precast concrete, manufacturing
562111 Garbage pick-up services
336211 Garbage truck bodies manufacturing
336120 Garbage trucks assembling on chassis of own manufacture
336211 Garbage trucks assembling on purchased chassis
111130 Garbanzo farming, dry, field and seed production
236116 Garden apartment construction general contractors
236117 Garden apartment for-sale builders
444220 Garden centers
813410 Garden clubs
811411 Garden equipment repair and maintenance services without retailing new garden equipment
327390 Garden furniture, precast concrete, manufacturing
327991 Garden furniture, stone, manufacturing
337122 Garden furniture, wood, manufacturing
326220 Garden hose, rubber or plastics, manufacturing
423820 Garden machinery and equipment merchant wholesalers
333112 Garden machinery and equipment, powered, manufacturing
561730 Garden maintenance services
541320 Garden planning services
327110 Garden pottery manufacturing
444210 Garden power equipment stores
424910 Garden supplies (e.g., fertilizers, pesticides) merchant wholesalers
811411 Garden tool sharpening and repair services
532490 Garden tractor rental or leasing
339999 Garden umbrellas manufacturing
712130 Gardens, zoological or botanical
111219 Garlic farming (except under cover), field, bedding plant and seed production 111419
Garlic farming, grown under cover 811490 Garment
alteration and/or repair shops without retailing new garments
812320 Garment cleaning (e.g., fur, leather, suede) services
321999 Garment hangers, wood, manufacturing
316110 Garment leather manufacturing
314910 Garment storage bags manufacturing
315280 Garments, leather or sheep-lined (except apparel contractors), manufacturing
315210 Garments, leather or sheep-lined, cut and sew apparel contractors

313320 Garments, oiling (i.e., waterproofing)
212399 Garnet mining and/or beneficiating
333249 Garnetting machinery for textiles manufacturing
314999 Garnetting of textile waste and rags
315210 Garter belts cut and sew apparel contractors
315240 Garter belts cut and sewn from purchased fabric (except apparel contractors)
315210 Garters cut and sew apparel contractors
315240 Garters, women's and girls', cut and sewn from purchased fabric (except apparel contractors)
334513 Gas analyzers, industrial process-type, manufacturing
334516 Gas analyzers, laboratory-type, manufacturing
334513 Gas and liquid analysis instruments, industrial process-type, manufacturing
334512 Gas burner automatic controls (except valves) manufacturing
333414 Gas burners, heating, manufacturing
334513 Gas chromatographic instruments, industrial process-type, manufacturing
334516 Gas chromatographic instruments, laboratory-type, manufacturing
423830 Gas detecting equipment and supplies (except household-type) merchant wholesalers
211130 Gas field development for own account
211130 Gas field exploration for own account
333414 Gas fireplaces manufacturing
423720 Gas fireplaces merchant wholesalers
238220 Gas fitting contractor
334513 Gas flow instrumentation, industrial process-type, manufacturing
333999 Gas generating machinery, general purpose-type, manufacturing
423720 Gas hot water heaters merchant wholesalers
334519 Gas leak detectors manufacturing
523999 Gas lease brokers' offices
335129 Gas lighting fixtures manufacturing
423990 Gas lighting fixtures merchant wholesalers
238220 Gas line installation, individual hookup, contractors
333249 Gas liquefying machinery manufacturing
237120 Gas main construction
339113 Gas masks manufacturing
561990 Gas meter reading services, contract
333318 Gas ranges, commercial-type, manufacturing
335220 Gas ranges, household-type, manufacturing
333999 Gas separating machinery manufacturing
333414 Gas space heaters manufacturing
332420 Gas storage tanks, heavy gauge metal, manufacturing
336390 Gas tanks assembled, automotive, truck, and bus, manufacturing
333611 Gas turbine generator set units manufacturing
333611 Gas turbines (except aircraft) manufacturing
336412 Gas turbines, aircraft, manufacturing
332911 Gas valves, industrial-type, manufacturing
333992 Gas welding equipment manufacturing
333992 Gas welding rods, coated or cored, manufacturing
213111 Gas well drilling on a contract basis
333132 Gas well machinery and equipment manufacturing
213112 Gas well rig building, repairing, and dismantling on a contract basis
213112 Gas, compressing natural, in the field on a contract basis
221210 Gas, manufactured, distribution
221210 Gas, mixed natural and manufactured, distribution
211130 Gas, natural liquefied petroleum, extraction
221210 Gas, natural, distribution
211130 Gas, natural, extraction
211130 Gas, natural, liquids, extraction
486210 Gas, natural, pipeline operation
211130 Gas, residue, extraction
424690 Gases, compressed and liquefied (except liquefied petroleum gas), merchant wholesalers
325120 Gases, industrial (i.e., compressed, liquefied, solid), manufacturing
211130 Gases, petroleum, liquefied, extraction
339991 Gasket, packing, and sealing devices manufacturing
339991 Gaskets manufacturing
423840 Gaskets merchant wholesalers 334514
Gasmeters, consumption registering, manufacturing
334514 Gasmeters, large capacity, domestic and industrial, manufacturing

424710 Gasohol bulk stations and terminals, merchant wholesalers
424720 Gasohol merchant wholesalers (except bulk stations, terminals)
333414 Gas-oil burners, combination, manufacturing
424710 Gasoline bulk stations and terminals, merchant wholesalers
334514 Gasoline dispensing meters (except pumps) manufacturing
336412 Gasoline engine parts (except carburetors, pistons, piston rings, valves), aircraft, manufacturing
336310 Gasoline engine parts, mechanical, automotive and truck, manufacturing
333618 Gasoline engines (except aircraft, automotive, truck) manufacturing
336310 Gasoline engines for hybrid automotive vehicles manufacturing
336412 Gasoline engines, aircraft, manufacturing
336310 Gasoline engines, automotive and truck, manufacturing
324110 Gasoline made in petroleum refineries
423120 Gasoline marketing equipment merchant wholesalers
333914 Gasoline measuring and dispensing pumps manufacturing
423120 Gasoline measuring and dispensing pumps merchant wholesalers
424720 Gasoline merchant wholesalers (except bulk stations, terminals)
486910 Gasoline pipeline transportation
238290 Gasoline pump, service station, installation
423120 Gasoline service station equipment merchant wholesalers
447110 Gasoline stations with convenience stores
447190 Gasoline stations without convenience stores
447110 Gasoline with convenience stores
211130 Gasoline, natural, production
313310 Gassing yarn (i.e., singeing)
621111 Gastroenterologists' offices (e.g., centers, clinics)
339112 Gastroscopes (except electromedical) manufacturing
334510 Gastroscopes, electromedical, manufacturing
333999 Gate and bridge lifting machinery manufacturing
423390 Gate and fence hardware merchant wholesalers
332911 Gate valves, industrial-type, manufacturing
332323 Gates, holding, sheet metal, manufacturing
332323 Gates, metal (except wire), manufacturing
237120 Gathering line, gas and oil field, construction
113210 Gathering of forest products (e.g., barks, gums, needles, seeds)
113210 Gathering, extracting, and selling tree seeds
332216 Gauge blocks, machinists' precision tools, manufacturing
334514 Gauges (e.g., oil pressure, water temperature, speedometer, tachometer), motor vehicle, manufacturing
334513 Gauges (i.e., analog, digital), industrial process-type, manufacturing
334514 Gauges for computing pressure-temperature corrections manufacturing
333314 Gauges, machinist's precision tool, optical, manufacturing
332216 Gauges, machinists' precision tools (except optical), manufacturing
424210 Gauze merchant wholesalers
339113 Gauze, surgical, made from purchased fabric
313210 Gauzes, surgical, made in broadwoven fabric mills
321999 Gavels, wood, manufacturing
333517 Gear cutting and finishing machines, metalworking, manufacturing
332216 Gear pullers, handtools, manufacturing
333517 Gear rolling machines, metalworking, manufacturing
333612 Gearmotors (i.e., power transmission equipment) manufacturing
336350 Gears (e.g., crown, pinion, spider), automotive, truck, and bus, manufacturing
423840 Gears merchant wholesalers 333612 Gears, power transmission (except aircraft, motor vehicle), manufacturing
112390 Geese production
311615 Geese, processing, fresh, frozen, canned, or cooked
311615 Geese, slaughtering and dressing
334519 Geiger counters manufacturing 325998 Gelatin (except dessert preparations) manufacturing
325998 Gelatin capsules, empty, manufacturing
311999 Gelatin dessert preparations manufacturing
311999 Gelatin for cooking manufacturing
424490 Gelatin, edible, merchant wholesalers

424690 Gelatin, inedible, merchant wholesalers
212399 Gem stone (e.g., amethyst, garnet, agate, ruby, sapphire, jade) mining and/or beneficiating
333249 Gem stone processing machinery manufacturing
448310 Gem stone shops, precious and semi-precious
423940 Gem stones merchant wholesalers 325414
Gene therapy preparations manufacturing 812990
Genealogical investigation services 921190 General accounting offices, government 811111 General automotive repair shops 112990 General combination animal farming 111998 General combination crop farming (except fruit and nut combinations, oilseed and
grain, vegetable)
926110 General economics statistical agencies
484110 General freight trucking, local 484122
General freight trucking, long-distance, less-than-truckload (LTL)
484121 General freight trucking, long-distance, truckload (TL)
541611 General management consulting services
622110 General medical and surgical hospitals
423990 General merchandise, durable goods, merchant wholesalers
424990 General merchandise, nondurable goods, merchant wholesalers
921190 General public administration
423830 General purpose industrial machinery and equipment merchant wholesalers
532310 General rental centers
921190 General services departments, government
452319 General stores
493110 General warehousing and storage
424210 General-line drugs merchant wholesalers
424410 General-line groceries merchant wholesalers
423840 General-line industrial supplies merchant wholesalers
423930 General-line scrap merchant wholesalers
336320 Generating apparatus and parts for internal combustion engines manufacturing
335312 Generating apparatus and parts, electrical (except internal combustion engine and welding), manufacturing
333992 Generating apparatus and parts, welding, electrical, manufacturing
335313 Generator control and metering panels, switchgear-type, manufacturing 532490
Generator rental or leasing 335312 Generator sets, prime mover (except
turbine generator sets), manufacturing
333611 Generator sets, turbine (e.g., gas, hydraulic, steam), manufacturing
335311 Generator voltage regulators, electric induction and step-type (except engine electrical equipment), manufacturing
335312 Generators and sets, electric (except internal combustion engine, welding, turbine generator sets), manufacturing
335312 Generators for gas-electric and oil-electric vehicles, manufacturing
336320 Generators for internal combustion engines manufacturing
335312 Generators for storage battery chargers (except internal combustion engine and aircraft) manufacturing
423610 Generators, electrical (except motor vehicle), merchant wholesalers
423120 Generators, motor vehicle electrical, new, merchant wholesalers
423140 Generators, motor vehicle electrical, used, merchant wholesalers
332994 Generators, smoke, manufacturing
334517 Generators, X-ray, manufacturing 621511
Genetic testing laboratories 541715 Genetics research and development laboratories or services (except biotechnology and nanotechnology
research and development)
541690 Geochemical consulting services
321992 Geodesic domes, prefabricated, wood, manufacturing
541370 Geodetic surveying services
541370 Geographic information system (GIS) base mapping services
541330 Geological engineering services 213112
Geological exploration (except surveying) for oil and gas on a contract basis
541715 Geological research and development laboratories or services (except nanotechnology research and development)
924120 Geological research program administration
541360 Geological surveying services
541330 Geophysical engineering services 213112
Geophysical exploration (except surveying) for oil and gas on a contract
basis
334519 Geophysical instruments manufacturing

541360 Geophysical mapping services
541360 Geophysical surveying services
541370 Geospatial mapping services
541380 Geotechnical testing laboratories or services
237110 Geothermal drilling
221116 Geothermal electric power generation
221330 Geothermal steam production
325199 Geraniol manufacturing
331492 Germanium recovering from scrap and/or alloying purchased metals
331410 Germanium refining, primary 335931
GFCI (ground fault circuit interrupters) manufacturing
711510 Ghost writers, independent
453220 Gift shops
453220 Gift stands, permanent location 322220
Gift wrap made from purchased materials 424120
Gift wrapping paper merchant wholesalers 561910
Gift wrapping services 212399 Gilsonite mining
and/or beneficiating 111219 Gingerroot farming
(except under cover), field, bedding plant and seed
production
111419 Gingerroot farming, grown under cover
115111 Ginning cotton
111219 Ginseng farming (except under cover), field, bedding plant and seed production
111419 Ginseng farming, grown under cover
113210 Ginseng gathering
327390 Girders and beams, prestressed concrete, manufacturing
327390 Girders, prestressed concrete, manufacturing
315190 Girdles and other foundation garments made in apparel knitting mills
315210 Girdles cut and sew apparel contractors
315240 Girdles, women's and girls', cut and sewn from purchased fabric (except apparel contractors)
813410 Girl guiding organizations
721214 Girls' camps (except day, instructional)
611620 Girls' camps, sports instruction 713990
Girls' day camps (except instructional) 315110
Girls' hosiery, sheer, full-length and knee-length,
knitting or knitting and finishing
315110 Girls' socks manufacturing
325411 Glandular derivatives, uncompounded, manufacturing
325412 Glandular medicinal preparations manufacturing
325612 Glass and tile cleaning preparations manufacturing
327215 Glass blanks for electric light bulbs made from purchased glass
327212 Glass blanks for electric light bulbs made in glass making plants
238140 Glass block laying
334290 Glass breakage detection and signaling devices
313210 Glass broadwoven fabrics weaving
238150 Glass cladding (i.e., curtain wall), installation
238150 Glass coating and tinting (except automotive) contractors
313220 Glass fabrics, narrow woven weaving
238310 Glass fiber insulation installation
327212 Glass fiber, optical, made in glass making plants
327212 Glass fiber, textile type, made in glass making plants
327212 Glass fiber, unsheathed, made in glass making plants
238150 Glass installation (except automotive) contractors
811122 Glass installation, automotive repair
327212 Glass making and blowing by hand
333249 Glass making machinery (e.g., blowing, forming, molding) manufacturing
327213 Glass packaging containers manufacturing
238150 Glass partitions, installation
327215 Glass products (except packaging containers) made from purchased glass
327212 Glass products (except packaging containers) made in a glass making plants
212322 Glass sand quarrying and/or beneficiating
423930 Glass scrap merchant wholesalers
811122 Glass shops, automotive
444190 Glass stores
811122 Glass tinting, automotive
238140 Glass unit (i.e., glass block) masonry
811122 Glass work, automotive
327215 Glass, automotive, made from purchased glass
327212 Glass, automotive, made in glass making plants
423120 Glass, automotive, merchant wholesalers
423390 Glass, block and brick, merchant wholesalers

327211 Glass, plate, made in glass making plants
423390 Glass, plate, merchant wholesalers
333314 Glasses, field or opera, manufacturing
423460 Glasses, optical, merchant wholesalers
327120 Glasshouse refractories manufacturing
322299 Glassine wrapping paper made from purchased paper
322121 Glassine wrapping paper made in paper mills
327215 Glassware for industrial, scientific, and technical use made from purchased glass
327212 Glassware for industrial, scientific, and technical use made in glass making plants
327215 Glassware for lighting fixtures made from purchased glass
327212 Glassware for lighting fixtures made in glass making plants
442299 Glassware stores
327215 Glassware, art decorative and novelty, made from purchased glass
327212 Glassware, art, decorative, and novelty made in glass making plants
327215 Glassware, cutting and engraving, made from purchased glass
423220 Glassware, household-type, merchant wholesalers
423450 Glassware, medical, merchant wholesalers
325180 Glauber's salt manufacturing
212391 Glauber's salt mining and/or beneficiating
325510 Glaziers' putty manufacturing
238150 Glazing contractors
315280 Glazing furs
332812 Glazing metals and metal products for the trade
334511 Glide slope instrumentation manufacturing
487990 Glider excursions
336411 Gliders (i.e., aircraft) manufacturing
334220 Global positioning system (GPS) equipment manufacturing
511130 Globe cover publishers
511130 Globe cover publishers and printing combined
323111 Globe covers and maps commercial printing (except screen) without publishing
323113 Globe covers and maps screen printing without publishing
332911 Globe valves, industrial-type, manufacturing
339999 Globes, geographical, manufacturing
316110 Glove leather manufacturing
315990 Glove linings (except fur) manufacturing
315280 Glove linings, fur (except apparel contractors), manufacturing
315210 Glove linings, fur, cut and sew apparel contractors
315210 Gloves and mittens (except athletic), leather, fabric, fur, or combinations, cut and sew apparel contractors
315990 Gloves and mittens (except athletic), leather, fabric, fur, or combinations, cut and sewn from purchased fabric (except apparel contractors)
315210 Gloves and mittens, woven or knit, cut and sew apparel contractors
315990 Gloves and mittens, woven or knit, cut and sewn from purchased fabric (except apparel contractors), manufacturing
315190 Gloves, knit, made in apparel knitting mills
315990 Gloves, leather (except athletic, cut and sewn apparel contractors), manufacturing
424320 Gloves, men's and boys', merchant wholesalers
326199 Gloves, plastics, manufacturing
339113 Gloves, rubber (e.g., electrician's, examination, household-type, surgeon's), manufacturing
339920 Gloves, sport and athletic (e.g., baseball, boxing, racketball, handball), manufacturing
424330 Gloves, women's, children's, and infants', merchant wholesalers
335110 Glow lamp bulbs manufacturing
339114 Glue, dental, manufacturing
325520 Glues (except dental) manufacturing
424690 Glues merchant wholesalers
311221 Gluten feed, flour, and meal, made by wet milling corn
311221 Gluten manufacturing
325611 Glycerin (i.e., glycerol), natural, manufacturing
325199 Glycerin (i.e., glycerol), synthetic, manufacturing
325411 Glycosides, uncompounded, manufacturing
212313 Gneiss crushed and broken stone mining and/or beneficiating
212311 Gneiss mining or quarrying
522294 GNMA (Government National Mortgage Association)
112420 Goat farming (e.g., meat, milk, mohair production)

424520 Goats merchant wholesalers
713990 Gocart raceways (i.e., amusement rides)
713990 Gocart tracks (i.e., amusement rides)
336999 Gocarts (except children's) manufacturing
423910 Gocarts merchant wholesalers
339930 Gocarts, children's, manufacturing
339115 Goggles (e.g., industrial, safety, sun, underwater) manufacturing
331491 Gold and gold alloy bar, sheet, strip, and tubing made from purchased metals or scrap
332813 Gold and silver plating metals and metal products for the trade
332999 Gold beating (i.e., foil, leaf)
331410 Gold bullion or dore bar produced at primary metal refineries
332999 Gold foil and leaf not made in rolling mills
331491 Gold foil made by rolling purchased metals or scrap
212221 Gold lode mining and/or beneficiating
212221 Gold ore mine site development for own account
212221 Gold ore mining and/or beneficiating plants
212221 Gold ores, concentrates, bullion, and/or precipitates mining and/or beneficiating
212221 Gold placer mining and/or beneficiating
325910 Gold printing inks manufacturing 331492
Gold recovering from scrap and/or alloying purchased metals
331410 Gold refining, primary
331491 Gold rolling and drawing purchased metals or scrap
323120 Gold stamping books for the trade
813410 Golden age clubs
112511 Goldfish production, farm raising
713910 Golf and country clubs
441228 Golf cart dealers, powered
532284 Golf cart rental
423910 Golf carts (except motorized passenger) merchant wholesalers
336999 Golf carts and similar motorized passenger carriers manufacturing
423860 Golf carts, motorized passenger, merchant wholesalers
336999 Golf carts, powered, manufacturing
237990 Golf course construction
541320 Golf course design services
713910 Golf courses (except miniature, pitch-n-putt)
713990 Golf courses, miniature
713990 Golf courses, pitch-n-putt
713990 Golf driving ranges
423910 Golf equipment and supplies merchant wholesalers
611620 Golf instruction, camps, or schools
713990 Golf practice ranges
451110 Golf pro shops
316210 Golf shoes, men's cleated, manufacturing
316210 Golf shoes, women's cleated, manufacturing
711219 Golfers, independent professional (i.e., participating in sports events)
339920 Golfing equipment (e.g., bags, balls, caddy carts, clubs, tees) manufacturing
335999 Gongs, electric, manufacturing
111334 Gooseberry farming
332216 Gouges, woodworking, manufacturing
445299 Gourmet food stores
561210 Government base facilities operation support services
522294 Government National Mortgage Association (GNMA)
522294 Government-sponsored enterprises providing secondary market financing
336310 Governors for automotive gasoline engines manufacturing
921110 Governors' offices
333618 Governors, diesel engine, manufacturing
333618 Governors, gasoline engine (except automotive), manufacturing
333611 Governors, steam, manufacturing
812331 Gown (e.g., doctors, nurses, hospital, beauticians) supply services
532281 Gown rental
315210 Gowns (e.g., academic, choir, clerical) cut and sew apparel contractors
315280 Gowns (e.g., academic, choir, clerical) cut and sewn from purchased fabric (except apparel contractors)
315210 Gowns, formal, cut and sew apparel contractors
315240 Gowns, formal, women's and girls', cut and sewn from purchased fabric (except apparel contractors)
315210 Gowns, hospital, surgical and patient, cut and sew apparel contractors
315280 Gowns, hospital, surgical and patient, cut and sewn from purchased fabric (except apparel contractors)

315210 Gowns, wedding, cut and sew apparel contractors
315240 Gowns, wedding, women's and girls', cut and sewn from purchased fabric (except apparel contractors)
334220 GPS (global positioning system) equipment manufacturing
333120 Grader attachments manufacturing
333120 Graders, road, manufacturing
238910 Grading construction sites
333241 Grading, cleaning, and sorting machinery (i.e., food manufacturing-type) manufacturing
333111 Grading, cleaning, and sorting machinery, farm-type, manufacturing
237310 Grading, highway, road, street and airport runway
334512 Gradual switches, pneumatic, manufacturing
532281 Graduation cap and gown rental 315210
Graduation caps and gowns cut and sew apparel contractors
315280 Graduation caps and gowns cut and sewn from purchased fabric (except apparel contractors)
311211 Graham flour manufacturing
311821 Graham wafers manufacturing
212399 Grahamite mining and/or beneficiating
312140 Grain alcohol, beverage, manufacturing
325193 Grain alcohol, nonpotable, manufacturing
236220 Grain bin construction
115114 Grain cleaning
333111 Grain drills manufacturing
115114 Grain drying
236220 Grain elevator construction
424510 Grain elevators merchant wholesalers
493130 Grain elevators, storage only
115114 Grain fumigation
115114 Grain grinding (except custom grinding for animal feed)
311119 Grain grinding, custom, for animal feed
484220 Grain hauling, local
484230 Grain hauling, long-distance
488210 Grain leveling and trimming in railroad cars
321999 Grain measures, wood, turned and shaped, manufacturing
424510 Grain merchant wholesalers
333241 Grain milling machinery manufacturing
311211 Grain mills (except animal feed, breakfast cereal, rice)
311119 Grain mills, animal feed
311230 Grain mills, breakfast cereal
311212 Grain mills, rice
333111 Grain stackers manufacturing
311230 Grain, breakfast cereal, manufacturing
312120 Grain, brewers' spent, manufacturing
115113 Grain, machine harvesting
327910 Grains, abrasive, natural and artificial, manufacturing
813410 Granges
212313 Granite beneficiating plants (e.g., grinding or pulverizing)
212313 Granite crushed and broken stone mining and/or beneficiating
212311 Granite mining or quarrying
238140 Granite, exterior, contractors
238340 Granite, interior, installation
311351 Granola bars and clusters, chocolate, made from cacao beans
311352 Granola bars and clusters, chocolate, made from purchased chocolate
311340 Granola bars and clusters, nonchocolate, manufacturing
311230 Granola, cereal (except bars and clusters), manufacturing
813211 Grantmaking foundations
311313 Granulated beet sugar manufacturing
311314 Granulated cane sugar manufacturing
333249 Granulator and pelletizer machinery for plastics manufacturing
212319 Granules, slate, mining and/or beneficiating
312130 Grape farming and making wine
111332 Grape farming without making wine
111320 Grapefruit groves
325998 Grapefruit oil manufacturing
311423 Grapes, artificially drying
541430 Graphic art and related design services
541430 Graphic artists, independent
325992 Graphic arts plates, sensitized, manufacturing
611519 Graphic arts schools
541430 Graphic design services
334515 Graphic recording meters, electric, manufacturing

335991 Graphite electrodes and contacts, electric, manufacturing
212399 Graphite mining and/or beneficiating
335991 Graphite specialties for aerospace use (except gaskets) manufacturing
335991 Graphite specialties for electrical use manufacturing
335991 Graphite specialties for mechanical use (except gaskets) manufacturing
327992 Graphite, natural (e.g., ground, pulverized, refined, blended), manufacturing
111940 Grass hay farming
333111 Grass mowing equipment (except lawn and garden) manufacturing
332216 Grass mowing equipment, nonpowered lawn and garden, manufacturing
333112 Grass mowing equipment, powered lawn and garden, manufacturing
111998 Grass seed farming 332323 Gratings (i.e., open steel flooring) manufacturing
333314 Gratings, diffraction, manufacturing
238910 Grave excavation contractors
484220 Gravel hauling, local
484230 Gravel hauling, long-distance
212321 Gravel quarrying and/or beneficiating
423320 Gravel, construction, merchant wholesalers
541360 Gravity geophysical surveying services
325910 Gravure inks manufacturing
323120 Gravure plate and cylinder preparation services
323111 Gravure printing (except books, grey goods)
333244 Gravure printing presses manufacturing
311422 Gravy canning
311942 Gravy mixes, dry, manufacturing
331511 Gray iron foundries
531190 Grazing land rental or leasing
311613 Grease rendering
339991 Grease seals manufacturing
562998 Grease trap cleaning
311225 Grease, inedible, animal and vegetable, refining and blending purchased oils
424990 Greases, inedible animal and vegetable, merchant wholesalers
324191 Greases, petroleum lubricating, made from refined petroleum
325998 Greases, synthetic lubricating, manufacturing
483113 Great Lakes freight transportation (including St. Lawrence Seaway)
483114 Great Lakes passenger transportation (including St. Lawrence Seaway)
111219 Green bean farming, field and seed production
111219 Green cowpea farming, field and seed production
111219 Green lima bean farming, field and seed production
111219 Green pea farming, field and seed production
332311 Greenhouses, prefabricated metal, manufacturing
212399 Greensand mining and/or beneficiating
212311 Greenstone mining or quarrying
511191 Greeting card publishers (except exclusive Internet publishing)
511191 Greeting card publishers and printing combined
519130 Greeting card publishers, exclusively on Internet
453220 Greeting card shops
323111 Greeting cards (e.g., birthday, holiday, sympathy) commercial printing (except screen) without publishing
323113 Greeting cards (e.g., birthday, holiday, sympathy) screen printing without publishing
424120 Greeting cards merchant wholesalers
332994 Grenade launchers manufacturing
332993 Grenades, hand or projectile, manufacturing
711212 Greyhound dog racetracks 335210 Griddles and grills, household-type portable electric, manufacturing
332618 Grilles and grillwork made from purchased wire
332323 Grills and grillwork, sheet metal, manufacturing
332323 Grillwork, ornamental metal, manufacturing
333991 Grinders, handheld power-driven, manufacturing
325411 Grinding and milling botanicals (i.e., for medicinal or dietary supplement use)
423510 Grinding balls merchant wholesalers 327910 Grinding balls, ceramic, manufacturing

333517 Grinding machines, metalworking, manufacturing
324191 Grinding oils, petroleum, made from refined petroleum
212399 Grinding pebbles mining and/or beneficiating
212322 Grinding sand quarrying and/or beneficiating
311942 Grinding spices
327910 Grinding wheels manufacturing
212399 Grindstones mining and/or beneficiating
326299 Grips and handles, rubber, manufacturing
311211 Grits and flakes, corn brewer's, manufacturing
212319 Grits crushed and broken stone mining and/or beneficiating
424410 Groceries, general-line, merchant wholesalers
322220 Grocers' bags and sacks made from purchased uncoated paper
326111 Grocery bags, plastics film, single wall or multiwall, manufacturing
333924 Grocery carts made from purchased wire
492210 Grocery delivery services (i.e., independent service from grocery store)
445110 Grocery stores
423840 Grommets merchant wholesalers
326299 Grommets, rubber, manufacturing
812910 Grooming services, animal
335931 Ground clamps (i.e., electric wiring devices) manufacturing
335931 Ground fault circuit interrupters (GFCI) manufacturing
335312 Ground Power Units (GPU) manufacturing
238910 Ground thawing for construction site digging
322122 Groundwood paper products (e.g., publication and printing paper, tablet stock, wallpaper base) made in newsprint mills
424110 Groundwood paper, bulk, merchant wholesalers
322121 Groundwood paper, coated, laminated, or treated in paper mills
322220 Groundwood paper, coated, made from purchased paper
322121 Groundwood paper, coated, made in paper mills
322122 Groundwood paper, newsprint, made in paper mills
322110 Groundwood pulp manufacturing
624410 Group day care centers, child or infant
623990 Group foster homes for children 623110
Group homes for the disabled with nursing care
623990 Group homes for the disabled without nursing care
623990 Group homes for the hearing impaired
623990 Group homes for the visually impaired
623210 Group homes, intellectual and developmental disability
621491 Group hospitalization plans providing health care services
524114 Group hospitalization plans without providing health care services
114111 Grouper fishing
238110 Grouting (i.e., reinforcing with concrete)
335122 Grow light fixtures (except residential) manufacturing
335121 Grow light fixtures, residential, electric, manufacturing
813910 Growers' associations
212393 Guano mining and/or beneficiating
111998 Guar farming
524127 Guaranteeing titles
561612 Guard dog services
812910 Guard dog training services
561612 Guard services
237310 Guardrail construction
332322 Guardrails, highway, sheet metal (except stampings), manufacturing
332323 Guards, bannisters, and railings, sheet metal, manufacturing
332618 Guards, wire, made from purchased wire
111339 Guava farming
721199 Guest houses
721214 Guest ranches with accommodation facilities
812910 Guide dog training services
713990 Guide services (i.e., fishing, hunting, tourist)
713990 Guide services, fishing
713990 Guide services, hunting
713990 Guide services, tourist
511130 Guide, street map, publishers (except exclusive Internet publishing)
511130 Guide, street map, publishers and printing combined
519130 Guide, street map, publishers, exclusively on Internet

336415 Guided missile and space vehicle engine manufacturing
541715 Guided missile and space vehicle engine research and development
336414 Guided missile and space vehicle manufacturing
336419 Guided missile and space vehicle parts (except engines) manufacturing
541715 Guided missile and space vehicle parts (except engines) research and development
423860 Guided missiles and space vehicles merchant wholesalers
336414 Guided missiles, complete, assembling
323111 Guides, street map, commercial printing (except screen) without publishing
323113 Guides, street map, screen printing without publishing
339992 Guitars and parts, electric and nonelectric, manufacturing
113210 Gum (i.e., forest product) gathering
325194 Gum and wood chemicals manufacturing
424690 Gum and wood chemicals merchant wholesalers
311340 Gum, chewing, manufacturing
424450 Gum, chewing, merchant wholesalers
322220 Gummed paper products (e.g., labels, sheets, tapes) made from purchased paper
424130 Gummed tapes (except cellophane) merchant wholesalers
424120 Gummed tapes, cellophane, merchant wholesalers
332994 Gun barrels manufacturing
332994 Gun cleaning kits manufacturing
325612 Gun cleaning preparations
713990 Gun clubs, recreational
813319 Gun control organizations
332111 Gun forgings made from purchased iron or steel, unfinished
331110 Gun forgings made in iron and steel mills
332994 Gun magazines manufacturing
811490 Gun repair and maintenance shops without retailing new guns
451110 Gun shops
333314 Gun sighting and fire control equipment and instruments, optical, manufacturing
333314 Gun sights, optical, manufacturing
332613 Gun springs, light gauge, made from purchased wire or strip, manufacturing
321912 Gun stock blanks manufacturing
332510 Gun trigger locks, metal, manufacturing
332994 Gun turrets manufacturing
238110 Gunite contractors
334413 Gunn effect devices manufacturing
238110 Gunning shotcrete
325920 Gunpowder manufacturing
423990 Guns (except sporting) merchant wholesalers
332994 Guns manufacturing
332994 Guns, BB and pellet, manufacturing
332216 Guns, caulking, nonpowered, manufacturing
423910 Guns, sporting equipment, merchant wholesalers
811490 Gunsmith shops without retailing new guns
238170 Gutter and downspout contractors
561790 Gutter cleaning services
423330 Gutters and down spouts (except wood) merchant wholesalers
332114 Gutters and down spouts sheet metal, custom roll formed, manufacturing
326199 Gutters and down spouts, plastics, manufacturing
238170 Gutters, seamless roof, formed and installed on site
332322 Gutters, sheet metal (except custom roll formed), manufacturing
339920 Gymnasium and playground equipment, manufacturing
423910 Gymnasium equipment merchant wholesalers
713940 Gymnasiums
611620 Gymnastics instruction, camps, or schools
713940 Gyms, physical fitness
339113 Gynecological supplies and appliances manufacturing
621111 Gynecologists' offices (e.g., centers, clinics)
212399 Gypsite mining and/or beneficiating
238310 Gypsum board installation
327420 Gypsum building products manufacturing
423390 Gypsum building products merchant wholesalers
212399 Gypsum mining and/or beneficiating
327420 Gypsum products (e.g., block, board, plaster, lath, rock, tile) manufacturing
327420 Gypsum statuary manufacturing
334511 Gyrocompasses manufacturing
334511 Gyrogimbals manufacturing
334511 Gyroscopes manufacturing

624310 Habilitation job counseling and training, vocational

114111 Haddock fishing

212299 Hafnium mining and/or beneficiating

424310 Hair accessories merchant wholesalers

326299 Hair care products (e.g., combs, curlers), rubber, manufacturing

424210 Hair care products merchant wholesalers

333111 Hair clippers for animal use, electric, manufacturing

332216 Hair clippers for animal use, nonelectric, manufacturing

335210 Hair clippers for human use, electric, manufacturing

332215 Hair clippers for human use, nonelectric, manufacturing

325620 Hair coloring preparations manufacturing

335210 Hair curlers, household-type electric, manufacturing

332999 Hair curlers, metal, manufacturing

333318 Hair dryers, beauty parlor-type, manufacturing

335210 Hair dryers, electric (except equipment designed for beauty parlor use), manufacturing

423620 Hair dryers, personal, merchant wholesalers

339999 Hair nets made from purchased netting

325620 Hair preparations (e.g., conditioners, dyes, rinses, shampoos) manufacturing

424210 Hair preparations (except professional) merchant wholesalers

423850 Hair preparations, professional, merchant wholesalers

812199 Hair removal (i.e., depilatory, electrolysis, laser, waxing) services

812199 Hair replacement services (except by offices of physicians)

325620 Hair sprays manufacturing

812112 Hair stylist salons or shops, unisex or women's

812111 Hair stylist services, men's

812112 Hair stylist services, unisex or women's

812111 Hair stylist shops, men's

812199 Hair weaving services

339994 Hairbrushes manufacturing

424990 Hairbrushes merchant wholesalers

812112 Hairdresser services

812112 Hairdressing salons or shops, unisex or women's

339999 Hairpieces (e.g., toupees, wigs, wiglets) manufacturing

424990 Hairpieces (e.g., toupees, wigs, wiglets) merchant wholesalers

339993 Hairpins (except rubber) manufacturing

326299 Hairpins, rubber, manufacturing 332613

Hairsprings (except clock, watch), light gauge, made from purchased wire or strip, manufacturing

114111 Hake fishing

623990 Halfway group homes for delinquents and ex-offenders

623220 Halfway houses for patients with mental health illnesses

623220 Halfway houses, substance abuse (e.g., alcoholism, drug addiction)

114111 Halibut fishing

531120 Hall and banquet room, nonresidential, rental or leasing

334413 Hall effect devices manufacturing

531120 Hall, nonresidential, rental or leasing

712110 Halls of fame

335110 Halogen light bulbs manufacturing

325194 Halogenated aromatic hydrocarbon derivatives manufacturing

325199 Halogenated hydrocarbon derivatives (except aromatic) manufacturing

311340 Halvah manufacturing

332111 Hammer forgings made from purchased iron or steel, unfinished

332112 Hammer forgings made from purchased nonferrous metals, unfinished

333120 Hammer mill machinery (i.e., rock and ore crushing machines), portable, manufacturing

333131 Hammer mill machinery (i.e., rock and ore crushing machines), stationary, manufacturing

332216 Hammers, handtools, manufacturing

339992 Hammers, piano, manufacturing

321999 Hammers, wood, meat, manufacturing

314999 Hammocks, fabric, manufacturing

337124 Hammocks, metal framed, manufacturing

337122 Hammocks, wood framed, manufacturing

326199 Hampers, laundry, plastics, manufacturing

337125 Hampers, laundry, reed, wicker, rattan, manufacturing

332322 Hampers, laundry, sheet metal (except stampings), manufacturing

311611 Hams (except poultry) produced in slaughtering plants

311612 Hams, canned, made from purchased carcasses
311615 Hams, poultry, manufacturing
311612 Hams, preserved (except poultry), made from purchased carcasses
327215 Hand blowing purchased glass
313240 Hand knitting lace or warp fabric products
812320 Hand laundries
325620 Hand lotions manufacturing
339940 Hand operated stamps (e.g., canceling, postmark, shoe, textile marking) manufacturing
325611 Hand soaps (e.g., hard, liquid, soft) manufacturing
334519 Hand stamps (e.g., date, time), timing mechanism operated, manufacturing
333924 Hand trucks manufacturing
313220 Hand weaving fabric, 12 inches or less (30cm)
313210 Hand weaving fabrics, more than 12 inches (30 cm) in width
316110 Handbag leather manufacturing
448150 Handbag stores
316998 Handbags (except metal), men's, manufacturing
424330 Handbags merchant wholesalers
339910 Handbags, precious metal, manufacturing
316992 Handbags, women's, all materials (except precious metal), manufacturing
713940 Handball club facilities
541870 Handbill direct distribution services
332999 Handcuffs manufacturing
332216 Handheld edge tools (except scissors-type), nonelectric, manufacturing
485991 Handicapped passenger transportation services
611110 Handicapped, schools for, elementary or secondary
611610 Handicrafts instruction
315210 Handkerchiefs (except paper) cut and sew apparel contractors
315990 Handkerchiefs (except paper) cut and sewn from purchased fabric
322291 Handkerchiefs, paper, made from purchased paper
321912 Handle blanks, wood, manufacturing
321912 Handle stock, sawed or planed, manufacturing
321999 Handles (e.g., broom, mop, handtool), wood, manufacturing
424990 Handles (e.g., broom, mop, paint) merchant wholesalers
326199 Handles (e.g., brush, tool, umbrella), plastics, manufacturing
316998 Handles (e.g., luggage, whip), leather, manufacturing
332999 Handles (e.g., parasol, umbrella), metal, manufacturing
327110 Handles, faucet, vitreous china and earthenware, manufacturing
541420 Handtool industrial design services
332216 Handtool metal blades (e.g., putty knives, scrapers, screw drivers) manufacturing
423710 Handtools (except motor vehicle mechanics', machinists' precision) merchant wholesalers
332216 Handtools, machinists' precision, manufacturing
423830 Handtools, machinists' precision, merchant wholesalers
332216 Handtools, motor vehicle mechanics', manufacturing
423120 Handtools, motor vehicle mechanics', merchant wholesalers
333991 Handtools, power-driven, manufacturing
444130 Handtools, power-driven, repair and maintenance services retailing new power-driven handtools
811411 Handtools, power-driven, repair and maintenance services without retailing new power-driven handtools
541990 Handwriting analysis services
541990 Handwriting expert services
236220 Handyman construction service, commercial and institutional building
236118 Handyman construction service, residential building
336411 Hang gliders manufacturing
236220 Hangar construction
332321 Hangar doors, metal, manufacturing
488119 Hangar rental, aircraft
321999 Hangers, wooden, garment, manufacturing
111422 Hanging basket plant growing
423610 Hanging devices, electrical, merchant wholesalers
237990 Harbor construction
488310 Harbor maintenance services (except dredging)
488310 Harbor operation
487210 Harbor sightseeing tours
488330 Harbor tugboat services

213112 Hard banding oil and gas field service on a contract basis
311340 Hard candies manufacturing
424820 Hard cider merchant wholesalers
212113 Hard coal (i.e., anthracite) surface mining
212113 Hard coal (i.e., anthracite) underground mining
334112 Hard disk drives manufacturing
334613 Hard drive media manufacturing
313210 Hard fiber fabrics, broadwoven, weaving
313110 Hard fiber spun yarns made from purchased fiber
313110 Hard fiber thread manufacturing
313220 Hard fiber, narrow woven, weaving
339113 Hard hats manufacturing
321219 Hardboard manufacturing
332811 Hardening (i.e., heat treating) metals and metal products for the trade
334519 Hardness testing equipment manufacturing
423710 Hardware (except motor vehicle) merchant wholesalers
332618 Hardware cloth, woven wire, made from purchased wire
444130 Hardware stores
423120 Hardware, motor vehicle, merchant wholesalers
326199 Hardware, plastics, manufacturing
335932 Hardware, transmission pole and line, manufacturing
423610 Hardware, transmission pole and line, merchant wholesalers
321912 Hardwood dimension lumber and stock, resawing purchased lumber
325194 Hardwood distillates manufacturing
444190 Hardwood flooring dealers
238330 Hardwood flooring, installation only
321211 Hardwood plywood composites manufacturing
321211 Hardwood veneer or plywood manufacturing
339992 Harmonicas manufacturing
334419 Harness assemblies for electronic use manufacturing
711219 Harness drivers
424910 Harness equipment merchant wholesalers
316110 Harness leather manufacturing
332999 Harness parts, metal, manufacturing
711212 Harness racetracks
316998 Harnesses and harness parts, leather, manufacturing
316998 Harnesses, dog, manufacturing
339992 Harps and parts manufacturing
339992 Harpsichords manufacturing
333111 Harrows (e.g., disc, spring, tine) manufacturing
315990 Harvest hats, straw, manufacturing 113210
Harvesting berries or nuts from native and non-cultivated plants
333111 Harvesting machinery and equipment, agriculture, manufacturing
423820 Harvesting machinery and equipment, agriculture, merchant wholesalers 335210
Hassock fans, electric, manufacturing 424310 Hat
and cap materials merchant wholesalers
448150 Hat and cap stores
339999 Hat blocks manufacturing 315210 Hat bod-
ies (e.g., fur-felt, straw, wool-felt) cut and sew apparel contractors
315990 Hat bodies (e.g., fur-felt, straw, wool-felt) cut and sewn from purchased fabric (except apparel contractors)
812320 Hat cleaning services
315210 Hat findings cut and sew apparel contractors
315990 Hat findings cut and sewn from purchased fabric (except apparel contractors)
315210 Hat linings and trimmings cut and sew apparel contractors
315990 Hat linings and trimmings cut and sewn from purchased fabric (except apparel contractors)
112511 Hatcheries, finfish
112340 Hatcheries, poultry
112512 Hatcheries, shellfish
236220 Hatchery construction
332216 Hatchets manufacturing
315210 Hats (e.g., cloth, fur, fur-felt, leather, straw, wool-felt) cut and sew apparel contractors
315990 Hats (except fur, knitting mill products, leather) cut and sewn from purchased fabric (except apparel contractors)
424320 Hats and caps, men's and boys', merchant wholesalers
424330 Hats and caps, women's, girls', and infants', merchant wholesalers
322299 Hats made from purchased paper
315190 Hats made in apparel knitting mills

315990 Hats, cloth, cut and sewn from purchased fabric (except apparel contractors)
315280 Hats, fur (except apparel contractors), manufacturing
315990 Hats, fur-felt, straw, and wool-felt, cut and sewn from purchased fabric (except apparel contractors)
315280 Hats, leather (except apparel contractors), manufacturing
315210 Hats, trimmed, cut and sew apparel contractors
315990 Hats, trimmed, cut and sewn from purchased fabric (except apparel contractors)
333111 Hay balers and presses manufacturing
111940 Hay farming (e.g., alfalfa hay, clover hay, grass hay)
424910 Hay merchant wholesalers
115113 Hay mowing, raking, baling, and chopping
111998 Hay seed farming
311119 Hay, cubed, manufacturing
333111 Haying machines manufacturing
423820 Haying machines merchant wholesalers
562910 Hazardous material storage tank removal and disposal services
562112 Hazardous waste collection services
562211 Hazardous waste disposal facilities
562211 Hazardous waste disposal facilities combined with collection and/or local hauling of hazardous waste
562211 Hazardous waste material disposal facilities
562211 Hazardous waste material treatment facilities
562211 Hazardous waste treatment facilities
562211 Hazardous waste treatment facilities combined with collection and/or local hauling of hazardous waste
111335 Hazelnut farming
334613 Head cleaners for magnetic tape equipment, manufacturing
551114 Head offices
311212 Head rice manufacturing
624410 Head start programs, separate from schools
315210 Headbands cut and sew apparel contractors
315990 Headbands, women's and girls', cut and sewn from purchased fabric (except apparel contractors)
337122 Headboards, wood, manufacturing
321920 Heading, barrel (i.e., cooperage stock), wood, manufacturing
551114 Headquarters offices
334419 Heads (e.g., recording, read/write) manufacturing
334511 Heads-up display (HUD) systems, aeronautical, manufacturing
236220 Health and athletic club construction
525120 Health and welfare funds
713940 Health club facilities, physical fitness
424490 Health foods (except fresh fruits, vegetables) merchant wholesalers
424480 Health foods, fresh fruits and vegetables, merchant wholesalers
524114 Health insurance carriers, direct
335110 Health lamp bulbs, infrared and ultraviolet radiation, manufacturing
621491 Health maintenance organization (HMO) medical centers and clinics
923120 Health planning and development agencies, government
813920 Health professionals' associations
926150 Health professions licensure agencies
923120 Health program administration
541715 Health research and development laboratories or services (except biotechnology and nanotechnology research and development)
813212 Health research fundraising organizations
621999 Health screening services (except by offices of health practitioners)
621111 Health screening services in physicians' offices
721110 Health spas (i.e., physical fitness facilities) with accommodations
713940 Health spas without accommodations, physical fitness
923120 Health statistics centers, government
713940 Health studios, physical fitness
446199 Hearing aid stores
423450 Hearing aids merchant wholesalers
334510 Hearing aids, electronic, manufacturing
621999 Hearing testing services (except by offices of audiologists)
621340 Hearing testing services by offices of audiologists
336211 Hearse bodies manufacturing
485320 Hearse rental with driver
532111 Hearse rental without driver
336111 Hearses assembling on chassis of own manufacture

336211 Hearses assembling on purchased chassis
334510 Heart-lung machine manufacturing
423830 Heat exchange equipment, industrial, merchant wholesalers
332410 Heat exchangers manufacturing
238220 Heat pump installation
333415 Heat pumps manufacturing
423730 Heat pumps merchant wholesalers
325992 Heat sensitized (i.e., thermal) paper made from purchased paper
335991 Heat shields, carbon or graphite, manufacturing
332811 Heat treating metals and metal products for the trade
333994 Heat treating ovens, industrial process-type, manufacturing
221330 Heat, steam, distribution
221330 Heated air distribution
335210 Heaters, portable electric space, manufacturing
423620 Heaters, portable electric, merchant wholesalers
333414 Heaters, space (except portable electric), manufacturing
333414 Heaters, swimming pool, manufacturing
335210 Heaters, tape, manufacturing 333415 Heating and air-conditioning combination units manufacturing
238220 Heating and cooling duct work installation
334512 Heating and cooling system controls, residential and commercial, manufacturing
238220 Heating and ventilation system component (e.g., air registers, diffusers, filters, grilles, sound attenuators) installation
238220 Heating boiler installation
423720 Heating boilers, steam and hot water, merchant wholesalers
238220 Heating contractors
541330 Heating engineering consulting services
238220 Heating equipment installation
333414 Heating equipment, hot water (except hot water heaters), manufacturing
423720 Heating equipment, hot water, merchant wholesalers
423730 Heating equipment, warm air (i.e. forced air), merchant wholesalers
333415 Heating equipment, warm air (i.e., forced air), manufacturing
424710 Heating oil bulk stations and terminals, merchant wholesalers
454310 Heating oil dealers, direct selling
324110 Heating oils made in petroleum refineries
335210 Heating pads, electric, manufacturing
334512 Heating regulators manufacturing
221330 Heating steam (suppliers of heat) providers
335210 Heating units for electric appliances manufacturing
333414 Heating units, baseboard, manufacturing
238220 Heating, ventilation and air-conditioning (HVAC) contractors
532412 Heavy construction equipment rental without operator
611519 Heavy equipment operation schools
611519 Heavy equipment repair training 811310 Heavy machinery and equipment repair and maintenance services
423130 Heavy truck tires and tubes merchant wholesalers
336120 Heavy trucks assembling on chassis of own manufacture
336211 Heavy trucks assembling on purchased chassis
325180 Heavy water (i.e., deuterium oxide) manufacturing
332216 Hedge shears and trimmers, nonelectric, manufacturing
333112 Hedge trimmers, powered, manufacturing
316998 Heel caps, leather or metal, manufacturing
316998 Heel lifts, leather, manufacturing
321999 Heels, boot and shoe, finished wood, manufacturing
316998 Heels, boot and shoe, leather, manufacturing
332613 Helical springs, hot wound heavy gauge metal, manufacturing
332613 Helical springs, light gauge, made from purchased wire or strip, manufacturing
481212 Helicopter carriers, freight, nonscheduled
481112 Helicopter freight carriers, scheduled
481211 Helicopter passenger carriers (except scenic, sightseeing), nonscheduled
481111 Helicopter passenger carriers, scheduled
487990 Helicopter ride, scenic and sightseeing, operation
336411 Helicopters manufacturing
325120 Helium manufacturing
325120 Helium recovery from natural gas

339113 Helmets (except athletic), safety (e.g., motorized vehicle crash helmets, space helmets), manufacturing
339920 Helmets, athletic (except motorized vehicle crash helmets), manufacturing
561320 Help supply services
212210 Hematite mining and/or beneficiating
334516 Hematology instruments manufacturing
325413 Hematology in-vitro diagnostic substances manufacturing
325412 Hematology in-vivo diagnostic substances manufacturing
325414 Hematology products (except diagnostic substances) manufacturing
325194 Hemlock extract manufacturing
113210 Hemlock gum gathering
621492 Hemodialysis centers and clinics
313110 Hemp bags made from purchased fiber
313110 Hemp ropes made from purchased fiber
313110 Hemp spun yarns made from purchased fiber
315210 Hemstitching apparel contractors on apparel
325110 Heptanes made from refined petroleum or liquid hydrocarbons
325110 Heptenes made from refined petroleum or liquid hydrocarbons
111419 Herb farming, grown under cover
111998 Herb farming, open field
111421 Herbaceous perennial growing
446191 Herbal supplement stores
424210 Herbal supplements merchant wholesalers
325412 Herbal supplements, compounded, manufacturing
325411 Herbal supplements, uncompounded, manufacturing
621399 Herbalists' offices (e.g., centers, clinics)
712110 Herbariums
325320 Herbicides manufacturing
424910 Herbicides merchant wholesalers
711310 Heritage festival managers with facilities
711320 Heritage festival managers without facilities
711310 Heritage festival organizers with facilities
711320 Heritage festival organizers without facilities
711310 Heritage festival promoters with facilities
711320 Heritage festival promoters without facilities
712120 Heritage villages 238150 Hermetically sealed window unit, commercial-type, installation
238350 Hermetically sealed window unit, residential-type, installation
114111 Herring fishing
325199 Heterocyclic chemicals, not specified elsewhere by process, manufacturing 325199 Hexadecanol manufacturing 325199 Hexamethylenediamine manufacturing 325199 Hexamethylenetetramine manufacturing 325199 Hexanol manufacturing
311221 HFCS (high fructose corn syrup) manufacturing
311611 Hides and skins produced in slaughtering plants
316110 Hides and skins, finishing on a contract basis
424590 Hides merchant wholesalers
316110 Hides, tanning, currying, dressing, and finishing
337122 High chairs, wood, children's, manufacturing
311221 High fructose corn syrup (HFCS) manufacturing
335110 High intensity lamp bulbs manufacturing
331110 High percentage nonferrous alloying elements (i.e., ferroalloys) manufacturing
611691 High school equivalency (e.g., GED) exam instruction
611110 High schools
611110 High schools offering both academic and technical courses
611110 High schools offering both academic and vocational courses
236116 High-rise apartment construction general contractors
236117 High-rise apartment for-sale builders
332312 Highway bridge sections, prefabricated metal, manufacturing
237310 Highway construction
332322 Highway guardrails, sheet metal (except stampings), manufacturing
333120 Highway line marking machinery manufacturing
237310 Highway line painting
922120 Highway patrols, police 336120 Highway tractors assembled on chassis of own manufacture
336211 Highway tractors assembling on purchased chassis

238210 Highway, street and bridge lighting and electrical signal installation
423710 Hinges merchant wholesalers
332510 Hinges, metal, manufacturing 541720 Historic and cultural preservation research and development services
813410 Historical clubs
712120 Historical forts
712110 Historical museums
712120 Historical ships
712120 Historical sites
336390 Hitches, trailer, automotive, truck, and bus, manufacturing
325413 HIV test kits manufacturing
621491 HMO (health maintenance organization) medical centers and clinics
423920 Hobby craft kits merchant wholesalers
451120 Hobby shops
339930 Hobbyhorses manufacturing
423920 Hobbyists' supplies merchant wholesalers
333515 Hobs (i.e., metal gear cutting tool) manufacturing
711211 Hockey clubs, professional or semiprofessional
713990 Hockey clubs, recreational
339920 Hockey equipment (except apparel) manufacturing
423910 Hockey equipment and supplies merchant wholesalers
611620 Hockey instruction, camps, or schools
339920 Hockey skates manufacturing
711211 Hockey teams, professional or semiprofessional
713990 Hockey teams, recreational
115112 Hoeing
332216 Hoes, garden and mason's handtools, manufacturing
112210 Hog and pig (including breeding, farrowing, nursery, and finishing activities) farming
333111 Hog feeding and watering equipment manufacturing
112210 Hog feedlots (except stockyards for transportation)
424520 Hogs merchant wholesalers
321920 Hogsheads, coopered wood, manufacturing
238290 Hoisting and placement of large-scale apparatus
333923 Hoists (except aircraft loading) manufacturing
423830 Hoists (except automotive) merchant wholesalers
333924 Hoists, aircraft loading, manufacturing
423120 Hoists, automotive, merchant wholesalers
551112 Holding companies (except bank, managing)
551114 Holding companies that manage
551111 Holding companies, bank (except managing)
333318 Holepunchers (except hand operated), office-type, manufacturing
339940 Holepunchers, hand operated, manufacturing
423220 Hollowware (except precious metal) merchant wholesalers
339910 Hollowware, precious metal, manufacturing
423940 Hollowware, precious metal, merchant wholesalers
332999 Hollowware, precious plated metal, manufacturing
316998 Holsters, leather, manufacturing
452319 Home and auto supply stores
532310 Home and garden equipment rental centers
238210 Home automation system installation
236116 Home builders (except for-sale), multifamily
236115 Home builders (except for-sale), single-family
236117 Home builders, for-sale
332119 Home canning lids and rings, metal stamping
621610 Home care of elderly, medical
624120 Home care of elderly, non-medical
444110 Home centers, building materials
624229 Home construction organizations, work (sweat) equity
454390 Home delivery newspaper routes, direct selling
337124 Home entertainment centers, metal, manufacturing
337122 Home entertainment centers, wood, manufacturing
522292 Home equity credit lending
423220 Home furnishings merchant wholesalers
442299 Home furnishings stores
621610 Home health agencies
611519 Home health aid schools

621610 Home health care agencies 423450 Home health care supplies merchant wholesalers
532283 Home health furniture and equipment rental
236118 Home improvement (e.g., adding on, remodeling, renovating)
236118 Home improvement (e.g., adding on, remodeling, renovating), multifamily building, for-sale builders
236118 Home improvement (e.g., adding on, remodeling, renovating), multifamily building, general contractors
236118 Home improvement (e.g., adding on, remodeling, renovating), single-family housing, for-sale builders
236118 Home improvement (e.g., adding on, remodeling, renovating), single-family housing, general contractors
444110 Home improvement centers
621610 Home infusion therapy services
541350 Home inspection services
621610 Home nursing services (except private practices)
621399 Home nursing services, private practice
236118 Home renovation
453998 Home security equipment stores
561920 Home show managers
561920 Home show organizers
561920 Home show promoters
334310 Home stereo systems manufacturing
334310 Home tape recorders and players (e.g., cartridge, cassette, reel) manufacturing
334310 Home theater audio and video equipment manufacturing
238210 Home theater installation
333517 Home workshop metal cutting machine tools (except handtools, welding equipment) manufacturing
624221 Homeless shelters
624120 Homemaker's service for elderly or disabled persons, non-medical
621399 Homeopaths' offices (e.g., centers, clinics)
813990 Homeowners' associations
813990 Homeowners' associations, condominium
524126 Homeowners' insurance carriers, direct
524128 Homeowners' warranty insurance carriers, direct
623990 Homes for children with health care incidental
623220 Homes for emotionally disturbed adults or children
623110 Homes for the aged with nursing care
623312 Homes for the aged without nursing care
623110 Homes for the elderly with nursing care
623312 Homes for the elderly without nursing care
623990 Homes for unwed mothers
623210 Homes with or without health care, intellectual and developmental disability
623220 Homes, psychiatric convalescent
311211 Hominy grits (except breakfast food), manufacturing
311230 Hominy grits, prepared as cereal breakfast food, manufacturing
311421 Hominy, canned, manufacturing
333241 Homogenizing machinery, food, manufacturing
311511 Homogenizing milk
212399 Hones mining and/or beneficiating
112910 Honey bee production
424490 Honey merchant wholesalers
311999 Honey processing
111219 Honeydew melon farming, field, bedding plant and seed production
333517 Honing and lapping machines, metal cutting type, manufacturing
333515 Honing heads (i.e., a machine tool accessory) manufacturing
922140 Honor camps, correctional 332313 Hoods, industrial, fabricated metal plate work, manufacturing
332322 Hoods, range (except household-type), sheet metal (except stampings), manufacturing
335210 Hoods, range, household-type, manufacturing
115210 Hoof trimming
339993 Hook and eye fasteners (i.e., sewing accessories) manufacturing
332722 Hook and eye latches, metal, manufacturing
313220 Hook and loop fastener fabric manufacturing
713990 Hookah lounges (except primarily selling food and beverages)
332722 Hooks (i.e., general purpose fasteners), metal, manufacturing
339920 Hooks, fishing, manufacturing

332216 Hooks, handtools (e.g., baling, bush, grass, husking), manufacturing
332722 Hooks, metal screw, manufacturing
331110 Hoops made in iron and steel mills 331110
Hoops, galvanized, made in iron and steel mills
332999 Hoops, metal (except wire), fabricated from purchased metal
321920 Hoops, sawed or split wood for tight or slack cooperage, manufacturing
311942 Hop extract manufacturing
424490 Hop extract merchant wholesalers
111998 Hop farming
333515 Hopper feed devices (i.e., a machine tool accessory) manufacturing
332313 Hoppers, fabricated metal plate work, manufacturing
332439 Hoppers, light gauge metal, manufacturing
424590 Hops merchant wholesalers 334511
Horizon situation instrumentation manufacturing
237990 Horizontal drilling (e.g., underground cable, pipeline, sewer installation)
325413 Hormone in-vitro diagnostic substances manufacturing
325412 Hormone preparations (except in-vitro diagnostics) manufacturing
325411 Hormones and derivatives, uncompounded, manufacturing
112920 Horse (including thoroughbreds) production
332999 Horse bits manufacturing
316998 Horse boots and muzzles manufacturing
711212 Horse racetracks
711219 Horse racing stables
713990 Horse rental services, recreational saddle
711310 Horse show managers with facilities
711320 Horse show managers without facilities
711310 Horse show organizers with facilities
711320 Horse show organizers without facilities
711310 Horse show promoters with facilities
711320 Horse show promoters without facilities
711190 Horse shows
441228 Horse trailer dealers
336214 Horse trailers (except fifth-wheel-type) manufacturing
336212 Horse trailers, fifth-wheel-type, manufacturing
713990 Horseback riding, recreational
487110 Horse-drawn carriage operation
311611 Horsemeat produced in slaughtering plants
311111 Horsemeat, processing, for dog and cat food
311421 Horseradish (except sauce) canning
311941 Horseradish, prepared sauce, manufacturing
115210 Horses (except racehorses), boarding
424590 Horses merchant wholesalers
115210 Horses, training (except racehorses)
331222 Horseshoe nails, iron or steel, made in wire drawing plants
115210 Horseshoeing
332111 Horseshoes, ferrous forged, made from purchased iron or steel
541690 Horticultural consulting services
424910 Horticultural products merchant wholesalers
332912 Hose assemblies for fluid power systems manufacturing
332722 Hose clamps, metal, manufacturing
332912 Hose couplings and fittings, fluid power, manufacturing
332919 Hose couplings, metal (except fluid power), manufacturing
313220 Hose fabrics, tubular, weaving
332999 Hose, flexible metal, manufacturing
423840 Hose, industrial, merchant wholesalers
326220 Hoses, reinforced, rubber or plastics, manufacturing
326220 Hoses, rubberized fabric, manufacturing
333249 Hosiery machines manufacturing
448190 Hosiery stores
424320 Hosiery, men's and boys', merchant wholesalers
339113 Hosiery, orthopedic support, manufacturing
315110 Hosiery, sheer, women's, misses', and girls' full-length and knee-length, knitting or knitting and finishing
424330 Hosiery, women's and girls', merchant wholesalers
424330 Hosiery, women's, children's, and infants', merchant wholesalers
315110 Hosiery, women's, girls', and infants', manufacturing
621610 Hospice care services, in-home
623110 Hospices, inpatient care
813920 Hospital administrators' associations

524114 Hospital and medical service plans, direct, without providing health care services
813910 Hospital associations
532283 Hospital bed rental and leasing (i.e., home use)
339113 Hospital beds manufacturing
423450 Hospital beds merchant wholesalers
236220 Hospital construction
423450 Hospital equipment and supplies merchant wholesalers
532283 Hospital equipment rental (i.e. home use)
532283 Hospital furniture and equipment rental (i.e. home use)
423450 Hospital furniture merchant wholesalers
339113 Hospital furniture, specialized (e.g., hospital beds, operating room furniture)
423450 Hospital gowns merchant wholesalers
926150 Hospital licensure agencies 611519 Hospital management schools (except academic)
611310 Hospital management schools offering baccalaureate or graduate degrees
315210 Hospital service apparel, washable, cut and sew apparel contractors
315220 Hospital service apparel, washable, men's and boys', cut and sewn from purchased fabric (except apparel contractors)
315240 Hospital service apparel, washable, women's and girls', cut and sewn from purchased fabric (except apparel contractors)
611519 Hospitality management schools (except academic)
611310 Hospitality management schools offering baccalaureate or graduate degrees
524114 Hospitalization insurance carriers, direct, without providing health care services
****** Hospitals -- see type 622210
Hospitals for alcoholics 622210 Hospitals, addiction 541940 Hospitals, animal
622110 Hospitals, general medical and surgical
622110 Hospitals, general pediatric
623210 Hospitals, intellectual and developmental disability
622210 Hospitals, mental (except intellectual and developmental disability)
622210 Hospitals, psychiatric (except convalescent)
623220 Hospitals, psychiatric convalescent
622210 Hospitals, psychiatric pediatric 622310 Hospitals, specialty (except psychiatric, substance abuse)
622210 Hospitals, substance abuse
721199 Hostels
487990 Hot air balloon ride, scenic and sightseeing, operation
333318 Hot beverage vending machines manufacturing
332812 Hot dip galvanizing metals and metal products for the trade
311612 Hot dogs (except poultry) made from purchased carcasses
311611 Hot dogs (except poultry) produced in slaughtering plants
311615 Hot dogs, poultry, manufacturing 332111 Hot forgings made from purchased iron or steel, unfinished
332112 Hot forgings made from purchased nonferrous metals, unfinished
213112 Hot oil treating of oil field tanks on a contract basis
213112 Hot shot service on a contract basis
333519 Hot strip mill machinery, metalworking, manufacturing
453998 Hot tub stores
423910 Hot tubs merchant wholesalers
321920 Hot tubs, coopered, manufacturing
326191 Hot tubs, plastics or fiberglass, manufacturing
326299 Hot water bottles, rubber, manufacturing
335220 Hot water heaters (including nonelectric), household-type, manufacturing
238220 Hot water heating system installation
238220 Hot water tank installation
531120 Hotel building rental or leasing, not operating hotel
236220 Hotel construction
423440 Hotel equipment and supplies (except furniture) merchant wholesalers
423210 Hotel furniture merchant wholesalers
561110 Hotel management services (except complete operation of client's business)
721110 Hotel management services (i.e., providing management and operating staff to run hotel)
561599 Hotel reservation services
327110 Hotel tableware and kitchen articles, vitreous china, manufacturing

721110 Hotels (except casino hotels) 721110 Hotels (except casino hotels) with golf courses, tennis courts, and/or other health spa facilities (i.e., resorts)
721120 Hotels, casino
721110 Hotels, membership
721120 Hotels, resort, with casinos
721110 Hotels, resort, without casinos
721120 Hotels, seasonal, with casinos
721110 Hotels, seasonal, without casinos
624190 Hotline centers
333318 Hotplates, commercial-type, manufacturing
335210 Hotplates, household-type electric, manufacturing
331110 Hot-rolling iron or steel products in iron and steel mills
333519 Hot-rolling mill machinery, metalworking, manufacturing
331221 Hot-rolling purchased steel
238910 House demolishing
238130 House framing
238990 House moving (i.e., raising from one site, moving, and placing on a new foundation)
238320 House painting
111422 House plant growing
238910 House razing
812990 House sitting services
316210 House slippers manufacturing
316210 House slippers, plastics or plastics soled fabric upper, manufacturing
316210 House slippers, rubber or rubber soled fabric upper, manufacturing
423330 House wrapping insulation materials merchant wholesalers
532284 Houseboat rental
315210 Housecoats cut and sew apparel contractors
315190 Housecoats made in apparel knitting mills
315240 Housecoats, women's, girls', and infants', cut and sewn from purchased fabric (except apparel contractors)
315210 Housedresses cut and sew apparel contractors
315240 Housedresses, women's and girls', cut and sewn from purchased fabric (except apparel contractors)
238220 Household oil storage tank installation
814110 Households, private, employing (e.g., cooks, maids, chauffeurs, gardeners)
814110 Households, private, employing domestic personnel
443141 Household-type appliance stores 423620 Household-type appliances (except water heaters, heating stoves (i.e., noncooking)), gas and electric, merchant wholesalers
327110 Household-type earthenware, semivitreous, manufacturing
423210 Household-type furniture merchant wholesalers
337121 Household-type furniture, upholstered, manufacturing
337122 Household-type furniture, wood, not upholstered (except TV and radio housings and sewing machine cabinets), manufacturing
325320 Household-type insecticides manufacturing
423620 Household-type laundry equipment (e.g., dryers, washers) merchant wholesalers
327110 Household-type tableware and kitchen articles, vitreous china, manufacturing
334519 Household-type timing mechanisms manufacturing
321999 Household-type woodenware manufacturing
721199 Housekeeping cabins
721199 Housekeeping cottages
561720 Housekeeping services (i.e., cleaning services)
922140 Houses of correction
531110 Houses rental or leasing
332311 Houses, prefabricated metal, manufacturing
321991 Houses, prefabricated mobile homes, manufacturing
321992 Houses, prefabricated, wood (except mobile homes), manufacturing
454390 House-to-house direct selling
423220 Housewares (except electric) merchant wholesalers
442299 Housewares stores
423620 Housewares, gas and electric, merchant wholesalers
624229 Housing assistance agencies
531110 Housing authorities owning and operating residential buildings
925110 Housing authorities, nonoperating
236117 Housing construction, for-sale builder
236117 Housing construction, merchant builder
922120 Housing police, government
925110 Housing programs, planning and development, government

624229 Housing repair organizations, volunteer
236116 Housing, multifamily, construction general contractors
236115 Housing, single-family, construction general contractors
336612 Hovercraft building
487210 Hovercraft sightseeing operation
332994 Howitzers manufacturing
321999 Hubs, wood, manufacturing
111334 Huckleberry farming
113210 Huckleberry greens, gathering of
334511 HUD (heads-up display) systems, aeronautical, manufacturing
212299 Huebnerite mining and/or beneficiating
115114 Hulling and shelling of nuts
333111 Hulling machinery, farm-type, manufacturing
621991 Human egg or ova banks
621991 Human embryo storage services
712110 Human history museums
541612 Human resource consulting services
813311 Human rights advocacy organizations
921190 Human rights commissions, government
813312 Humane societies
541720 Humanities research and development services
423730 Humidifiers and dehumidifiers (except portable) merchant wholesalers
423620 Humidifiers and dehumidifiers, portable, merchant wholesalers
335210 Humidifiers, portable electric, manufacturing
333415 Humidifying equipment (except portable) manufacturing
334512 Humidistats (e.g., duct, skeleton, wall) manufacturing
238210 Humidity control system installation
334512 Humidity controls, air-conditioning-type, manufacturing
334519 Humidity instruments (except industrial process and air-conditioning type) manufacturing
334513 Humidity instruments, industrial process-type, manufacturing
212399 Humus, peat, mining and/or beneficiating
112390 Hungarian partridge production
721214 Hunting camps with accommodation facilities
713990 Hunting clubs, recreational
315210 Hunting coats and vests cut and sew apparel contractors
315220 Hunting coats and vests, men's and boys', cut and sewn from purchased fabric (except apparel contractors)
423910 Hunting equipment and supplies merchant wholesalers
713990 Hunting guide services
332215 Hunting knives manufacturing
114210 Hunting preserves
813319 Hunting, fishing, and sport shooting advocacy organizations
238220 HVAC (heating, ventilation and air-conditioning) contractors
423730 HVAC equipment merchant wholesalers
334111 Hybrid computers manufacturing
334413 Hybrid integrated circuits manufacturing
112511 Hybrid striped bass production
237110 Hydrant and flushing hydrant installation
327410 Hydrated lime (i.e., calcium hydroxide) manufacturing
332912 Hydraulic aircraft subassemblies manufacturing
333995 Hydraulic cylinders, fluid power, manufacturing
811310 Hydraulic equipment repair and maintenance services
324110 Hydraulic fluids made in petroleum refineries
324191 Hydraulic fluids, petroleum, made from refined petroleum
325998 Hydraulic fluids, synthetic, manufacturing
213112 Hydraulic fracturing wells on a contract basis
332912 Hydraulic hose fittings, fluid power, manufacturing
326220 Hydraulic hoses (without fitting), rubber or plastics, manufacturing
423830 Hydraulic power transmission equipment merchant wholesalers
423830 Hydraulic pumps and parts merchant wholesalers
333996 Hydraulic pumps, fluid power, manufacturing
336340 Hydraulic slave cylinders, automotive, truck, and bus clutch, manufacturing
333611 Hydraulic turbine generator set units manufacturing
333611 Hydraulic turbines manufacturing
332912 Hydraulic valves, fluid power, manufacturing

325180 Hydrazine manufacturing
325180 Hydrochloric acid manufacturing
325180 Hydrocyanic acid manufacturing
238910 Hydrodemolition (i.e., demolition with pressurized water) contractors
237990 Hydroelectric generating facility construction
221111 Hydroelectric power generation
325180 Hydrofluoric acid manufacturing
325180 Hydrofluosilicic acid manufacturing
336611 Hydrofoil vessel building and repairing in shipyard
325120 Hydrogen manufacturing
325180 Hydrogen peroxide manufacturing
325180 Hydrogen sulfide manufacturing
311225 Hydrogenating purchased oil
541370 Hydrographic mapping services
323111 Hydrographic printing
541370 Hydrographic surveying services
541690 Hydrology consulting services
334519 Hydrometers (except industrial process-type) manufacturing
334513 Hydrometers, industrial process-type, manufacturing
334512 Hydronic circulator control, automatic, manufacturing
423720 Hydronic heating equipment and supplies merchant wholesalers
333414 Hydronic heating equipment manufacturing
238220 Hydronic heating system installation
334512 Hydronic limit control manufacturing
334512 Hydronic limit, pressure, and temperature controls, manufacturing
334511 Hydrophones manufacturing
111419 Hydroponic crop farming
325194 Hydroquinone manufacturing
561730 Hydroseeding services (e.g., decorative, erosion control purposes)
333996 Hydrostatic drives manufacturing
541380 Hydrostatic testing laboratories or services
333996 Hydrostatic transmissions manufacturing
325180 Hydrosulfites manufacturing
339113 Hydrotherapy equipment manufacturing
424210 Hygiene products, oral, merchant wholesalers
334519 Hygrometers (except industrial process-type) manufacturing
334513 Hygrometers, industrial process-type, manufacturing
334519 Hygrothermographs manufacturing
621399 Hypnotherapists' offices (e.g., centers, clinics)
325411 Hypnotic drugs, uncompounded, manufacturing
325180 Hypochlorites manufacturing
339112 Hypodermic needles and syringes manufacturing
325180 Hypophosphites manufacturing
312113 Ice (except dry ice) manufacturing
424990 Ice (except dry ice) merchant wholesalers
238170 Ice apron, roof, installation
334512 Ice bank controls manufacturing
335220 Ice boxes, household-type, manufacturing
326199 Ice buckets, plastics (except foam), manufacturing
326140 Ice buckets, polystyrene foam, manufacturing
326150 Ice buckets, urethane or other plastics foam (except polystyrene), manufacturing
332439 Ice chests or coolers, light gauge metal, manufacturing
326199 Ice chests or coolers, plastics (except plastics foam), manufacturing
326140 Ice chests or coolers, polystyrene foam, manufacturing
326150 Ice chests or coolers, urethane or other plastics foam (except polystyrene) manufacturing
445299 Ice cream (i.e., packaged) stores
424430 Ice cream and ices merchant wholesalers
311821 Ice cream cones manufacturing
424490 Ice cream cones merchant wholesalers
333241 Ice cream making machinery manufacturing
311520 Ice cream manufacturing
424430 Ice cream merchant wholesalers
311514 Ice cream mix manufacturing
722515 Ice cream parlors
311520 Ice cream specialties manufacturing
722330 Ice cream truck vendors
333318 Ice cream vending machines manufacturing
335210 Ice crushers, household-type electric, manufacturing
333999 Ice crushers, industrial and commercial-type, manufacturing

711211 Ice hockey clubs, professional or semiprofessional
713990 Ice hockey clubs, recreational
334512 Ice maker controls manufacturing
333415 Ice making machinery manufacturing
423740 Ice making machines merchant wholesalers
311520 Ice milk manufacturing
424430 Ice milk merchant wholesalers
311514 Ice milk mix manufacturing
311520 Ice milk specialties manufacturing
237990 Ice rink (except indoor) construction
236220 Ice rink, indoor, construction
339920 Ice skates manufacturing
711190 Ice skating companies
713940 Ice skating rinks
711190 Ice skating shows
312130 Ice wine
325120 Ice, dry, manufacturing
424690 Ice, dry, merchant wholesalers
312111 Iced coffee manufacturing
312111 Iced tea manufacturing
212399 Iceland spar (i.e., optical grade calcite), mining and/or beneficiating
311520 Ices, flavored sherbets, manufacturing
332999 Identification plates, metal, manufacturing
423410 Identity recorders merchant wholesalers
812990 Identity theft protection services
332993 Igniters, ammunition tracer (i.e., more than 30 mm., more than 1.18 inch), manufacturing
811118 Ignition and battery repair shops, automotive
334512 Ignition controls for gas appliances and furnaces, automatic, manufacturing
336320 Ignition points and condensers for internal combustion engines manufacturing
334515 Ignition testing instruments manufacturing
336320 Ignition wiring harness for internal combustion engines manufacturing 321213 I-joists, wood, fabricating 335122 Illuminated indoor lighting fixtures (e.g., directional, exit) manufacturing
541430 Illustrators, independent commercial
212299 Ilmenite ores mining and/or beneficiating
327420 Images, small gypsum, manufacturing
327999 Images, small papier-mache, manufacturing
323120 Imagesetting services, prepress
312230 Imitation tobacco cigarettes, manufacturing
335210 Immersion heaters, household-type electric, manufacturing
624230 Immigrant resettlement services
928120 Immigration services
923120 Immunization program administration
621111 Immunologists' offices (e.g., centers, clinics)
334516 Immunology instruments, laboratory, manufacturing
333991 Impact wrenches, handheld power-driven, manufacturing
334515 Impedance measuring equipment manufacturing
334514 Impeller and counter driven flow meters manufacturing
339113 Implants, surgical, manufacturing
213112 Impounding and storing salt water in connection with petroleum production
221310 Impounding reservoirs, irrigation
339114 Impression material, dental, manufacturing
711110 Improvisational theaters
334512 In-built thermostats, filled system and bimetal types, manufacturing
335110 Incandescent filament lamp bulbs, complete, manufacturing
325998 Incense manufacturing 334512 Incinerator control systems, residential and commercial-type, manufacturing
236210 Incinerator, mass-burn type, construction
236210 Incinerator, municipal waste disposal, construction
333994 Incinerators (except precast concrete) manufacturing
238290 Incinerators, building equipment type, installation
562211 Incinerators, hazardous waste, operating
562213 Incinerators, nonhazardous solid waste
327390 Incinerators, precast concrete, manufacturing
541213 Income tax compilation services
541213 Income tax return preparation services
333318 Incoming mail handling equipment (e.g., opening, scanning, sorting) manufacturing
339113 Incubators, infant, manufacturing
339113 Incubators, laboratory-type, manufacturing
333111 Incubators, poultry, manufacturing
325998 Indelible inks manufacturing

488190 Independent pilot, air (except owner-operators)
711510 Independent technical writers
488490 Independent truck driver (except owner-operators)
333515 Indexing, rotary tables (i.e., a machine tool accessory) manufacturing
325998 India inks manufacturing
921190 Indian affairs programs, government
334515 Indicating instruments, electric, manufacturing
334519 Indicator testers, turntable, manufacturing
334513 Indicators, industrial process control-type, manufacturing
325180 Indium chloride manufacturing
624190 Individual and family social services, multi-purpose
523910 Individuals investing in financial contracts on own account
541850 Indoor display advertising services
713120 Indoor play areas
236220 Indoor swimming pool construction
333994 Induction heating equipment, industrial process-type, manufacturing
334416 Inductors, electronic component-type (e.g., chokes, coils, transformers), manufacturing
813910 Industrial associations
522190 Industrial banks (i.e., known as), depository
522298 Industrial banks (i.e., known as), nondepository
314994 Industrial belting reinforcement, cord and fabric, manufacturing
236210 Industrial building (except warehouses) construction
236210 Industrial building (except warehouses) construction, for-sale builders
236210 Industrial building (except warehouses) construction, general contractors
531120 Industrial building rental or leasing
722310 Industrial caterers (i.e., providing food services on a contractual arrangement (except single-event basis))
424690 Industrial chemicals merchant wholesalers
423840 Industrial containers merchant wholesalers
335314 Industrial controls (e.g., pushbutton, selector, and pilot switches) manufacturing
423610 Industrial controls, electrical, merchant wholesalers
541420 Industrial design consulting services
533110 Industrial design licensing
541420 Industrial design services 926110
Industrial development program administration
423840 Industrial diamonds merchant wholesalers
541330 Industrial engineering services 811310 Industrial equipment and machinery repair and maintenance services
315210 Industrial garments cut and sew apparel contractors
315220 Industrial garments, men's and boys', cut and sewn from purchased fabric (except apparel contractors)
315240 Industrial garments, women's and girls', cut and sewn from purchased fabric (except apparel contractors)
325120 Industrial gases manufacturing
424690 Industrial gases merchant wholesalers
327212 Industrial glassware and glass products, pressed or blown, made in glass making plants
327215 Industrial glassware made from purchased glass
813930 Industrial labor unions
541320 Industrial land use planning services
812332 Industrial launderers
423840 Industrial leather products merchant wholesalers
335122 Industrial lighting fixtures, electric, manufacturing
522298 Industrial loan companies, nondepository
336510 Industrial locomotives and parts manufacturing
423830 Industrial machinery and equipment (except electrical) merchant wholesalers
561110 Industrial management services
335122 Industrial mercury lighting fixtures, electric, manufacturing
333511 Industrial molds (except steel ingot) manufacturing
331511 Industrial molds, steel ingot, manufacturing
332999 Industrial pattern manufacturing
423840 Industrial pottery products merchant wholesalers
334513 Industrial process control instruments manufacturing
238220 Industrial process piping installation
325510 Industrial product finishes and coatings (i.e., paint) manufacturing
541715 Industrial research and development laboratories or services (except biotechnology and nanotechnology research and development)

423450 Industrial safety devices (e.g., eye shields, face shields, first-aid kits) merchant wholesalers
325998 Industrial salt manufacturing
424690 Industrial salts merchant wholesalers
212322 Industrial sand beneficiating (e.g., screening, washing)
212322 Industrial sand sandpits and dredging
333997 Industrial scales manufacturing 423840 Industrial supplies (except disposable plastics, paper) merchant wholesalers
424130 Industrial supplies, disposable plastics, paper, merchant wholesalers
541380 Industrial testing laboratories or services
621340 Industrial therapists' offices (e.g., centers, clinics)
811310 Industrial truck (e.g., forklifts) repair and maintenance services
532490 Industrial truck rental or leasing
333924 Industrial trucks and tractors manufacturing
423830 Industrial trucks, tractors, or trailers merchant wholesalers
812332 Industrial uniform supply services
423930 Industrial wastes to be reclaimed merchant wholesalers
311611 Inedible products (e.g., hides, skins, pulled wool, wool grease) produced in slaughtering plants
334511 Inertial navigation systems, aeronautical, manufacturing
311422 Infant and junior food canning
311230 Infant cereals, dry, manufacturing
624410 Infant day care centers 624410 Infant day care services 339113 Infant incubators manufacturing 315240 Infants' apparel cut and sewn from purchased fabric (except apparel contractors)
424330 Infants' clothing merchant wholesalers
315210 Infants' cut and sew apparel contractors
311514 Infant's formulas manufacturing 316210 Infant's shoes manufacturing 315240 Infants' water resistant outerwear cut and sewn from purchased fabric (except apparel contractors)
336612 Inflatable plastic boats, heavy-duty, manufacturing
336612 Inflatable rubber boats, heavy-duty, manufacturing
541512 Information management computer systems integration design services
334516 Infrared analytical instruments, laboratory-type, manufacturing
334511 Infrared homing systems, aeronautical, manufacturing
334513 Infrared instruments, industrial process-type, manufacturing
335110 Infrared lamp bulbs manufacturing
335129 Infrared lamp fixtures manufacturing
333994 Infrared ovens, industrial, manufacturing
334413 Infrared sensors, solid-state, manufacturing
621498 Infusion therapy centers and clinics, outpatient
331318 Ingot made by rolling purchased aluminum
331110 Ingot made in iron and steel mills
331318 Ingot, aluminum, made in integrated secondary smelting and rolling mills
331492 Ingot, nonferrous metals (except aluminum, copper), secondary smelting and refining
331313 Ingot, primary aluminum, manufacturing
331410 Ingot, primary, nonferrous metals (except aluminum), manufacturing
423510 Ingots (except precious) merchant wholesalers
423940 Ingots, precious, merchant wholesalers
621399 Inhalation therapists' offices (e.g., centers, clinics)
339112 Inhalation therapy equipment manufacturing
339112 Inhalators, surgical and medical, manufacturing
325998 Inhibitors (e.g., corrosion, oxidation, polymerization) manufacturing
454390 In-home sales of merchandise, direct selling
333249 Injection molding machinery for plastics manufacturing
325612 Ink eradicators manufacturing
424120 Ink, writing, merchant wholesalers
339940 Inked ribbons manufacturing
424120 Inked ribbons merchant wholesalers
325910 Inkjet cartridges manufacturing
325910 Inkjet inks manufacturing
424120 Inks, pastes, and solvents, office, merchant wholesalers
325910 Inks, printing, manufacturing
423840 Inks, printing, merchant wholesalers

325998 Inks, writing, manufacturing
316998 Inner soles, leather, manufacturing
326211 Inner tubes manufacturing
337910 Innerspring cushions manufacturing
721191 Inns, bed and breakfast
424690 Inorganic chemicals merchant wholesalers
325130 Inorganic pigments (except bone black, carbon black, lamp black) manufacturing
334118 Input/output equipment, computer, manufacturing
423620 Insect control devices, electric, merchant wholesalers
115112 Insect control for crops
335129 Insect lamps, electric, manufacturing
332618 Insect screening made from purchased wire
424690 Insecticides (except lawn and agricultural) merchant wholesalers
325320 Insecticides manufacturing
424910 Insecticides, agricultural, merchant wholesalers
333515 Inserts, cutting tool, manufacturing
541350 Inspection bureaus, building
926150 Inspection for labor standards
488490 Inspection or weighing services, truck transportation
488190 Inspection services, aircraft
541350 Inspection services, building or home
238210 Installation of photovoltaic panels
213112 Installing production equipment at the oil or gas field on a contract basis
522220 Installment sales financing
311920 Instant coffee manufacturing
311230 Instant hot cereals manufacturing
323111 Instant printing (i.e., quick printing) (except books)
311920 Instant tea manufacturing
236220 Institutional building construction 236220
Institutional building construction for-sale builders
236220 Institutional building construction general contractors
337127 Institutional furniture manufacturing
335122 Institutional lighting fixtures, electric, manufacturing
454110 Institutional pharmacies, off-site, exclusively on Internet
454110 Institutional pharmacies, off-site, mail-order
446110 Institutional pharmacies, on-site
522120 Institutions, savings

****** Instruction -- see type of training 512110
Instructional video production 336320 Instrument control panels (i.e., assembling purchased gauges), automotive, truck, and
bus, manufacturing
334511 Instrument landing system instrumentation, airborne or airport, manufacturing
333314 Instrument lenses manufacturing
334514 Instrument panels, assembling gauges made in the same establishment
334515 Instrument shunts manufacturing
332613 Instrument springs, precision (except clock, watch), light gauge, made from purchased wire or strip, manufacturing
335311 Instrument transformers (except complete instruments) for metering or protective relaying use manufacturing
334519 Instrumentation for reactor controls, auxiliary, manufacturing
423830 Instruments (except electrical) (e.g., controlling, indicating, recording) merchant wholesalers
334513 Instruments for industrial process control manufacturing
334515 Instruments for measuring electrical quantities manufacturing
334511 Instruments, aeronautical, manufacturing
423450 Instruments, dental and medical, merchant wholesalers
334515 Instruments, electric (i.e., testing electrical characteristics), manufacturing
423610 Instruments, electric measuring, merchant wholesalers
339112 Instruments, mechanical microsurgical, manufacturing
339992 Instruments, musical, manufacturing
423990 Instruments, musical, merchant wholesalers
423490 Instruments, professional and scientific, merchant wholesalers
331420 Insulated wire or cable made from purchased copper in wire drawing plants
331318 Insulated wire or cable made in aluminum wire drawing plants
423610 Insulated wire or cable merchant wholesalers
331420 Insulated wire or cable, copper, made in integrated secondary smelting and wire drawing plants
322299 Insulating batts, fills, or blankets made from purchased paper

327993 Insulating batts, fills, or blankets, fiberglass, manufacturing
327120 Insulating firebrick and shapes, clay, manufacturing
327215 Insulating glass, sealed units, made from purchased glass
327211 Insulating glass, sealed units, made in glass making plants
321999 Insulating materials, cork, manufacturing
325998 Insulating oils manufacturing
335929 Insulating purchased nonferrous wire
326150 Insulation and cushioning, foam plastics (except polystrene), manufacturing
326140 Insulation and cushioning, polystyrene foam plastics, manufacturing
321219 Insulation board, cellular fiber or hard pressed wood, manufacturing
238310 Insulation contractors 423330 Insulation materials (except wood) merchant wholesalers
238290 Insulation, boiler, duct and pipe, installation
335932 Insulators, electrical (except glass, porcelain), manufacturing
327110 Insulators, electrical porcelain, manufacturing
327215 Insulators, electrical, glass, made from purchased glass
327212 Insulators, electrical, glass, made in glass making plants
423610 Insulators, electrical, merchant wholesalers
325412 Insulin preparations manufacturing
325411 Insulin, uncompounded, manufacturing
524298 Insurance actuarial services
524298 Insurance advisory services
524210 Insurance agencies
524210 Insurance brokerages
531120 Insurance building rental or leasing
524113 Insurance carriers, disability, direct
524126 Insurance carriers, fidelity, direct
524114 Insurance carriers, health, direct
524113 Insurance carriers, life, direct
524126 Insurance carriers, property and casualty, direct
524126 Insurance carriers, surety, direct
524127 Insurance carriers, title, direct
524291 Insurance claims adjusting
524291 Insurance claims investigation services
524292 Insurance claims processing services, third party
926150 Insurance commissions, government
524298 Insurance coverage consulting services
524298 Insurance exchanges
524292 Insurance fund, third party administrative services (except claims adjusting only)
551112 Insurance holding companies 524298 Insurance investigation services (except claims investigation)
524298 Insurance loss prevention services
524292 Insurance plan administrative services (except claims adjusting only), third party
522220 Insurance premium financing
524298 Insurance rate making services
524298 Insurance reporting services
524291 Insurance settlement offices
524298 Insurance underwriters laboratories and standards services
524113 Insurance underwriting, disability, direct
524114 Insurance underwriting, health and medical, direct
524113 Insurance underwriting, life, direct
524126 Insurance underwriting, property and casualty, direct
524127 Insurance underwriting, title, direct
813910 Insurers' associations
323111 Intaglio printing (except books)
335312 Integral horsepower electric motors manufacturing
423690 Integrated circuits merchant wholesalers
334413 Integrated microcircuits manufacturing
512250 Integrated record companies (i.e., releasing, promoting, distributing)
512250 Integrated record production and distribution
334515 Integrated-circuit testers manufacturing
334515 Integrating electricity meters manufacturing
334514 Integrating meters, nonelectric, manufacturing
623210 Intellectual and developmental disability facilities (e.g., homes, hospitals, intermediate care facilities), residential
623210 Intellectual and developmental disability homes
623210 Intellectual and developmental disability hospitals
623210 Intellectual and developmental disability intermediate care facilities

813311 Intellectually and developmentally disabled advocacy groups
712110 Interactive museums
485210 Intercity bus line operation 483113 Intercoastal freight transportation to and from domestic ports
483114 Intercoastal transportation of passengers to and from domestic ports
334290 Intercom systems and equipment manufacturing
238210 Intercommunication (intercom) system installation
332410 Intercooler shells manufacturing
333314 Interferometers manufacturing
541410 Interior decorating consultant services
541410 Interior decorating consulting services
541410 Interior design consulting services
541410 Interior design services
541410 Interior designer services
561730 Interior landscaping services
811121 Interior repair shops, automotive
238990 Interlocking brick and block installation
623210 Intermediate care facilities, intellectual and developmental disability
334515 Internal combustion engine analyzers (i.e., testing electrical characteristics) manufacturing
333618 Internal combustion engines (except aircraft, nondiesel automotive, nondiesel truck) manufacturing
423830 Internal combustion engines (except aircraft, nondiesel automotive, nondiesel truck) merchant wholesalers
333618 Internal combustion engines for hybrid drive systems (except automotive) manufacturing
336412 Internal combustion engines, aircraft, manufacturing
336310 Internal combustion engines, automotive and truck gasoline, manufacturing
921130 Internal Revenue Service
928120 International Monetary Fund
522293 International trade financing
454110 Internet auctions, retail
519130 Internet book publishers
519130 Internet broadcasting
561439 Internet cafes (i.e., not serving food and beverages)
519130 Internet comic book publishing
519130 Internet entertainment sites
561311 Internet job listing services
519130 Internet magazine publishing
519130 Internet news publishers
519130 Internet newsletter publishing
519130 Internet newspaper publishing
519130 Internet periodical publishers
519130 Internet radio stations
561311 Internet resume listing services
454110 Internet retail sales sites
519130 Internet search portals
519130 Internet search Web sites
517919 Internet service providers, using client-supplied telecommunications (e.g., dial-up ISPs)
517311 Internet service providers, using own operated wired telecommunications infrastructure (e.g., cable, DSL)
519130 Internet sports sites
519130 Internet video broadcast sites
621111 Internists' offices (e.g., centers, clinics)
541940 Internists' offices, veterinary
541930 Interpretation services, language
712190 Interpretive centers, nature
711120 Interpretive dance companies
711510 Interpretive dancers, independent
485210 Interstate bus line operation
485210 Interurban bus line operation
339113 Intra ocular lenses manufacturing
483211 Intracoastal transportation of freight
483212 Intracoastal transportation of passengers
339113 Intrauterine devices manufacturing
325412 Intravenous (IV) solution preparations manufacturing
812990 Introduction services, social
532283 Invalid equipment rental (i.e., home use)
561990 Inventory computing services 541614 Inventory planning and control management consulting services
561990 Inventory taking services 311314
Invert sugar manufacturing
335312 Inverters, rotating electrical, manufacturing
335999 Inverters, solid-state, manufacturing
561611 Investigation services (except credit), private

561450 Investigation services, credit
561611 Investigators, private
523930 Investment advice consulting services, customized, fees paid by client
523930 Investment advice counseling services, customized, fees paid by client
523930 Investment advisory services, customized, fees paid by client
523110 Investment banking
331524 Investment castings, aluminum, unfinished, manufacturing
331529 Investment castings, nonferrous metal (except aluminum), unfinished, manufacturing
331512 Investment castings, steel, unfinished, manufacturing
523910 Investment clubs
525990 Investment funds, closed-end
525910 Investment funds, open-ended
523920 Investment management
325413 In-vitro diagnostic substances manufacturing
325412 In-vivo diagnostic substances manufacturing
325180 Iodides manufacturing
325412 Iodinated in-vivo diagnostic substances manufacturing
325180 Iodine, crude or resublimed, manufacturing
334519 Ion chambers manufacturing
325211 Ion exchange resins manufacturing
325211 Ionomer resins manufacturing
325199 Ionone manufacturing
331491 Iridium bar, rod, sheet, strip and tubing made from purchased metals or scrap
212299 Iridium mining and/or beneficiating
331492 Iridium recovering from scrap and/or alloying purchased metals
331410 Iridium refining, primary 423390 Iron and steel architectural shapes merchant wholesalers
325130 Iron based pigments manufacturing
331511 Iron castings, unfinished, manufacturing
325180 Iron compounds, not specified elsewhere by process, manufacturing
332111 Iron forgings made from purchased iron, unfinished
331511 Iron foundries
339113 Iron lungs manufacturing 212210 Iron ore (e.g., hematite, magnetite, siderite, taconite) mining and/or beneficiating
212210 Iron ore agglomerates mining and/or beneficiating
212210 Iron ore beneficiating plants (e.g., agglomeration, sintering)
212210 Iron ore mine site development for own account
331110 Iron ore recovery from open hearth slag
212210 Iron ore, blocked, mining and/or beneficiating
331110 Iron sinter made in iron and steel mills
325180 Iron sulphate manufacturing
238120 Iron work, structural, contractors
331110 Iron, pig, manufacturing
335220 Ironers and mangles, household-type (except portable irons), manufacturing
423220 Ironing boards merchant wholesalers
332999 Ironing boards, metal, manufacturing
321999 Ironing boards, wood, manufacturing
335210 Irons, household-type electric, manufacturing
423620 Irons, household-type, electric, merchant wholesalers
334517 Irradiation apparatus and tubes (e.g., industrial, medical diagnostic, medical therapeutic, research, scientific), manufacturing
334517 Irradiation equipment manufacturing
115114 Irradiation of fruits and vegetables
926130 Irrigation districts, nonoperating
423820 Irrigation equipment merchant wholesalers
333111 Irrigation equipment, agriculture, manufacturing
327332 Irrigation pipe, concrete, manufacturing
332322 Irrigation pipe, sheet metal (except stampings), manufacturing
237110 Irrigation project construction (except lawn)
221310 Irrigation system operation
325110 Isobutane made from refined petroleum or liquid hydrocarbons
211130 Isobutane recovered from oil and gas field gases
325110 Isobutene made from refined petroleum or liquid hydrocarbons
325211 Isobutylene polymer resins manufacturing
325212 Isobutylene-isoprene rubber manufacturing
325212 Isocyanate rubber manufacturing
325194 Isocyanates manufacturing
335311 Isolation transformers manufacturing

211130 Isopentane recovered from oil and gas field gases
325110 Isoprene made from refined petroleum or liquid hydrocarbons
325199 Isopropyl alcohol manufacturing
522210 Issuing, credit card
311422 Italian foods canning
339112 IV apparatus manufacturing
333120 Jack hammers manufacturing
315220 Jackets (except fur, leather, sheep-lined), men's and boys', cut and sewn from purchased fabric (except apparel contractors)
315240 Jackets (except fur, leather, sheep-lined), women's, girls', and infants', cut and sewn from purchased fabric (except apparel contractors)
315210 Jackets cut and sew apparel contractors
315190 Jackets made in apparel knitting mills 332992
Jackets, bullet (i.e., 30 mm. or less, 1.18 inch or less), manufacturing
315280 Jackets, fur (except apparel contractors), manufacturing
315210 Jackets, fur, cut and sew apparel contractors
332313 Jackets, industrial, fabricated metal plate work, manufacturing
315280 Jackets, leather (except welders') or sheep-lined (except apparel contractors), manufacturing
315210 Jackets, leather (except welders') or sheep-lined, cut and sew apparel contractors
315210 Jackets, service apparel (e.g., laboratory, medical), cut and sew apparel contractors
315220 Jackets, service apparel (e.g., laboratory, medical), men's and boys', cut and sewn from purchased fabric (except apparel contractors)
315240 Jackets, service apparel (e.g., laboratory, medical), women's and girls', cut and sewn from purchased fabric (except apparel contractors)
315210 Jackets, ski, cut and sew apparel contractors
315220 Jackets, ski, men's and boys', cut and sewn from purchased fabric (except apparel contractors)
315240 Jackets, ski, women's, girls', and infants', cut and sewn from purchased fabric (except apparel contractors)
315220 Jackets, tailored (except fur, leather, sheep-lined), men's and boys', cut and sewn from purchased fabric (except apparel contractors)
316998 Jackets, welder's, leather, manufacturing
332216 Jacks (except hydraulic, pneumatic) manufacturing
333999 Jacks, hydraulic and pneumatic, manufacturing
333249 Jacquard card cutting machinery manufacturing
313210 Jacquard woven fabrics weaving
212399 Jade mining and/or beneficiating
611620 Jai alai instruction, camps, or schools
711211 Jai alai teams, professional or semiprofessional
236220 Jail construction
561210 Jail operation on a contract or fee basis
922140 Jails (except private operation of)
561210 Jails, privately operated
332321 Jalousies, metal, manufacturing
424690 Janitorial chemicals merchant wholesalers
423850 Janitorial equipment and supplies merchant wholesalers
453998 Janitorial equipment and supplies stores
561720 Janitorial services
561720 Janitorial services, aircraft
332812 Japanning metals and metal products for the trade
316110 Japanning of leather
333994 Japanning ovens manufacturing 327213 Jars
for packaging, bottling, and canning, glass, manufacturing
326199 Jars, plastics, manufacturing
711120 Jazz dance companies
711510 Jazz dancers, independent
711130 Jazz musical artists, independent
711130 Jazz musical groups
315210 Jean-cut casual slacks cut and sew apparel contractors
315220 Jean-cut casual slacks, men's and boys', cut and sewn from purchased fabric (except apparel contractors)
315240 Jean-cut casual slacks, women's and girls', cut and sewn from purchased fabric (except apparel contractors)
315210 Jeans cut and sew apparel contractors
315240 Jeans, women's, girls', and infants', cut and sewn from purchased fabric (except apparel contractors)

311421 Jellies and jams manufacturing 424490 Jellies and jams merchant wholesalers 311340 Jelly candies manufacturing 315210 Jerseys cut and sew apparel contractors 315190 Jerseys made in apparel knitting mills 315220 Jerseys, men's and boys', cut and sewn from purchased fabric (except apparel contractors)
315240 Jerseys, women's and girls', cut and sewn from purchased fabric (except apparel contractors)
424710 Jet fuel bulk stations and terminals, merchant wholesalers
454310 Jet fuel bulk stations, selling for consumption
324110 Jet fuels manufacturing 336412 Jet propulsion and internal combustion engines and parts, aircraft, manufacturing
332993 Jet propulsion projectiles (except guided missiles) manufacturing
423910 Jet skis merchant wholesalers
237990 Jetty construction
339910 Jewel settings and mountings, precious metal, manufacturing
339910 Jeweler's findings and materials manufacturing
423940 Jewelers' findings merchant wholesalers
332216 Jeweler's handtools, nonelectric, manufacturing
424990 Jewelry boxes merchant wholesalers
541490 Jewelry design services
423940 Jewelry merchant wholesalers
811490 Jewelry repair shops without retailing new jewelry
448150 Jewelry stores, costume
448310 Jewelry stores, precious
339910 Jewelry, costume, manufacturing
339910 Jewelry, natural or cultured pearls, manufacturing
339910 Jewelry, precious metal, manufacturing
333514 Jigs (e.g., checking, gauging, inspection) manufacturing
333514 Jigs and fixtures for use with machine tools manufacturing
423830 Jigs merchant wholesalers 333991 Jigsaws, handheld power-driven, manufacturing
333243 Jigsaws, woodworking-type, stationary, manufacturing
624310 Job counseling, vocational rehabilitation or habilitation
323111 Job printing (except screen, books)
323111 Job printing, engraving (except books)
323111 Job printing, flexographic (except books)
323111 Job printing, gravure (except books)
323111 Job printing, letterpress (except books)
323111 Job printing, lithographic (except books)
323111 Job printing, offset (except books)
323113 Job printing, screen
336370 Job stampings, automotive, metal, manufacturing
624310 Job training, vocational rehabilitation or habilitation
711219 Jockeys, horse racing
339920 Jogging machines, manufacturing
315210 Jogging suits cut and sew apparel contractors
315190 Jogging suits made in apparel knitting mills
315220 Jogging suits, men's and boys', cut and sewn from purchased fabric (except apparel contractors)
315240 Jogging suits, women's, girls', and infants', cut and sewn from purchased fabric (except apparel contractors)
325520 Joint compounds (except gypsum base) manufacturing
327420 Joint compounds, gypsum based, manufacturing
333243 Jointers, woodworking-type, manufacturing
333613 Joints, swivel (except aircraft, motor vehicle), manufacturing
333613 Joints, universal (except aircraft, motor vehicle), manufacturing
336413 Joints, universal, aircraft, manufacturing
336350 Joints, universal, automotive, truck, and bus, manufacturing
332312 Joists, fabricated bar, manufacturing 332322 Joists, sheet metal (except stampings), manufacturing
111998 Jojoba farming
711510 Journalists, independent (freelance)
334118 Joystick devices manufacturing
611620 Judo instruction, camps, or schools
326150 Jugs, vacuum, foam plastics (except polystyrene), manufacturing
332439 Jugs, vacuum, light gauge metal, manufacturing

326140 Jugs, vacuum, polystyrene foam plastics, manufacturing
333241 Juice extractors (i.e., food manufacturing-type) manufacturing
335210 Juice extractors, household-type electric, manufacturing
311520 Juice pops, frozen, manufacturing
424490 Juices, canned or fresh, merchant wholesalers
424420 Juices, frozen, merchant wholesalers
311411 Juices, fruit or vegetable concentrates, frozen, manufacturing
311421 Juices, fruit or vegetable, canned manufacturing
311421 Juices, fruit or vegetable, fresh, manufacturing
311411 Juices, fruit or vegetable, frozen, manufacturing
713990 Jukebox concession operators (i.e., supplying and servicing in others' facilities)
334310 Jukeboxes manufacturing
315210 Jumpsuits cut and sew apparel contractors
315240 Jumpsuits, women's and girls', cut and sewn from purchased fabric (except apparel contractors)
335932 Junction boxes, electrical wiring, manufacturing
813910 Junior chambers of commerce
611210 Junior colleges
611210 Junior colleges offering a wide variety of academic and technical training
611110 Junior high schools
423140 Junk yards, auto, merchant wholesalers
541199 Jury consulting services
313210 Jute bags made in broadwoven mills
424310 Jute piece goods (except burlap) merchant wholesalers
337124 Juvenile furniture (except upholstered), metal manufacturing
337122 Juvenile furniture (except upholstered), wood, manufacturing
337125 Juvenile furniture, rattan and reed, manufacturing
337121 Juvenile furniture, upholstered, manufacturing
623990 Juvenile halfway group homes
511120 Juvenile magazine and periodical publishers (except exclusive Internet publishing)
511120 Juvenile magazine and periodical publishers and printing combined
519130 Juvenile magazine and periodical publishers, exclusively on Internet
323111 Juvenile magazines and periodicals commercial printing (except screen) without publishing
323113 Juvenile magazines and periodicals screen printing without publishing
111219 Kale farming, field, bedding plant and seed production
212324 Kaolin mining and/or beneficiating
327992 Kaolin, processing beyond beneficiation
611620 Karate instruction, camps or schools
713990 Kayaking, recreational
327420 Keene's cement manufacturing
321920 Kegs, wood, coopered, manufacturing
311119 Kelp meal and pellets, animal feed manufacturing
334515 Kelvin bridges (i.e., electrical measuring instruments) manufacturing
111998 Kenaf farming
112990 Kennels, breeding and raising stock for sale
711219 Kennels, dog racing
812910 Kennels, pet boarding
212391 Kernite mining and/or beneficiating
211120 Kerogen processing
424710 Kerosene bulk stations and terminals, merchant wholesalers
324110 Kerosene manufacturing
424720 Kerosene merchant wholesalers (except bulk stations, terminals)
333414 Kerosene space heaters manufacturing
311421 Ketchup manufacturing
325199 Ketone compounds, not specified elsewhere by process, manufacturing
332420 Kettles, heavy gauge metal, manufacturing
332510 Key blanks, metal, manufacturing
316998 Key cases (except metal) manufacturing
339910 Key cases, precious metal, manufacturing
333517 Key cutting machines, metal cutting type, manufacturing
811490 Key duplicating shops
332618 Key rings made from purchased wire
334118 Keyboards, computer peripheral equipment, manufacturing
423430 Keyboards, computer, merchant wholesalers
339992 Keyboards, piano or organ, manufacturing

336320 Keyless entry systems, automotive, truck, and bus, manufacturing
423710 Keys and locks merchant wholesalers
334210 Keysets, telephone, manufacturing
621492 Kidney dialysis centers and clinics
236210 Kiln construction
321999 Kiln drying lumber
327120 Kiln furniture, clay, manufacturing 333994
Kilns (except cement, chemical, wood) manufacturing
333249 Kilns (i.e., cement, chemical, wood) manufacturing
423830 Kilns, industrial, merchant wholesalers
611110 Kindergartens
611110 Kindergartens, combined with preschools
334519 Kinematic test and measuring equipment manufacturing
561910 Kit assembling and packaging services
336211 Kit car bodies manufacturing 423440 Kitchen appliances, commercial (except refrigerated), merchant wholesalers
423620 Kitchen appliances, household-type, gas and electric, merchant wholesalers
327110 Kitchen articles, coarse earthenware, manufacturing
444190 Kitchen cabinet (except custom) stores
337110 Kitchen cabinets (except freestanding), stock or custom wood, manufacturing
238350 Kitchen cabinets and counters, constructed on site
423310 Kitchen cabinets, built-in, merchant wholesalers
337122 Kitchen chairs (e.g., upholstered), wood, manufacturing
337124 Kitchen chairs (including upholstered), metal, manufacturing
337125 Kitchen chairs (including upholstered), plastics manufacturing
332215 Kitchen cutlery, nonprecious and precious plated metal, manufacturing
325612 Kitchen degreasing and cleaning preparations manufacturing
337124 Kitchen furniture, household-type, metal, manufacturing
337124 Kitchen furniture, metal household-type, manufacturing
337122 Kitchen furniture, wood household-type, manufacturing
238220 Kitchen sink and hardware installation
423440 Kitchen utensils, commercial, merchant wholesalers
332215 Kitchen utensils, fabricated metal (e.g., colanders, garlic presses, ice cream scoops, spatulas), manufacturing
423220 Kitchen utensils, household-type, merchant wholesalers
326199 Kitchen utensils, plastics, manufacturing
442299 Kitchenware stores
327110 Kitchenware, commercial and household-type, vitreous china, manufacturing
327110 Kitchenware, semivitreous earthenware, manufacturing
321999 Kitchenware, wood, manufacturing
339930 Kites manufacturing
111339 Kiwi fruit farming
334419 Klystron tubes manufacturing
423690 Klystron tubes merchant wholesalers
314910 Knapsacks (e.g., backpacks, book bags) manufacturing
314910 Knapsacks, made from purchased woven or knitted materials
315210 Knickers cut and sew apparel contractors
315220 Knickers, men's and boys', cut and sewn from purchased fabric (except apparel contractors)
315240 Knickers, women's, girls', and infants', cut and sewn from purchased fabric (except apparel contractors)
337122 Knickknack shelves, wood, manufacturing
332215 Knife blades manufacturing
332215 Knife blanks manufacturing
335313 Knife switches, electric power switchgear-type, manufacturing
311812 Knishes (except frozen) made in commercial bakeries
311813 Knishes, frozen, manufacturing
315210 Knit gloves cut and sew apparel contractors
315990 Knit gloves cut and sewn from purchased fabric (except apparel contractors)
315190 Knit gloves made in apparel knitting mills
313110 Knitting and crocheting thread manufacturing
313240 Knitting and finishing lace
313240 Knitting and finishing warp or weft fabric
313240 Knitting lace
333249 Knitting machinery manufacturing 313110
Knitting spun yarns (e.g., cotton, manmade fiber, silk, wool) made from purchased fiber
313240 Knitting warp or weft fabric

332215 Knives (e.g., hunting, pocket, table non-precious, table precious plated) manufacturing
423710 Knives (except disposable plastics) merchant wholesalers
333515 Knives and bits for metalworking lathes, planers, and shapers manufacturing
332216 Knives and bits for woodworking lathes, planers, and shapers manufacturing
424130 Knives, disposable plastics, merchant wholesalers
335210 Knives, household-type electric carving, manufacturing
339112 Knives, surgical, manufacturing
339992 Knobs, organ, manufacturing
321999 Knobs, wood, manufacturing
333249 Knot tying machinery for textiles manufacturing
333517 Knurling machines, metalworking, manufacturing
322130 Kraft linerboard manufacturing
322121 Kraft paper stock manufacturing
212325 Kyanite mining and/or beneficiating
339940 Label making equipment, handheld, manufacturing
333993 Labeling (i.e., packaging) machinery manufacturing
423420 Labeling machines merchant wholesalers
561910 Labeling services
313220 Labels weaving
323111 Labels, commercial printing (except screen), on a job-order basis
424310 Labels, textile, merchant wholesalers
561320 Labor (except farm) contractors (i.e., personnel suppliers)
561320 Labor (except farm) pools
115115 Labor contractors, farm
813930 Labor federations
561330 Labor leasing services
926150 Labor management negotiations boards, government
541612 Labor relations consulting services
926110 Labor statistics agencies
813930 Labor unions (except apprenticeship programs)
****** Laboratories -- see specific type
621512 Laboratories, dental X-ray 621511 Laboratories, medical (except radiological, X-ray)
621512 Laboratories, medical radiological or X-ray
334516 Laboratory analytical instruments (except optical) manufacturing
333314 Laboratory analytical optical instruments (e.g., microscopes) manufacturing 311119
Laboratory animal feed manufacturing 112990 Laboratory animal production (e.g., guinea pigs, mice, rats)
315210 Laboratory coats cut and sew apparel contractors
315220 Laboratory coats, men's and boys', cut and sewn from purchased fabric (except apparel contractors)
315240 Laboratory coats, women's and girls', cut and sewn from purchased fabric (except apparel contractors)
236220 Laboratory construction
423490 Laboratory equipment (except dental, medical, ophthalmic) merchant wholesalers
423450 Laboratory equipment, dental and medical, merchant wholesalers
238390 Laboratory furniture and equipment installation
327215 Laboratory glassware (e.g., beakers, test tubes, vials) made from purchased glass
327212 Laboratory glassware (e.g., beakers, test tubes, vials) made in glass making plants
811219 Laboratory instrument repair and maintenance services
512199 Laboratory services, motion picture
334515 Laboratory standards testing instruments (e.g., capacitance, electrical resistance, inductance) manufacturing
541380 Laboratory testing (except medical, veterinary) services
621511 Laboratory testing services, medical (except radiological, X-ray)
621512 Laboratory testing services, medical radiological or X-ray
541940 Laboratory testing services, veterinary
339113 Laboratory-type evaporation apparatus manufacturing
333415 Laboratory-type freezers manufacturing
337127 Laboratory-type furniture (e.g., benches, cabinets, stools, tables) (except dental) manufacturing
339113 Laboratory-type sample preparation apparatus manufacturing
333249 Lace and net making machinery manufacturing
316110 Lace leather manufacturing

313240 Lace manufacturing 313240 Lace products (except apparel) made in lace mills
314999 Lace, burnt-out, manufacturing
316998 Laces (e.g., shoe), leather, manufacturing
313220 Laces (e.g., shoe), textile, manufacturing
332812 Lacquering metals and metal products for the trade
333994 Lacquering ovens manufacturing
325510 Lacquers manufacturing
424950 Lacquers merchant wholesalers
325199 Lactic acid manufacturing
311514 Lactose manufacturing
332999 Ladder jacks, metal, manufacturing
321999 Ladder jacks, wood, manufacturing
321912 Ladder rounds or rungs, hardwood, manufacturing
423830 Ladders merchant wholesalers
321999 Ladders, extension, wood, manufacturing
326199 Ladders, fiberglass, manufacturing
332323 Ladders, metal chain, manufacturing
332323 Ladders, permanently installed, metal, manufacturing
332999 Ladders, portable metal, manufacturing
332313 Ladle bails, fabricated metal plate work, manufacturing
332313 Ladles, fabricated metal plate work, manufacturing
312120 Lager brewing
237110 Lagoon, sewage treatment construction
483211 Lake freight transportation (except on Great Lakes system)
483113 Lake freight transportation, Great Lakes (including St. Lawrence Seaway)
562998 Lake maintenance and cleaning services
483212 Lake passenger transportation (except on Great Lakes system)
483114 Lake passenger transportation, Great Lakes (including St. Lawrence Seaway)
325130 Lakes (i.e., organic pigments) manufacturing
311611 Lamb carcasses, half carcasses, primal and sub-primal cuts, produced in slaughtering plants
112410 Lamb feedlots (except stockyards for transportation)
311612 Lamb, primal and sub-primal cuts, made from purchased carcasses
327215 Laminated glass made from purchased glass
327211 Laminated glass made in glass making plants
326130 Laminated plastics plate, rod, and sheet, manufacturing
321213 Laminated structural wood members (except trusses) manufacturing
321213 Laminated veneer lumber (LVL) manufacturing
423310 Laminates, wood, merchant wholesalers
322220 Laminating foil for flexible packaging applications
332813 Laminating metals and metal formed products without fabricating
322220 Laminating purchased foil sheets for nonpackaging applications
322220 Laminating purchased paperboard
322220 Laminating purchased papers for nonpackaging applications
322220 Laminating purchased papers for packaging applications
313320 Laminating purchased textiles
335311 Lamp ballasts manufacturing
327110 Lamp bases, pottery, manufacturing
325180 Lamp black manufacturing
335110 Lamp bulb parts (except glass blanks), electric, manufacturing
335110 Lamp bulbs and tubes, electric (i.e., fluorescent, incandescent filament, vapor), manufacturing
335110 Lamp bulbs and tubes, health, infrared and ultraviolet radiation, manufacturing
332618 Lamp frames, wire, made from purchased wire
335931 Lamp holders manufacturing
332999 Lamp shade frames, metal, manufacturing
335121 Lamp shades (except glass, plastics), residential, manufacturing
327215 Lamp shades made from purchased glass
327212 Lamp shades made in glass making plants
326199 Lamp shades, plastics, manufacturing
442299 Lamp shops, electric
335931 Lamp sockets and receptacles (i.e., electric wiring devices) manufacturing
423220 Lamps (i.e., lighting fixtures) merchant wholesalers
335122 Lamps (i.e., lighting fixtures), commercial, industrial, and institutional, manufacturing

335121 Lamps (i.e., lighting fixtures), residential, electric, manufacturing
335129 Lamps, insect, electric fixture, manufacturing
334517 Lamps, X-ray, manufacturing
237210 Land (except cemeteries) subdividers
237210 Land acquisition, assembling and subdividing
238910 Land clearing
237210 Land developers (i.e., subdividing and installing infrastructure)
237990 Land drainage contractors
238910 Land leveling contractors
924120 Land management program administration
423820 Land preparation machinery, agricultural, merchant wholesalers
333120 Land preparation machinery, construction, manufacturing
423810 Land preparation machinery, construction, merchant wholesalers
925120 Land redevelopment agencies, government
531190 Land rental or leasing 237210 Land subdividing and utility installation (e.g., electric, sewer and water)
541370 Land surveying services 335312 Land transportation motors and generators manufacturing
541320 Land use design services
541320 Land use planning services
562212 Landfills
332312 Landing mats, aircraft, metal, manufacturing
531390 Landman services
541320 Landscape architects' offices
541320 Landscape architects' private practices
541320 Landscape architectural services
561730 Landscape care and maintenance services
541320 Landscape consulting services
561730 Landscape contractors (except construction)
541320 Landscape design services
561730 Landscape installation services
541320 Landscape planning services
561730 Landscaping services (except planning)
541930 Language interpretation services
541720 Language research and development services
611630 Language schools
541930 Language services (e.g., interpretation, sign, translation)
541930 Language translation services
335129 Lanterns (e.g., carbide, electric, gas, gasoline, kerosene) manufacturing
423840 Lapidary equipment, industrial, merchant wholesalers
339910 Lapidary work manufacturing
334111 Laptop computers manufacturing
311613 Lard made from purchased fat
424470 Lard merchant wholesalers
311611 Lard produced in slaughtering plants
333517 Laser boring, drilling, and cutting machines, metalworking, manufacturing
334413 Laser diodes manufacturing
532282 Laser disc, video, rental 334614 Laser disks, prerecorded video, mass reproducing
334510 Laser equipment, electromedical, manufacturing
621493 Laser surgery centers, freestanding 334510 Laser systems and equipment, medical, manufacturing
333992 Laser welding equipment manufacturing
316998 Lashes (i.e., whips) manufacturing
321999 Last sole patterns, all materials, manufacturing
212325 Laterite mining and/or beneficiating
326299 Latex foam rubber manufacturing
326299 Latex foam rubber products manufacturing
325510 Latex paint (i.e., water based) manufacturing
325212 Latex rubber, synthetic, manufacturing
332323 Lath, expanded metal, manufacturing
321219 Lath, fiber, manufacturing
327420 Lath, gypsum, manufacturing
321912 Lath, wood, manufacturing
333517 Lathes, metalworking, manufacturing
333243 Lathes, woodworking-type, manufacturing
238310 Lathing contractors
321912 Lathmills, wood
316110 Latigo leather manufacturing
812332 Laundered mat and rug supply services
812332 Launderers, industrial
812310 Launderettes

812320 Laundries (except coin-operated, linen supply, uniform supply)
812310 Laundries, coin-operated or similar self-service
812331 Laundries, linen and uniform supply
812310 Laundromats
812320 Laundry and drycleaning agents 314910
Laundry bags made from purchased woven or knitted materials
325612 Laundry bluing manufacturing
812320 Laundry drop-off and pick-up sites 335220
Laundry equipment (e.g., dryers, washers), household-type, manufacturing
333318 Laundry extractors manufacturing
332439 Laundry hampers, light gauge metal, manufacturing
337125 Laundry hampers, rattan, reed, wicker or willow, manufacturing
812310 Laundry machine routes (i.e., concession operators), coin-operated or similar self-service
333318 Laundry machinery and equipment (except household-type) manufacturing
423620 Laundry machinery and equipment, household-type (e.g., dryers, washers), merchant wholesalers
423850 Laundry machinery, equipment, and supplies, commercial, merchant wholesalers
314999 Laundry nets made from purchased materials
333318 Laundry pressing machines (except household-type) manufacturing
812320 Laundry services (except coin-operated, linen supply, uniform supply)
812310 Laundry services, coin-operated or similar self-service
812332 Laundry services, industrial
812331 Laundry services, linen supply 325611
Laundry soap, chips, and powder manufacturing
424690 Laundry soap, chips, and powder, merchant wholesalers
332999 Laundry tubs, metal, manufacturing
326191 Laundry tubs, plastics, manufacturing
325199 Lauric acid esters and amines manufacturing
332999 Lavatories, metal, manufacturing
327110 Lavatories, vitreous china, manufacturing
423720 Lavatory fixtures merchant wholesalers
423850 Law enforcement equipment (except safety) merchant wholesalers
922190 Law enforcement statistics centers, government
541110 Law firms
541110 Law offices
541110 Law practices
611310 Law schools
333112 Lawn and garden equipment manufacturing 811411 Lawn and garden equipment repair and maintenance services without retailing new lawn and garden equipment
713990 Lawn bowling clubs
561730 Lawn care services (e.g., fertilizing, mowing, seeding, spraying)
424910 Lawn care supplies (e.g., chemicals, fertilizers, pesticides) merchant wholesalers
332216 Lawn edgers, nonpowered, manufacturing
333112 Lawn edgers, powered, manufacturing
561730 Lawn fertilizing services
337125 Lawn furniture (except concrete, metal, stone, wood) manufacturing
337124 Lawn furniture, metal, manufacturing
337122 Lawn furniture, wood, manufacturing
332919 Lawn hose nozzles and lawn sprinklers manufacturing
423820 Lawn maintenance machinery and equipment merchant wholesalers
561730 Lawn maintenance services
561730 Lawn mowing services
561730 Lawn mulching services
444210 Lawn power equipment stores
561730 Lawn seeding services
561730 Lawn spraying services
238220 Lawn sprinkler system installation
444220 Lawn supply stores
562219 Lawn waste disposal facilities
532490 Lawnmower rental or leasing
811411 Lawnmower repair and maintenance shops without retailing new lawnmowers
333112 Lawnmowers (except agricultural-type), powered, manufacturing
423820 Lawnmowers merchant wholesalers 333111
Lawnmowers, agricultural-type, powered, manufacturing
332216 Lawnmowers, nonpowered, manufacturing

541110 Lawyers' offices
541110 Lawyers' private practices
325412 Laxative preparations manufacturing
112310 Layer-type chicken production
334419 LCD (liquid crystal display) unit screens manufacturing
212291 Leaching of uranium, radium, or vanadium ores
335911 Lead acid storage batteries manufacturing
331491 Lead and lead alloy bar, pipe, plate, rod, sheet, strip, and tubing made from purchased metals or scrap
325130 Lead based pigments manufacturing
331529 Lead castings (except die-castings), unfinished, manufacturing
331523 Lead die-castings, unfinished, manufacturing
332999 Lead foil not made in rolling mills
238390 Lead lining walls for X-ray room contractors
212230 Lead ore mine site development for own account
212230 Lead ore mining and/or beneficiating
325180 Lead oxides (except pigments) manufacturing
562910 Lead paint abatement services
562910 Lead paint removal contractors
325130 Lead pigments manufacturing
423510 Lead primary forms merchant wholesalers
331492 Lead recovering from scrap and/or alloying purchased metals
331491 Lead rolling, drawing, or extruding purchased metals or scrap
325180 Lead silicate manufacturing
331410 Lead smelting and refining, primary
327992 Lead, black (i.e., natural graphite), ground, refined, or blended, manufacturing
335110 Lead-in wires, electric lamp, made from purchased wire
212230 Lead-zinc ore mining and/or beneficiating
333112 Leaf blowers manufacturing 332216 Leaf skimmers and rakes, nonpowered swimming pool, manufacturing
332613 Leaf springs, heavy gauge metal, manufacturing
424590 Leaf tobacco merchant wholesalers
332999 Leaf, metal, manufacturing
334519 Leak detectors, water, manufacturing
813920 Learned societies
611691 Learning centers offering remedial courses
541720 Learning disabilities research and development services
213112 Lease tank cleaning and repairing on a contract basis
316998 Leashes, dog, manufacturing
****** Leasing -- see type of property or article being leased
522220 Leasing in combination with sales financing
315280 Leather apparel (e.g., capes, coats, hats, jackets) (except apparel contractors) manufacturing
315210 Leather apparel (e.g., capes, coats, hats, jackets) cut and sew apparel contractors
316998 Leather belting manufacturing
315280 Leather clothing (except apparel contractors) manufacturing
315210 Leather clothing cut and sew apparel contractors
448190 Leather coat stores
316110 Leather coloring, cutting, embossing, and japanning
316110 Leather converters
424990 Leather cut stock (except boot, shoe) merchant wholesalers
316998 Leather cut stock for shoe and boot manufacturing
424340 Leather cut stock for shoe and boot merchant wholesalers
316210 Leather footwear manufacturing
316210 Leather footwear, men's, manufacturing
316210 Leather footwear, slippers, manufacturing
316210 Leather footwear, women's, manufacturing
812320 Leather garment cleaning services
315210 Leather gloves or mittens (except athletic) cut and sew apparel contractors
315990 Leather gloves or mittens (except athletic, cut and sewn apparel contractors) manufacturing
339920 Leather gloves, athletic, manufacturing
424990 Leather goods (except belting, footwear, handbags, gloves, luggage) merchant wholesalers
811430 Leather goods repair shops without retailing new leather goods
448320 Leather goods stores
316998 Leather goods, small personal (e.g., coin purses, eyeglass cases, key cases), manufacturing
316992 Leather handbags and purses manufacturing

316210 Leather house slippers manufacturing
316998 Leather luggage manufacturing
316110 Leather tanning, currying, and finishing
316210 Leather upper athletic footwear manufacturing
316998 Leather welting manufacturing
333249 Leather working machinery manufacturing
313320 Leather, artificial, made from purchased fabric
322220 Leatherboard (i.e., paperboard based) made from purchased paperboard
322130 Leatherboard (i.e., paperboard based) made in paperboard mills
311225 Lecithin made from purchased oils
311224 Lecithin, cottonseed, made in crushing mills
311224 Lecithin, soybean, made in crushing mills
711410 Lecture bureaus 711510
Lecturers, independent
334413 LED (light emitting diode) manufacturing
111219 Leek farming, field, bedding plant and seed production
541110 Legal aid services
922130 Legal counsel offices, government 315210
Leggings cut and sew apparel contractors 315110
Leggings knitting or knitting and finishing 316998
Leggings, welder's, leather, manufacturing 315240
Leggings, women's, girls', and infants', cut and sewn
from purchased fabric (except apparel contractors)
921140 Legislative and executive office combinations
921120 Legislative assemblies
921120 Legislative bodies (e.g., federal, local, and state)
921120 Legislative commissions
111320 Lemon groves
325998 Lemon oil manufacturing
519120 Lending libraries
423460 Lens blanks, ophthalmic, merchant wholesalers
327215 Lens blanks, optical and ophthalmic, made from purchased glass
327212 Lens blanks, optical and ophthalmic, made in glass making plants
326199 Lens blanks, plastics ophthalmic or optical, manufacturing
333314 Lens coating (except ophthalmic)
339115 Lens coating, ophthalmic
333314 Lens grinding (except ophthalmic) 339115
Lens grinding, ophthalmic (except in retail stores)
446130 Lens grinding, ophthalmic, in retail stores
333316 Lens hoods, camera, manufacturing
333314 Lens mounting (except ophthalmic)
339115 Lens mounts, ophthalmic, manufacturing
333314 Lens polishing (except ophthalmic)
339115 Lens polishing, ophthalmic
333314 Lenses (except ophthalmic) manufacturing
339115 Lenses, ophthalmic, manufacturing
423460 Lenses, optical, merchant wholesalers
111130 Lentil farming, dry, field and seed production
315210 Leotards cut and sew apparel contractors
315190 Leotards made in apparel knitting mills
315240 Leotards, women's and girls', cut and sewn
from purchased fabric (except apparel contractors)
212393 Lepidolite mining and/or beneficiating
622310 Leprosy hospitals
****** Lessors -- see specific type of asset or property being rented or leased
531130 Lessors of miniwarehouses 531120 Lessors
of nonresidential buildings (except miniwarehouses)
531110 Lessors of residential buildings and dwellings
531130 Lessors of self-storage units
423420 Letter and envelope handling machines merchant wholesalers
333318 Letter folding, stuffing, and sealing machinery manufacturing
333515 Letter pins (e.g., gauging, measuring) manufacturing
561410 Letter writing services
325910 Letterpress inks manufacturing
323120 Letterpress plate preparation services
333244 Letterpress printing presses manufacturing
339950 Letters for signs manufacturing
322230 Letters, die-cut, made from purchased cardboard
111219 Lettuce farming, field, bedding plant and seed production
237990 Levee construction 334513 Level and bulk measuring instruments, industrial process-type, manufacturing

334519 Level gauges, radiation-type, manufacturing
334519 Levels and tapes, surveying, manufacturing
332216 Levels, carpenter's, manufacturing 524126
Liability insurance carriers, direct 519120 Libraries (except motion picture stock footage, motion picture commercial distribution)
512199 Libraries, motion picture stock footage film
512199 Libraries, video tape, stock footage
236220 Library construction
561990 License issuing services (except government), motor vehicle
621399 Licensed practical nurses' (LPNs) offices (e.g., centers, clinics)
926130 Licensing and inspecting of utilities
926150 Licensing and permit issuance for business operations, government
926150 Licensing and permit issuance for professional occupations, government
926120 Licensing of transportation equipment, facilities, and services
311340 Licorice candy manufacturing
332431 Lids and ends, can, light gauge metal, manufacturing
332119 Lids, jar, metal, stamping
561611 Lie detection services
334519 Lie detectors manufacturing
611699 Life guard training
524210 Life insurance agencies
524113 Life insurance carriers, direct
339113 Life preservers manufacturing
336612 Life rafts, inflatable, manufacturing
524130 Life reinsurance carriers
541715 Life sciences research and development laboratories or services (except biotechnology and nanotechnology research and development)
423830 Lift trucks, industrial, merchant wholesalers
316998 Lifts, heel, leather, manufacturing
333249 Light bulb and tube (i.e., electric lamp) machinery manufacturing
335110 Light bulbs manufacturing
423610 Light bulbs merchant wholesalers 335110
Light bulbs, sealed beam automotive, manufacturing
334413 Light emitting diodes (LED) manufacturing
333316 Light meters, photographic, manufacturing
336510 Light rail cars and equipment manufacturing
237990 Light rail system construction
485119 Light rail systems (except mixed mode), commuter
334511 Light reconnaissance and surveillance systems and equipment manufacturing
334512 Light responsive appliance controls manufacturing
441110 Light utility truck dealers, new only or new and used
441120 Light utility truck dealers, used only
336112 Light utility trucks assembling on chassis of own manufacture
325998 Lighter fluids (e.g., charcoal, cigarette) manufacturing
483211 Lighterage (i.e., freight transportation except vessel supply services)
339999 Lighters, cigar and cigarette (except motor vehicle, precious metal), manufacturing
339910 Lighters, cigar and cigarette, clad with precious metal, manufacturing
424990 Lighters, cigar and cigarette, merchant wholesalers
488310 Lighthouse operation
335991 Lighting carbons manufacturing
541490 Lighting design services
423990 Lighting equipment, gas, merchant wholesalers
444190 Lighting fixture stores
335129 Lighting fixtures, airport (e.g., approach, ramp, runway, taxi), manufacturing
335122 Lighting fixtures, commercial electric, manufacturing
423610 Lighting fixtures, electric, merchant wholesalers
335122 Lighting fixtures, industrial electric, manufacturing
335122 Lighting fixtures, institutional electric, manufacturing
335129 Lighting fixtures, nonelectric (e.g., propane, kerosene, carbide), manufacturing
335121 Lighting fixtures, residential electric, manufacturing
561790 Lighting maintenance services (e.g., bulb and fuse replacement and cleaning)
238210 Lighting system installation 711510
Lighting technicians, theatrical, independent
335311 Lighting transformers manufacturing

335311 Lighting transformers, street and airport, manufacturing
335931 Lightning arrestors and coils manufacturing
423610 Lightning arrestors merchant wholesalers
238290 Lightning protection equipment (e.g., lightning rod) installation
335931 Lightning protection equipment manufacturing
238290 Lightning rod and conductor installation
325211 Lignin plastics manufacturing 213113
Lignite mining services (except site preparation and related construction contractor activities) on a contract basis
212111 Lignite surface mining and/or beneficiating
111130 Lima bean farming, dry, field and seed production
339113 Limbs, artificial, manufacturing 423320
Lime (except agricultural) merchant wholesalers
111320 Lime groves
325998 Lime oil manufacturing
327410 Lime production
212312 Lime rock, ground, mining and/or beneficiating
424910 Lime, agricultural, merchant wholesalers
212312 Limestone (except bituminous) crushed and broken stone mining and/or beneficiating
212312 Limestone beneficiating plants (e.g., grinding or pulverizing)
212311 Limestone mining or quarrying
212319 Limestone, bituminous, mining and/or beneficiating
325320 Lime-sulfur fungicides manufacturing
334512 Limit controls (e.g., air-conditioning, appliance, heating) manufacturing
511199 Limited editions art print publishers (except exclusive Internet publishing)
452319 Limited price variety stores
212210 Limonite mining and/or beneficiating
532111 Limousine rental without driver
485320 Limousine services (except shuttle services)
485320 Limousines for hire with driver (except taxis)
325320 Lindane pesticides manufacturing
334512 Line or limit control for electric heat manufacturing
561730 Line slash (i.e., rights of way) maintenance services
238910 Line slashing or cutting (except maintenance)
335311 Line voltage regulators (i.e., electric transformers) manufacturing
335999 Linear accelerators manufacturing
332991 Linear ball bearings manufacturing
334514 Linear counters manufacturing
325220 Linear esters fibers and filaments manufacturing
332991 Linear roller bearings manufacturing
442299 Linen stores 812331 Linen supply services
423220 Linens (e.g., bath, bed, table) merchant wholesalers
314120 Linens made from purchased materials
327120 Liner brick and plates, vitrified clay, manufacturing
332313 Liners, industrial, fabricated metal plate work, manufacturing
114111 Lingcod fishing
315210 Lingerie cut and sew apparel contractors
424330 Lingerie merchant wholesalers
448190 Lingerie stores
315240 Lingerie, women's and girls', cut and sewn from purchased fabric (except apparel contractors)
316110 Lining leather manufacturing
316998 Linings, boot and shoe, leather, manufacturing
314999 Linings, casket, manufacturing 315210
Linings, hat, cut and sew apparel contractors
315990 Linings, hat, men's, cut and sewn from purchased fabric (except apparel contractors)
314999 Linings, luggage, manufacturing
332999 Linings, metal safe and vault, manufacturing
332994 Links, ammunition, manufacturing
325199 Linoleic acid esters and amines manufacturing
326199 Linoleum floor coverings manufacturing
238330 Linoleum, installation only
333244 Linotype machines manufacturing
311225 Linseed oil made from purchased oils
311224 Linseed oil, cake and meal, made in crushing mills

327390 Lintels, concrete, manufacturing
325412 Lip balms manufacturing
325620 Lipsticks manufacturing
424690 Liquefied gases (except LP) merchant wholesalers
488999 Liquefied natural gas (LNG) plants
424710 Liquefied petroleum gas (LPG) bulk stations and terminals, merchant wholesalers
332420 Liquefied petroleum gas (LPG) cylinders manufacturing
454310 Liquefied petroleum gas (LPG) dealers, direct selling
221210 Liquefied petroleum gas (LPG) distribution through mains
324110 Liquefied petroleum gas (LPG) made in refineries
424720 Liquefied petroleum gas (LPG) merchant wholesalers (except bulk stations, terminals)
211130 Liquefied petroleum gases (LPG), natural
325120 Liquid air manufacturing
334513 Liquid analysis instruments, industrial process-type, manufacturing
311313 Liquid beet syrup manufacturing
334516 Liquid chromatographic instruments, laboratory-type, manufacturing
334513 Liquid concentration instruments, industrial process-type, manufacturing
423690 Liquid crystal displays merchant wholesalers
334514 Liquid flow meters manufacturing
211130 Liquid hydrocarbons recovered from oil and gas field gases
334512 Liquid level controls, residential and commercial heating-type, manufacturing
334513 Liquid level instruments, industrial process-type, manufacturing
332420 Liquid oxygen tanks manufacturing
311313 Liquid sugar made from beet sugar
311314 Liquid sugar manufacturing
211130 Liquids, natural gas (e.g., ethane, isobutane, natural gasoline, propane) recovered from oil and gas field gases
445310 Liquor stores, package
311351 Liquor, chocolate, made from cacao beans
311352 Liquor, chocolate, made from purchased chocolate
424820 Liquors merchant wholesalers
312130 Liquors, brandy, distilling and blending
424820 Liquors, distilled, merchant wholesalers
312140 Liquors, distilling and blending (except brandy)
339940 List finders and roledex address files manufacturing
531390 Listing services, real estate
711410 Literary agents
325130 Litharge manufacturing
335912 Lithium batteries, primary, manufacturing
335911 Lithium batteries, storage, manufacturing
325180 Lithium compounds, not specified elsewhere by process, manufacturing
212393 Lithium mineral mining and/or beneficiating
325910 Lithographic inks manufacturing
323120 Lithographic plate preparation services
323111 Lithographic printing (except books, grey goods)
333244 Lithographic printing presses manufacturing
325130 Lithopone manufacturing
334510 Lithotripters manufacturing
711310 Live arts center operators
424990 Live bait merchant wholesalers
711310 Live theater operators
332994 Livens projectors (i.e., ordnance) manufacturing
424520 Livestock (except horses, mules, and feedlots) merchant wholesalers
541690 Livestock breeding consulting services
115210 Livestock breeding services (except consulting)
424910 Livestock feeds merchant wholesalers
311119 Livestock feeds, supplements, concentrates and premixes, manufacturing
541940 Livestock inspecting and testing services, veterinary
115210 Livestock spraying
484220 Livestock trucking, local
484230 Livestock trucking, long-distance
541940 Livestock veterinary services
337124 Living room furniture (except upholstered), metal, manufacturing
337122 Living room furniture (except upholstered), wood, manufacturing
337121 Living room furniture, upholstered, manufacturing
112990 Llama production
334418 Loaded computer boards manufacturing

423430 Loaded computer boards merchant wholesalers
423810 Loaders merchant wholesalers
333120 Loaders, shovel, manufacturing
332993 Loading and assembling bombs
488490 Loading and unloading at truck terminals
488320 Loading and unloading services at ports and harbors
488210 Loading and unloading services at rail terminals
333131 Loading machines, underground mining, manufacturing
334418 Loading printed circuit boards
522310 Loan brokerages
522310 Loan brokers' or agents' offices (i.e., independent)
522291 Loan companies (i.e., consumer, personal, small, student)
522292 Loan correspondents (i.e., lending funds with real estate as collateral)
522390 Loan servicing
541820 Lobbying services
541820 Lobbyists' offices
114112 Lobster fishing
334210 Local area network (LAN) communications equipment (e.g., bridges, gateways, routers) manufacturing
541512 Local area network (LAN) computer systems integration design services
611420 Local area network (LAN) management training
485113 Local bus services (except mixed mode)
561421 Local call centers
492210 Local letter and parcel delivery services (except as part of intercity courier network, U.S. Postal Service)
492110 Local letter and parcel delivery services as part of intercity courier network
485112 Local passenger rail systems (except mixed mode)
813940 Local political organizations
517311 Local telephone carriers, wired
485111 Local transit systems, mixed mode (e.g., bus, commuter rail, subway combinations)
561990 Locating underground utility lines prior to digging
237990 Lock and waterway construction
561622 Lock rekeying services
332722 Lock washers, metal, manufacturing
454390 Locker meat provisioners, direct selling
337215 Lockers (except refrigerated) manufacturing
423440 Lockers (except refrigerated) merchant wholesalers
812990 Lockers, coin-operated, rental
333415 Lockers, refrigerated, manufacturing
423740 Lockers, refrigerated, merchant wholesalers
332510 Locks (except coin-operated, time locks), metal, manufacturing
333318 Locks, coin-operated, manufacturing
423710 Locks, security, merchant wholesalers
423850 Locksmith equipment and supplies merchant wholesalers
561622 Locksmith services
561622 Locksmith services with or without sales of locking devices, safes, and security vaults
561622 Locksmith shops
488210 Locomotive and rail car repair (except factory conversion, factory overhaul, factory rebuilding)
336320 Locomotive and railroad car light fixtures manufacturing
333923 Locomotive cranes manufacturing
333618 Locomotive diesel engines manufacturing
336510 Locomotives manufacturing
423860 Locomotives merchant wholesalers
336510 Locomotives rebuilding
212221 Lode gold mining and/or beneficiating
321992 Log cabins, prefabricated wood, manufacturing
333120 Log debarking machinery, portable, manufacturing
333243 Log debarking machinery, stationary, manufacturing
113310 Log harvesting
484220 Log hauling, local
484230 Log hauling, long-distance
236115 Log home construction general contractors
236117 Log home for-sale builders
333120 Log splitters, portable, manufacturing
333243 Log splitters, stationary, manufacturing
111334 Loganberry farming
113310 Logging
236220 Logging camp construction
541330 Logging engineering services
423810 Logging equipment merchant wholesalers

532412 Logging equipment rental or leasing without operator

482112 Logging railroads

237310 Logging road construction

336212 Logging trailers manufacturing

213112 Logging wells on a contract basis

334515 Logic circuit testers manufacturing

541614 Logistics and integrated supply chain management consulting services

541614 Logistics management consulting services

423990 Logs merchant wholesalers

333414 Logs, gas fireplace, manufacturing

325194 Logwood extract manufacturing

517911 Long-distance telecommunication resellers (except satellite)

517311 Long-distance telephone carriers, wired

517410 Long-distance telephone satellite communication carriers

488320 Longshoremen services

333249 Loom bobbins manufacturing

333249 Loom reeds manufacturing

333249 Looms for textiles manufacturing

333249 Loopers for textiles manufacturing

323111 Looseleaf binders and devices manufacturing

424120 Looseleaf binders merchant wholesalers

322230 Looseleaf fillers and paper made from purchased paper

322121 Looseleaf fillers and paper made in paper mills

524291 Loss control consultants

325620 Lotions (e.g., body, face, hand) manufacturing

713290 Lottery control boards (i.e., operating lotteries)

921130 Lottery control boards, nonoperating

713290 Lottery corporations 713290 Lottery ticket sales agents (except retail stores)

334118 Lottery ticket sales terminals manufacturing

713290 Lottery ticket vendors (except retail stores)

334310 Loudspeakers manufacturing

722410 Lounges, cocktail

315210 Lounging robes and dressing gowns cut and sew apparel contractors

315190 Lounging robes and dressing gowns made in apparel knitting mills

315220 Lounging robes and dressing gowns, men's and boys', cut and sewn from purchased fabric (except apparel contractors)

315240 Lounging robes and dressing gowns, women's, girls', and infants', cut and sewn from purchased fabric (except apparel contractors)

333314 Loupes (e.g., jewelers) manufacturing

321911 Louver windows and doors, made from purchased glass with wood frame

332321 Louver windows, metal, manufacturing

332322 Louvers, sheet metal (except stampings), manufacturing

236117 Low income housing construction for-sale builders

236116 Low income housing, multifamily, construction general contractors

236115 Low income housing, single-family, construction general contractors

238160 Low slope roofing installation

238210 Low voltage electrical work 335121

Low voltage lighting equipment, residential, electric, manufacturing

236116 Low-rise apartment construction general contractors

236117 Low-rise apartment for-sale builders

311340 Lozenges, nonmedicated, candy, manufacturing

621399 LPNs' (licensed practical nurses) offices (e.g., centers, clinics)

484122 LTL (less-than-truckload) long-distance freight trucking

424710 Lubricating oils and greases bulk stations and terminals, merchant wholesalers

324110 Lubricating oils and greases made in petroleum refineries

424720 Lubricating oils and greases merchant wholesalers (except bulk stations, terminals)

324191 Lubricating oils and greases, petroleum, made from refined petroleum

325998 Lubricating oils and greases, synthetic, manufacturing

811191 Lubrication shops, automotive

336510 Lubrication systems, locomotive (except pumps), manufacturing

332510 Luggage hardware, metal, manufacturing

314999 Luggage linings manufacturing

423990 Luggage merchant wholesalers

336390 Luggage racks, car top, automotive, truck, and bus, manufacturing

811430 Luggage repair shops without retailing new luggage
448320 Luggage stores
316998 Luggage, all materials, manufacturing
335931 Lugs and connectors, electrical, manufacturing
423610 Lugs and connectors, electrical, merchant wholesalers
423310 Lumber (e.g., dressed, finished, rough) merchant wholesalers
321113 Lumber (i.e., rough, dressed) made from logs or bolts
561990 Lumber grading services
444190 Lumber retailing yards 493190
Lumber storage terminals
321113 Lumber, hardwood dimension, made from logs or bolts
321912 Lumber, hardwood dimension, resawing purchased lumber
321999 Lumber, kiln drying
321213 Lumber, parallel strand, manufacturing
321113 Lumber, softwood dimension, made from logs or bolts
321912 Lumber, softwood dimension, resawing purchased lumber
335122 Luminous panel ceilings, electric, manufacturing
335311 Luminous tube transformers manufacturing
332439 Lunch boxes, light gauge metal, manufacturing
722330 Lunch wagons
311612 Luncheon meat (except poultry) made from purchased carcasses
311611 Luncheon meat (except poultry) produced in slaughtering plants
311615 Luncheon meat, poultry, manufacturing
337127 Lunchroom tables and chairs manufacturing
532111 Luxury automobile rental without driver
485320 Luxury automobiles for hire with driver (except taxis)
321213 LVL (laminated veneer lumber) manufacturing
325612 Lye, household-type, manufacturing
111335 Macadamia farming
424490 Macaroni merchant wholesalers
311824 Macaroni, dry, manufacturing
311991 Macaroni, fresh, manufacturing
311412 Macaroni, frozen, manufacturing
332216 Machetes manufacturing
332999 Machine bases, metal, manufacturing
332322 Machine guards, sheet metal (except stampings), manufacturing
332994 Machine gun belts manufacturing
332994 Machine guns manufacturing
332722 Machine keys, metal, manufacturing
332216 Machine knives (except metal cutting) manufacturing
333515 Machine knives, metal cutting, manufacturing
238290 Machine rigging
332710 Machine shops
333515 Machine tool attachments and accessories manufacturing
335311 Machine tool transformers manufacturing
423830 Machine tools and accessories merchant wholesalers
811310 Machine tools repair and maintenance services
333517 Machine tools, metal cutting, manufacturing
333517 Machine tools, metal forming, manufacturing
238290 Machinery and equipment, large-scale, installation
522220 Machinery finance leasing
238910 Machinery, construction (except cranes), rental with operator
423420 Machines, office, merchant wholesalers
332216 Machinists' precision measuring tools (except optical) manufacturing
423830 Machinists' precision measuring tools merchant wholesalers
334511 Machmeters manufacturing
114111 Mackerel fishing
315210 Mackinaws cut and sew apparel contractors
315220 Mackinaws, men's and boys', cut and sewn
from purchased fabric (except apparel contractors)
315240 Mackinaws, women's, girls', and infants', cut and sewn from purchased fabric (except apparel contractors)
541840 Magazine advertising representatives (i.e., independent of media owners)
511120 Magazine publishers (except exclusive Internet publishing)
511120 Magazine publishers and printing combined
519130 Magazine publishers, exclusively on Internet

337122 Magazine racks, wood, manufacturing
451212 Magazine stands (i.e., permanent)
323111 Magazines and periodicals commercial printing (except screen) without publishing
323113 Magazines and periodicals screen printing without publishing
424920 Magazines merchant wholesalers
711190 Magic shows
451120 Magic supply stores
711510 Magicians, independent
327120 Magnesia refractory cement manufacturing
325411 Magnesia, medicinal, uncompounded, manufacturing
212325 Magnesite mining and/or beneficiating
327992 Magnesite, crude (e.g., calcined, dead-burned, ground), manufacturing
331491 Magnesium and magnesium alloy bar, rod, shape, sheet, strip, and tubing made from purchased metals or scrap
325180 Magnesium carbonate manufacturing
331529 Magnesium castings (except die-castings), unfinished, manufacturing
325180 Magnesium chloride manufacturing
325180 Magnesium compounds, not specified elsewhere by process, manufacturing
331523 Magnesium die-castings, unfinished, manufacturing
331491 Magnesium foil made by rolling purchased metals or scrap
332999 Magnesium foil not made in rolling mills
423520 Magnesium ores merchant wholesalers
331492 Magnesium recovering from scrap and/or alloying purchased metals
331410 Magnesium refining, primary 331491 Magnesium rolling, drawing, or extruding purchased metals or scrap
331420 Magnet wire, insulated, made from purchased copper in wire drawing plants
331318 Magnet wire, insulated, made in aluminum wire drawing plants
331491 Magnet wire, nonferrous metals (except aluminum, copper), made from purchased nonferrous metals (except aluminum, copper) in wire drawing plants
334613 Magnetic and optical media, blank, manufacturing
423690 Magnetic bubble memories merchant wholesalers
334514 Magnetic counters manufacturing
334513 Magnetic flow meters, industrial process-type, manufacturing
333517 Magnetic forming machines, metalworking, manufacturing
541360 Magnetic geophysical surveying services
334118 Magnetic ink recognition devices, computer peripheral equipment, manufacturing
334613 Magnetic recording media for tapes, cassettes, and disks, manufacturing
621512 Magnetic resonance imaging (MRI) centers
334510 Magnetic resonance imaging (MRI) medical diagnostic equipment manufacturing
334516 Magnetic resonance imaging (MRI) type apparatus (except medical diagnostic) manufacturing
334613 Magnetic tapes, cassettes and disks, blank, manufacturing
423690 Magnetic tapes, cassettes, and disks, blank, merchant wholesalers
334112 Magnetic/optical combination storage units for computers manufacturing
334519 Magnetometers manufacturing
334419 Magnetron tubes manufacturing 327110 Magnets, permanent, ceramic or ferrite, manufacturing
332999 Magnets, permanent, metallic, manufacturing
339115 Magnifiers, corrective vision-type, manufacturing
333314 Magnifying glasses (except corrective vision-type) manufacturing
423460 Magnifying glasses merchant wholesalers
333314 Magnifying instruments, optical, manufacturing
114111 Mahimahi fishing
561311 Maid registries
561720 Maid services (i.e., cleaning services)
238990 Mail box units, outdoor, multiple box-type, erection
337215 Mail carrier cases and tables, wood, manufacturing
332322 Mail chutes, sheet metal (except stampings), manufacturing
561499 Mail consolidation services 333318 Mail handling machinery, post office-type, manufacturing
561499 Mail presorting services
561431 Mailbox rental centers, private

561431 Mailbox rental services combined with one or more other office support services, private
423990 Mailboxes merchant wholesalers
332439 Mailboxes, light gauge metal, manufacturing
322219 Mailing cases and tubes, paper fiber (i.e., all-fiber, nonfiber ends of any material), made from purchased paperboard
532420 Mailing equipment rental or leasing
511140 Mailing list publishers (except exclusive Internet publishing)
423420 Mailing machines merchant wholesalers
454110 Mail-order houses
334111 Mainframe computers manufacturing
488190 Maintenance and repair services, aircraft (except factory conversion, factory overhaul, factory rebuilding)
561730 Maintenance of plants and shrubs in buildings
488210 Maintenance of rights of way and structures, railway
488119 Maintenance services, runway
488310 Maintenance services, waterfront terminal (except dredging)
711211 Major league baseball clubs
812112 Makeup (except permanent) salons
325620 Makeup (i.e., cosmetics) manufacturing
812199 Makeup salons, permanent
523110 Making markets for securities
337125 Malacca furniture (except upholstered), household-type, manufacturing
325320 Malathion insecticides manufacturing 325194 Maleic anhydride manufacturing 531120 Mall property operation (i.e., not operating contained businesses) rental or leasing
331511 Malleable iron foundries
332216 Mallets (e.g., rubber, wood) manufacturing
321999 Mallets, wood, manufacturing
325199 Malonic dinitrile manufacturing
524126 Malpractice insurance carriers, direct
311942 Malt extract and syrups manufacturing
424490 Malt extract merchant wholesalers
311213 Malt flour manufacturing
312120 Malt liquor brewing
424810 Malt liquor merchant wholesalers
311213 Malt manufacturing
424490 Malt merchant wholesalers
333241 Malt milling machinery manufacturing
311213 Malt sprouts manufacturing
311514 Malted milk manufacturing
311213 Malting (germinating and drying grains)
311221 Maltodextrins manufacturing
621512 Mammogram (i.e., breast imaging) centers
711410 Management agencies for artists, entertainers, and other public figures
611430 Management development training
525910 Management investment offices, open-ended
561110 Management services (except complete operation of client's business)
115116 Management services, farm
711310 Managers of agricultural fairs with facilities
711320 Managers of agricultural fairs without facilities
711310 Managers of arts events with facilities
711320 Managers of arts events without facilities
711310 Managers of festivals with facilities
711320 Managers of festivals without facilities
711310 Managers of live performing arts productions (e.g., concerts) with facilities
711320 Managers of live performing arts productions (e.g., concerts) without facilities
711310 Managers of sports events with facilities
711320 Managers of sports events without facilities
531312 Managers' offices, commercial condominium
531312 Managers' offices, commercial real estate
531312 Managers' offices, nonresidential real estate
531311 Managers' offices, residential condominium
531311 Managers' offices, residential real estate
711410 Managers, authors'
711410 Managers, celebrities'
561920 Managers, convention
711410 Managers, entertainers'
711410 Managers, public figures'
711410 Managers, sports figures'
561920 Managers, trade fair or show
531312 Managing commercial condominiums
531312 Managing commercial real estate
531311 Managing cooperative apartments
523920 Managing investment funds

523920 Managing mutual funds
561110 Managing offices of dentists
561110 Managing offices of physicians and surgeons
561110 Managing offices of professionals (e.g., dentists, physicians, surgeons)
523920 Managing personal investment trusts
531311 Managing residential condominiums
531311 Managing residential real estate
523920 Managing trusts
111320 Mandarin groves
339992 Mandolins manufacturing
333515 Mandrels (i.e., a machine tool accessory) manufacturing
212299 Manganese concentrates beneficiating
325180 Manganese dioxide manufacturing
331110 Manganese metal ferroalloys manufacturing
212299 Manganese ores mining and/or beneficiating
212210 Manganiferous ores valued for iron content, mining and/or beneficiating
212299 Manganiferousares ores (not valued for iron content) mining and/or beneficiating
212299 Manganite mining and/or beneficiating
111339 Mango farming
325194 Mangrove extract manufacturing
331511 Manhole covers, cast iron, manufacturing
237120 Manhole, oil and gas, construction
812113 Manicure and pedicure salons
611511 Manicure and pedicure schools
325620 Manicure preparations manufacturing
812113 Manicurist services
423850 Manicurists supplies merchant wholesalers
424120 Manifold business forms merchant wholesalers
323111 Manifold business forms printing
336310 Manifolds (i.e., intake and exhaust), automotive and truck gasoline engine, manufacturing
332996 Manifolds, pipe, made from purchased metal pipe
322230 Manila folders, die-cut, made from purchased paper or paperboard
327999 Manmade and engineered proppants (e.g., resin-coated sand, ceramic materials) manufacturing
325220 Manmade cellulosic fibers manufacturing
313220 Manmade fabric, narrow woven, weaving
313210 Manmade fabrics, broadwoven, weaving
313110 Manmade fiber thread manufacturing
424690 Manmade fibers merchant wholesalers
325220 Manmade noncellulosic fibers and filaments manufacturing
313110 Manmade staple spun yarns made from purchased fiber
541890 Mannequin decorating services
339999 Mannequins manufacturing
423440 Mannequins merchant wholesalers
325920 Mannitol hexanitrate explosive materials manufacturing
334513 Manometers, industrial process-type, manufacturing
561320 Manpower pools
238340 Mantel, marble or stone, installation
621399 Manual-arts therapists' offices (e.g., centers, clinics)
423390 Manufactured (i.e., mobile) homes merchant wholesalers
321991 Manufactured (mobile) buildings for commercial use (e.g., banks, offices) manufacturing
321991 Manufactured (mobile) classrooms manufacturing
453930 Manufactured (mobile) home dealers
531190 Manufactured (mobile) home parks 238990
Manufactured (mobile) home set up and tie-down work
531190 Manufactured (mobile) home sites rental or leasing
321991 Manufactured (mobile) homes manufacturing
221210 Manufactured gas distribution
813910 Manufacturers' associations
236210 Manufacturing building construction
531120 Manufacturing building rental or leasing
532490 Manufacturing machinery and equipment rental or leasing
423830 Manufacturing machinery and equipment, industrial, merchant wholesalers
541614 Manufacturing management consulting services
541614 Manufacturing operations improvement consulting services
511130 Map publishers (except exclusive Internet publishing)

511130 Map publishers and printing combined
519130 Map publishers, exclusively on Internet
111998 Maple sap concentrating (i.e., producing pure maple syrup in the field)
111998 Maple sap gathering
111998 Maple syrup (i.e., maple sap reducing)
424490 Maple syrup merchant wholesalers
311999 Maple syrup mixing into other products
541370 Mapping (except geophysical) services
541360 Mapping services, geophysical
424920 Maps (except globe, school, wall) merchant wholesalers
323111 Maps commercial printing (except screen) without publishing
323113 Maps screen printing without publishing
212319 Marble crushed and broken stone mining and/or beneficiating
212311 Marble mining or quarrying
238140 Marble, granite and slate, exterior, contractors
238340 Marble, granite, and slate, interior installation contractors
339930 Marbles manufacturing
212393 Marcasite mining and/or beneficiating
325199 Margaric acid manufacturing
311221 Margarine and other corn oils made by wet milling corn
424490 Margarine merchant wholesalers
311225 Margarine-butter blend made from purchased fats and oils
311225 Margarines (including imitation) made from purchased fats and oils
424590 Marijuana merchant wholesalers
453998 Marijuana stores, medical or recreational
111998 Marijuana, grown in an open field
111419 Marijuana, grown under cover
713930 Marinas
335314 Marine and navy auxiliary controls, manufacturing
713930 Marine basins, operation of
488390 Marine cargo checkers and surveyors
488320 Marine cargo handling services
237990 Marine construction
928110 Marine Corps
541330 Marine engineering services
333618 Marine engines manufacturing
541990 Marine forecasting services
332510 Marine hardware, metal, manufacturing
332999 Marine horns, compressed air or steam, metal, manufacturing
524126 Marine insurance carriers, direct
712110 Marine museums
611519 Marine navigational schools
325510 Marine paints manufacturing
332410 Marine power boilers manufacturing
334220 Marine radio communications equipment manufacturing
524130 Marine reinsurance carriers
488330 Marine salvaging services
447190 Marine service stations
488510 Marine shipping agency
335911 Marine storage batteries manufacturing
423860 Marine supplies (except pleasure) merchant wholesalers
423910 Marine supplies, pleasure, merchant wholesalers
441222 Marine supply dealers
541990 Marine surveyor (i.e., ship appraiser) services
488330 Marine vessel traffic reporting services
339999 Marionettes (i.e., puppets) manufacturing
541330 Maritime technology engineering services
339940 Marker boards (i.e., whiteboards) manufacturing
523110 Market making for securities
541910 Marketing analysis services
541613 Marketing consulting services
541613 Marketing management consulting services
541910 Marketing research services
339940 Marking devices manufacturing
424120 Marking devices merchant wholesalers
333519 Marking machines, metal, manufacturing
212312 Marl crushed and broken stone mining and/or beneficiating
311421 Marmalade manufacturing
424490 Marmalade merchant wholesalers 321999 Marquetry, wood, manufacturing 624190 Marriage counseling services (except by offices of mental health practitioners)
922120 Marshals' offices
311340 Marshmallow creme manufacturing
311340 Marshmallows manufacturing
611620 Martial arts instruction, camps, or schools

311340 Marzipan (i.e., candy) manufacturing 335999 Maser (i.e., microwave amplification by stimulated emission of radiation) amplifiers manufacturing
321999 Mashers, potato, wood, manufacturing
322220 Masking tape made from purchased paper
444190 Masonry (e.g., block, brick, stone) dealers
238140 Masonry contractors
238140 Masonry pointing, cleaning or caulking
332216 Mason's handtools manufacturing
423320 Mason's materials merchant wholesalers
334516 Mass spectrometers manufacturing
334516 Mass spectroscopy instrumentation manufacturing
423850 Massage equipment merchant wholesalers
335210 Massage machines, electric (except designed for beauty and barber shop use), manufacturing
812199 Massage parlors
611519 Massage therapist instruction 621399 Massage therapists' offices (e.g., centers, clinics)
512250 Master recording leasing and licensing
424690 Mastics (except construction) merchant wholesalers
423390 Mastics, construction, merchant wholesalers
321999 Masts, wood, manufacturing
812332 Mat and rug supply services
325998 Matches and match books manufacturing
424990 Matches and match books merchant wholesalers
238290 Material handling equipment installation
811310 Material handling equipment repair and maintenance services
423830 Material handling machinery and equipment merchant wholesalers
532490 Material handling machinery and equipment rental or leasing
541614 Materials management consulting services
562920 Materials recovery facilities (MRF)
236210 Materials recovery facility construction
923120 Maternity and child health program administration
315210 Maternity bras and corsets cut and sew apparel contractors
315240 Maternity bras and corsets, women's and girls', cut and sewn from purchased fabric (except apparel contractors)
622310 Maternity hospitals
448120 Maternity shops
541715 Mathematics research and development laboratories or services
332618 Mats and matting made from purchased wire
332216 Mattocks (i.e., handtools) manufacturing
326299 Mattress protectors, rubber, manufacturing
332613 Mattress springs and spring units, light gauge, made from purchased wire or strip
442110 Mattress stores (including waterbeds)
337910 Mattresses (i.e., box spring, innerspring, noninnerspring) manufacturing
337910 Mattresses made from felt, foam rubber, urethane and similar materials
423210 Mattresses merchant wholesalers
326199 Mattresses, air, plastics, manufacturing
326299 Mattresses, air, rubber, manufacturing
311812 Matzo baking made in commercial bakeries
332216 Mauls, metal, manufacturing
321999 Mauls, wood, manufacturing
236220 Mausoleum (i.e., building) construction
812220 Mausoleums
311941 Mayonnaise manufacturing
921110 Mayor's offices
321219 MDF (medium density fiberboard) manufacturing
621112 MDs' (medical doctors), mental health, offices (e.g., centers, clinics)
621111 MDs' (medical doctors, except mental health) offices (e.g., centers, clinics)
624210 Meal delivery programs
311119 Meal, alfalfa, manufacturing
311119 Meal, bone, prepared as feed for animals and fowls, manufacturing
311211 Meal, corn, for human consumption made in flour mills
423830 Measuring and testing equipment (except electric measuring and automotive) merchant wholesalers
333515 Measuring attachments (e.g., sine bars) for machine tool manufacturing
334515 Measuring equipment for electronic and electrical circuits and equipment manufacturing
811219 Measuring instrument repair and maintenance services
334515 Measuring instruments and meters, electric, manufacturing

334513 Measuring instruments, industrial process control-type, manufacturing
332216 Measuring tools, machinist's (except optical), manufacturing
334514 Measuring wheels manufacturing 311613
Meat and bone meal and tankage, produced in rendering plant
333241 Meat and poultry processing and preparation machinery
311612 Meat canning (except baby, pet food, poultry), made from purchased carcasses
311611 Meat canning (except poultry) produced in slaughtering plants
311422 Meat canning, baby food, manufacturing
311111 Meat canning, dog and cat, pet food, made from purchased carcasses
311615 Meat canning, poultry (except baby and pet food), manufacturing
311612 Meat extracts made from purchased carcasses
333241 Meat grinders, food-type, manufacturing
445210 Meat markets
311615 Meat products (e.g., hot dogs, luncheon meats, sausages) made from a combination of poultry and other meats
311612 Meat products canning (except baby, pet food, poultry) made from purchased carcasses
311111 Meat products, dog and cat, pet food, canning, made from purchased carcasses
311612 Meats (except poultry), cured or smoked, made from purchased carcasses
424470 Meats and meat products (except canned, packaged frozen) merchant wholesalers
311611 Meats fresh, chilled or frozen (except poultry and small game), produced in slaughtering plants
424490 Meats, canned, merchant wholesalers
424470 Meats, cured or smoked, merchant wholesalers
311611 Meats, cured or smoked, produced in slaughtering plants
311612 Meats, fresh or chilled (except poultry and small game), frozen, made from purchased carcasses
424470 Meats, fresh, merchant wholesalers
424470 Meats, frozen (except packaged), merchant wholesalers
424420 Meats, packaged frozen, merchant wholesalers
238220 Mechanical contractors
541330 Mechanical engineering services
238290 Mechanical equipment insulation
313310 Mechanical finishing of fabrics
316110 Mechanical leather manufacturing
334513 Mechanical measuring instruments, industrial process-type, manufacturing
339940 Mechanical pencil refills manufacturing
339940 Mechanical pencils manufacturing 811310
Mechanical power transmission equipment repair and maintenance services
423840 Mechanical power transmission supplies (e.g., gears, pulleys, sprockets) merchant wholesalers
326291 Mechanical rubber goods (i.e., extruded, lathe-cut, molded) manufacturing
423840 Mechanical rubber goods merchant wholesalers
541380 Mechanical testing laboratories or services
611513 Mechanic's apprenticeship training
333924 Mechanic's creepers manufacturing
325611 Mechanic's hand soaps and pastes manufacturing
332216 Mechanic's handtools, nonpowered, manufacturing
611519 Mechanic's schools (except apprenticeship)
423120 Mechanic's tools merchant wholesalers
333318 Mechanisms for coin-operated machines manufacturing
334519 Mechanisms, clockwork operated device, manufacturing
423940 Medallions merchant wholesalers 541840
Media advertising representatives (i.e., independent of media owners)
541830 Media buying agencies
541830 Media buying services
541840 Media representatives (i.e., independent of media owners)
518210 Media streaming services
926150 Mediation and conciliation services, government
541990 Mediation product services (except by lawyer, attorney, paralegal offices, family and social services)
624190 Mediation, social service, family, agencies
811219 Medical and surgical equipment repair and maintenance services
541430 Medical art services
541430 Medical artists, independent
923130 Medical assistance programs administration, government

813920 Medical associations
531120 Medical building rental or leasing
621999 Medical care management services
621999 Medical case management services
334510 Medical cleaning equipment, ultrasonic, manufacturing
541219 Medical coding services combined with accounting services (except CPA services)
524298 Medical cost evaluation services 621112
Medical doctors' (MDs), mental health, offices (e.g., centers, clinics)
621111 Medical doctors' (MDs, except mental health) offices (e.g., centers, clinics)
532490 Medical equipment (except home health furniture and equipment) rental or leasing
446199 Medical equipment and supplies stores
423450 Medical equipment merchant wholesalers
423450 Medical furniture merchant wholesalers
424690 Medical gases merchant wholesalers
327215 Medical glassware made from purchased glass
327212 Medical glassware made in glass making plants
423450 Medical glassware merchant wholesalers
541430 Medical illustration services
541430 Medical illustrators, independent
423450 Medical instruments merchant wholesalers
524114 Medical insurance carriers, direct
511120 Medical journal and periodical publishers (except exclusive Internet publishing)
511120 Medical journal and periodical publishers and printing combined
519130 Medical journal and periodical publishers, exclusively on Internet
621511 Medical laboratories (except radiological, X-ray)
621512 Medical laboratories, radiological or X-ray
541611 Medical office management consulting services or consultants
561110 Medical office management services
621511 Medical pathology laboratories
541922 Medical photography services
334517 Medical radiation therapy equipment manufacturing
621512 Medical radiological laboratories
524130 Medical reinsurance carriers 541715
Medical research and development laboratories or services (except biotechnology and nanotechnology research and development)
611310 Medical schools
315210 Medical service apparel cut and sew apparel contractors
315220 Medical service apparel, men's and boys', cut and sewn from purchased fabric (except apparel contractors)
315240 Medical service apparel, women's and girls', cut and sewn from purchased fabric (except apparel contractors)
524114 Medical service plans without providing health care services
424210 Medical sundries, rubber, merchant wholesalers
423450 Medical supplies (except household first-aid kits and non-surgical bandages) merchant wholesalers
611519 Medical technician schools
339112 Medical thermometers manufacturing
334510 Medical ultrasound equipment manufacturing
562211 Medical waste treatment facilities, hazardous
621512 Medical X-ray laboratories
923130 Medicare and Medicaid administration
325411 Medicinal chemicals, uncompounded, manufacturing
325411 Medicinal gelatins manufacturing
337110 Medicine cabinets (except freestanding), wood household-type, manufacturing
337124 Medicine cabinets, metal household-type, manufacturing
321219 Medium density fiberboard (MDF) manufacturing
212399 Meerschaum mining and/or beneficiating
531120 Meeting hall and room rental or leasing
325211 Melamine resins manufacturing 111219
Melon farming (e.g., cantaloupe, casaba, honeydew, watermelon), field, bedding plant and seed production
111419 Melon farming, grown under cover
313230 Melt blown nonwoven fabrics manufacturing
315210 Melton jackets cut and sew apparel contractors
315220 Melton jackets, men's and boys', cut and sewn from purchased fabric (except apparel contractors)
315240 Melton jackets, women's, girls', and infants', cut and sewn from purchased fabric (except apparel contractors)
813410 Membership associations, civic or social
721110 Membership hotels

812220 Memorial gardens (i.e., burial places)
334418 Memory boards manufacturing
423430 Memory boards merchant wholesalers
712130 Menageries
114111 Menhaden fishing
424320 Men's and boys' clothing merchant wholesalers
424320 Men's and boys' furnishings (except shoes) merchant wholesalers
315110 Men's socks knitting or knitting and finishing
622210 Mental (except intellectual and developmental disability) hospitals
621420 Mental health centers and clinics (except hospitals), outpatient
623220 Mental health facilities, residential
623220 Mental health halfway houses
622210 Mental health hospitals
621112 Mental health physicians' offices (e.g., centers, clinics)
923120 Mental health program administration
561450 Mercantile credit reporting bureaus
333249 Mercerizing machinery manufacturing
313310 Mercerizing textile products and fabrics
326111 Merchandise bags, plastics film, single wall or multiwall, manufacturing
423440 Merchandising machines, coin-operated, merchant wholesalers
236117 Merchant builders (i.e., building on own land, for sale), residential
926120 Merchant Marine (except academy)
813910 Merchants' associations
335912 Mercuric oxide batteries manufacturing
212299 Mercury (quicksilver) mining and/or beneficiating
335999 Mercury arc rectifiers (i.e., electrical apparatus) manufacturing
325180 Mercury chloride manufacturing 325180
Mercury compounds, not specified elsewhere by process, manufacturing
325920 Mercury fulminate explosive materials manufacturing
335110 Mercury halide lamp bulbs manufacturing
212299 Mercury ores mining and/or beneficiating
325180 Mercury oxide manufacturing
332618 Mesh made from purchased wire
331420 Mesh, wire, made from purchased copper in wire drawing plants
331318 Mesh, wire, made in aluminum wire drawing plants
331110 Mesh, wire, made in iron and steel mills
331222 Mesh, wire, made in wire drawing mills
331491 Mesh, wire, nonferrous metals (except aluminum, copper), made from purchased nonferrous metals (except aluminum, copper) in wire drawing plants
561421 Message services, telephone answering
492210 Messenger service
325412 Metabolite in-vivo diagnostic substances manufacturing
423390 Metal buildings merchant wholesalers
332431 Metal cans, light gauge metal, manufacturing
333249 Metal casting machinery and equipment manufacturing
333517 Metal cutting machine tools manufacturing
332216 Metal cutting saw blades manufacturing
424690 Metal cyanides merchant wholesalers
333517 Metal deposit forming machines manufacturing
334519 Metal detectors manufacturing
339113 Metal fabric and mesh safety gloves manufacturing
332999 Metal foil containers (except bags) manufacturing
333517 Metal forming machine tools manufacturing
337121 Metal framed furniture, household-type, upholstered, manufacturing
238190 Metal furring contractors
339940 Metal hand stamps manufacturing
333994 Metal melting furnaces, industrial, manufacturing
213114 Metal mining support services (shaft sinking, tunneling, blasting) (except site preparation and related construction contractor activities)
336370 Metal motor vehicle body parts stamping
423520 Metal ores merchant wholesalers 334413
Metal oxide silicon (MOS) devices manufacturing
423510 Metal pipe merchant wholesalers
325612 Metal polishes (i.e., tarnish removers) manufacturing
331314 Metal powder and flake made from purchased aluminum
331420 Metal powder and flake made from purchased copper

331221 Metal powder and flake made from purchased iron or steel
331492 Metal powder and flake nonferrous (except aluminum, copper) made from purchased metal
236210 Metal processing plant construction
423510 Metal products (e.g., bars, ingots, plates, rods, shapes, sheets) merchant wholesalers
423930 Metal scrap and waste merchant wholesalers
238170 Metal siding installation
332119 Metal stampings (except automotive, cans, coins), unfinished, manufacturing
335991 Metal-graphite products manufacturing
423520 Metallic concentrates merchant wholesalers
325130 Metallic pigments, inorganic, manufacturing
325199 Metallic soap manufacturing
313320 Metallizing purchased textiles 541380
Metallurgical testing laboratories or services
423510 Metals sales offices
423510 Metals service centers 423510 Metals,
ferrous and nonferrous, merchant wholesalers
423940 Metals, precious, merchant wholesalers
424690 Metalworking compounds merchant wholesalers
333517 Metalworking lathes manufacturing
423830 Metalworking machinery and equipment merchant wholesalers
532490 Metalworking machinery and equipment rental or leasing
423830 Metalworking tools (drills, taps, dies, grinding wheels) merchant wholesalers
334519 Meteorologic tracking systems manufacturing
811219 Meteorological instrument repair and maintenance services
334519 Meteorological instruments manufacturing
541990 Meteorological services
561990 Meter reading services, contract
334514 Metering devices (except electrical and industrial process control) manufacturing
335313 Metering panels, electric, manufacturing
334514 Meters (except electrical and industrial process control) manufacturing
423830 Meters (except electrical, parking) merchant wholesalers
334515 Meters, electrical (i.e., graphic recording, panelboard, pocket, portable), manufacturing
423610 Meters, electrical, merchant wholesalers
334513 Meters, industrial process control-type, manufacturing
334514 Meters, parking, manufacturing
423850 Meters, parking, merchant wholesalers
334515 Meters, power factor and phase angle, manufacturing
325320 Methoxychlor insecticides manufacturing
325194 Methyl acetone manufacturing
325211 Methyl acrylate resins manufacturing
325199 Methyl alcohol (i.e., methanol), synthetic, manufacturing
325194 Methyl alcohol (methanol), natural, manufacturing
325211 Methyl cellulose resins manufacturing
325199 Methyl chloride manufacturing
325211 Methyl methacrylate resins manufacturing
325199 Methyl perhydrofluorine manufacturing
325199 Methyl salicylate manufacturing
325130 Methyl violet toners manufacturing
325199 Methylamine manufacturing
325199 Methylene chloride manufacturing
311422 Mexican foods canning
311412 Mexican foods, frozen, manufacturing
212399 Mica mining and/or beneficiating
327992 Mica processing beyond beneficiation
327999 Mica products manufacturing
212319 Mica schist crushed and broken stone mining and/or beneficiating
212311 Mica schist mining or quarrying
311119 Micro and macro premixes, livestock, manufacturing
334516 Microbiology instruments manufacturing
325413 Microbiology, virology, and serology in-vitro diagnostic substances manufacturing
334111 Microcomputers manufacturing
334413 Microcontroller chip manufacturing
333316 Microfiche equipment (e.g., cameras, projectors, readers) manufacturing
518210 Microfiche recording and imaging services
333316 Microfilm equipment (e.g., cameras, projectors, readers) manufacturing
423420 Microfilm equipment and supplies merchant wholesalers

518210 Microfilm recording and imaging services
212299 Microlite mining and/or beneficiating
333242 Micro-lithography equipment, semiconductor, manufacturing
332216 Micrometers, machinist's precision tools, manufacturing
334310 Microphones (except broadcast and studio equipment) manufacturing
334220 Microphones, broadcast and studio equipment, manufacturing
334516 Microprobes (e.g., electron, ion, laser, X-ray) manufacturing
334413 Microprocessor chip manufacturing
423430 Microprocessors merchant wholesalers
333314 Microscopes (except electron, proton) manufacturing
334516 Microscopes, electron and proton, manufacturing
237990 Microtunneling contractors
334220 Microwave communications equipment manufacturing
334419 Microwave components manufacturing
811412 Microwave oven, household-type, repair and maintenance services, without retailing new microwave ovens
335220 Microwave ovens (including portable), household-type, manufacturing
423440 Microwave ovens, commercial, merchant wholesalers
333318 Microwave ovens, commercial-type, manufacturing
423620 Microwave ovens, household-type, merchant wholesalers
237130 Microwave relay tower construction
517911 Microwave telecommunication resellers
334515 Microwave test equipment manufacturing
326199 Microwaveware, plastics, manufacturing
315210 Middies cut and sew apparel contractors
315240 Middies, women's, girls', and infants', cut and sewn from purchased fabric (except apparel contractors)
611110 Middle schools
621399 Midwives' offices (e.g., clinics)
721310 Migrant workers' camps
611310 Military academies, college level
611110 Military academies, elementary or secondary
561210 Military base support services
928110 Military bases and camps
315210 Military dress uniforms cut and sew apparel contractors
315220 Military dress uniforms, men's and boys', cut and sewn from purchased fabric (except apparel contractors)
315240 Military dress uniforms, tailored, women's and girls', cut and sewn from purchased fabric (except apparel contractors)
611512 Military flight instruction training
332999 Military insignia, metal, manufacturing
314999 Military insignia, textile, manufacturing
712110 Military museums
928110 Military police
928110 Military reserve armories and bases
611310 Military service academies (college)
928110 Military training schools (except academies)
423860 Military vehicles (except trucks) merchant wholesalers
311511 Milk based drinks (except dietary) manufacturing
311514 Milk based drinks, dietary, manufacturing
322130 Milk carton board made in paperboard mills
322220 Milk carton board stock made from purchased paperboard
322219 Milk cartons made from purchased paper or paperboard
311511 Milk drink, chocolate, manufacturing
484220 Milk hauling, local
311511 Milk pasteurizing
311511 Milk processing (e.g., bottling, homogenizing, pasteurizing, vitaminizing) manufacturing
333241 Milk processing (except farm-type) machinery manufacturing
112120 Milk production, dairy cattle
311511 Milk substitutes manufacturing
115210 Milk testing for butterfat and milk solids
311511 Milk, acidophilus, manufacturing
424490 Milk, canned or dried, merchant wholesalers
311514 Milk, concentrated, condensed, dried, evaporated, and powdered, manufacturing
311511 Milk, fluid (except canned), manufacturing
424430 Milk, fluid (except canned), merchant wholesalers
311514 Milk, malted, manufacturing
311514 Milk, powdered, manufacturing
311514 Milk, ultra high temperature, manufacturing

112120 Milking dairy cattle
112420 Milking dairy goat
112410 Milking dairy sheep
423820 Milking machinery and equipment merchant wholesalers
333111 Milking machines manufacturing
311514 Milkshake mixes manufacturing
314999 Mill menders, contract, woven fabrics
316998 Mill strapping for textile mills, leather, manufacturing
423840 Mill supplies merchant wholesalers 315210
Millinery cut and sew apparel contractors 315990
Millinery cut and sewn from purchased fabric (except apparel contractors)
424330 Millinery merchant wholesalers
424310 Millinery supplies merchant wholesalers
315210 Millinery trimmings cut and sew apparel contractors
315990 Millinery trimmings cut and sewn from purchased fabric (except apparel contractors)
333517 Milling machines, metalworking, manufacturing
311212 Milling rice
212399 Millstones mining and/or beneficiating
238350 Millwork installation
423310 Millwork merchant wholesalers
337212 Millwork, custom architectural, manufacturing
321114 Millwork, treating
238290 Millwrights
111199 Milo farming, field and seed production
711110 Mime theaters
333922 Mine conveyors manufacturing 213114
Mine development (except site preparation and related construction contractor activities) for metal mining on a contract basis
213115 Mine development for nonmetallic minerals mining (except fuels) on a contract basis
236210 Mine loading and discharging station construction
321114 Mine props, treating
562910 Mine reclamation services, integrated (e.g., demolition, hazardous material removal, soil remediation, revegetation)
213113 Mine shaft sinking services for coal mining on a contract basis
213114 Mine shaft sinking services for metal mining on a contract basis
213115 Mine shaft sinking services for nonmetallic minerals (except fuels) on a contract basis
238910 Mine site preparation and related construction activities, construction contractors
321114 Mine ties, wood, treated, manufacturing
213113 Mine tunneling services for coal mining on a contract basis
213114 Mine tunneling services for metal mining on a contract basis
213115 Mine tunneling services for nonmetallic minerals (except fuels) on a contract basis
325130 Mineral colors and pigments manufacturing
311119 Mineral feed supplements (except cat, dog) manufacturing
212393 Mineral pigments, natural, mining and/or beneficiating
333131 Mineral processing and beneficiating machinery manufacturing
523910 Mineral royalties or leases dealing (i.e., acting as a principal in dealing royalties or leases to investors)
311119 Mineral supplements, animal (except cat, dog), manufacturing
424910 Mineral supplements, animal, merchant wholesalers
238310 Mineral wool insulation installation
327993 Mineral wool insulation materials manufacturing
327993 Mineral wool products (e.g., board, insulation, tile) manufacturing
423520 Minerals (except construction materials, petroleum) merchant wholesalers
335129 Miner's lamps manufacturing
332993 Mines, ammunition, manufacturing
713990 Miniature golf courses
337920 Miniblinds manufacturing
334111 Minicomputers manufacturing
331110 Mini-mills, steel
926150 Minimum wage program administration
****** Mining -- see type
813910 Mining associations
333131 Mining cars manufacturing
423810 Mining cranes merchant wholesalers
541330 Mining engineering services
336510 Mining locomotives and parts manufacturing

423810 Mining machinery and equipment (except petroleum) merchant wholesalers
532412 Mining machinery and equipment rental or leasing
811310 Mining machinery and equipment repair and maintenance services
423830 Mining machinery and equipment, petroleum, merchant wholesalers
531190 Mining property leasing
813110 Ministries, religious
423110 Minivan merchant wholesalers
336112 Minivans assembling on chassis of own manufacture
531130 Miniwarehouse rental or leasing
112930 Mink production
112511 Minnow production, farm raising
711211 Minor league baseball clubs
111998 Mint farming
238150 Mirror installation
423220 Mirrors (except automotive) merchant wholesalers
423120 Mirrors, automotive, merchant wholesalers
327215 Mirrors, framed (except automotive) or unframed, made from purchased glass
333314 Mirrors, optical, manufacturing
237990 Missile facility construction
332993 Missile warheads manufacturing
561611 Missing person tracing services
813110 Missions, religious organization
332216 Miter boxes manufacturing
315210 Mittens (e.g., leather, woven or knit) cut and sew apparel contractors
315990 Mittens cut and sewn from purchased fabric (except apparel contractors)
315190 Mittens, knit, made in apparel knitting mills
315990 Mittens, leather (except apparel contractors), manufacturing
315990 Mittens, woven or knit, cut and sewn from purchased fabric (except apparel contractors)
311230 Mix grain breakfast manufacturing
311514 Mix, ice cream, manufacturing
312140 Mixed drinks, alcoholic, manufacturing
111940 Mixed hay farming
485111 Mixed mode transit systems (e.g., bus, commuter rail, subway combinations)
333120 Mixers, concrete, portable, manufacturing
423810 Mixers, construction and mining, merchant wholesalers
424490 Mixes (e.g., cake, dessert, pie) merchant wholesalers
311211 Mixes, flour (e.g., biscuit, cake, doughnut, pancake) made in flour mills
311824 Mixes, flour (e.g., biscuit, cake, doughnut, pancake), made from purchased flour
325314 Mixing purchased fertilizer materials
531190 Mobile (manufactured) home parks 531110
Mobile (manufactured) home rental or leasing, on-site
531190 Mobile (manufactured) home sites rental or leasing
811111 Mobile automotive and truck repair services
621512 Mobile breast imaging centers
811192 Mobile car and truck washes 334220
Mobile communications equipment manufacturing
311119 Mobile feed mill
722330 Mobile food stands
453930 Mobile home dealers, manufactured
532120 Mobile home rental, off-site
484220 Mobile home towing services, local
484230 Mobile home towing services, long-distance
321991 Mobile homes manufacturing
712110 Mobile museums
532490 Mobile office building rental or leasing, off-site
531120 Mobile office building rental or leasing, on-site
517312 Mobile phone stores, primarily selling mobile phone service plans
624210 Mobile soup kitchens
333924 Mobile straddle carriers manufacturing
517312 Mobile telephone communication carriers (except satellite)
621512 Mobile X-ray facilities (medical)
316210 Moccasins manufacturing
325220 Modacrylic fibers and filaments manufacturing
313110 Modacrylic spun yarns made from purchased fiber
339930 Model kits manufacturing
423920 Model kits merchant wholesalers
339930 Model railroad manufacturing
561311 Model registries

561320 Model supply services
711410 Modeling agents
339940 Modeling clay manufacturing
611519 Modeling schools
711410 Models' agents or managers
339999 Models, anatomical, manufacturing
711510 Models, independent
339930 Models, toy and hobby (e.g., airplane, boat, ship), manufacturing
423690 Modems merchant wholesalers
334210 Modems, carrier equipment, manufacturing
711120 Modern dance companies
532490 Modular building rental or leasing, off-site
238390 Modular furniture system attachment and installation
337214 Modular furniture systems (except wood frame), office-type, manufacturing
337211 Modular furniture systems, wood frame office-type, manufacturing
236117 Modular housing, residential, assembled on site by for-sale builders
236115 Modular single-family housing assembled on site by general contractors
334519 Modules for clocks and watches manufacturing
112420 Mohair farming
313110 Mohair yarn twisting or winding of purchased yarn
424590 Mohair, raw, merchant wholesalers
334516 Moisture analyzers, laboratory-type, manufacturing
334513 Moisture meters, industrial process-type, manufacturing
311313 Molasses made from sugar beets
311314 Molasses manufacturing 424490 Molasses merchant wholesalers 311314 Molasses, blackstrap, manufacturing 562910 Mold remediation services
339991 Molded packings and seals manufacturing
322299 Molded pulp products (e.g., egg cartons, food containers, food trays) manufacturing
423310 Molding (e.g., sheet metal, wood) merchant wholesalers
332321 Molding and trim (except motor vehicle), metal, manufacturing
238350 Molding or trim, wood or plastic, installation
212322 Molding sand quarrying and/or beneficiating
336370 Moldings and trim, motor vehicle, stamping
321918 Moldings, clear and finger joint wood, manufacturing
321918 Moldings, wood and covered wood, manufacturing
333511 Molds (except steel ingot), industrial, manufacturing
331511 Molds for casting steel ingots manufacturing
333511 Molds for forming materials (e.g., glass, plastics, rubber) manufacturing
333511 Molds for metal casting (except steel ingot) manufacturing
333511 Molds for plastics and rubber working machinery manufacturing
331511 Molds, steel ingot, industrial, manufacturing
112512 Mollusk production, farm raising 212299 Molybdenite mining and/or beneficiating 331491 Molybdenum and molybdenum alloy bar, plate, pipe, rod, sheet, tubing, and wire made from purchased metals or scrap
212299 Molybdenum ores mining and/or beneficiating
331491 Molybdenum rolling, drawing, or extruding purchased metals or scrap
331110 Molybdenum silicon ferroalloys manufacturing
212299 Molybdite mining and/or beneficiating
813110 Monasteries (except schools)
212299 Monazite mining and/or beneficiating
521110 Monetary authorities, central bank
332999 Money chests, metal, manufacturing
525990 Money market mutual funds, closed-end
525910 Money market mutual funds, open-ended
522390 Money order issuance services
522390 Money transmission services
423430 Monitor screen projection devices merchant wholesalers
334118 Monitors, computer peripheral equipment, manufacturing
423430 Monitors, computer, merchant wholesalers
325120 Monochlorodifluoromethane manufacturing
334516 Monochrometers, laboratory-type, manufacturing
334413 Monolithic integrated circuits (solid-state) manufacturing

325199 Monomethylparaminophenol sulfate manufacturing
237990 Monorail construction
333923 Monorail systems (except passenger-type) manufacturing
485119 Monorail transit systems (except mixed mode), commuter
487110 Monorail, scenic and sightseeing, operation
325199 Monosodium glutamate manufacturing
611110 Montessori schools, elementary or secondary
236220 Monument (i.e., building) construction
453998 Monument (i.e., burial marker) dealers
423990 Monuments and grave markers merchant wholesalers
327991 Monuments and tombstone, cut stone (except finishing or lettering to order only), manufacturing
333318 Mop wringers manufacturing
441228 Moped dealers
423110 Moped merchant wholesalers
532284 Moped rental
336991 Mopeds and parts manufacturing
339994 Mops, floor and dust, manufacturing
423220 Mops, household, merchant wholesalers
423850 Mops, industrial, merchant wholesalers
325130 Mordant dyes manufacturing
325613 Mordants manufacturing
325411 Morphine and derivatives (i.e., basic chemicals) manufacturing
522190 Morris Plans (i.e., known as), depository
522298 Morris Plans (i.e., known as), nondepository
333120 Mortar mixers, portable, manufacturing
332993 Mortar shells manufacturing
327120 Mortar, nonclay refractory, manufacturing
332994 Mortars manufacturing
327120 Mortars, clay refractory, manufacturing
522292 Mortgage banking (i.e., nondepository mortgage lending)
522310 Mortgage brokerages 522310 Mortgage brokers' or agents' offices (i.e., independent)
522292 Mortgage companies
523910 Mortgage dealers, buying and selling
524126 Mortgage guaranty insurance carriers, direct
525990 Mortgage real estate investment trusts (REITs)
525990 Mortgage-backed securities
812210 Mortician services 333243 Mortisers, woodworking-type, manufacturing
812210 Mortuaries
334413 MOS (metal oxide silicon) devices manufacturing
327120 Mosaic tile, ceramic, manufacturing
238340 Mosaic work
813110 Mosques, religious
926130 Mosquito eradication districts
561710 Mosquito eradication services
113210 Moss gathering
531120 Motel building rental or leasing, not operating motel
236220 Motel construction
561110 Motel management services (except complete operation of client's business)
721110 Motels
325320 Moth repellents manufacturing 423430 Motherboards, loaded, merchant wholesalers
334290 Motion alarms (e.g., swimming pool, perimeter) manufacturing
334290 Motion detectors, security system, manufacturing
512110 Motion picture and video production
512110 Motion picture and video production and distribution
512191 Motion picture animation, postproduction
512199 Motion picture booking agencies
333316 Motion picture cameras manufacturing
423410 Motion picture cameras, equipment, and supplies merchant wholesalers
541690 Motion picture consulting services
711510 Motion picture directors, independent
512120 Motion picture distribution exclusive of production
532490 Motion picture equipment rental or leasing
512131 Motion picture exhibition
512131 Motion picture exhibitors for airlines
512131 Motion picture exhibitors, itinerant
512120 Motion picture film distributors
512199 Motion picture film laboratories
512120 Motion picture film libraries
519120 Motion picture film libraries, archives

512199 Motion picture film libraries, stock footage
325992 Motion picture film manufacturing
512199 Motion picture film reproduction for theatrical distribution
512199 Motion picture laboratories
512191 Motion picture or video editing services
512191 Motion picture or video postproduction services
512191 Motion picture or video titling
711510 Motion picture producers, independent
512110 Motion picture production
512110 Motion picture production and distribution
512191 Motion picture production special effects, postproduction
333316 Motion picture projectors manufacturing
512110 Motion picture studios, producing motion pictures
512132 Motion picture theaters, drive-in
512131 Motion picture theaters, indoor 532281 Motion picture wardrobe and costume rental
711510 Motivational speakers, independent
926120 Motor carrier licensing and inspection offices
485210 Motor coach operation, interurban and rural
335314 Motor control accessories (including overload relays) manufacturing
335314 Motor control centers, manufacturing
335314 Motor controls, electric, manufacturing
423610 Motor controls, electric, merchant wholesalers
721110 Motor courts
484110 Motor freight carrier, general, local
484122 Motor freight carrier, general, long-distance, less-than-truckload (LTL)
484121 Motor freight carrier, general, long-distance, truckload (TL)
484210 Motor freight carrier, used household goods
335312 Motor generator sets (except automotive, turbine generator sets) manufacturing
333611 Motor generator sets, turbo generators, manufacturing
441210 Motor home dealers
423110 Motor home merchant wholesalers
532120 Motor home rental, off-site
336213 Motor homes, self-contained, assembling on purchased chassis
336120 Motor homes, self-contained, mounted on heavy truck chassis of own manufacture
336112 Motor homes, self-contained, mounted on light duty truck chassis of own manufacture
721110 Motor hotels without casinos
721110 Motor inns 721110
Motor lodges
324191 Motor oils, petroleum, made from refined petroleum
325998 Motor oils, synthetic, manufacturing
811310 Motor repair and maintenance services, commercial or industrial
441228 Motor scooters dealers
336991 Motor scooters manufacturing 335314 Motor starters, contractors, and controllers, industrial, manufacturing
561599 Motor travel clubs
333997 Motor truck scales manufacturing
236210 Motor vehicle assembly plant construction
326220 Motor vehicle belts, rubber or plastics, manufacturing
238290 Motor vehicle garage and service station mechanical equipment (e.g., gasoline pumps, hoists) installation
332510 Motor vehicle hardware, metal, manufacturing
326220 Motor vehicle hoses, rubber or plastics, manufacturing
334514 Motor vehicle instruments (e.g., fuel level gauges, oil pressure, speedometers, tachometers, water temperature) manufacturing
423120 Motor vehicle instruments, electric, merchant wholesalers
336360 Motor vehicle interior systems (e.g., headliners, panels, seats, trims) manufacturing
561990 Motor vehicle license issuing services, private franchise
926120 Motor vehicle licensing offices, government
423110 Motor vehicle merchant wholesalers
336370 Motor vehicle metal bumper stampings
336370 Motor vehicle metal parts stamping
336370 Motor vehicle metal stampings (e.g., body parts, fenders, hub caps, tops, trim) manufacturing
326199 Motor vehicle moldings and extrusions, plastics, manufacturing
325510 Motor vehicle paints manufacturing

423120 Motor vehicle parts and accessories, new, merchant wholesalers

423140 Motor vehicle parts, used, merchant wholesalers

336360 Motor vehicle seats manufacturing

336360 Motor vehicle seats, metal framed, manufacturing

423130 Motor vehicle tire and tube merchant wholesalers

326211 Motor vehicle tires manufacturing

488410 Motor vehicle towing services

336360 Motor vehicle trimmings manufacturing

441228 Motorbike dealers

811490 Motorboat (i.e., inboard and outboard) repair and maintenance services

336612 Motorboat, inboard or outboard, building

441228 Motorcycle dealers

611692 Motorcycle driving schools

423110 Motorcycle merchant wholesalers

441228 Motorcycle parts and accessories dealers

423120 Motorcycle parts, new, merchant wholesalers

711212 Motorcycle racetracks

711219 Motorcycle racing teams

532284 Motorcycle rental

811490 Motorcycle repair shops without retailing new motorcycles

336991 Motorcycles and parts manufacturing

423860 Motorized passenger golf carts merchant wholesalers

335312 Motors, electric (except engine starting motors, gearmotors, outboard), manufacturing

423610 Motors, electric, merchant wholesalers

333996 Motors, fluid power, manufacturing

333612 Motors, gear, manufacturing

333618 Motors, outboard, manufacturing

423910 Motors, outboard, merchant wholesalers

336320 Motors, starter, for internal combustion engines, manufacturing

713990 Mountain hiking, recreational

561910 Mounting merchandise on cards 334118

Mouse devices, computer peripheral equipment, manufacturing

213112 Mouse hole and rat hole drilling at oil and gas fields on a contract basis

339992 Mouthpieces for musical instruments manufacturing

325620 Mouthwashes (except medicinal) manufacturing

325412 Mouthwashes, medicated, manufacturing

334519 Movements, watch or clock, manufacturing

423620 Movie apparatus, home, merchant wholesalers

512110 Movie production and distribution

512131 Movie theaters (except drive-in)

512132 Movie theaters, drive-in

238290 Moving sidewalk installation

561730 Mowing services (e.g., highway, lawn, road strip)

562920 MRF (materials recovery facilities)

621512 MRI (magnetic resonance imaging) centers

334510 MRI (magnetic resonance imaging) medical diagnostic equipment manufacturing

325520 Mucilage adhesives manufacturing

213112 Mud service for oil field drilling on a contract basis

238110 Mud-jacking contractors

811112 Muffler repair and replacement shops 336390

Mufflers and resonators, automotive, truck, and buses manufacturing

315210 Mufflers cut and sew apparel contractors

315990 Mufflers cut and sewn from purchased fabric (except apparel contractors)

315190 Mufflers made in apparel knitting mills

423120 Mufflers, exhaust, merchant wholesalers

424910 Mulch merchant wholesalers

333112 Mulchers, lawn and garden-type, manufacturing

112920 Mule production

424590 Mules merchant wholesalers

114111 Mullet fishing

517311 Multichannel multipoint distribution services (MMDS)

712110 Multidisciplinary museums

236116 Multifamily building construction general contractors

236117 Multifamily building for-sale builders

334515 Multimeters manufacturing 334210

Multiplex equipment, telephone, manufacturing

624190 Multiservice centers, neighborhood

212391 Muriate of potash, mining 325412

Muscle relaxant preparations manufacturing

212399 Muscovite mining and/or beneficiating

561990 Museum cataloging services
236220 Museum construction
712110 Museums
111411 Mushroom farming
111411 Mushroom spawn farming
311421 Mushrooms canning
519120 Music archives
711510 Music arrangers, independent 512230
Music book (i.e., bound sheet music) publishers
512230 Music book (i.e., bound sheet music) publishers and printing combined
323117 Music books printing or printing and binding without publishing
339999 Music boxes manufacturing
512230 Music copyright authorizing use
512230 Music copyright buying and licensing
711510 Music directors, independent
711310 Music festival managers with facilities
711320 Music festival managers without facilities
711310 Music festival organizers with facilities
711320 Music festival organizers without facilities
711310 Music festival promoters with facilities
711320 Music festival promoters without facilities
611610 Music instruction (e.g., guitar, piano)
515112 Music program distribution (except exclusively on Internet), radio
517311 Music program distribution, cable or satellite
512290 Music program distribution, prerecorded
512230 Music publishers
339992 Music rolls, perforated, manufacturing
611610 Music schools (except academic)
443142 Music stores (e.g., cassette, compact disc, record, tape)
453310 Music stores (e.g., cassette, instrument, record, tape), used
451140 Music stores (i.e., instrument)
621340 Music therapists' offices (e.g., centers, clinics)
512110 Music video production
512110 Music video production and distribution
323111 Music, sheet, commercial printing (except screen) without publishing
424990 Music, sheet, merchant wholesalers
512230 Music, sheet, publishers and printing combined
323113 Music, sheet, screen printing without publishing
711130 Musical artists, independent
711130 Musical groups (except musical theater groups)
339992 Musical instrument accessories (e.g., mouthpieces, reeds, stands, traps) manufacturing
423990 Musical instrument accessories and supplies merchant wholesalers
316998 Musical instrument cases, all materials, manufacturing
532289 Musical instrument rental
811490 Musical instrument repair shops without retailing new musical instruments
451140 Musical instrument stores
339992 Musical instruments (except toy) manufacturing
423990 Musical instruments merchant wholesalers
339930 Musical instruments, toy, manufacturing
711130 Musical productions (except musical theater productions), live
512250 Musical recording, releasing, promoting, and distributing
423990 Musical recordings (e.g., compact discs, records, tapes) merchant wholesalers
711110 Musical theater companies or groups
711110 Musical theater productions, live
711130 Musicians, independent
111219 Muskmelon farming, field, bedding plant and seed production
114112 Mussel fishing
112512 Mussel production, farm raising
111120 Mustard seed farming, field and seed production
311941 Mustard, prepared, manufacturing
523120 Mutual fund agencies (i.e., brokerages)
523120 Mutual fund agents' (i.e., brokers') offices
523920 Mutual fund managing
525990 Mutual funds, closed-end
525910 Mutual funds, open-ended
522120 Mutual savings banks
621511 Mycology health laboratories
325194 Myrobalans extract manufacturing
333991 Nail guns, handheld power-driven, manufacturing
333517 Nail heading machines manufacturing
325620 Nail polish remover manufacturing
325620 Nail polishes manufacturing

812113 Nail salons
333991 Nailers and staplers, handheld power-driven, manufacturing
423510 Nails merchant wholesalers
331318 Nails, aluminum, made in wire drawing plants
332618 Nails, brads, and staples made from purchased wire
331222 Nails, iron or steel, made in wire drawing plants
331491 Nails, nonferrous metals (except aluminum, copper), made from purchased nonferrous metals (except aluminum, copper) in wire drawing plants
332999 Name plate blanks, metal, manufacturing
541713 Nanobiotechnologies research and experimental development laboratories
334513 Nanofluidic measurement and control devices manufacturing
333242 Nanoindentation equipment, semiconductor, manufacturing
334516 Nanomanipulator equipment manufacturing
334516 Nanosensor instruments manufacturing
541713 Nanotechnology research and development laboratories or services, all fields of science
325998 Napalm manufacturing
325194 Naphtha made by distillation of coal tar
324110 Naphtha made in petroleum refineries
325194 Naphtha, solvent, made by distillation of coal tar
325194 Naphthalene made from refined petroleum or natural gas
325194 Naphthalenesulfonic acid manufacturing
325199 Naphthenic acid soaps manufacturing
325194 Naphthenic acids made from refined petroleum or natural gas
324110 Naphthenic acids made in petroleum refineries
325194 Naphthol sulfonic acids manufacturing
325194 Naphthol, alpha and beta, manufacturing
423220 Napkins (except paper) merchant wholesalers
314120 Napkins made from purchased fabrics
424130 Napkins, paper, merchant wholesalers
322291 Napkins, table, made from purchased paper
322121 Napkins, table, made in paper mills
333249 Napping machinery for textiles manufacturing
313310 Napping textile products and fabrics
313220 Narrow fabrics weaving
927110 National Aeronautics and Space Administration
522110 National commercial banks
522298 National Credit Union Administration (NCUA)
928110 National Guard
712190 National parks
926120 National Transportation Safety Board
311422 Nationality specialty foods canning
311412 Nationality specialty foods, frozen, manufacturing
212399 Native asphalt mining and/or beneficiating
327310 Natural (i.e., calcined earth) cement manufacturing
212399 Natural abrasives (e.g., emery, grindstones, hones, pumice) (except sand) mining and/or beneficiating
313110 Natural fiber (i.e., hemp, linen, ramie) thread manufacturing
313210 Natural fiber fabrics (i.e., jute, linen, hemp, ramie), broadwoven, weaving
313220 Natural fiber fabrics (i.e., jute, linen, hemp, ramie), narrow woven, weaving
313110 Natural fiber spun yarns (i.e., hemp, jute, ramie, flax) made from purchased fiber
221210 Natural gas brokers
423690 Natural gas detectors, electronic, merchant wholesalers
221210 Natural gas distribution systems
221210 Natural gas distribution with transmission
333618 Natural gas engines manufacturing
211130 Natural gas liquid lease condensate production
211130 Natural gas liquids (e.g., ethane, isobutane, natural gasoline, propane) recovered from oil and gas field gases
486910 Natural gas liquids pipeline transportation
221210 Natural gas marketers
237120 Natural gas pipeline construction
486210 Natural gas pipeline transportation
238220 Natural gas piping installation
237120 Natural gas processing plant construction
211130 Natural gas production
486210 Natural gas transmission (i.e., processing plants to local distribution systems)
211130 Natural gas, offshore production

211130 Natural gasoline recovered from oil and gas field gases
712110 Natural history museums
325199 Natural nonfood coloring manufacturing
813312 Natural resource preservation organizations
712110 Natural science museums
712190 Natural wonder tourist attractions (e.g., caverns, waterfalls)
312112 Naturally carbonated water, purifying and bottling
712190 Nature centers
712190 Nature parks
712190 Nature preserves
712190 Nature reserves
621399 Naturopaths' offices (e.g., centers, clinics)
334511 Nautical systems and instruments manufacturing
332994 Naval artillery manufacturing
336611 Naval ship building
325194 Naval stores, gum or wood, manufacturing
811219 Navigational instruments (e.g., radar, sonar) repair and maintenance services
423860 Navigational instruments (except electronic) merchant wholesalers
334511 Navigational instruments manufacturing
423690 Navigational instruments, electronic (e.g., radar, sonar), merchant wholesalers
928110 Navy
312120 Near beer brewing
311613 Neatsfoot oil rendering
315280 Neckpieces, fur (except apparel contractors), manufacturing
315210 Neckpieces, fur, cut and sew apparel contractors
315210 Neckties cut and sew apparel contractors
315990 Neckties cut and sewn from purchased fabric (except apparel contractors)
315190 Neckties made in apparel knitting mills
424320 Neckties, men's and boys', merchant wholesalers
315210 Neckwear cut and sew apparel contractors
315990 Neckwear cut and sewn from purchased fabric (except apparel contractors)
315190 Neckwear made in a apparel knitting mills
448150 Neckwear stores
111339 Nectarine farming
332991 Needle roller bearings manufacturing
451130 Needlecraft sewing supply stores
339993 Needles (except hypodermic, phonograph, styli) manufacturing
333249 Needles for knitting machinery manufacturing
339112 Needles, hypodermic and suture, manufacturing
334419 Needles, phonograph and styli, manufacturing
424310 Needles, sewing, merchant wholesalers
314999 Needlework art contractors on apparel
315210 Negligees cut and sew apparel contractors
315190 Negligees made in apparel knitting mills
315240 Negligees, women's and girls', cut and sewn from purchased fabric (except apparel contractors)
813319 Neighborhood development advocacy organizations
325120 Neon manufacturing
339950 Neon signs manufacturing
325212 Neoprene manufacturing
212325 Nepheline syenite mining and/or beneficiating
334516 Nephelometers (except meteorological) manufacturing
334519 Nephoscopes manufacturing
621111 Nephrologists' offices (e.g., centers, clinics)
333249 Net and lace making machinery manufacturing
424310 Net goods merchant wholesalers
313210 Nets and nettings, more than 12 inches in width, weaving
313240 Netting made in warp or weft knitting mills
313240 Netting made on a lace or net machine
326199 Netting, plastics, manufacturing
332618 Netting, woven, made from purchased wire
515111 Network broadcasting service, radio
515111 Network radio broadcasting
541512 Network systems integration design services, computer
515120 Network television broadcasting
515210 Networks, cable television
622310 Neurological hospitals
621111 Neurologists' offices (e.g., centers, clinics)
621111 Neuropathologists' offices (e.g., centers, clinics)
312140 Neutral spirit, beverages (except fruit), manufacturing

424820 Neutral spirits merchant wholesalers
334516 Neutron activation analysis instruments manufacturing
441110 New car dealers
541613 New product development consulting services
321918 Newel posts, wood, manufacturing
519190 News clipping services
711510 News correspondents, independent (freelance)
451212 News dealers
519110 News picture gathering and distributing services
519110 News reporting services
519110 News service syndicates
519110 News ticker services
511120 Newsletter publishers (except exclusive Internet publishing)
511120 Newsletter publishers and printing combined (except Internet)
519130 Newsletter publishers, exclusively on Internet
323111 Newsletters commercial printing (except screen) without publishing
323113 Newsletters screen printing without publishing
541840 Newspaper advertising representatives (i.e., independent of media owners)
424920 Newspaper agencies merchant wholesalers
511110 Newspaper branch offices
711510 Newspaper columnists, independent (freelance)
519110 Newspaper feature syndicates
333244 Newspaper inserting equipment manufacturing
511110 Newspaper publishers (except exclusive Internet publishing)
511110 Newspaper publishers and printing combined
519130 Newspaper publishing, exclusively on Internet
323111 Newspapers commercial printing (except screen) without publishing
424920 Newspapers merchant wholesalers
323113 Newspapers screen printing without publishing
424110 Newsprint merchant wholesalers
322122 Newsprint mills
322122 Newsprint paper, manufacturing
451212 Newsstands (i.e., permanent)
339940 Nibs (i.e., pen points) manufacturing
331523 Nickel alloy die-castings, unfinished, manufacturing
325180 Nickel ammonium sulfate manufacturing
331491 Nickel and nickel alloy pipe, plate, sheet, strip, and tubing made from purchased metals or scrap
423510 Nickel and nickel alloy primary forms merchant wholesalers
325180 Nickel carbonate manufacturing
331529 Nickel castings (except die-castings), unfinished, manufacturing
325180 Nickel compounds, not specified elsewhere by process, manufacturing
212230 Nickel concentrates recovery
331523 Nickel die-castings, unfinished, manufacturing
332999 Nickel foil not made in rolling mills
212230 Nickel ore beneficiating plants
212230 Nickel ore mine site development for own account
212230 Nickel ores mining and/or beneficiating
331492 Nickel recovering from scrap and/or alloying purchased metals
331410 Nickel refining, primary
331491 Nickel rolling, drawing, or extruding purchased metals or scrap
325180 Nickel sulfate manufacturing
335911 Nickel-cadmium storage batteries manufacturing
325411 Nicotine and derivatives (i.e., basic chemicals) manufacturing
325320 Nicotine insecticides manufacturing
337122 Night stands, wood, manufacturing
333314 Night vision optical devices manufacturing
713990 Nightclubs without alcoholic beverages
722410 Nightclubs, alcoholic beverage
315210 Nightgowns cut and sew apparel contractors
315190 Nightgowns made in apparel knitting mills
315220 Nightgowns, men's and boys', cut and sewn from purchased fabric (except apparel contractors)
315240 Nightgowns, women's, girls', and infants', cut and sewn from purchased fabric (except apparel contractors)
315210 Nightshirts cut and sew apparel contractors
315190 Nightshirts made in apparel knitting mills

315220 Nightshirts, men's and boys', cut and sewn from purchased fabric (except apparel contractors)
315240 Nightshirts, women's, girls', and infants', cut and sewn from purchased fabric (except contractors)
315210 Nightwear cut and sew apparel contractors
315190 Nightwear made in apparel knitting mills
315220 Nightwear, men's and boys', cut and sewn from purchased fabric (except apparel contractors)
424320 Nightwear, men's and boys', merchant wholesalers
424330 Nightwear, women's, children's, and infants', merchant wholesalers
315240 Nightwear, women's, girls', and infants', cut and sewn from purchased fabric (except apparel contractors)
331410 Niobium refining, primary
326299 Nipples and teething rings, rubber, manufacturing
332996 Nipples, metal, made from purchased pipe
325194 Nitrated hydrocarbon derivatives manufacturing
325311 Nitric acid manufacturing
325212 Nitrile rubber manufacturing
325212 Nitrile-butadiene rubber manufacturing
325212 Nitrile-chloroprene rubbers manufacturing
325194 Nitroaniline manufacturing
325194 Nitrobenzene manufacturing
325211 Nitrocellulose (i.e., pyroxylin) resins manufacturing
325920 Nitrocellulose explosive materials manufacturing
325220 Nitrocellulose fibers manufacturing
325120 Nitrogen manufacturing
325311 Nitrogenous fertilizer materials manufacturing
325314 Nitrogenous fertilizers made by mixing purchased materials
325920 Nitroglycerin explosive materials manufacturing
325194 Nitrophenol manufacturing
325194 Nitrosated hydrocarbon derivatives manufacturing
325130 Nitroso dyes manufacturing
325920 Nitrostarch explosive materials manufacturing
325199 Nitrous ether manufacturing
325120 Nitrous oxide manufacturing
325411 N-methylpiperazine manufacturing
924110 NOAA (National Oceanic and Atmospheric Administration)
339113 Noise protectors, personal, manufacturing
312120 Nonalcoholic beer brewing
312130 Nonalcoholic wines manufacturing
551112 Nonbank holding companies (except managing)
325220 Noncellulosic fibers and filaments manufacturing
325220 Noncellulosic filament yarn manufacturing
325220 Noncellulosic staple fibers and filaments manufacturing
111339 Noncitrus fruit farming
327120 Nonclay refractories (e.g., block, brick, mortar, tile) manufacturing
311514 Nondairy creamers, dry, manufacturing
311511 Nondairy creamers, liquid, manufacturing
541380 Nondestructive testing laboratories or services
425120 Nondurable goods agents and brokers, wholesale trade
425110 Nondurable goods business to business electronic markets, wholesale trade
325110 Nonene made from refined petroleum or liquid hydrocarbons
311514 Nonfat dry milk manufacturing
331492 Nonferrous alloys (except aluminum, copper) made from purchased nonferrous metals
331492 Nonferrous alloys (except aluminum, copper) made in integrated secondary smelting and alloying plants
331523 Nonferrous die-casting foundries
331410 Nonferrous metal (except aluminum) shapes made in primary nonferrous metal smelting and refining mills
331491 Nonferrous metal shapes (except aluminum, copper) made by rolling, drawing, or extruding purchased nonferrous metal
331491 Nonferrous metal shapes (except aluminum, copper) made in integrated secondary smelting and extruding mills
331491 Nonferrous metal shapes (except aluminum, copper) made in integrated secondary smelting and rolling mills
331491 Nonferrous metal shapes (except aluminum, copper) made in integrated secondary smelting mills and wire drawing plants

331529 Nonferrous metals (except aluminum) foundries (except die-casting)
331410 Nonferrous metals (except aluminum) made in primary nonferrous metal smelting and refining mills
331410 Nonferrous metals (except aluminum) smelting and refining, primary
331529 Nonferrous metals (except aluminum) unfinished castings (except die-castings) manufacturing
331492 Nonferrous metals (except aluminum, copper) secondary smelting and refining
423510 Nonferrous metals (except precious) merchant wholesalers
331491 Nonferrous wire (except aluminum, copper) made from purchased nonferrous metals (except aluminum, copper) in wire drawing plants
331491 Nonferrous wire (except aluminum, copper) made in integrated secondary smelting mills and wire drawing plants
511130 Nonfiction book publishers (except exclusive Internet publishing)
511130 Nonfiction book publishers and printing combined
519130 Nonfiction book publishers, exclusively on Internet
323120 Nonfiction bookbinding without printing
323117 Nonfiction books printing and binding without publishing
323117 Nonfiction books printing without publishing
562219 Nonhazardous waste treatment and disposal facilities (except combustors, incinerators, landfills, sewer systems, sewage treatment facilities)
423510 Noninsulated wire merchant wholesalers
423520 Nonmetallic minerals (except precious and semiprecious stones and minerals used in construction, such as sand and gravel)
213115 Nonmetallic minerals mining support services (e.g., blasting, shaft sinking, tunneling) (except site preparation and related construction contractor activities) on a contract basis
423520 Nonmetallic ores merchant wholesalers
325412 Nonprescription drug preparations manufacturing
424210 Nonprescription drugs merchant wholesalers
531120 Nonresidential building (except miniwarehouse) rental or leasing
531312 Nonresidential property managing
481212 Nonscheduled air freight transportation
481211 Nonscheduled air passenger transportation
332215 Nonstick metal cooking utensils
337122 Nonupholstered, household-type, custom wood furniture, manufacturing
313230 Nonwoven fabric tapes manufacturing
313230 Nonwoven fabrics manufacturing
313230 Nonwoven felts manufacturing
311999 Noodle mixes made from purchased dry ingredients
311423 Noodle mixes made in dehydration plants
311824 Noodle mixes made in dry pasta plants
311824 Noodles, dry, manufacturing 311991 Noodles, fresh, manufacturing 311999 Noodles, fried, manufacturing 339113 Nose and ear plugs manufacturing 541199 Notary public services 541199 Notary publics' private practices 334111 Notebook computers manufacturing 322230 Notebooks (including mechanically bound by wire, or plastics) made from purchased paper
424120 Notebooks merchant wholesalers
424310 Notions merchant wholesalers 332999 Novelties and specialties, nonprecious metal and precious plated, manufacturing
424990 Novelties merchant wholesalers
316998 Novelties, leather (e.g., cigarette lighter covers, key fobs), manufacturing
339999 Novelties, not specified elsewhere, manufacturing
339910 Novelties, precious metal (except precious plated), manufacturing
321999 Novelties, wood fiber, manufacturing
453220 Novelty shops
314999 Novelty stitching contractors on apparel
326199 Nozzles, aerosol spray, plastics, manufacturing
332919 Nozzles, firefighting, manufacturing
332919 Nozzles, lawn hose, manufacturing
325212 N-type rubber manufacturing
332911 Nuclear application valves manufacturing
332410 Nuclear control drive mechanisms manufacturing
541690 Nuclear energy consulting services 926130 Nuclear energy inspection and regulation offices

325180 Nuclear fuel scrap reprocessing

325180 Nuclear fuels, inorganic, manufacturing

334519 Nuclear instrument modules manufacturing

334517 Nuclear irradiation equipment manufacturing

325412 Nuclear medicine (e.g., radioactive isotopes) preparations manufacturing

237130 Nuclear power plant construction 332410

Nuclear reactor steam supply systems manufacturing

332410 Nuclear reactors control rod drive mechanisms manufacturing

332410 Nuclear reactors manufacturing

332313 Nuclear shielding, fabricated metal plate work, manufacturing

332420 Nuclear waste casks, heavy gauge metal, manufacturing

237990 Nuclear waste disposal site construction

541714 Nucleic acid chemistry research and experimental development laboratories

721214 Nudist camps with accommodation facilities

713990 Nudist camps without accommodations

335314 Numerical controls, manufacturing 333517

Numerically controlled metal cutting machine tools manufacturing

812990 Numerology services

423940 Numismatic goods merchant wholesalers

621610 Nurse associations, visiting

621399 Nurse practitioners' offices (e.g., centers, clinics)

561311 Nurse registries

113210 Nurseries for reforestation growing trees

444220 Nurseries, retail, stock primarily grown off premises

444220 Nursery and garden centers without tree production

337122 Nursery furniture (except upholstered), wood, manufacturing

337124 Nursery furniture, metal, manufacturing

624410 Nursery schools

424930 Nursery stock (except plant bulbs, seeds) merchant wholesalers

111421 Nursery stock growing

111421 Nursery with tree production (except for reforestation)

611519 Nurse's aides schools

813920 Nurses' associations

621399 Nurses', licensed practical or registered, offices (e.g., centers, clinics)

621610 Nursing agencies, primarily providing home nursing services

621399 Nursing call centers

623110 Nursing homes

611519 Nursing schools (except academic)

445292 Nut (i.e., packaged) stores

115114 Nut hulling and shelling

331221 Nut rods, iron or steel, made in cold rolling mills

331110 Nut rods, iron or steel, made in iron and steel mills

333111 Nut shellers, farm-type, manufacturing

446191 Nutrition (i.e., food supplement) stores

621399 Nutritionists' offices (e.g., centers, clinics)

424450 Nuts (e.g., canned, roasted, salted) merchant wholesalers

311351 Nuts, chocolate covered, made from cacao beans

311352 Nuts, chocolate covered, made from purchased chocolate

311340 Nuts, covered (except chocolate covered), manufacturing

311911 Nuts, kernels and seeds, roasting and processing

115113 Nuts, machine harvesting

332722 Nuts, metal, manufacturing 311911 Nuts, salted, roasted, cooked, canned, manufacturing

424590 Nuts, unprocessed or shelled only, merchant wholesalers

325220 Nylon fibers and filaments manufacturing

424690 Nylon fibers merchant wholesalers 315110

Nylon hosiery, sheer, women's, misses', and girls' full-length and knee-length, knitting or knitting and finishing

325211 Nylon resins manufacturing

424610 Nylon resins merchant wholesalers 313110

Nylon spun yarns made from purchased fiber

313110 Nylon thread manufacturing

313110 Nylon yarn twisting or winding of purchased yarn

315110 Nylons, sheer, women's, misses', and girls' full-length and knee-length, knitting or knitting and finishing

325194 Oak extract manufacturing

321999 Oars, wood, manufacturing

111199 Oat farming, field and seed production

311211 Oat flour manufacturing 311230 Oatmeal (i.e., cereal breakfast food) manufacturing
311230 Oats, breakfast cereal, manufacturing
311230 Oats, rolled (i.e., cereal breakfast food), manufacturing
812910 Obedience training services, pet
339992 Oboes manufacturing
713990 Observation towers
712110 Observatories (except research institutions)
541715 Observatories, research institutions
622310 Obstetrical hospital
621111 Obstetricians' offices (e.g., centers, clinics)
339992 Ocarinas manufacturing
926150 Occupational safety and health administration
926150 Occupational safety and health standards agencies
813920 Occupational therapists' associations
621340 Occupational therapists' offices (e.g., centers, clinics)
541715 Oceanographic research and development laboratories or services
212393 Ocher mining and/or beneficiating
325130 Ocher pigments manufacturing
339992 Octophones manufacturing
114112 Octopus fishing
621399 Ocularists' offices (e.g., centers, clinics)
621320 ODs' (doctors of optometry) offices (e.g., centers, clinics)
332994 Oerlikon guns manufacturing
721310 Off campus dormitories
624190 Offender self-help organizations
336999 Off-highway tracked vehicles (except construction, armored military) manufacturing
333120 Off-highway trucks manufacturing
561110 Office administration services 541512 Office automation computer systems integration design services
236220 Office building construction
531120 Office building rental or leasing
561720 Office cleaning services
423420 Office equipment merchant wholesalers
337214 Office furniture (except wood), padded, upholstered, or plain (except wood), manufacturing
423210 Office furniture merchant wholesalers
532420 Office furniture rental or leasing
442110 Office furniture stores
238390 Office furniture, modular system, installation
337211 Office furniture, padded, upholstered, or plain wood, manufacturing
561320 Office help supply services
811212 Office machine repair and maintenance services (except communication equipment)
532420 Office machinery and equipment rental or leasing
423420 Office machines merchant wholesalers
561110 Office management services 322121 Office paper (e.g., computer printer, photocopy, plain paper) made in paper mills
322230 Office paper (e.g., computer printer, photocopy, plain paper), cut sheet, made from purchased paper
424120 Office supplies (except furniture, machines) merchant wholesalers
322230 Office supplies, die-cut paper, made from purchased paper or paperboard
561320 Office supply pools
453210 Office supply stores
551111 Offices of bank holding companies
441228 Off-road all-terrain vehicles (ATVs), wheeled or tracked, dealers
336999 Off-road all-terrain vehicles (ATVs), wheeled or tracked, manufacturing
325910 Offset inks manufacturing
323120 Offset plate preparation services
323111 Offset printing (except books, grey goods)
333244 Offset printing presses manufacturing
211120 Offshore crude petroleum production
211130 Offshore natural gas production
713290 Off-track betting parlors
334515 Ohmmeters manufacturing
324110 Oil (i.e., petroleum) refineries
325998 Oil additive preparations manufacturing
324110 Oil additives made in petroleum refineries
424690 Oil additives merchant wholesalers
237120 Oil and gas field distribution line construction
484220 Oil and gas field equipment trucking, local
484230 Oil and gas field equipment trucking, long-distance

811310 Oil and gas field machinery and equipment repair and maintenance services
213112 Oil and gas field services (except contract drilling, site preparation and related construction contractor activities) on a contract basis
333132 Oil and gas field-type drilling machinery and equipment (except offshore floating platforms) manufacturing
336611 Oil and gas offshore floating platforms manufacturing
213111 Oil and gas well drilling services (redrilling, spudding, tailing) on a contract basis
238220 Oil burner installation
333414 Oil burners, heating, manufacturing
423720 Oil burners, heating, merchant wholesalers
811191 Oil change and lubrication shops, automotive
424690 Oil drilling muds merchant wholesalers
211120 Oil field development for own account
423830 Oil field equipment merchant wholesalers
213112 Oil field exploration (except surveying) on a contract basis
211120 Oil field exploration for own account
532412 Oil field machinery and equipment rental or leasing
237310 Oil field road construction
423120 Oil filters, automotive, merchant wholesalers
336390 Oil filters, automotive, truck, and bus, manufacturing
424590 Oil kernels merchant wholesalers
523999 Oil lease brokers' offices
211130 Oil line drip, natural gas liquid
333914 Oil measuring and dispensing pumps manufacturing
424590 Oil nuts merchant wholesalers
237120 Oil pipeline construction
237120 Oil refinery construction
533110 Oil royalty companies
523910 Oil royalty dealing (i.e., acting as a principal in dealing royalties to investors)
533110 Oil royalty leasing
533110 Oil royalty traders (except for own account)
213112 Oil sampling services on a contract basis
339991 Oil seals manufacturing
211120 Oil shale mining and/or beneficiating
562910 Oil spill cleanup services
332420 Oil storage tanks, heavy gauge metal, manufacturing
333318 Oil water separators manufacturing
333914 Oil well and oil field pumps manufacturing
532412 Oil well drilling machinery and equipment rental or leasing
213111 Oil well drilling on a contract basis
213112 Oil well logging on a contract basis
423830 Oil well machinery and equipment merchant wholesalers
213112 Oil well rig building, repairing, and dismantling, on a contract basis
423830 Oil well supply houses merchant wholesalers
311613 Oil, animal, rendering
311221 Oil, corn crude and refined, made by wet milling corn
311225 Oil, olive, made from purchased oils
424710 Oil, petroleum, bulk stations and terminals, merchant wholesalers
424720 Oil, petroleum, merchant wholesalers (except bulk stations, terminals)
311225 Oil, vegetable stearin, made from purchased oils
423930 Oil, waste, merchant wholesalers 324199
Oil-based additives made from refined petroleum
313320 Oilcloth manufacturing
313320 Oiling of purchased textiles and apparel
325998 Oils (e.g., cutting, lubricating), synthetic, manufacturing
325194 Oils made by distillation of coal tar
424490 Oils, cooking and salad, merchant wholesalers
324110 Oils, fuel, manufacturing
424990 Oils, inedible, animal or vegetable, merchant wholesalers
324191 Oils, lubricating petroleum, made from refined petroleum
325998 Oils, lubricating, synthetic, manufacturing
324191 Oils, petroleum lubricating, re-refining used
325613 Oils, soluble (i.e., textile finishing assistants), manufacturing
325411 Oils, vegetable and animal, medicinal, uncompounded, manufacturing
325194 Oils, wood, made by distillation of wood
111191 Oilseed and grain combination farming, field and seed production
424990 Oilseed cake and meal merchant wholesalers

333241 Oilseed crushing and extracting machinery manufacturing
111120 Oilseed farming (except soybean), field and seed production
424590 Oilseeds merchant wholesalers
212399 Oilstones mining and/or beneficiating
111219 Okra farming, field, bedding plant and seed production
623312 Old age homes without nursing care
923130 Old age survivors and disability programs
623312 Old soldiers' homes without nursing care
325220 Olefin fibers and filaments manufacturing
325110 Olefins made from refined petroleum or liquid hydrocarbons
325199 Oleic acid (i.e., red oil) manufacturing
325199 Oleic acid esters manufacturing 325180
Oleum (i.e., fuming sulfuric acid) manufacturing
111339 Olive farming
311225 Olive oil made from purchased oils
311224 Olive oil made in crushing mills
311421 Olives brined
311423 Olives, dried, made in dehydration plants
212325 Olivine, non-gem, mining and/or beneficiating
334511 Omnibearing instrumentation manufacturing
621111 Oncologists' offices (e.g., centers, clinics)
812922 One-hour photofinishing services 111219
Onion farming, field, bedding plant and seed production
311421 Onions pickled
517919 On-line access service providers, using client-supplied telecommunications (e.g., dial-up ISPs)
517311 On-line access service providers, using own operated wired telecommunications infrastructure
561422 On-line customer service centers
212319 Onyx marble crushed and broken stone mining and/or beneficiating
212311 Onyx marble mining or quarrying
512132 Open air motion picture theaters
711110 Opera companies
315210 Opera hats cut and sew apparel contractors
315990 Opera hats cut and sewn from purchased fabric (except apparel contractors)
711130 Opera singers, independent
927110 Operating and launching government satellites
213112 Operating condensate gasoline field gathering lines on a contract basis
211120 Operating crude petroleum field gathering lines, except on a contract basis
211130 Operating natural gas liquid field gathering lines, except on a contract basis
339113 Operating room tables manufacturing
511210 Operating systems software, computer, packaged
541614 Operations research consulting services
325411 Ophthalmic agents, uncompounded, manufacturing
423460 Ophthalmic goods (except cameras) merchant wholesalers
339112 Ophthalmic instruments and apparatus (except laser surgical) manufacturing
621111 Ophthalmologists' offices (e.g., centers, clinics)
339112 Ophthalmometers and ophthalmoscopes manufacturing
541910 Opinion research services
325411 Opium and opium derivatives (i.e., basic chemicals) manufacturing
333314 Optical alignment and display instruments (except photographic) manufacturing
334112 Optical disk drives manufacturing 423460
Optical goods (except cameras) merchant wholesalers
446130 Optical goods stores (except offices of optometrists)
212399 Optical grade calcite mining and/or beneficiating
333314 Optical gun sighting and fire control equipment and instruments manufacturing
811219 Optical instrument repair and maintenance services (e.g., microscopes, telescopes)
333249 Optical lens making and grinding machinery manufacturing
334118 Optical readers and scanners manufacturing
518210 Optical scanning services 333314 Optical
test and inspection equipment manufacturing
334413 Optoelectronic devices manufacturing
339112 Optometers manufacturing
423460 Optometric equipment and supplies merchant wholesalers
813920 Optometrists' associations

621320 Optometrists' offices (e.g., centers, clinics)
621210 Oral and maxillofacial surgeons' offices (e.g., centers, clinics)
325412 Oral contraceptive preparations manufacturing
621210 Oral pathologists' offices (e.g., centers, clinics)
111310 Orange groves
325998 Orange oil manufacturing 115112 Orchard cultivation services (e.g., bracing, planting, pruning, removal, spraying, surgery)
111998 Orchard grass seed farming
711510 Orchestra conductors, independent
711130 Orchestras
561422 Order-taking for clients over the Internet
454110 Order-taking offices of mail-order houses
423990 Ordnance and accessories merchant wholesalers
236210 Ore and metal refinery construction
423520 Ore concentrates merchant wholesalers
333131 Ore crushing, washing, screening, and loading machinery manufacturing
423520 Ores (e.g., gold, iron, lead, silver, zinc) merchant wholesalers
621991 Organ banks, body
621991 Organ donor centers, body
424690 Organic chemicals merchant wholesalers
325220 Organic noncellulosic fibers and filaments manufacturing
325130 Organic pigments, dyes, lakes, and toners manufacturing
541612 Organization development consulting services
928120 Organization for Economic Cooperation and Development
928120 Organization of American States
326199 Organizers for closets, drawers, and shelves, plastics, manufacturing
711310 Organizers of agricultural fairs with facilities
711320 Organizers of agricultural fairs without facilities
711310 Organizers of arts events with facilities
711320 Organizers of arts events without facilities
711310 Organizers of festivals with facilities
711320 Organizers of festivals without facilities
711310 Organizers of live performing arts productions (e.g., concerts) with facilities
711320 Organizers of live performing arts productions (e.g., concerts) without facilities
711310 Organizers of sports events with facilities
711320 Organizers of sports events without facilities
325199 Organo-inorganic compound manufacturing
325320 Organo-phosphate based insecticides manufacturing
321219 Oriented strandboard (OSB) manufacturing
327420 Ornamental and architectural plaster work (e.g., columns, mantels, molding) manufacturing
327390 Ornamental and statuary precast concrete products manufacturing
112511 Ornamental fish production, farm raising
423390 Ornamental ironwork merchant wholesalers
238190 Ornamental metal work installation
332323 Ornamental metalwork manufacturing
111422 Ornamental plant growing
424930 Ornamental plants and flowers merchant wholesalers
561730 Ornamental tree and shrub services
321918 Ornamental woodwork (e.g., cornices, mantels) manufacturing
339999 Ornaments, Christmas tree (except electric, glass), manufacturing
335129 Ornaments, Christmas tree, electric, manufacturing
327212 Ornaments, Christmas tree, glass, made in glass making plants
327215 Ornaments, Christmas tree, made from purchased glass
623990 Orphanages
325998 Orris oil manufacturing
325194 Orthodichlorobenzene manufacturing
339116 Orthodontic appliance, custom made in dental laboratories
339114 Orthodontic appliances manufacturing
621210 Orthodontists' offices (e.g., centers, clinics)
339113 Orthopedic canes manufacturing
339113 Orthopedic device manufacturing and sale in retail environment
339113 Orthopedic devices manufacturing
423450 Orthopedic equipment and supplies merchant wholesalers
339113 Orthopedic extension shoes manufacturing
339113 Orthopedic hosiery, elastic, manufacturing
622310 Orthopedic hospitals

621111 Orthopedic physicians' offices (e.g., centers, clinics)
327420 Orthopedic plaster, gypsum, manufacturing
316210 Orthopedic shoes (except extension shoes), children's, manufacturing
316210 Orthopedic shoes (except extension shoes), men's, manufacturing
316210 Orthopedic shoes (except extension shoes), women's, manufacturing
448210 Orthopedic shoes stores 621111 Orthopedic surgeons' offices (e.g., centers, clinics)
621399 Orthotists' offices (e.g., centers, clinics)
321219 OSB (oriented strandboard) manufacturing
334515 Oscillators (e.g., instrument type audiofrequency and radiofrequency) manufacturing
334515 Oscilloscopes manufacturing
212299 Osmium mining and/or beneficiating
334516 Osmometers manufacturing
325998 Ossein manufacturing
622110 Osteopathic hospitals
621111 Osteopathic physicians' (except mental health) offices (e.g., centers, clinics)
112390 Ostrich production
621111 Otolaryngologists' offices (e.g., centers, clinics)
334510 Otoscopes, electromedical, manufacturing
337121 Ottomans, upholstered, manufacturing
441222 Outboard motor dealers 811490 Outboard motor repair shops 333618 Outboard motors manufacturing 423910 Outboard motors merchant wholesalers 713990 Outdoor adventure operations (e.g., white water rafting) without accommodations
721214 Outdoor adventure retreats with accommodation facilities
541850 Outdoor display advertising services
423210 Outdoor furniture merchant wholesalers
423620 Outdoor grills merchant wholesalers
237990 Outdoor recreation facility construction
451110 Outdoor sporting equipment stores
315190 Outerwear handknitted for the trade
424320 Outerwear, men's and boys', merchant wholesalers
424330 Outerwear, women's, children's, and infants', merchant wholesalers
713990 Outfitters (i.e., providing trips and equipment)
335932 Outlet boxes, electrical wiring, manufacturing
335931 Outlets (i.e., receptacles), electrical, manufacturing
335931 Outlets, convenience, electrical, manufacturing
541850 Out-of-home media (i.e., display) advertising services
621420 Outpatient mental health centers and clinics (except hospitals)
621420 Outpatient treatment centers and clinics (except hospitals) for substance abuse (i.e., alcoholism, drug addiction)
621420 Outpatient treatment centers and clinics for alcoholism
621420 Outpatient treatment centers and clinics for drug addiction
561320 Outplacement consulting services
561320 Outplacement services
325612 Oven cleaners manufacturing
334512 Oven temperature controls, nonindustrial, manufacturing
811412 Oven, household-type, repair and maintenance services without retailing new ovens
236210 Oven, industrial plant, construction
333241 Ovens, bakery, manufacturing
333318 Ovens, commercial-type, manufacturing
423440 Ovens, commercial-type, merchant wholesalers
335220 Ovens, freestanding household-type, manufacturing
423620 Ovens, gas and electric, household-type, merchant wholesalers
333994 Ovens, industrial process and laboratory-type, manufacturing
423830 Ovens, industrial, merchant wholesalers
335210 Ovens, portable household-type (except microwave and convection ovens), manufacturing
335220 Ovens, portable household-type convection and microwave, manufacturing
327215 Ovenware made from purchased glass
327212 Ovenware, glass, made in glass making plants
315210 Overall jackets, work, cut and sew apparel contractors
315220 Overall jackets, work, men's and boys', cut and sewn from purchased fabric (except apparel contractors)

315210 Overalls, work, cut and sew apparel contractors
315220 Overalls, work, men's and boys', cut and sewn from purchased fabric (except apparel contractors)
213113 Overburden removal for coal mining on a contract basis
213114 Overburden removal for metal mining on a contract basis
213115 Overburden removal for nonmetallic minerals mining (except fuels) on a contract basis
315210 Overcoats cut and sew apparel contractors
315220 Overcoats, men's and boys', cut and sewn from purchased fabric (except apparel contractors)
315240 Overcoats, women's and girls', cut and sewn from purchased fabric (except apparel contractors)
333922 Overhead conveyors manufacturing
238290 Overhead door, commercial- or industrial-type, installation
238350 Overhead door, residential-type, installation
333316 Overhead projectors (except computer peripheral) manufacturing
334118 Overhead projectors, computer peripheral-type, manufacturing
333923 Overhead traveling cranes manufacturing
237310 Overpass construction 316210 Overshoes, plastics or plastics soled fabric upper, manufacturing
316210 Overshoes, rubber, or rubber soled fabric, manufacturing
325199 Oxalates (e.g., ammonium oxalate, ethyl oxalate, sodium oxalate) manufacturing
325199 Oxalic acid manufacturing
532283 Oxygen equipment rental (i.e., home use)
325120 Oxygen manufacturing
339112 Oxygen tents manufacturing
114112 Oyster dredging
112512 Oyster production, farm raising
212399 Ozokerite mining and/or beneficiating
333318 Ozone machines for water purification manufacturing
621999 Pacemaker monitoring services
334510 Pacemakers manufacturing
326299 Pacifiers, rubber, manufacturing
713990 Pack trains (i.e., trail riding), recreational
445310 Package stores (i.e., liquor)
511210 Packaged computer software publishers
424440 Packaged poultry (except canned and frozen) merchant wholesalers
326112 Packaging film, plastics, single-web or multiweb, manufacturing
115114 Packaging fresh or farm-dried fruits and vegetables
541420 Packaging industrial design services
333993 Packaging machinery manufacturing
423840 Packaging materials merchant wholesalers
561910 Packaging services (except packing and crating for transportation)
326150 Packaging, foam plastics (except polystyrene), manufacturing
326199 Packaging, plastics (e.g., blister, bubble), manufacturing
325998 Packer's fluids manufacturing
488991 Packing and preparing goods for shipping
321920 Packing cases, wood, nailed or lock corner, manufacturing
321920 Packing crates, wood, manufacturing
115114 Packing fruits and vegetables
423830 Packing machinery and equipment merchant wholesalers
423840 Packing materials merchant wholesalers
813940 PACs (Political Action Committees) 316210 Pacs, plastics or plastics soled fabric upper, manufacturing
316210 Pacs, rubber or rubber soled fabric upper, manufacturing
322230 Padded envelopes manufacturing 314999 Padding and wadding (except nonwoven fabric) manufacturing
423850 Padding, upholstery filling, merchant wholesalers
424310 Paddings, apparel, merchant wholesalers
321999 Paddles, wood, manufacturing
332510 Padlocks, metal, manufacturing
314120 Pads and protectors (e.g., ironing board, mattress, table), textile, made from purchased fabrics or felts
313230 Pads and wadding, nonwoven, manufacturing
322211 Pads, corrugated and solid fiberboard, made from purchased paper or paperboard
322230 Pads, desk, made from purchased paper
321999 Pads, excelsior, wood, manufacturing
322291 Pads, incontinent and bed, manufacturing

332999 Pads, soap impregnated scouring, manufacturing
321999 Pads, table, rattan, reed, and willow, manufacturing
334220 Pagers manufacturing
517312 Paging services (except satellite)
321920 Pails, coopered wood, manufacturing
326199 Pails, plastics, manufacturing
321920 Pails, plywood, manufacturing
321920 Pails, wood, manufacturing
621498 Pain therapy centers and clinics, outpatient
325510 Paint and varnish removers manufacturing
238320 Paint and wallpaper stripping
333994 Paint baking and drying ovens manufacturing
424950 Paint removers merchant wholesalers
339994 Paint rollers manufacturing
424950 Paint rollers merchant wholesalers
811121 Paint shops, automotive
333991 Paint spray guns, handheld pneumatic, manufacturing
333912 Paint sprayers (i.e., compressor and spray gun unit) manufacturing
332999 Paint sticks, metal, manufacturing
326199 Paint sticks, plastics, manufacturing
321999 Paint sticks, wood, manufacturing
444120 Paint stores
325510 Paint thinner and reducer preparations manufacturing
424950 Paint thinners merchant wholesalers 713990
Paintball, laser tag, and similar fields and arenas
325510 Paintbrush cleaners manufacturing
339994 Paintbrushes manufacturing
424950 Paintbrushes merchant wholesalers
711510 Painters (i.e., artists), independent
424950 Painter's supplies (except artists', turpentine) merchant wholesalers
238320 Painting (except roof) contractors
238320 Painting and wallpapering
611610 Painting instruction
237310 Painting lines on highways, streets and bridges
332812 Painting metals and metal products for the trade
711510 Painting restorers, independent
237310 Painting traffic lanes or parking lots
238160 Painting, spraying, or coating, roof

325510 Paints (except artist's) manufacturing
424950 Paints (except artists') merchant wholesalers
339940 Paints, artist's, manufacturing
424990 Paints, artist's, merchant wholesalers
325510 Paints, emulsion (i.e., latex paint), manufacturing
325510 Paints, oil and alkyd vehicle, manufacturing
315210 Pajamas cut and sew apparel contractors
315190 Pajamas made in apparel knitting mills
315220 Pajamas, men's and boys', cut and sewn
from purchased fabric (except apparel contractors)
315240 Pajamas, women's, girls', and infants', cut and sewn from purchased fabric (except apparel contractors)
339940 Palettes, artist's, manufacturing
212299 Palladium mining and/or beneficiating
321920 Pallet containers, wood or wood and metal
combination, manufacturing 333924
Pallet movers manufacturing 333924 Pallet or
skid jacks manufacturing 332999 Pallet parts,
metal, manufacturing 321920 Pallet parts,
wood, manufacturing 532490 Pallet rental or
leasing
423830 Pallets and skids merchant wholesalers
322211 Pallets, corrugated and solid fiber, made
from purchased paper or paperboard
332999 Pallets, metal, manufacturing
321920 Pallets, wood or wood and metal combination, manufacturing
812990 Palm reading services
325199 Palmitic acid esters and amines manufacturing
311225 Palm-kernel oil made from purchased oils
311224 Palm-kernel oil, cake, and meal made in crushing mills
323120 Pamphlet binding without printing
511130 Pamphlet publishers (except exclusive Internet publishing)
511130 Pamphlet publishers and printing combined
519130 Pamphlet publishers, exclusively on Internet
424920 Pamphlets merchant wholesalers
323117 Pamphlets printing and binding without publishing

323117 Pamphlets printing without publishing
315210 Panama hats cut and sew apparel contractors
315990 Panama hats cut and sewn from purchased fabric (except apparel contractors)
311824 Pancake mixes made from purchased flour
311999 Pancake syrups (except pure maple) manufacturing
311412 Pancakes, frozen, manufacturing 238310
Panel or rigid board insulation installation 321918
Panel work, wood millwork, manufacturing 238390
Panel, metal, installation 334513 Panelboard indicators, recorders, and controllers, receiver industrial
process-
type, manufacturing
335313 Panelboards, electric power distribution, manufacturing
423610 Panelboards, electric power distribution, merchant wholesalers
238350 Paneling installation
423310 Paneling merchant wholesalers 236117 Pan-
elized housing, residential, assembled on site by for-sale builders
236117 Panelized multifamily housing assembled on site by for-sale builders
236116 Panelized multifamily housing assembled on site by general contractors
236115 Panelized single-family housing assembled on site by general contractors
335313 Panels, generator control and metering, manufacturing
321211 Panels, hardwood plywood, manufacturing
332311 Panels, prefabricated metal building, manufacturing
321992 Panels, prefabricated wood building, manufacturing
321212 Panels, softwood plywood, manufacturing
423440 Pans, commercial, merchant wholesalers 315210 Panties cut and sew apparel contractors 315190 Panties made in apparel knitting mills
315240 Panties, women's, girls', and infants', cut
and sewn from purchased fabric (except apparel contractors)
315210 Pants (e.g., athletic, dress, leather, sweat, waterproof outerwear, work) cut and sew apparel contractors
315220 Pants (e.g., athletic, dress, sweat, work), men's and boys', cut and sewn from purchased fabric (except apparel contractors)
315210 Pants outfits cut and sew apparel contractors
315240 Pants outfits, women's and girls', cut and sewn from purchased fabric (except apparel contractors)
315190 Pants, athletic, made in apparel knitting mills
315240 Pants, athletic, women's, girls', and infants', cut and sewn from purchased fabric (except apparel contractors)
315280 Pants, leather (except apparel contractors), manufacturing
315190 Pants, outerwear, made in apparel knitting mills
315280 Pants, rubber and rubberized fabric, made in the same establishment as the basic material
315240 Pants, sweat, women's, girls', and infants', cut and sewn from purchased fabric (except apparel contractors)
315280 Pants, vulcanized rubber, manufacturing
315280 Pants, waterproof outerwear, cut and sewn from purchased fabric (except apparel contractors)
315240 Pants, women's, girls', and infants', cut and sewn from purchased fabric (except apparel contractors)
315210 Pantsuits cut and sew apparel contractors
315240 Pantsuits, women's, girls', and infants', cut and sewn from purchased fabric (except apparel contractors)
315210 Panty girdles cut and sew apparel contractors
315240 Panty girdles, women's and girls', cut and sewn from purchased fabric (except apparel contractors)
315110 Panty hose, women's and girls', knitting or knitting and finishing
111339 Papaya farming
327910 Paper (e.g., aluminum oxide, emery, garnet, silicon carbide), abrasive-coated, made from purchased paper
424110 Paper (e.g., fine, printing, writing), bulk, merchant wholesalers
322121 Paper (except newsprint, uncoated groundwood) manufacturing
322121 Paper (except newsprint, uncoated groundwood) products made in paper mills
322121 Paper (except newsprint, uncoated groundwood), coated, laminated or treated, made in paper mills
424130 Paper (except office supplies, printing paper, stationery, writing paper) merchant wholesalers

333243 Paper and paperboard coating and finishing machinery manufacturing
333243 Paper and paperboard converting machinery manufacturing
333243 Paper and paperboard corrugating machinery manufacturing
333243 Paper and paperboard cutting and folding machinery manufacturing
333243 Paper and paperboard die-cutting and stamping machinery manufacturing
423830 Paper and pulp industries manufacturing machinery merchant wholesalers
333243 Paper bag making machinery manufacturing
424130 Paper bags merchant wholesalers 322220
Paper bags, coated, made from purchased paper
322220 Paper bags, uncoated, made from purchased paper
212324 Paper clay mining and/or beneficiating
332618 Paper clips made from purchased wire
331222 Paper clips, iron or steel, made in wire drawing plants
322219 Paper cups made from purchased paper or paperboard
339940 Paper cutters, office-type, manufacturing
322299 Paper dishes (e.g., cups, plates) made from molded pulp
322219 Paper dishes (e.g., cups, plates) made from purchased paper or paperboard
315210 Paper dresses cut and sew apparel contractors
315240 Paper dresses, women's and girls', cut and sewn from purchased fabric (except apparel contractors)
313220 Paper fabric, narrow woven, weaving
313210 Paper fabrics, broadwoven, weaving
332618 Paper machine wire cloth made from purchased wire
333243 Paper making machinery manufacturing
811310 Paper making machinery repair and maintenance services
322121 Paper mills (except newsprint, uncoated groundwood paper mills)
322122 Paper mills, newsprint
322122 Paper mills, uncoated groundwood
322291 Paper napkins and tablecloths made from purchased paper
322299 Paper novelties made from purchased paper
236210 Paper or pulp mill construction 322219 Paper
plates made from purchased paper or paperboard
322299 Paper products (except office supply), die-cut, made from purchased paper or paperboard
322230 Paper products, die-cut office supply, made from purchased paper or paperboard
332992 Paper shells (i.e., 30 mm. or less, 1.18 inch or less) manufacturing
423420 Paper shredders merchant wholesalers
322121 Paper stock for conversion into paper products (e.g., bag and sack stock, envelope stock, tissue stock, wallpaper stock) manufacturing
322291 Paper towels made from purchased paper
322121 Paper towels made in paper mills
424130 Paper towels merchant wholesalers
313110 Paper yarn manufacturing
322121 Paper, asphalt, made in paper mills
423390 Paper, building, merchant wholesalers
339940 Paper, carbon, manufacturing
322211 Paper, corrugated, made from purchased paper or paperboard
523110 Paper, dealing of commercial (i.e., acting as principal in dealing securities to investors)
322122 Paper, newsprint and uncoated groundwood, manufacturing
424120 Paper, office (e.g., carbon, computer, copier, typewriter), merchant wholesalers
325992 Paper, photographic sensitized, manufacturing
423930 Paper, scrap, merchant wholesalers
339940 Paper, stencil, manufacturing 322130 Paper-
board (e.g., can/drum stock, container board, corrugating medium, folding carton
stock, linerboard, tube) manufacturing
424130 Paperboard and paperboard products (except office supplies) merchant wholesalers
333243 Paperboard box making machinery manufacturing
322130 Paperboard coating, laminating, or treating in paperboard mills
333243 Paperboard making machinery manufacturing
322130 Paperboard mills
322130 Paperboard products (e.g., containers) made in paperboard mills

322220 Paperboard, pasted, lined, laminated, or surface coated, made from purchased paperboard
238320 Paperhanging and removal contractors
238320 Paperhanging or removal contractors
327999 Papier-mache statuary and related art goods (e.g., urns, vases) manufacturing
713990 Para sailing, recreational
314999 Parachutes manufacturing
213112 Paraffin services, oil and gas field, on a contract basis
324110 Paraffin waxes made in petroleum refineries
325110 Paraffins made from refined petroleum or liquid hydrocarbons
541199 Paralegal services
321213 Parallel strand lumber manufacturing
621399 Paramedics' offices (e.g., centers, clinics)
325130 Pararosaniline dyes manufacturing
621511 Parasitology health laboratories
339999 Parasols manufacturing
325320 Parathion insecticides manufacturing
485991 Paratransit transportation services
561431 Parcel mailing services combined with one or more other office support services, private
561431 Parcel mailing services, private
561910 Parcel packing services
333997 Parcel post scales manufacturing
316110 Parchment leather manufacturing
922150 Pardon boards and offices
624190 Parenting support services
813410 Parent-teachers' associations
325320 Paris green insecticides manufacturing
237990 Park and recreational open space improvement construction
922120 Park police
332812 Parkerizing metals and metal products for the trade
236220 Parking garage construction
812930 Parking garages, automobile
561790 Parking lot cleaning (e.g., power sweeping, washing) services
237310 Parking lot marking and line painting
238990 Parking lot paving and sealing
812930 Parking lots, automobile
334514 Parking meters manufacturing
561612 Parking security services
488119 Parking services, aircraft
812930 Parking services, valet
713110 Parks (e.g., theme, water), amusement
924120 Parks and recreation commission, government
712190 Parks, national
712190 Parks, nature
712130 Parks, wild animal
237310 Parkway construction
611310 Parochial schools, college level
611110 Parochial schools, elementary or secondary
624190 Parole offices, privately operated
922150 Parole offices, publicly administered
238330 Parquet flooring installation
321918 Parquet flooring, hardwood, manufacturing
321918 Parquetry, hardwood, manufacturing
111219 Parsley farming, field, bedding plant and seed production
111219 Parsnip farming, field, bedding plant and seed production
335999 Particle accelerators, high-voltage, manufacturing
334516 Particle beam excitation instruments, laboratory-type, manufacturing
334516 Particle size analyzers manufacturing
321219 Particleboard manufacturing
423310 Particleboard merchant wholesalers
238390 Partition (e.g., office, washroom), metal, installation
238390 Partition, moveable and/or demountable, installation
337215 Partitions for floor attachment, prefabricated, manufacturing
423440 Partitions merchant wholesalers
322211 Partitions, corrugated and solid fiber, made from purchased paper or paperboard
337215 Partitions, freestanding, prefabricated, manufacturing
332323 Partitions, ornamental metal, manufacturing
112390 Partridge production
441310 Parts and accessories dealers, automotive
423120 Parts, new, motor vehicle, merchant wholesalers
423140 Parts, used, motor vehicle, merchant wholesalers
532289 Party (i.e., banquet) equipment rental

453220 Party goods (e.g., paper supplies, decorations, novelties) stores
454390 Party plan merchandisers, direct selling
812990 Party planning services 532289
Party rental supply centers
481211 Passenger air transportation, nonscheduled
481111 Passenger air transportation, scheduled
333922 Passenger baggage belt loaders (except industrial truck) manufacturing
532112 Passenger car leasing
532111 Passenger car rental
481211 Passenger carriers, air, nonscheduled
481111 Passenger carriers, air, scheduled
485320 Passenger limousine rental with driver (except shuttle service, taxi)
482111 Passenger railways, line-haul
336611 Passenger ship building 483114 Passenger
transportation, coastal or Great Lakes (including St.
Lawrence Seaway)
483114 Passenger transportation, deep sea, to and from domestic ports (including Puerto Rico)
483112 Passenger transportation, deep sea, to or from foreign ports
483212 Passenger transportation, inland waters (except on Great Lakes system)
532112 Passenger van leasing
532111 Passenger van rental
532111 Passenger van rental agencies
485320 Passenger van rental with driver (except shuttle service, taxi)
532112 Passenger vehicle fleet leasing
111339 Passion fruit farming
928120 Passport issuing services
541921 Passport photography services
311422 Pasta based products canning
333241 Pasta making machinery (i.e., food manufacturing-type) manufacturing
311999 Pasta mixes made from purchased dry ingredients
311824 Pasta, dry, manufacturing
311991 Pasta, fresh, manufacturing
331314 Paste made from purchased aluminum
331420 Paste made from purchased copper
331221 Paste made from purchased iron or steel
331110 Paste, iron or steel, made in iron and steel mills
331492 Paste, nonferrous metals (except aluminum, copper), made from purchased metal
325520 Pastes, adhesive, manufacturing
311421 Pastes, fruit and vegetable, canning
333241 Pasteurizing equipment, food, manufacturing
311511 Pasteurizing milk
311612 Pastrami made from purchased carcasses
311812 Pastries (e.g., Danish, French), fresh, made in commercial bakeries
311813 Pastries (e.g., Danish, French), frozen, manufacturing
311824 Pastries, uncooked, manufacturing
321999 Pastry boards, wood, manufacturing 541199
Patent agent services (i.e., patent filing and searching services)
541110 Patent attorneys' offices
541110 Patent attorneys' private practices
541990 Patent broker services (i.e., patent marketing services)
533110 Patent buying and licensing
533110 Patent leasing
316110 Patent leather manufacturing
325412 Patent medicine preparations manufacturing
621511 Pathological analysis laboratories
621111 Pathologists' (except oral, speech, voice) offices (e.g., centers, clinics)
621111 Pathologists', forensic, offices (e.g., centers, clinics)
621111 Pathologists', neuropathological, offices (e.g., centers, clinics)
621210 Pathologists', oral, offices (e.g., centers, clinics)
621340 Pathologists', speech or voice, offices (e.g., centers, clinics)
621111 Pathologists', surgical, offices (e.g., centers, clinics)
621511 Pathology laboratories, medical 334510
Patient monitoring equipment (e.g., intensive
care, coronary care unit)
manufacturing
423450 Patient monitoring equipment merchant wholesalers
327331 Patio block, concrete, manufacturing
238990 Patio construction
336611 Patrol boat building
561612 Patrol services, security

541990 Patrolling (i.e., visual inspection) of electric transmission or gas lines
511199 Pattern and plan (e.g., clothing patterns) publishers (except exclusive Internet publishing)
511199 Pattern and plan (e.g., clothing patterns) publishers and printing combined
519130 Pattern and plan (e.g., clothing patterns) publishers, exclusively on Internet
332999 Patterns (except shoe), industrial, manufacturing
423830 Patterns (except shoe), industrial, merchant wholesalers
323111 Patterns and plans (e.g., clothing patterns) commercial printing (except blueprinting, screen) without publishing
323113 Patterns and plans (e.g., clothing patterns) screen printing without publishing
339999 Patterns, shoe, manufacturing
423850 Patterns, shoe, merchant wholesalers 237310 Pavement, highway, road, street, bridge or airport runway, construction
238990 Paver, brick (e.g., driveway, patio, sidewalk), installation
423810 Pavers merchant wholesalers
212399 Pavers mining and/or beneficiating 324121 Paving blocks and mixtures made from purchased asphaltic materials
327331 Paving blocks, concrete, manufacturing
327120 Paving brick, clay, manufacturing
333120 Paving machinery manufacturing
423320 Paving mixtures merchant wholesalers
238990 Paving, residential and commercial driveway and parking lot
522298 Pawnshops
812990 Pay telephone equipment concession operators
515210 Pay television networks
522390 Payday lending services
515210 Pay-per-view cable programming
541214 Payroll processing services
334210 PBX (private branch exchange) equipment manufacturing
111219 Pea (except dry) farming, field and seed production
111130 Pea farming, dry, field and seed production
813319 Peace advocacy organizations
928120 Peace Corps
111339 Peach farming
325130 Peacock blue lake manufacturing
311911 Peanut butter blended with jelly manufacturing
311911 Peanut butter manufacturing
311224 Peanut cake, meal, and oil made in crushing mills
333111 Peanut combines (i.e., diggers, packers, threshers) manufacturing
111992 Peanut farming
311225 Peanut oil made from purchased oils
333241 Peanut roasting machines (i.e., food manufacturing-type) manufacturing
115114 Peanut shelling
115113 Peanut, machine harvesting 424590 Peanuts, bulk, unprocessed, merchant wholesalers
111339 Pear farming
339910 Pearl drilling, peeling, or sawing
325130 Pearl essence pigment, synthetic, manufacturing
331511 Pearlitic castings, malleable iron, unfinished, manufacturing
423940 Pearls merchant wholesalers
339910 Pearls, costume, manufacturing
212399 Peat grinding
212399 Peat humus mining and/or beneficiating
212399 Peat mining and/or beneficiating
327999 Peat pots, molded pulp, manufacturing
212321 Pebbles (except grinding) mining and/or beneficiating
212399 Pebbles grinding
111335 Pecan farming
115114 Pecan hulling and shelling
311942 Pectin manufacturing
621111 Pediatricians' (except mental health) offices (e.g., centers, clinics)
621112 Pediatricians', mental health, offices (e.g., centers, clinics)
812113 Pedicure and manicure salons
812113 Pedicurist services 115210 Pedigree (i.e., livestock, pets, poultry) record services
812910 Pedigree record services, pet
334514 Pedometers manufacturing
621399 Pedorthics' offices (e.g., centers, clinics)
813920 Peer review boards
212325 Pegmatite, feldspar, mining and/or beneficiating

316998 Pegs, leather shoe, manufacturing
332994 Pellet guns manufacturing
333131 Pellet mills machinery, mining-type, manufacturing
332992 Pellets, air rifle and pistol, manufacturing
316110 Pelts bleaching, currying, dyeing, scraping, and tanning
424590 Pelts, raw, merchant wholesalers
339112 Pelvimeters manufacturing
339940 Pen refills and cartridges manufacturing
339940 Pencil leads manufacturing
339940 Pencil sharpeners manufacturing
321999 Pencil slats, wood, manufacturing
339940 Pencils manufacturing
424120 Pencils merchant wholesalers
335122 Pendant lamps (except residential), electric, manufacturing
335121 Pendant lamps fixtures, residential electric, manufacturing
325613 Penetrants manufacturing
325998 Penetrating fluids, synthetic, manufacturing
325412 Penicillin preparations manufacturing
325411 Penicillin, uncompounded, manufacturing
922140 Penitentiaries
236220 Penitentiary construction
212113 Pennsylvania anthracite mining and/or beneficiating
339940 Pens manufacturing
424120 Pens, writing, merchant wholesalers
523920 Pension fund managing
524292 Pension fund, third party administrative services
525110 Pension funds
525110 Pension plans (e.g., employee benefit, retirement)
332313 Penstocks, fabricated metal plate, manufacturing
325194 Pentachlorophenol manufacturing
325199 Pentaerythritol manufacturing 325110 Pentanes made from refined petroleum or liquid hydrocarbons
325110 Pentenes made from refined petroleum or liquid hydrocarbons
325920 Pentolite explosive materials manufacturing
561330 PEO (professional employer organizations)
111219 Pepper (e.g., bell, chili, green, hot, red, sweet) farming
311942 Pepper (i.e., spice) manufacturing
325998 Peppermint oil manufacturing
313210 Percales weaving
114111 Perch fishing
325180 Perchloric acid manufacturing
325199 Perchloroethylene manufacturing
335210 Percolators, household-type electric, manufacturing
332992 Percussion caps (i.e., 30 mm. or less, 1.18 inch or less), ammunition, manufacturing
339992 Percussion musical instruments manufacturing
423420 Perforating machines merchant wholesalers
213112 Perforating oil and gas well casings on a contract basis
533110 Performance rights, licensing of
711510 Performers (i.e., entertainers), independent
711510 Performing artists, independent
711310 Performing arts center operators
611610 Performing arts schools (except academic)
561599 Performing arts ticket offices
325199 Perfume materials (i.e., basic synthetic chemicals, such as terpineol) manufacturing
446120 Perfume stores
325620 Perfumes manufacturing
424210 Perfumes merchant wholesalers
511120 Periodical publishers (except exclusive Internet publishing)
511120 Periodical publishers and printing combined
519130 Periodical publishers, exclusively on Internet
323111 Periodicals commercial printing (except screen) without publishing
424920 Periodicals merchant wholesalers
323113 Periodicals screen printing without publishing
621210 Periodontists' offices (e.g., centers, clinics)
334418 Peripheral controller boards manufacturing
423430 Peripheral equipment, computer, merchant wholesalers
333314 Periscopes manufacturing
327992 Perlite aggregates manufacturing
212399 Perlite mining and/or beneficiating
327992 Perlite, expanded, manufacturing

331524 Permanent mold castings, aluminum, unfinished, manufacturing
331529 Permanent mold castings, nonferrous metal (except aluminum), unfinished, manufacturing
325620 Permanent wave preparations manufacturing
238130 Permanent wood foundation installation
325180 Peroxides, inorganic, manufacturing
325199 Peroxides, organic, manufacturing
325130 Persian orange lake manufacturing
111339 Persimmon farming
423620 Personal care appliances, electric, merchant wholesalers
812990 Personal chef services
334418 Personal computer modems manufacturing
334111 Personal computers manufacturing
522291 Personal credit institutions (i.e., unsecured cash loans)
611699 Personal development schools
525920 Personal estates (i.e., managing assets)
522291 Personal finance companies (i.e., unsecured cash loans)
611519 Personal fitness instructor training
812990 Personal fitness training services
339910 Personal goods, metal, manufacturing
551112 Personal holding companies
525920 Personal investment trusts
523991 Personal investments trust administration
523920 Personal investments trusts, managing
316998 Personal leather goods (e.g., coin purses, eyeglass cases, key cases), small, manufacturing
446199 Personal mobility scooter dealers
812990 Personal organizer services 561612 Personal protection services (except security systems services)
339113 Personal safety devices, not specified elsewhere, manufacturing
424130 Personal sanitary paper products merchant wholesalers
812990 Personal shopping services
525920 Personal trusts
441228 Personal watercraft dealers
336999 Personal watercraft manufacturing
532284 Personal watercraft rental
561320 Personnel (e.g., industrial, office) suppliers
813920 Personnel management associations
541612 Personnel management consulting services
921190 Personnel offices, government
325320 Pest (e.g., ant, rat, roach, rodent) control poison manufacturing
561710 Pest (e.g., termite) inspection services
561710 Pest control (except agricultural, forestry) services
926140 Pest control programs, agriculture, government
115112 Pest control services, agricultural
115310 Pest control services, forestry 424690 Pesticides (except agricultural) merchant wholesalers
325320 Pesticides manufacturing
424910 Pesticides, agricultural, merchant wholesalers
334510 PET (positron emission tomography) scanners manufacturing
812910 Pet boarding services
812220 Pet cemeteries
311119 Pet food (except cat, dog) manufacturing
424490 Pet food merchant wholesalers
311111 Pet food, dog and cat, manufacturing
812910 Pet grooming services
524128 Pet health insurance carriers, direct
541940 Pet hospitals
926150 Pet licensing
453910 Pet shops
812910 Pet sitting services
424990 Pet supplies (except pet food) merchant wholesalers
453910 Pet supply stores
812910 Pet training services
485991 Pet transportation services
324110 Petrochemical feedstocks made in petroleum refineries
237120 Petrochemical plant construction
324110 Petrochemicals made in petroleum refineries
424710 Petroleum and petroleum products bulk stations and terminals, merchant wholesalers
424720 Petroleum and petroleum products merchant wholesalers (except bulk stations, terminals)
425120 Petroleum brokers
324110 Petroleum coke made in petroleum refineries
424720 Petroleum coke merchant wholesalers

324110 Petroleum cracking and reforming
324110 Petroleum distillation
541330 Petroleum engineering services
211130 Petroleum gases, liquefied, recovering from oil and gas field gases
324199 Petroleum jelly made from refined petroleum
324110 Petroleum jelly made in petroleum refineries
324191 Petroleum lubricating oils made from refined petroleum
324110 Petroleum lubricating oils made in petroleum refineries
486110 Petroleum pipelines, crude 486910 Petroleum pipelines, refined 325211 Petroleum polymer resins manufacturing 423830 Petroleum production machinery and equipment merchant wholesalers
324110 Petroleum refineries
237120 Petroleum refinery construction
333249 Petroleum refining machinery manufacturing
332420 Petroleum storage tanks, heavy gauge metal, manufacturing
324199 Petroleum waxes made from refined petroleum
211120 Petroleum, crude, production (i.e., extraction)
424990 Pets merchant wholesalers
712130 Petting zoos
337127 Pews, church, manufacturing
339910 Pewter ware manufacturing
236210 Pharmaceutical manufacturing plant construction
325412 Pharmaceutical preparations (e.g., capsules, liniments, ointments, tablets) manufacturing
424210 Pharmaceuticals merchant wholesalers
446110 Pharmacies
813920 Pharmacists' associations
334515 Phase angle meters manufacturing
335312 Phase converters (i.e., electrical equipment) manufacturing
112390 Pheasant production
325194 Phenol manufacturing
325211 Phenol-formaldehyde resins manufacturing
325211 Phenol-furfural resins manufacturing
325211 Phenolic resins manufacturing
325211 Phenoxy resins manufacturing
813211 Philanthropic trusts, awarding grants
212399 Phlogopite mining and/or beneficiating
334510 Phonocardiographs manufacturing
334614 Phonograph records manufacturing
423990 Phonograph records merchant wholesalers
423440 Phonographs, coin-operated, merchant wholesalers
325199 Phosgene manufacturing
212392 Phosphate rock mining and/or beneficiating
424910 Phosphate rock, ground, merchant wholesalers
325312 Phosphatic fertilizer materials manufacturing
325314 Phosphatic fertilizers made by mixing purchased materials
325130 Phosphomolybdic acid lakes and toners manufacturing
325199 Phosphoric acid esters manufacturing
325312 Phosphoric acid manufacturing 325180 Phosphorus compounds, not specified elsewhere by process, manufacturing
325180 Phosphorus oxychloride manufacturing
325130 Phosphotungstic acid lakes and toners manufacturing
323111 Photo albums and refills manufacturing
424120 Photo albums merchant wholesalers
323120 Photocomposition services, for the printing trade
424120 Photocopy supplies merchant wholesalers
811212 Photocopying machine repair and maintenance services without retailing new photocopying machines
333316 Photocopying machines manufacturing
561439 Photocopying services (except combined with printing services)
325992 Photocopying toner cartridges manufacturing
334413 Photoelectric cells, solid-state (e.g., electronic eye), manufacturing
333244 Photoengraving machinery manufacturing
323120 Photoengraving plate preparation services
423410 Photofinishing equipment merchant wholesalers
812921 Photofinishing labs (except one-hour)
812922 Photofinishing labs, one-hour
812921 Photofinishing services (except one-hour)
812922 Photofinishing services, one-hour

335110 Photoflash and photoflood lamp bulbs and tubes manufacturing
333316 Photoflash equipment manufacturing
541370 Photogrammetric mapping services 322299 Photograph folders, mats, and mounts manufacturing
541922 Photographers specializing in aerial photography
711510 Photographers, independent artistic
325992 Photographic chemicals manufacturing
333316 Photographic equipment (except lenses) manufacturing
423410 Photographic equipment and supplies merchant wholesalers
532210 Photographic equipment rental
811211 Photographic equipment repair shops without retailing new photographic equipment
423410 Photographic film and plates merchant wholesalers
325992 Photographic film, cloth, paper, and plate, sensitized, manufacturing
333314 Photographic lenses manufacturing
812990 Photographic machine concession operators, coin-operated
443142 Photographic supply stores 326113 Photographic, micrographic, and X-ray plastics, sheet, and film (except sensitized), manufacturing
611610 Photography schools, art
611519 Photography schools, commercial
541922 Photography services, commercial
541921 Photography services, portrait (e.g., still, video)
541922 Photography studios, commercial
541921 Photography studios, portrait
711510 Photojournalists, independent (freelance)
327212 Photomask blanks, glass, made in glass making plants
325992 Photomasks manufacturing
334516 Photometers (except photographic exposure meters) manufacturing
334516 Photonexcitation analyzers manufacturing
334413 Photonic integrated circuits manufacturing
541715 Photonics research and development services (except nanotechnology research and development)
325992 Photosensitized paper manufacturing
323120 Phototypesetting services
334413 Photovoltaic cells manufacturing
334413 Photovoltaic devices, solid-state, manufacturing
335999 Photovoltaic panels made from purchased cells
325199 Phthalate acid manufacturing
325211 Phthalic alkyd resins manufacturing
325194 Phthalic anhydride manufacturing
325211 Phthalic anhydride resins manufacturing
325130 Phthalocyanine pigments manufacturing
541614 Physical distribution consulting services
713940 Physical fitness centers
621999 Physical fitness evaluation services (except by offices of health practitioners)
713940 Physical fitness facilities
713940 Physical fitness studios 334519 Physical properties testing and inspection equipment manufacturing
622310 Physical rehabilitation hospitals
541715 Physical science research and development laboratories or services (except biotechnology and nanotechnology research and development)
621340 Physical therapists' offices (e.g., centers, clinics)
621340 Physical therapy offices (e.g., centers, clinics)
621340 Physical-integration practitioners' offices (e.g., centers, clinics)
621111 Physicians' (except mental health) offices (e.g., centers, clinics)
621399 Physicians' assistants' offices (e.g., centers, clinics)
423450 Physicians' equipment and supplies merchant wholesalers
621112 Physicians', mental health, offices (e.g., centers, clinics)
541690 Physics consulting services
541715 Physics research and development laboratories or services (except nanotechnology research and development)
621340 Physiotherapists' offices (e.g., centers, clinics)
339112 Physiotherapy equipment (except electrotherapeutic) manufacturing
325411 Physostigmine and derivatives (i.e., basic chemicals) manufacturing
332510 Piano hardware, metal, manufacturing
339992 Piano parts and materials (except piano hardware) manufacturing
532289 Piano rental
451140 Piano stores

339992 Piccolos and parts manufacturing
333249 Picker machinery for textiles manufacturing
333249 Picker sticks for looms manufacturing
311710 Picking crab meat 333519 Picklers and pickling machinery, metalworking, manufacturing
311421 Pickles manufacturing
311421 Pickling fruits and vegetables
332813 Pickling metals and metal products for the trade
332216 Picks (i.e., handtools) manufacturing
812320 Pick-up and drop-off sites for drycleaners and laundries
336214 Pick-up canopies, caps, or covers manufacturing
336112 Pick-up trucks, light duty, assembling on chassis of own manufacture
713990 Picnic grounds
326199 Picnic jugs, plastics (except foam), manufacturing
325920 Picric acid explosive materials manufacturing
334511 Pictorial situation instrumentation manufacturing
442299 Picture frame shops, custom 311824 Pie crust shells, uncooked, made from purchased flour
424310 Piece goods (except burlap, felt) merchant wholesalers
451130 Piece goods stores
424990 Piece goods, burlap and felt, merchant wholesalers
237990 Pier construction
531120 Piers and associated building rental or leasing
713110 Piers, amusement
424420 Pies (e.g., fruit, meat, poultry), frozen, merchant wholesalers
311812 Pies, fresh, made in commercial bakeries
311813 Pies, frozen, manufacturing
334419 Piezoelectric crystals manufacturing
334419 Piezoelectric devices manufacturing
112210 Pig farming
331110 Pig iron manufacturing
423510 Pig iron merchant wholesalers
325130 Pigment, scarlet lake, manufacturing
325130 Pigments (except animal black, bone black), organic, manufacturing
325130 Pigments (except bone black, carbon black, lamp black), inorganic, manufacturing
212393 Pigments, natural, mineral, mining and/or beneficiating
424950 Pigments, paint, merchant wholesalers 311612 Pig's feet, cooked and pickled, made from purchased carcasses
114111 Pilchard fishing
238910 Pile driving, building foundation
237990 Pile driving, marine
313240 Pile fabrics made in warp or weft knitting mills
332313 Pile shells, fabricated metal plate, manufacturing
332322 Pile shells, sheet metal (except stampings), manufacturing
333120 Pile-driving equipment manufacturing 238910 Piling (i.e., bored, cast-in-place, drilled), building foundation, contractors
321114 Pilings, foundation and marine construction, treating
331110 Pilings, iron or steel plain sheet, made in iron and steel mills
423510 Pilings, metal, merchant wholesalers
321114 Pilings, round wood, cutting and treating
321114 Pilings, wood, treating
332991 Pillow blocks with ball or roller bearings manufacturing
812320 Pillow cleaning services
314120 Pillowcases, bed, made from purchased fabrics
314120 Pillows, bed, made from purchased materials
488490 Pilot car services (i.e., wide load warning services)
488330 Piloting services, water transportation
713120 Pinball arcades
713990 Pinball machine concession operators (i.e., supplying and servicing in others' facilities)
339999 Pinball machines, coin-operated, manufacturing
113210 Pine gum extracting
325194 Pine oil manufacturing
111339 Pineapple farming
325194 Pinene manufacturing
713990 Ping pong parlors
212325 Pinite mining and/or beneficiating 339993 Pins (except precious) manufacturing

339910 Pins and brooches, precious metal, manufacturing
712120 Pioneer villages
331210 Pipe (e.g., heavy riveted, lock joint, seamless, welded) made from purchased iron or steel
423720 Pipe and boiler coverings merchant wholesalers
332996 Pipe and pipe fittings made from purchased metal pipe
331511 Pipe and pipe fittings, cast iron, manufacturing
333519 Pipe and tube rolling mill machinery, metalworking, manufacturing
332323 Pipe bannisters, metal, manufacturing
326299 Pipe bits and stems, tobacco, hard rubber, manufacturing
339999 Pipe cleaners manufacturing
332996 Pipe couplings made from purchased metal pipe
331511 Pipe couplings, cast iron, manufacturing
238290 Pipe covering
333517 Pipe cutting and threading machines, metalworking, manufacturing
332996 Pipe fabricating (i.e., bending, cutting, threading) made from purchased metal pipe
238220 Pipe fitting contractors
423840 Pipe fittings and valves (except plumbing) merchant wholesalers
423720 Pipe fittings and valves, plumbers', merchant wholesalers
326122 Pipe fittings, rigid plastics, manufacturing
332323 Pipe guards, metal, manufacturing
332999 Pipe hangers and supports, metal, manufacturing
332996 Pipe headers made from purchased metal pipe
237120 Pipe lining (except thermal insulating) contractors
331318 Pipe made by extruding purchased aluminum
332323 Pipe railings, metal, manufacturing
325520 Pipe sealing compounds manufacturing
213112 Pipe testing services, oil and gas field, on a contract basis
424940 Pipe tobacco merchant wholesalers
312230 Pipe tobacco, prepared, manufacturing
331318 Pipe, aluminum, made in integrated secondary smelting and extruding mills
327332 Pipe, concrete, manufacturing
238290 Pipe, duct and boiler insulation
331420 Pipe, extruded and drawn, brass, bronze, and copper, made from purchased copper or in integrated secondary smelting and rolling, drawing or extruding plants
332313 Pipe, fabricated metal plate, manufacturing
331110 Pipe, iron or steel, made in iron and steel mills
423510 Pipe, metal, merchant wholesalers
331491 Pipe, nonferrous metals (except aluminum, copper), made from purchased metals or scrap
326122 Pipe, rigid plastics, manufacturing
332322 Pipe, sheet metal (except stampings), manufacturing
515112 Piped-in music services, radio transmitted
237990 Pipe-jacking contractors
237120 Pipeline construction on oil and gas field gathering lines to point of distribution on a contract basis
541990 Pipeline inspection (i.e., visual) services
423830 Pipeline machinery and equipment merchant wholesalers
237120 Pipeline rehabilitation contractors
488999 Pipeline terminal facilities, independently operated
486990 Pipeline transportation (except crude oil, natural gas, refined petroleum products)
486110 Pipeline transportation, crude oil
486910 Pipeline transportation, gasoline and other refined petroleum products
486210 Pipeline transportation, natural gas
237120 Pipeline wrapping contractors
237120 Pipeline, gas and oil, construction
339992 Pipes, organ, manufacturing
339999 Pipes, smoker's, manufacturing
212399 Pipestones mining and/or beneficiating
111335 Pistachio farming
332994 Pistols manufacturing
336310 Pistons and piston rings manufacturing
423120 Pistons and valves, automotive, merchant wholesalers
423840 Pistons and valves, industrial, merchant wholesalers
423830 Pistons, hydraulic and pneumatic, merchant wholesalers
325194 Pitch made by distillation of coal tar
324122 Pitch, roofing, made from purchased asphaltic materials
325194 Pitch, wood, manufacturing
212291 Pitchblende mining and/or beneficiating

334519 Pitometers manufacturing 325411 Pituitary gland derivatives, uncompounded, manufacturing
325412 Pituitary gland preparations manufacturing
722513 Pizza delivery shops
311824 Pizza doughs made from purchased flour
722511 Pizza parlors, full service
722513 Pizza parlors, limited-service
424490 Pizzas (except frozen) merchant wholesalers
311991 Pizzas, fresh, manufacturing
311412 Pizzas, frozen, manufacturing
424420 Pizzas, frozen, merchant wholesalers
722511 Pizzerias, full service
722513 Pizzerias, limited-service (e.g., takeout)
314120 Placemats, all materials, made from purchased materials
561311 Placement agencies or services, employment
621991 Placenta banks
212221 Placer gold mining and/or beneficiating
212222 Placer silver mining and/or beneficiating
813110 Places of worship
238120 Placing and tying reinforcing rod at a construction site
334417 Planar cable connectors manufacturing
333243 Planers woodworking-type, stationary, manufacturing
333120 Planers, bituminous, manufacturing
333991 Planers, handheld power-driven, manufacturing
333517 Planers, metalworking, manufacturing
332216 Planes, handheld, nonpowered, manufacturing
712110 Planetariums
321912 Planing mills (except millwork)
321918 Planing mills, millwork
321912 Planing purchased lumber
525120 Plans, health- and welfare-related employee benefit
522190 Plans, Morris (i.e., known as), depository
522298 Plans, Morris (i.e., known as), nondepository
525110 Plans, pension
561730 Plant and shrub maintenance in buildings
112519 Plant aquaculture
424910 Plant bulbs merchant wholesalers
424990 Plant food merchant wholesalers 325311 Plant foods, mixed, made in plants producing nitrogenous fertilizer materials
325312 Plant foods, mixed, made in plants producing phosphatic fertilizer materials
325320 Plant growth regulants manufacturing
561730 Plant maintenance services
111422 Plant, ornamental, growing
111422 Plant, potted flower and foliage, growing
111339 Plantain farming
115112 Planting crops
423820 Planting machinery and equipment, farm-type, merchant wholesalers
333111 Planting machines, farm-type, manufacturing
424930 Plants, potted, merchant wholesalers
621991 Plasma collection services
333517 Plasma jet spray metal forming machines manufacturing
333517 Plasma process metal cutting machines (except welding equipment) manufacturing
333992 Plasma welding equipment manufacturing
621991 Plasmapheresis centers
325414 Plasmas manufacturing
424210 Plasmas, blood, merchant wholesalers
327420 Plaster and plasterboard, gypsum, manufacturing
423320 Plaster merchant wholesalers
327420 Plaster of paris manufacturing 327420 Plaster of paris products (e.g., columns, statuary, urns) manufacturing
327420 Plaster, gypsum, manufacturing 238310 Plastering (i.e., ornamental, plain) contractors
212325 Plastic fire clay mining and/or beneficiating
621111 Plastic surgeons' offices (e.g., centers, clinics)
325510 Plastic wood fillers manufacturing
332813 Plastic, glass, or other media blasting services
325199 Plasticizers (i.e., basic synthetic chemicals) manufacturing
424610 Plasticizers merchant wholesalers
337125 Plastics (including fiberglass) furniture (except upholstered), household-type, manufacturing
326220 Plastics and rubber belts and hoses (without fittings) manufacturing

325211 Plastics and synthetic resins regenerating, precipitating, and coagulating
424130 Plastics bags merchant wholesalers
424610 Plastics basic shapes (e.g., film, rod, sheet, sheeting, tubing) merchant wholesalers 313320 Plastics coating of textiles and apparel 326113 Plastics film and unlaminated sheet (except packaging) manufacturing
424610 Plastics foam merchant wholesalers
423840 Plastics foam packing and packaging materials merchant wholesalers
424990 Plastics foam products (except disposable and packaging) merchant wholesalers
424130 Plastics foam products, disposable (except packaging, packing), merchant wholesalers
315210 Plastics gowns cut and sew apparel contractors
315280 Plastics gowns cut and sewn from purchased fabric (except apparel contractors)
423830 Plastics industries machinery, equipment, and supplies merchant wholesalers
337110 Plastics laminated over particleboard (e.g., fixture tops) manufacturing
424610 Plastics materials merchant wholesalers
315210 Plastics rainwear cut and sew apparel contractors
315280 Plastics rainwear cut and sewn from purchased fabric (except apparel contractors)
325991 Plastics resins compounding from recycled materials
424610 Plastics resins merchant wholesalers 325991 Plastics resins, custom compounding of purchased
423930 Plastics scrap merchant wholesalers
333249 Plastics working machinery manufacturing
325510 Plastisol coating compounds manufacturing
524126 Plate glass insurance carriers, direct
423390 Plate glass merchant wholesalers
333519 Plate rolling mill machinery, metalworking, manufacturing
332313 Plate work (e.g., bending, cutting, punching, shaping, welding), fabricated metal, manufacturing
331315 Plate, aluminum, made by continuous casting purchased aluminum
331315 Plate, aluminum, made by flat rolling purchased aluminum
331315 Plate, aluminum, made in integrated secondary smelting and continuous casting mills
331315 Plate, aluminum, made in integrated secondary smelting and flat rolling mills
331420 Plate, copper and copper alloy, made from purchased copper or in integrated secondary smelting and rolling, drawing or extruding plants
331110 Plate, iron or steel, made in iron and steel mills
326130 Plate, laminated plastics, manufacturing
331491 Plate, nonferrous metals (except aluminum, copper), made from purchased metals or scrap
332215 Plated metal cutlery manufacturing
423940 Plated metal cutlery or flatware merchant wholesalers
332215 Plated metal flatware manufacturing
332999 Plated ware (e.g., ecclesiastical ware, hollowware, toilet ware) manufacturing
335932 Plates (i.e., outlet or switch covers), face, manufacturing
322299 Plates, molded pulp, manufacturing
326140 Plates, polystyrene foam, manufacturing
332813 Plating metals and metal products for the trade
331491 Platinum and platinum alloy rolling, drawing, or extruding from purchased metals or scrap
331491 Platinum and platinum alloy sheet and tubing made from purchased metals or scrap
332999 Platinum foil and leaf not made in rolling mills
212299 Platinum mining and/or beneficiating
331492 Platinum recovering from scrap and/or alloying purchased metals
331410 Platinum refining, primary
237990 Playground construction 423910 Playground equipment and supplies merchant wholesalers
238990 Playground equipment installation
423920 Playing cards merchant wholesalers 337124
Playpens, children's metal, manufacturing 337122
Playpens, children's wood, manufacturing 315210
Playsuits cut and sew apparel contractors 315240
Playsuits, women's, girls', and infants', cut and sewn from purchased fabric (except apparel contractors)
711510 Playwrights, independent
811490 Pleasure boat maintenance services (e.g., cleaning, scaling, waxing)
532284 Pleasure boat rental

336612 Pleasure boats manufacturing
423910 Pleasure boats merchant wholesalers
315210 Pleating contractors on apparel
332216 Pliers, handtools, manufacturing
327331 Plinth blocks, precast terrazzo, manufacturing
334418 Plotter controller boards manufacturing
423430 Plotters merchant wholesalers
334118 Plotters, computer, manufacturing
115112 Plowing
333120 Plows, construction (e.g., excavating, grading), manufacturing
423820 Plows, farm, merchant wholesalers
333111 Plows, farm-type, manufacturing
111422 Plug (i.e., floriculture products) growing
332911 Plug valves, industrial-type, manufacturing
213112 Plugging and abandoning wells on a contract basis
335931 Plugs, electric cord, manufacturing
332999 Plugs, magnetic metal drain, manufacturing
321999 Plugs, wood, manufacturing
111339 Plum farming
238220 Plumbers
611513 Plumbers' apprenticeship training
423720 Plumbers' brass goods merchant wholesalers
332216 Plumbers' handtools, nonpowered, manufacturing
325520 Plumbers' putty manufacturing
423710 Plumbers' tools and equipment merchant wholesalers
238220 Plumbing and heating contractors
332919 Plumbing and heating inline valves (e.g., check, cutoffs, stop) manufacturing
423720 Plumbing and heating valves merchant wholesalers
238220 Plumbing contractors
423720 Plumbing equipment merchant wholesalers 532490 Plumbing equipment rental or leasing
332913 Plumbing fittings and couplings (e.g., compression fittings, metal elbows, metal unions) manufacturing
332913 Plumbing fixture fittings and trim, all materials, manufacturing
238220 Plumbing fixture installation
326191 Plumbing fixtures (e.g., shower stalls, toilets, urinals), plastics or fiberglass, manufacturing
423720 Plumbing fixtures merchant wholesalers
332999 Plumbing fixtures, metal, manufacturing
327110 Plumbing fixtures, vitreous china, manufacturing
423720 Plumbing supplies merchant wholesalers
444190 Plumbing supply stores
423310 Plywood merchant wholesalers
321211 Plywood, faced with nonwood materials, hardwood, manufacturing
321212 Plywood, faced with nonwood materials, softwood, manufacturing
321211 Plywood, hardwood faced, manufacturing
321211 Plywood, hardwood, manufacturing
321212 Plywood, softwood faced, manufacturing
321212 Plywood, softwood, manufacturing
332912 Pneumatic aircraft subassemblies manufacturing
334513 Pneumatic controllers, industrial process type, manufacturing
333995 Pneumatic cylinders, fluid power, manufacturing
326220 Pneumatic hose (without fittings), rubber or plastics, manufacturing
332912 Pneumatic hose fittings, fluid power, manufacturing
423830 Pneumatic pumps and parts merchant wholesalers
333996 Pneumatic pumps, fluid power, manufacturing
334512 Pneumatic relays, air-conditioning-type, manufacturing
238290 Pneumatic tube conveyor system installation
333922 Pneumatic tube conveyors manufacturing
332912 Pneumatic valves, fluid power, manufacturing
322230 Pocket folders made from purchased paper or paperboard
332215 Pocket knives manufacturing
339910 Pocketbooks, precious metal, men's or women's, manufacturing
315210 Pockets (e.g., coat, suit) cut and sew apparel contractors
621391 Podiatrists' offices (e.g., centers, clinics)
813410 Poetry clubs
711510 Poets, independent
334118 Point of sale terminals manufacturing
423420 Point of sale terminals merchant wholesalers

334118 Pointing devices, computer peripheral equipment, manufacturing
315280 Pointing furs
339114 Points, abrasive dental, manufacturing
334516 Polariscopes manufacturing
334516 Polarizers manufacturing
334516 Polarographic equipment manufacturing
238990 Pole (e.g., telephone) removal
237130 Pole line construction
423610 Pole line hardware merchant wholesalers
327390 Poles, concrete, manufacturing
423510 Poles, metal, merchant wholesalers
321114 Poles, round wood, cutting and treating
321113 Poles, wood, made from log or bolts
321114 Poles, wood, treating
922120 Police academies
922120 Police and fire departments, combined
315210 Police caps and hats (except protective head gear) cut and sew apparel contractors
315990 Police caps and hats (except protective head gear) cut and sewn from purchased fabric (except apparel contractors)
922120 Police departments (except American Indian or Alaska Native)
315220 Police dress uniforms, men's, cut and sewn from purchased fabric (except apparel contractors)
315240 Police dress uniforms, women's, cut and sewn from purchased fabric (except apparel contractors)
453998 Police supply stores
611519 Police training schools 315210 Police uniforms cut and sew apparel contractors
921150 Police, American Indian or Alaska Native tribal
311212 Polished rice manufacturing
333991 Polishers, handheld power-driven, manufacturing
325612 Polishes (e.g., automobile, furniture, metal, shoe) manufacturing
424690 Polishes (e.g., automobile, furniture, metal, shoe, stove) merchant wholesalers
333517 Polishing and buffing machines, metalworking, manufacturing
332813 Polishing metals and metal products for the trade
325612 Polishing preparations manufacturing
327910 Polishing wheels manufacturing
813940 Political action committees (PACs)
813940 Political campaign organizations
711510 Political cartoonists, independent
541820 Political consulting services
541910 Political opinion polling services
813940 Political organizations or clubs
813940 Political parties
115112 Pollinating
114111 Pollock fishing
423830 Pollution control equipment (except air) merchant wholesalers
423730 Pollution control equipment, air, merchant wholesalers
924110 Pollution control program administration
541380 Pollution testing (except automotive emissions testing) services
315210 Polo shirts cut and sew apparel contractors
315190 Polo shirts made in apparel knitting mills
315220 Polo shirts, men's and boys', cut and sewn from purchased fabric (except apparel contractors)
315240 Polo shirts, women's and girls', cut and sewn from purchased fabric (except apparel contractors)
325211 Polyacrylonitrile resins manufacturing
325211 Polyamide resins manufacturing
325211 Polycarbonate resins manufacturing
325220 Polyester fibers and filaments manufacturing
424690 Polyester fibers merchant wholesalers
313110 Polyester filament yarn throwing, twisting, texturizing, or winding of purchased yarn
326113 Polyester film and unlaminated sheet (except packaging) manufacturing
325211 Polyester resins manufacturing
424610 Polyester resins merchant wholesalers
313110 Polyester spun yarns made from purchased fiber
313110 Polyester thread manufacturing
326113 Polyethylene film and unlaminated sheet (except packaging) manufacturing
325211 Polyethylene resins manufacturing
325212 Polyethylene rubber manufacturing
325220 Polyethylene terephthalate (PET) fibers and filaments manufacturing
325211 Polyethylene terephthalate (PET) resins manufacturing
334519 Polygraph machines manufacturing

561611 Polygraph services 325211 Polyhexamethylenediamine adipamide resins manufacturing
325199 Polyhydric alcohol esters and amines manufacturing
325199 Polyhydric alcohols manufacturing
325211 Polyisobutylene resins manufacturing
325212 Polyisobutylene rubber manufacturing
325212 Polyisobutylene-isoprene rubber manufacturing
325211 Polymethacrylate resins manufacturing
325212 Polymethylene rubber manufacturing
325220 Polyolefin fibers and filaments manufacturing
313110 Polypropylene filament yarn throwing, twisting, texturizing, or winding of puchased yarn
326113 Polypropylene film and unlaminated sheet (except packaging) manufacturing
325211 Polypropylene resins manufacturing
313110 Polypropylene spun yarns made from purchased fiber
238310 Polystyrene board insulation installation
326140 Polystyrene foam packaging manufacturing
325211 Polystyrene resins manufacturing
325212 Polysulfide rubber manufacturing
325211 Polytetrafluoroethylene resins manufacturing
325510 Polyurethane coatings manufacturing
326150 Polyurethane foam products manufacturing
325211 Polyurethane resins manufacturing
325211 Polyvinyl alcohol resins manufacturing
325211 Polyvinyl chloride (PVC) resins manufacturing
325220 Polyvinyl ester fibers and filaments manufacturing
326113 Polyvinyl film and unlaminated sheet (except packaging) manufacturing
325211 Polyvinyl halide resins manufacturing
325211 Polyvinyl resins manufacturing
325220 Polyvinylidene chloride (i.e., saran) fibers and filaments manufacturing
111339 Pomegranate farming
315210 Ponchos and similar waterproof raincoats cut and sew apparel contractors
315280 Ponchos and similar waterproof raincoats cut and sewn from purchased fabric (except apparel contractors)
562998 Pond maintenance and cleaning services
112920 Pony production 423910 Pool (billiards) tables and supplies merchant wholesalers
423910 Pool (swimming) and equipment merchant wholesalers
713990 Pool halls
713990 Pool parlors
713990 Pool rooms
312111 Pop, soda, manufacturing
311919 Popcorn (except candy covered), popped, manufacturing
311999 Popcorn (except popped) manufacturing
311340 Popcorn balls manufacturing
111150 Popcorn farming, field and seed production
424450 Popcorn merchant wholesalers
335210 Popcorn poppers, household-type electric, manufacturing
311340 Popcorn, candy covered popped, manufacturing
313210 Poplins weaving
621391 Popopediatricians' offices (e.g., centers, clinics)
711130 Popular musical artists, independent
711130 Popular musical groups
532120 Popup camper rental
327110 Porcelain parts, electrical and electronic device, molded, manufacturing
327110 Porcelain, chemical, manufacturing
236118 Porch construction, residential-type 337122 Porch furniture (except upholstered), wood, manufacturing
337920 Porch shades, wood slat, manufacturing
337124 Porch swings, metal, manufacturing 321918 Porch work (e.g., columns, newels, rails, trellises), wood, manufacturing
114111 Porgy fishing 311422 Pork and beans canning
311611 Pork carcasses, half carcasses, and primal and sub-primal cuts produced in slaughtering plants
311919 Pork rinds manufacturing
311612 Pork, primal and sub-primal cuts, made from purchased carcasses
926120 Port authorities and districts, nonoperating
237990 Port facility construction
488310 Port facility operation
332311 Portable buildings, prefabricated metal, manufacturing

332999 Portable chemical toilets, metal, manufacturing
334111 Portable computers manufacturing
335210 Portable cooking appliances (except convection, microwave ovens), household-type electric, manufacturing
335210 Portable electric space heaters manufacturing
335210 Portable hair dryers, electric, manufacturing
335210 Portable humidifiers and dehumidifiers manufacturing
334290 Portable intrusion detection and signaling devices manufacturing
334310 Portable stereo systems manufacturing
334515 Portable test meters manufacturing
562991 Portable toilet pumping (i.e., cleaning) services
562991 Portable toilet renting and/or servicing
326191 Portable toilets, plastics, manufacturing
519130 Portals, web search
312120 Porter brewing
424810 Porter merchant wholesalers
812990 Porter services
523920 Portfolio fund managing
541921 Portrait photography services
541921 Portrait photography studios
334511 Position indicators (e.g., for landing gear, stabilizers), airframe equipment, manufacturing
336310 Positive crankcase ventilation (PCV) valves, engine, manufacturing
334514 Positive displacement meters manufacturing
621512 Positron emission tomography (PET) scanner centers
334510 Positron emission tomography (PET) scanners manufacturing
238130 Post framing contractors
332216 Post hole diggers, nonpowered, manufacturing
333120 Post hole diggers, powered, manufacturing
236220 Post office construction
333997 Post office-type scales manufacturing
333318 Postage meters manufacturing
423420 Postage meters merchant wholesalers
333318 Postage stamp vending machines manufacturing
491110 Postal delivery services, local, operated by U.S. Postal Service
491110 Postal delivery services, local, operated on a contract basis
337215 Postal service lock boxes manufacturing
491110 Postal services operated by U.S. Postal Service
491110 Postal stations operated by U.S. Postal Service
491110 Postal stations operated on a contract basis
511199 Postcard publishers (except exclusive Internet publishing)
511199 Postcard publishers and printing combined
519130 Postcard publishers, exclusively on Internet
323111 Postcards commercial printing (except screen) without publishing
424120 Postcards merchant wholesalers
323113 Postcards screen printing without publishing
511199 Poster publishers (except exclusive Internet publishing)
511199 Poster publishers and printing combined
519130 Poster publishers, exclusively on Internet
323111 Posters commercial printing (except screen) without publishing
323113 Posters screen printing without publishing
238990 Posthole digging
323120 Postpress services (e.g., beveling, bronzing, folding, gluing, edging, foil stamping, gilding) on printed materials
512191 Postproduction facilities, motion picture or video
327390 Posts, concrete, manufacturing
423510 Posts, metal, merchant wholesalers
321114 Posts, round wood, cutting and treating
321114 Posts, wood, treating
512191 Post-synchronization sound dubbing
311412 Pot pies, frozen, manufacturing
212391 Potash mining and/or beneficiating
325314 Potassic fertilizers made by mixing purchased materials
325180 Potassium aluminum sulfate manufacturing
325180 Potassium bichromate and chromate manufacturing
325199 Potassium bitartrate manufacturing
325180 Potassium bromide manufacturing
212391 Potassium bromide, natural, mining and/or beneficiating
325180 Potassium carbonate manufacturing
325180 Potassium chlorate manufacturing
325180 Potassium chloride manufacturing

212391 Potassium chloride mining and/or beneficiating
212391 Potassium compounds prepared at beneficiating plants
212391 Potassium compounds, natural, mining and/or beneficiating
325180 Potassium cyanide manufacturing
325180 Potassium hydroxide (i.e., caustic potash) manufacturing
325180 Potassium hypochlorate manufacturing
325180 Potassium inorganic compounds, not specified elsewhere by process, manufacturing
325180 Potassium iodide manufacturing
325180 Potassium nitrate manufacturing 325199
Potassium organic compounds, not specified elsewhere by process,
manufacturing
325180 Potassium permanganate manufacturing
325180 Potassium salts manufacturing 212391
Potassium salts, natural, mining and/or beneficiating
325180 Potassium sulfate manufacturing 424450
Potato chips and related snacks merchant wholesalers
311919 Potato chips manufacturing
115114 Potato curing
333111 Potato diggers, harvesters, and planters manufacturing
111211 Potato farming, field and seed potato production
311211 Potato flour manufacturing
332215 Potato mashers manufacturing 311999
Potato mixes made from purchased dry ingredients
311423 Potato products (e.g., flakes, granules) dehydrating
311221 Potato starches manufacturing 311919
Potato sticks manufacturing 311991 Potatoes, peeled or cut, manufacturing 334515 Potentiometric instruments (except industrial process-type) manufacturing
334513 Potentiometric instruments (except X-Y recorders), industrial process-type, manufacturing
237310 Pothole filling, highway, road, street or bridge
339999 Potpourri manufacturing
332420 Pots (e.g., annealing, melting, smelting), heavy gauge metal, manufacturing
332215 Pots and pans, fabricated metal, manufacturing
327120 Pots, glasshouse, clay refractory, manufacturing
311612 Potted meats made from purchased carcasses
451120 Pottery (unfinished pottery to be painted by customer on premises) stores
327110 Pottery made and sold on site
327110 Pottery products manufacturing
424990 Pottery, novelty, merchant wholesalers
325314 Potting soil manufacturing
311615 Poultry (e.g., canned, cooked, fresh, frozen) manufacturing
311615 Poultry (e.g., canned, cooked, fresh, frozen) processing
424440 Poultry and poultry products (except canned, packaged frozen) merchant wholesalers
333111 Poultry brooders, feeders, and waterers manufacturing
311615 Poultry canning (except baby, pet food)
115210 Poultry catching services
445210 Poultry dealers
423820 Poultry equipment merchant wholesalers
311119 Poultry feeds, supplements, and concentrates
manufacturing
112340 Poultry hatcheries
332618 Poultry netting made from purchased wire
424440 Poultry pies (except packaged frozen) merchant wholesalers
423830 Poultry processing machinery merchant wholesalers
311615 Poultry slaughtering, dressing, and packing
424490 Poultry, canned, merchant wholesalers
424440 Poultry, live and dressed, merchant wholesalers
424420 Poultry, packaged frozen, merchant wholesalers
333991 Powder actuated handheld power tools manufacturing
332812 Powder coating metals and metal products for the trade
325510 Powder coatings manufacturing
331314 Powder made from purchased aluminum
331420 Powder made from purchased copper
331221 Powder made from purchased iron or steel
333517 Powder metal forming presses manufacturing

332117 Powder metallurgy products manufactured on a job or order basis
314999 Powder puffs and mitts manufacturing
331110 Powder, iron or steel, made in iron and steel mills
331492 Powder, nonferrous metals (except aluminum, copper), made from purchased metal
311999 Powdered drink mixes (except chocolate, coffee, tea, milk based) manufacturing
311514 Powdered milk manufacturing
325620 Powders (e.g., baby, body, face, talcum, toilet) manufacturing
311999 Powders, baking, manufacturing
333912 Power (i.e., pressure) washer units manufacturing
441222 Power boat dealers
238290 Power boiler, installation only
332410 Power boilers manufacturing
335313 Power circuit breakers manufacturing
335313 Power connectors manufacturing
335999 Power converter units (i.e., AC to DC), static, manufacturing
444210 Power equipment stores, outdoor
334515 Power factor meters manufacturing
335313 Power fuses (i.e., 600 volts and over) manufacturing
238290 Power generating equipment installation
221117 Power generation, biomass
221112 Power generation, fossil fuel (e.g., coal, gas, oil), electric
221116 Power generation, geothermal
221111 Power generation, hydroelectric
562213 Power generation, nonhazardous solid waste combustor or incinerator electric
221113 Power generation, nuclear electric
221114 Power generation, solar electric
221118 Power generation, tidal electric
221115 Power generation, wind electric
335312 Power generators manufacturing
423710 Power handtools (e.g., drills, sanders, saws) merchant wholesalers
812320 Power laundries, family
541990 Power line inspection (i.e., visual) services
237130 Power line stringing
334515 Power measuring equipment, electrical, manufacturing
237130 Power plant (except hydroelectric) construction
423830 Power plant machinery (except electrical) merchant wholesalers
237990 Power plant, hydroelectric, construction
238910 Power shovel, construction, rental with operator
336330 Power steering hose assemblies manufacturing
336330 Power steering pumps manufacturing
335999 Power supplies, regulated and unregulated, manufacturing
335313 Power switchboards manufacturing
335313 Power switching equipment manufacturing
335311 Power transformers, electric, manufacturing
423610 Power transmission equipment, electrical, merchant wholesalers
423840 Power transmission supplies (e.g., gears, pulleys, sprockets), mechanical, merchant wholesalers
333318 Power washer cleaning equipment manufacturing
532490 Power washer rental or leasing
561790 Power washing building exteriors
336320 Power window and door lock systems, automotive, truck, and bus, manufacturing
238910 Power, communication and pipe line right of way clearance (except maintenance)
333991 Power-driven handtools manufacturing
212399 Pozzolana mining and/or beneficiating
621399 Practical nurses' offices (e.g., centers, clinics), licensed
315210 Prayer shawls cut and sew apparel contractors
315280 Prayer shawls cut and sewn from purchased fabric (except apparel contractors)
315190 Prayer shawls made in apparel knitting mills
327331 Precast concrete block and brick manufacturing
238120 Precast concrete panel, slab, or form installation
327332 Precast concrete pipe manufacturing
327390 Precast concrete products (except brick, block, pipe) manufacturing
423940 Precious and semiprecious stones merchant wholesalers
331491 Precious metal bar, rod, sheet, strip, and tubing made from purchased metals or scrap
423520 Precious metal ores merchant wholesalers
423940 Precious metals merchant wholesalers

331492 Precious metals recovering from scrap and/or alloying purchased metals
331410 Precious metals refining, primary
212399 Precious stones mining and/or beneficiating
811219 Precision equipment calibration
332216 Precision tools, machinist's (except optical), manufacturing
332721 Precision turned product manufacturing
488999 Precooling of fruits and vegetables in connection with transportation
236117 Precut housing, residential, assembled on site by for-sale builders
236116 Precut multifamily housing assembled on site by general contractors
236115 Precut single-family housing assembled on site by general contractors
334514 Predetermined counters manufacturing
444190 Prefabricated building dealers
423390 Prefabricated buildings (except wood) merchant wholesalers
332311 Prefabricated buildings, metal, manufacturing
326199 Prefabricated buildings, plastics, manufacturing
423310 Prefabricated buildings, wood, merchant wholesalers
236220 Prefabricated commercial building erection
321992 Prefabricated homes (except mobile homes), wood, manufacturing
332311 Prefabricated homes, metal, manufacturing
236210 Prefabricated industrial building (except warehouses) erection
236220 Prefabricated institutional building erection
238350 Prefabricated kitchen and bath cabinet, residential-type, installation
238350 Prefabricated sash and door installation
321992 Prefabricated wood buildings manufacturing
238130 Prefabricated wood frame component (e.g., trusses) installation
321211 Prefinished hardwood plywood manufacturing
321212 Prefinished softwood plywood manufacturing
621410 Pregnancy counseling centers
325413 Pregnancy test kits manufacturing
624410 Pre-kindergarten centers (except part of elementary school system)
236117 Premanufactured housing assembled on site by for-sale builders
236115 Premanufactured single-family housing assembled on site by general contractors
334614 Prepackaged software, mass reproducing
424990 Pre-paid calling card distribution, merchant wholesalers
517911 Pre-paid calling cards, telecommunications resellers
213112 Preparation of oil and gas field drilling sites (except site preparation and related construction contractor activities) on a contract basis
212113 Preparation plants, anthracite
611110 Preparatory schools, elementary or secondary
311824 Prepared flour mixes made from purchased flour
311211 Prepared flour mixes made in flour mills
424490 Prepared foods (except frozen) merchant wholesalers
424420 Prepared foods, frozen (except dairy products), merchant wholesalers
424430 Prepared foods, frozen dairy, merchant wholesalers
311991 Prepared meals, perishable, packaged for individual resale
311941 Prepared sauces (except gravy, tomato-based) manufacturing
237210 Preparing and subdividing land for sale
488991 Preparing goods for transportation (i.e., crating, packing)
323120 Prepress printing services (e.g., color separation, imagesetting, photocomposition, typesetting)
541350 Prepurchase home inspection services
423990 Prerecorded audio and video tapes and discs merchant wholesalers
512250 Prerecorded audio tapes and compact discs integrated manufacture, release, and distribution
334614 Prerecorded magnetic audio tapes and cassettes mass reproducing
454110 Prerecorded tape, compact disc, and record mail-order houses
624410 Preschool centers
424210 Prescription drugs merchant wholesalers
111421 Preseeded mat farming
311421 Preserves (e.g., imitation) canning
321114 Preserving purchased wood and wood products
313310 Preshrinking textile products and fabrics
921110 President's office, United States
325611 Presoaks manufacturing

333517 Press brakes, metalworking, manufacturing
519190 Press clipping services
332111 Press forgings made from purchased iron or steel, unfinished
332112 Press forgings made from purchased nonferrous metals, unfinished
424130 Pressed and molded pulp goods (e.g., egg cartons, shipping supplies) merchant wholesalers
313230 Pressed felts manufacturing
321999 Pressed logs of sawdust and other wood particles, nonpetroleum binder, manufacturing
333517 Presses (e.g., bending, punching, shearing, stamping), metal forming, manufacturing
333241 Presses (i.e., food manufacturing-type) manufacturing
333243 Presses for making composite woods (e.g., hardboard, medium density fiberboard (MDF), particleboard, plywood) manufacturing
333111 Presses, farm-type, manufacturing
333999 Presses, metal baling, manufacturing
333244 Presses, printing (except textile), manufacturing
321999 Pressing blocks, wood, tailor's, manufacturing
336350 Pressure and clutch plate assemblies, automotive, truck, and bus, manufacturing
334519 Pressure and vacuum indicators, aircraft engine, manufacturing
332911 Pressure control valves (except fluid power), industrial-type, manufacturing
332912 Pressure control valves, fluid power, manufacturing
334512 Pressure controllers, air-conditioning system-type, manufacturing
332215 Pressure cookers, household-type, manufacturing
334513 Pressure gauges (e.g., dial, digital), industrial process-type, manufacturing
334513 Pressure instruments, industrial process-type, manufacturing
327332 Pressure pipe, reinforced concrete, manufacturing
322220 Pressure sensitive paper and tape (except medical) made from purchased materials
334519 Pressure transducers manufacturing 321113 Pressure treated lumber made from logs or bolts and treated
321114 Pressure treated lumber made from purchased lumber
423850 Pressure washers merchant wholesalers
561790 Pressure washing (e.g., buildings, decks, fences)
334512 Pressurestats manufacturing
238120 Prestressed concrete beam, slab or other component installation
327331 Prestressed concrete blocks or bricks manufacturing
327332 Prestressed concrete pipes manufacturing
327390 Prestressed concrete products (except blocks, bricks, pipes) manufacturing
722515 Pretzel shops, on premise baking and carryout service
424490 Pretzels (except frozen) merchant wholesalers
311919 Pretzels (except soft) manufacturing
424420 Pretzels, frozen, merchant wholesalers
311812 Pretzels, soft, manufacturing
335129 Prewired poles, brackets, and accessories for electric lighting, manufacturing
926150 Price control agencies
111339 Prickly pear farming 331313 Primary aluminum production and manufacturing aluminum alloys
331313 Primary aluminum production and manufacturing aluminum shapes (e.g., bar, ingot, rod, sheet)
335912 Primary batteries manufacturing
334513 Primary elements for process flow measurement (i.e., orifice plates) manufacturing
334512 Primary oil burner controls (e.g., cadmium cells, stack controls) manufacturing
334513 Primary process temperature sensors manufacturing
331313 Primary refining of aluminum
331410 Primary refining of copper 331410 Primary refining of nonferrous metals (except aluminum)
611110 Primary schools
331313 Primary smelting of aluminum
331410 Primary smelting of copper
331410 Primary smelting of nonferrous metals (except aluminum)
335312 Prime mover generator sets (except turbine generator sets) manufacturing
332993 Primers (i.e., more than 30 mm., more than 1.18 inch), ammunition, manufacturing
325510 Primers, paint, manufacturing

323111 Print shops, digital (except printing books)
323111 Print shops, engraving (except printing books)
323111 Print shops, flexographic (except printing books)
323111 Print shops, gravure (except printing books)
323111 Print shops, letterpress (except printing books)
323111 Print shops, lithographic (offset) (except printing books)
323111 Print shops, quick (except printing books)
323113 Print shops, screen
334418 Printed circuit assemblies manufacturing
334418 Printed circuit boards loading
423690 Printed circuit boards merchant wholesalers
334412 Printed circuit boards, bare, manufacturing
334419 Printed circuit laminates manufacturing
333249 Printer machinery, 3D, manufacturing
334118 Printers, computer, manufacturing
423430 Printers, computer, merchant wholesalers
323117 Printing and binding books without publishing
323111 Printing apparel (except screen printing)
323117 Printing books without publishing
561990 Printing brokers
313310 Printing fabric grey goods
325910 Printing inks manufacturing
423840 Printing inks merchant wholesalers
333249 Printing machinery for textiles manufacturing
323111 Printing manifold business forms
424120 Printing paper (except bulk) merchant wholesalers
424110 Printing paper, bulk, merchant wholesalers
236210 Printing plant construction
333244 Printing plate engraving machinery manufacturing
323120 Printing plate preparation services
333244 Printing plates, blank (except photosentive), manufacturing
323120 Printing postpress services (e.g., beveling, bronzing, folding, gluing, edging, foil stamping) to printed products (e.g., books, cards, paper)
323120 Printing prepress services (e.g., color separation, imagesetting, photocomposition, typesetting)
333244 Printing press rollers manufacturing
333244 Printing presses (except textile) manufacturing
313310 Printing textile banners (except screen printing)
313310 Printing textile products (except screen and apparel printing)
811310 Printing trade machinery repair and maintenance services
423830 Printing trade machinery, equipment, and supplies merchant wholesalers
323111 Printing, digital (e.g., billboards, other large format graphical materials, high resolution) (except books, grey goods)
323111 Printing, engraving, on paper products
323111 Printing, flexographic (except books, grey goods)
323111 Printing, gravure (except books, grey goods)
323111 Printing, letterpress (except books, grey goods)
323111 Printing, lithographic (except books, grey goods)
323111 Printing, photo-offset (except books, grey goods)
323111 Printing, quick (except books, grey goods)
323113 Printing, screen (except books, manifold business forms, grey goods)
423410 Printmaking apparatus, photographic, merchant wholesalers
333314 Prisms, optical, manufacturing
337127 Prison bed manufacturing
236220 Prison construction
922140 Prison farms
922140 Prisons
522190 Private banks (i.e., unincorporated)
334210 Private branch exchange (PBX) equipment manufacturing
611310 Private colleges (except community or junior college)
561611 Private detective services
238210 Private driveway or parking area lighting contractors
523920 Private equity fund managing
525920 Private estates (i.e., administering on behalf of beneficiaries)
814110 Private households employing domestic personnel
814110 Private households with employees
561611 Private investigation services (except credit)

561431 Private mail centers 561431 Private mailbox rental centers 611110 Private schools, elementary or secondary 561990 Private volunteer firefighting 493190 Private warehousing and storage (except farm products, general merchandise, refrigerated)
493130 Private warehousing and storage, farm products (except refrigerated)
493110 Private warehousing and storage, general merchandise
493120 Private warehousing and storage, refrigerated
451110 Pro shops (e.g., golf, skiing, tennis)
624190 Probation offices, privately operated
922150 Probation offices, publicly administered
212391 Probertite mining and/or quarrying
334510 Probes, electric medical, manufacturing
339112 Probes, surgical, manufacturing
325411 Procaine and derivatives (i.e., basic chemicals) manufacturing
334513 Process control instruments, industrial, manufacturing
238220 Process piping installation
541199 Process server services
541199 Process serving services
311513 Processed cheeses manufacturing
424470 Processed meats (e.g., luncheon, sausage) merchant wholesalers
311612 Processed meats manufacturing
424440 Processed poultry (e.g., luncheon) merchant wholesalers
311615 Processed poultry manufacturing
423410 Processing and finishing equipment, photographic, merchant wholesalers
522320 Processing financial transactions
314999 Processing of textile mill waste and recovering fibers
621111 Proctologists' offices (e.g., centers, clinics)
424910 Produce containers merchant wholesalers
445230 Produce markets
445230 Produce stands, permanent
454390 Produce stands, temporary
424480 Produce, fresh, merchant wholesalers
813910 Producers' associations
711510 Producers, independent
512290 Producers, recorded radio shows (except independent producers)
561910 Product sterilization and packaging services
541380 Product testing laboratories or services
524128 Product warranty insurance carriers, direct
334514 Production counters manufacturing
541614 Production planning and control consulting services
541614 Productivity improvement consulting services
813920 Professional associations
711219 Professional athletes, independent (i.e., participating in sports events)
711211 Professional baseball clubs
511130 Professional book publishers (except exclusive Internet publishing)
511130 Professional book publishers and printing combined
519130 Professional book publishers, exclusively on Internet
323120 Professional bookbinding without printing
323117 Professional books printing and binding without publishing
323117 Professional books printing without publishing
611430 Professional development training
561330 Professional employer organizations (PEO)
423490 Professional equipment and supplies (except dental, medical, ophthalmic) merchant wholesalers
423460 Professional equipment and supplies, optical, merchant wholesalers
611691 Professional examination review instruction
711211 Professional football clubs
423490 Professional furniture (except dental, metal, ophthalmic, and school) merchant wholesalers
423490 Professional instruments merchant wholesalers
511120 Professional magazine and periodical publishers (except exclusive Internet publishing)
511120 Professional magazine and periodical publishers and printing combined
519130 Professional magazine and periodical publishers, exclusively on Internet
323111 Professional magazines and periodicals commercial printing (except screen) without publishing
323113 Professional magazines and periodicals screen printing without publishing

813920 Professional membership associations
531120 Professional office building rental or leasing
611310 Professional schools (e.g., business administration, dental, law, medical)
315210 Professional service apparel, washable, cut and sew apparel contractors
315220 Professional service apparel, washable, men's and boys', cut and sewn from purchased fabric (except apparel contractors)
315240 Professional service apparel, washable, women's and girls', cut and sewn from purchased fabric (except apparel contractors)
611620 Professional sports (e.g., golf, skiing, swimming, tennis) instructors (i.e., not participating in sporting events)
711211 Professional sports clubs
711310 Professional sports promoters with facilities
711320 Professional sports promoters without facilities
813920 Professional standards review boards
326130 Profile shapes (e.g., plate, rod, sheet), laminated plastics, manufacturing
326121 Profile shapes (e.g., rod, tube), nonrigid plastics, manufacturing
525990 Profit-sharing funds
512110 Program producing, television
334513 Programmers, process-type, manufacturing
511210 Programming language and compiler software publishers, packaged
541511 Programming services, custom computer
332993 Projectiles (except guided missile), jet propulsion, manufacturing
333316 Projection equipment (e.g., motion picture, slide), photographic, manufacturing
423410 Projection equipment (e.g., motion picture, slide), photographic, merchant wholesalers
333314 Projection lenses manufacturing 333316
Projection screens (i.e., motion picture, overhead, slide) manufacturing
334310 Projection television manufacturing
332994 Projectors (e.g., antisub, depth charge release, grenade, livens, rocket), ordnance, manufacturing
711310 Promoters of agricultural fairs with facilities
711320 Promoters of agricultural fairs without facilities
711310 Promoters of arts events with facilities
711320 Promoters of arts events without facilities
561920 Promoters of conventions with or without facilities
711310 Promoters of festivals with facilities
711320 Promoters of festivals without facilities
711310 Promoters of live performing arts productions (e.g., concerts) with facilities
711320 Promoters of live performing arts productions (e.g., concerts) without facilities
711310 Promoters of sports events with facilities
711320 Promoters of sports events without facilities
561920 Promoters of trade fairs or shows with or without facilities
561410 Proofreading services
111421 Propagation material farming 424710
Propane bulk stations and terminals, merchant wholesalers
324110 Propane gases made in petroleum refineries
424720 Propane merchant wholesalers (except bulk stations, terminals)
211130 Propane recovered from oil and gas field gases
333519 Propeller straightening presses manufacturing
334514 Propeller type meters with registers manufacturing
332999 Propellers, ship and boat, made from purchased metal
524126 Property and casualty insurance carriers, direct
524130 Property and casualty reinsurance carriers
524126 Property damage insurance carriers, direct
531312 Property managers' offices, commercial real estate
531312 Property managers' offices, nonresidential real estate
531311 Property managers' offices, residential real estate
531312 Property managing, commercial real estate
531312 Property managing, nonresidential real estate
531311 Property managing, residential real estate
813990 Property owners' associations 561612
Property protection services (except armored car, security systems)
921130 Property tax assessors' offices
326299 Prophylactics manufacturing
112910 Propolis production, bees

423860 Propulsion systems, marine, merchant wholesalers
336415 Propulsion units and parts, guided missile and space vehicle, manufacturing
325199 Propylcarbinol manufacturing 324110
Propylene (i.e., propene) made in petroleum refineries
325199 Propylene glycol manufacturing
325110 Propylene made from refined petroleum or liquid hydrocarbons
325211 Propylene resins manufacturing
213113 Prospect and test drilling services for coal mining on contract basis
213114 Prospect and test drilling services for metal mining on contract basis
213115 Prospect and test drilling services for non-metallic mineral mining (except fuels) on a contract basis
339113 Prosthetic appliances and supplies manufacturing
423450 Prosthetic appliances and supplies merchant wholesalers
446199 Prosthetic stores
621399 Prosthetists' offices (e.g., centers, clinics)
621210 Prosthodontists' offices (e.g., centers, clinics)
561612 Protection services (except armored car, security systems), personal or property
812332 Protective apparel supply services
523999 Protective committees, security holders
316210 Protective footwear, plastics or plastics soled fabric upper, manufacturing
316210 Protective footwear, rubber or rubber soled fabric upper, manufacturing
561612 Protective guard services
339920 Protectors, sports (e.g., baseball, basketball, hockey), manufacturing
334516 Protein analyzers, laboratory-type, manufacturing
541714 Protein engineering research and experimental development laboratories
325220 Protein fibers and filaments manufacturing
325211 Protein plastics manufacturing
712190 Provincial parks
334511 Proximity warning (i.e., collision avoidance) equipment manufacturing
111339 Prune farming
332216 Pruners manufacturing
311423 Prunes, dried, made in dehydration plants
115112 Pruning of orchard trees and vines
561730 Pruning services, ornamental tree and shrub
325130 Prussian blue pigments manufacturing
332216 Pry (i.e., crow) bars manufacturing
212299 Psilomelane mining and/or beneficiating
621420 Psychiatric centers and clinics (except hospitals), outpatient
623220 Psychiatric convalescent homes or hospitals
622210 Psychiatric hospitals (except convalescent)
621112 Psychiatrists' offices (e.g., centers, clinics)
812990 Psychic services
621330 Psychoanalysts' (except MDs or DOs) offices (e.g., centers, clinics)
621112 Psychoanalysts' (MDs or DOs) offices (e.g., centers, clinics)
813920 Psychologists' associations 621330 Psychologists' offices (e.g., centers, clinics), clinical
541720 Psychology research and development services
621330 Psychotherapists' (except MDs or DOs) offices (e.g., centers, clinics)
621112 Psychotherapists' (MDs or DOs) offices (e.g., centers, clinics)
541211 Public accountants' (CPAs) offices, certified
541211 Public accountants' (CPAs) private practices, certified
541219 Public accountants' (except CPAs) offices
541219 Public accountants' (except CPAs) private practices
238210 Public address system installation
532490 Public address system rental or leasing
811213 Public address system repair and maintenance services
334310 Public address systems and equipment manufacturing
423690 Public address systems and equipment merchant wholesalers
423210 Public building furniture merchant wholesalers
922130 Public defenders' offices
711410 Public figures' agents or managers 923120
Public health program administration, nonoperating
541910 Public opinion polling services
541910 Public opinion research services
922150 Public parole offices
922150 Public probation offices

921190 Public property management services, government
922130 Public prosecutors' offices
541820 Public relations agencies
541820 Public relations consulting services
541820 Public relations services
813319 Public safety advocacy organizations
922190 Public safety bureaus and statistics centers, government
922190 Public safety statistics centers, government
611110 Public schools, elementary or secondary
926130 Public service (except transportation) commissions, nonoperating
813410 Public speaking improvement clubs
611699 Public speaking training
561492 Public stenography services
926120 Public transportation commissions, nonoperating
926130 Public utility (except transportation) commissions, nonoperating
813910 Public utility associations
551112 Public utility holding companies 236220
Public warehouse construction 493190 Public warehousing and storage (except farm products, general merchandise,
refrigerated, self-storage)
493110 Public warehousing and storage (except self-storage), general merchandise
493130 Public warehousing and storage, farm products (except refrigerated)
493120 Public warehousing and storage, refrigerated
****** Publishers -- see specific type 511130
Publishers (except exclusive Internet publishing), book
511140 Publishers (except exclusive Internet publishing), directory
511191 Publishers (except exclusive Internet publishing), greeting card
511120 Publishers (except exclusive Internet publishing), magazine
511130 Publishers (except exclusive Internet publishing), map
511120 Publishers (except exclusive Internet publishing), periodical
511199 Publishers (except exclusive Internet publishing), racing form
541840 Publishers' advertising representatives (i.e., independent of media owners)
* Publishers and printing combined -- see specific type of publisher
* Publishers or publishing -- see specific type
511130 Publishers, book, combined with printing
511191 Publishers, greeting card, combined with printing
519130 Publishers, Internet greeting card
519130 Publishers, Internet map
519130 Publishers, Internet racing form
511120 Publishers, magazine, combined with printing
512230 Publishers, music
511110 Publishers, newspaper (except exclusive Internet publishing)
511110 Publishers, newspaper, combined with printing
511210 Publishers, packaged computer software
511120 Publishers, periodical, combined with printing
311520 Pudding pops, frozen, manufacturing
311999 Puddings, canned dessert, manufacturing
311999 Puddings, dessert, manufacturing
333923 Pulleys (except power transmission), metal, manufacturing
333613 Pulleys, power transmission, manufacturing
321999 Pulleys, wood, manufacturing 213112 Pulling oil and gas field casings, tubes, or rods on a contract basis
621111 Pulmonary specialists' offices (e.g., centers, clinics)
322122 Pulp and newsprint combined manufacturing
322121 Pulp and paper (except groundwood, newsprint) combined manufacturing
322130 Pulp and paperboard combined manufacturing
333243 Pulp making machinery manufacturing
322110 Pulp manufacturing (i.e., chemical, mechanical, or semichemical processes)
without making paper
322110 Pulp manufacturing (made from bagasse, linters, rags, straw, wastepaper, or wood) without making paper
322122 Pulp mills and groundwood paper,
uncoated and untreated, manufacturing
322110 Pulp mills not making paper or paperboard
322122 Pulp mills producing newsprint paper 322121
Pulp mills producing paper (except groundwood, newsprint)

322130 Pulp mills producing paperboard
322299 Pulp products, molded, manufacturing
333243 Pulp, paper, and paperboard molding machinery manufacturing
212399 Pulpstones, natural, mining and/or beneficiating
113310 Pulpwood logging camps
423990 Pulpwood merchant wholesalers
334515 Pulse (i.e., signal) generators manufacturing
334519 Pulse analyzers, nuclear monitoring, manufacturing
423830 Pulverizing machinery and equipment, industrial, merchant wholesalers
327992 Pumice (except abrasives) processing beyond beneficiation
327910 Pumice and pumicite abrasives manufacturing
212399 Pumice mining and/or beneficiating
212399 Pumicite mining and/or beneficiating
562991 Pumping (i.e., cleaning) cesspools and septic tanks
562991 Pumping (i.e., cleaning) portable toilets
213112 Pumping oil and gas wells on a contract basis
213113 Pumping or draining coal mines on a contract basis
213114 Pumping or draining metal mines on a contract basis
213115 Pumping or draining nonmetallic mineral mines (except fuel) on a contract basis
237120 Pumping station, gas and oil transmission, construction
237110 Pumping station, water and sewage system, construction
238220 Pumping system, water, installation
111219 Pumpkin farming, field and seed production
423120 Pumps (e.g., fuel, oil, power steering, water), automotive, merchant wholesalers
336310 Pumps (e.g., fuel, oil, water), mechanical, automotive and truck gasoline engine (except power steering), manufacturing
333914 Pumps (except fluid power), general purpose, manufacturing
316210 Pumps (i.e., dress shoes) manufacturing
423830 Pumps and pumping equipment, industrial-type, merchant wholesalers
333914 Pumps for railroad equipment lubrication systems manufacturing
333996 Pumps, fluid power, manufacturing
333914 Pumps, industrial and commercial-type, general purpose, manufacturing
333914 Pumps, measuring and dispensing (e.g., gasoline), manufacturing
333914 Pumps, oil field or well, manufacturing
333914 Pumps, sump or water, residential-type, manufacturing
313230 Punched felts manufacturing
332216 Punches (except paper), nonpowered handtool, manufacturing
333514 Punches for use with machine tools manufacturing
333517 Punching machines, metalworking, manufacturing
711110 Puppet theaters
339999 Puppets manufacturing 921190 Purchasing and supply agencies, government
522298 Purchasing of accounts receivable
332323 Purlins, metal, manufacturing 316998
Purses (except precious metal), men's, manufacturing
316992 Purses (except precious metal), women's, manufacturing
424330 Purses merchant wholesalers
339910 Purses, precious metal or clad with precious metal, manufacturing
333515 Pushers (i.e., a machine tool accessory) manufacturing
332216 Putty knives manufacturing
423920 Puzzles merchant wholesalers
326122 PVC pipe manufacturing
325320 Pyrethrin insecticides manufacturing
334519 Pyrheliometers manufacturing
212393 Pyrite concentrates mining and/or beneficiating
212393 Pyrite mining and/or beneficiating
325194 Pyroligneous acids manufacturing
212299 Pyrolusite mining and/or beneficiating
327110 Pyrometer tubes manufacturing
334513 Pyrometers, industrial process-type, manufacturing
327110 Pyrometric cones, earthenware, manufacturing
212399 Pyrophyllite mining and/or beneficiating
327992 Pyrophyllite processing beyond beneficiation
332994 Pyrotechnic pistols and projectors manufacturing

325998 Pyrotechnics (e.g., flares, flashlight bombs, signals) manufacturing
325211 Pyroxylin (i.e., nitrocellulose) resins manufacturing
212393 Pyrrhotite mining and/or beneficiating
112390 Quail production
611430 Quality assurance training
541990 Quantity surveyor services
327120 Quarry tiles, clay, manufacturing
333131 Quarrying machinery and equipment manufacturing
423810 Quarrying machinery and equipment merchant wholesalers
316998 Quarters (i.e., shoe cut stock), leather, manufacturing
212399 Quartz crystal, pure, mining and/or beneficiating
334419 Quartz crystals, electronic application, manufacturing
212319 Quartzite crushed and broken stone mining and/or beneficiating
212311 Quartzite dimension stone mining or quarrying
325194 Quebracho extracts manufacturing
112910 Queen bee production
325194 Quercitron extracts manufacturing
323111 Quick printing (except books)
327410 Quicklime (i.e., calcium oxide) manufacturing
811191 Quick-lube shops
212299 Quicksilver ores and metal mining and/or beneficiating
314999 Quilting of textiles
314120 Quilts made from purchased materials
111339 Quince farming
325411 Quinine and derivatives (i.e., basic chemicals) manufacturing
523999 Quotation services, securities
523999 Quotation services, stock
311119 Rabbit food manufacturing
112930 Rabbit production
311615 Rabbits processing (i.e., canned, cooked, fresh, frozen)
311615 Rabbits slaughtering and dressing
711219 Race car drivers
711219 Race car owners (i.e., racing cars)
336999 Race cars manufacturing
711219 Race dog owners (i.e., racing dogs)
711219 Racehorse owners (i.e., racing horses)
711219 Racehorse trainers
711219 Racehorse training
332991 Races, ball or roller bearings, manufacturing
511199 Racetrack program publishers (except Internet)
511199 Racetrack program publishers and printing combined
519130 Racetrack program publishers, exclusively on Internet
323111 Racetrack programs commercial printing (except screen) without publishing
323113 Racetrack programs screen printing without publishing
711212 Racetracks (e.g., automobile, dog, horse)
713990 Racetracks, slot car (i.e., amusement devices)
335932 Raceways manufacturing
713990 Raceways, gocart (i.e., amusement rides)
511199 Racing form publishers (except exclusive Internet publishing)
511199 Racing form publishers and printing combined
519130 Racing form publishers, exclusively on Internet
323111 Racing forms commercial printing (except screen) without publishing
323113 Racing forms screen printing without publishing
711219 Racing stables, horse
711219 Racing teams (e.g., automobile, motorcycle, snowmobile)
334417 Rack and panel connectors manufacturing
336330 Rack and pinion steering assemblies manufacturing
336390 Racks (e.g., bicycle, luggage, ski, tire), automotive, truck, and buses manufacturing
332313 Racks (e.g., trash), fabricated metal plate, manufacturing
332618 Racks, household-type, made from purchased wire
713940 Racquetball club facilities
811219 Radar and sonar equipment repair and maintenance services
334511 Radar detectors manufacturing
423690 Radar equipment merchant wholesalers
517919 Radar station operations
334511 Radar systems and equipment manufacturing

334515 Radar testing instruments, electric, manufacturing
334519 RADIAC (radioactivity detection, identification, and computation) equipment manufacturing
238220 Radiant floor heating equipment installation
334519 Radiation detection and monitoring instruments manufacturing
541380 Radiation dosimetry (i.e., radiation testing) laboratories or services
812332 Radiation protection garment supply services
339113 Radiation shielding aprons, gloves, and sheeting manufacturing
541380 Radiation testing laboratories or services
325998 Radiator additive preparations manufacturing
326220 Radiator and heater hoses, rubber or plastics, manufacturing
811118 Radiator repair shops, automotive 332322
Radiator shields and enclosures, sheet metal (except stampings), manufacturing
333414 Radiators (except motor vehicle, portable electric) manufacturing
336390 Radiators and cores manufacturing
423720 Radiators, heating, nonelectric, merchant wholesalers
423120 Radiators, motor vehicle, merchant wholesalers
335210 Radiators, portable electric, manufacturing
811211 Radio (except two-way radio) repair and maintenance services without retailing new radios
541840 Radio advertising representatives (i.e., independent of media owners)
236220 Radio and television broadcast studio construction
443142 Radio and television stores
332312 Radio and television tower sections, fabricated structural metal, manufacturing
488330 Radio beacon (i.e., ship navigation) services
515112 Radio broadcasting (except exclusively on Internet) stations (e.g., AM, FM, shortwave)
515111 Radio broadcasting network services
515111 Radio broadcasting networks
515111 Radio broadcasting syndicates
711510 Radio commentators, independent
541690 Radio consulting services
334419 Radio frequency identification (RFID) devices manufacturing
423690 Radio frequency identification (RFID) equipment merchant wholesalers
511120 Radio guide publishers (except exclusive Internet publishing)
511120 Radio guide publishers and printing combined
519130 Radio guide publishers, exclusively on Internet
323111 Radio guides commercial printing (except screen) without publishing
323113 Radio guides screen printing without publishing
334310 Radio headphones manufacturing
326199 Radio housings, plastics, manufacturing
334511 Radio magnetic instrumentation (RMI) manufacturing
517312 Radio paging services communications carriers
423690 Radio parts and accessories (e.g., transistors, tubes) merchant wholesalers
512290 Radio program recording production (except independent producers)
334310 Radio receiving sets manufacturing
811211 Radio repair, automotive, without retailing new
511120 Radio schedule publishers (except exclusive Internet publishing)
511120 Radio schedule publishers and printing combined
519130 Radio schedule publishers, exclusively on Internet
323111 Radio schedules commercial printing (except screen) without publishing
323113 Radio schedules screen printing without publishing
236220 Radio station construction
515112 Radio stations (except exclusively on Internet)
561410 Radio transcription services
334220 Radio transmitting antennas and ground equipment manufacturing
237130 Radio transmitting tower construction
325180 Radioactive elements manufacturing
541360 Radioactive geophysical surveying services
325412 Radioactive in-vivo diagnostic substances manufacturing
325180 Radioactive isotopes manufacturing
424210 Radioactive pharmaceutical isotopes merchant wholesalers
562112 Radioactive waste collecting and/or local hauling

562211 Radioactive waste collecting and/or local hauling in combination with disposal and/or treatment facilities
562211 Radioactive waste disposal facilities
484230 Radioactive waste hauling, long-distance
562211 Radioactive waste treatment facilities
334519 Radioactivity detection, identification, and computation (RADIAC) equipment manufacturing
334515 Radiofrequency measuring equipment manufacturing
334515 Radiofrequency oscillators manufacturing
541380 Radiographic testing laboratories or services
541380 Radiographing welded joints on pipes and fittings
541380 Radiography inspection services
621512 Radiological laboratories, medical
621512 Radiological laboratory services, medical
621111 Radiologists' offices (e.g., centers, clinics)
424210 Radiopharmaceuticals merchant wholesalers
423690 Radios (except household-type) merchant wholesalers
423620 Radios, household-type, merchant wholesalers
111219 Radish farming, field and seed production
325180 Radium chloride manufacturing
334517 Radium equipment manufacturing
325180 Radium luminous compounds manufacturing
212291 Radium ores mining and/or beneficiating
238990 Radon gas alleviation contractors
541380 Radon testing laboratories or services
326299 Rafts, swimming pool-type, rubber inflatable, manufacturing
423930 Rags merchant wholesalers
335931 Rail bonds, propulsion and signal circuit electric, manufacturing
331110 Rail joints and fastenings made in iron and steel mills
336510 Rail laying and tamping equipment manufacturing
485112 Rail transportation (except mixed mode), commuter
332323 Railings, metal, manufacturing
321918 Railings, wood stair, manufacturing
423310 Railings, wood, merchant wholesalers
926120 Railroad and warehouse commissions, nonoperating
333613 Railroad car journal bearings, plain, manufacturing
532411 Railroad car rental or leasing
336510 Railroad cars and car equipment manufacturing
423860 Railroad cars merchant wholesalers
336510 Railroad cars, self-propelled, manufacturing
237990 Railroad construction
331110 Railroad crossings, iron or steel, made in iron and steel mills
423860 Railroad equipment and supplies merchant wholesalers
551112 Railroad holding companies
336510 Railroad locomotives and parts (except diesel engines) manufacturing
339930 Railroad models, hobby and toy, manufacturing
923130 Railroad Retirement Board
531190 Railroad right of way leasing
336510 Railroad rolling stock manufacturing
336360 Railroad seating manufacturing
238210 Railroad signaling equipment installation
334290 Railroad signaling equipment manufacturing
488210 Railroad switching services
488210 Railroad terminals, independent operation
561599 Railroad ticket offices
321114 Railroad ties (i.e., bridge, cross, switch) treating
423990 Railroad ties, wood, merchant wholesalers
333997 Railroad track scales manufacturing
482111 Railroad transportation, line-haul
487110 Railroad transportation, scenic and sightseeing
482112 Railroad transportation, short-line or beltline
487110 Railroad, scenic and sightseeing, operation
482111 Railroads, line-haul
482112 Railroads, short-line or beltline
321999 Rails (except rough), wood fence, manufacturing
423510 Rails and accessories, metal, merchant wholesalers
331318 Rails made by rolling or drawing purchased aluminum
331110 Rails rerolled or renewed in iron and steel mills

331318 Rails, aluminum, made in integrated secondary smelting and drawing plants
331318 Rails, aluminum, made in integrated secondary smelting and rolling mills
331110 Rails, iron or steel, made in iron and steel mills
113310 Rails, rough wood, manufacturing
332312 Railway bridge sections, prefabricated metal, manufacturing
237990 Railway construction (e.g., interlocker, roadbed, signal, track)
335312 Railway motors and control equipment, electric, manufacturing
237990 Railway roadbed construction
236220 Railway station construction
485112 Railway systems (except mixed mode), commuter
488210 Railway terminals, independent operation
482111 Railway transportation, line-haul 487110
Railway transportation, scenic and sightseeing
482112 Railway transportation, short-line or beltline
334519 Rain gauges manufacturing
315210 Raincoats (e.g., water resistant, waterproof, water-repellent) cut and sew apparel contractors
313320 Raincoats waterproofing (i.e., oiling)
315280 Raincoats, rubber or rubberized fabric, manufacturing
315220 Raincoats, water resistant, men's and boys', cut and sewn from purchased fabric (except apparel contractors)
315240 Raincoats, water resistant, women's, girls', and infants', cut and sewn from purchased fabric (except apparel contractors)
315280 Raincoats, waterproof, cut and sewn from purchased fabric (except apparel contractors)
315220 Raincoats, water-repellent, men's and boys', cut and sewn from purchased fabric (except apparel contractors)
315240 Raincoats, water-repellent, women's, girls', and infants', cut and sewn from purchased fabric (except apparel contractors)
111332 Raisin farming
112990 Raising swans, peacocks, flamingos, or other adornment birds
311423 Raisins made in dehydration plants
333111 Rakes, hay, manufacturing 332216
Rakes, nonpowered handtool, manufacturing
313110 Ramie spun yarns made from purchased fiber
423690 Random access memory (RAM) chips merchant wholesalers
316998 Rands (i.e., shoe cut stock), leather, manufacturing
333316 Range finders, photographic, manufacturing
335210 Range hoods with integral lighting fixtures, household-type, manufacturing
335210 Range hoods, household-type, manufacturing
333318 Ranges, commercial-type, manufacturing
423620 Ranges, gas and electric, merchant wholesalers
335220 Ranges, household-type cooking, manufacturing
624190 Rape crisis centers
311225 Rapeseed (i.e., canola) oil made from purchased oils
311224 Rapeseed (i.e., canola) oil made in crushing mills
111120 Rapeseed farming, field and seed production
336510 Rapid transit cars and equipment manufacturing
325180 Rare earth compounds, not specified elsewhere by process, manufacturing
212299 Rare earth metal concentrates beneficiating
212299 Rare earth metal ores mining and/or beneficiating
325180 Rare earth salts manufacturing
453310 Rare manuscript stores
111334 Raspberry farming
332216 Rasps, handheld, manufacturing
332216 Ratchets, nonpowered, manufacturing
524298 Ratemaking services, insurance
334511 Rate-of-climb instrumentation manufacturing
213112 Rathole and mousehole drilling at oil and gas fields on a contract basis
112390 Ratite production 337125 Rattan furniture, household-type, manufacturing
321999 Rattan ware (except furniture) manufacturing
112990 Rattlesnake production
311313 Raw beet sugar manufacturing 424590 Raw farm products (except field beans, grains) merchant wholesalers

424430 Raw milk merchant wholesalers
316110 Rawhide manufacturing
114111 Ray fishing
325220 Rayon fibers and filaments manufacturing
313110 Rayon spun yarns made from purchased fiber
313110 Rayon thread manufacturing
313110 Rayon yarn throwing, twisting, texturizing, or winding purchased filament
331221 Razor blade strip steel made in cold rolling mills
332215 Razor blades manufacturing
424210 Razor blades merchant wholesalers
316998 Razor strops manufacturing
332215 Razors (except electric) manufacturing
424210 Razors (except electric) merchant wholesalers
335210 Razors, electric, manufacturing
423620 Razors, electric, merchant wholesalers
332313 Reactor containment vessels, fabricated metal plate, manufacturing
332410 Reactors, nuclear, manufacturing
333316 Readers, microfilm or microfiche, manufacturing
327320 Ready-mix concrete manufacturing and distributing
336211 Ready-mix concrete trucks assembling on purchased chassis
531190 Real estate (except building) rental or leasing
237210 Real estate (except cemeteries) subdividers
531210 Real estate agencies
531210 Real estate agents' offices
531320 Real estate appraisal services
531320 Real estate appraisers' offices
531390 Real estate asset management services (except property management)
813910 Real estate boards
531210 Real estate brokerages
531210 Real estate brokers' offices
531390 Real estate consultants' (except agents, appraisers) offices
522292 Real estate credit lending
531390 Real estate escrow agencies
531390 Real estate escrow agents' offices
531390 Real estate fiduciaries' offices
541110 Real estate law offices
531390 Real estate listing services 525990 Real estate mortgage investment conduits (REMICs)
522294 Real estate mortgage investment conduits (REMICs) issuing, private
531312 Real estate property managers' offices, commercial
531311 Real estate property managers' offices, residential
531130 Real estate rental or leasing of miniwarehouses and self-storage units
531120 Real estate rental or leasing of nonresidential building (except miniwarehouse)
531110 Real estate rental or leasing of residential building
611519 Real estate schools
524127 Real estate title insurance carriers, direct
237210 Real property (except cemeteries) subdivision
561492 Real-time (i.e., simultaneous) closed captioning of live television performances, meetings, conferences, and so forth
333515 Reamers (i.e., a machine tool accessory) manufacturing
333517 Reaming machines, metalworking, manufacturing
238120 Rebar contractors
323120 Rebinding books, magazines, or pamphlets
515112 Rebroadcast radio stations (except exclusively on Internet)
336310 Rebuilding automotive and truck gasoline engines
326212 Rebuilding tires
423130 Recapped tires merchant wholesalers
423830 Recapping machinery, tire, merchant wholesalers
326212 Recapping tires
424120 Receipt books merchant wholesalers
334220 Receiver-transmitter units (i.e., transceivers) manufacturing
335931 Receptacles (i.e., outlets), electrical, manufacturing
423610 Receptacles, electrical, merchant wholesalers
531120 Reception hall rental or leasing
335122 Recessed lighting housings and trim (except residential), electric, manufacturing
335121 Recessed lighting housings and trim, residential electric, manufacturing
335911 Rechargeable battery packs made from purchased battery cells and housings

335911 Rechargeable nickel-cadmium (NICAD) batteries manufacturing

314999 Reclaimed wool processing

326299 Reclaiming rubber from waste or scrap

337121 Recliners, upholstered, manufacturing

332994 Recoil mechanisms, gun, manufacturing

332994 Recoilless rifles manufacturing

541714 Recombinant DNA research and experimental development laboratories

423840 Reconditioned barrels and drums merchant wholesalers

213111 Reconditioning oil and gas field wells on a contract basis

811310 Reconditioning shipping barrels and drums

321219 Reconstituted wood panels manufacturing

321219 Reconstituted wood sheets and boards manufacturing

312230 Reconstituting tobacco

512250 Record producers (except independent)

711510 Record producers, independent 512250 Record production (except independent record producers) without duplication or distribution

512250 Record releasing, promoting, and distributing combined with mass duplication

443142 Record stores, new

453310 Record stores, used

423620 Recorders (e.g., tape, video), household-type, merchant wholesalers

334513 Recorders, industrial process control-type, manufacturing

334515 Recorders, oscillographic, manufacturing

512290 Recording books on tape or disc (except publishers)

512290 Recording seminars and conferences, audio

512240 Recording studios, sound, operating on a contract or fee basis

711510 Recording technicians, independent

541611 Records management consulting services

314999 Recovered fibers processing 331492 Recovering and refining of nonferrous metals (except aluminum, copper) from scrap

331492 Recovering silver from used photographic film or X-ray plates

237990 Recreation area, open space, construction

621340 Recreational (e.g., art, dance, music) therapists' offices (e.g., centers, clinics)

721214 Recreational camps with accommodation facilities (except campgrounds)

713990 Recreational camps without accommodations

713990 Recreational day camps (except instructional)

423910 Recreational equipment and supplies (except vehicles) merchant wholesalers

236220 Recreational facility building construction

532284 Recreational goods rental 924120 Recreational programs administration, government

713940 Recreational sports club facilities 713990 Recreational sports clubs (i.e., sports teams) not operating sports facilities

713990 Recreational sports teams and leagues

532120 Recreational trailer rental

441210 Recreational vehicle (RV) dealers

441210 Recreational vehicle (RV) parts and accessories stores

532120 Recreational vehicle (RV) rental or leasing

423110 Recreational vehicle merchant wholesalers 237990 Recreational vehicle park construction

721211 Recreational vehicle parks 335999 Rectifiers (except electronic component-type, semiconductor) manufacturing

334419 Rectifiers, electronic component-type (except semiconductor), manufacturing

423690 Rectifiers, electronic, merchant wholesalers

334413 Rectifiers, semiconductor, manufacturing

333249 Rectifying equipment, chemical, manufacturing

562111 Recyclable material collection services

562111 Recyclable material hauling, local

484230 Recyclable material hauling, long-distance

423930 Recyclable materials (e.g., glass, metal, paper) merchant wholesalers

562920 Recyclable materials recovery facilities

325612 Recycling drycleaning fluids

811212 Recycling inkjet cartridges

325998 Recycling services for degreasing solvents (e.g., engine, machinery) manufacturing

325199 Red oil (i.e., oleic acid) manufacturing

925120 Redevelopment land agencies, government

334516 Redox (i.e., oxidation-reduction potential) instruments manufacturing

333612 Reducers, speed, manufacturing

333612 Reduction gears and gear units (except aircraft power transmission equipment, automotive) manufacturing
337125 Reed furniture (except upholstered), household-type, manufacturing
212399 Reed peat mining and/or beneficiating
321999 Reed ware (except furniture) manufacturing
339992 Reeds, musical instrument, manufacturing
339920 Reels, fishing, manufacturing
332999 Reels, metal, manufacturing
326199 Reels, plastics, manufacturing
321999 Reels, plywood, manufacturing
321999 Reels, wood, manufacturing
711219 Referees and umpires
519120 Reference libraries
561311 Referral agencies or services, employment
624190 Referral services for personal and social problems
486910 Refined petroleum products pipeline transportation
324110 Refineries, petroleum
324110 Refinery gases made in petroleum refineries
423830 Refinery machinery and equipment merchant wholesalers
237120 Refinery, petroleum, construction
331313 Refining aluminum, primary
331314 Refining aluminum, secondary
331410 Refining copper, primary
331420 Refining copper, secondary
331410 Refining nonferrous metals and alloys (except aluminum), primary
331492 Refining nonferrous metals and alloys (except aluminum, copper), secondary
335129 Reflectors for lighting equipment, metal, manufacturing
333314 Reflectors, optical, manufacturing
326199 Reflectors, plastics, manufacturing
115310 Reforestation
922140 Reformatories
325991 Reformulating plastics resins from recycled plastics products
334513 Refractometers, industrial process-type, manufacturing
334516 Refractometers, laboratory-type, manufacturing
327120 Refractories (e.g., block, brick, mortar, tile), clay, manufacturing
327120 Refractories (e.g., block, brick, mortar, tile), nonclay, manufacturing
238140 Refractory brick contractors
327120 Refractory cement, nonclay, manufacturing
423840 Refractory materials (e.g., block, brick, mortar, tile) merchant wholesalers
212325 Refractory minerals mining and/or beneficiating
722515 Refreshment stands, fixed location
722330 Refreshment stands, mobile 423740 Refrigerated display cases merchant wholesalers
311824 Refrigerated doughs made from purchased flour
333415 Refrigerated lockers manufacturing
484220 Refrigerated products trucking, local
484230 Refrigerated products trucking, long-distance
493120 Refrigerated warehousing
333415 Refrigeration compressors manufacturing
334512 Refrigeration controls, residential and commercial-type, manufacturing
423740 Refrigeration equipment and supplies, commercial-type, merchant wholesalers
811310 Refrigeration equipment repair and maintenance services, industrial and commercial-type
333415 Refrigeration equipment, industrial and commercial-type, manufacturing
238220 Refrigeration system (e.g., commercial, industrial, scientific) installation
334512 Refrigeration thermostats manufacturing
423740 Refrigeration units, motor vehicle, merchant wholesalers
333415 Refrigeration units, truck-type, manufacturing
334512 Refrigeration/air-conditioning defrost controls manufacturing
532210 Refrigerator rental
811412 Refrigerator, household-type, repair and maintenance services without retailing new refrigerators
335220 Refrigerator/freezer combinations, household-type, manufacturing
335220 Refrigerators (e.g., absorption, mechanical), household-type, manufacturing
423740 Refrigerators (e.g., reach-in, walk-in), commercial-type, merchant wholesalers
423620 Refrigerators, household-type, merchant wholesalers

624230 Refugee settlement services 562212 Refuse collecting and operating solid waste landfills
562111 Refuse collection services
562213 Refuse disposal combustors or incinerators
562212 Refuse disposal landfills
236210 Refuse disposal plant (except sewage treatment) construction
562111 Refuse hauling, local
484230 Refuse hauling, long-distance
325220 Regenerated cellulosic fibers manufacturing
925120 Regional planning and development program administration
621399 Registered nurses' (RNs) offices (e.g., centers, clinics)
334514 Registers, linear tallying, manufacturing
332323 Registers, metal air, manufacturing
561311 Registries, employment
561311 Registries, teacher
335311 Regulating transformers, power system-type, manufacturing
926140 Regulation and inspection of agricultural products
926130 Regulation of utilities
335311 Regulators (i.e., electric transformers), feeder voltage, manufacturing
336320 Regulators, motor vehicle voltage for internal combustion engines manufacturing
335313 Regulators, power, manufacturing 423610 Regulators, voltage (except motor vehicle), merchant wholesalers
624190 Rehabilitation agencies for offenders
622310 Rehabilitation hospitals (except alcoholism, drug addiction)
622210 Rehabilitation hospitals, alcoholism and drug addiction
624310 Rehabilitation job counseling and training, vocational
922150 Rehabilitation services, correctional, government
423510 Reinforcement mesh and wire merchant wholesalers
332618 Reinforcing mesh, concrete, made from purchased wire
238120 Reinforcing rod, bar, mesh and cage installation
238120 Reinforcing steel contractors
524130 Reinsurance carriers
334515 Relays (except electrical, electronic), instrument, manufacturing
423610 Relays merchant wholesalers 335314 Relays, electrical and electronic, manufacturing
624230 Relief services, disaster
624230 Relief services, emergency 511130 Religious book publishers (except exclusive Internet publishing)
511130 Religious book publishers and printing combined
519130 Religious book publishers, exclusively on Internet
451211 Religious book stores
323120 Religious bookbinding without printing
323117 Religious books printing and binding without publishing
323117 Religious books printing without publishing
236220 Religious building (e.g., church, synagogue, mosque, temple) construction
337127 Religious furniture manufacturing 423210 Religious furniture merchant wholesalers 453998 Religious goods (except books) stores 511120 Religious magazine and periodical publishers (except exclusive Internet publishing)
511120 Religious magazine and periodical publishers and printing combined
519130 Religious magazine and periodical publishers, exclusively on Internet
323111 Religious magazines and periodicals commercial printing (except screen) without publishing
323113 Religious magazines and periodicals screen printing without publishing
813110 Religious organizations
423490 Religious supplies merchant wholesalers
311421 Relishes canning
562910 Remediation and cleanup of contaminated buildings, mine sites, soil, or ground water
562910 Remediation services, environmental
525990 REMICs (real estate mortgage investment conduits)
522294 REMICs (real estate mortgage investment conduits) issuing, private
424310 Remnants, piece goods, merchant wholesalers
236118 Remodeling and renovating for-sale builders
236118 Remodeling and renovating general contractors, multifamily building

236118 Remodeling and renovating general contractors, residential
236118 Remodeling and renovating general contractors, single-family housing
236118 Remodeling and renovating single-family housing
236118 Remodeling and renovating, residential building
334290 Remote control units (e.g., garage door, television) manufacturing
541360 Remote sensing geophysical surveying services
238910 Removal of dams, dikes, and other heavy and civil engineering constructions
213113 Removal of overburden for coal mining on a contract basis
213114 Removal of overburden for metal mining on a contract basis
213115 Removal of overburden for nonmetallic minerals mining (except fuels) on a contract basis
562920 Removal of recyclable materials from a waste stream
621492 Renal dialysis centers and clinics
311613 Rendering animals (carrion) for feed
311613 Rendering fats
311613 Rendering plants
424990 Rennets merchant wholesalers
926150 Rent control agencies
* Rental -- see type of article or property being rented
532310 Rent-all centers
532490 Renting coin-operated amusement devices (except concession operators)
531210 Renting real estate for others (i.e., agents, brokers)
541611 Reorganizational consulting services
522294 Repackaging loans for sale to others (i.e., private conduits)
* Repair -- see type of article being repaired
237310 Repair, highway, road, street, bridge or airport runway
323120 Repairing books
334210 Repeater and transceiver equipment, carrier line, manufacturing
711110 Repertory companies, theatrical
322230 Report covers made from purchased paper or paperboard
711510 Reporters, independent (freelance)
561491 Repossession services
512199 Reproduction of motion picture films for theatrical distribution
115210 Reproductive flushing services for animals
621410 Reproductive health services centers
561439 Reprographic services
712130 Reptile exhibits, live
324191 Re-refining used petroleum lubricating oils
321912 Resawing purchased lumber
621910 Rescue services, air
621910 Rescue services, medical
517410 Resellers, satellite telecommunication
517911 Resellers, telecommunication (except satellite)
325411 Reserpines (i.e., basic chemicals) manufacturing
561599 Reservation (e.g., airline, car rental, hotel, restaurant) services
522320 Reserve and liquidity services (except central bank)
237110 Reservoir construction
562998 Reservoir maintenance and cleaning services
721310 Residence clubs, organizational
531110 Residential building rental or leasing
561720 Residential cleaning services
721310 Residential clubs
236116 Residential construction, multifamily, general contractors
236115 Residential construction, single-family, general contractors
236117 Residential for-sale builders 623220
Residential group homes for the emotionally disturbed
531110 Residential hotel rental or leasing
531311 Residential property managing
531210 Residential real estate agencies
531210 Residential real estate agents' offices
531210 Residential real estate brokerages
531210 Residential real estate brokers' offices
531311 Residential real estate property managers' offices
531190 Residential trailer parks
211130 Residue gas production 326199 Resilient
floor coverings (e.g., sheet, tile) manufacturing
238330 Resilient floor tile or sheet (e.g., linoleum, rubber, vinyl), installation only

325211 Resins, plastics (except custom compounding purchased resins), manufacturing
424610 Resins, plastics, merchant wholesalers
424690 Resins, synthetic rubber, merchant wholesalers
334515 Resistance measuring equipment manufacturing
334513 Resistance thermometers and bulbs, industrial process-type, manufacturing
333992 Resistance welding equipment manufacturing
334416 Resistors, electronic, manufacturing
423690 Resistors, electronic, merchant wholesalers
335312 Resolvers manufacturing
334516 Resonance instruments (i.e., laboratory-type) manufacturing
334419 Resonant reed devices, electronic, manufacturing
325194 Resorcinol manufacturing
721120 Resort hotels with casinos
721110 Resort hotels without casinos
531311 Resort or vacation property managers' offices
334510 Respiratory analysis equipment, electromedical, manufacturing
339113 Respiratory protection mask manufacturing
621399 Respiratory therapists' offices (e.g., centers, clinics)
623110 Rest homes with nursing care
623312 Rest homes without nursing care
561720 Rest room cleaning services
812990 Rest room operation
813910 Restaurant associations
236220 Restaurant construction
423440 Restaurant equipment (except furniture) merchant wholesalers
337127 Restaurant furniture (e.g., carts, chairs, foodwagons, tables) manufacturing
423210 Restaurant furniture merchant wholesalers
561720 Restaurant kitchen cleaning services 611519
Restaurant management schools (except academic)
492210 Restaurant meals delivery services (i.e., independent delivery services)
722513 Restaurants, carryout
722513 Restaurants, fast-food
722511 Restaurants, full service
811420 Restoration and repair of antique furniture
811121 Restoration shops, antique and classic automotive
339113 Restraints, patient, manufacturing
561410 Resume writing services
238330 Resurfacing hardwood flooring
237310 Resurfacing, highway, road, street, bridge or airport runway
****** Retail -- see type of dealer, shop, or store
333997 Retail scales (e.g., butcher, delicatessen, produce) manufacturing
813910 Retailers' associations
238110 Retaining wall (except anchored earth), poured concrete, construction
238140 Retaining wall, masonry (i.e., block, brick, stone), construction
237990 Retaining walls, anchored (e.g., with piles, soil nails, tieback anchors), construction
325998 Retarders (e.g., flameproofing agents, mildewproofing agents) manufacturing
339112 Retinoscopes (except electromedical) manufacturing
334510 Retinoscopes, electromedical, manufacturing
813410 Retirement associations, social
623311 Retirement communities, continuing care
623110 Retirement homes with nursing care
623312 Retirement homes without nursing care
531110 Retirement hotel rental or leasing
525110 Retirement pension plans
332420 Retorts, heavy gauge metal, manufacturing
339112 Retractors, medical, manufacturing
326211 Retreading materials, tire, manufacturing
326212 Retreading tires
813110 Retreat houses, religious
115114 Retting flax
811420 Reupholstery shops, furniture
522292 Reverse mortgage lending
237990 Revetment construction
332994 Revolvers manufacturing
238290 Revolving door installation
811310 Rewinding armatures (except on an assembly line or factory basis)
213111 Reworking oil and gas wells on a contract basis
331410 Rhenium refining, primary
335931 Rheostats (i.e., dimmer switches), current-carrying wiring device, manufacturing
334419 Rheostats, electronic, manufacturing

335314 Rheostats, industrial control, manufacturing
212299 Rhodium mining and/or beneficiating
212299 Rhodochrosite mining and/or beneficiating
111219 Rhubarb farming, field and seed production
111419 Rhubarb, grown under cover
339940 Ribbons (e.g., cash register, printer, typewriter), inked, manufacturing 314999
Ribbons made from purchased fabrics 313220 Rib-
bons made in narrow woven fabric mills
313230 Ribbons made in nonwoven fabric mills
339940 Ribbons, inked, manufacturing
424120 Ribbons, inked, merchant wholesalers
424310 Ribbons, textile, merchant wholesalers
111160 Rice (except wild rice) farming, field and seed production
311212 Rice bran, flour, and meals, manufacturing
311230 Rice breakfast foods manufacturing
311212 Rice cleaning and polishing
115114 Rice drying
311212 Rice flour manufacturing
311213 Rice malt manufacturing
311212 Rice meal manufacturing
311212 Rice milling
311999 Rice mixes (i.e., uncooked and packaged with other ingredients) made from purchased rice and dry ingredients
311423 Rice mixes (i.e., uncooked and packaged with other ingredients) made in dehydration plants
311212 Rice mixes (i.e., uncooked and packaged with other ingredients) made in rice mills
311221 Rice starches manufacturing
311212 Rice, brewer's, manufacturing
311212 Rice, brown, manufacturing
424490 Rice, polished, merchant wholesalers
424510 Rice, unpolished, merchant wholesalers
315210 Riding clothes cut and sew apparel contractors
315220 Riding clothes, men's and boys', cut and sewn from purchased fabric (except apparel contractors)
315240 Riding clothes, women's and girls', cut and sewn from purchased fabric (except apparel contractors)
713990 Riding clubs, recreational
316998 Riding crops manufacturing
611620 Riding instruction academies or schools
713990 Riding stables
713990 Rifle clubs, recreational
332994 Rifles (except toy) manufacturing
332994 Rifles, BB and pellet, manufacturing
332994 Rifles, pneumatic, manufacturing
332994 Rifles, recoilless, manufacturing
339930 Rifles, toy, manufacturing
333517 Rifling machines, metalworking, manufacturing
213112 Rig skidding, oil and gas field, on a contract basis
238290 Rigging large-scale equipment
238910 Right of way cutting (except maintenance)
336612 Rigid inflatable boats (RIBs) manufacturing
336390 Rims, automotive, truck, and bus wheel, manufacturing
336310 Rings, piston, manufacturing
713940 Rinks, ice or roller skating 212319 Riprap (except granite, limestone) preparation plants
212319 Riprap (except limestone and granite) mining or quarrying
237990 Riprap installation
212313 Riprap, granite, mining or quarrying
212313 Riprap, granite, preparation plants
212312 Riprap, limestone, mining or quarrying
212312 Riprap, limestone, preparation plants
483211 River freight transportation
483212 River passenger transportation
713990 River rafting, recreational
713210 Riverboat casinos
333991 Riveting guns, handheld power-driven, manufacturing
333517 Riveting machines, metalworking, manufacturing
332722 Rivets, metal, manufacturing 621399 RNs'
(registered nurses) offices (e.g., centers, clinics)
325320 Roach poisons manufacturing
711110 Road companies, theatrical
237310 Road construction
423810 Road construction and maintenance machinery merchant wholesalers
238910 Road decommissioning

324199 Road oils made from refined petroleum
324110 Road oils made in petroleum refineries
311911 Roasted nuts and seeds manufacturing
112320 Roaster chicken production
335210 Roasters (i.e., cooking appliances), household-type electric, manufacturing
311920 Roasting coffee
333241 Roasting machinery manufacturing
315210 Robes, lounging, cut and sew apparel contractors
315190 Robes, lounging, made in apparel knitting mills
315220 Robes, lounging, men's and boys', cut and sewn from purchased fabric (except apparel contractors)
315240 Robes, lounging, women's, girls', and infants', cut and sewn from purchased fabric (except apparel contractors)
333120 Rock crushing machinery, portable, manufacturing
333131 Rock crushing machinery, stationary, manufacturing
333132 Rock drill bits, oil and gas field-type, manufacturing
333120 Rock drills, construction and surface mining-type, manufacturing
333131 Rock drills, underground mining-type, manufacturing
711130 Rock musical artists, independent
711130 Rock musical groups
237990 Rock removal, underwater
212393 Rock salt mining and/or beneficiating
336310 Rocker arms and parts, automotive and truck gasoline engine, manufacturing
337122 Rockers (except upholstered), wood, manufacturing
337121 Rockers, upholstered, manufacturing
332313 Rocket casings, fabricated metal work, manufacturing
336412 Rocket engines, aircraft, manufacturing
336415 Rocket engines, guided missile, manufacturing
332994 Rocket launchers manufacturing
336414 Rockets (guided missiles), space and military, complete, manufacturing
332993 Rockets, ammunition (except guided missiles, pyrotechnic), manufacturing
114111 Rockfish fishing
339930 Rocking horses manufacturing
331318 Rod made by extruding purchased aluminum
331318 Rod made by rolling purchased aluminum
333519 Rod rolling mill machinery, metalworking, manufacturing
331318 Rod, aluminum, made in integrated secondary smelting and extruding mills
331318 Rod, aluminum, made in integrated secondary smelting and rolling mills
331420 Rod, copper and copper alloy, made from purchased copper or in integrated secondary smelting and rolling, drawing or extruding plants
326130 Rod, laminated plastics, manufacturing
331491 Rod, nonferrous metals (except aluminum, copper), made from purchased metals or scrap
326121 Rod, nonrigid plastics, manufacturing
325320 Rodent poisons manufacturing
325320 Rodenticides manufacturing
711310 Rodeo managers with facilities
711320 Rodeo managers without facilities
711310 Rodeo organizers with facilities
711320 Rodeo organizers without facilities
711310 Rodeo promoters with facilities
711320 Rodeo promoters without facilities
339920 Rods and rod parts, fishing, manufacturing
326299 Rods, hard rubber, manufacturing
331110 Rods, iron or steel, made in iron and steel mills
423510 Rods, metal (except precious), merchant wholesalers
334519 Rods, surveyor's, manufacturing
238160 Roll roofing installation
332991 Roller bearings manufacturing
711211 Roller hockey clubs, professional or semiprofessional
316110 Roller leather manufacturing
339920 Roller skates manufacturing
713940 Roller skating rinks
333120 Rollers, road construction and maintenance machinery, manufacturing
321999 Rollers, wood, manufacturing
332321 Rolling doors for industrial buildings and warehouses, metal, manufacturing
333519 Rolling mill machinery and equipment, metalworking, manufacturing
423830 Rolling mill machinery merchant wholesalers
333519 Rolling mill roll machines, metalworking, manufacturing

331511 Rolling mill rolls, iron, manufacturing
331513 Rolling mill rolls, steel, manufacturing
321999 Rolling pins, wood, manufacturing
336510 Rolling stock, railroad, rebuilding
311812 Rolls and buns (including frozen) made in commercial bakeries
326299 Rolls and roll coverings, rubber (e.g., industrial, papermill, painters', steelmill) manufacturing
111219 Romaine lettuce farming, field and seed production
315210 Rompers cut and sew apparel contractors
315240 Rompers, infants', cut and sewn from purchased fabric (except apparel contractors)
541690 Roof consulting services
332322 Roof deck, sheet metal (except stampings), manufacturing
238310 Roof insulation contractor
238160 Roof membrane installation
238160 Roof painting, spraying, or coating
238130 Roof truss (wood) installation
321214 Roof trusses, wood, manufacturing
326299 Roofing (i.e., single ply rubber membrane) manufacturing
324122 Roofing cements, asphalt, made from purchased asphaltic materials
324122 Roofing coatings made from purchased asphaltic materials
238160 Roofing contractors 324122 Roofing felts made from purchased asphaltic materials
444190 Roofing material dealers
423330 Roofing materials (except wood) merchant wholesalers
423310 Roofing materials, wood, merchant wholesalers
327120 Roofing tile, clay, manufacturing
327390 Roofing tile, concrete, manufacturing
238160 Roofing, built-up tar and gravel, installation
332322 Roofing, sheet metal (except stampings), manufacturing
333415 Room air-conditioners manufacturing
423620 Room air-conditioners merchant wholesalers
337122 Room dividers, wood household-type, manufacturing
333414 Room heaters (except portable electric) manufacturing
335210 Room heaters, portable electric, manufacturing
334512 Room thermostats manufacturing
721310 Rooming and boarding houses
325320 Root removing chemicals manufacturing
311221 Root starches manufacturing
332999 Rope fittings manufacturing
332618 Rope, wire, made from purchased wire
314994 Ropes (except wire rope) manufacturing
423840 Ropes (except wire rope) merchant wholesalers
423510 Ropes, wire (except insulated), merchant wholesalers
339910 Rosaries and other small religious articles, precious metal, manufacturing
212291 Roscoelite (vanadium hydromica) mining and/or beneficiating
111421 Rose bush growing 325211 Rosins (i.e., modified resins) manufacturing
325194 Rosins made by distillation of pine gum or pine wood
424690 Rosins merchant wholesalers
333111 Rotary hoes manufacturing
333111 Rotary tillers, farm-type, manufacturing
334514 Rotary type meters, consumption registering, manufacturing
325320 Rotenone insecticides manufacturing
323111 Rotogravure printing (except books)
323120 Rotogravure printing plates and cylinders preparation services
335312 Rotor retainers and housings manufacturing
335312 Rotors (i.e., for motors) manufacturing
325620 Rouge, cosmetic, manufacturing 321920 Round stave baskets (e.g., fruit, vegetable) manufacturing
321912 Rounds or rungs, furniture, hardwood, manufacturing
331110 Rounds, tube, steel, made in iron and steel mills
423990 Roundwood merchant wholesalers
213112 Roustabout mining services, on a contract basis
333991 Routers, handheld power-driven, manufacturing
333249 Roving machinery for textiles manufacturing
236115 Row house (i.e., single-family type) construction general contractors

236117 Row house construction for-sale builders
532284 Rowboat rental
336612 Rowboats manufacturing
713990 Rowing clubs, recreational
112910 Royal jelly production, bees
326220 Rubber and plastics belts and hoses (without fittings) manufacturing
326299 Rubber bands manufacturing
325520 Rubber cements manufacturing
212324 Rubber clay mining and/or beneficiating
238290 Rubber door installation
326199 Rubber floor coverings manufacturing
326291 Rubber goods, mechanical (i.e., extruded, lathe-cut, molded), manufacturing
423840 Rubber goods, mechanical (i.e., extruded, lathe-cut, molded), merchant wholesalers
424210 Rubber goods, medical, merchant wholesalers
325998 Rubber processing preparations (e.g., accelerators, stabilizers) manufacturing
423930 Rubber scrap and scrap tires merchant wholesalers
339940 Rubber stamps manufacturing
424120 Rubber stamps merchant wholesalers
313220 Rubber thread and yarns, fabric covered, manufacturing
326299 Rubber tubing manufacturing
333249 Rubber working machinery manufacturing
424990 Rubber, crude, merchant wholesalers
325212 Rubber, synthetic, manufacturing
313320 Rubberizing purchased capes
313320 Rubberizing purchased cloaks
313320 Rubberizing purchased clothing
313320 Rubberizing purchased coats
313320 Rubberizing purchased textiles and apparel
212399 Rubbing stones mining and/or beneficiating
562111 Rubbish (i.e., nonhazardous solid waste) hauling, local
562111 Rubbish collection services
562213 Rubbish disposal combustors or incinerators
562212 Rubbish disposal landfills
484230 Rubbish hauling without collection or disposal, truck, long-distance
562119 Rubble hauling, local
562119 Rubble removal services
212399 Ruby mining and/or beneficiating
532289 Rug and carpet rental
561740 Rug cleaning plants
325612 Rug cleaning preparations manufacturing
561740 Rug cleaning services
442210 Rug stores
314110 Rugs and carpets made from textile materials
423220 Rugs merchant wholesalers
321999 Rulers and rules (except slide), wood, manufacturing
332216 Rulers, metal, manufacturing
326199 Rulers, plastics, manufacturing
334519 Rules, slide, manufacturing
624221 Runaway youth shelters
488119 Runway maintenance services
237310 Runway, airport, line painting (e.g., striping)
485210 Rural bus services
324191 Rust arresting petroleum compounds made from refined petroleum
325998 Rust preventive preparations manufacturing
325612 Rust removers manufacturing
238320 Rustproofing (except automotive)
332812 Rustproofing metals and metal products for the trade
811198 Rustproofing shops, automotive
111219 Rutabaga farming, field and seed production
212299 Ruthenium ore mining and/or beneficiating
212299 Rutile mining and/or beneficiating
721211 RV (recreational vehicle) parks
532120 RV (recreational vehicle) rental or leasing
441210 RV dealers
111199 Rye farming, field and seed production
311211 Rye flour manufacturing
311213 Rye malt manufacturing
111998 Ryegrass seed farming
114111 Sablefish fishing
325199 Saccharin manufacturing
325620 Sachet, scented, manufacturing
322220 Sacks, multiwall, made from purchased uncoated paper
424130 Sacks, paper, merchant wholesalers
713990 Saddle horse rental services, recreational
325612 Saddle soaps manufacturing

321999 Saddle trees, wood, manufacturing
316110 Saddlery leather manufacturing
424910 Saddlery merchant wholesalers
332999 Saddlery parts, metal, manufacturing
811430 Saddlery repair shops without retailing new saddlery
451110 Saddlery stores
316998 Saddles and parts, leather, manufacturing
332999 Safe deposit boxes and chests, metal, manufacturing
332999 Safe doors and linings, metal, manufacturing
332999 Safes, metal, manufacturing
423420 Safes, security, merchant wholesalers 332911
Safety (i.e., pop-off) valves, industrial-type, manufacturing
316998 Safety belts, leather, manufacturing
541690 Safety consulting services
423990 Safety deposit boxes merchant wholesalers
423990 Safety devices (e.g., eye shields, face shields) merchant wholesalers
325920 Safety fuses, blasting, manufacturing
327215 Safety glass (including motor vehicle) made from purchased glass
238990 Safety net system, erecting and dismantling at construction site
339993 Safety pins manufacturing
332215 Safety razor blades manufacturing
332215 Safety razors manufacturing
111120 Safflower farming, field and seed production
311225 Safflower oil made from purchased oils
311224 Safflower oil made in crushing mills
339920 Sailboards manufacturing
336612 Sailboat building, not done in shipyards
441222 Sailboat dealers
532284 Sailboat rental
713930 Sailing clubs with marinas
713990 Sailing clubs without marinas
336611 Sailing ships, commercial, manufacturing
314910 Sails made from purchased fabrics
312130 Sake manufacturing
325180 Sal soda (i.e., washing soda) manufacturing
311423 Salad dressing mixes, dry, made in dehydration plants
311942 Salad dressing mixes, dry, manufacturing
311941 Salad dressings manufacturing
424490 Salad dressings merchant wholesalers
424490 Salad oils merchant wholesalers
311991 Salads, fresh or refrigerated, manufacturing
424480 Salads, prepackaged, merchant wholesalers
424120 Sales books merchant wholesalers
323111 Sales books, manifold, printing
522220 Sales financing
541613 Sales management consulting services
325199 Salicylic acid (except medicinal) manufacturing
325411 Salicylic acid, medicinal, uncompounded, manufacturing
212391 Salines (except common salt) mining and/or beneficiating
114111 Salmon fishing
236220 Salon construction
311421 Salsa canning
325998 Salt (except table) manufacturing
311942 Salt substitute manufacturing
213112 Salt water disposal systems, oil and gas field, on a contract basis
212393 Salt, common, mining and/or beneficiating
212393 Salt, rock, mining and/or beneficiating
311942 Salt, table, manufacturing
424490 Salt, table, merchant wholesalers
311612 Salted meats made from purchased carcasses
311821 Saltines manufacturing
424210 Salts, bath, merchant wholesalers
424690 Salts, industrial, merchant wholesalers
423930 Salvage, scrap, merchant wholesalers
334516 Sample analysis instruments (except medical) manufacturing
316998 Sample cases, all materials, manufacturing
334519 Sample changers, nuclear radiation, manufacturing
541870 Sample direct distribution services
323120 Samples mounting
541910 Sampling services, statistical
423320 Sand (except industrial) merchant wholesalers
212321 Sand and gravel quarrying (i.e., construction grade) and/or beneficiating
331524 Sand castings, aluminum, unfinished, manufacturing
331529 Sand castings, nonferrous metals (except aluminum), unfinished, manufacturing
484220 Sand hauling, local

484230 Sand hauling, long-distance
333120 Sand mixers manufacturing
212322 Sand, blast, quarrying and/or beneficiating
212321 Sand, construction grade, quarrying and/or beneficiating
212322 Sand, industrial (e.g., engine, filtration, glass grinding, proppant), quarrying and/or beneficiating
423840 Sand, industrial, merchant wholesalers
316210 Sandals, children's, manufacturing
316210 Sandals, men's footwear, manufacturing
316210 Sandals, plastics or plastics soled fabric upper, manufacturing
316210 Sandals, rubber or rubber soled fabric upper, manufacturing
316210 Sandals, women's footwear, manufacturing
332813 Sandblasting metals and metal products for the trade
213112 Sandblasting pipelines on lease, oil and gas field on a contract basis
238990 Sandblasting, building exterior
333991 Sanders, handheld power-driven, manufacturing
333318 Sanding machines, floor, manufacturing
333243 Sanding machines, woodworking-type, stationary, manufacturing
333243 Sandpaper making machines manufacturing
327910 Sandpaper manufacturing 212319 Sandstone crushed and broken stone mining
212311 Sandstone mining or quarrying
722513 Sandwich shops, limited-service
311612 Sandwich spreads, meat, made from purchased carcasses
311941 Sandwich spreads, salad dressing based, manufacturing
335210 Sandwich toasters and grills, household-type electric, manufacturing
424490 Sandwiches merchant wholesalers 311991
Sandwiches, fresh (i.e., assembled and packaged for wholesale market), manufacturing
322212 Sanitary food container, folding, made from purchased paperboard
424130 Sanitary food containers (e.g., disposable plastics, paper, paperboard) merchant wholesalers
322219 Sanitary food containers (except folding) made from purchased paper or paperboard
562212 Sanitary landfills
322291 Sanitary napkins and tampons made from purchased paper or textile fiber
322121 Sanitary napkins and tampons made in paper mills
322121 Sanitary paper products (except newsprint, uncoated groundwood) made in paper mills
424130 Sanitary paper products merchant wholesalers
322121 Sanitary paper stock manufacturing
322291 Sanitary products made from purchased sanitary paper stock
322121 Sanitary products made in paper mills
237110 Sanitary sewer construction 332999 Sani-
tary ware (e.g., bathtubs, lavatories, sinks), metal, manufacturing
238220 Sanitary ware installation
423720 Sanitary ware, china or enameled iron, merchant wholesalers
541620 Sanitation consulting services
926130 Sanitation districts, nonoperating
924110 Sanitation engineering agencies, government
212399 Sapphire mining and/or beneficiating
325220 Saran (i.e., polyvinylidene chloride) fibers and filaments manufacturing
332613 Sash balance springs, light gauge, made from purchased wire or strip
332321 Sash, door and window, metal, manufacturing
321911 Sash, door and window, wood and covered wood, manufacturing
316998 Satchels, all materials, manufacturing
334220 Satellite antennas manufacturing
334220 Satellite communications equipment manufacturing
238290 Satellite dish, household-type, installation
517311 Satellite master antenna television service (SMATV)
515111 Satellite radio networks
237130 Satellite receiving station construction
517410 Satellite telecommunication carriers
517410 Satellite telecommunication resellers
517919 Satellite telemetry operations on a contract or fee basis
517311 Satellite television distribution systems
515210 Satellite television networks
517919 Satellite tracking stations

325130 Satin white pigments manufacturing
335311 Saturable transformers manufacturing
324122 Saturated felts made from purchased paper
322121 Saturated felts made in paper mills
311423 Sauce mixes, dry, made in dehydration plants
311942 Sauce mixes, dry, manufacturing
311941 Sauces (except tomato-based) manufacturing
311941 Sauces for meat (except tomato-based) manufacturing
311941 Sauces for seafood (except tomato-based) manufacturing
311941 Sauces for vegetable (except tomato-based) manufacturing
311421 Sauces, tomato-based, canning
311421 Sauerkraut manufacturing
335210 Sauna heaters, electric, manufacturing
321992 Sauna rooms, prefabricated, wood, manufacturing
812199 Saunas
311612 Sausage and similar cased products made from purchased carcasses
424490 Sausage casings merchant wholesalers
311612 Sausage casings, collagen, made from purchased hides
311611 Sausage casings, natural, produced in slaughtering plant
326121 Sausage casings, plastics, manufacturing
522120 Savings and loan associations (S&L)
551112 Savings and loan holding companies
524113 Savings bank life insurance carriers, direct
522120 Savings banks
522120 Savings institutions
332216 Saw blades, all types, manufacturing
811411 Saw repair and maintenance (except sawmills) without retailing new saws
321113 Sawdust and shavings (i.e., sawmill byproducts) manufacturing
424990 Sawdust merchant wholesalers
321999 Sawdust, regrinding
321113 Sawed lumber made in sawmills
321912 Sawed lumber, resawing purchased lumber
333517 Sawing machines, metalworking, manufacturing
333243 Sawmill equipment manufacturing
532490 Sawmill machinery rental or leasing
423830 Sawmill machinery, equipment, and supplies merchant wholesalers
321113 Sawmills
333243 Saws, bench and table, power-driven, woodworking-type, manufacturing
332216 Saws, hand, nonpowered, manufacturing
333991 Saws, handheld power-driven, manufacturing
423830 Saws, industrial, merchant wholesalers
339112 Saws, surgical, manufacturing
339992 Saxophones and parts manufacturing
238990 Scaffold erecting and dismantling
423810 Scaffolding merchant wholesalers
532490 Scaffolding rental or leasing
332323 Scaffolds, metal, manufacturing
334519 Scalers, nuclear radiation, manufacturing
333997 Scales, including laboratory-type, manufacturing
423490 Scales, laboratory (except dental and medical), merchant wholesalers
114112 Scallop fishing
812199 Scalp treating services
423430 Scanners, computer, merchant wholesalers
518210 Scanning services, optical
334516 Scanning tunneling microscopes manufacturing
333243 Scarfing machines, woodworking-type, manufacturing
333519 Scarfing units, rolling mill machinery, metalworking, manufacturing 333120
Scarifiers, road, manufacturing 325130 Scarlet 2 R
lake manufacturing 315210 Scarves cut and sew apparel contractors 315990 Scarves cut and sewn from
purchased fabric (except apparel contractors)
315190 Scarves made in apparel knitting mills
336350 Scattershield, engine, manufacturing
711510 Scenery designers, independent theatrical
532490 Scenery, theatrical, rental or leasing
487990 Scenic and sightseeing excursions, aerial
487110 Scenic and sightseeing excursions, land
487210 Scenic and sightseeing excursions, water
481112 Scheduled air freight carriers
481112 Scheduled air freight transportation
481111 Scheduled air passenger carriers
481111 Scheduled air passenger transportation

212299 Scheelite mining and/or beneficiating
313220 Schiffli machine embroideries manufacturing
333249 Schiffli machinery manufacturing
212319 Schist, mica, crushed and broken stone, mining and/or beneficiating
212311 Schist, mica, mining or quarrying
511120 Scholarly journal publishers (except exclusive Internet publishing)
511120 Scholarly journal publishers and printing combined
519130 Scholarly journal publishers, exclusively on Internet
323111 Scholarly journals commercial printing (except screen) without publishing
323113 Scholarly journals screen printing without publishing
813211 Scholarship trusts (i.e., grantmaking, charitable trust foundations)
511120 Scholastic magazine and periodical publishers (except exclusive Internet publishing)
511120 Scholastic magazine and periodical publishers and printing combined
519130 Scholastic magazine and periodical publishers, exclusively on Internet
323111 Scholastic magazines and periodicals commercial printing (except screen) without publishing
323113 Scholastic magazines and periodicals screen printing without publishing
611110 School boards, elementary and secondary
511130 School book publishers (except exclusive Internet publishing)
511130 School book publishers and printing combined
519130 School book publishers, exclusively on Internet
323117 School books printing and binding without publishing
323117 School books printing without publishing
236220 School building construction
611710 School bus attendant services
423110 School bus merchant wholesalers
532120 School bus rental or leasing
485410 School bus services
336211 School buses assembling on purchased chassis
611110 School districts, elementary or secondary
423490 School equipment and supplies (except books, furniture) merchant wholesalers
337127 School furniture manufacturing
423210 School furniture merchant wholesalers
541921 School photography (i.e., portrait photography) services
453210 School supply stores
511130 School textbook publishers (except exclusive Internet publishing)
511130 School textbook publishers and printing combined
519130 School textbook publishers, exclusively on Internet
323120 School textbooks binding without printing
448190 School uniform stores
611110 Schools for the handicapped, elementary or secondary
611110 Schools for the intellectually and developmentally disabled (except preschool, job training, vocational rehabilitation)
611110 Schools for the physically disabled, elementary or secondary
611512 Schools, aviation
611511 Schools, barber
611511 Schools, beauty
611410 Schools, business, not offering academic degrees
611310 Schools, correspondence, college level
611511 Schools, cosmetology
611610 Schools, drama (except academic)
611110 Schools, elementary
611210 Schools, junior college
611210 Schools, junior college vocational
611630 Schools, language
611310 Schools, medical
611310 Schools, music (colleges or universities)
611610 Schools, music (except academic)
611310 Schools, professional (colleges or universities)
611110 Schools, secondary
611620 Schools, sports instruction
712110 Science and technology museums
339930 Science kits (e.g., chemistry sets, microscopes, natural science sets) manufacturing
423920 Science kits and sets merchant wholesalers
327215 Scientific apparatus glassware made from purchased glass
813920 Scientific associations
327215 Scientific glassware made from purchased glass

327212 Scientific glassware, pressed or blown, made in glass making plants
423490 Scientific instruments merchant wholesalers
511120 Scientific journal and periodical publishers (except exclusive Internet publishing)
511120 Scientific journal and periodical publishers and printing combined
519130 Scientific journal and periodical publishers, exclusively on Internet
423490 Scientific laboratory equipment merchant wholesalers
334519 Scintillation detectors manufacturing
335210 Scissors, electric, manufacturing
332215 Scissors, nonelectric, manufacturing
332216 Scoops, metal (except kitchen-type), manufacturing
321999 Scoops, wood, manufacturing
339930 Scooters, children's, manufacturing
339950 Scoreboards manufacturing
212399 Scoria mining and/or beneficiating
313310 Scouring and combing textile fibers
325611 Scouring cleansers (e.g., pastes, powders) manufacturing
332999 Scouring pads, soap impregnated, manufacturing
813410 Scouting organizations 423930 Scrap materials (e.g., automotive, industrial) merchant wholesalers
323111 Scrapbooks and refills manufacturing
424120 Scrapbooks merchant wholesalers 333131 Scraper loaders, underground mining-type, manufacturing
333120 Scrapers, construction-type, manufacturing
332321 Screen doors, metal frame, manufacturing
323120 Screen for printing, preparation services
323113 Screen printing (except books, manifold business forms, grey goods)
323113 Screen printing apparel and textile products (e.g., caps, napkins, placemats, T-shirts, towels) (except grey goods)
313310 Screen printing fabric grey goods
323113 Screen printing textile banners
325910 Screen process inks manufacturing
333999 Screening and sifting machinery for general industrial use manufacturing
423830 Screening machinery and equipment, industrial, merchant wholesalers
333120 Screening machinery, portable, manufacturing
333131 Screening machinery, stationary, manufacturing
212399 Screening peat
212113 Screening plants, anthracite
212111 Screening plants, bituminous coal or lignite
326199 Screening, window, plastics, manufacturing
711510 Screenplay writers, independent 334419 Screens for liquid crystal display (LCD) manufacturing
332321 Screens, door and window, metal frame, manufacturing
321911 Screens, door and window, wood framed, manufacturing
333316 Screens, projection (i.e., motion picture, overhead, slide), manufacturing
423310 Screens, window and door, merchant wholesalers
333517 Screw and nut slotting machines, metalworking, manufacturing
333922 Screw conveyors manufacturing
332216 Screw drivers, nonelectric, manufacturing
332722 Screw eyes, metal, manufacturing
333519 Screwdowns and boxes machinery, metal, manufacturing
333991 Screwdrivers and nut drivers, handheld power-driven, manufacturing
333519 Screwdriving machines manufacturing
332216 Screwjacks manufacturing
332722 Screws, metal, manufacturing
711510 Script writers, independent
238220 Scrubber, air purification, installation
339920 Scuba diving equipment manufacturing
611620 Scuba instruction, camps, or schools
711510 Sculptors, independent
611610 Sculpture instruction
327420 Sculptures (e.g., gypsum, plaster of paris) manufacturing
327110 Sculptures, architectural, clay, manufacturing
332216 Scythes manufacturing
212399 Scythestones mining and/or beneficiating
114111 Sea bass fishing
114111 Sea herring fishing
713990 Sea kayaking, recreational
112519 Sea plant agriculture
114111 Sea trout fishing

114112 Sea urchin fishing
424460 Seafood (except canned, packaged frozen) merchant wholesalers
311710 Seafood and seafood products canning
311710 Seafood and seafood products curing
311710 Seafood and seafood products manufacturing
311710 Seafood dinners, frozen, manufacturing
445220 Seafood markets
424490 Seafood, canned, merchant wholesalers
424420 Seafoods, packaged frozen, merchant wholesalers
339940 Seal presses (e.g., notary), hand operated, manufacturing
424690 Sealants merchant wholesalers
335110 Sealed beam automotive light bulbs manufacturing
325520 Sealing compounds for pipe threads and joints manufacturing
423840 Seals merchant wholesalers
339991 Seals, grease or oil, manufacturing
333992 Seam welding equipment manufacturing
334511 Search and detection systems and instruments manufacturing
519130 Search portals, Internet 335129 Searchlights, electric and nonelectric, manufacturing
453220 Seasonal and holiday decoration stores
721110 Seasonal hotels without casinos
561730 Seasonal property maintenance services (i.e., snow plowing in winter, landscaping during other seasons)
311942 Seasoning salt manufacturing
336360 Seat belts, motor vehicle and aircraft, manufacturing
423120 Seat belts, motor vehicle, merchant wholesalers
423120 Seat covers, automotive, merchant wholesalers
321999 Seat covers, rattan, manufacturing
326150 Seat cushions, foam plastics (except polystyrene), manufacturing
316998 Seatbelts, leather, manufacturing
336360 Seats for public conveyances, manufacturing
336360 Seats, railroad, manufacturing
321999 Seats, toilet, wood, manufacturing
237990 Seawall, wave protection, construction
488310 Seaway operation
112519 Seaweed farming
114119 Seaweed gathering
311710 Seaweed processing (e.g., dulse)
325199 Sebacic acid esters manufacturing 325199 Sebacic acid manufacturing 611630 Second language instruction 522294 Secondary market financing (i.e., buying, pooling, repackaging loans for sale to others)
331492 Secondary refining of nonferrous metals (except aluminum, copper)
611110 Secondary schools offering both academic and technical courses
331492 Secondary smelting of nonferrous metals (except aluminum, copper)
453310 Secondhand merchandise stores
611410 Secretarial schools
561410 Secretarial services
332311 Sections for prefabricated metal buildings manufacturing
321992 Sections, prefabricated wood building, manufacturing
523120 Securities brokerages
523120 Securities brokers' offices
523991 Securities custodians
523110 Securities dealers (i.e., acting as a principal in dealing securities to investors)
523110 Securities dealing (i.e., acting as a principal in dealing securities to investors)
523110 Securities distributing (i.e., acting as a principal in dealing securities to investors)
523210 Securities exchanges 523120 Securities floor brokers
523110 Securities floor traders (i.e., acting as a principal in dealing securities to investors)
523110 Securities flotation companies 523999 Securities holders' protective services 523110 Securities originating (i.e., acting as a principal in dealing securities to investors)
926150 Securities regulation commissions
523910 Securities speculators for own account
523110 Securities trading (i.e., acting as a principal in dealing securities to investors)
523999 Securities transfer agencies
523110 Securities underwriting

561621 Security alarm systems sales combined with installation, repair, or monitoring services
238210 Security and fire system, installation only
541690 Security consulting services
561612 Security guard services
611519 Security guard training
561612 Security patrol services
423420 Security safes merchant wholesalers
561621 Security system monitoring services
423610 Security systems merchant wholesalers
325412 Sedative preparations manufacturing
212399 Sedge peat mining and/or beneficiating
237990 Sediment control system construction
333131 Sedimentary mineral machinery manufacturing
314910 Seed bags made from purchased woven or knitted materials
115112 Seed bed preparing
115114 Seed cleaning
322230 Seed packets made from purchased paper
115114 Seed processing, postharvest for propagation
541380 Seed testing laboratories or services
325320 Seed treatment preparations manufacturing
333111 Seeders, farm-type, manufacturing
333112 Seeders, lawn and garden-type, manufacturing
115112 Seeding crops
561730 Seeding lawns
424450 Seeds (e.g., canned, roasted, salted) merchant wholesalers
424910 Seeds (e.g., field, flower, garden) merchant wholesalers
311911 Seeds, snack (e.g., canned, cooked, roasted, salted) manufacturing
541360 Seismic geophysical surveying services
213112 Seismograph exploration (except surveying) for oil and gas on a contract basis
334519 Seismographs manufacturing
334519 Seismometers manufacturing 334519 Seismoscopes manufacturing 212399 Selenite mining and/or beneficiating 331491 Selenium bar, rod, sheet, strip, and tubing made from purchased metals or scrap
325180 Selenium compounds, not specified elsewhere by process, manufacturing
325180 Selenium dioxide manufacturing 331492 Selenium recovering from scrap and/or alloying purchased metals
331410 Selenium refining, primary
611699 Self defense (except martial arts) instruction
624190 Self-help organizations (except for disabled persons, the elderly, persons diagnosed with intellectual and developmental disabilities)
624120 Self-help organizations for disabled persons, the elderly, and persons diagnosed with intellectual and developmental disabilities
624110 Self-help organizations, youth
525190 Self-insurance funds (except employee benefit funds)
811192 Self-service car washes
812310 Self-service drycleaners and laundries
531130 Self-storage unit rental or leasing
531130 Self-storage warehousing
531210 Selling real estate for others (i.e., agents, brokers)
531210 Selling time-share condominiums for others (i.e., agents, brokers)
115210 Semen collection
424590 Semen, bovine, merchant wholesalers
212111 Semianthracite surface mining and/or beneficiating
212112 Semianthracite underground mining or mining and beneficiating
212111 Semibituminous coal surface mining and/or beneficiating
212112 Semibituminous coal underground mining or mining and beneficiating
333242 Semiconductor assembly and packaging machinery manufacturing
335999 Semiconductor battery chargers manufacturing
334413 Semiconductor circuit networks (i.e., solid-state integrated circuits) manufacturing
334413 Semiconductor devices manufacturing
423690 Semiconductor devices merchant wholesalers
334413 Semiconductor dice and wafers manufacturing
335999 Semiconductor high-voltage power supplies manufacturing
333242 Semiconductor making machinery manufacturing

334413 Semiconductor memory chips manufacturing
334515 Semiconductor test equipment manufacturing
333618 Semidiesel engines manufacturing 423510
Semi-finished metal products merchant wholesalers
611110 Seminaries, below university grade
611310 Seminaries, theological, offering baccalaureate or graduate degrees
212399 Semiprecious stones mining and/or beneficiating
711211 Semiprofessional baseball clubs
711211 Semiprofessional football clubs
711211 Semiprofessional sports clubs
331511 Semisteel foundries
532120 Semi-trailer rental or leasing
336212 Semi-trailers manufacturing
311211 Semolina flour manufacturing
624120 Senior citizens activity centers
813311 Senior citizens advocacy organizations
813410 Senior citizens' associations, social
624120 Senior citizens centers
623312 Senior citizens' homes without nursing care
485991 Senior citizens transportation services
561312 Senior executive search services
325992 Sensitized cloth or paper (e.g., blueprint, photographic) manufacturing
333316 Sensitometers, photographic, manufacturing
334510 Sentinel, cardiac, manufacturing
238910 Septic system contractors
238910 Septic tank and weeping tile installation
562991 Septic tank cleaning services
562991 Septic tank pumping (i.e., cleaning) services
423390 Septic tanks (except concrete) merchant wholesalers
423320 Septic tanks, concrete, merchant wholesalers
332420 Septic tanks, heavy gauge metal, manufacturing
326199 Septic tanks, plastics or fiberglass, manufacturing
334512 Sequencing controls for electric heating equipment manufacturing
335999 Series capacitors (except electronic) manufacturing
212319 Serpentine crushed and broken stone mining and/or beneficiating
212311 Serpentine mining or quarrying
325414 Serums (except diagnostic substances) manufacturing
315210 Service apparel, washable, cut and sew apparel contractors
315220 Service apparel, washable, men's and boys', cut and sewn from purchased fabric (except apparel contractors)
315240 Service apparel, washable, women's and girls', cut and sewn from purchased fabric (except apparel contractors)
423850 Service establishment equipment and supplies merchant wholesalers 813910
Service industries associations 237120 Service line, gas and oil, construction 811310 Service machinery and equipment repair and maintenance services
561720 Service station cleaning and degreasing services
236220 Service station construction
447190 Service stations, gasoline
213111 Service well drilling on a contract basis
213112 Servicing oil and gas wells on a contract basis
337124 Serving carts, metal household-type, manufacturing
337122 Serving carts, wood household-type, manufacturing
335312 Servomotors manufacturing
111120 Sesame farming, field and seed production
711510 Set designers, independent theatrical
541191 Settlement offices, real estate
525920 Settlement trust funds
322219 Setup (i.e., not shipped flat) boxes made from purchased paperboard
322130 Setup boxboard stock manufacturing
237110 Sewage collection and disposal line construction
237110 Sewage disposal plant construction
221320 Sewage disposal plants 333318
Sewage treatment equipment manufacturing
237110 Sewage treatment plant construction
221320 Sewage treatment plants or facilities
562998 Sewer cleaning and rodding services
562998 Sewer cleanout services
237110 Sewer construction

238220 Sewer hookup and connection, building

237110 Sewer main, pipe and connection, construction

327120 Sewer pipe and fittings, clay, manufacturing

331511 Sewer pipe, cast iron, manufacturing

423320 Sewer pipe, clay (except refractory), merchant wholesalers

327332 Sewer pipe, concrete, manufacturing

423510 Sewer pipe, metal, merchant wholesalers

221320 Sewer systems

424310 Sewing accessories merchant wholesalers

339999 Sewing and mending kits assembling

316998 Sewing cases (except metal) manufacturing

339910 Sewing cases, precious metal, manufacturing

315210 Sewing fabric owned by others for apparel

321999 Sewing machine cabinets, wood, manufacturing

443141 Sewing machine stores, household-type

811412 Sewing machine, household-type, repair shops without retailing new sewing machines

333249 Sewing machines (including household-type) manufacturing

423620 Sewing machines, household-type, merchant wholesalers

423830 Sewing machines, industrial, merchant wholesalers

451130 Sewing supply stores

313110 Sewing threads manufacturing

334511 Sextants (except surveying) manufacturing

334519 Sextants, surveying, manufacturing

337920 Shade pulls, window, manufacturing

335121 Shades, lamp (except glass, plastics), residential-type, manufacturing

337920 Shades, window (except outdoor canvas awnings), manufacturing

213113 Shaft sinking for coal mines on a contract basis

213114 Shaft sinking for metal mines on a contract basis

238160 Shake and shingle, roof, installation

321113 Shakes (i.e., hand split shingles) manufacturing

212325 Shale (except oil shale) mining and/or beneficiating

327992 Shale, expanded, manufacturing 211120

Shale, oil, mining and/or beneficiating

111219 Shallot farming, field and seed production

325620 Shampoos and conditioners, hair, manufacturing

316998 Shanks, shoe, leather, manufacturing

333243 Shapers, woodworking-type, manufacturing

114111 Shark fishing

339994 Shaving brushes manufacturing 333517

Shaving machines, metalworking, manufacturing

325620 Shaving preparations (e.g., creams, gels, lotions, powders) manufacturing

424210 Shaving preparations merchant wholesalers

333517 Shearing machines, metal forming, manufacturing

316110 Shearling (i.e., prepared sheepskin) manufacturing

333991 Shears and nibblers, handheld power-driven, manufacturing

332215 Shears, nonelectric, household-type (e.g., kitchen, barber, tailor) manufacturing

332216 Shears, nonelectric, tool-type (e.g., garden, pruners, tinsnip), manufacturing

333111 Shears, powered, for use on animals, manufacturing

322121 Sheathing paper (except newsprint, uncoated groundwood) made in paper mills

324122 Sheathing, asphalt saturated, made from refined petroleum

238130 Sheathing, wood, installation 333613

Sheaves, mechanical power transmission, manufacturing

332311 Sheds (e.g., garden, storage, utility), prefabricated metal, manufacturing

321992 Sheds (e.g., garden, storage, utility), prefabricated wood, manufacturing

115210 Sheep dipping and shearing 112410 Sheep

farming (e.g., meat, milk, wool production)

424520 Sheep merchant wholesalers

333111 Sheep shears, powered, manufacturing

326140 Sheet (i.e., board), polystyrene foam insulation, manufacturing

423730 Sheet metal duct work (heating and air-conditioning) merchant wholesalers

238220 Sheet metal duct work installation

333517 Sheet metal forming machines manufacturing

238160 Sheet metal roofing installation

423330 Sheet metal roofing materials merchant wholesalers
332322 Sheet metal work (except stampings) manufacturing
611513 Sheet metal workers' apprenticeship training
323111 Sheet music commercial printing (except screen) without publishing
424990 Sheet music merchant wholesalers
512230 Sheet music publishers 512230 Sheet music publishers and printing combined
323113 Sheet music screen printing without publishing
451140 Sheet music stores
331110 Sheet pilings, plain, iron or steel, made in iron and steel mills
331315 Sheet, aluminum, made by flat rolling purchased aluminum
331315 Sheet, aluminum, made in integrated secondary smelting and flat rolling mills
331420 Sheet, copper and copper alloy, made from purchased copper or in integrated secondary smelting and rolling, drawing or extruding plants
326130 Sheet, laminated plastics (except flexible packaging), manufacturing
326113 Sheet, plastics, unlaminated (except packaging), manufacturing
326299 Sheeting, rubber, manufacturing 314120 Sheets and pillowcases made from purchased fabrics
313210 Sheets and pillowcases made in broadwoven fabric mills
331110 Sheets, steel, made in iron and steel mills
311119 Shell crushing and grinding for animal feed
311119 Shell crushing for feed
332993 Shell loading and assembly plants
212399 Shell mining and/or beneficiating
339999 Shell novelties
331110 Shell slugs, steel, made in iron and steel mills
325510 Shellac manufacturing
424950 Shellac merchant wholesalers
311710 Shellfish and shellfish products canning
311710 Shellfish and shellfish products manufacturing
311710 Shellfish curing
114112 Shellfish fishing (e.g., clam, crab, oyster, shrimp)
112512 Shellfish hatcheries
332993 Shells, artillery, manufacturing
332992 Shells, small arms (i.e., 30 mm. or less, 1.18 inch or less), manufacturing
624310 Sheltered workshops (i.e., work experience centers)
624221 Shelters (except for victims of domestic or international disasters or conflicts), emergency
624230 Shelters for victims of domestic or international disasters or conflicts, emergency
624221 Shelters, battered women's
624221 Shelters, homeless
624221 Shelters, runaway youth
624221 Shelters, temporary (e.g., battered women's, homeless, runaway youth)
337215 Shelving (except wire) manufacturing
423440 Shelving, commercial, merchant wholesalers
238390 Shelving, metal, constructed on site
332618 Shelving, wire, made from purchased wire
238350 Shelving, wood, constructed on site
332812 Sherardizing of metals and metal products for the trade
311520 Sherbets manufacturing
922120 Sheriffs' offices (except court functions only)
922110 Sheriffs' offices, court functions only
332999 Shims, metal, manufacturing
321113 Shingle mills, wood
423330 Shingles (except wood) merchant wholesalers
324122 Shingles made from purchased asphaltic materials
423310 Shingles, wood, merchant wholesalers
321113 Shingles, wood, sawed or hand split, manufacturing
331529 Ship and boat propellers, cast brass, bronze and copper (except die-casting), unfinished, manufacturing
424990 Ship chandler merchant wholesalers
483113 Ship chartering with crew, coastal or Great Lakes freight transportation (including St. Lawrence Seaway)
483114 Ship chartering with crew, coastal or Great Lakes passenger transportation (including St. Lawrence Seaway)
483111 Ship chartering with crew, deep sea freight transportation to or from foreign ports

483112 Ship chartering with crew, deep sea passenger transportation to or from foreign ports
483211 Ship chartering with crew, freight transportation, inland waters (except on Great Lakes system)
483212 Ship chartering with crew, passenger transportation, inland waters (except on Great Lakes system)
333923 Ship cranes and derricks manufacturing
561311 Ship crew employment agencies 561311
Ship crew registries 423930 Ship dismantling (except at floating drydocks and shipyards) merchant wholesalers
488390 Ship dismantling at floating drydock
336611 Ship dismantling at shipyards
337127 Ship furniture manufacturing
488320 Ship hold cleaning services
238350 Ship joinery contractors
238320 Ship painting contractors
532411 Ship rental or leasing without crew
336611 Ship repair done in a shipyard
336611 Ship scaling services done at a shipyard
488390 Ship scaling services not done at a shipyard
332312 Ship sections, prefabricated metal, manufacturing
331420 Shipboard cable made from purchased copper in wire drawing plants
331318 Shipboard cable made in aluminum wire drawing plants
488510 Shipping agents (freight forwarding)
314910 Shipping bags made from purchased woven or knitted materials
332439 Shipping barrels, drums, kegs, and pails, light gauge metal, manufacturing
321920 Shipping cases and drums, wood, wirebound, manufacturing
321920 Shipping cases, wood, nailed or lock corner, manufacturing
813910 Shipping companies' associations 423840
Shipping containers (except disposable plastics, paper) merchant wholesalers
322211 Shipping containers made from purchased paperboard
322211 Shipping containers, corrugated, made from purchased paper or paperboard
321920 Shipping crates, wood, manufacturing
483113 Shipping freight to and from domestic ports (i.e., coastal, deep sea (including Puerto Rico), Great Lakes system (including St. Lawrence Seaway))
483111 Shipping freight to or from foreign ports, deep sea
483211 Shipping freight, inland waters (except on Great Lakes system)
326150 Shipping pads and shaped cushioning, foam plastics (except polystyrene), manufacturing
326140 Shipping pads and shaped cushioning, polystyrene foam, manufacturing
423840 Shipping pails, metal, merchant wholesalers
323111 Shipping registers commercial printing (except screen) without publishing
323113 Shipping registers screen printing without publishing
424130 Shipping supplies, paper and disposable plastics, merchant wholesalers
336611 Ships (i.e., not suitable or intended for personal use) manufacturing
423860 Ships merchant wholesalers 517312 Ship-
to-shore broadcasting communication carriers (except satellite)
336611 Shipyard (i.e., facility capable of building ships)
315210 Shirts, outerwear, cut and sew apparel contractors
315190 Shirts, outerwear, made in apparel knitting mills
315220 Shirts, outerwear, men's and boys', cut and sewn from purchased fabric (except apparel contractors)
315220 Shirts, outerwear, unisex (i.e., sized without regard to gender), cut and sewn from purchased fabric (except apparel contractors)
315240 Shirts, outerwear, women's, girls', and infants', cut and sewn from purchased fabric (except apparel contractors)
315210 Shirts, underwear, cut and sew apparel contractors
315190 Shirts, underwear, made in apparel knitting mills
315220 Shirts, underwear, men's and boys', cut and sewn from purchased fabric (except apparel contractors)
315240 Shirts, underwear, women's, girls', and infants', cut and sewn from purchased fabric (except apparel contractors)
111411 Shitake mushroom farming

336330 Shock absorbers, automotive, truck, and bus, manufacturing
448210 Shoe (except bowling, golf, spiked) stores
424340 Shoe accessories merchant wholesalers
326299 Shoe and boot parts (e.g., heels, soles, soling strips), rubber, manufacturing
322212 Shoe boxes, folding, made from purchased paperboard
322219 Shoe boxes, setup, made from purchased paperboard
541490 Shoe design services 321999 Shoe display forms, all materials, manufacturing
316998 Shoe kits (i.e., cases), all materials, manufacturing
333249 Shoe making and repairing machinery manufacturing
423830 Shoe manufacturing and repairing machinery merchant wholesalers
326199 Shoe parts (e.g., heels, soles), plastics, manufacturing
335210 Shoe polishers, household-type electric, manufacturing
325612 Shoe polishes and cleaners manufacturing
423850 Shoe repair materials merchant wholesalers
811430 Shoe repair shops without retailing new shoes
316998 Shoe soles, leather, manufacturing
448210 Shoe stores, orthopedic 451110 Shoe stores, specialty sports footwear (e.g., bowling, golf, spiked)
321999 Shoe stretchers manufacturing
321999 Shoe trees manufacturing
424340 Shoes merchant wholesalers
316210 Shoes, athletic, manufacturing
316210 Shoes, ballet, manufacturing
316210 Shoes, children's and infant's (except orthopedic extension), manufacturing
316210 Shoes, cleated or spiked, all materials, manufacturing
316210 Shoes, men's (except orthopedic extension), manufacturing
339113 Shoes, orthopedic extension, manufacturing
316210 Shoes, plastics or plastics soled fabric upper, manufacturing
316210 Shoes, rubber or rubber soled fabric upper, manufacturing
316210 Shoes, theatrical, manufacturing
316210 Shoes, women's (except orthopedic extension), manufacturing
316210 Shoes, wooden, manufacturing
812990 Shoeshine parlors
812990 Shoeshine services
321920 Shook, box, manufacturing
713990 Shooting clubs, recreational
713990 Shooting galleries
713990 Shooting ranges
423120 Shop equipment, service station, merchant wholesalers
424130 Shopping bags, paper and plastics, merchant wholesalers
531120 Shopping center (i.e., not operating contained businesses) rental or leasing
236220 Shopping center construction
236220 Shopping mall construction
812990 Shopping services, personal
****** Shops -- see type
238990 Shoring, construction
111421 Short rotation woody tree growing (i.e., growing and harvesting cycle ten years or less)
311225 Shortening made from purchased fats and oils
311224 Shortening made in crushing mills
424490 Shortening, vegetable, merchant wholesalers
482112 Short-line railroads
315210 Shorts, outerwear, cut and sew apparel contractors
315190 Shorts, outerwear, made in apparel knitting mills
315220 Shorts, outerwear, men's and boys', cut and sewn from purchased fabric (except apparel contractors)
315240 Shorts, outerwear, women's, girls', and infants', cut and sewn from purchased fabric (except apparel contractors)
315210 Shorts, underwear, cut and sew apparel contractors
315190 Shorts, underwear, made in apparel knitting mills
315220 Shorts, underwear, men's and boys', cut and sewn from purchased fabric (except apparel contractors)
522298 Short-term inventory credit lending
213112 Shot hole drilling, oil and gas field, on a contract basis
332811 Shot peening metal and metal products for the trade
332992 Shot, BB, manufacturing

332992 Shot, lead, manufacturing
332992 Shot, pellet, manufacturing
332992 Shot, steel, manufacturing
238110 Shotcrete contractors
332992 Shotgun shells manufacturing
332994 Shotguns manufacturing
333120 Shovel loaders manufacturing
332216 Shovels, handheld, manufacturing
333120 Shovels, power, manufacturing
423810 Shovels, power, merchant wholesalers
337215 Showcases (except refrigerated) manufacturing
423440 Showcases (except refrigerated) merchant wholesalers
333415 Showcases, refrigerated, manufacturing
423740 Showcases, refrigerated, merchant wholesalers
314120 Shower and bath curtains, all materials, made from purchased fabric or sheet goods
332913 Shower heads, plumbing, manufacturing
332999 Shower receptors, metal, manufacturing
332999 Shower rods, metal, manufacturing
316210 Shower sandals or slippers, rubber, manufacturing
332999 Shower stalls, metal, manufacturing
326191 Shower stalls, plastics or fiberglass, manufacturing
115210 Showing of cattle, hogs, sheep, goats, and poultry
333111 Shredders, farm-type, manufacturing
212399 Shredding peat mining and/or beneficiating
114112 Shrimp fishing
112512 Shrimp production, farm raising 813110
Shrines, religious 561910 Shrink wrapping services 313310 Shrinking textile products and fabrics
561730 Shrub services (e.g., bracing, planting, pruning, removal, spraying, surgery,
trimming)
111421 Shrubbery farming
311710 Shucking and packing fresh shellfish
488490 Shunting of trailers in truck terminals
488210 Shunting trailers in rail terminals
334515 Shunts, instrument, manufacturing
238190 Shutter installation
332321 Shutters, door and window, metal, manufacturing
321918 Shutters, door and window, wood and covered wood, manufacturing
326199 Shutters, plastics, manufacturing
321918 Shutters, wood, manufacturing
485999 Shuttle services (except employee bus)
333249 Shuttles for textile weaving machinery manufacturing
446199 Sick room supply stores
332216 Sickles manufacturing
212210 Siderite mining and/or beneficiating
238990 Sidewalk construction, residential and commercial
237310 Sidewalk, public, construction
238170 Siding (e.g., vinyl, wood, aluminum) installation
423330 Siding (except wood) merchant wholesalers
238170 Siding contractors
444190 Siding dealers
324122 Siding made from purchased asphaltic materials
321113 Siding mills, wood
321113 Siding, dressed lumber, manufacturing
326199 Siding, plastics, manufacturing
332322 Siding, sheet metal (except stampings), manufacturing
423310 Siding, wood, merchant wholesalers
212393 Sienna mining and/or beneficiating
325130 Sienna pigment manufacturing
333241 Sieves and screening equipment (i.e., food manufacturing-type) manufacturing
333249 Sieves and screening equipment, chemical preparation-type, manufacturing
333999 Sieves and screening equipment, general purpose-type, manufacturing
333131 Sieves and screening equipment, mineral beneficiating, manufacturing
332618 Sieves, made from purchased wire, manufacturing
333241 Sifting machine (i.e., food manufacturing-type) manufacturing
333314 Sights, telescopic, manufacturing
487210 Sightseeing boat operation
487110 Sightseeing bus operation
487110 Sightseeing operation, human-drawn vehicle
238990 Sign (except on highways, streets, bridges and tunnels) erection

237310 Sign erection, highway, road, street, or bridge
611630 Sign language instruction
611630 Sign language schools
541930 Sign language services
541890 Sign lettering and painting services
238990 Sign, building, erection
331420 Signal and control cable made from purchased copper in wire drawing plants
331318 Signal and control cable made in aluminum wire drawing plants
334515 Signal generators and averagers manufacturing
423610 Signal systems and devices merchant wholesalers
335311 Signaling transformers, electric, manufacturing
334290 Signals (e.g., highway, pedestrian, railway, traffic) manufacturing
423990 Signs (except electrical) merchant wholesalers
339950 Signs and signboards (except paper, paperboard) manufacturing
423440 Signs, electrical, merchant wholesalers
325180 Silica gel manufacturing
212322 Silica mining and/or beneficiating
212322 Silica sand quarrying and/or beneficiating
325180 Silica, amorphous, manufacturing
325180 Silicofluorides manufacturing
331110 Silicomanganese ferroalloys manufacturing
327910 Silicon carbide abrasives manufacturing
334413 Silicon wafers, chemically doped, manufacturing
334413 Silicon wave guides manufacturing
327992 Silicon, ultra high purity, manufacturing
325199 Silicone (except resins) manufacturing
325211 Silicone resins manufacturing
325212 Silicone rubber manufacturing
313210 Silk fabrics, broadwoven, weaving
541430 Silk screen design services
333249 Silk screens for textile fabrics manufacturing
313110 Silk spun yarns made from purchased fiber
313110 Silk thread manufacturing 313110 Silk throwing, spooling, twisting, or winding of purchased yarn
424590 Silk, raw, merchant wholesalers
212325 Sillimanite mining and/or beneficiating
327390 Sills, concrete, manufacturing
236220 Silo construction
327390 Silos, prefabricated concrete, manufacturing
332311 Silos, prefabricated metal, manufacturing
423390 Silt fence and other fabrics (e.g., for erosion control) merchant wholesalers
331491 Silver and silver alloy bar, rod, sheet, strip, and tubing made from purchased metals or scrap
332999 Silver beating (i.e., foil, leaf)
325180 Silver bromide manufacturing 331410 Silver bullion or dore bar produced at primary metal refineries
325180 Silver chloride manufacturing
325180 Silver compounds, not specified elsewhere by process, manufacturing
332999 Silver foil and leaf not made in rolling mills
331491 Silver foil made by rolling purchased metals or scrap
325180 Silver nitrate manufacturing
212222 Silver ores mining and/or beneficiating
325612 Silver polishes manufacturing
331492 Silver recovering from scrap and/or alloying purchased metals
331492 Silver recovering from used photographic film or X-ray plates
331410 Silver refining, primary 331491 Silver rolling, drawing, or extruding purchased metals or scrap
532289 Silverware rental
423940 Silverware, precious and plated, merchant wholesalers
333515 Sine bars (i.e., a machine tool accessory) manufacturing
711130 Singers, independent
611610 Singing instruction
813410 Singing societies
812990 Singing telegram services
621512 Single photon emission computerized tomography (SPECT) centers
236115 Single-family attached housing construction general contractors
236115 Single-family detached housing construction general contractors
236115 Single-family homes built on land owned by others, general contractors of
236115 Single-family house construction by general contractors

531110 Single-family house rental or leasing
236117 Single-family housing built on own land for sale (i.e., for-sale builders)
236117 Single-family housing construction for-sale builders
213113 Sinking shafts for coal mining on a contract basis
213114 Sinking shafts for metal mining on a contract basis
423720 Sinks merchant wholesalers
332999 Sinks, metal, manufacturing
326191 Sinks, plastics, manufacturing
327110 Sinks, vitreous china, manufacturing
212210 Sintered iron ore produced at the mine
212392 Sintered phosphate rock mining and/or beneficiating
334290 Sirens (e.g., air raid, industrial, marine, vehicle) manufacturing
541611 Site location consulting services
541620 Site remediation consulting services
562910 Site remediation services
541611 Site selection consulting services
812990 Sitting services, house
812910 Sitting services, pet
313310 Sizing of fabrics
339920 Skateboards manufacturing
339920 Skates and parts, ice and roller, manufacturing
713990 Skeet shooting facilities
331110 Skelp, iron or steel, made in iron and steel mills
711510 Sketch artists, independent
321999 Skewers, wood, manufacturing
541320 Ski area design services
541320 Ski area planning services
532284 Ski equipment rental
713920 Ski lift and tow operators
721110 Ski lodges and resorts with accommodations
315210 Ski pants cut and sew apparel contractors
315190 Ski pants made in apparel knitting mills
315220 Ski pants, men's and boys', cut and sewn from purchased fabric (except apparel contractors)
315240 Ski pants, women's, girls', and infants', cut and sewn from purchased fabric (except apparel contractors)
713920 Ski resorts without accommodations
315210 Ski suits cut and sew apparel contractors
315190 Ski suits made in apparel knitting mills
315220 Ski suits, men's and boys', cut and sewn from purchased fabric (except apparel contractors)
315240 Ski suits, women's, girls', and infants', cut and sewn from purchased fabric (except apparel contractors)
237990 Ski tow construction
532490 Skid rental or leasing
213112 Skidding of rigs, oil and gas field, on a contract basis
321920 Skids and pallets, wood or wood and metal combination, manufacturing
423830 Skids merchant wholesalers
332999 Skids, metal, manufacturing
711219 Skiers, independent (i.e., participating in sports events)
423910 Skiing equipment and supplies merchant wholesalers
713920 Skiing facilities, cross country, without accommodations
713920 Skiing facilities, downhill, without accommodations
611620 Skiing instruction, camps, or schools
623110 Skilled nursing facilities
561910 Skin blister packaging services
424210 Skin care preparations merchant wholesalers
611620 Skin diving instruction, camps, or schools
339112 Skin grafting equipment manufacturing
424990 Skins, dressed, merchant wholesalers
424590 Skins, raw, merchant wholesalers
316110 Skins, tanning, currying and finishing
561611 Skip tracing services
316110 Skirting leather manufacturing
315210 Skirts cut and sew apparel contractors
315190 Skirts made in apparel knitting mills
315240 Skirts, tennis, women's and girls', cut and sewn from purchased fabric (except apparel contractors)
315240 Skirts, women's, girls', and infants', cut and sewn from purchased fabric (except apparel contractors)
339920 Skis and skiing equipment (except apparel) manufacturing
316110 Skivers, leather, manufacturing
611620 Sky diving instruction, camps, or schools
238160 Skylight installation

332321 Skylights, metal, manufacturing 331410
Slab, nonferrous metals (except aluminum) primary
331313 Slab, primary aluminum, manufacturing
331110 Slab, steel, made in iron and steel mills
315210 Slacks cut and sew apparel contractors
315190 Slacks made in apparel knitting mills
315210 Slacks, jean-cut casual, cut and sew apparel contractors
315190 Slacks, jean-cut casual, made in apparel knitting mills
315220 Slacks, jean-cut casual, men's and boys', cut and sewn from purchased fabric (except apparel contractors)
315240 Slacks, jean-cut casual, women's, girls', and infants', cut and sewn from purchased fabric (except apparel contractors)
315220 Slacks, men's and boys', cut and sewn from purchased fabric (except apparel contractors)
315240 Slacks, women's, girls', and infants', cut and sewn from purchased fabric (except apparel contractors)
333120 Slag mixers, portable, manufacturing
238140 Slate (i.e., masonry) contractors
423320 Slate and slate products merchant wholesalers
212319 Slate crushed and broken stone mining and/or beneficiating
212311 Slate mining or quarrying
327991 Slate products manufacturing
238340 Slate, interior, installation
311611 Slaughtering, custom
311991 Slaw, cole, fresh, manufacturing
332216 Sledgehammers manufacturing
339930 Sleds, children's, manufacturing
621498 Sleep disorder centers and clinics, outpatient
337215 Sleeper mechanisms, convertible bed, manufacturing
314999 Sleeping bags manufacturing
424320 Sleepwear, men's and boys', merchant wholesalers
424330 Sleepwear, women's, children's, and infants', merchant wholesalers
316998 Sleeves, welder's, leather, manufacturing
333241 Slicing machinery (i.e., food manufacturing-type) manufacturing
339993 Slide fasteners (i.e., zippers) manufacturing
332618 Slings, lifting, made from purchased wire
212324 Slip clay mining and/or beneficiating 335312
Slip rings for motors and generators manufacturing
423220 Slipcovers merchant wholesalers
314120 Slipcovers, all materials, made from purchased materials
316210 Slipper socks made from purchased socks
315110 Slipper socks made in sock mills 424340
Slippers merchant wholesalers 316210 Slippers,
ballet, manufacturing 316210 Slippers, house, manufacturing 315210 Slips cut and sew apparel contractors 315190 Slips made in apparel knitting mills
315240 Slips, women's and girls', cut and sewn from
purchased fabric (except apparel contractors)
522294 SLMA (Student Loan Marketing Association)
713990 Slot car racetracks (i.e., amusement devices)
713290 Slot machine concession operators (i.e., supplying and servicing in others' facilities)
713290 Slot machine parlors
339999 Slot machines manufacturing 333517
Slotting machines, metalworking, manufacturing
562212 Sludge disposal sites
333999 Sludge tables manufacturing
327331 Slumped brick manufacturing
486990 Slurry pipeline transportation
213112 Slush pits and cellars, excavation of, on a contract basis
541940 Small animal veterinary services
332992 Small arms ammunition (i.e., 30 mm. or less, 1.18 inch or less) manufacturing
332994 Small arms manufacturing
926110 Small business development agencies
811411 Small engine repair and maintenance shops
311615 Small game, processing, fresh, frozen, canned or cooked
311615 Small game, slaughtering, dressing and packing
522291 Small loan companies (i.e., unsecured cash loans)
423490 Smartboards merchant wholesalers
334220 Smartphones manufacturing
423690 Smartphones merchant wholesalers
236210 Smelter construction

331492 Smelting and refining of nonferrous metals (except aluminum, copper), secondary
423830 Smelting machinery and equipment merchant wholesalers
331492 Smelting nonferrous metals (except aluminum, copper), secondary
331410 Smelting of nonferrous metals (except aluminum), primary
333994 Smelting ovens manufacturing
332420 Smelting pots and retorts manufacturing
212230 Smithsonite mining and/or beneficiating
238210 Smoke detection system, installation only
334290 Smoke detectors manufacturing
423620 Smoke detectors, household-type, merchant wholesalers
332994 Smoke generators manufacturing
311612 Smoked meats made from purchased carcasses
424990 Smokers' supplies merchant wholesalers
453991 Smokers' supply stores 332313 Smokestacks, fabricated metal boiler plate, manufacturing
621999 Smoking cessation programs
312230 Smoking tobacco (e.g., cigarette, pipe) manufacturing
333318 Snack and confection vending machines manufacturing
722515 Snack bars (e.g., cookies, popcorn, pretzels), fixed location
722330 Snack stands, mobile 111219 Snap bean farming (i.e., bush and pole), field and seed production
335931 Snap switches (i.e., electric wiring devices) manufacturing
114111 Snapper fishing
488490 Snow clearing, highways and bridges, road transportation
321912 Snow fence lath manufacturing
321999 Snow fence, sections or rolls, manufacturing
333415 Snow making machinery manufacturing
238210 Snow melting cable, electric, installation
238220 Snow melting system (e.g., hot water, glycol) installation
111219 Snow pea farming, field and seed production
333120 Snow plow attachments (except lawn, garden-type) manufacturing
333112 Snow plow attachments, lawn and garden-type, manufacturing
561790 Snow plowing driveways and parking lots (i.e., not combined with any other service)
561730 Snow plowing services combined with landscaping services (i.e., seasonal property maintenance services)
423810 Snow plows merchant wholesalers
488490 Snow removal, highway
532284 Snow ski equipment rental
423810 Snowblowers (except household-type) merchant wholesalers
333112 Snowblowers and throwers, residential-type, manufacturing
423820 Snowblowers, household-type, merchant wholesalers
441228 Snowmobile dealers
423110 Snowmobile merchant wholesalers 711212 Snowmobile racetracks 711219 Snowmobile racing teams 336999 Snowmobiles and parts manufacturing 713990 Snowmobiling, recreational 339920 Snowshoes manufacturing 315210 Snowsuits cut and sew apparel contractors 315190 Snowsuits made in apparel knitting mills 315220 Snowsuits, men's and boys', cut and sewn from purchased fabric (except apparel contractors)
315240 Snowsuits, women's, girls, and infants', cut and sewn from purchased fabric (except apparel contractors)
312230 Snuff manufacturing
424940 Snuff merchant wholesalers 327110 Soap dishes, vitreous china and earthenware, manufacturing
332999 Soap dispensers, metal, manufacturing
325611 Soaps (e.g., bar, chip, powder) manufacturing
212399 Soapstone mining and/or beneficiating
711211 Soccer clubs, professional or semiprofessional
713990 Soccer clubs, recreational
611620 Soccer instruction, camps, or schools
711211 Soccer teams, professional or semiprofessional
923130 Social assistance cost-sharing, government
813319 Social change advocacy organizations
813410 Social clubs
812990 Social escort services
519130 Social networking sites, Internet

813410 Social organizations, civic and fraternal
541720 Social science research and development services
923130 Social Security Administration (SSA), federal
813319 Social service advocacy organizations
624190 Social service agencies, family
624190 Social service centers, multi-purpose
424120 Social stationery merchant wholesalers
813920 Social workers' associations
621330 Social workers', mental health, offices (e.g., centers, clinics)
541720 Sociological research and development services
541720 Sociology research and development services
448190 Sock shops
332216 Sockets and socket sets manufacturing
335931 Sockets, electric, manufacturing
315110 Socks knitting or knitting and finishing
315110 Socks, men's and boy's, manufacturing
424320 Socks, men's and boys', merchant wholesalers
316210 Socks, slipper, made from purchased socks
315110 Socks, slipper, made in sock mills 424330
Socks, women's, children's, and infants', merchant wholesalers
111421 Sod farming
333111 Sod harvesting machines manufacturing
561730 Sod laying services
424590 Sod merchant wholesalers
325180 Soda ash manufacturing
212391 Soda ash mining and/or beneficiating
212391 Soda ash, natural, mining and/or beneficiating
327213 Soda bottles, glass, manufacturing
312111 Soda carbonated, manufacturing
311821 Soda crackers manufacturing
333415 Soda fountain cooling and dispensing equipment manufacturing
423440 Soda fountain fixtures (except refrigerated) merchant wholesalers
423740 Soda fountain fixtures, refrigerated, merchant wholesalers
311930 Soda fountain syrups manufacturing
312111 Soda pop manufacturing
325199 Sodium acetate manufacturing
325199 Sodium alginate manufacturing
325180 Sodium aluminate manufacturing
325180 Sodium aluminum sulfate manufacturing
325180 Sodium antimoniate manufacturing
325180 Sodium arsenite (except insecticides) manufacturing
325320 Sodium arsenite insecticides manufacturing
325199 Sodium benzoate manufacturing
325180 Sodium bicarbonate manufacturing
325180 Sodium bichromate and chromate manufacturing
325180 Sodium borate manufacturing 212391 Sodium borates, natural, mining and/or beneficiating
325180 Sodium borohydride manufacturing
325180 Sodium bromide manufacturing
325180 Sodium carbonate (i.e., soda ash) manufacturing
212391 Sodium carbonates, natural, mining and/or beneficiating
325180 Sodium chlorate manufacturing
325412 Sodium chloride pharmaceutical preparations manufacturing
212393 Sodium chloride, rock salt, mining and/or beneficiating
212391 Sodium compounds prepared at beneficiating plants
212391 Sodium compounds, natural (except common salt), mining and/or beneficiating
325180 Sodium cyanide manufacturing
325199 Sodium glutamate manufacturing
325180 Sodium hydrosulfite manufacturing
325180 Sodium hydroxide (i.e., caustic soda) manufacturing
325180 Sodium hypochlorite manufacturing
325180 Sodium inorganic compounds, not specified elsewhere by process, manufacturing
325180 Sodium molybdate manufacturing
325199 Sodium organic compounds, not specified elsewhere by process, manufacturing
325199 Sodium pentachlorophenate manufacturing
325180 Sodium perborate manufacturing
325180 Sodium peroxide manufacturing
325180 Sodium phosphate manufacturing
325180 Sodium polyphosphate manufacturing
325412 Sodium salicylate preparations manufacturing

325180 Sodium silicate (i.e., water glass) manufacturing
325180 Sodium silicofluoride manufacturing
325180 Sodium stannate manufacturing
325180 Sodium sulfate manufacturing
212391 Sodium sulfate, natural, mining and/or beneficiating
325199 Sodium sulfoxalate formaldehyde manufacturing
325180 Sodium tetraborate manufacturing
325180 Sodium thiosulfate manufacturing
325180 Sodium tungstate manufacturing
325180 Sodium uranate manufacturing
335110 Sodium vapor lamp bulbs manufacturing
337121 Sofa beds and chair beds, upholstered, manufacturing
337121 Sofas, convertible (except futons), manufacturing
337121 Sofas, upholstered, manufacturing
423330 Soffit, building (except wood), merchant wholesalers
722515 Soft drink beverage bars, nonalcoholic, fixed location
332431 Soft drink cans manufacturing
311930 Soft drink concentrates (i.e., syrup) manufacturing
445299 Soft drink stores, bottled
333318 Soft drink vending machines manufacturing
312111 Soft drinks manufacturing
424490 Soft drinks merchant wholesalers
311812 Soft pretzels made in a commercial bakery
325613 Softeners, leather or textile, manufacturing
541511 Software analysis and design services, custom computer
611420 Software application training
511210 Software computer, packaged, publishers
541519 Software installation services, computer
541511 Software programming services, custom computer
511210 Software publishers
511210 Software publishers, packaged
443142 Software stores, computer
423430 Software, computer, packaged, merchant wholesalers
334614 Software, packaged, mass reproducing
321912 Softwood dimension lumber and stock, resawing purchased lumber
325194 Softwood distillates manufacturing
321212 Softwood plywood composites manufacturing
321212 Softwood veneer or plywood manufacturing
238910 Soil compacting
924120 Soil conservation services, government
331511 Soil pipe, cast iron, manufacturing
562910 Soil remediation services
238910 Soil test drilling
325998 Soil testing kits manufacturing
541380 Soil testing laboratories or services
424930 Soil, top and potting, merchant wholesalers
334413 Solar cells manufacturing
423690 Solar cells merchant wholesalers
926130 Solar energy regulation
333414 Solar energy heating equipment manufacturing
221114 Solar farms
238220 Solar heating equipment installation
423720 Solar heating panels and equipment merchant wholesalers
333414 Solar heating systems manufacturing
335122 Solar lighting fixtures (except residential), electric, manufacturing
335121 Solar lighting fixtures, residential, electric, manufacturing
238210 Solar panel installation 237130 Solar power structure construction 238160 Solar reflecting coating, roof, application 423330 Solar reflective film merchant wholesalers 334519 Solarimeters manufacturing 331491 Solder wire, nonferrous metals (except aluminum, copper), made from purchased metals or scrap
333992 Soldering equipment (except handheld) manufacturing
332216 Soldering guns and irons, handheld (including electric), manufacturing
332216 Soldering iron tips and tiplets manufacturing
335931 Solderless connectors (electric wiring devices) manufacturing
316110 Sole leather manufacturing 335314 Solenoid switches, industrial, manufacturing
332911 Solenoid valves (except fluid power), industrial-type, manufacturing

332912 Solenoid valves, fluid power, manufacturing
334419 Solenoids for electronic applications manufacturing
316998 Soles, boot and shoe, leather, manufacturing
922130 Solicitors' offices, government
541110 Solicitors' offices, private
541110 Solicitors' private practices
325180 Solid fuel propellants, inorganic, not specified elsewhere by process, manufacturing
562213 Solid waste combustors or incinerators, nonhazardous
562212 Solid waste landfills combined with collection and/or local hauling of nonhazardous waste materials
562212 Solid waste landfills, nonhazardous
711130 Soloists, independent musical
325130 Solvent dyes manufacturing
324110 Solvents made in petroleum refineries
334511 Sonabuoys manufacturing
423690 Sonar equipment merchant wholesalers
334511 Sonar fish finders manufacturing
334511 Sonar systems and equipment manufacturing
512230 Song publishers
512230 Song publishers and printing combined
711510 Song writers, independent
325612 Soot removing chemicals manufacturing
325199 Sorbitol manufacturing
111199 Sorghum farming, field and seed production
311211 Sorghum flour manufacturing
111998 Sorghum sudan seed farming
311999 Sorghum syrup manufacturing
813410 Sororities (except residential)
721310 Sorority houses
115114 Sorting, grading, cleaning, and packing of fruits and vegetables
532490 Sound and lighting equipment rental or leasing
423430 Sound boards, computer, merchant wholesalers
512191 Sound dubbing services, motion picture
238210 Sound equipment installation 423620
Sound equipment, household-type, merchant wholesalers
423330 Sound insulation merchant wholesalers
512240 Sound recording studios (except integrated record companies)
512250 Sound recording, integrated production, reproduction, release, and distribution
512250 Sound recording, releasing, promoting, and distributing
238310 Soundproofing contractors 332431
Soup cans, light gauge metal, manufacturing
624210 Soup kitchens
311423 Soup mixes made in dehydration plants
311999 Soup mixes, dry, made from purchased dry ingredients
424490 Soups (except frozen) merchant wholesalers
311422 Soups (except seafood) canning
311412 Soups, frozen (except seafood), manufacturing
424420 Soups, frozen, merchant wholesalers
311710 Soups, seafood, manufacturing
311511 Sour cream manufacturing
311511 Sour cream substitutes manufacturing
453220 Souvenir shops
311941 Soy sauce manufacturing
311224 Soybean cakes and meal manufacturing
311225 Soybean cooking oil made from purchased oils
111110 Soybean farming, field and seed production
325220 Soybean fibers and filaments manufacturing
311224 Soybean flour and grits manufacturing
311224 Soybean millfeed made in oil mills
311224 Soybean oil mills
311224 Soybean oil, cake, and meal, made in crushing mills
311224 Soybean oil, crude, manufacturing
311224 Soybean oil, deodorized, made in oil mills
311224 Soybean oil, refined, made in crushing mills
325211 Soybean plastics manufacturing
311224 Soybean protein concentrates made in crushing mills
311224 Soybean protein isolates made in crushing mills
424510 Soybeans merchant wholesalers
423720 Spa equipment merchant wholesalers
336419 Space capsules manufacturing

927110 Space flight operations, government 333414
Space heaters (except portable electric) manufacturing
423860 Space propulsion units and parts merchant wholesalers
927110 Space research services, government
334220 Space satellites, communications, manufacturing
332313 Space simulation chambers, fabricated metal plate work, manufacturing
339113 Space suits manufacturing
481212 Space transportation, freight, nonscheduled
334511 Space vehicle guidance systems and equipment manufacturing
336414 Space vehicles, complete, manufacturing
332216 Spades and shovels, handheld, manufacturing
311422 Spaghetti canning
424490 Spaghetti merchant wholesalers
311421 Spaghetti sauce canning
111219 Spaghetti squash farming, field, bedding plant and seed production
311824 Spaghetti, dry, manufacturing
313210 Spandex broadwoven fabrics
325220 Spandex fiber, filaments, and yarn manufacturing
113210 Spanish moss gathering
212399 Spar, iceland, mining and/or beneficiating
327110 Spark plug insulators, porcelain, manufacturing
334515 Spark plug testing instruments, electric, manufacturing
336320 Spark plugs for internal combustion engines manufacturing
312130 Sparkling wines manufacturing
321999 Spars, wood, manufacturing
713940 Spas without accommodations, fitness
316998 Spats, leather, manufacturing
326299 Spatulas, rubber, manufacturing
321999 Speaker cabinets (i.e., housings), wood, manufacturing
334310 Speaker systems manufacturing
423620 Speaker systems merchant wholesalers
711410 Speakers' bureaus
813410 Speakers' clubs
711510 Speakers, independent
325998 Spearmint oil manufacturing
711510 Special effect technicians, independent
512191 Special effects for motion picture production, postproduction
519130 Special interest portals (e.g., parents sharing information about child rearing, etc.), Internet
485991 Special needs passenger transportation services
525990 Special purpose financial vehicles
336211 Special purpose highway vehicle (e.g., fire-fighting vehicles) assembling on purchased chassis
336211 Special purpose highway vehicle (e.g., firefighting vehicles) bodies manufacturing
423110 Special purpose highway vehicle merchant wholesalers
336120 Special purpose highway vehicles (e.g., fire-fighting vehicles) assembling on heavy chassis of own manufacture
423830 Special purpose industrial machinery and equipment merchant wholesalers
611519 Specialized military training (except flight instruction, academies, and basic training)
445299 Specialty food stores
316110 Specialty leathers manufacturing 515210
Specialty television (e.g., music, sports, news) cable networks
335311 Specialty transformers, electric, manufacturing
423710 Specialty-line hardware merchant wholesalers
424210 Specialty-line pharmaceuticals merchant wholesalers
334516 Specific ion measuring instruments, laboratory-type, manufacturing 238390 Spectator seating installation 334516 Spectrofluorometers manufacturing 334516 Spectrographs manufacturing 334516
Spectrometers (e.g., electron diffraction, mass, NMR, Raman) manufacturing
334519 Spectrometers (e.g., liquid scintillation, nuclear) manufacturing
334516 Spectrophotometers (e.g., atomic absorption, atomic emission, flame, fluorescence, infrared, Raman, visible) manufacturing
334515 Spectrum analyzers manufacturing
236220 Speculative builders (i.e., building on own land, for sale), commercial and institutional building
236210 Speculative builders (i.e., building on own land, for sale), industrial building (except warehouses)

236117 Speculative builders (i.e., building on own land, for sale), multifamily housing
236117 Speculative builders (i.e., building on own land, for sale), residential
236117 Speculative builders (i.e., building on own land, for sale), single-family housing
339112 Speculums manufacturing
541930 Speech (i.e., language) interpretation services
621340 Speech clinicians' offices (e.g., centers, clinics)
621340 Speech defect clinics
621340 Speech pathologists' offices (e.g., centers, clinics)
621340 Speech therapists' offices (e.g., centers, clinics)
333612 Speed changers (i.e., power transmission equipment) manufacturing
423840 Speed changers merchant wholesalers
611699 Speed reading instruction
333612 Speed reducers (i.e., power transmission equipment) manufacturing
441310 Speed shops
334511 Speed, pitch, and roll navigational instruments and systems manufacturing
711212 Speedways
621991 Sperm banks, human
113210 Sphagnum moss gathering
212230 Sphalerite mining and/or beneficiating
339112 Sphygmomanometers manufacturing
111998 Spice farming
111419 Spice farming, grown under cover
311942 Spice grinding and blending
311942 Spice mixtures manufacturing
445299 Spice stores
311942 Spices and spice mix manufacturing
424490 Spices merchant wholesalers
424590 Spices, raw, merchant wholesalers
331110 Spiegeleisen ferroalloys manufacturing
332913 Spigots, plumbing fixture fitting, manufacturing
321999 Spigots, wood, manufacturing
331110 Spike rods made in iron and steel mills
332618 Spikes made from purchased wire
331222 Spikes, iron or steel, made in wire drawing plants
423510 Spikes, metal, merchant wholesalers
237990 Spillway, floodwater, construction
111219 Spinach farming, field, bedding plant and seed production
333249 Spindles for textile machinery manufacturing
313110 Spinning carpet and rug yarn from purchased fiber
333249 Spinning machinery for textiles manufacturing
333517 Spinning machines, metalworking, manufacturing
332119 Spinning unfinished metal products
313110 Spinning yarn from purchased fiber
332618 Spiral cloth made from purchased wire
312140 Spirits, distilled (except brandy), manufacturing
424820 Spirits, distilled, merchant wholesalers
333517 Spline rolling machines, metalworking, manufacturing
321920 Splint baskets for fruits and vegetables, manufacturing
339113 Splints manufacturing
316110 Splits, leather, manufacturing
212393 Spodumene mining and/or beneficiating
321999 Spokes, wood, manufacturing
114119 Sponge gathering
331110 Sponge iron
424990 Sponges merchant wholesalers
332999 Sponges, metal scouring, manufacturing
326199 Sponges, plastics, manufacturing
326299 Sponges, rubber, manufacturing
313310 Sponging textile products and fabrics
313110 Spooling of yarn
313110 Spooling of yarns for the trade
321999 Spools (except for textile machinery), wood, manufacturing
333249 Spools for textile machinery manufacturing
332215 Spoons, table, nonprecious and precious plated metal, manufacturing
315220 Sport coats (except fur, leather), men's and boys', cut and sewn from purchased fabric (except apparel contractors)
315210 Sport coats cut and sew apparel contractors
315280 Sport coats, fur (except apparel contractors), manufacturing
315210 Sport coats, fur, cut and sew apparel contractors
315280 Sport coats, leather (including artificial and tailored) (except apparel contractors), manufacturing

315210 Sport coats, leather (including artificial and tailored), cut and sew apparel contractors
424490 Sport energy drinks merchant wholesalers
315210 Sport shirts cut and sew apparel contractors
315220 Sport shirts, men's and boys', cut and sewn from purchased fabric (except apparel contractors)
532112 Sport utility vehicle leasing
423110 Sport utility vehicle merchant wholesalers
532111 Sport utility vehicle rental
336112 Sport utility vehicles assembling on chassis of own manufacture
811490 Sporting equipment repair and maintenance without retailing new sports equipment
423910 Sporting firearms and ammunition merchant wholesalers
339920 Sporting goods (except ammunition, clothing, footwear, small arms) manufacturing
423910 Sporting goods and supplies merchant wholesalers
532284 Sporting goods rental
451110 Sporting goods stores
453310 Sporting goods stores, used
711510 Sports announcers, independent
448190 Sports apparel stores (except uniforms)
711310 Sports arena operators
611620 Sports camps (e.g., baseball, basketball, football), instructional
315220 Sports clothing (except team uniforms), men's and boys', cut and sewn from purchased fabric (except apparel contractors)
315240 Sports clothing (except team uniforms), women's and girls', cut and sewn from purchased fabric (except apparel contractors)
315210 Sports clothing cut and sew apparel contractors
315190 Sports clothing made in apparel knitting mills
315280 Sports clothing, team uniforms, cut and sewn from purchased fabric (except apparel contractors)
713940 Sports club facilities, physical fitness
713990 Sports clubs (i.e., sports teams) not operating sports facilities, recreational
711211 Sports clubs, professional or semiprofessional
423910 Sports equipment and supplies merchant wholesalers
532284 Sports equipment rental
711310 Sports event managers with facilities
711320 Sports event managers without facilities
711310 Sports event organizers with facilities
711320 Sports event organizers without facilities
711310 Sports event promoters with facilities
711320 Sports event promoters without facilities
237990 Sports field construction
711410 Sports figures' agents or managers
451110 Sports gear stores (e.g., outdoors, scuba, skiing)
813990 Sports governing bodies
712110 Sports halls of fame
611620 Sports instruction, camps, or schools
611620 Sports instructors, independent (i.e., not participating in sporting events)
813990 Sports leagues (i.e., regulating bodies)
621340 Sports physical therapists' offices (e.g., centers, clinics)
711219 Sports professionals, independent (i.e., participating in sports events)
315190 Sports shirts made in apparel knitting mills
711310 Sports stadium operators
713990 Sports teams and leagues, recreational or youth
711211 Sports teams, professional or semiprofessional
561599 Sports ticket offices
711219 Sports trainers, independent
424320 Sportswear, men's and boys', merchant wholesalers
325612 Spot removers (except laundry presoaks) manufacturing
333992 Spot welding equipment manufacturing
335129 Spotlights (except vehicular) manufacturing
336320 Spotlights, vehicular, manufacturing
332322 Spouts, sheet metal (except stampings), manufacturing
424950 Spray painting equipment (except industrial-type) merchant wholesalers
423830 Spray painting equipment, industrial-type, merchant wholesalers
333111 Sprayers and dusters, farm-type, manufacturing
423820 Sprayers, farm-type, merchant wholesalers
333912 Sprayers, manual pump, general purpose-type, manufacturing
115112 Spraying crops

561730 Spraying lawns
811198 Spray-on bedliner installation for trucks
333111 Spreaders, farm-type, manufacturing
423820 Spreaders, fertilizer, merchant wholesalers
333112 Spreaders, lawn and garden-type, manufacturing
115112 Spreading lime for crops
311513 Spreads, cheese, manufacturing
332722 Spring pins, metal, manufacturing
332722 Spring washers, metal, manufacturing
312112 Spring waters, purifying and bottling
333517 Spring winding and forming machines, metalworking, manufacturing
332613 Springs and spring units for seats, light gauge, made from purchased wire or strip
337910 Springs, assembled bed and box, made from purchased springs
334519 Springs, clock and watch, made from purchased wire
332613 Springs, heavy gauge metal, manufacturing
332613 Springs, light gauge (except clock, watch), made from purchased wire or strip
332613 Springs, precision (except clock, watch), light gauge, made from purchased wire or strip
423510 Springs, steel, merchant wholesalers
238220 Sprinkler system, building, installation
333999 Sprinkler systems, automatic fire, manufacturing
423850 Sprinkler systems, fire, merchant wholesalers
423820 Sprinklers, agricultural, merchant wholesalers
423820 Sprinklers, garden, merchant wholesalers
332919 Sprinklers, lawn, manufacturing
423840 Sprockets merchant wholesalers
333613 Sprockets, power transmission equipment, manufacturing
113210 Spruce gum gathering
213111 Spudding in oil and gas wells on a contract basis
313230 Spunbonded fabrics manufacturing
332216 Squares, carpenters', metal, manufacturing
713940 Squash club facilities
339920 Squash equipment (except apparel) manufacturing
111219 Squash farming, field, bedding plant and seed production
114112 Squid fishing
424610 Stabilizers, plastic, merchant wholesalers
332999 Stabilizing bars, cargo, metal, manufacturing
711219 Stables, horse racing
713990 Stables, riding
423830 Stackers, industrial, merchant wholesalers
333924 Stackers, industrial, truck-type, manufacturing
333924 Stackers, portable (except farm), manufacturing
236220 Stadium and arena construction
711310 Stadium operators
531120 Stadium rental or leasing without promotion of events
337127 Stadium seating manufacturing 561330 Staff leasing services 335129 Stage lighting equipment manufacturing 711510 Stage set (e.g., concert, motion picture, television) erecting and dismantling, independent
327211 Stained glass and stained glass products made in glass making plants
238150 Stained glass installation
327215 Stained glass products made from purchased glass
331513 Stainless steel castings (except investment), unfinished, manufacturing
331110 Stainless steel made in iron and steel mills
423510 Stainless steel merchant wholesalers 325510 Stains (except biological) manufacturing 424950 Stains merchant wholesalers 325130 Stains, biological, manufacturing 332323 Stair railings, metal, manufacturing 321918 Stair railings, wood, manufacturing 332323 Stair treads, metal, manufacturing 326299 Stair treads, rubber, manufacturing 332323 Staircases, metal, manufacturing 332323 Stairs, metal, manufacturing 423310 Stairs, wood, merchant wholesalers 238190 Stairway, metal, installation 238120 Stairway, precast concrete, installation 238350 Stairway, wood, installation 333921 Stairways, moving, manufacturing 321918 Stairwork (e.g., newel posts, railings, staircases, stairs), wood, manufacturing
321999 Stakes, surveyor's, wood, manufacturing

333111 Stalk choppers (i.e., shredders) manufacturing
332323 Stalls, metal, manufacturing
325998 Stamp pad ink manufacturing
339940 Stamp pads manufacturing
339910 Stamping coins
339940 Stamping devices, hand operated, manufacturing
333517 Stamping machines, metalworking, manufacturing
336370 Stamping metal motor vehicle body parts
336370 Stamping metal motor vehicle moldings and trims
332119 Stampings (except automotive, cans, coins), metal, unfinished, manufacturing
423920 Stamps, philatelist, merchant wholesalers
713210 Stand-alone casinos (except slot machine parlors)
334515 Standards and calibration equipment for electrical measuring manufacturing
813920 Standards review committees, professional
926150 Standards, setting and management, agencies, government
334515 Standing wave ratio measuring equipment manufacturing
337215 Stands (except wire), merchandise display, manufacturing
711510 Standup comedians, independent
325180 Stannic and stannous chloride manufacturing
339940 Staple removers manufacturing
333991 Staplers and nailers, handheld power-driven, manufacturing
339940 Staplers manufacturing
332618 Staples made from purchased wire
423710 Staples merchant wholesalers
331222 Staples, iron or steel, made in wire drawing plants
423420 Stapling machines merchant wholesalers
325520 Starch glues manufacturing
311221 Starches (except laundry) manufacturing
325612 Starches, laundry, manufacturing
112310 Started pullet production
336320 Starter and starter parts for internal combustion engines manufacturing
522110 State commercial banks
522130 State credit unions
928120 State Department
923110 State education departments 561311 State operated employment job services offices
922120 State police
522120 State savings and loan associations
522120 State savings banks
921130 State tax commissions
334413 Static converters, integrated circuits, manufacturing
334512 Static pressure regulators manufacturing
332410 Stationary power boilers manufacturing
327110 Stationery articles, pottery, manufacturing
322230 Stationery made from purchased paper
453210 Stationery stores
424120 Stationery supplies merchant wholesalers
323111 Stationery, commercial printing (except screen), on a job-order basis
323113 Stationery, screen printing, on a job-order basis
335312 Stators for motors manufacturing
327420 Statuary (e.g., gypsum, plaster of paris) manufacturing
424990 Statuary (except religious) merchant wholesalers
327110 Statuary, clay and ceramic, manufacturing
327991 Statuary, marble, manufacturing
423490 Statuary, religious, merchant wholesalers
327999 Statuary, vases, and urns, papier-mache, manufacturing
238990 Statue erection
212399 Staurolite mining and/or beneficiating
321920 Staves, barrel, sawed or split, manufacturing
316998 Stays, shoe, leather, manufacturing
722511 Steak houses, full service
722513 Steak houses, limited-service
812199 Steam baths
561790 Steam cleaning building exteriors 213112 Steam cleaning oil and gas wells on a contract basis
332410 Steam condensers manufacturing
333318 Steam cookers, commercial-type, manufacturing
335210 Steam cookers, household-type, manufacturing
611513 Steam fitters' apprenticeship training
238220 Steam fitting contractors
332919 Steam fittings, metal, manufacturing

221330 Steam heat distribution
333414 Steam heating equipment manufacturing
221330 Steam heating systems (i.e., suppliers of heat)
334512 Steam pressure controls, residential and commercial heating-type, manufacturing
221330 Steam production and distribution
333999 Steam separating machinery manufacturing
221330 Steam supply systems, including geothermal
333318 Steam tables manufacturing
487110 Steam train excursions
332911 Steam traps, industrial-type, manufacturing
333611 Steam turbine generator set units manufacturing
333611 Steam turbines manufacturing
532411 Steamship rental or leasing without crew
325199 Stearic acid esters manufacturing
325199 Stearic acid manufacturing
325199 Stearic acid salts manufacturing
311613 Stearin, animal, rendering
212399 Steatite mining and/or beneficiating
327110 Steatite porcelain insulators manufacturing
331110 Steel balls made in iron and steel mills
332431 Steel cans, light gauge metal, manufacturing
331513 Steel castings (except investment), unfinished, manufacturing
332111 Steel forgings made from purchased steel, unfinished
331513 Steel foundries (except investment)
238130 Steel framing contractors
331512 Steel investment castings, unfinished, manufacturing
331512 Steel investment foundries
332312 Steel joists manufacturing
331110 Steel manufacturing
423510 Steel merchant wholesalers
236210 Steel mill construction
331110 Steel mill products (e.g., bar, plate, rod, sheet, structural shapes) manufacturing
331110 Steel mills
332312 Steel railroad car racks manufacturing
238120 Steel reinforcing contractors
327910 Steel shot abrasives manufacturing
423510 Steel wire cloth (screening) merchant wholesalers
332999 Steel wool manufacturing
423510 Steel wool merchant wholesalers
331110 Steel, from pig iron, manufacturing
238160 Steep slope roofing installation
238990 Steeplejack work
311221 Steepwater concentrate manufacturing
336330 Steering boxes, manual and power assist, manufacturing
336330 Steering columns, automotive, truck, and bus, manufacturing
336330 Steering wheels, automotive, truck, and bus, manufacturing
327215 Stemware made from purchased glass
327212 Stemware, glass, made in glass making plants
325910 Stencil inks manufacturing
339940 Stencil paper manufacturing
339940 Stencils for painting and marking (e.g., cardboard, metal) manufacturing
561410 Stenographic services (except court or stenographic reporting)
333318 Stenography machinery manufacturing
561492 Stenography services, public
561492 Stenotype recording services
332999 Stepladders, metal, manufacturing
321999 Stepladders, wood, manufacturing
321999 Stereo cabinets (i.e., housings), wood, manufacturing
423620 Stereo equipment merchant wholesalers
532210 Stereo equipment rental
811211 Stereo equipment repair shops without retailing new stereo equipment
325212 Stereo rubber manufacturing
443142 Stereo stores (except automotive)
441310 Stereo stores, automotive
339114 Sterilizers, dental, manufacturing
339113 Sterilizers, hospital and surgical, manufacturing
339113 Sterilizers, laboratory-type (except dental), manufacturing
332313 Sterilizing chambers, fabricated metal plate work, manufacturing
325411 Steroids, uncompounded, manufacturing
339112 Stethoscopes manufacturing
488320 Stevedoring services
339920 Sticks, sports (e.g., hockey, lacrosse), manufacturing

325130 Stilbene dyes manufacturing

324110 Still gases made in petroleum refineries

332420 Stills, heavy gauge metal, manufacturing

333244 Stitchers and trimmers bookbinding equipment manufacturing

314999 Stitching, decorative and novelty, contractors on apparel

314999 Stitching, decorative and novelty, on textile articles and apparel

523120 Stock brokerages

523120 Stock brokers' offices

711212 Stock car racetracks

711219 Stock car racing teams

711110 Stock companies, theatrical

523210 Stock exchanges

512199 Stock footage film libraries

512290 Stock music and other audio services

523120 Stock options brokerages

523110 Stock options dealing (i.e., acting as a principal in dealing securities to investors)

523210 Stock or commodity options exchanges

519190 Stock photo agencies

523999 Stock quotation services

512290 Stock sound library (e.g., general background sounds, stock music)

523999 Stock transfer agencies 321912 Stock, chair, unfinished hardwood, manufacturing

112111 Stocker calf production

315110 Stockings, sheer, manufacturing

315110 Stockings, sheer, women's, misses', and girls', full-length and knee-length, knitting or knitting and finishing

488999 Stockyards (i.e., not for fattening or selling livestock), transportation

212319 Stone (except limestone and granite) beneficiating plants (e.g., grinding)

333131 Stone beneficiating machinery manufacturing

332216 Stone cutting saw blades manufacturing

238340 Stone flooring installation

313310 Stone washing textile products, apparel, and fabrics

333249 Stone working machinery manufacturing

423320 Stone, building or crushed, merchant wholesalers

212319 Stone, crushed and broken (except granite or limestone), mining and/or beneficiating

212311 Stone, dimension, mining or quarrying

332216 Stonecutters' handtools, nonpowered, manufacturing

212399 Stones, abrasive (e.g., emery, grindstones, hones, pumice), mining and/or beneficiating

423940 Stones, precious and semiprecious, merchant wholesalers

327999 Stones, synthetic, for gem stones and industrial use, manufacturing

327110 Stoneware (i.e., pottery products) manufacturing

212325 Stoneware clay mining and/or beneficiating

238140 Stonework (i.e., masonry) contractors

337124 Stools, metal household-type (except upholstered), manufacturing

337122 Stools, wood household-type (except upholstered), manufacturing

621999 Stop smoking clinics

332911 Stop valves, industrial-type, manufacturing

332913 Stopcock drains, plumbing, manufacturing

321999 Stoppers, cork, manufacturing

326299 Stoppers, rubber, manufacturing

423610 Storage batteries (except automotive) merchant wholesalers

335911 Storage batteries manufacturing

335312 Storage battery chargers (except internal combustion engine-type) manufacturing

423390 Storage bins merchant wholesalers

334112 Storage devices, computer, manufacturing

236220 Storage elevator construction

486210 Storage of natural gas

237120 Storage tank, natural gas or oil, tank farm or field, construction

332420 Storage tanks, heavy gauge metal, manufacturing

423510 Storage tanks, metal, merchant wholesalers

236220 Store construction

541850 Store display advertising services

337215 Store display fixtures manufacturing

423440 Store equipment (except furniture) merchant wholesalers

423440 Store fixtures (except refrigerated) merchant wholesalers

423210 Store furniture merchant wholesalers

238190 Storefront, metal or metal frame, installation

****** Stores -- see type

562998 Storm basin cleanout services

332321 Storm doors and windows, metal, manufacturing
321911 Storm doors and windows, wood framed, manufacturing
237110 Storm sewer construction
711510 Storytellers, independent
312120 Stout brewing
332322 Stove boards, sheet metal (except stampings), manufacturing
327120 Stove lining, clay, manufacturing
332322 Stove pipes and flues, sheet metal (except stampings), manufacturing
811412 Stove, household-type, repair and maintenance services without retailing new stoves
423720 Stoves (i.e., noncooking), heating, merchant wholesalers
335220 Stoves, ceramic disk element, household-type, manufacturing
333318 Stoves, commercial-type, manufacturing
423620 Stoves, cooking, household-type, merchant wholesalers
335220 Stoves, household-type cooking, manufacturing
333924 Straddle carriers, mobile, manufacturing
332215 Straight razors manufacturing 332911
Straightway (i.e., Y-type) valves, industrial-type, manufacturing
333999 Strainers, pipeline, manufacturing
321219 Strandboard, oriented, manufacturing
332618 Stranded wire, uninsulated, made from purchased wire
316110 Strap leather manufacturing
332999 Strappings, metal, manufacturing
316998 Straps, leather, manufacturing
316998 Straps, watch (except metal), manufacturing
339910 Straps, watch, precious metal, manufacturing
541611 Strategic planning consulting services
213112 Stratigraphic drilling, oil and gas field exploration on a contract basis
321999 Straw baskets manufacturing
315990 Straw hats manufacturing
424910 Straw merchant wholesalers
111333 Strawberry farming
488490 Street cleaning service
237310 Street construction
335129 Street lighting fixtures (except traffic signals) manufacturing
519130 Street map and guide publishers, exclusively on Internet
511130 Street map guide publishers (except exclusive Internet publishing)
485119 Street railway systems (except mixed mode), commuter
423810 Street sweeping and cleaning equipment merchant wholesalers
454390 Street vendors (except food)
722330 Street vendors, food 238990 Street,
interlocking brick (i.e., not mortared), installation
237990 Streetcar line construction
485119 Streetcar systems (except mixed mode), commuter
336510 Streetcars and car equipment, urban transit, manufacturing
713940 Strength development centers 336211
Stretch limousines assembling on purchased chassis
321999 Stretchers, curtain, wood, manufacturing
339113 Stretchers, medical, manufacturing
333517 Stretching machines, metalworking, manufacturing
111219 String bean farming, field and seed production
314994 Strings (except musical instrument) manufacturing
339992 Strings, musical instrument, manufacturing
212113 Strip mining, anthracite, on own account
212111 Strip mining, bituminous coal or lignite, on own account
212111 Strip mining, lignite, on own account
331420 Strip, copper and copper alloy, made from purchased copper or in integrated secondary smelting and rolling, drawing or extruding plants
331110 Strip, galvanized iron or steel, made in iron and steel mills
331110 Strip, iron or steel, made in iron and steel mills
331491 Strip, nonferrous metals (except aluminum, copper), made from purchased metals or scrap
211130 Stripper gas well production
211120 Stripper oil well production
213113 Stripping overburden services for coal mining on a contract basis

213114 Stripping overburden services for metal mining on a contract basis
213115 Stripping overburden services for nonmetallic minerals mining (except fuels) on a contract basis
423510 Strips, metal (except precious), merchant wholesalers
334515 Stroboscopes manufacturing
335110 Strobotrons manufacturing
424330 Strollers merchant wholesalers
339930 Strollers, baby, manufacturing
212393 Strontianite mining and/or beneficiating
325180 Strontium carbonate manufacturing
325180 Strontium compounds, not specified elsewhere by process, manufacturing
212393 Strontium mineral mining and/or beneficiating
325180 Strontium nitrate manufacturing
423510 Structural assemblies, metal, merchant wholesalers
423390 Structural assemblies, prefabricated (except wood), merchant wholesalers
423310 Structural assemblies, prefabricated wood, merchant wholesalers
423320 Structural clay tile (except refractory and clay roofing tile) merchant wholesalers
327120 Structural clay tile manufacturing
321114 Structural lumber and timber, treating
321213 Structural members, glue laminated or pre-engineered wood, manufacturing
333519 Structural rolling mill machinery, metalworking, manufacturing
331318 Structural shapes made by rolling purchased aluminum
331318 Structural shapes, aluminum, made in integrated secondary smelting and rolling mills
331110 Structural shapes, iron or steel, made in iron and steel mills
238120 Structural steel erecting or iron work contractors
332312 Structural steel, fabricated, manufacturing
339930 Structural toy sets manufacturing 321213
Structural wood members (except trusses), fabricated, manufacturing
336330 Struts, automotive, truck, and bus, manufacturing
325411 Strychnine and derivatives (i.e., basic chemicals) manufacturing
327999 Stucco and stucco products manufacturing
238140 Stucco contractors
423320 Stucco merchant wholesalers
321113 Stud mills
115210 Stud services
238130 Stud wall (e.g., wood, steel) installation
813410 Student clubs
611710 Student exchange programs
522291 Student loan companies
522294 Student Loan Marketing Association (SLMA)
813410 Students' associations
813410 Students' unions
334220 Studio equipment, radio and television broadcasting, manufacturing
541430 Studios, commercial art
321912 Studs, resawing purchased lumber
332322 Studs, sheet metal (except stampings), manufacturing
611710 Study abroad programs
921120 Study commissions, legislative
339930 Stuffed toys (including animals) manufacturing
333241 Stuffer, sausage machinery, manufacturing
113310 Stump removing in the field
325212 S-type rubber manufacturing
325920 Styphnic acid explosive materials manufacturing
325110 Styrene made from refined petroleum or liquid hydrocarbons
324110 Styrene made in petroleum refineries 325211
Styrene resins manufacturing 325211 Styrene-acrylonitrile resins manufacturing 325212 Styrene-butadiene rubber containing less than 50 percent styrene manufacturing
325212 Styrene-chloroprene rubber manufacturing
325212 Styrene-isoprene rubber manufacturing
238310 Styrofoam insulation installation
722513 Sub shops, limited-service
212111 Subbituminous coal surface mining and/or beneficiating
212112 Subbituminous coal underground mining or mining and beneficiating
237210 Subdividers, real estate
237210 Subdividing and preparing land owned by others
237210 Subdividing real estate
332994 Submachine guns manufacturing

336611 Submarine building
333514 Subpresses, machine tool, manufacturing
334210 Subscriber loop equipment, telephone, manufacturing
515210 Subscription television networks
551114 Subsidiary management offices 623220
Substance abuse (i.e., alcoholism, drug addiction) halfway houses
623220 Substance abuse facilities, residential
813319 Substance abuse prevention advocacy organizations
621420 Substance abuse treatment centers and clinics (except hospitals), outpatient
237130 Substation and switching station, power transmission line, construction
335311 Substation transformers, electric power distribution, manufacturing
512191 Subtitling of motion picture film or video
485113 Suburban bus line services (except mixed mode)
485112 Suburban commuter rail systems (except mixed mode)
485111 Suburban transit systems, mixed mode (e.g., bus, commuter rail, subway combinations)
541850 Subway card display advertising services
336510 Subway cars manufacturing
423860 Subway cars merchant wholesalers
237990 Subway construction
485119 Subway systems (except mixed mode), commuter
339112 Suction therapy apparatus manufacturing
812320 Suede garment cleaning services 313310
Sueding textile products and fabrics 111991 Sugar beet farming 115113 Sugar beets, machine harvesting 311221 Sugar made by wet milling corn 333241
Sugar refining machinery manufacturing 325998
Sugar substitutes (i.e., synthetic sweeteners blended with other ingredients) made from purchased synthetic sweeteners
325199 Sugar substitutes (i.e., synthetic sweeteners blended with other ingredients) made in synthetic sweetener establishments
311314 Sugar, cane, manufacturing
311314 Sugar, clarified, granulated, and raw, manufacturing
311313 Sugar, confectionery, made from sugar beets
311314 Sugar, confectionery, manufacturing
311313 Sugar, granulated, made from sugar beets
311314 Sugar, granulated, manufacturing
311313 Sugar, invert, made from sugar beets
311314 Sugar, invert, manufacturing
311313 Sugar, liquid, made from sugar beets
311314 Sugar, raw, manufacturing
424590 Sugar, raw, merchant wholesalers
311314 Sugar, refined, manufacturing
424490 Sugar, refined, merchant wholesalers
111930 Sugarcane farming, field production
311314 Sugarcane mills
311314 Sugarcane refining
115113 Sugarcane, machine harvesting
624190 Suicide crisis centers
532281 Suit rental
315210 Suit trimmings cut and sew apparel contractors
315990 Suit trimmings cut and sewn from purchased fabric (except apparel contractors)
332510 Suitcase hardware, metal, manufacturing
423990 Suitcases merchant wholesalers 316998
Suitcases, all materials, manufacturing 315240 Suits (e.g., jogging, snowsuit, warmup), women's, girls', and infants', cut and sewn from purchased fabric (except apparel contractors)
315210 Suits (i.e., nontailored, tailored, work) cut and sew apparel contractors
315190 Suits made in apparel knitting mills
339113 Suits, firefighting, manufacturing
424320 Suits, men's and boys', merchant wholesalers
315220 Suits, nontailored (e.g., jogging, snow, ski, warmup), men's and boys', cut and sewn from purchased fabric (except apparel contractors)
339113 Suits, space, manufacturing
315220 Suits, tailored, men's and boys', cut and sewn from purchased fabric (except apparel contractors)
315240 Suits, tailored, women's and girls', cut and sewn from purchased fabric (except apparel contractors)
325411 Sulfa drugs, uncompounded, manufacturing
212391 Sulfate, sodium, mining and/or beneficiating
325180 Sulfides and sulfites manufacturing

325180 Sulfocyanides manufacturing 325411
Sulfonamides, uncompounded, manufacturing
325194 Sulfonated naphthalene manufacturing
325180 Sulfur and sulfur compounds, not specified elsewhere by process, manufacturing
325180 Sulfur chloride manufacturing
325180 Sulfur dioxide manufacturing
325180 Sulfur hexafluoride gas manufacturing
325320 Sulfur insecticides manufacturing
212393 Sulfur mining and/or beneficiating
211130 Sulfur recovered from natural gas
325180 Sulfur recovering or refining (except from sour natural gas)
212393 Sulfur, native, mining and/or beneficiating
325180 Sulfuric acid manufacturing
424690 Sulfuric acid merchant wholesalers
325194 Sulphonated derivatives manufacturing
311423 Sulphured fruits and vegetables manufacturing
325194 Sumac extract manufacturing
721214 Summer camps (except day, instructional)
713990 Summer day camps (except instructional)
721110 Summer resort hotels without casinos
711110 Summer theaters
238220 Sump pump installation
333914 Sump pumps, residential-type, manufacturing
115114 Sun drying of dates, prunes, raisins, and olives
115114 Sun drying of fruits and vegetables
115114 Sun drying of tomatoes
812199 Sun tanning salons
111120 Sunflower farming, field and seed production
311224 Sunflower seed oil, cake and meal, made in crushing mills
446130 Sunglass stores
339115 Sunglasses and goggles manufacturing
423460 Sunglasses merchant wholesalers
336390 Sunroofs and parts, automotive, truck, and bus, manufacturing
236118 Sunroom additions, residential
325620 Sunscreen lotions and oils manufacturing
315240 Sunsuits, infants', cut and sewn from purchased fabric (except apparel contractors)
325620 Suntan lotions and oils manufacturing
331110 Superalloys, iron or steel, manufacturing
331492 Superalloys, nonferrous based, made from purchased metals or scrap
452311 Supercenters
445110 Supermarkets
325312 Superphosphates manufacturing 452311
Superstores (i.e., food and general merchandise)
921190 Supply agencies, government
332913 Supply line assemblies, plumbing (i.e., flexible hose with fittings), manufacturing
624190 Support group services
339113 Supports, orthopedic (e.g., abdominal, ankle, arch, kneecap), manufacturing
325412 Suppositories manufacturing
524126 Surety insurance carriers, direct
325613 Surface active agents manufacturing
424690 Surface active agents merchant wholesalers
334516 Surface area analyzers manufacturing
334512 Surface burner controls, temperature, manufacturing
322220 Surface coating purchased paperboard
333120 Surface mining machinery (except drilling) manufacturing
333242 Surface mount machinery for making printed circuit boards manufacturing
237310 Surfacing, highway, road, street, bridge or airport runway
532284 Surfboard rental
339920 Surfboards manufacturing
335999 Surge suppressors manufacturing
621111 Surgeons' (except dental) offices (e.g., centers, clinics)
541940 Surgeons' offices, veterinary
621210 Surgeons', dental, offices (e.g., centers, clinics)
115112 Surgery on trees and vines
541940 Surgery services, veterinary
423450 Surgical appliances merchant wholesalers
339112 Surgical clamps manufacturing
339113 Surgical dressings manufacturing
423450 Surgical dressings merchant wholesalers
339113 Surgical implants manufacturing
811219 Surgical instrument repair and maintenance services
423450 Surgical instruments and apparatus merchant wholesalers

339112 Surgical knife blades and handles manufacturing
621111 Surgical pathologists' offices (e.g., centers, clinics)
339112 Surgical stapling devices manufacturing
339113 Surgical supplies (except medical instruments) manufacturing
423450 Surgical supplies merchant wholesalers
334510 Surgical support systems (e.g., heart-lung machines) (except iron lungs) manufacturing
423450 Surgical towels merchant wholesalers
311710 Surimi manufacturing
238210 Surveillance system, installation only
213112 Surveying (except seismographic) oil or gas wells on a contract basis
541370 Surveying and mapping services (except geophysical)
423490 Surveying equipment and supplies merchant wholesalers
811219 Surveying instrument repair and maintenance services
334519 Surveying instruments manufacturing
541360 Surveying services, geophysical
321999 Surveyor's stakes, wood, manufacturing
611699 Survival training instruction
238310 Suspended ceiling installation
315210 Suspenders cut and sew apparel contractors
315990 Suspenders cut and sewn from purchased fabric (except apparel contractors) 811118
Suspension repair shops, automotive 339113 Sutures, surgical, manufacturing 213112 Swabbing oil or gas wells on a contract
basis
333517 Swaging machines, metalworking, manufacturing
487210 Swamp buggy operation
323120 Swatches and samples, mounting for the trade
332999 Swatters, fly, metal, manufacturing
315210 Sweat bands cut and sew apparel contractors
315280 Sweat bands cut and sewn from purchased fabric (except apparel contractors)
315190 Sweat bands made in apparel knitting mills
315210 Sweat pants cut and sew apparel contractors
315190 Sweat pants made in apparel knitting mills
315220 Sweat pants, men's, boys', and unisex (i.e., sized without regard to gender), cut and sewn from purchased fabric (except apparel contractors)
315240 Sweat pants, women's, girls', and infants', cut and sewn from purchased fabric (except apparel contractors)
315210 Sweat suits cut and sew apparel contractors
315190 Sweat suits made in apparel knitting mills
315220 Sweat suits, men's and boys', cut and sewn
from purchased fabric (except apparel contractors)
315240 Sweat suits, women's, girls', and infants', cut and sewn from purchased fabric (except apparel contractors)
316110 Sweatband leather manufacturing
315210 Sweater jackets cut and sew apparel contractors
315190 Sweater jackets made in apparel knitting mills
315220 Sweater jackets, men's and boys', cut and sewn from purchased fabric (except apparel contractors)
315240 Sweater jackets, women's, girls', and infants', cut and sewn from purchased fabric (except apparel contractors)
315210 Sweater vests cut and sew apparel contractors
315190 Sweater vests made in apparel knitting mills
315220 Sweater vests, men's and boys', cut and sewn from purchased fabric (except apparel contractors)
315240 Sweater vests, women's, girls', and infants', cut and sewn from purchased fabric (except apparel contractors)
315210 Sweaters cut and sew apparel contractors
315190 Sweaters made in apparel knitting mills
315220 Sweaters, men's and boys', cut and sewn from
purchased fabric (except apparel contractors)
315240 Sweaters, women's, girls', and infants', cut and sewn from purchased fabric (except apparel contractors)
315210 Sweatshirts cut and sew apparel contractors
315190 Sweatshirts made in apparel knitting mills
315220 Sweatshirts, men's and boys', cut and sewn
from purchased fabric (except apparel contractors)
315220 Sweatshirts, outerwear, unisex (sized without regard to gender), cut and sewn from purchased fabric (except apparel contractors)
315240 Sweatshirts, women's, girls', and infants', cut and sewn from purchased fabric (except apparel contractors)
334515 Sweep generators manufacturing

334515 Sweep oscillators manufacturing 335210
Sweepers, household-type electric vacuum, manufacturing
325612 Sweeping compounds, absorbent, manufacturing
111219 Sweet corn farming, field and seed production
111219 Sweet pepper farming, field, bedding plant and seed production
115114 Sweet potato curing
111211 Sweet potato farming, field and seed potato production
311812 Sweet yeast goods (except frozen) manufacturing
311813 Sweet yeast goods, frozen, manufacturing
311999 Sweetening syrups (except pure maple) manufacturing
236220 Swimming facility, indoor, construction
611620 Swimming instruction 325998 Swimming
pool chemical preparations manufacturing
561790 Swimming pool cleaning and maintenance services
326199 Swimming pool covers and liners, plastics, manufacturing
333318 Swimming pool filter systems manufacturing
333414 Swimming pool heaters manufacturing
335129 Swimming pool lighting fixtures manufacturing
238990 Swimming pool screen enclosure construction
453998 Swimming pool supply stores
238990 Swimming pool, outdoor, construction
713940 Swimming pools
423910 Swimming pools and equipment merchant wholesalers
339920 Swimming pools, above ground, manufacturing
326199 Swimming pools, fiberglass, manufacturing
315210 Swimsuits cut and sew apparel contractors
315190 Swimsuits made in apparel knitting mills
315220 Swimsuits, men's and boys', cut and sewn
from purchased fabric (except apparel contractors)
315240 Swimsuits, women's, girls', and infants', cut and sewn from purchased fabric (except apparel contractors)
448190 Swimwear stores
424320 Swimwear, men's and boys', merchant wholesalers
424330 Swimwear, women's, children's, and infants', merchant wholesalers
112210 Swine farming
311119 Swine feed, complete, manufacturing 311119
Swine feed, supplements, concentrates, and premixes, manufacturing
424520 Swine merchant wholesalers
335932 Switch boxes, electrical wiring, manufacturing
335931 Switch cutouts manufacturing
335313 Switchboards and parts, power, manufacturing
423610 Switchboards, electrical distribution, merchant wholesalers
335931 Switches for electrical wiring (e.g., pressure, pushbutton, snap, tumbler) manufacturing
334419 Switches for electronic applications manufacturing
335313 Switches, electric power (except pushbutton, snap, solenoid, tumbler), manufacturing
423610 Switches, electrical, merchant wholesalers
423690 Switches, electronic, merchant wholesalers
335931 Switches, outlet box mounting-type, manufacturing
334512 Switches, pneumatic positioning remote, manufacturing
334512 Switches, thermostatic, manufacturing
335313 Switchgear and switchgear accessories manufacturing
335313 Switching equipment, power, manufacturing
334210 Switching equipment, telephone, manufacturing
488210 Switching services, railroad
114111 Swordfish fishing
332215 Swords, nonprecious and precious plated metal, manufacturing
212313 Syenite (except nepheline) crushed and broken stone mining and/or beneficiating
212311 Syenite (except nepheline) mining or quarrying
212325 Syenite, nepheline, mining and/or beneficiating
212221 Sylvanite mining and/or beneficiating
711130 Symphony orchestras
813110 Synagogues
335312 Synchronous condensers and timing motors, electric, manufacturing
335312 Synchronous motors manufacturing

334515 Synchroscopes manufacturing
519110 Syndicates, news
339992 Synthesizers, music, manufacturing
311340 Synthetic chocolate manufacturing
314110 Synthetic or artificial turf manufacturing
325212 Synthetic rubber (i.e., vulcanizable elastomers) manufacturing
424690 Synthetic rubber merchant wholesalers
327999 Synthetic stones, for gem stones and industrial use, manufacturing
325199 Synthetic sweeteners (i.e., sweetening agents) manufacturing
339112 Syringes, hypodermic, manufacturing
424490 Syrup (except fountain) merchant wholesalers
311313 Syrup made from sugar beets
311930 Syrup, beverage, manufacturing
311314 Syrup, cane, manufacturing
311351 Syrup, chocolate, made from cacao beans
311352 Syrup, chocolate, made from purchased chocolate
311999 Syrup, corn (except wet milled), manufacturing
311221 Syrup, corn, made by wet milling
311930 Syrup, flavoring (except coffee based), manufacturing
311920 Syrup, flavoring, coffee based, manufacturing
111998 Syrup, pure maple (i.e., maple syrup reducing)
311999 Syrup, sweetening (except pure maple), manufacturing
311999 Syrup, table, artificially flavored, manufacturing
424450 Syrups, fountain (except soft drink), merchant wholesalers
541512 Systems integration design consulting services, computer
541512 Systems integration design services, computer
532289 Table and banquet accessory rental
327110 Table articles, coarse earthenware, manufacturing
327110 Table articles, earthenware, manufacturing
327110 Table articles, fine earthenware (i.e., whiteware), manufacturing
327110 Table articles, vitreous china, manufacturing
332215 Table cutlery, nonprecious and precious plated metal, manufacturing
339910 Table cutlery, precious metal, manufacturing
335121 Table lamps (i.e., lighting fixtures) manufacturing
812331 Table linen supply services
311225 Table oil made from purchased oils
311221 Table oil, corn, made by wet milling
311942 Table salt manufacturing
327991 Table tops, marble, manufacturing
337215 Table tops, wood, manufacturing
314120 Tablecloths (except paper) made from purchased materials
313210 Tablecloths made in broadwoven fabric mills
313240 Tablecloths made in lace mills
313240 Tablecloths made in warp or weft knitting mills
322291 Tablecloths, paper, made from purchased paper
337214 Tables (except wood), office-type, manufacturing
337124 Tables, metal household-type, manufacturing
337122 Tables, wood household-type, manufacturing
337211 Tables, wood, office-type, manufacturing
334111 Tablet computers manufacturing 322230
Tablets (e.g., memo, note, writing) made from purchased paper
322121 Tablets (e.g., memo, note, writing) made in paper mills
332999 Tablets, metal, manufacturing
423220 Tableware (except disposable, plated, precious) merchant wholesalers
327215 Tableware made from purchased glass
327212 Tableware made in glass making plants
532289 Tableware rental
424130 Tableware, disposable, merchant wholesalers
423940 Tableware, precious and plated, merchant wholesalers
327110 Tableware, vitreous china, manufacturing
334515 Tachometer generators manufacturing
424910 Tack (e.g., harnesses, saddlery) merchant wholesalers
451110 Tack (e.g., harnesses, saddlery) shops
321999 Tackle blocks, wood, manufacturing
451110 Tackle shops (i.e., fishing)
339920 Tackle, fishing (except line, nets, seines), manufacturing

423710 Tacks merchant wholesalers
331222 Tacks, iron or steel, made in wire drawing plants
332618 Tacks, metal, made from purchased wire
212210 Taconite concentrates or agglomerates beneficiating
212210 Taconite ores mining and/or beneficiating
334511 Taffrail logs manufacturing
213111 Tailing in oil and gas field wells on a contract basis
811490 Tailor shops, alterations only
315210 Tailored dress and sport coats cut and sew apparel contractors
315220 Tailored dress and sport coats, men's and boys', cut and sewn from purchased fabric (except apparel contractors)
****** Tailors -- see specific apparel manufacturing
332215 Tailors' scissors, nonelectric, manufacturing
423850 Tailors' supplies merchant wholesalers
445299 Take-and-bake meal stores
445299 Take-and-bake pizza shops
722513 Takeout eating places
212399 Talc mining and/or beneficiating
327992 Talc processing beyond beneficiation
325620 Talcum powders manufacturing
711410 Talent agencies
711410 Talent agents
541214 Talent payment services
325194 Tall oil (except skimmings) manufacturing
311611 Tallow produced in a slaughtering plant
311613 Tallow produced in rendering plant
334514 Tally counters manufacturing
334514 Tallying meters (except clocks, electricity meters, watches) manufacturing
333120 Tampers, powered, manufacturing
332994 Tampion guns manufacturing
111320 Tangelo groves
111320 Tangerine groves
332994 Tank artillery manufacturing
336211 Tank bodies for trucks manufacturing
562998 Tank cleaning and disposal services, commercial or industrial
562991 Tank cleaning services, septic
238990 Tank lining contractors
315210 Tank tops cut and sew apparel contractors
315190 Tank tops, outerwear, made in apparel knitting mills
315220 Tank tops, outerwear, men's and boys', cut and sewn from purchased fabric (except apparel contractors)
315190 Tank tops, underwear, made in apparel knitting mills
315220 Tank tops, underwear, men's and boys', cut and sewn from purchased fabric (except apparel contractors)
315240 Tank tops, women's, girls', and infants', cut and sewn from purchased fabric (except apparel contractors)
336212 Tank trailers, liquid and dry bulk, manufacturing
334514 Tank truck meters manufacturing
336211 Tank trucks (e.g., fuel oil, milk, water) assembling on purchased chassis
532411 Tanker (boat) rental or leasing without crew
484220 Tanker trucking (e.g., chemical, juice, milk, petroleum), local
484230 Tanker trucking (e.g., chemical, juice, milk, petroleum), long-distance
423860 Tanks and tank components merchant wholesalers
327390 Tanks, concrete, manufacturing
327110 Tanks, flush, vitreous china, manufacturing
332420 Tanks, heavy gauge metal, manufacturing
336992 Tanks, military (including factory rebuilding), manufacturing
333316 Tanks, photographic developing, fixing, and washing, manufacturing
423830 Tanks, pressure, merchant wholesalers
423510 Tanks, storage metal, merchant wholesalers
326199 Tanks, storage, plastics or fiberglass, manufacturing
321920 Tanks, wood, coopered, manufacturing
316110 Tannery leather manufacturing
333249 Tannery machinery manufacturing
325194 Tannic acid (i.e., tannins) manufacturing
325180 Tanning agents, inorganic, manufacturing
325199 Tanning agents, synthetic organic, manufacturing
316110 Tanning and currying furs
325194 Tanning extracts and materials, natural, manufacturing
812199 Tanning salons
212299 Tantalite mining and/or beneficiating
212299 Tantalum ores mining and/or beneficiating
331410 Tantalum refining, primary

711120 Tap dance companies
722410 Tap rooms (i.e., drinking places)
339940 Tape dispensers manufacturing
423420 Tape dispensing machines merchant wholesalers
512120 Tape distribution for television
332216 Tape measures, metal, manufacturing
334310 Tape players and recorders, household-type, manufacturing
423620 Tape players and recorders, household-type, merchant wholesalers
532210 Tape recorder rental
561990 Tape slitting (e.g., cutting plastic or leather into widths) for the trade
334112 Tape storage units (e.g., drive backups), computer peripheral equipment, manufacturing
512191 Tape transfer service
332991 Tapered roller bearings manufacturing
322230 Tapes (e.g., adding machine, calculator, cash register) made from purchased paper
313220 Tapes weaving
423690 Tapes, blank, audio and video, merchant wholesalers
424120 Tapes, cellophane, merchant wholesalers
334613 Tapes, magnetic recording (i.e., audio, data, video), blank, manufacturing
339113 Tapes, medical adhesive, manufacturing
423450 Tapes, medical and surgical, merchant wholesalers
313230 Tapes, nonwoven fabric, manufacturing
423990 Tapes, prerecorded, audio or video, merchant wholesalers
322220 Tapes, pressure sensitive (e.g., cellophane, masking), gummed, made from purchased paper or other materials
334519 Tapes, surveyor's, manufacturing
424310 Tapes, textile, merchant wholesalers
313320 Tapes, varnished and coated (except magnetic), made from purchased fabric
238310 Taping and finishing drywall
311221 Tapioca manufacturing 333517 Tapping machines, metalworking, manufacturing
333515 Taps and dies (i.e., a machine tool accessory) manufacturing
335931 Taps, current, attachment plug and screw shell types, manufacturing
316998 Taps, shoe, leather, manufacturing
325211 Tar acid resins manufacturing
324121 Tar and asphalt paving mixtures made from purchased asphaltic materials
325194 Tar and tar oils made by distillation of wood
325194 Tar made by distillation of coal tar
324110 Tar made in petroleum refineries 324122 Tar paper made from purchased asphaltic materials and paper
324122 Tar paper, building and roofing, made from purchased paper
322121 Tar paper, building and roofing, made in paper mills
324122 Tar roofing cements and coatings made from purchased asphaltic materials
211120 Tar sands mining
336411 Target drones, aircraft, manufacturing
336413 Targets, trailer type, aircraft, manufacturing
541614 Tariff rate consulting services
541614 Tariff rate information services
111219 Taro farming, field and seed production
314910 Tarpaulins made from purchased fabrics
423330 Tarred felts merchant wholesalers
237310 Tarring roads
311941 Tartar sauce manufacturing
325199 Tartaric acid manufacturing
325199 Tartrates, not specified elsewhere by process, manufacturing
314999 Tassels manufacturing
812199 Tattoo parlors
722410 Taverns (i.e., drinking places)
561440 Tax collection services on a contract or fee basis
541110 Tax law attorneys' offices
541110 Tax law attorneys' private practices 523910 Tax liens dealing (i.e., acting as a principal in dealing tax liens to investors)
541213 Tax return preparation services
921130 Taxation departments
541850 Taxicab card advertising services
485310 Taxicab dispatch services
485310 Taxicab fleet operators
423110 Taxicab merchant wholesalers
485310 Taxicab organizations
485310 Taxicab owner-operators
485310 Taxicab services
711510 Taxidermists, independent

423850 Taxidermy supplies merchant wholesalers
334514 Taximeters manufacturing
813319 Taxpayers' advocacy organizations
311920 Tea (except herbal) manufacturing
445299 Tea and coffee (i.e., packaged) stores
311920 Tea blending
111998 Tea farming
424490 Tea merchant wholesalers
311920 Tea, herbal, manufacturing
312111 Tea, iced, manufacturing
311920 Tea, instant, manufacturing
113210 Teaberries gathering
923110 Teacher certification bureaus
561311 Teacher registries
333318 Teaching machines (e.g., flight simulators) manufacturing
423490 Teaching machines (except computers), electronic, merchant wholesalers
332215 Teakettles and coffee pots, fabricated metal (except electric, glass), manufacturing
335210 Teakettles, electric, manufacturing
327212 Teakettles, glass and glass ceramic, made in glass making plants
315210 Team athletic uniforms cut and sew apparel contractors
315280 Team athletic uniforms cut and sewn from purchased fabric (except apparel contractors)
325199 Tear gas manufacturing
313310 Teaseling fabrics 325412 Technetium medicinal preparations manufacturing
561410 Technical editing services
327212 Technical glassware and glass products, pressed or blown, made in glass making plants
327215 Technical glassware made from purchased glass
511120 Technical magazine and periodical publishers (except exclusive Internet publishing)
511120 Technical magazine and periodical publishers and printing combined
519130 Technical magazine and periodical publishers, exclusively on Internet
323111 Technical magazines and periodicals commercial printing (except screen) without publishing
323113 Technical magazines and periodicals screen printing without publishing
511130 Technical manual and paperback book publishers (except exclusive Internet publishing)
511130 Technical manual and paperback book publishers and printing combined
323120 Technical manual paper (books) binding without printing
511130 Technical manual publishers (except exclusive Internet publishing)
519130 Technical manual publishers, exclusively on Internet
323117 Technical manuals and papers (books) printing and binding without publishing
323117 Technical manuals and papers (books) printing without publishing
711510 Technical writers, independent
315210 Teddies cut and sew apparel contractors
315240 Teddies, women's and girls', cut and sewn from purchased fabric (except apparel contractors)
624110 Teen outreach services
339114 Teeth (except customized) manufacturing
325611 Teeth whiteners (e.g., pastes, gels) manufacturing
339116 Teeth, custom made in dental laboratories
423450 Teeth, dental, merchant wholesalers
517312 Telecommunications carriers, cellular telephone
517311 Telecommunications carriers, wired 238210 Telecommunications equipment and wiring (except transmission line) installation contractors
423690 Telecommunications equipment merchant wholesalers
532490 Telecommunications equipment rental or leasing
541618 Telecommunications management consulting services
517911 Telecommunications resellers 423690 Teleconferencing equipment, audio or video, merchant wholesalers
561499 Teleconferencing services
812990 Telegram services, singing
423690 Telegraph equipment merchant wholesalers
561422 Telemarketing bureaus
561422 Telemarketing services on a contract or fee basis
334513 Telemetering instruments, industrial process-type, manufacturing
517919 Telemetry and tracking system operations on a contract or fee basis

334416 Telephone and telegraph transformers, electronic component-type, manufacturing
334210 Telephone answering machines manufacturing
423620 Telephone answering machines merchant wholesalers
561421 Telephone answering services
337215 Telephone booths manufacturing
561422 Telephone call centers
561421 Telephone call forwarding services
334210 Telephone carrier line equipment manufacturing
334210 Telephone carrier switching equipment manufacturing
517410 Telephone communications carriers, satellite
517312 Telephone communications carriers, wireless (except satellite)
517911 Telephone communications resellers (except satellite)
624190 Telephone counseling services
323111 Telephone directories commercial printing (except screen) without publishing
323113 Telephone directories screen printing without publishing
541870 Telephone directory distribution services, door-to-door
511140 Telephone directory publishers (except exclusive Internet publishing)
511140 Telephone directory publishers and printing combined
519130 Telephone directory publishers, exclusively on Internet
238210 Telephone equipment and building wiring installation
423690 Telephone equipment merchant wholesalers
811213 Telephone equipment repair and maintenance services without retailing new telephone equipment
238210 Telephone installation contractors
237130 Telephone line construction
237130 Telephone line stringing
561422 Telephone solicitation services on a contract or fee basis
519190 Telephone-based recorded information services
334210 Telephones (except cellular telephone) manufacturing
423690 Telephones merchant wholesalers
334220 Telephones, cellular, manufacturing
334210 Telephones, coin-operated, manufacturing
334118 Teleprinters (i.e., computer terminals) manufacturing
512191 Teleproduction services
333314 Telescopes manufacturing
334310 Television (TV) sets manufacturing
541840 Television advertising representatives (i.e., independent of media owners) 443142
Television and radio stores 515120 Television broad-
casting networks 515120 Television broadcasting
stations 321999 Television cabinets (i.e., housings),
wood,
manufacturing
423410 Television cameras merchant wholesalers
512110 Television commercial production
561311 Television employment agencies
511120 Television guide publishers (except exclusive Internet publishing)
511120 Television guide publishers and printing combined
519130 Television guide publishers, exclusively on Internet
323111 Television guides commercial printing (except screen) without publishing
323113 Television guides screen printing without publishing
326199 Television housings, plastics, manufacturing
517311 Television operations, closed-circuit
454110 Television order, home shopping
334419 Television picture tubes manufacturing
711510 Television producers, independent
532210 Television rental
811211 Television repair services without retailing new televisions
423620 Television sets merchant wholesalers
512110 Television show production
512120 Television show syndicators
236220 Television station construction
515210 Television subscription services
332312 Television tower sections, fabricated structural metal, manufacturing
334220 Television transmitting antennas and ground equipment manufacturing
237130 Television transmitting tower construction
334220 Television, closed-circuit equipment, manufacturing

212221 Telluride (gold) mining and/or beneficiating
331410 Tellurium refining, primary
813319 Temperance organizations 238210 Temperature control system installation 334512 Temperature controls, automatic, residential and commercial-types, manufacturing
334513 Temperature instruments, industrial process-type (except glass and bimetal thermometers), manufacturing
334512 Temperature sensors for motor windings manufacturing
327215 Tempered glass made from purchased glass
332811 Tempering metals and metal products for the trade
331110 Template, made in iron and steel mills, manufacturing
334519 Templates, drafting, manufacturing
339115 Temples and fronts (i.e., eyeglass frames), ophthalmic, manufacturing
813110 Temples, religious
561320 Temporary employment services
561320 Temporary help services
624221 Temporary housing for families of medical patients
624221 Temporary shelters (e.g., battered women's, homeless, runaway youth)
561320 Temporary staffing services
713950 Ten pin bowling alleys
713950 Ten pin bowling centers
813319 Tenants' advocacy associations
813990 Tenants' associations (except advocacy)
813319 Tenants' associations, advocacy
713940 Tennis club facilities
236220 Tennis court, indoor, construction
713940 Tennis courts
237990 Tennis courts, outdoor, construction 423910 Tennis equipment and supplies merchant wholesalers
339920 Tennis goods (e.g., balls, frames, rackets) manufacturing
611620 Tennis instruction, camps, or schools
711219 Tennis professionals, independent (i.e., participating in sports events)
315210 Tennis shirts cut and sew apparel contractors
315190 Tennis shirts made in apparel knitting mills
315220 Tennis shirts, men's and boys', cut and sewn from purchased fabric (except apparel contractors)
315240 Tennis shirts, women's, girls', and infants', cut and sewn from purchased fabric (except apparel contractors)
315210 Tennis skirts cut and sew apparel contractors
315190 Tennis skirts made in apparel knitting mills
315240 Tennis skirts, women's, girls', and infants', cut and sewn from purchased fabric (except apparel contractors)
334510 TENS (transcutaneous electrical nerve stimulator) manufacturing
334519 Tensile strength testing equipment manufacturing
321999 Tent poles, wood, manufacturing
336214 Tent trailers (hard top and soft top) manufacturing
532284 Tent, camping, rental
532289 Tent, party, rental
424990 Tents (except camping) merchant wholesalers
314910 Tents made from purchased fabrics
335931 Terminals and connectors for electrical devices manufacturing
334118 Terminals, computer, manufacturing
424710 Terminals, petroleum, merchant wholesalers
561710 Termite control services
325320 Termite poisons manufacturing
331110 Terneplate made in iron and steel mills
423510 Terneplate merchant wholesalers
331110 Ternes, iron or steel, long or short, made in iron and steel mills
325199 Terpineol manufacturing
423320 Terra cotta merchant wholesalers
114119 Terrapin fishing
238340 Terrazzo and tile refinishing
238340 Terrazzo contractors
327390 Terrazzo products, precast (except brick, block and pipe), manufacturing
313210 Terry broadwoven fabrics weaving
325199 Tert-butylated bis (p-phenoxyphenyl) ether fluid manufacturing
238910 Test boring for construction
611710 Test development and evaluation services, educational
213114 Test drilling for metal mining on a contract basis
213115 Test drilling for nonmetallic minerals mining (except fuel) on a contract basis

334515 Test equipment for electronic and electrical circuits and equipment manufacturing
334515 Test sets, ignition harness, manufacturing
525920 Testamentary trusts
334519 Testers for checking hydraulic controls on aircraft manufacturing
423830 Testing and measuring equipment, electrical (except automotive), merchant wholesalers
423120 Testing and measuring equipment, electrical, automotive, merchant wholesalers
334519 Testing equipment (e.g., abrasion, shearing strength, tensile strength, torsion) manufacturing
541380 Testing laboratories (except medical, veterinary)
621511 Testing laboratories, medical
541940 Testing laboratories, veterinary
541940 Testing services for veterinarians
488190 Testing services, aircraft
611710 Testing services, educational
333993 Testing, weighing, inspecting, packaging machinery manufacturing
325199 Tetrachloroethylene manufacturing
325411 Tetracycline, uncompounded, manufacturing
325199 Tetraethyl lead manufacturing
325920 Tetryl explosive materials manufacturing
424920 Textbooks merchant wholesalers
323117 Textbooks printing and binding without publishing
323117 Textbooks printing without publishing
314910 Textile bags made from purchased woven or knitted materials
424990 Textile bags merchant wholesalers
313210 Textile broadwoven fabrics mills
561990 Textile cutting services
541490 Textile design services
325613 Textile finishing assistants manufacturing
333249 Textile finishing machinery (e.g., bleaching, dyeing, mercerizing, printing) manufacturing
314999 Textile fire hose made from purchased material
561910 Textile folding and packaging services
327212 Textile glass fibers made in glass making plants
327110 Textile guides, porcelain, manufacturing
316998 Textile leathers (e.g., apron picker leather, mill strapping) manufacturing
423830 Textile machinery and equipment merchant wholesalers
532490 Textile machinery rental or leasing
811310 Textile machinery repair and maintenance services
333249 Textile making machinery manufacturing
236210 Textile mill construction
313210 Textile mills, broadwoven fabrics
313220 Textile mills, narrow woven fabric
313220 Textile narrow woven fabric mills
325910 Textile printing inks manufacturing
333249 Textile printing machinery manufacturing
313210 Textile products (except apparel) made in broadwoven fabric mills
313240 Textile products (except apparel) made in lace mills
313220 Textile products (except apparel) made in narrow woven fabric mills
313240 Textile products (except apparel) made in warp or weft knitting mills
313310 Textile products finishing
325613 Textile scouring agents manufacturing
423930 Textile waste merchant wholesalers
313320 Textile waterproofing
424310 Textiles (except burlap, felt) merchant wholesalers
325220 Texturizing cellulosic yarn made in the same establishment
333249 Texturizing machinery for textiles manufacturing
325220 Texturizing noncellulosic yarn made in the same establishment
313110 Texturizing purchased yarn
212299 Thallium mining and/or beneficiating
711110 Theater companies (except dance)
711110 Theater companies (except dance), amateur
711120 Theater companies, dance
236220 Theater construction
423410 Theater equipment (except seats) merchant wholesalers
711310 Theater festival managers with facilities
711320 Theater festival managers without facilities
711310 Theater festival organizers with facilities
711320 Theater festival organizers without facilities
711310 Theater festival promoters with facilities

711320 Theater festival promoters without facilities
711310 Theater operators
531120 Theater property rental or leasing, not operating theater
611610 Theater schools
337127 Theater seating manufacturing
423210 Theater seats merchant wholesalers
711120 Theaters, dance
711110 Theaters, dinner
711110 Theaters, live theatrical production (except dance)
512131 Theaters, motion picture (except drive-in)
512132 Theaters, motion picture, drive-in
512131 Theaters, motion picture, indoor
711110 Theaters, musical
512132 Theaters, outdoor motion picture
711320 Theatrical booking agencies (except motion picture)
315210 Theatrical costumes cut and sew apparel contractors
315280 Theatrical costumes cut and sewn from purchased fabric (except apparel contractors)
711120 Theatrical dance productions, live
561311 Theatrical employment agencies 532490 Theatrical equipment (except costumes) rental or leasing
711310 Theatrical production managers with facilities
711320 Theatrical production managers without facilities
711310 Theatrical production organizers with facilities
711320 Theatrical production organizers without facilities
711310 Theatrical production promoters with facilities
711320 Theatrical production promoters without facilities
711110 Theatrical repertory companies
711110 Theatrical road companies
339999 Theatrical scenery manufacturing
711110 Theatrical stock companies
711410 Theatrical talent agents
561599 Theatrical ticket offices
532281 Theatrical wardrobe and costume rental
334290 Theft prevention signaling devices (e.g., door entrance annunciation, holdup signaling devices, personal duress signaling devices), manufacturing
713110 Theme parks, amusement 325411 Theobromine and derivatives (i.e., basic chemicals) manufacturing
333314 Theodolites manufacturing
334519 Theodolites, surveying, manufacturing
611310 Theological seminaries offering baccalaureate or graduate degrees
334517 Therapeutic X-ray apparatus and tubes (e.g., medical, industrial, research) manufacturing
****** Therapists' offices -- see type
423450 Therapy equipment merchant wholesalers
334516 Thermal analysis instruments, laboratory-type, manufacturing
334516 Thermal conductivity instruments and sensors manufacturing
334513 Thermal conductivity instruments, industrial process-type, manufacturing
326140 Thermal insulation, polystyrene foam, manufacturing
237130 Thermal power plant construction
541380 Thermal testing laboratories or services
423330 Thermal wrap, house, merchant wholesalers
334416 Thermistors manufacturing
334513 Thermistors, industrial process-type, manufacturing
334519 Thermocouples (except industrial process, aircraft type, glass vacuum) manufacturing
334512 Thermocouples, glass vacuum, manufacturing
334513 Thermocouples, industrial process-type, manufacturing
335999 Thermoelectric generators manufacturing
333993 Thermoform, blister, and skin packaging machinery manufacturing
333249 Thermoforming machinery for plastics manufacturing
334516 Thermogravimetric analyzers manufacturing
334519 Thermometer, liquid-in-glass and bimetal types (except medical), manufacturing
423450 Thermometers merchant wholesalers
334513 Thermometers, filled system industrial process-type, manufacturing
339112 Thermometers, medical, manufacturing
325211 Thermoplastic resins and plastics materials manufacturing

325211 Thermosetting plastics resins manufacturing
325212 Thermosetting vulcanizable elastomers manufacturing
332911 Thermostatic traps, industrial-type, manufacturing
334512 Thermostats (e.g., air-conditioning, appliance, comfort heating, refrigeration) manufacturing
336390 Thermostats, automotive, truck, and bus, manufacturing
334519 Thickness gauging instruments, ultrasonic, manufacturing
332999 Thimbles for wire rope manufacturing
334413 Thin film integrated circuits manufacturing
333242 Thin layer deposition equipment, semiconductor, manufacturing
115112 Thinning of crops, mechanical and chemical
325180 Thiocyanate manufacturing
325199 Thioglycolic acid manufacturing
325212 Thiol rubber manufacturing
212299 Thorite mining and/or beneficiating
212299 Thorium ores mining and/or beneficiating
711212 Thoroughbred racetracks
424310 Thread (except industrial) merchant wholesalers
333515 Thread cutting dies (i.e., a machine tool accessory) manufacturing
313310 Thread finishing
333249 Thread making machinery manufacturing
313110 Thread mills
333517 Thread rolling machines, metalworking, manufacturing
313110 Thread, all fibers, manufacturing
423840 Thread, industrial, merchant wholesalers
326299 Thread, rubber (except fabric covered), manufacturing
333517 Threading machines, metalworking, manufacturing
423830 Threading tools merchant wholesalers
115113 Threshing service
551112 Thrift holding companies
453310 Thrift shops, used merchandise
333249 Through-hole machinery, printed circuit board loading, manufacturing
325220 Throwing cellulosic yarn made in the same establishment
325220 Throwing noncellulosic yarn made in the same establishment
313110 Throwing purchased yarn 334519 Thrust power indicators, aircraft engine, manufacturing
332991 Thrust roller bearings manufacturing
334413 Thyristors manufacturing
325412 Thyroid preparations manufacturing
325320 Tick powders or sprays manufacturing
561599 Ticket (e.g., airline, bus, cruise ship, sports, theatrical) offices
561599 Ticket (e.g., airline, bus, cruise ship, sports, theatrical) sales offices
561599 Ticket (e.g., amusement, sports, theatrical) agencies
561599 Ticket (e.g., amusement, sports, theatrical) sales agencies
561599 Ticket agencies, amusement
561599 Ticket agencies, sports
561599 Ticket agencies, theatrical
561599 Ticket offices for foreign cruise ship companies
331110 Tie plates, iron or steel, made in iron and steel mills
448150 Tie shops
331222 Tie wires made in wire drawing plants
315210 Ties cut and sew apparel contractors 315190 Ties made in apparel knitting mills 327390 Ties, concrete, railroad, manufacturing 315990 Ties, men's and boys' hand sewn (except apparel contractors), manufacturing
321113 Ties, railroad, made from logs or bolts
321114 Ties, wood railroad bridge, cross, and switch, treating
321113 Ties, wood, made from logs or bolts
423990 Ties, wood, merchant wholesalers
315110 Tights knitting or knitting and finishing
112511 Tilapia production
238340 Tile (except resilient) contractors
238340 Tile (except resilient) laying and setting
325520 Tile adhesives manufacturing
333249 Tile making machinery (except kilns) manufacturing
444190 Tile stores, ceramic
327120 Tile, ceramic wall and floor, manufacturing
327120 Tile, clay, refractory, manufacturing
327120 Tile, clay, structural, manufacturing
321999 Tile, cork, manufacturing
327120 Tile, roofing and drain, clay, manufacturing

327120 Tile, sewer, clay, manufacturing
423320 Tile, structural clay (except refractory and clay roofing tile) merchant wholesalers
114111 Tilefish fishing
333994 Tilemaking kilns manufacturing
326199 Tiles, floor (i.e., linoleum, rubber, vinyl), manufacturing
423820 Tillers, farm and garden, merchant wholesalers
333112 Tillers, lawn and garden-type, manufacturing
423990 Timber and timber products (except lumber) merchant wholesalers
113310 Timber piling
113310 Timber pole cutting
237990 Timber removal, underwater
113110 Timber tract operations
115310 Timber valuation
321114 Timber, structural, treating
321113 Timbers, made from logs or bolts
321213 Timbers, structural, glue laminated or pre-engineered wood, manufacturing
334519 Time clocks and time recording devices manufacturing
334513 Time cycle and program controllers, industrial process-type, manufacturing
334519 Time locks manufacturing
323111 Time planners/organizers and refills manufacturing
334512 Time program controls, air-conditioning systems, manufacturing
423420 Time recording machines merchant wholesalers
334519 Time stamps containing clock mechanisms manufacturing
335313 Time switches, electrical switchgear apparatus, manufacturing
334519 Timers for industrial use, clockwork mechanism, manufacturing
236117 Time-share condominium construction for-sale builders
236115 Time-share condominium construction general contractors
561599 Time-share exchange services, condominium
326220 Timing belt, rubber or plastics, manufacturing
335314 Timing devices, mechanical and solid-state (except clockwork), manufacturing
336310 Timing gears and chains, automotive and truck gasoline engine, manufacturing
334519 Timing mechanisms, clockwork, manufacturing
335312 Timing motors, synchronous, electric, manufacturing
331491 Tin and tin alloy bar, pipe, rod, sheet, strip, and tubing made from purchased metals or scrap
423510 Tin and tin alloy primary forms merchant wholesalers
331410 Tin base alloys made in primary tin smelting and refining mills
325180 Tin chloride manufacturing
325180 Tin compounds, not specified elsewhere by process, manufacturing
212299 Tin metal concentrates beneficiating
212299 Tin metal ores mining and/or beneficiating
325180 Tin oxide manufacturing
332431 Tin plate cans, light gauge metal, manufacturing
423510 Tin plate merchant wholesalers
331492 Tin recovering from scrap and/or alloying purchased metals
331410 Tin refining, primary
331491 Tin rolling, drawing, or extruding purchased metals or scrap
325180 Tin salts manufacturing
325412 Tincture of iodine preparations manufacturing
332999 Tinfoil not made in rolling mills
331110 Tin-free steel made in iron and steel mills
332216 Tinners' snips manufacturing
331110 Tinplate made in iron and steel mills
339999 Tinsel manufacturing
325998 Tint and dye preparations, household-type (except hair), manufacturing
325620 Tints, dyes, and rinses, hair, manufacturing
212111 Tipple operation, bituminous coal mining and/or beneficiating
236210 Tipple, mining, construction
316998 Tips, shoe, leather, manufacturing
423130 Tire and tube repair materials merchant wholesalers
332618 Tire chains made from purchased wire
314994 Tire cord and fabric, all materials, manufacturing
336360 Tire covers made from purchased fabric
441320 Tire dealers, automotive
325998 Tire inflators, aerosol, manufacturing

333249 Tire making machinery manufacturing
333318 Tire mounting machines, motor vehicle, manufacturing
333249 Tire recapping machinery manufacturing
423830 Tire recapping machinery merchant wholesalers
326211 Tire repair materials manufacturing
811198 Tire repair shops (except retreading), automotive
326212 Tire retreading, recapping or rebuilding
333249 Tire shredding machinery manufacturing
423130 Tire tubes, motor vehicle, merchant wholesalers
326211 Tires (e.g., pneumatic, semi-pneumatic, solid rubber) manufacturing
423130 Tires, new, motor vehicle, merchant wholesalers
326199 Tires, plastics, manufacturing
423930 Tires, scrap, merchant wholesalers
423130 Tires, used (except scrap), merchant wholesalers
111421 Tissue culture farming
322121 Tissue paper stock manufacturing 424130
Tissue paper, toilet and facial, merchant wholesalers
327110 Titania porcelain insulators manufacturing
212299 Titaniferous-magnetite ores, valued chiefly for titanium content, mining and/or beneficiating
331491 Titanium and titanium alloy bar, billet, rod, sheet, strip, and tubing made from purchased metals or scrap
325130 Titanium based pigments manufacturing
331529 Titanium castings (except die-castings), unfinished, manufacturing
212299 Titanium concentrates beneficiating
331523 Titanium die-castings, unfinished, manufacturing
325180 Titanium dioxide manufacturing
332112 Titanium forgings made from purchased metals, unfinished
212299 Titanium ores mining and/or beneficiating
331410 Titanium refining, primary 331491 Titanium
rolling, drawing, or extruding purchased metals or scrap
541191 Title abstract companies, real estate
541191 Title companies, real estate
524127 Title insurance carriers, real estate, direct
541191 Title search companies, real estate
519190 Title search services (except real estate)
512191 Titling of motion picture film or video
334516 Titrimeters manufacturing
325920 TNT (trinitrotoluene) manufacturing
335210 Toaster ovens, household-type electric, manufacturing
423620 Toasters, electric, merchant wholesalers
335210 Toasters, household-type electric, manufacturing
424940 Tobacco (except leaf) merchant wholesalers
111910 Tobacco farming, field and seed production
115114 Tobacco grading
333111 Tobacco harvester machines manufacturing
321920 Tobacco hogshead stock, manufacturing
321920 Tobacco hogsheads, manufacturing
312230 Tobacco leaf processing and aging
339999 Tobacco pipes manufacturing
316998 Tobacco pouches (except metal) manufacturing
339910 Tobacco pouches, precious metal, manufacturing
333249 Tobacco processing machinery (except farm-type) manufacturing
312230 Tobacco products (e.g., chewing, smoking, snuff) manufacturing
424940 Tobacco products merchant wholesalers
312230 Tobacco products, imitation, manufacturing
312230 Tobacco sheeting services
312230 Tobacco stemming and redrying
453991 Tobacco stores
424590 Tobacco, leaf, merchant wholesalers
339920 Toboggans manufacturing
316998 Toe caps, leather, manufacturing
311340 Toffee manufacturing
311991 Tofu (i.e., bean curd) (except frozen desserts) manufacturing
311520 Tofu frozen desserts manufacturing
332722 Toggle bolts, metal, manufacturing
325612 Toilet bowl cleaners manufacturing
423720 Toilet bowls and tanks merchant wholesalers
332999 Toilet fixtures, metal, manufacturing
326191 Toilet fixtures, plastics, manufacturing
327110 Toilet fixtures, vitreous china, manufacturing

316998 Toilet kits and cases (except metal) manufacturing
339910 Toilet kits and cases, precious metal, manufacturing
322291 Toilet paper made from purchased paper
322121 Toilet paper made in paper mills
325620 Toilet preparations (e.g., cosmetics, deodorants, perfumes) manufacturing
424210 Toilet preparations merchant wholesalers
562991 Toilet renting and/or servicing, portable
321999 Toilet seats, wood, manufacturing
325611 Toilet soaps manufacturing
424210 Toilet soaps merchant wholesalers
424130 Toilet tissue merchant wholesalers
332999 Toilet ware, precious plated metal, manufacturing
325620 Toilet water manufacturing
424210 Toiletries merchant wholesalers
488490 Toll road operations, highway
334210 Toll switching equipment, telephone, manufacturing
325110 Toluene made from refined petroleum or liquid hydrocarbons
324110 Toluene made in petroleum refineries
325194 Toluidines manufacturing 111219 Tomato farming (except under cover), field, bedding plant and seed production
111419 Tomato farming, grown under cover
333111 Tomato harvesting machines manufacturing
423990 Tombstones merchant wholesalers
325992 Toner cartridges manufacturing
424120 Toner cartridges merchant wholesalers
325992 Toner cartridges rebuilding
325130 Toners (except electrostatic, photographic) manufacturing
325992 Toners, electrostatic and photographic, manufacturing
339113 Tongue depressors manufacturing
316998 Tongues, boot and shoe, leather, manufacturing
339112 Tonometers, medical, manufacturing
332439 Tool boxes, light gauge metal, manufacturing
321920 Tool chests, wood, manufacturing
321999 Tool handles, wood, turned and shaped, manufacturing
541420 Tool industrial design services
532289 Tool rental or leasing for home use
337127 Tool stands, factory, manufacturing
331110 Tool steel made in iron and steel mills
444130 Tool stores, power and hand (except outdoor)
811411 Tool, home and garden, sharpening and repair services without retailing new home and garden tools
333515 Toolholders (i.e., a machine tool accessory) manufacturing
333515 Tools and accessories for machine tools manufacturing
423120 Tools and equipment, motor vehicle, merchant wholesalers
339114 Tools, dentists', manufacturing
423710 Tools, hand (except motor vehicle, machinists' precision tools), merchant wholesalers
332216 Tools, hand, metal blade (e.g., putty knives, scrapers, screwdrivers)
333991 Tools, handheld power-driven, manufacturing
332216 Tools, handheld, nonpowered (except kitchen-type), manufacturing
423830 Tools, machinists' precision, merchant wholesalers
332216 Tools, woodworking edge (e.g., augers, bits, countersinks), manufacturing
339994 Toothbrushes (except electric) manufacturing
424210 Toothbrushes (except electric) merchant wholesalers
335210 Toothbrushes, electric, manufacturing
423620 Toothbrushes, electric, merchant wholesalers
424210 Toothpastes merchant wholesalers
325611 Toothpastes, gels, and tooth powders manufacturing
321999 Toothpicks, wood, manufacturing
316998 Top lifts, boot and shoe, leather, manufacturing
212325 Topaz, non-gem, mining and/or beneficiating
315210 Topcoats cut and sew apparel contractors
315220 Topcoats, men's and boys', cut and sewn from purchased fabric (except apparel contractors)
541370 Topographic mapping services
541370 Topographic surveying services 424490 Toppings (except fountain) merchant wholesalers

424450 Toppings, fountain, merchant wholesalers
336390 Tops, convertible automotive, manufacturing
484220 Top-soil hauling, local
332994 Torpedo tubes manufacturing
332993 Torpedoes manufacturing
336350 Torque converters, automotive, truck, and bus, manufacturing
335312 Torque motors, electric, manufacturing
332613 Torsion bar, heavy gauge metal, manufacturing
334519 Torsion testing equipment manufacturing
311919 Tortilla chips manufacturing
311830 Tortillas manufacturing
334514 Totalizing fluid meters manufacturing
334514 Totalizing meters (except aircraft), consumption registering, manufacturing
339999 Toupees manufacturing
424990 Toupees merchant wholesalers
487110 Tour bus, scenic and sightseeing, operation
561520 Tour operators (i.e., arranging and assembling tours)
561591 Tourism bureaus
926110 Tourism development offices, government
721199 Tourist courts
713990 Tourist guide services
721199 Tourist homes
561591 Tourist information bureaus
721110 Tourist lodges
336413 Tow targets, aircraft, manufacturing
488410 Tow truck services
336211 Tow trucks (including tilt and load) assembling on purchased chassis
336611 Towboat building and repairing
532411 Towboat rental or leasing without crew
812331 Towel (except shop, wiping) supply services
327110 Towel bar holders, vitreous china and earthenware, manufacturing
812332 Towel supply services, shop or wiping
325620 Towelettes, premoistened, manufacturing
313210 Towels and washcloths made in broadwoven fabric mills
313240 Towels and washcloths made in warp or weft knitting mills
423220 Towels and washcloths merchant wholesalers
314120 Towels or washcloths made from purchased fabrics
423840 Towels, industrial, merchant wholesalers
322291 Towels, paper, made from purchased paper
322121 Towels, paper, made in paper mills
423450 Towels, surgical, merchant wholesalers
237130 Tower, power distribution and communication, construction
336390 Towing bars and systems manufacturing
483211 Towing service, inland waters (except on Great Lakes system)
488410 Towing services, motor vehicle
236115 Town house (i.e., single-family type) construction by general contractors
236117 Town house construction for-sale builders
531110 Town house rental or leasing
541320 Town planners' offices
541320 Town planning services
562910 Toxic material abatement services
562910 Toxic material removal contractors
621511 Toxicology health laboratories
325414 Toxoids (e.g., diphtheria, tetanus) manufacturing
339930 Toy furniture and household-type equipment manufacturing
423920 Toy furniture merchant wholesalers
451120 Toy stores 451120 Toy
stores, electronic
423920 Toys (including electronic) merchant wholesalers
339930 Toys manufacturing
333515 Tracer and tapering machine tool attachments manufacturing
332993 Tracer igniters, ammunition (i.e., more than 30 mm., more than 1.18 inch), manufacturing
339920 Track and field athletic equipment (except apparel, footwear) manufacturing
335121 Track lighting fixtures and equipment, residential, electric, manufacturing
484220 Tracked vehicle freight transportation, local
484230 Tracked vehicle freight transportation, long-distance
487110 Tracked vehicle sightseeing operation
339113 Traction apparatus manufacturing 811310
Tractor, farm or construction equipment repair and maintenance services
532490 Tractor, farm, rental or leasing

532490 Tractor, garden, rental or leasing 811411
Tractor, lawn and garden, repair and maintenance services without retailing new lawn and garden tractors
333120 Tractors and attachments, construction-type, manufacturing
333111 Tractors and attachments, farm-type, manufacturing
333112 Tractors and attachments, lawn and garden-type, manufacturing
333120 Tractors, crawler, manufacturing
423820 Tractors, farm and garden, merchant wholesalers
423110 Tractors, highway, merchant wholesalers
333924 Tractors, industrial, manufacturing
423830 Tractors, industrial, merchant wholesalers
336120 Tractors, truck for highway use, assembled on chassis of own manufacture
813910 Trade associations
522293 Trade banks (i.e., international trade financing)
323120 Trade binding services
926110 Trade commissions, government
926110 Trade development program administration
561920 Trade fair managers
561920 Trade fair organizers
561920 Trade fair promoters
522293 Trade financing, international
511120 Trade journal publishers (except exclusive Internet publishing)
511120 Trade journal publishers and printing combined
519130 Trade journal publishers, exclusively on Internet
323111 Trade journals commercial printing (except screen) without publishing
323113 Trade journals screen printing without publishing
511120 Trade magazine and periodical publishers (except exclusive Internet publishing)
511120 Trade magazine and periodical publishers and printing combined
519130 Trade magazine and periodical publishers, exclusively on Internet
323111 Trade magazines and periodicals commercial printing (except screen) without publishing
323113 Trade magazines and periodicals screen printing without publishing
238390 Trade show exhibit installation and dismantling contractors
561920 Trade show managers
561920 Trade show organizers
561920 Trade show promoters
611513 Trade union apprenticeship training programs
813930 Trade unions (except apprenticeship programs)
813930 Trade unions, local 533110
Trademark licensing
423920 Trading cards merchant wholesalers
523130 Trading companies, commodity contracts
452319 Trading posts, general merchandise
523110 Trading securities (i.e., acting as a principal in dealing securities to investors)
561990 Trading stamp promotion and sale to stores
561990 Trading stamp redemption services 334290
Traffic advisory and signalling systems manufacturing
922110 Traffic courts
541330 Traffic engineering consulting services
237310 Traffic lane painting
519110 Traffic reporting services
238210 Traffic signal installation
334290 Traffic signals manufacturing
237990 Trail construction
721214 Trail riding camps with accommodation facilities
713990 Trail riding, recreational
336390 Trailer hitches, motor vehicle, manufacturing
531190 Trailer park or court, residential
423120 Trailer parts, new, merchant wholesalers
532120 Trailer rental or leasing
336214 Trailers for transporting horses (except fifth-wheel-type) manufacturing 336214
Trailers, camping, manufacturing 336212 Trailers, fifth-wheel-type, for transporting horses, manufacturing
423830 Trailers, industrial, merchant wholesalers
423110 Trailers, motor vehicle, merchant wholesalers
115210 Training horses (except racehorses)
315210 Training pants (i.e., underwear) cut and sew apparel contractors
315240 Training pants (i.e., underwear), infants', cut and sewn from purchased fabric (except apparel contractors)
711219 Training race dogs

711219 Training racehorses 339930 Trains and equipment, toy, electric or mechanical, manufacturing
713990 Trampoline facilities, recreational
485119 Tramway systems (except mixed mode), commuter
487990 Tramway, aerial, scenic and sightseeing operation
332994 Tranquilizer guns, manufacturing
325412 Tranquilizer preparations manufacturing
336350 Transaxles, automotive, truck, and bus, manufacturing
334220 Transceivers (i.e., transmitter-receiver units) manufacturing
561410 Transcription services
334510 Transcutaneous electrical nerve stimulators (TENS) manufacturing
334419 Transducers (except pressure) manufacturing
334519 Transducers, pressure, manufacturing
325199 Transesterification of vegetable oils to produce fuels or fuel additives
484110 Transfer (trucking) services, general freight, local
523999 Transfer agencies, securities 237130 Transformer station and substation, electric power, construction
423610 Transformers (except electronic) merchant wholesalers
335311 Transformers, electric power, manufacturing
334416 Transformers, electronic component-types, manufacturing
423690 Transformers, electronic, merchant wholesalers
335311 Transformers, ignition, for use on domestic fuel burners, manufacturing
335311 Transformers, reactor, manufacturing
335311 Transformers, separate solid-state arc-welding, manufacturing
335912 Transistor radio batteries manufacturing
334413 Transistors manufacturing
423690 Transistors merchant wholesalers
541850 Transit advertising services
922120 Transit police
926120 Transit systems and authorities, nonoperating
485111 Transit systems, mixed mode (e.g., bus, commuter rail, subway combinations)
624229 Transitional housing agencies
327320 Transit-mixed concrete manufacturing
334519 Transits, surveying, manufacturing
541930 Translation services, language
237130 Transmission and distribution line construction
335311 Transmission and distribution voltage regulators manufacturing
316998 Transmission belting, leather, manufacturing
326220 Transmission belts, rubber, manufacturing
336390 Transmission coolers manufacturing
423610 Transmission equipment, electrical, merchant wholesalers
324191 Transmission fluids, petroleum, made from refined petroleum
325998 Transmission fluids, synthetic, manufacturing
221121 Transmission of electric power
486210 Transmission of natural gas via pipeline (i.e., processing plants to local distribution systems)
335932 Transmission pole and line hardware manufacturing
811113 Transmission repair shops, automotive
332312 Transmission tower sections, fabricated structural metal, manufacturing
336350 Transmissions and parts, automotive, truck, and bus, manufacturing
423690 Transmitters merchant wholesalers
334513 Transmitters, industrial process control-type, manufacturing
333111 Transplanters, farm-type, manufacturing
115112 Transplanting services
****** Transportation -- see mode
481212 Transportation by spacecraft, freight
926120 Transportation departments, nonoperating
423860 Transportation equipment and supplies (except marine pleasure craft, motor vehicles) merchant wholesalers
336360 Transportation equipment seating manufacturing
423110 Transportation equipment, motor vehicle, merchant wholesalers
423860 Transportation machinery, equipment, and supplies (except marine pleasure craft, motor vehicles) merchant wholesalers
541614 Transportation management consulting services
926120 Transportation regulatory agencies
926120 Transportation safety programs, government

483111 Transporting freight to or from foreign ports, deep sea

483112 Transporting passengers to or from foreign ports, deep sea

212319 Trap rock crushed and broken stone mining and/or beneficiating

212311 Trap rock mining or quarrying

332618 Traps, animal and fish, made from purchased wire

332919 Traps, water, manufacturing

423910 Trapshooting equipment and supplies merchant wholesalers

713990 Trapshooting facilities, recreational

333318 Trash and garbage compactors, commercial-type, manufacturing

335220 Trash and garbage compactors, household-type, manufacturing

326111 Trash bags, plastics film, single wall or multiwall, manufacturing 562111 Trash collection services 423620 Trash compactors, household-type, merchant wholesalers

326199 Trash containers, plastics, manufacturing

562213 Trash disposal combustors or incinerators

562212 Trash disposal landfills

562111 Trash hauling, local

484230 Trash hauling, long-distance

332313 Trash racks, fabricated metal plate work, manufacturing

621493 Trauma centers (except hospitals), freestanding

561510 Travel agencies

511130 Travel guide book publishers (except exclusive Internet publishing)

511130 Travel guide book publishers and printing combined

519130 Travel guide book publishers, exclusively on Internet

323117 Travel guide books printing and binding without publishing

323117 Travel guide books printing without publishing

561510 Travel management services

561520 Travel tour operators

423110 Travel trailer (e.g., tent trailers) merchant wholesalers

721211 Travel trailer campsites

441210 Travel trailer dealers

336214 Travel trailers, recreational, manufacturing

624190 Travelers' aid centers

522390 Travelers' check issuance services 316998 Traveling bags, all materials, manufacturing

712110 Traveling museum exhibits

711190 Traveling shows, carnival

334419 Traveling wave tubes manufacturing

212312 Travertine crushed and broken stone mining and/or beneficiating

212311 Travertine mining or quarrying

337127 Tray trucks, restaurant, manufacturing

321920 Trays, carrier, wood, manufacturing

322299 Trays, food, molded pulp, manufacturing

333316 Trays, photographic printing and processing, manufacturing

332618 Trays, wire, made from purchased wire

321999 Trays, wood, wicker, and bagasse, manufacturing

326211 Tread rubber (i.e., camelback) manufacturing

332323 Treads, metal stair, manufacturing

921130 Treasurers' offices, government

321114 Treating purchased wood and wood products

238160 Treating roofs (by spraying, painting or coating)

321114 Treating wood products with creosote or other preservatives

561730 Tree and brush trimming, overhead utility line

113310 Tree chipping in the field

111421 Tree crop farming (except forestry), short rotation growing and harvesting cycle

111335 Tree nut farming

311225 Tree nut oils (e.g., tung, walnut) made from purchased oils

311224 Tree nut oils (e.g., tung, walnut) made in crushing mill

561730 Tree pruning services

561730 Tree removal services

113210 Tree seed extracting

113210 Tree seed gathering

113210 Tree seed growing for reforestation 561730 Tree services (e.g., bracing, planting, pruning, removal, spraying, surgery, trimming)

333111 Tree shakers (e.g., citrus, nut, soft fruit) manufacturing

561730 Tree surgery services 561730 Tree trimming services

339999 Trees and plants, artificial, manufacturing
424930 Trees merchant wholesalers
321918 Trellises, wood, manufacturing
238910 Trenching (except underwater)
333120 Trenching machines manufacturing
237990 Trenching, underwater
237310 Trestle construction
321114 Trestle parts, wood, treating
325220 Triacetate fibers and yarns manufacturing
541199 Trial consulting services
921150 Tribal chief's or chairman's office, American Indian or Alaska Native
921150 Tribal councils, American Indian or Alaska Native
921150 Tribal courts, American Indian or Alaska Native
325199 Trichloroethylene manufacturing
325199 Trichlorophenoxyacetic acid manufacturing
325199 Tricresyl phosphate manufacturing
339930 Tricycles (except metal) manufacturing
336991 Tricycles, metal, adult and children's, manufacturing
325199 Tridecyl alcohol manufacturing
238350 Trim and finish carpentry contractors 332321 Trim and molding (except motor vehicle), metal, manufacturing
332321 Trim, metal, manufacturing
321918 Trim, wood and covered wood, manufacturing
333112 Trimmers, hedge, electric, manufacturing
332216 Trimmers, hedge, nonelectric, manufacturing
333112 Trimmers, string, lawn and garden-type, manufacturing
315280 Trimmings, fur (except apparel contractors), manufacturing
315210 Trimmings, fur, cut and sew apparel contractors
316998 Trimmings, shoe, leather, manufacturing
325920 Trinitrotoluene (TNT) manufacturing
325199 Triphenyl phosphate manufacturing
333316 Tripods, camera and projector, manufacturing
212399 Tripoli mining and/or beneficiating
339112 Trocars manufacturing 485119 Trolley systems (except mixed mode), commuter
487110 Trolley, scenic and sightseeing, operation
339992 Trombones and parts manufacturing
212391 Trona mining and/or beneficiating
423940 Trophies merchant wholesalers
332999 Trophies, nonprecious and precious plated metal, manufacturing
339910 Trophies, precious metal (except precious plated), manufacturing
453998 Trophy (including awards and plaques) shops
321999 Trophy bases, wood, manufacturing
424990 Tropical fish merchant wholesalers
112511 Tropical fish production, farm raising
561730 Tropical plant maintenance services
335129 Trouble lights manufacturing
332322 Troughs, elevator, sheet metal (except stampings), manufacturing
332313 Troughs, industrial, fabricated metal plate work, manufacturing
335210 Trouser pressers, household-type electric, manufacturing
315210 Trousers cut and sew apparel contractors
315190 Trousers made in apparel knitting mills
315220 Trousers, men's and boys', cut and sewn from purchased fabric (except apparel contractors)
114111 Trout fishing
112511 Trout production, farm raising
332216 Trowels manufacturing
532120 Truck (except industrial) rental or leasing
811192 Truck and bus washes
336211 Truck bodies and cabs manufacturing
336211 Truck bodies assembling on purchased chassis
336214 Truck campers (i.e., slide-in campers) manufacturing
441310 Truck cap stores
611519 Truck driving schools 111219 Truck farming, field, bedding plant and seed production
522220 Truck finance leasing
423120 Truck parts, new, merchant wholesalers
811310 Truck refrigeration repair and maintenance services
811111 Truck repair shops, general
447190 Truck stops
236220 Truck terminal construction

441320 Truck tires and tubes dealers (except heavy truck)
532120 Truck tractor rental or leasing without driver
336120 Truck tractors for highway use, assembling on chassis of own manufacture
336211 Truck tractors for highway use, assembling on purchased chassis
423110 Truck tractors, road, merchant wholesalers
811121 Truck trailer body shops 423110 Truck trailer merchant wholesalers 811121 Truck trailer paint and body repair 336212 Truck trailers manufacturing
488490 Truck weighing station operation 532490 Truck, industrial, rental or leasing 488490 Trucking terminals, independently operated 484210 Trucking used household, office, or institutional furniture and equipment
484110 Trucking, general freight, local 484122 Trucking, general freight, long-distance, less-than-truckload (LTL)
484121 Trucking, general freight, long-distance, truckload (TL)
484220 Trucking, specialized freight (except used goods), local
484230 Trucking, specialized freight (except used goods), long-distance
327320 Truck-mixed concrete manufacturing 336120 Trucks, heavy, assembling on chassis of own manufacture
333924 Trucks, industrial, manufacturing
423830 Trucks, industrial, merchant wholesalers
336112 Trucks, light duty, assembling on chassis of own manufacture
333120 Trucks, off-highway, manufacturing
423110 Trucks, road, merchant wholesalers
111419 Truffles farming, grown under cover
339992 Trumpets and parts manufacturing
316998 Trunks (i.e., luggage), all materials, manufacturing
332313 Truss plates, metal, manufacturing
321214 Trusses, glue laminated or pre-engineered wood, manufacturing
321214 Trusses, wood roof or floor, manufacturing
321214 Trusses, wood, glue laminated or metal connected, manufacturing
523991 Trust administration, personal investment
523991 Trust companies, nondepository
813211 Trusts, charitable, awarding grants
813211 Trusts, educational, awarding grants
525920 Trusts, estates, and agency accounts
813211 Trusts, religious, awarding grants
448190 T-shirt shops
315210 T-shirts, outerwear, cut and sew apparel contractors
315190 T-shirts, outerwear, made in apparel knitting mills
315220 T-shirts, outerwear, men's and boys', cut and sewn from purchased fabric (except apparel contractors)
315220 T-shirts, outerwear, unisex (i.e., sized without regard to gender), cut and sewn from purchased fabric (except apparel contractors)
315240 T-shirts, outerwear, women's, girls', and infants', cut and sewn from purchased fabric (except apparel contractors)
315210 T-shirts, underwear, cut and sew apparel contractors
315190 T-shirts, underwear, made in apparel knitting mills
315220 T-shirts, underwear, men's and boys', cut and sewn from purchased fabric (except apparel contractors)
315240 T-shirts, underwear, women's, girls', and infants', cut and sewn from purchased fabric (except apparel contractors)
334519 T-squares (drafting) manufacturing
325612 Tub and tile cleaning preparations manufacturing
331210 Tube (e.g., heavy riveted, lock joint, seamless, welded) made from purchased iron or steel
332912 Tube and hose fittings, fluid power, manufacturing
331318 Tube blooms made by extruding purchased aluminum
331318 Tube blooms, aluminum, made in integrated secondary smelting and extruding mills
331318 Tube made by drawing or extruding purchased aluminum
333519 Tube rolling mill machinery, metalworking, manufacturing
331110 Tube rounds, iron or steel, made in iron and steel mills
331318 Tube, aluminum, made in integrated secondary smelting and drawing plants
331318 Tube, aluminum, made in integrated secondary smelting and extruding mills

331110 Tube, iron or steel, made in iron and steel mills
326121 Tube, nonrigid plastics, manufacturing
331315 Tube, welded, aluminum, made by flat rolling purchased aluminum
331315 Tube, welded, aluminum, made in integrated secondary smelting and flat rolling mills
325414 Tuberculin (i.e., tuberculo-protein derived) manufacturing
622310 Tuberculosis and other respiratory illness hospitals
332996 Tubes made from purchased metal pipe
334419 Tubes, cathode ray, manufacturing
334419 Tubes, electron, manufacturing 423690
Tubes, electronic (e.g., industrial, receiving,
transmitting), merchant wholesalers
334419 Tubes, electronic, manufacturing
334419 Tubes, klystron, manufacturing 334517
Tubes, X-ray, manufacturing 331420 Tubing, copper
and copper alloy, made from purchased copper or in
integrated secondary smelting and rolling, drawing or extruding plants
332999 Tubing, flexible metal, manufacturing
331210 Tubing, mechanical and hypodermic sizes, cold-drawn stainless steel, made from purchased steel
423510 Tubing, metal, merchant wholesalers
331491 Tubing, nonferrous metals (except aluminum, copper), made from purchased metals or scrap
331110 Tubing, seamless steel, made in iron and steel mills
331110 Tubing, wrought iron or steel, made in iron and steel mills
332999 Tubs, laundry and bath, metal, manufacturing
238140 Tuck pointing contractors 212312 Tufa,
calcareous, crushed and broken
stone, mining and/or beneficiating 212311
Tufa, calcareous, mining or quarrying 333249 Tufting machinery for textiles manufacturing
336611 Tugboat building
532411 Tugboat rental or leasing without crew
488330 Tugboat services, harbor operation 326199
Tumblers, plastics, manufacturing 332813 Tumbling
(i.e., cleaning and polishing) metal and metal products for the trade
114111 Tuna fishing
811118 Tune-up shops, automotive
325180 Tungstates (e.g., ammonium tungstate, sodium tungstate) manufacturing
331491 Tungsten bar, rod, sheet, strip, and tubing made by rolling, drawing, or extruding purchased metals or scrap
331492 Tungsten carbide powder made by metallurgical process
325180 Tungsten compounds, not specified elsewhere by process, manufacturing
212299 Tungsten concentrates beneficiating
212299 Tungsten ores mining and/or beneficiating
811490 Tuning and repair of musical instruments
339992 Tuning forks manufacturing
237990 Tunnel construction
238210 Tunnel lighting contractors
332313 Tunnel lining, fabricated metal plate work, manufacturing
213113 Tunneling services for coal mining on a contract basis
332313 Tunnels, wind, fabricated metal plate work, manufacturing
334513 Turbidity instruments, industrial process-type, manufacturing
334516 Turbidometers, laboratory-type, manufacturing
334513 Turbine flow meters, industrial process-type, manufacturing
333611 Turbine generator set units manufacturing
334514 Turbine meters, consumption registering, manufacturing
333611 Turbines (except aircraft) manufacturing
423830 Turbines (except transportation) merchant wholesalers
423860 Turbines, transportation, merchant wholesalers
561730 Turf (except artificial) installation services
111421 Turf farming
238990 Turf, artificial, installation
424440 Turkey and turkey products (except canned and packaged frozen) merchant wholesalers
112330 Turkey egg production
311119 Turkey feeds, prepared, manufacturing
112340 Turkey hatcheries
112330 Turkey production
325613 Turkey-red oil manufacturing

311615 Turkeys, processing, fresh, frozen, canned, or cooked
311615 Turkeys, slaughtering and dressing
812199 Turkish bathhouses
812199 Turkish baths
332722 Turnbuckles, metal, manufacturing
333517 Turning machines (i.e., lathes), metalworking, manufacturing
321912 Turnings, furniture, unfinished wood, manufacturing
111219 Turnip farming, field, bedding plant and seed production
325194 Turpentine made by distillation of pine gum or pine wood
424690 Turpentine merchant wholesalers
212399 Turquoise mining and/or beneficiating
333517 Turret lathes, metalworking, manufacturing
332994 Turrets, gun, manufacturing
114119 Turtle fishing
112519 Turtle production, farm raising
611691 Tutoring, academic
532281 Tuxedo rental
315210 Tuxedos cut and sew apparel contractors
315220 Tuxedos cut and sewn from purchased fabric (except apparel contractors)
334310 TV (television) sets manufacturing
443142 TV (television) stores 532490 TV broadcasting and studio equipment rental or leasing
337124 TV stands and similar stands for consumer electronics, metal, manufacturing
337125 TV stands and similar stands for consumer electronics, plastics, manufacturing
337122 TV stands and similar stands for consumer electronics, wood, manufacturing
313210 Twills weaving
423840 Twine merchant wholesalers
314994 Twines manufacturing
423830 Twist drills merchant wholesalers
517312 Two-way paging communication carriers (except satellite)
811213 Two-way radio repair and maintenance services
323120 Typesetting (i.e., computer controlled, hand, machine)
333244 Typesetting machinery manufacturing
424120 Typewriter paper merchant wholesalers
811212 Typewriter repair and maintenance services
339940 Typewriter ribbons manufacturing
333318 Typewriters manufacturing
423420 Typewriters merchant wholesalers
561410 Typing services
212291 Tyuyamunite mining and/or beneficiating
922130 U.S. attorneys' offices
311514 UHT (ultra high temperature) milk manufacturing
339992 Ukuleles and parts manufacturing
212391 Ulexite mining and/or beneficiating
531130 U-lock storage
336411 Ultra light aircraft manufacturing 325130 Ultramarine pigments manufacturing 333517 Ultrasonic boring, drilling, and cutting machines, metalworking, manufacturing
335999 Ultrasonic cleaning equipment (except dental, medical) manufacturing
339114 Ultrasonic dental equipment manufacturing
335999 Ultrasonic generators sold separately for inclusion in tools and equipment manufacturing
339113 Ultrasonic medical cleaning equipment manufacturing
334510 Ultrasonic medical equipment manufacturing
333517 Ultrasonic metal forming machines manufacturing
334510 Ultrasonic scanning devices, medical, manufacturing
334519 Ultrasonic testing equipment (except medical) manufacturing
333992 Ultrasonic welding equipment manufacturing
423450 Ultrasound equipment, medical, merchant wholesalers
621512 Ultrasound imaging centers
335110 Ultraviolet lamp bulbs manufacturing
335129 Ultraviolet lamp fixtures manufacturing
334516 Ultraviolet-type analytical instruments manufacturing
325130 Umber manufacturing
212393 Umber mining and/or beneficiating
339999 Umbrellas manufacturing
424320 Umbrellas, men's and boys', merchant wholesalers
424330 Umbrellas, women's and girls', merchant wholesalers

322122 Uncoated groundwood paper mills
811198 Undercoating shops, automotive
237130 Underground cable (e.g., cable television, electricity, telephone) laying
333131 Underground mining machinery manufacturing
238910 Underground tank (except hazardous material) removal
237310 Underpass construction
238990 Underpinning, construction
812210 Undertaker services
423850 Undertakers' equipment and supplies merchant wholesalers
335129 Underwater lighting fixtures manufacturing
334511 Underwater navigational systems manufacturing
336612 Underwater remotely operated vehicles (ROVs) manufacturing in boat yards
336611 Underwater remotely operated vehicles (ROVs) manufacturing in shipyards
315210 Underwear cut and sew apparel contractors
315190 Underwear made in apparel knitting mills
315210 Underwear shirts cut and sew apparel contractors
315190 Underwear shirts made in apparel knitting mills
315220 Underwear shirts, men's and boys', cut and sewn from purchased fabric (except apparel contractors)
315240 Underwear shirts, women's, girls', and infants', cut and sewn from purchased fabric (except apparel contractors)
315210 Underwear shorts cut and sew apparel contractors
315190 Underwear shorts made in apparel knitting mills
315220 Underwear shorts, men's and boys', cut and sewn from purchased fabric (except apparel contractors)
315240 Underwear shorts, women's, girls', and infants', cut and sewn from purchased fabric (except apparel contractors)
315220 Underwear, men's and boys', cut and sewn from purchased fabric (except apparel contractors)
424320 Underwear, men's and boys', merchant wholesalers
424330 Underwear, women's, children's, and infants', merchant wholesalers
315240 Underwear, women's, girls', and infants', cut and sewn from purchased fabric (except apparel contractors)
523110 Underwriting securities
923130 Unemployment insurance program administration
812331 Uniform (except industrial) supply services
315210 Uniform hats and caps cut and sew apparel contractors
315990 Uniform hats and caps cut and sewn from purchased fabric (except apparel contractors)
315220 Uniform shirts (except team athletic), men's and boys', cut and sewn from purchased fabric (except apparel contractors)
315240 Uniform shirts (except team athletic), women's and girls', cut and sewn from purchased fabric (except apparel contractors)
315210 Uniform shirts cut and sew apparel contractors
315280 Uniform shirts, team athletic, cut and sewn from purchased fabric (except apparel contractors)
448190 Uniform stores (except athletic)
451110 Uniform stores, athletic
812332 Uniform supply services, industrial
315240 Uniforms (except team athletic), nontailored, women's and girls', cut and sewn from purchased fabric (except apparel contractors)
315210 Uniforms, band, cut and sew apparel contractors
315280 Uniforms, band, cut and sewn from purchased fabric (except apparel contractors)
315220 Uniforms, dress (e.g., fire fighter, military, police), men's, cut and sewn from purchased fabric (except apparel contractors)
315210 Uniforms, dress (e.g., military, police, fire fighter), cut and sew apparel contractors
315240 Uniforms, dress, tailored (e.g., fire fighter, military, police), women's and girls', cut and sewn from purchased fabric (except apparel contractors)
424320 Uniforms, men's and boys', merchant wholesalers
315210 Uniforms, nontailored, cut and sew apparel contractors
315190 Uniforms, nontailored, made in apparel knitting mills
315220 Uniforms, nontailored, men's and boys', cut and sewn from purchased fabric (except apparel contractors)
315210 Uniforms, team athletic, cut and sew apparel contractors

315280 Uniforms, team athletic, cut and sewn from purchased fabric (except apparel contractors)
424330 Uniforms, women's, children's, and infants', merchant wholesalers
335999 Uninterruptible power supplies (UPS) manufacturing
525120 Union health and welfare funds
525110 Union pension funds
315210 Union suits cut and sew apparel contractors
315190 Union suits made in apparel knitting mills
315220 Union suits, men's and boys', cut and sewn from purchased fabric (except apparel contractors)
315240 Union suits, women's, girls', and infants', cut and sewn from purchased fabric (except apparel contractors)
813930 Unions (except apprenticeship programs), labor
522130 Unions, credit
332919 Unions, pipe, metal (except made from purchased pipe), manufacturing
424330 Unisex clothing merchant wholesalers
448140 Unisex clothing stores
812112 Unisex hair stylist shops
333414 Unit heaters (except portable electric) manufacturing
335210 Unit heaters, portable electric, manufacturing
525990 Unit investment trust funds
323111 Unit set forms (e.g., manifold credit card slips) printing
423610 Unit substations, electrical, merchant wholesalers
813219 United fund councils
813219 United funds for colleges
928120 United Nations
333613 Universal joints (except aircraft, motor vehicle) manufacturing
336413 Universal joints, aircraft, manufacturing
336350 Universal joints, automotive, truck, and bus, manufacturing
611310 Universities
813410 University clubs
511130 University press publishers (except exclusive Internet publishing)
519130 University press publishers, exclusively on Internet
923110 University regents or boards, government
311812 Unleavened bread made in commercial bakeries
423690 Unloaded computer boards merchant wholesalers
336411 Unmanned and robotic aircraft manufacturing
336111 Unmanned and robotic automobiles manufacturing
336612 Unmanned and robotic watercraft manufacturing in boat yards
336611 Unmanned and robotic watercraft manufacturing in shipyards
337121 Upholstered furniture, household-type, custom, manufacturing
337121 Upholstered furniture, household-type, on frames of any material, manufacturing
423850 Upholsterers' equipment and supplies (except fabrics) merchant wholesalers
314999 Upholstering filling (except nonwoven fabric) manufacturing
811420 Upholstery (except motor vehicle) repair services
561740 Upholstery cleaning on customers' premises
561740 Upholstery cleaning services
424310 Upholstery fabrics merchant wholesalers
316110 Upholstery leather manufacturing
451130 Upholstery materials stores
811121 Upholstery shops, automotive
332613 Upholstery springs and spring units, light gauge, made from purchased wire or strip
316110 Upper leather manufacturing
316998 Uppers (i.e., shoe cut stock), leather, manufacturing
335999 UPS (uninterruptible power supplies) manufacturing
332111 Upset forgings made from purchased iron or steel, unfinished
332112 Upset forgings made from purchased nonferrous metals, unfinished
333517 Upsetters (i.e., forging machines) manufacturing
212291 Uraninite (pitchblende) mining and/or beneficiating
325180 Uranium compounds, not specified elsewhere by process, manufacturing
212291 Uranium ores mining and/or beneficiating
325180 Uranium oxide manufacturing
331410 Uranium refining, primary
325180 Uranium, enriched, manufacturing
212291 Uranium-radium-vanadium ore mine site development for own account

212291 Uranium-radium-vanadium ores mining and/or beneficiating
485113 Urban bus line services (except mixed mode)
485112 Urban commuter rail systems (except mixed mode)
541320 Urban planners' offices
925120 Urban planning commissions, government
541320 Urban planning services
485111 Urban transit systems, mixed mode (e.g., bus, commuter rail, subway combinations)
325311 Urea manufacturing
325211 Urea resins manufacturing
325211 Urea-formaldehyde resins manufacturing
238310 Urethane foam insulation application
326150 Urethane foam products manufacturing
325212 Urethane rubber manufacturing
238190 Urethane slabjacking contractors
238190 Urethane soil stabilization contractors
621493 Urgent medical care centers and clinics (except hospitals), freestanding
423720 Urinals merchant wholesalers
332999 Urinals, metal, manufacturing
326191 Urinals, plastics, manufacturing
327110 Urinals, vitreous china, manufacturing
621511 Urinalysis laboratories
327420 Urns (e.g., gypsum, plaster of paris) manufacturing
335210 Urns, household-type electric, manufacturing
621111 Urologists' offices (e.g., centers, clinics)
441228 Used aircraft dealers
441310 Used automotive parts stores
441320 Used automotive tire dealers
453310 Used bicycle (except motorized) shops
441222 Used boat dealers
441120 Used car dealers
423110 Used car merchant wholesalers
484210 Used household and office goods moving
453930 Used manufactured (mobile) home dealers
453310 Used merchandise dealers (except motor vehicles and parts)
453310 Used merchandise stores
441228 Used motorcycle dealers
423140 Used parts, motor vehicle, merchant wholesalers
453310 Used rare collectors' items (e.g., autograph, coin, card, stamps) shops
441210 Used recreational vehicle (RV) dealers
441320 Used tire dealers
423130 Used tires, motor vehicle, merchant wholesalers
441228 Used utility trailer dealers
541618 Utilities management consulting services
332311 Utility buildings, prefabricated metal, manufacturing
326199 Utility containers (e.g., baskets, bins, boxes, buckets, dishpans, pails), plastics (except foam), manufacturing
237130 Utility line (i.e., communication, electric power), construction
237110 Utility line (i.e., sewer, water), construction
511210 Utility software, computer, packaged
441228 Utility trailer dealers
423110 Utility trailer merchant wholesalers
532120 Utility trailer rental or leasing
336214 Utility trailers manufacturing
531190 Vacant lot rental or leasing
531190 Vacation and recreation land rental or leasing
721214 Vacation camps (except campgrounds, day, instructional)
236115 Vacation home, single-family, construction by general contractors
236117 Vacation housing construction for-sale builders
115210 Vaccinating livestock (except by veterinarians)
541940 Vaccination services, veterinary
325414 Vaccines (i.e., bacterial, virus) manufacturing
424210 Vaccines merchant wholesalers 332439
Vacuum bottles and jugs, light gauge metal, manufacturing
336340 Vacuum brake booster, automotive, truck, and bus, manufacturing
326220 Vacuum cleaner belts, rubber or plastics, manufacturing
443141 Vacuum cleaner stores, household-type
335210 Vacuum cleaners (e.g., canister, handheld, upright) household-type electric, manufacturing
335210 Vacuum cleaners and sweepers, household-type electric, manufacturing
423620 Vacuum cleaners, household-type, merchant wholesalers

333318 Vacuum cleaners, industrial and commercial-type, manufacturing
238290 Vacuum cleaning system, built-in, installation
423850 Vacuum cleaning systems, commercial, merchant wholesalers
333912 Vacuum pumps (except laboratory) manufacturing
423830 Vacuum pumps merchant wholesalers
339113 Vacuum pumps, laboratory-type, manufacturing
335314 Vacuum relays manufacturing 332420
Vacuum tanks, heavy gauge metal, manufacturing
327215 Vacuum tube blanks, glass, made from purchased glass
327212 Vacuum tube blanks, glass, made in glass making plants
334419 Vacuum tubes manufacturing
488119 Vacuuming of airport runways
333112 Vacuums, yard, manufacturing
812930 Valet parking services
316998 Valises, all materials, manufacturing
325194 Valonia extract manufacturing
333517 Valve grinding machines, metalworking, manufacturing
423840 Valves (except hydraulic, plumbing, pneumatic) merchant wholesalers
332911 Valves for nuclear applications manufacturing
332911 Valves for water works and municipal water systems manufacturing
336310 Valves, engine, intake and exhaust, manufacturing
332912 Valves, hydraulic and pneumatic, fluid power, manufacturing
423830 Valves, hydraulic and pneumatic, merchant wholesalers
332911 Valves, industrial-type (e.g., check, gate, globe, relief, safety), manufacturing
332919 Valves, inline plumbing and heating (e.g., cutoffs, stop), manufacturing
423720 Valves, plumbing and heating, merchant wholesalers
316998 Vamps, leather, manufacturing
532120 Van (except passenger) rental or leasing without driver
532112 Van (passenger) leasing
532111 Van (passenger) rental
336213 Van and minivan conversions on purchased chassis
811121 Van conversion shops (except on assembly line or factory basis)
484210 Van lines, moving and storage services
212291 Vanadium ores mining and/or beneficiating
325199 Vanillin, synthetic, manufacturing
337110 Vanities (except freestanding), stock or custom wood, manufacturing
337122 Vanities, freestanding, wood, manufacturing
337124 Vanities, metal household-type, manufacturing
316998 Vanity cases, leather, manufacturing 337110
Vanity tops, wood or plastics laminated on wood, manufacturing
485999 Vanpool operation
488999 Vanpools, arrangement of
336112 Vans, commercial and passenger light duty, assembling on chassis of own manufacture
333242 Vapor deposition equipment, semiconductor, manufacturing
334512 Vapor heating controls manufacturing
335110 Vapor lamps, electric, manufacturing
333999 Vapor separating machinery manufacturing
335210 Vaporizers, household-type electric, manufacturing
334513 Variable control instruments, industrial process-type, manufacturing
311612 Variety meats, edible organs, made from purchased meats
311611 Variety meats, edible organs, made in slaughtering plants
452319 Variety stores
334416 Varistors manufacturing
325510 Varnishes manufacturing
424950 Varnishes merchant wholesalers
332812 Varnishing metals and metal products for the trade
313320 Varnishing purchased textiles and apparel
327420 Vases (e.g., gypsum, plaster of paris) manufacturing
327215 Vases, glass, made from purchased glass
327212 Vases, glass, made in glass making plants
327110 Vases, pottery (e.g., china, earthenware, stoneware), manufacturing
325130 Vat dyes, synthetic, manufacturing
332420 Vats, heavy gauge metal, manufacturing

332439 Vats, light gauge metal, manufacturing
711110 Vaudeville companies
332999 Vault doors and linings, metal, manufacturing
238290 Vault, safe and banking machine installation
332999 Vaults (except burial), metal, manufacturing
339995 Vaults (except concrete) manufacturing
326220 V-belts, rubber or plastics, manufacturing
334310 VCR (video cassette recorder) manufacturing
112111 Veal calf production
311611 Veal carcasses, half carcasses, primal and sub-primal cuts, produced in slaughtering plants
311612 Veal, primal and sub-primal cuts, made from purchased carcasses
325411 Vegetable alkaloids (i.e., basic chemicals) (e.g., caffeine, codeine, morphine, nicotine), manufacturing
111211 Vegetable and melon farming, potato dominant crop, field and seed production
111219 Vegetable and melon farming, vegetable (except potato) and melon dominant crops, field, bedding plants and seed production
111211 Vegetable and potato farming, potato dominant crop, field and seed potato production
111219 Vegetable and potato farming, vegetable (except potato) dominant crops, field, bedding plants and seed production
321920 Vegetable baskets, veneer and splint, manufacturing
311421 Vegetable brining
424990 Vegetable cake and meal merchant wholesalers
311421 Vegetable canning
321920 Vegetable crates, wood, wirebound, manufacturing
424910 Vegetable dusts and sprays merchant wholesalers
111419 Vegetable farming, grown under cover
311211 Vegetable flour manufacturing 311211 Vegetable flour, meal, and powders, made in flour mills
311411 Vegetable juice concentrates, frozen, manufacturing
311421 Vegetable juices canning
311421 Vegetable juices, fresh, manufacturing
445230 Vegetable markets
333241 Vegetable oil processing machinery manufacturing
424990 Vegetable oils (except cooking) merchant wholesalers
311225 Vegetable oils made from purchased oils
311224 Vegetable oils made in crushing mills
115114 Vegetable precooling
115114 Vegetable sorting, grading, and packing
311221 Vegetable starches manufacturing
115114 Vegetable sun drying
115114 Vegetable vacuum cooling
311423 Vegetables dehydrating
311421 Vegetables pickling
424490 Vegetables, canned, merchant wholesalers
311991 Vegetables, cut or peeled, fresh, manufacturing
424480 Vegetables, fresh, merchant wholesalers
311411 Vegetables, frozen, manufacturing
424420 Vegetables, frozen, merchant wholesalers
115113 Vegetables, machine harvesting
238290 Vehicle lift installation
333997 Vehicle scales manufacturing
321912 Vehicle stock, hardwood, manufacturing
336991 Vehicle, children's, metal manufacturing
339930 Vehicles, children's (except bicycles and metal tricycles), manufacturing
423920 Vehicles, children's (except bicycles), merchant wholesalers
423110 Vehicles, recreational, merchant wholesalers
336320 Vehicular lighting fixtures manufacturing
316110 Vellum leather manufacturing
313210 Velvets, manmade fiber and silk, weaving
238290 Vending machine installation
454210 Vending machine merchandisers, sale of products
532490 Vending machine rental
333318 Vending machines manufacturing
423440 Vending machines merchant wholesalers
333243 Veneer and plywood forming machinery manufacturing
321920 Veneer baskets, for fruits and vegetables, manufacturing
321211 Veneer mills, hardwood
321212 Veneer mills, softwood
321999 Veneer work, inlaid, manufacturing
423310 Veneer, wood, merchant wholesalers

561720 Venetian blind cleaning services 811490

Venetian blind repair and maintenance shops without retailing new venetian blinds

321918 Venetian blind slats, wood, manufacturing

337920 Venetian blinds manufacturing 238390

Ventilated wire shelving (i.e., closet organizing-type) installation

238220 Ventilating contractors 423730 Ventilating

equipment and supplies (except household-type fans)

merchant wholesalers

333413 Ventilating fans, industrial and commercial-type, manufacturing

335210 Ventilating kitchen fans, household-type electric, manufacturing

335210 Ventilation and exhaust fans (except attic fans), household-type, manufacturing

561790 Ventilation duct cleaning services 332322

Ventilators, sheet metal (except stampings), manu-

facturing 523910 Venture capital companies 212319

Verde' antique crushed and broken stone mining and/or beneficiating

212311 Verde' antique mining or quarrying

212399 Vermiculite mining and/or beneficiating

327992 Vermiculite, exfoliated, manufacturing

325412 Vermifuge preparations manufacturing

325130 Vermilion pigments manufacturing

312130 Vermouth manufacturing

337920 Vertical blinds manufacturing

332420 Vessels, heavy gauge metal, manufacturing

315210 Vestments, academic and clerical, cut and sew apparel contractors

315280 Vestments, academic and clerical, cut and sewn from purchased fabric (except apparel contractors)

423490 Vestments, religious, merchant wholesalers

315210 Vests cut and sew apparel contractors 315280

Vests, leather, fur, or sheep-lined (except apparel contractors), manufacturing

315210 Vests, leather, fur, or sheep-lined, cut and sew apparel contractors

315220 Vests, men's and boys', cut and sewn from purchased fabric (except apparel contractors)

315240 Vests, women's and girls', cut and sewn from purchased fabric (except apparel contractors)

813410 Veterans' membership organizations

923140 Veterans' affairs offices

923140 Veterans' benefits program administration, government

813311 Veterans' rights organizations

423490 Veterinarians' equipment and supplies merchant wholesalers

339112 Veterinarians' instruments and apparatus manufacturing

424210 Veterinarians' medicines merchant wholesalers

541940 Veterinarians' offices

541940 Veterinarians' practices

541940 Veterinary clinics

325412 Veterinary medicinal preparations manufacturing

541715 Veterinary research and development laboratories or services (except biotechnology and nanotechnology research and development)

541940 Veterinary services

541940 Veterinary services, livestock 541940 Veteri-

nary services, pets and other animal specialties

541940 Veterinary testing laboratories

523910 Viatical settlement companies

339992 Vibraphones manufacturing

238390 Vibration isolation contractors

334519 Vibration meters, analyzers, and calibrators, manufacturing

541380 Vibration testing laboratories or services

333120 Vibrators, concrete, manufacturing

518210 Video and audio streaming services

423430 Video boards merchant wholesalers

519130 Video broadcasting, exclusively on Internet

334220 Video cameras (except household-type) manufacturing

423410 Video cameras (except household-type) merchant wholesalers

334310 Video cameras, household-type, manufacturing

423620 Video cameras, household-type, merchant wholesalers

811211 Video cassette recorder (VCR) repair services without retailing new video cassette recorders

532210 Video cassette recorder rental

334310 Video cassette recorders (VCR) manufacturing

334613 Video cassettes, blank, manufacturing

334614 Video cassettes, prerecorded, mass reproducing

512191 Video conversion services (i.e., between formats)
532210 Video disc player rental
532282 Video disc rental for home electronic equipment (e.g., DVD)
713290 Video gambling device concession operators (i.e., supplying and servicing in others' facilities)
713120 Video game arcades (except gambling)
339930 Video game machines (except coin-operated) manufacturing
532282 Video game rental
443142 Video game software stores
423920 Video games merchant wholesalers
713290 Video gaming device concession operators (i.e., supplying and servicing in others' facilities)
541921 Video photography services, portrait
512191 Video postproduction services
512110 Video production
512110 Video production and distribution
532210 Video recorder rental
512199 Video tape libraries, stock footage
334614 Video tape or disk mass reproducing
532210 Video tape player rental
532282 Video tape rental for home electronic equipment (e.g., VCR)
532282 Video tape rental stores
443142 Video tape stores
334613 Video tapes, blank, manufacturing
423690 Video tapes, blank, merchant wholesalers
423990 Video tapes, prerecorded, merchant wholesalers
541922 Video taping services for legal depositions
541921 Video taping services, special events (e.g., birthdays, weddings)
334290 Video-based stadium displays manufacturing
561499 Videoconferencing services 311941 Vinegar manufacturing 115112 Vineyard cultivation services
325199 Vinyl acetate (except resins) manufacturing
325211 Vinyl acetate resins manufacturing 326113 Vinyl and vinyl copolymer film and unlaminated sheet (except packaging) manufacturing
325211 Vinyl chloride resins manufacturing
313320 Vinyl coated fabrics manufacturing
325220 Vinyl fibers and filaments manufacturing
326199 Vinyl floor coverings manufacturing
238330 Vinyl flooring contractors
325211 Vinyl resins manufacturing
423330 Vinyl siding merchant wholesalers
238170 Vinyl siding, soffit and fascia, installation
316210 Vinyl upper athletic footwear manufacturing
325220 Vinylidene chloride fiber and filament manufacturing
325211 Vinylidene resins manufacturing
339992 Violas and parts manufacturing
339992 Violins and parts manufacturing
325413 Viral in-vitro diagnostic test substances manufacturing
523130 Virtual currency exchange services (i.e., selling to the public)
325414 Virus vaccines manufacturing 325220 Viscose fibers, bands, strips, and yarn manufacturing
334519 Viscosimeters (except industrial process type) manufacturing
334513 Viscosimeters, industrial process-type, manufacturing
334513 Viscosity instruments, industrial process-type, manufacturing
332216 Vises (except machine tool attachments) manufacturing
621610 Visiting nurse associations
561591 Visitor information centers
561591 Visitors bureaus
325412 Vitamin preparations manufacturing
446191 Vitamin stores
424210 Vitamins merchant wholesalers
325411 Vitamins, uncompounded, manufacturing
711130 Vocalists, independent
611513 Vocational apprenticeship training
624310 Vocational habilitation job counseling
624310 Vocational habilitation job training facilities (except schools)
624310 Vocational rehabilitation agencies
624310 Vocational rehabilitation job counseling
624310 Vocational rehabilitation job training facilities (except schools)
624310 Vocational rehabilitation or habilitation services (e.g., job counseling, job training, work experience)

611610 Voice instruction 561421
Voice mailbox services
621340 Voice pathologists' offices (e.g., centers, clinics)
423430 Voice recognition equipment merchant wholesalers
517919 VoIP service providers, using client-supplied telecommunications connections
517311 VoIP service providers, using own operated wired telecommunications infrastructure
212399 Volcanic ash mining and/or beneficiating
212319 Volcanic rock crushed and broken stone mining and/or beneficiating
212311 Volcanic rock, mining or quarrying
335311 Voltage regulating transformers, electric power, manufacturing
423610 Voltage regulators (except motor vehicle) merchant wholesalers
336320 Voltage regulators for internal combustion engines manufacturing
334413 Voltage regulators, integrated circuits, manufacturing
423120 Voltage regulators, motor vehicle, merchant wholesalers
335311 Voltage regulators, transmission and distribution, manufacturing
334515 Voltmeters manufacturing
813212 Voluntary health organizations
624229 Volunteer housing repair organizations
333318 Voting machines manufacturing
423850 Voting machines merchant wholesalers
322219 Vulcanized fiber products made from purchased paperboard
325212 Vulcanized oils manufacturing
333249 Vulcanizing machinery manufacturing
332992 Wads, ammunition, manufacturing
333242 Wafer processing equipment, semiconductor, manufacturing
321219 Waferboard manufacturing 334413
Wafers (semiconductor devices) manufacturing
335210 Waffle irons, household-type electric, manufacturing
311412 Waffles, frozen, manufacturing
926150 Wage control agencies, government
339930 Wagons, children's (e.g., coaster, express, and play), manufacturing
333111 Wagons, farm-type, manufacturing
333112 Wagons, lawn and garden-type, manufacturing
321918 Wainscots, wood, manufacturing
561421 Wakeup call services
532283 Walker, invalid, rental
339930 Walkers, baby (vehicles), manufacturing
621111 Walk-in physicians' offices (e.g., centers, clinics)
333921 Walkways, moving, manufacturing
238310 Wall cavity and attic space insulation installation
334519 Wall clocks manufacturing
238130 Wall component (i.e., exterior, interior), prefabricated, installation
238320 Wall covering or removal contractors
424950 Wall coverings (e.g., fabric, plastics) merchant wholesalers
335122 Wall lamps (i.e., lighting fixtures), commercial, institutional, and industrial electric, manufacturing
335121 Wall lamps (i.e., lighting fixtures), residential electric, manufacturing 423490 Wall maps merchant wholesalers 327120 Wall tile, ceramic, manufacturing 423310 Wallboard merchant wholesalers 327420 Wallboard, gypsum, manufacturing 316998 Wallets (except metal) manufacturing
339910 Wallets, precious metal, manufacturing
444120 Wallpaper and wall coverings stores 325612 Wallpaper cleaners manufacturing 238320 Wallpaper hanging and removal contractors
322220 Wallpaper made from purchased papers or other materials
424950 Wallpaper merchant wholesalers
238320 Wallpaper stripping
111335 Walnut farming
115114 Walnut hulling and shelling
712110 War museums
316998 Wardrobe bags (i.e., luggage) manufacturing
532281 Wardrobe rental
337124 Wardrobes, metal household-type, manufacturing
337122 Wardrobes, wood household-type, manufacturing
452311 Warehouse clubs (i.e., food and general merchandise)
236220 Warehouse construction (e.g., commercial, industrial, manufacturing, private)

238220 Warehouse refrigeration system installation
236220 Warehouse, commercial and institutional, construction
236220 Warehouse, industrial, construction
332311 Warehouses, prefabricated metal, manufacturing
493190 Warehousing (except farm products, general merchandise, refrigerated)
493110 Warehousing (including foreign trade zones), general merchandise
493110 Warehousing and storage, general merchandise
813910 Warehousing associations
493130 Warehousing, farm products (except refrigerated)
493120 Warehousing, refrigerated
531130 Warehousing, self-storage 334511 Warfare countermeasures equipment manufacturing
423730 Warm air heating equipment merchant wholesalers
238220 Warm air heating system installation
335210 Warming trays, electric, manufacturing
315210 Warmup suits cut and sew apparel contractors
315190 Warmup suits made in apparel knitting mills
315220 Warmup suits, men's and boys', cut and sewn from purchased fabric (except apparel contractors)
315240 Warmup suits, women's, girls', and infants', cut and sewn from purchased fabric (except apparel contractors)
313240 Warp or weft fabrics knitting
333249 Warping machinery manufacturing 524128 Warranty insurance carriers (e.g., appliance, automobile, homeowners', product), direct
333318 Wash water recycling machinery manufacturing
315210 Washable service apparel (e.g., barbers', hospital, professional) cut and sew apparel contractors
315220 Washable service apparel (e.g., barbers', hospital, professional), men's and boys', cut and sewn from purchased fabric (except apparel contractors)
315240 Washable service apparel, women's and girls', cut and sewn from purchased fabric (except apparel contractors)
321999 Washboards, wood and part wood, manufacturing
532210 Washer, clothes, rental 212113 Washeries, anthracite
212111 Washeries, bituminous coal or lignite 333131 Washers, aggregate and sand, stationary, manufacturing
332722 Washers, metal, manufacturing
236210 Washery, mining, construction 811412 Washing machine, household-type, repair and maintenance services without retailing new washing machine
335220 Washing machines, household-type, manufacturing
423620 Washing machines, household-type, merchant wholesalers
333318 Washing machines, laundry (except household-type), manufacturing
561720 Washroom sanitation services
562219 Waste (except sewage) treatment facilities, nonhazardous
562119 Waste (except solid and hazardous) collection services
562119 Waste (except solid and hazardous) hauling, local
562112 Waste collection services, hazardous
562111 Waste collection services, nonhazardous solid
221320 Waste collection, treatment, and disposal through a sewer system
562213 Waste disposal combustors or incinerators, nonhazardous solid
562211 Waste disposal facilities, hazardous
562212 Waste disposal landfills, nonhazardous solid
236210 Waste disposal plant (except sewage treatment) construction
484230 Waste hauling, hazardous, long-distance
562112 Waste hauling, local, hazardous
562111 Waste hauling, local, nonhazardous solid
484230 Waste hauling, nonhazardous, long-distance
924110 Waste management program administration
423930 Waste materials merchant wholesalers
562920 Waste recovery facilities
562112 Waste transfer stations, hazardous
562111 Waste transfer stations, nonhazardous solid
562211 Waste treatment facilities, hazardous
562211 Waste treatment plants, hazardous
322219 Wastebaskets, fiber made from purchased paperboard

316998 Watch bands (except metal) manufacturing

339910 Watch bands, metal, manufacturing

335912 Watch batteries manufacturing

327215 Watch crystals made from purchased glass

326199 Watch crystals, plastics, manufacturing

334519 Watch jewels manufacturing

811490 Watch repair shops without retailing new watches

448310 Watch shops

334519 Watchcase manufacturing

423940 Watchcases merchant wholesalers

334519 Watches and parts (except crystals) manufacturing

423940 Watches and parts merchant wholesalers

333415 Water (i.e., drinking) coolers, mechanical, manufacturing

325412 Water (i.e., drinking) decontamination or purification tablets manufacturing

337124 Water bed frames, metal, manufacturing

337122 Water bed frames, wood, manufacturing

337910 Water bed mattresses manufacturing

327110 Water closet bowls, vitreous china, manufacturing

332999 Water closets, metal, manufacturing

339940 Water colors, artist's, manufacturing

924110 Water control and quality program administration

423740 Water coolers, mechanical, merchant wholesalers

237110 Water desalination plant construction

221310 Water distribution (except irrigation)

221310 Water distribution for irrigation 237110 Water filtration plant construction 221310 Water filtration plant operation 334512 Water heater controls manufacturing 238220 Water heater installation 811412 Water heater repair and maintenance services without retailing new water heaters

333318 Water heaters (except boilers), commercial-type, manufacturing

335220 Water heaters (including nonelectric), household-type, manufacturing

423720 Water heaters, gas and electric, merchant wholesaler

326220 Water hoses, rubber or plastics, manufacturing

213111 Water intake well drilling, oil and gas field on a contract basis

334519 Water leak detectors manufacturing

237110 Water main and line construction

238220 Water meter installation

713110 Water parks, amusement

238290 Water pipe insulating

331511 Water pipe, cast iron, manufacturing 335210 Water pulsating devices, household-type electric, manufacturing

237110 Water pumping or lift station construction

333318 Water purification equipment manufacturing

423720 Water purification equipment, household-type, merchant wholesalers

334513 Water quality monitoring and control systems manufacturing

315210 Water resistant apparel cut and sew apparel contractors

315220 Water resistant jackets and windbreakers, nontailored, men's and boys', cut and sewn from purchased fabric (except apparel contractors)

315240 Water resistant jackets and windbreakers, not tailored, women's and girls', cut and sewn from purchased fabric (except apparel contractors)

315210 Water resistant outerwear cut and sew apparel contractors

315220 Water resistant outerwear, men's and boys', cut and sewn from purchased fabric (except apparel contractors)

315240 Water resistant outerwear, women's, girls', and infants', cut and sewn from purchased fabric (except apparel contractors)

315220 Water resistant overcoats, men's and boys', cut and sewn from purchased fabric (except apparel contractors)

315240 Water resistant overcoats, women's and girls', cut and sewn from purchased fabric (except apparel contractors)

237110 Water sampling station installation

332911 Water sampling station manufacturing

316210 Water shoes, plastics or plastics soled fabric upper, manufacturing

316210 Water shoes, rubber or rubber soled fabric upper, manufacturing

483212 Water shuttle services

532284 Water ski rental

238220 Water softener installation

454390 Water softener service providers, direct selling

423720 Water softening and conditioning equipment merchant wholesalers
561990 Water softening and conditioning services
424690 Water softening compounds merchant wholesalers
333318 Water softening equipment manufacturing
445299 Water stores, bottled
221310 Water supply systems
238220 Water system balancing and testing contractors
237110 Water system storage tank and tower construction
332420 Water tanks, heavy gauge metal, manufacturing
483212 Water taxi services
332919 Water traps manufacturing
221310 Water treatment and distribution
333318 Water treatment equipment manufacturing
423830 Water treatment equipment, industrial, merchant wholesalers
423850 Water treatment equipment, municipal, merchant wholesalers
237110 Water treatment plant construction
221310 Water treatment plants
333611 Water turbines manufacturing
333132 Water well drilling machinery manufacturing
237110 Water well drilling, digging, boring or sinking (except water intake wells in oil and gas fields)
237110 Water well pump and well piping system installation
312111 Water, artificially carbonated, manufacturing
424490 Water, bottled (except water treating), merchant wholesalers
325998 Water, distilled, manufacturing
312111 Water, flavored, manufacturing 312112 Water, naturally carbonated, purifying and bottling
712190 Waterfalls (i.e., natural wonder tourist attractions)
488310 Waterfront terminal operation (e.g., docks, piers, wharves)
326199 Watering cans, plastics, manufacturing
238220 Waterless fire suppression system installation
238220 Waterless fire suppression system installation and repair
811310 Waterless fire suppression system repair and maintenance, without installation
541990 Waterless fire suppression system testing and/or inspection, without sales, service, or installation
325611 Waterless hand soaps manufacturing
111219 Watermelon farming, field, bedding plant and seed production
334514 Watermeters, consumption registering, manufacturing
541690 Waterproof consulting services 424320 Waterproof garments, men's and boys', merchant wholesalers
424330 Waterproof garments, women's, children's, and infants', merchant wholesalers
315210 Waterproof outerwear cut and sew apparel contractors
315280 Waterproof outerwear cut and sewn from purchased fabric (except apparel contractors)
315280 Waterproof outerwear, rubberizing fabric and manufacturing outerwear
313320 Waterproofing apparel, fabrics and textile products (e.g., oiling, rubberizing, waxing, varnishing)
238390 Waterproofing contractors
325510 Water-repellent coatings for wood, concrete and masonry manufacturing
315210 Water-repellent outerwear cut and sew apparel contractors
315220 Water-repellent outerwear, men's and boys', cut and sewn from purchased fabric (except apparel contractors)
315240 Water-repellent outerwear, women's, girls', and infants', cut and sewn from purchased fabric (except apparel contractors)
315220 Water-repellent overcoats, men's and boys', cut and sewn from purchased fabric (except apparel contractors)
315240 Water-repellent overcoats, women's and girls', cut and sewn from purchased fabric (except apparel contractors)
713990 Waterslides (i.e., amusement rides) 332911 Waterworks and municipal water system valves manufacturing
334515 Watt-hour and demand meters, combined, manufacturing
334515 Watt-hour and time switch meters, combined, manufacturing
334515 Watt-hour meters, electric, manufacturing
325194 Wattle extract manufacturing
334515 Wattmeters manufacturing
713940 Wave pools
334515 Waveform measuring and/or analyzing equipment manufacturing

713990 Wax figure exhibitions, amusement

339999 Wax figures (i.e., mannequins) manufacturing

712110 Wax museums

325612 Wax removers manufacturing 322220

Waxed paper for nonpackaging applications made

from purchased paper

322220 Waxed paper for packaging applications made from purchased paper

424130 Waxed paper merchant wholesalers

424690 Waxes (except petroleum) merchant wholesalers

324199 Waxes, petroleum, made from refined petroleum

324110 Waxes, petroleum, made in petroleum refineries

325612 Waxes, polishing (e.g., floor, furniture), manufacturing

313320 Waxing purchased textiles and apparel

115114 Waxing, fruits or vegetables

112210 Weaning pig operations

336992 Weapons, self-propelled, manufacturing

541990 Weather forecasting services

924120 Weather research program administration

321918 Weather strip, wood, manufacturing

238390 Weather stripping installation

423330 Weather stripping merchant wholesalers

334519 Weather tracking equipment manufacturing

333999 Weather vanes manufacturing

331420 Weatherproof wire or cable made from purchased copper in wire drawing plants

331318 Weatherproof wire or cable made in aluminum wire drawing plants

238390 Weatherproofing concrete

332321 Weatherstrip, metal, manufacturing

314999 Weatherstripping made from purchased textiles

313220 Weaving and finishing narrow fabrics

313210 Weaving and finishing of broadwoven fabrics (except rugs, tire fabric)

313210 Weaving broadwoven fabrics (except rugs, tire fabrics)

313210 Weaving broadwoven felts

313220 Weaving fabric less than 12 inches (30cm)

313210 Weaving fabrics more than 12 inches (30cm) in width

333249 Weaving machinery manufacturing

313220 Weaving narrow fabrics

314110 Weaving rugs, carpets, and mats 541511

Web (i.e., Internet) page design services, custom

519130 Web broadcasting

519130 Web communities

518210 Web hosting

454110 Web retailers

519130 Web search portals

313220 Webbing weaving

321999 Webbing, cane, reed, and rattan, manufacturing

812990 Wedding chapels (except churches)

315210 Wedding dresses cut and sew apparel contractors

315240 Wedding dresses, women's and girls', cut and sewn from purchased fabric (except apparel contractors)

541921 Wedding photography services

812990 Wedding planning services 561730 Weed

control and fertilizing services (except crop)

115112 Weed control services for crops

926140 Weed control, agriculture, government

424910 Weed killers merchant wholesalers

333111 Weeding machines, farm-type, manufacturing

238910 Weeping tile installation

811219 Weighing equipment (e.g., balance, scales)

repair and maintenance services 812191

Weight loss centers, non-medical 812191 Weight re-

ducing centers, non-medical 713940 Weight training

centers 541890 Welcoming services (i.e., advertising services)

331222 Welded iron or steel wire fabric made in wire drawing plants

316998 Welders' aprons, leather, manufacturing

339113 Welder's hoods manufacturing

316998 Welders' jackets, leggings, and sleeves, leather, manufacturing

333992 Welding equipment manufacturing

532412 Welding equipment rental or leasing

424690 Welding gases merchant wholesalers

423830 Welding machinery and equipment merchant wholesalers

333514 Welding positioners (i.e., jigs) manufacturing

811310 Welding repair services (e.g., automotive, general)

331491 Welding rod, uncoated, nonferrous metals (except aluminum, copper), made from purchased metals or scrap
423840 Welding supplies (except welding gases) merchant wholesalers
333992 Welding wire or rods (i.e., coated, cored) manufacturing
238190 Welding, on-site, contractors
332313 Weldments manufacturing
923130 Welfare administration, nonoperating
923130 Welfare programs administration
624190 Welfare service centers, multi-program
213112 Well casing running, cutting and pulling, oil and gas field on a contract basis
331210 Well casings (e.g., heavy riveted, lock joint, welded, wrought) made from purchased iron or steel
331110 Well casings, iron or steel, made in iron and steel mills
213111 Well drilling (i.e., oil, gas, water intake wells) on a contract basis
532412 Well drilling machinery and equipment rental or leasing
333132 Well logging equipment manufacturing
213112 Well logging, oil and gas field, on a contract basis
213112 Well plugging, oil and gas field, on a contract basis
213112 Well pumping, oil and gas field, on a contract basis
213112 Well servicing, oil and gas field, on a contract basis
213112 Well surveying, oil and gas field, on a contract basis
332322 Wells, light, sheet metal (except stampings), manufacturing
316110 Welting leather manufacturing
448140 Western wear stores
316110 Wet blues manufacturing
313230 Wet laid nonwoven fabrics manufacturing
322130 Wet machine board mills
311221 Wet milling corn and other vegetables
339920 Wet suits manufacturing
541620 Wetland restoration planning services
325613 Wetting agents manufacturing
487210 Whale watching excursions
237990 Wharf construction
488310 Wharf operation
311211 Wheat bran manufacturing
311230 Wheat breakfast cereal manufacturing
111140 Wheat farming, field and seed production
311211 Wheat flour manufacturing
311211 Wheat germ manufacturing
311213 Wheat malt manufacturing
424510 Wheat merchant wholesalers
334515 Wheatstone bridges (i.e., electrical measuring instruments) manufacturing
811118 Wheel alignment shops, automotive
532283 Wheel chair rental
334511 Wheel position indicators and transmitters, aircraft, manufacturing
332216 Wheel pullers, handtools, manufacturing
333924 Wheelbarrows manufacturing
339113 Wheelchairs manufacturing
423450 Wheelchairs merchant wholesalers
336390 Wheels (i.e., rims), automotive, truck, and bus, manufacturing
327910 Wheels, abrasive, manufacturing
331110 Wheels, car and locomotive, iron or steel, made in iron and steel mills
423120 Wheels, motor vehicle, new, merchant wholesalers
327910 Wheels, polishing and grinding, manufacturing
336330 Wheels, steering, automotive, truck, and bus, manufacturing
327910 Whetstones manufacturing
212399 Whetstones mining and/or beneficiating
311512 Whey butter manufacturing
311514 Whey, condensed, dried, evaporated, and powdered, manufacturing
311513 Whey, raw, liquid, manufacturing
311511 Whipped topping (except dry mix, frozen) manufacturing
311514 Whipped topping, dry mix, manufacturing
311412 Whipped topping, frozen, manufacturing
335210 Whippers, household-type electric, manufacturing
311511 Whipping cream manufacturing
316998 Whips, horse, manufacturing
316998 Whipstocks manufacturing
339113 Whirlpool baths (i.e., hydrotherapy equipment) manufacturing
423450 Whirlpool baths, hospital, merchant wholesalers
493190 Whiskey warehousing
325130 White extender pigments (e.g., barytes, blanc fixe, whiting) manufacturing

331529 White metal castings (except die-castings), unfinished, manufacturing
713990 White water rafting, recreational
238320 Whitewashing contractors
212312 Whiting crushed and broken stone, mining and/or beneficiating
114111 Whiting fishing
325130 Whiting manufacturing
334519 Whole body counters, nuclear, manufacturing
****** Wholesale -- see type of product
561520 Wholesale tour operators
813910 Wholesalers' associations
337125 Wicker furniture (except upholstered), household-type, manufacturing
313220 Wicks manufacturing
334210 Wide area network communications equipment (e.g., bridges, gateways, routers) manufacturing
448150 Wig and hairpiece stores
424990 Wigs merchant wholesalers
339999 Wigs, wiglets, toupees, hairpieces, manufacturing
712130 Wild animal parks
111199 Wild rice farming, field and seed production
721214 Wilderness camps
711510 Wildlife artists, independent
924120 Wildlife conservation agencies
813312 Wildlife preservation organizations
712190 Wildlife sanctuaries
212230 Willemite mining and/or beneficiating
337125 Willow furniture (except upholstered), household-type, manufacturing
321999 Willow ware (except furniture) manufacturing
333923 Winches manufacturing
423830 Winches merchant wholesalers
924120 Wind and water erosion control agencies, government
334519 Wind direction indicators manufacturing
926130 Wind generated electrical power regulation
237130 Wind power structure construction
333611 Wind powered turbine generator sets manufacturing
333611 Wind turbines (i.e., windmill) manufacturing
315210 Windbreakers cut and sew apparel contractors
315220 Windbreakers, men's and boys', cut and sewn from purchased fabric (except apparel contractors)
315240 Windbreakers, women's, girls', and infants', cut and sewn from purchased fabric (except apparel contractors)
333249 Winding machinery for textiles manufacturing
313110 Winding purchased yarn
313110 Winding, spooling, beaming and rewinding of purchased yarn
333611 Windmills, electric power, generation-type, manufacturing
333111 Windmills, farm-type, manufacturing
238350 Window and door (residential-type) of any material, prefabricated, installation
325612 Window cleaning preparations manufacturing
561720 Window cleaning services
423440 Window display equipment merchant wholesalers
541890 Window dressing or trimming services, store
332321 Window frames and sash, metal, manufacturing
321911 Window frames and sash, wood and covered wood, manufacturing
238350 Window installation
238150 Window pane or sheet installation
326199 Window sashes, vinyl, manufacturing
332618 Window screening, woven, made from purchased wire
332321 Window screens, metal frame, manufacturing
321911 Window screens, wood framed, manufacturing
238390 Window shade and blind installation
811490 Window shade repair and maintenance shops
337920 Window shade rollers and fittings manufacturing
337920 Window shades (except awnings) manufacturing
423220 Window shades and blinds merchant wholesalers
444190 Window stores
811122 Window tinting, automotive
442291 Window treatment stores

321918 Window trim, wood and covered wood moldings, manufacturing
321911 Window units, wood and covered wood, manufacturing
238350 Window, metal frame residential-type, installation
238350 Window, wood, installation
423310 Windows and window frames merchant wholesalers
326199 Windows and window frames, plastics, manufacturing
326199 Windows and window frames, vinyl, manufacturing
321911 Windows, louver, wood, manufacturing
332321 Windows, metal, manufacturing
321911 Windows, wood and covered wood, manufacturing
811122 Windshield repair shops, automotive
325612 Windshield washer fluid manufacturing
336320 Windshield washer pumps, automotive, truck, and bus, manufacturing
336390 Windshield wiper blades and refills manufacturing
336320 Windshield wiper systems, automotive, truck, and bus, manufacturing
326199 Windshields, plastics, manufacturing
312130 Wine coolers manufacturing 424820
Wine coolers, alcoholic, merchant wholesalers
453998 Wine making supply stores
445310 Wine shops, packaged
312130 Wineries
312130 Wines manufacturing
424820 Wines merchant wholesalers
312130 Wines, cooking, manufacturing
325998 Wintergreen oil manufacturing
336390 Wipers, windshield, automotive, truck, and bus, manufacturing
313230 Wipes, nonwoven fabric, manufacturing
423840 Wiping cloths merchant wholesalers
423510 Wire (except insulated) merchant wholesalers
423510 Wire and cable (except electrical) merchant wholesalers
333249 Wire and cable insulating machinery manufacturing
331222 Wire cages, iron or steel, made in wire drawing plants
331222 Wire carts (e.g., grocery, household, industrial), iron or steel, made in wire drawing plants
331420 Wire cloth made from purchased copper in wire drawing plants
331318 Wire cloth made in aluminum wire drawing plants
331420 Wire cloth, copper, made in integrated secondary smelting and wire drawing plants
331222 Wire cloth, iron or steel, made in wire drawing plants
331491 Wire cloth, nonferrous metals (except aluminum, copper), made from purchased metals or scrap
333519 Wire drawing and fabricating machinery and equipment (except dies) manufacturing
333514 Wire drawing and straightening dies manufacturing
423390 Wire fencing and fencing accessories merchant wholesalers
331222 Wire garment hangers, iron or steel, made in wire drawing plants
519110 Wire photo services
331110 Wire products, iron or steel, made in iron and steel mills
331222 Wire products, iron or steel, made in wire drawing plants
423510 Wire rope (except insulated) merchant wholesalers
333923 Wire rope hoists manufacturing
423510 Wire screening merchant wholesalers 331318
Wire screening, aluminum, made in integrated secondary smelting and drawing plants
331491 Wire screening, nonferrous metals (except aluminum, copper), made from purchased nonferrous metals (except aluminum, copper) in wire drawing plants
561422 Wire services (i.e., telemarketing services), floral
519110 Wire services, news
331318 Wire, armored, made in aluminum wire drawing plants
331318 Wire, bare, made in aluminum wire drawing plants
331420 Wire, copper (e.g., armored, bare, insulated), made from purchased copper in wire drawing plants
331420 Wire, copper (e.g., armored, bare, insulated), made in integrated secondary smelting and wire drawing plants
331221 Wire, flat, rolled strip, made in cold rolling mills
331318 Wire, insulated, made in aluminum wire drawing plants
423610 Wire, insulated, merchant wholesalers

331222 Wire, iron or steel (e.g., armored, bare, insulated), made in wire drawing plants
331420 Wire, mechanical, copper and copper alloy, made from purchased copper or in integrated secondary smelting and rolling, drawing or extruding plants
331491 Wire, nonferrous metals (except aluminum, copper), made from purchased nonferrous metals (except aluminum, copper) in wire drawing plants
331491 Wire, nonferrous metals (except aluminum, copper), made in integrated secondary smelting mills and wire drawing plants
517911 Wired telecommunication resellers
517312 Wireless data communication carriers (except satellite)
517312 Wireless Internet service providers (except satellite)
517312 Wireless phone stores, primarily selling wireless phone service plans
517911 Wireless telecommunication resellers (except satellite)
517312 Wireless telephone communications carriers (except satellite)
517312 Wireless video services (except satellite)
213112 Wireline services, oil and gas field, on a contract basis
336320 Wiring harness and ignition sets for internal combustion engines manufacturing
423610 Wiring supplies merchant wholesalers
325194 Witch hazel extract manufacturing
212299 Wolframite mining and/or beneficiating
212399 Wollastonite mining and/or beneficiating
424330 Women's and children's clothing accessories merchant wholesalers
813410 Women's auxiliaries
923130 Women's bureaus
424330 Women's clothing merchant wholesalers
813410 Women's clubs
624221 Women's shelters, battered
325194 Wood alcohol, natural, manufacturing
325199 Wood alcohol, synthetic, manufacturing
424990 Wood carvings merchant wholesalers
113310 Wood chipping in the field
321113 Wood chips made in sawmills
332216 Wood cutting saw blades manufacturing
325194 Wood distillates manufacturing
321911 Wood door frames and sash manufacturing
333249 Wood drying kilns manufacturing
321114 Wood fence (i.e., pickets, poling, rails), treating
423310 Wood fencing merchant wholesalers
325510 Wood fillers manufacturing 238330
Wood floor finishing (e.g., coating, sanding)
321918 Wood flooring manufacturing
423310 Wood flooring merchant wholesalers
238330 Wood flooring, installation only
321999 Wood flour manufacturing
238130 Wood frame component (e.g., truss) fabrication on site
337121 Wood framed furniture, upholstered, household-type, manufacturing 321999
Wood heel blocks manufacturing 321999 Wood heels, finished, manufacturing 321213 Wood I-joists manufacturing 321918 Wood moldings (e.g., prefinished, unfinished), clear and finger joint,
manufacturing
325194 Wood oils manufacturing
424950 Wood paste merchant wholesalers
321999 Wood pellets manufacturing
423990 Wood products (e.g., chips, posts, shavings, ties) merchant wholesalers
321114 Wood products, creosoting purchased wood products
322110 Wood pulp manufacturing
424990 Wood pulp merchant wholesalers
423310 Wood shingles merchant wholesalers
321918 Wood shutters manufacturing
423310 Wood siding merchant wholesalers
238170 Wood siding, installation
333414 Wood stoves manufacturing
424690 Wood treating preparations merchant wholesalers
333243 Wood veneer laminating and gluing machines manufacturing
321911 Wood window frames and sash manufacturing
321999 Wood wool (excelsior) manufacturing
442299 Wood-burning stove stores
423440 Woodenware, commercial, merchant wholesalers
321999 Woodenware, kitchen and household, manufacturing
532490 Woodworking machinery and equipment rental or leasing

423830 Woodworking machinery merchant wholesalers
333243 Woodworking machines (except handheld) manufacturing
333249 Wool and worsted finishing machinery manufacturing
313210 Wool fabrics, broadwoven, weaving
313220 Wool fabrics, narrow woven, weaving
313110 Wool spun yarn made from purchased fiber
313310 Wool tops and noils manufacturing
424590 Wool tops and noils merchant wholesalers
314999 Wool waste processing
313110 Wool yarn, twisting or winding of purchased yarn
424590 Wool, raw, merchant wholesalers
311941 Worcestershire sauce manufacturing 333318
Word processing equipment, dedicated, manufacturing
561410 Word processing services
624229 Work (sweat) equity home construction organizations
337127 Work benches manufacturing
812332 Work clothing and uniform supply services, industrial
424320 Work clothing, men's and boys', merchant wholesalers
315210 Work coats and jackets cut and sew apparel contractors
315220 Work coats and jackets, men's and boys', cut and sewn from purchased fabric (except apparel contractors)
624310 Work experience centers (i.e., sheltered workshops)
315190 Work gloves and mittens, knit, made in apparel knitting mills
315990 Work gloves, leather (except apparel contractors), manufacturing
315210 Work gloves, leather, cut and sew apparel contractors
315210 Work pants cut and sew apparel contractors
315220 Work pants, men's and boys', cut and sewn from purchased fabric (except apparel contractors)
315210 Work shirts cut and sew apparel contractors
315220 Work shirts, men's and boys', cut and sewn from purchased fabric (except apparel contractors)
316210 Work shoes manufacturing
721310 Workers' camps
525190 Workers' compensation insurance funds
524126 Workers' compensation insurance underwriting
923130 Workers' compensation program administration
721310 Workers' dormitories
812910 Working, sporting, and service dog training services
213111 Workover of oil and gas wells on a contract basis
624310 Workshops for persons with disabilities
334111 Workstations, computer, manufacturing
928120 World Bank
813319 World peace and understanding advocacy organizations
112990 Worm production
424990 Worms merchant wholesalers
313210 Worsted fabrics weaving
321999 Wrappers, excelsior, manufacturing
333993 Wrapping (i.e., packaging) machinery manufacturing
424130 Wrapping paper (except gift wrap) merchant wholesalers
339999 Wreaths, artificial, manufacturing
488410 Wrecker services (i.e., towing services), motor vehicle
238910 Wrecking, building or other structure
332216 Wrenches, handtools, nonpowered, manufacturing
333991 Wrenches, impact, handheld power-driven, manufacturing
711219 Wrestlers, independent professional
711310 Wrestling event managers with facilities
711320 Wrestling event managers without facilities
711310 Wrestling event organizers with facilities
711320 Wrestling event organizers without facilities
711310 Wrestling event promoters with facilities
711320 Wrestling event promoters without facilities
711510 Writers of advertising copy, independent
711510 Writers, independent (freelance)
813410 Writing clubs
325998 Writing inks manufacturing 424120 Writing paper (except bulk) merchant wholesalers
322230 Writing paper and envelopes, boxed sets, made from purchased paper
322121 Writing paper made in paper mills
322230 Writing paper, cut sheet, made from purchased paper

332323 Wrought iron fences manufacturing
337124 Wrought iron furniture (except upholstered), household-type, manufacturing
332996 Wrought iron or steel pipe and tubing made from purchased metal pipe
331110 Wrought iron or steel pipe and tubing made in iron and steel mills
212299 Wulfenite mining and/or beneficiating
212399 Wurtzilite mining and/or beneficiating
325320 Xanthone insecticides manufacturing
335110 X-mas tree light bulbs manufacturing
334517 X-ray apparatus and tubes (e.g., control, industrial, medical, research) manufacturing
325992 X-ray film and plates, sensitized, manufacturing
334517 X-ray generators manufacturing
541380 X-ray inspection services
334517 X-ray irradiation equipment manufacturing
621512 X-ray laboratories, medical or dental
423450 X-ray machines and parts, medical and dental, merchant wholesalers
334517 X-ray tubes manufacturing
334515 X-Y recorders (i.e., plotters (except computer peripheral equipment)) manufacturing
325110 Xylene made from refined petroleum or liquid hydrocarbons
324110 Xylene made in petroleum refineries
339992 Xylophones and parts manufacturing
713930 Yacht basins
336612 Yacht building, not done in shipyards
713930 Yacht clubs with marinas
713990 Yacht clubs without marinas
532284 Yacht rental without crew
423860 Yachts (except pleasure) merchant wholesalers
336611 Yachts built in shipyards
423910 Yachts, pleasure, merchant wholesalers
111211 Yam farming, field and seed production
424310 Yard goods, textile (except burlap, felt), merchant wholesalers
335121 Yard lights, residential electric, manufacturing
332216 Yardsticks, metal, manufacturing
321999 Yardsticks, wood, manufacturing
313110 Yarn spinning mills
313110 Yarn spun from purchased fiber
333249 Yarn texturizing machines manufacturing
313110 Yarn throwing, twisting, and winding of purchased yarn
313110 Yarn, carpet and rug, spun from purchased fiber
325220 Yarn, cellulosic filament, manufacturing
325220 Yarn, cellulosic filament, manufacturing and texturizing
327212 Yarn, fiberglass, made in glass making plants
325220 Yarn, noncellulosic fiber and filament, manufacturing
325220 Yarn, noncellulosic fiber and filament, manufacturing and texturizing
424310 Yarns (except industrial) merchant wholesalers
424990 Yarns, industrial, merchant wholesalers
511199 Yearbook (e.g., high school, college, university) publishers (except exclusive Internet publishing)
511199 Yearbook (e.g., high school, college, university) publishers and printing combined
519130 Yearbook (e.g., high school, college, university) publishers, exclusively on Internet
323111 Yearbooks commercial printing (except screen) without publishing
323113 Yearbooks screen printing without publishing
311999 Yeast manufacturing
424490 Yeast merchant wholesalers
611699 Yoga instruction, camps, or schools
611519 Yoga instructor training
311511 Yogurt (except frozen) manufacturing
424430 Yogurt merchant wholesalers
311514 Yogurt mix manufacturing
311520 Yogurt, frozen, manufacturing
111334 Youngberry farming
624110 Youth centers (except recreational only)
813410 Youth civic clubs
813410 Youth clubs (except recreational only)
813410 Youth farming organizations
624110 Youth guidance organizations
721199 Youth hostels
813410 Youth scouting organizations
624110 Youth self-help organizations
813410 Youth social clubs

713990 Youth sports league teams

325220 Zein fibers and filaments manufacturing

325180 Zinc ammonium chloride manufacturing

331491 Zinc and zinc alloy bar, plate, pipe, rod, sheet, tubing, and wire made from purchased metals or scrap

423510 Zinc and zinc alloy primary forms merchant wholesalers

325130 Zinc based pigments manufacturing

335912 Zinc carbon batteries manufacturing

331529 Zinc castings (except die-castings), unfinished, manufacturing

325180 Zinc chloride manufacturing 325180 Zinc compounds, not specified elsewhere by process, manufacturing

331523 Zinc die-castings, unfinished, manufacturing

331492 Zinc dust reclaiming

332999 Zinc foil and leaf not made in rolling mills

325180 Zinc hydrosulfite (i.e., zinc dithionite) manufacturing

212230 Zinc ore mine site development for own account

212230 Zinc ores mining and/or beneficiating

325180 Zinc oxide (except pigments) manufacturing

325412 Zinc oxide medicinal preparations manufacturing

331492 Zinc recovering from scrap and/or alloying purchased metals

331410 Zinc refining, primary 331491 Zinc rolling, drawing, or extruding purchased metals or scrap

325180 Zinc sulfide manufacturing

212230 Zinc-blende (sphalerite) mining and/or beneficiating

212230 Zincite mining and/or beneficiating

333249 Zipper making machinery manufacturing

313220 Zipper tape weaving

339993 Zippers (i.e., slide fasteners) manufacturing 424310 Zippers merchant wholesalers 331491 Zirconium and zirconium alloy bar, rod, billet, sheet, strip, and tubing made from purchased metals or scrap

212299 Zirconium concentrates beneficiating

212299 Zirconium ores mining and/or beneficiating

331410 Zirconium refining, primary

331491 Zirconium rolling, drawing, or extruding purchased metals or scrap

339992 Zithers and parts manufacturing

925120 Zoning boards and commissions

712130 Zoological gardens

712130 Zoos

111219 Zucchini farming, field, bedding plant and seed production

U.S. Small Business Administration
Table of Size Standards
matched to the 2017 NAICS
SBA size standards date August 19, 2019

U.S. Small Business Administration

U. S. Small Business Administration

Table of Small Business Size Standards Matched to North American Industry Classification System Codes

This table lists small business size standards matched to industries described in the North American Industry Classification System (NAICS), as modified by the Office of Management and Budget, effective January 1, 2017. The latest NAICS codes are referred to as NAICS 2017.

The size standards are for the most part expressed in either millions of dollars (those preceded by "$") or number of employees (those without the "$"). A size standard is the largest that a concern can be and still qualify as a small business for Federal Government programs. For the most part, size standards are the average annual receipts or the average employment of a firm. How to calculate average annual receipts and average employment of a firm can be found in 13 CFR § 121.104 and 13 CFR § 121.106, respectively.

SBA also includes the table of size standards in the Small Business Size Regulations, 13 CFR § 121.201. This table includes size standards that have changed since the last publication of 13 CFR § 121.

For more information on these size standards, please visit SBA's Size Standards webpage.

If you have any other questions concerning size standards, contact a Size Specialist at your nearest SBA Government Contracting Area Office (list at the end of the table), or contact the Office of Size Standards by email at *sizestandards@sba.gov* or by phone at (202) 205-6618.

Important Notice: Businesses registered in the System for Award Management (SAM.gov) must update their SAM registration in order to have their small business status updated based on the new size standards effective August 19, 2019. Until the SAM registration is updated, the SAM profiles will continue to display the small business status under the old size standards.

These size standards are effective

August 19, 2019

Sector 11 – Agriculture, Forestry, Fishing and Hunting

NAICS codes	NAICS U.S. industry title	Size standards in millions of dollars	Size standards in number of employees
111110	Soybean Farming	$1.0	
111120	Oilseed (except Soybean) Farming	$1.0	
111130	Dry Pea and Bean Farming	$1.0	
111140	Wheat Farming	$1.0	
111150	Corn Farming	$1.0	
111160	Rice Farming	$1.0	
111191	Oilseed and Grain Combination Farming	$1.0	
111199	All Other Grain Farming	$1.0	
111211	Potato Farming	$1.0	
111219	Other Vegetable (except Potato) and Melon Farming	$1.0	
111310	Orange Groves	$1.0	
111320	Citrus (except Orange) Groves	$1.0	
111331	Apple Orchards	$1.0	
111332	Grape Vineyards	$1.0	
111333	Strawberry Farming	$1.0	
111334	Berry (except Strawberry) Farming	$1.0	
111335	Tree Nut Farming	$1.0	
111336	Fruit and Tree Nut Combination Farming	$1.0	
111339	Other Noncitrus Fruit Farming	$1.0	
111411	Mushroom Production	$1.0	
111419	Other Food Crops Grown Under Cover	$1.0	
111421	Nursery and Tree Production	$1.0	
111422	Floriculture Production	$1.0	
111910	Tobacco Farming	$1.0	
111920	Cotton Farming	$1.0	
111930	Sugarcane Farming	$1.0	
111940	Hay Farming	$1.0	
111991	Sugar Beet Farming	$1.0	
111992	Peanut Farming	$1.0	
111998	All Other Miscellaneous Crop Farming	$1.0	
112111	Beef Cattle Ranching and Farming	$1.0	
112112	Cattle Feedlots	$8.0	
112120	Dairy Cattle and Milk Production	$1.0	
112210	Hog and Pig Farming	$1.0	

NAICS codes	NAICS U.S. industry title	Size standards in millions of dollars	Size standards in number of employees
112310	Chicken Egg Production	$16.5	
112320	Broilers and Other Meat Type Chicken Production	$1.0	
112330	Turkey Production	$1.0	
112340	Poultry Hatcheries	$1.0	
112390	Other Poultry Production	$1.0	
112410	Sheep Farming	$1.0	
112420	Goat Farming	$1.0	
112511	Finfish Farming and Fish Hatcheries	$1.0	
112512	Shellfish Farming	$1.0	
112519	Other Aquaculture	$1.0	
112910	Apiculture	$1.0	
112920	Horses and Other Equine Production	$1.0	
112930	Fur-Bearing Animal and Rabbit Production	$1.0	
112990	All Other Animal Production	$1.0	
113110	Timber Tract Operations	$12.0	
113210	Forest Nurseries and Gathering of Forest Products	$12.0	
113310	Logging		500
114111	Finfish Fishing	$22.0	
114112	Shellfish Fishing	$6.0	
114119	Other Marine Fishing	$8.0	
114210	Hunting and Trapping	$6.0	
115111	Cotton Ginning	$12.0	
115112	Soil Preparation, Planting, and Cultivating	$8.0	
115113	Crop Harvesting, Primarily by Machine	$8.0	
115114	Postharvest Crop Activities (except Cotton Ginning)	$30.0	
115115	Farm Labor Contractors and Crew Leaders	$16.5	
115116	Farm Management Services	$8.0	
115210	Support Activities for Animal Production	$8.0	
115310	Support Activities for Forestry	$8.0	
Except,	Forest Fire Suppression[17]	$20.5[17]	
Except,	Fuels Management Services[17]	$20.5[17]	

Sector 21 – Mining, Quarrying, and Oil and Gas Extraction

NAICS codes	NAICS U.S. industry title	Size standards in millions of dollars	Size standards in number of employees
211120	Crude Petroleum Extraction		1,250
211130	Natural Gas Extraction		1,250
212111	Bituminous Coal and Lignite Surface Mining		1,250
212112	Bituminous Coal Underground Mining		1,500
212113	Anthracite Mining		250
212210	Iron Ore Mining		750
212221	Gold Ore Mining		1,500
212222	Silver Ore Mining		250
212230	Copper, Nickel, Lead, and Zinc Mining		750
212291	Uranium-Radium-Vanadium Ore Mining		250
212299	All Other Metal Ore Mining		750
212311	Dimension Stone Mining and Quarrying		500
212312	Crushed and Broken Limestone Mining and Quarrying		750
212313	Crushed and Broken Granite Mining and Quarrying		750
212319	Other Crushed and Broken Stone Mining and Quarrying		500
212321	Construction Sand and Gravel Mining		500
212322	Industrial Sand Mining		500
212324	Kaolin and Ball Clay Mining		750
212325	Clay and Ceramic and Refractory Minerals Mining		500
212391	Potash, Soda, and Borate Mineral Mining		750
212392	Phosphate Rock Mining		1,000
212393	Other Chemical and Fertilizer Mineral Mining		500
212399	All Other Nonmetallic Mineral Mining		500
213111	Drilling Oil and Gas Wells		1,000
213112	Support Activities for Oil and Gas Operations	$41.5	
213113	Support Activities for Coal Mining	$22.0	
213114	Support Activities for Metal Mining	$22.0	
213115	Support Activities for Nonmetallic Minerals (except Fuels)	$8.0	

Sector 22 – Utilities

NAICS codes	NAICS U.S. industry title	Size standards in millions of dollars	Size standards in number of employees
221111	Hydroelectric Power Generation		500
221112	Fossil Fuel Electric Power Generation		750
221113	Nuclear Electric Power Generation		750
221114	Solar Electric Power Generation		250
221115	Wind Electric Power Generation		250
221116	Geothermal Electric Power Generation		250
221117	Biomass Electric Power Generation		250
221118	Other Electric Power Generation		250
221121	Electric Bulk Power Transmission and Control		500
221122	Electric Power Distribution		1,000
221210	Natural Gas Distribution		1,000
221310	Water Supply and Irrigation Systems	$30.0	
221320	Sewage Treatment Facilities	$22.0	
221330	Steam and Air-Conditioning Supply	$16.5	

Sector 23 – Construction

NAICS codes	NAICS U.S. industry title	Size standards in millions of dollars	Size standards in number of employees
236115	New Single-family Housing Construction (Except For-Sale Builders)	$39.5	
236116	New Multifamily Housing Construction (except For-Sale Builders)	$39.5	
236117	New Housing For-Sale Builders	$39.5	
236118	Residential Remodelers	$39.5	
236210	Industrial Building Construction	$39.5	
236220	Commercial and Institutional Building Construction	$39.5	
237110	Water and Sewer Line and Related Structures Construction	$39.5	
237120	Oil and Gas Pipeline and Related Structures Construction	$39.5	

NAICS codes	NAICS U.S. industry title	Size standards in millions of dollars	Size standards in number of employees
237130	Power and Communication Line and Related Structures Construction	$39.5	
237210	Land Subdivision	$30.0	
237310	Highway, Street, and Bridge Construction	$39.5	
237990	Other Heavy and Civil Engineering Construction	$39.5	
Except,	Dredging and Surface Cleanup Activities[2]	$30.0[2]	
238110	Poured Concrete Foundation and Structure Contractors	$16.5	
238120	Structural Steel and Precast Concrete Contractors	$16.5	
238130	Framing Contractors	$16.5	
238140	Masonry Contractors	$16.5	
238150	Glass and Glazing Contractors	$16.5	
238160	Roofing Contractors	$16.5	
238170	Siding Contractors	$16.5	
238190	Other Foundation, Structure, and Building Exterior Contractors	$16.5	
238210	Electrical Contractors and Other Wiring Installation Contractors	$16.5	
238220	Plumbing, Heating, and Air-Conditioning Contractors	$16.5	
238290	Other Building Equipment Contractors	$16.5	
238310	Drywall and Insulation Contractors	$16.5	
238320	Painting and Wall Covering Contractors	$16.5	
238330	Flooring Contractors	$16.5	
238340	Tile and Terrazzo Contractors	$16.5	
238350	Finish Carpentry Contractors	$16.5	
238390	Other Building Finishing Contractors	$16.5	
238910	Site Preparation Contractors	$16.5	
238990	All Other Specialty Trade Contractors	$16.5	
Except,	Building and Property Specialty Trade Services [13]	$16.5[13]	

Sector 31 – 33 – Manufacturing

NAICS codes	NAICS U.S. industry title	Size standards in millions of dollars	Size standards in number of employees
311111	Dog and Cat Food Manufacturing		1,000
311119	Other Animal Food Manufacturing		500
311211	Flour Milling		1,000
311212	Rice Milling		500
311213	Malt Manufacturing		500
311221	Wet Corn Milling		1,250
311224	Soybean and Other Oilseed Processing		1,000
311225	Fats and Oils Refining and Blending		1,000
311230	Breakfast Cereal Manufacturing		1,000
311313	Beet Sugar Manufacturing		750
311314	Cane Sugar Manufacturing		1,000
311340	Nonchocolate Confectionery Manufacturing		1,000
311351	Chocolate and Confectionery Manufacturing from Cacao Beans		1,250
311352	Confectionery Manufacturing from Purchased Chocolate		1,000
311411	Frozen Fruit, Juice and Vegetable Manufacturing		1,000
311412	Frozen Specialty Food Manufacturing		1,250
311421	Fruit and Vegetable Canning[3]		1,000[3]
311422	Specialty Canning		1,250
311423	Dried and Dehydrated Food Manufacturing		750
311511	Fluid Milk Manufacturing		1,000
311512	Creamery Butter Manufacturing		750
311513	Cheese Manufacturing		1,250
311514	Dry, Condensed, and Evaporated Dairy Product Manufacturing		750
311520	Ice Cream and Frozen Dessert Manufacturing		1,000
311611	Animal (except Poultry) Slaughtering		1,000
311612	Meat Processed from Carcasses		1,000
311613	Rendering and Meat Byproduct Processing		750
311615	Poultry Processing		1,250
311710	Seafood Product Preparation and Packaging		750
311811	Retail Bakeries		500
311812	Commercial Bakeries		1,000

NAICS codes	NAICS U.S. industry title	Size standards in millions of dollars	Size standards in number of employees
311813	Frozen Cakes, Pies, and Other Pastries Manufacturing		750
311821	Cookie and Cracker Manufacturing		1,250
311824	Dry Pasta, Dough, and Flour Mixes Manufacturing from Purchased Flour		750
311830	Tortilla Manufacturing		1,250
311911	Roasted Nuts and Peanut Butter Manufacturing		750
311919	Other Snack Food Manufacturing		1,250
311920	Coffee and Tea Manufacturing		750
311930	Flavoring Syrup and Concentrate Manufacturing		1,000
311941	Mayonnaise, Dressing and Other Prepared Sauce Manufacturing		750
311942	Spice and Extract Manufacturing		500
311991	Perishable Prepared Food Manufacturing		500
311999	All Other Miscellaneous Food Manufacturing		500
312111	Soft Drink Manufacturing		1,250
312112	Bottled Water Manufacturing		1,000
312113	Ice Manufacturing		750
312120	Breweries		1,250
312130	Wineries		1,000
312140	Distilleries		1,000
312230	Tobacco Manufacturing		1,500
313110	Fiber, Yarn, and Thread Mills		1,250
313210	Broadwoven Fabric Mills		1,000
313220	Narrow Fabric Mills and Schiffli Machine Embroidery		500
313230	Nonwoven Fabric Mills		750
313240	Knit Fabric Mills		500
313310	Textile and Fabric Finishing Mills		1,000
313320	Fabric Coating Mills		1,000
314110	Carpet and Rug Mills		1,500
314120	Curtain and Linen Mills		750
314910	Textile Bag and Canvas Mills		500
314994	Rope, Cordage, Twine, Tire Cord, and Tire Fabric Mills		1,000

NAICS codes	NAICS U.S. industry title	Size standards in millions of dollars	Size standards in number of employees
314999	All Other Miscellaneous Textile Product Mills		500
315110	Hosiery and Sock Mills		750
315190	Other Apparel Knitting Mills		750
315210	Cut and Sew Apparel Contractors		750
315220	Men's and Boys' Cut and Sew Apparel Manufacturing		750
315240	Women's, Girls', and Infants' Cut and Sew Apparel Manufacturing		750
315280	Other Cut and Sew Apparel Manufacturing		750
315990	Apparel Accessories and Other Apparel Manufacturing		500
316110	Leather and Hide Tanning and Finishing		500
316210	Footwear Manufacturing		1,000
316992	Women's Handbag and Purse Manufacturing		750
316998	All Other Leather Good and Allied Product Manufacturing		500
321113	Sawmills		500
321114	Wood Preservation		500
321211	Hardwood Veneer and Plywood Manufacturing		500
321212	Softwood Veneer and Plywood Manufacturing		1,250
321213	Engineered Wood Member (except Truss) Manufacturing		750
321214	Truss Manufacturing		500
321219	Reconstituted Wood Product Manufacturing		750
321911	Wood Window and Door Manufacturing		1,000
321912	Cut Stock, Resawing Lumber, and Planing		500
321918	Other Millwork (including Flooring)		500
321920	Wood Container and Pallet Manufacturing		500
321991	Manufactured Home (Mobile Home) Manufacturing		1,250
321992	Prefabricated Wood Building Manufacturing		500
321999	All Other Miscellaneous Wood Product Manufacturing		500
322110	Pulp Mills		750
322121	Paper (except Newsprint) Mills		1,250

NAICS codes	NAICS U.S. industry title	Size standards in millions of dollars	Size standards in number of employees
322122	Newsprint Mills		750
322130	Paperboard Mills		1,250
322211	Corrugated and Solid Fiber Box Manufacturing		1,250
322212	Folding Paperboard Box Manufacturing		750
322219	Other Paperboard Container Manufacturing		1,000
322220	Paper Bag and Coated and Treated Paper Manufacturing		750
322230	Stationery Product Manufacturing		750
322291	Sanitary Paper Product Manufacturing		1,500
322299	All Other Converted Paper Product Manufacturing		500
323111	Commercial Printing (except Screen and Books)		500
323113	Commercial Screen Printing		500
323117	Books Printing		1,250
323120	Support Activities for Printing		500
324110	Petroleum Refineries[4]		1,500[4]
324121	Asphalt Paving Mixture and Block Manufacturing		500
324122	Asphalt Shingle and Coating Materials Manufacturing		750
324191	Petroleum Lubricating Oil and Grease Manufacturing		750
324199	All Other Petroleum and Coal Products Manufacturing		500
325110	Petrochemical Manufacturing		1,000
325120	Industrial Gas Manufacturing		1,000
325130	Synthetic Dye and Pigment Manufacturing		1,000
325180	Other Basic Inorganic Chemical Manufacturing		1,000
325193	Ethyl Alcohol Manufacturing		1,000
325194	Cyclic Crude, Intermediate, and Gum and Wood Chemical Manufacturing		1,250
325199	All Other Basic Organic Chemical Manufacturing		1,250
325211	Plastics Material and Resin Manufacturing		1,250

NAICS codes	NAICS U.S. industry title	Size standards in millions of dollars	Size standards in number of employees
325212	Synthetic Rubber Manufacturing		1,000
325220	Artificial and Synthetic Fibers and Filaments Manufacturing		1,000
325311	Nitrogenous Fertilizer Manufacturing		1,000
325312	Phosphatic Fertilizer Manufacturing		750
325314	Fertilizer (Mixing Only) Manufacturing		500
325320	Pesticide and Other Agricultural Chemical Manufacturing		1,000
325411	Medicinal and Botanical Manufacturing		1,000
325412	Pharmaceutical Preparation Manufacturing		1,250
325413	In-Vitro Diagnostic Substance Manufacturing		1,250
325414	Biological Product (except Diagnostic) Manufacturing		1,250
325510	Paint and Coating Manufacturing		1,000
325520	Adhesive Manufacturing		500
325611	Soap and Other Detergent Manufacturing		1,000
325612	Polish and Other Sanitation Good Manufacturing		750
325613	Surface Active Agent Manufacturing		750
325620	Toilet Preparation Manufacturing		1,250
325910	Printing Ink Manufacturing		500
325920	Explosives Manufacturing		750
325991	Custom Compounding of Purchased Resins		500
325992	Photographic Film, Paper, Plate and Chemical Manufacturing		1,500
325998	All Other Miscellaneous Chemical Product and Preparation Manufacturing		500
326111	Plastic Bag and Pouch Manufacturing		750
326112	Plastics Packaging Film and Sheet (including Laminated) Manufacturing		1,000
326113	Unlaminated Plastics Film and Sheet (except Packaging) Manufacturing		750
326121	Unlaminated Plastics Profile Shape Manufacturing		500
326122	Plastics Pipe and Pipe Fitting Manufacturing		750
326130	Laminated Plastics Plate, Sheet (except Packaging), and Shape Manufacturing		500

NAICS codes	NAICS U.S. industry title	Size standards in millions of dollars	Size standards in number of employees
326140	Polystyrene Foam Product Manufacturing		1,000
326150	Urethane and Other Foam Product (except Polystyrene) Manufacturing		750
326160	Plastics Bottle Manufacturing		1,250
326191	Plastics Plumbing Fixture Manufacturing		750
326199	All Other Plastics Product Manufacturing		750
326211	Tire Manufacturing (except Retreading)[5]		1,500[5]
326212	Tire Retreading		500
326220	Rubber and Plastics Hoses and Belting Manufacturing		750
326291	Rubber Product Manufacturing for Mechanical Use		750
326299	All Other Rubber Product Manufacturing		500
327110	Pottery, Ceramics, and Plumbing Fixture Manufacturing		1,000
327120	Clay Building Material and Refractories Manufacturing		750
327211	Flat Glass Manufacturing		1,000
327212	Other Pressed and Blown Glass and Glassware Manufacturing		1,250
327213	Glass Container Manufacturing		1,250
327215	Glass Product Manufacturing Made of Purchased Glass		1,000
327310	Cement Manufacturing		1,000
327320	Ready-Mix Concrete Manufacturing		500
327331	Concrete Block and Brick Manufacturing		500
327332	Concrete Pipe Manufacturing		750
327390	Other Concrete Product Manufacturing		500
327410	Lime Manufacturing		750
327420	Gypsum Product Manufacturing		1,500
327910	Abrasive Product Manufacturing		750
327991	Cut Stone and Stone Product Manufacturing		500
327992	Ground or Treated Mineral and Earth Manufacturing		500
327993	Mineral Wool Manufacturing		1,500
327999	All Other Miscellaneous Nonmetallic Mineral Product Manufacturing		500

NAICS codes	NAICS U.S. industry title	Size standards in millions of dollars	Size standards in number of employees
331110	Iron and Steel Mills and Ferroalloy Manufacturing		1,500
331210	Iron and Steel Pipe and Tube Manufacturing from Purchased Steel		1,000
331221	Rolled Steel Shape Manufacturing		1,000
331222	Steel Wire Drawing		1,000
331313	Alumina Refining and Primary Aluminum Production		1,000
331314	Secondary Smelting and Alloying of Aluminum		750
331315	Aluminum Sheet, Plate and Foil Manufacturing		1,250
331318	Other Aluminum Rolling, Drawing, and Extruding		750
331410	Nonferrous Metal (except Aluminum) Smelting and Refining		1,000
331420	Copper Rolling, Drawing, Extruding, and Alloying		1,000
331491	Nonferrous Metal (except Copper and Aluminum) Rolling, Drawing and Extruding		750
331492	Secondary Smelting, Refining, and Alloying of Nonferrous Metal (except Copper and Aluminum)		750
331511	Iron Foundries		1,000
331512	Steel Investment Foundries		1,000
331513	Steel Foundries (except Investment)		500
331523	Nonferrous Metal Die-Casting Foundries		500
331524	Aluminum Foundries (except Die-Casting)		500
331529	Other Nonferrous Metal Foundries (except Die-Casting)		500
332111	Iron and Steel Forging		750
332112	Nonferrous Forging		750
332114	Custom Roll Forming		500
332117	Powder Metallurgy Part Manufacturing		500
332119	Metal Crown, Closure, and Other Metal Stamping (except Automotive)		500

NAICS codes	NAICS U.S. industry title	Size standards in millions of dollars	Size standards in number of employees
332215	Metal Kitchen Cookware, Utensil, Cutlery, and Flatware (except Precious) Manufacturing		750
332216	Saw Blade and Handtool Manufacturing		750
332311	Prefabricated Metal Building and Component Manufacturing		750
332312	Fabricated Structural Metal Manufacturing		500
332313	Plate Work Manufacturing		750
332321	Metal Window and Door Manufacturing		750
332322	Sheet Metal Work Manufacturing		500
332323	Ornamental and Architectural Metal Work Manufacturing		500
332410	Power Boiler and Heat Exchanger Manufacturing		750
332420	Metal Tank (Heavy Gauge) Manufacturing		750
332431	Metal Can Manufacturing		1,500
332439	Other Metal Container Manufacturing		500
332510	Hardware Manufacturing		750
332613	Spring Manufacturing		500
332618	Other Fabricated Wire Product Manufacturing		500
332710	Machine Shops		500
332721	Precision Turned Product Manufacturing		500
332722	Bolt, Nut, Screw, Rivet and Washer Manufacturing		500
332811	Metal Heat Treating		750
332812	Metal Coating, Engraving (except Jewelry and Silverware), and Allied Services to Manufacturers		500
332813	Electroplating, Plating, Polishing, Anodizing and Coloring		500
332911	Industrial Valve Manufacturing		750
332912	Fluid Power Valve and Hose Fitting Manufacturing		1,000
332913	Plumbing Fixture Fitting and Trim Manufacturing		1,000

NAICS codes	NAICS U.S. industry title	Size standards in millions of dollars	Size standards in number of employees
332919	Other Metal Valve and Pipe Fitting Manufacturing		750
332991	Ball and Roller Bearing Manufacturing		1,250
332992	Small Arms Ammunition Manufacturing		1,250
332993	Ammunition (except Small Arms) Manufacturing		1,500
332994	Small Arms, Ordnance, and Ordnance Accessories Manufacturing		1,000
332996	Fabricated Pipe and Pipe Fitting Manufacturing		500
332999	All Other Miscellaneous Fabricated Metal Product Manufacturing		750
333111	Farm Machinery and Equipment Manufacturing		1,250
333112	Lawn and Garden Tractor and Home Lawn and Garden Equipment Manufacturing		1,500
333120	Construction Machinery Manufacturing		1,250
333131	Mining Machinery and Equipment Manufacturing		500
333132	Oil and Gas Field Machinery and Equipment Manufacturing		1,250
333241	Food Product Machinery Manufacturing		500
333242	Semiconductor Machinery Manufacturing		1,500
333243	Sawmill, Woodworking, and Paper Machinery Manufacturing		500
333244	Printing Machinery and Equipment Manufacturing		750
333249	Other Industrial Machinery Manufacturing		500
333314	Optical Instrument and Lens Manufacturing		500
333316	Photographic and Photocopying Equipment Manufacturing		1,000
333318	Other Commercial and Service Industry Machinery Manufacturing		1,000
333413	Industrial and Commercial Fan and Blower and Air Purification Equipment Manufacturing		500

NAICS codes	NAICS U.S. industry title	Size standards in millions of dollars	Size standards in number of employees
333414	Heating Equipment (except Warm Air Furnaces) Manufacturing		500
333415	Air-Conditioning and Warm Air Heating Equipment and Commercial and Industrial Refrigeration Equipment Manufacturing		1,250
333511	Industrial Mold Manufacturing		500
333514	Special Die and Tool, Die Set, Jig and Fixture Manufacturing		500
333515	Cutting Tool and Machine Tool Accessory Manufacturing		500
333517	Machine Tool Manufacturing		500
333519	Rolling Mill and Other Metalworking Machinery Manufacturing		500
333611	Turbine and Turbine Generator Set Unit Manufacturing		1,500
333612	Speed Changer, Industrial High-Speed Drive and Gear Manufacturing		750
333613	Mechanical Power Transmission Equipment Manufacturing		750
333618	Other Engine Equipment Manufacturing		1,500
333912	Air and Gas Compressor Manufacturing		1,000
333914	Measuring, Dispensing, and Other Pumping Equipment Manufacturing		750
333921	Elevator and Moving Stairway Manufacturing		1,000
333922	Conveyor and Conveying Equipment Manufacturing		500
333923	Overhead Traveling Crane, Hoist and Monorail System Manufacturing		1,250
333924	Industrial Truck, Tractor, Trailer and Stacker Machinery Manufacturing		750
333991	Power-Driven Hand Tool Manufacturing		500
333992	Welding and Soldering Equipment Manufacturing		1,250
333993	Packaging Machinery Manufacturing		500
333994	Industrial Process Furnace and Oven Manufacturing		500

NAICS codes	NAICS U.S. industry title	Size standards in millions of dollars	Size standards in number of employees
333995	Fluid Power Cylinder and Actuator Manufacturing		750
333996	Fluid Power Pump and Motor Manufacturing		1,250
333997	Scale and Balance Manufacturing		500
333999	All Other Miscellaneous General Purpose Machinery Manufacturing		500
334111	Electronic Computer Manufacturing		1,250
334112	Computer Storage Device Manufacturing		1,250
334118	Computer Terminal and Other Computer Peripheral Equipment Manufacturing		1,000
334210	Telephone Apparatus Manufacturing		1,250
334220	Radio and Television Broadcasting and Wireless Communications Equipment Manufacturing		1,250
334290	Other Communications Equipment Manufacturing		750
334310	Audio and Video Equipment Manufacturing		750
334412	Bare Printed Circuit Board Manufacturing		750
334413	Semiconductor and Related Device Manufacturing		1,250
334416	Capacitor, Resistor, Coil, Transformer, and Other Inductor Manufacturing		500
334417	Electronic Connector Manufacturing		1,000
334418	Printed Circuit Assembly (Electronic Assembly) Manufacturing		750
334419	Other Electronic Component Manufacturing		750
334510	Electromedical and Electrotherapeutic Apparatus Manufacturing		1,250
334511	Search, Detection, Navigation, Guidance, Aeronautical, and Nautical System and Instrument Manufacturing		1,250
334512	Automatic Environmental Control Manufacturing for Residential, Commercial and Appliance Use		500
334513	Instruments and Related Products Manufacturing for Measuring, Displaying, and Controlling Industrial Process Variables		750

NAICS codes	NAICS U.S. industry title	Size standards in millions of dollars	Size standards in number of employees
334514	Totalizing Fluid Meter and Counting Device Manufacturing		750
334515	Instrument Manufacturing for Measuring and Testing Electricity and Electrical Signals		750
334516	Analytical Laboratory Instrument Manufacturing		1,000
334517	Irradiation Apparatus Manufacturing		1,000
334519	Other Measuring and Controlling Device Manufacturing		500
334613	Blank Magnetic and Optical Recording Media Manufacturing		1,000
334614	Software and Other Prerecorded Compact Disc, Tape, and Record Reproducing		1,250
335110	Electric Lamp Bulb and Part Manufacturing		1,250
335121	Residential Electric Lighting Fixture Manufacturing		750
335122	Commercial, Industrial and Institutional Electric Lighting Fixture Manufacturing		500
335129	Other Lighting Equipment Manufacturing		500
335210	Small Electrical Appliance Manufacturing		1,500
335220	Major Household Appliance Manufacturing		1,500
335311	Power, Distribution and Specialty Transformer Manufacturing		750
335312	Motor and Generator Manufacturing		1,250
335313	Switchgear and Switchboard Apparatus Manufacturing		1,250
335314	Relay and Industrial Control Manufacturing		750
335911	Storage Battery Manufacturing		1,250
335912	Primary Battery Manufacturing		1,000
335921	Fiber Optic Cable Manufacturing		1,000
335929	Other Communication and Energy Wire Manufacturing		1,000
335931	Current-Carrying Wiring Device Manufacturing		500
335932	Noncurrent-Carrying Wiring Device Manufacturing		1,000
335991	Carbon and Graphite Product Manufacturing		750

NAICS codes	NAICS U.S. industry title	Size standards in millions of dollars	Size standards in number of employees
335999	All Other Miscellaneous Electrical Equipment and Component Manufacturing		500
336111	Automobile Manufacturing		1,500
336112	Light Truck and Utility Vehicle Manufacturing		1,500
336120	Heavy Duty Truck Manufacturing		1,500
336211	Motor Vehicle Body Manufacturing		1,000
336212	Truck Trailer Manufacturing		1,000
336213	Motor Home Manufacturing		1,250
336214	Travel Trailer and Camper Manufacturing		1,000
336310	Motor Vehicle Gasoline Engine and Engine Parts Manufacturing		1,000
336320	Motor Vehicle Electrical and Electronic Equipment Manufacturing		1,000
336330	Motor Vehicle Steering and Suspension Components (except Spring) Manufacturing		1,000
336340	Motor Vehicle Brake System Manufacturing		1,250
336350	Motor Vehicle Transmission and Power Train Parts Manufacturing		1,500
336360	Motor Vehicle Seating and Interior Trim Manufacturing		1,500
336370	Motor Vehicle Metal Stamping		1,000
336390	Other Motor Vehicle Parts Manufacturing		1,000
336411	Aircraft Manufacturing		1,500
336412	Aircraft Engine and Engine Parts Manufacturing		1,500
336413	Other Aircraft Part and Auxiliary Equipment Manufacturing[7]		1,250[7]
336414	Guided Missile and Space Vehicle Manufacturing		1,250
336415	Guided Missile and Space Vehicle Propulsion Unit and Propulsion Unit Parts Manufacturing		1,250
336419	Other Guided Missile and Space Vehicle Parts and Auxiliary Equipment Manufacturing		1,000
336510	Railroad Rolling Stock Manufacturing		1,500
336611	Ship Building and Repairing		1,250
336612	Boat Building		1,000

NAICS codes	NAICS U.S. industry title	Size standards in millions of dollars	Size standards in number of employees
336991	Motorcycle, Bicycle and Parts Manufacturing		1,000
336992	Military Armored Vehicle, Tank and Tank Component Manufacturing		1,500
336999	All Other Transportation Equipment Manufacturing		1,000
337110	Wood Kitchen Cabinet and Counter Top Manufacturing		750
337121	Upholstered Household Furniture Manufacturing		1,000
337122	Nonupholstered Wood Household Furniture Manufacturing		750
337124	Metal Household Furniture Manufacturing		750
337125	Household Furniture (except Wood and Metal) Manufacturing		750
337127	Institutional Furniture Manufacturing		500
337211	Wood Office Furniture Manufacturing		1,000
337212	Custom Architectural Woodwork and Millwork Manufacturing		500
337214	Office Furniture (Except Wood) Manufacturing		1,000
337215	Showcase, Partition, Shelving, and Locker Manufacturing		500
337910	Mattress Manufacturing		1,000
337920	Blind and Shade Manufacturing		1,000
339112	Surgical and Medical Instrument Manufacturing		1,000
339113	Surgical Appliance and Supplies Manufacturing		750
339114	Dental Equipment and Supplies Manufacturing		750
339115	Ophthalmic Goods Manufacturing		1,000
339116	Dental Laboratories		500
339910	Jewelry and Silverware Manufacturing		500
339920	Sporting and Athletic Goods Manufacturing		750
339930	Doll, Toy, and Game Manufacturing		500
339940	Office Supplies (except Paper) Manufacturing		750
339950	Sign Manufacturing		500

NAICS codes	NAICS U.S. industry title	Size standards in millions of dollars	Size standards in number of employees
339991	Gasket, Packing, and Sealing Device Manufacturing		500
339992	Musical Instrument Manufacturing		1,000
339993	Fastener, Button, Needle and Pin Manufacturing		750
339994	Broom, Brush and Mop Manufacturing		500
339995	Burial Casket Manufacturing		1,000
339999	All Other Miscellaneous Manufacturing		500

Sector 42 – Wholesale Trade

(These NAICS codes shall not be used to classify Government acquisitions for supplies. They also shall not be used by Federal government contractors when subcontracting for the acquisition for supplies. The applicable manufacturing NAICS code shall be used to classify acquisitions for supplies. A Wholesale Trade or Retail Trade business concern submitting an offer or a quote on a supply acquisition is categorized as a nonmanufacturer and deemed small if it has 500 or fewer employees and meets the requirements of 13 CFR 121.406.)

NAICS codes	NAICS U.S. industry title	Size standards in millions of dollars	Size standards in number of employees
423110	Automobile and Other Motor Vehicle Merchant Wholesalers		250
423120	Motor Vehicle Supplies and New Parts Merchant Wholesalers		200
423130	Tire and Tube Merchant Wholesalers		200
423140	Motor Vehicle Parts (Used) Merchant Wholesalers		100
423210	Furniture Merchant Wholesalers		100
423220	Home Furnishing Merchant Wholesalers		100
423310	Lumber, Plywood, Millwork, and Wood Panel Merchant Wholesalers		150
423320	Brick, Stone, and Related Construction Material Merchant Wholesalers		150

NAICS codes	NAICS U.S. industry title	Size standards in millions of dollars	Size standards in number of employees
423330	Roofing, Siding, and Insulation Material Merchant Wholesalers		200
423390	Other Construction Material Merchant Wholesalers		100
423410	Photographic Equipment and Supplies Merchant Wholesalers		200
423420	Office Equipment Merchant Wholesalers		200
423430	Computer and Computer Peripheral Equipment and Software Merchant Wholesalers		250
423440	Other Commercial Equipment Merchant Wholesalers		100
423450	Medical, Dental, and Hospital Equipment and Supplies Merchant Wholesalers		200
423460	Ophthalmic Goods Merchant Wholesalers		150
423490	Other Professional Equipment and Supplies Merchant Wholesalers		150
423510	Metal Service Centers and Other Metal Merchant Wholesalers		200
423520	Coal and Other Mineral and Ore Merchant Wholesalers		100
423610	Electrical Apparatus and Equipment, Wiring Supplies, and Related Equipment Merchant Wholesalers		200
423620	Household Appliances, Electric Housewares, and Consumer Electronics Merchant Wholesalers		200
423690	Other Electronic Parts and Equipment Merchant Wholesalers		250
423710	Hardware Merchant Wholesalers		150
423720	Plumbing and Heating Equipment and Supplies (Hydronics) Merchant Wholesalers		200
423730	Warm Air Heating and Air-Conditioning Equipment and Supplies Merchant Wholesalers		150
423740	Refrigeration Equipment and Supplies Merchant Wholesalers		100

NAICS codes	NAICS U.S. industry title	Size standards in millions of dollars	Size standards in number of employees
423810	Construction and Mining (except Oil Well) Machinery and Equipment Merchant Wholesalers		250
423820	Farm and Garden Machinery and Equipment Merchant Wholesalers		100
423830	Industrial Machinery and Equipment Merchant Wholesalers		100
423840	Industrial Supplies Merchant Wholesalers		100
423850	Service Establishment Equipment and Supplies Merchant Wholesalers		100
423860	Transportation Equipment and Supplies (except Motor Vehicle) Merchant Wholesalers		150
423910	Sporting and Recreational Goods and Supplies Merchant Wholesalers		100
423920	Toy and Hobby Goods and Supplies Merchant Wholesalers		150
423930	Recyclable Material Merchant Wholesalers		100
423940	Jewelry, Watch, Precious Stone, and Precious Metal Merchant Wholesalers		100
423990	Other Miscellaneous Durable Goods Merchant Wholesalers		100
424110	Printing and Writing Paper Merchant Wholesalers		200
424120	Stationary and Office Supplies Merchant Wholesalers		150
424130	Industrial and Personal Service Paper Merchant Wholesalers		150
424210	Drugs and Druggists' Sundries Merchant Wholesalers		250
424310	Piece Goods, Notions, and Other Dry Goods Merchant Wholesalers		100
424320	Men's and Boys' Clothing and Furnishings Merchant Wholesalers		150
424330	Women's, Children's, and Infants' Clothing and Accessories Merchant Wholesalers		100
424340	Footwear Merchant Wholesalers		200
424410	General Line Grocery Merchant Wholesalers		250

NAICS codes	NAICS U.S. industry title	Size standards in millions of dollars	Size standards in number of employees
424420	Packaged Frozen Food Merchant Wholesalers		200
424430	Dairy Product (except Dried or Canned) Merchant Wholesalers		200
424440	Poultry and Poultry Product Merchant Wholesalers		150
424450	Confectionery Merchant Wholesalers		200
424460	Fish and Seafood Merchant Wholesalers		100
424470	Meat and Meat Product Merchant Wholesalers		150
424480	Fresh Fruit and Vegetable Merchant Wholesalers		100
424490	Other Grocery and Related Products Merchant Wholesalers		250
424510	Grain and Field Bean Merchant Wholesalers		200
424520	Livestock Merchant Wholesalers		100
424590	Other Farm Product Raw Material Merchant Wholesalers		100
424610	Plastics Materials and Basic Forms and Shapes Merchant Wholesalers		150
424690	Other Chemical and Allied Products Merchant Wholesalers		150
424710	Petroleum Bulk Stations and Terminals		200
424720	Petroleum and Petroleum Products Merchant Wholesalers (except Bulk Stations and Terminals)		200
424810	Beer and Ale Merchant Wholesalers		200
424820	Wine and Distilled Alcoholic Beverage Merchant Wholesalers		250
424910	Farm Supplies Merchant Wholesalers		200
424920	Book, Periodical, and Newspaper Merchant Wholesalers		200
424930	Flower, Nursery Stock, and Florists' Supplies Merchant Wholesalers		100
424940	Tobacco and Tobacco Product Merchant Wholesalers		250

NAICS codes	NAICS U.S. industry title	Size standards in millions of dollars	Size standards in number of employees
424950	Paint, Varnish, and Supplies Merchant Wholesalers		150
424990	Other Miscellaneous Nondurable Goods Merchant Wholesalers		100
425110	Business to Business Electronic Markets		100
425120	Wholesale Trade Agents and Brokers		100

Sector 44 - 45 – Retail Trade

(These NAICS codes shall not be used to classify Government acquisitions for supplies. They also shall not be used by Federal government contractors when subcontracting for the acquisition for supplies. The applicable manufacturing NAICS code shall be used to classify acquisitions for supplies. A Wholesale Trade or Retail Trade business concern submitting an offer or a quote on a supply acquisition is categorized as a nonmanufacturer and deemed small if it has 500 or fewer employees and meets the requirements of 13 CFR 121.406.)

NAICS codes	NAICS U.S. industry title	Size standards in millions of dollars	Size standards in number of employees
441110	New Car Dealers		200
441120	Used Car Dealers	$27.0	
441210	Recreational Vehicle Dealers	$35.0	
441222	Boat Dealers	$35.0	
441228	Motorcycle, ATV, and All Other Motor Vehicle Dealers	$35.0	
441310	Automotive Parts and Accessories Stores	$16.5	
441320	Tire Dealers	$16.5	
442110	Furniture Stores	$22.0	
442210	Floor Covering Stores	$8.0	
442291	Window Treatment Stores	$8.0	
442299	All Other Home Furnishings Stores	$22.0	
443141	Household Appliance Stores	$12.0	
443142	Electronics Stores	$35.0	

NAICS codes	NAICS U.S. industry title	Size standards in millions of dollars	Size standards in number of employees
444110	Home Centers	$41.5	
444120	Paint and Wallpaper Stores	$30.0	
444130	Hardware Stores	$8.0	
444190	Other Building Material Dealers	$22.0	
444210	Outdoor Power Equipment Stores	$8.0	
444220	Nursery and Garden Centers	$12.0	
445110	Supermarkets and Other Grocery (except Convenience) Stores	$35.0	
445120	Convenience Stores	$32.0	
445210	Meat Markets	$8.0	
445220	Fish and Seafood Markets	$8.0	
445230	Fruit and Vegetable Markets	$8.0	
445291	Baked Goods Stores	$8.0	
445292	Confectionery and Nut Stores	$8.0	
445299	All Other Specialty Food Stores	$8.0	
445310	Beer, Wine and Liquor Stores	$8.0	
446110	Pharmacies and Drug Stores	$30.0	
446120	Cosmetics, Beauty Supplies and Perfume Stores	$30.0	
446130	Optical Goods Stores	$22.0	
446191	Food (Health) Supplement Stores	$16.5	
446199	All Other Health and Personal Care Stores	$8.0	
447110	Gasoline Stations with Convenience Stores	$32.0	
447190	Other Gasoline Stations	$16.5	
448110	Men's Clothing Stores	$12.0	
448120	Women's Clothing Stores	$30.0	
448130	Children's and Infants' Clothing Stores	$35.0	
448140	Family Clothing Stores	$41.5	
448150	Clothing Accessories Stores	$16.5	
448190	Other Clothing Stores	$22.0	
448210	Shoe Stores	$30.0	
448310	Jewelry Stores	$16.5	
448320	Luggage and Leather Goods Stores	$30.0	
451110	Sporting Goods Stores	$16.5	
451120	Hobby, Toy and Game Stores	$30.0	
451130	Sewing, Needlework and Piece Goods Stores	$30.0	
451140	Musical Instrument and Supplies Stores	$12.0	

NAICS codes	NAICS U.S. industry title	Size standards in millions of dollars	Size standards in number of employees
451211	Book Stores	$30.0	
451212	News Dealers and Newsstands	$8.0	
452210	Department Stores	$35.0	
452311	Warehouse Clubs and Supercenters	$32.0	
452319	All Other General Merchandise Stores	$35.0	
453110	Florists	$8.0	
453210	Office Supplies and Stationery Stores	$35.0	
453220	Gift, Novelty and Souvenir Stores	$8.0	
453310	Used Merchandise Stores	$8.0	
453910	Pet and Pet Supplies Stores	$22.0	
453920	Art Dealers	$8.0	
453930	Manufactured (Mobile) Home Dealers	$16.5	
453991	Tobacco Stores	$8.0	
453998	All Other Miscellaneous Store Retailers (except Tobacco Stores)	$8.0	
454110	Electronic Shopping and Mail-Order Houses	$41.5	
454210	Vending Machine Operators	$12.0	
454310	Fuel Dealers		100
454390	Other Direct Selling Establishments	$8.0	

Sector 48 - 49 – Transportation and Warehousing

NAICS codes	NAICS U.S. industry title	Size standards in millions of dollars	Size standards in number of employees
481111	Scheduled Passenger Air Transportation		1,500
481112	Scheduled Freight Air Transportation		1,500
481211	Nonscheduled Chartered Passenger Air Transportation		1,500
481212	Nonscheduled Chartered Freight Air Transportation		1,500
481219	Other Nonscheduled Air Transportation	$16.5	
482111	Line-Haul Railroads		1,500
482112	Short Line Railroads		1,500

NAICS codes	NAICS U.S. industry title	Size standards in millions of dollars	Size standards in number of employees
483111	Deep Sea Freight Transportation		500
483112	Deep Sea Passenger Transportation		1,500
483113	Coastal and Great Lakes Freight Transportation		750
483114	Coastal and Great Lakes Passenger Transportation		500
483211	Inland Water Freight Transportation		750
483212	Inland Water Passenger Transportation		500
484110	General Freight Trucking, Local	$30.0	
484121	General Freight Trucking, Long-Distance, Truckload	$30.0	
484122	General Freight Trucking, Long-Distance, Less Than Truckload	$30.0	
484210	Used Household and Office Goods Moving	$30.0	
484220	Specialized Freight (except Used Goods) Trucking, Local	$30.0	
484230	Specialized Freight (except Used Goods) Trucking, Long-Distance	$30.0	
485111	Mixed Mode Transit Systems	$16.5	
485112	Commuter Rail Systems	$16.5	
485113	Bus and Other Motor Vehicle Transit Systems	$16.5	
485119	Other Urban Transit Systems	$16.5	
485210	Interurban and Rural Bus Transportation	$16.5	
485310	Taxi Service	$16.5	
485320	Limousine Service	$16.5	
485410	School and Employee Bus Transportation	$16.5	
485510	Charter Bus Industry	$16.5	
485991	Special Needs Transportation	$16.5	
485999	All Other Transit and Ground Passenger Transportation	$16.5	
486110	Pipeline Transportation of Crude Oil		1,500
486210	Pipeline Transportation of Natural Gas	$30.0	
486910	Pipeline Transportation of Refined Petroleum Products		1,500
486990	All Other Pipeline Transportation	$40.5	

NAICS codes	NAICS U.S. industry title	Size standards in millions of dollars	Size standards in number of employees
487110	Scenic and Sightseeing Transportation, Land	$8.0	
487210	Scenic and Sightseeing Transportation, Water	$8.0	
487990	Scenic and Sightseeing Transportation, Other	$8.0	
488111	Air Traffic Control	$35.0	
488119	Other Airport Operations	$35.0	
488190	Other Support Activities for Air Transportation	$35.0	
488210	Support Activities for Rail Transportation	$16.5	
488310	Port and Harbor Operations	$41.5	
488320	Marine Cargo Handling	$41.5	
488330	Navigational Services to Shipping	$41.5	
488390	Other Support Activities for Water Transportation	$41.5	
488410	Motor Vehicle Towing	$8.0	
488490	Other Support Activities for Road Transportation	$8.0	
488510	Freight Transportation Arrangement[10]	$16.5[10]	
Except,	Non-Vessel Owning Common Carriers and Household Goods Forwarders	$30.0	
488991	Packing and Crating	$30.0	
488999	All Other Support Activities for Transportation	$8.0	
491110	Postal Service	$8.0	
492110	Couriers and Express Delivery Services		1,500
492210	Local Messengers and Local Delivery	$30.0	
493110	General Warehousing and Storage	$30.0	
493120	Refrigerated Warehousing and Storage	$30.0	
493130	Farm Product Warehousing and Storage	$30.0	
493190	Other Warehousing and Storage	$30.0	

Sector 51 – Information

NAICS codes	NAICS U.S. industry title	Size standards in millions of dollars	Size standards in number of employees
511110	Newspaper Publishers		1,000
511120	Periodical Publishers		1,000
511130	Book Publishers		1,000
511140	Directory and Mailing List Publishers		1,250
511191	Greeting Card Publishers		1,500
511199	All Other Publishers		500
511210	Software Publishers[20]	$41.5[20]	
512110	Motion Picture and Video Production	$35.0	
512120	Motion Picture and Video Distribution	$34.5	
512131	Motion Picture Theaters (except Drive-Ins)	$41.5	
512132	Drive-In Motion Picture Theaters	$8.0	
512191	Teleproduction and Other Postproduction Services	$34.5	
512199	Other Motion Picture and Video Industries	$22.0	
512230	Music Publishers		750
512240	Sound Recording Studios	$8.0	
512250	Record Production and Distribution		250
512290	Other Sound Recording Industries	$12.0	
515111	Radio Networks	$35.0	
515112	Radio Stations	$41.5	
515120	Television Broadcasting	$41.5	
515210	Cable and Other Subscription Programming	$41.5	
517311	Wired Telecommunications Carriers		1,500
517312	Wireless Telecommunications Carriers (except Satellite)		1,500
517410	Satellite Telecommunications	$35.0	
517911	Telecommunications Resellers		1,500
517919	All Other Telecommunications	$35.0	
518210	Data Processing, Hosting, and Related Services	$35.0	
519110	News Syndicates	$30.0	
519120	Libraries and Archives	$16.5	
519130	Internet Publishing and Broadcasting and Web Search Portals		1,000
519190	All Other Information Services	$30.0	

Sector 52 – Finance and Insurance

NAICS codes	NAICS U.S. industry title	Size standards in millions of dollars	Size standards in number of employees
522110	Commercial Banking[8]	$600 million in assets[8]	
522120	Savings Institutions[8]	$600 million in assets[8]	
522130	Credit Unions[8]	$600 million in assets[8]	
522190	Other Depository Credit Intermediation[8]	$600 million in assets[8]	
522210	Credit Card Issuing[8]	$600 million in assets[8]	
522220	Sales Financing	$41.5	
522291	Consumer Lending	$41.5	
522292	Real Estate Credit	$41.5	
522293	International Trade Financing	$41.5	
522294	Secondary Market Financing	$41.5	
522298	All Other Nondepository Credit Intermediation	$41.5	
522310	Mortgage and Nonmortgage Loan Brokers	$8.0	
522320	Financial Transactions Processing, Reserve, and Clearinghouse Activities	$41.5	
522390	Other Activities Related to Credit Intermediation	$22.0	
523110	Investment Banking and Securities Dealing	$41.5	
523120	Securities Brokerage	$41.5	
523130	Commodity Contracts Dealing	$41.5	
523140	Commodity Contracts Brokerage	$41.5	
523210	Securities and Commodity Exchanges	$41.5	
523910	Miscellaneous Intermediation	$41.5	
523920	Portfolio Management	$41.5	
523930	Investment Advice	$41.5	
523991	Trust, Fiduciary and Custody Activities	$41.5	
523999	Miscellaneous Financial Investment Activities	$41.5	
524113	Direct Life Insurance Carriers	$41.5	
524114	Direct Health and Medical Insurance Carriers	$41.5	

NAICS codes	NAICS U.S. industry title	Size standards in millions of dollars	Size standards in number of employees
524126	Direct Property and Casualty Insurance Carriers		1,500
524127	Direct Title Insurance Carriers	$41.5	
524128	Other Direct Insurance (except Life, Health and Medical) Carriers	$41.5	
524130	Reinsurance Carriers	$41.5	
524210	Insurance Agencies and Brokerages	$8.0	
524291	Claims Adjusting	$22.0	
524292	Third Party Administration of Insurance and Pension Funds	$35.0	
524298	All Other Insurance Related Activities	$16.5	
525110	Pension Funds	$35.0	
525120	Health and Welfare Funds	$35.0	
525190	Other Insurance Funds	$35.0	
525910	Open-End Investment Funds	$35.0	
525920	Trusts, Estates, and Agency Accounts	$35.0	
525990	Other Financial Vehicles	$35.0	

Sector 53 – Real Estate and Rental and Leasing

NAICS codes	NAICS U.S. industry title	Size standards in millions of dollars	Size standards in number of employees
531110	Lessors of Residential Buildings and Dwellings[9]	$30.0[9]	
531120	Lessors of Nonresidential Buildings (except Miniwarehouses)[9]	$30.0[9]	
531130	Lessors of Miniwarehouses and Self Storage Units[9]	$30.0[9]	
531190	Lessors of Other Real Estate Property[9]	$30.0[9]	
531210	Offices of Real Estate Agents and Brokers[10]	$8.0[10]	
531311	Residential Property Managers	$8.0	
531312	Nonresidential Property Managers	$8.0	
531320	Offices of Real Estate Appraisers	$8.0	
531390	Other Activities Related to Real Estate	$8.0	

NAICS codes	NAICS U.S. industry title	Size standards in millions of dollars	Size standards in number of employees
532111	Passenger Car Rental	$41.5	
532112	Passenger Car Leasing	$41.5	
532120	Truck, Utility Trailer, and RV (Recreational Vehicle) Rental and Leasing	$41.5	
532210	Consumer Electronics and Appliances Rental	$41.5	
532281	Formal Wear and Costume Rental	$22.0	
532282	Video Tape and Disc Rental	$30.0	
532283	Home Health Equipment Rental	$35.0	
532284	Recreational Goods Rental	$8.0	
532289	All Other Consumer Goods Rental	$8.0	
532310	General Rental Centers	$8.0	
532411	Commercial Air, Rail, and Water Transportation Equipment Rental and Leasing	$35.0	
532412	Construction, Mining and Forestry Machinery and Equipment Rental and Leasing	$35.0	
532420	Office Machinery and Equipment Rental and Leasing	$35.0	
532490	Other Commercial and Industrial Machinery and Equipment Rental and Leasing	$35.0	
533110	Lessors of Nonfinancial Intangible Assets (except Copyrighted Works)	$41.5	

Sector 54 – Professional, Scientific and Technical Services

NAICS codes	NAICS U.S. industry title	Size standards in millions of dollars	Size standards in number of employees
541110	Offices of Lawyers	$12.0	
541191	Title Abstract and Settlement Offices	$12.0	
541199	All Other Legal Services	$12.0	
541211	Offices of Certified Public Accountants	$22.0	
541213	Tax Preparation Services	$22.0	
541214	Payroll Services	$22.0	
541219	Other Accounting Services	$22.0	

NAICS codes	NAICS U.S. industry title	Size standards in millions of dollars	Size standards in number of employees
541310	Architectural Services	$8.0	
541320	Landscape Architectural Services	$8.0	
541330	Engineering Services	$16.5	
Except,	Military and Aerospace Equipment and Military Weapons	$41.5	
Except,	Contracts and Subcontracts for Engineering Services Awarded Under the National Energy Policy Act of 1992	$41.5	
Except,	Marine Engineering and Naval Architecture	$41.5	
541340	Drafting Services	$8.0	
541350	Building Inspection Services	$8.0	
541360	Geophysical Surveying and Mapping Services	$16.5	
541370	Surveying and Mapping (except Geophysical) Services	$16.5	
541380	Testing Laboratories	$16.5	
541410	Interior Design Services	$8.0	
541420	Industrial Design Services	$8.0	
541430	Graphic Design Services	$8.0	
541490	Other Specialized Design Services	$8.0	
541511	Custom Computer Programming Services	$30.0	
541512	Computer Systems Design Services	$30.0	
541513	Computer Facilities Management Services	$30.0	
541519	Other Computer Related Services	$30.0	
Except,	Information Technology Value Added Resellers[18]		150[18]
541611	Administrative Management and General Management Consulting Services	$16.5	
541612	Human Resources Consulting Services	$16.5	
541613	Marketing Consulting Services	$16.5	
541614	Process, Physical Distribution and Logistics Consulting Services	$16.5	
541618	Other Management Consulting Services	$16.5	
541620	Environmental Consulting Services	$16.5	
541690	Other Scientific and Technical Consulting Services	$16.5	
541713	Research and Technology in Nanotechnology[11]		1,000[11]

NAICS codes	NAICS U.S. industry title	Size standards in millions of dollars	Size standards in number of employees
541714	Research and Technology in Biotechnology (except Nanobiotechnology) [11]		1,000[11]
541715	Research and Development in the Physical, Engineering, and Life Sciences (except Nanotechnology and Biotechnology) [11]		1,000[11]
Except,	Aircraft, Aircraft Engine and Engine Parts[11]		1,500[11]
Except,	Other Aircraft Parts and Auxiliary Equipment[11]		1,250[11]
Except,	Guided Missiles and Space Vehicles, Their Propulsion Units and Propulsion Parts[11]		1,250[11]
541720	Research and Development in the Social Sciences and Humanities	$22.0	
541810	Advertising Agencies[10]	$16.5[10]	
541820	Public Relations Agencies	$16.5	
541830	Media Buying Agencies	$16.5	
541840	Media Representatives	$16.5	
541850	Outdoor Advertising	$16.5	
541860	Direct Mail Advertising	$16.5	
541870	Advertising Material Distribution Services	$16.5	
541890	Other Services Related to Advertising	$16.5	
541910	Marketing Research and Public Opinion Polling	$16.5	
541921	Photography Studios, Portrait	$8.0	
541922	Commercial Photography	$8.0	
541930	Translation and Interpretation Services	$8.0	
541940	Veterinary Services	$8.0	
541990	All Other Professional, Scientific and Technical Services	$16.5	

Sector 55 – Management of Companies and Enterprises

NAICS codes	NAICS U.S. industry title	Size Standards in millions of dollars	Size standards in number of employees
551111	Offices of Bank Holding Companies	$22.0	
551112	Offices of Other Holding Companies	$22.0	

Sector 56 – Administrative and Support, Waste Management and Remediation Services

NAICS codes	NAICS U.S. industry title	Size standards in millions of dollars	Size standards in number of employees
561110	Office Administrative Services	$8.0	
561210	Facilities Support Services[12]	$41.5[12]	
561311	Employment Placement Agencies	$30.0	
561312	Executive Search Services	$30.0	
561320	Temporary Help Services	$30.0	
561330	Professional Employer Organizations	$30.0	
561410	Document Preparation Services	$16.5	
561421	Telephone Answering Services	$16.5	
561422	Telemarketing Bureaus and Other contact Centers	$16.5	
561431	Private Mail Centers	$16.5	
561439	Other Business Service Centers (including Copy Shops)	$16.5	
561440	Collection Agencies	$16.5	
561450	Credit Bureaus	$16.5	
561491	Repossession Services	$16.5	
561492	Court Reporting and Stenotype Services	$16.5	
561499	All Other Business Support Services	$16.5	
561510	Travel Agencies[10]	$22.0[10]	
561520	Tour Operators[10]	$22.0[10]	
561591	Convention and Visitors Bureaus	$22.0	
561599	All Other Travel Arrangement and Reservation Services	$22.0	
561611	Investigation Services	$22.0	
561612	Security Guards and Patrol Services	$22.0	

NAICS codes	NAICS U.S. industry title	Size standards in millions of dollars	Size standards in number of employees
561613	Armored Car Services	$22.0	
561621	Security Systems Services (except Locksmiths)	$22.0	
561622	Locksmiths	$22.0	
561710	Exterminating and Pest Control Services	$12.0	
561720	Janitorial Services	$19.5	
561730	Landscaping Services	$8.0	
561740	Carpet and Upholstery Cleaning Services	$6.0	
561790	Other Services to Buildings and Dwellings	$8.0	
561910	Packaging and Labeling Services	$12.0	
561920	Convention and Trade Show Organizers[10]	$12.0[10]	
561990	All Other Support Services	$12.0	
562111	Solid Waste Collection	$41.5	
562112	Hazardous Waste Collection	$41.5	
562119	Other Waste Collection	$41.5	
562211	Hazardous Waste Treatment and Disposal	$41.5	
562212	Solid Waste Landfill	$41.5	
562213	Solid Waste Combustors and Incinerators	$41.5	
562219	Other Nonhazardous Waste Treatment and Disposal	$41.5	
562910	Remediation Services	$22.0	
Except,	Environmental Remediation Services[14]		750[14]
562920	Materials Recovery Facilities	$22.0	
562991	Septic Tank and Related Services	$8.0	
562998	All Other Miscellaneous Waste Management Services	$8.0	

Sector 61 – Educational Services

NAICS codes	NAICS U.S. industry title	Size standards in millions of dollars	Size standards in number of employees
611110	Elementary and Secondary Schools	$12.0	
611210	Junior Colleges	$22.0	

NAICS codes	NAICS U.S. industry title	Size standards in millions of dollars	Size standards in number of employees
611310	Colleges, Universities and Professional Schools	$30.0	
611410	Business and Secretarial Schools	$8.0	
611420	Computer Training	$12.0	
611430	Professional and Management Development Training	$12.0	
611511	Cosmetology and Barber Schools	$8.0	
611512	Flight Training	$30.0	
611513	Apprenticeship Training	$8.0	
611519	Other Technical and Trade Schools	$16.5	
Except,	Job Corps Centers[16]	$41.5[16]	
611610	Fine Arts Schools	$8.0	
611620	Sports and Recreation Instruction	$8.0	
611630	Language Schools	$12.0	
611691	Exam Preparation and Tutoring	$8.0	
611692	Automobile Driving Schools	$8.0	
611699	All Other Miscellaneous Schools and Instruction	$12.0	
611710	Educational Support Services	$16.5	

Sector 62 – Health Care and Social Assistance

NAICS codes	NAICS U.S. industry title	Size standards in millions of dollars	Size standards in number of employees
621111	Offices of Physicians (except Mental Health Specialists)	$12.0	
621112	Offices of Physicians, Mental Health Specialists	$12.0	
621210	Offices of Dentists	$8.0	
621310	Offices of Chiropractors	$8.0	
621320	Offices of Optometrists	$8.0	
621330	Offices of Mental Health Practitioners (except Physicians)	$8.0	

NAICS codes	NAICS U.S. industry title	Size standards in millions of dollars	Size standards in number of employees
621340	Offices of Physical, Occupational and Speech Therapists and Audiologists	$8.0	
621391	Offices of Podiatrists	$8.0	
621399	Offices of All Other Miscellaneous Health Practitioners	$8.0	
621410	Family Planning Centers	$12.0	
621420	Outpatient Mental Health and Substance Abuse Centers	$16.5	
621491	HMO Medical Centers	$35.0	
621492	Kidney Dialysis Centers	$41.5	
621493	Freestanding Ambulatory Surgical and Emergency Centers	$16.5	
621498	All Other Outpatient Care Centers	$22.0	
621511	Medical Laboratories	$35.0	
621512	Diagnostic Imaging Centers	$16.5	
621610	Home Health Care Services	$16.5	
621910	Ambulance Services	$16.5	
621991	Blood and Organ Banks	$35.0	
621999	All Other Miscellaneous Ambulatory Health Care Services	$16.5	
622110	General Medical and Surgical Hospitals	$41.5	
622210	Psychiatric and Substance Abuse Hospitals	$41.5	
622310	Specialty (except Psychiatric and Substance Abuse) Hospitals	$41.5	
623110	Nursing Care Facilities (Skilled Nursing Facilities)	$30.0	
623210	Residential Intellectual and Developmental Disability Facilities	$16.5	
623220	Residential Mental Health and Substance Abuse Facilities	$16.5	
623311	Continuing Care Retirement Communities	$30.0	
623312	Assisted Living Facilities for the Elderly	$12.0	
623990	Other Residential Care Facilities	$12.0	
624110	Child and Youth Services	$12.0	
624120	Services for the Elderly and Persons with Disabilities	$12.0	
624190	Other Individual and Family Services	$12.0	

NAICS codes	NAICS U.S. industry title	Size standards in millions of dollars	Size standards in number of employees
624210	Community Food Services	$12.0	
624221	Temporary Shelters	$12.0	
624229	Other Community Housing Services	$16.5	
624230	Emergency and Other Relief Services	$35.0	
624310	Vocational Rehabilitation Services	$12.0	
624410	Child Day Care Services	$8.0	

Sector 71 – Arts, Entertainment and Recreation

NAICS codes	NAICS U.S. industry title	Size standards in millions of dollars	Size standards in number of employees
711110	Theater Companies and Dinner Theaters	$22.0	
711120	Dance Companies	$12.0	
711130	Musical Groups and Artists	$12.0	
711190	Other Performing Arts Companies	$30.0	
711211	Sports Teams and Clubs	$41.5	
711212	Race Tracks	$41.5	
711219	Other Spectator Sports	$12.0	
711310	Promoters of Performing Arts, Sports and Similar Events with Facilities	$35.0	
711320	Promoters of Performing Arts, Sports and Similar Events without Facilities	$16.5	
711410	Agents and Managers for Artists, Athletes, Entertainers and Other Public Figures	$12.0	
711510	Independent Artists, Writers, and Performers	$8.0	
712110	Museums	$30.0	
712120	Historical Sites	$8.0	
712130	Zoos and Botanical Gardens	$30.0	
712190	Nature Parks and Other Similar Institutions	$8.0	
713110	Amusement and Theme Parks	$41.5	
713120	Amusement Arcades	$8.0	
713210	Casinos (except Casino Hotels)	$30.0	
713290	Other Gambling Industries	$35.0	
713910	Golf Courses and Country Clubs	$16.5	

NAICS codes	NAICS U.S. industry title	Size standards in millions of dollars	Size standards in number of employees
713920	Skiing Facilities	$30.0	
713930	Marinas	$8.0	
713940	Fitness and Recreational Sports Centers	$8.0	
713950	Bowling Centers	$8.0	
713990	All Other Amusement and Recreation Industries	$8.0	

Sector 72 – Accommodation and Food Services

NAICS Codes	NAICS U.S. industry title	Size standards in millions of dollars	Size standards in number of employees
721110	Hotels (except Casino Hotels) and Motels	$35.0	
721120	Casino Hotels	$35.0	
721191	Bed-and-Breakfast Inns	$8.0	
721199	All Other Traveler Accommodation	$8.0	
721211	RV (Recreational Vehicle) Parks and Campgrounds	$8.0	
721214	Recreational and Vacation Camps (except Campgrounds)	$8.0	
721310	Rooming and Boarding Houses, Dormitories, and Workers' Camps	$8.0	
722310	Food Service Contractors	$41.5	
722320	Caterers	$8.0	
722330	Mobile Food Services	$8.0	
722410	Drinking Places (Alcoholic Beverages)	$8.0	
722511	Full-Service Restaurants	$8.0	
722513	Limited-Service Restaurants	$12.0	
722514	Cafeterias, Grill Buffets, and Buffets	$30.0	
722515	Snack and Nonalcoholic Beverage Bars	$8.0	

Sector 81 – Other Services

NAICS codes	NAICS U.S. industry title	Size standards in millions of dollars	Size standards in number of employees
811111	General Automotive Repair	$8.0	
811112	Automotive Exhaust System Repair	$8.0	
811113	Automotive Transmission Repair	$8.0	
811118	Other Automotive Mechanical and Electrical Repair and Maintenance	$8.0	
811121	Automotive Body, Paint and Interior Repair and Maintenance	$8.0	
811122	Automotive Glass Replacement Shops	$12.0	
811191	Automotive Oil Change and Lubrication Shops	$8.0	
811192	Car Washes	$8.0	
811198	All Other Automotive Repair and Maintenance	$8.0	
811211	Consumer Electronics Repair and Maintenance	$8.0	
811212	Computer and Office Machine Repair and Maintenance	$30.0	
811213	Communication Equipment Repair and Maintenance	$12.0	
811219	Other Electronic and Precision Equipment Repair and Maintenance	$22.0	
811310	Commercial and Industrial Machinery and Equipment (except Automotive and Electronic) Repair and Maintenance	$8.0	
811411	Home and Garden Equipment Repair and Maintenance	$8.0	
811412	Appliance Repair and Maintenance	$16.5	
811420	Reupholstery and Furniture Repair	$8.0	
811430	Footwear and Leather Goods Repair	$8.0	
811490	Other Personal and Household Goods Repair and Maintenance	$8.0	
812111	Barber Shops	$8.0	
812112	Beauty Salons	$8.0	
812113	Nail Salons	$8.0	
812191	Diet and Weight Reducing Centers	$22.0	

NAICS codes	NAICS U.S. industry title	Size standards in millions of dollars	Size standards in number of employees
812199	Other Personal Care Services	$8.0	
812210	Funeral Homes and Funeral Services	$8.0	
812220	Cemeteries and Crematories	$22.0	
812310	Coin-Operated Laundries and Drycleaners	$8.0	
812320	Drycleaning and Laundry Services (except Coin-Operated)	$6.0	
812331	Linen Supply	$35.0	
812332	Industrial Launderers	$41.5	
812910	Pet Care (except Veterinary) Services	$8.0	
812921	Photofinishing Laboratories (except One-Hour)	$22.0	
812922	One-Hour Photofinishing	$16.5	
812930	Parking Lots and Garages	$41.5	
812990	All Other Personal Services	$8.0	
813110	Religious Organizations	$8.0	
813211	Grantmaking Foundations	$35.0	
813212	Voluntary Health Organizations	$30.0	
813219	Other Grantmaking and Giving Services	$41.5	
813311	Human Rights Organizations	$30.0	
813312	Environment, Conservation and Wildlife Organizations	$16.5	
813319	Other Social Advocacy Organizations	$8.0	
813410	Civic and Social Organizations	$8.0	
813910	Business Associations	$8.0	
813920	Professional Organizations	$16.5	
813930	Labor Unions and Similar Labor Organizations	$8.0	
813940	Political Organizations	$8.0	
813990	Other Similar Organizations (except Business, Professional, Labor, and Political Organizations)	$8.0	

Sector 92 – Public Administration[19]

(Small business size standards are not established for this Sector. Establishments in the Public Administration Sector are Federal, state, and local government agencies which administer and oversee government programs and activities that are not performed by private establishments.)

Footnotes

1. [Reserved].

2. NAICS code 237990 – Dredging: To be considered small for purposes of Government procurement, a firm must perform at least 40 percent of the volume dredged with its own equipment or equipment owned by another small dredging concern.

3. NAICS code 311421 – For purposes of Government procurement for food canning and preserving, the standard of 1,000 employees excludes agricultural labor as defined in section 3306(k) of the Internal Revenue Code, 26 U.S.C. 3306(k).

4. NAICS code 324110 – To qualify as small for purposes of Government procurement, the petroleum refiner, including its affiliates, must be a concern that has either no more than 1,500 employees or no more than 200,000 barrels per calendar day total Operable Atmospheric Crude Oil Distillation capacity. Capacity includes all domestic and foreign affiliates, all owned or leased facilities, and all facilities under a processing agreement or an arrangement such as an exchange agreement or a throughput. To qualify under the capacity size standard, the firm, together with its affiliates, must be primarily engaged in refining crude petroleum into refined petroleum products. A firm's "primary industry" is determined in accordance with 13 CFR § 121.107.

5. NAICS code 326211 – For Government procurement, a firm is small for bidding on a contract for pneumatic tires within Census NAICS Product Classification codes 3262111 and 3262113, provided that:

a) The value of tires within Census NAICS Product Classification codes 3262113 that it manufactured in the United States during the previous calendar year is more than 50 percent of the value of its total worldwide manufacture,

b) The value of pneumatic tires within Census Classification codes 30111 and 30112 comprising its total worldwide manufacture during the preceding calendar year was less than 5 percent of the value of all such tires manufactured in the United States during that period, and

c) The value of the principal product that it manufactured, produced, or sold worldwide during the preceding calendar year is less than 10 percent of the total value of such products manufactured or otherwise produced or sold in the United States during that period.

6. NAICS Subsectors 333, 334, 335 and 336 – For rebuilding machinery or equipment on a factory basis, or equivalent, use the NAICS code for a newly manufactured product. Concerns performing major rebuilding or overhaul activities do not necessarily have to meet the criteria for being a "manufacturer" although the activities may be classified under a manufacturing NAICS code. Ordinary repair services or preservation are not considered rebuilding.

7. NAICS code 336413 – Contracts for the rebuilding or overhaul of aircraft ground support equipment on a contract basis are classified under NAICS code 336413.

8. NAICS Codes 522110, 522120, 522130, 522190, and 522210 – A financial institution's assets are determined by averaging the assets reported on its four quarterly financial statements for the preceding year. "Assets" for the purposes of this size standard means the assets defined according to the Federal Financial Institutions Examination Council 041 call report form for NAICS Codes 522110, 522120, 522190, and 522210 and the National Credit Union Administration 5300 call report form for NAICS code 522130.

9. NAICS codes 531110, 531120, 531130, and 531190 – Leasing of building space to the Federal Government by Owners: For Government procurement, a size standard of $41.5 million in gross receipts applies to the owners of building space leased to the Federal Government. The standard does not apply to an agent.

10. NAICS codes 488510, 531210, 541810, 561510, 561520 and 561920 – As measured by total revenues, but excluding funds received in trust for an unaffiliated third party, such as bookings or sales subject to commissions. The commissions received are included as revenue.

11. NAICS code 541713, 541714 and 541715:

a) "Research and Development" means laboratory or other physical research and development. It does not include economic, educational, engineering, operations, systems, or othe nonphysical research; or computer programming, data processing, commercial and/or medical laboratory testing.

b) For research and development contracts requiring the delivery of a manufactured product, the appropriate size standard is that of the manufacturing industry.

c) For purposes of the Small Business Innovation Research (SBIR) and Small Business Transfer Technology (STTR) programs, the term "research" or "research and development" means any activity which is (A) a systematic, intensive study directed toward greater knowledge or understanding of the subject studied; (B) a systematic study directed specifically toward applying new knowledge to meet a recognized need; or (C) a systematic application of knowledge toward the production of useful materials, devices, and systems or methods, including design, development, and improvement of prototypes and new processes to meet specific requirements. See 15 U.S.C. § 638(e)(5) and section 3 of the SBIR and STTR policy directives available at www.sbir.gov. For size eligibility requirements for the SBIR and STTR programs, see § 121.702 of these regulations.

d) Research and Development for guided missiles and space vehicles includes evaluations and simulation, and other services requiring thorough knowledge of complete missiles and spacecraft.

1. NAICS 561210 – Facilities Support Services:

a) ~~If one or more~~ activities of Facilities Support Services as defined in paragraph (b) (below in this footnote) can be identified with a specific industry and that industry accounts for 50% or more of the value of an entire procurement, then the proper classification of the procurement is that of the specific industry, not Facilities Support Services.

b) "Facilities Support Services" requires the performance of three or more separate activities in the areas of services or specialty trade contractors industries. If services are performed, these service activities must each be in a separate NAICS industry. If the procurement requires the use of specialty trade contractors (plumbing, painting, plastering, carpentry, *etc.*), all such specialty trade contractors activities are considered a single activity and classified as "Building and Property Specialty Trade Services." Since "Building and Property Specialty Trade Services" is only one activity, two additional activities of separate NAICS industries are required for a procurement to be classified as "Facilities Support Services."

1. NAICS code 238990 – Building and Property Specialty Trade Services: If a procurement requires the use of multiple specialty trade contractors (i.e., plumbing, painting, plastering, carpentry, etc.), and no specialty trade accounts for 50% or more of the value of the procurement, all such specialty trade contractors activities are considered a single activity and classified as Building and Property Specialty Trade Services.

2. NAICS 562910 – Environmental Remediation Services:

a) For SBA assistance as a small business concern in the industry of Environmental Remediation Services, other than for Government procurement, a concern must be engaged primarily in furnishing a range of services for the remediation of a contaminated environment to an acceptable condition including, but not limited to, preliminary assessment, site inspection, testing, remedial investigation, feasibility studies, regulatory compliance, remedial design, containment, remedial action, removal of contaminated materials, nuclear remediation, storage of contaminated materials and security and site closeouts. If one of such activities accounts for 50 percent or more of a concern's total revenues, employees, or other related factors, the concern's primary industry is that of the particular industry and not the Environmental Remediation Services Industry.

b) For purposes of classifying a Government procurement as Environmental Remediation Services, the general purpose of the procurement must be to restore or directly support the restoration of a contaminated environment. This includes activities such as preliminary assessment, site inspection, testing, remedial investigation, feasibility studies, regulatory compliance, remedial design, remediation services, containment, nuclear remediation, and removal of contaminated materials or security and site closeouts. The general purpose of the procurement need not necessarily include remedial actions. Also, the procurement must be composed of activities in three or more separate industries with separate NAICS codes or, in some instances (e.g., engineering), smaller sub-components of NAICS codes with separate and distinct size standards. These activities may include, but are not limited to, separate activities in industries such as: Heavy Construction; Special Trade Contractors; Engineering Services; Architectural Services; Management Consulting Services; Hazardous and Other Waste Collection; Remediation Services; Testing Laboratories; and Research and Development in the Physical, Engineering, and Life Sciences. If any activity in the procurement can be identified with a separate NAICS code, or component of a code with a separate distinct size standard, and that industry accounts for 50 percent or more of the value of the entire procurement, then the proper size standard is the one for that particular industry, and not the Environmental Remediation Service size standard.

16. NAICS code 611519 – Job Corps Centers. For classifying a Federal procurement, the purpose of the solicitation must be for the management and operation of a U.S. Department of Labor Job Corps Center. The activities involved include admissions activities, life skills training, educational activities, comprehensive career preparation activities, career development activities, caree transition activities, as well as the management and support functions and services needed to operate ~~and maintain the fac~~ility. For SBA assistance as a small business concern, other than for Federal Government procurements, a concern must be

primarily engaged in providing the services to operate and maintain Federal Job Corps Centers.

1. NAICS code 115310 – Support Activities for Forestry. Forest Fire Suppression and Fuels Management Services are two components of Support Activities for Forestry. Forest Fire Suppression includes establishments which provide services to fight forest fires. These firms usually have fire-fighting crews and equipment. Fuels Management Services firms provide services to clear land of hazardous materials that would fuel forest fires. The treatments used by these firms may include prescribed fire, mechanical removal, establishing fuel breaks, thinning, pruning, and piling.

2. NAICS code 541519 – An Information Technology Value Added Reseller (ITVAR) provides a total solution to information technology acquisitions by providing multi-vendor hardware and software along with significant value added services. Significant value added services consist of, but are not limited to, configuration consulting and design, systems integration, installation of multi-vendor computer equipment, customization of hardware or software, training, product technical support, maintenance, and end user support. For purposes of Government procurement, an information technology procurement classified under this exception and 150-employee size standard must consist of at least 15% and not more than 50% of value added services, as measured by the total contract price. In addition, the offeror must comply with the manufacturing performance requirements, or comply with the non-manufacturer rule by supplying the products of small business concerns, unless SBA has issued a class or contract specific waiver of the non-manufacturer rule. If the contract consists of less than 15% of value added services, then it must be classified under a NAICS manufacturing industry. If the contract consists of more than 50% of value added services, then it must be classified under the NAICS industry that best describes the predominate service of the procurement.

3. NAICS Sector 92 – Small business size standards are not established for this sector. Establishments in the Public Administration sector are Federal, State, and local government agencies which administer and oversee government programs and activities that are not performed by private establishments. Concerns performing operational services for the administration of a government program are classified under the NAICS private sector industry based on the activities performed. Similarly, procurements for these types of services are classified under the NAICS private sector industry that best describes the activities to be performed. For example, if a government agency issues a procurement for law enforcement services, the requirement would be classified using one of the NAICS industry codes under NAICS industry 56161, Investigation, Guard, and Armored Car Services.

4. NAICS code 511210 – For purposes of Government procurement, the purchase of software subject to potential waiver of the nonmanufacturer rule pursuant to §121.1203(d) should be classified under this NAICS code.

Contacts SBA's Office of Government Contracting has six area offices with an employee designated as a Size Specialist. Below are the office addresses and telephone numbers.	
Area I Office of Government Contracting **Boston Area Office** U.S. Small Business Administration 10 Causeway Street Room 265 Boston, MA 02222-1093 Tel: (617) 565-5622	**Area IV** Office of Government Contracting **Chicago Area Office** U.S. Small Business Administration 500 West Madison Street Suite 1250 Chicago, IL 60661-2511 Tel: 312.353.7674
Area II Office of Government Contracting **Philadelphia Area Office** U.S. Small Business Administration Parkview Tower 1150 First Avenue Suite 1001 King of Prussia, PA 19406 Tel: (610) 382-3190	**Area V** Office Government Contracting **Dallas Area Office** U.S. Small Business Administration 4300 Amon Carter Boulevard, Suite 116 Fort Worth, TX 76155 Tel: (817) 684-5303
Area III Office of Government Contracting **Atlanta Area Office** U.S. Small Business Administration 233 Peachtree Street, NE Suite 1805 Atlanta, GA 30309 Tel: (404) 331-7587	**Area VI** Office of Government Contracting **San Francisco Area Office** U.S. Small Business Administration 455 Market Street 6th Floor San Francisco, CA 94105 Tel: (415) 744-8429
IN WASHINGTON, DC, THERE ARE TWO OFFICES THAT YOU MAY CONTACT	
Office of Size Standards U.S. Small Business Administration 409 3rd Street, SW Washington, DC 20416 Tel: (202) 205-6618	**Office of Government Contracting** U.S. Small Business Administration 409 3rd Street, SW Washington, DC 20416 Tel: (202) 205-6460

www.ingramcontent.com/pod-product-compliance
Lightning Source LLC
Chambersburg PA
CBHW080412030426
42335CB00020B/2425